Comparative Constitutional Law

Comparative Constitutional Law

A Study of the Principles of Constitutional Law

HAMID KHAN
M. WAQAR RANA

OXFORD
UNIVERSITY PRESS

OXFORD
UNIVERSITY PRESS

Oxford University Press is a department of the University of Oxford.
It furthers the University's objective of excellence in research, scholarship,
and education by publishing worldwide. Oxford is a registered trade mark of
Oxford University Press in the UK and in certain other countries

Published in Pakistan by
Oxford University Press
No. 38, Sector 15, Korangi Industrial Area,
PO Box 8214, Karachi-74900, Pakistan

This Paperback Edition published in 2022

ISBN 978-0-19-070972-3

Second Impression 2025

Typeset in Minion Pro
Printed on 63gsm Offset Paper

Printed by The Times Press (Pvt.) Ltd., Karachi

This work is dedicated to
the Legal Fraternity of Pakistan
who continue to struggle for the
Rule of Law, Supremacy of the Constitution, and
Independence of the Judiciary

Contents

Table of Cases xxi
Preface xlix

Part I
INTRODUCTION

1. **Definition and Scope of Constitutional Law** 2
   - Definition 2
   - Constitution and Constitutional Law 2
   - Development of Public Law: Constitutional and Administrative Law 3
   - Classification of Constitutions 3
2. **State and the Citizen** 6
   - Meaning of State 6
   - Citizenship 7
     - Britain 7
     - Pakistan 8
     - India 9
   - Citizenship of India after Commencement of the Constitution 12
     - The Citizenship Act 1955 12
     - Termination of Citizenship of India 14
     - United States of America 16
   - Rights of the Citizen 17
     - Civil Rights under the British Constitution 17
     - Human Rights in International Law 17

Part II
BASIC CONSTITUTIONAL CONCEPTS

3. **Constitutional Conventions** 24
   - Introduction 24
   - Development of Constitutional Convention 24
   - Constitutional Conventions in India 28
   - Constitutional Conventions in Pakistan 29
4. **The Rule of Law** 32
   - Introduction 32
   - History of the Rule of Law 32
   - Dicey's Exposition of the Rule of Law 32
   - Dicey's Three Parts of the Rule of Law 33
   - English Cases 35
     - M v. Home Office 35

X Ltd v. Morgan-Grampian 35
Bennett v. Horseferry Road Magistrates' Court 36
A v. Secretary Home 37
R v. Secretary Home 37
Modern Concept of The Rule of Law 37
The Rule of Law in USA 38
The Rule of Law in India 38
The Rule of Law in Pakistan 39

5. Due Process of Law **43**
Introduction 43
History of Due Process in American Constitutions 43
The Distinction Between Procedural and Substantive Due Process 45
Definitions 45
Substantive Due Process 46
Substantive Due Process of the 14th Amendment: Judicial Definition of the Boundaries of State Authority to Regulate Economic Activity 46
The Development of Substantive Due Process 47
Substantive Due Process and Freedom to Contract 48
The Controversy over Substantive Due Process 48
Procedural Due Process 49
Due Process in India 52
Due Process in Pakistan 53
Old American Case 55
Munn v. Illinois 94 U.S.113 (1876)
Mr Chief Justice Waite delivered the opinion of the Court: 55
English Cases on 'Due Process of Law' 58

6. Equality before Law and Equal Protection of Laws **62**
Equality Before Law Under English Law 63
Equality Under French Law 64
Equal Protection of Laws Under American Law 64
Introduction 64
'Equal Protection Component' of the 5th Amendment 65
The Rational Basis Test 65
Introduction
Formulation of Rational Basis Test 65
Underlying Issues 66
Classification 67
What is the Appropriate Level of Scrutiny? 68
Does the Government Action Meet the Level of Scrutiny? 69
Reasonable, Invidious and Suspect Classification 70
The Suspect Classification Doctrine 72
Racial Discrimination 73
The Little Rock Crisis 76
Desegregation Cases 77
The Affirmative Action Controversy 79
Gender-Based Discrimination 81
Equality Right in Pakistan and India 86
Legislative Classification 86
Legislation Affecting Individuals 88
Ex Facie And Not *Ex Facie* Discriminatory Laws 90

Special Mode of Trial 92
Discrimination Amongst Pensioners 95
Inequality on Ground of Tax Exemption 96
Inequality on Basis of Sex 97
Special Provision For Protection Of Women And Children 99
Enactment of Progressive Application 100
New Test of Reasonableness of Classification 101
Unreasonableness Of Subordinate Legislation 102
Absence of Show Cause Notice 102
Places reserved for public entertainment and public resort 102
Government contracts 102
Concept of Equality (*Musawat*) In Islam 103

Part III
CONSTITUTIONAL STRUCTURES

7. Parliamentary Form of Government **114**
Parliamentary Supremacy (Sovereignty) 114
(i) The Source and Scope of Parliamentary Supremacy 115
(ii) Parliamentary Supremacy and Political Reality 116
(iii) Can Parliament bind its Successors? 118
The House of Commons and The House of Lords 119
Parliamentary Democracy In Germany 120
Election and Removal of other Federal Officeholders 121
Parliamentary Government in Japan 122
Parliamentary System in India 122
Parliamentary System in Pakistan 123
Constitution of 1956 124

8. Federalism **129**
Introduction 129
Development of Federalism 130
10th Amendment to The US Constitution and Federalism 133
Federalism in Pakistan 133
Federalism in India 136
Federalism under the Canadian Constitution 138
Federalism under the US Constitution 139
Federation and Judicial Power 142
Special Functions of the Judiciary in a Federation 142
(a) USA 143
(b) Australia 145
(c) Canada 146
(d) Germany 146
(e) Switzerland 146
(f) India 147
(g) Pakistan 148

9. Separation of Powers **152**
Introduction 152
Constitutional Background and US Constitution 154

Separation of powers in Pakistan 157
Separation of powers in India 160
Some Leading Cases on Separation of Powers 162

10. Presidential Form of Government **169**
INTRODUCTION 169
Structural aspects of the Presidency 169
The Electoral College 170
Presidential Succession and Disability 171
Removal of the President 171
The Veto Power 173
Under Article 1, Section 7: 173
The Power to Grant Pardons 174
Appointment and Removal of Officers 175
Presidential Immunity 176
Foreign Policy and International Relations 176
War Powers 178
Presidential Power and the War on Terrorism 181
Detentions 181
Conclusion 184
Presidential System in Pakistan 184

Part IV
JUDICIARY AS GUARDIAN OF CONSTITUTION

11. Independence of Judiciary **190**
INTRODUCTION 190
THE SEPARATION OF JUDICIAL POWER 190
COMPARATIVE ANALYSIS OF JUDICIAL INDEPENDENCE 192
INDEPENDENCE OF JUDICIARY IN USA 195
THE APPOINTMENT PROCESS 195
TENURE AND REMOVAL 196
INDEPENDENCE OF JUDICIARY IN THE UNITED KINGDOM 197
(i) *Tenure of judicial office* 197
(ii) *Procedure for removal* 197
(iii) *Judicial impartiality* 198
(iv) *Judicial Immunity* 198
CONSTITUTIONAL REFORMS IN THE UNITED KINGDOM 198
INTRODUCTION 198
OVERVIEW 198
INDEPENDENCE OF JUDICIARY IN INDIA 202
Introduction 202
APPOINTMENT PROCESS IN INDIA 202
TENURE AND REMOVAL 203
Conclusion 204
INDEPENDENCE OF JUDICIARY IN PAKISTAN 205
Introduction 205
PROCESS OF APPOINTMENT OF JUDGES 206
TENURE OF JUDGES AND THEIR REMOVAL 208
CONCLUSION 208

12. Judicial Power and the Doctrine of Judicial Review 212
Introduction 212
The American Contribution for Judicial Review 212
Early Establishment of Judcial Review 213
Marbury v. Madison: The Authority for Judicial Review of Congressional and Presidential Actions. 214
Facts 214
Findings 214
Issue 1: *Does Marbury Have a Right to the Commission?* 215
Issue 2: *Do the Laws Afford Marbury a Remedy?* 215
Issue 3: *Can the Supreme Court Issue this Remedy? Is Mandamus an Appropriate Remedy?* 216
Does the Law Authorize Mandamus on Original Jurisdiction? 216
Does Mandamus on Original Jurisdiction Violate Article III? 217
Can the Supreme Court Declare Laws Unconstitutional? 217
Reaction to *Marbury v. Madison* 218
Judicial Activism and Restraint: Differing Exercise of Judicial Review 219
Limiting Doctrines 220
(i) The Doctrine of Strict Necessity 220
(ii) The Doctrine of Saving Construction 221
(iii) The Presumption of Constitutionality 221
(iv) The Narrowness Doctrine 222
(v) Avoiding the Creation of New Principles 222
(vi) Stare Decisis 222
(vii) The Severability Doctrine 223
(viii) Unconstitutional as Applied 223
Principles of Judicial Restraint 224
The Political Question Doctrine. 224
(i) Definition 224
(ii) Why Is the Political Question Doctrine Confusing? 224
(iii) The Baker Criteria 225
(iv) Justifications for the Political Question Doctrine 226
(v) Justiciability of *Bush v. Gore* 227
(vi) Issues to Consider concerning *Bush v. Gore* 229
Racial Discrimination in Voting Rights. 229
Doctrine of Political Question in Pakistan 230
Judicial Review in the United Kingdom, Pakistan, India and other countries 230
(i) Purposive approach 231
(ii) Progressive approach 233
(iii) Sociological construction 233
(iv) Change in approach by Commonwealth Courts 234
(v) Approach of Pakistan Supreme Court 234
(vi) Approach of Indian Supreme Court 237
Judicial Activism in India and Pakistan 239

13. Theories of Constitutional Interpretation 244
Judicial Interpretation of the Constitution 244
The Doctrine of 'Implied Powers' 244
Jefferson countered Hamilton's views with the following statement: 245
McCulloch v. Maryland and The Scope of Congressional Powers 246
Factual Background of *McCulloch* 246
Congress's Authority to Create the Bank of the United States 247
The Constitutionality of Maryland's Tax 248

Comments 249
Problems relating to Constitutional Interpretation 250
Doctrine of Originalism and Non-originalism 251
Other theories of Constitutional interpretation 251
Doctrine of Original intent 252
The Doctrine of Strict Necessity 253
The Doctrine of Saving Construction 253
The Presumption of Constitutionality 254
Doctrine of Original Package 254
The Rise and Fall of the Doctrine of Original Package 255
Doctrine of Pith and Substance and Incidental Trespass 255
Doctrine of Occupied Field 257

14. Precedents **259**
Doctrine of Precedents in USA 262
Doctrine of Precedent in India 263
Doctrine of Precedents in Pakistan 264

Part V
FUNDAMENTAL HUMAN RIGHTS

15. Right to Life and Liberty **270**
Deprivations of 'Life' 270
Deprivations of 'Liberty' 270
Deportation and Exclusion Proceedings 272
Liberty Interests for Prisoners 273
The Freedom of a Person in the UK 277
A. Personal Freedom 277
No Constitutional Guarantees 277
Trial by Jury 277
International Aspect 277
Justification for Imprisonment 278
Arrest with Warrant 278
Arrest without Warrant 278
Questioning of Suspected Persons 279
General Warrant Cases 279
Search Warrants 280
Civil Detention 281
Protection of Life and Personal Liberty in India 281
Article 21 of the Indian Constitution 281
Introduction 281
Right to education a fundamental right 282
Prior to *Maneka Gandhi* Decision 282
Right to Travel Abroad 283
Maneka Gandhi Case – A New Dimension 284
Natural Justice 285
Right to Liberty 293
Right against solitary confinement 294
Right to speedy trial 294
Compensation for violation of Article 21 299

Safeguards against Arbitrary Arrest and Detention 299
(Article 22) 299
Introduction 299
Preventive Detention 300
Rights of arrested persons under ordinary laws: 300
Preventive Detention Laws 302
Right to life and liberty under Pakistan's Constitution 310
Right to life 310
Arrest and detention under Pakistan's Constitution 311
Nature of provisions of Article 10 312
Rights of arrested persons 313
Arrest under a warrant 313
Right to counsel 314
Appraisal of procedure adopted by Trial Court 314
Trial in absentia 314
Preventive detention 314
Justification for detention 315
Basic Principles governing preventive detention 316
Review Boards 317
Grounds of detention and representation 317
Objective or subjective satisfaction of detaining authority 317
Vague grounds 319
Maximum period of detention 320

16. Right to Property **326**
Property as an 'Entitlement' in the USA 326
Government Benefits 327
B. Enjoyment of Property Rights in the United Kingdom 328
Public Control of Land 328
Compulsory Purchase; Powers and Procedure 328
Compensation 329
Acquisition for defence 330
General Restrictions on Use of Property and Freedom of Contract 330
Right to Property in India 331
Right to Acquire and Dispose of Property in Pakistan 333
Subject to the Constitution 333
Property rights under Pakistan's Constitution 334
Restrictions on Property Rights 334
Taxation 335
Protection of property rights 335
Act of State 335
Eminent domain 336
Exceptions 336

17. Freedom of Conscience and Religion **339**
Freedom of Religion under the US Constitution 339
Introduction 339
What Constitutes Religion for First Amendment Purposes? 340
Religion Broadly Defined 340
(i) *A Working Definition of Religion* 341
The Establishment Clause 341
Introduction 341

The wall of separation 342
(i) *Competing Interpretations of the Establishment Clause* 342
(ii) *Traditional Government Practices* 342
(iii) *The Lemon Test* 343
Religion and public education 343
Release Time Programs and Equal Access Policies 344
Government Efforts to assist Religious Schools 344
The School Prayer Controversy 347
The Evolution-Creationism Conflict 348
Discrimination against Religious Expression in the Public Educational Arena 349
Government affirmations of religious belief 350
Religious Displays on Public Property 350
The Free Exercise of Religion 351
Introduction 351
Religious belief and the right to proselytize 351
(i) *Religious Solicitation* 352
(ii) *Time, Place, and Manner Regulations* 352
Unconventional religious practices 352
(i) *The Mormon Polygamy Case* 353
(ii) *The Warren Court Establishes the Compelling Interest Test* 353
(iii) *The Oregon Peyote Case* 353
(iv) *Is the Denial of Funding a Violation of the Free Exercise Clause?* 355
(v) *The Religious Freedom Restoration Act* 356
(v) *Is Animal Sacrifice 'Free Exercise of Religion'?* 356
Freedom of Religion in India 356
Article 25 of the Indian Constitution 356
Article 26 of the Indian Constitution 357
Sanskrit language not anti-secular 358
Freedom of Conscience and Religion under the Indian Constitution 359
Restrictions on freedom of religion 362
(1) *Religious liberty subject to public order, morality and health* 362
(2) *Regulation of economic, financial, political, and secular activities associated with religious practices – Clause (2)(a)* 363
(3) *Social Welfare and Social Reforms – Clause (2)(b)* 364
(a) *Freedom to manage religious affairs – (Article 26)* 364
Freedom from taxes for promotion of any particular religion. – Article 27 367
Prohibition of Religious Instruction in State-aided Institution. – Article 28 367
Freedom of Religion in Pakistan 368
Subject to public order and morality 368
Subject to law 369
XIV. *Safeguards against taxation for purposes of any particular religion* 370
Levy must be tax 370
Distinction between tax and fee 370
XV. *Safeguards as to educational institutions in respect of religion etc.* 371
Leading cases: 371
Everson v. Board of Education 372
Justice Hugo Black delivered the opinion of the US Supreme Court 372
Abington School District v. Schempp 374

18. Right to Privacy Including Searches and Seizures **381**
Introduction 381
US Constitution and Right of Privacy 381

Philosophical Foundations of the Right of Privacy 381
Constitutional foundations of the right of privacy 382
The abortion controversy: *Roe v. Wade* 383
The Debate over *Roe v. Wade* 385
Decisions after *Roe v. Wade* 386
The *Webster* Decision 387
Rust v. Sullivan: Restricting Information about Abortion 387
The Court Reaffirms *Roe v. Wade* 387
Undue Burden test on the Right to Abortion? 389
No Requirement for Government Funding for Abortions 389
Latest Verdict of US Supreme Court 390
Searches and Seizures 391
Reasonable Expectations of Privacy 391
Probable Cause 393
The Warrant Requirement 393
Confidential and Anonymous Informants 394
Execution of Search Warrants 394
Warrantless Searches 395
Police Powers of Search and Entry in the UK 396
Post Interception and Telephone Tapping 397
Right of Privacy in Pakistan and India 397

19. Self-Incrimination **402**
Historical background and rationale 402
The development of the privilege against self-incrimination in the UK 402
Privilege against Self Incrimination in the USA 403
The 5th Amendment 403
The purposes of the privilege against Self-Incrimination 405
Exchanging immunity from criminal prosecution for the privilege against Self-Incrimination 406
Leading Cases: 406
Brown v. Walker 406
Justice Brown...delivered the opinion of the court 407
Justice Field dissenting 408
Later Developments in the USA 408
Miranda v. Arizona and Later Rulings 409
Decision 410
Concerns about *Miranda's* Future 411
The Reaffirmation of *Miranda* 411
Miranda Warnings 411
Conclusion: *Miranda* has survived 412
Self-Incrimination in India 412
(i) *Person accused of an offence* 413
(ii) *Protection Against compulsion to be a Witness* 414
To be a Witness – Furnishing Evidence 414
Section 27 of Evidence Act 1872 and Article 20(3) 415
(iii) *Compulsion to give Evidence 'against himself'* 415
Tape-recording of Statements made by the accused 416
Scope of the Protection contained in Article 20(3) 416
Protection Against Self-Incrimination in Pakistan 416
Section 340(2) Cr.P.C. is inconsistent with Article 13(b) or not 417
Person accused of an offence 418
Compulsion to be a witness 418

20. Double Jeopardy 421
SUCCESSIVE STATE AND FEDERAL PROSECUTIONS 421
MISTRIALS 422
CONFINEMENT OF SEXUAL PREDATORS IN MENTAL INSTITUTIONS 422
CIVIL FORFEITURES, DOUBLE JEOPARDY, AND EXCESSIVE FINES 423
DOUBLE JEOPARDY IN INDIA 423
DOUBLE JEOPARDY AND ISSUE ESTOPPELS 426
DOUBLE JEOPARDY IN PAKISTAN 427

Part VI
POLITICAL RIGHTS AND CIVIL LIBERTIES

21. Freedom of Speech and Press 434
INTERPRETIVE FOUNDATIONS OF EXPRESSIVE FREEDOM 434
(i) *Incorporation of the Freedoms of Speech and Press* 434
(ii) *Preferred Freedoms?* 435
(iii) *Are the Protections of the First Amendment Absolute?* 435
RESTRICTIONS ON FREEDOM OF SPEECH 436
(i) *The clear and present danger doctrine* 436
(ii) *The Bad Tendency Test* 437
(iii) *Clear and Probable Danger* 439
(iv) *Fighting words* 440
(v) *Hate Speech* 440
(vi) *Profanity* 441
SYMBOLIC SPEECH AND EXPRESSIVE CONDUCT 442
(i) *The Flag Salute Controversy* 442
(ii) *Symbolic Speech in the Vietnam Era* 442
(iii) *Flag Burning* 443
PRIOR RESTRAINT OR CENSORSHIP 444
(i) *The Court Adopts the Rule against Prior Restraint* 444
(ii) *The Pentagon Papers Case* 445
(iii) *May the Government Prevent Publication of How to Make a Hydrogen Bomb?* 445
(iv) *Does the Prior Restraint Doctrine Apply to Student Newspapers?* 445
THE OBSCENITY PROBLEM 446
(i) *The Prurient Interest Test* 446
(ii) *The Miller Test* 447
(iii) *Pornography on the Internet* 447
(iv) *Child Pornography* 448
(v) *Nude Dancing* 448
(vi) *Speech materially assisting a Foreign Terrorist Organization* 449
ELECTRONIC MEDIA AND THE FIRST AMENDMENT 449
(i) *Restrictions of 'Indecent' Programming on Television and Radio* 450
(ii) *Indecent Programming on Cable Television* 450
(iii) *Editorializing by Public Television and Radio Stations* 451
COMMERCIAL SPEECH 451
(i) *A Test for Judging Regulations of Commercial Speech* 451
(ii) *Conflicting Applications of the Test* 452
(iii) *Commercial advertising of Alcoholic Beverages* 452
(iv) *Restrictions on Advertising of Tobacco Products* 452
(v) *Attorney Advertising and Solicitation* 453

Freedom of Speech and Press in the United Kingdom 454
Freedom of Speech and Press in India 455
New dimension to freedom of speech and expression – Government has no monopoly on electronic media 457
Commercial Advertisement – Part of freedom of speech and expression 458
Telephone Tapping – Invasion on right to privacy 459
Calling for and holding '*Bandh*' illegal and unconstitutional being violative of fundamental Rights of Citizens 460
Decency or morality 463
Reasonableness of restrictions 463
Government cannot impose prior-restraint on publication of defamatory material against its officials- Auto Shankar case 464
Freedom of Speech and Press in Pakistan 471
Freedom of Press 471
Reasonableness of restrictions 472
(a) *Security of State* 472
(b) *Friendly relations with Foreign States* 473
(c) *The Glory of Islam* 473
(d) *Decency or Morality* 473
(e) *Public Order* 474
Contempt of Court 475
(f) *Defamation* 479
(g) *Incitement to an offence* 479
Leading Cases: 479
Schenck v. United States 479
New York Times Company v. United States (The Pentagon Papers Case) 481
Per Curiam. 481
Roth v. United States 484

22. Freedom of Association **490**
Introduction: 490
Protection as a fundamental right 490
Issues Concerning Freedom of Association 490
Laws Prohibiting or Punishing Membership 490
Public Employment 491
Bar Membership 492
Laws Requiring Disclosure of Membership 492
Campaign Finance Disclosure 493
Laws Prohibiting Discrimination 493
Freedom of Association Generally Does Not Protect Discrimination 493
Freedom of Association in United Kingdom 496
Right to Form 'Union' in United Kingdom 496
Freedom to Form Associations or Unions in India 496
Scope of the right to form associations or unions 497
Right To Be a Member Voluntarily 497
Right of the State to Nominate Members to Societies 497
Right subjected to Reasonable Restrictions [Article 19(4)] 498
Right Not to be a Member of an Association 498
No right to continue in Government Service 499
No Prior Restraint on the Right to Form Association 499
No Right to Recognition by State 499
No Right to Achieve the Objects of Association 500

Freedom of Association in Pakistan 500
Freedom of Association 501
Right to form Unions 502
Right under Article 17 is not absolute 502
Compulsory registration of and rendition of accounts by political parties 503
Denial of election symbols to political parties 503
Acts completed and continuing 504

23. Freedom of Assembly **507**
Freedom of Assembly in India and Pakistan 509
In the interest of 'public order' 510
Right to take out processions 512

24. Freedom of Movement **514**
Introductory 514
Externment or Internment Orders 515
Public Interest 516
Inter-Provincial Travel 517
Right to Enter, Remain and Reside anywhere in the Country 517
Right to Travel Abroad 519
'Reasonable Restrictions' their Nature and Justiciability 520
Power to Impose Restrictions is Legislative 520
'Reasonableness' – Its Connotation and Test 520

25. Right to Counsel **524**
Introductory 524
The *Gideon* Decision 524
When can the right to counsel invoked. 525
Effectiveness of Appointed Counsel 526
Self-Representation 527
Right to Counsel in India 527
Right to be represented by a Lawyer before Review Board 528
Right to Counsel in Pakistan 529
Right of a government servant to counsel in Inquiry Proceedings 529

Part VII
EVOLVING CONSTITUTIONAL CONCEPTS

26. Doctrine of Necessity **534**
Introductory 534
doctrine of necessity and military take overs; the case of Pakistan 537
Doctrine of Necessity and The Indian Supreme Court 546
Doctrine of Civil Necessity in England 546
Doctrine of Civil Necessity in The United States 548
Attorney General of Cyprus v. Mustafa Ibrahim 549
Doctrine of Necessity in Canada 550
Conclusions 550

27. Theory of Basic Structure of Constitution **553**
Introduction 553
Power of Amendment of Constitution 553

Concept of Basic Structure or framework of the Constitution in India 556
99th Constitutional Amendment Declared 558
Basic Structure Theory in Pakistan 560
Basic Structure Theory in Bangladesh 565
Basic Structure Theory in Malaysia 566
Criticism of the Concept of Basic Structure of Constitution 566
Conclusions 567

Index 571

Table of Cases

A

A.A. Mulla v. State of Maharashtra, AIR 1997 SC 1441
A.D.M. Jabalpur v. Shivakant Shukla, AIR 1976 S.C. 1207
A.G. for Ontario v. A.G. for Canada, (1912) A.C. 571 (581) P.C.
A.K. Ghose v. E.X. Joseph, AIR 1963 S.C. 812
A.K. Gopalan v. State of Madras, AIR 1950 S.C. 27
A.K. Roy v. Union of India, AIR 1982 S.C. 710
A.L. Kolra v. P&E. Corp. of India Ltd., AIR 1984 S.C. 1361
A.P. v. Kokkilagada Meerayya, AIR 1970 S.C. 771
A.S. Narayan v. State of Andhra Pradesh, AIR 1006 S.C. 1765
Abdul Aziz v. Delhi Administration, AIR 1981 SC 1389
Abdul Aziz v. Province of West Pakistan, PLD 1958 SC 499
Abdul Baqi Baloch v. Government of Pakistan, PLD 1968 S.C. 313
Abdul Gaffar v. State of West Bengal, AIR 1975 SC 1496
Abdul Ghani v. Pakistan, PLD 1958 Lahore 584
Abdul Hakim v. State of Bihar, AIR 1961 S.C. 448
Abdul Hameed Qadri v. D.M. Lahore, PLD 1957 Lahore 263
Abdul Hameed Qadri v. District Magistrate, PLD 1959 Lah 213
Abdul Hameed v. District Magistrate, PLD 1957 (WP) Lah 213
Abdul Latif v. B.K. Jha, AIR 1987 S.C. 725
Abdul Rehman Antuley v. R.S. Nayak, AIR 1992 SC 1630
Abdul Sattar Ibrahim Manik v. Union of India, AIR 1991 SC 2261
Abdul Sattar v. State of Gujrat, AIR 1965 SC 810
Abdus Samad v. State of West Bengal, AIR 1973 SC 505
Abington School District v. Schempp, 374, U.S. 203 (1963)
Abrams v. United States, 250 U.S. 616 (1919)
Abrar Hassan v. Government of Pakistan, PLD 1976 S.C. 315
Abul Ala Maududi, PLD 1964 S.C. 673 at p. 700
Abul A'la Maudoodi v. Government of West Pakistan, PLD 1964 S.C. 673.
Abul A'la Maudoodi v. The State Bank of Pakistan, PLD 1969 Lahore 908
Acchan Rizvi v. State of U.P., (1994) 6 SCC 751
Acharya Jagdishwaranand Avadhuta v. Commissioner of Police, Calcutta, (1984) 4 SCC 522
Addington v. Texas, 441 U.S. 418 (1979)
Advocates-on-Record Association v. Union of India, AIR 1994 S.C. 268
Adeladie Co. v. Commonwealth, (1943) 67 CLC 116
Afroyim v. Rusk, 387 U.S. 253 (1967)
Aftab Shahban Mirani v. President of Pakistan, 1998 SCMR 1863
Agostini v. Felton, 521 U.S. 203 (1997)
Aguilar v. Felton, 473 U.S. 402 (1985)
Aguilar v. Texas, 375 U.S. 812 (1963)
Ahmad Tariq Rahim v. Federation of Pakistan, PLD 1992 S.C. 646
Air India Statutory Corpn. V. United Labour Union, AIR 1997 S.C. 645
Air Canada v. Secretary of State for Trade, (1983) AC. 394 (HL)

Airlines of N.S.W. v. N.S.W., (1964–65) 113 C.L.R. 54 (112, 115, 116–17) F.C.
Ajay Hasia v. Khalid Mujib, AIR 1981 S.C. 487
Akhtar Hamid Ghori v. Saima Estate Developer, 1989 CLC 2173
Akron v. Akron Center for Reproductive Health, 462 U.S. 416 (1983)
Alabama v. White, 496 U.S. 325 (1990)
Alamdar Hussain Shah v. Abdul Basir Qureshi, PLD 1978 S.C. 121
Alexander v. Holmes County, 396 U.S. 19 (1969)
Al-jehad Trust v. Federation of Pakistan, 1999 SCMR 1379
Al-Jehad Trust v. Federation of Pakistan, PLD 1996 S.C. 324
All India Bank Employees Association v. National Industries Tribunal, AIR 1962 SC 171
All India Imam Organization v. Union of India, AIR 1993 SC 2086
All India Sainik Schools Employees Association v. Sainik Schools Society, AIR 1989 SC 88 at 92
Allah Ditta v. Fetah Ali Khan, PLD 1970 Lah. 168
Allegheny Pittsburgh Coal Co. v. County Commission, 488 U.S. 336 (1989)
Allgeyer v. Louisiana, 165 U.S. 578 (1897)
Allied Stores v. Bowers, 358 U.S. 522 (1959)
Ambard v. Attorney-General for Trinidad and Tobago, (1946) AC 335
Ameerunnisa Begum v. Mehboob Begum, AIR 1953 SC 91
Amendment of the Constitution of Canada, re (1982) 125 DLR (3d) 1,84
American Communications v. Douds, 339 US 382 (1950)
American Manufacturers Mutual Insurance Company v. Sullivan, 526 U.S. 40 (1999)
Ames v. Kansas, 111 U.S. 449 (1884)
Amir Khatoon v. Faiz Ahmad, PLD 1991 S.C. 787
Amin v. State of U.P., AIR 1958 All 293
Amrit Singh v. State of Punjab, AIR 2007 S.C. 132, (2006) 12 SCC 79
Amrut Sonia Kumbi v. State of Bombay, AIR 1960 Bom 488
Anastaplo, in re, 366 U.S. 82 (1961)
Anderson v. Celebrezze, 460 US 780, (1983)
Anderson v. Gorrie, (1895) 1 Q.B. 668
Andre Paul Terence v. Att. Gen. Of Trinidad, AIR 1936 P.C. 141
Anisminic Ltd. v. Foreign Compensation Commission, (1969) 2 AC 147
Anti-Inflation Act, re, (1976) 68 D.L.R. (3d) 452
Anwar v. Crown, PLD 1955 F.C. 185
Aptheker v. Secretary of State, 378 U.S. 500 (1964)
Arbab Khan v. The State, 2010 SCMR 755
Ardeshir Cowasji v. Multiline Associates, Karachi, PLD 1993 Karachi 237
Argersinger v. Hamlin, 407 U.S. 25 (1972)
Argil v. Argyll, (1967) Ch 302
Arkansas v. Sanders, 442 U.S. 573 (1979)
Arnit Das v. State of Bihar, (2000) 5 SCC 488
Arshad Ali Khan (Mrs) v. Government of the Punjab, 1994 SCMR 1532
Arshad Ali Khan v. Govt. of the Punjab, 1994 SCMR 1532
Arshad Mahmood v. Government of Punjab, PLD 2005, S.C. 193.
Arshad Mahmood v. Government of Punjab, 2006 PSC 324
Article 143, Constitution of India, in re, AIR 1965 S.C. 745
Asad All v. Federation of Pakistan, PLD 1998 S.C. 161 nt 344
Ashcroft v. Free Speech Coalition Supra Note 1, p. 448
Ashfaque Ahmad Sheikh v. The State, PLD 1972 S.C. 39
Ashok Kumar v. Delhi Administration, AIR 192 SC 1143
Ashwander v. Tennessee Valley Authority, 297 U.S. 288 (1936)
Aslam Ali Shah v. Collector, 1983 P.L.C. (C.S.) 498

Asma Jillani v. Government of the Punjab, PLD 1972 S.C. 139
Assam Railway and Trading Co. Ltd. v. Commissioner of Inland Revenue, (1935) A.C. 445
Assit Collector v. Malwani, AIR 1970 SC 962
Athiest Society of India v. Government of A.P., AIR 1992 AP 310
Atiabari Tea Co. v. State of Assam, AIR. 1961 S.C. 232
Attorney General for Australia v. The Queen & the Boilermaker's Society of Australia, (1957) AC 288
Attorney General v. Colonial Sugar Refining Co. Ltd., (1913) 17 CR 644
Attorney General for Canada v. Attorney General of Ontario, (1937), A.C. 326.
Attorney General for Commonwealth of Australia v. Colonial Sugar Refining, Co Ltd., (1914) A.C. 237, 253
Attorney General of Alberta v. Attorney General for Canada, (1943) A.C. 356
Attorney General of Canada v. Attorney General of Ontario, (1937) A.C. 326
Attorney General of Cyprus v. Mustafa Ibrahim, 1994 CLR 195
Attorney General v. De Keyser's Royal Hotel Ltd., 1920 A.C. 508
Attorney General v. Jonathan Cape Ltd., (1976) QB 752
Attorney-General of Saskatchewan v. The Attorney General of Canada, AIR 1949 P.C. 190
Austin v. United States, 509 U.S. 602 (1993)
Automobile Transport v. State of Rajasthan, AIR 1962 S.C. 140
Azeez Basha v. Union of India, AIR 1968 SC 662

B

Babar Hussain Shah v. Mujeeb Ahmad Khan, 2012 SCMR 1235
Babu Lal Parate v. State of Maharashtra, AIR 1991 SC 884
Babu Sing v. State of U.P., AIR 1978 SC 527
Babulal Parate v. State of Madras, AIR 1961 SC 884
Babulal v. State of West Bengal, AIR 1973 SC 606
Bachan Singh v. State of Punjab, AIR 1980 S.C. 898
Baij Nath v. State of Bhopal, AIR 1957 SC 494
Baird v. State Bar of Arizona, 401 U.S. 1 (1971)
Bajoe Emmanual v. State of Kerala, (1984)1 SCC 615
Baker v. Carr, 369 U.S. 186 (1962)
Balchand Chorasia v. Union of India, AIR 1978 SC 297
Balkishan v. State of Maharashtra, AIR 1981 SC 379
Balkrishna v. Shree D.M. Sansthan, AIR 1959 SC 798
Ball v. U.S., 163 U.S. 82 (1896)
Bankatlal v. State of Rajasthan, AIR 1975 SC 522
Baradakant v. Registrar, Orissa, AIR 1974 SC 710
Barbier v. Connolly, 113 U.S. 27 (1885)
Barenblatt v. United States, 360 U.S. 109 (1959)
Barium Chemicals v. Company Law Bd., AIR 1967 S.C. 295
Barnes v. Glen Theatre, Inc., 501 U.S. 560 (1991)
Basudev v. Rex, AIR 1949 All 513 (FB)
Bates v. State Bar of Arizona, 433 U.S. 350 (1977)
Baxter v. Commissioner of Taxation, (1907) 4 C.L.R. 1087 (1110)
Bazal Ahmed Ayubi v. The West Pakistan Province, PLD 1957 (W.P.) Lah 388
Begum Shamim Afridi v. Province of the Punjab, PLD 1973 Lahore 120
Begum Zeb-un-Nissa Hamidullah v. Pakistan, PLD 1958 SC 35
Belfast Corporation v. O.D. Cars Ltd., (1960) A.C. 490
Benazir Bhutto v. Farooq Ahmad Khan Leghari, PLD 1998 S.C. 388
Benazir Bhutto v. Federation of Pakistan, PLD 1988 SC 416
Benazir Bhutto v. Federation of Pakistan, PLD 1989 S.C. 66

Benazir Bhutto v. Federation, PLD 1988 SC 416 at p. 518
Benazir Bhutto v. President of Pakistan, PLD 1998 S.C. 388
Benazir Bhutto v. The Federation of Pakistan, PLD 1988 S.C. 416
Bengal Immunity Co. v. State of Bihar, AIR. 1955 S.C. 661
Bengal Iron Corporation v. Commercial Tax Officer, AIR 1993 SC 2414
Bennet Colman and Co. v. Union of India, AIR 1973 SC 106
Bennett v. Horseferry Road Magistrates' Court and another, (1993) 3 All E.R. 138
Benton v. Maryland, 395 U.S. 784 (1969)
Betty v. Gillabanks, (1882) 9 Q. B.D. 308
Bhanwaroo Khan v. Union of India, 2002 (3) SCC 464
Bharat Petroleum Management State Pensioners v. B.P.C. Ltd., (1988) 3 SCC 32
Bhim Singh v. State of J.K, AIR 1986 S.C. 494, (1985) 4 SCC 677
Bijayalakshmi Tripathy v. Managing Committee of Working Women Hostel, AIR 1992 Ori 242
Bijoe Emmanual v. State of Kerala, AIR 1987 S.C. 748
Bijoe Emmanuel v. State of Kerala, (1986) 3 SCC 615
Billing v. Sharpe, 347 U.S. 497 (1954)
Bira Kishore Dev v. State of Orissa, AIR 1964 SC 1501
Board of Directors of Rotary International v. Rotary Club of Duarte, 481 U.S. 537 (1987)
Board of Education v. Allen, 389 U.S. 1031 (1968)
Board of Education v. Dowell, 498 U.S. 237 (1991)
Board of Education v. Mergens, 496 U.S. 226 (1990)
Board of Pardons v. Allen, 482 U.S. 369 (1987)
Bobby Art International v. Om Pal Singh Hoon, (1996) 4 SCC 1
Bognor Regis D.C. v. Champion ,(1972) 2 Q.B. 169
Bolan Medical College v. Miss Safia Hamid, 1979 SCMR 529
Boldwin v. Missouri, 281 U.S. 586 (1930)
Bombay Dyeing Co. v. State of Bombay, AIR 1958 SC 328
Bowles v. Willingham, 321 U.S. 503 (1944)
Boy Scouts of America v. Dale, 530 U.S. 640 (2000)
Boyd v. United States, 116 U.S. 616 (1886)
Bradley v. United States, 410 U.S. 605 (1973)
Bradwell v. Illnois, 83 U.S. 130 (1872)
Bragg v. Crossville Motor Services Lt, (1959) 1 All ER 613
Bramchari Sidheswar Shai v. State of W.B., (1995) 4 SCC 646
Brandenburg v. Ohio, 396 U.S. 444 (1969)
Bribery Commissioners v. Ranasinghe, (1965) AC 172
Brig. Imitiaz Ahmad v. Govt. of Pakistan, 1994 SCMR 2142, 2160
Brij Bhushan v. State of Delhi, AIR 1950 SC 129
Brinegar v. United States, 338 U.S. 160 (1949)
British Coal Corporation v. The King, (1935) A.C. 500
Brown v. Board of Education of Topeka, 347 U.S. 483 (1954)
Brown v. Maryland ,25 U.S. 419 (1827)
Brown v. Socialist Workers'74 Campaign Committee, 459 U.S. 87 (1982)
Brown v. Walker, 161 U.S. 591 (1896)
Browsher v. Synar, 478 U.S. 714 (1986)
Buchan Singh v. State of Punjab, AIR 1980 S.C. 898
Buckley v. Valeo, 424 U.S. 1 (1976)
Burke v. U.S., 437 U.S. 1 (1978)
Burmah Oil Company, Ltd. v. Lord Advocate, (1965) A.C. 75
Burnett v. Coronado Oil Company, 285 U.S. 393 (1932)
Bush v. Gore, 531 U.S. 98 (2000)

C

C. Sampath Kumar v. E.O. Enforcement Directorate, Madras, AIR 1998 SC 16
C.B.I. v. Anupam J. Kulkarni, (1992) 3 SCC 141
C.N. Rudramurthy v. K. Barkatullah Khan, (1998) 8 SCC 275
Calder v. Bull, 3 U.S. 386 (1798)
Califano v. Aznavorian, 439 US 170 (1978)
Califano v. Goldfarb, 430 U.S. 199 (1977)
Cantwell v. Connecticut, 310 U.S. 296 (1940)
Carltona Ltd. v. Commissioners of Works, (1943) All. E.R. 560
Carroll v. United States, 267 U.S. 132 (1925)
Carter v. Carter Coal Co., 298 U.S. 238 (1936)
Central Bank of India v. Ram Narayan, AIR 1955 SC 36
Central Hudson Gas and Electric Corporation v. Public Service Commission of New York, 447 U.S. 557 (1980)
Central Inland Water Transport Corp. v. Brojo Nath Ganguli, (1986) 3 SCC 156
Champlin Refining Company v. Corporation Commission of Oklahoma, 286 U.S. 210 (1932)
Chandra Raja Kumari v. Police Commissioner Hyderabad, AIR 1998 AP 302
Chaplinsky v. New Hampshire, 315 U.S. 568 (1942)
Charanjit Lal v. Union of India, AIR 1951 SC 41
Charanlal v. Union of India, AIR 1990 S.C. 1480
Charles Sobhraj v. Superintendent Jail, Tihar, AIR 1978 S.C. 1514, (1978) 4 SCC 104
Chemeli Singh v. State of U.P., (1996) 2 SCC 549, AIR 1996 S.C. 1051
Chenna Jagadeeswar v. State of AP, 1988 Cr. LJ 549
Chew v. Colding, 344 U.S. 590 (1953)
Chic Fashions (East Wales) Ltd. v. Jones, (1968) 2 QB 299, (1968) 1 All ER 229
Chicago, Milwaukee and St. Paul R. Co. v. Minnesota, 134 U.S. 418 (1890)
Chief Justice of Pakistan Iftikhar Muhammad Chaudhry v. President of Pakistan, PLJ 2007 S.C. 814, PLD 2010 S.C. 61
Chief Settlement Commr. v. Om Parkash, AIR 1969 SC 33
Chimel v. California, 395 U.S. 752 (1969)
Chinese Exclusion Case, 130 U.S. 581 (1889)
Chiranjit and Chaudhury v. India, AIR 1951 SC 41
Chisholm v. Georgia, 2 U.S. 419 (1793)
Christie v. Leachinsky, (1947) A.C. 573
Church of the Lukumi Babalu Aye v. City of Hialeah, 508 U.S. 520 (1993)
Citizen for Democracy v. State of Assam, (1995) 3 SCC 743
Citizen Insurance Co. of Canada v. Parson, (1981) 7 A.C. 96
City of Boerne v. Flores, 521 U.S. 507 (1997)
City of Cleburne, Texas v. Cleburne Living Center, Inc., 473 U.S. 432 (1985)
City of Dallas v. Stanglin, 490 U.S. 19 (1989)
Civil Rights Cases, 109 U.S. 3 (1883)
Cleburne v. Cleburne Living Center, 473 U.S. 432 (1985)
Cohen v. California, 403 U.S. 15 (1971)
Colcheser Estates (Cardiff) v. Carlton Industries, (1984) 2 All ER 601
Collector, Central Excise and Land Customs v. Aslam Ali Shah, PLD 1985 S.C. 82
Commissioner of Income Tax v. Sun Engineering Works Ltd., AIR 1993 SC 43
Commissioner Wealth Tax v. Suresh Seth, AIR 1981 SC 1106
Commissioner, Hindu Religious Endowment, v. Sri Lakshmindra Thirtha Swamiar, AIR 1954 S.C. 282
Committee for Public Education v. Nyquist, 413 U.S. 756 (1973)
Commr. Hindu Religious Endowments, Madras v. L.T. Swamiar, AIR 1956 SC 282
Commr., H.R.E. v. LT. Swamiar, AIR 1954 SC 282
Communist Party of India (M) v. Bharat Kumar and Others, AIR 1998 SC 184

Communist Party of Indiana v. Whitcomb, 414 U.S. 441 (1974),
Communist Party of the United States v. Subversive Activities, Control Board, 351 US. 115 (1956)
Communist Party of the United States v. Subversive Activities, Control Board, 367 U.S. 1 (1961)
Communist Party v. Subversive Activities Control Board, 367 U.S. 1 (1961)
Confederation of Ex-servicemen Association v. Union of India, AIR 2006 S.C. 2945, (2006) 8 SCC 399
Connecticut Board of Pardons v. Dumschat, 452 U.S. 458 (1981)
Consumer Education and Research Centre v. Union of India, AIR 1995 S.C. 922
Contempt Proceedings against Chief Secretary, Sindh, 2013 SCMR 1752
Conway v. Rimmer, (1968) 1 All ER 283
Coolidge v. New Hampshire, 403 U.S. 443 (1971)
Cooper v. Aaron, 358 U.S. 1 (1958)
Cooper v. Union of India, AIR 1970 S.C. 564
Corfield v. Coryell, 6 Fed. Cas. 546 (C.C.Pa.1823)
Costello v. United States, 365 U.S. 265 (1961) (27 years)
Council for Enviro-legal Action v. Union of India, (1996) 5 SCC 281
Counsel-man v. Hitchcock, 142 U.S. 547 (1892)
County of Allegheny v. American Civil Liberties Union, 492 U.S. 573 (1989)
Cox v. Louisiana, 379 US 536, (1965)
Craig v. Boren, 429 U.S. 190 (1976)
Crown v. Saadat Hassan Minto, PLD 1952 Lahore 384
Cruzan v. Director, Mo. Dept. of Health, 497 U.S. 261 (1990)
Curtis Moffat v. Wheeler, (1929) 2 Ch. 224
Curtiss-Wright Export Corporation v. United States, 299 U.S. 304 (1936)

D

D.A. Kelshikar v. State of Bombay, AIR 1960 Born 225
D.B.M. Patnaik v. State of A.P., AIR 1974 SC 2092
D.C. Wadhwa v. State of Bihar, AIR 1987 S.C. 579
D.K. Basu v. State of W.B., AIR 1997 SC 610
D.K. Yadav v. J.M.A. Industries, (1993) 3 SCC 258
D.O. Vyas v. Ghaziabad Development Authority, AIR 1993 All 57
Dada Amir Haider Khan, PLD 1987 SC 504
Dallas v. Stanglin, 490 U.S. 19 (1989)
Dames & Moore v. Regan, 453 U.S. 654 (1981)
Damyanti v. Union of India, AIR 1971 SC 966
Dargah Committee, Ajmer v. Hussain Ali, AIR 1961 SC 1402
Dastagir v. State of Madras, AIR 1960 SC 756
Davidson v. New Orleans, 96 U.S. 97 (1877)
Davis v, Beason, 133 U.S. 333 (1890)
Davis v. Johnson, (1979) A.C. 264
Davis v. Lisle, (1936) 2 KB 434, (1936) 2 All ER 213
DeFunis v. Odep-narci, 416 I T S 312 (1974)
Delhi Development Horticulture Employee's Union v. Delhi Administration, AIR 1992 SC 789
Delhi Judicial Service Association v. State of Gujarat, AIR 1991 SC 2176
Delhi Laws Act, in re, (1951) S.C.R. 747
Delhi Police Non-Gazetted Karmchari Sangh v. Union of India, (1987) 1 SCC 115
D'Emden v. Pedder, (1904) HCA 1, (1904) 1 CLR 91
Dennis v. United States, 341 U.S. 494 (1951)
Denver Area Educational Telecommunications Consortium v. Federal Communications Commission, 518 U.S. 727 (1996)

Deokinandan Prasad v. State of Bihar, AIR 1971 SC 1409
Department of Revenue of Montana v. Kurth Ranch, 511 U.S. 767 (1994)
Devi Saren v. State, AIR 1954 Patna 254
Dhananjoy Dad v. District Magistrate, AIR 1982 S.C. 1315
Director of Film Festivals v. Gaura Ashwin Jain, AIR 2007 S.C. 1640, (2007) 4 SCC 737
District Bar Association, Rawalpindi v. Federation of Pakistan, PLD 2015 S.C. 401
Donogue v. Stevenson, (1932) AC 562
Dosso, PLD 1958 SC 543
Douglas v. City of Jeanette, 319 U.S. 157 (1943)
Dr Bonham, (1610) 8 Co. Rep. 114, 118
Dr Ram Manohar Lohia v. State of Bihar, AIR 1966 SC 740
Dr Suresh Chandra v. Panbit Goala, AIR 1958 Cal. 176
Dred Scott v. Sandford, 60 U.S. 393 (1857)
Drummond v. Drummond, LR 2 Equity cases 335
DTC v. DTC Mazdoor Union, AIR 1991 SC 101
Duncan v. Cammell, Laird & Co. Ltd., (1942) AC 624
Duncan v. Jones, (1936) 1 K.B. 218
Duncan v. Kahanamoku, 327 U.S. 304 (1946)
Dushyani Somal v. Sushma Samal, AIR 1981 SC 1027
Dutton v. Bognor Regis UDC (1972) 1 All ER 462
Dwarkadas Shrinivas v. Shohlapur Spinning and Weaving Mills, AIR 1954 SC 119

E

E.P. Royappa v. State of T.N., AIR 1974 S.C. 555
Eakin v. Raub, 12 Serg & Rauls 330 (Pa 1825)
East and West Steamship Co v. Pakistan, PLD 1958 S.C. 41
Eastman Photographic Materials Co. Ltd. v. Comptroller-General of Patents, Designs and Trademarks, (1898) A.C. 571
Ebrahim Wazir v. State of Bombay, AIR 1954 S.C. 229
Edwards v. Aguillard, 482 U.S. 578 (1987)
Edwards v. California, 314 US 160 (1941)
Edwards v. United States, 358 U.S. 847 (1958)
Eisenstadt v. Baird, 405 U.S. 438 (1972)
Elahi Cotton Mills v. Federation, PLD 1997 SC 582
Elfbrandt v. Russell, 384 U.S. 11 (1966)
Elias v. Pasmore, (1934) 2 K.B. 164
Ellen Street Estates v. Minister of Health, (1934) 1 KB 590
Emperor v. Chhotalal Amarchand, AIR 1937 Bom 1
Employees of Pakistan Law Commission v. Ministry of Works, 1994 SCMR 1548
Employment Division v. Smith, 494 U.S. 872 (1990)
Engel v. Vitale, 370 U.S. 421 (1962)
Entick v. Carrington, (1765) 19 St. Tr. 1030: K. & L. 174
Epperson v. Arkansas, 393 U.S. 97 (1968)
Erusian Equipment & Chemical Ltd. v. State of West Bengal, AIR 1975 SC 266
Everson v. Board of Education, 330 U.S. 1 (1947)
Executive Privilege: United States v. Nixon, 418 U.S. 683 (1974)
Express Newspaper Pvt Ltd. v. Union of India, (1986)1 SCC 133
Express Newspapers v. Union of India, AIR 1958 SC 578

F

F.B. Ali v. The State, P.L.D. 1975 S.C. 506
F.R.J. Swami v. State of Tamil Nadu, AIR 1972 SC 1585
FPC v. Hope Natural Gas Company, 320 U.S. 591 (1944)
Fairfax v. Commr. of Taxation, (1965) 114 C.L.R. 1(7)
Faretta v. California, 422 U.S. 806 (1975)
Farooq Ahmad Khan Leghari v. Federation of Pakistan, PLD 1999 S.C. 57
Fauji Foundation v. Shamimur Rahman, PLD 1983 S.C. 457
Fazal Jan v. Roshan Din, PLD 1990 SC 661
Fazalul Qadir Chaudhery v. Muhammad Abdul Haq, PLD 1963 S.C. 486
Fazalul Quader Chowdhary v. Syed Shah Nawaz, PLD 1966 SC 105
Fazlul Quader Chowdhry v. Abdul Haque, PLD 1963 S.C. 486
Fecto Belarus Tractor Ltd. v. Government of Pakistan, PLD 2005 SC 605
Federal Communications Commission v. League of Women Voters, 468 U.S. 364 (1984)
Federal Communications Commission v. Pacifica Foundation, 438 U.S. 726 (1978)
Federation of Pakistan v. Ghulam Mustafa Khar, PLD 1989 SC 26
Federation of Pakistan v. Haji Mohammad Saifullah Khan, PLD 1989 S.C. 166
Federation of Pakistan v. Mohammad Akram Sheikh, PLD 1989 S.C. 689
Federation of Pakistan v. Moulvi Tamizuddin Khan, PLD 1955 F.C. 240
Federation of Pakistan v. Mrs Amatul Jalil Khawaja, PLD 2003 S.C. 442
Federation of Pakistan v. Saeed Ahmad Khan, PLD 1974 S.C. 151
Federation of Pakistan v. United Sugar Mills Ltd., PLD 1977 S.C. 397
Federation v. Saeed Ahmad, PLD 1974 S.C. 151
Felker v. Turpin, 518 U.S. 651 (1996)
Fiske v. Kansas, 274 U.S. 380 (1927)
Florida Bar v. Went for It, Inc., 515 U.S. 618 (1995)
Florida v. Bostick, 501 U.S. 429 (1991)
Fogla & S.K. Jalil v. State of West Bengal, AIR 1975 SC 245
Foster v. Chief Adjudication Officer, (1993) 2 W.L.R. 292, (1993) 1 All E.R. 705
Fothergill v. Monarch Airlines Ltd., (1981) A.C. 251
FPC v. Hope Natural Gas Company, 320 U.S. 591 (1944)
France Fenwick and Co. v. The King, (1927) 1 K.B. 458
Francis Coralie v. Union Territory of Delhi, AIR 1981 SC 746
Frank v. Magnum, 237 U.S. 309 (1915)
Freeman v. Pitts, 503 U.S. 467 (1992)
Frohwerk v. U.S., 249 U.S. 204 (1919)
Frontiero v. Richardson, 11 U.S. 677 (1973)
Fry v. U.S., 421 U.S. 542 (1975)
Fullilove v. Klutznick, 448 U.S. 448, 496 (1980)
Furman v. Georgia, 408 U.S. 238 (1972)

G

Gagnon v. Scarpelli, 411 U.S. 778 (1973)
Ganapati K. Reddy v. Nafisul Hasan, AIR 1954 SC 636
Garcia v. San Antonio Metropolitan Authority, 469 US 528 (1985)
Garland, ex parte, 71 U.S. 333 (1866)
Gault, in re, 387 U.S. 1 (1967)
Geduldig v. Aiello, 417 U.S. 484 (1974)
Geelong Harber Trust Cors v. Gibbs Bright & Co., (1972) 2 WLR 507

Ghani v. Jones, (1970) 1 QB 693, (1969) 3 All ER 1700
Ghazi v. State of U.P., AIR 1966 All 142
Ghulam Abbas v. State of U.P., (1984) 1 SCC 81
Ghulam Ali Shah v. State, P.L.D. 1990 S.C. 253
Ghulam Jilani v. Government of Pakistan, PLD 1967 S.C. 373
Ghulam Muhammad Khan Lundkhawar v. The State, PLD Lahore 497?
Ghulam Nabi v. State, AIR 1957 J&K 44
Ghulam Sarwar Awan v. Government of Sindh, PLD 1988 Karachi 414
Gian Kaur v. State of Punjab, (1996) 2 SCC 648
Gibbons v. Ogden, 22 U.S. 1 (1824)
Gideon (Douglas v. California), 407 U.S. 25 (1972)
Gideon v. Wainwright, 372 U.S. 335 (1963)
Gilligan v. Morgan, 413 U.S. 1 (1973)
Gitlow v. New York, 268 U.S. 652 (1925)
Gobind v. State of MP, (1975) 2 SCC 148
Golak Nath v. State of Punjab, AIR 1967 S.C. 1643
Goldwater v. Carter, 444 U.S. 996 (1979)
Good News Club v. Milford Central School 533 U.S. 98 (2001)
Gopalan, (1950) S.C.R. 88
Gopalan v. State of Madras, (1950) S.C.R. 88
Government of Balochistan v. Azizullah Memon, PLD 1993 S.C. 341
Government of Balochistan v. Rifat Parveen, 1981 SCMR 1002
Government of Pakistan v. Akhlaque Hussain, PLD 1965 SC 527
Government of Pakistan v. Dada Amir Haider Khan, PLD 1987 SC 504
Government of Sindh v. Dr Nadeem Rizvi, 2019 SCMR 556
Government of West Pakistan v. Begum Agha Abdul Karim Shorish Kashmiri, PLD 1969 SC 14
Govind v. State of M.P., AIR 1975 SC 1379
Govt. of East Pakistan v. Mrs Rowshan Bijya Shaukat, PLD 1966 SC 286
Graham v. Connor, 490 U.S. 386 (1989)
Graham v. Richardson, 403 U.S. 365 (1971)
Grand Rapids School District v. Ball, 473 U.S. 373 (1985)
Great Western Rly Co v. Mostyn (Owners), (1928) AC 57
Gregg & Georgia, 428 U.S. 153 (1975)
Griswold v. Connecticut, 381 U.S. 479 (1965)
Gulam Kadar Ahmadbhai Memon v. Surat Municipal Corporation, AIR 1998 Gujarat 234
Gulam Nabi v. State, AIR 1957 J & K 44
Gupta v. Union of India, AIR 1982 S.C. 149
Gurdatta Sharma v. State of Bihar, AIR 1961 S.C. 1684

H

Habiba Jilani v. Federation of Pakistan, PLD 1974 Lahore 153
Hack v. London Provident Society, (1883) 23 Ch D 103 at 112
Hadmor Production Ltd. v. Hamilton, (1983) 1 A.C. 191
Hague v. Congress of Industrial Organization, 307 US 496 (1939)
Haji Mohd. v. District Board Malda, AIR 1958 Cal 401
Hakim Khan v. Government of Pakistan, PLD 1992 SC 595
Hamdard Dwakhana v. Union of India, AIR 1960 SC 554
Hamdi v. Rumsfeld, 542 U.S. 507 (2004)
Hamid Sarfraz v. Federation of Pakistan, PLD 1979 S.C. 991
Hammer v. Dagenhart, 247 U.S. 251 (1918)

Hammood v. Howell, (1677) 2 Mod. 210
Hampton v. Mow Sun Wong, 426 U.S. 88 (1976)
Hansmukh v. State of Gujarat, AIR 1981 SC 28
Hansraj v. State of U.P., AIR 1956 All 641
Hanumanthappa v. Special Officer, District Board, AIR 1960 AP 342
Hardy v. Stumpf, 21 Ca1.3d 1 (1978)
Hari Shankar Jain v. Sonia Gandhi, (2001) 8 SCC 233
Harisiades v. Shaughnessy, 342 U.S. 580 (1952)
Harkrishan v. State of Maharashtra, AIR 1962 SC 911
Harminder Singh Arora v. Union of India, (1986) 3 SCC 247
Harris v. Minister of the Interior (1952), (2) SA 429(AD)
Hashim v. State, PLD 1963 SC 82
Hayburn's Case, 2 U.S. 409 (1792)
Hazelwood School District v. Kuhlmeier, 484 U.S. 260 (1988)
Heffron v. International Society for Krishna Consciousness, 452 U.S. 640 (1981)
Helvering v. Davis, 301 U.S. 619 (1937)
Herndon v. Lowry, 301 U.S. 242 (1937)
Herrietta Muir Edward v. Attorney-General for Canada, 1930 PC 124
Hidayatullah v. State, 2006 SCMR 1920 at 1926
High Court of Australia in Mathews v. Chicory Marketing Board, 60 CLR 263
Himat Lal K. Shah v. Commissioner of Police Bombay, AIR 1973 S.C. 87
Hirabayshi v. U.S., 320 U.S. 81 (1943)
Hirsh v. INS, 308 F. 2nd 562 (9th Cir.1962)
Hobbie v. Unemployment Appeals Division, 480 U.S. 136 (1987)
Model v. Indiana, 452 U.S. 314, 331–332 (1981)
Home Office v. Harman, (1981) Q.B. 534
Hosenball, ex parte, (1977) 1 VVLR 766
Hoskot v. State of Maharashtra, AIR 1978 S.C. 1548
Huddart Parker v. Moorehead, (1908) 8 C.L.R. 330 (409–12)
Hudson Bay Co. v. Maclav, (1920), 36 T.L.R. 469
Human Rights Case No. 17599 of 2018, 2019 SCMR 247
Humphrey's Executor v. United States, 295 U.S. 602 (1934)
Hunter v. Underwood, 471 U.S. 222 (1985)
Hurd v. Hodge, 334 U.S. 24 (1948)
Hurley v. Irish American Gay, Lesbian, and Bisexual Group of Boston, 515 U.S. 557 (1995)
Hurtado v. California, 110 U.S. 516 (1884)
Hussain Ahmad v. Pervez Musharraf, PLD 2002 S.C. 853
Husainara Khatoon (No. 1) v. Home Secretary, State of Bihar, AIR 1979 SC 1360
Husainara Khatoon (No. 2) v. Home Secretary, State of Bihar, AIR 1979 SC 1369
Husainara Khatoon (No. 3) v. Home Secretary, State of Bihar, AIR 1979 SC 1377

I

I.A. Sharawani v. Government of Pakistan, 1991 SCMR 1041
I.T. Commissioner v. Shirinbal, AIR 1965 Bombay 586
Illinois v. Gates, 462 U.S. 213 (1983)
Immigration and Naturalization Service v. Chadha, 462 U.S 919 (1983)
In re: P. Bapanaiah v. Unknown, AIR 1970 AP 47
In re Special Courts Bill, AIR 1979 SC 478 at 508
In re. Winship, 397 U.S. 358 (1970)
In the matter of public hanging, PLD 1994 S.C. 219

Inamur Rehman v. Federation of Pakistan, 1992 SCMR 563
Inderdeo Singh v. The State, AIR 1951 Patna 242
Indian Council for Enviro-Legal Action v. Union of India, (1966) 3 SCC 212
Indian Express Newspaper v. Union of India, (1985) 1 SCC 641
Indian Oil Corporation Limited v. Municipal Corporation, AIR 1995 SC 1480
Indira Gandhi v. Raj Narain, AIR 1975 S.C. 2299
Indra Sawhney v. Union of India, AIR 2000 SC 498
Indra Sawhney v. Union of India, AIR 1993 S.C. 477
Industrial Properties (Barton Hill) Ltd. v. Associated Electrical Industries, (1977) 2 All ER 293
International Airport Authority, AIR 1979 SC 1628
Iowa C.R. Co. v. Iowa, 160 U.S. 389 (1896)
Islamic Republic of Pakistan v. Abdul Wali Khan, PLD 1976 S.C. 57
Ismail Farooqui v. Union of India, AIR 1995 S.C. 604, (1994) 6 SCC 360
Iswarlal v. State of Gujarat, AIR 1968 S.C. 870
Izhar Ahmed v. Union of India, AIR 1962 SC 1052

J

J.N. Roy v. State of W.B., AIR 1972 SC 2142
Jackson v. Metropolitan Edison Co., 419 U.S. 345 (1974)
Jacobellis v. Ohio, 378 U.S. 184 (1964)
Jai Singh v. State of Haryana, AIR 1995 P. & H. 243
Jaisinghani v. Union of India, AIR 1967 SC 1427
Jamal Shah v. Member Election Commission, PLD 1966 SC 1
Jamat-e-Islami v. Federation of Pakistan, PLD 2009 S.C. 549
Javed Ahmad v. State of Maharashtra, AIR 1985 SC 231
Jayanarayan Sukul v. State of West Bengal, AIR 1979 SC 675
Jenkins v. Georgia, 418 U.S. 153 (1974)
Jibendra Kishore v. the Province of East Pakistan, PLD 1957 SC 9
Jilabhai Nanbhai Khachar v. State of Gujarat, AIR 1995 SC 142
Jogindar Kumar v. State of U.P., (1994) 4 SCC 260
John Vallamattom v. Union of India, AIR 2003 S.C. 2902, (2003) 6 SCC 611
Johnstone v. Pedlar, (1921) AC 262
Johnson v. Agnew, (1978) 3 All ER 314
Joginder Kumar v. State of U.P., AIR 1994 SC 1349
Jones v. A.G. of Canada, (1974) 45 D.L.R. (3d) 583
Jones v. German, (1896) 2 Q.B. 418
Jones v. Owen, (1870) 34 JP 759
Jones v. United States, 463 U.S. 354, (1983)
Joseph Augusthi v. M.A. Narayanan, AIR 1964 SC 1552
Joseph v. R.B.I., AIR 1962 S.C. 1371
Joseph v. Reserve Bank of India, AIR 1962 S.C. 1371

K

K. Kunhikoman v. State of Kerala, AIR 1962 S.C. 723
K. Veeraswami v. Union of India, (1991) 3 SCC 655
K.A Kundi v. Padiya Purryil, AIR 1956 Madras 685
K.A. Abbas v. Union of India, AIR 1971 SC 481
K.A. Nair v. Union of India, AIR 1976 SC 1179

Kadra Pahadiya v. State of Bihar, AIR 1982 SC 1167
Kahn v. Shevin, 416 U.S. 351 (1974)
Kalawati v. State of Himachal Pradesh, AIR 1953 SC 131
Kamal China v. The State, AIR 1963 Punjab 36
Kamala Kant Mishra v. State of Bihar, AIR 1971 S.C. 1667
Kamalakar Prasad Chaturvedi v. State of M.P., (1983) 4 SCC 442
Kameshwar Singh v. Sate of Bihar, AIR 1962 SC 1166
Kameshwar Singh v. State of Bihar, AIR 1951 Patna 91
Kameshwar v. State of Bihar, AIR 1962 S.C. 1166
Kamla v. State of Maharashtra, AIR 1981 SC 814
Kansas v. Crane, 534 U.S. 407 (2002)
Kansas v. Hendricks, 521 U.S. 346 (1997)
Kanu Biswas v. State of W.B., AIR 1972 SC 1656
Kapildeo Singh v. The King, AIR 1950 FC 80
Kastigar v. United States, 406 U.S. 441 (1972)
Karam Narain Daulat Ram v. Valkart Bros, AIR 1946 Lahore 116 (F.B.)
Karimun Nisa v. State of Madhya Pradesh, AIR 1955 Nag 6
Karnataka STDC v. Karnataka State, (1986)4 SCC 421
Kartar Singh v. State of Punjab, (1994) 3 SCC 569
Kasturi Lal v. State of J.K., AIR 1980 SC 1992
Katz v. United States, 389 U.S. 347 (1967)
Kaushaliaya v. The State, AIR 1963 Allahabad 71
Kedar Nath Bajoria v. West Bengal, AIR 1953 S.C. 404 at 406
Kedar Nath v. State of Bihar, AIR 1962 SC 955
Kennedy v. Mendoza-Martinez, 372 U.S. 144 (1963)
Kentucky Department of Corrections v. Thompson, 490 U.S. 454 (1989)
Kepner v. United States, 195 U.S. 100 (1905)
Kesavananda Bharati v. State of Kerala, AIR 1973 S.C. 1461 (1584, 1535)
Keshar Singh v. Speaker of U.P. Assembly, AIR 1965 Allahabad 349
Kesavananda Bharati v. Kerala, AIR 1973 S.C. 1461
Kewal Pati v. State of Uttar Pradesh, (1995) 3 SCC 600
Keyes v. Denver School District, 413 U.S. 189 (1973)
Keyishian v. Board of Regents, 385 U.S. 589 (1967)
Khan Abdul Ghaffar Khan v. D.C. Peshawar, PLD 1965 Peshawar 100
Kharaiti Ram Samras v. United States, 125 F.2d 879 (9th Cir. 1942), certificate denied 317 U.S. 634 (1942)
Kharak Singh v. State of U.P., AIR 1963 S.C. 1295
Khare v. State of Delhi, (1950) S.C.R. 519 (524)
Khatri v. State of Bihar, AIR 1981 S.C. 928, (1981) 1 SCC 735
Khatoon Begum v. Union of India, AIR 1981 SC 1077
Khawaja Ahmad Tariq Rahim v. Federation of Pakistan, PLD 1992 S.C. 646
Khawaja Muhammad Safdar v. West Pakistan, PLD 1964 Lahore 718
Khudiram Das v. State of W.B., AIR 1975 SC 550
King v. R, (1969) AC 304, (1968) 2 All ER 610
Kinsella v. Krueger, 354 U.S. 1 (1957)
Kinsella v. Singleton, 361 U.S. 234 (1960)
Kiryas Joel School District v. Grumet, 512 U.S. 687 (1994)
Kishore Singh v. State of Rajasthan, AIR 1981 SC 625
Kishori Mohan v. State of W.B., AIR 1972 SC 1749
Kissinger v. Halperin, 452 U.S. 713 (1981)
Knauer v. United States, 328 U.S. 654 (1946)
Konigsberg v. State Bar of California, 366 U.S. 36 (1961)

Korematsu v. United States, 323 U.S. 214 (1944)
Kotch v. Board of River Port Pilot Commissioners, 330 U.S. 552 (1947)
Kubic Dariusz v. Union of India, (1990) 1 SCC 568
Kuruma v. R, (1955) AC 197, (1955) 1 All ER 236
Kyllo v. United States, 533 U.S. 27 (2001)

L

L.N. Mishra Institute of E.D. & Social Change v. State of Bihar, AIR 1988 S.C. 1136
Lal Babu Hussain v. Electoral Registration Officer, AIR 1995 SC 1189
Lallubhai Jogibhai Patel v. Union of India, (1981) 2 BCC 427
Lamb's Chapel v. Center Moriches Union Free School District, 508 U.S. 384 (1993)
Law Students Civil Rights Research Council v. Wadmond, 401 U.S. 154 (1971)
Lawrence J. D'Souza v. Bombay State, AIR 1956 S.C. 531
Leach v. Money, (1765) 19 St.Tr.1002
Lee v. Welslman, 505 U.S. 577 (1992)
Lehr v. Robertson, 463 U.S. 248 (1983)
Lemon v. Kurtzman, 403 U.S. 602 (1971)
Leo Roy Frey v. Superintendent District Jail, AIR 1958 SC 119
Liaquat Hussain v. Federation of Pakistan, PLD 1999 SC 504
Life Insurance Corporation of India v. Manubhai D. Shah, (1992) 3 SCC 637
Lindsley v. Natural Carbonic Gas Co., 220 U.S. 61 (1911)
Liquormat, Inc. v. Rhode Island, 517 U.S. 484 (1996)
Liversidge v. Anderson, (1942) 3 ALL E.R. 33
Liversidge v. Anderson, (1942) A.C. 206
Liyanage v. Reginam, (1966) 1 All E.R. 650
Liyanage v. The Queen, (1967) 1 AC 259
Loan Association v. City of Topeka, 87 U.S. 655 (1874)
Lochner v. New York, 198 U.S. 45 (1905)
London Artists Limited v. Littler, (1969) 2 All ER 193
Lord Mansfield Jones v. Randle, (1774) 1 Cowp, 37
Lord Porter in London Graving Dock Co v. Horton, (1951) 2 All ER 1
Lorillard Tobacco Company v. Reilly, 533 U.S. 525 (2001)
Louis De Raedt v. Union of India, AIR 1991 SC 1886
Louisville Joint Stock Land Bank v. Radford, 295 U.S. 555 (1935)
Louisville & N.R. Co. v. Schmidt, (1879)
Lovell v. Griffin, 303 U.S. 444 (1938)
Loving v. Virginia, 388 U.S. 1 (1967)
Lowe v. Austin, 80 U.S. 29 (1871)
Luther v. Borden, 48 U.S. (7 How.) 1 (1849)
Lynch v. Donnelly, 465 U.S. 668 (1984)

M

M. Chhaganlal v. Greater Bombay Municipality, AIR 1974 S.C. 2009
M. David, in re, AIR 1959 AP 137
M. Inayat Khan v. M. Anwar, PLD 1976 S.C. 354 at 368
M. Ismail Faruqui v. Union of India, AIR 1995 S.C. 605
M.C. Mehta (2) v. Union of India, (1988) 1 SCC 471
M.C. Mehta v. Union of India, (1987) 4 SCC 463

M.C. Mehta v. Union of India, (1996) 4 SCC 750
M.C. Mehta v. Union of India, AIR 1987 S.C. 1086
M.C. Mehta v. Union of India, (1986) 2 SCC 176
M.H. Devendrappa v. The Karnataka State Small Industries Development Corpn., AIR 1998 SC 1064
M.M. Gandhi v. State of Mysore, AIR 1960 Mys. 1112
M.P. Lohia v. State of West Bengal, AIR 2005 S.C. 790, (2005) 2 SCC 686
M.P. Sharma v. Satish Chandra, AIR 1954 S.C. 300
McCreary Connty, Ky v. ACLU of Ky, 545 U.S. 844 (2005)
MacCormick v. Lord Advocate, 1953 SC 396, 411–13
Madhav Rao v. Union of India, AIR 1971 S.C. 530
Madhu Lal v. Emperor, AIR 1951 Bombay 513
Madzimbamuto v. Lardner-Bruke, (1969) 1 AC 645
Mahabir Auto Stores v. Indian Oil Corporation, AIR 1990 SC 1031
Mahendra v. State of U.P., AIR 1963 S.C. 1019
Mahmood Khan Achakzai v. Federation of Pakistan, PLD 1997 S.C. 426
Majid Nizami v. Sheikh Muhammad Rashid, PLD 1996 Lahore 410
Makashi v. Menon, AIR 1982 S.0
Makhan v. State of Punjab, AIR 1964 SC 381
Malik Ghulam Jilani v. The Government of West Pakistan, PLD 1967 S.C. 373
Malkiat Singh v. State of Punjab, AIR 1959 Punjab 250
Malone v. Metropolitan Police Commissioner, (1979) Cr. 344
Malone v. Metropolitan Police Comr, (1980) QB 49, (1979) 1 All ER 256
Maneka Gandhi v. Union of India, AIR 1978 S.C. 597
Manipur Administration v. Thokchom Bira Singh, AIR 1964 S.C. 87
Manzoor Ellahi v. Federation of Pakistan, PLD 1975 S.C. 66
Manzar Hasan v. Syed Muhammad Zaman, AIR 1925 PC 36
Manzoor Ahmad Wattoo v. Federation of Pakistan, PLD 1997 Lahore 38
Manzoor Hussain Bukhari v. S.P. City, Lahore, 1990 MLD 1807
Maqbool Hussain v. State of Bombay, AIR 1953 SC 325
Marbury v. Madison, 2 L. Ed. 60 (1803)
Marbury v. Madison, 5 U.S. 137 (1803)
Marsh v. Chambers, 463 U.S. 783 (1983)
Martin & Co. v. Faiyaz, AIR 1944 PC 33
Martin v. Struthers, 319 U.S. 141 (1943)
Maryland v. Wirtz, 392 U.S. 183 (1968)
Masroor Ahsan v. Ardeshir Cowasjee, PLD 1998 S.C. 823
Massachusetts v. Laird, 400 U.S. 886 (1970)
Matajog v. Bhari, (1955) 2 S.C.R. 925
Mathews v. De Castro, 429 U.S. 181 (1976)
Maulvi Iqbal Haider v. Capital Development Authority, PLD 2006 S.C. 394
Maulvi Tameezuddin Khan v. Federation of Pakistan, PLD 1955 Sindh 96.
Maxwell v. Dow, 176 U.S. 581 (1900).
McCardle, ex parte, 74 U.S. 506 (1869)
McCollum v. Board of Education, 333 U.S. 203 (1948)
McCulloch v. Maryland, 17 U.S. 316 (1819)
McCulloch v. Maryland, 4 Wheat 1316 (1819)
McDaniel v. Paty, 435 U.S. 618 (1978)
McGowan v. Maryland, 366 U.S. 420 (1961)
McKay v. R., (1965) S.C.R. 798
McLaughlin v. Florida, 379 U.S. 184 (1964)
Mclaurin v. Oklahama State Regents, 339 U.S. 637 (1950)

Mcleord v. St. Aubyn, (1899) A.C. 549
M'Culloch v. Maryland, 17 U.S. 316 (1819)
Meachum v. Fano, 427 U.S. 215 (1976)
Mehram Ali v. Federation of Pakistan, PLD 1958 S.C. 1445
Mehtab Jan v. Municipal Committee, PLD 1958 Lah 929
Melbourne Corpn. v. Commonwealth, (1947) 74 C.L.R. 31
Memoirs v. Massachusetts, 383 U.S. 413 (1966)
Memphis Light, Gas & Water Division v. Craft, 436 U.S. 1 (1978)
Meritor Savings Bank v. Vinson, 477 U.S. 57 (1986)
Metropolitan Life Insurance Company v. Ward, 470 U.S. 869 (1985)
Meyer v. Nebraska, 262 U.S. 390 (1923)
Mian Fazal Din v. Lahore Improvement Trust, PLD 1969 S.C. 223
Michelin Tire Corporation v. Wages, 423 U.S. 276 (1976)
Michigan v. Tyler, 436 U.S. 499 (1978)
Miller v. California, 413 U.S. 15 (1973)
Miller v. Taylor, (1769) 4 Burr. 2303
Milligan, ex parte, 71 U.S. 2 (1866)
Milliken v. Bradley, 418 U.S. 717 (1974)
Minersville School District v. Gobitis, 310 U.S. 586 (1940)
Minerva Mills Ltd v. Union of India, AIR 1980 S.C. 1789
Minor v. Happersett, 88 U.S. 162 (1875)
Mir Ali Nawaz Bugti v. Superintendent Jail, PLD 1966 SC 357
Mir Ikhlaq Khan v. The State, 2008 SCMR 951
Miranda v. Arizona, 384 U.S. 436 (1966).
Mishri Lal v. Dhirendra Nath, AIR 1999 SC 1958
Mississippi University for Women v. Hogan, 458 U.S. 718 (1982)
Missouri ex rel. Gaines v. Canada, 305 U.S. 337 (1938)
Missouri v. Holland, 252 U.S. 416 (1920)
Missouri v. Jenkins, 515 U.S. 70 (1995)
Mitchell v. Helms, 530 U.S. 793 (2000)
Mithu v. Punjab, AIR 1983 S.C. 473
Mohabat Khan v. Road Transport Board, 1993 SCMR 833
Mohammad Khan v. Sanaullah, PLD 1971 SC 324 at 329
Mohammad Safdur v. Province, PLD 1964 Lah. 718
Mohd. Ali v. Sri Ram Swarup, AIR 1965 All 161
Mohd. Dastagir v. State of Madras, AIR 1960 S.C. 756
Mohd. Hanif Quareshi v. State of Bihar, AIR 1958 SC 731
Mohd. Yousuf v. State of J & K., AIR 1979 SC 1925
Mohinder Singh v. State of Punjab, AIR 1999 SC 211
Mohinder Singh v. State of Punjab, AIR 1965 S.C. 79
Mohini Jain v. State of Karnataka, (1992) 3 SCC 666
Mohsin Tirmizy v. The State, PLD 1965 S.C. 28
Molasses Trading & Export (Pvt) Ltd. v. Federation of Pakistan, 1993 SCMR 1905
Montanye v. Haymes, 427 U.S. 236 (1976)
Morrison v. California, 291 U.S. 82 (1934)
Morrissey v. Brewer, 408 U.S. 471 (1972)
Moslemuddin Sikadar v. Chief Secretary, PLD 1957 Dacca 101
Moti Bai v. State of Rajasthan, AIR 1954, Raj 241
Motising Chhagasing Vaghela v. S.D. Mehta, AIR 1966 Guj 233
Moulana Mufti Sayeed Mohd. Noorur Rehman Barkariq v. State of West Bengal, AIR 1999 Calcutta 15
Moulvi Tamizuddin Khan v. Federation of Pakistan, PLD 1955 Sindh 96

Mozert v. Hawkins County Public Schools, 484 U.S. 1066 (1988)
Mrs Arshad Ali Khan v. Government of the Punjab, 1994 SCMR 1532
Mst Fazal Jan v. Roshan Din, PLD 1990 S.C. 661
Mudhu Limaye v. D.M. Monghyr, AIR 1971 SC 2486
Muhammad Anwar v. Pakistan, PLD 1963 Lahore 109
Muhammad Ashraf v. The State, 1995 SCMR 626
Muhammad Ayub v. Chairman, Area Electricity Board, and WAPDA, PLD 1987 S.C. 195
Muhammad Ghafoor v. N.W.F.P., PLD 1974 Peshawar 28
Muhammad Ilyas v. Ijaz Ahmad Butt, 1992 SCMR 1857
Muhammad Ismail and Company v. Chief Cotton Inspector, PLD 1966 S.C. 388
Muhammad Nasrullah v. M.C. Karachi, PLD 1960 S.C. 24
Muhammad Nawaz Sharif v. President, PLD 1993 S.C. 473
Muhammad Nurullah v. M.C. Karachi, PLD 1990 S.C. 253
Muhammad Saeed Ahmad Khan v. Secetary, PLD 1983 Lahore 206
Muhammad Safi v. State of West Bengal, AIR 1966 S.C. 69
Muhammad Shahbaz Sharif v. Federation of Pakistan, PLD 2004 SC 583
Muhammad Sharif v. Federation of Pakistan, PLD 1988 Lahore 725
Muhammad Siddique v. Government of Pakistan, PLD 2005 SC 1
Muhammad Siddique v. State, PLD 1983 FSC 173
Muhammad Usman v. State, PLD 1957 Lahore 388
Muhammad Usman v. The State, PLD 1965 Lahore 229
Muhammad Yar Khan v. Deputy Commissioner, 1980 SCMR 456
Muhammad Younis v. Province of Sindh, PLD 1973 Karachi 694
Mukhtar Ahmad Ansari v. State (NCT of Delhi), AIR 2005 S.C. 2804, (2005) SCC 258
Mumtaz Ali Bhutto v. Government of Pakistan, PLD 1981 Kar 98
Munir Hussain Bhatti v. Federation of Pakistan, PLD 2011 S.C. 407
Munn v. Illinois, 94 U.S. 113 (1876)
Munn v. Illinois, 96 U.S. 97 (1877)
Munshi Singh Gautam v. State of M.P., AIR 2005 S.C. 402, (2005) 9 SCC 631
Munro v. National Capital Commn., (1966) S.C.R. 663
Murdock v. Pennsylvania, 319 U.S. 105 (1943)
Murray v. Curlett, 374 U.S. 203 (1963)
Murray's Lessee v. Hoboken Land & Improvement. Co., 59 U.S. 272 (1856)
Mushtaq Awan v. Government of Pakistan, PLD 1999 Lah 372
Muzaffar Qadir v. District Magistrate, PLD 1975 Lahore 1198 (1204)
Myers v. United States, 272 U.S. 52 (1926)

N

NAACP v. Alabama, 357 U.S. 449 (1958)
Nadeem Ahmed v. Federation of Pakistan, PLD 2010 S.C. 1165
Naeem Mahmood v. Principal, King Edward Medical College, PLD 1965 Lahore 272
Nagarajan v. State of Karnataka, AIR 1976 S.C. 1976
Naimat v. Summary Military Court, PLD 1979 Lahore 279
Nainmal Pratapmal v. Union of India, AIR 1980 SC 2129
Nand Lal v. State of Punjab, AIR 1981 SC 2041
Nandini Satpathy v. P.L. Dani, AIR 1978 SC 1025
Nandoli Muhammad Rafeeq v. Union of India, (2004) SCC 218
Narayan Lal v. M.P. Mistry, AIR 1961 SC 29
Nasrullah Khan v. District Magistrate, PLD 1965 Lah 642, 692
Nasrullah Khan Henjra v. Government of Pakistan, PLD 1994 S.C. 23, PLD 1998 SCMR 1072

National Labor Relations Board v. Jones & Laughlin Steel Corporation, 301 U.S. 1 (1937)
National League of Cities v. Usery, 426 U.S. 833 (1976)
Navinchand v. Commissioner of Income Tax, Bombay, AIR 1955 S.C. 58
Nawabzada Nasrullah Khan v. Government of West Pakistan, PLD 1965 Lahore 642
Nawaz Sharif v. President of Pakistan, PLD 1993 S.C. 473
Nawbazada Nasrullah Khan v. Government of West Pakistan, PLD 1965 Lahore 642
Nazir Ahmad v. Muhammad Shafi, PLD 1980 S.C. 6
Near v. Minnesota, 283 U.S. 697 (1931)
NESPAK v. Kamil Khan Mumtaz, 2018 SCMR 211
New Jubilee Insurance v. National Bank of Pakistan, PLD 1999 SC 1126
New Orleans v. Dukes, 427 U.S. 297 (1976)
New Reviera Coop. Housing Society v. Special Land Acquisition Officer, (1996) 1 SCC 731
New York ex rel. Bryant v. Zimmerman, 278 U.S. 63 (1928)
New York State Club Association, Inc. v. City of New York, 487 U.S. 1 (1988)
New York Times Company v. United States (The Pentagon Papers Case), 403 U.S. 713 (1971)
New York Times Company v. United States, 403 U.S. 713 (1971)
New York Transit Authority v. Beazer 440 U.S. 568 (1979)
New York v. Ferber, 458 U.S. 747 (1982)
Newcastle Breweries v. The King, (1920) 1 K.B. 854
Ng Fung Ho v. White, 259 U.S. 276, 281 (1922)
Niemotko v. Maryland, 340 U.S. 268 (1951)
Niharendu v. Emperor, AIR 1942 F.C. 22
Nilabati Behera v. State of Orissa, (1993) 2 SCC 746
Niranjan Prasad v. State, AIR 1960 All 323
Nixon v. Administrator of General Services, 433 U.S. 425 (1977)
Nixon v. Condon, 286 U.S. 73 (1932)
Nixon v. Fitzgerald, 457 U.S. 731 (1982)
Nixon v. Herndon, 273 U.S. 536 (1927)
Nixon v. United States, 506 U.S. 224 (1993)
Noor Mohammad v. Rex., AIR 1949 A11120
Noor Muhammad v. Commissioner Sargodha, PLD 1968 Lahore 1441
Nordlinger v. Hahn, 505 U.S. 1 (1992)
Noto v. United States, 367 U.S. 290 (1961)
Nusrat Bhutto v. Chief of Army Staff, PLD 1977 S.C. 657

O

O.K. Ghose v. E.X. Joseph., AIR 1963 SC 812
O.P. Dahiya v. Union of India, AIR 2003 S.C. 4464, (2003) 1 SCC 122
O'Bannon v. Town Court Nursing Center, 447 U.S. 773 (1980)
O'Connor v. Donaldson, 422 U.S. 563, (1975)
Odyssey Communication Pvt. Ltd. v. Lokvidayan Sanghatana, (1988) 3 SCC 410
Ohio v. Robinette, 519 U.S. 33 (1996)
Okanogan Indians v. United States, 279 U.S. 655 (1929)
Olga Tellis v. Bombay Municipal Corporation, AIR 1986 SC 180, (1985) 3 SCC 545
Oliver v. United States, 466 U.S. 170 (1984)
Olmstead v. United States, 277 U.S. 438 (1928)
Om Prakash Gupta v. State of U.P., AIR 1957 SC 458
Om Prakash v. Emperor, AIR 1948 Nag. 199
Omnia Commercial Co. v. US, 261 US 502 (1923)
Oregon v. Mitchell, 400 US 112 (1970)

Orr v. Orr, 440 U.S. 268 (1979)
Osborne v. Rowlett, (1880) 13 Ch D 774 at 785
Ozawa v. United States, 260 U.S. 178 (1922)

P

P.A. Jacob v. Supdt. Of Police, Kottayams, AIR 1993 Ker 1
P. Balakothiah v. Union of India, AIR 1958 SC 232
PMDC v. Federation of Pakistan, 2018 SCMR 1956
PUCL v. Union of India, AIR 2003 S.C. 2363, (2003) 4 SCC 399
P. Rathinam v. Union of India, (1994) 3 SCC 394
P.L. Shamdassni v. Central Bank, AIR 1962 SC 59
P.V. Mohammad v. Director of Enforcement, AIR 1993 SC 1188
Padilla v. Hanft, 547 U.S. 1062 (2006)
Pakistan Lawyers Forum v. Federation of Pakistan, PLD 2005 S.C. 719
Pakistan Muslim League v. Federation of Pakistan, PLD 2007 S.C. 642
Palko v. Connecticut, 302 U.S. 319 (1937)
Pankaj Kumar v. State of Bengal, AIR 1970 SC 97.
Palmore v. Sidoti, 466 U.S. 429 (1984)
Parikaj Kumar v. State of Bengal, AIR 1970 SC 97
Papethi Anmal, in re, AIR 1959 Mad 241
Parham v. J.R., 442 U.S. 584 (1979)
Parshadi v. State of U.P., AIR 1957 S.C. 211
Partap Singh v. State of Punjab, AIR 1964 S.C. 72
Paul v. Davis, 424 U.S. 693 (1976)
Pennell v. City of San Jose, 485 U.S. 1 (1988)
Pennsylvania v. Finley, 440 U.S. 367 (1979)
Peoples Union for Civil Liberties Union v. Union of India, AIR 1997 SC 568
Peoples Union for Civil Liberties v. Union of India, AIR 1997 S.C. 1203
Peoples Union for Civil liberties v. Union of India, (2004) 9 SCC 580
Peoples Union for Democratic Rights v. Police Commissioner, Delhi Headquarters, (1989) 4 SCC 730
Peoples Union for Democratic Rights v. Union of India, AIR 1982 SC 1473
Perez v. Brownell, 356 U.S. 44 (1958)
Perkins v. Elg., 307 U.S. 325 (1939)
Personnel Administrator of Massachusetts v. Feeney, 442 U.S. 256 (1979)
Phillips Chem. Co. v. Dumas School Dist., 361 U.S. 376 (1960)
Piara Singh v. State of Punjab, AIR 1969 SC 961
Piare Dusadh v. Emperor, AIR 1944 F.C. 1
Pickstone v. Freemans, (1989) A.C. 66
Pierce v. Society of Sisters, 268 U.S. 510 (1925)
Planned Parenthood of Southeastern Pennsylvania v. Casey, 505 U.S. 833 (1992)
Plessy v. Ferguson, 163 U.S. 537 (1896)
Plyler v. Doe, 457 U.S. 202 (1982)
Polites v. United States, 364 U.S. 426 (1960)
Pope v. Illinois, 481 U.S. 497(1987)
Popular Bank Ltd. v. K. Madhava Naik, AIR 1965 SC 654
Posadas de Puerto Rico Associates v. Tourism Company, 478 U.S. 328 (1986)
Powell v. Alabama, 287 U.S. 45 (1932)
Powell v. McCormack, 395 U.S. 486 (1969)
Prabhu Dutt v. Union of India, AIR 1982 SC 6
Prafulla Kumar v. Bank of Commerce Ltd., Khulna, AIR 1947 P.C. 60

Prag Oil Mill v. Union of India, AIR 1978 S.C. 1296
Prem Chand v. Union of India, (1981) Cr. LJ. 5
Prem Lala Sharma v. District Magistrate Mathura, AIR 1998 SC 2212
Prem Sankar v. Delhi Administration, AIR 1980 SC 1535
Printers (Mysore) Ltd. v. Asstt. Commercial Tax Officer, (1994) 2 SCC 434
Pritam Singh v. State of Punjab, AIR 1956 S.C. 415
Progress of Pakistan Co. Ltd. v. Registrar, Joint Stock Companies, PLD 1958 Lahore 887
Province of East Pakistan v. Hasan Askari, PLD 1971 SC 82
Prudential Insurance Company v. Cheek, 259 U.S. 530 (1922)
Punkaj Kumar v. State of W.B., AIR 1970 SC 97
Purunlal Lakhanpal v. India, AIR 1958 S.C. 163
Purushottam Lal v. Union of India, AIR 1958 S.C. 36
Pushka Mukerjee v. State of West Bengal, AIR 1970 S.C. 582

Q

Qadir Qureshi v. The Crown, PLD 1953 Lahore 588
Qazalbash Trust v. Chief Land Commissioner, PLD 1990 SC 99
Quareshi v. State of Bihar, AIR 1958 S.C. 731
Queen v. Brown (1841). Car. & M., 314: K. & L. 428
Queen v. Jackson, (1891) 1 Q.B. 671
Quinn v. Leathen, (1901) A C 495
Quinn v. United States, 349 U.S. 155 (1955)

R

R v. Leatham, (1861) 8 Cox CC 498
R v. Metropolitan Police Commission, (1968) 2 AER 319
R v. Sang, (1980) AC 402, (1979) 2 All ER 1222
R v. Sullivan, (1868) 11 Cox CC 44
R v. Warwickshire County Council, ex p. Johnson, (1993) 2 W.L.R. 1, (1993) 1 All E.R. 299
R. Rajagopal v. State of T.N., (1994) 6 SCC 632
R. v. Hicklin, (1868) L.R. 3 Q.B.D. 360
R. v. New Statesman, (1928) 44 T.L.R. 301
R. v. Public Vehicles Appeal Tribunal, (1964) 113 CLR 225
R. v. Reiter, (1954) All E.R. 741 (C.C.A.)
R. Vasan v. Union of India, AIR 1983 SC 658
R.A.V. v. City of St. Paul, 505 U.S. 377 (1992)
R.C. Cooper v. Union of India, AIR 1978 SC 597
R.C. Cooper v. Union of India, AIR 1970 SC 564
R.K. Gupta v. Union of India, AIR 1981 S.C. 2138
R. v. Brislan, (1935) 54 CLR 262
R. v. Jordan, (1967) Crim. L Rev. 483
Radha Mohan Lal v. Rajasthan High Court, AIR 2003 S.C. 1467, (2003) 3 SCC 427
Radhey Shyam v. P.M.G. Nagpur, AIR 1965 SC 311
Raghavendra Singh v. Superintendent District Jail, Kanpur, AIR 1986 SC 356
Raghubai Dayal v. Union of India, AIR 1962 SC 263
Raghubir Singh v. State of Bihar, (1986) 4 SCC 481
Rahmatullah v. State of Bihar, AIR 1981 SC 2069
Railroad Commission Cases, 116 U.S. 307 (1886)

Railway express Agency, Inc. v. New York, 336 U.S. 106 (1949)
Raj Bahadur Gond v. State of Hyderabad, AIR 1953 Hyd 124
Raj Bahadur Singh v. Legal Remembrancer, AIR 1955 Cal 522
Raja Kulkarni v. State of Bombay, AIR 1954 S.C. 73
Rajangam v. State of Madras, AIR 1959 Mad 294
Raj kishore Prasad v. State of Bihar, AIR 1983 SC 320
Ram & Shyam Co. v. State of Haryana, (1985) SCC 267
Ram Bahadur v. State of Bihar, AIR 1975 SC 223
Ram Halbani v. State of Maharashtra, AIR 1973 SC 157
Ram Jawaya Kapur v. The State of Punjab, AIR 1955 S.C. 549
Ram Krishan v. State of Delhi, AIR 1953 S.C. 318
Ram Krishna v. Tendolkar, AIR 1958 S.C. 538
Ram Prasad v. State of Bihar, AIR 1953 SC 215
Ram Swamp v. Union of India, AIR 1965 SC 247
Ramana Dayaram Shetty v. The International Airport Authority of India, AIR 1979 S.C. 1628
Ramanlal Bhogilal Shah v. D.K. Gupta, AIR 1973 SC 1196
Ramesh Thapper v. State of Madras, AIR 1950 SC 124
Ramesh v. Union of India, (1988) 1 SCC 668
Ramjilal Modi v. State of U.P., AIR 1957 SC 622
Ranjit D. Udeshi v. State of Moharashtra, AIR 1965 SC 881
Rao Mahroz Akhtar v. District Magistrate, D.G. Khan, PLD 1957 (W.P.) Lah 676
Rati Lal v. State of Bombay, AIR 1954 S.C. 388
Ravinder Singh v. State of Haryana, AIR 1975 S.C. 856
Re-Amendment of the Constitution of Canada, (1981) 125 DIR (3d)
Reed v. Reed, 404 U.S. 71 (1971)
Reference by His Excellency the Governor General, PLD 1955 S.C. 435
Reg v. Secretary of State for Transport, (1990) 2 A.C. 85
Reg v. Warner, (1969) 2 A.C. 256
Regents of the University of California v. Bakke, 438 U.S. 265 (1978)
Regina v. Hicklin, (1868) L.R.3 Q.B 360
Rehmat Illahi v. West Pakistan, PLD 1965 Lahore 112
Reid v. CoVert, 351 U.S. 487 (1956)
Reno v. American Civil Liberties Union, 521 U.S. 844 (1997)
Rev. Stainislaus v. State of Madhya Pradesh, AIR 1977 SC 908
Rex v. Amir Hussain, AIR 1949 PC 152
Rex v. Halliday, (1917) A.C. 260
Reynolds v. Sims, 377 U.S. 533 (1964)
Reynolds v. Times Newspapers, (1999) 4 All ER 609
Reynolds v. United States, 98 U.S. 145 (1878)
Richards v. Wisconsin, 520 U.S. 385 (1997)
Roberts v. United States Jaycees, 468 U.S. 609 (1984)
Robinson v. The King, (1921) 3 K.B. 183
Rochin v. California, 342 U.S. 165 (1952)
Roe v. Wade, 410 U.S. 113 (1973)
Rogers v. Bellei, 401 U.S. 815 (1971)
Romer v. Evans, 517 U.S. 620 (1996)
Romesh Chandra Metha v. State of W.B., AIR 1970 SC 940
Romesh Thapar v. State of Madras, AIR 1950 S.C. 124
Roncarelli v. Duplessis, (1959) SCR 121: 16 DLR (2d) 689
Rosenberger v. University of Virginia, 515 U.S. 819 (1995)
Ross v. Registrar, (1974) 42 D.L.R. (3d) 69

Rostker v. Goldberg, 453 U.S. 57 (1981)
Roth v. Board of Regents, 408 U.S. 564 (1972)
Roth v. United States, 354 U.S. 476 (1957)
Rowshan Bijaya Shaukat (Mrs) v. Govt. of East Pakistan, PLD 1965 Dacca 241
Roy v. Union of India, AIR 1982 S.C. 710
Royster Guano Co. v. Virginia, 253 U.S. 412 (1920)
Rudal Shah v. State of Bihar, (1983) 4 SCC 141
Rural Litigation and Entitlement Kendra v. State of U.P., (1985) 2 SCC 431
Russel v. Queen, 46. L.T. 889
Rust v. Sullivan, 500 U.S. 173 (1991)
Rustom Cowasjee Cooper v. Union of India, AIR 1970 S.C. 564

S

S. Jagannath v. Union of India, AIR 1997 SC 811
S.A. Venkataraman v. Union of India, AIR 1954 SC 375
S.K. Sakawat v. State of W.B., AIR 1975 SC 64
S.K. Singh v. V.V. Giri, AIR 1970 SC 2097
S.N. Sarkar v. Union of India, AIR 1973 SC 1425
S.P. Gupta v. Union of India, AIR 1982 S.C. 149
S.P. Mittal v. Union of India, AIR 1983 SC 1
S.R. Bommai v. Union of India, (1994) 3 SCC 1
S.R. Bommai v. Union of India, AIR 1994 S.C. 1918
S.R. Kapoor v. Union of India, AIR 1990 SC 752
Sabir Shah v. Federation of Pakistan, PLD 1994 S.C. 738
Sabir Shah v. Shad Muhammad Khan, PLD 1995 S.C. 66
Sadho Samsher v. State of Pepsu, AIR 1954 SC 276
Saeed Ahmad v. The Province, PLD 1993 Lahore 218
Saenz v. Roe, 526 U.S. 489 (1999)
Saharanpur Municipality v. K. Ram, AIR 1965 All 160
Saheli v. Commr. of Police, AIR 1990 SC 513
Sahib Ram Jawaya Kapur v. Punjab, AIR 1955 S.C. 549
Saifuddin Saheb v. State of Bombay, AIR 1962 SC 853
Saifuddin v. State of Bombay, AIR 1963 SC 853
Sajjan Singh v. Rajasthan, A.I.R. 1965 S.C. 845
Sajjan Singh v. State of Rajasthan, AIR 1965 S.C. 845
Sakal Papers Ltd. v. Union of India, AIR 1962 S.C. 305
Sakhi Daler Khan v. Superintendent, Recovery of Abducted women, PLD 1957 Lahore 813
Salkeld v. Johnson, (1948) 2 Exch. 256
San Antonio Indep. School/Dist. v. Rodriguez, 411 U.S. 1 (1973)
Sandin v. Conner, 515 U.S. 472 (1995)
Sanjeev Coke Manufacturing Co. v. Bharat Coking Coal Ltd., AIR 1983 S.C. 239
Sankari Prasad Singh v. Union of India, AIR 1951 S.C. 458
Santa Fe Independent School District v. Doe, 530 U.S. 290 (2000)
Santosh Kumar v. Secy. Ministry of Human Resources Development, AIR 1995 S.C. 293
Saraswathi Seshagiri v. State of Kerala, AIR 1982 SC 1165
Sardar Begum Faruqui v. Rashida Khatoon, 1990 CLC 83
Sardar Ram v. Haji Abdul Majid, AIR 1960 Pb 196
Sarojini Ramaswamy v. Union of India, AIR 1992 S.C. 2219
Satwant Singh v. Assistant Passport Officer, New Delhi, AIR 1967 SC 1836
Satya Deo Prasad v. State of Bihar, AIR 1957 SC 367

Scales v. United States, 367 U.S. 203 (1961)
Schenck v. United States, 249 U.S. 47 (1919)
Schering Chemical Ltd v. Falkman Ltd, (1982) Q.B. 1
Schick v. Reed, 419 U.S. 256 (1974)
Schmerber v. California, 384 U.S. 757 (1966)
Schneckloth v. Bustamonte, 412 U.S. 218 (1973)
Schneider v. Rusk, 377 U.S. 163 (1964)
Schweiker v. Wilson, 450 U.S. 221 (1981)
Scott v. Illinois, 440 US. 367 (1979)
Scott v. Scott, (1913) A.C. 417
Sebastian M. Hongray v. Union of India, AIR 1984 SC 1026
Secretary, Ministry of I&B v. Cricket Association of Bengal (CAB), (1955) 2 SCC 161
Serfass v. Jenkins, 420 U.S. 377 (1975)
Sh. Liaqat Hussain v. Federation of Pakistan, PLD 1999 SC 504
Sh. Riaz-ul-Haq v. Federation of Pakistan, PLD 2013 SC 501
Shafqat v. the State, 2019 SCMR 43
Shafique Ahmad v. District Magistrate, Meerut, AIR 1990 SC 220
Shahal H. Musaliar v. State of Kerala, (1993) 4 SCC 112
Shahid Pervez v. Ejaz Ahmed, 2017 SCMR 206
Shakuntala Devi v. Delhi Electric Supply Undertaking, (1995) 2 SCC 369
Shankari Prasad Singh v. Union of India, AIR 1951 S.C. 458
Sharaf Faridi v. The Government of Pakistan, PLD 1989 Karachi 404
Shaughnessy v. Mezei, 345 U.S. 206, 212 (1953)
Shaughnessy v. United States ex rel. Mezei, 345 U.S. 206 (1953)
Sheela Barse v. State of Moharashtra, AIR 1983 SC 96, (1983) 2 SCC 96
Sheela Devi v. Mohan Sarup, (1987) 3 SCC 234
Shehla Zia v. WAPDA, PLD 1994 S.C. 693
Shehla Zia v. Wapda, PLD 1994 SC 693
Shelley v. Kraemer, 334 U.S. 1 (1948)
Shelton v. Tucker, 364 U.S. 479 (1960)
Sher Singh v. State of Punjab, AIR 1983 SC 465
Sherbert v. Verner, 374 U.S. 398 (1963)
Shewpujanrai v. Collector of Customs, AIR 1958 S.C. 845
Shibban Lai v. State of U.P., AIR 1954 SC 179, 198
Shirin Munir v. Government of the Punjab, PLJ 1990 S.C. 159
Shirin Munir v. Govt. of the Punjab, PLD 1990 S.C. 295
Shri Raghunathrao Ganpatrao v. Union of India, AIR 1993 S.C. 1267
Shrilekha Vidyarathi v. State of U.P., AIR 1991 S.C. 537
Shukar Din v. Govt. of West Pakistan, PLD 1965 Lahore 521
Shyam Sunder Chowkham v. Kajal Kanti Biswas, AIR 1999 Gauheti 101
Shyam Sunder v. Kajal Kanti, AIR 1999 Gau 101
Sindh Employees' Social Security Institution v. Mumtaz Ali Taj, PLD 1975 S.C. 450
Sipuel v. Oklahama Board of Regents, 199 Okl. 586 (Okl. 1948)
Sirajuddin v. State, PLD 1957 Lahore 962
Sitaramacharya v. Senior Dy. Inspector, AIR 1958 A.P. 78
Skinners v. Oklahoma, 316 U.S. 535 (1942)
Slaughterhouse, 83 U.S. 36 (1873)
Smt. Begum v. The State, AIR 1963 Bombay 17
Smt. Triveni Ben v. State of Gujarat, AIR (1989) SC 142
Smit v. Allwright, 321 U.S. 649 (1944)
Smyth v. Ames, 169 U.S. 466 (1898)

Snajder v. INS, 29 F.3d 1203 (7th Cir. 1994)
Sobbo Gyanchandani v. The Crown, PLD 1952 F.C. 29
Sodan Singh v. New Delhi Municipal Committee, AIR 1989 SC 1988
Southwest, (1951) 1 BVerfGe 14
Specht v. Patterson, 386 U.S. 605 (1967)
Special Courts Bill, in re 1978, AIR 1979 S.C. 478
Special Courts Bill, in re 1979, 2 SCR 476
Special Reference No. 1 of 1957, PLD 1957 S.C. 219
Special Reference, PLD 1955 S.C. 219
Special Reference No. 1 of 1998, AIR 1999 S.C. 1
Spinelli v. United States, 393 U.S. 410 (1969)
Springer v. Govt. of Philippine Islands, 277 U.S. 189 (1928)
Sreenivasa General Traders v. State of A.P., 1983 SCR (3) 843
Sri Jagannath v. State of Orissa, AIR 1954 SC 400
Sri Jayendra Saraswathy v. State of T.N., AIR 2006 S.C. 6, (2005) 8 SCC 771
Sri Srinavesa Theater v. Govt. of T.N., AIR 1992 S.C. 999
Sri F.R.J Swami v. State of Tamil Nadu, AIR 1972 S.C. 1585
Srikant Upadhya v. Union of India, AIR 1963 Pat.38
Srilal Shaw v. State of West Bengal, AIR 1975 SC 393
Srinivas v. State of Madras, AIR 1931 Mad. 70
St. James Evening Post, (1772) 2 Atk.469
St. Stephen's College v. University of Delhi, (1992) 1 SCC 558
St. Xavier's College v. State of Gujrat, AIR 1974 SC 1389 at 1414
Standard Printing Press v. Sindh Employees Social Security Institution, 1988 SCMR 1991
Stanford v. Texas, 380 U.S. 926 (1965)
Stanley v. Georgia, 394 U.S. 557 (1969)
State of A.P. v. Kokkilagada Meerayya, AIR 1970 SC 771
State of Andhra Pradesh v. Khader, AIR 1961 SC 1468
State of Bihar v. Kameshwar Singh, AIR 1952 SC 252
State of Bihar v. Shailabala Devi, AIR 1952 S.C. 329
State of Bombay v. Atma Ram, AIR 1951 SC 157
State of Bombay v. Balsora, AIR 1951 SC 318
State of Bombay v. Kathi Kalu Oghad, AIR 1961 SC 1808
State of Bombay v. Varasu Bapamali, AIR 1953 Bom. 8,1
State of Gujarat v. Shamlal, AIR 1965 SC 1251
State of Gujrat v. Ibrahim, AIR 1974 SC 645
State of Haryana v. Ghaseeta Ram, AIR 1997 SC 1868
State of Haryana v. Balwant Singh, AIR 2003 S.C. 1253, (2003) 3 SCC 414
State of Karnataka v. Nagarajaswamy, AIR 2005 S.C. 4308, (2005) 8 SCC 370
State of Kerala v. M. Padmanabhan Nair, (1985) 1 SCC 429
State of M.P. v. Baldeo Prasad, AIR 1961 S.C. 293
State of M.P. v. Bharat Singh, AIR 1967 S.C. 1170
State of M.P. v. Shobharam, AIR 1966 SC 1910
State of M.P. v. Veereshwar Rao Agnihotry, AIR 1957 SC 592
State of Madhya Pradesh v. Peer Mohd., AIR 1963 SC 645
State of Madras v. V.G. Row, AIR 1952 S.C. 597
State of Madras v. V.G. Row, AIR 1952 S.C. 196
State of Maharashtra v. Champalal, AIR 1981 S.C. 1675
State of Maharashtra v. Chandrabhall, (1983) 3 SCC 387
State of Maharashtra v. Maruti Shripati Dubal, 1986 Mah LJ 913
State of Maharashtra v. N.E. & P. Co., AIR 1951 Bom 242

State of Maharashtra v. Shriram, (1991) Cr Lj 1613
State of Mahrashtra v. Ramdas Shrinivas Nayak, AIR 1982 SC 1249
State of Moharashtra v. Ravikant S. Patil, (1991) 2 SCC 373
State of (NCT of Delhi) v. Navjot Sandhu, AIR 2005 S.C. 3820, (2005) 11 SCC 600
State of Punjab v. Ajab Singh, AIR 1953 SC 10
State of Punjab v. Ajaib Singh, AIR 1952 SC 16
State of Punjab v. Sansari Mal, AIR 1968 S.C. 331
State of Punjab v. Surrender Kumar, AIR 1992 SC 1593
State of Rajasthan v. Union of India, AIR 1977 S.C. 1361
State of Rajasthan v. Daulat Ram, AIR 1980 SC 1314
State of Tamil Nadu v. Senthil Kumar, AIR 1999 S.C. 971, (1999) 2 SCC 646
State of Uttar Pradesh v. Abdul Samad, AIR 1962 S.C. 1506
State of U.P. v. Boota Singh, AIR 1978 SC 1770
State of U.P. v. COD Chheoki Employees Cooperative Society, AIR 1997 SC 1413
State of U.P. v. Kaushaliya, AIR 1964 S.C. 416
State of U.P. v. Rehamatullah, AIR 1971 SC 1382
State of U.P. v. Synthetics and Chemicals Ltd., (1991) 4 SCC 139
State of W.B. v. Ashutosh Lahiri, AIR 1995 SC 464: (1995) 1 SCC 189
State of West Bengal v. Union of India, AIR 1963 S.C. 1241
State of West Bengal v. Anwar Ali Sarkar, AIR 1952 S.C. 75
State Trading Corporation v. C.T.O., AIR 1963 SC 1811
State v. Abdul Latif, PLD 1961 Lahore 51
State v. Charita, AIR 1999 SC 1379
State v. Dosso, PLD 1958 S.C. 533
State v. Justice Sheikh Shaukat Ali, PLD 1971 S.C. 585
State v. Zia-ur-Rehman, PLD 1973 S.C. 49, 66, 70
Stockdale v. Hansard, (1839)9 Ad. & E
Stolar, in re, 401 U.S. 23 (1971)
Stone v. Graham, 449 U.S. 39 (1980)
Strauder v. West Virginia, 100 U.S. 303 (1879)
Stuart v. Laird, 5 U.S. 298 (1803)
Street v. New York, 394 U.S. 576 (1969)
Strickland v. Washington, 466 U.S. 668 (1984)
Stubbings v. Webb, (1993) 2 W.L.R. 120, (1993) 1 All E.R. 322
Sub Committee of Judicial Accountability v. Union of India, (1991) 4 Supreme Court Cases, 699
Sub Committee of Judicial Accountability v. Union of India, AIR 1992 S.C. 320
Subhas Kumar v. State of Bihar, AIR 1991 SC 420
Sudhir Chandra, AIR 1952 Calcutta 258
Sudhir Chandra Sarkar v. Tata Iron and Steel Co. Ltd., (1984) 3 SCC 369
Suleman Mala v. Karachi Building Control Authority, 1990 CLC 448
Sung v. McGrath, 339 U.S. 33 (1950)
Sunil Batra (No. 1) v. Delhi Administration, AIR 1978 S.C. 1575
Sunil Batra (No. 2) v. Delhi Administration, AIR 1980 SC 1579
Sunil Batra v. Delhi Administration, AIR 1978 SC 1675
Sunil Gupta v. State of M.P., (1990) 3 SCC 119
Sunil v. Delhi Admn, AIR 1978 S.C. 1675
Sunil v. Delhi Admn, AIR 1980 S.C. 1579
Suo Motu Case No. 4 of 2010, PLD 2012 S.C. 553
Suo Motu Case No. 13 of 2009, PLD 2011 S.C. 619
Suo Moto Case No. 15 of 2006, PLD 2012 S.C. 610

Suo Motu Constitutional Petition, 1994 SCMR 1028
Superintendent of Police v. Abubakar, 1972 SCMR 154
Superintendent, Central Prison v. Ram Manohar Lohia, AIR 1960 SC 633
Supreme Court Advocates on Record Association v. Union of India, AIR 1994 SC 268
Supreme Court Advocates-on-Record v. Union of India, (2016) 5 SCC 1
Supreme Court Bar Association v. Union of India, (1998) 4 SCC 409
Surjeet Singh v. Union of India, AIR 1981 SC 1153
Surya Pal v. State of U.P., AIR 1951 All 674
Swadeshi Cotton Mills v. S.I. Tribunal, AIR 1961 S.C. 1381
Swann v. Charlotte-Mecklenburg Board of Education, 402 U.S. 1 (1971)
Sweatt v. Painter, 339 U.S. 629 (1950)
Syed Ali Gul Shah v. Government of Sindh, 1999 SCMR 988 at 994
Syed Mahmood Akhtar Naqvi v. Federation of Pakistan, PLD 2012 S.C. 1089

T

T. Subbiah v. S.K.D. Ramaswamy Nadar, AIR 1970 Mad. 85
T.D. Abdul Rahman v. State of Kerala, AIR 1990 SC 434
T.M.A. Pai Foundation v. State of Karnataka, AIR 2003 S.C. 355, (2002) 8 SCC 481
T.V. Vatheeswaran v. State of Tamil Nadu, AIR 1981 SC 361
Tajamal Hussain Malik v. Federal Government of Pakistan, PLD 1981 Lahore 462
Tamil Nadu Assocn. v. State of T.N., AIR 1980 S.C. 379
Tamizuddin Ahmed v. The Government of East Pakistan, PLD 1964 Dhaka 795
Tamizuddin, PLD 1955 FC 240
Tarapada v. State of West Bengal, AIR 1951 SC 174
Tasawar Hussain v. State, 1986 P. Cr. L.J. 2218
Tata Press Ltd. v. Mahanagar Telephone Nigam Ltd., (1995) 5 SCC 139
Taylor v. Kentucky, 436 U.S. 478 (1978)
Tennessee v. Garner, 471 U.S. 1 (1985)
Terry v. Adams, 345 U.S. 461 (1953)
Texas v. Johnson, 491 U.S. 397 (1989)
Thomas Dana v. State of Punjab, AIR 1959 S.C. 375
Thomas v. Review Board, 450 U.S. 707 (1981)
Thomas v. Sawkins, (1935) 2 K.B. 249
Thomson v. Catherine's College Cambridge, (1919) AC 468
Thornburgh v. American College of Obstetricians and Gynecologists, 476 U.S. 747 (1986)
Thornhill v. Alabama, 310 U.S. 88 (1940)
Tika Iqbal Muhammad Khan v. General Pervez Musharrif, PLD 2008 SC 178,
Tika Iqbal Muhammad Khan v. General Pervez Musharrif, PLD 2008 S.C. 615
Tika Ramji v. State of U.P., AIR 1956 SC 676
Tinker v. Des Moines Independent Community School District, 383 U.S. 503 (1969)
Toguru Sudhakar Keddy v. Government of Andhra Pradesh, (1993) Supp (4) SCC 439
Torcaso v. Watkins, 367 U.S. 488 (1961)
Toti Khan v. D.M. Sibi, PLD 1957 (W.P.) Quetta 1
Toyota v. United States, 268 U.S. 402 (1925)
Trapada v. State of West Bengal, AIR 1951 S.C. 174.
Trop v. Dulles, 356 U.S. 86 (1958)
Twining v. New Jersey, 211 U.S. 78 (1908)

U

U. Hetwe v. U. Tun, (1948) BLR 541
U.N. Rao v. Indira Gandhi, AIR 1971 S.C. 1002
U.P. Avas Evam Vikas Parishad v. Friends Co-operative Housing Society Ltd., AIR 1996 SC 114
U.S. ex rel. Knauff v. Shaughnessy, 338 U.S. 537 (1950)
U.S. Retirement Board v. Fritz, 449 U.S. 166 (1980)
Union Carbide v. Union of India, AIR 1992 S.C. 248
Union Council, Ali Wahan v. Associated Cement, 1993 SCMR 468
Union of India v. Dudh Nath Prasad, AIR 2000 SC 525
Union of India v. Jyoti Prakash, AIR 1971 S.C. 1093
Union of India v. Sankal Chand, AIR 1977 S.C. 2328
Union of India v. Subedar Ram Narain, AIR 1998 SC 3225
Union of India v. Sunil Kumar, AIR 2001 SC 1092
Union of India v. Tulsiram Patel, (1985) 3 SCC 398
United States Department of Agriculture v. Moreno, 413 U.S. 528 (1973)
United States ex rel. Cuff v. Shaughnessy, 338 U.S. 537 (1950)
United States ex rel. Toth v. Quarles, 350 U.S. 11 (1955)
United States Term Limits v. Thornton, 514 U.S. 779 (1995)
United States v. Belmont, 301 U.S. 324(1937)
United States v. Bhagat Singh Thind, 261 U.S. 204 (1923)
United States v. Carolene Products Co., 304 U.S. 144 (1938)
United States v. Causby, 328 US 256 (1946)
United States v. Chemical Foundation, 272 U.S. 1 (1926)
United States v. Cruikshank, (1875) 92 U.S. 542
United States v. Eichman, 496 U.S. 310 (1990)
United States v. Ju Toy, 198 U.S. 253, 263 (1905)
United States v. Lanza, 260 U.S. 377 (1922)
United States v. Lopez, 115 S Ct. 1624 (1995)
United States v. Macintosh, 283 U.S. 605, 615 (1931)
United States v. Moreno, 413 U.S. 528 (1973)
United States v. Nixon, 418 U.S. 683 (1974)
United States v. O'Brien, (1968) 391 U.S. 367 (1968)
United States v. Pink, 315 U.S. 203 (1942)
United States v. Progressive, 467 F. Supp. 990 (D.C. Wis. 1979)
United States v. Robel, 389 U.S. 258 (1967)
United States v. Ross, 456 U.S. 798 (1982)
United States v. S.E. Underwriters Association, 322 U.S. 533 (1944)
United States v. Seeger, 380 U.S. 163 (1965)
United States v. United Foods, 533 U.S. 405 (2001)
United States v. United States District Court, 407 U.S. 297 (1972)
United States v. Ursery, 518 U.S. 267 (1996)
United States v. Virginia, 518 U.S. 515 (1996)
United States v. Wunderlich, 342 US 98 (1951)
University of Alabama v. Garrett, 531 U.S. 356
Unni Krishnan J.P. v. State of A.P., (1993) 4 SCC 111
Unni Krishnan v. State of A.P., (1993) 1 SCC 645
US v. Cruikshank, 92 US 542 (1875)
US v. Guest, 383 US 745 (1966)
Usha Agarwal v. Union of India, 2006 Cri LJ 2934
Usif Patel v. Crown, PLD 1955 S.C. 387

V

V.C. Misra, In re, (1995) 2 SCC 584
V.K. Agarwal v. Vasantaraj, AIR 1988 SC 1106
V.S. Kuttan Pillai v. Ramakrishanan, AIR 1980 S.C. 185
Vaguapurushcdji v. Muldas, AIR 1966 SC 1119
Vallandigham, Ex parte 1 Wall. 243 (1864)
Vance v. Bradley, 440 U.S. 93 (1979)
Vasudev v. Vamanji, ILR 1881 Bom. 80
Veera Ibrahim v. State of Maharashtra, AIR 1976 SC 1167
Vellore Citizen. Welfare Forum v. Union of India, (1966) 5 SCC 647,
Venkataraman v. Union of India, AIR 1954 S.C. 375
Venkataramana Devaru v. State of Mysore, AIR 1958 SC 255
Verral v. Great Yarmouth, B.C. (1981) Q.B. 202
Vice Chancellor Osmania University v. Chancellor, AIR 1967 S.C. 1305
Vikram Deo Singh Tomar v. State of Bihar, AIR 1988 SC 1782
Vimal Chand v. Pradhan, AIR 1979 S.C. 1501, (1979) 4 SCC 401
Vincent Parikurlangara v. Union of India, (1987) 2 SCC 165
Vineet Narayan v. Union of India, (1998) 1 SCC 226
Virendra v. State of Punjab, AIR 1957 S.C. 896
Virindra Singh v. U.P., AIR 1954 S.C. 447
Virginia State Board of Pharmacy v. Virginia Citizens Consumer Council, 425 U.S. 748 (1976)
Vitek v. Jones, 445 U.S. 480 (1980)

W

W.T. Commissioner v. Suresh Seth, AIR 1981 SC 1106
Wagon Mond, (No. 2) (1966) 2 All ER 709
Wajid Shamsul Hassan v. Federation of Pakistan, PLD 1997 Lah 617
Walker v. City of Birmingham, 388 US 307 (1967)
Wallace v. Jaffree, 472 U.S. 38 (1985)
Walters v. W.H. Smith & Son, Ltd., (1914) 1 K.B. 595
Waman Rao v. Union of India, AIR 1981 S.C. 272
Ward-Smith v. Jebb, (1965) 3 All ER 358
Warden v. Hayden, 387 U.S. 294 (1967)
Waris Meah v. The State, PLD 1957 S.C. 157
Washington v. Davis, 426 U.S. 229 (1976)
Washington v. Glucksberg, 521 U.S. 702 (1997)
Washington v. Harper, 494 U.S. 210 (1990)
Wasi Uddin Ahmad v. District Magistrate, Aligarh, AIR 1981 SC 2166
Wasim Sajjad v. Federation of Pakistan, PLD 2001 SC 233
Wattan Party v. Federation of Pakistan, PLD 2006 S.C. 697
Wattan Party v. Federation of Pakistan, PLD 2012 S.C. 292
Wayman v. Southard, 23 U.S. 1 (1825)
Wazir Chand v. State of H.P., AIR 1954 SC 415
Webster v. Reproductive Health Services, 492 U.S. 490 (1989)
Weinberger v. Wiesenfeld, 420 U.S. 636 (1975)
West Virginia State Board of Education v. Barnette, 319 U.S. 624 (1943)
Western Union tel. Co. V. Pennsylvania R. Co., 195 US 540 (1904)
Whitney v. California, 274 U.S. 357 (1927)
Widmar v. Vincent, 454 U.S. 263 (1981)

Wiener v. U.S., 357 U.S. 349 (1958)
Wilkes v. Wood, (1763), 19 St. Tr. 1153
Wilkes v. Woods, (1769) 19 St. Tr. 1406
Williamson v. Lee Optical, 348 U.S. 483 (1955)
Wilson v. Arkansa, 514 U.S. 927 (1995)
Wilson v. Girard, 354 U.S. 524 (1957)
Winship, in re, 397 U.S. 358 (1970)
Wisconsin v. Mitchell, 508 U.S. 476 (1993)
Woodby v. INS, 385 U.S. 276, 285 (1966)
Wooley v. Maynard, 430 U.S. 705 (1977)

Y

Yakus v. U.S., 321 U.S. 414 (1944)
Yamashita, 327 U.S. 1 (1946)
Yates v. United States, 354 U.S. 298 (1957)
Young v. Bristol Aeroplane Co Ltd., (1944) 2 All ER 193
Youngstown Sheet & Tube Co. v. Sawyer, 343 U.S. 579 (1952)
Yousaf Ali Khan v. The State, PLD 1977 S.C. 482
Yousufalli v. State of Maharashtra, AIR 1960 SC 756
Yumnam Mangibabu siungh v. State of Manipur, AIR 1983 SC 300
Yusufalli Esmail Nagree v. State of Maharashtra, AIR 1968 SC 147
Yusufalli Esmail Nagree v. State of Maharashtra, AIR 1967 SCR (3) 720

Z

Zadvydas v. Davis, 533 U.S. 678
Zafar Ali Shah v. Chief of Army Staff, PLD 2000 S.C. 869
Zafar Ali Shah v. General Pervez Musharraf, PLD 2000 S.C. 673
Zafar Ali Shah v. Pervez Musharraf, PLD 2000 S.C. 821
Zaheeruddin v. The State, 1993 SCMR 1718
Zahur Elahi v. Z.A. Bhutto, PLD 1975 SC 383
Zia-ur-Rehman, P.L.D. 1973 S.C. 49
Zobel v. Williams, 457 U.S. 55 (1982)
Zorach v. Clauson, 343 U.S. 306 (1952)

Preface

Writers on constitutional law have generally focused on the Constitutions of their respective countries particularly in case of written Constitutions. However, authors writing commentaries on Constitutions refer to leading constitutional cases of other countries for comparative purposes. Such commentaries generally follow the scheme of the Constitution, article by article, which is helpful for legal practitioners in finding relevant precedents.

However, there are very few writers on comparative constitutional law. During the last twenty years or so that I have been teaching constitutional law to the LL.M students at the Punjab University Law College, I realized that there is acute deficiency of materials for LLM students in Pakistan and India studying principles and concepts of constitutional law on comparative basis.

We, in Pakistan and India, derive our concepts on constitutional law mainly from English and American jurisprudence developed by leading authors and superior courts in these countries. Keeping that in mind I have endeavoured to explain these concepts and to show how they have been adopted, applied, extended and developed by the superior courts in India and Pakistan. Therefore, the basic effort in this work is to identify the universally established principles and concepts of constitutional law and to analyse and discuss them in the light of the judgments of the superior courts of the USA, UK, India and Pakistan. At places, judgments rendered by the superior courts in Australia, Canada and Germany have also been mentioned.

The book is divided into seven parts. Part I is introductory and discusses definition and scope of the Constitutional Law. It also discusses interaction between the principal actors who set the constitutional law machinery into motion, i.e., State and Citizen. Part II relates to the basic constitutional concepts like constitutional conventions, the rule of law, due process of law, and equality before law. Part III relates to certain basic constitutional structures like parliamentary and presidential forms of government and concepts of separation of powers and federalism. Part IV relates to judiciary and includes subjects like independence of judiciary, judicial review, precedents and theories of interpretations of Constitution. The fundamental rights included in various constitutions are divided into two parts: Human Rights and Civil Liberties. Part V deals with human rights like rights to life, liberty, privacy and property, freedom of religion and safeguards against self incrimination and double jeopardy. Part VI pertains to civil liberties like freedoms of speech, press, association, assembly and movement. Certain evolving concepts like doctrines of state necessity and basic structure of Constitution are dealt with in Part VII of the book.

I hope that this book will be of utility in areas not frequently treaded upon in the past by many authors. The cases and materials in this book could meet the needs of the students of constitutional law studying for the degree of LL.M, being offered by the universities in India and Pakistan. It can also be of assistance to lawyers practising before the superior courts particularly in India and Pakistan.

I am deeply indebted to Mr Muhammad Waqar Rana, LL.M. (Harvard) who contributed the chapters on the 'doctrine of necessity' and 'precedents'. He has gone through the remaining manuscript and made very valuable suggestions which have been duly incorporated. These changes would hopefully enhance the utility and value of the book. I am delighted to have him as co-author of the book.

I express my gratitude to Max-Planck Institute for International and Comparative Law in Heidelberg, Germany where I initially worked on the book during the summer of the year 2004. The cooperation extended to me by the Institute to utilize the materials in its library and has been extremely helpful to me in my research on the book. I am thankful to my law firm 'Cornelius, Lane & Mufti' for use of its library and secretarial services. I owe debt of gratitude to Messrs Akbar Chauhan and Asghar Baig, who typed the entire manuscript.

It is a matter of gratification for me that the book has been well received by the lawyers, law teachers and law students in Pakistan. It has been used as textbook for the LL.M. students in Pakistan studying 'Constitutional Law'.

This is an updated edition in which latest laws and judgments have been included and discussed. One of the chapters, 'Independence of Judiciary', has incorporated the judicial reforms introduced in the United Kingdom under the Constitutional Reforms Act of 2005.

I am grateful to Mr. Arshad Saeed Husain, Managing Director, Oxford University Press Karachi for accepting the book for publication. I am also thankful to Mr. Samuel Ray, Editor, Higher Education, Academic and Reference books for supervising the publication and for excellent editorial work done on the manuscript.

HAMID KHAN

Part I

Introduction

1 Definition and Scope of Constitutional Law

Definition

There is no single comprehensive definition of Constitutional Law. It has different meanings in different systems of law. Essentially it must have reference to that branch of law which is concerned with the constitution of a country. The significance of the definition is relevant because in the first instance for the reader to understand what constitutes the Constitutional Law and secondly, it is important to differentiate between Constitutional Law and other laws in the field especially where judicial review is developed. This second aspect, however, is not present in the British Constitution where there is no such distinction between the Constitutional Law and other laws. In a great majority of the nations of the civilized world, it is possible to discover a single document or bundle of documents which embody the constitution of a country, however, in Britain there is no such guide. The provisions of British constitution must be gleaned from among the vast mass of source material which together forms the whole body of English, Scots, and Northern Ireland law.[1]

Owen Hood Phillips (1907–1986)[2] has defined the constitution of a state as the system of laws, customs, and conventions which define the composition and powers of organs of the state, and regulate the relations of the various state organs to one another and to the private citizen.[3] In the generally accepted use of the term, it means the rules which regulate the structure of the principal organs of government and their relationship to each other, and determine their principal functions. These rules consist both of legal rules in strict sense and of usages, commonly called conventions, which without being enacted are accepted as binding by all who are concerned with government. Though the constitutional law is concerned primarily with the legal aspects of government, but it is required for an understanding of constitutional law that there is some knowledge of the main features of constitutional history and of the working of the political institutions. The 'Constitutional Law' also deals with the relationship between the citizen and the state, and more particularly, with what may be called political relationship rather than economic relationship.[4]

A.K. Brohi (1915–1987)[5] attempted the definition of Constitutional Law as 'that branch of public law which deals with questions relating to the legal character of the state, describe the power-relations that subsist between the several organs of its sovereign power, and sets forth its morphology, its structural peculiarities and the principles of inner dynamism, growth and movement.[6]

Constitution and Constitutional Law

The concepts of 'Constitution' and 'Constitutional Law' have been frequently confused by the scholars of Constitutional Law. These terms are commonly and interchangeably used and at times given the same or similar meanings. However, the distinction between these two concepts is of utmost importance.

A 'Constitution', in a written form, means there is a fundamental instrument that deals with the legislature, the executive, and the judiciary; the fundamental rights of the citizens; and states the provisions for its own amendment. In other words, the constitution is a statement or a collection of statements in relation to the above factors and the interaction between these factors. It is an inert document which can be brought into motion by the working, collaboration and interaction of such factors. Constitutional Law, on the other hand, deals with the transformation of this inert document into a living document by setting into motion these factors. Such transformation is made possible by the role and rulings of the judiciary. In the words of Justice Charles Evans Hughes (1862–1948),

> 'We are under a Constitution, but the Constitution is what the judges, say it is'.[7]

Noel T. Dowling (1885–1969)[8] says that

> 'the study of Constitutional Law...may be described in general terms as a study of the doctrine of judicial review in action.'[9]

These definitions/descriptions emphasize the role of the judiciary in converting the Constitution into Constitutional Law. Thus, constitutional law is a judge made constitution. The Constitution is an abstract form of fundamental law and constitutional law is its practical shape. Thus, Constitutional Law is the constitution as interpreted or construed by the superior courts of the country.

Development of Public Law: Constitutional and Administrative Law

Constitutional Law is an important branch of Public Law which is generally divided into three sub-branches: Public International Law, Constitutional Law and Administrative Law. For a long time, administrative law was not considered as an independent field of study and in particular, the British authors regarded it as part of the study of Constitutional Law. However, in the 20th century with the state-functions becoming more complex and having undertaken diverse activities especially in public welfare and the public sector of the economy, administrative law has assumed greater importance and is now universally recognized as an independent field of study.

The term 'public law' is used in contradistinction to 'private law'. The latter pertains to that area which deals with law, persons, things and obligations among persons, while public law is the law of the state. Whereas the old legal order had encompassed every one, both governors and the governed, modern law has produced a new system, containing two co-existing legal worlds, that of the relations between monarch and subjects, and that of the relations among the citizens mutually. It is because of these political overtones that the distinction between public and private law is even today much debated and in no way evident to everyone.[10]

Classification of Constitutions

According to Kenneth Wheare (1907–79)[11], the word Constitution is commonly used in at least two senses. Firstly, it is used to describe the whole system of government of a country, the collection of rules. These rules are partly legal, in the sense that courts of law will recognize and apply them, and partly non-legal or extra-legal, taking the form of images, understandings, customs, or conventions which courts do not recognize as law, but which are no less effective in regulating the government than the rules of law strictly so called. Secondly, it is used in a narrower sense to describe not the whole collection of rules, legal or non-legal, but rather a selection of them which has usually been embodied in one document or in a few closely related documents. This selection is almost invariably a selection of legal rules which governs the government of that country and which has been embodied in a document.[12]

These two different meanings given to the word 'constitution' became a basis for classifying constitutions into written and unwritten constitutions with Britain as the sole surviving example of an unwritten constitution.

Constitutions may also be classified according to the method by which they may be amended. One category is of those constitutions which may be amended by legislation through the same process as any other ordinary law. The other category requires a special process for its amendment. The first category, also called 'flexible constitutions' is very small and includes the Constitution of New Zealand. The other category which has most of the constitutions of the world including USA, India, Pakistan, Switzerland etc. This category is also classified as 'rigid constitutions.

Within the category of rigid constitutions, there can be two further classifications, one more rigid than the other. The more rigid class is where the constitution cannot be amended by the single legislature. The US Constitution provides in its Article V that the Congress with a two-third majority of each house can propose an amendment to the constitution and that such amendment can only become part of the constitution when ratified by three-fourths of the legislatures or conventions of the total number of states. The Congress, thus, does not have the power to amend the constitution but can only propose such amendments. In Belgium, whenever an incumbent parliament proposes an amendment in the constitution, dissolution of both houses follows. After the general election, the amendment is carried if at least two-thirds of the members of each house are present and two-thirds of those present vote in favour of the proposed amendment. Although, the amendment is made by the legislature, but not the one that proposed it. In Switzerland, no constitutional amendment can take place unless the amendment proposed by the federal assembly is duly assented to both by a majority of Swiss citizens and a majority of the cantons. Such a class of 'rigid' constitutions can be called supreme over the legislature.[13]

The Constitution in Pakistan can be amended by a two-thirds (Article 239) majority of each house of the parliament. While the Constitution of India requires that an amendment in the constitution can be passed by a majority of the total membership of each house and by not less than two-thirds of the members of the house present and voting (Article 368). These constitutions would fall within the meaning of less 'rigid' constitution where legislature is supreme over the constitution. It is however, noticeable in the Indian constitution that an amendment in provisions relating to the election of the president, executive power of the union and the states, dealing with constitution, powers and jurisdiction of the supreme court and the high courts, legislative relations between union and states requires special majority of each house of parliament and ratification by resolutions of not less than one-half of the states. The Indian constitution in respect of above referred matter falls in the class of more 'rigid' where the constitution is supreme over the legislature.

Constitutions may be classified also in terms of the method by which the powers of government are distributed between the central government and the governments of the units. These powers are the executive, legislative, and judicial powers. On this basis, constitutions are classified as 'federal' or 'unitary'. In a federal constitution, the powers of government are divided between a government for the whole country and governments of the constituent parts or the federating units of the country and the latter in turn exercise their powers without being controlled by the central government. Thus, both the central as well as the provincial or state legislatures have limited powers. Neither is subordinate to the other; both are co-ordinate. In a unitary constitution, on the other hand, the legislature of the whole country is the supreme law-making body in the country. It may permit other legislatures to exist and to exercise their powers, but it has the right in law, to overrule them; they are subordinate to it.[14]

The examples of federal constitutions include the United States, Switzerland, Germany, India, Pakistan, and Australia. The category of unitary constitutions includes Britain, France, New Zealand, Sweden, Norway, and Denmark. In each of the federal constitutions, the subjects upon which the central legislature may make laws are set out and the residuary subjects are left to the provincial or state legislatures to legislate. Within the federal constitutions, there can be a category which can be described as quasi-federal. This would include a constitution where the central government/legislature, under certain special circumstances like emergency, can take over the functions of the provincial or state government/legislature and legislate for the province or state. India and Pakistan are examples of quasi-federal constitutions. Another example of quasi-federal constitutions is that constitution which provides for a common list of subjects for legislation by the central and provincial legislature and in case of conflict between the legislation on the same subject by both the legislatures, the legislation of the central legislature would prevail over the provincial legislature to the extent of the conflict or inconsistency.

Constitutions can also be classified on the basis of the form of government as parliamentary or presidential. The point of distinction is that in a parliamentary system, the executive branch including prime minister and other ministers are taken from the parliament but in the presidential system the executive including the president and his cabinet are from outside the parliament.

Notes

1. D.C.M. Yardley, *Introduction to British Constitutional Law*, 6th ed. (London: Butterworths, 1984), p. 3.
2. Owen Hood Phillips was one of the most eminent constitutional lawyer and leading figure in the University and City of Birmingham.
3. Ibid., pp. 3–4.
4. E.C.S. Wade and A.W. Bradley, *Constitutional Law*, 7th ed. (London: Longmans, 1965), p. 3.
5. A.K. Brohi was a prominent Pakistani politician and lawyer.
6. A.K. Brohi, *Fundamental Law of Pakistan* (Karachi: Din Muhammad Press, 1958), p. 3.
7. Charles Evans Hughes was the 11th Chief Justice of the USA from 1930 to 1941.
8. Noel T. Dowling was Columbia University's principal teacher of constitutional law.
9. Noel T. Dowling and Gerald Gunther, *Cases and Materials on Constitutional Law*, 7th ed. (Foundation Press, USA, 1965), p. 19.
10. R.C. van Caenegem, *An Historical Introduction to Western Constitutional Law* (Cambridge: Cambridge University Press, 1995), p. 5.
11. Kenneth C. Wheare was an Australian academic at Oxford University, and an expert on the constitutions of the British Commonwealth.
12. K.C. Wheare, *Modern Constitutions* (London: Oxford University Press, 1951), pp. 1–2.
13. Ibid., p. 25.
14. Ibid., pp. 26–7.

2 State and the Citizen

Meaning of State

The concept of allegiance presupposes a State.[1] The State is as old as human association. Republic, commonwealth, and *'almulk'*[2] are recognized concepts in Western and Islamic political thought. The modern nation state with a constitution and citizens is a phenomenon starting with the Treaty of Westphalia (1648)[3] and ultimately culminating in the present concept of state after the American and French revolutions. Unless a political society is instituted, i.e. in a state there is no administration of justice and no concept of rights. Since the state is supreme and all embracing, the concept of rights and duties are built around it. The state has a monopoly over the coercive power. In a society, the promotion of virtue and the highest good and complete happiness of the individual can only be realized in the state. Therefore, it is necessary to enquire into the best constitution and the best system of legislation in a state for the said purposes. The state is much more than an alliance, which the individuals can join or leave without effect, for the independent or cityless man is unscrupulous and savage something essentially different from a citizen. The members of state are numerous, and they differ in their personal qualities; it is by the cooperation of its various parts in the performance of their proper functions, and by the reciprocal equality of these parts, that the state is constituted in an organic whole and its preservation secured.[4]

The state has been variously defined by different authorities from different viewpoints. It may shortly be described as an independent political society, occupying a definite territory, and having for its primary object, the defence of the territory against external aggression and the maintenance of order and justice within the community itself.[5] This definition has been expanded to include the furtherance of common welfare through an original role of government. A modern state is expected to deal with a vast mass of social problems, either by direct activity or by supervision or regulation. In order to perform these functions, the state must have agents or organs through which to operate. The appointment or establishment of these agents or organs, the general nature of their functions and powers, their relationship *inter se* and between them and the citizen form a large part of the constitution of a state.[6] The authority of the state, being supreme within its territory and independent of any external control, is called its sovereignty.[7] Apart from the nature of 'State' as a sovereign entity, the term is sometimes used to refer to a federating unit or province in a federation as is the case in the constitutions of United States of America, India and Australia.

Britain is a unitary state. The United States, Pakistan, India, and Germany are federal states. In the USA, the term 'United States' is used in contradistinction to the term 'State'.[8]

The State of Pakistan is known as Islamic Republic of Pakistan (Article 1). This is the legal character of the State of Pakistan established by the Constitution of Pakistan. Islam is the state religion of Pakistan. It is a republic which means that the government established under the constitution will be of representative character, the representatives having been chosen by the people through a process of election. The preamble to the Constitution of Pakistan which is a beacon light for the constitution makers[9] lays down that –

> 'State shall exercise its powers and authority through the chosen representatives of the people'.

The principle of Republicanism enjoins that the whole body of the people should be admitted to political privileges irrespective of any consideration based on caste, colour, creed, race, status etc. It is for this reason that the idea of equality is the foundation of any republican form of government. A republican form of government necessarily implies that sovereignty vests in the people and that all the constitutional process within the state is regulated and controlled by such decisions as the people make. In Pakistan, however, a unique concept was introduced. Sovereignty over the universe belongs to Allah Almighty and the authority of the state is to be exercised by the people as a sacred trust.[10] (preamble to the Constitution).

According to the Constitution of Pakistan, 'the State' means the federal government, Parliament, a provincial government, a provincial assembly and such local or other authorities in Pakistan as are by law empowered to impose any tax or cess.[11]

The Indian Constitution defines the term 'State' as used in different Articles of Part III of its constitution, which states that unless the context otherwise requires, the term 'State' includes the following:

1. The Government and Parliament of India, i.e. Executive and Legislature of the Union.
2. The Government and the Legislature of each State, i.e. Executive and Legislatures of States.
3. All local or other authorities within the territory of India.
4. All local and other authorities under the control of the Government of India.

The term 'State' thus includes the executive as well as the legislative organs of the union and the states. It is, therefore, the actions of these bodies that can be challenged before the courts as violating fundamental rights.

It may be noted that in the definition of the 'State' given in Article 7 of the Constitution, the judiciary has been excluded because it is the custodian of the fundamental rights charged with the duty to enforce them and to see that none of the fundamental rights are abridged or taken away as provided in Article 8 of the Constitution.[12] The judicature is a state organ and its function is to decide whether a fundamental right has been violated or not and in the hierarchy of courts, the Supreme Court being at the apex whose decisions are binding on all other courts and authorities in Pakistan. The last portion of Article 7 was not there in the earlier Constitutions of 1956 or 1962 (Articles 3 and 5 respectively) and the question arose whether the judiciary was included in the definition of the State? These words were therefore added to exclude the superior judiciary from the definition of the State for the apparent reason that the judiciary was charged with the obligation to enforce fundamental rights and to interpret the constitution. However, for the limited purpose of Article 25(3) the Supreme Court has held that the definition of State would include the judiciary.[13]

The relationship between the State and its citizens is very important especially in the context of fundamentals rights. The Constitution of Pakistan envisages a distinct scheme. In the first instance, it enjoins that loyalty to the State is the basic duty of every citizen and obedience to the constitution and law is an inviolable obligation of every citizen and every other person in Pakistan.[14] Fundamental Rights come only after this loyalty is owed. In the context of the Constitution of Pakistan, there are certain rights which have been conferred on the citizens only:

Fundamental Rights of Freedom of Movement	Article 15
Freedom of Assembly	Article 16
Freedom of Association	Article 17
Freedom of Trade and Business	Article 18
Freedom of Speech	Article 19
Freedom of Religion and to establish religious institutions	Article 20
Right to have Property	Article 23
Right to the claim equality before law and to have equal protection of law	Article 25

Since the blessings of citizenship are great and also its relevance to the fundamental rights is obvious, it is therefore imperative to treat the subject of citizenship in detail.

CITIZENSHIP

Britain

The British Nationality Act 1981, repealed the Nationality Act 1948, except sections 3, 32, and 34 of the later Act.[15] This new British Act provides for citizenship, nationality and issues relating to immigration. Earlier, UK nationality laws were founded on the common law doctrine of 'allegiance'. Allegiance was defined by Blackstone as 'the tie, or ligament, which binds the subject to the king, in return for that protection which the king affords the subject.' Allegiance is no longer a source of British nationality although it may be a consequence of it. It must be regarded henceforth as relevant to the law of treason rather than nationality.

In 1870, Naturalization Act was passed by the British Parliament to enable aliens to acquire British nationality by the executive grant of the home secretary. The British Nationality and Status of Aliens Act 1914 repealed the Naturalization Act 1870 and provided a comprehensive code for the acquisition and loss of British nationality. Further acts passed dealing notably with the status were of married women, and this legislation was known as the British Nationality and Status of Aliens Acts of 1914 and 1943. These acts were almost entirely repealed by the British Nationality Act 1948.

A Commonwealth legal conference was held in London in 1947 and it was decided to accept the principles of the Canadian Citizenship Act, 1946 for general application throughout the Commonwealth. The British Nationality Act 1948 gave effect to these principles as far as the United Kingdom and British colonies were concerned. It provided a new method of giving effect to the principle that people of each of the self-governing countries within the Commonwealth have both a particular status as citizens of their own country and a common status as members of the wider association of peoples comprising the Commonwealth.

Friendly aliens are citizens of countries with which the Crown is not at war, and who have the right to contract, to own and dispose of personal property, and to bring and defend actions. They may now own and dispose of real property. Resident aliens owe allegiance to the Crown and are subject to the general civil and criminal law. They do not enjoy the parliamentary or local government franchise, they may not sit in either house of Parliament or hold any public office; but they may be employed in any civil capacity under the Crown (a) outside the United Kingdom, or (b) under a certificate issued by a Minister with the Treasury's approval.[16]

The object of the British Nationality Act 1981 is to distinguish clearly a category of citizenship which carries with it the right of entry and residence from other categories.

The act recognizes three categories of citizenship:

(i) British;
(ii) British Dependent Territories;
(iii) British Overseas. It also recognizes the special status of
  a. British protected persons; and
  b. British subjects without citizenships (British Subjects).

The term Commonwealth citizen embraces all categories (apart from that of British Protected Persons) and citizens of independent Commonwealth countries.

British citizenship may be acquired by—

(i) Birth in the United Kingdom provided that one parent was at the time of birth a British citizen or was settled in the United Kingdom. A person who does not acquire citizenship by birth in the United Kingdom may, however, be subsequently entitled to citizenship, for example, if one of his parents later acquires citizenship or he spends the first ten years of his life in the United Kingdom.
(ii) Descent; when birth occurs abroad but one parent is a British citizen other than by descent, it allows acquisition by descent for one generation only.

British citizenship may be acquired by naturalization and by registration.

Pakistan

Unlike the Indian Constitution, 1950, the Constitution of Pakistan leaves the matters of citizenship, nationality and naturalization to Parliament.[17] Under the Pakistan Citizenship Act 1951, there are altogether ten types of Pakistani citizenships, four under Section 3 and six under Sections 4 to 9.

1. By birth in the territories constituting Pakistan before 14 August 1947.

2. By birth in India having domicile in Pakistan.
3. By naturalization as British subject in Pakistan.
4. By migration to Pakistan from India before 13 April 1951 to be proved by means of a certificate issued under the Rules.
5. By birth in Pakistan after 13 April 1951.
6. By descent if born after 13 April 1951 if father was a citizen of Pakistan at the time of his birth.
7. By migration from India between 13 April 1951 and 1 January 1952 acquired by registration granted by federal government.
8. By migration to India from Pakistan after 1 March 1947 and returning to Pakistan under a permit for re-settlement.
9. By registration of a person whose father or father's father was born in India and was resident outside Pakistan before 13 April 1951 and have obtained a certificate of domicile.
10. By naturalization under the Naturalization Act 1926 and registration as a citizen of Pakistan.

A Pakistan citizen loses citizenship on acquisition of citizenship of a foreign country except in the case of married women, minors or where dual nationality is allowed by the Act.[18] With citizenship, several constitutional, political, and civil rights are associated. Under Article 63(1) (c) of Pakistan's Constitution, in order to be qualified to be elected to Parliament, or to hold or be elected to a constitutional office, a person has to be a citizen of Pakistan. A person is disqualified to become or from being a member of Parliament if he acquires the citizenship of a foreign State.[19] Moreover recently, it has been held that a civil servant who acquires nationality of another State during his service has to choose between the service and his foreign nationality.[20]

The Pakistan Citizenship Act 1951, also deals with domicile. Domicile relates to person's permanent dwelling and nationality of a country and is different from permanent residence.[21] Article 27 of the Constitution prohibits against discrimination *inter alia* on the basis of residence but since there was a huge disparity amongst different parts of Pakistan, it was permitted for a period of forty years to provide for a quota system on regional basis in jobs and admission to various educational institutions and therefore, domicile becomes necessary.

India

On partition of the country, some people were living in India, some people came from Pakistan, and some others were living abroad. The problem relating to the citizenship of India, is therefore, tackled by three-fold provisions. A person at the commencement of the Indian Constitution could be a citizen of India in the following ways–

(1) by domicile,
(2) by migration, and
(3) by registration.

1. Citizenship by Domicile (Article 5)

According to Article 5 of the Indian Constitution, a person shall be a citizen of India if he fulfils the following two conditions.

1. He must, at the commencement of the Constitution, have his domicile in the territory of India; and
2. Such persons must fulfil any one of the following three conditions
    a. he was born in the territory of India; or
    b. either of his parents was born in the territory of India; or
    c. he must have been ordinarily resident in the territory of India for not less than five years immediately preceding the commencement of the Constitution.

Conditions contained in (a), (b) and (c) are alternative and any one of them needs to be fulfilled by a person having domicile in India, to be a citizen of India.

The expression *territory of India*, meant the territory of India as is defined under Article 1(3) of the constitution, at the commencement of the constitution.

Domicile

The term 'domicile' is not defined in the Indian Constitution. Ordinarily, it means the home or the place where a person resides with the intention to remain there permanently and without any present intention to remove himself therefrom. It is a place which a person fixes as a habitation for himself and his family, for not a mere special or temporary purpose but with a present intention of making it his permanent home.[22]

Domicile is not the same thing as residence, for, residence implies the purely physical fact, fact of just being and living at a particular place. But domicile is not residence, it is residence coupled with intention to live indefinitely at the place.[23]

There are two kinds of domicile:

— 'domicile of origin' and
— 'domicile of choice'.

Every person is born with a domicile of origin. It is the domicile which he receives at the time of his birth. The domicile of origin of every person of legitimate birth is the place where, at the time of his birth, his father is domiciled. The domicile of origin of the illegitimate child is the place where, at the time of his birth, his mother is domiciled.[24] Therefore, the domicile of origin, though received at the time of birth, need not be either the country in which the child is born or the country in which his parents are residing or the country to which his father belongs by race or allegiance.[25] The domicile of origin is a concept of law and it clings to the man until he abandons it and has a domicile of choice.[26] A married woman takes the domicile of her husband on her marriage.[27] A widow retains the domicile of her deceased husband until she changes it.

Every person of full age and capacity can acquire a domicile of choice by abandoning his domicile of origin. He can acquire the domicile of choice by moving from the place of his residence to another place and settling down there with a definite intention to remain there permanently. The onus to prove that he has changed his domicile lies on him. It depends on his conduct and for this purpose, the course of his conduct, both before and after the material time, is relevant.[28]

2. Citizenship by Migration (Article 6)

On partition of the country, people residing in Pakistan and migrating to the territory of India, could not be regarded Indian citizens under the provisions of Article 6. Special provisions under Articles 6 and 7 had, therefore, been made for them.

Article 6 is applicable to persons of Indian origin, i.e. those who themselves were born within the territory of India as defined in the Government of India Act 1935, or either of their parents was born in India so defined, or any of their grandparents was born in the territory of India so defined.

Any of such persons migrating from Pakistan to India could acquire Indian citizenship, under this provision. Article 6 has classified such persons migrating from Pakistan to India, into two categories—

(i) those who came to India before 19 July 1948, and
(ii) those who came to India on or after 19 July 1948.

Article 6 provides that a person of Indian origin shall be deemed to be a citizen of India at the commencement of the constitution if he, having migrated from Pakistan to India before 19 July 1948, has been ordinarily resident in the territory of India since the date of his migration.

A person of Indian origin shall be deemed to be a citizen of India if he migrated from Pakistan to India on or after 19 July 1948 and only when he has been registered as a citizen of India by an officer appointed on behalf by the Government of the Dominion of India. His application could be accepted for registration only if he had been resident in the territory of India for at least 6 months immediately preceding the date of his application.[29]

Article 6 specifies 19 July 1948 for determining the acquisition of citizenship by migrants from Pakistan. It was on this date that the Influx from Pakistan (Control) Ordinance 1948, promulgated by the Governor General of India, came into force. The ordinance was promulgated for regulating the movements of people from Pakistan to India. Under this ordinance, permit system was introduced for the entry to India from Pakistan. Therefore, people migrating from Pakistan to India on or after 19 July 1948, could enter Indian territory under a permit issued by the officer appointed by the Government of India for the purpose. The ordinance was replaced by the Influx from Pakistan (Control) Act 1949.

Article 7 provides that a citizen of India, whether by domicile or by migration, ceased to be a citizen of India, if he had migrated to Pakistan after 1 March 1947.[30] Article 7 overrides Article 5, for even if a person was a citizen of India by virtue of Article 5, he would cease to be a citizen of India, if he migrated to Pakistan after 1 March 1947. Similarly, a person acquiring the citizenship of India under Article 6 would cease to be a citizen of India, if he had migrated to Pakistan after this date.

Proviso to Article 7 contains an exception in favour of persons who having migrated to Pakistan, returned to India. It provides that a person, who after having migrated to Pakistan, returned to the territory of India, under a permit for resettlement or permanent return to India, issued by or under the authority of any law, could be registered as a citizen of India.

Such a person would be deemed to have migrated from Pakistan to India after 19 July 1948. Therefore, it required that such a person was to make an application for his registration as a citizen of India, to an officer appointed by the Government of India. He could be so registered only if he had resided in the territory of India for at least six months immediately preceding the date of his application. On his registration, he would be deemed to be a citizen of India.[31]

3. Citizenship by Registration (Article 8)

Article 8 deals with the right of citizenship of persons of Indian origin residing outside undivided India. It provides that:

> 'any person who or either of his parents or any of his grand-parents was born in the territory of India as defined in the Government of India Act 1935, and who was ordinary resident in any country outside India as so defined, would be deemed to be a citizen of India, if he was registered as a citizen of India, by the Diplomatic or Consular Representative of India in the country where, for the time being, he was residing.'

What was required under Article 8 was that a person of Indian origin residing abroad, at the commencement of the constitution, could register himself as a citizen of India, by making an application to the diplomatic or consular representative of India in the country where he was for the time being residing. Such an application could be made before or after the commencement of the constitution, i.e. 26 January 1950. The application could be made in the form and manner prescribed by the Government of the Dominion of India or the Government of India.

Article 8 is to covers overseas Indians having no domicile in the territory of India. Under Article 8, unlike Articles 5 and 6, a person could become a citizen of India, not only at the commencement of the constitution but also subsequent to such commencement.[32]

Article 9 enacts that –

> 'a person who has voluntarily acquired the citizenship of a foreign State shall not be deemed to be a citizen of India.'

This article deals with the voluntary acquisition by a citizen of India, of citizenship of a foreign State before the commencement of the constitution. Cases of acquisition of foreign citizenship, after the commencement of the constitution, are dealt with under the Citizenship Act 1955.[33]

Article 9 recognizes the principle that no Indian citizen can claim a dual or plural citizenship. The question whether an Indian citizen has acquired the citizenship of a foreign country, is one for the determination by the central government and not by the court.[34]

Mere proof of the fact that a person has obtained a passport from a foreign country, is not sufficient, to order his deportation from India or prosecute him, unless there has been a decision of the central government in this respect. The enquiry by the central government in such a matter is quasi-judicial.[35]

Pakistan is not a foreign State under Article 9 by reason of the Declaration as in Foreign State Order 1950, made under Article 367(3) read with Article 392(3) of the Constitution. The words 'Foreign State' do not occur in Article 7, and Article 9 has no reference to Article 7. Hence, a person who migrated to Pakistan after 1 March 1947, and acquired Pakistan citizenship cannot claim to be a citizen of India. Such a person ceases to be a citizen of India under Article 7. Article 9 would have no application to such a case.[36]

Article 10 provides that:

> 'every person who is or is deemed to be a citizen of India under the provisions of Articles 5 to 8, shall continue to be a citizen of India, subject, however, to the provisions of any law that may be made by the Parliament.'

It thus enacts that the right to citizenship of India given under the provisions of the constitution can only be taken away by an express law made by the union Parliament for the purpose. Therefore, a citizen of India cannot be denied the right to citizenship indirectly.[37]

Citizenship of India after Commencement of the Constitution

The Citizenship Act 1955

Article 11 of the Indian Constitution expressly empowers the Union Parliament to make a law with respect to the acquisition or termination of citizenship of India after the commencement of the constitution and all other related matters. In the exercise of this power, Parliament has enacted the Citizenship Act 1955. The Act recognizes formally the concept of Commonwealth citizenship. The Act does not apply to a company, association or body of individuals whether incorporated or not.[38] The Citizenship Act 1955 provides the following modes of acquiring Indian citizenship after the commencement of the Constitution:

(i) Citizenship by Birth (Section 3)

Section 3 of the Citizenship Act 1955, provides that every person born in India on or after 26 January 1950, shall be a citizen of India by birth. However, such a person shall not be a citizen of India, if at the time of his birth:

(a) his father possesses such immunity from suits and legal processes as is accorded to an envoy of a foreign sovereign power and is not an Indian citizen; or
(b) his father is an enemy alien and his birth takes place in a territory under enemy occupation.

The Citizenship Act 1955, has been amended by the Citizenship (Amendment) Act 1986 with the object of making the acquisition of citizenship of India somewhat difficult. The object is to prevent persons coming to India from Bangladesh, Sri Lanka or African countries, from becoming citizens of India.

The Amendment Act 1986, amends Section 3 of the Citizenship Act 1955, and provides that citizenship by birth can be acquired only by such persons whose either of the parents is a citizen of India at the time of his birth. This amendment came into force on 26 November 1986, and therefore is applicable to the cases occurring after this date. Therefore, a person born within the territory of India on or after 26 November 1986, would become a citizen of India under Section 3 only if at the time of his birth either of his parents is a citizen of India.

(ii) Citizenship by Descent (Section 4)

Section 4 of the Citizenship Act 1955, provides that a person born outside India on or after 26 January 1950, shall be a citizen of India by descent, if, at the time of his birth, his father is a citizen of India. However, if the father of such a person is himself a citizen of India by descent, then, such a person shall not be a citizen of India unless:

(a) his birth is registered at the Indian consulate, or
(b) his father is, at the time of his birth, in the service under the Government of India.

The birth of such a person can be registered, with the Indian consulate, within one year of its occurrence or within one year of the commencement of the Citizenship Act 1955, or within such period as extended by the Government of India.

(iii) Citizenship by Registration (Section 5)

Section 5 of the Citizenship Act 1955 provides for the registration of certain categories of persons as citizens of India. This section lays down that the prescribed authority may, on application made in this behalf, register as citizen of India, any person, who is not a citizen by virtue of any provision of the constitution or by virtue of any other provisions of the Citizenship Act 1955, and belongs to any of the following categories:

(a) Persons of Indian origin, who are ordinarily resident in India and have been so resident for six months (five years);[39]
(b) Persons of Indian origin who are ordinarily resident in any country or place outside undivided India;
(c) Women, who are or have been married to citizens of India.[40] After the passing of the Citizenship (Amendment) Act 1986, this provision read as 'persons who are, or have been, married to citizens of India and are ordinarily resident in India and have been so resident for five years immediately before making an application for registration';
(d) Minor children of persons who are citizens of India; and
(e) Persons of full age and capacity who are citizens of a country mentioned in the First Schedule[41] to the Citizenship Act 1955.

Section 5 further provides that the central government may lay down conditions and restrictions subject to which the above categories of persons may be registered. The government has framed the following rules for the purpose:

(i) a person shall be deemed to be of Indian origin if he or either of his parents or any of his grandparents was born in undivided India;
(ii) a person of full age shall not be registered as a citizen of India unless he takes an oath of allegiance to the Constitution of India;
(iii) a person who has renounced or has been deprived of his Indian citizenship has been terminated, shall not be registered as a citizen except by order of the central government;
(iv) a minor may be registered as a citizen if the central government is satisfied that there are special circumstances justifying such a registration; and
(v) a person so registered shall be a citizen of India by registration, as from the date he is so registered.

(iv) Citizenship by Naturalization (Section 6)

Naturalization means to adopt, to introduce to any other country, to admit to citizenship, or to naturalize as a citizen of a State. In the context of citizenship, naturalization is 'the act by which rights of citizenship are conferred by a State upon a person who was before an alien to that State'[42] Section 6 of the Citizenship Act 1955, provides for the acquisition of citizenship of India by naturalization. It is applicable to person of full age and capacity who are not citizens of the countries mentioned in the First Schedule to the Act.[43]

The Government of India may, if satisfied that the applicant is qualified for naturalization, grant him a certificate of naturalization. The qualifications for naturalization of a person are as follows:

(i) that he must not be a citizen of a country where Indian citizens are prevented from becoming citizens of that country by naturalization;
(ii) that he has renounced the citizenship of his own country according to the law of that country and has notified such renunciation to the central government;
(iii) that he has either resided in India or has been in service of Government of India for twelve months immediately preceding the date of making the application for naturalization;
(iv) that during seven years (twelve years)[44] immediately preceding the above period of twelve months, he has either resided in India or has been in the service of government or partly the one and partly the other, for period amounting in aggregate to not less than four years (nine years);[45]
(v) that he is of good character;
(vi) that he has adequate knowledge of at least one language recognized by the Constitution of India;[46] and
(vii) that in the event of a certificate of naturalization being granted to him, he intends to reside in India or to serve under a government in India or under an International organization or under a society, company or body of persons established in India.

The Government of India may waive all or any of the above conditions for naturalization, in the case of a person who, in its opinion, has rendered distinguished service for the cause of science, philosophy, art, literature, world peace or human progress generally.

(v) Citizenship by Incorporation of Territory (Section 7)

Section 7 of the Citizenship Act 1955, provides that if any territory, not being part of the territory of India, becomes a part of the territory of India, the Government of India may, by order, notified in the official gazette, specify the persons, who are residents of such territory, to be citizens of India from the date to be specified in the order.

Termination of Citizenship of India

Article 9 of the Constitution as already discussed, lays down that a citizen of India whether by virtue of Article 5 or Article 6 or Article 8, shall cease to be a citizen of India, if he has voluntarily acquired the citizenship of any foreign State. Under this provision, a citizen of India shall cease to be a citizen of India, if he had voluntarily acquired the citizenship of a foreign State, prior to or at the commencement of the constitution.

As regards the termination of citizenship of India subsequent to the commencement of the constitution, the Citizenship Act 1955 provides the following ways:[47]

(a) by renunciation;
(b) by termination; or
(c) by deprivation.

(a) Renunciation of Citizenship (Section 8)

Section 8 of the Citizenship Act 1955 provides that a citizen of India of full age and capacity, who is also a citizen or a national of any other country, may renounce his Indian citizenship, by making a declaration to the effect, and having it registered with the prescribed authority. Upon such registration, that person shall cease to be a citizen of India. But if, such a declaration is made during any war in which India is engaged, the registration of such declaration shall be withheld until the central government otherwise directs.

Clause (2) of Section 8 provides that where a male person renounces his citizenship, every minor child of that person shall also cease to be a citizen of India. However, such a child may resume Indian citizenship by making a declaration to that effect, within one year of his attaining majority/maturity. For the purpose of renunciation, any woman, who is or has been married, shall be deemed to be of full age. The Citizenship (Amendment) Act 1992 has amended Sub-section (2) of Section 8 to the effect that in place of the words 'a male person' the words 'a person' shall be substituted. Thus, the minor children of a person, whether male or female, who renounces his/her Indian citizenship, shall also cease to be citizens of India.

(b) Termination of Citizenship (Section 9)

Section 9 of the Citizenship Act 1955 provides that if a citizen of India voluntarily acquires the citizenship of any other country subsequent to the commencement of the constitution; he shall cease to be a citizen of India. But it will not apply to a citizen of India who, during any war in which India may be engaged, voluntarily acquires the citizenship of any other country. If a question arises as to whether, when, or how any person has acquired the citizenship of any other country, it is to be determined by such authority and in such a manner as may be prescribed by the rules.

Cases that would ordinarily arise about loss of Indian citizenship by acquisition of foreign citizenship would be of three kinds:

(a) Indian citizen who voluntarily acquires the citizenship of any other State or country prior to the commencement of the constitution;
(b) Indian citizen who voluntarily acquires the citizenship of any other State or country between 26 January 1950 and 30 December 1955, i.e. the date of commencement of the Citizenship Act 1955;
(c) Indian citizen who voluntarily acquires foreign citizenship after the date of commencement of the Citizenship Act, i.e. 30 December 1955.

As regards the first category, it would be dealt with under Article 9 of the Constitution. The second and third categories would be covered by the provisions of Section 9 of the Citizenship Act 1955.

(c) Deprivation of Citizenship (Section 10)

Section 10 of the Citizenship Act 1955, provides that a citizen of India, whether by naturalization or by registration or by domicile or by residence, may be deprived of his citizenship of India by an order of the Central Government, if it is satisfied:

(i) that the registration or certificate of naturalization was obtained by him by means of fraud, false representation or concealment of any material fact; or
(ii) that he has shown himself, by act or speech, to be disloyal or disaffected towards the Constitution of India; or
(iii) that he, during a war in which India may be engaged, unlawfully traded or communicated with the enemy; or
(iv) that within five years of his registration or naturalization, he has been sentenced to imprisonment for not less than two years; or
(v) that he has been ordinarily resident out of India for seven years continuously and during that period, he has neither been at any time a student of any educational institution in a country outside India, nor in the service of government of India, or of an International organization of which India is a member nor registered annually in the prescribed manner, at an Indian consulate, his intention to retain his citizenship of India.

Before making an order depriving a person of his Indian citizenship, the central government is to give to him a written notice containing the grounds on which the order is proposed to be made. If the order is made on any of the above mentioned grounds specified in (i) to (iv) clauses, that person might have his case referred to a committee of inquiry. The government shall then refer the case to a committee of inquiry consisting of a chairman and two other members. The chairman shall be a person who has held any judicial office within the territory of India for not less than ten years. The committee of inquiry shall hold the enquiry and the central government shall ordinarily be guided by its report in making the order.

United States of America

Citizenship in the US is defined and conferred by Section 1 of the 14th Amendment to the Constitution which states:

> 'All persons born or naturalized in the United States, and subject to jurisdiction thereof, are citizens of the United States and of the State wherein they reside.'

The congressional ability to set standards for naturalization of aliens has never been significantly limited by the court. The 14th Amendment's grant of citizenship contains no provision for termination of citizenship. Thus problems have arisen as to expatriation—the termination of a person's citizenship. Voluntary expatriation is permissible so that a person may renounce his citizenship.[48] The court, however, has struck down several congressional attempts to provide for involuntary termination of citizenship. Thus, the court has held that a person could not be deprived of his citizenship for an act totally opposed to that status, such as service in the armed forces or for voting in a foreign election.[49] However, there may still be a question as to whether Congress might by statue require a person to elect to reject his citizenship for an act totally opposed to that status, such as service in the armed forces of a nation at war with the United States. While the court has taken the position that Congress was without power to deprive a person of citizenship since the 14th Amendment was meant to be an irrevocable grant of citizenship to certain persons,[50] it might be argued that at some point a person's actions might constitute voluntary expatriation.[51]

A person who has not been born in the country may be a naturalized citizen if he or she complies with the conditions for naturalization set by Congress.[52] Following naturalization in this country the naturalized citizen is not subject to involuntary expatriation to any greater extent than a natural born citizen with an exception; if the person engages in fraud or misrepresentation in the naturalization process later discovery of the fraud will annul the grant of citizenship.[53] Congress may also attach reasonable conditions to the original grant of citizenship under which the person might later be divested of citizenship, if the person is naturalized outside of the United States. Thus, in *Rogers v. Bellei*,[54] the court upheld the requirement for children born abroad with only one parent of United States citizenship that granted them citizenship on the condition that they later spend five continuous years in the United States between the ages of 14 and 28. Since these persons were not born in the United States or finally naturalized there, they were not granted citizenship by the 14th Amendment. The Congress could grant conditional citizenship just as it could have refused to make any grant of citizenship until they fulfilled the residence requirement.[55]

Congress also has virtually unrestricted power to set the terms for alien immigration[56] and this power may be delegated in part to the executive.[57] The immigration acts have set conditions and quotas for entry into this country.[58] Whether the alien seeks entry for a temporary visit or to establish residence he has no right to entry and Congress may exclude any alien or group as it pleases. For many years, Congress set quotas for immigration based on nationality.[59] And, despite the racial-national origin classification, the law was never seriously questioned.[60] The executive branch also has been given the authority to exclude individual aliens whom are either unqualified for immigration or who may present some moral or social danger.[61] Not only are these general powers subject to no significant limitation, the individuals who are refused entry do not have a right to a hearing to determine the basis for their exclusion.[62] Indeed the Supreme Court upheld the refusal to grant a hearing to an alien who sought re-entry to the country after a temporary absence even though no other country would accept this person.[63] While the person seemed harmless and remained an indefinite *de facto* prisoner on Ellis Island, the Supreme Court would not order the Justice Department to disclose to a judge the reason for refusing him re-entry. This decision should now be considered constitutionally infirm even though it has never been overruled, but it demonstrates the historic refusal of the court to review immigration decisions. Absent imprisonment by United States officials, persons will have no right to a hearing to determine their eligibility to enter the country.

The congressional power to regulate immigration and naturalization includes the power to regulate the behaviour of aliens who are in this country.[64] Pursuant to statute, aliens may be deported for a variety of activities deemed harmful to this country.[65] These conditions will be upheld as within the power of Congress for the court defers to the legislature in such matters. But the resident alien will have right to a hearing prior to the deportation.[66] The hearing will determine whether the person is an alien or a citizen, and, if he is an alien, whether the conditions for continuing residence have been violated. While the procedural aspects of the due process clause requires this hearing to establish the basis for the deportation, an alien who has violated the statutes or conditions of entry has no right to continued residence in this country.[67]

Rights of the Citizen

Civil Rights under the British Constitution

Under the Constitution of the United Kingdom, [because of the supremacy of Parliament and in the absence of a written constitution] there are no basic, fundamental, or inalienable rights. There is no judicial review of acts of Parliament. Yet, no other country in history has made a greater contribution than Britain to the recognition of the rights of the individual and their protection by an independent judiciary against government authorities. In the political context, such rights are often called civil rights in contrast with social, economic, or cultural rights such as the right to work, holidays with pay, medical services, and social security. In international law such rights are described as human rights, universal in place as well as time, and imposing international obligations on States to protect them. In the United Kingdom, civil rights such as freedom of expression and association are residual that is, whatever freedom is left over after the imposition of limitation by the statutes and common law.

Human Rights in International Law

Human rights, now an international term, which is not defined in any act or international law, was introduced by the United States Declaration of Independence of 1776 and the Declaration of the Rights of the Man and of the Citizen passed by France's National Constituent Assembly in August 1789, is a fundamental document of the French Revolution. The term was adopted by the US Constitution and extended in 1913 by its 16th Constitutional Amendment. It is the subject of international declarations, the first being the Declaration of Human Rights and Duties worked out in 1929 by the New York Institute of International Law and submitted to Inter-American Legal Committees.

In Article 1, the 1929 Declaration proclaimed that it is a duty of every State to recognize equal rights of an individual to life, freedom, and property and to fully grant and protect these rights on its entire territory regardless of nationality, sex, race, language, or religion.

In Article 2, it provided that it is a duty of every State to recognize equal rights of an individual to the execution whether in public or in private, of any faith, religion or worship, the practice of which is not in violation of public order and good manners. This declaration together with the resolution of Inter-American Conference in Chapultepec of 8 March 1945 on the need to establish International protection of human rights, laid the foundations for a draft of the Universal Declaration of Human Rights.

Human Rights provisions are made in the preamble and 6 articles of the UN Charter, the most important being Articles 55 and 56. Article 55 calls for

> 'Universal respect, for, and observance of, human rights and fundamental freedoms for all...'

and Article 56 makes it obligatory on all UN member nations:

> 'to take joint and separate action in cooperation with organization for the achievement of (these) purposes....'

The UN has gradually built up a large body of laws and precedents of human rights. These fall into three main categories; conventions, covenants (treaties), and non-binding declarations. The UN lists 19 major conventions on human rights and over 20 declarations. Others have been adopted by the UN specialized agencies. The most important of all is, of course, the Universal Declaration of Human Rights adopted by the General Assembly in 1948. It was drafted in the UN Commission on Human Rights under the leadership of Eleanor Roosevelt. It is based in part on the United States Bill of rights. It has 30 articles, 22 of which cover a range of civil and political rights and 5 articles cover the economic, social, and cultural rights.

The General Assembly of the UN proclaimed the declaration as a 'common standard of achievement for all nations'. But in practice, it is not so? Perceptions of human rights vary widely among the members of the UN. The Western concept tends to emphasize individual political freedoms such as the right to vote and hold public office and the rights of free speech and assembly. In the developing countries the achievement of economic and social rights, such as the meeting of basic human needs for adequate food, clothing, and shelter, are necessarily seen to be at least as important as the political rights if not more.

The comparison of the Universal Declaration of Human Rights 1948 with the US Declaration of Independence 1776, the Declaration of Rights of the Man and of the Citizen, a fundamental document of the of the French Revolution in 1789, the 16th Amendment of 1913 in the American Constitution, the Declaration of Human Rights and Duties worked out in 1929 by the New York Institute of International Law shows their *inter se* close similarity. The Universal Declaration proclaims to have elevated the principles of government of Western civilization to the international level. The American Declaration of Independence or the French Declaration of the Rights of the Man and of the Citizen could not be confined only to the American and the French people. The American and the French Declarations adopted more than two centuries ago were meant to be operative throughout the world.

The human rights are

(i) civil and political and
(ii) economic and social rights.

The human rights of the first category are in fact limitations on the government. To comply with these limitations, the only action that is required on the part of the government is its inaction. If it refrains from taking actions that limit these rights, the rights are enforced. The Universal Declaration contains 30 Rights all together, of which 23 are civil and political rights and the remaining 7 are economic, social, and cultural rights.[68]

- Right to life, liberty, and security of person;
- prohibition against slavery and servitude;
- prohibition against torture, cruel, inhuman or degrading treatment or punishment;
- right to effective remedy by competent tribunal in respect of fundamental rights;
- prohibition against arbitrary arrest and detention;
- right to fair and public hearing;
- right to be presumed innocent until proved guilty and protection against retrospective punishment;
- protection against arbitrary interference with privacy, family, home etc.,;
- right to freedom of movement;
- right to seek political asylum;
- right to nationality;
- right to marriage;
- right to own property and not to be deprived of it arbitrarily;
- right to freedom of opinion;
- right to freedom of assembly and association;
- right to take part in government and equal access to public office are the civil and political rights.
- The right to work and equal pay for equal work;
- right to form and join trade union and right to rest and leisure;
- right to social security and economic, social and cultural rights indispensable for dignity and free development of personality;

- right to standard of living adequate for health and well-being including food, clothing, housing and medical care and necessary social services;
- the right to security in the event of unemployment, sickness, disability, widowhood, old age or other lack of livelihood in circumstances beyond his/her control;
- right to special care and assistance during motherhood and childhood;
- right to education and right to participate in the cultural life of the community are the economic, social and cultural rights.

These rights involve the positive tasks of government which requires skill, thought, and resources.

It is true that some of the rights enumerated in the Universal Declaration are not the particular property of any single culture or civilization. They should be deemed generally applicable to humanity. The right to life, liberty, and security of person; the prohibition of slavery, torture, and cruel, inhuman and degrading treatment or punishment; equality before the law and equal protection of the law; the rule against arbitrary interference with a person's privacy, family home, or correspondence; freedom of movement within one's country and across international borders; freedom of expression, thought, conscience and religion and the right to choose one's government in free elections are the rights which should be guaranteed to all citizens of every country the world over and cannot be deemed to be confined to the inhabitants of the western civilization only. After all we are members of the human race and in that capacity there are many things in common. But it is also true that we all live in different cultures and are rooted in different civilizations. We live at different levels of economic and social development. In Western societies emphasis is on individual's initiative whereas in the developing countries the collective values are considered to be paramount. For Asians, Africans and Latin Americans assured employment, housing and medical care is the pre-eminent human right whereas in the Western world freedom of press, freedom of association, freedom of movement, protection against retrospective punishment, freedom to profess religion, freedom to acquire and hold property etc., are treated as basic fundamental and unalterable rights. Much of the Muslim world believes that an individual's freedoms should not threaten the interests of the community.

Like other known and great civilization of the world, Islam which is the religion of over one billion people all over the world has immensely contributed towards fundamental or human rights. The Quran ensures equality of mankind (49:13), freedom of conscience (2:256), freedom of trade (4:29), rule of law (4:58), privacy of homes (24:27), no liability for the actions of others (6:164). The Prophet Muhammad (PBUH) in his famous last sermon at Mount Arafat on 6 March 623 AD laid out a complete charter of fundamental rights that provided a whole range of freedoms and protection:

> 'your lives and property are sacred and inviolable as the sacred inviolability of this very day.'[69]

According to the *Shariah,*

> 'it is the State's duty to enhance human dignity and alleviate conditions'.

Article 14 of the 1973 Constitution of Pakistan lays down that 'the dignity of man is inviolable.' The preamble to this Constitution provides that Pakistan would be a democratic state based on Islamic principles of social justice. Article 3 lays down that 'the State shall ensure the elimination of all forms of exploitation and the gradual fulfilment of the fundamental principle, from each according to his ability to each according to his work'. Article 39 lays down that the State shall:

(a) secure the well-being of the people irrespective of sex, caste, creed, or race, by raising their standard of living, by preventing the concentration of wealth and means of production and distribution in the hands of a few to the detriment of general interest and by ensuring equitable adjustment of rights between employers and employees, and landlords and tenants;
(b) provide for all citizens, within the available resources of the country, facilities for work and adequate livelihood with reasonable rest and leisure;
(c) provide for all persons employed in the service of Pakistan or otherwise, social insurance or other means;

(d) provide basic necessities of life, such as food, clothing, housing, education and medical relief, for all such citizens, irrespective of sex, caste, creed or race, as are permanently or temporarily unable to earn their livelihood on account of infirmity, sickness or unemployment; and
(e) reduce disparity in incomes and earnings of individuals, including persons in the various classes of the service of Pakistan.

Although, the Constitution of Pakistan recognizes in unmistakable terms the supremacy of an individual's political rights, it also lays great emphasis on the economic and social rights of the people.

In view of these provisions of the Constitution, Pakistan has its own standards of human rights. Similarly, other developing countries are making endeavours to stake out distinctive positions in line with their own cultures, histories, and special circumstances. It is noticeable that there is a general discontent throughout these countries with the purely Western interpretation of human rights. The catalogue of rights and freedoms in international law of human rights now generally encompasses such matters as pay, working conditions, trade unions, standard of living, rest and leisure, welfare and social security, women's and children's rights and the environment. The pressures to link economic concerns with human rights are on the rise.

The hard core of rights that are truly universal is smaller than many in the West would acknowledge. More than half a century after the adoption of the universal declaration, many of its thirty articles are still subject to debate over interpretation and application not just between Asia and the West, but within the West itself. The American and some European human rights activists place more emphasis on civil and political rights than on economic, social and cultural rights. They do not realize that poverty, insecurity, and instability breed abuses of human rights, while wealth creates security and stability. Wealth also renders the well-being and happiness of the poor, irrelevant. On the other hand, the governments of the developing countries are struggling to protect and advance the human dignity of their citizens, within the constraints of their economic circumstances. In any case the world has long way to go before it can universalize the concepts and meaning of human rights.

Notes

1. Article 5 of the Constitution of Pakistan, 1973.
2. Al-Quran 3:26.
3. http://www.newworldencyclopedia.org/entry/Nation-State#The_History_of_the_Nation-State.
4. Jean-Jacques Rousseau, *The Social Contract or Principles of Political Right*, trans. H. J. Tozzer, introduction by Derek Matravers (Wordsworth Classics of World Literature; Hertfordshire: Wordsworth Editions Limited, 1998), pp. 4–5.
5. Owen Hood Philips, *Constitutional and Administrative Law*, 5th ed. (London: Sweet & Maxwell, 1973), p. 5.
6. A.G. Chaudhry, *Lectures on Constitutional Law* (Lahore: Irfan Law Book House, 1994), p. 11.
7. Durga Das Basu, *Comparative Constitutional Law* (New Delhi: Prentice-Hall of India Pvt. Ltd, 1984), p. 155.
8. 10th Amendment to the US Constitution.
9. *District Bar Association Rawalpindi v. Federation of Pakistan* PLD 2015 SC 401.
10. Muhammad Asad, *The Principles of State and Government in Islam*, New Edition (Gibraltar: Dar al-Andalus, 1980), p. 39.
11. 'The State' is defined in similar terms in the Constitutions of 1962 and 1956. However, the test of power to impose tax or cess was not there in the earlier constitutions.
12. *Sharaf Faridi v. The Government of Pakistan* PLD 1989 Karachi 404.
13. *Fazal Jan v. Roshan Din* PLD 1990 SC 661.
14. *Watan Party v. Federation of Pakistan* PLD 2012 SC 292, *Suo Moto* Case No. 15 of 2009, PLD 2012 SC 610.
15. Schedule 9 of the British Nationality Act, 1981.
16. Supra Note 6, p. 89.
17. Entry 4 of the Fourth Schedule of the Constitution.
18. Section 14 A of the Citizenship Act, 1951, pp. 90–1.
19. *Syed Mehmood Akhtar Naqvi v. Federation of Pakistan* PLD 2012 SC 1089.
20. Suo Motu Case No. 3 of 2018 (Dual Nationality Case) decided on 15 December 2018.
21. *Muhammad Yar Khan v. Deputy Commissioner* 1980 SCMR 456.

22. *Abdus Samad v. State of West Bengal*, AIR 1973 SC 505. Also see *Union of India v. Dudh Nath Prasad*, AIR 2000 SC 525, wherein the Supreme Court held that domicile and residence were relative concepts and had to be understood in the context in which they were used.
23. *Central Bank of India v. Ram Narayan*, AIR 1955 SC 36.
24. *Malkiat Singh v. State of Punjab*, AIR 1959 Punjab 250.
25. A.V. Dicey, *Conflict of Laws* (6th ed.), p. 78, cited in V.N. Shukla, *The Constitution of India*, 9th ed., ed. Mahendra P. Singh (Lucknow: Eastern Book Co., 1994), p. 12.
26. *Louis De Raedt v. Union of India*, AIR 1991 SC 1886.
27. *Karimun Nisa v. State of Madhya Pradesh*, AIR 1955 Nag 6.
28. After the partition of the country, a person who continued to reside and carry on business in Pakistan, would not be deemed to have acquired Indian domicile by simply sending his family to India without himself coming to reside in India. See *Central Bank of India v. Ram Narayan*, AIR 1955 SC 36.
29. Article 6(b)(ii).
30. It was on this day that communal riots started in India and migration of Muslims from India to Muslim majority areas began.
31. Narender Kumar, *Constitutional Law of India*, 3rd ed. (Faridabad, Haryana: Pioneer Publication, 2002), pp. 43–7.
32. Ibid., p. 48.
33. *State of Madhya Pradesh v. Peer Mohd.*, AIR 1963 SC 645; *Izhar Ahmed v. Union of India*, AIR 1962 SC 1052. See also *Bhanwaroo Khan v. Union of India* 2002 (3) SCC 464. *Hari Shankar Jain v. Sonia Gandhi* 2001 (8) SCC 233.
34. *State of Andhra Pradesh v. Khader*, AIR 1961 SC 1468.
35. *Lal Babu Hussain v. Electoral Registration Officer*, AIR 1995 SC 1189; *State of U.P. v. Rehamatullah*, AIR 1971 SC 1382; *State of Gujrat v. Ibrahim*, AIR 1974 SC 645.
36. *Abdul Sattar v. State of Gujrat*, AIR 1965 SC 810.
37. *Ebrahim Wazir v. State of Bombay*, AIR 1954 SC 229.
38. Section 2(f) of the Citizenship Act, 1955. See also *State Trading Corporation v. C.T.O.* AIR 1963 SC 1811.
39. The Citizenship (Amendment) Act 1986 has extended this period of six months to five years w.e.f. 26 November 1986.
40. The Citizenship (Amendment) Act 1986, now requires that a woman married to a citizen of India must have resided in India at least for five years before she is registered as a citizen of India under Section 5, w.e.f. 26 November 1986.
41. This Schedule includes the Commonwealth countries and the Republic of Ireland.
42. Durga Das Basu, *Commentary on the Constitution of India*, Volume A, 6th ed. (Calcutta: S.C. Sarkar and Sons Ltd., 1982), p. 222.
43. The Schedule includes Commonwealth countries.
44. This change is incorporated by the Citizenship (Amendment) Act 1986, w.e.f. 26 November 1986.
45. This change is incorporated by the Citizenship (Amendment) Act 1986, w.e.f. 26 November 1986.
46. See the Eighth Schedule to the Constitution, which includes 18 languages.
47. Supra Note 28, p. 53.
48. By the Act of 27 July 1868 [15 Stat. L. 223, Chap. 249] Congress declared that the right of expatriation is a natural and inherent right of all people. Expatriation is the voluntary renunciation or abandonment of nationality and allegiance.' *Perkins v. Elg.* 307 U.S. 325 (1939). The Act has since been repeated and the right of expatriation is covered by 8 U.S.C.A. 1482, 1483. See also *Kennedy v. Mondoza-Martinez*, 372 U.S. 144 (1963) where Court states there is no disagreement that citizenship may be voluntarily relinquished either expressly or by conduct.
49. *Kennedy v. Mendoza-Martinez*, 372 U.S. 144 (1963) (Expatriation of one who departed from or remained outside the United States in time of War or during a period of national emergency for the purpose of evading military service found unconstitutional); *Trop v. Dulles*, 356 U.S. 86 (1958). Expatriation for desertion of military services during war held unconstitutional as applied to native born (citizen); *Afroyim v. Rusk*, 387 U.S. 253 (1967). Expatriation of citizen for voting in foreign election found unconstitutional, overruling *Perez v. Brownell*, 356 U.S. 44 (1958).
50. *Afroyim v. Rusk*, 387 U.S. 253 (1967).
51. See *e.g.* Chief Justice Warren's dissent in *Perez v. Brownell*, 356 U.S. 44 (1958), with which the *Afroyim* majority declared its agreement. *Afroyim* overruled *Perez.*
52. The constitution vests Congress with the power 'to establish a Uniform Rule of Naturalization.' Art. I, 8, cl. 4. The Supreme Court has given Congress great latitude in selecting the appropriate conditions. *United States v. Macintosh*, 283 U.S. 605 (1931); Congress has provided by statute that the right to become a citizen may not be denied on the basis of race, sex, or marital status 311, 66 Stat. 239 (1952), 8 U.S.C.A. 1422. The right will be denied where, for example, a person is or has been a member of an organization advocating the violent overthrow of the government 313(a) and (c), 66 Stat. 240 (1952), 8 U.S.C.A. 1424(a) and (c). 'Good moral character' is also a prerequisite, 316(a)(3), 66 Stat. 242, 8 U.S.C.A. 1427(a)(3).

53. 340(a), 66 Stat. 260 (1952), 8 U.S.C.A. 1451(a). Proof of fraud or misrepresentation may be proved and result in loss of citizenship at any time regardless of how long ago person became a citizen. *Costello v. United States*, 365 U.S. 265 (1961) (27 years); *Polites v. United States*, 364 U.S. 426 (1960) (10 years); *Knauer v. United States*, 328 U.S. 654 (1946) (6 years). Affiliation with an organization which advocates violent over throw of the government within five years after becoming a citizen is prima facie evidence of fraud. 340, 66 Stat. 261 (1952), 8 U.S.C.A. 1451(c). *Schneider v. Rusk*, 377 U.S. 163 (1964). (Court struck down provision that naturalized citizen lost his citizenship if he resided continuously for three years in the country of which he was formerly a national or in which he was born).
54. 401 U.S. 815 (1971).
55. Justice Black, Brennan, Douglas, and Marshall dissented. But see *Schneider v. Rusk*, 377 U.S. 163 (1964).
56. Congress does not derive its power to regulate immigration from a specific constitutional grant. It is simply regarded as a power inherent to sovereignty. See *Chinese Exclusion Case.* 130 U.S. 581 (1889). For a further discussion of congressional authority and foreign affair, see Louis Henkin, *Foreign Affairs and the Constitution* (Mineola, New York: The Foundation Press, 1972).
57. *U.S. ex rel. Knauff v. Shaughnessy*, 338 U.S. 537 (1950).
58. Aliens presently excludable are listed in 8 U.S. C.A. 1182. The method of allocation of immigration is found in 8 U.S.C.A. 1153.
59. The first Congressional act limiting immigration on the basis of race or nationality was the Chinese Exclusion Act of 1882. Act of 6 May 1882, 22 Stat. 58, which remained in effect until 1943. In 1924, Congress set up the national origin quota system, Act of 26 May 1924, 43 Stat. 153, which remained into effect until 1965. Act of 3 October 1965, P.L. 89-236, 79 Stat. 911. 8 U.S.C.A. 1152(a) now prohibits the use of race national origin, sex, place of birth, or place of residence to determine the eligibility of an alien to immigrate.
60. See *Ozawa v. United States*, 260 U.S. 178 (1922); *United States v. Bhagat Singh Thind*, 261 U.S. 204 (1923); *Toyota v. United States*, 268 U.S. 402 (1925); *Morrison v. California*, 291 U.S. 82 (1934). The court refused to review the only case in which the constitutional issue was raised and rejected, *Kharaiti Ram Samras v. United States* 125 F.2d 879 (9th Cir. 1942), cert. denied 317 U.S. 634 (1942).
61. 8 U.S.C.A. 1103, 1104.
62. To aliens who have never been naturalized nor acquired residence in the US, the decision of an executive or administrative officer, acting within the powers conferred by Congress is due process. *United States v. Ju Toy.* 198 U.S. 253, 263 (1905). See, *Hart and Wechsler's The Federal Courts and the Federal System*, 2nd ed. (1973) (the 'Dialogue'), pp. 352–3.
63. *Shaughnessy v. United States ex rel. Mezei*, 345 U.S. 206 (1953).
64. See the dissenting opinion of Justice Rehnquist in *Hampton v. Mow Sun Wong*, 426 U.S. 88 (1976).
65. 8 U.S.C.A. 1251. Reasons for deportation include non-compliance with eligibility requirements for entrance, a conviction of a crime of moral turpitude within five years after entry, and membership in proscribed organizations. The latter provision was upheld as to aliens who had become members of the communist party before the law was established. See *Harisiades v. Shaughnessy*, 342 U.S. 580 (1952).
66. 8 U.S.C.A. 1252(b). A person arrested and held for deportation who claims to be a citizen is entitled to his day in court. *Ng Fung Ho v. White* 259 U.S. 276, 281 (1922).
67. John E. Nowak, Ronald D. Rotunda, Young J. Nelson, *Handbook on Constitutional Law* (West Publishing Co., 1978), pp. 589–92.
68. Supra Note 6, pp. 93–4.
69. *Qazalbash Trust v. Chief Land Commissioner*, PLD 1990 SC 99.

Part II

Basic Constitutional Concepts

3 Constitutional Conventions

Introduction

By 'convention' means a binding rule, a rule of behaviour accepted as obligatory by those concerned in the working of the Constitution.[1] Conventions appear to arise from at least two sources; one as just indicated, a course of conduct that might have persisted over a long period of time and gradually attain first persuasive and then obligatory force. It is common to call conventions of this kind as 'customs'. The second source of a convention may arise more quickly than this. There may be an agreement among the people concerned to work in a particular way and to adopt a particular rule of conduct. This rule is immediately binding and it is a convention. It has not arisen from custom; it has had no previous history as a usage. It springs from agreement. Its basis is indeed like that of the conventions which are drawn up in international relations. They are held to be morally and politically binding, but until they are enacted by the appropriate machinery of a state they do not in most countries alter the law or form part of the law.

The conventions which arise from agreements might take the form of an agreement signed by the leaders of political parties, or of a memorandum issued after discussions between ministers. Conventions are not necessarily unwritten rules, though those which have grown up by custom often are. It is important to stress this fact for it illustrates once again how unsatisfactory are distinctions among constitutional rules between 'written' and 'un-written'. It is a distinction which is seldom applied accurately and is seldom, if ever, profitable.[2]

Development of Constitutional Convention

One prominent characteristic of the British Constitution is the role played by conventions. These rules, sometimes known as 'rules of constitutional morality', create powers and impose obligations which are not legally enforceable, but which are nevertheless regarded as binding. It is improper, in a sense unconstitutional, to violate a convention, though it is not illegal. The most important conventions in the United Kingdom limit of the legal powers of the monarch and to regulate the relationship of the government of Parliament; they are crucial to the modern constitution.

Conventions may be found in other countries. For example, under Article II of the US Constitution the president and vice president are chosen by a college, comprising electors from each state. By convention, however, the president and vice president are elected by popular vote, the electors automatically casting their vote in the Electoral College for the candidates who win the election in that state. Another important convention forbade a president from serving more than two terms of four years each, but after its breach by Franklin D. Roosevelt (1882–1945)[3] in 1940, the rule of two terms became law by a formal amendment to the Constitution. Similarly, there are some important conventions in France, particularly concerning the division of authority between the president of the republic and the prime minister when they come from different political parties. The text of the Constitution of 1958 does not make plain, for example, whether it is for the president or the prime minister to determine foreign policy. But it was agreed in 1986–88 during the period of 'cohabitation' as it was termed, between President François Mitterrand (1916–96)[4] a socialist, and Jacques Chirac (1932–2019)[5], his Gaullist prime minister, that the president had responsibility for the broad direction of foreign policy. Mitterrand was therefore able to veto the appointment of a foreign minister, although the Constitution provides that the President appoints ministers on the recommendation of the prime minister.[6]

A. V. Dicey (1835–1922)[7] went so far as to claim that conventions were as important to the United States Constitution as they were to the English.[8] Whatever its merits, at the end of the 19th century that view is quite implausible now. A student conversant with the text of the United States Constitution, and the decisions of the US Supreme Court interpreting it, would have a reasonable idea of how it works in practice. This is also true of the German Constitution, where the notion of constitutional conventions is virtually unknown. All constitutional questions are in principle questions of law for resolution by the constitutional court. In both these systems, there is some correspondence between the scope of constitutional law and the operation of the constitution in daily life.

In contrast, an equally knowledgeable observer of United Kingdom constitutional law, but ignorant of its conventions, would be totally at sea. He would, for instance, believe that the Queen has unfettered discretionary power to give or refuse royal assent to legislation after its passage through the parliament. In addition, the Queen has a free choice in deciding whom to invite to form a government. He would also not know anything about the significance of a vote by the House of Commons of no confidence in the government (a matter covered by the text of both the French and German Constitutions).[9] In terms of strict constitutional law, the monarch does have discretion to refuse royal assent and choose the prime minister, while the law says nothing about the responsibility of government and ministers to the House of Commons. But all these matters are to a greater or lesser extent regulated by constitutional conventions, which, to use Sir Ivor Jennings's (1903–65)[10] graphic description, 'provide the flesh which clothes the dry bones of the law'.[11] Some of them are as well-established and as clear as any rule of law. For instance, the convention requiring the Crown to assent to measures passed by both houses of parliament has evolved over the last two to three centuries since the royal assent was last refused by Queen Anne (1665–1714)[12] in 1707. Others are less firmly established. For instance, there is now in most circumstances a clear convention requiring the monarch to appoint as prime minister the person chosen by the majority party as its leader under its current rules. It is, however, of recent origin. But it is unclear how it would apply in the unusual circumstances of a hung parliament where no party had a clear majority. Further, there is real controversy about the scope of another convention where the Crown is required to dissolve parliament at the request of the prime minister.

What then are constitutional conventions and what is their relationship to constitutional law? And to pose a less familiar question: is it good that conventions play such an important role in the constitution? Writers on constitutional law offer various definitions. Generally, they can be described as non-legal rules stating the powers and obligations of the branches of government, in particular the executive, and their relations with each other. Thus, a number of conventions impose obligations on the monarch, for example, as already mentioned, to assent to legislation, to choose the leader of the majority party in the commons as her prime minister (at least in most circumstances), and generally to act on his and other ministers' advice.

Other conventions are concerned with the working of the cabinet, but these are now less clear. The principles of collective cabinet responsibility, under which all its members must observe the confidentiality of cabinet discussion and support its decisions, are regarded as constitutional conventions. But prime ministers now claim a power to dispense with the requirement of cabinet solidarity in certain circumstances, and this may have reformulated the convention. This power was illustrated by the Labour cabinet's agreement to disagree in 1975 over the question whether it was right to stay in the European community and gave cabinet ministers the freedom to campaign in the referendum for withdrawal from the community against the majority decision. The new convention, if that is what it is, was formulated by James Callaghan (1919–2005)[13] in 1977 when, as prime minister, he tolerated similar dissent with regard to passage of the European Assembly Elections Bill. For Prime Minister Callaghan, the doctrine of collective responsibility applied 'except in case where I announce that it does not'.

According to the Supreme Court of Canada, the purpose of conventions is:

> 'to ensure that the legal framework of the Constitution will be operated in accordance with the prevailing constitutional values or principles of the period', in particular the democratic principle of a responsible government.[14]

For many of the legal rules of the constitution, particularly those concerned with the fundamental discretionary powers that are still in law and exercisable by the monarch personally, have become antiquated since the English constitutional settlement of 1689 (aka Bill of Rights, 1689). The constitutional law of United Kingdom says very little about the prime minister and the cabinet. A crucial role of constitutional conventions is, therefore, to limit the vast powers of the monarch. They also recognize the status of the prime minister and other ministers when they impose an obligation on the monarch to exercise these powers on their advice. This general obligation to act on ministerial advice constitutes perhaps the most important constitutional convention. The conventions of collective and individual ministerial responsibility enforce the accountability of government to the elected legislature, a central principle of a liberal democracy.

In other countries, conventions provide an informal method of constitutional amendment. This is important where it is difficult to amend, because it is necessary, for instance, to obtain the approval of the people through a referendum or in a federal constitution, the consent of a large majority of the states. That may partly explain why the development of conventions has not occurred in Germany; the Basic Law[15] is relatively easy to alter and amendments have been made frequently. Conversely, though the United Kingdom constitutional arrangements are flexible in theory, the basic legal structure has rarely been amended by statute over the last 300 years. (Only two or three statutes, the Parliament Acts 1911 and 1949 and the European Communities Act 1972, have brought about radical constitutional reform, although the measure devolving legislative and executive power to Scotland may prove to be equally significant.) The gradual change effected by the constitutional conventions mentioned in the previous paragraphs has been much more important in altering the balance of power between the Crown, the ministers, and the legislature.

There is much debate about how conventions are created or arise. Unlike rules of law, they are not instituted by the legislature or by the courts. A practice of compliance with the rule is often important, as it creates a series of precedents on which reliance can be placed. If a convention has been observed, and accepted as binding, over a long period of time, it is hard to dispute its existence. The reason it can be said with confidence that it is the constitutional duty of the Crown to give royal assent to bills because the royal assent has not been refused since 1707. In normal circumstances, everyone accepts it as a rule of the constitution. But precedent may neither be necessary nor sufficient. It is unnecessary, because conventions may arise simply from the agreement of those affected by the rule.

This is illustrated by the Balfour Declaration of 1926, which established the convention that the Westminster Parliament could not legislate for Canada, Australia, and the other dominions of the Empire without their consent. The convention was subsequently incorporated in the Statute of Westminster 1931. More importantly, practice alone is not enough. A convention arises only when its content is accepted as a binding rule by the institution affected e.g. the monarch or members of the cabinet or government. This point is fundamental. Conventions must be distinguished from mere practices or usages which are only adopted out of habit. Finally, Sir Ivor Jennings argued that a convention must be supported by reason, in the rather limited sense that it must be in accord with contemporary political philosophy. That perhaps was rather a way of making the point that a convention which is inconsistent with contemporary attitudes is unlikely to be accepted as a binding standard. Like other legal rules, the terms of a constitution may survive in force even when they no longer enjoy public support. In contrast, a convention which becomes outdated can no longer be regarded as part of the constitution.[16]

The most interesting question for a constitutional lawyer is the relationship between conventions and law. Dicey sharply distinguished them. Constitutional conventions are not laws, because the courts cannot enforce them. This view may be broadly correct. It has been supported by the Canadian Supreme Court. It is inconceivable, for example, that the courts would issue an order to enforce the monarch's duty to give royal assent to bills or the government's obligation to resign following a defeat on a confidence motion. Conventions are enforceable politically, either by parliament or by public opinion. For instance, if the monarch persistently failed to take her ministers' advice and insisted on exercising her legal powers, steps would be taken to curtail them by statute.

Though not directly enforceable, conventions may have some legal significance. The courts may use them as a foundation for a principle of common law. That was what happened in the *Crossman Diaries* case,[17] when Lord Chief Justice John Widgery (1911–81)[18], considered whether to grant an injunction to restrain publication of a former cabinet minister's diaries. He held that the remedy would be appropriate when publication amounted to a breach of confidence. The relationships of confidence between members of the cabinet arose under the convention of collective cabinet responsibility. The courts are also competent to determine whether a convention exists, at least when this jurisdiction is expressly conferred by statute. On that basis a majority of the Canadian Supreme Court held that there was a convention requiring the consent of the provinces before the federal parliament presented proposals to the United Kingdom parliament to amend the British North America Act 1867. This ruling was more significant than the court's decision that the consent of the provinces was not required as a matter of constitutional law. In the light of this decision, the Canadian government accepted an obligation to seek the provinces' approval before proceeding with its constitutional reform.

Does it matter that conventions play such an enormous part in the working of the United Kingdom constitution? Commentators such as Sir Ivor Jennings have tended to emphasize their role in keeping the constitution up to date with contemporary political values. Against the background of archaic legal rules, their role is entirely beneficial. However, it is also sensible to ask whether there are disadvantages to reliance on conventions, compared to the adoption of a codified constitution and its periodic amendment. It goes without saying that the conventions are frequently vague. This is particularly true of the major conventions of collective and individual ministerial responsibility. They have become so unclear at times that it is hard to determine how far they really exist in any significant sense. The weakness of these conventions, if not of those regulating the monarch's discretionary powers, is that they are not enforceable. Nor are the courts generally able to determine their scope or their application to a particular set of circumstances; the *Crossman Diaries* case was exceptional in this respect. Instead, these questions are decided by politicians and political parties, as James Callaghan cheerfully claimed when, as Prime Minister, he reformulated the principle of collective responsibility.

The central part played by conventions in the constitutional arrangements of the United Kingdom indicates a preference for self-regulation by governments and politicians over a system of legal checks and balances enforceable by the courts, which is much more characteristic of modern codified liberal constitutions. That conventions are so important to the working of the constitution in the United Kingdom should occasion no surprise. They are an integral feature of the 'political constitution'.[19]

In the United States, it became a convention that a president should not seek a third term of office. It was based on the example set by the first President, George Washington (1732–99)[20] who served for two terms from 1789–97, but refused to run for re-election as president for third term. This became a convention for American presidents until 1940, when Franklin D. Roosevelt was elected for the third term and in 1944 when he was elected for a fourth term. President Roosevelt standing for re-election for a third term was justified by the need for continuity in the direction of the affairs of the United States when the danger of war was imminent, an argument which in 1944 was still stronger for the United States as by then the US was fully involved in the war. The re-election of President Roosevelt for a third and then a fourth term has indeed confirmed the belief among politicians in the United States that the rule embodied in this convention was good and steps were taken to turn this convention into law. After Franklin D. Roosevelt's death, a constitutional amendment was moved in 1947 which was finally approved in 1951 as the 22nd Amendment to the US Constitution. Under this amendment, no person can be elected to the office of the president for more than two terms. Even a person who was elected as vice president but acted as president due to the death or resignation of the president for more than two years of a term cannot be elected to the office of the president more than once. This is a remarkable example of a constitutional convention becoming a constitutional amendment.

Conventions can become law also by judicial recognition. In the ordinary law of the land it is often within the province of courts to recognize customs, under certain conditions, as part of the law. The same thing is possible in constitutional law. When a convention is so recognized it becomes a part of the law; it is no longer a convention.[21]

Certain cases concerning constitutional conventions are discussed below:

(i) In *Liversidge v. Anderson* (1942) A.C. 206, the House of Lords refused jurisdiction to go into the reasonableness and sufficiency of grounds of detention on the ground *inter alia* that the home secretary was responsible to parliament.

(ii) In *British Coal Corporation v. The King* (1935) A.C. 500, the Judicial Committee of the Privy Council mentioned that the conventions regulating dominion statutes and the crown invariably accept the Judicial Committee's advice.

(iii) In *Carltona Ltd. v. Commissioners of Works* (1943) All. E.R. 560, Lord Green M.R. referred to the convention of a minister's responsibility to parliament for the acts of his officials.

(iv) In *Attorney General v. Jonathan Cape Ltd.* (1976) QB 752 Lord Chief Justice John Widgery referred to the doctrine of joint responsibility within the cabinet, cabinet meetings, the secretary to the cabinet and the prime minister.

(v) *Ex.p. Hosenball* (1977) 1 WLR 766, Lord Denning M.R. referred to the responsibility of the home secretary to parliament for the exercise of his power to deport persons on grounds of national security.

(vi) In *Air Canada v. Secretary of State for Trade* (1983) AC. 394 (HL) there were a number of references to the convention which prohibits ministers of one party from having access to the papers of their predecessors of other parties without the agreement of the previous administration.

(vii) In *Re-Amendment of the Constitution of Canada* (1981) 125 DIR (3d) I, in addition to the legal question whether the consent of the provinces was required before the Canadian parliament could request the United Kingdom to amend the Canadian Constitution (British North America Act 1867, as amended), the Supreme Court accepted the appellate jurisdiction to determine whether such consent was required by constitutional convention and, if so, whether the convention had been observed in that case. Both the existence and content of the alleged convention being disputed, the Supreme Court's decision involved an analysis of the general nature of constitutional conventions. A majority held in the first place that a constitution convention cannot crystallize into law. They said:

> No instance of an explicit recognition of a convention as having matured into a rule of law was produced. The very nature of a convention as political in inception and as depending on a persistent course of political recognition by those for whose benefit and to whose detriment (if any) the convention developed over a considerable period of time, is inconsistent with its legal enforcement....
>
> The attempted assimilation of the growth or a convention to the growth of the common law is misconceived. The latter is the product of judicial effect, based on justiciable issues which attained legal formulation and are subject to modification and even reversal by the Courts which gave them their birth.... No such parental role is played by the Courts if there is a conflict between conventions and law, the Courts must enforce the law. The sanctions for conventions are political though the violation of conventions is 'unconstitutional'.

Constitutional Conventions in India

The fact that the Indian Constitution, with its 395 articles and 9 schedules, is one of the most elaborate in the world does not imply that it does not have in addition certain tacit provisions. It is based on the recognized conventions of a parliamentary form of government which it establishes both at the centre and in the states.

For a long time some people, politicians and others, professed not to see anything but the written word, and rejected the conventions altogether. This was particularly done with regard to the president's powers which laid bare the political motivation underlying the arid intellectual exercise. It is however grossly improper to tinker with the constitution and distort its meaning in order to achieve personal political objectives. The Supreme Court delivered a judgment, on 17 March 1971, which gave impetus to these efforts by recognizing the force and relevance of the essential constitutional conventions concerning parliamentary government.[22]

A petition had been filed in the Madras High Court for a writ of *quo warranto* against Prime Minister Indira Gandhi (1917–84)[23], for a declaration that she had no constitutional authority to hold the office of Prime Minister of India. The reason was that Article 75(3) of the constitution laid down that

> 'the council of ministers shall be collectively responsible to the house of the people.'

And how could it be so responsible after the house has been dissolved? The alternative was for the president to exercise executive power directly or through officers subordinate to him.

The Madras High Court was not impressed by these arguments and rejected the petition. The petitioner appealed to the Supreme Court and lost again, but the Supreme Court made some pertinent observations on constitutional interpretation and very clearly gave legal recognition to constitutional conventions concerning the parliamentary system of government. The Supreme Court observed:

> It was said that we must interpret Article 75(3) according to its own terms regardless of the convention that prevail in the United Kingdom. If the words of an article are clear, notwithstanding any relevant convention, effect will no doubt be given to the words. But it must be remembered that we are interpreting a Constitution and not an Act of parliament, a Constitution which establishes a parliamentary system of government with a cabinet. In trying to understand one may well keep in mind the conventions prevalent at the time the Constitution was framed.

In plain words, the court recognized that the provisions of Indian constitution were based on certain British conventions regarding the cabinet and that to ignore the latter would be to misinterpret the former. According to Granville Austin (1927–2014)[24], the framers of the constitution had to initially face this question:

> Should the well-known conventions of cabinet government, as practiced in England be included in the Constitution in the form of written provisions, or could India rely on the honesty of her leaders and their grounding in the traditional behaviour demanded by the parliamentary system to protect the democratic working of her political institutions?[25]

The constitution-framers chose the latter course and the Supreme Court has given effect to their intention. At one stage they had decided to codify some of the conventions in the form of an instrument of instructions but later changed their mind. It may be mentioned that as early as 1955 the Supreme Court held that:

> Under Article 53(1) of our Constitution, the executive power of the union is vested in the president but under Article 75 there is to be a council of ministers with the prime minister at the head to aid and advice the president in the exercise of his functions. The president has thus been made a formal or constitutional head of the executive and the real executive powers are vested in the ministers or the cabinet. The same provisions obtain in regard to the government of States; the governor or the *rajpramukh*, as the case may be, occupies the position of the head of the executive in the State but it is virtually the council of ministers in each State that carried on the executive government. In the Indian Constitution, therefore, we have the same system of parliamentary executive, as in England and the council of ministers consisting, as it does, of the members of the legislature is, like the British cabinet, 'a hyphen which joints a buckle which fastens the legislative part of a State to the executive part.[26]

The existence of a council of ministers to aid and advise the president is mandatory. The president cannot act except on its advice. Rejecting the appellant's contention that after the dissolution of the *Lok Sabha* the council of ministers should go and the president should govern directly, the Supreme Court said:

> The constituent assembly did not choose the presidential system of government. If we were to give effect to this contention of the appellant we would be changing the whole concept of the executive. It would mean that the president need not have a prime minister and ministers to aid and advise him in the exercise of his functions. As there would be no council of ministers, nobody would be responsible to the house of the people. With the aid of advisers he would be able to rule the country at least until he was impeached under Article 61.[27]

Constitutional Conventions in Pakistan

In Pakistan, the Supreme Court recognized the force of conventions for interpretation and understanding of the provisions of the constitution. Relying upon certain longstanding conventions about the working of the judiciary in Pakistan and India, it decided a case concerning appointment of judges of the superior courts and gave the following directions based on constitutional conventions recognized as part of the constitution itself.[28]

(1) Appointment of ad hoc judges against permanent vacancies of the Supreme Court violated the constitution.
(2) Appointment of acting chief justice can only be a stopgap arrangement for a short period and not, in any case, exceeding a period of ninety days.
(3) An acting chief justice cannot be a consultee for the purposes of appointment of judges, and the appointments made on the recommendation of an acting chief justice were invalid and unconstitutional.
(4) An additional judge of a High Court acquires a reasonable expectancy to be considered for appointment as permanent judge, and if he is recommended by the chief justice of Pakistan, he is to be appointed as such in the absence of strong reasons to the contrary to be recorded by the president/executive which would any way be justiciable.
(5) All permanent vacancies in the judiciary, particularly those of the chief justices, should be filled in advance if they are normal ones (like arising out of retirement) and in any case, not later than thirty days after their occurrence. If a vacancy occurs on account of death or for any unforeseen cause, it should be filled, at the most, within ninety days.
(6) The senior most judge of a High Court has a legitimate expectancy to be considered for appointment as chief justice. He is entitled to be appointed as chief justice of that court in the absence of very strong reasons to the contrary to be recorded by the president/executive.

(7) That sending of a Supreme Court judge to a High Court as an acting chief justice would be undesirable.
(8) The words 'after consultation' occurring in Articles 177 and 193 of the constitution involve a participatory consultative process between the consultees and the executive. It should be effective, meaningful, purposive, and consensus oriented, leaving no room for complaint of arbitrariness or unfair play. The chief justice of a High Court and the chief justice of Pakistan are well equipped to assess the knowledge and suitability of a candidate for judgeship of the superior courts. The opinion of the chief justices as constitutional consultees was held to be binding on the executive, and if the executive disagreed with the view of the chief justice of Pakistan and the chief justice of a High Court, it should record strong reasons which would be justiciable. The court found it to be a consistent practice that has acquired the status of convention during the pre-partition days of India as well as the post-partition period, that the recommendations of the chief justice of a High Court and the chief justice of the Supreme Court, in India as well as in Pakistan, have been consistently accepted and acted upon except in very rare cases.
(9) The requirement of ten years practice as an advocate of the High Court for appointment as judge of the High Court does not mean mere enrolment for that period as an advocate, but actual practice/experience as an advocate of the High Court for such period.
(10) If a person of unimpeachable integrity and sound knowledge of law is recommended by the chief justice of the High Court and the chief justice of Pakistan, his past political affiliation would not be disqualification because a person of integrity and sound knowledge normally severs his past connections with the political party with which he had affiliation and decides the matter purely on merits. However, it would be desirable not to appoint a person who is a strong activist in a political party and for him, it would not be possible to erase an unconscious tilt in favour his party.
(11) The power to transfer judges from one High Court to another cannot be invoked by the president/executive for any purpose other than public interest, and that too only after consultation with the chief justice of Pakistan. The power of transfer cannot be pressed into service for the purpose of inflicting punishment on a judge or for any other extraneous consideration.

This judgment in Pakistan is a precedent for use of consistent past practice maturing into a Constitutional convention for interpretation of the provisions of the constitution. In another case, the Supreme Court of Pakistan gave a comprehensive explanation of what is described as 'constitutional convention'.[29]

> We are inclined to agree with the conclusion that a Constitutional convention once established has the same binding effect as a Constitutional provision. We may, however, add that in the case of an unwritten Constitution, conventions play a more prominent and dominant role in the interpretation of Constitutional provisions than in the case of written Constitution. Therefore, while explaining the Constitutional provision of a written Constitution on the basis of a convention, it must be shown that either a convention has developed with the passage of time side by side with the enforcement and interpretation of the Constitution or a convention already existing on the date of enforcement of a written Constitution, has either received a statutory recognition in the Constitutional document or has been established as a Constitutional convention on account of conscious and deliberate obedience of the convention by those who are charged with the duty of interpreting or enforcing the Constitution. Therefore, when an already existing convention is followed in interpreting a provision of a written Constitution consistently and consciously over a length of time by those who are responsible under the Constitutional mandate to interpret and enforce the said provision of Constitution, the convention is established as a Constitutional convention and may breach thereof may be treated by the Courts as a breach of the provision of the Constitution to which the convention relates.

NOTES

1. K.C. Wheare, *Modern Constitutions* (London: Oxford University Press, 1951), p. 179.
2. Ibid., p. 180.
3. Franklin D. Roosevelt was the 32nd President of the United States from 1933 until his death in 1945.
4. François Mitterrand was President of France from 1981 to 1995, the longest serving President in the history of France.
5. Jacques Chirac was President of France from 1995 to 2007.
6. The Constitution of the Fifth Republic of France, Article 8.
7. A.V. Dicey was a British Whig jurist and constitutional theorist.
8. A.V. Dicey, *Introduction to the Study of the Law of the Constitution*, 10th ed. (London: Macmillan; New York: St. Martin's Press, 1961), pp. 28–9.
9. Supra Note 3, Articles 49–50, German Basic Law, Articles 67–8.
10. Ivor Jennings was a British lawyer and academic.
11. Ivor Jennings, *The Law and the Constitution*, 5th ed. (London: University of London Press, 1959), p. 81.
12. Queen Anne was Queen of England, Scotland and Ireland from 8 March 1702 and 1 May 1707.
13. James Callaghan was a British Labour Party politician, who was Prime Minister from 1976 to 1979.
14. *Re: Amendment of the Constitution of Canada* (1982) 125 DLR (3d) 1, 84.
15. The Basic Law is the constitution of the Federal Republic of Germany.
16. Eric Barendt, *An Introduction to Constitutional Law*, Clarendon Law Series (Oxford: Oxford University Press,1998), pp. 40–4.
17. *Attorney General v. Jonathan Cape Ltd.*, (1976) QB 752.
18. John Widgery was a Lord Chief Justice of England and Wales from 1971 to 1980.
19. Supra Note 16, pp. 44–5.
20. George Washington was the 1st President of the United States of America.
21. Supra Note 1, p. 199.
22. *U.N. Rao v. Indira Gandhi*, AIR 1971 S.C. 1002.
23. Indira Gandhi was the 3rd Prime Minister of India, first female Prime Minister of India.
24. Granville Austin was an American historian of the Indian Constitution.
25. Granville Austin, *The Indian Constitution: Cornerstone of a Nation* (Clarendon Press: Oxford University Press, 1966), p. 132.
26. *Ram Jawaya Kapur v. The State of Punjab*, AIR 1955 S.C. 549.
27. A.G. Noorani, *Constitutional Questions in India: The President, Parliament and the States* (New Delhi: Oxford University Press, 2000), pp. 53–5.
28. *Al-Jehad Trust v. Federation of Pakistan*, PLD 1996 S.C. 324.
29. *Asad Ali v. Federation of Pakistan*, PLD 1998 S.C. 161, p. 314.

4 The Rule of Law

Introduction

The phrase 'rule of law' has been used since the time of Aristotle (385–322 BC)[1] in the 4th century BC. It has meant different things to different authors and theorists. Aristotle's concept of rule of law is contained in his simple saying: 'the rule of law is to be preferred to that of any individual'. In other words, the rule of law is anathema to the rule of men. In the words of the Constitution of the State of Massachusetts, it means 'a government of law and not of men'. In brief, it means the supremacy of law.[2]

The supremacy or rule of law has always been a principle of the constitution. It means that the exercise of powers of government should be conditioned by law and that the subject should not be exposed to the arbitrary will of the ruler. There is much truth in the statement that 'principles of the constitution' are only 'political principles'. The rule of law had a different interpretation under weak Lancastrian monarchs (1267–1361) than under the Tudors (1485–1603). It has been said that 'unconstitutional' may mean merely 'contrary to tradition,' but 'the principles of 1689 have become part of the accepted theory of democracy' and 'in the political sphere there is much in the Whig[3] philosophy with which any democrat will agree, and which is, therefore, an accepted and, one might almost say, permanent part of the constitution.' But the rule of law is a concept of greater antiquity, although admittedly it had to be reconciled with the doctrine of parliamentary supremacy in the course of the 17th century contest with the Crown.[4]

History of the Rule of Law

In the Middle Ages (500–1500 AD) the theory was accepted that there was a universal law which ruled the world. Henry de Bracton (1210–68)[5], writing in the first half of the 13th century, deduced from this theory the proposition that rulers were subject to law. It is a matter of historical experience that the alliance between common lawyers and Parliament had a decisive effect upon the contest between the crown and the Parliament. That alliance had its roots in the later Middle Ages. Mediaeval lawyers never denied the wide scope of the royal prerogative, but the king could do certain things only in certain ways. It was not until the 17th century that Parliament established its supremacy, but Chief Justice John Fortescue (1394–1479)[6] writing in the reign of Henry VI (1421–71), had applied what later became the two major principles of the constitution—the rule of law and the supremacy of the Parliament—and relied upon the rule of law to justify the contention that taxation could not be imposed without the consent of Parliament. With the rise in the 16th century of the modern territorial state, the mediaeval conception of a universal law which ruled the world gave place to the conception of the supremacy of the common law. The abolition in 1640 of the Court of Star Chamber ensured that the principles of the common law should apply to public as well as private law. The 'rule of law' mean the supremacy of all parts of the law of England, both enacted and un-enacted. The supremacy of the law together with the supremacy of Parliament was finally established by the Bill of Rights in 1688.[7]

Dicey's Exposition of the Rule of Law

Of all the writers of the constitution since William Blackstone (1723–80)[8] the most influential has been A.V. Dicey (1835–1923)[9].

His lectures delivered as Vinerian Professor of English Law at Oxford and first published in 1885 under the title *Introduction to the Study of the Law of the Constitution*,[10] have been studied by successive generations of statesmen, lawyers and a large section of those interested in public life. The constitutional law of today differs in many respects from that of 1885, but the influence of Dicey remains a real force. There is no better way of distinction between the permanent and impermanent features of British Constitution than by examining the principles of the constitution as expounded by Dicey and to determine how far they hold good today. Of those principles which Dicey expounded and those which have had most influence and at the same time has received most modern criticism was his exposition of the rule of law.

Dicey's Three Parts of the Rule of Law

Dicey divided the 'rule of law' into three parts,[11] explained by the following extracts:

1. '...no man is punishable or can be lawfully made to suffer in body or goods except for a distinct breach of law established in the ordinary legal manner before the ordinary Courts of the land. In this sense the rule of law is contrasted with every system of government based on the exercise by persons in authority of wide, arbitrary, or discretionary powers of constraint.... It means, in the first place, the absolute supremacy or predominance of regular law as opposed to the influence of arbitrary power, and excludes the existence of arbitrariness, of prerogative or even a wide discretionary authority on the part of the government.'[12]
2. '...every man, whatever be his rank or condition, is subject to the ordinary law of the realm and amenable to the jurisdiction of the ordinary tribunals.'[13]
3. '...the general principles of the constitution (as for example the right to personal liberty or the right of public meeting) are with us the result of judicial decisions determining the rights of private persons in particular cases brought before the Courts; whereas under many foreign constitutions the security (such as it is) given to the rights of individuals results, or appears to result, from the general principles of the constitution.... Our constitution, in short, is a judge-made constitution....'[14]

In other words, the 'rule of law', according to Dicey, included the following three[15] conceptions:

(i) The absence of arbitrary power. No man is above the law. No man is punishable except for distinct breach of law, established in the ordinary legal manner before the ordinary courts.

(ii) Equality before the law. Every man, whatever his rank or condition, is subject to the ordinary law and jurisdiction of ordinary tribunals. Dicey contrasted this principle with the French *droit administratif*, under which the responsibility of public officers for their official acts is decided by a distinct system of administrative courts.

(iii) The general principles of the British Constitution especially the liberties of the individuals, such as personal liberty, freedom of speech and public meeting are the result of judicial decisions in particular cases. The constitution is judge-made law.

It can be seen that the first two parts of the rule are closely linked, and may be said to amount to the concept of equality before the law for all citizens.[16]

Dicey did in fact go on to compare English law with French public law, as there existed (and still exists today) a separate system of administrative courts, which had jurisdiction over all disputes between the state and individuals, to the exclusion of the ordinary courts of law. Many critics of Dicey have believed that he was asserting that no such thing as administrative law existed in his country, but such criticism has been unjust, for he intended to say no more than that England had any separate *droit administratif* with its own special courts. It was clear to him and to all English lawyers that there must always be a branch of law amounting to administrative law, because no country can survive without an administration, and any such administration must possess certain legal rights, powers, and duties which impinge in some way upon the lives and rights of the ordinary citizens of the land. In 1915, Dicey t published a paper in the *Law Quarterly Review* entitled, 'The Development of Administrative Law in England',[17] and that he only intended to declare that in the United Kingdom the ordinary courts had jurisdiction over questions of administrative law, just as over all branches of the law, whatever the rules of those branches may be. Where he was wrong was in believing that the French system favoured the state to the detriment of the rights of the ordinary citizens of France, and that thus the existence of the administrative courts conflicted with the rule of law. If one accepts Dicey's distinction between the two systems as correct, with the exception of his mistaken distrust of the French administrative courts, and that the ordinary courts dealt with English administrative law problems, then there is one way at least in which the laws of the United Kingdom may have progressed away from the concept of the 'rule of law' because since the time of his writing, a large number of administrative tribunals have been created and these tribunals have jurisdiction over much of the litigation of all types in the field of administrative law. Their existence may be strictly contrary to Dicey's first branch of the rule, but at least none of them ought to favour the executive to the derogation of the rights of individuals, and all are subject to control by the ordinary courts of the land.[18]

It is not hard to find several other examples in English laws which must be exceptions to the first two branches of Dicey's concept. Foreign sovereigns and diplomats enjoy special immunity from criminal prosecution or civil action, and judges can never be held civilly liable for anything done or said during their office. Members of both houses of Parliament enjoy extensive privileges, while peers are disqualified from voting in parliamentary elections. Trade unions occupy a specially privileged position in that they cannot normally be rendered liable in tort at all, although this legal immunity was only conferred for the first time by the Trades Disputes Act 1906, some twenty years after Dicey first published his theory, and it has been somewhat reduced by provisions in the Employment Act 1982. Police powers of arrest without warrant may be regarded as infringements upon individual liberty, even though they are unlikely to be used in an entirely arbitrary manner in the United Kingdom. Discretionary powers may always be conferred upon the executive, or indeed upon anyone, by act of Parliament, the most usual example being the power to make delegated legislation, and powers of a somewhat similar nature may be conferred also by the royal prerogative. But at the time of Dicey's writing probably the most glaring exception from his rule was the immunity from the ordinary process of law which had been accorded to the crown because of the royal prerogative, an immunity in which Parliament had acquiesced, for it could be useful to the government or to any future government. This exception has been largely eliminated by the passage of the Crown Proceedings Act 1947 and it is now true to say that in one very important respect, British law has approached more nearly to the concept of the 'rule of law' which Dicey had propounded.[19]

It would be impossible to iron out all the inequalities. Perhaps the clearest example of all inequalities, which are essential in civilized communities, is provided by the age for criminal responsibility. It is unthinkable that a new born baby or a very young child should bear full criminal responsibility for his activities. So, the 'rule of law, even for Dicey, cannot have meant equal treatment for all before the law. It is enough that the same law covers everyone, even though it makes different provisions for different groups of people—and it is of course always possible for the ordinary citizen to join a trade union or become a member of Parliament. Yet, the fact that the law in a totalitarian state may recognize the various exceptions within the law is not enough to satisfy the principle of the rule of law. The International Commission of Jurists has repeatedly stressed that a legal system must also provide for a proper balance, with judicial safeguards, between the interests of the state and of individuals, an independent judiciary and bar, and social institutions allowing for the dignity of man.

The third branch of Dicey's rule is largely true, provided it is accepted that the concept of the sovereignty of Parliament is based on the decisions of the courts to that effect.

Certainly, it is true that the constitution in United Kingdom is part of the ordinary law of the land and is not contained in any special instrument or instruments. The sovereignty of Parliament renders the first two branches of Dicey's rule subject to a possible enormous practical exception.

The great value of Dicey's work in this field has been to provide lawyers and jurists with an ideal. It is not possible to formulate a satisfactory definition of the rule of law, and indeed it cannot seriously be contended that any one 'rule' as such has any place in the law of the United Kingdom, which depends primarily on the rules laid down by Parliament and secondarily upon the concrete decisions of the courts. If such a theoretical 'rule' has no place among the detailed statutes and decisions from which English law is drawn, then it cannot be considered as a basic tenet of British constitutional law. But as a guide to law-makers and reformers it can be of inestimable value, and for this purpose it is of little importance whether one accepts the views of Dicey or of any other jurist, or constructs an entirely new idea concerning its identity. Providing the aim is the preservation of the liberty and rights of all members of the community, and that only such exceptions from this aim are allowed as are essential to the administration of the nation in an orderly fashion (such as judicial and parliamentary privilege, with proper safeguards), the purpose of the 'rule of law' will have been fulfilled. In short, the 'rule of law' is not a rule or a law, but a persuasive guide for the legislature, the executive and the judiciary, linked in practice, in the United Kingdom, with the working of many of the conventions which mitigate the theoretical deficiencies in the constitution, and mould it into a living democratic entity.[20]

Lord Tom Bingham (1933–2010)[21] in his book *The Rule of Law* explores the ingredients of the rule of law by identifying what the rule of law' really means[22]:

1. The law must be accessible and so far as possible intelligible, clear, and predictable.
2. Questions of legal right and liability should ordinarily be resolved by application of the law and not the exercise of discretion.
3. The laws of the land should apply equally to all, save to the extent that objective differences justify differentiation.
4. Ministers and public officers at all levels must exercise the powers conferred on them in good faith, fairly, for the purpose for which the powers were conferred, without exceeding the limits of such powers and not unreasonably.
5. The law must afford adequate protection of fundamental human rights.
6. Means must be provided for resolving, without prohibitive cost or inordinate delay, *bona fide* civil disputes which the parties themselves are unable to resolve.
7. Adjudicative procedures provided by the state should be fair.
8. The rule of law requires compliance by the state with its obligations in international law as in national law.

English Cases

'The rule of law' is, obviously, an English expression, and the English judges have frequently invoked it in their judgments, without, however, devising its definition. The following recent cases will shed some light on the meaning of the expression.[23]

M v. Home Office

This was the first case in United Kingdom's history in which a minister of the Crown was convicted for contempt of court and for which Dicey's historic principle was called in aid:

> when we speak of the rule of law as a characteristic of our country, we mean not only that with us no man is above the law, but what is a different thing, that here every man, whatever be his rank or condition, is subject to the ordinary law of the realm and amenable to the jurisdiction of the ordinary tribunals.

This was the idea of legal equality. It was held,

> the Sovereign could do no wrong did not mean that a servant of the Crown could do no wrong, and that there appears no reason in principle why, if a statute places a duty on a specified minister or other official which creates a course of action, an action cannot be brought for a breach of statutory duty claiming damages or for an injunction....[24]

X Ltd v. Morgan-Grampian

This case illustrates the duty to obey the law and the courts' power to interpret the legal aspects of the rule of law. William Robin Goodwin, a young journalist, was ordered by the judge to disclose the notes of the conversation during which he had come into possession of information relating to a confidential business plan. Mr Goodwin declined to do so and relying upon professional ethics offered to pay the penalty for breach of law. When that case was in the Court of Appeal, the Master of the Rolls, Lord John Donaldson (1920–2005)[25] said:

> The constitutional position is clear. Parliament makes the law and it is the duty of the court to enforce that law, whether or not they agree with it. Every citizen, every corporate body and every authority, whether national or local, is entitled to campaign to change the law, but until the law is changed it is their duty to obey it. That is what parliamentary democracy and the rule of law is all about. Each one of us surrenders a part of his

> personal freedom of action and choice and in return is protected by the law from the consequences of other seeking to exercise an unfettered freedom of action and choice.[26]

Dealing with the offer to pay the penalty, Lord Donaldson described it as pernicious nonsense.

> 'His right to disobey the law is not obtainable by the payment of a penalty or license fee…'.

The House of Lords emphasized the importance of the maintenance of the 'rule of law' as follows:

> The maintenance of the rule of law is in every way as important in a free society as the democratic franchise. In our society the rule of law rests on twin foundations: the sovereignty of the Queen in Parliament in making the law and the sovereignty of the Queen's courts in interpreting and apply the law.[27]

As Goodwin had disobeyed the order of the court and had thereby disobeyed the law, the Court of Appeal refused to hear him in support of his appeal and the House of Lords upheld that decision. 'Certainly in a case where a contemnor,' so observed Lord Nigel Bridge (1917–2007)[28],

> 'not only fails wilfully and contumaciously to comply with an order of the court but makes it clear that he will continue to defy court's authority, if the order should be affirmed on appeal, the court must, in my opinion, have a discretion to decline to entertain his appeal against the order.'

Bennett v. Horseferry Road Magistrates' Court[29]

This is an example of the principle that lawlessness anywhere is a threat to the 'rule of law' everywhere. The *Bennett* case stands out as an outstanding illustration of enforcement of 'rule of law' in the UK in modern times. In this case, the House of Lords overruled a long line of cases in which the view taken was that the English courts had jurisdiction to try a criminal without going into the legality or illegality of his arrest and the circumstances in which he had been brought to England.

The appellant, Paul James Bennett, was a New Zealand citizen who was wanted for criminal offences alleged to have been committed by him in connection with the purchase of a helicopter in England in 1989. The English police tracked him down in South Africa and in collusion with the South African police had arrested him there, and then had him forcibly brought to England against his will. It was in these facts that the question arose whether the appellant Bennett could be tried by the magistrate. In taking the view that the 'rule of law' must prevail, Lord Bridge held as under:

> Whatever differences there may be between the legal systems of South Africa, the United States, New Zealand and this country, many of the basic principles to which they seek to give effect stem from common roots. There is, I think, no principle more basic to any proper system of law than the maintenance of the rule of law itself. When it is shown that the law enforcement agency responsible for bringing a prosecution has only been enabled to do so by participating in violations of international law and of the laws of another state in order to secure the presence of the accused within the territorial jurisdiction of the court, I think that respect for the rule of law demands that the court take cognizance of that circumstance. To hold that the court may turn a blind eye to executive lawlessness beyond the frontiers of its own jurisdiction is, to my mind, an insular and unacceptable view. Having then taken cognizance of the lawlessness it would again appear to me to be a wholly inadequate response for the court to hold that the only remedy lies in civil proceedings at the suit of the defendant or in disciplinary or criminal proceedings against the individual officers of the law enforcement agency who were concerned in the illegal action taken. Since the prosecution could never have been brought if the defendant had not been illegally abducted, the whole proceeding is tainted. If a resident in another country is properly extradited here, the time when the prosecution commences is the time when the authorities here set the extradition process in motion. By parity of reasoning, if the authorities, instead of proceeding by way of extradition, have resorted to abduction, which is the effective commencement of the prosecution process and is the illegal foundation on which it rests.

A v. Secretary Home[30]

In this case, the question was whether an English court may receive evidence which has or may have been procured by torture inflicted, to obtain evidence, by officials of a foreign state without the complicity of the British authorities. In that connection, Lord Bingham referred to Bennett and the judiciary's responsibility for the maintenance of the 'rule of law' and the international and constitutional aspects of torture and observed:

> 'It trivializes the issue before the House to treat it as an argument about the law of evidence. The issue is one of constitutional principle, whether evidence be admitted against a party to proceedings in a British Court, irrespective of where, or by whom, or on whose authority the torture was inflicted.'

To that question, said Lord Bingham,

> 'I would give a very clear negative answer.'

And this is what Lord David Hope (b. 1938)[31] had to say:

> 'The temptation to use it (torture) in times of emergency will be controlled by the law whenever the rule of law is allowed to operate. But where the rule of law is absent or is reduced to a mere form of words to which those in authority pay no more than lip service, the temptation to use torture is unrestrained....'.

R v. Secretary Home[32]

In this case, Lord Steyn, (1932–2017)[33] said:

> 'Unless there is the clearest provision to the contrary, Parliament must be presumed not to legislate contrary to the rule of law. And the rule of law enforces minimum standards of fairness, both substantive and procedural.'

Modern Concept of The Rule of Law

The principle of the 'rule of law' has since the end of the Second World War (1939–45) been a matter of universal discussion and endeavour to formulate the basic elements of the rule. So far from the principle being confined to the common law jurisdictions, the 'rule of law' is now considered as a basic idea which can serve to unite lawyers of many differing systems, all of which aim at protecting the individual from arbitrary government. In this way, the rule has come to be identified with the concept of the rights of man. Most countries accept that the rule has a positive content, no matter how much that content may differ in various countries. If justice is to be done in the process of harmonizing the opposing notions of individual liberty and public order, that is achieved ultimately but not exclusively by the ordinary courts. There are, however other methods of making a government submit to the law, such as adjudication by administrative tribunals and action in the legislature at the instance of private members, and even in the case of action by subordinate authority by higher administrative control. All these methods play their part in securing the observance of the law and orderly government in the United Kingdom.[34]

In the modern sense, the 'rule of law' means supremacy of the Constitution in the countries with written Constitution. It also means observance with the law existing or to be framed which is not repugnant to the Constitution. It also means conforming to the developed modern concepts of constitutional law which have attained universal acceptance. These concepts involve due process of law, equality before law, independence of judiciary, separation of powers and enforceability and justiciability of human rights and civil liberties as propounded in every Constitution under the chapter of 'Fundamental Rights'. The 'rule of law' is an all-pervading concept which can only be understood in the modern World by adherence to universal values of democratic dispensation which in its wake brings to life the concepts of constitutional law enumerated above. These concepts are discussed in the following chapters and the principles of 'rule of law' would have to be read in each of the principle of constitutional law.

The Rule of Law in USA

According to the American jurists, the Constitution is the embodiment of the founders' belief in the 'rule of law'. The idea is that government and society can be regulated by law, not subjected to the whims of powerful but potentially capricious rulers. The Constitution rests on the belief that no one in power should be above the law. Even the legislature, the people's elected representatives, should be bound to respect the principles and limitations contained in the 'supreme law of the Land'. The subordination of government to law was seen by the framers as a means of protecting individual rights to life, liberty, and property.

It must be understood that the Constitution imposes limits on government action. Private actions are beyond the scope of constitutional law. Individuals are subject to the constraints of the civil and criminal law. In addition to imposing constitutional limitations on government, the 'rule of law' requires that citizens who are wronged by others have opportunities to seek justice through the courts. It also means that persons who offend society's rules are brought into court to answer for their crimes. Of course, the 'rule of law' is a two-way street: Defendants in civil and criminal cases are entitled to procedural fairness.[35]

The Rule of Law in India

The absence of arbitrary power is the first essential of the 'rule of law' upon which the whole of Indian constitutional system is based. In a system governed by the rule of law, discretion, when conferred upon executive authorities, must be confined within clearly defined limits.[36] The 'rule of law' from this point of view means that decisions should be made by application of known principles and rules, and, in general, such decisions should be predictable and the citizen should know where he is.[37] The 'rule of law' means the authority of the law courts to test all administrative actions by the standard of legality. The administrative or executive action that does not meet the standard would be set aside, if the aggrieved person brings the appropriate action in competent court. The 'rule of law' rejects the conception of dual State in which government action is pleaded in a privileged position of immunity from control by law.[38]

The 'rule of law' in India cannot be better described than in the following words of Justice N. Rajagopala Ayyangar in relation to the duty of the superior courts when an allegation is properly raised and established.

> The Constitution enshrines and guarantees the rule of law and Article 226 is designed to ensure that each and every authority in the State, including the government, acts *bonafide* and within the limits of its power and we consider that when a court is satisfied that there is an abuse or misuse of power and its jurisdiction is invoked, it is incumbent on the court to afford justice to the individual.[39]

The presumption that when discretionary powers are conferred upon high officials or the government and that such high officials or government would exercise the power reasonably or honestly without adversely affecting the fundamental rights might not be sound.[40] The Indian Supreme Court observed:

> The plea of constitutionality of a statute infringing a fundamental right cannot be negative on the assumption that the autocratic power of imposing penalty or punishment is entrusted to the executive authority which will exercise it only in the proper cases and there will be no abuse of power. In the larger interest, our Constitution makers have been averse to conferral of autocratic power and have tried to protect the citizen against the exercise of such power by guaranteeing him the fundamental freedoms against infringement of these freedoms by legislative or executive action.[41]

The Rule of Law in Pakistan

The Government in Pakistan is under a written Constitution; therefore, the written Constitution is the rule of law.
Article 4 of the Constitution of 1973 embodies the essence of the rule of law. It reads:

4. Right of individuals to be dealt with in accordance with law, etc.
   (1) To enjoy the protection of law and to be treated in accordance with law is the inalienable right of every citizen, wherever he may be, and of every other person for the time being within Pakistan.
   (2) In particular—
      (a) No action detrimental to the life, liberty, body, reputation or property of any person shall be taken except in accordance with law;
      (b) No person shall be prevented from or be hindered in doing that which is not prohibited by law; and
      (c) No person shall be compelled to do that which the law does not require him to do.

It was observed by Chief Justice Muhammad Haleem (1925–2006)[42] in *Benazir Bhutto v. Federation of Pakistan*,[43] that any application of a principle of Anglo-Saxon jurisprudence, which might be 'destructive of the rule of law which is so worded in Article 4 of the Constitution as to give protection to all citizens,' has to be discouraged, 'but regard should be had to the object and the purpose for which this Article is enacted, that is, that this interpretative approach must receive inspiration from the triad of provisions which saturate and invigorate the entire Constitution, namely the Objectives Resolution, …, the fundamental rights and the directive principles of State policy so as to achieve democracy, tolerance, equity and social justice according to Islam' so that 'national integration and social cohesion by creating an egalitarian society through a new legal order' is achieved.

Article 4 is an original contribution to the constitutional law.[44] It embodies the rule of law.[45] 'It prevents the government from taking any action in this country for which there is no legal sanction and it at the same time debars the legislature from creating an authority whose actions are not subject to law. The legislature cannot enact that whatever action a particular person may take shall be immune from challenge. All persons exercising authority in Pakistan must do so only in accordance with law.'[46] It is 'intended to negate any claim by the Government that any category of its acts in relation to citizens and other persons in Pakistan are not subject to law at all.'[47] So predominant is the position of Article 4 that it furnishes the only guarantee or assurance to the citizens when the fundamental rights stand suspended, for example, during martial law, so that 'no action detrimental to life, liberty, body, reputation or property of any person shall be taken except in accordance with law.'[48]

The former Chief Justice Muhammad Munir (1895–1979)[49] in his commentary on the 1973 Constitution of Pakistan,[50]

> 'confers a right which is more basic than fundamental rights because while the fundamental rights can be suspended, the right given by Article 4 cannot.'

The right to access to justice has been held as part of the rule of law, as derived from Article 4, read with Article 9. This includes the right to have a fair and proper trial and the right to have an impartial court or tribunal, as also to have a reasonable opportunity to defend, and all this depends on the independence of judiciary.[51]

In *Zahur Elahi v. Z.A. Bhutto*,[52] reference made by the Government of Pakistan against the National Awami Party (NAP) and its leaders under Section 6(2) of the Political Parties Act 1962, was pending, before the Supreme Court when Zulfikar Ali Bhutto (1928–79)[53], Prime Minister of Pakistan, made a speech, in which he was alleged to have said that:

> 'if the Supreme Court in its wisdom or according to its own understanding gives a decision against us then it will not be my decision or that of the people but will be a decision of the Supreme Court. We will accept this decision but the responsibility for the consequences will be that of the Supreme Court….'

The Supreme Court was moved for taking action against Zulfikar Ali Bhutto (1928–79), on the ground that the speech amounted to contempt of the Supreme Court. One of the grounds raised in defence was based upon Article 248 of the Constitution; which grants immunity to the President, a Governor, the Prime Minister and others, so that, among others, they

> 'shall not be answerable to any court for the exercise of powers and performance of functions of their respective offices or for any act done or purported to be done in the exercise of those powers and performance of those functions.'

Speaking for the Supreme Court, Chief Justice Hamoodur Rehman (1910–81)[54] was not in a position to draw a firm line between the functions of the Prime Minister in a parliamentary democracy, and his role as the leader of the political party in power and to say on which side of the line the speech in question could fall.

> 'It is not uncommon,' he observed 'these days for leaders of political parties, leading a Government as Prime Minister, to address public meetings for explaining or justifying the policies of his Government with regard to the state of affairs prevailing in the country, particularly when public opinion is disturbed by drastic actions of the Government in power as in the present case.'

The Prime Minister was therefore held entitled to the immunity given by Article 248. However, dealing with the argument that the provisions of Article 248 should be construed strictly 'because under the Islamic system, which the Constitution professes to adopt, no one is above the law and no immunity is granted even to a '*Khalifa*', the Chief Justice Hamoodur Rehman observed:

> Since we are bound by the Constitution and have to give effect to its provisions, it is necessary that we should express our view with regard to the scope of Article 248. Learned counsel for the petitioner has conceded that under a system of parliamentary democracy, where a leader of a political party becomes also the Prime Minister, it is not easy to define the exact scope of his powers and functions, but this much is certain that his powers and functions are derived from the Constitution and must, therefore, be referable to the Constitution. Hence, since neither the Constitution nor any law can possibly authorize him to commit a criminal act or does anything which is contrary to law, the immunity cannot extend to illegal or unconstitutional acts. Even a Prime Minister is under clause (2) of Article 5 of the Constitution, bound to obey the Constitution and Law as that is the basic obligation of every citizen. The scope of the powers and functions of a Prime Minister cannot possibly extend to the committing of contempt of court which is punishable under the Constitution itself and, therefore, by necessary implication prohibited. If his speech did prejudice the pending proceedings against the NAP and also contained a veiled threat to this Court, then it amounted to contempt and was not protected by Article 248. The Constitution itself declares by Article 190 that all executive and judicial authorities throughout Pakistan shall act in aid of the Supreme Court. The Prime Minister is, therefore, duty-bound to give effect to the decisions of this Court. He had, therefore, no right to say that he would not accept responsibility for the decision of the Court *if* it goes against his decision. This amounted to deliberately flouting the Court's authority or, at least, attempting to influence its decision.
>
> As to the scope of Article 248, we are in agreement with the learned counsel for the petitioners that each and every act done, or action taken by the Prime Minister is not necessarily covered by this Article. The Article necessarily refers to his official acts and not to acts done by him in his private capacity. Only those acts are covered which he does in exercise of his powers as Prime Minister and in the performance of his functions as Prime Minister. If he has any other capacity, then he cannot claim immunity for act done in that capacity if it has no relation whatsoever to the office of the Prime Minister. It is true that the immunity cannot possibly extend to anything done illegally, nor does the immunity protect the Prime Minister in respect of any criminal proceeding. In order to avail of this immunity, it must be shown that whatever was done had some co-relation to the official functions or duties or powers of the Prime Minister.
>
> We are also in agreement with the learned counsel for the petitioners that the immunity provisions must, in accordance with the accepted principles of interpretation, be construed strictly and unless persons claiming the immunity come strictly within the terms of the provisions granting the immunity, the immunity cannot be extended. The immunity is in the nature of an exception to the general rule that no one is above the law. It is, nevertheless, not possible to lay down any hard and fast rule as to what is or what is not within the powers and functions of a Minister or a Prime Minister, but each case will have to be judged on its own facts and circumstances.

In *Brig. Imtiaz Ahmad v. Govt. of Pakistan*,[55] it was sought to be argued that the appellant, a former Director, Intelligence Bureau, who had challenged the registration of some criminal cases against him by means of a petition under Article 199 of the Constitution, was not an ordinary man, the Supreme Court thought it necessary to recall, 'for the benefit of all concerned,' the following observations of Chief Justice Sir John Eardley Wilmot (1709–92),[56] in that historic case, *Wilkes v. Woods*,

> 'The law makes no difference between great and petty officers; thank God, they are all amenable to justice.'[57]

NOTES

1. Aristotle was an Ancient Greek philosopher and scientist.
2. Justice Fazal Karim, *Judicial Review of Public Actions*, 3 vols. (Karachi: Pakistan Law House, 2006), p. 46.
3. Whigs were a political faction and then a political party in the Parliaments of England, Scotland, Great Britain, Ireland and the United Kingdom. Between the 1680s and 1850s.
4. E.C.S. Wade and A.W. Bradley, *Constitutional Law*, 7th ed. (London: Longmans, 1965), p. 60.
5. Henry de Bracton was a leading English jurist and cleric.
6. John Fortescue was Chief Justice of the King's Bench and was the author of *De Laudibus Legum Angliae*.
7. Supra Note 4, p. 61.
8. William Blackstone was an English jurist, judge and Tory politician of the 18th century.
9. A.V. Dicey was a British jurist and constitutional theorist.
10. A.V. Dicey, *Introduction to the Study of the Law of the Constitution*, 10th ed. (London: MacMillan, 1959).
11. D.C.M. Yardley, *Introduction to British Constitutional Law*, 6th ed. (London: Butterworths, 1984), p. 70.
12. Supra Note 4, pp. 188, 202.
13. Ibid., p. 193.
14. Ibid., pp. 195–6.
15. A.G. Chaudhry, *Lectures on Constitutional Law* (Lahore: Irfan Law Book House, 1994), p. 65.
16. Supra Note 10, pp. 70–1.
17. 31 LQR 148.
18. Supra Note 10, pp. 71–2.
19. Ibid., pp. 72–3.
20. Ibid., pp. 73–4.
21. Lord Tom Bingham a British judge was Master of the Rolls, Lord Chief Justice and Senior Law Lord.
22. Justice Fazal Karim, *Judicial Review of Public Actions*, vol. 1, 2nd ed. (Karachi: Pakistan Law House, 2018), p. 57.
23. Ibid., pp. 58–62.
24. (1993) 3 All ER 537.
25. John Donaldson a senior British judge, served as Master of the Rolls from 1982–92.
26. (1990) 1 All E.R. 616.
27. (1990) 2 All E. R 1.
28. Nigel Bridge was a British judge, who served as Lord of Appeal in Ordinary from 1980–92.
29. (1993) 3 All E.R. 138.
30. (2006) 2 AC 221.
31. David Hope was the first Deputy President of the Supreme Court of the United Kingdom from 2009 until his retirement in 2013.
32. (1998) AC 591.
33. Johan Steyn was a South African-British judge and until September 2005, a Law Lord.
34. Supra Note 10, pp. 72–3.
35. Otis H. Stephens, Jr and John M. Scheb II, *American Constitutional Law*, 3rd ed. (Belmont: Thomson/West, 2003), p. 8.
36. H. K. Saharay, *The Constitution of India: An Analytical Approach*, 3rd ed. (New Delhi: Eastern Law House, 2002), p. 60
37. *Jaisinghani v Union of India* AIR 1967 SC 1427 relying upon *United States v Wunderlich* 342 US 98 (1951).
38. *Chief Settlement Commr. v. Om Parkash* AIR 1969 SC 33 relying upon *Youngstown Sheet & Tube Co. v. Sawyer* 343 US 579 (1952).
39. *Partap Singh v. State of Punjab*, AIR 1964 S.C. 72.
40. Durga Das Basu, *Human Rights in Constitutional Law* (New Delhi: Prentice Hall of India, 1994), p. 252.
41. *Joseph Kuruvilla v. R.B.I.*, AIR 1962 S.C. 1371.
42. Muhammad Haleem was the 10th Chief Justice of Pakistan from 1981–1989.

43. PLD 1988 SC 416 at p. 489.
44. Muhammad Munir in his commentary on the Constitution of Pakistan, 1973 (Edition 1975).
45. *Manzoor Ellahi v. Federation of Pakistan* PLD 1975 S.C. 66.
46. Justice Badi-uz-Zaman Kaikaus in *Jamal Shah v. Member Election Commission* PLD 1966 SC 1.
47. *Mir Ali Nawaz Bugti v. Superintendent Jail* PLD 1966 SC 357.
48. Justice Saad Saood Jan in *Federation of Pakistan v. Ghulam Mustafa Khar* PLD 1989 SC 26 at p. 53.
49. Muhammad Munir was the 2nd Chief Justice of Pakistan from 1954 to 1960.
50. Supra Note 35.
51. Supra note 2, p. 52 relying on the cases titled *Government of Baluchistan v. Aziz Ullah Memon*, PLD 1993 SC 341; *Liaqat Hussain v. Federation of Pakistan* PLD 1999 SC 504 at p. 632, *Aftab Shahban Mirani v. President of Pakistan*, 1998 SCMR 1863 at p. 1875 and *New Jubilee Insurance v. National Bank of Pakistan*, PLD 1999 SC 1126. There, the meanings of 'in accordance with law' have also been explained.
52. PLD 1975 SC 383.
53. Zulfikar Ali Bhutto was a barrister and politician who served as the 9th Prime Minister of Pakistan from 1973 to 1977.
54. Hamoodur Rehman was the 7th Chief Justice of Pakistan from 1968 to 1975.
55. 1994 SCMR 2142, 2160.
56. Sir John Eardley Wilmot was an English Judge and Chief Justice of the Common Pleas from 1766 to 1771.
57. (1769) 19 St. Tr. 1406.

5 Due Process of Law

Introduction

The *Magna Carta*[1] (1215) was not a statute but was merely a personal treaty between King John (1166–1216)[2] and the enraged upper classes. Consequently, when Henry III (1207–72) ascended the throne in 1216 at the age of 9, the regents of the kingdom re-issued the charter in the name of the boy king. The following year there was another re-issue, and in 1225, Henry III transcribed it, with some alterations, into the final form which the *Magna Carta* was to take. It then became the custom for each successive king to reaffirm the charters at each political crisis during his reign. This practice continued for two centuries and in that period Sir Edward Coke (1552–1634)[3] has counted over thirty confirmations.

It is in connection with one of these confirmations (1354) that the phrase 'due process of law' probably was first used.

> 'That no man of what estate or condition that he be, shall be put out of Land or Tenement, nor taken, nor imprisoned, nor disinherited, nor put to Death, without being brought to Answer by due Process of the Law.'[4]

Three years before a similar phrase had been used:

> From henceforth none shall be taken by Petition or Suggestion made to our Lord the King or to his Council, unless it be by Indictment or Presentment of his good and lawful People of the same neighbourhood, where such Deeds be done, in due Manner, or by Process made by writ original at the Common Law, nor that none be ousted of his Franchises, nor of his Freehold, unless he be duly brought to answer and forejudged of the same by the Course of the law.[5]

The context in which this phrase is found, i.e. the protection against illegal deprivations of liberties, is strikingly similar to Section 39 of *Magna Carta*, as transcribed into the statutes by Henry III. Indeed the natural inference that the phrases 'law of the land' and 'due process of law' were intended to be synonymous is given additional weight by a direct implication in a statute issued by the same king 9 years later. With the authority of Sir Edward Coke supporting it, this interpretation has been generally accepted, and is now the law in the United States.[6] The Privy Council, in one of its recent judgments, traced the history of the phrase 'due process of law' to *Magna Carta* to show its English origin.[7]

History of Due Process in American Constitutions

Virginia was the first colony to draw up a Bill of Rights although two other colonies had framed constitutions before her. The celebrated Virginia Declaration of Rights was drafted by George Mason (1725–92)[8] and after being adopted by the Virginia Constitutional Convention (12 June 1776), it was made a part of the first Constitution of Virginia. Article 8 contained the 'law of the land' provision but presents an innovation in that the terms of Section 39 of *Magna Carta* in an abridged form are added as a postscript to an article safeguarding criminal procedure. This protection applies only to 'liberty' and was followed in this respect by the state of Vermont; but two other states, in framing their Declaration of Rights during the revolutionary period, considered Mason's terse statement adequate in the main, but made it clear that 'life' and 'property' were also to be protected. Some of the other states, on the other hand, preferred the variable statement of *Magna Carta* as transcribed into the statutes of England by Henry III. The long Declaration of Rights of Maryland, Article 21 which closely followed the *Magna Carta*, became a model in this respect, as in many others, for the Constitution of North Carolina. The only other Constitution, framed during this period, which contained this provision, was that of New York. The wording of paragraph 13 of the Constitution of New York represents a compromise between the two tendencies which had developed in that, while as in Virginia, much of the feudal phraseology of *Magna Carta* was omitted, it is nevertheless, as in Maryland, given an independent place in the constitution.

As first adopted, the federal Constitution contained no article guaranteeing the citizens of the new federal union the rights of 'due process of law'. In fact it contained only a very few guarantees of the personal rights of citizens in any form and one of the most frequently advanced objections to the document, when its ratification was urged, was the lack of a formal Bill of Rights. Indeed seven of the ratifying states proposed amendments covering this defect. To this end, on 25 September 1789, the First Federal Congress of the United States, under the leadership of James Madison, passed twelve proposals for amendments and by December 1791, ten of these were ratified by the requisite number of state legislatures.[9]

The wording of the 5th Amendment contains the first use of the phrase 'due process of law' in an American Constitution. The general arrangement follows Article 8 of the Virginia Declaration of Rights although there are wide differences in content. It reads:

> No person shall be held to answer for a capital, or otherwise infamous crime, unless on a presentment or indictment of a Grand Jury, except in cases arising in the land or naval forces, or in the militia, when in actual service in time of War or public danger; nor shall any person be subject for the same offence to be twice put in jeopardy of life or limb; nor shall be compelled in any criminal case to be a witness against himself, nor be deprived of life, liberty, or property, without due process of law; nor shall private property be taken for public use, without just compensation.

It should be noted that this article deals in general with the subject of criminal procedure and that the phrase 'due process of law' comes immediately after the protection against forced self-incrimination. In both of these important respects, the article resembles Mason's section, which was, one may almost say, the textual forerunner of the 5th Amendment.

Although in general arrangement the two sections are comparable, in specific wording they are very different. Mason's section had only protected the citizen against deprivation of his liberty, nothing having been said about life or property, although it was doubtless expected that it would be included in the larger term, 'liberty'. In the 5th Amendment, however, there is a reiteration of the three fundamental rights of man in such a manner that the scope of the protection in this regard is perfectly clear. Still more important is the substitution of the terse phrase 'due process of law', as used in the statute of 28 Edward III (1363), chapter 18, for the older, more ambiguous, and rather cumbersome wording of *Magna Carta*. This alteration was an innovation in America, for all the former Declarations of Rights of the revolutionary or colonial period had used the time honoured phrase 'law of the land' from *Magna Carta*. The innovation was, however, destined to prevail, as since that time the general tendency of American constitutional draftsmen has been, to follow the wording of the 5th Amendment. This portion of the 5th Amendment may thus be regarded as containing phraseology of the purest gold mined under the stress of heated constitutional crises, refined by the fire of violent revolutions, proved by the acid test of centuries of struggle, and moulded by the hand of one of America's greatest constitutional draftsmen.[10]

The 5th Amendment, however, did not apply to state action but was solely limited to the federal government. It was probably this fact, together with a desire to protect the loyal citizens in the southern states who were freed, the Congress proposed that 14th Amendment to the Constitution; its Section 1 reads as under:

> All persons born or naturalized in the United States, and subject to the jurisdiction thereof, are citizens of the United States and of the State wherein they reside. No state shall make or enforce any law which shall abridge the privileges or immunities of citizens of the United States; nor shall any State deprive any person of life, liberty, or property, without due process of law; nor deny to any person within its jurisdiction the equal protection of the laws.

Three-fourths of the states had ratified this amendment by July 1868. The wording of the due process portion of this article is practically identical with the phrases used in the 5th Amendment, the single exception being that the later article expressly applies only to the States. The context, in which the phrase appears, however, is totally different. In the 5th Amendment it follows immediately after a provision protecting persons accused of crime from arbitrary punishment and precedes the limitation on the use of the power of eminent domain.

In the 14th Amendment neither of these restrictions appears. The amendment opens by defining citizenship in the US, and the second sentence prohibits the abridgment of the privileges of that citizenship by the States. Then, as if to define the greatest of the privileges of citizenship, or at least the one uppermost in the minds of the framers of the section, follows the due process phrase. Furthermore, the phrase is followed by the additional limitation that no one is to be denied the equal protection of the law evidencing the fact that it was this specific protection of due process that congress had most in mind when the article was framed. The language used, however, is so general that its scope has become very wide and protects not only the Negro race but also all citizens of the country.[11] The US Supreme Court has held that a mob or media trial is denial of due process of law, for here the trial is not by the court, but in actuality, by the mob, or as the case may be, by media.[12]

The Distinction Between Procedural and Substantive Due Process

Definitions

The 5th and 14th Amendments, respectively, provide that neither the United States nor the state governments shall deprive any person 'of life, liberty, or property without due process of law'. This clause has been interpreted as imposing two separate limits on government, usually called 'procedural due process' and 'substantive due process'.

Procedural due process, as the phrase implies, refers to the procedures that the government must follow before it deprives a person of life, liberty, or property. Classic procedural due process issues concern what kind of notice and what form of hearing the government must provide when it takes a particular action.

Substantive due process, as that phrase implies, asks whether the government has an adequate reason for taking away a person's life, liberty, or property. In other words, substantive due process requires as to whether there is a sufficient justification for the government's action. Whether there is such a justification depends very much on the level of scrutiny used. For example, if a law is in an area where only rational basis review is applied, substantive due process is met so long as the law is rationally related to a legitimate government purpose. However, if it is in an area where strict scrutiny is used, such as for protecting fundamental rights, then the government will meet substantive due process only if it can prove that the law is necessary to achieve a compelling government purpose.[13]

An example can be found in the constitutional right of parents to custody of their children. The US Supreme Court has held that parents have a liberal interest in the custody of their children. Therefore, procedural due process requires that the government provide notice and a hearing, and that there be clear and convincing evidence of a need to terminate custody, before parental rights are permanently ended. Because the right to custody is deemed a fundamental right, substantive due process requires that the government prove that terminating custody is necessary to achieve a compelling purpose, such as the need to prevent abuse or neglect of the child.

Another example of the distinction between procedural and substantive due process can be found in challenges to large punitive damages awards. Procedural due process requires that there be safeguards such as instructions to the jury to guide their discretion, and judicial review to ensure the reasonableness of the awards. Substantive due process prevents excessive punitive damages awards, regardless of the procedures followed.

Thus, it is possible to distinguish procedural and substantive due process based on the remedy sought. If the plaintiff is seeking to have a government action declared unconstitutional as violating a constitutional right, substantive due process is involved. But when a person or a group is seeking to have a government action declared unconstitutional because of the lack of adequate safeguards, such as notice and a hearing, procedural due process is the issue.

Procedural and substantive due process can involve some of the same questions. For example, for both, it often is necessary to define what is 'liberty' or 'property'. If there is not a denial of life, liberty, or property, then the government does not have to provide procedural or substantive due process.[14]

In *US v. Salerno*, the contention was that the enactment in question –

> 'violates substantive Due Process because the pre-trial detention (of a person accused of a criminal offence) authorizes constitutes impermissible punishment before trial.'

The contention was repelled because pre-trial detention was not punishment. For that purpose Chief Justice William Rehnquist (1924–2005)[15] pointed out the distinction between procedural and substantive 'due process', observing that 'Due Process clause' under the 5th Amendment –

> 'protects individuals against two types of government action. So-called 'substantive Due Process' prevents the government from engaging in conduct that 'shocks the conscience' or interferes with rights 'implicit in the concept of ordered liberty'. When government action depriving a person of life, liberty or property survives substantive Due Process scrutiny, it must still be implemented in a fair manner. This requirement has traditionally been referred to as Procedural Due Process.'[16]

So, 'substantive due process' means that an unreasonable law, even if properly passed and properly applied would be unconstitutional.

Substantive Due Process

Substantive due process refers to the interpretation of the due process clauses of the 14th and 5th Amendments to include protections of property and individual rights that are not explicitly part of the constitution. The courts apply value judgments to constitutional interpretation in defining substantive due process. Under the substantive due process, doctrine courts examine the actual content of laws instead of the procedures by which they are adopted and carried out. When substantive due process is applied, the fairness of the law is judged much as it would be by a legislature.

In defining the due process clauses subjectively, for example to include economic rights nowhere mentioned in the constitution, the courts were not adopting a new method of constitutional interpretation. Judges had always more or less injected their values into their decisions. Moreover, the additions to the constitution that resulted from substantive due process interpretations were no more extreme than had occurred on numerous occasions through judicial interpretations of other parts of the constitution. Certainly the opinion in the *Dred Scott* case,[17] which held that Congress could not 'infringe upon local rights of person or rights of property' by prohibiting slavery in the territories, was an example of the court injecting its own values into its decision, for the first time declaring a congressional act both unconstitutional and essentially unfair. Although, the court did not explicitly apply a 'substantive due process' doctrine in *Dred Scott*, its method was much the same, involving the substitution of judicial for legislative values. In the economic sphere, the court during the New Deal supplanted legislative values with its own concerning the constitutionality of a large part of the economic program of President Franklin D. Roosevelt. The New Deal legislation was rejected by the court not on the basis of 'due process' violations but as transgressions of the commerce clause and the delegation of powers doctrine.[18]

Substantive Due Process of the 14th Amendment: Judicial Definition of the Boundaries of State Authority to Regulate Economic Activity

Substantive due process was primarily developed and applied by the courts under the 14th Amendment to invalidate state economic regulation. Although the Court rejected a 'substantive due process' challenge to a Louisiana law in the *Slaughterhouse Cases*,[19] Justice Samuel Freeman Miller's (1816–90)[20] majority opinion implied that there were constitutional limits to State economic regulation derived from natural and common law standards. Miller's opinion, which rejected any explicit constitutional limitations upon the States under the 14th Amendment, left the way clear for the Court to impose boundaries upon State action on the basis of a subjective interpretation of natural and common law criteria. Thus at the same time that he was seeking to limit the application of the 14th Amendment to the States, Miller in fact was paving the way for the imposition of even greater constraints upon state action than were stated in the US Constitution.

Judicial interpretation, wrote Justice Miller, defines the 'due process' clause. Although he found that past judicial interpretation of the 'due process' clause of the 14th Amendment did not support invalidating the Louisiana law, his method placed no obstacle in the path of judicial interpretation restraining state action. Miller quoted with approval the opinion of Justice Bushrod Washington (1762–1829)[21] in *Corfield v. Coryell*,[22] that the privileges and immunities clause of Article 4 protects against State action such fundamental privileges and immunities as,

> 'the right to acquire and possess property of every kind, and to pursue and obtain happiness and safety, subject, nevertheless, to such restraints as the government may prescribe for the general good of the whole.'

Ironically, at the same time Miller was rendering the privileges and immunities clause impotent, he implied that circumstances might make it necessary for the court to determine what privileges and immunities were 'fundamental' and balance these against the 'general good of the whole'.

The substantive limits on state action implied in the *Slaughterhouse* opinion were defined by Miller himself a year later in *Loan Association v. City of Topeka*.[23] He wrote the opinion of the court invalidating a city ordinance that authorized the issuance of municipal bonds to raise money to support private industry, stating,

> 'There are rights in every free government beyond the control of the state.... There are limitations on such power which grow out of the essential nature of all free governments.'

The states are limited in the exercise of their power to the promotion of the general public welfare. The ordinance under review violated this limit and was therefore void.

In *Davidson v. New Orleans*,[24] Justice Miller warned against judicial acquiescence to the onslaught of demands that the due process clause be interpreted to include broad protections against the state invasion of private property rights. At the same time, he recognized that judicial inclusion and exclusion could give meaning to the due process clause. In the same year, the court squarely faced the issue of the limits upon State economic regulation imposed by the due process clause in *Munn v. Illinois*,[25] in which a state statute regulating the rates of grain elevators was challenged in part on the grounds that it violated the due process clause of the 14th Amendment. The regulation was upheld by the Supreme Court being not repugnant to the US Constitution.

The Development of Substantive Due Process

While the opinion in the *Munn* case upheld the State statute as a legitimate regulation in the public interest, it recognized that the 14th Amendment due process clause 'prevents the states from doing that which will operate as...a deprivation [of private property].' While giving deference to State legislative judgment in the determination of what concerned the public interest and was a reasonable regulation thereof, the court was careful to point out that 'in mere private contracts, relating to matters in which the public has no interest, what is reasonable must be ascertained judicially.'

Chief Justice Morrison Waite (1816–88)[26] warned against in *The Railroad Commission Cases*[27] that State legislative judgments concerning economic regulation might be subject to judicial control. Waite wrote for the Court,

> This power to regulate is not a power to destroy, and limitation is not the equivalent of confiscation. Under pretense of regulating fares and freights, the state cannot require a railroad corporation to carry persons or property without reward; neither can it do that which in law amounts to a taking of private property for public use without just compensation, or without due process of law.

The importance the court attached to judicial rather than legislative or administrative determination of the reasonableness of government regulation affecting property interests was illustrated in *Chicago, Milwaukee, and St. Paul R. Co. v. Minnesota*.[28] The decision overturned a State law that authorized administrative ratemaking without judicial review, because it violated both procedural and substantive due process. The law was deficient in its failure to provide adequate procedural protection for the railroads which could only be achieved through judicial review. The court concluded that judicial review was necessary to determine the reasonableness of rates, which is 'eminently a question for judicial investigation.' Administrative regulation of the reasonableness of rates is 'in substance and effect' a deprivation of property without due process of law. In a dissenting opinion, Justice Joseph P. Bradley (1813–92)[29] declared that the court had overruled the *Munn v. Illinois* decision.

The *Chicago, Milwaukee and St. Paul* case placed the courts squarely in the centre of the rate-making process. Neither administrative agencies nor legislatures could set rates without judicial scrutiny which did not conform to judicial views of fairness. Substantive due process review of rates became complete in *Smyth v. Ames*,[30] which voided a Nebraska statute setting intrastate freight rates. The court investigated in detail the earning power of the railroads and concluded that the rates were unreasonable and therefore a deprivation of property without due process of law.[31]

In *Washington v. Glucksberg* case, a State law made promoting a suicide attempt a felony and made a person who knowingly caused or aided another person to attempt suicide guilty of that crime. The respondents, who were physicians who treated terminally ill, brought a suit seeking a declaration that the ban was, on its face, unconstitutional because it placed an undue burden on the exercise of the constitutionally protected liberty interest—liberty to die—protected by the 14th Amendment Due Process clause of a mentally competent, terminally ill adult. The Supreme Court held that the ban did not violated the Due Process clause; in so holding, Chief Justice William Rehnquist, speaking for the court, observed that due process guarantees more than fair procedure, and the liberty it protects includes more than the absence of physical restraint. It protects individual liberty against certain government actions regardless of the fairness of the procedures used to implement them.[32]

Substantive Due Process and Freedom to Contract

The line of cases from *Munn* in 1877 *to Smyth v. Ames* in 1898 applied substantive due process review based upon property rights and held unreasonable deprivations of private property to be violations of the due process clause of the 14th Amendment. The court extended the substantive due process doctrine beyond the standard of deprivation of property to deprivation of liberty into which it incorporated the freedom to contract. *Barbier v. Connolly*,[33] while upholding a San Francisco ordinance prohibiting laundries to operate at night, put the States on notice that the due process clause protected common law liberties and the freedom to contract.

The Supreme Court finally overturned a state law as a violation of the substantive right of freedom to contract under the due process clause of the 14th Amendment in *Allgeyer v. Louisiana*.[34] The Louisiana statute prohibited non-licensed companies from selling marine insurance contracts within the State. The court broadly defined liberty to include,

> 'not only the right of the citizen to be free from the mere physical restraint of his person, as by incarceration, but the term is deemed to embrace the right of the citizen to be free in the enjoyment of all of his faculties; to be free to use them in all lawful ways; to live and work where he will; to earn his livelihood by any lawful calling; to pursue any livelihood or avocation, and for that purpose to enter into all contracts which may be proper, necessary, and essential to his carrying out to a successful conclusion the purposes above mentioned.'

By substituting its judgment for that of State legislatures in determining the fairness of regulations of property and liberty under the due process clause of the 14th Amendment, the court was acting contrary to the public opinion that had spurred State regulation. Political pressures upon State legislatures throughout the country had resulted in laws regulating business which the courts were unwilling to sustain.[35]

The Controversy over Substantive Due Process

The concept of procedural due process has never been controversial, although, there certainly have been major disputes over what constitutes liberty and property interests and what procedures should be required.[36] However, at times, the very idea of substantive due process has been contested. The argument has been that due process actually denotes procedures and that it is incorrect to use the due process clause as the concept meant for protecting substantive rights. This argument, as has been discussed above, has been repelled by the Supreme Court in a number of cases.

The criticism of substantive due process has many facets. In part, critics argue that due process is the wrong provision to use to protect substantive rights. The arguments is that within the 14th Amendment, the privileges or immunities clause—the provision that states that no state 'shall abridge the privileges or immunities of citizens of the United States'—is the appropriate phrase for safeguarding substantive rights.

However, as in the *Slaughterhouse Cases*, in 1872, the court gave the clause an extremely narrow interpretation that has prevented it from being used to safeguard individual liberties.[37] As a result, the court turned to the due process clause to protect substantive rights. Critics argue that this is inappropriate. Also, the objections to substantive due process inevitably are combined with arguments against the Supreme Court protecting rights that are not expressly enumerated in the constitution. In other words, the objections generally are not only to the place in the constitution where the rights are found, but also to the court's finding and protecting the rights at all. Critics argue that the court acts illegitimately when it protects rights that are not explicitly stated in the constitution or intended by its framers.

Finally, the criticism of substantive due process cannot be separated from attacks on how the Supreme Court has used the doctrine over the course of American history. There have been two major uses of substantive due process. Early in the 20th century, before 1937, the court used it to safeguard economic liberties and to protect freedom of contract as a fundamental right. The paradigm case of this era was *Lochner v. New York*,[38] where the court declared unconstitutional a law that imposed a limit on the number of hour's bakers could work.

In the more contemporary era, substantive due process has been used to protect rights of privacy and personal autonomy. *Roe v. Wade*,[39] which legalized abortion, is the most famous example of this modern substantive due process. Both sets of cases are controversial, and often the criticisms are presented as attacks on the idea of substantive due process.

In response to these criticisms, defenders argue that 'due process' does denote substantive limits on government. Over a century ago, the Supreme Court declared that due process

> 'is a restraint on the legislative as well as on the executive and judicial powers of the government, and cannot be so construed as to leave congress free to make any "due process of law" by its mere will.'[40]

The clause does not speak solely of due process but, rather, of 'due process of law', and it is argued that an action is not in accord with the law of the land if it violates the substantive guarantees of the US Constitution.

Thus, the due process clause has been found to incorporate provisions of the Bill of Rights that are deemed fundamental and to protect these rights from State and local interference. This is substantive due process in that it uses the due process clause to protect rights and only allows interference if there is a sufficient justification.

Supporters of substantive due process also defend the legitimacy of the court protecting rights that are not expressly stated or implied in the constitution. This approach to 'judicial review', often called 'non originalism', points that it is desirable for the Supreme Court to identify and safeguard unenumerated rights. Of course, *Roe v. Wade* has its defenders, as well as its critics, and this is a part of the debate over substantive due process.[41]

The dilemma about substantive due process has been explained by Justice Lewis F. Powell Jr (1907–98)[42] in *Moose v. City of East Cleveland* in the following words:

> Substantive due Process has at times been a treacherous field for this Court. There are risks when the judicial branch gives enhanced protection to certain substantive liberties without the guidance of the more specific provisions of the Bill of Rights.... There is reason for concern lest the only limits to such judicial intervention become the predilections of those who happen at the time to be members of this Court.... That history counsels caution and restraint. But it does not counsel abandonment of substantive Due Process.[43]

Procedural Due Process

On a national level, the standards of procedural due process were explicitly stated in the Bill of Rights. However, after the adoption of the 14th Amendment, the court decided not to incorporate the Bill of Rights under the due process clause, but to determine on a selective and case-by-case basis what standards of due process it would apply. In effect, by selectively determining what procedural rights were to be guaranteed by the due process clause of the 14th Amendment, the court was subjectively defining non-economic substantive due process. It was giving procedural content or substance to the due process clause that was based on its own view of the government's fairness.

While the Bill of Rights is used as the primary source to determine standards of procedural due process at the national level, the fact that there is a separate due process clause of the 5th Amendment suggests that the framers did not confine 'due process' to the express provisions of the Bill of Rights. Due process had a meaning separate from the Bill of Rights. In *Murray's Lessee v. Hoboken Land and Improvement Company*[44] Justice Benjamin R. Curtis (1809–74)[45] defined the meaning of the due process clause of the 5th Amendment.

> The words 'due process of law', were undoubtedly intended to convey the same meaning as the words, 'by the law of the land', in Magna Carta....The Constitution contains no description of those processes which it was intended to allow or forbid. It does not even declare what principles are to be applied to ascertain whether it be due process. It is manifest that it was not left to the legislative power to enact any process which might be devised. The article is a restraint on the legislative as well as on the executive and judicial powers of government, and cannot be so construed as to leave Congress free to make any process 'due process of law' by its mere will. To what principles then, are we to resort to ascertain whether this process, enacted by Congress, is due process? To this the answer must be twofold. We must examine the Constitution itself, to see whether this process be in conflict with any of its provisions [such as the Bill of Rights]. If not found to be so, we must look to those settled usages and modes of proceeding existing in the common and statute law of England, before the emigration of our ancestors, and which are shown not to have been unsuited to their civil and political condition by having been acted on by them after the settlement of this country.... [T]hough 'due process of law' generally implies and includes regular allegations, opportunity to answer, and a trial according to some settled course of judicial proceedings, yet this is not universally true.

The due process standards laid down by Justice Curtis in *Murray's Lessee*, allow the court broad discretion in the development of the criteria of due process. In defining standards of procedural due process, the court at the national level had drawn upon the provisions of the Bill of Rights and had not expanded procedural protections beyond those that were enumerated in the first eight amendments.

The court applied its own values in interpreting the extent to which the rights under the Bill of Rights would be incorporated under the due process clause of the 14th Amendment. When the court first confronted challenges to state action for being in violation of due process under the 14th Amendment, it limited the due process clause to 'those settled usages and modes of proceeding existing in the common law and statute law of England' that were brought to America by the settlers and that were adopted by colonial governments.

The threshold decision of the court to define procedural due process under the 14th Amendment separately from the Bill of Rights introduced an element of subjectivity that produced 100 years of debate over what procedural rights should be included under due process—an issue that is still not finally settled. The Bill of Rights was used as a reference point only insofar as it explicated what the court considered historical and fundamental rights in English and Colonial history. How judges defined due process depended upon their views of what constituted fundamental and historical rights. Differing views of history led to contrasting interpretations of the due process clause. Other reflections as well entered into a judge's determination of procedural due process, particularly considerations of federalism. Judges favouring judicial self-restraint on the basis of considerations of 'federalism' and allowed the States more leeway to adopt procedures under their laws than judges who favoured an active role for the Supreme Court in establishing national standards of procedural due process.

A contrasting view of the reach of the due process clause of the 14th Amendment surfaced in *Hurtado v. California*.[46] Joseph Hurtado was convicted of murder in California and sentenced to be hanged. California law provided for indictment by 'information' prepared by the prosecuting attorney, rather than by a grand jury. Joseph Hurtado claimed that due process included the right to grand jury indictment to which he would be entitled under common law and under the Bill of Rights.

Justice Thomas Stanley Matthews' (1824–89)[47] majority opinion facilely disposed of this argument by holding that the due process clause of the 14th Amendment did not exclusively require grand jury indictment. Matthews reasoned that:

> 'Any legal proceeding enforced by public authority, whether sanctioned by age and custom, or newly devised in the discretion of the legislative power, in furtherance of the general public good, which regards and preserves... principles of liberty and justice, must be held to be due process of law....'

The Court concluded:

> Tried by these principles [of liberty and justice], we are unable to say that the substitution for a presentment or indictment by a grand jury of the proceeding by information, after examination and commitment by a magistrate, certifying to the probable guilt of the defendant, with the right on his part to the aid of counsel, and to the cross examination of the witnesses produced for the prosecution, is not due process of law. It is, as we have seen, an ancient proceeding at common law, which might include every case of an offense of less grade than a felony, except misprision or treason; and in every circumstance of its administration, as authorized by the statute of California, it carefully considers and guards the substantial interest of the prisoner. It is merely a preliminary proceeding, and can result in no final judgment, except as the consequence of a regular judicial trial, conducted precisely as in cases of indictments.[48]

Even though the common law required indictment by a grand jury in felony cases, the court in its *Hurtado* opinion held that the less stringent procedure of indictment by information conformed to due process.

Justice John M. Harlan (1833–1911)[49] dissented in *Hurtado*, stating that:

> 'I cannot agree that the state may, consistently with due process of law, require a person to answer for a capital offense, except upon the presentment of indictment of a grand jury.'

Justice Harlan concluded that the settled usages and modes of proceeding of the common law precluded the use of indictment by information in capital cases.

The scope of the due process clause of the 14th Amendment was again raised in *Twining v. New Jersey*.[50] The defendants argued that their criminal conviction by New Jersey Court was unlawful because the trial procedure did not conform to the 5th Amendment requirement that:

> 'No person…shall be compelled in any criminal case to be a witness against himself…'.

While the New Jersey Constitution included protection against compulsory self-incrimination in its own Bill of Rights, the state permitted an inference of guilt to be drawn from the failure of a defendant to testify in his own behalf.

In the *Twining case*, the judge had charged the jury that:

> 'because a man does not go upon the stand you are not necessarily justified in drawing an inference of guilt. But you have a right to consider the fact that he does not go upon the stand where a direct accusation is made against him.'

Undeterred by Justice Samuel F. Miller's (1816–90) majority opinion in the *Slaughterhouse Cases*, and encouraged by the dissenting views in that case, the defendants argued that the New Jersey procedure violated their fundamental rights guaranteed under the privileges and immunities and due process clauses of the 14th Amendment. The brief for the defendants stated that it was still open to question

> '[whether or not the 14th Amendment has extended the application of [the protection against self-incrimination embodied in the 5th Amendment] to the several states….'

Where such fundamental rights as the protection against self-incrimination are violated, the brief argued, the court should intervene to protect the individual.

In its defence, New Jersey pointed out that its constitution contained the right against compulsory self-incrimination but that:

> 'it has never been considered that this right was abridged or infringed by the submission to a trial jury the right to draw an inference, if they saw fit to do so, from the fact of the silence of an accused person in the face of a direct criminal accusation.'

The State courts declared that under the doctrine of the *Slaughterhouse Cases* establishing dual citizenship, the procedures followed by the state disclosed:

> 'no fundamental right or immunity guaranteed to the plaintiffs in error as citizens of the United States by the 14th Amendment of the Federal Constitution which has been abridged by the decision of the court of last resort of New Jersey' [which upheld the defendants' conviction].

The US Supreme Court upheld the conviction of the defendants on the rationale that this privilege of self-incrimination was not immutable principle of justice. It was not an inalienable right of every citizen and did not rank equal with the rights like hearing before condemnation, the immunity from arbitrary power not acting by general laws or the inviolability of private property.[51]

In *Powell v. Alabama*, US Supreme Court held that notice and hearing are preliminary steps essential to the passing of an enforceable judgment and they, together with a legally competent tribunal having jurisdiction of the case, constitute basic elements of the constitutional requirement of due process of law.[52] In this case, it was held that right of hearing include right to the aid of counsel when desired and provided by the party asserting the right. The right to be heard would be of little avail if it did not comprehend the right to be heard by counsel.

Due Process in India

There is importation of the concept of due processes into Article 21 of the Indian Constitution, which has not even the word 'reasonable' in its text. On the other hand, in relation to this provision, the makers of Indian Constitution expressly sought to exclude due processes.[53] It is on this basis that the majority of the Supreme Court, in its earliest pronouncement in *Gopalan*'s case,[54] simply denied the possibility of admitting into Article 21, any ingredient of American 'due process', or even of the 'reasonableness' concept from Article 19 of the constitution itself,—to arrive at the proposition that whatever was laid down by the Legislature in a penal law would satisfy Article 21; and that the court could not intervene even where the procedure laid down was arbitrary or 'harsh, unreasonable, archaic or odious.'[55]

But the fundamental point of the thesis that the very word 'procedure' in Article 21 means a procedure which is not arbitrary but gives to the person condemned 'the right to be heard before he is condemned'—which as Justice Sir Saiyid Fazal Ali (1886–1959)[56], demonstrated, was an ingredient of 'due process',[57] is to be found in the judgments of some of the judges in *Gopalan*'s case. Most illuminating were the words of Justice Mehr Chand Mahajan (1889–1967)[58] who otherwise sided with the majority conclusions:[59]

> Article 21...gives also a further guarantee that in its true concept there should be some form of proceeding before a person can be condemned.... It negatives the idea of fantastic, arbitrary and oppressive forms of proceedings.

In subsequent decisions, this view has prevailed, highlighting the concept of 'fairness' being inherent in Article 21. It may be pointed out that

(a) absence of arbitrariness and
(b) fairness are both essentials of the concept of 'due process';

as explained in leading American decisions.

In the *Bank Nationalization Case*,[60] the majority of an eleven judges Bench overruled the *Gopalan* thesis that Articles 19 and 21 constituted watertight compartments so that nothing in Article 19 could be imported to test the validity of a penal law to which Article 21 was attracted. Nevertheless, the condition of 'reasonableness' in Article 19(1)(d) could be imported into Article 21 only if the other part of the majority decision in *Gopalan* was demolished, namely, that the scope of the freedom of movement in Article 19(1)(d) was limited by the territorial import conveyed by the words 'throughout the territory of India'.

The *Bank Nationalization* decision did not go so far; and that this narrow interpretation of Article 19(1)(d) has not been authority[61] is evidenced by the clear statements made in the later Constitution Bench judgment in *Bachan Singh's* case.[62] Later on, in *Bachan Singh*'s case the majority relied upon the doctrine of 'direct and inevitable effect' to exclude the applicability of Article 19(1) to the interpretation of Article 21.

However, even if in any particular case, there was a direct impact of a penal law on any of the fundamental rights enumerated in Article 19(1), Sub-clause (d) of that provision could never possibly be invoked so long as the right to 'move freely' were not extracted from the succeeding words 'throughout the territory of India' and construed to mean 'personal liberty' in the widest sense, lifted from its territorial constraint, in which case the sweep of Article 19(1)(d) would have been co-extensive with Article 21, dealing with deprivation of 'personal liberty'.

So, some other device had to be invented if the 'due process' concept was to be admitted into the 'prohibited area' of Article 21. This the Supreme Court has done in a number of decisions[63] following the observation in *Maneka's case* that the very words 'procedure' and 'established' in Article 21 indicated that the procedure should be 'fair, just and reasonable' and not arbitrary or whimsical. In short, 'the component of fairness' is implicit in Article 21. If this broad proposition is acknowledged, there is no need to appeal to Article 19(1)(d) at all, to strike down a law of criminal procedure which the court thinks as unfair.

This line of reasoning, to appeal to 'fairness', even where no principle of natural justice was violated, has been followed in numerous decisions later on. The most prominent amongst these cases is the Reference on the Special Courts Bill[64] where the court castigated some provisions of the Special Courts Bill, as originally drafted, on the ground that they were lacking in fairness, because—

a) there was no provision for transfer of any case from the Special Court, on any ground,
b) the Special Court was to be presided over by a retired High Court Judge whose appointment could be terminated at the will of the government, and
c) in the selection of such judge, the concurrence of the Chief Justice of India was not required, so that the accused was to be tried by a judge whose tenure depended upon the pleasure of the government and would therefore be lacking in independence.

Before parting with this aspect of the concept of 'due process' it is noticeable that in *Bachan Singh*'s case, the Constitution Bench did not question the implication of 'fairness and reasonableness' in Article 21 (as had been launched by *Maneka*'s case), but came to hold that there was nothing unfair in hanging a man for a heinous offence like murder, and that, accordingly, Section 302, Indian Penal Code, did not violate the 'unfairness' concept which is implicit in Article 21.

The 'unfairness' implication of Article 21 has thus come to stay.[65] Is it not going to the opposite pole from *Gopalan*, and would a legal analyst be wrong to say that this somersault has been possible only because the concept of 'due process' had been working in the minds of new judges of the Supreme Court who bear indelible impress of the American influence not only in ideas but even in language and diction.[66]

The most outspoken confession regarding the importation of the concept of 'due process', without directly overruling *Gopalan*, is to be found in the following words of Justice V.R. Krishna Iyer (1915–2014)[67]

> True, our Constitution has no 'due process' clause or the VIth Amendment; but, in this branch of law, after *Cooper* [AIR 1970 S.C. 1318] and *Maneka Gandhi* [AIR 1978 S.C. 597] the consequence is the same. For what is punitively outrageous, scandalizingly unusual or cruel and rehabilitatingly counterproductive, is unarguably unreasonable and arbitrary and is shot down by Art. 14 and 19 and if inflicted with procedural unfairness, falls foul of Art. 21.[68]

Due Process in Pakistan

Article 4 of the Constitution of 1973 is *para materia* with Article 2 of the Constitution of 1962. These two articles provide *inter alia* that no person shall be deprived of his life, liberty and property except in accordance with law.

These articles are not part of the chapter containing fundamental rights. But, these articles contain enough content and had the judiciary in Pakistan truly interpreted and enforced these Articles, they would have proved loftier than the whole *Magna Carta* and more comprehensive than many bills of rights. It never happened.

Chief Justice Hamoodur Rahman (1910–81)[69] speaking for the Court in *Begum Shorish Kashmiri*'s case[70] stated:

> The words 'in unlawful manner' in Sub-clause (b) of Article 98(2) have been used deliberately to give meaning and content to the solemn declaration under Article 2 of the Constitution itself that it is the inalienable

> right of every citizen to be treated in accordance with law and only in accordance with law. Therefore, in determining as to how and in what circumstances a detention would be detention in unlawful manner one would inevitably have first to see whether the action is in accordance with law, and if not, then it is an action in unlawful manner. Law is here not confined to statute law but is used in its generic sense as connoting all that is treated as law in this country including even the judicial principles laid down from time to time by the Superior Courts. It means according to the accepted norms of the legal process and postulates as strict performance of all the functions and duties laid down by law. It may well be, as has been suggested in some quarters that in this sense it is as comprehensive as the American 'due process' clause in a new garb.[71]

Almost 14 years later, the Supreme Court while again discussing the concept of the 'due process' in *Fauji Foundation*'s case[72] came to somewhat unusual conclusion and refused to accept the applicability of this doctrine in Pakistan. Justice Muhammad Haleem (1925–2006)[73] speaking for the court observed:

> Now coming to the crucial observations of Hamoodur Rahman, C.J., as reproduced earlier, what he meant to emphasize was the scope of expression 'in accordance with law' in Article 2 as to be comparable to the American 'due process' clause, which embraced within its concept, like in English common Law, the principles of natural justice and so also what S.A. Rehman, J. had emphatically stated in *Fardison*'s case, namely, a duty to act judicially which Hamoodur Rahman, C.J., put it in *Begum Shorish Kashmiri*'s case, as 'according to the accepted norms of legal process and strict performance of all the functions and duties laid down by law'. Hamoodur Rahman C.J. did not affirmatively hold by using the word 'comprehensive' to mean that the word 'Law' in Article 2 has the same substantive connotation as the 'due process' clause in the American Constitution, but he only meant to emphasize the principles of natural justice as obtaining in the judicial procedures of the 'due process' clause for judging actions against persons in regard to their life, liberty or property. From a review of the judgments, this is the only conclusion I can draw; and as the procedural aspect of 'due process' was to an assimilable as an element of natural justice, in Article 2 of the Constitution, it was, therefore, described as to have been enacted in a new garb, as no such provision existed in any earlier Constitution. The word comprehensive, in my view could not have meant the natural Law-cum-due process clause limitation power as is contended for that concept is not obtainable under our Constitutional system.

It would be seen that there was a fundamental difference in both the cases. In *Begum Shorish Kashmiri*'s case an executive action was challenged, while in *Fauji Foundation*'s case it was the legislative instrument that was sought to be challenged on the basis of 'due process' doctrine. It may therefore be stated that despite the fact that in the later case, the Supreme Court did not follow the due process doctrine, one could still argue on the basis of *Begum Kashmiri*'s case that an administrative action was unlawful.

The fact of the matter is that courts in Pakistan have not bothered to emancipate the people from the tyranny of the executive particularly the military dictators who under the garb of so-called legitimacy conferred on them by the courts have flouted civil liberties.

The Constitution (18th Amendment) Act 2010, added Article 10A to the Constitution which reads as:

> 'For the determination for his civil rights and obligations or in any criminal charge against him a person shall be entitled to a fair trial and due process.'

The expression 'due process' is yet to be judicially determined by the superior courts in Pakistan. This question is at present pending in a number of cases before the Supreme Court and the High Courts in Pakistan for authoritative adjudication.

It has been held that although from the very inception the concept of fair trial and due process has always been the golden principle of administration of justice, yet after inclusion of Article 10A in Pakistan's Constitution, it has been more important that due process should be adopted for conducting a fair trial and that order passed in violation of due process be considered to be void.[74] It has been noticed in another case that right to fair trial is now a constitutionally guaranteed fundamental right and has been raised to a higher pedestal, consequently a law or custom or usage having the force of law, which is inconsistent with the right to 'fair trial' would be void.[75] In *All Pakistan Newspapers Society v. Federation of Pakistan*,[76] it was held that:

> It is true that denial of right of appeal is violative of the due process of law in matters where judicial powers are being exercised by a functionary discharging judicial or quasi-judicial function, if the same are being

exercised by the executive or the administration.... And as per Injunctions of Islam, denial of right of appeal in adversarial proceedings, both civil and criminal, is considered against the due process of law and norms of justice, but in exercise of legislative powers or legislative activities, no right of appeal can be extended before the forums, higher in status, within the legislative body which had passed the order....

Old American Case

Munn v. Illinois 94 U.S. 113 (1876)
Mr Chief Justice Waite delivered the opinion of the Court:

The question to be determined in this case is whether the General Assembly of Illinois can, under the limitations upon the legislative power of the States imposed by the Constitution of the United States, fix by law the maximum of charges for the storage of grain in warehouses at Chicago and other places in the State....

It is claimed that such a law is repugnant...[t]o that part of Amendment XIV, which ordains that no state shall 'Deprive any person of life, liberty or property, without due process of law, nor deny to any person within its jurisdiction the equal protection of the laws...'

Every statute is presumed to be constitutional. The courts ought not to declare one to be unconstitutional, unless it is clearly so. If there is doubt, the expressed will of the legislature should be sustained. The constitution contains no definition of the word 'deprive', as used in the 14th Amendment. To determine its signification, therefore, it is necessary to ascertain the effect which usage given it, when employed in the same like connection....

....[I]t is apparent that, down to the time of the adoption of the 14th Amendment, it was not supposed that statutes regulating the use, or even the price of the use, of private property necessarily deprived an owner of his property without due process of law. Under some circumstances they may, but not under all. The Amendment does not change the law in this particular; it simply prevents the States from doing that which will operate as such a deprivation.

This brings us to ask, as to the principles upon which this power of regulation rests, in order that we may determine, what is within and what is without its operative effect. Looking, then, to the common law, from whence came the right which the constitution protects, we discover that when private property is 'affected with a public interest, it ceases to be *juris privati* only.' This was said by Lord Chief Justice Sir Matthew Hale (1609–76)[77] more than 200 years ago, in his treatise *De Portibus Maris*, ... and has been accepted without objection as an essential element in the law of property ever since. Property does become clothed with a public interest when used in a manner to make it of public consequence, and affect the community at large. When, therefore, one devotes his property to a use in which the public has an interest, he, in effect, grants to the public an interest in that use, and must submit to be controlled by the public for the common good, to the extent of the interest he has thus created. He may withdraw his grant by discontinuing the use; but, so long as he maintains the use, he must submit to the control....

....[W]hen private property is devoted to a public use; it is subject to public regulation. It remains only to ascertain whether the warehouses of these plaintiffs in error, and the business which is carried on there, come within the operation of this principle....

...[T]hese plaintiffs in error....stand....in the very 'gateway of commerce,' and take toll from all who pass. Their business most certainly 'tends to a common charge, and has become a thing of public interest and use.' ....Certainly, if any business can be clothed 'with a public interest, and cease to be *juris privati* only,' this has been. It may not be made so by the operation of the Constitution of Illinois or this statute, but it is by the facts.

We also are not permitted to overlook the fact that, for some reason, the people of Illinois, when they revised their Constitution in 1870, saw fit to make it the duty of the General Assembly to pass laws 'for the protection of producers, shippers and receivers of grain and produce,' Art. XIII., Sec. 7; and by Sec. 5 of the same article, to require all railroad companies receiving and transporting grain in bulk or otherwise to deliver the same at any elevator to which it might be consigned, that could be reached by any track that was or could be used by such company, and that all railroad companies should permit connections to be made with their tracks, so that any public warehouse, etc., might be reached by the cars on their railroads. This indicates very clearly that during the 20 years in which this peculiar business had been assuming its present 'immense proportions', something had occurred which led the whole body of the people to suppose that remedies such as are usually employed to prevent abuses by virtual monopolies might not be inappropriate here.

For our purposes we must assume that, if a state of facts could exist that would justify such legislation, it actually did exist when the statute now under consideration was passed. For us the question is one of power, not of expediency. If no state of circumstances could exist to justify such a statute, then we may declare this one void, because in excess of the legislative power of the state. But if it could, we must presume it did. Of the propriety of the legislative interference within the scope of the legislative power, the Legislature is the exclusive judge.

Neither is it a matter of any moment that no precedent can be found for a statute precisely like this. It is conceded that the business is one of recent origin, that its growth has been rapid, and that it is already of great importance. And it must also be conceded that it is a business in which the whole public has a direct and positive interest. It presents, therefore, a case for the application of a long known and well established principle in social science, and this statute simply extends the law so as to meet this new development of commercial progress. There is no attempt to compel these owners to grant the public an interest in their property, but to declare their obligations, if they use it in this particular manner.

It matters not in this case that these plaintiffs in error had built their warehouses and established their business before the regulations complained of were adopted. What they did was, from the beginning, subject to the power of the body politic to require them to conform to such regulations as might be established by the proper authorities for the common good. They entered upon their business and provided themselves with the means to carry it on subject to this condition. If they did not wish to submit themselves to such interference, they should not have clothed the public with an interest in their concerns....

It is insisted, however, that the owner of property is entitled to a reasonable compensation for its use, even though it be clothed with a public interest, and that what is reasonable is a judicial and not a legislative question.

As has already been shown, the practice has been otherwise. In countries where the Common Law prevails, it has been customary from time immemorial for the legislature to declare what shall be a reasonable compensation under such circumstances, or, perhaps more properly speaking, to fix a maximum beyond which any charge made would be unreasonable. Undoubtedly, in mere private contracts, relating to matters in which the public has no interest, what is reasonable must be ascertained judicially. But this is because the legislature has no control over such a contract. So, too, in matters which do affect the public interest, and as to which legislative control may be exercised, if there are no statutory regulations upon the subject, the courts must determine what is reasonable. The controlling fact is the power to regulate at all. If that exists, the right to establish the maximum of charge, as one of the means of regulation, is implied. In fact, the common law rule, which requires the charge to be reasonable, is itself a regulation as to price. Without it the owner could make his rates at will, and compel the public to yield to his terms, or forego the use.

But a mere common law regulation of trade or business may be changed by statute. A person has no property, no vested interest, in any rule of the common law. This is only one of the forms of municipal law, and is no more sacred than any other. Rights of property which have been created by the common law cannot be taken away without due process; but the law itself, as a rule of conduct, may be changed at the will, or even at the whim, of the Legislature, unless prevented by constitutional limitations. Indeed, the great office of statutes is to remedy defects in the common law as they are developed, and to adapt it to the changes of time and circumstances. To limit the rate of charge for services rendered in a public employment, or for the use of property in which the public has an interest, is only changing a regulation which existed before. It establishes no new principle in the law, but only gives a new effect to an old one.

We know that this is a power which may be abused; but that is no argument against its existence. For protection against abuses by Legislatures the people must resort to the polls, not to the courts....

We conclude, therefore, that the statute in question is not repugnant to the Constitution of the United States, and that there is no error in the judgment.

The judgment is affirmed.

Mr Justice Stephen Johnson Field (1816–99)[78], dissenting:

I am compelled to dissent from the decision of the Court in this case, and from the reasons upon which that decision is founded. The principle upon which the opinion of the majority proceeds is, in my judgment, subversive of the rights of private property, heretofore believed to be protected by constitutional guarantees against legislative interference, and is in conflict with the authorities cited in its support...

The declaration of the [Illinois] Constitution of 1870, that private buildings used for private purposes shall be deemed public institutions, does not make them so. The receipt and storage of grain in a building erected by private means for that purpose does not constitute the building a public warehouse. There is no magic in the language, though used by a constitutional convention, which can change a private business into a public one, or alter the character of the building in which the business is transacted....

...The doctrine declared is that property 'becomes clothed with a public interest when used in a manner to make it of public consequence, and affect the community at large' and from such clothing the right of the legislature is deducted to control the use of the property, and to determine the compensation which the owner may receive for it.

When Sir Matthew Hale, and the sages of the law in his day, spoke of property as affected by a public interest, and ceasing from that cause to be *juris private* solely, that is, ceasing to be held merely in private right, they referred to property dedicated by the owner to public uses, or to property the use of which was granted by the government, or in connection with which special privileges were conferred. Unless the property was thus dedicated, or some right bestowed by the government was held with the property, either by specific grant or by prescription of so long a time as to imply a grant originally, the property was not affected by any public interest so as to be taken out of the category of property held in private right.

But it isn't in any such sense that the terms 'clothing property with a public interest': are used in this case. From the nature of the business under consideration—the storage of grain—which, in any sense in which the words can be used, is a private business in which the public are interested only as they are interested in the storage of other products of the soil, or in articles of manufacture, it is clear that the court intended to declare that, whenever one devotes his property to a business which is useful to the public, 'affects the community at large', the legislature can regulate the compensation which the owner may receive for its use, and for his own services in connection with it....

If this be sound law, if there be no protection, either in the principles upon which our republican government is founded, or in the prohibitions of the constitution against such invasion of private rights, all property and all business in the State are held at the mercy of a majority of its legislature...

No State 'shall deprive any person of life, liberty or property without due process of law', says the 14th Amendment to the Constitution....

The term 'liberty', as used in the provision, something more is meant than mere freedom from physical restraint or the bounds of a prison. It means freedom to go where one may choose, and to act in such manner, not inconsistent with the equal rights of others, as his judgment may dictate for the promotion of his happiness; that is, to pursue such callings and avocations as may be most suitable to develop his capacities, and give to them their highest enjoyment.

The same liberal construction which is required for the protection of life and liberty, in all particulars in which life and liberty are of any value, should be applied to the protection of private property. If the Legislature of a State, under pretence of providing for the public good, or for any other reason, can determine against the consent of the owner, the uses to which private property shall be devoted, or the prices which the owner shall receive for its uses, it can deprive him of the property as completely as by a special Act for its confiscation or destruction.

If, for instance, the owner is prohibited from using his building for the purposes for which it was designed, it is of little consequence that he is permitted to retain the title and possession; or, if he is compelled to take as compensation for its use less than the expenses to which he is subjected by its ownership, he is, for all practical purposes, deprived of the property, as effectually as if the legislature had ordered his forcible dispossession. If it be admitted that the legislature has any control over the compensation, the extent of that compensation becomes a mere matter of legislative discretion....

There is nothing in the character of the business of the defendants as warehousemen which called for the interference complained of in this case. Their buildings are not nuisances; their occupation of receiving and storing grain infringes upon no rights of others, disturb no neighbourhood, infects not the air, and in no respect prevents others from using and enjoying their property as to them may seen best. The legislation in question is nothing less than a bold assertion of absolute power by the State to control, at its discretion, the property and business of the citizen, and fix the compensation he shall receive....

...I deny the power of any Legislature under our government to fix the price which one shall receive for his property of any kind. If the power can be exercised as to one article, it may as to all articles, and the prices of everything, from a calico gown to a city mansion, may be the subject of legislative direction...

I am of opinion that the judgment of the Supreme Court of Illinois should be reversed.

Mr Justice William Strong (1808–95)[79] concurred in this dissent.

English Cases on 'Due Process of Law'[80]

The Republic of Trinidad and Tobago had a 'Due Process' clause in its 1962 Constitution; and it has a 'Due Process' clause in its 1976 Constitution. It was under those constitutions that the Privy Council of England, as a Court of Appeal, had had occasion to consider and apply the 'Due Process of Law' concept in the following cases.

In *Maharaj v. AG of Trinidad and Tobago*,[81] a judge of the High Court of the Republic made an order committing the appellant, a barrister, to prison for seven days for contempt of court, on the ground that the appellant had said in the face of the judge that his conduct was unjudicial.

The appellant applied for a motion under Section 6 of the 1962 Constitution for redress for alleged contravention of his right under Section 1(a) of that Constitution, namely the right not to be deprived of liberty except by due process of law. The redress claimed was, *inter alia*, an order for immediate release from prison pending final determination of his motion and damages for wrongful detention and false imprisonment. When the matter reached the Privy Council, the contempt order was set aside on the ground that the judge who made the committal order had failed to specify sufficiently the nature of the contempt charged against the appellant before committing him to prison and consequently the committal order was invalid.

In the second case also titled *Maharaj v. AG of Trinidad and Tobago*,[82] the question was whether the failure to observe 'a fundamental rule of natural justice that a person accused of an offence should be told what he is said to have done plainly enough to give him an opportunity to put forward any explanation or excuse that he may wish to advance' amounted to deprivation of liberty, within the meaning of Section 1(a) of the Constitution, otherwise than by due process of law, for which the appellant was entitled to redress by way of monetary compensation under Section 6 of the Constitution. The answer was yes; the failure of the judge 'to inform the appellant of the specific nature of the contempt of court with which he was charged did contravene a constitutional right of the appellant in respect of which he was entitled to protection under Section 1(a)', that is, 'the right of the individual to life, liberty, security of the person and enjoyment of property, and the right not to be deprived thereof except by due process of law...'.

The facts in *Darrin Roger Thomas v. Cipriani Baptiste*,[83] were as follows: on 28 May 1999, the Government of Trinidad and Tobago ratified the American Convention on Human Rights, 1969. The Convention established two institutions, the Inter-American Commission on Human Rights (IAHCR) and its autonomous judicial organ the Inter-American Court of Human Rights, to which the Commission could refer disputes. By ratifying the Commission, the Government of Trinidad and Tobago, recognized the Commission's competence to entertain petitions from individuals complaining of violations of the Convention and to make reports and recommendations in respect thereof. It also recognized the compulsory jurisdiction of the Inter-American Court to give binding rulings on the interpretation and application of the Convention. Darrin Roger Thomas was arrested on 12 February 1993 on a murder charge. He remained in custody until trial. He was convicted and sentenced to death on 15 November 1995. His appeal was dismissed on 20 June 1997, and his application for leave to appeal was dismissed by the Privy Council on 11 March 1998. On 31 March 1998, that is after the publication of Instructions issued by the government relating to applications from persons under the sentence of death to the commission, Thomas lodged a petition to the commission, alleging violation of his human rights by the excessive delay in bringing him to trial etc. That petition was pending when a warrant was read for his execution.

One of the questions before the Privy Council was whether the execution of the death sentence pending Thomas's petition before the commission would violate his due process of law right. He sought a stay of execution until his petition before the commission was determined.

This primarily turned on the meaning of 'law' in the phrase 'due process of law', and it was on that meaning that there was a difference of opinion. The majority, speaking through Lord Peter Millett (1932)[84], was of the view that 'the due process clause must be...broadly interpreted' so that it is not 'a synonym for common law or statute. Rather it invokes the concept of rule of law itself and the universally accepted standards of justice....'. But, the minority, Lord Robert Goff (1923–2016)[85] and Lord John Hobhouse (1932–2004)[86], thought that as a Court of the Republic, 'it is the laws of the Republic alone which their Lordships are under a duty and at liberty to apply. It is upon these laws alone which the appellants are entitled to rely in support of their motions....' Due Process of law, in their view, was a synonym for the expression 'law of the land', and as the treaty was an unincorporated international treaty, a treaty which had not been adopted as law by the Republic, Darrin Roger Thomas was not entitled to invoke it. The minority, would thus have adopted the original meaning of the phrase, 'due process of law'.

One remarkable feature of both the majority and minority judgments, it may be noticed, is that both trace the history of the phrase back to *Magna Carta* to show its English origin, and, both call to their aid the meaning ascribed to the phrase in the United States of America.

Notes

1. The Magna Carta ('Great Charter') is a document guaranteeing English political liberties. It established for the first time the principle that everybody, including the king, was subject to the law. It was drafted at Runnymede, a meadow by the River Thames, and signed by King John (r. 1199–1216) on 15 June 1215, under pressure from his rebellious barons.
2. King John ruled England from 1199 to 1216. He is remembered for granting the Magna Carta in June 1215.
3. Sir Edward Coke was an English barrister, judge and politician and is considered to be the greatest jurist of the Elizabethan and Jacobean eras.
4. Statute of 28 Edward III, sometimes called 'the Statute of Westminster of the Liberties of London', Ch. iii, 1 *Statutes of the Realm*, p. 345.
5. Statute of 25 Edward III, Statutes 5, Ch. IV (1351), *Statutes of the Realm*, p. 321.
6. Rodney. L. Mott, *Due Process of Law: A Historical and Analytical Treatise of the Principles and Methods Followed by Courts in the Application of the Concept of the Law of the Land* (New York: Da Capo Press, 1973 [1926]), pp. 4–5.
7. *Darin Rogar Thomas v. Cipriani Baptiste*, (2000) 2 AC 1. The case is discussed in *Judicial Review of Public Action* by Justice Fazal Karim, Vol. 2, 2nd ed. (Karachi: Pakistan Law House, 2018), pp. 896–900.
8. George Mason was a delegate to the US Constitutional Convention in 1787, one of three delegates who refused to sign the Constitution.
9. Supra Note 6, pp. 14–6.
10. Ibid.
11. Ibid., pp. 16–9.
12. *Frank v. Mangum*, (1915) 237 U.S. 309.
13. Erwin Chemerinsky, *Constitutional Law: Principles and Policies*, 2nd ed. (New York: Aspen Law & Business, 2002), pp. 523–4.
14. Ibid., p. 524.
15. William Rehnquist was the 16th Chief Justice of the US Supreme Court from 1986 to 2005.
16. (1987) 481 US 739.
17. *Dred Scott v. Sanford*, 60 U.S. 393 (1857).
18. Peter Woll, *Constitutional Law: Cases and Comments* (Englewood Cliffs, NJ: Prentice-Hall, Inc., 1981), pp. 471–2.
19. 83 U.S. 36 (1873).
20. Samuel Freeman Miller was Associate Justice of the US Supreme Court from 1862–90.
21. Bushrod Washington was Associate Justice of the US Supreme Court from 1798–1829.
22. 6 Fed. Cas. 546 (C.C.Pa.1823).
23. 87 U.S. 655 (1874).
24. 96 U.S. 97 (1877).
25. 94 U.S. 113 (1876).
26. Morrison Waite was the 7th Chief Justice of the US Supreme Court from 1874 to 1888.
27. 116 U.S. 307 (1886).
28. 134 U.S. 418 (1890).
29. Joseph P. Bradley was Associate Justice of the US Supreme Court from 1870–92.
30. 169 U.S. 466 (1898).

31. *Smyth v. Ames* was overruled in *FPC v. Hope Natural Gas Company*, 320 U.S. 591 (1944).
32. (1997) 521 US 702.
33. 113 U.S. 27 (1885).
34. 165 U.S. 578 (1897).
35. Supra Note 18, pp. 485–6.
36. Chief Justice Rehnquist observed in *Washington v. Gluckburg* that in a long line of cases, apart from specific freedoms protected by the Bill of Rights (first nine Amendments to the US Constitution), the 'liberty' specifically protected by the 'due process clause' includes: (1) the right to marry – *Loving v. Virginia*, (1967) 388 US 1; (2) the right to have children – *Skinner v. Oklahoma*, (1942) 316 US 535; (3) the right to direct the education and upbringing of one's children – *Meyer v. Nebraska*, (1923) 262 US 390; *Pierce v. Society of Sisters*, (1925) 268 US 510; (4) the right to marital privacy – *Grisword v. Connecticut*, (1965) 381 US 479; (5) the right to use contraception – *Eisenstadt v. Baird*, (1972) 405 US 438; (6) the right to bodily integrity – *Rochin v. California*, (1952) 342 US 165; and (7) the right to abortion – *Planned Parenthood v. Casey*, (1992) 505 US 833.
37. In 1999, for the first time in American history, the Court used the privileges and immunities clause to invalidate a State law. *Saenz v. Roe*, 526 U.S. 489 (1999).
38. 198 U.S. 45 (1905).
39. 410 U.S. 113 (1973).
40. *Murray's Lessee v. Hoboken Land & Improvement Co.*, 59 U.S. 272 (1856).
41. Supra Note 13, pp. 525–6.
42. Lewis F. Powell Jr., was Associate Justice of the US Supreme Court from 1971–87.
43. (1977) 431 US 494.
44. 59 U.S. 272 (1856).
45. Benjamin R. Curtis was Associate Justice of the US Supreme Court from 1851–57.
46. 110 U.S. 516 (1884).
47. Thomas Stanley Matthews was Associate Justice of the US Supreme Court from 1881–89.
48. Supra Note 46., p. 538.
49. John M. Harlan was Associate Justice of the US Supreme Court from 1877–1911.
50. 211 U.S. 78 (1908).
51. 211 U.S. 78 (1908). The opinion of the court was written by Justice William Henry Moody.
52. (1932) 287 US 45.
53. Durga Das Basu, *Comparative Constitutional Law* (New Delhi: Prentice Hall, 1984), p. 19.
54. *Gopalan v. State of Madras*, AIR 1950 S.C. 27.
55. Cf. *Khare v. State of Delhi*, (1950) S.C.R. 519 (524); *Maneka v. Union of India*, AIR. 1978 S.C. 597.
56. Sir Saiyid Fazal Ali, OBE, served as Judge of the Supreme Court of India from 1950–51.
57. AIR 1950 S.C. 27.
58. Mehr Chand Mahajan was the 3rd Chief Justice of the Supreme Court of India.
59. Ibid., p. 230.
60. *Cooper V. Union of India*, AIR 1970 S.C. 564.
61. In *Maneka's case* [AIR 1978 S.C. 597], it was said: 'The decision in *Gopalan's* case gave rise to the theory that Arts. 19, 21 and 22...are exclusive-each article enacting a code relating to the protection of distinct rights, but this theory was overturned in *R.C. Cooper's* case'. It was nowhere stated that *Gopalan* had been overruled in toto had that been the position; nothing of *Gopalan* would have been left for *Bachan Singh* [AIR. 1980 S.C. 898] to fall back upon.
62. *Bachan Singh v. State of Punjab*, AIR 1980 S.C. 898.
63. *Hussainara v. Home Secy.*, AIR 1979 S.C. 1360; *Hoskot v. State of Maharashtra*, AIR 1978 S.C. 1548; *Sunil v. Delhi Admn.*, AIR 1978 S.C. 1675; *State of Maharashtra v. Champalal*, AIR 1981 S.C. 1675.
64. In re *Special courts Bill*, 1978, AIR 1979 S.C. 478.
65. Supra Note 53, pp. 21–2.
66. Ibid., p. 22. None of the decisions condemned unfairness in a criminal law upon an express reliance upon the concept of 'due process', but the same result has been achieved by either falling back upon Article 19 or reading Article 21 together with Article 19 [*Prem Chand v. Union of India* (1981) Cr. LJ 5; *Sunil v. Delhi Admn.*, AIR.1980 S.C. 1579; *Nand Lal v. State of Punjab*, AIR 1981 S.C. 2041]. This is a position which would never have been countenanced by the majority in *Gopalan*'s case, (1950) S.C.R. 88, who would exclude the application of Article 19 to a penal law as to which, according to them, Article 21 offered an exclusive code. The round-about-turn has been possible only because later Judges, some of whom had American legal education, have been inspired by the concept of 'due process' which, of course, they could not openly confess because of the deliberate exclusion of that expression from Article 21, by the makers of the Constitution [vide *Roy v. Union of India*, AIR 1982 S.C. 710].

67. V.R. Krishna Iyer was a Judge of Kerala High Court, and was appointed as Judge of the Supreme Court of India from 1973.
68. *Sunil v. Delhi Admn.* AIR 1978 S.C. 1675.
69. Justice Hamoodur Rahman was 7th Chief Justice of Pakistan from 1968 to 1975.
70. *Government of West Pakistan v. Begum Agha Abdul Karim Shorish Kashmiri* PLD 1969 SC 14.
71. Ibid., p. 31.
72. *Fauji Foundation v. Shamimur Rehman* PLD 1983 SC 457.
73. Justice Muhammad Haleem served as 10th Chief Justice of Pakistan from 1981 to 1989.
74. *Babar Hussain Shah v. Mujeeb Ahmad Khan*, 2012 SCMR 1235.
75. *Suo moto* Case No. 4 of 2010, PLD 2012 S.C. 553.
76. PLD 2012 S.C. 1.
77. Sir Matthew Hale was first Chief Baron of the Exchequer and then Chief Justice of the King's Bench.
78. Stephen Johnson Field was Associate Justice of the US Supreme Court from 1863–97, the second longest tenure of any justice.
79. Justice William Strong was a justice of the Supreme Court of Pennsylvania and was successfully appointed as an Associate Justice of the US Supreme Court.
80. These cases have been taken from the book by Justice Fazal Karim, Vol. 2, 2nd ed. (Karachi: Pakistan Law House, 2018), pp. 895–7.
81. (1977) 1 All ER 411.
82. (1978) 2 All ER 670.
83. (2000) 2 AC 1.
84. Lord Peter Millett is a non-permanent judge of the Hong Kong Court of Final Appeal and a former Lord of Appeal in Ordinary and barrister of the United Kingdom.
85. Lord Robert Goff was an English barrister and judge who served as Senior Lord of Appeal in Ordinary.
86. Lord John Hobhouse was a British judge and Law Lord.

6 Equality before Law and Equal Protection of Laws

The first expression 'equality before law', which is taken from English common law seems to have been borrowed from the Constitution of Eire and West Germany by Indian constitution-makers. It was first used by A.V. Dicey as one of three aspects of his doctrine of the rule of law which was long after the American Constitution and the 14th Amendment had been adopted. As propounded by Dicey, the theory of 'equality before law' means that no man is above the law, and that every man, whatever be his rank or position/condition, is subject to the ordinary law of the realm and amenable to the jurisdiction of the ordinary tribunals/courts. Explaining the concept of legal equality, as operating in England, Dicey said:

> 'With us every official, from the Prime Minister down to a constable or a collector of taxes, is under the same responsibility for every act done without any legal justification as any other citizen.'[1]

The second expression, 'equal protection of laws', which is rather a corollary of the first expression, and is based on the 14th Amendment to the American Constitution, directs that people are entitled to equal protection in the enjoyment of their rights and privileges without favouritism or discrimination. It has been said that 'equal protection of law' is a pledge of protection or guarantee of equal laws. The Supreme Court of India said in *Sri Srinivasa Theatre v. Govt. of Tamil Nadu*,[2] that it is difficult to imagine any violation of 'equal protection of law' which would not also be a violation of 'equality before law'. However, the court clarified that even if there is much in common between the two expressions they do not mean the same thing.

The word 'laws' in the 'equal protection of laws' denotes specific laws. Thus, two rules are clearly deducible from the 'equality before the law' provision:[3]

1. the provision does not mean that all laws must apply to all the subjects or that all subjects must have the same rights and liabilities; and
2. that a citizen's rights as a human being are not affected by reason of his descent, religion, social or official status, economic condition, or place of birth or residence, and further that all citizens are equally subject to the general law of the land.

The 'equal protection of laws' means that:

1. No person or class of persons shall be denied the same protection of laws which is enjoyed by other persons or other classes in like circumstances in their lives, liberty, property, and pursuit of happiness. (The guiding principle, most often stated by the courts, is that this constitutional guarantee requires that all persons shall be treated alike under like circumstances and conditions, both in the privileges conferred and, in the liabilities, imposed.)
2. In similar circumstances the same law will apply, that two sets of circumstances shall not have different legal effects unless the difference of circumstances between the two sets is sufficient, in reason, to justify difference in effect or that if a law applies to one set of circumstances and does not apply to another, the difference between the two sets shall be material enough to support the discrimination.

In *Nasrullah Khan v. District Magistrate*,[4] it was held that where a law confers wide, naked, and uncontrolled power on an official so that he is entitled arbitrarily to interfere with private rights granted by the constitution, the law would be void on the grounds that it enables him to discriminate at his sweet will.

Equality Before Law Under English Law

The classic statement of 'equality before the law,' as one of the fundamental characteristics of the United Kingdom Constitution, is the one given by Dicey. He proposed that one of three meanings of a fundamental principle of the United Kingdom Constitution is known as the 'rule of law'. This, he explained in the following terms:

> [E]quality before the law, or the equal subjection of all classes to the ordinary law of the land, administered by the ordinary law courts; the 'rule of law' in this sense excludes the idea of any exemption of officials or others from the duty of obedience to the law which governs other citizens or from the jurisdiction of the ordinary tribunals....

Dicey further states that, as a result, unlike France, the United Kingdom knew nothing of 'administrative law' or 'administrative tribunals'. In other words, his reference to 'equality before the law' as part of the 'rule of law' was to show that unlike the continental situation in the United Kingdom, the government and its servants were not to be dealt with by special official bodies, but rather within the sphere of civil courts. Subsequent development of 'administrative law' in the United Kingdom and Canada has disproved this distinction.

A more modern, although somewhat closely related variant of the Dicey definition of 'equality before the law', is the one suggested by John Marshall,[5] i.e. that the doctrine implies 'equality of state and individual before the law'. Although the state and citizens cannot really be equals, and while state servants might in fact be given specific powers, nevertheless, the doctrine requires that rules granting powers to officials should be precise, and that it is the duty of the courts to hold an equal balance between citizens and officials.

One of the most famous applications of this view of 'equality before the law' as part of 'the rule of law' was the decision of the Supreme Court of Canada in *Roncarelli v. Duplessis*.[6] The essence of this decision was probably most concisely set out by one of Roncarelli's counsel, Frank Scott, who suggested that the essence of the 'rule of law', which includes 'equality before the law', could be stated in 'two basic rules underlying our constitutional structure, which entitles us to say that we live in a free society'.

> First, is that the individual may do anything he pleases, in any circumstances anywhere, unless there is some provision of law prohibiting him. Freedom is thus presumed, and is the general rule. All restrictions are exceptions. Second rule defines the authority of the state, and places the public official (including the policeman) in exactly the opposite situation from the private individual; the public officer can do nothing in his public capacity unless the law permits it. His incapacity is presumed, and authority to act is an exception. Duplessis, for instance, could not find any legal authority to justify his order to cancel Roncarelli's liquor licence: so he paid personally.

Some of Dicey's modern critics, for example Sir Ivor Jennings,[7] have extended this concept somewhat, to require a basic procedural equality in the sense that there shall be impartiality before the ordinary law courts as well as other adjudicatory tribunals. Sir Ivor Jennings described 'equality before the law' thus:

> It assumes that among equals the laws should be equal and should be equally administered, that like should be treated alike. The right to sue and be sued, to prosecute and be prosecuted, for the same kind of action should be the same for all citizens of full age and understanding, and without distinction of race, religion, wealth, social status or political influence. Nevertheless, even this view of 'equality before the law' basically restricts it to a procedural concept relating only to the even handed operation of the legal system in its application and enforcement of the law.[8]

Over the years, the UN General Assembly has adopted conventions to promote equality such as the International Convention on the Elimination of All Forms of Racial Discrimination[9] (ICERD) was adopted in 1966; and a Convention on the Elimination of All Forms of Discrimination against Women (CEDAW) was adopted in 1979. The International Labour Organization adopted a Convention concerning Equal Remuneration for Men and Women Workers for Work of Equal Value in 1951. Article 14 of the European Convention of Human Rights provides that 'the enjoyment of the rights and freedoms set forth in this convention shall be secured without discrimination on any ground such as sex, race, color, language, religion, political, or other opinion, national or social origin, association with a national minority, property, birth or other status.' Following these international precedents, the Equal Pay Act 1970, the Sex Discrimination Act 1975, the Race Relations Act 1976, prohibited, in certain circumstances, discrimination against the members of groups identifiable by sex, color, race, nationality or ethnic or national origins. According to the Sex Discrimination Act 1975, in the field of employment, discrimination is also prohibited against married persons.[10]

Equality Under French Law

Since the French Revolution of 1789, equality has been at the core of the French republican tradition. That event also played an important part in giving equality its central place in the western, liberal political tradition as a whole. Reaffirmed in subsequent constitutions, it is enshrined in Article 2 of the Fifth Republic Constitution of 1958, which proclaims that the French Republic ensures equality before the law for all citizens, without distinction as to origin, race, or religion'. Given its long-standing prominence, it is not surprising that equality should have been of constitutional value that has been frequently invoked before the *Conseil Constitutionnel*.[11] A large number of case-law that were developed since the *Conseil* first invoked equality in December 1973 reveals both the conception of equality current in the French republican tradition and the extent to which the *Conseil* engages in the review of *lois* on substantive grounds.

Although 'equality' occurs alongside 'liberty' and 'fraternity' in the motto of the French Republic, it does not feature prominently in leading treatises on French constitutional or administrative law. Even in works on fundamental rights it has a limited place. Constitutional texts have focused predominantly on the institutional arrangements of the Constitution, not on its political values. Indeed, constitutional writers have been much vexed with the question of whether values such as equality have any constitutional status at all. Ambiguity of such an idea has deterred many from treating it as a legally enforceable value rather than just a piece of political rhetoric. It is the attitude of the *Conseil* that has stirred interest in the question of equality as a constitutional value, and has caused leading writers to revise some of their opinions. While drawing on the republican tradition, the *Conseil* is, in a real sense, engaged in the process of defining the substantive content of the Constitution.

Arguably the *Conseil's* notion of equality is quite limited. Rather than a value of general application, equality is mainly concerned with non-discrimination in relation to specific constitutional values. Here, and in the wider range of cases where it is invoked, the concern of the *Conseil* seems predominantly to ensure a rational relationship between the provisions of a *loi* and the constitutional or legislative objectives that they are intended to achieve. The conception of equality in keeping with the ideology of 1789, is limited and essentially formal. Equality before the law is concerned with the rejection of irrelevant differences and with the recognition of relevant differences in the categories in which the law places citizens and in the rules that it applies to them, rather than with requiring the legislator to seek substantive equality of outcomes, resources, or opportunities. The existence of substantive inequalities may be accepted by the *Conseil* as an adequate reason for formal differences in treatment in a *loi*, but they are not used by the *Conseil* to require action by Parliament. Such a limited theory merits attention not merely because of the checks that it reveals on French constitutional review, but also for the light that it sheds on the value of equality in the liberal political tradition. That equality seems almost reducible to more specific constitutional values or to a requirement of rationality in legislation would give support to those political writers who reject egalitarianism as part of the liberal political ideal.[12]

Equal Protection of Laws Under American Law

Introduction

American democracy is based upon philosophical idea that all individuals are equal before the law. This ideal is expressed both in the Declaration of Independence and in the Equal Protection Clause of the 14th Amendment, which provides that

> no state shall 'deny to any person within its jurisdiction the equal protection of the laws.'

The Equal Protection Clause prohibits states from denying any person or class of persons the same protection and rights that the law extends to other similarly situated persons or classes of persons.

Post-Civil War (1861–1865), like other rights guaranteed by the amendments, the Equal Protection Clause was motivated in large part by a desire to protect the civil rights of African-Americans recently freed from slavery. However, the clause makes no mention of race; rather, it refers to 'any person' within the jurisdiction of a state. Although the Supreme Court attempted initially to limit the scope of the Equal Protection Clause to discrimination claims brought by African-Americans (see *The Slaughter-House* cases[13] and *Strauder v. West Virginia*),[14] it has developed into a broad prohibition against unreasonable governmental discrimination directed at any identifiable group.

In the late 19th century, the Supreme Court declared that the word 'person' in the 'equal protection clause' included corporations. Occasionally, the clause was employed as a basis for invalidating discriminatory business regulation. In the modern era, the 'equal protection clause' has been invoked successfully to challenge discrimination against racial and ethnic minorities, as well as discrimination against women, the poor, illegitimate children, the mentally retarded, illegal aliens, and, most recently, gay men and lesbians. Under the new Equal Protection, the Supreme Court has used the 'equal protection clause' to scrutinize closely any State law or practice that discriminates among groups in their enjoyment of fundamental rights. Without question, the scope of the 'equal protection clause' has been expanded far beyond the expectations of its authors. Along with the 'due processes clause' of the 14th Amendment, the 'equal protection clause' has become the principal basis for challenging the constitutionality of a broad range of state laws, action, and policies.[15]

The 'Equal Protection Component' of the 5th Amendment

The 14th Amendment applies only to the states, and because the Bill of Rights contains no explicit equal protection provisions, does it follow, that the national government is under no constitutional obligation to provide equal protection of the laws? The Supreme Court has answered this question emphatically in the negative, 'finding' an 'equal protection component' in the 'due process clause' of the 5th Amendment. The Court has concluded that the values underlying the equal protection guarantee are embraced within the broad definition of due process of law. Since the 14th Amendment contains a 'due process clause' virtually identical to that found in the 5th Amendment, one might conclude that the equal protection clause of the 14th Amendment is superfluous. Although this may be true in a formal, logical sense, the 'equal protection clause' was the historic basis for judicial scrutiny of governmental policies challenged as discriminatory. In the absence of the 'equal protection clause', such scrutiny would have been more difficult to justify.[16]

The Rational Basis Test

Introduction
Formulations of the Rational Basis Test

The rational basis test is the minimal level of scrutiny that all government actions challenged under equal protection clause must meet. In other words, unless government action is a type of discrimination that warrants the application of intermediate or strict scrutiny, rational basis review is used.

The rational basis test has been phrased in varying ways by the Supreme Court. For example, in *Lindsley v. Natural Carbonic Gas Co.*,[17] the court declared:

> 'When the classification in such a law is called in question, if any state of facts reasonably can be conceived that would sustain it, the existence of that state of facts at the time the law was enacted must be assumed.... one who assails the classification in such a law must carry the burden of showing that it does not rest upon any reasonable basis, but is essentially arbitrary.'

A similar definition of the rational basis test was articulated by the court in *McGowan v. Maryland*.[18]

> '[t]he court has held that the 14th Amendment permits the state a wide scope of discretion in enacting laws which affect some groups of citizens differently from others. The constitutional safeguard is offended only if a classification rests on grounds wholly irrelevant to the achievement of the state's objective. State legislatures are presumed to have acted within their constitutional power despite the fact that, in practice, their laws result in some inequality. Statutory discrimination will not be set aside if any state of facts reasonably may be conceived to justify it'.

Afterwards, the court has phrased the rational basis test in more rigorous terms. For example, in *Royster Guano Co. v. Virginia*[19], the court said:

> '[T]he classification must be reasonable, not arbitrary and must rest upon some ground of difference having a fair and substantial relation to the object of the legislation, so that all persons similarly situated shall be treated alike.

Although, the court has phrased the test in different ways, the basic requirement is that a law meets rational basis review if it is rationally related to a legitimate government purpose. For instance, in *New Orleans v. Dukes*[20], and in many other cases, the court said that the equal protection clause is satisfied so long as the classification is 'rationally related to a legitimate state interest.' Also, the court has been consistent that the challenger has the burden of proof where rational basis review is applied. There is a strong presumption in favour of laws that are challenged under the rational basis test.[21]

As the court declared in *Hodel v. Indiana:*[22]

> 'social and economic legislation .... that does not employ suspect classifications or impinge on fundamental rights must be upheld against equal protection attack when the legislative means are rationally related to a legitimate government purpose. Moreover, such legislation carries with it a presumption of rationality that can only be overcome by a clear showing of arbitrariness and irrationality.'

In other words, the law will be upheld unless the challenger can prove that it has no legitimate purpose or that the means used are not a reasonable way to accomplish the goal.

Underlying Issues

The Supreme Court in most cases has been extremely deferential to the government when applying the rational basis test. The court has often said that a law should be upheld if it is possible to conceive any legitimate purpose for the law, even if it was not the government's actual purpose. And so the Supreme Court rarely found that a law fails the rational basis test.

This raises important questions. First, is this appropriate deference to the legislative process or is it an undue judicial abdication? Since 1937, the court has made it clear that it will defer to government's economic and social regulations unless they infringe on a fundamental right or discriminate against a group that warrants special judicial protection.[23] This can be defended as proper judicial restraint, as the court allows the more democratic branches of government to make decisions except in areas where there is reason for heightened judicial scrutiny.

> 'Unless a statute employs a classification that is inherently invidious or that impinges on fundamental rights, areas in which the judiciary has a duty to intervene in the democratic process, this court properly exercises only a limited review power over Congress, the appropriate representative body through which the public makes democratic choices among alternative solutions to social and economic problems.'[24]

Legislation often involves arbitrary choices favouring some over others, and judicial defence leaves these decisions to the political process.[25]

But it can also be argued that the court has gone too far in its deference under the rational basis test. Unfair laws are allowed to stand because a conceivable legitimate purpose can be identified for virtually any law. Frequently these are laws enacted to help a particular group with political clout at the expense of others who are less politically powerful. For example, in *Kotch v. Board of River Port Pilot Commissioners*,[26] the court upheld a Louisiana law that conditioned receiving a harbour pilot's license on completion of an apprenticeship term, even though

> 'with occasional exception, only relatives and friends' of pilots were selected as apprentices. The court said that it was sufficient that 'the benefits to morale and *esprit de corps*...might have prompted the legislature to permit Louisiana pilot officers to select those whom they serve.'

Critics of the rational basis test argue that in *Kotch*, and many other similar cases, the court is upholding unfair, discriminatory laws because of its almost complete deference to the legislative process.

Another underlying issue in considering the rational basis test is whether the court has been consistent in applying it. Even though the court has been extremely deferential, there have been several cases where laws have been declared unconstitutional under rational basis review. For example, in *City of Cleburne v. Cleburne Living Centre*,[27] the court used rational basis review to invalidate a zoning ordinance that prevented the operation of a home for the mentally disabled. In *Metropolitan Life Insurance Company v. Ward*,[28] the court declared unconstitutional a state law that attempted to encourage growth of an in-state insurance industry by taxing in-state companies at much lower rates than out-of-state companies doing business in the State.

In *United States Department of Agriculture v. Moreno*,[29] the court invalidated, as violating the rational basis test, a federal law that prevented a household from receiving food stamps if it included individuals who were not related to one another. In *Romer v. Evans*,[30] the court found that a voter initiative in Colorado that repealed laws prohibiting discrimination based on sexual orientation and that precluded the adoption of new protections failed rational basis review.

Many argue that the court in these cases applied a different, more rigorous version of the rational basis test. They claim that there is not a singular rational basis test but one that varies between complete deference and substantial rigor. Instead, it might be argued that the test is consistent and that the court is simply deciding that certain laws lack a legitimate purpose or are arbitrary so as to be unreasonable.[31]

Classification

The principle of 'equal protection of laws' depends upon classification, its fairness, and reasonableness. It is therefore, important to understand classification and its scrutiny by courts: To be more specific, all equal protection issues can be broken down into three questions:

1. What is the classification?
2. What level of scrutiny should be applied?
3. Does the particular government action meet the level of scrutiny?

The first question is: What is the government's classification? How is the government drawing a distinction among people?

Equal protection analysis always must begin by identifying how the government is distinguishing among people. Sometimes it is clear; sometimes it is the focus of the litigation.

There are two basic ways of establishing a classification. First is where the classification exists on the face of the law, that is, where the law in its very terms draws a distinction among people based on a particular characteristic. For example, a law that prohibits blacks from serving on juries is an obvious racial classification on the face of it.[32] A law that says that only those 16 and older can have drivers' licenses is obviously an age classification.

Second is sometimes laws are prima facie facially neutral, but there is a discriminatory impact to the law or discriminatory effects from its administration. For instance, a law that requires that all police officers be at least 5'10' tall and weigh 150 pounds is, on its face, only a height and weight classification. Statistics, however, show that 40 per cent of men, but only 2 per cent of women, will meet this requirement. The result is that the law has a discriminatory impact against women in hiring for the police force.

The Supreme Court has made it clear that discriminatory impact is insufficient to prove a racial or gender classification. If a law is facially neutral, demonstrating a race or gender classification requires proof that there is a discriminatory purpose behind the law.[33] Thus, women challenging the height and weight requirements for the police force must show that the government's purpose was to discriminate based on gender. In other words, there are two alternative ways of proving the existence of a classification: showing that it exists on the face of the law or demonstrating that a facially neutral law has a discriminatory impact and a discriminatory purpose.[34]

What is the Appropriate Level of Scrutiny?

When the classification is identified, the next step in analysis, is to identify the level of scrutiny to be applied. The US Supreme Court has made it clear that differing levels of scrutiny will be applied depending on the type of discrimination.

Discrimination based on race or national origin is subjected to strict scrutiny. Also, generally, discrimination against aliens is subjected to strict scrutiny; although there are several exceptions where less than strict scrutiny is used. Under strict scrutiny a law is upheld if it is proved necessary to achieve a compelling government purpose.[35] The government must have a truly significant reason for discriminating, and it must show that it cannot achieve its objective through any less discriminatory alternative.

The government has the burden of proof under strict scrutiny, and the law will be upheld only if the government persuades the court that it is necessary to achieve a compelling purpose. Strict scrutiny is virtually always fatal to the challenged law. In *Miller-El v. Dretke*,[36] the court found that the defendant proved the prosecutor violated equal protection by showing that the prosecutor's office had a policy of striking off black prospective jurors when there was a black defendant; that blacks were struck off while whites with similar circumstances were not; that blacks were asked different questions than whites; and that prosecutor 'shuffled' the jury when prospective black jurors were coming up. Justice David Souter (1939)[37] opinion in a 6 to 3 decision sent a clear message to trial and appellate courts dealing with this issue; they are required to examine the record closely, as the Supreme Court did, to see if race or gender was being impermissibly used in such matters. In *Grutter v. Bollinger*[38] *and Grtaz v. Bolliner*[39] the US Supreme Court reaffirmed that,

> 'all racial classifications imposed by government must be analyzed by a reviewing court under strict scrutiny.'

The court explained:

> we apply strict scrutiny to all racial classifications to 'smoke out' illegitimate use of race by assuring that [government] is pursuing a goal important enough to warrant use of a highly suspect tool.[40]

Intermediate scrutiny is used for discrimination based on gender and for discrimination against non marital children. Under intermediate scrutiny a law is upheld if it is substantially related to an important government purpose. In other words, the court need not find the government's purpose 'compelling, but it must characterize the objective as 'important.' The means used need not be necessary, but must have a 'substantial relationship' to the end being sought. Under intermediate scrutiny, the government has the burden of proof. The Supreme Court explained that the 'burden of justification is demanding and that it rests entirely on the state.'[41] Many questions remain unanswered concerning intermediate scrutiny. For example, it is unclear whether less restrictive alternative analysis ever should be used for intermediate scrutiny.[42]

Finally, there is the rational basis test. Rational basis review is the minimum level of scrutiny that all laws challenged under equal protection must meet. All laws not subjected to strict or intermediate scrutiny are evaluated under the rational basis test. Under rational basis review a law will be upheld if it is rationally related to a legitimate government purpose.[43] The government's objective need not be compelling or important, but just something that the government legitimately may do. The means chosen only need be a rational way to accomplish the end. The challenger has the burden of proof under rational basis review. The rational basis test is enormously deferential to the government, and only rarely have laws been declared unconstitutional for failing to meet this level of review.[44]

How has the court decided which level of scrutiny to use for particular classification? Although the court has shown little willingness in the past to subject additional classifications to strict or intermediate scrutiny, how will it evaluate such requests? Several criteria are applied in determining the level of scrutiny. For example, the court has emphasized that immutable characteristic like race, national origin, gender, and the marital status of one's parents warrant heightened scrutiny.[45] The notion is, that it is unfair to penalize a person for characteristics that the person did not choose and that the individual cannot change. The court also considers the ability of the group to protect itself through the political process. Women, for example, are more than half the population, but traditionally they have been severely underrepresented in political offices. Aliens do not have the ability to vote, and thus the political process cannot be trusted to represent their interests.[46]

The history of discrimination against the group also is relevant to the court in determining the level of scrutiny. A related issue is the court's judgement concerning the likelihood that the classification reflects prejudice as opposed to a permissible government purpose.[47] For example, the court's choice of strict scrutiny for racial classifications reflects its judgement that race is virtually never an acceptable justification for government action. In contrast, the court's use of intermediate scrutiny for gender classifications reflects its view that the biological differences between men and women mean that there are more likely to be instances where sex is a justifiable basis for discrimination.[48]

Although the levels of scrutiny are firmly established in constitutional law and especially in equal protection analysis, there are many who criticize the rigid tiers of review. For example, Justices Thurgood Marshall (1908–93)[49] and John Paul Stevens (1920–2019)[50], among others, have argued that there should be a sliding scale of review rather than the three levels of scrutiny.[51] They maintain that the court should consider such factors as the constitutional and social importance of the interests adversely affected and the invidiousness of the basis on which the classification was drawn. They contend that under the rigid tiers of review the choice of the level of scrutiny is usually decisive and unduly limits the scope of judicial analysis. Those who favour a sliding scale believe that it would lead to more candid discussion of the competing interests and therefore provide overall better decision making.

Critics suggest that although the court speaks in terms of three tiers of review, in reality there is a spectrum of standards of review.[52] They claim that in some cases where the court says that it is using rational basis review, it is actually employing a test with more 'bite' than the customarily very deferential rational basis review. Similarly, it is argued that in some cases intermediate scrutiny is applied in a very deferential manner that is essentially rational basis review, while in other cases intermediate scrutiny seems indistinguishable from strict scrutiny. Argument is, that although the court articulates three tiers of review, the reality is a range of standards.

Does the Government Action Meet the Level of Scrutiny?

The level of scrutiny is the rule of law that is applied to the particular government action being challenged as denying equal protection. In evaluating the constitutionality of a law, the court evaluates both the law's ends and its means.

For strict scrutiny the end must be deemed compelling for the law to be upheld; for intermediate scrutiny the end has to be regarded as important; and for the rational basis test there just has to be a legitimate purpose.

In evaluating the relationship of the means of the particular law to the end, the US Supreme Court often focuses on the degree to which a law is underinclusive and/or overinclusive. A law is underinclusive if it does not apply to individuals who are similar to those to whom the law applies. For example, a law that excludes those under age 16 from having drivers' licenses is somewhat underinclusive because some younger drivers undoubtedly have the physical ability and the emotional maturity to be effective drivers.[53]

A law is overinclusive if it applies to those who need not be included in order for the government to achieve its purpose. In other words, the law unnecessarily applies to a group of people. For example, the government's decision to evacuate and intern all Japanese-Americans on the West Coast during World War II was radically overinclusive.[54] The government's purported interest was in preventing espionage, individuals were evacuated and interned without any determination of their threat. The law was enormously overinclusive because it harmed a large number of people unnecessarily.

A law can be both underinclusive and overinclusive. The decision to evacuate Japanese-Americans during World War II was certainly both. If the goal was to isolate those who were a threat to security, interning only Japanese-Americans was underinclusive in that it did not identify those of other races who posed a danger. At the same time, as explained above, the federal government's action was extremely overinclusive because few, if any, Japanese-Americans posed any threat. In fact, not a single Japanese-American during World War II was ever charged with espionage.

The fact that a law is underinclusive and/or overinclusive does not mean that it is sure to be invalidated. Quite the contrary, virtually all laws are underinclusive, overinclusive, or both. The court has recognized that laws often are underinclusive because the government may choose to proceed 'one step at a time.'[55] 'But underinclusiveness and overinclusiveness are used by courts in evaluating the relationship between the government's means and its ends.' If strict scrutiny is used, a relatively close relationship is required; in fact, the government will have to show that the means is necessary - the least restrictive alternative—to achieve the goal. Under intermediate scrutiny a closer relationship, less underinclusive or overinclusive, will be required than under the rational basis test.

Thus, equal protection analysis involves three questions:

1. What is the classification?
2. What level of scrutiny should be applied?
3. Does the particular government action meet the level of scrutiny?

Cases posing an equal protection issue always involve a dispute over one or more of these questions.[56]

Reasonable, Invidious and Suspect Classification

Under rational basis review, the court also must decide 'whether the classifications drawn in a statute are reasonable in light of its purposes.'[57] However, the court repeatedly has expressed that this is 'the most relaxed and tolerant form of judicial scrutiny.'[58] Thus, the court has said that

> under the rational basis test, laws will be upheld unless the government's action is 'clearly wrong, a display of arbitrary power, not an exercise of judgement.'[59]

(i) Underinclusiveness

As a result, under the rational basis test the court will allow laws that are both significantly underinclusive and overinclusive. Mentioned earlier, laws are underinclusive when they do not regulate all who are similarly situated.

Underinclusive laws raise the concern that the government has enacted a law that targets a particular politically powerless group or that exempts those with more political clout. But the Supreme Court has said that

> when rational basis review is used, even substantial under inclusiveness is allowed because the government 'may take one step at a time, addressing itself to the phase of the problem which seems most acute to the legislative mind.'[60]

For example, in *Railway Express Agency, Inc. v. New York*[61], the court upheld an ordinance that banned all advertising on the sides of trucks unless the ad was for the business of the truck's owner. It was argued that this distinction was irrational as a way to achieve the government's purpose of decreasing distractions for drivers and promoting traffic safety. The court concluded that the government might have perceived some difference among the ads and that it was immaterial whether the government failed to deal with even greater distractions to motorists. The court declared:

> 'It is no requirement of equal protection that all evils of the same genus be eradicated or none at all.'

(ii) Overinclusiveness

Likewise, even substantial overinclusiveness is tolerated under rational basis review. A law is overinclusive if it regulates individuals who are not similarly situated, that is, if it covers more people than it needs to in order to accomplish its purpose.

Overinclusive laws are unfair to those who are unnecessarily regulated, and they risk 'burden[ing] a politically powerless group which would have been spared if it had enough clout to compel normal attention to the relevant costs and benefits.'[62]

Nevertheless, the Supreme Court has indicated that even significant overinclusiveness is allowed under rational basis review. For example, in *New York Transit Authority v. Beazer*[63] the Supreme Court upheld a city's regulation that prevented those in methadone maintenance programs from holding positions with the Transit Authority. The court noted that:

> '[t]he evidence indicates that methadone is an effective cure for the physical aspects of heroin addiction and that "the strong majority" of patients who have been on methadone maintenance for at least a year are free from illicit drug use.'

Therefore, the exclusion of all methadone addicts was substantially overinclusive relative to the goal of safety. The vast majority of those in methadone programs posed no safety risk. But the Supreme Court upheld the law under the rational basis test. The court said that any alternative rule is likely to be less precise 'and will assuredly be more costly' than the total ban on those using drugs.

(iii) Laws That are Both Underinclusive and Overinclusive

Many laws are both underinclusive and overinclusive. Yet, these laws, too, are usually tolerated under the rational basis test. The Supreme Court has declared:

> 'Even if the classification involved here is to some extent both underinclusive and overinclusive, and hence the law drawn by Congress imperfect, it is nevertheless the rule that...perfection is by no means required.'[64]

For example, in *Beazer*, the law prohibiting methadone addicts from working for the Transit Authority was upheld even though it was both overinclusive and underinclusive. The law was overinclusive in excluding from employment the vast majority of methadone users who posed no safety risk, and it was underinclusive in that it allowed employment of others who would be a safety threat.

In *Vance v. Bradley*,[65] the Supreme Court upheld a mandatory retirement age of 60 for those in the Foreign Service. The court recognized that the law was overinclusive in that it applied to many who were capable of continuing to work effectively, and it was underinclusive in that it did not apply to many who were under that age and were no longer capable of performing adequately. Nonetheless, the Supreme Court held that age discrimination receives only rational basis review under the equal protection clause and upheld the law even though the 'classification involved here is to some extent both underinclusive and overinclusive.

(iv) Cases where Laws are deemed arbitrary and unreasonable

The Supreme Court decisions indicate that it is extremely deferential under the rational basis test and usually will find that laws are reasonable. There are, however, a few cases where the court has found that laws are very arbitrary and fail rational basis review. For example, in *City of Cleburne, Texas v. Cleburne Living Center, Inc.*,[66] The Supreme Court declared unconstitutional a city ordinance that required a special permit for the operation of a group home for the mentally disabled.

The court expressly held that rational basis review was the appropriate standard for evaluating government action discriminating against the mentally disabled. The court nevertheless declared the ordinance unconstitutional. The city offered a number of justifications for the law; the court concluded either that they were not legitimate purposes or that the ordinance was not a reasonable way of accomplishing the goals. For example, the city argued that property owners in the area opposed having a facility for the mentally disabled, and the city expressed concern that students from a junior high school across the street might harass occupants of a group home. The court held that these justifications were based on prejudices against the mentally disabled and that indulging such private biases is not a legitimate government purpose. The city also contended that the home was located on a 'five hundred year flood plain'. The court dismissed this concern because in the same area the city allowed facilities such as nursing homes, homes for convalescents and the aged, hospitals, and sanatoriums. Therefore, the court rejected the city's concern over the number who would live in the home because no similar restrictions on size existed for nursing homes, boarding houses, fraternities, or others.[67]

Although the court expressly declared that it was applying rational basis review, it appears that there was more 'bite' to the court's approach than usual for this level of scrutiny. The court usually has declared that the rational basis test allows the government to proceed one step at a time; substantial underinclusiveness is tolerated.

Therefore, under usual rational basis review the government would be able to regulate homes for the mentally disabled, but not apply the standards to hospitals or nursing homes. But the Supreme Court's decision also can be seen as a straightforward application of rational basis review: Drawing a distinction between a home for the mentally disabled and all other facilities is based on nothing other than irrational prejudices and thus fails even deferential scrutiny. In a subsequent decision, *University of Alabama v. Garrett*,[68] the court declared that Cleburne held that only rational basis review is to be used for disability discrimination.

Another instance where the court declared unconstitutional a government action because of its irrationality is *Allegheny Pittsburgh Coal Co. v. County Commission*.[69] The court unanimously invalidated a county tax assessor's practice of valuing real property at 50 per cent of its most recent sale price. Property would not be reassessed until it was again sold. The result was that properties with identical values would have widely divergent assessments depending on the timing of the sales. The plaintiff's property was assessed at a value of 8 to 35 times more than similar property in the county, even though the West Virginia constitution ensured that taxes would be 'equal and uniform.' The court said that although the judiciary should generally defer to distinctions drawn in tax laws, the county assessor's practices were arbitrary and unsupported by state law. The court concluded that

> '[t]he relative undervaluation of comparable property in Webster County over time therefore denies petitioners the equal protection of the law.'

However, just a few years later, in *Nordlinger v. Hahn*,[70] the Supreme Court upheld a California law that was very similar in its effects to what was declared unconstitutional in *Allegheny Pittsburgh Coal*. Proposition 13, adopted by California voters as an initiative in 1976, limits real property taxes to 1 per cent of assessed valuation of the property as of 1975–1976 and permits reassessment only when sold. The result is enormous disparities in the property taxes for otherwise identical property. A person who purchased property in the 1970s when property values were low would pay little property taxes; but a person who bought the identical house next door in the 1980s, when property values were high, would pay far more in property taxes.[71]

Nonetheless, the court upheld Proposition 13 as being rationally related to a legitimate government purpose. The court said that there were many conceivable purposes for the law including encouraging stable neighbourhoods by offering an economic disincentive for people to move, avoiding taxes on appreciation that was the result of inflation, and allowing people to know their tax burden at the time of purchase.

The Suspect Classification Doctrine

In *Korematsu v. United States*[72] provided the first real indication that the US Supreme Court was embarking on a new approach to the equal protection clause. In *Korematsu*, the court upheld the constitutionality of the 'relocation' of Japanese-Americans living on West Coast during the Second World War (1939–45). In his majority opinion, Justice Hugo Black (1886–1971)[73] stated that

> 'all legal restrictions which curtail the civil rights of a single group are immediately suspected. That is not to say that all such restrictions are unconstitutional. It is to say that courts must subject them to the most rigid scrutiny. Pressing public necessity may sometimes justify the existence of such restrictions; racial antagonism never can.'

It is now widely recognized that no compelling justification supported the relocation order. However, the majority in *Korematsu* apparently did not have full access to information, which was later made public, clearly indicating that the relocation order stemmed more from racial prejudice rather than from military necessity.

Although on its face the *Korematsu* decision was hardly a victory for civil rights, it marked the inception of the suspect classification doctrine, which holds that certain kinds of discrimination are inherently suspect and therefore must be subjected to strict judicial scrutiny. Included among those laws that are inherently suspect are those that classify persons based on race, religion, or ethnicity, as well as those that impinge on fundamental rights.

Operationally speaking, strict judicial scrutiny means that the ordinary presumption of constitutionality is reversed; the government carries the burden of proof that its challenged policy is constitutional. To carry that burden, government must show that its policy is necessary to the achievement of a compelling interest and that it is 'narrowly tailored' to further that interest.[74]

Although judicial tests are far from precise, in that courts seldom define the terms that comprise these tests, the compelling interest test is generally understood to be far more stringent than the traditional rational basis test.

Using the suspect classification doctrine, the court has invalidated, explicitly or implicitly, virtually all public policies that overtly discriminate among persons on the basis of their race, for example, *Loving v. Virginia*.[75] In the court's view, it is virtually impossible for government to have a compelling interest that would require or justify racial or ethnic discrimination.

Racial Discrimination

Although the 'equal protection clause' is now recognized as a broad shield against arbitrary government action, little doubt exists that the 14th Amendment was adopted primarily to protect the rights of the newly freed former slaves. Specifically, the 14th Amendment was designed to provide constitutional authority for newly enacted federal civil rights legislation aimed at ending discrimination against African-Americans. Section 5 of the 14th Amendment gives Congress the power to enforce, 'by appropriate legislation,' the abstract promises of the 'equal protection clause' and other provisions of the amendment.

(i) Early Interpretations of the Equal Protection Clause

Shortly before the ratification of the 14th Amendment, Congress passed the Civil Rights Act of 1866, which, among other things, protected the right of African-Americans to inherit, own, and convey property. In the wake of the Civil War (1861–65), many of the Southern states had adopted Black Codes, which denied such basic economic rights to former slaves.

Under the new Civil Rights Act, violation of these rights was made a federal offense where it could be shown that the violator was acting 'under color of state law'. Apparently, having some reservations about the constitutionality of this law, Congress rushed to adopt the 14th Amendment, believing that the Equal Protection Clause of Section 1 together with the enforcement provisions of section 5 would provide an adequate constitutional basis for far-ranging civil rights legislation.

(ii) The Civil Rights Cases (1883)

The Supreme Court's early view of congressional authority in the field of civil rights was much more restrictive. But present-day Supreme Court recognizes broad congressional power under the 14th Amendment.

In adopting the *Civil Rights Act of 1875*, Congress made a serious attempt to eradicate racial discrimination in *places of public accommodation*, including hotels, taverns, restaurants, theatres, and 'public conveyance'. In *The Civil Rights Cases*,[76] however, the Supreme Court struck down the key provisions of this Act, ruling that the 14th Amendment limited congressional action to the prohibition of official, state-sponsored discrimination as distinct from discrimination practiced by privately owned places of public accommodation.

The Supreme Court's decision in '*The Civil Rights Cases*' may have been motivated by a desire to promote reconciliation between North and South and between the federal and state governments. Unfortunately, any such reconciliation was achieved at the expense of African-Americans.

(iii) Adoption of Jim Crow Laws

The court's decision in '*The Civil Rights Cases*' preserve widespread practices of racial discrimination in restaurants, hotels, etc., but it was also regarded as a green light for the passage of legislation mandating strict racial segregation.

The so-called Jim Crow laws adopted in the aftermath '*The Civil Rights Cases*' required segregation in virtually every area of public life. They required blacks and whites to attend separate schools, to use separate parks, to ride in separate railroad cars, and even to be buried in separate cemeteries. Perhaps the most ludicrous of the many Jim Crow laws required white and black witnesses in court to take their oaths on separate Bibles.[77]

(iv) The Separate but Equal Doctrine

In *Plessy v. Ferguson*[78] the Supreme Court upheld racial segregation in the context of public transportation. The court's ruling provided a rationale for government-mandated segregation on a broad scale. The issue regarding *Plessy*, was a 1890 Louisiana law requiring passenger trains operating within the state to provide 'equal but separate' accommodations for the 'white and colored races.' Homer Plessy, who was considered 'colored' under Louisiana law because one of his great-grandparents was black, was ordered to leave a railroad car reserved for whites. Plessy, who intended to challenge the constitutionality of the law, refused to vacate his seat and was arrested. Dividing 7 to 1 (Justice David Josiah Brewer (1837–1910)[79] not participating), the court sustained the Louisiana statute. Writing for the majority, Justice Henry Billings Brown (1836–1913)[80] asserted that

> 'in the nature of things, [the 14th Amendment] could not have been intended to abolish distinctions based upon color, or to enforce social, as distinguished from political, equality, or a commingling of the two races upon terms unsatisfactory to either.'

In one of the most widely quoted opinions in American constitutional law, Justice John Marshall Harlan (1833–1911)[81] dissented vehemently. For Justice Harlan, ironically a former Kentucky slave owner, the 'arbitrary separation of citizens on the basis of race' was tantamount to imposing a 'badge of servitude' on the Negro race. He asserted that

> 'our Constitution is color-blind, and neither knows nor tolerates classes among citizens.'

The 'separate but equal doctrine' approved in *Plessy* remained the authoritative interpretation of the 'equal protection clause' for 58 years. Ultimately, of course, it was repudiated by the Supreme Court in *Brown v. Board of Education of Topeka.*[82]

The state action doctrine announced in '*The Civil Rights Cases*' remains authoritative to this day—and in fact, not until the 1960s was Congress willing or able to prohibit discrimination in places of public accommodation. When Congress did finally act in passing the Civil Rights Act of 1964, it chose to rely primarily on its broad powers under the Commerce clause, rather than on Section 5 of the 14th Amendment.

The effect of '*The Civil Rights Cases*' and *Plessy v. Ferguson*, were to delay legal and political equality for African-Americans for nearly a century after ratification of the 14th Amendment. During this period, racial discrimination was simply a way of life for many Americans, both black and white. Even today, although considerable progress toward racial equality has been achieved, racial discrimination and hatred have by no means disappeared from American society.[83]

(v) The Decline of deJure Racial Segregation

The Court's decision in *Plessy v. Ferguson* rested on two obvious fictions:

(1) that racial segregation conveyed no negative statement about the status of African-Americans and
(2) that separate accommodations and facilities for blacks were in fact equal to those reserved for whites.

The American people, blacks or whites, were sensible enough to know better. As time went by, it became increasingly obvious to the Supreme Court that the separate but equal doctrine was a mere rationalization for relegating African-Americans to second-class citizenship.

In a series of cases decided between 1938 and 1950, the Supreme Court chipped away at the separate but equal doctrine, as applied to higher-education, without repudiating the doctrine altogether.

In *Missouri ex rel. Gaines v. Canada*,[84] the court mandated the admission of a qualified African-American resident of Missouri to the state university law school. The court held that a state could not escape its obligation by making provision for its African-American students to attend out-of-state law schools.

The Supreme Court reaffirmed its holding in *Gaines* a decade later in *Sipuel v. Oklahoma Board of Regents*.[85] Two years later, in *Mclaurin v. Oklahoma State Regents*,[86] the court disallowed an attempt by the University of Oklahoma to segregate a black graduate student from his white colleagues after he was admitted pursuant to a court order.

In class, the student, McLaurin, was required to sit in a row of desks restricted to blacks. In the cafeteria, he was required to eat alone at a particular table. He was restricted to a designated table in the library. He was even prohibited from visiting his professors during their regular office hours in order to minimize his interactions with white students. In the court's view, this isolation significantly detracted from McLaurin's educational experience and thus could not be justified under the separate but equal doctrine.

In *Sweatt v. Painter*,[87] the court considered an attempt by the state of Texas to provide a separate law school for African-Americans. The court found that the newly created law school at the Texas College for Negroes was substantially inferior, in terms of both measurable and intangible factors, to the white-only law school at the University of Texas.

(vi) Desegregation

By the early 1950s, it was clear that the Supreme Court would no longer tolerate the provision of demonstrably inferior educational services or facilities to African-Americans under the aegis of the 'separate but equal doctrine'.

But considerable uncertainty remained, both within and outside the court, as to whether the justices would, or should, abandon the *Plessy* doctrine altogether.

The National Association for the Advancement of Colored People (NAACP) mounted a major challenge to segregated public schools, instituting lawsuits in four states and the district of Columbia. These cases were first argued before the Supreme Court in 1952, but because of the political magnitude of the issue presented, the court directed that the cases be re-argued in 1953.

Before the second round of oral argument, Chief Justice Fred Moore Vinson (1890–1953)[88] died and was succeeded by Justice Earl Warren (1891–1974).[89]

The Brown Decision and its Implementation

Finally, on 17 May 1954, the court handed down its landmark decision in *Brown v. Board of Education*. In one of the most important decisions in its history. The court unanimously struck down racial segregation in the public schools of Kansas, South Carolina, Delaware, and Virginia. Speaking for the court in *Brown*, Chief Justice Warren declared that

> 'in the field of public education, the doctrine of 'separate but equal' has no place. Separate educational facilities are inherently unequal.'

The Warren Court abandoned a long-standing constitutional precedent and precipitated a revolution in public education.

In a companion case, *Billing v. Sharpe*,[90] the court held that the operation of segregated schools by the District of Columbia violated the 'due process clause' of the 5th Amendment. Here the court recognized 'equal protection component' in the 5th Amendment due process requirement, indicating that uniform anti-discrimination mandates were to be applied to the federal government as well as the states.

The Brown decision of 1954 left open the question how and when desegregation would have to be achieved. In a follow-up decision in 1955, the court blunted the revolutionary potential of the original decision by adopting a formula calling for implementation of desegregation with 'all deliberate speed.'

Recognizing that compliance would be more difficult to achieve in the South than in other sections of the country, the court left it to federal district judges to apply this formula, taking into account the particular circumstances characterizing race relations within their respective jurisdictions.

This approach ensured great diversity in the implementation of Brown and invited the use of delaying tactics by state and local officials. Despite its concern for the difficulties public officials would face in bringing about desegregation, the court was reviled in many quarters for 'meddling' in state and local affairs. Some of the court's harsher critics went so far as to call for the impeachment of Chief Justice Warren.

Some of the more extreme critics of school desegregation called for militant non-compliance with the court's directive. John Kasper, a well-known white supremacist and self-styled protégé of the fascist poet Ezra Pound (1885–1972), went around the country preaching the use of violence and intimidation to prevent black students from entering formerly all-white public schools. In the summer of 1956, Kasper went to Clinton, Tennessee, where he succeeded in fomenting violent resistance to court-ordered integration of Clinton High School. In August, Kasper was ordered by federal judge Robert Taylor 'to cease hindering, obstructing, or in any wise interfering' with court-ordered integration. Kasper persisted in his efforts, and Clinton experienced a turbulent fall replete with riots, beatings, death threats directed at various school officials, and harassment of African-American students. After the US National Guard was called in to restore order, Kasper was arrested and convicted for violating the federal court injunction. Ultimately, peace returned to Clinton, and desegregation proceeded swiftly.

The Little Rock Crisis

In one of the best known and most dramatic efforts to resist the Supreme Court's desegregation decisions, Arkansas Governor Orval Faubus (1970–94) called out the US National Guard in 1957 to prevent 9 African-American students from entering Little Rock Central High School. US National Guard was soon withdrawn, but an angry mob of whites continued to harass the black students. President Dwight D. Eisenhower (1890–1969), who had expressed serious reservations about the *Brown* decision, nevertheless intervened with federal troops to quell the violence and enforce the court-ordered integration.

In *Cooper v. Aaron*,[91] the court delivered a sharp rebuke to Arkansas officials who had attempted to frustrate the court's mandate.

After the Little Rock incident, the state and local governments that were intent on avoiding desegregation adopted a strategy of 'legislate and litigate', this delayed universal compliance with *Brown* for well over a decade. But in *Alexander v. Holmes County*,[92] the Supreme Court finally abandoned the permissive 'all deliberate speed' policy and ordered desegregation 'at once.' This set the stage for the busing controversy of the 1970s.

(vii) The Busing Controversy

The Supreme Court had left the implementation of school desegregation largely to the discretion of federal district judges. These judges employed various measures in dismantling dual school systems, but 'forced busing' was by far the most controversial.

In *Swann v. Charlotte-Mecklenburg Board of Education*,[93] the Supreme Court unanimously approved the use of court-ordered busing to achieve the goal of desegregation. In 1973, the court turned its attention to school desegregation outside the South. In *Keyes v. Denver School District*,[94] the court, with only Justice William Rehnquist (1924–2005) dissenting, found *de jure* discrimination where a series of administrative decisions in the 1960s had helped to maintain racially segregated public schools in the city of Denver. Thus, in *Keyes*, as in *Swann*, the Supreme Court upheld a busing plan imposed by a federal district court.

Busing eventually became more pervasive and it erupted into a major political issue. In the 1972 presidential campaign, candidate George Wallace (1919–98) exploited the busing issue quite successfully, goading incumbent Richard Nixon (1913–94) into taking a stronger anti-busing posture than he had previously maintained.

Perhaps, as a reaction to widespread criticism of *Swann* and *Keyes*, as well as anti-busing rumblings in Congress, the Supreme Court withdrew from busing in the case of *Milliken v. Bradley*.[95] *Milliken* involved a challenge to a court-ordered desegregation plan for greater Detroit that involved busing students across school district lines within the metropolitan area.

Although, *Milliken* by no means overturned *Swann* and *Keyes*, a 5 to 4 majority of the justices held that court-ordered busing of students across school district lines is permissible only if all affected districts had been guilty of past discriminatory practices. By thus limiting inter-district busing plans, the Supreme Court placed substantial limits on this approach to school desegregation in metropolitan areas.

To the proponents of racial busing, the decision in *Milliken* was an unfortunate retreat from the court's long concession to public opinion, which was generally negative toward busing. Clearly, the effect of the *Milliken* decision was to defuse much of the harsh criticism that had previously been directed at the court over the busing issue. Nevertheless, inter-district busing schemes continued to be ordered by federal judges where inter-district violations were uncovered. In the unfortunate case of Boston, inter-district busing in 1974 produced intense hostility and violence.[96]

The use of busing to achieve desegregation continues to this day, although, it is not as pervasive as it was in the early 1970s. Indeed, African-American intellectuals and educators no longer uniformly support busing. Some reject what they regard as a racist implication that black children cannot improve themselves without exposure to white children. Clearly, the political and intellectual impetus behind racial busing has diminished dramatically. Consequently, busing is no longer a salient political issue.

The Supreme Court continues to hear cases in this area, but the major thrust of litigation is toward the termination, rather than the continued implementation, of busing and related desegregation plans. In a significant 1991 decision, *Board of Education v. Dowell*,[97] the court granted federal district courts clear authority to terminate desegregation orders provided that two conditions are met:

(1) that the local school board in question has complied in good faith with the desegregation decree, and
(2) that all vestiges of prior discrimination have been effectively removed.

The *Dowell* decision left many questions unanswered, but the court made it clear that judicial supervision of school desegregation is, after all, temporary in nature.

In *Freeman v. Pitts*[98] the Supreme Court amplified its decision in *Dowell* by permitting a federal district court, for many years had supervised desegregation of the DeKalb County, Georgia. Schools to relinquish supervision over certain aspects of school administration.

The court held that district judges have discretion to relinquish supervision of school systems where racial imbalances stemming from *de jure* segregation have disappeared, even if schools remain 'racially identifiable' due to demographic factors. Under the approach taken in *Dowell* and *Freeman*, local school districts that show good-faith efforts to comply with court-mandated desegregation plans would eventually regain full control of their school systems.

Desegregation Cases

In *Missouri v. Jenkins*,[99] the Supreme Court reviewed a federal district judge's effort to desegregate the Kansas City school system. The plan would redistribute the students within the system, and also included magnet schools to attract non-minority students from outside the Kansas City Metropolitan School District.

Splitting 5 to 4, the Supreme Court invalidated the judge's order, finding inter-district reassignment to be excessive and abusive of the district court's remedial orders under the stricter level of scrutiny articulated in *Freeman v. Pitts*. Writing for the court, Chief Justice William Rehnquist reminded the district court

> 'that its end purpose is not only "to remedy the violation" to the extent practicable, but also "to restore state and local authorities to the control of a school system that is operating in compliance with the Constitution."'

In her concurring opinion in *Jenkins*, Justice Sandra Day O'Connor (1930)[100] emphasized the narrowness of the court's holding. In contrast, Justice Clarence Thomas's (1948)[101] concurring opinion launched a broadside against desegregation jurisprudence:

> 'Given that desegregation has not produced the predicted leaps forward in black educational achievement, there is no reason to think that black students cannot learn as well when surrounded by members of their own race as when they are in an integrated environment.'

Thomas also attacked the 'virtually unlimited' power of federal district judges to craft desegregation remedies:

> 'Federal courts simply cannot gather sufficient information to render an effective decree, have limited resources to induce compliance, and cannot seek political and public support for their remedies. When we presume to have the institutional ability to set effective educational, budgetary, or administrative policy, we transform the least dangerous branch into the most dangerous one.'

Dissenting in *Jenkins*, Justice David Souter (1939) noted that state and local officials 'intentionally created this segregated system of education, and subsequently failed to correct it. Clearly, in Souter's view, officials 'defaulted in their obligation to uphold the Constitution.' In remedying the violation, the district court must be accorded broad latitude. It must be 'authorized to remedy all conditions flowing directly from the constitutional violations committed by state or local officials, including the educational deficits that result from a segregated school system.' Justice Souter was joined in this view by Justices Ruth Bader Ginsburg (1933–2020)[102], Stephen Breyer (1938)[103], and John Paul Stevens (1920–2019). In her separate dissent, Justice Ginsburg sounded a cautionary note:

> 'Given the deep, inglorious history of segregation in Missouri, to curtail desegregation at this time and in this manner is an action at once too swift and too soon.'

The Supreme Court in its recent decision on the subject of school segregation, *Parents involved in Community Schools v. Seattle School Dist. No. 1*,[104] limits the ability of school boards to remedy racial separation. The case involved public school systems in Louisville, Kentucky and Seattle, Washington; had adopted plans which used race as one factor in assigning students to schools to achieve greater racial diversity.

Louisville, which had a program that included all students from kindergarten through 12th grade. Previously, it had been a system segregated by law and had been subject to a judicial desegregation order which had been lifted not long before it adopted its own desegregation plan. Seattle had never been segregated by law and had a plan that used race as a factor in assigning students to high schools to achieve greater racial diversity.

The court, in a 5 to 4 decision found both plans to be unconstitutional. Chief Justice John Roberts' (1955)[105] opinion was joined in its entirety only by Justices Antonin Scalia (1936–2016)[106], Clarence Thomas and Samuel Alito (1950)[107]. Justice Anthony Kennedy (1936)[108] concurred in part, but also concurred only in the judgment in part, and has separate opinion is thus crucial to determining the scope of impact of the decision.

All five justices to the majority agreed that the government must meet strict scrutiny–its actions must be necessary to achieve a compelling purpose – even if it is using race to achieve school desegregation. Chief Justice Roberts, writing for the majority, declared

> 'it is well established that when the government distributes burdens or benefits on the basis of individual racial classifications, that action is reviewed under strict scrutiny.'

Chief Justice Roberts, writing for a plurality of four, found that Seattle and Louisville lacked a compelling interest for their desegregation efforts. Roberts stressed that the school systems were not seeking to scrutiny constitutional violations and he rejected the argument that diversity in classification was an interest sufficient to meet strict scrutiny. Roberts, writing for the plurality stated:

> 'However closely related race-based assignments may be so achieving racial balance, that itself cannot be the goal, whether labeled racial diversity or anything else. To the extent the objective is sufficient diversity so that students see fellow students as individuals rather than solely as members of a racial group, using means that treat students solely as members of a racial group is fundamentally at cross-purposes with that end.

By contrast, Justice Kennedy and the four dissenters said that desegregating schools is a compelling government interest. Justice Kennedy stated:

> 'In the administration of public schools by the state and local authorities it is permissible to consider the racial makeup of schools and to adopt general policies to encourage a diverse student body, one aspect of which is its racial composition.

Justice Breyer wrote a lengthy dissent joined by Justices Stevens, Souter, and Ginsburg. He described how American public schools are increasingly racially segregated and lamented that the court's decision will have the effect of placing many effective desegregation plans in jeopardy. Justice Breyer attached an appendix to his dissent which listed the many voluntary desegregation plans that will be in jeopardy in light of the invalidation of the Louisville and Seattle programs. The dissent questioned whether these efforts can be in achieving meaningful desegregation.

The majority and the dissent have dramatically different views about the importance of diversity in public schools and the meaning of *Brown v. Board of Education*. Chief Justice Roberts sees in the Constitution a command for color blindness and concluded his opinion by declaring:

> 'Before *Brown*, school-children were told where they could and could not go to school based on the color of their skin. The school districts in these cases have not carried the heavy burden of demonstrating that we should allow this once again-even for very different reasons. For schools that never segregated on the basis of race, such as Seattle, or they have removed the vestiges of past segregation, such as Jefferson Country, the way to achieve a system of determining admission to the public schools on a non-racial basis, is to stop assigning students on a racial basis. The way to stop discrimination on the basis of race is to stop discriminating on the basis of race.'

By contrast, Justice Breyer and the dissent express the need for deference to school boards in desegregating schools and see the majority as abandoning the promise of *Brown v. Board of Education*. Justice Breyer concludes his dissent by stating:

> 'The last half century has witnessed great strides toward racial equality, but we have not yet realized the promise of *Brown*. To invalidate the plans under review is to threaten the promise of *Brown*. The plurality's position, I fear, would break that promise. This is a decision that the Court and the Nation will come to regret.[109]

The Affirmative Action Controversy

The 1970s controversy over the court-ordered busing had largely subsided by the late 1980s. A new controversy of 'affirmative action' emerged in American politics to take its place. The controversy involves 'affirmative action', a broad term referring to a variety of efforts designed to assist members of traditionally disfavoured minority groups.

The 'affirmative action' concept is manifested in three major areas of distributive policy: employment, government contracts, and higher education. Affirmative action actually emerged through executive orders handed down during the Kennedy, Johnson, and Nixon administrations of the 1960s and early 1970s. Initially, it was limited to the requirement that federal government contractors make increased efforts to recruit minority employees. Thereafter, state higher education programs were subjected to affirmative action guidelines as a condition of accepting federal subsidies.

Thereafter, the federal and state courts were adopting race conscience remedies (for example, racial busing) in resolving desegregation lawsuits. Eventually, what began as little more than a public exhortation became a series of goals, quotas, and timetables designed to integrate African-Americans, Hispanics, Native Americans, and other traditionally disfavoured minorities into the economic and educational mainstream.

Although, the ultimate objective of affirmative action was, and is, universally applauded, the means of achieving it—quotas, formulas, and ratios based on immutable racial characteristics—are distasteful to many and appear downright unjust to others. To many critics, affirmative action represents and unfortunate degeneration of the noble ideal of equality of opportunity into statistical parity.

For some legal critics, affirmative action is a violation of the color-blind constitution idealized by Justice Marshall Harlan's (1833–1911) dissent in *Plessy v. Ferguson*. Still others, some of them members of non preferred ethnic minorities, object to affirmative action not on principle but because they have not been given preferred status. Yet, the many defenders of affirmative action characterize it as the only practicable means of realizing the American dream for those who have been traditionally locked out.[110]

(i) Competing Models of Justice

Affirmative action is problematic legally, because it involves two competing models of racial justice. One theory views race discrimination and its appropriate remedies in terms of identifiable groups. Under this theory, all individuals belonging to a traditionally disfavoured minority are entitled to partake of a remedy.

The competing individualistic theory holds that remedies are to be provided only to those individuals who can show that they have been the targets of invidious discrimination. The conflict can also be viewed as one between contemporary politics and traditional principles of law.

In the contemporary pluralistic political process, the people are accustomed to thinking in terms of group interests. However, American system of law rests on a foundation of individualism and does not easily accommodate the concept of group rights.

Naturally, people on all sides of the affirmative action controversy looked to the Supreme Court for settlement of issues. The Supreme Court initially avoided the constitutionality of affirmative action when it decided *DeFunis v. Odegaard*,[111] holding that the question presented in this case was moot.

(ii) The Bakke and Fullilove Cases

The Supreme Court eventually, did hand down a ruling on affirmative action, but *Regents of the University of California v. Bakke*[112] could hardly be regarded as a definitive resolution of the issue.

Alan Bakke, a 37 year old white male engineer, brought suit to challenge the affirmative action policy of the medical school at the University of California, Davis. Bakke had been denied admission to the medical school, although his objective indicators i.e. Medical College Admission Test (MCAT) score and grade point average (GPA), were better than those of several of the 16 minority students admitted under a set-aside policy. The California Supreme Court found this to be a violation of equal protection and ordered Bakke to be admitted to the medical school. Seeking a more authoritative resolution of the issue, the university appealed. Bakke ultimately won the appeal and completed his medical school program.

In a fragmented decision, the court voted 5 to 4 invalidate the Cal–Davis quota system and admit Alan Bakke to medical school. However, also by a 5 to 4 margin, the court endorsed affirmative action in the abstract, by recognizing race as a legitimate criterion of admission to medical school. According to Justice Lewis Franklin Powell's (1907–98)[113] controlling opinion in *Bakke*,

> the state has a compelling interest in achieving diversity in its medical school, and this interest justifies the use of race as one of several criteria of admission.

However, the use of a rigid quota system

> 'tells applicants who are not Negro, Asian or Chicano that they are totally excluded from a specific percentage of the seats in an entering class. No matter how strong their qualifications, quantitative and extracurricular, including their own potential for contribution to educational diversity, they are never afforded the chance to compete with applicants from the preferred groups for the special admissions seats.'

For Justice Powell, this was the fatal flaw in the Davis affirmative action plan. Powell's brethren were less equivocal. Four members of the court–Warren E. Burger (1907–95)[114], Potter Stewart (1915–85)[115], William Rehnquist, and John Paul Stevens–would have declared the entire policy to be in violation of the Civil Rights Act, which, in their judgement, requires government to observe a standard of colour blindness. On the other hand, Justices William J. Brennan Jr (1906–97)[116], Thurgood Marshall (1908–93), Byron White (1917–2002)[117], and Harry Blackmun

(1908–99)[118] found no statutory or constitutional violation in the minority 'set-aside' policy. According to Justice William Brennan Jr,

> '[g]overnment may take race into account when it acts not to demean or insult any racial group, but to remedy disadvantages cast on minorities by past racial prejudice.'

An equally equivocal endorsement of affirmative action was provided by the Supreme Court in *Fullilove v. Klutznic*.[119] In *Fullilove*, the court upheld a federal public works program that provided a 10 per cent set-aside of federal funds for 'minority business enterprises.' Because this case involved an act of Congress, rather than state action, the set-aside policy was challenged as a violation of the equal protection component of the 5th Amendment 'due process clause'. The Supreme Court upheld the minority set-aside by a vote of 6 to 3. Unfortunately, as in *Bakke*, the court was unable to produce a majority opinion. Chief Justice Warren E. Burger's plurality opinion stressed Congress's broad powers under Section 5 of the 14th Amendment but stopped far short of providing a wholesale endorsement of affirmative action. In a concurring opinion, Justice Brennan echoed the strong pro-affirmative action position he had taken in *Bakke*:

> '[The] principles outlawing the irrelevant or pernicious use of race [are] inapposite to racial classifications that provide benefits to minorities for the purpose of remedying the present effects of past racial discrimination. Such classifications may disadvantage some whites, but whites as a class lack the "traditional indicia of suspectness: the class is not saddled with such disabilities or subjected to such a history of purposeful unequal treatment or relegated to such a position of political powerlessness as to command extraordinary protection from the majoritarian political process."'

Justice Stewart, joined by Justice Rehnquist, cited Justice Harlan's *Plessy* dissent as a barrier to any sort of race preferences, while Justice Stevens's dissenting opinion focused on Congress's failure to demonstrate that remedial preferences were being bestowed on a truly disadvantaged class. The court's failure to produce majority opinions in *Bakke* and *Fullilove* compounded the uncertainties surrounding the myriad affirmative action policies in effect by the early 1980s.[120]

Gender-Based Discrimination

Women are hardly a 'discrete and insular minority'. In fact, they comprise a majority of the adult population. Nevertheless, women have been historically subjected to considerable legal discrimination. Some of this discrimination was ostensibly benign, reflecting the paternalism of a patriarchal society. Not only were women once thought unfit to vote or hold public office, they were also regarded as in need of special protection from a cruel world.

Therefore, some gender-based classifications actually benefited females and burdened males. For example, number of state and also the federal government, for a short period maintained minimum wage requirements for women but not for men. Most graphically, women have traditionally been exempted from compulsory military service.

The Supreme Court for quite some time, refused to recognize even the most blatant forms of sex discrimination as constitutionally offensive. In *Bradwell v. Illnois*[121], the court upheld an Illinois law that prohibited women from practicing law. Similarly, in *Minor v. Happersett*,[122] the court held that women had no constitutional right to vote. In 1948, the court upheld a Michigan law that prohibited women from serving as bartenders. These decisions reflected broader societal attitudes that relegated women, much like African-Americans, to a position of social inferiority and second-class citizenship.

The Second World War (1939–45) did much to change the social status of women. Women in great numbers left the home and entered the industrial workplace, often taking jobs many thought they were incapable of handling. By the 1970s, women had begun to compete with men for managerial and professional positions.

Although, women are still on average paid less than men, even for equal work. American society has come to accept women in the workplace. Society is also learning to accept women in political roles: in Congress, in state legislatures, as mayors, governors, presidential candidates, and as justices of the Supreme Court. Naturally, the changing role of women is accompanied by demands for legal equality.[123]

(i) Congressional Responses to demands for Sexual Equality

The Congress responded to growing demands for legal equality between the sexes by passing the Equal Pay Act of 1963, the 1972 Amendments to Title VII of the Civil Rights Act of 1964, and Title IX of the Federal Education Act of 1972.

The first and second of these statutes were aimed at eliminating sex discrimination in the workplace. The third authorized the withholding of federal funds from educational institutions that engaged in sex discrimination. These statutes have been an important source of civil rights for women and have given rise to a number of significant Supreme Court decisions. For example, in *Meritor Savings Bank v. Vinson*,[124] the court held that Title VII of the Civil Rights Act of 1964, bars sexual harassment on the job.

(ii) The Equal Rights Amendment

The Congress in 1972 attempted to broaden legal protection of women's rights by adopting a constitutional amendment that read as follows:

> Section 1. Equality of rights under the law shall not be denied or abridged by the United States or by any State on account of sex.
>
> Section 2. The Congress shall have the power to enforce, by appropriate legislation, the provisions of this article.
>
> Section 3. This amendment shall take effect two years after the date of ratification.

Like all constitutional amendments, the Equal Rights Amendment (ERA) had to be ratified by at least three-fourths of the states to become part of the Constitution. Initially, the ERA met with much enthusiasm and little controversy in the state legislatures. By 1976, it had been ratified by 35 of the necessary 38 states.

But, in late 1970s, opposition to the ERA crystallized in those states that had yet to ratify. Although Congress extended the period for ratification until 1982, the amendment ultimately failed to win approval by the requisite number of states.

(iii) Judicial Scrutiny of Gender-Based Discrimination

The demise of the Equal Rights Amendment left constitutional interpretation in the field of sex discrimination largely in the domain of the 14th Amendment. In the early 1970s, it appeared that the Supreme Court was going to add sex to the list of 'suspect classifications' under the 14th Amendment. In *Reed v. Reed*[125] the court struck down a provision of the Idaho Probate Code that required probate judges to prefer males to females in appointing administrators of estates. Writing for the majority in *Reed*, Chief Justice Warren E. Burger noted that

> 'to give a mandatory preference to members of either sex over members of the other .... is to make the very kind of arbitrary legislative choice forbidden by the Equal Protection Clause.'

In *Frontiero v. Richardson*,[126] the Supreme Court divided 8 to 1 (Justice Rehnquist dissenting) in upholding Lieutenant Sharron Frontiero's claim that the Air Force violated the equal protection component of the 5th Amendment in requiring women, but not men, to demonstrate that their spouses were in fact dependents for the purpose of receiving medical and dental benefits. While the court was receptive to the equal protection claim, it was unable to achieve majority support for the proposition that sex is a suspect classification. Expressing the views of four members of the court, Justice Brennan's plurality opinion was unequivocal in declaring gender-based discrimination to be inherently suspect and thus presumptively unconstitutional.

[S]ince sex, like race and national origin, is an immutable characteristic determined solely by the accident of birth, the imposition of special disabilities upon the member of a particular sex because of their sex would seem to violate 'the basic concept of our system that legal burdens should bear some relationship to individual responsibility'.

The remaining four members of the majority were not prepared to go so far. In an opinion concurring in the judgement only, Justice Powell wrote that

> '[i]t is unnecessary for the court in this case to characterize sex as a suspect classification, with all of the far-reaching implications of such a holding.'

(iv) Heightened Scrutiny

The Supreme Court still has not recognized sex discrimination as inherently suspect. It should be noted, however, that some state courts have applied strict scrutiny analysis to gender-based classifications (see, for example, the California Supreme Court's decision in *Hardy v. Stumpf*).[127] While it has not adopted strict scrutiny for gender discrimination cases, the US Supreme Court has invalidated a number of gender-based policies under a 'heightened scrutiny' of 'intermediate scrutiny' approach. For example, in *Weinberger v. Wiesenfeld*,[128] the court unanimously voided a provision of the Social Scrutiny Act that authorized survivors' benefits for the widows of deceased workers but withheld them for men in the same situation.

Similarly, in *Califano v. Goldfarb*,[129] a sharply divided court struck down another Social Security requirement that widowers, but not widows, had to demonstrate their financial dependence on their deceased spouses as a condition for obtaining survivors' benefits.

In *Craig v. Boren*[130], the court articulated a test for judging gender-based policies under the intermediate standard of review. According to this test, a gender-based policy must be substantially related to an important government objective. Presumably, this test is stricter than the rational basis test but less strict than the compelling state interest test.

In *Craig v. Boren*, the court struck down an Oklahoma law that forbade the sale of '3.2' beer to females under the age of 18 and males under 21. Oklahoma attempted to justify the statute as a means of promoting its interest in traffic safety, citing data that were purported to show that men in the 18–21 age brackets were more likely to be arrested for drunk driving than were women in the same age bracket. Unconvinced by the statistical evidence, the court held that the state had failed to demonstrate a substantial relationship between its sexually discriminatory policy and its admittedly important interest in traffic safety. In a sharp dissent, Justice William Rehnquist challenged the new intermediate standard of equal protection review. In Rehnquist's view the terms 'important objective' and 'substantial relation' were so 'elastic as to invite subjective judicial preferences or prejudices.' Despite this criticism, the court has maintained the intermediate standard of review for gender-based policies.

In *Orr v. Orr*,[131] the court considered the question of differential alimony requirements for men and women. The Alabama law in question required divorced men, under certain circumstances, to make alimony payments to their ex-wives, but exempted women in the same circumstances from paying alimony to their ex-husbands. The state deceitfully, argued that its gender-based alimony policy was designed to compensate women for economic discrimination produced by the institution of marriage. The court accepted the state's asserted interest as both legitimate and important but rejected the argument that its alimony policy was substantially related to the achievement of this objective. Writing for the court, Justice Brennan asserted that

> 'Alabama's alleged compensatory purpose may be effectuated without placing burdens solely on husbands. Progress toward fulfillment of such a purpose would not be hampered, and it would cost the state nothing more, if it were to treat men and women equally by making alimony burdens independent of sex .... Thus, "[t]he [wives] who benefit from the disparate treatment are those who were .... non-dependent on their husbands ...." They are precisely those who are not "needy spouses" and who are the "least likely to have been victims of discrimination" by the institution of marriage.'

These cases are not meant to suggest that the Supreme Court's sex-discrimination decisions have uniformly cut in one direction. On the contrary, the flexible approach to sex discrimination employed by the court has resulted in a number of decisions upholding challenged gender-based policies. For example, in *Kahn v. Shevin*,[132] the court let stand a Florida statute that gave property tax exemptions to widows but not widowers. According to Justice William O. Douglas's (1898–1980)[133] majority opinion, the distinction was

> 'reasonably designed to further the state policy of cushioning the financial impact of spousal loss upon the sex for which that loss imposes a disproportionately heavy burden…The financial difficulties confronting the lone woman in Florida or any other state exceed those facing the man'.

The same year, in *Geduldig v. Aiello*,[134] the court upheld a state health insurance policy that excluded pregnancy from the list of disabilities for which a state employee could be compensated. In approving the policy, the court concluded that:

> it did not discriminate 'against any definable group or class in terms of the aggregate risk protection derived by the group or class from the program. There is no risk from which men are protected and women are not. Likewise, there is no risk from which women are protected and men are not.'

Not surprisingly, several observers took issue with the court's assumption that a state's refusal to extend its disability policy to include pregnancy was gender–neutral.

One of the most controversial issues in the area of sex discrimination is the role that women should play in military service. Opponents of the Equal Rights Amendment argued that adoption of the amendment would result in women being drafted into combat, a prospect that many people still find unacceptable.

In *Rostker v. Goldberg*,[135] the Supreme Court considered the constitutionality of the male-only draft registration law. Emphasizing its traditional deference to Congress in the area of military affairs, the court upheld the challenged policy by a vote of 6 to 3. Writing for the majority, Justice Rehnquist asserted that exclusion of women from the draft

> 'was not an "accidental by-product of a traditional way of thinking about women."'

According to Justice Rehnquist, 'men and women are simply not similarly situated for purposes of a draft or registration for a draft.' No doubt many women and men would challenge Rehnquist's assumption.

Under the intermediate scrutiny approach, it is difficult to say what principles have guided the court's treatment of sex discrimination cases. Perhaps each decision rests on each justice's intuitive sense of whether the challenged discrimination is 'benign' or 'invidious.' As Justice Oliver Wendell Holmes Jr pointed out in his dissent in *Lochner v. New York*,[136] judicial decisions often 'depends on a judgement or intuition subtler than any articulate major premise.' What Holmes was suggesting was that judicial decision making is pre-eminently political behaviour: that any exercise in legal methodology is subordinate to the assertion of judicial values. While this position can be overstated, one cannot examine the history of American constitutional decision making, and deny the essential validity of Holmes's observation.[137]

(v) Sex Discrimination by Educational Institutions

In perhaps the most significant of its sex discrimination decisions, the Burger Court voted 5 to 4 to require the Mississippi University for Women (MUW) to admit a male student to its nursing school (*Mississippi University for Women v. Hogan*).[138]

Joe Hogan, was a registered nurse working in Columbus, where MUW is located. Lacking a bachelor's degree, he applied for admission to the MUW nursing program and was denied solely on account of his sex. Although the school did inform him that he could register on a non-credit basis. Rather than quit his job to enrol in another state institution, Hogan filed suit.

The state of Mississippi argued that operating a school solely for women compensated for sex discrimination in the past. Additionally, the state argued that the presence of men would detract from the performance of female students. Writing for the Supreme Court, Justice Sandra Day O'Connor gave both of the state's arguments short shrift. Justice O'Connor rejected the 'compensation' argument as contrived since the state had made no showing that women had historically lacked opportunities in the field of nursing. Justice O'Connor then pointed out that the state's argument that male students would adversely affect the performance of females was undermined by the university's willingness to accept male students as auditors. In Justice O'Connor's view, the principal effect of the female-only nursing program was to 'perpetuate the stereotyped view of nursing as an exclusively women's job.'

In a strongly worded dissent, Justice Lewis F. Powell Jr[139] asserted that the court's decision adversely affected the opportunities of women by forbidding the,

> 'states from providing women with an opportunity to choose the type of university they prefer.' Powell further suggested that the court's decision 'bows deeply to conformity.'

The *Hogan* decision addressed the question of whether state-operated professional schools could limit enrolment to one sex. It did not address the broader question of whether publicly operated or supported educational institutions generally may constitutionally impose such restrictions.

Only two state-supported institutions of higher education that limited enrolment to members of one sex were military schools: the Citadel in Charleston, South Carolina, and Virginia Military Institute (VMI) in Lexington. In the wake of the *Hogan* decision, young women seeking admission to these institutions sued in the federal court. Ultimately, they prevailed.

In one of the most widely anticipated decisions of the 1990s, *United States v. Virginia*,[140] the Supreme Court struck down VMI's male-only admission policy. In so doing, the court closed the book on a case that had been in litigation for nearly six years. The suit had been brought by the Justice Department, after a complaint was filed by a female high school student who wanted to go to VMI but was barred from doing so by the Institute's prohibition against admitting women.

In a 7 to 1 decision, the Supreme Court, speaking through Justice Ruth Bader Ginsburg, ruled that the state of Virginia had –

> 'fallen far short of establishing the 'exceedingly persuasive justification,' that must be the solid base for any gender-defined classification.'

Although, the court rejected the argument advanced by the Clinton administration that sex discrimination should be subjected to the same 'strict scrutiny' the courts apply to race discrimination, Justice Ginsburg's opinion suggested that the current court has increased the level of scrutiny applied to policies that treat men and women differently. According to Ginsburg, the court should apply a 'sceptical scrutiny' under which government must demonstrate an 'exceedingly persuasive justification' for any gender discrimination. 'The justification must be genuine, not hypothesized or invented *post hoc* in response to litigation,' said Ginsburg. Moreover, it must not rely on 'overbroad generalizations about the different talents, capacities, or preferences of males and females.'

Although, technically applicable only to the VMI case, the decision in *United States v. Virginia* affected the resolution of a similar widely publicized case involving the Citadel in South Carolina. In fact, within days after the VMI decision was announced, the Citadel's governing board voted unanimously to eliminate sex as a criterion for admission, ending a 154-year tradition of admitting only men.

The sweeping character of the court's opinion seemed to imply that it would be extremely difficult for any State to defend any single-sex educational institution. Chief Justice Rehnquist, who concurred in the judgment only, adopted a more restrained position. For Rehnquist, the State had failed in its obligation to provide equal protection because it had not demonstrated any serious effort to provide comparable opportunities to women who were interested in the kind of 'citizen-soldier' training that men receive at VMI. According to Rehnquist,

> it was 'not the 'exclusion of women' that violate[d] the Equal Protection Clause, but the maintenance of an all-men school without providing any-much less a comparable-institution for women.'

Rehnquist's opinion opens the possibility that single-sex public higher education might, under certain circumstances, pass constitutional muster. Of course, Rehnquist's concurrence is just one person's opinion. Six justices representing the court's liberal and moderate blocs clearly wanted to make a stronger and a more definitive statement.

In one other of his scathing dissent, Justice Antonin Scalia asserted that the majority's 'amorphous "exceedingly persuasive justification" phrase' was an unwarranted departure from the 'heightened scrutiny' test used by the court in gender-discrimination cases. Scalia concluded by lamenting the fact that, in his view, 'single-sex public education is functionally dead.' Scalia expressed his regret that the court had, in his view, 'shut down an institution that has served the people of the commonwealth of Virginia with pride and distinction for over a century and a half.' He ended by observing that 'I do not think any of us, women included, will be better off for its destruction.'

Not surprisingly, Justice Scalia's sentiments were shared by students, faculty, and administrators at VMI. Major General Josiah Bunting III, the superintendent of VMI, described the court's decision as a 'savage disappointment.' Of course, women's rights groups hailed the decision as a major victory.[141]

(vi) Gender Equity in Collegiate Athletics

Intercollegiate athletics, once the sole province of men, has witnessed considerable change in recent years. Under the rubric of gender equity, state colleges and universities have been putting more resources into women's athletic programs. Still, there are some who believe that forbidding women to participate in male-only athletic programs at state institutions constitutes invidious discrimination.

- Is the separate but equal doctrine appropriate when considering collegiate athletics?

Suppose a female student wants to play football at a state university. Since the university does not have a women's football program, does the Equal Protection Clause require the university to let the woman try out for the men's team? While some may feel that such issues trivialize the Constitution, these matters tend to be far from trivial in the minds of plaintiffs.[142]

Equality Right in Pakistan and India

Article 25 of 1973 Constitution of Pakistan, provides that–

(1) All citizens are equal before law and are entitled to equal protection of law.
(2) There shall be no discrimination on the basis of sex alone.
(3) Nothing in this Article shall prevent the state from making any special provision for the protection of women and children.

Articles 14 to 18 of the Indian Constitution guarantee the right to equality to every citizen of India. Article 14 embodies the general principles of equality before law and prohibits unreasonable discrimination between persons. Article 14 embodies the idea of equality expressed in the Preamble. The succeeding Article 15, 16, 17 and 18 lay down specific application of the general rules laid down in Article 14. Article 15 relates to prohibition of discrimination on grounds of religion, race, caste, sex or place of birth. Article 16 guarantees equality of opportunity in matters of public employment. Article 17 abolishes 'Untouchability'. Article 18 abolishes title. Article 14 declares that

> 'the state shall not deny to any person equality before the law or the equal protection of the laws within the territory of India.'

Therefore, Article 14 uses two expressions 'equality before the law' and 'equal protection of the law.' The phrase 'equality before the law' finds a place in almost all written constitutions that guarantees fundamental rights. Both these expressions have, however, been used in the Universal Declaration of Human Rights. The first expression 'equality before law' is of English origin and the second expression has been taken from the American Constitution. Both these expressions aim at establishing what is called 'equality of status' as postulated in the Preamble of the Constitution.[143]

Legislative Classification

Sir Ivor Jennings in his book *The Law and the Constitution* states 'equality before law', which means that amongst equals the law should be equal and should be equally administered and that like should be treated alike. Hence, what it forbids, is discrimination between persons who are substantially in similar circumstances or conditions. It does not forbid different treatment of un-equals. The rule rather is that like should be treated alike and that unlike should be treated differently.

The Indian Supreme Court in *All India Sainik Schools Employees Association v. Sainik Schools Society*,[144] said,

> equal treatment of un-equals is as bad as unequal treatment of equals. All persons are not alike or equal in all respects. Application of the same laws uniformly to all of them will therefore to be inconsistent with the principle of equality.

To eliminate this situation, laws must distinguish between those who are equals and to whom they must apply and those who are different and to whom they should not apply. This leads to classifications between persons made by laws. Persons may be classified into groups and such groups may differently be treated if there is a reasonable basis for such difference.

The 'equality clause' does not prohibit legislation which is limited either in the objects to which it is directed or by the territory within which it is to operate. The rule of differentiation is that in enacting laws differentiating between different persons or things in different circumstances which govern one set of persons or objects such laws may not necessarily be the same as those governing another set of persons, or objects so that the question of unequal treatment does not really arise between persons governed by different conditions and different set of circumstances.

The principle of equality does not mean that every law must have universal application for all persons who are not by nature, attainment or circumstances in the same position. The varying needs of different classes of persons require different treatment. The Indian Supreme Court in *Kedar Nath Bajoria* v. *West Bengal*,[145] has observed that –

> 'the equal protection of the laws guaranteed by Article 14 of the Constitution does not mean that all the laws must be general in character and universal in application and that the State is no longer to have the power of distinguishing and classifying persons or things for the purposes of legislation.'

A classification to be valid must be reasonable. It must always rest upon some real and substantial distinction bearing reasonable and just relation to the needs in respect of which the classification is made. In order to pass the test of permissible classification two conditions must be fulfilled, namely:

(1) the classification must be founded on an intelligible differentia which distinguishes persons or things that are grouped together from others left out of the group, and
(2) the differentia must have a rational relation to the object sought to be achieved by the statute in question.

This test was laid down by Justice Sudhi Ranjan Das (1894–1977)[146] of the Indian Supreme Court in *State of West Bengal v. Anwar Ali Sarkar*,[147] and has been repeated in all subsequent cases of the Indian jurisdiction. The test has also been adopted by the Supreme Court of Pakistan in a number of cases, for example in *I.A. Sharawani v. Government of Pakistan*,[148] *Mohabat Khan v. Road Transport Board*,[149] and *Government of Balochistan v. Azizullah Memon*,[150]

The Supreme Court of India in *Re Special Courts Bill*,[151] has re-stated the following principles relating to permissible classification:

(a) A law may be constitutional even though it relates to a single individual if, on account of some special circumstances, or reasons applicable to him and not applicable to others, that single individual may be treated as a class by himself.
(b) There is always a presumption in favour of the constitutionality of an enactment and the burden is upon him who attacks it to show that there has been a clear transgression of the constitutional principles. The person, therefore, who pleads that the Article has been violated, must make out that not only has he been treated differently from others but he has been so treated from persons similarly circumstanced without any reasonable basis and such differential treatment has been unjustifiably made.

(c) It must be presumed that the legislature understands and correctly appreciates the needs of its own people, that its laws are directed to problems made manifest by experience, and that its discriminations are based on adequate grounds.
(d) The legislature is free to recognize the degrees of harm and may confine its restriction to those cases where the need is deemed to be the clearest.
(e) In order to sustain the presumption of constitutionality, the court may take into consideration matters of common knowledge, matters of common report, the history of the times and may assume every state of facts which can be conceived existing at the time of legislation.
(f) While good faith and knowledge of the existing conditions on the part of the legislature are to be presumed, if there is nothing on the face of the law or the surrounding circumstances brought to the notice of the court on which the classification may reasonably be regarded as based, the presumption of the constitutionality cannot be carried to the extent of always holding that there must be some undisclosed and unknown reasons for subjecting certain individuals or corporations to hostile or discriminating legislation.
(g) A classification need not be scientifically perfect or logically complete.
(h) The validity of a rule has to be judged by assessing its overall effect and not by picking up exceptional cases. What the court has to see is whether the classification made is just taking all aspects into consideration.
(i) The court must look beyond the ostensible classification and to the purpose of the law and apply the test of 'palpable arbitrariness' in the context of the needs of the times and social exigencies informed by experience to determine reasonableness of classification.

Legislation Affecting Individuals

The Supreme Court of India, in a number of cases has decided that a law affecting single persons or specified individuals may be constitutional and valid. In *Chiranjit v. India*,[152] the validity of the Sholpur Spinning and Weaving Company (Emergency Provisions) Act 1950, was challenged on the ground that it infringed the rule of equal protection of the laws because single company and the shareholders, thereof, were being subjected to disabilities *vis-à-vis* other companies and the shareholders thereof.

The Indian Supreme Court dismissed the petition and held the legislation valid. It laid down that:

> a law may be constitutional even though it applies to a single individual if, on account of some special circumstances or reasons applicable to him and not applicable to others, that single individual may be treated as a class by himself and that unless it was shown that there were other companies similarly circumstanced, the legislation must be presumed to be constitutional.

The Sholapur Company formed a class by itself because the mismanagement of the Company's affairs prejudicially affected the production of an essential commodity and had caused serious unemployment amongst a section of the community.

In two subsequent cases, namely, *Ameerunnisa Begum v. Mehboob Begum*[153] and *Ram Prasad v. State of Bihar*,[154] Indian Supreme Court again had to decide the validity of the legislation affecting specified individuals.

The facts in *Ameerunnisa* were that a dispute between two rival parties regarding succession to the estate of the deceased Nawab of Hyderabad had been going on since 1938, and after several vicissitudes for which the Nizam himself or his legal advisers were primarily responsible, a report was prepared by the legal advisers to the state in a particular way which, contrary to the opinion given by an earlier special commission, negatived the claim of one party, namely, two ladies and their children. To give effect to the report, the Nizam, who at that time exercised the powers of the Hyderabad legislature, passed an Act, the *Wali-ud-Dowla* Act 1950.

By this Act the claim of the two ladies was dismissed and the property adjudged to the other party. Obviously, the effect of the Act was that the two ladies and their children were deprived of the right to enforce their claim in a court of law in accordance with the Muslim law. They, in fact, were discriminated against the rest of the community in respect of a valuable right which the law secures to all, namely, the right of free access to the court. The discrimination made against the two ladies could only be valid if there were some reasonable grounds for the differentiation made by the law. Two reasons were put in justification of the classification or differentiation made by the Act. First, that there was an adverse report against them by the state legal advisers and, second, that the dispute was of a long standing. The Supreme Court held that –

> neither of these grounds could serve as a reasonable basis of the differentiation made by the law. As regards the first, the dispute regarding succession to the estate of the Nawab was a legal dispute, pure and simple, and without determination of the points in issue by a properly constituted Tribunal of law, a legislation based upon the reports of a non-judicial authority and made applicable to specific individuals, who were deprived thereby of valuable rights, which were enjoyed by all other persons occupying the same position as themselves, did plainly come within the constitutional inhibition of Article 14. If the legislature makes the report of the legal adviser as the ground on which it deprives one specific person of his rights to have his say in a court of law that would be arbitrary and unreasonable.

The second ground put in support of the classification was also rejected. The court pointed out that

> the continuance of a dispute even for a long period of time between two sets of rival claimants to the property of a private person is not a circumstance of such an unusual nature as would invest a case with special or exceptional features and make it a class by itself justifying its differentiation from all other cases of succession dispute. Thus, there was nothing to distinguish the dispute between the parties under the *Wali-ud-Dowla* Act which is not found in any other dispute between private parties.

The Attorney-General who appeared in support of the Hyderabad legislation, also argued the case on the ground of presumption laid down in *Chiranjit Lal* case. He contended that the presumption is always in favour of constitutionality of an enactment and unless the person who attacks it clearly proves that the law is discriminatory (the burden of which is cast upon him), the court must not disturb the classification made by the legislature which, presumably understands the needs of its own people. The court explained that

> the presumption laid down in *Chiranjit Lal* case is not absolute in its application but would depend upon the facts and circumstances of the case.

In *Chiranjit Lal* case the majority justified their decision because the action of one company had affected the production of an essential commodity and caused serious unemployment amongst labourers. Where the legislation affects the interest of the community as a whole, the court will assume the existence of any state of facts which can reasonably be conceived of as existing at the date of legislation and capable of sustaining the classification made by it. The Act in this case professedly concerned a private dispute and no interest of the community was involved.

In *Ram Prasad v. Bihar,*[155] the two appellants in 1946 had obtained a settlement of two hundred *bighas* of land from the Bettiah Estate in Bihar. For some reasons there was an agitation amongst the tenants of the locality against the leasehold by the appellants, the matter was brought to the notice of the Congress Working Committee and in its view the settlement was illegal and against public interest. The lessees, therefore, were asked to vacate the land which they refused, and thereupon the Bihar State Legislature passed the impugned Act, the Bihar Sathi Lands (Restoration) Act 1950.

The Act terminated the contract of lease and directed the lessees to quit the land immediately. The lessees (appellants) contended that the Act was unconstitutional because it denied to them the equal protection of laws. The Indian Supreme Court accepted the appellants' contention and held the act *ultra vires* the Bihar Legislature because it appeared that there were numerous persons occupying the same position as the appellants, who were not subjected to the impugned ex-proprietary legislation. Further, the dispute being between private parties, it was a matter for determination by duly constituted courts in accordance with the normal procedure. But what the legislature had done was to single out the two individuals and denied them the right which every Indian citizen possesses to have his rights adjudicated in accordance with the laws which applied to his case.

The reasons given for the extraordinary procedure were indeed remarkable for 'their disturbing implications'. It was said that the agitation amongst the tenantry of the locality, and opposition on the part of persons living in the locality against the appellants' possession of the land had led to breach of the peace and institution of criminal cases. This could not be a rational basis to discriminate against the two named individuals. When on the face of a statute there is no classification at all, and no attempt has been made to select any individual or group with reference to any differentiating attribute peculiar to that individual or group and not possessed by others, this presumption is of little or no assistance.

Singling out was found unconstitutional by the Indian Supreme Court in *Vice Chancellor Osmania University v. Chancellor*[156] when it was done for the purpose of hostile discrimination. However, in *S.P. Mittal v. Union of India*[157] relying on its earlier rulings the Supreme Court upheld the provisions of the Auroville (Emergency Provisions) Act 1980, which provided for the taking over of the management of Auroville in Pondicherry for a limited period. Similarly in *L.N. Mishra Institute of E.D. & Social Change v. State of Bihar*[158] the court upheld a Bihar legislation which provided for phased nationalization of private educational institutions, but, initially mentioned only one institution for such nationalization.

Ex Facie And Not *Ex Facie* Discriminatory Laws

Actual proof of discrimination is not required to be given when the *vires* of the *ex facie* discriminatory provision of an Act is challenged. Where, however, the provision is not *ex facie* discriminatory but is capable of being administered in discriminatory manner, than the party challenging it has to show that it has actually been administered in a partial, unjust and oppressive manner.

A legislation, may immediately on its commencement, take away or abridge the fundamental rights of a person by its very terms and without any further overt act being done. In such a case the infringement of the fundamental rights is complete *coinstanti*, the passing of the legislation and, therefore, there can be no reason why the person so prejudicially affected by the law should not be entitled immediately to avail himself of the constitutional remedy.

The infractions alleged cannot be regarded as seeking a declaration in the air or asking the court to decide in abstract and for that matter hypothetical or contingent question. In *Benazir Bhutto v. Federation of Pakistan*,[159] by a constitutional petition filed under Article 184(3) of the 1973 Constitution of Pakistan, the petitioner, a Co-chairperson of the Pakistan Peoples' Party sought to challenge the amendments made in the Political Parties Act 1962, as violative of Articles 17 and 25 of the Constitution. The *vires* of the Freedom of Association Order 1978 (President's Order No. 20 of 1978) was also challenged as being unconstitutional. The Supreme Court of Pakistan accepted the petition and declared a number of the provisions of the Political Parties Act 1962, as void and of no legal effect.

Where a statute is not *ex facie* discriminatory but is capable of being administered in a discriminatory manner, it must be shown that it has actually been administered to the detriment of a particular class and in partial, unjust and oppressive manner.

Equal protection of the laws means that no person or class of persons shall be denied the same protection of the laws which is enjoyed by other persons or other classes in like circumstances, in their lives, liberty and property and in pursuit of happiness. Another generalization more frequently stated is that the guarantee of equal protection of the laws requires that all persons shall be treated alike, under like circumstances and conditions, both in the privileges conferred and, in the liabilities, imposed.

In the application of these principles, however, it has always been recognized that classification of persons or things is in no way repugnant to the equality doctrine provided the classification is not arbitrary or capricious, is natural and reasonable and bears a fair and substantial relation to the object of the legislation. In *Jibendra Kishore v. Province of East Pakistan*,[160] the East Bengal State Acquisition and Tenancy Act 1950, was passed by the Provincial Assembly of East Bengal to provide for acquisition by the state of the interests of rent receivers in East Bengal. The Section 3(1) the Act enabled the provincial government to acquire by notification in the official Gazette all interests of such of the rent receivers as were specified in that notification. Section 3(2) empowered the government, also to acquire in a similar manner all or any of the lands in the *khas* possession of such rent receivers. The rent receiver thus expropriated were declared by section 37 of the Act entitled to receive compensation on their net incomes on a sliding scale, that is to say, the rate of compensation decreasing as the income increased.

The provincial government by several notifications acquired the interests of certain rent receivers and the lands in their *khas* possession before the Constitution of 1956 came into force. On 2 April 1956, that government issued further notifications, district wise, purporting to acquire the interests of the remaining rent receivers under Section 3(1) and the lands in their *khas* possession under section 3(2) of the Act, with effect from 14 April 1956. On the

13 of April 1956 eighty-three petitions for writs of *mandamus* or in the nature of *mandamus* was moved in the High Court of Dacca against the provincial government directing them to withdraw or rescind the notifications.

The principal attack on the notifications was on the strength of Article 5 of the Constitution which provides that

> 'All citizens are equal before law and are entitled to equal protection of law'.

Furthermore, in the case of *wakf* and debutter property reliance was placed on that of Article 18, which declared that subject to law, public order and morality,

(a) every citizen has the right to profess, practice and propagate any religion; and
(b) every religious denomination and every sect thereof has the right to establish, maintain and manage its religious institutions.

The petitioners argued that Section 3 of the Act, which enabled the government to pick and choose rent receivers whose interests were to be acquired conferred on that government, a naked arbitrary power which being capable of being used in a discriminatory manner was void by reason of Article 5, which guaranteed equal protection of law, and that since in the matter of compensation under Section 37 of the Act drew a distinction between income earning groups of rent receivers, the provision was *ex facie* discriminatory and therefore void.

In the case of acquisition of *wakf* and debutter properties the contention raised was that since the effect of the Act was to transfer the ownership of such properties to the provincial government and to dispossess the *mutawallis* (the administrators of religious foundations) and *shebait* of possession, the Act adversely affected religious institutions and consequently trenched upon the right guaranteed by Article 18 of the Constitution. The full Bench of the Dacca High Court repelled all the constitutional objections to the notifications.

In case of acquisition of lands in the *khas* possession of managers of *waqf* and debutter properties, however, rules *nisi* issued earlier were made absolute on the ground that the notifications contravened the provisions of Section 20 of the Act.[161] The rent receivers, thereupon, appealed to the Pakistan Supreme Court and contended that Sections 3 and 37 of the Act were void, the former because it conferred upon the provincial government an arbitrary power to pick for expropriation any rent receiver that it liked, and could thus, lead to discrimination between one rent receiver and another, and the latter because it provided different rates of compensation for rent receivers with different amounts of net income.

The objection to the acquisition of *waqf* and debutter estates was founded on Article 18 of the Constitution further on the ground that a *mutawalli* or a *shebait* was not a proprietor, and therefore, not a 'rent receiver' as defined in the Act. The Supreme Court dismissed all the appeals except 8 holding that Sections 3 and 37 of the Act, did not offend against Article 5, and/or so far as *waqf* or debutter estates were concerned it was held that they were not against Article 18 of the Constitution, and were, therefore, not void or inoperative.

The eight petitions made a challenge to the Act on the basis of Article 18 and succeeded. It was further held that where a statute is not *ex facie* discriminatory but is capable of being administered in a discriminatory manner, the party challenging its constitutionality has to show that it has actually been administered to his determent or in a partial, unjust and oppressive manner. Equality is not violated by the mere conferment of unguided power, but only by its arbitrary exercise by that authority upon whom it is conferred.

In *East and West Steamship Co v. Pakistan*,[162] the Pakistan Supreme Court held that the Control of Shipping Act 1947, proceeds on a definite policy and is not *ex facie* bad either on the ground of excessive delegation of legislative authority or on the ground that the Shipping Authority, if it were so minded, could administer it in a discriminatory manner.

The Supreme Court further held that the carriage of goods for purposes of commerce is essentially a trade activity which may be permitted only under a licence. Prohibition of a trade by licencing system, if its effect be such, is not prohibited by Article 12 of the 1956 Constitution, under which power to regulate means the power to limit, control and restraint and to foster and protect.

In 1956, the petitioner–Company filed a writ petition under Article 22 of the Constitution, in Pakistan Supreme Court praying for the issuance of writs of *mandamus* and prohibition against the Government of Pakistan, the Shipping Authority functioning under the Control of Shipping Act 1947, and the District Magistrate of Karachi;

on the ground that certain prosecutions under the Control of Shipping Act launched by the Shipping Authority against the petitioners were in contravention of fundamental rights.

The Company owned six ships which had been operating under the licensing system introduced by the Control of Shipping Act 1947. Four ships were alleged to have rendered themselves liable to prosecution under Section 8 of the Act by engaging in unauthorized voyages. Each of these ships sailed from a home port under a valid licence granted by the Shipping Authority under Section 3 of the Act, but on reaching its destination, it was alleged to have sailed for a foreign port either under a charter–party with foreigners or otherwise without a licence and was further alleged to have contravened certain directions or orders given by Authority and two of them were stated not to have returned the licences as required by law on completion of their licensed voyages.

The Shipping Authority, therefore, instituted a separate complaint against the petitioners in respect of each of these ships under Section 8 of the Act, which was pending for trial in the Court of the District Magistrate, Karachi. The petition was presented against this action of the Shipping Authority on the allegation that the provisions of the law under which action had been taken against the petitioners were *ultra vires* because they impinged upon the fundamental rights guaranteed by Articles 5, 11, 12, and 15 of the 1956 Constitution, namely, Equality of Law (Article 5); Freedom of movement (Article 11); Freedom of trade, business or profession (Article 12); and Protection of Property Rights (Article 15). The Supreme Court did not find any provisions of the Control of Shipping Act 1947, violative of any of these fundamental rights and therefore dismissed the petition.[163]

A law that prescribes three different punishing authorities each with different power and procedure and entailing punishments of unequal nature and description without any discernible principle guiding the choice of forum is *ex facie* discriminatory infringing the 'equality before law' and 'equal protection of law' clauses.

Conferment of power on the Central Government or the State Bank of Pakistan to determine whether an offender was to be tried under the ordinary law or by an Adjudication Officer or by a tribunal/court was not invalid on the ground of excessive delegation of legislative authority. It was so held in *Waris Meah v. The State*,[164] therefore, the appellants exported fish to India but did not, as required by law, repatriate the sale proceeds to Pakistan through an authorized dealer and thus committed an offence under Section 22-A of the Foreign Exchange Regulation Act 1947.

The appellants pleaded guilty and were convicted by the tribunal/court constituted under Section 23-B of the Regulation Act. Their appeals having been dismissed by the High Court, they were granted leave to appeal by the Pakistan Supreme Court, to consider the question raised before the Supreme Court for the first time that Section 23-B of the Foreign Exchange Regulation Act 1947 was unconstitutional inasmuch as it offended against Article 5 of the 1956 Constitution; which makes all citizens equal before the law and declares them to be entitled to equal protection of the laws.

Section 23 of the Foreign Exchange Regulation 1947; provided that the offences created by the Act should be tried by a Court of Sessions, a Presidency Magistrate or a Magistrate of the 1st or 2nd Class, in accordance with the procedure laid down by the Code of Criminal Procedure, Section 23-A provided the trial by an Adjudication Officer and Section 23-B provided the trial by a tribunal/court.

The Pakistan Supreme Court allowed the appeals and set aside their convictions and sentences on the ground that the appellants were tried by an incompetent tribunal/courts because the Foreign Exchange Regulation Act, 1947 being *ex facie* discriminatory.

Special Mode of Trial

In Criminal trials, the person accused, under the general law have the following important rights:

(1) the right to know before the trial the charge and the evidence against him;
(2) the right to cross-examine the prosecution witnesses;
(3) the right to certain presumptions and defences;
(4) the right to produce evidence in defence;
(5) the right to appeal or to apply for revision;
(6) the right to be represented by counsel;
(7) the right to have the case decided by the judge who heard the evidence; and
(8) the right to apply for transfer of the case to another court.

A law may bring about a substantial change in procedure and as against the general law such change would *prima facie* be violative of the guarantee of equal protection of the laws unless it can be brought within the rule of permissible classification.

A law conferring unfettered power on the executive to administer criminal justice in a part of the country is discriminatory because in other areas of the country criminal justice is administered by courts. The mere existence of a tribal society or a tribal culture in that part of the country cannot be considered a rational basis for classification.

In *Government of Balochistan v. Azizullah Memon,*[165] such mode of criminal trial was held violative of 'equality clause'. The facts of this case were that in Balochistan, Frontier Crimes Regulation 1901 (FCR), was promulgated to try Pathans and Balochis by the council of elders headed by the executive officer in whom vested the power to give the final judgement.

The regulation laid down a special procedure for a criminal trial and was different from the trials under the ordinary law of the land. The applicability of the law of evidence and criminal procedure was specifically excluded. The High Court struck down the discriminatory provisions of the regulation as violative of 'equality clause' in *Toti Khan v. District Magistrate Sibi and Ziarat,*[166] and *Khan Abdul Ghaffar Khan v. Deputy Commissioner Peshawar.*[167]

The Frontier Crimes Regulation (FCR) was replaced by the West Pakistan Criminal Law (Amendment) Act 1963, which was also declared *ultra vires*, the 'equality clause' in *Muhammad Usman v. The State.*[168] Then came the Quetta and Kalat (Civil and Criminal law) Ordinance 1965, which was extended in the first instance to the divisions of Quetta and Kalat and areas specified in its first Schedule.

The provisions of this Ordinance regarding trial of offences were almost the same as those of its predecessors. This Ordinance remained in operation till its replacement by the Civil Procedure (Special Provisions) Ordinance 1968; and the Criminal Law (Special Provisions) Ordinance 1968. The former Ordinance relating to civil disputes was repealed and civil disputes in Balochistan came to be adjudicated upon by the courts established under the ordinary law.

The constitutionality of the Criminal law (Special Provisions) Ordinance 1968, which is in reality the reproduction of its predecessors with somewhat legislative ornamentation, was challenged before the Balochistan High Court in a number of constitutional petitions which were accepted by a detailed judgement passed on 2 August 1990.

The Government of Balochistan preferred an appeal which was dismissed by the Supreme Court declaring the Ordinance as violative of Article 9 (Security of Persons), Article 25 (Equality before Law), Article 175 (separation of judiciary from executive) and Article 203 (superintendence of subordinate courts by High Court); and directing the Government of Balochistan to amend the Ordinance in order to bring it in conformity with these constitutional provisions within a period of 6 months and to appoint Judicial Magistrates for trial of offences under the Ordinance.

The provisions of an Act designed to subject to a particular class of persons, who had illegally kept foreign exchange outside the country and were compelled to repatriate such foreign exchange under threat of punishment, to a special procedure before a special tribunal/court, so that if any other person was deprived of such money, he may establish his claim to the foreign exchange kept abroad before such a special tribunal/court, are violative of 'equality before Law' and 'equal protection of law' clauses.

In *Inamur Rehman v. Federation of Pakistan,*[169] the appellant declared and repatriated two sums of foreign exchange under the Foreign Exchange Repatriation 1972 (MLR 104). The State Bank of Pakistan acting under the Foreign Exchange (Prevention of Payments) Act 1972, subsequently amended by the Foreign exchange (Prevention of Payments) (Amendments) Act 1974, directed the concerned Banks, where the repatriated sums of money were deposited, to deposit with the State Bank of Pakistan, the rupees equivalent of the repatriated amount.

The banks accordingly deposited the amount in the State Bank of Pakistan. The appellant challenged the direction of the State Bank by filing a writ petition in the High Court of Sindh, which was dismissed by a Division Bench of that court. The appellant preferred an appeal by special leave in the Supreme Court contending that the proceedings pending under the Act were liable to be declared without lawful authority. In that—

(i) Since restoration of fundamental rights on 31 December 1985, the Act became void in terms of Article 8 of the Constitution, being discriminatory and arbitrary. In other words, the Act was violative of Article 25 of the Constitution guaranteeing 'equality before the law' and 'equal protection of law' to citizens of Pakistan.

(ii) Since the lifting of Emergency on 31 December 1985, and the expiry of six months thereafter, i.e., on 30 June 1986; the Act ceased to have effect in terms of clause (6) of Article 234 of the Constitution, because the Act was an inroad by the Parliament into the provincial field of legislation.

It was further contended by the appellant that the appointment of authorized officer under Section 2(3) of the Act for disposal of applications of claims filed against the appellant was violative of equality clause. The Federation of Pakistan submitted that the fundamental rights remained suspended till 31 December 1985, that is, till the filing of the petition for leave to appeal in the Supreme Court, therefore, the question of violation of fundamental rights could not be agitated in the Supreme Court. The Supreme Court allowed the appeal of the appellant holding that:

(i) Acts done and completed before the coming into existence of the fundamental rights cannot be reopened on the ground of inconsistency, nor can proceedings already commenced be stopped. But the position would be different if the right was still subsisting and capable of being enforced or there was something still left to be done to complete the extinction of the right after the conferment of the fundamental rights. Thus, if a person is detained under a law before the coming into existence of the fundamental rights, he would be entitled to challenge the detention order, if his detention continues after the coming into force of the fundamental rights on the ground that the law under which his detention was ordered is inconsistent with the security of person guaranteed to him. Where rights are still capable of being in force and there is something still left to be done under the impugned legislation after the restoration of fundamental rights, the court is bound to give effect to such fundamental rights. *Abul A'laMaudoodi v. Government of West Pakistan*,[170] was relied upon.

(ii) The following propositions sum up the content of classification under 'equality before law':
   (1) The State can make a reasonable classification.
   (2) The classification, in order to be reasonable, must satisfy two tests:
      a) Classification must be founded on intelligible differentia.
      b) Differentia must have rational nexus with the object sought to be achieved by the legislation.
   (3) The object must be lawful and must not be discriminatory.
   (4) The object is discriminatory when there is a choice for selecting the person to whom the law may apply.

(iii) The mere fact that a person has repatriated certain foreign exchange under the Martial Law Regulation, he cannot be put into a separate class, and any claim, which would have gone to ordinary court of law with all the advantages of the procedure applicable to the trial of suits, cannot be treated differently by applying special procedure by a non-judicial Tribunal presided over by a *persona designata*. There is no rational basis for such a classification and the classification does not rest on any intelligible differentia, as there is no indication whatsoever that such claim has any nexus with the foreign exchange repatriated.

(iv) Not only the impugned provisions are *per se* arbitrary and discriminatory but have also been put into operation in a discriminatory manner.

(v) Equal protection to all is the basis principle on which rests justice under the law.

(vi) The provisions of Sections 2, 6 and 6-A of the Act being violative of Article 25 of the 1973

(vii) If a classification made by an impugned law can reasonably be conceived and sustained, the burden of showing that it does not rest upon any reasonable basis lies upon one who assails the classification.[171]

'Equality before law' and 'equal protection of law' means that no person or class of persons shall be denied the same protection of laws which is enjoyed by other persons or class of persons in like circumstances in respect of their life, liberty, property or pursuits of happiness.

However, reasonable classification may be made by law resting it on a real or substantial difference or distinction. Therefore, a category of civilians who seduce the personnel of Armed Forces from allegiance to the government may be selected by law to be tried along with the armed personnel under the Army Act.

In *Brig. (Retd.) F.B. Ali and another v. The State*,[172] two appellants, who had retired from the Army, were charged by the court martial to be tried along with a number of other army officers

(i) for having committed the offence of conspiracy to wage war against Pakistan under Section 121-A of the Pakistan Penal Code; in that they together, between the period of August 1972 and 30 March 1973, at Rawalpindi, Jhelum, Lahore and elsewhere, formed a plot to overthrow the government established by law in Pakistan. By conspiring to put under arrest with the help of troops at their disposal, the President, the Governor of Punjab, the Ministers, all the Generals assembled in a conference and other officials holding key position in the administration. And thereby to assume power in the country for themselves, by means of criminal force.

(ii) for attempting to seduce members of the Armed Forces of Pakistan from their allegiance to the Government of Pakistan, in order to enlist their support for furthering the design of conspiracy.

They objected to the jurisdiction of the court martial exercisable under the Pakistan Army Act 1952; on the ground that they were no longer subject to the Pakistan Army Act. Therefore, they could not be tried by a General Court Martial. The objection was overruled and consequently they filed a writ petition in the Lahore High Court. During the pendency of the writ petition, the appellants contested their prosecution before the court martial which ultimately resulted in their convictions on both the charges. They were awarded a single sentence of transportation for life as required by Rule 54 of the Rules framed under the Army Act.

The writ petition was accordingly amended. It was argued before the High Court that the Pakistan Army Act applied only to persons who are subject to the discipline of the Pakistan Army and that the inclusion of the categories of persons to whom the Pakistan Army Act was sought to be made applicable by the two Ordinances promulgated in 1967, was of no effect. As the Ordinances themselves were, firstly, *ultra vires* the powers of the President under the 1962 Constitution. Secondly, in any event, were discriminatory and violative of the Fundamental Right No. 15 of the 1962 Constitution, relating to equality of citizens before law.

Hence, their arguments were *ab initio* void and of no legal effect by reason of the provisions of Article 6 of the Constitution. It was further argued that the Order made by the President under Article 233, Clause (2) of the 1973 Constitution, suspending the enforcement of fundamental rights has also ceased to have any validity. Since, the state of emergency continued by Article 280 of the 1973 Constitution, had itself come to an end on the 14 February 1974. The joint resolution of the two Houses, passed on the 5 March 1974, purporting to extend the emergency was, therefore, an exercise in futility.

The High Court dismissed the writ petition *in limine* holding that the Ordinances of 1967 were competently made by the President, as the subject was expressly covered by items 1, 48 and 49 of the Third Schedule to the Constitution of 1962. The contention that the Ordinances were violative of Fundamental Right No. 15 of the 1962 Constitution, pertaining to the equality of citizens before the law, was also repelled on the ground that a challenge of a law on account of its being in conflict with a fundamental right was in reality an attempt to enforce a fundamental right, which could not be done during the subsistence of a proclamation of emergency.

The contention that the joint resolution of both Houses of the Legislature, passed on 5 March 1974, was an exercise in futility as the proclamation of emergency had already expired on the 14 February 1974, was held by the High Court to be fallacious, because upon a true construction of Article 232, Clause (7)(b), the calculation was to be made after excluding the period of two months during which the proclamation was to last. The appeal preferred by the appellants against the judgment of the High Court was unanimously dismissed by the Supreme Court.

Discrimination Amongst Pensioners

A pensionary benefit granted to pensioners who retire from service after a particular date cannot be declined to those pensioners who retire before that date. In *I. A. Sharwani v. Govt. of Pakistan*,[173] the four appellants retired civil servants and judges, who were pensioners of the government, moved direct petitions under Article 184(3) of the 1973 Constitution; in Pakistan Supreme Court contending that they were discriminated in payment of enhanced pension in violation of Article 25 of the Constitution, inasmuch as certain increases in the pension have been denied to them on the ground that they had retired prior to a specified date.

The Government of Pakistan contended that no discriminatory treatment had been meted out to the petitioners and they were being paid pensions according to the rules applicable to them. The Supreme Court held that a pension is a periodical allowance of money granted by the government in consideration or recognition of meritorious past services, or of loss or injury sustained in the public service.

The right to a pension depends upon statutory provisions and therefore, the existence of such right is determinable primarily from the terms of the statute under which the right or privilege is granted. The pension is earned by rendering long and efficient service and therefore can be said to be a deferred portion of the compensation for services rendered.

The most practical *raison d'etre* for pension is the inability to provide for oneself, due to old age. Pension like salary of a civil servant is no longer a bounty but is a right acquired after putting in satisfactory service for the prescribed minimum period. *A fortiori*, it cannot be reduced or refused arbitrarily except to the extent and in the manner provided by the relevant rules. The Supreme Court held:

(i) It will be a reasonable classification if all the pensioners as a group are to be treated as one class and all serving civil servants as a group as a separate class. If the pay scales of serving civil servants are raised, the civil servants, who have by then already retired cannot have any legitimate grievance to agitate for national revision of their pay scales for re-computing their pension amounts, and here cannot be any uniformity in the amounts of pension among the civil servants despite the fact that they have equal rank and equal length of service, if they retire not on one date but on different dates and in between such dates pay scales have been revised.

(ii) However, a pensioner may have a legitimate grievance if he is not treated alike with other pensioners. For example, if the government increases amount of pension by 10% on 1.1.1991 but provide that this benefit will be available only to those pensioners who have retired after 1.1.1989, and the pensioners who retire prior to 1.1.1989 are deprived of this benefit, this would be violative of Article 25 of the Constitution, unless the Government can demonstrate that this sub-classification within the class of pensioners is based on an intelligible differentia. And that the differentia has rational nexus to the object sought to be achieved by the relevant sub-classification.

(iii) It cannot be laid down as a general proposition that in no case a specified date can be made basis for classification. It will depend on the facts of each case and if the specification of a particular date is based on an intelligible differentia, which in turn has nexus to the object for which the relevant statute has been enacted, such classification will be legal and valid. But if the specification of a date is arbitrary or whimsical, it cannot be made the basis of classification.

(iv) The pensionary benefits cannot be denied to those judges who retired from service before 1 of July 1981. No discrimination can be made between judges who retire after and those who retire prior to 1 of July 1981. Similarly, the additional pensionary benefits allowed to civil servants retiring after 1 July 1986 cannot be denied to those who retire before the said date.

Inequality on Ground of Tax Exemption

A private limited company, the total shares of which are owned and controlled by the Government of Pakistan, cannot take the benefit of exemption from payment of tax under Article 165 of the Constitution 1993 by lifting the veil of its incorporation, for it would place the company in any advantageous position to the detriment of other companies which are also engaged in the manufacture and sale of same commodity as it would be violative of equality of law and equal protection of law. In *Union Council, Ali Wahan v. Associated Cement*,[174] by the Associated Cement (Vesting) Ordinance, 1974, the Associated Cement (Pvt) Ltd. was vested in the State Cement Corporation of Pakistan (Pvt) Ltd., a private limited company, the total shares of which were owned and controlled by the Government of Pakistan. The appellant demanded payment of octroi on all goods of the respondent which was resisted by the respondent on the ground that as it was owned by the Government of Pakistan, it was exempted from payment of octroi under Article 165 of the 1973 Constitution. Since the appellant persisted on the demand, the respondent filed a writ petition in the Sindh High Court, which was accepted on the ground that though

> from the juristic point of view the company is a legal personality entirely from its members and the company is capable of enjoying rights and being subjected to duties... in certain exceptional cases, the Court is entitled

> to lift the veil of corporate entity and to pay regard to the economic realities behind the legal façade' .... The company was clearly entitled to the exemption germane to the property of the Federal Government as provided by Article 165 of the Constitution and all goods imported by the petitioner for its consumption is exempt from payment of octroi tax.

The appellant preferred an appeal before the Supreme Court of Pakistan which was allowed holding that invoking the doctrine of lifting the veil of incorporation in such as case to enable the company to have the benefit of Article 165 would place the company in an advantageous position to the detriment of the other companies, which were also engaged in manufacture and sale of cement, as they would not be entitled to the benefit of exemption of octroi which would be violative of, inter alia, Article 25 of the 1973 Constitution. The Supreme Court on particular points held that:

(i) There should be a justifiable reason warranting the lifting of veil of incorporation, which depends on particular facts of each case.
(ii) Where government owns, controls and manages a corporation which is engaged in a commercial activity competing with private companies engaged in similar business, such corporation cannot claim any privilege or immunity to the disadvantage of its competitors.
(iii) The octroi is levied by the Union Council in order to raise funds for the development of the rural area which is under developed and badly needs funds. Grant of exemption to the company by lifting the veil of incorporation would not, in any way, foster the cause of justice but in fact retard the development of the rural area.
(iv) To grant exemption to the respondent-company by lifting the veil of incorporation to the detriment of private cement companies would be violative of 'equality of law' and 'equal protection of law' clauses of the Constitution.

Inequality on Basis of Sex

Where an educational institution admits students of both sexes and is not reserved for one sex alone, the fixation of quota for admission in the ratio of 4:1 for male and female students respectively is violative of the 'equality before law' Clause contained in Article 25(2) of the Constitution which provides:

> 'there shall be no discrimination on the basis of sex alone'.

Article 25(3) implies that while the difference on the basis of sex can be created and maintained, it shall be done only in those cases where it operates favourably as a protective measure for and not against women and children.

Article 22(3)(b) which states that:

> 'no citizen shall be denied admission to any educational institution receiving aid from public revenues on the ground only of race, religion caste or place of birth,'

is not inconsistent with or repugnant to Article 25(2), notwithstanding the generality of the latter and the particularity of the other, for the reason that classification based on intelligent and reasonable standards is permissible within the framework of Article 25(2) on the ground of sex alone.

There is no conflict between the two provisions as the word 'sex' does not appear in Article 22(3)(b). If the word 'sex' had also been introduced in Article 22(3)(b) then there would have occurred a conflict instead of consistency, between the two inasmuch as the classification permissible under Article 25 would have become impermissible in educational institutions with regard to admission.

In *Shirin Munir v. Govt. of the Punjab,*[175] the appellants, girl students who obtained such marks in F.Sc (Medical) examination which would have entitled them on merits to admission in one of the seven medical colleges but because of quota fixed for them, they could not get admission. Out of the total 1085 seats, after excluding 227 reserved seats, the remaining 858 open seats were divided between boys and girls. Inasmuch as 677 seats were allocated to boys and 181 seats to girls. As the girls were required to compete within their own quota. Therefore, the boys could get admission on as low as 731 marks.

The girls students filed writ petitions in the Lahore High Court challenging the fixation of quota as violative of 'equality before law' enshrined in Article 25 of the Constitution, 1973. The petitions were accepted by the single judge of the High Court, holding that first the discrimination has been meted out to the girl students on the basis of sex and therefore the quota was violative of Article 25 of the Constitution. Second, Article 22 of the 1973 Constitution, was not applicable as the medical college were government institutions and not private institutions 'receiving aid from public revenue'. Third, although the provisions of Article 22(3)(b) being special provisions would prevail against the general provisions of Article 25(2) the special provisions have to be applied in their own terms, and anyhow, both the provisions must be allowed to co-exist under the elementary rule of interpretation of Constitution. And fourth, classification was unreasonable.

The intra-court appeals preferred by the Government of the Punjab were allowed and judgment of the single Bench set aside on the ground that Article 22(3)(b) confers a special right on the citizens regarding admission into educational institutions. It is, therefore, legitimate to treat Article 22(3)(b) as a special provision and Article 25(2) as general provision. The comparison of these two provisions brings two questions in the forefront, first, what is the effect of the omission of the word 'sex' from Article 22(3)(b) and secondly, can the word 'sex' be imported into it from Article 25(2), being a special provision. Article 22(3)(b) overrides the general provision of Article 25(2).

On the strength of Chairman, Selection Committee, *Bolan Medical College v. Miss Safia Hamid*,[176] and *Government of Baluchistan v. Rifat Parveen*,[177] the Appeal Bench held that addition to the sanctioned seats could not have been ordered by the single Bench while allowing the constitutional petitions. The girl students challenged the decision of the intra-court appeal before the Supreme Court contending that the Constitution of Pakistan, should be considered as an organic whole, no part of it being treated as redundant, cancelling, curtailing or diminishing the utility of another provision of equal dignity and equal standing, and the treatment of one fundamental right as general. The other as special, and further to limit one on the strength of other is not warranted by any principle of interpretation. It is only in extreme cases of repugnancy and irreconciliation that one provision may be limited as against the other. The Supreme Court allowed the appeals holding that—

(i) by the principles of interpretation of Constitution as stated in *Special Reference*[178], and as explained in *State v. Zia-ur-Rahman*[179], and summarized in *Federation v. Saeed Ahmad*[180], and by the Comments made in paras 2.11 & 2.12 in *Constitutional Law of India* by H.M. Seeravi, 1968 Ed., the words 'discrimination' and 'alone' occurring in Article 25(2) saying 'there shall be no discrimination on the basis of sex alone' have to be given their due weight.

(ii) Article 25(2) prohibits distinction on the basis of sex alone. However, Article 25(3) controls the rest of Article 25. It implies, therefore, while the difference on the basis of sex can be created and maintained, it shall be done only in those cases where it operates favourably as a protective measure for and not against women and children.

(iii) Discrimination against a group or an individual implies making an adverse distinction about some benefit, advantage or facility.

(iv) The harmony and the consistency between Article 25 and Article 22 of the Constitution is obvious notwithstanding the generality of the one and the particularity of the other, only if one keeps this important fact in view that classification based on intelligible and reasonable standards is permissible within the framework of Article 25 the word 'sex' had also been introduced then there would have occurred a conflict instead of consistency between Article 25 and Article 22 inasmuch as the classification permissible under Article 25 would have become impermissible in educational institutions with regard to admission therein.

(v) Both Articles 25 and 22 have to be read harmoniously, there being no repugnancy between them. No discrimination on the ground of sex alone can be permitted except on the ground of reasonable and intelligible classification. Such classification in Pakistan permits for the present, establishment of education institutions exclusively for the females or exclusively for the males. Where, however, co-education is permitted, and the institution is not reserved for one sex alone, the fixation of number on the ground of sex will directly be opposed to the requirement of Article 25(2) unless it is justified as a protective measure for women and children under Article 25(3).

(vi) As the two Articles 25 and 22 stands at present, the general rule is that 'sex' cannot be adopted as the sole criteria for discrimination except for advancing the cause of women and children as permitted by clause (3) of Article 25. On the principle of reasonable and intelligible classification it is possible to have educational institutions exclusively catering to the needs of the male population and also educational institutions catering exclusively to the female population in our context and in our society. However, when an educational institution is thrown open for co-education, then a further restriction of numbers on the ground of sex is permissible only as a protective measure of women and children but in no case so as to protect comparatively less meritorious boys to the prejudice and exclusion of women. This amounts to gross violation of constitutional mandate.

(vii) Classification based on intelligible and reasonable standards is permissible within the framework of Article 25 on the ground of sex and sex alone.

(viii) Prohibition in Article 8 is against the law which discriminates. If the instructions or the statutory instruments challenged qualify as law then it is liable to be struck down under Article 8, if found discriminatory; and who takes the action under it, is immaterial.

(ix) Article 22 is subject to law. If the public revenues are coming to the aid of an institution either wholly or in part, then the institution comes within the purview of Article 22(3)(b) and it is immaterial whether the State is managing it or some one else.

(x) Principles of policy have to be considered to be a part of the Constitution and other provisions of the Constitution should not be interpreted totally losing sight of it. Harmony should be struck as far as possible without, of course, enforcing in positive terms the basic principles of policy or allowing them to supersede the Fundamental Rights or in any manner curtailing what is mandated in the Constitution.[181]

Special Provision For Protection Of Women And Children

Though the word 'State' occurring in Article 25(3) and as defined by Article 7 of the 1973 Constitution, does not include 'judiciary', yet in the peculiar context of Article 25(3), the word 'State' would also include judicial functionaries.

The definition in Article 7 would not prevent a court from directing the state to perform the function visualized in Article 25(3). Thus in both senses, namely, contextually as well as by statutory definition, the women can be provided with legal assistance through engagement of a competent counsel.

In *Mst. Fazal Jan v. Roshan Din*[182], the petitioner, a lady, instituted a suit for declaration to the effect that she was entitled to the suit land as she has inherited it through her father from her father's paternal uncle, the original owner. The case was very badly conducted on her behalf. She lost the suit and also failed in her revision petition before the High Court. In her petition for leave to appeal, the Supreme Court found that all the relevant documents were not brought on the record of the suit. The record of the trial court was a miserable jumble of papers. A strong possibility could not be excluded that a woman like the petitioner being unable to manage and protect her property and rights could be taken undue advantage of by others and the proceedings resulted in miscarriage of justice.

The Supreme Court granted leave to appeal and provided the services of a competent civil lawyer to the petitioner at state expenses invoking the provisions of Article 25(3) of the 1973 Constitution, which state that –

> 'nothing... shall prevent the state from making any special provision for the protection of women and children'

holding that though the word 'State' used in Article 25(3) and as defined in Article 7 of the Constitution does not include 'judiciary'. Yet in the peculiar context of Article 25(3), the word 'State' would also include the judicial functionaries. The question of protection of the women and children arises almost in every case wherein they are involved. Accordingly the word 'State' would include the presiding judge who hear and decide such like cases.

Enactment of Progressive Application

A provision of an Act saying that it 'shall apply only to such areas, classes of persons, industries or establishments as Government may, by notification specify in this behalf', is not violative of the 'equality before law' clause if it is made applicable to one particular establishment leaving the other similar establishments in the same area provided the Act is conditional and envisages its application and extension progressively.

In *Standard Printing Press v. Sindh Employees Social Security Institution*,[183] the applicant a small printing press, employing about 10 workers at a time, was subjected to certain specified provisions of the West Pakistan Employee's Social Security Ordinance 1965, by issuing a notification on 24 January 1977 under Section 1(3) of the Ordinance, and accordingly a notice of demand dated 21 May 1977 was served on the appellant, which the appellant challenged by filing an appeal under Section 59 of the Ordinance before the Sindh Social Security Court on the sole ground that the notification was discriminatory and violative of Article 25 of the Constitution, inasmuch as similar other establishments in the locality were not subjected to these provisions of the Ordinance.

The appeal was dismissed on the ground that the point raised was not covered by Section 57 of the Ordinance and that the government was not made a party to the proceedings. In the second appeal filed before the Sindh High Court under Section 64 of the Ordinance, the appellant urged 3 points of law.

- The first was that the notification was *ultra vires* section 1(3) of the Ordinance as it individualized and particularized the establishment of the appellant for the reason that the section on its own words, permitted such an action only in respect of class of establishments, or class of industries and not in respect of individual establishment or individuals industry.
- The second contention was that even if section 1(3) of the Ordinance permitted such individualized action, the Government under its cover by issuance of a notification cannot, without reasonable classification, discriminate against any individual industry or establishment in violation of Article 25 of the Constitution.
- The third ground was that these two grounds could lawfully be raised before the Social Security Court in view of clause (f) of Section 57 of the Ordinance.

The learned judge in the High Court, while dismissing the appeal, held that Clause (f) of Section 57 of the Ordinance must be given a restricted meaning as held in *Sindh Employee's Social Security Institution v. Mumtaz Ali Taj*[184], and it cannot be extended 'to include the fundamental question whether the Ordinance itself was legally applicable to a particular establishment'.

The Social Security Court being a tribunal/court of limited jurisdiction was held not competent to adjudicate on the *vires* of the notification. It was further held that the language of Section 1(3) of the Ordinance permitted application of Ordinance by notification to individual establishment or industry and class requirement was confined to persons and did not extend to industry or establishment. As regards to the violation of Article 25 of the constitution, the High Court did not advert to it. The appellant came up in appeal, by leave, to the Supreme Court and reiterated the three questions argued before the High Court. The Supreme Court dismissed the appeal holding that—

> 'Although Section 1(3) of the Ordinance says that it shall apply only to such areas, classes of persons industries or establishments as Government may, by notification, specify in this behalf, on its plain language there is no scope for contending that the expression 'classes of' should be carried forward to govern not only the persons but also the 'industries' and 'establishments'.

The Ordinance envisages progressive application and extension which is left to the Government. Conditional legislation is possible as ruled in *Sobbo Gyanchandani v. The Crown*.[185] Therefore, the applicability of the Ordinance to some of the establishments does not violate the 'equality before law', applying the dicta in *Jabindra Kishore v. East Pakistan*,[186] and *East and West Steamship Co. v. Pakistan*,[187] and therefore Section 1(3) of the Ordinance is not *ultra vires* Article 25 of the constitution.

New Test of Reasonableness of Classification

The Supreme Court of India has replaced the nexus test by the test of arbitrariness. In *E.P. Royappa v. State of T.N.*,[188] propounded a new approach to Article 14 in the following words:

> 'Equality is a dynamic concept with many aspects and dimensions and it cannot be "cribbed, cabined and confined" within traditional and doctrinaire limits, from a positivistic point of view, equality is antithetic to arbitrariness. In fact, equality and arbitrariness are sworn enemies; one belongs to the rule of law in a republic while the other, to the whim and caprice of an absolute monarch. Where an act is arbitrary, it is implicit in it that it is unequal both according to political logic and Constitutional Law and is therefore violative of Article 14.'

A few months later in *Maganlal Chhaganlal v. Greater Bombay Municipality*',[189] Justice P.N. Bhagwati (1921–2017)[190], in a concurring opinion, speaking for himself and Justice V.R. Krishna Iyer (1915–2014)[191], emphasized:

> 'Article 14 enunciates a vital principle which lies at the core of our republicanism and shines like a beacon light pointing towards the goal of classless egalitarian socio-economic order which were promised to build for ourselves when we made a tryst with destiny on that fateful day when we adopted our Constitution. If we have to choose between fanatical devotion to this great principle of equality and feeble allegiance to it, we would unhesitatingly prefer to err on the side of the former as against the latter.'

And further he said:

> 'What the equality clause is intended to strike at are real and substantial disparities .... and arbitrary or capricious actions of the executive and it would be contrary to the object and intendment of the equality clause to exalt delicate distinctions, shades of harshness and theoretical possibilities of prejudice into legislative inequality or executive discrimination'.

In the famous *Maneka Gandhi v. Union of India*,[192] quoting himself from *Royappa* case, Justice Bhagwati, very clearly read the principle of reasonableness in Article 14. He said:

> 'Article 14 strikes at arbitrariness in State action and ensures fairness and equality of treatment. The principle of reasonableness, which logically as well as philosophically, is an essential element of equality or non-arbitrariness pervades Article 14 like a brooding omnipresence'.

Finally, in *Ajay Hasia v. Khalid Mujib*,[193] he stamped the new approach with a unanimous opinion of a Constitution Bench of the Court in the following words:

> 'It must .... Now be taken to be well settled that what Article 14 strikes at is arbitrariness because an action that is arbitrary, must necessarily involve negation of equality. The doctrine of classification which is evolved by the Courts is not paraphrase of Article 14 nor is it the objective end of that Article. It is merely a judicial formula for determining whether the legislative or executive action in question is arbitrary and therefore constituting denial of equality. If the classification is not reasonable and does not satisfy the two conditions referred to above (i) intelligible differentia, and (ii) rational relation between the differentia and the object sought, the impugned legislation or executive action would plainly be arbitrary and the guarantee of equality under Article 14 would be breached. Wherever, therefore is arbitrariness in state action whether it is of the legislature or of the executive or of an "authority" under Article 12, Article 14 immediately springs into action and strikes down such State action.'

Again, in *Mithu v. Punjab*,[194] Section 303 of the Indian Penal Code, which provided for mandatory death penalty for murder committed by a life convicts was invalidated. The court framed two issues:

(i) whether there is any intelligible basis for giving differential treatment to an accused who commits the offence of murder whilst under a sentence of life imprisonment and
(ii) is such a law just and fair?

It answered both the issues in the negative. Earlier in *Bachan Singh v. State of Punjab*,[195] (Justice Bhagwati, dissenting), however, the court refused to invalidate Section 302 of the Indian Penal Code on the ground that it was unreasonable in so far as it gave discretion to the judge to choose between life imprisonment and death sentence.

The Supreme Court of India in *Karnataka STDC v. Karnataka State*,[196] invalidated clause (iv) of the proviso to Section 63(7) of the Motor Vehicles Act 1939. Clause (iv) required the Regional Transport Authority to give preference to certain kinds of applicants approved by the Central Ministry of Tourism in granting permits for motor vehicles. Invalidating the clause under Article 14, the court held:

> 'We find it difficult to sustain this clause and uphold its validity. The very idea that a Tribunal (Regional Transport Authority) created by a statute for the purpose of considering rival claims and granting permits, on merits should be compelled to give preference to persons securing the approval of the executive government appears to us to be arbitrary and unreasonable.'

Unreasonableness Of Subordinate Legislation

In *Sudhir Chandra Sarkar v. Tata Iron and Steel Co. Ltd.*[197] Rule 10 of the Retiring Gratuity Rules 1937, which gave absolute discretion to the employer company to grant or refuse payment of gratuity to an employee, was invalidated as an unreasonable provision.

Similarly, in *Central Inland Water Transport Corp. v. Brojo Nath Ganguly*,[198] the court invalidated Rule 9(i) of the Corporation's Rules which provided for termination of service on three month's notice or on payment of three month's salary in lieu of notice. Holding the corporation 'State' within the meaning of Article 12 and its Rules, the court decided:

> 'Rule 9(i) is both arbitrary and unreasonable and it also wholly ignores and sets aside the *audialterm partem* rule. It, therefore, violates Article 14 of the Constitution.'

Absence of Show Cause Notice

In *Maneka Gandhi v. Union of India*,[199] and more clearly in *Union of India v. Tulsiram Patel*,[200] the court had held that non-observance of the principles of the natural justice in state action violates Article 14.

Places reserved for public entertainment and public resort

If a particular place is reserved for certain public use in a master plan of a city, it cannot put to some other use. It was held by the Supreme Court of Pakistan that plots in a housing scheme for public use cannot be converted to other uses.[201] Where a public park, reserved in the master plan for public entertainment, was leased out to a commercial use as a mini golf course, the leased agreement was declared unlawful.[202] In a *suo moto* case, where a part of Fatima Jinnah Park, Islamabad was leased out for establishment of McDonald restaurant, contrary to the master plan, the Supreme Court declared the lease unlawful.[203]

The rationale in these cases has been that putting places of public entertainment to commercial use would deny access to the public at large to these places permanently or temporarily which would be denial of equal access to the people at large under Article 26 of the Constitution.

Government contracts

Public or government contracts have been the most fertile area for the evolution and application of the new approach to Article 14. *International Airport Authority case*[204] and *Kasturi Lal* case[205] were government contract case where Justice Bhagwati, very elaborately discussed the need of reasonableness in state action reading its source in Article 14.

Earlier in *Erusian Equipment & Chemical Ltd. v. State of West Bengal*,[206] the court rejecting the right privilege dichotomy for purposes of fair play, held that the state could not blacklist and debar a person from government contracts without giving him an opportunity to be heard. Duty to act fairly in *Erusian Equipment* case was extended to duty to act reasonably in the *International Airport Authority* and *Kasturi Lal* cases.

Subsequently in *Ram & Shyam Co. v. State of Haryana*,[207] the court invalidated a grant of lease to a person who made a higher offer through private negotiations with the Chief Minister than the highest bid made by the appellant in the public auction. Refusal to grant lease to the appellant without affording it any opportunity to raise the bid was found unreasonable and violative of Article 14.

Similarly, in *Harminder Singh Arora v. Union of India*,[208] where contrary to the terms of tender, the government for no valid reasons granted the contract to supply milk to a person other than the one who submitted valid tender for the invalidated, the government action relying upon the supplying of quality milk at much lower price, the court relied on law laid down in *International Airport Authority* case.

In *Mahabir Auto Stores v. Indian Oil Corporation*,[209] even though there was no formal contract between the petitioner and the respondent, the court found the decision of the respondent to suddenly stop the supply of lubricants to the petitioner, which it had been supplying for the last 18 years, to be unreasonable and arbitrary because there existed no good reasons for the action of the respondent.

Again, in *Shrilekha Vidyarathi v. State of U.P.*,[210] the court invalidated the UP Government Order terminating *en masse* the appointments of all Government Counsel in the state. The court held that even if the appointments of counsel were contractual they had to be governed by the requirements of reasonableness and non-arbitrariness, inherent in Article 14, and the principle of the rule of law which apply to all state action whatsoever.

Concept of Equality (*Musawat*) in Islam

In *Dr Mobashir Hassan v. Federation*,[211] the Supreme Court observed that 'the principle of equality *(Musawat)*, as enshrined in Article 25 of the Constitution, has its origin in the Islamic teachings. The judgment also quested from the Last Sermon of the Prophet Muhammad (PBUH) as under:

> 'O ye people, Allah says, O people, We created you from one male and one female and made you into tribes and nations, so as to be known to one another. Verily in the sight of Allah, the most honoured amongst you is the one who is most God fearing. There is no superiority for an Arab over a non-Arab and for a non-Arab over an Arab, nor for the white over the black...'.

Leading Cases

Certain leading cases of the US Supreme Court on the interpretation of equal protection clause are discussed below:

Plessy v. Ferguson[212]

In this case, in response to a challenge to racial segregation in railroad cars, the US Supreme Court propounded the dubious doctrine of 'separate but equal' while interpreting equal protection clause.

Justice Henry Billings Brown (1836–1913) delivered the opinion of the court:

...... The object of the 14th Amendment was undoubtedly to enforce the absolute equality of the two races before the law but in the nature of things it could not have been intended to abolish distinctions based upon color, or to enforce social, as distinguished from political, equality, or a commingling of the two races upon terms unsatisfactory to either, Laws permitting, and even requiring their separation in places where they are liable to be brought into contact do not necessarily imply the inferiority of either race to the other, and have been generally, if not universally recognized as within the competency of the state legislatures in the exercise of their police power. The most common instance of this is connected with the establishment of separate schools for white and colored children, which have been held to be a valid exercise of the legislative power even by courts of states where the political rights of the colored race have been longest and most earnestly enforced.

One of the earliest of these cases is that of *Roberts v. Boston*[213], in which the supreme judicial court of Massachusetts held that he general school committee of Boston had power to make provision for the instruction of coloured children in separate schools established exclusively for them, and to prohibit their attendance upon the other schools …. Similar laws have been enacted by Congress under its general power of legislation over the District of Columbia…. As well as by legislatures of many of the states, and have been generally, if not uniformly, sustained by the courts.

Laws forbidding the intermarriage of the two races may be said in a technical sense to interfere with the freedom of contract, and yet have been universally recognized as within the police power of the state ….

The distinction between laws interfering with the political equality of the Negro and those requiring the separation of the two races in schools, theatres, and railways carriages, has been frequently drawn by this court ….

In this connection it is also suggested by the learned counsel for the plaintiff in error that the same argument that will justify the state legislature in requiring railways to provide separate accommodations for the two races will also authorize them to require separate cars to be provided for people whose hair is of a certain color, or who are aliens, or who belong to certain nationalities, or to enact laws requiring coloured people to walk upon one side of and white people the other, or requiring white men's houses to be painted white, and coloured men's black or their vehicles or business sights to be of different colors, upon the theory that, one side of the street is as good as the other, or that a house or vehicle of one color is as good as one of another color. The answer to all this, is that every exercise of the police power must be reasonable, and extend only to such laws as are enacted in good faith for the promotion of the public good, and not for the annoyance or oppression of a particular class ….

So far, then, as a conflict with the 14th Amendment is concerned, the case reduces itself – to the question whether the statute of Louisiana is a reasonable regulation, and with respect to this there must necessarily be a large discretion on the part of the legislature. In determining the question of reasonableness, it is liberty to act with reference to the established usages, customs, and traditions of the people, and with a view to the promotion of their comfort, and the preservation of public peace and good order. Gauged by this standard, we cannot say that a law which authorizes or even requires the separation of the two races in public conveyances is unreasonable or more obnoxious to the 14th Amendment than the acts of Congress requiring separate schools for coloured children in the District of Columbia, the constitutionality of which does not seem to have been questioned, or the corresponding acts of state legislatures.

We consider the underlying fallacy of the plaintiff's argument to consist in the assumption that the enforced separation of the two races stamps the coloured race with a badge of inferiority. If this be so, it is not by reason of anything found in the act, but solely because the coloured race chooses to put that construction upon it.

The argument necessarily assumes that if, as has been more than once the case, and is not unlikely to be so again, the coloured race should become the dominant power in the state legislature, and should enact a law in precisely similar terms, it would thereby relegate the white race to an inferior position. We imagine that the white race, at least, would not acquiesce in this assumption. The argument also assumes that social prejudices may be overcome by legislation, and that equal rights cannot be secured to the negro except by an enforced commingling of the two races. We cannot accept this proposition. If the two races are to meet on terms of social equality, it must be the result of natural affinities, a mutual appreciation of each other's merits and a voluntary consent of individuals… Legislation is powerless to eradicate racial instincts or to abolish distinctions based upon physical differences, and the attempt to do so can only result in accentuating the difficulties of the present situation. If the civil and political rights of both races be equal, one cannot be inferior to the other civilly or politically. If one race be inferior to the other socially, the United States Constitution cannot put them upon the same plane …. The judgment of the court below is therefore affirmed, Mr Justice John M. Harlan, dissenting:

… While there may be in Louisiana persons of different races who are not citizens of the United States, the words in the act, 'white and colored races' necessarily include all citizens of the United States of both races residing in that state. So that we have before us a state enactment that compels, under penalties, the separation of the two races in railroad passenger coaches, and makes it rime for a citizen of either race to enter a coach that has been assigned to citizens of the other race. Thus the state regulates the use of a public highway by citizens of the United States solely upon the basis of race.

However, apparent the injustice of such legislation may be, we have only to consider whether it is consistent with the American Constitution.

In respect of civil rights, common to all citizens, the United States Constitution does not, I think, permit any public authority to know the race of those entitled to be protected in the enjoyment of such rights. Every true man has pride of race, and under appropriate circumstances, when the rights of others, his equals before the law, are not to be affected, it is his privilege to express such pride and to take such action based it as to him seems proper. But I deny that any legislative body or judicial tribunal may have regard to the race of citizens when the civil rights of those citizens are involved. Indeed such legislation as that here in question is inconsistent, not only with that equality of rights, which pertains to citizenship, national and state, but with the personal liberty enjoyed by everyone within the United States....

The white race deems itself to be the dominant race in this country. And so it is, in prestige, in achievements, in education, in wealth. and in power. So, I doubt not that it will continue to be for all times, if it remains true to its great heritage and holds fast to the principles of constitutional liberty. But in view of the Constitution, in the eye of the law, there is in this country no superior, dominant. ruling class of citizens. There is no caste here. Our Constitution is color-blind. and neither knows nor tolerates classes among citizens. In respect of civil rights, all citizens are equal before the law. The humblest is the peer of the most powerful. The law regards man as man and takes no account of his surroundings or of his color when his civil rights as guaranteed by the supreme law of the land are involved. It is therefore to be regretted that this high tribunal, the final expositor of the fundamental law of the land, has reached the conclusion that it is competent for a state to regulate the enjoyment by citizens of their civil rights solely upon the basis of race.

In my opinion, the judgment this day rendered will, in time, prove to be quite as pernicious as the decision made by this tribunal in the *Dred Scott*[214] case. It was adjudged in that case that the descendants of Africans who were imported into this country and sold as slaves were not included nor intended to be included under the word 'citizens' in the Constitution, and could not claim any of the rights and privileges which that instrument provided for and secured to citizens of the United States; that at the time of the adoption of the Constitution they were

> 'considered as a subordinate and inferior class of beings, who had been subjugated by the dominant race, and whether emancipated or not, yet remained subject to their authority, and had no rights or privileges but such as those who held the power and the government might choose to grant them.'

The recent amendments of the Constitution, it was supposed had eradicated these principles from our institutions. But it seems that we have yet, in some of the states, a dominant race, a superior class of citizens, which assumes to regulate the enjoyment of civil rights, common to all citizens, upon the basis of race. The present decision, it may well be apprehended, will not stimulate aggressions, more or less brutal and irritating, upon the admitted rights of coloured citizens, but will encourage the belief that it is possible, by means of state enactments, to defeat the beneficent purposes which the people of the United States had in view when they adopted the recent amendments of the Constitution, by one of which the blacks of this country were made citizens of the United States and of the states in which they respectively reside and whose privileges and immunities, as citizens, the states are forbidden to abridge. Sixty millions of whites are in no danger from the presence here of eight millions of blacks. The destinies of the two races in this country are indissolubly linked together, and the interests of both require that the common government of all shall not permit the seeds of race hate to be planted under the sanction of law, What can more certainly arouse race hate, what more certainly create and perpetuate a feeling of distrust between these races, than state enactments which in fact proceed on the ground that coloured citizens are so inferior and degraded that they cannot be allowed to sit in public coaches occupied by white citizens? That, as all will admit, is the real meaning of such legislation as was enacted in Louisiana.

The sure guaranty of the peace and security of each race is the clear, distinct, and unconditional recognition by our governments, national and state, of every light that inheres in civil freedom, and of the equality before the law of all citizens of the United States without regard to race. State enactments, regulating the enjoyment of civil rights, upon the basis of race, and cunningly devised to defeat legitimate results of the war, under the pretence of recognizing equality of rights, can have no other result than to render permanent peace impossible and to keep alive a conflict of races, the continuance of which must do harm to all concerned. This question is not met by the suggestion that social equality cannot exist between the white and black races in this country. That argument, if it can he properly regarded as one, is scarcely worthy of consideration, for social equality no more exists between two races when travelling in a passenger coach or a public highway than when members of the same races sit by each other in a street car or in the jury box, or stand or sit with each other in a political assembly, or when they use in common the streets of a city or town, or when they are in the same room for the purpose of having their names placed on the registry of voters, or when they approach the ballot box in order to exercise the high privilege of voting.

The arbitrary separation of citizens, on the basis of race, while they are on a public highway, is a badge of servitude wholly inconsistent with the civil freedom and the equality before the law established by the US Constitution. It cannot be justified upon any legal grounds.

If evils will result from the commingling of the two races upon public highways established for the benefit of all, they will be infinitely less than those that will surely come from state legislation regulating the enjoyment of civil right upon the basis of race. We boast of the freedom enjoyed by our people above all other peoples. But it is difficult to reconcile that boast with a state of the law which practically puts the brand of servitude and degradation upon a large class of our fellow citizens, our equals before the law. The thin disguise of 'equal- accommodations for passengers in railroad coaches will not mislead anyone, or atone for the wrong this day done…

I am of opinion that the statute of Louisiana is inconsistent with the personal liberty of citizens, white and black, in that state, and hostile to both the spirit and letter of the Constitution of the United States. If laws of like character should be enacted in the several states of the Union, the effect would be in the highest degree mischievous. Slavery as an institution tolerated by law would have disappeared from our country but there would remain a power in the states, by sinister legislation, to interfere with the full enjoyment of the blessings of freedom: to regulate civil rights common to all citizens, upon the basis of race: and to place in a condition of legal inferiority a large body of American citizens, now constituting a part of the political community, called the people of the United States, for whom and by whom, through representatives, our government is administered. Such a system is inconsistent with guarantee given by the constitution to each state of a republican form of government and may be stricken down by congressional action or by the courts in the discharge of their solemn duty to maintain the supreme law of the land, anything in the Constitution of laws of any state to the contrary notwithstanding.

For the reasons stated, I am constrained to withhold my assent from the opinion and judgement of the majority.

Brown v. Board of Education of Topeka[215]

In what has been dubbed 'the case of the century,' the Supreme Court `invalidates compulsory racial segregation in the public schools.

Chief Justice Earl Warren delivered the opinion of the court:

> These cases come to us from the States of Kansas, South Carolina, Vïrginia, and Delaware. They are premised on different facts and different local conditions, but a common legal question justifies their consideration in this consolidated opinion.

In each of the cases, minors of the Negro race, through their legal representatives, seek the aid of the courts in obtaining admission to the public schools of their community on a non-segregated basis. In each instance, they had been denied admission to schools attended by white children under laws requiring or permitting segregation according to race. This segregation was alleged to deprive the plaintiffs of the equal protection of the laws under the 14th Amendment. In each of the cases other than the Delaware case, a three-judge federal district court denied relief to the plaintiffs on the so-called 'separate but equal' doctrine announced by this court in *Plessy v. Ferguson*…. Under that doctrine, equality of treatment is accorded when the races are provided substantially equal facilities, even though these facilities are separate. In the Delaware case, the Supreme Court of Delaware adhered to that doctrine, but ordered that the plaintiffs be admitted to the white schools because of their superiority to the Negro schools ….

Because of the obvious importance of the question presented, the court took jurisdiction. Argument was heard in the 1952 Term, and reargument was heard this term on certain questions propounded by the court.

Reargument was largely devoted to the circumstances surrounding the adoption of the 14th Amendment in 1868. It covered exhaustively consideration of the Amendment in Congress, ratification by the states, then existing practices in racial segregation, and the views of proponents and opponents of the Amendment. This discussion and our own investigation convince us that, although these sources cast some light, it is not enough to resolve the problem with which we are faced. At best, they are inconclusive. The most avid proponents of the post-War Amendments undoubtedly intended them to remove all legal distinctions among 'all persons born or naturalized in the United States.' Their opponents, just as certainly, were antagonistic to both the letter and the spirit of the Amendments and wished them to have the most limited effect. What others in Congress and the state legislatures had in mind cannot be determined with any degree of certainty.

An additional reason for the inconclusive nature of the Amendment's history, with respect to segregated schools, is the status of public education at that time. In the South, the movement toward free common schools, supported by general taxation, had not yet taken hold. Education of white children was largely in the hands of private groups. Education of Negroes was almost nonexistent, and practically all of the races were illiterate. In fact, any education of Negroes was forbidden by law in some states. Today, in contrast, many Negroes have achieved outstanding success in the arts and sciences as well as in the business and professional world. It is true that public education had already advanced further in the North, but the effect of the Amendment on Northern states was generally ignored in the Congressional debates. Even in the North, the conditions of public education did not approximate those existing today. The curriculum was rudimentary; upgraded schools were common in rural areas; the school term was but three months a year in many states; and compulsory school attendance was virtually unknown. As a consequence, it is not surprising that there should be so little in the history of the 14th Amendment relating to its intended effect on public education.

In the first cases in this court construing the 14th Amendment, decided shortly after its adoption, the court interpreted it as proscribing all state-imposed discriminations against the Negro race. The doctrine of 'separate but equal' did not make its appearance in this court until 1896 in the case of *Plessy v. Ferguson*… involving not education but transportation. American courts have since laboured with the doctrine for over half a century. In this court, there have been six cases involving the 'separate but equal' doctrine in the field of public education. In *Cumming v. Richmond County Board of Education*[216] … and *Gong Lum v. Rice*[217]… the validity of the doctrine itself was not challenged. In more recent cases, all on the graduate school level, inequality was found in that specific benefits enjoyed by white students were denied to Negro students of the same educational qualifications. In none of these cases was it necessary to re-examine the doctrine to grant relief to the Negro plaintiff. And in *Sweatt v. Painter*[218], …the court expressly reserved decision on the question whether *Plessy v. Ferguson* should be held inapplicable to public education.

In the instant cases, that question is directly presented. Here, unlike *Sweatt v. Painter*, there are findings below that the Negro and white schools involved have been equalized, or are being equalized, with respect to buildings, curricula, qualifications and salaries of teachers, and other 'tangible' factors. Our decision, therefore, cannot turn on merely a comparison of these tangible factors in the Negro and white schools involved in each of the cases. We must look instead to the effect of segregation itself on public education.

In approaching this problem, we cannot turn the clock back to 1868 when the Amendment was adopted, or even to 1896 when *Plessy v. Ferguson* was written. We must consider public education in the light of its full development and its present place in American life throughout the nation. Only in this way can it be determined if segregation in public schools deprives these plaintiffs of the equal protection of the laws.

Today, education is perhaps the most important function of state and local governments. Compulsory school attendance laws and the great expenditures for education both demonstrate our recognition of the importance of education to our democratic society. It is required in the performance of our most basic public responsibilities, even service in the armed forces. It is the very foundation of good citizenship. Today it is a principal instrument in awakening the child to cultural values, in preparing him for later professional training, and in helping him to adjust normally to his environment. In these days, it is doubtful that any child may reasonably be expected to succeed in life if he is denied the opportunity of an education. Such an opportunity, where the state has undertaken to provide it, is a right which must be made available to all on equal terms.

We come then to the question presented: Does segregation of children in public schools solely on the basis of race, even though the physical facilities and other 'tangible' factors may be equal, deprive the children of the minority group of equal educational opportunities? We believe that it does.

In *Sweatt v. Painter*, in finding that a segregated law school for Negroes could not provide them equal educational opportunities, this court relied in large part on 'those qualities which are incapable of objective measurement but which make for greatness in a law school.' In *McLaurin v. Oklahoma State Regents....*[219] the court, in requiring that a Negro admitted to a white graduate school be treated like all other students, again resorted to intangible considerations: '... his ability to study, to engage in discussions and exchange views with other students, and, in general, to learn his profession.' Such considerations apply with added force to children in grade and high schools. To separate them from others of similar age and qualifications solely because of their race generates a feeling of inferiority as to their status in the community that may affect their hearts and minds in a way unlikely ever to be undone. The effect of this separation on their educational opportunities was well stated by a finding in the Kansas case by a court which nevertheless felt compelled to rule against the Negro plaintiffs.

Segregation of white and coloured children in public schools has a detrimental effect upon the coloured children. The impact is greater when it has the sanction of the law; for the policy of separating the races is usually interpreted as denoting the inferiority of the Negro group. A sense of inferiority affects the motivation of a child to learn. Segregation with the sanction of law, therefore, has a tendency to retard the educational and mental development of Negro children and to deprive them of some of the benefits they would receive in a racially integrated school system.

Whatever may have been the extent of psychological knowledge at the time of *Plessy v. Ferguson*, this finding is amply supported by modern authority. Any language in *Plessy v. Ferguson* contrary to this finding is rejected.

We conclude that in the field of public education the doctrine of 'separate but equal' has no place. Separate educational facilities are inherently unequal. Therefore, we hold that the plaintiffs and others similarly situated for whom the actions have been brought are, by reason of the segregation complained of, deprived of the equal protection of the laws guaranteed by the 14th Amendment. This disposition makes unnecessary any discussion whether such segregation also violates the Due Process Clause of the 14th Amendment.

NOTES

1. A.V. Dicey, *Law of the Constitution*, 10th ed. (London: MacMillan, 1959), p. 193.
2. AIR 1992 SC 999.
3. A.G. Chaudhry, *Lectures on Constitutional Law* (Lahore: Irfan Law Book House, 1994), pp. 229–30.
4. PLD 1965 Lahore 642.
5. Justice John Marshall was the 4th Chief Justice of the US Supreme Court from 1801 to 1835.
6. (1959) SCR 121; 16 DLR (2d) 689.
7. Sir William Ivor Jennings was a British lawyer and academic and former Vice Chancellor of the University of Cambridge.
8. Patrick Macklem, R.C.B. Risk, Carol Rogerson, Katherine E. Swinton, Lorraine E. Weinrib, John D. Whyte., *Canadian Constitutional Law*, 2nd ed. (Toronto: Emond Montgomery Publications, 1997), pp. 974–5.
9. The Convention was adopted by the General Assembly of the United Nations in resolution 2106 (XX)2 of 21 December 1965.
10. Supra Note 3, pp. 228–9.
11. *Conseil Constitutionnel* was established by the Constitution of the Fifth Republic adopted on 4 October 1958. It is a court vested with various powers, including in particular the review of the constitutionality of legislation.
12. John Bell, *French Constitutional Law* (Clarendon Press: Oxford University Press, 1995) pp. 199–200.
13. 83 U.S. 36 (1873).
14. 100 U.S. 303 (1879).
15. Otis H. Stephens, John M. Scheb, *American Constitutional Law*, 3rd ed. (Belmont, California: Thomson West, 2003) p. 721.
16. Ibid.
17. 220 U.S. 61 (1911).
18. 366 U.S. 420 (1961).
19. 253 U.S. 412 (1920).
20. 427 U.S. 297 (1976).
21. *McGowan v. Maryland*, 366 U.S. 420 (1961) ("State legislatures are presumed to have acted within their constitutional power despite the fact that, in practice, their laws, result in some inequality.").
22. 452 U.S. 314, 331-332 (1981).

23. This, of course, was the philosophy articulated in the famous Carolene Products footnote four. *United States v. Carolene Products Co.*, 304 U.S. 144, (1938).
24. *Schweiker v. Wilson*, 450 U.S. 221 (1981).
25. Erwin Chemerinsky, *Constitutional Law: Principles and Policies*, 2nd ed. (New York: Aspen Law & Business, 2005), pp. 651–2.
26. 330 U.S. 552 (1947).
27. 473 U.S. 432 (1985).
28. 470 U.S. 869 (1985).
29. 413 U.S. 528 (1973).
30. 517 U.S. 620 (1996).
31. Supra Note 25, p. 653.
32. *Strauder v. West Virginia*, 100 U.S. 303 (1879) (invalidating state law limiting jury service to 'white male persons').
33. *Personnel Administrator of Massachusetts v. Feeney*, 442 U.S. 256 (1979) (discriminatory impact is insufficient to prove a gender classification; there must be proof of discriminatory purpose); *Washington v. Davis*, 426 U.S. 229 (1976) (discriminatory impact is insufficient to prove a racial classification; there must be proof of discriminatory purpose).
34. Supra Note 25, pp. 644–5.
35. *Palmore v. Sidoti*, 466 U.S. 429 (1984).
36. 545 U.S. 731 (2005).
37. David Souter was Associate Justice of the US Supreme Court from 1990 to 2009.
38. 539 U.S. 306 (2003).
39. 539 U.S. 244 (2003).
40. *Craig v. Boren*, 429 U.S. 190 (1976); *Lehr v. Robertson*, 463 U.S. 248 (1983).
41. *United States v. Virginia*, 518 U.S. 515 (1996).
42. Supra Note 25, p. 645.
43. *Pennell v. City of San Jose*, 485 U.S. 1 (1988); *U.S.Retirement Board v. Fritz*, 449 U.S. 166 (1980); *Allied stores v. Bowers*, 358 U.S. 522 (1959).
44. *Romer v. Evans*, 517 U.S. 620 (1996); *City of Cleburne v. Cleburne Living Center, Inc.*, 473 U.S. 432 (1985); *Zobel v. Williams*, 457 U.S. 55 (1982); *United States v. Moreno*, 413 U.S. 528 (1973).
45. *Fullilove v. Klutznick*, 448 U.S. 448, 496 (1980); *Kahn v. Shevin*, 416 U.S. 351 (1974).
46. *Graham v. Richardson*, 403 U.S. 365 (1971).
47. *Cleburne v. Cleburne Living Center*, 473 U.S. 432 (1985) ('[W]hen a statute classifies by race, lineage, or national origin, [t]hese factors are so seldom relevant to the achievement of any legitimate state interest that laws grounded in which considerations are deemed to reflect prejudice and antipathy...For these reasons and because such discrimination is unlikely to be soon rectified by legislative means, these laws are subjected to strict scrutiny and will be sustained only if they are suitably tailored to serve a compelling state interest.').
48. Supra Note 25, p. 646.
49. Thurgood Marshall, was Associate Justice of the US Supreme Court from 1967 to 1991.
50. John Paul Stevens, was Associate Justice of the US Supreme Court from 1975 to 2010.
51. *Plyler v. Doe*, 457 U.S. 202 (1982) (Marshall, J., concurring); *Craig v. Boren*, 429 U.S. 190 (1976) (Stevens, J., concurring); *San Antonio Indep. School/Dist. V. Rodriguez*, 411 U.S. 1 (1973) (Marshall, J., dissenting).
52. Jeffrey M. Shaman, *Cracks in the Structure: The Coming Breakdown of the Levels of Scrutiny* (Ohio: Ohio State University, College of Law, 1984).
53. Supra Note 25, p. 647.
54. *Korematsu v. United States*, 323 U.S. 214 (1944).
55. *Williamson v. Lee Optical*, 348 U.S. 483 (1955).
56. In a provocative article, Professor Peter Westen argued that equality 'is an ideal that should be banished from moral and legal discourse as an explanatory norm.' Peter Westen, *The Empty Idea of Equality*, vol. 95, No. 3. (Harvard: Harvard Law Review, 1982) pp. 537, 542. Professor Westen argues that equality is unnecessary as a concept because it always is necessary to develop standards to decide which inequalities are acceptable and which intolerable. Westen says that once these standards exist, they can be the basis for decisions, making the concept of equality superfluous. Moreover, he claims that equality is an undesirable concept that distorts legal analysis.

    Many commentators wrote replies to Professor Westen. See, e.g., Steven Burton, *Comment on 'Empty Ideas'. Logical Positivist Analysis of Equality and Rules*, vol. 81, No. 6. (Yale: Yale Law Journal Company, 1982) pp. 1136–1152; Erwin Chemerinsky, *In Defense of Equality: A Reply to Professor Westen*, vol. 81 (Michigan: Michigan Law Review, 1983) pp. 575. Critics of Professor Westen argue, in part, that he demonstrates only that equality is insufficient because other concepts are needed; he does not prove that equality is unnecessary. Moreover, critics argue that equality serves many

important purposes, such as to remind us to care about how people are treated relative to one another and to create a presumption in favour of treating people alike and placing a burden on those who would discriminate. These comments are taken from the book of Chemerinsky, Supra Note 22, p. 648.
57. *McLaughlin v. Florida*, 379 U.S. 184 (1964).
58. *Dallas v. Stanglin*, 490 U.S. 19 (1989).
59. *Mathews v. De Castro*, 429 U.S. 181 (1976), quoting *Helvering v. Davis*, 301 U.S. 619 (1937).
60. *Williamson v. Lee Optical*, 348 U.S. 483 (1955).
61. 336 U.S. 106 (1949).
62. Supra Note 25, pp. 659–60.
63. 440 U.S. 568 (1979).
64. *Vance v. Bradley*, 440 U.S. 93 (1979), quoting *Phillips Chem. Co. v. Dumas School Dist.*, 361 U.S. 376 (1960).
65. 440 U.S. 93 (1979).
66. 473 U.S. 432 (1985).
67. Supra Note 25, p. 661.
68. 531 U.S. 356 (2001). In *Garrett*, the court held that Congress lacked the authority to authorize suits against the states for employment discrimination based on disability under Title I of the Americans with Disabilities Act.
69. 488 U.S. 336 (1989).
70. 505 U.S. 1 (1992).
71. Supra Note 25, p. 662.
72. 323 U.S. 214 (1944).
73. Hugo Black was Associate Justice of the US Supreme Court from 1937–1971.
74. Supra Note. 15, p. 723.
75. 388 U.S. 1 (1967).
76. 109 U.S. 3 (1883).
77. Supra Note 15, pp. 724–6.
78. 163 U.S. 537 (1896).
79. David Josiah Brewer was Associate Justice of the US Supreme Court.
80. Henry Billings Brown was Associate Justice of the US Supreme Court.
81. John Marshall Harlan was Associate Justice of the US Supreme Court.
82. 347 U.S. 483 (1954).
83. Supra Note 15, pp. 726–7.
84. 305 U.S. 337 (1938).
85. 199 Okl. 586 (Okl. 1948).
86. 339 U.S. 637 (1950).
87. 339 U.S. 629 (1950).
88. Fred Moore Vinson, was the 13th Chief Justice of the US Supreme Court.
89. Supra Note 15, p. 727.
90. 347 U.S. 497 (1954).
91. 358 U.S. 1 (1958).
92. 396 U.S. 19 (1969).
93. 402 U.S. 1 (1971).
94. 413 U.S. 189 (1973).
95. 418 U.S. 717 (1974).
96. Supra Note 15, p. 729.
97. 498 U.S. 237 (1991).
98. 503 U.S. 467 (1992).
99. 515 U.S. 70 (1995).
100. Sandra Day O'Connor was the first woman Associate Justice of the US Supreme Court from 1981 to 2006.
101. Clarence Thomas is an Associate Justice of the US Supreme Court since 1991.
102. Ruth Bader Ginsburg was an Associate Justice of the US Supreme Court from 1993 to 2020.
103. Stephen Breyer is Associate Justice of the US Supreme Court since 1994.
104. 551 U.S. 701 (2007).
105. John Roberts is the 17th Chief Justice of the US Supreme Court since 2005.
106. Antonin Scalia was Associate Justice of the US Supreme Court from 1986 to 2016.
107. Samuel Alito is an Associate Justice of the US Supreme Court since 2006.
108. Anthony Kennedy was Associate Justice of the US Supreme Court from 1988 to 2018.

109. Erwin Chemerinsky, *Constitutional Law*. 4th ed. (New York: Walter Kluwer Law & Business, 2011) pp. 749–51.
110. Supra Note 15, p. 731.
111. 416 U.S. 312 (1974).
112. 438 U.S. 265 (1978).
113. Lewis Franklin Powell was an Associate Justice of the US Supreme Court from 1972 to 1987.
114. Warren E. Burger was the 15th Chief Justice of the US Supreme Court from 1969 to 1986.
115. Potter Stewart was an Associate Justice of the US Supreme Court from 1958 to 1981.
116. William J Brennan Jr. was an Associate Justice of the US Supreme Court from 1956 to 1990.
117. Byron White was an Associate Justice of the US Supreme Court from 1962 to 1993.
118. Harry Blackmun was an Associate Justice of the US Supreme Court from 1970 to 1994.
119. 448 U.S. 448 (1980).
120. Supra Note 15, pp. 732–3.
121. 83 U.S. 130 (1872).
122. 88 U.S. 162 (1875).
123. Supra Note 15, p. 737.
124. 477 U.S. 57 (1986).
125. 404 U.S. 71 (1971).
126. 11 U.S. 677 (1973).
127. 21 Cal. 3d 1 (1978).
128. 420 U.S. 636 (1975).
129. 430 U.S. 199 (1977).
130. 429 U.S. 190 (1976).
131. 440 U.S. 268 (1979).
132. 416 U.S. 351 (1974).
133. William O. Douglas was an Associate Justice of the US Supreme Court from 1939 to 1975.
134. 417 U.S. 484 (1974).
135. 453 U.S. 57 (1981).
136. 198 U.S. 45 (1905).
137. Supra Note 12, pp. 738–40.
138. 458 U.S. 718 (1982).
139. Lewis F. Powell Jr was Associate Justice of the US Supreme Court from 1971 to 1987.
140. 518 U.S. 515 (1996).
141. Supra Note 15, pp. 741–2.
142. Ibid., p. 742.
143. J.N. Pandey, *Constitutional Law of India*, 38th ed. (Allahabad: Central Law Agency, 2002) p. 69.
144. AIR 88, 1988 SCR Supl. (3) 398.
145. AIR 1953 S.C. 404 at 406.
146. Sudhi Ranjan Das was the 5th Chief Justice of the Supreme Court of India.
147. AIR 1952 S.C. 75.
148. 1991 SCMR 1041.
149. 1993 SCMR 833.
150. PLD 1993 S.C. 341.
151. AIR 1979 SC 478 at 508.
152. AIR 1951 SC 41.
153. AIR 1953 SC 91.
154. AIR 1953 SC 215.
155. Ibid.
156. AIR 1967 S.C. 1305.
157. AIR 1983 S.C. 1.
158. AIR 1988 S.C. 1136.
159. PLD 1988 S.C. 416.
160. PLD 1957 S.C. 9.
161. Supra Note 3, pp. 237–9.
162. PLD 1958 S.C. 41.
163. Supra Note 3, p. 240.
164. PLD 1957 S.C. 157.

165. PLD 1993 SC 341.
166. PLD 1957 West Pakistan Quetta 1.
167. PLD 1957 (W.P) Peshawar 100.
168. PLD 1965 Lahore 229.
169. 1992 SCMR 563.
170. PLD 1964 S.C. 673.
171. Supra Note 3, pp. 244–6.
172. PLD 1975 S.C. 506.
173. 1991 SCMR 1041.
174. 1993 SCMR 468.
175. PLD 1990 S.C. 295.
176. 1979 SCMR 529.
177. 1981 SCMR 1002.
178. PLD 1955 S.C. 219.
179. PLD 1973 S.C. 49.
180. PLD 1974 S.C. 151.
181. Supra Note 3, pp. 251–5.
182. PLD 1990 S.C. 661.
183. 1988 SCMR 1991.
184. PLD 1975 S.C. 450.
185. PLD 1952 F.C. 29.
186. PLD 1957 S.C. 9.
187. PLD 1958 S.C. 41.
188. AIR 1974 S.C. 555.
189. AIR 1974 S.C. 2009 at 2029.
190. P.N. Bhagwati was the 17th Chief Justice of India.
191. V.R. Krishna lyer was judge of the Supreme Court of India on 17 July 1973.
192. AIR 1978 S.C. 597.
193. AIR 1981 S.C. 487.
194. AIR 1983 S.C. 473.
195. AIR 1980 S.C. 898.
196. (1986)4 SCC 421.
197. (1984) 3 SCC 369.
198. (1986) 3 SCC 156.
199. AIR 1978 SC 597.
200. (1985) 3 SCC 398.
201. *Mian Fazal Din v. Lahore Improvement Trust*, PLD 1969 S.C. 223.
202. *Moulvi Iqbal Haider v. Capital Development Authority*, PLD 2006 S.C. 394.
203. PLD 2010 S.C. 759.
204. AIR 1979 SC 1628.
205. AIR 1980 SC 1992.
206. AIR 1975 SC 266.
207. (1985) SCC 267.
208. (1986) 3 SCC 247.
209. AIR 1990 SC 1031.
210. AIR 1991 S.C. 537.
211. The short order is reported as PLD 2010 S.C. 1. The detailed reasons are reported as PLD 2010 S.C. 265. This case was decided by all seventeen judges of the Supreme Court of Pakistan.
212. 163 U.S. 537 (1896).
213. 59 Mass. (5 Cush.) 198 (1850).
214. 60 U.S. 393 (1857).
215. 347 U.S. 483 (1954).
216. 175 U.S. 528 (1899).
217. 275 U.S. 78 (1927).
218. 339 U.S. 629 (1950).
219. 339 U.S. 637 (1950).

Part III

Constitutional Structures

7 Parliamentary Form of Government

The British Parliament is the mother of all Parliaments and the unwritten constitution of Britain and its peculiar constitutional evolution has given birth to the concept of parliamentary supremacy. The parliamentary system of government has been adopted by several countries and prominent among them are Germany, Italy, Japan, Canada, Australia, Pakistan and India. To understand the parliamentary form of government, the British model is discussed below.

The government generally has three distinct powers, executive, legislative and judicial powers. Parliamentary form of government may be described as form of government wherein the executive branch of the government is elected or chosen from the legislative branch (called the Parliament in UK) and the executive is responsible to the Parliament. The Parliamentary form of government evolved in England owing to its peculiar constitutional history. Indeed, the development of this parliamentary form of government is a journey from absolute monarchy to a notional monarchy spanning over nine hundred years. British Parliament is therefore the mother of all Parliaments. The Parliamentary form of government has been adopted by several countries particularly in those countries, which formed part of the British Empire (with the exception of the United States which parted ways from the British Empire by declaration of its independence in 1776). To understand the parliamentary form of government a general understanding of the British model is necessary which is discussed below.

When Parliament is spoken of today, it is commonly understood to refer to the two chambers, the House of Commons and the House of Lords and the institution called the Executive or the Government. The latter is understood to mean the Queen's Minister, the Cabinet and the Central Departments and, in short is called Whitehall. The shorthand for the Houses of Parliament is Westminster. The two institutions are rightly seen as separate both geographically and functionally and this separation is not weakened by the constitutional requirement that Ministers should also be members of one or the other Houses. There is some duality of membership, but each institution is distinct.

All this is clear but is inadequate in explaining the nature of a formal relationship between the Queen, the Ministers and the two Houses. It suggests what is not true: that Parliament is merely a single word to describe what is called the two Houses of Parliament. From earliest times and after the Norman conquest (1066–75), the sovereign (the King or Queen) sought counsel from the most powerful subjects and during the 13th century under Edward I (1239–1307), the Knights of the Shires and representatives from the towns were also invited to attend what was called the King's Council in his Parliament. The King wanted more than advice. He wanted money and he needed to gather around him those who could supply it through taxes. Soon the Knights and the burgesses from the town began to meet separately in what became the House of Commons and the powerful baron and church leaders became the House of Lords. By the reign of Edward III (1312–77) it was established that taxation was illegal without of the two Houses and that the concurrence of the Houses was necessary for all statutory legislation.[1] The next few hundred years saw a further transfer of actual sovereign power from the King to the Parliament.

Another development, which concomitantly took place, was that the Executive (which comprised mostly undefined areas and was explained in terms of prerogatives) authority of the Sovereign King started to be exercised by some other persons called Ministers. These Ministers, for their act, were to be responsible to Parliament and that is why it is called a responsible government. Later, the Executive further evolved into the form that these Ministers would be chosen from the Parliament.

Parliamentary Supremacy (Sovereignty)

A.V. Dicey and other writers on the English Constitution have generally referred to the Parliament's legislative supremacy as Parliamentary sovereignty. The word sovereignty has always been confusing owing to historical reasons. The words 'Parliament' and 'Sovereignty' can have different meanings when used for different purposes and therefore, it is necessary to explain the different meanings they have here. The word 'Parliament' would be used in its usual legal sense, meaning the King in Parliament.

When we talk about Parliamentary Sovereignty, we use it in its legal sense and not in its political sense. Therefore, the word 'sovereignty' is interchangeable with the word 'supremacy'. 'Sovereignty' is much more difficult to define partly because it depends on meaning of 'law' which is notoriously problematic. Dicey defines the supremacy or sovereignty of the Parliament in terms of two criteria, one positive and the other negative. The positive criterion is that Parliament has right to make and unmake any law whatever; the negative one is that no person or body is recognized by the law of England as having a right to override or set aside the legislation of the Parliament.[2]

There is another unique characteristic of the English Constitution, which is not found elsewhere the parliamentary form of government is established. The highest court of appeal under the English Judicial system is the House of Lords. The true significance of this aspect of the English Constitution in the context of supremacy of the Parliament has to be seen. Although, as stated herein before power paradigm has shifted completely and the King and Lords are now considered only dignified and efficient part lies in the hand of the Commons. The characteristic merit of the English Constitution is that its dignified parts are very complicated and somewhat imposing, very old and rather venerable; while its efficient part, at least when in great and critical action, is decidedly simple and rather modern.[3]

One consequence of the absence of a codified constitution in the United Kingdom is that the legislative powers of Parliament have never been set out in any definitive form. The Bill of Rights 1689, still the most important statute on the powers of Parliament, was primarily concerned with the protection of its rights against interference by the monarch: Among other things, it declared that it was illegal for the Crown to levy taxes without parliamentary consent and to suspend the application of parliamentary enactments. Other significant legislation, the Parliament Acts of 1911 and 1949, removed the requirement that the House of Lords consent to legislation. But these statutes assume that Parliament is entitled to enact legislation, that is, rules of general application. They do not establish its right to legislate.

In contrast, codified constitutional texts spell out the powers of the legislature quite explicitly, as well as its composition and methods for its election. For instance, Article I, Section 1 of the US Constitution states clearly that –

> 'all Legislative Powers herein granted shall be vested in a Congress of the United States, which shall consist of a Senate and House of Representatives.'

Other Sections of the Article prescribe the composition of the Senate and House and the procedure for enacting legislation, as well as enumerating a number of specific legislative and other powers, such as the power to 'lay and collect Taxes' and the power to regulate inter-state commerce.

Similarly, Article 34 of the Constitution of the Fifth French Republic spells out the legislative powers of Parliament, while Article 77 of the German Basic Law states that Bills must be adopted by the *Bundestag*[4] if they are to become federal laws.[5]

(i) The Source and Scope of Parliamentary Supremacy

What is the source of the United Kingdom Parliament's legislative authority and what is the scope of that power? The short answer is that the source of its legislative authority is Common law, the uncodified rules of law formulated by judges when they decide cases. Furthermore, it is for the courts to determine the scope of that authority. They must decide, for instance, whether parliamentary legislative authority prevails over it or gives way to inconsistent rules of European Community law.

It is largely for this reason the Constitution of the United Kingdom can be described, as a Common Law constitution. The law reports are full of statements that it is the duty of the courts to give effect to enactments of Parliament, or that they cannot be challenged for infringing some fundamental right or the rules of international law. For example, a court easily rejected the argument that it was unconstitutional for Parliament to introduce the offence of incitement to racial hatred, because the law limited the fundamental right to freedom of speech.[6] Judges have emphasized that the UK Parliament has unlimited legislative supremacy and that it is sovereign.

It is therefore the courts, rather than Parliament itself, which have formulated the principle which is the cornerstone of the uncodified constitution of the United Kingdom. Naturally, Parliament could declare by an Act of Parliament that it is legally sovereign and that it has unlimited entitlement to enact any legislation it likes.[7] But such a declaratory statute would not add anything to its legislative capacity. Parliament can hardly confer constitutional authority on itself by its own enactment.

There was a time when the judges were unclear whether there are limits to the scope of parliamentary legislative supremacy. Early in the 17th century, Chief Justice Sir Edward Coke (1552–1634)[8] wrote that

> Acts of Parliament contrary to common right and reason should be regarded as of no effect.[9]

But it is very rare to find anyone saying that after the Glorious Revolution of 1688. Judges gradually accepted parliamentary rule, and during the 18th century the principle of its legislative supremacy became firmly established. It has generally been welcomed by politicians and ministers, for they can employ it to secure compliance with their policies, at least when they control the Parliament. Significant reservations have, however, been expressed by some Scottish judges.[10] Legislative supremacy was not an established feature of the Scottish Parliament, before it was merged with the English Parliament, under the Act of Union in 1707. But, their doubts have rarely, if ever, been shared by English judges.[11]

The courts have recognized/formulated the principle of parliamentary supremacy, it is also for them to decide what amounts to an Act of Parliament. The common law rule is that Parliament consists of the House of Commons, the House of Lords, and the Crown. Together they constitute the Queen in Parliament. Subject to the changes made by the Parliament Acts 1911 and of 1949, each House sitting separately, and the monarch must assent to a Bill, for it to become a statute. As a matter of constitutional law, legislative supremacy means the supremacy of the Queen in Parliament, not just the House of Commons. A resolution of the House of Commons may be binding on members of Parliament, but it cannot change the law of the land.[12]

As with other aspects of constitutional law the formulation of the principle of parliamentary supremacy has largely been left to writers on the constitution. The doctrine of parliamentary supremacy is particularly associated with one of the greatest of these scholars, A. V. Dicey. For him, it was the dominant legal principle of the constitution. Indeed, it does play much the same role in United Kingdom constitutional law as the codified constitutional text does in other countries: it lies at the root of most, if not all, other important aspects of the constitution. It is, of course, in isolation not as comprehensive as, say, the United States or French Constitutions. But the principle is as fundamental as a codified constitution. Since Parliament enjoys legislative supremacy, it is entitled, for instance, to alter the powers of the Crown or to establish new courts. In other countries, the powers of these institutions would be derived from the constitution itself.

Dicey and other writers on the constitution have generally referred to Parliament's legislative supremacy as 'parliamentary sovereignty'. This is a rather confusing description, and it is better to avoid it. It is confusing because the concept of 'sovereignty' is more often used in political discourse either to refer to the ultimate sovereign power of the electorate or alternatively to the sovereignty, that is the independence of the nation state. Parliament may be legally sovereign, but it is misleading to use a word which can be understood to suggest it also enjoys ultimate political control. It certainly does not carry that implication.

Firstly, voters elect the members of Parliament and, therefore, in a sense choose the government every few years. Secondly, as a matter of political reality, in normal circumstances the government controls Parliament through the power of the Prime Minister to dissolve Parliament, if the government is not supported by members of the majority political party. As a matter of constitutional law, the legislative supremacy of Parliament means simply that the Queen in Parliament has unlimited capacity to enact laws, parliamentary legislative supremacy means no more than that.

(ii) Parliamentary Supremacy and Political Reality

The discussion above has mainly focused on the supremacy of the Parliament in the legal sense. Regarding political sovereignty, we will now examine the transformation of a system of government from absolute monarchy to a representative government. Prior to this transformation, the King or Queen were the absolute repository of what is now called the executive powers. Walter Bagehot[13] describes this transformation in these words,

> 'The efficient secret of the English constitution may be described as the close union, the nearly complete fusion of the executive and legislative powers. According to the traditional theory, as it exists in all the books, the goodness of our constitution consists in the entire separation of legislative and executive authorities, but in truth its merits consist in their singular approximation. The connecting link is *the Cabinet*. By that new word we mean a committee of the legislative body selected to be the executive body. The legislature has many committees, but this is its greatest. It chooses for this, its main committee, the men in whom they has most confidence. It does not, it is true, choose them directly; but it is nearly *omnipotent* in choosing them indirectly. A century ago the Crown had a real choice of ministers, though it had no longer a choice in policy. During the long reign of Sir Robert Walpole[14] he was obliged not only to manage Parliament but also to manage the palace. He was obliged to take care that some court intrigue did not expel him from his place. The nation then selected the English policy, but the Crown chose the English ministers. They were not only in name, as now, but in fact, the Queen's servants. Remnants, important remnants, of this great prerogative still remain. The discriminating favour of William IV made Lord Melbourne head of the Whig Party, when he was only one of several rivals. At the death of Lord Palmerston, it is very likely that the Queen may have the opportunity of freely choosing between two, if not three statesmen. But as a rule, the nominal Prime Minister is chosen by the legislature—and the real Prime Minister for most purposes—the leader of the House of commons almost without exception is so. There is nearly always someone man plainly selected by the voice of the predominant party in the predominant house of the legislature to head that party, and consequently to rule the nation. We have in England an elective first magistrate as truly as the Americans have an elective first magistrate. The Queen is only at the head of the dignified part of the constitution. The Prime Minister is at the head of the efficient part. The Crown is, according to the saying, the 'fountain of honour;' but the Treasury is the spring of the business.'[15]
>
> The first and the cardinal consideration is the definition of a Cabinet. A cabinet is a combining committee – a *hyphen* which joins, a *buckle* which fastens the legislative part of the State to the executive part of the State. In its origin it belongs to the one, in its functions it belongs to the other.[16]

Taken to its logical limits, the supremacy of Parliament could have absurd implication. The European Parliament, it has been said, could as a matter of law make it a crime for French citizens to smoke on the streets of Paris. Strictly, English courts would have to apply such a rule, and could fine a Frenchman who is arrested and charged with the offence, while resident or on holiday in England. The law can depart from reality in circumstances of this sort.

Such problems were, however, far from hypothetical at the time when Dicey formulated his theory. At the end of the 19th century and in the first three decades of this, it was unclear whether the British Parliament was still entitled to legislate for the Dominions, for example, Canada, Australia, New Zealand, and South Africa. Legislation such as the British North America Act 1867 (the first Canadian Constitution) had given the local Parliaments freedom to enact laws, provided their provisions were not incompatible with United Kingdom statutes. It followed that the British Parliament was still entitled to legislate for the Dominions, as it had at least in theory been for the American colonies before the United States became independent. This possibility was only removed as a matter of law in 1931, when the Statute of Westminster enacted the convention that the United Kingdom Parliament could not legislate for a Dominion without the request and consent of the country.[17]

The relationship of the principle of parliamentary legislative supremacy to political reality is perhaps, best illustrated by the 1969 ruling of the Privy Council in *Madzimbamuto v. Lardner-Burke*.[18] Immediately after the Unilateral Declaration of Independence (UDI) by the minority White regime in Southern Rhodesia, the UK Parliament enacted the Southern Rhodesia Act 1965. This repealed an earlier enactment which had given full authority to the Rhodesian Parliament; it also empowered the Crown to introduce Orders in Council to regulate that country. The Privy Council decided that Parliament's legislative power was not limited by the established convention that it should not legislate for Rhodesia without its consent. Lord James Reid (1890–1975)[19] added:

> 'It is often said that it would be unconstitutional for the United Kingdom Parliament to do certain things, meaning that the moral, political and other reasons against doing them are so strong that most people would regard it as highly improper if Parliament did these things. But that does not mean that it is beyond the power of Parliament to do such things.'

In other words, the legislative supremacy of Parliament and political reality may part company. This did not happen in Rhodesia's case because at the time of the Privy Council judgement, a few years after UDI (Unilateral Declaration of Independence), it was unclear whether the attempts of the British government to exercise effective control over Rhodesia were successful. But, constitutional law would certainly depart from reality if Parliament were to enact legislation which purported to amend United States criminal law or to proscribe smoking on the streets of Paris.

(iii) Can Parliament bind its Successors?

The relationship to political reality of constitutional law in general, and the principle of parliamentary supremacy in particular, is usually of only theoretical interest. Of potentially more practical significance is the question whether it is possible for Parliament to enact legislation which effectively binds its successors, that is, later Parliaments.

The answer might be important, because it would determine whether Parliament could enact, for example, a Bill of Rights or a measure devolving power to a Scottish Parliament, and effectively preclude the repeal of these measures by a later Parliament. The question is generally put in this way: is it possible for Parliament to entrench legislation against repeal, or amendment, by a subsequent enactment passed in the traditional way?

Dicey denied that Parliament could do this.[20] He said that Parliament must as a matter of logic always retain its sovereign capacity to repeal its earlier laws and that England has always been ruled by an absolute legislator, at one time the King and now the Parliament.

Admittedly, some cases do establish that Parliament cannot fetter itself simply by stating that a legislative provision is to endure 'forever' or that a section in a subsequent act should not have any effect if inconsistent with it.[21] In these circumstances there are no strong reasons for applying the provisions in the earlier statute in preference to those in the later one. It is reasonable for the courts to apply the later statute which is taken impliedly to repeal the inconsistent provisions of the earlier one. But it would be wrong for them to reach the same conclusion, if Parliament were to provide, say, in a Bill of Rights statute that any future legislation infringing these fundamental rights, or repealing the Bill of Rights itself, must secure a two-thirds majority in the House of Commons or be approved by a referendum. It would be dogmatic in these circumstances to insist that the Bill of Rights could be repealed (or any right set out in it infringed) by the traditional simple majority procedure. For there are obviously good reasons why Parliament might intend fundamental human rights to be guaranteed against interference in a Bill only approved by a simple majority of a subsequent Parliament. The requirement of a two-thirds majority or approval at a referendum provides some safeguard against a government decision, approved by its supporters in the Commons, to restrict the exercise of fundamental rights. In the absence of powerful counter arguments, one would expect the courts to respect that guarantee.

Yet, defenders of Dicey's views argue that entrenchment of a Bill of Rights or other fundamental legislation in this way is constitutionally impossible.[22] Their case is that the principle of parliamentary legislative supremacy necessarily means that the Houses of Parliament (or more specifically the House of Commons) must be able to pass laws by simple majority and that the Parliament cannot change this rule, even for the enactment of certain types of important legislation. The rule is said to be quite different from any other rule of the common law, in that it alone cannot be modified by statute. Any amendment to that rule, it is claimed, would amount to a legal revolution.

The argument is not very convincing. In the first place, the common law rule does not require Parliament to enact legislation by simple majority. The Houses happen to use that procedure, but there is no reason to believe that the practice is sacrosanct or could not be changed by an Act of Parliament. And in the second place, Parliament has changed the rules for the enactment of legislation in the Parliament Acts 1911 and 1949 by reducing the powers of the House of Lords. If there is no difficulty in accepting a change in the composition of Parliament which strengthens the prerogatives of the

> 'House of Commons, there should not be any problem in accepting a change in the manner of enacting legislation which reduces those prerogatives—either by the introduction of the requirements of a two-thirds majority or by requiring certain legislation to be approved at a referendum. Some cases from other countries show that legislation can be entrenched in these ways.[23]'

One implication of the traditional Dicey perspective is that the United Kingdom constitutional arrangements would have to be regarded as rigid in practice. For its defenders claim that the common law rule of parliamentary supremacy is so fundamental that it cannot be modified. As a result, it would be impossible to amend the present constitutional arrangements by entrenching a Bill of Rights, let alone introduce a federal or non-federal constitution. In contrast, the vast majority of codified constitutions, generally characterized as more rigid than the flexible constitution of the United Kingdom, can be amended by a procedure set out in the text.[24] It is hard to accept that the Constitution of United Kingdom is so rigid that the principle of parliamentary supremacy can never be modified without a legal revolution.

What is clear is that the judiciary is as much the guardian of the UK Constitution as it is of codified constitutions. It would be for the courts to determine whether Parliament can bind its successors by making radical amendments to the procedure for enacting legislation, just as they have decided, that Parliament is free to bind itself not to enact legislation contrary to European Community law. As a matter of prediction, it is uncertain whether they would accept that Parliament can entrench, say, a Bill of Rights in preference to the traditional Diceyan view. But there can be no doubt that they should uphold the entrenchment of a Bill of Rights or of a measure devolving power to Scotland or other parts of the United Kingdom.[25]

The House of Commons and The House of Lords

Like many other countries the United Kingdom has a bi-cameral legislature, that is, there are two Houses of Parliament, the House of Commons and the House of Lords. Until about the end of the 18th century the House of Lords, frequently referred to as the Upper Chamber to denote its seniority, was at least an equal partner to the Commons in the 'balanced constitution',[26] But with the gradual extension during the 19th century of the right to vote and the advent of democratic politics, its legitimacy has increasingly been called into question. At first by constitutional convention, and now by law under the Parliament Acts 1911 and 1949, its legislative role has been significantly curtailed. In effect, the Lords must assent to a Bill certified by the Speaker of the House of Commons as a Money Bill within a month after it has been sent to the Upper Chamber, while, with one exception, they can only delay other Public Bills for one year.[27] This reduction in the Lords' powers does not apply to a Bill to extend the life of a Parliament, or, to put it another way, to postpone a General Election, beyond the 5 year period established in 1911 for the duration of Parliaments. However, even in this context the legislative power of the Lords is not entrenched, for the House could only delay for a year a Bill to remove this last vestige of the 'veto power'.

The Parliament Acts 1911 and 1949 have established the dominance of the House of Commons. There were unsuccessful attempts during the passage of the 1911 law to exempt Bills dealing with 'constitutional issues' from the new procedure, so retaining the Lords' right to veto major changes to the existing arrangements[28]. Not surprisingly there was little agreement over which measures should be given constitutional status for this purpose, while the Liberal government was anxious to exclude the courts from any jurisdiction to determine these matters. The supremacy of the Commons is ensured by giving the last word on the question of what amounts to a Money Bill and other issues arising under the Parliament Acts to the Speaker of the House of Commons, hardly a neutral umpire if there were a serious disagreement between the two Houses.

What is the significance of this reform, one of the most important amendments made to the uncodified constitution in the course of this century? In the first place it gave legal expression to the gradual change in the balance of powers between the Commons and Lords which had occurred over the previous century. Parliamentary legislative supremacy now clearly means the supremacy of the elected House of Commons, a development which alarmed its great apostle, Dicey. It even prompted him in his later writings to urge use of the referendum to act as a constraint on the Commons' potentially dictatorial powers. Whatever the weaknesses of the House of Lords, at least in theory, it could check abuses of power by the stronger branch of the legislature. The constitutional value of checks and balances was sacrificed in 1911 and 1949 in the interests of democracy.[29]

In the second place the Parliament's Acts have altered the common law rule which provides the basis of the informal UK Constitution. When the Speaker certifies that a Bill is a Money Bill or that it satisfies other requirements of the Parliament's Acts, the courts must apply it even if the consent of the House of Lords to the measure had not been obtained. Acceptance of legislation enacted under the procedure prescribed by the Parliament

Acts 1911 and 1949 shows that there is nothing immutable or sacrosanct in the common law formulation of the principle of parliamentary supremacy.

It is now taken for granted that the abolition of the peers' veto power was a reasonable step in the context of their obstruction of David Lloyd George's (1863–1945)[30] 'People's Budget' in 1909 and of the illegitimacy of the composition of the Upper Chamber. At that time the House was composed more or less entirely of hereditary peers, the only other members being some Bishops of the Church of England and the Law Lords, given life peerages to sit as Lords of Appeal. Now about a third of the House is life peers, appointed by the Prime Minister, albeit some times on the nomination of Opposition parties. But that has done little to enhance its legitimacy. In effect, recent Crown appointees have been added to the more substantial numbers of hereditary peers, themselves the heirs of dukes and other nobles given their titles in previous centuries.

The Preamble to the Parliament Act 1911, refers to the desirability of replacing the hereditary House with a Second Chamber constituted on a popular basis, that is, by election. But, nothing has been done to bring this about. Reform of the composition of the House of Lords remains one of the most intractable problems of constitutional reform.[31] The central difficulty is that it would be difficult to establish an elected Second Chamber without undermining the democratic legitimacy of the Commons. One possibility would be for the members of the Second Chamber to be elected to represent Scotland, Wales, and separate English regions; that would be a sensible step if the United Kingdom were eventually to adopt something like a federal constitution. In this context, it is important to note that the most influential Upper Houses are found in federal constitutions; the United States and Australian Senates and the German *Bundesrat*[32] are good examples. If successful reform of the Upper Chamber's composition could be achieved, it might also be appropriate to consider strengthening its functions, for example, by restoring its power to veto certain types of Bill, such as those affecting fundamental rights or amending the constitution.

The positions of the House of Lords and its members have been further weakened by constitutional conventions. Though there is no legal bar to a peer becoming Prime Minister or Chancellor of the Exchequer, such an appointment is almost certainly precluded by convention. Even if George V's (1865–1936) appointment of Stanley Baldwin (1867–1947)[33] as Prime Minister in preference to Lord Curzon (1859–1925)[34] in 1923 does not afford a wholly persuasive precedent for the existence of the convention,[35] the fact that Sir Alec Douglas Home (1903–1995)[36] renounced his peerage on the invitation to succeed Harold MacMillan (1894–1986)[37] as Prime Minister in 1964 indicates that a rule of this kind is now generally accepted. The possibility that a political party (or its Members of Parliament) would elect a Peer as its leader can safely be discounted.

There is also arguably a convention to the effect that, except in extreme cases, the House of Lords should not exercise its legal power to delay the passage of legislation, at least when an intention to introduce the measure has been stated in the governing party's manifesto. Whether this is so or not, only one Bill has been delayed by the House since 1949; that was the War Crimes Bill, a non-party measure conferring jurisdiction on United Kingdom Courts to try certain Second World War (1939–45) crimes, even when committed outside the country.

In practice, whatever the political colour of the government, the House is extremely reluctant to assert its view against that of the Commons. The key point is that with its present composition, and with its weak legal authority further restricted by convention, the Upper Chamber is not an effective check on the legislative supremacy of the House of Commons.[38]

Parliamentary Democracy In Germany

The form of government established by the Basic Law (Grundgesetz)[39] is that of parliamentary democracy.[40] This means that the Federal Government is dependent upon the *Bundestag* (German federal Parliament)[41] and that its formation and removal fall within the latter's competence.

The Federal Government consists of the Federal Chancellor and the Federal Ministers.[42] According to the Basic Law, the *Bundestag* elects the Federal Chancellor[43] but not the Federal Government as a whole. The Federal Ministers are appointed by the Federal President upon the proposal of the Federal Chancellor.[44] In practice, the decision on who will become the Federal Chancellor, or a Federal Minister is largely predetermined by the outcome of the popular election of the *Bundestag*. The parties which can expect to overcome the five-percent threshold of the popular vote not only present their candidates for membership in the *Bundestag* to the electorate but also their candidates for Federal Chancellor and Federal Ministers. The party or coalition of parties winning the election will therefore be politically bound to elect its candidate for Federal Chancellor, while the latter will likewise be bound to propose the designated persons for appointment as Federal Ministers.

Despite its dependence upon the *Bundestag*, the Federal Government is not envisaged by the Basic Law as a kind of parliamentary committee but as a separate governmental organ within the system of distribution of powers at the national level. In order to secure a stable and viable Federal Government, the Basic Law provides for several mechanisms.

Firstly, the election of the Federal Chancellor requires in general the votes of the majority of the members of the *Bundestag*; if no candidate obtains an absolute majority which entitles him to be appointed by the Federal President, a relative majority of the votes is sufficient, but in this case the Federal President is free to either appoint the candidate or to dissolve the *Bundestag*.[45] Furthermore, the removal of the Federal Chancellor and consequently of the Federal Ministers[46] requires a 'constructive' vote of no-confidence, i.e. the *Bundestag* can express its lack of confidence in the Federal Chancellor only by electing a successor with the majority of its members. In other words, the vote on a motion of no-confidence has dual purpose: it removes a Chancellor and at the same time elects his successor. The successful candidate must then be appointed by the Federal President.[47]

Finally, the Federal Chancellor can ask the *Bundestag* for a vote of confidence; if his motion is not carried by the majority of its members, the *Bundestag* can be dissolved by the Federal President upon the proposal of the Federal chancellor provided that it does not elect-with the same majority- a successor.[48]

Taken together, these mechanisms are aimed at providing an adequate balance between the necessary dependence and autonomy of the Federal Government in relation to the *Bundestag*. They have an additional effect on the internal structure of the *Bundestag*. On the one hand, they compel the members to form the required majority, instituting and supporting the Federal Government, or face the dissolution of the *Bundestag*. On the other hand, they give the minority a chance to distinguish itself as the opposition and as a possible alternative to the Federal Government in power. The traditional distribution of powers between the *Bundestag* and the Federal Government is thus supplemented, but not abolished, by a further distribution of powers between the political forces supporting the Federal Government and those opposing it. The latter distinction can be found not only in the *Bundestag* but also among the electorate due to the concentration of political preferences within the various political parties.[49]

Election and Removal of other Federal Officeholders

The *Bundestag* participates further in the election and removal of other federal officeholders, especially the Federal President and the members of the Federal Constitutional Court.

The Federal President is elected by the Federal Assembly (*Bundesversammlung*)[50] which consists of the members of the Federal Parliament (*Bundestag*) and an equal number of members elected by the state parliaments. Election requires the votes of the majority of the Assembly members in the first two ballots or the largest number of votes in the subsequent ballot.[51] Removal of the Federal President is only possible by a decision of the Federal Constitutional Court upon impeachment which requires a two-thirds majority of the members of the Bundestag or of the votes of the Federal Council (*Bundesrat*).[52]

The *Bundestag* elects one-half of the members of the Federal Constitutional Court, while the other half is elected by the Federal Council.[53] In implementing this constitutional provision, the Statute on the Federal Constitutional Court delegates election by the *Bundestag* to a committee of twelve members chosen by proportional ballot and requires a two-thirds majority of the committee members or of the votes of the *Bundesrat* for election. The delegation of the electoral competence from the plenum to a small committee of the *Bundestag* raises serious doubts as to its constitutionality. The requirement of a two-thirds majority can be justified by the need to ensure a broad basis of support for the members of the court who have the final word in constitutional controversies. Removal of a member of the court from office is only possible by the Federal President upon authorization by a two-thirds majority of the full court.

In contrast to its exclusive competence regarding the formation and removal of the Federal Government, the *Bundestag* shares its powers in the election and removal of the Federal President and the members of the federal Constitutional Court with other governmental organs, especially the state parliaments and the Federal Council.

Legitimisation and stabilisation of government are therefore major functions of the *Bundestag*, even though they are partially shared by other governmental organs at the national and state levels.[54]

Parliamentary Government in Japan

The Constitution of Japan is the supreme law in the state, it was promulgated in 1946 and came in to force in 3 May 1947, replacing the Meiji Constitution (1889–1947)[55]. It also recognizes judicial review as an ingredient of checks and balances. While this might be an unusual combination of British and American prototypes, there have been no serious political deadlocks between the legislative and judicial branches since the introduction of the system.

Under the parliamentary system, the Cabinet may hold office as long as it is given confidence by the Lower House of Parliament. The Prime Minister has to be a member of the *Diet*[56] and a majority of the Ministers of State should also be members of the *Diet*[57].

The text of the *Meiji* Constitution provided that the Ministers were appointed solely by the Emperor and were individually responsible only to the Emperor. Nevertheless, even under the old Constitution, the parliamentary system had evolved as a 'regular constitutional course', as part of sound political practice during the period prior to the pre-World War II national emergency. In accordance with the widely-accepted ideas of constitutional monarchy and party government, it was understood that cabinet members were appointed by the Emperor but were jointly responsible to the Parliament because the sovereign could do no wrong.[58]

Under the present Japanese Constitution,[59] it has generally been accepted that the cabinet system is based on the British model. Now, the Cabinet is collectively responsible to the Lower House (the House of Representatives) for the general conduct of affairs and is concerned with political matters but not legal matters. The offices of the individual Ministers are not impeachable. The political responsibility of the Cabinet consists in its being obliged to resign *en masse* when it loses the confidence of the Lower house. Article 69 of the Constitution provides that, in case the House of Representatives passes a no confidence resolution or rejects a confidence resolution, all the Cabinet members must resign, unless the House is dissolved within 10 days. If the House is dissolved, a new election must take place within 40 days of the dissolution…

The House of Representatives may be dissolved at any time by the Emperor with the advice and approval of the Cabinet as stated in Article 7. The power of the Lower House to express no confidence in the Cabinet is thus balanced with the power of the Cabinet to dissolve the House of Representatives at its will.

The political party in power in the two Houses of the Diet can nominate the Prime Minister by majority vote. Thus, the leading party can control both the law making and administrative processes. As for the selection of the Prime Minister, Article 67 of the Constitution provides that in case the House of Representatives and the House of Councillors disagree and no agreement is reached even through a joint committee of both Houses, or the House of Councillors fails to reach a decision within ten days, the decision of the House of Representatives as to who shall be the Prime Minister shall be that of the *Diet.*[60] It establishes not only the supremacy of the Lower House over the Upper House but also the crucial political importance of securing a majority in the Lower House.

Parliamentary System in India

In India, there is a parliamentary form of government both at the Center and the States. The executive power of the Union is vested in the President, who exercises his powers and functions with the aid and advice of the Council of Ministers headed by a Prime Minister. The only exception is that under Article 103, the President has to act according to the opinion of the Election Commission.

The Council of Ministers is responsible for every executive act and accountable for their actions to the Parliament. Their responsibility is collective. Wherever the Constitution requires the satisfaction of the President for the exercise of any power or function, that satisfaction is not his personal satisfaction but in the constitutional sense that of the Council of Ministers. The same is the position of a Governor of a State who is required to act as a constitutional head and act according to the advice of his ministers except when he acts in his discretion.

There were many reasons why the framers of the Constitution preferred the parliamentary system of government to the presidential system. The people of India were already familiar with the working of the parliamentary system.

A parliamentary system could provide effective leadership in emergencies. Cabinet system ensures harmony between the executive and the legislature. Parliamentary system gives more responsibility. The assessment of the responsibility of the executive is both on daily as well as periodic basis. The members of parliament can make the ministers responsible by putting those questions, moving resolutions and no-confidence motions, adjournment motions and debates on address by the President. Elections are held after regular intervals and that gives the voters an opportunity to express their approval or dissatisfaction with the Government in power.[61]

However, the federal parliamentary character of the Indian Constitution has been recognized by the Supreme Court of India as part of the basic structure of the Constitution. In *Kesavananda Bharati v. State of Kerala*,[62] the Supreme Court of India held the principles on which the basic structure or framework of the Indian Constitution depends as under:

(i) the supremacy of the Constitution;
(ii) the republican and democratic form of government;
(iii) the secular character of the Constitution;
(iv) the separation of powers between the legislature, the executive and the judiciary; and
(v) the federal character of the Constitution.

Although while enumerating the basic structure of the Constitution, parliamentary form of government has not been mentioned, yet what Supreme Court meant by the republican and democratic form of government was in fact parliamentary system of government. However, one of the judges, namely P. Jaganmohan Reddy (1910–99), while agreeing with the majority in the *Kesavanada* case specifically included parliamentary democracy as one of the elements forming the basic structure of the Constitution.

In *Indira Nehru Gandhi v. Raj Narain*,[63] the Supreme Court of India accepted the majority opinion in *Kesavanada Bharati*'s case. In this case the Supreme Court identified four unamendable features as forming part of the basic structure of the constitution, namely:

(i) sovereign democratic republic status;
(ii) equality of status and opportunity of an individual;
(iii) secularism and freedom of conscience and religion; and
(iv) government of laws and not of men.

In this case as well, by sovereign democratic republic status, the Supreme Court meant the parliamentary democracy.

Despite many drawbacks, the parliamentary system in India has worked successfully over the last more than 70 years. In this period, parliamentary traditions and conventions have taken roots and people of India have grown familiar with the parliamentary democracy.

According to critics, the parliamentary system in India has failed because of multiplicity of political parties, evil of defections, lack of cohesiveness and leadership in national parties, illiteracy of voters, large growth of regional parties, and criminalization of politics.[64] Despite such factors, the parliamentary system has given the huge electorate in India a voice and opportunity to change governments which it has done a number of times.

Parliamentary System in Pakistan

Prior to Independence, the territories which now constitute Pakistan were governed as part of India under the Government of India Act, 1935, which was the constitutional instrument then in force. Under the Indian Independence Act 1947, (the law creating the Dominions of Pakistan and India), the Governor General, till 31 March 1948, was empowered to make by Order such provisions as appeared to him to be necessary to bring the provisions of that Act into effective operation and to make necessary adaptations of the Government of India Act 1935, in its application to the Dominion of Pakistan.

In exercise of this authority, the Governor General promulgated the Pakistan (Provisional Constitution) Order 1947. Thus, the Government of India Act 1935, was adapted by that Order, and by subsequent such Orders and/or

Acts of the Constituent Assembly, remained the Constitution of Pakistan till the framing and enforcement of the first Constitution of Pakistan in 1956.

Constitution of 1956

The 1956 Constitution was founded on the concept of parliamentary democracy and some of its main features were:[65]

1. The President was to be elected for a period of five years by an Electoral College consisting of the members of the National Assembly and the Provincial assemblies.
2. The Prime Minister was to be appointed by the President in his discretion who, in his opinion, was likely to command the confidence of the majority of the members of the National Assembly. Prime Minister was to hold office during the pleasure of the President but the President could not exercise power of removal unless he was satisfied that Prime Minister had lost the confidence of majority of the members of the National Assembly.
3. The President was required to act on the advice of the cabinet or the concerned minister in exercise of his functions, except in cases where President could act in his own discretion.
4. The President had the power to dissolve the National Assembly sooner than the expiration of its term of five years.
5. The executive authority of the Federation vested in the President who had the power to appoint and remove ministers.
6. A detailed and comprehensive list of fundamental rights had been provided for in the constitution. These fundamental rights were later adopted in the Constitutions of 1962 and 1973, with slight variations and modifications here and there.
7. There was distribution of subjects between the centre and the provinces, East and West Pakistan. The Federal list, the concurrent list and provincial list were given in the constitution under its 5th Schedule. The residuary powers belonged to the Provinces with a few limitations.
8. The constitution provided for uni-cameral legislature with only one House of Parliament, the National Assembly. There was equal representation from both the Provinces in the National Assembly which was based on the principle of parity agreed to by the Constituent Assembly that framed the Constitution.
9. The Constitution had provided for two national languages, Urdu for West Pakistan and Bengali for East Pakistan. This decision for two national languages was also taken by the Constituent Assembly.
10. The Constitution was given an Islamic character. The name adopted for the Republic in the constitution was Islamic Republic of Pakistan. This name was subsequently adopted by the constitutions of 1962 and 1973. The Constitution provided for setting up an organization for Islamic research and instructions in advance studies to assist in the reconstruction of Muslim society on a truly Islamic basis.

The 1956 Constitution did not last long and was abrogated on 8 October 1958, on the imposition of Martial Law. The 1962 Constitution[66] is not discussed here because it did not give parliamentary form of government. The present constitution was enacted in 1973, and, again introduced parliamentary form of government. Some of its main features in its original form were as under:

1. Prime Minister was not an appointee of the President, but was to be elected by the National Assembly.
2. Prime Minister was designated as the Chief Executive.
3. Prime Minister could not be removed, except through a vote of no-confidence.
4. Bi-cameral legislature was introduced for the first time in Pakistan. The parliament consists of the Senate (having equal representation from each Province) as the Upper House and the National Assembly (with representation on the basis of population) as the Lower House.
5. The President was to be elected for 5 years by the parliament in a joint session.
6. The President could not veto or withhold assent for more than seven days to any Bill passed by the Parliament.

7. The President had no power to dissolve the National Assembly in his discretion. The National Assembly would stand dissolved on the expiry of its term of five years. The National Assembly could only be dissolved prior to the expiry of its term on the advice of the Prime Minister and on tendering of such advice, the National Assembly stood dissolved in forty-eight hours.
8. On the dissolution of the National Assembly, the Prime Minister would continue in office along with the Ministers of his choice until the new elections were held to the National Assembly and his successor was elected and entered upon his Office.
9. The Chiefs of the Armed Forces were to be appointed by the President on advice of the Prime Minister and not in his discretion.
10. Islamic provisions included the declaration of Islam as state religion and establishment of Islamic Ideology Council.
11. Elections to the National and Provincial Assemblies were to be held on the basis of joint electorate. Special seats for women and minorities were reserved in these Assemblies in addition to the general seats, which were open to women and minorities alone.

The 1973 Constitution was suspended in July 1977, on declaration of Martial Law by General Ziaul Haq (1924–88).[67] Before lifting the Martial Law, he made extensive changes in the constitution by promulgating Revival of the Constitution of 1973 Order 1985 (RCO), in March 1985. The RCO was made part of the constitution by Constitution (8th) Amendment Act, 1985, passed in November 1985.

The 8th Amendment empowers the President with vast powers, including

- the discretionary dissolution of the National Assembly and
- dismissal of the Prime Minister and his federal cabinet.
- He could appoint, in his discretion, Chiefs of all armed forces including Chief of Army, Navy and Air Force and the Chief Election Commissioner.

The Prime Minister had nothing to do with such appointments. It made the system tilted in favour of the President and the Prime Minister, the cabinet and the Parliament were weakened. Thus, the 8th Amendment undermined the parliamentary system in Pakistan.

The President of Pakistan exercised his discretionary power to dissolve the National Assembly and to dismiss the Prime Minister on no less than four occasions, that is, in 1988, for the first time it was used by President General Ziaul Haq to dismiss Muhammad Khan Junejo's (1932–93)[68] government. In 1990, for the second time, President Ghulam Ishaq Khan (1915–2006)[69] dismissed Benazir Bhutto's (1953–2007)[70] first government. In 1993, President Ghulam Ishaq Khan once again exercised his power to dissolve Nawaz Sharif's (1949)[71] first government. In 1996, President Farooq Leghari (1940–2010)[72] dismissed Benazir Bhutto's second government.

The Supreme Court of Pakistan upheld the action of the President twice, in 1990 and 1996 and both were Benazir Bhutto's government.[73] In another case, the action of the President to dissolve Muhammad Khan Junejo's government was held to be justiciable and was declared as invalid. Despite the Court's declaration, the National Assembly was not revived, and the federal government was not reinstated on the ground that general elections had already been announced and the people were geared to take part in the elections.[74]

Only in one case not only the order of the President was set aside but the National Assembly was restored, and the Prime Minister and his cabinet were reinstated.[75] The Supreme Court, in this case, stated, reaffirmed and emphasized that:

> the Constitution of Pakistan establishes parliamentary system of the government. The Prime Minister, in administering the affairs of the government, is neither answerable to the President nor is in any way subordinate to him. He is answerable only to the National Assembly. It is the President who is bound by the advice of the Prime Minister or the Cabinet in all matters concerning formulation of policies and administration of the affairs of the government and not the other way about.

This judgment strengthened, for the time being, the parliamentary system of government in Pakistan.

In a case where the 8th Amendment of the Constitution was challenged as invalid, the Supreme Court of Pakistan held that incorporation of 8th Amendment in Constitution did not change parliamentary form of government.[76] Although, the Supreme Court, in this case, did not accept the theory of basic structure of the Constitution, yet, it accepted certain basic features of the Constitution which cannot be changed through normal process of amendment of the Constitution. The Supreme Court enunciated fundamental rights, independence of judiciary, federal parliamentary form of government and Islamic provisions as basic features of the Constitution.

In 1997, the 13th Amendment in the Constitution was enacted which withdrew the discretionary power of the President to dissolve the National Assembly and the provincial assemblies in Pakistan. The power of the President to appoint chiefs of armed forces was also withdrawn and their appointment could only be made on the advice of the Prime Minister.

The 13th Amendment restored the full parliamentary character of the constitution. But it was not to be for a long time. Prime Minister Nawaz Sharif was deposed in military coup in October 1999 and the Constitution was suspended. The military ruler, General Pervez Musharraf (1943),[77] forced all the independent judges in the Supreme Court to resign and later the Supreme Court with a pliable Chief Justice and judges validated the military takeover and suspension of the Constitution,[78] thus allowing General Musharraf to amend the Constitution. However, he was forbidden from amending the salient features of the Constitution, i.e. the independence of judiciary, federation, parliamentary form of government blended with Islamic provisions.

General Musharraf, on the pretext of the power to amend the Constitution granted to him by the Supreme Court, promulgated a Legal Framework Order (LFO) in August 2002, altering the Constitution extensively, thus, weakening the position of the Parliament and the Prime Minister and conferring, once again, discretionary power on the President to dissolve the National Assembly and dismiss the Prime Minister and the Cabinet. The President was once again given discretionary power to appoint chiefs of armed forces.

After more than one year of resistance against the LFO, some opposition parties reached a compromise with General Musharraf and passed 17th Amendment to the Constitution in December 2003.

In this Amendment, the discretionary power of the President to dissolve the National Assembly and dismiss the Prime Minister and the Cabinet was affirmed. The only condition imposed by the 17th Amendment on this power is that within fifteen days of the passing of the order of dissolution, he will have to refer the matter to the Supreme Court for its opinion. The Supreme Court can either affirm or set aside such order. The Supreme Court upheld the 17th Amendment as valid.[79] The Supreme Court has declared 'parliamentary form of government' as a salient feature of the Constitution forming the basic structure of the Constitution.[80]

In a nutshell, due to the 8th Amendment, and later, the 17th Amendment, the parliamentary character of the Constitution of Pakistan was seriously undermined. The office of the President became too powerful in relation to the Parliament, the Prime Minister and the Cabinet. However, 18th Amendment passed in 2010 largely restored the Parliamentary character of the Constitution with the President becoming once again the titular head of the State.

Notes

1. J.A. Griffith, Michael Ryle, *Parliament Functions, Practice and Procedures* (Sweet & Maxwell,1989), page 3.
2. Jeffery Goldsworthy, *The Sovereignty of Parliament, History and Philosophy,* (Oxford University Press, 2001), chapter 2, page 10.
3. Walter Bagehot, *The English Constitution* (Chapman and Hall, 1867), page 67.
4. *Bundestag,* is the German federal parliament. It is the only body that is directly elected by the German people at the Federal level. It can be compared to the lower house similar to the United States House of Representatives or the House of Commons of the United Kingdom.
5. *Eric Barendt, An Introduction to Constitutional Law (Oxford: Oxford University Press, 1998), p. 86.*
6. *R v. Jordan,* (1956) 40 Cr. App. R. 152.
7. There is a precedent for such a statute, since the Bill of Rights 1689, is a measure, declaring the rights and liberties of Parliament against the 'pretended' powers of the Monarch.
8. Sir Edward Coke was an English barrister, judge, and Member of Parliament.
9. *Dr Bonham's case* (1610) 8 Co. Rep. 114, 118.
10. *MacCormick v. Lord Advocate,* 1953 SC 396, 411–13.
11. Supra Note 5, p. 88.

12. See *Stockdale v. Hansard* (1839) 9 Ad. & E: which held that a Resolution of the House could not protect Hansard from a libel action in respect of his reports of Parliamentary proceedings.
13. Walter Bagehot was a British journalist, businessman, and essayist, who wrote extensively about government, economics, literature and race.
14. Robert Walpole (1676 –1745) is generally regarded as the first British Prime Minister.
15. Supra Note 3, p. 68.
16. *Ibid.*
17. The Statute of Westminster is a British law that was passed on 11 December 1931. The Statute of Westminster gave Canada and the other Commonwealth Dominions legislative equality with Britain. They now had full legal freedom except in areas of their choosing.
18. (1969) 1 AC 645.
19. James Reid was a Scottish Unionist politician and judge. He is considered as one of the most outstanding judges of the 20th century.
20. A.V. Dicey, *The Law of the Constitution*, page 64–70.
21. *Ellen Street Estates v. Minister of Health* (1934) 1 KB 590.
22. The classic exposition of this case is by H.W.R. Wade, '*The Basis of Legal Sovereignty*' (1955) Cambridge LJ 172.
23. See in particular *Harris v. Minister of the Interior* (1952), (2) SA 429(AD), and *Bribery Commissioners v. Ranasinghe* (1965) AC 172 (Privy Council appeal from Sri Lanka). The Israeli Supreme Court has held that when the Knesset, a sovereign legislature, enacts Basic Laws on human rights, it binds itself not to enact ordinary legislation which infringes those rights.
24. Supra Note 5, p. 92.
25. *Ibid.*
26. *Ibid*, p. 93.
27. Under the 1911 Act, it could delay Public Bills for two years, but this was reduced to one year by the 1949 year measure, itself enacted under the 1911 Act procedure.
28. See J. Jaconelli, '*The Parliament Bill 1910–1911: The Mechanics of Constitutional Protection*" vol. 10, issue 2, Parliamentary History,(1991) 277.
29. Supra Note 5, p. 94.
30. David Lloyd George was a Welsh statesman who served as Prime Minister of the United Kingdom from 1916–22.
31. Supra Note 5, p. 95.
32. *Bundesrat* (Federal Council) is a legislative body that represents the 16 Länder (federated states) of Germany.
33. Stanley Baldwin was a British Conservative politician and three times Prime Minister between 1923–37.
34. Lord Curzon was a British Conservative statesman who served as Viceroy of India from 1899 to 1905.
35. Vernon Bogdanor, *The Monarchy and the Constitution* (USA: Oxford University Press, 1995), 89–93.
36. Sir Alec Douglas–Home was Prime Minister of the United Kingdom from 1963 to 1964.
37. Harold MacMillan was a Conservative statesman. He was Prime Minister of the United Kingdom from 1957–63.
38. Supra Note 5, pp. 95–6.
39. Basic Law [*Grundgesetz*] is the Constitution of Federal Republic of Germany.
40. Christian Starck, *Studies in German Constitutionalism* (Baden-Baden, Germany: Nomos, 1995), p. 152.
41. *Bundestag* (federal Parliament) It is the only body that is directly elected by the German people on the Federal level.
42. Article 62 of the Basic Law for the Federal Republic of Germany.
43. Article 63 of the Basic Law for the Federal Republic of Germany.
44. Article 64 Sec. 1 of the Basic Law for the Federal Republic of Germany.
45. Article 63 of the Basic Law for the Federal Republic of Germany.
46. Article 69 Sec. 2 of the Basic Law for the Federal Republic of Germany.
47. Article 67 of the Basic Law for the Federal Republic of Germany.
48. Article 68 of the Basic Law for the Federal Republic of Germany.
49. Supra Note 40, p. 154.
50. Is the largest parliamentary assembly in the Federal Republic of Germany. Its only job is to elect the Federal President.
51. Article 54 of the Basic Law for the Federal Republic of Germany.
52. Article 61, of the Bundesrat is the upper house of the parliament.
53. Article 94.
54. Supra Note 40, p. 155.
55. Meiji Constitution was the first constitution of the Empire of Japan, which was promulgated by the Emperor in 1889.
56. *Diet* is the Parliament of Japan with two Houses, the House of Representatives (Lower House) and the House of Councilors (Upper House).

57. Articles 67 and 68 of the Constitution of Japan.
58. Hiroyuki Hata, Gō Nakagawa, *Constitutional Law of Japan* (The Hague: Kluwer Law International,1997), p. 44.
59. The Constitution of Japan is the supreme law in the state. It replaced the Meiji Constitution on 3 May 1947.
60. Supra Note 45, p. 58.
61. V.D. Mahajan, *Constitutional Law of India*. 6th ed. (Delhi: Eastern Book Co.,1991), p. 25.
62. AIR 1973 S.C. 1461.
63. AIR 1975 S.C. 2299.
64. Narender Kumar, *Constitutional Law of India*, 3rd ed. (Faridabad, Haryana: Pioneer Publications, 2002), p. 4.
65. Hamid Khan, *Eighth amendment: Constitutional & political crisis in Pakistan* (Lahore: Wajidalis, 1994) pp. 236.
66. The 1962 Constitution provided for a federal state and a presidential system of government with a unicameral legislature.
67. General Ziaul Haq was Pakistan's Chief of Army Staff and Chief Martial-Law administrator, and President of Pakistan (1978–88).
68. Muhammad Khan Junejo was the 10th Prime Minister of Pakistan. From 24 March 1985–29 May 1988.
69. Ghulam Ishaq Khan was a Pakistani bureaucrat who served as the 7th President of Pakistan, elected in 1988 until his resignation in 1993.
70. Benazir Bhutto became the first woman leader of a Muslim nation in modern history. She served two terms as Prime Minister.
71. Nawaz Sharif served as the Prime Minister of Pakistan for three non-consecutive terms.
72. Farooq Leghari served as the 8th President of Pakistan from 14 November 1993 until resigning on 2 December 1997.
73. *Khawaja Ahmad Tariq Rahim v. Federation of Pakistan*, PLD 1992 SC 646 and *Benazir Bhutto v. Farooq Ahmad Khan Leghari*, PLD 1998 SC 388.
74. *Federation of Pakistan v. Haji Mohammad Saifullah Khan* PLD 1989 SC 166.
75. *Muhammad Nawaz Sharif v. Federation of Pakistan*, PLD 1993 S.C. 473.
76. *Mahmood Khan Achakzai v. Federation of Pakistan*. PLD 1997 S.C. 426.
77. Pervez Musharraf served as the 10th President of Pakistan after a military coup. From 2001 to 2008.
78. *Zafar Ali Shah v. General Parvez Musharaf*, PLD 2000 S.C. 673.
79. *Pakistan Lawyers Forum v. Federation of Pakistan*, PLD 2005 S.C. 719.
80. *District Bar Association, Rawalpindi v. Federation of Pakistan*, PLD 2015 S.C. 401 at 745.

8 Federalism

Introduction

In a federal system, power is divided between a central government and a set of regional governments. A unitary system, by contrast, vests all authority in the central government[1] the formal distribution of powers between the national government and the states proved to be subject of diverse interpretation in the US. Those who strived to safeguard state sovereignty also feared a broad construction of national powers; those who viewed the continuance of state power as the enemy of national strength, tended to, for tactical reasons, attach their satisfaction with the increased scope of national authority.[2]

The federal form of government was adopted by the framers of the US Constitution to accommodate the state interests while assuming that the national government would be able to exercise sufficient power to deal with common concerns of the nation. Those supporting 'federalism' in the 18th century were nationalist of their time, advancing 'federalism' as a form of government that would permit the exercise of national power over the states.[3] The concept of 'federalism' quickly spread all over the world and leading states like the US, Germany, Canada, Australia, Pakistan, and India are now federal States.

The federal form of government may be defined as a form of government where powers and authority of the state are distributed between the central government and the regional governments which may be called either provinces or states or federating units. There may be multiple reasons for adopting a federal form of government. Diverse cultural and regional nationalities who volunteer to form a federation, as in the case of the US, where after the failure of a confederation, it was thought that it was essential to have a strong central government in order have better security and the blessings of freedom.

In a colonial context, however, in Pakistan, India, Canada and Australia it was more for historical reasons that there was a demand for provincial autonomy that necessitated the demand for a federal form of government.

The federal form is usually adopted for good administration as the regional issues are dealt with at the state level. On the other hand, by distributing the powers between the federal and provincial entities, the liberty of the citizens is secured.

The best federal system however proved to be that of the US. For the development and strength of the federal system in the United States, it was the Federal Supreme Court, which under the leadership of Chief Justice John Marshall (1755–1835),[4] laid down solid foundations of the federation by extending the federal judicial authority to the actions of the states.[5]

In the constitutions of Canada and Australia, the problem of the distribution of legislative powers has been partially solved by conferring upon the provinces power to legislate on certain specified subjects while reserving the residual power of legislation for the federation. Thus, under the British North America Act 1867, which established a federal government for Canada, the legislative activities of the provinces are strictly defined, the residuary legislative power had been vested in the Dominion Government. In Australia, on the other hand, the states enjoy the residuary power, while the Commonwealth Parliament has power to make laws with respect to the 39 enumerated subjects.

Experience has shown that such distribution of powers tends to promote litigation on the questions whether the legislation on a particular subject falls within the competence of one legislature or the other. It has also shown that there are certain matters which cannot be allocated exclusively either to the federal/central legislature or to a provincial legislature, and for which, though it is often desirable that the provincial legislature should make provision, it is equally necessary that the central legislature should also have legislative jurisdiction, to enable it in some cases to secure uniformity in main principles of law throughout the country.[6]

While the British Parliament was giving a new constitution to India in the 1930s, a new experiment in the light of above difficulties experienced in Canada and Australia was undertaken by providing two sets of lists of the subjects, one in relation to which the federation and provinces had their respective exclusive legislative jurisdiction; and the other was a third list of subjects in relation to which the federal and provincial legislatures were possessed of concurrent legislative entitlement. If on the same subject, there is legislation by the provincial as well the federal legislature[7] then the federal law would prevail and the provincial law would be struck down to the extent of inconsistency.[8]

Development of Federalism

The best-known federal constitution is that of the United States of America. A short exposition of its origins and some of its principal features make a good introduction to the topic. Following the War of Independence, the newly independent states adopted the Articles of Confederation, the first American Constitution, in force from 1781 to 1788. It made no provision for a central government or judiciary; the Continental Congress, consisting of delegates from the states such as Massachusetts and Virginia, had some legislative power over the states, but no authority to impose taxes or to regulate commerce between the states. Moreover, it had no legislative authority over individuals in the states. Article II declared that:

> each state kept its sovereignty and independence. Moreover, changes to the Articles of Confederation had to be approved by all thirteen state legislatures.[9]

The Continental Congress was too weak to resolve conflicts over boundaries, trade, and tariffs. Many states printed their own currency. There were even occasional military skirmishes. Eventually, at the prompting of James Madison (1751–1836)[10] and Alexander Hamilton (1755/57–1804)[11]; a convention was gathered of delegates from all the states to consider reform of these unsatisfactory arrangements. The Constitutional Congress in Philadelphia drafted the Federal Constitution, which under its own terms (Article VII) came into force when it had been ratified by conventions held in nine states.

The principal object of the new constitution was to strengthen power at the centre, principally by the establishment of a federal Congress with broad legislative powers, including the power to tax, and, impose other obligations on individuals and to regulate inter-state commerce. It also provided for the election of a president with significant executive powers, and the institution of the United States Supreme Court.

Two provisions of the US Constitution are particularly important. Article VI, known as the 'Supremacy Clause', establishes the supremacy of the Constitution, laws, and treaties of the United States over the state constitutions and laws. State judges are expressly required by the Clause to apply the federal constitution and laws in their courts, whatever the state constitution and laws provide. When, therefore, an Act of Congress grants rights or imposes duties directly on the citizens of the states, the 'Supremacy Clause' requires judges in the states to enforce it, notwithstanding any inconsistent provision in state law. (There is now a similar principle in the constitutional law of the European Community; some rules of community law have supremacy over inconsistent national law) In the United States the institution of federal courts, with a right of appeal to the Supreme Court established by Article III of the US Constitution, further helped to secure the effective supremacy of federal law.[12]

Secondly, Article V, provides for amendments to the Constitution to come into force when proposals have been ratified by three-quarters of the state. The only qualification is that each state may veto an amendment to deprive it of its equal representation in the Senate, the branch of Congress which represents the states. Constitutional amendment is therefore difficult. But, it may be achieved without the unanimous consent of the states, a significant difference from the requirement in the Articles of Confederation. The US Constitution was drafted to bring closer together the 'People of the United States'.[13]

Integration is often a function of federations where some degree of union, rather than complete political and legal unity, is desired: the federal Swiss Constitution and the German Constitution of 1871 provide other examples. These constitutions strengthened the powers of the central or federal Parliament and government at the expense of previously more powerful bodies in the Cantons or States. Equally, in the other direction, federal constitutions (or constitutions with some federal characteristics) may be adopted to loosen the grip of central power in countries which have previously had unitary constitutions. That has recently happened in Belgium and Spain, where a measure of constitutional autonomy has been granted to particular communities (Flemish, Walloon, Basque, and Catalan) without the dissolution of those countries into separate independent states. Clearly, any eventual

European Union federal constitution would belong to the first group of integrating constitutions, while a federal constitution of the second type might conceivably result from the devolution of power to Scotland and Wales.

What is common to both types of federal constitutions is the distribution of legal power between central or federal authorities and a number of state (or regional) institutions. Put simply, the intention is to avoid a concentration of power. Before developing this idea, it would be useful to mention some standard aspects of federal constitutions, almost all of which are found in the United States Constitution.[14]

The Constitution divides legislative authority between the federation and the states (or provinces or regions). Neither federation nor state is legally supreme or sovereign, as the Westminster Parliament is in the United Kingdom. It is quite impossible to locate legal supremacy anywhere, for both federal and state institutions must act in accordance with the constitution. The term 'sovereign' is indeed not to be found in the text of the US Constitution; it belongs perhaps to the people of the United States who established it in the conventions held in the states to ratify the Philadelphia draft.[15]

Normally a federal constitution prescribes the powers given to the federation, while the states retain all residual powers. For example, the German Basic Law (*Grundgesetz*)[16] provides that the *Lander* (states) such as Bavaria and Hesse; have the right to legislate so long as it does not confer legislative power on the Federation.[17] The Canadian Constitution Act 1867 (formerly) known as the British North America (Act) is much less typical as it gives general law-making power to the Federal Parliament, assigning competence to legislate only on specified matters to the Province.[18]

It is standard for some important powers to be reserved for the federal authorities, especially in defense and foreign affairs, the raising of income and other taxes, the regulation of inter-state commerce, and the printing of currency. Presently, environmental protection, transport, and immigration control is also added to this list. The interests of the states or regions are often protected politically by their representation in a Second Chamber or Senate. This is the case, for instance, in the US, Australia, and Germany. In the first two countries, each state, whatever its population, is represented in the Senate by an equal number of directly elected representatives. In contrast, the German Federal Council (*Bundesrat*) is composed of members of the states' (*Lander*) governments; the more populous states have more votes in the Council than those with fewer inhabitants.[19]

Another test of a federation as laid down by Lord Richard Haldane (1856–1928),[20] is that the word "federal" applies to those cases in which states, while agreeing on a measure of delegation of their powers to a common government, continue to preserve their original constitutions. Where a constitution not only creates a new common government but also new provincial governments whose powers are confined exclusively to a list of subjects, it is not a true "federation". Regardless of what Haldane has to say about them, such federations are very common these days particularly after the Second World War (1939–45). Pakistan and India are examples of such federations.

Another common feature is that disputes between the central and regional institutions about their respective legislative and other competences are resolved by a supreme or constitutional court. Judicial review of the constitutionality of legislation may also be a feature of those unitary constitutions such as those of France or Italy, where a court may intervene to adjudicate separation of powers disputes between the legislature and the executive or so protect fundamental rights. But judicial review is not essential for the effective working of a unitary constitution; further, the practice may be considered wrong in principle, on the ground that it is counter to majoritarian democracy. In a federal constitution, on the other hand, courts must be able to strike down state legislation for infringing the competence of the central government, otherwise federal law would apply in some states, but not in those others were inconsistent state legislation had been enacted. In a famous aphorism, Oliver Wendell Holmes Jr (1841–1935)[21], one of greatest American judges, wrote:

> 'I do not think the United States would come to an end if we lost our power to declare an Act of Congress void. I do think the Union would be imperiled if we could not make that declaration as to the laws of the several States.'[22]

The Supremacy Clause of Article VI of the US Constitution provides a firm basis in the Constitution for the supremacy of federal over state law; the courts must hold the latter invalid when it conflicts with the federal rule.[23]

However, judicial review of federal legislation on the ground that it infringes the competence of the states or regions may not be so essential. The Swiss Federal Tribunal reviews the constitutionality of Cantonal, but not federal, legislation. Recently, the United States Supreme Court has sometimes been reluctant to entertain challenges to congressional statutes on federalism grounds. In one case the court, by a majority of 5 to 4 judges, rejected a challenge by state public transit authority to the application to its employees of a federal statute regulating minimum wages and other work conditions.[24] The main ground for the court's decision was that the States should protect their interest through the political process, in particular their representatives in the senate. However, the court has invalidated an Act of Congress which made it an offence to possess a gun within 1000 feet of school premises. The measure bore no relation to the power of Congress to regulate inter-state commerce; moreover, it interfered with the traditional responsibility of the states over education and schools.[25] While the United States Supreme Court has fluctuated in its approach to the review of federal laws, the German Constitutional Court has generally had little hesitation in striking them down when they exceed the powers conferred by the Basic Law on the *Bundestag* (German Federal Parliament).[26]

Federal constitutions, in fact, vary considerably. They differ in their allocation of particular powers to the federation and the states, and in the extent to which the courts are prepared to control federal laws. Moreover, it would be wrong to conclude that they establish a rigid boundary between the fields of competence belonging to federal and state authorities; the system sometimes termed 'dual federalism' to refer to a strict division of powers. The position is almost always much more flexible than that. Under the United States Constitution, for example, the states may be free to legislate even in an area where Congress has power, unless this is specifically forbidden by the terms of the constitution or unless state legislation would affect inter-state commerce.[27] Under the German Basic Law (*Grundgesetz*), the federation and the *Lander* have concurrent authority to legislate on a vast range of matters; the entitlement of the states lapses only when, and to the extent that, the *Bundestag* has exercised its right to legislate on the matter.[28] In both these countries, and in other federations, the system is broadly one of 'co-operative federalism' under which the federal government may in some circumstances allow the states to act on their own, or may authorize them to act on the federal government's behalf to implement a national policy. In the course of this century the trend has been for the effective power and influence of the centre to expand, largely because of its greater financial resources. But this process has not been even or uniform.

The capacity of federal constitutions to evolve in response to different political and social needs is one of their merits.[29] Moreover, they enable variety and diversity to flourish, while the Bill of Rights guarantees the uniform enjoyment of some basic rights throughout the federation and the central government ensures that the states provide a minimum standard of welfare. In that event the constitution provides a degree of uniformity, while tolerating greater differences than have usually been allowed in a unitary system like that of the United Kingdom. It is difficult to improve on the conclusion of a leading American scholar Richard B. Stewart;

> '(f)ederation seeks to maintain political decentralization and social diversity while simultaneously promoting national measures to meet national needs and prevent localized oppression'[30]

At the same time, more traditional arguments for 'federalism', classically formulated in the *Federalist Papers*[31], should not be ignored. James Madison and Alexander Hamilton were worried by the growth of what they termed 'factions', that is, sectional groups which had dominated the conduct of state legislatures under the confederation. The formation of a strong central government was intended to limit their influence. Nowadays there is probably more anxiety about the growth of central power under unitary constitution where local authorities are entirely subordinate to central government. In this context one merit of a federal constitution is that it safeguards the interests of regional communities; state or provincial assemblies are more likely to take account of their needs than a remote central Parliament which may be dominated by the representatives of other geographical areas or of national groups.

In short, federal constitution, like the separation of powers principle, reduces the risk of a concentration of power and the danger of arbitrary government. The former distributes authority vertically between the centre and the states or regions, while the separation principle operates on the horizontal level to allocate powers between different institutions or organs of government. Both therefore, serve the value of constitutionalism in similar ways.

Nevertheless, there is a case against federal constitution. For small, homogeneous societies they would be too complex and cumbersome. Dicey was very critical of them, albeit largely in the context of the argument for a federal constitution for the British Empire which was made sometime towards the end of the 19th century. In his view, 'federal government was always weak government'.[32] Moreover, 'federalism means legalism'; judges determine the balance of power between the federation and the states. That of course explains why federal constitutions are unpopular with politicians accustomed to working with the lesser constraints of a unitary one. The charge that, federal government is weak can hardly be taken too seriously in the light of the experience of the United States and modern Germany, while 'federalism' works well in other countries as diverse as Austria and Australia.

However, 'federalism' is not a popular or easily comprehensible form of government. Whatever the merits of his other points, Dicey rightly concluded in 1915 (in his Introduction to the 8th edition of *Law of the Constitution*) that there was little desire for it in England. His observation is as accurate now as it was at that time. It is a far less exciting cause or value than, say, human rights or political equality. Until recently, it has not been easy to envisage circumstances in which a unitary constitution with a long tradition, such as that of the United Kingdom or France, would transform itself into a federation. Nevertheless, the devolution of legislative powers to a Parliament in Scotland may mean that this development is not now as inconceivable as it has been. The difference, as we will see, between federalism and legislative devolution may be greater in theory than it turns out to be in practice.[33]

10TH AMENDMENT TO THE US CONSTITUTION AND FEDERALISM

The 10th Amendment to the US Constitution states:

> 'The powers not delegated to the United States by the Constitution, nor prohibited by it to the States, are reserved to the States respectively, or to the people.'

The key question about the 10th Amendment is whether it is a judicially enforceable limit on Congress's powers: can federal laws be declared unconstitutional as violating this constitutional provision? Over the course of American history, the Court has been inconsistent in answering this question and has shifted between two different approaches.[34]

One approach is that the 10th Amendment is not a separate constraint on Congress, but, rather is simply a reminder that Congress may only legislate if it has authority under the Constitution. Under this approach, a federal law would never be found unconstitutional as violating the 10th Amendment, but it could be invalidated as exceeding the scope of Congress's powers under Article I of the US Constitution or for violating another constitutional provision.

The alternate approach is that the 10th Amendment protects state sovereignty from federal intrusion. Under this approach, the 10th Amendment is a key protection of states' rights and federalism. The 10th Amendment reserves a zone of activity to the states for their exclusive control, and federal laws intruding into this zone should be declared unconstitutional by the courts.

In the 19th century, the court took the former position and held that a federal law was constitutional so long as Congress was acting within the scope of- its authority. In the first third of the 20th century until 1937, the court adopted the latter view and found that the 10th Amendment reserved to the states control over production and that the federal laws attempting to regulate production were unconstitutional.

From 1937 until the 1990s, the court went back to the former approach. In fact, during this period, there was only one case where a federal law was found to violate the 10th Amendment and this case was later expressly overruled.[35] Since the 1990s, however, the Court resurrected the 10th Amendment as a limit on congressional power.[36]

Federalism in Pakistan

When Pakistan came into being on 14 August 1947, there was almost unanimous demand for a federal form of the constitution for at least two reasons. One being historical and the other practical. All India Muslim League, the founding party of Pakistan, in its historic resolution adopted at the Lahore session of 1940, demanded Pakistan on the ground that states in the North West of India and in the East of India (the province of Bengal) be constituted into the State of Pakistan. In the Delhi Session of Muslim League in 1946, the resolution of 1940 was amended and the word 'States' used in Lahore Resolution was converted to a 'State'.[37]

After Pakistan came into being, East Bengal that was separated from the United Bengal, the Bengalis, who had a different culture and language demanded a federal form of government, for an additional reason that East Bengal was not contiguous to the provinces forming part of the West Pakistan. It is in this context that the

Objectives Resolution was passed on 23 March 1949 by the First Constituent Assembly. Later on, this Resolution served as the preamble to the Constitutions of 1956 and 1962. The Objective Resolution was also adopted as the preamble to the 1973 Constitution, and which was made a substantive part of the Constitution in 1985. The Objective Resolution, however, does not stand on a higher pedestal than any other provision of the Constitution in Pakistan, and, no provision of the Constitution can be declared void on the ground that it was repugnant to the Objective Resolution.[38]

The preamble of the 1973 Constitution, lays down that the territories of Pakistan shall form a federation, wherein the units would be autonomous with such boundaries and limitation on their powers and authority as may be prescribed. As discussed above, the essence of federation, whether based on agreement or imposed by a paramount authority, is that there is a distribution of powers between the units and the center in such a way that both are, within their respective spheres, coordinate and independent, neither being subordinate to the other. It is immaterial that the powers of the center are specified and all other powers vest in the units or vice versa or whether the residuary powers vest in the units or vice versa or whether the residuary powers vest in the units or the center, the determining factor being that the powers so divided vest exclusively in the recipients, making them supreme in the exercise of those powers.

Article 1 of the Pakistan Constitution lays down that –

> 'Pakistan shall be a Federal Republic'.

A Republic is a state with a form of government, not a monarchy, in which the Supreme Power is vested in the people and is exercised through their elected representatives. A Federal Republic implies that there are units in the state, whether they are called states, provinces or units, which in the legislative, executive, financial and judicial spheres enjoy powers which the Constitution assigned to them and with the exercise of which, generally speaking, the center does not interfere. The centre or the federation enjoys only those powers which the Constitution has marked for it.

Northern Areas consisting of Gilgit Baltistan, as is clear from Article 1, Clause (2), do not form part of the territories of Pakistan. They are said to be disputed areas like Kashmir. Pakistan is administering them under a United Nations mandate.[39]

Article 70(4) of the Pakistan Constitution divided the legislative subjects into 'federal legislative list' and 'concurrent legislative list'. The federal legislature that is, the Parliament has power to legislate on the subjects in both the lists. The provincial legislatures have the powers to legislate on the subjects included in the concurrent list and the residuary subjects.[40]

The 4th Schedule to the Constitution gives the legislative lists which include Federal Legislative List consisting of 67 subjects and Concurrent Legislative List consisting of 47 subjects. The Parliament has exclusive powers to make laws with respect to any other covered under the subjects mentioned in Federal Legislative List [Article 142(a)]. A Provincial Assembly can exclusively legislate on any matter or subject not enumerated in either of the Lists [Article 142(c)].

In other words all the residuary subjects belong to the exclusive legislative competence of the Provinces. If provisions of any Act of Parliament and an Act of a Provincial Assembly on a subject under the competence of both the legislatives (from Concurrent List), are inconsistent, then the federal law would prevail over the provincial laws to the extent of inconsistency [Article 43]. However, such a declaration can only be made by the superior Courts in Pakistan (i.e. the Supreme Court or the High Courts).

Pakistan is a Federal Republic with a parliamentary form of government both at the Centre and in the Provinces. The system of 'federalism' is so designed as to accommodate the parliamentary form of government to suit the conditions in Pakistan. Speaking broadly, wrote Justice Zafar Hussain Mirza (1926–2015)[41] in *Benazir Bhutto v. Pakistan*,[42]

> 'our Constitution is a federal constitution based on the model of parliamentary form of representative government prevalent in United Kingdom'.

The constitution embodies in itself all the important, formal, institutional, conditions necessary for the success of a constitutional representative democracy such as:[43]

(1) Popular election for limited terms of most of the constitutional institutions and offices, e.g. the office of the President, National and Provincial Legislative Assemblies;
(2) Universal adult suffrage, for example, election to the National Assembly and Provincial Assemblies are to be by direct and free vote (Articles 51 and 106 of the Constitution) and all elections under the Constitution are to be by secret ballot (Article 226 of the Constitution).
(3) Free entry of citizens to candidacy for elective offices with only minimal restrictions;
(4) Freedom of political communication, that is to say, freedom of association and freedom of expression guaranteed by Articles 17 and 19 of the Constitution respectively.

The executive authority of the federation and the provinces is also divided on the same lines. The executive authority of the federation extends to the matters over which the Parliament has the power to legislate [Article 97]. Similarly, the executive authority of a province extends to the matter with respect to which its Provincial Assembly has power to legislate [Article 137].

There was a marked dominance or pre-eminence of Federation over the Provinces. In times of emergency, which only the Federal Government has the power to proclaim, the Parliament can legislate for Provinces, with respect to matters in the exclusive legislative competence of the Provincial Assemblies [Article 232(2)(a)]. During such emergency, the Federal Government can give direction to a Province as to the manner in which it should exercise its executive authority [Article 232(2)(b)]. The Federal Government can even order a Governor of a Province, during the emergency, to assume all the executive authority of the Province and exercise it under its directions [Article 232(2)(c)]. The Federal Government can also proclaim emergency in a Province and take over all the legislative and executive authority of that Province during the period such emergency continues [Article 234]. The Federal Government can also proclaim financial emergency and can make direction to the Provinces to adopt financial measures prescribed by the Federal Government during the course of such emergency [Article 235].[44]

However, the 18th Amendment to the Constitution of Pakistan, adopted in 2010, attempts to bring about paradigm change to 'federalism' in Pakistan. Certain steps like deletion of Concurrent List of subjects for legislation, division of revenue and assets between the Federation and Provinces, devolution of various subjects like education, health and labour matters are meant to emphasis the federal character of the Constitution. The Supreme Court of Pakistan is yet to determine the nature and extent of devolution brought about by the 18th Amendment. In a recent case involving devolution of 3 hospitals and medical institutes in Karachi and one such institute in Lahore, the Supreme Court held that, devolution of health sector to Provinces does not mean that the federation cannot establish or run such institutes in the Provinces. The devolution of such hospitals and institutes was set aside.[45] The Supreme Court held:

> 'We find that the power of the Federation to set up, run and operate projects including hospitals and related research facilities where enforcement of fundamental rights is involved is an obligation of the Federal Government under the Constitution. In the instant case, enforcement of right to life is involved which is one of the most fundamental of the fundamental rights. To curtail or circumscribe the power of the Federal Government to enforce Fundamental Rights guaranteed by the Constitution would be anathema for the concept of Federalism. The performance of its positive obligations under the fundamental rights for example right to life, prevention of slavery, forced labour, human trafficking, etc., constitute a "purpose" of the Federation for which it can carry out projects throughout Pakistan. For performance of the said purpose, it is not necessary to look into the legislative list when the main body of the Constitution provides the requisite Powers. Refer to Province of Sindh v. MQM (PLD 2014 SC 531). We, however, reiterate that in doing so in the territorial jurisdiction of a Province, the projects and institutes of the Federal Government shall be subject to the Provincial Laws and regulatory control. Consequently, neither the legislative nor executive authority of the Provinces in relation to the subject of hospitals is encroached upon.'

The Supreme Court is yet to determine 'federalism' and the relations between the Federation and the Provinces under the Constitution after the 18th Amendment.

Federalism in India

There is a difference of opinion among the constitutional jurists about the nature of the Indian Constitution. One view is that it is a quasi-federal Constitution and has more unitary features than federal features. The other view is that it is a federal Constitution but, changes have been made in it to suit the requirements of the country. In the words of Dr B. R. Ambedkar (1891–1956)[46],

> 'I think it is agreed that our Constitution, notwithstanding the many provisions which are contained in it, whereby the Centre has been given powers to override the provisions, nonetheless, is a federal Constitution'.

However, if the essentials of a federal constitution like the supremacy of the constitution, division of powers between the federal government and the units, a written constitution, rigidity in respect of amendments in the Constitution and the authority of courts to judicially review and declare *ultra vires* and invalid the laws passed by the federal legislative or provincial legislative, are taken into consideration, there is no doubt that the Indian Constitution is a federal constitution.

However, there are certain distinctive features of the Indian federal system which are discussed as under:—[47]

(i) In the United States, there is dual citizenship. An American is a citizen of the United States and also of the State in which he lives. The result is that each State has the right to grant its citizens or residents a number of rights which it may legally deny or grant on more difficult terms to those who are not its citizens or residents. In India, there is a dual polity but single citizenship. To quote, there is only one citizenship for the whole of India. It is the Indian citizenship. There is no State citizenship. Every Indian has the same rights of citizenship, no matter in what State he resides.

(ii) Every State in the United States has the right to make or amend its own Constitution. The Federal Government has not the power to change the Constitution of any State. In India, no state has the power to amend its own Constitution although the central legislature (Parliament) has the power to amend the state Constitution under certain circumstances. The Constitution of the Union and of the States is a single frame from which neither can get out and within which they must work.

(iii) The residuary powers in India are given to the Union Government and the Indian Parliament can make laws with regard to them. In the United States, the residuary powers are with the States.

(iv) Rigidity and legalism are considered to be the two evils of a federal polity. A federal Constitution has to be a written Constitution which is usually rigid. Moreover, the people in a federal polity always talk in terms of legality or illegality of a measure, irrespective of its merits. However, the Indian Constitution has adopted certain methods to avoid the evils of rigidity and legalism. It has provided a long list of concurrent subjects. A large number of provisions have been made which are to remain in force until Parliament provides otherwise by law. Power has also been given to Parliament to legislate on matters in the State List under certain circumstances. This is so when a subject assumes national importance. The same is the case when an emergency is declared by President. The Centre can exercise powers within a State with the consent of the State or States concerned. Greater facility is given for the amendment of the Constitution than that given in foreign countries.

(v) The Constitution becomes unitary in times of emergency. All federal systems are placed in a tight mold of federalism. In no circumstances can it change its form and shape. It can never be unitary. On the other hand, the Indian Constitution can be both unitary as well as federal, according to requirement of time and circumstances.

(vi) The Indian federation maintains unity in all basic matters. The federation being a dual polity based on divided authority with separate legislative, executive and judicial powers for each of the two polities is bound to produce diversities in laws, in administration and in judicial protection. Up to a certain point, this diversity does not matter. It may be welcomed as being an attempt to accommodate the powers of government to local needs and circumstances. But this diversity when it goes beyond a certain point is capable of producing chaos and has actually produced chaos in many federating states.

(vii) The Indian Constitution does not set up the States as rivals to one another or to the Union. Each is intended to work harmoniously in its own sphere without impediment by the other, with an overriding power of the Union where it is necessary in the public interest. It has a nice balance of jurisdiction which has worked out successfully so far and would continue to work so in times to come with good sense prevailing in all States.

(viii) The Supreme Court of India and the High Courts form a single integrated judiciary having jurisdiction over all cases arising under various laws – central as well as State laws and include constitutional, civil and criminal laws. To eliminate diversity of laws, codes of civil and criminal law are placed in the Concurrent List. To maintain uniformity in administration, the Constitution provides that there should be All-India services recruited on an All-India basis which would be common to the Union and the States.

Nevertheless, there are certain federal principles that have been modified by the Indian Constitution which are discussed below:[48]

(i) Article 249 provides that if the Council of States has declared by resolution supported by not less than two-thirds of the members present and voting that it is necessary or expedient in the national interest that Parliament should make laws with respect to the matter enumerated in the State List specified in the resolution, it shall be lawful for Parliament to make laws for the whole or any part of the territory of India with respect to that matter while the resolution remains in force. Such a resolution would remain in force for period as may be specified but not exceeding one year. Whenever a resolution approving the continuance in force of any such resolution is passed, such resolution would continue in force for a further period of one year from the date on which it would otherwise have ceased to be in force.

(ii) Article 250 provides that Parliament should, while a Proclamation of Emergency is in operation, have power to make laws for the whole or any part of the territory of India with respect to any of the matters enumerated in the State List. A law so made by Parliament would cease to have effect on the expiration of a period of 6 months after the Proclamation ceases to operate.

(iii) Article 252 provides that if it appears to the legislatures of two or more States to be desirable that any of the matters with respect to which Parliament has no power to make laws for the States should be regulated in such States by the Parliament by law, and if resolution to that effect are passed by all the Houses of the legislatures of those States, it would be lawful for Parliament to pass an Act for regulating that matter accordingly and any Act so passed shall apply to such states and to any other State by which it is adopted afterwards by resolution passed in that behalf by the House or Houses of the legislature of that State.

(iv) Article 253 provides that Parliament has power to make any law for the whole or any part of the territory of India for implementing any treaty, agreement or convention with any other country or countries or any decision made at any international conference, association or other body.

(v) Article 256 provides that the executive power of every State should be so exercised as to ensure compliance with the laws made by Parliament and any existing laws which apply in that State, and the executive power of the Union shall extend to the giving of such directions to a State as may appear to the Government of India to be necessary for that purpose.

(vi) Article 257 lays down that the executive power of every state shall be so exercised as not to impede or prejudice the exercise of the executive power of the Union, and the executive power of the Union shall extend to the giving of such directions to a State as may appear to the Government of India to be necessary for that purpose. The executive power of the Union shall also extend to the giving of directions to a State as to the construction and maintenance of means of communication declared in that direction to be of national or military importance. Parliament has power to declare highways or waterways to be national highways or national waterways. The executive power of the Union shall also extend to the giving of directions to a State as to the measures to be taken for the protection of the railways within the State.

(vii) Article 353 provides that while a Proclamation of Emergency under Article 352 is in operation, the executive power of the Union shall extend to the giving of directions to any State as to the manner in which its executive power would be exercised.

(viii) Article 356 provides that if the President of India is satisfied that a situation has arisen in which the Government of the State cannot be carried on in accordance with the provisions of the Constitution, he may by Proclamation assume to himself all or any of the functions of the government of the State and all or any of the powers vested in or exercisable by the Governor or anybody or authority in the State other than the legislature of the State. He may declare that the powers of the legislature of the State shall be exercisable by or under the authority of Parliament. He may make such incidental and consequential provisions which he considers necessary or desirable for giving effect to the objects of the Proclamation. However, he cannot assume any of the powers vested in or exercisable by the High Court.

(ix) Article 357 provides that where it has been declared under Article 356 that the powers of the legislature of the State shall be exercisable by or under the authority of Parliament, it would be competent for Parliament to confer on the President the power of the Legislature of the State to make laws and to authorize him to delegate the powers so conferred to any other authority to be specified by him in that behalf. It would be competent for the President to authorize when the House of the People is not in session, expenditure from the Consolidated Fund of the State pending the sanction of such expenditure by Parliament.

(x) Article 360 lays down that if the President of India is satisfied that a situation has arisen whereby the financial stability or credit of India or any part of its territory is threatened, he may by a Proclamation make a declaration to that effect. During the period when financial emergency is in operation, the executive authority of the Union shall extend to the giving of directions to any State to observe such canons of financial propriety as may be specified in the directions and to the giving of such other directions as the President may deem necessary and adequate for the purpose. Any such direction may include a provision requiring the reduction of salaries and allowances of all or any class of persons serving in connection with the affairs of a State and a provision requiring all Money Bills or other Bills to which the provisions of Article 207 apply to be reserved for the consideration of the President after they are passed by the legislature of the State.

(xi) Article 3 provides that Parliament may by law form a new State by separation of territory from any State or by uniting two or more States or parts of States or by uniting any territory to be a part of any State. Parliament may also increase or diminish the area of any State. It may alter the boundaries of any State or the name of any State. Where the proposal contained in the Bill affects the area, boundaries or name of any of the States, the Bill has to be referred by the President to the legislature of that State for expressing its views thereon within a specified period. The power conferred on Parliament includes the power to form a new State or Union Territory by uniting a part of any State or Union Territory to any other State or Union Territory.

(xii) Laws passed by the State Legislature concerning certain matters do not become valid unless they have been reserved for the consideration of the President and received his assent.

(xiii) The Governors of the States are appointed by the President and to the extent they exercise their powers in their discretion, they are answerable to the President.

(xiv) Some additional powers were given to the Union Parliament by the Constitution (42nd Amendment) Act, 1976.

The view of Dr Kenneth Clinton Wheare (1907–79)[49], is that the –

> Indian Constitution has established a system of government which is at the most quasi-federal, almost devolutionary in character, a unitary State with subsidiary federal features rather than a federal state with subsidiary unitary features.

Federalism under the Canadian Constitution

As discussed, the general feature of a federal constitution is that in the division of subjects, specified subjects are given to the federation to legislate and exercise its executive powers upon; the residuary subjects that are left to the provinces for legislation and executive authority. The Canadian Constitution is an exception to this usual feature of the federal constitution.

It was on account of a different situation in Canada at the time of framing of the federal constitution. In 1865, the representatives of Canada met in Quebec, known as the Quebec Conference. The conference objective was to discuss the distribution of powers between the federal government and the provincial government. There was a desire to keep a strong Federal Government.

In any case Canada, being a prized colony of the British Empire, the provinces in Canada could not be empowered to the extent that they constitute a threat to the power of the colonial empire who controlled the affairs of Canada. Besides the patriots of Canada were not prepared to ignore the lessons which the American Civil War 1860–65, seemed to teach them. It was felt that if there had been a powerful Central Government in the United States, the Southern States would not have dared to revolt. No wonder, while distributing the powers between the Federal Government and the provinces in Canada, more powers were granted to the Federal Government and the provinces were made relatively weak.

Analysis of Sections 91 of the British North American Act 1867 (now called the Constitution Act, 1867) would reveal the following main propositions, in the light of which, the distribution of legislative powers between the Canadian Parliament and the Provincial Legislatures can be understood.

(1) It is lawful for the Dominion Parliament to make laws for peace, order and good government of Canada in relation to all matters other than those assigned exclusively to the legislatures of the Provinces. Under Section 92, sixteen subjects have been enumerated with respect to which the Provincial legislatures have exclusive power to make laws. If upon an enquiry by a court, directed upon the question whether a particular enactment is one which comes under the purview of Section 92, it is found that the answer is in the negative, then the impugned enactment must be deemed to fall within the scope of legislation competent to Dominion Parliament under Section 91.[50]

(2) The subjects, as have been mentioned in Section 91, have been specified merely to secure greater certainty in the matter of defining the sphere of Dominion Legislation. The generality of power expressly asserted in favour of Dominion Legislature in Section 91 cannot be restricted. Section 91 provides 'to make laws for peace, order and good government of Canada in relation to all matters not coming within classes of subjects by this Act assigned exclusively to the legislature of the Provinces, and for greater certainty but not so as to restrict the generality of the foregoing terms of the section'. It would appear that this provision is not in the nature of a vesting provision, for the power is affirmed broadly and then illustrated to provide greater certainty in the matter of fixing boundaries of the legislative power of the Dominion Legislature.[51] In other words, in addition to the subjects enumerated in Section 91, it also exemplifies the species of general power admissible to the Dominion Legislature, 'to legislate for the peace, order and good government of Canada.'

(3) Any matter enumerated in Section 91 should not be so construed so as to enable the Dominion Parliament to enact laws of a local or private nature in respect of matters which have been reserved exclusively to the legislature of the Provinces.[52]

(4) The Judicial Committee of the Privy Council, which was the highest legal authority in terms of the Canadian Constitution, proceeded on the assumption that categories in Sections 91 and 92 were mutually exclusive. The Canadian ship of state, in Lord Atkins (1867–1944)[53] celebrated metaphor, retains the 'water tight compartments which are essential part of her original structure.'[54] This assumption meant that the categories in Sections 91 and 92 should be interpreted so as to avoid, to the greatest extent possible, any overlapping between them. The compartments approach seemed to follow from the fact that the twenty-nine enumerated categories in Section 91 and the sixteen enumerated categories in Section 92 were each described as conferring 'exclusive' legislative jurisdiction.

Federalism under the US Constitution

Federalism is one of the two basic structural characteristics of the American constitutional system, the other being separation of powers among branches of the national government. During the two centuries since the republic was founded, the relationship between the national government and the states has changed dramatically. Today, there is no question of the dominance of the national government in most areas of policy making. Yet, states remain viable actors in the political system and in recent years may have become even more important. Thus, as a constitutional principle, federalism retains considerable vitality.

As an applied principle of government, federalism requires an ongoing effort by legislators, chief executives, and judges to balance many competing interests and values–among them individual liberty and public order, local diversity and the national interest, limited government, and social justice. The constitutional basis and evolving meaning of federalism owe much to the contribution of the US Supreme Court in defining the relationships and marking the boundaries between national and state functions.

Prior to the ratification of the Constitution of 1787, the United States was a confederation of sovereign states. Each state was vested with the necessary powers of government, limited only by the terms of state constitutions and the traditional common law rights and immunities of individuals. States had broad taxing and spending powers, of course, but they also issued their own currency and regulated the terms of their commercial relationships with other states and foreign countries. Moreover, the states possessed police power: the authority to make laws to protect the public safety, health, and welfare, and even to foster the morality of their citizens.

There was never any real prospect that the Constitution of 1787 would provide for a unitary system. The states existed as autonomous political entities from the time of the American Revolution (1775–78) and were not about to surrender to the national government their rights and powers to which they had become accustomed. Moreover, there was widespread fear of concentrating too much power in the national government. The smaller states, in particular, were concerned about how their interests would be protected under the new Constitution. The solution was twofold. First, all states would enjoy equal representation in the US Senate. Second, the national government would be one of definite and limited powers. In addition, the 10th Amendment, ratified in 1791, specifically recognized the reserved powers of the states in the following words:

> 'The powers not delegated to the United States by the Constitution, nor prohibited by it to the States, are reserved to the States respectively, or to the people.'

The clear implication was (made explicit in the 10th Amendment) that the states retained autonomy in other areas. The original Constitution, however, was ambiguous on the question of where ultimate sovereign power resided. Federalist Party leaders, including Alexander Hamilton (1755/57–1804), John Marshall (1755–1835), and John Adams (1735–1826), argued eloquently that the issue must be resolved in favor of the national government.

The Democratic-Republicans, most notably Thomas Jefferson (1743–1826), argued on behalf of states' rights. In proposing the Virginia and Kentucky Resolution of 1798, Jefferson went so far as to argue that the 'sovereign and independent states' had the right to nullify acts of Congress that they deemed to be unconstitutional. This was the origin of the doctrines of 'nullification and interposition', later employed by the New England states during the War of 1812 and by South Carolina in opposition to federal tariff legislation in 1832. These doctrines were most fully developed in the writings of the South Carolina statesman and political theorist John C. Calhoun (1782–1850).[55] States' rights doctrines even figured prominently in the desegregation battles of the 1950s and 1960s.

Chisholm v. Georgia[56]

The US Supreme Court rendered its first major constitutional decision in 1793. The case, *Chisholm v. Georgia*, dealt specifically with the issue of state sovereignty. An essential aspect of sovereignty in the Anglo-American tradition has been sovereign immunity, the doctrine that the government may be sued only with its consent. Article III of the US Constitution granted to federal courts jurisdiction over 'controversies between a state and citizens of another state'. In response to criticism from the Anti-Federalists, proponents of the Constitution argued that this provision did not authorize a private individual to sue a state without its consent.

Nevertheless, shortly after the Constitution was adopted, several such suits were filed in federal court. One of these cases was *Chisholm v. Georgia*, in 1792, Alexander Chisholm attempted to sue the state of Georgia in the US Supreme Court over payments due to him for goods that Robert Farquhar had supplied to the state of Georgia during the American War of Independence. The defendant, state of Georgia, refused to appear, claiming that as a sovereign state, it could not be sued without consenting to the suit. Georgia filed a strong protest denying the court's jurisdiction. In addition, a resolution was introduced in the Georgia legislature asserting that federal judicial authority to entertain such suits 'would effectually destroy the retained sovereignty of the states.'

By a 4 to 1 majority, the Supreme Court rejected the State of Georgia's argument, strongly endorsing the authority of the federal judiciary in relation to the states. This decision drew an intense reaction from states' rights advocates.

The result was adoption of the 11th Amendment in 1798, in effect barring a citizen from suing a state government in a federal court without the state's consent. Specifically, the amendment provides:

> 'The judicial power of the United States shall not be construed to extend to any suit in law or equity, commenced or prosecuted against one of the United States by Citizens of another State, or by Citizens or Subjects of any Foreign State.'

Although, ratification of the 11th Amendment was a major victory for states' rights forces, the amendment has not proved to be an insurmountable barrier to federal court review of most state policies. However, the 14th Amendment, authorizes Congress to enforce certain basic civil rights guarantees against the states. Congress has used this power to limit the states' sovereign immunity with respect to certain civil rights lawsuits. However, since the mid-1990s, a determined five-member majority of the Rehnquist Court (1986–2005) has placed substantial limits on the power of Congress to abrogate state sovereign immunity.

Gibbons v. Ogden[57]

The first major decision of the Supreme Court involving state versus federal regulation of commerce was *Gibbons v. Ogden* (1824). The Gibbons case resulted from an attempt by the state of New York to create and protect a monopoly issued to a private steamboat company. A competing company, operating under a federal license, was enjoined by a New York court from operating on waters within the borders of New York State. The Supreme Court held that –

(1) the licensing of steamboats by the federal government was a valid exercise of the national power to regulate interstate commerce and
(2) the attempt by New York to enforce a steamboat monopoly within its waters was a violation of the Supremacy Clause of the Constitution.

In terms of 'federalism', the thrust of *Gibbons v. Ogden* was that states could not impede the efforts of Congress to regulate commerce among the States. But, the Court stopped short of holding that states had no power, whatsoever, to regulate interstate commerce. Suppose Congress has not acted on a matter covered by state commercial legislation. Or suppose state law merely complements existing national policy. Under such circumstances, are the states free to act, even if their actions have an impact on interstate commerce? The *Gibbons* decision left these questions unanswered.

Taking into account both the constitutional basis and the political dimensions of American federalism, it is possible to identify five basic characteristics of this system of government.

1. *The continuing division of legal authority between two levels of government: national and state*: Each level has an independent mechanism of government through which it enacts, interprets, and administers law. Considerable overlapping occurs, of course, but the structure of two legally distinct spheres of government – each with its own constitution, legislature, chief executive, judiciary, and administrative bureaucracy – remains intact.
2. *Direct simultaneous authority over persons within their jurisdictions*: The national government and the states exercise authority over persons within their jurisdiction. Dual citizenship is a fundamental part of the federal system, and rights, privileges, and immunities derive their validity from both types of citizenship.
3. *National supremacy*: Both the Supremacy Clause of Article VI and the 14th Amendment mandate the subordination of state to national authority in instances where the national government is constitutionally empowered to act.
4. *Cooperative federalism*: The modern era has been characterized by a high level of interaction between federal and state authorities. Today, the national government and the states work cooperatively in the areas of law enforcement, domestic security, education, highway construction, public health, social welfare, and environmental protection, among others. While the term 'cooperative federalism' is often used to describe these relationships, the role of the national government is clearly dominant.

5. *The Supreme Court as 'umpire of the federal system'*: Throughout its history, the Supreme Court has played a leading role in allocating constitutional power between the national government and the states and in refereeing interstate relations. Federalism encompasses a set of complex and dynamic relationships between the States and the national government and among the States themselves. These relationships are defined and redefined through the process of judicial interpretation. In performing its role as umpire of the federal system, the Supreme Court has attempted over the years to give expression to the contending values of national unity and local diversity.

Although, the role of the national government became dominant during the second half of the 20th century, the states continue to be viable and important governmental entities. They have by no means become mere administrative units of the national government. Indeed, as a result of the 'Reagan Revolution' of the 1980s and the Republican Congress's 'devolution' of power to the states in the 1990s, states have had to shoulder greater policy making and fiscal responsibilities.

Since the mid-1990s, the Supreme Court, in a series of closely divided and highly controversial decisions, has buttressed the constitutional standing of the states within the federal system. Whether the recent reallocation of power toward the states represents a long-term trend remains to be seen. American federalism, after all, is highly dynamic.

Federation and Judicial Power

As discussed above, the written constitution is a law which imposes limitations upon all other organs of the state, the task of acting as the guardian of this constitution has been assumed by the Judiciary in the US and provided for in other constitutions which have followed the American model, such as India and Pakistan.

Whenever a constitution is justiciable, i.e., enforceable in a court of law, the judiciary becomes the guardian of the constitution, having the power as well as the duty to see that any of the organs of the state does not transgress the limits to its powers as have been prescribed by the constitution. From this generic point of view, therefore, judicial review or guardianship of the constitution follows from the nature of a written constitution, provided it is treated as a legal instrument, and exists even in unitary constitutions such as those of Ireland or Japan.

The guardianship of the judiciary, in enforcing the constitution, expands where there is a constitutional division of powers not only as between the three branches of the government,—executive, legislative and judicial, but the state itself is divided into two units,—national and state, with a consequential distribution of powers as between the two units as laid down in the constitution; that is to say where the constitution is federal. In short, a federal constitution imposes an additional duty and foundation for judicial review.

Special Functions of the Judiciary in a Federation

Broadly speaking, the special functions of a federal judiciary would fall under the following heads:[58]

I. Maintaining the supremacy of the Constitution.
II. Determining controversies between the parties to the federation.
III. Securing uniformity in the interpretation and application of the Constitution as amongst the States which mean –
   (a) Appellate; and
   (b) Advisory jurisdiction.

These may be discussed as under:

Every federal Constitution, whatever the degree of cohesion it aims at establishing, involves a distribution of powers between the Union and the units composing the Union, and both Union and state governments derive their authority from, and are limited by, the same constitution. In a unitary constitution, there is no such problem to solve, for, there the local administrative or legislative bodies are mere subordinate bodies under the central authority. Hence, there is no problem of judicially determining disputes between the central and local authorities.

But, in a federal constitution, since the powers are divided between the national and the state governments, it becomes necessary that there must be some authority to determine disputes between the Union and the states or the states *inter se* and to maintain the distribution of powers as made by the constitution. This authority must necessarily be judicial if the provisions of the constitution which effect the division of powers between the federation and the units of the federation are to constitute legal limitations upon the respective parties to the federation.

Hence, in a federal constitution, the judiciary has an additional problem, apart from guarding the constitution against transgression by the organs of the national government, namely, to maintain the distribution of powers prescribed by the constitution as against encroachments by the Union and the state governments *inter se*. It is, in short, the 'umpire' or the arbiter in the federal system.

This function of acting as the guardian of the constitution is known as 'judicial review' because it involves the responsibility of determining the constitutional validity of both federal[59] and state laws and executive actions so that they may not transgress the limitations imposed upon them by the constitution. The power of 'judicial review' to maintain the supremacy of the constitution is generally vested in the highest federal court of the land, called the Supreme Court (in USA, Pakistan, India), or the High Court (in Australia).

While the subject of 'judicial review' will be accorded separate treatment in another chapter, broad features under the leading federal constitutions may be discussed in the present context.

(a) USA

In the American Constitution, this duty of the federal Court is accentuated by the fact that the Constitution is in the nature of a treaty between component units and that the Constitution sets up a double government and a double allegiance.[60]

As to its duties as a federal court, the Supreme Court itself has observed—

> 'This Court has no more important function than that which devolves upon it, the obligation to preserve inviolate the constitutional limitations upon the exercise of authority. Federal and State, to the end that each may continue to discharge harmoniously with the other, the duties entrusted to it by the Constitution.[61]

But, as has been stated earlier, in the United States, the Constitution itself does not specifically vest in the judiciary any power to declare laws enacted by the legislature to be unconstitutional. This power has been deduced by the Supreme Court from its power to determine—

> 'All cases arising under the Constitution' [Article III, Section 2(1)], read with Article VI(2) which says—'This Constitution ...shall be the supreme law of the land.'

But, while the power to pronounce upon the unconstitutionality of a statute was originally asserted as incidental to the judicial power, since the case of *Marbury v. Madison*,[62] it has come to be considered a duty of every judge in the United States to treat as void any enactment which violates the constitution. The courts cannot properly decline to exercise this power.[63]

The radical application of the above reasoning has, in the United States, led to the establishment of the doctrine of judicial supremacy. This means that no act of the government or of any official is valid unless it is supported by some law and no law is valid in the United States which is not recognized as such by the courts. And no act either of the executive or of the legislature is upheld by the courts unless it is in conformity with or warranted by the provisions of the Constitution from which the executive or the legislature derives its powers.

Of course, the power to invalidate laws has not been so frequently used[64] by the US Supreme Court as may be supposed. Nevertheless, it is by a radical application of this doctrine combined with that of 'due process' that the American Supreme Court has come to be 'the balance wheel' of the Constitution. Under the American Constitution,

> 'everything which may pass under the form of an enactment is not to be considered the law of the land',

so long as the Supreme Court does not uphold it as valid, and thus the key to any social and economic progress has been placed at the hands of the Supreme Court.

The pre-eminent position of the Supreme Court in the American Constitution is due to this power of judicial review in its hands. Its subsequent evolution has given the Supreme Court a position in relation to the executive and the legislature which was not envisaged by the fathers of the constitution. Thus, while Alexander Hamilton thought that,

> 'the judiciary is beyond comparison the weakest of the three departments of power',

today it has gained a position of 'supremacy' inasmuch as it has the last word as to the constitutionality of the acts of the other two branches of the government.

The word 'federal' was not mentioned anywhere in the US Constitution. But the words 'a more perfect Union' in the Preamble suggest that the Union sought to be established by the Constitution was to be more federal than the loose confederation which existed prior to 1787. This was supported by the fact that the Constitution divided all governmental powers between the Union and the States, by granting only enumerated powers to the federal Congress [Article I, section 8], while the powers not so granted to the Union nor prohibited to the States, were 'reserved to the States' by the 10th Amendment. If the Constitution rested here, much of the judicial controversy as to the borderline between federal and state powers would hardly have arisen. But, the picture has been mystified by another provision which has justly been called 'the Supremacy Clause' in Article VI, which declares not only the supremacy of the federal constitution over State Constitutions and laws, but also, the supremacy of 'laws of the United States, made in pursuance of the (federal) Constitution' as against the constitution or laws of the states, in case they are inconsistent with the provisions of federal laws.

In *McCulloch v. Maryland,*[65] Chief Justice John Marshall (1755–1835), applied his theory earlier propounded in the case of *Marbury* that the constitution was the higher law, ordained by the people themselves, so that it would prevail over laws made by the legislatures set up by the constitution. It followed, as held in *McCulloch's* case, that in case of any conflict between the federal constitution and a law made by a state, the constitution would prevail and also that it was the concern and duty of the Supreme Court to decide any such dispute.

The foregoing position has not been questioned since then. The power of the court to strike down a law made by the Congress in case it is beyond the powers granted to it by the constitution had been asserted in *Marbury's* case[66] itself, where the provision in the Judiciary Act 1789, which conferred original jurisdiction upon the Supreme Court to issue the writ of *mandamus* was held unconstitutional because it was beyond the powers granted to the Supreme Court, as its original jurisdiction, by Article III, Section 2. It was held that though the Supreme Court could issue the writ in the exercise of its appellate jurisdiction, it could not issue the writ directly to a party, in its original jurisdiction, which, under Article III (2), was confined to cases involving ambassadors and states. Since then, up to 1970, the court has actually invalidated some 20 Acts of Congress, as violative of the constitutional distribution of powers.

The balance of power between the federation and the states in the United States, at any point of time, thus, depends upon the contemporary interpretation given by the Supreme Court to the Constitution of which it has assumed the role of a guardian. It is quite natural that the Supreme Court, as the guardian of the Constitution, has been wavering between the two provisions in Article VI and the 10th Amendment, in short, between federal powers and state rights. In this controversy, the Supreme Court has more often inclined in favour of federal powers, building a stronger federal government than had been intended by the fathers of the constitution by granting only enumerated powers to the Union.

Naturally, there are critics who opine that, in performing its task of maintaining the 'dual polity' set up by the American Constitution, the American Supreme Court has failed to act as the 'guardian of the Constitution' in so far as it has expanded the federal power at the cost of the states, in the interest of national strength, beyond what was envisaged by the fathers of the federal constitution. However, the Supreme Court has stood against the tide of expansion of federal commerce power by holding that it could not be applied to extend federal minimum wage provisions to employees of state and local governments. However, plenary the federal power over interstate commerce might be, the court observed, it must not abrogate:

> 'Functions essential to separate and independent existence of the States'[67]

In 1976, thus, the court seems to have harkened back to the dissenting voice of Justice William O. Douglas (1898–1980) in *Maryland v. Wirtz*[68] or of Justice William Rehnquist (1924–2005) in *Fry v. US*[69], that though the situation under the war power[70] might be otherwise, the power over inter-State commerce would not enable the Federal Government 'to devour the essentials of State sovereignty,' which was reserved to the States by the 10th Amendment.

(b) Australia

The Constitution of Australia being federal, it is the duty of the judiciary to see that the 'indissoluble Federal Commonwealth' which was established by the Constitution Act (Preamble) is not impaired by any encroachment on the part of the Commonwealth:

> 'The Constitution predicates their (i.e. the States) continued existence as independent entities'[71]

The covering Article V, further, says that the Constitution Act shall be

> 'binding on the courts, judges, and people of every State ....'

There are also some substantive provisions which assume the federal nature of the constitutional system and their enforceability by the courts, e.g. mutual immunity of the Commonwealth and the states from taxation (Article 114); the distribution of legislative powers (ss. 51–52), with predominance of federal law, in case of inconsistency (Article 109); financial relations between the Commonwealth and the States (Articles 87, 93–96, 99, 105).

The Judiciary has derived the power of judicial review from the foregoing express provisions of the Constitution itself, without having to rely on general principles, as in the US. Though, in its role of guardianship of the federal constitution, the High Court and, on appeal, the Privy Council has, in different periodic waves inclined sometimes in favour of state autonomy and sometimes in favour of federal power to cope with national problems, the following broad trends may be discernable:

(1) The Court will not allow any federal action as would tend to annihilate the States. A corollary from this proposition is that the Federal Legislature shall not be allowed to so exercise its taxing power as to impose a special burden upon a State as a State. In the *Melbourne Corporation* case, the Australian High Court observed—
   (a) '... the federal power of taxation will not support a law which places a special burden upon the States. They cannot be singled out and taxed as States in respect of some exercise of their functions .... The federal system itself is the foundation of the restraint upon the use of the power to control the States'.[72]

(2) The Court will not allow the federal government to discriminate between States.

(3) A federal law, in order to be valid, must—
   (a) relate to one or more of the enumerated subjects within the federal power under Section 51 of the Constitution Act; which means that it must be a law on that enumerated subject, according to the doctrine of pith and substance and[73]
   (b) relate to a matter which is incidental to an enumerated power.

(4) If, however, a subject-matter cannot be brought under a federal enumerated power or anything incidental to it, it cannot so operate as to restrict a State power or activity, merely, because State activity might prejudicially affect some activity within federal power. The reason is:

> 'The Australian union is one of dual federalism, and until the Parliament and the people see fit to change it, a true federation it must remain'[74]

The Australian High Court thus acts as a federal court like the American Supreme Court, through, its original jurisdiction under Section 75 of the Australian Constitution Act to decide cases between the Commonwealth and the states, and between the states *inter se* (Article 131). The scope of appeal to the Privy Council from decisions of the High Court on constitutional questions has been reduced by the Privy Council (Limitation of Appeals) Act 1968.

(c) Canada

The British North America Act 1867 set up a federal system, it did not expressly provide for 'judicial review'. Nevertheless, since that Act limited the powers of both the Dominion and Provincial Legislatures.[75] The judiciary assumed the power to enforce those limitations, applying the general principle of *ultra vires*.

But until of late, the role of the Canadian Supreme Court to act as a federal arbiter was not much effective, owing to the reason that having no original jurisdiction, the Canadian Supreme Court lacks any direct power to act as an 'arbiter' in the federal system, and, until 1949, its position as an appellate court was eclipsed by the Privy Council. After the abolition of appeals to the Privy Council in 1949, it can be naturally expected that it will gain importance and will have to act as a federal court through the indirect means of reviewing the constitutionality of Dominion and Provincial laws, in appeal.[76]

(d) Germany

In Germany, the power to determine constitutionality of laws belongs to the Federal Constitutional Court (*Bundesverfassungsgericht*). This Court decides questions relating to the interpretation of the 'Basic Law', in the event of disputes concerning the rights and duties of the supreme federal organs and it also decides on the compatibility of a state law with a federal law, on the application of the federal government, or of a state government, or of one-third of the members of the *Bundestag* [Article 93].

Any Court before which the violation of the Basic Law is alleged, and the decision of the case involves a decision of the constitutional question, is bound to refer such question to the Federal Constitutional Court. Besides, every citizen can make a constitutional complaint to the Federal Constitutional Court whenever his basic rights are violated [Article 100].

It is to be noted that the Federal Constitutional Court is an institution created by the Constitution [Article 92], separate from the Federal Court of Justice, which stands at the head of the ordinary system of courts [Article 95] and, that the decisions of the Constitutional Court, according to a federal law of 1951, are binding upon all authorities and courts of the federation as well as the states. There is thus no uncertainty on this point that has existed in America. even the today. The paramountcy of the federal law over the law of the states is also secured by the Constitution itself. Article 31 says—

> 'Federal Law shall override Land (i.e., State) law'

This provision obviously narrows down the function of the Constitutional Court as an interpreter of the Constitution and makes it much easier than in America. The Constitutional Court has, however, saved the *Lander* (States) from legal extinction by holding that their authority is derived from the Constitution and not from the federation, and that, within the sphere allotted by the Constitution, the states exercise 'sovereign power', so long as it does not violate the 'federal constitutional order' [Article 28(1)].

The Constitutional Court, it has been held, is bound to hold a state law 'null and void' if it is inconsistent with the provisions of the 'Basic Law', i.e., the Constitution.[77]

(e) Switzerland

The Swiss Constitution empowers the Federal Supreme Court to declare an Act of the Cantonal Legislature to be invalid, if repugnant to the provision of the federal constitution, but, the court is given no such powers as regards laws passed by the Federal Legislature. On the other hand, Article 113 of the Swiss Constitution directs the federal tribunal/court to give effect to the laws passed by the Federal Assembly, and Article 71 states that –

> 'the supreme authority of the Confederation is exercised by the Federal Assembly'.

The result is that the Federal Legislature may encroach on cantonal subjects, without interference from the courts. Switzerland thus, offers a partial exception to the theory so far propounded that in a Federal Constitution; the guardianship of the constitution is vested in a federal court with power to invalidate laws passed by any legislature which is subject to the distribution of powers or other limitations imposed thereon by the constitution.

In the Swiss Constitution, the power to determine the validity of federal laws is given to the people themselves. If 30000 voters or 8 cantons demand, a federal law must be submitted to the people who have the final power to determine whether it shall go into effect or not [Article 89]. Subject to this, the guardianship of the constitution is vested in the Federal Executive, by Article 102(2) which says—

> 'The Federal Council ensures observance of the Constitution ....'

The result is that, the Swiss Supreme Court has no power of 'judicial review' against acts of the federal executive or legislature, on the ground of unconstitutionality.

(f) India

Though the word 'federation' or 'federal' is nowhere mentioned in the Constitution of India, the Constitution sets up a federal system, with provisions relating to the 'Union' in Part V, and provisions relating to the states in Part VI. The legislative powers as between these two units (i.e., the Union Parliament and the State Legislature) are divided by numerous Entries in the three Lists included in the 7th Schedule to the Constitution. The division of executive power as between the Union and State Governments, in general, follows the division of legislative powers [Articles 73, 162].

Though, there are points of difference on matters of details, it may be stated, broadly, that the duty of the judiciary in India, as in the United States, is to annul any Union or State action which transgresses the foregoing limitations[78] as well as the general mandatory limitations imposed by other substantive provisions of the constitution, e.g., Articles 286,[79] 301, 304,[80] or the Fundamental Rights in Part III. The Supreme Court, in short, acts as the policemen of federalism in India, as in the United States, by exercising its powers under Articles 32, 131 to 136 of the Indian Constitution.

Though Indian federation is not in the nature of a treaty or compact between the component units, there is nevertheless, a division of legislative as well as administrative powers between the Union and the States. Article 131 of Indian Constitution, therefore, vests the Supreme Court with original and exclusive jurisdiction to determine justiciable disputes between the Union and the States or between the States *inter se*. This provision, however, differs from that of Article III, Section 2(1) of the United States Constitution as well as of Section 75 of the Australian Constitution; in this that Indian Supreme Court shall have no original jurisdiction to decide disputes between residents of different states or between a state and a resident of another state. Such disputes would, under Indian Constitution, come up to the Supreme Court only in appeal, if the provisions relating thereto are satisfied.

Of course, in the case of disputes between the Union and the States, the nature of the jurisdiction of the Indian Supreme Court may differ considerably from that of the US Supreme Court, owing to the difference in the very nature of the federation in the two countries. The absence in Indian Constitution of the theories of 'State right', 'Immunity of Instrumentalities', 'dual Government', 'divided sovereignty', on the one hand, and the vesting in the Union of residuary powers and the power of issuing administrative directions and overriding powers in emergencies, on the other, would no doubt tend to minimize litigation between the Union and the States in India.[81]

Nevertheless, as the experience under the Government of India Act 1935, has shown, the very elaborateness of the legislative lists and the attempt at exhaustiveness leads to the growth of justiciable doubts and disputes as to legislative powers, at least so long as the principles of interpretation applied by the Supreme Court are not well settled. Though, Indian Constitution has strengthened the Union more than in any other federal country, nevertheless, it is not a unitary system that has been set up by the constitution. Hence, it is the interpretation of the Supreme Court in particular cases that hold the centripetal and centrifugal forces in the balance and saves the original distribution of powers from any aggressive encroachment on the part of the Union. As Alladi Krishnaswamy Iyer (1883–1953)[82] observed—

> 'The future evolution of the Indian Constitution will thus depend to a large extent upon the work of the Supreme Court and the direction given to it by that Court. From time to time, in the interpretation of the Constitution, the Supreme Court will be confronted with apparently contradictory forces at work in the society for the time being. While its function may be one of interpreting the Constitution as contained in the instrument of Government, it cannot in the discharge of its duties afford to ignore the social, economic and political tendencies of the time which furnish the necessary background. It has to keep the poise between the seemingly contradictory forces. In the process of the interpretation of the constitution, on certain occasions, it may appear to strengthen the Union at the expense of the Units and at another time it may appear to champion the cause of provincial autonomy and regionalism.'

It must be observed, however, that during the first three decades of its work, the Supreme Court has favoured the Union to further accentuate the central bias of the constitution.

The first suit under the Original Jurisdiction of Supreme Court had been instituted by the State of West Bengal in the year 1961, for a declaration that Parliament was not competent to make a law authorizing the Union Government to acquire coal-bearing lands vested in the state. The conclusion arrived at by the majority of the Supreme Court in that case, in short, is that though the power to 'acquire' property, which belongs concurrently to the Union and the States, under Entry 42, List III of the 7th Schedule, the Union has the power to acquire lands vested in a state though a state cannot draw a similar power from the same Entry to acquire property belonging to the Union. The reasoning on which this conclusion was arrived at by the majority was an assumption of pre-eminence of the Union vis-a-vis the states, underlying the Constitution. Thus, it was observed—

> 'It would be difficult to hold that the parliament which is competent to destroy a State is on account of some assumption as to absolute sovereignty of the State incompetent effectively to acquire by legislation designed for that purpose the property owned by the State for governmental purpose'.[83]

If the Supreme Court is to act as the 'guardian of the Constitution' as the final interpreter of the fundamental law embodied in the written Constitution[84], it must enforce the division of powers laid down in the Constitution against the Union as against the states, instead of applying the court's own ideology apart from the express provisions of the Constitution providing for Union supremacy under specified circumstances.

It can never be overlooked there is no 'Supremacy Clause' in the Indian Constitution like Article VI(2) of the American Constitution, and that, wherever the framers of the Indian Constitution desired that the federal interest or power should prevail, they have provided so in express terms, e.g., Articles 3, 246(1)- (3), 248–251, 254. The judiciary has not been empowered to add to these provisions. After having elevated federalism as a basic feature of the constitution, it is time that the Supreme Court should re-examine its earlier theory of 'national pre-eminence', over and above the specific provisions in the constitution itself, in this behalf.

(g) Pakistan

Like India, Pakistan is also a federation. Article 1 of the Constitution declares Pakistan to be a Federal Republic comprising of four provinces. The Supreme Court of Pakistan is the guardian of the Federation and has original jurisdiction to resolve any dispute between the Federal Government and a Provincial Government or between two Provincial Governments [Article 184]. The superior Courts (the Supreme Court and the High Courts) can declare any law passed by the Parliament as *ultra vires* of the law falls outside the subjects enumerated in the Federal Legislative List or Concurrent Legislative List.

Such a law would be deemed to have been passed on a subject exclusively within the competence of the Provincial Assembly thus violative of the principle of federation. Similarly, the superior courts can declare any provincial law as *ultra vires*, if it pertains to the subject enumerated in the Federal Legislative List. Thus, it is the function of the superior courts in Pakistan to keep the federal and provincial legislatives and government within their respective areas of competence according to the subjects allocated to them by the constitution.

The Supreme Court of Pakistan has been sensitive about the federal character of the Constitution. Although, the Supreme Court did not initially accept the theory of the basic structure of the constitution but, has recognized certain basic features of the Constitution. Federalism and federal parliamentary form of the government have been recognized by the Supreme Court amongst the basic features of the Constitution, which cannot be altered through ordinary amendment procedure of the constitution.[85] The Supreme Court of Pakistan, like the Indian Supreme Court, has conferred the status of constitutional preeminence to the federal character of the Constitution.

The earlier view of the Supreme Court of Pakistan regarding basic structure and features has undergone change in its subsequent judgment titled '*District Bar Association, Rawalpindi v. Federation of Pakistan*'.[86] The case was heard by all 17 judges of the Supreme Court in which parts of the 18th and 21st Amendments to the Constitution were challenged. The Court recognized the salient features of the Constitution as unamendable in the following paras of the judgment.[87]

(a) The Constitution contains a scheme reflecting its Salient Features which define the Constitution. Such Salient Features are obvious and self-evident upon a harmonious and wholistic interpretation of the Constitution. In an effort to discover such Salient Features, material outside the Constitution cannot be safely relied upon.
(b) The Salient Features as are ascertainable from the Constitution including Democracy, Parliamentary Form of Government, and Independence of the Judiciary.
(c) The amendatory powers of the Parliament are subject to implied limitations. The Parliament, in view of Article 238 and 239 is vested with the power to amend the Constitution as long as the Salient Features of the Constitution are not repealed, abrogated or substantively altered.
(d) This Court is vested with the jurisdiction to interpret the Constitution in order to ascertain and identify its defining Salient Features. It is equally vested with jurisdiction to examine the vires of any Constitutional Amendment so as to determine whether any of the Salient Features of the constitution has been repealed, abrogated or substantively altered as a consequence thereof.

Although the Court did not give exhaustive list of the Salient Features of the Constitution, yet all the features that are ascertainable from the Constitution form part of the Salient Features. 'Federalism', without any shadow of doubt, is clearly ascertainable from the Constitution as one of its basic features of the Constitution and thus unamendable.

Notes

1. Otis H. Stephens Jr, John M. Scheb, *American Constitutional Law*, 3rd ed. (Belmont, California: Thomson West, 2003), p. 265.
2. Alpheus Thomas Mason, William Merritt Beaney, Donald Grier Jr Stéphenson; *American Constitutional Law*, 7th ed. (New Jersey: Prentice – Hall, Inc 1983), p. 142.
3. Peter Woll, *Constitutional Law: Cases and Comments*, (Englewood Cliffs, N.J.: Prentice-Hall, 1981), p. 254.
4. John Marshall was the 4th Chief Justice of the US Supreme Court from 1801 to 1835.
5. *McCulloch v. Maryland* 17 U.S. 316 (1819).
6. J P Eddy, Frederick Horace Lawton, *India's New Constitution: a survey of the Government of India Act, 1935* (London: Macmillan, 1935).
7. Seventh Schedule to the Government of India Act, 1935.
8. *Muhammad Siddique v. Government of Pakistan* PLD 2005 S.C 1.
9. Eric Barendt, *An Introduction to Constitutional Law*, (Clarendon: Oxford University Press, 1998), p. 54.
10. James Madison was a founding father who was the 4th President of the United States.
11. Alexander Hamilton was one of the founding fathers of the United States, a legal scholar, military commander, lawyer, banker, and economist.
12. Supra Note 9, p. 53.
13. Preamble in the Constitution. By contrast, the Treaties of Rome and Maastricht refer to the 'Peoples [plural] of Europe', while the European Parliament consists of 'representation of the peoples of the States brought together in the Community….' Article 137 of the Treaty of Rome.
14. Geoffry Sawyer, *Modern Federalism*, 2nd ed, (Carlton, Vic: Pitman Australia, 1976).
15. Akhil. R. Amar, *Of Sovereignty and Federalism*', Yale Law Journal 96, 1987.
16. The Basic Law (constitution) of Germany is divided into Artikel or articles, not sections. To cite the Basic Law a notation like "Artikel 1 GG" or "Article 1 GG", where GG stands for Grundgesetz, basic law, is used.
17. Art. 70(1). Also see Art. 30: '[t]he exercise of governmental powers and the discharge of governmental functions shall be incumbent on the Lander in so far as this Basic Law does not otherwise prescribe or permit.'

18. Sections 91–92 of the Canada Constitution Act 1867.
19. Article 51 GG. The delegates of each Land must vote as a block (see Art. 51(3), which means that the *Bundesrat* will be in opposition to the *Bundestag* if the governments of a majority of the, or of the more populous, *Lander* have a different political composition from that of the federal government.
20. *Attorney General for Common Wealth of Australia v. Colonial Sugar Refining Co. Ltd.* (1914) A.C. 237, 253.
21. Oliver Wendell Holmes Jr was Associate Justice of the US Supreme Court from 1902 to 1932.
22. Oliver Wendell Holmes Jr., *The Collected Legal Papers* (London: Constable & Robinson, 1920), pp. 295.
23. Article 31 GG; provides for the supremacy of federal law.
24. *Garcia v. San Antonio Metropolitan Authority*, 469 US 528 (1985).
25. *United States v. Lopez*, 115 S Ct. 1624 (1995).
26. *e.g.* the court struck down a federal order instituting a national television channel, since cultural matters are reserved for *the Lander*: 12 BVerfGE 205 (1961).
27. Martin H. Redish, *The Constitution As Political Structure*, 1st ed., (Oxford University Press, 1995) Chapter 2–3.
28. Article 72 GG and Article 74 GG, German Basic Law.
29. Geoffery Sawyer, Supra Note 14 refers to the 'stages of federalism' in *Modern Federalism*, ch. 8.
30. Richard B. Stewart, *Federalism and Rights*, 19 Ga. L. Rev. 917 (1984–1985).
31. *The Federalist Papers* were collection of essays written by John Jay, James Madison, and Alexander Hamilton in 1788.
32. A.V. Dicey, *The Law of the Constitution*, (Oxford: Oxford University Press, 2013) pp. 171–5, but see the criticism of his analysis by Sawyer, Supra Note 14 above, 124–5.
33. Ibid, p. 58.
34. Erwin Chemerinsky, *Constitutional Law: Principles and Policies*, 4th ed. (New York: Wolters Kluwer Law & Business, 2011), p. 319.
35. *National League of cities v. Usery*, 426 U.S. 833 (1976); overruled in *Garcia v. San Antonio Metro Transit Auth.*, 469 U.S. 528 (1985).
36. Supra Note 34, pp. 319–20.
37. Syed Sharifuddin Pirzada, *Foundations of Pakistan, 1906–1947*, (Karachi: National Publishing House, 1990).
38. *Hakim Khan v. Government of Pakistan* PLD 1992 SC 595.
39. *Al-Jehad Trust v. Federation of Pakistan*, 1999 SCMR 1379.
40. The Constitution (18th Amendment) Act, 2010 has omitted the Concurrent List.
41. Zafar Hussain Mirza served as judge of the Supreme Court of Pakistan from 1981 to 1991.
42. PLD 1988 SC 416.
43. Justice Fazal Karim, *Judicial Review of Public Action, Vol. 1* (Karachi: Pakistan Law House, 2018), 27–8.
44. For details see Articles 232 to 237 of the Constitution of Pakistan.
45. *Government of Sindh v. Dr. Nadeem Rizvi* decided on 17-01-2019 by a bench of 5 judges of the Supreme Court of Pakistan. It was decided by 4 to 1 majority with Justice Ijaz-ul-Ahsan writing for the majority and Justice Maqbool Baqar writing his dissenting note. 2019 S C M R 556.
46. Dr B.R. Ambedkar served as independent India's first Minister of Law and Justice, the chief architect of the Constitution of India, and a founding father of the Republic of India.
47. V.D. Mahajan, *Constitutional Law of India*, 7th ed., (Lucknow: Eastern Book Company, 1991), pp. 22–23.
48. *Ibid*, pp. 17–9.
49. Kenneth Clinton Wheare was an Australian academic at Oxford Univeristy. He was an expert on the constitutions of the British Commonwealth.
50. *Attorney General of Alberta v. Attorney General of Canada*; (1943) A.C. 356.
51. *Citizen Insurance Co. of Canada v. Parson* (1881) 7 A.C. 96.
52. A. K. Brohi, *Fundamental Law of Pakistan*, (Karachi: Din Muhammadi Press, 1958), p. 225.
53. Lord Atkin was a lawyer and judge of Irish, Welsh and Australian origin, who practiced in England and Wales.
54. *Attorney General for Canada v. Attorney General of Ontario*, (1937) A.C. 326 at 354 (Lord Atkins).
55. John C. Calhoun was the 7th Vice-President of the United States from 1825 to 1832.
56. 2 U.S. 419 (1793).
57. 22 U.S. 1 (1824).
58. Durga Das Basu, *Comparative Constitutional Law*, 2nd ed. (New Delhi: Prentice Hall of India, 1984) pp. 481–2.
59. This is subject to an exception in the case of Switzerland where federal laws are not subject to judicial review and the Federal Court can examine the constitutionality only of State (Cantonal) Laws.
60. *Baxter v. Commissioner of Taxation*, (1907) 4 C.L.R. 1087 (1110).
61. *Hammer v. Dagenhart*, 247 U.S. 251 (1918).
62. *Marbury v. Madison*, 5 U.S. 137 (1803).

63. *Carter v. Carter Coal Co.*, 298 U.S. 238 (1936).
64. During a period of 180 years (1790–1970), the Supreme Court has invalidated some 92 Acts of Congress The power of judicial review has, however been more frequently used in annulling State Laws.
65. 17 U.S. 316 (1819).
66. *Marbury v. Madison*, 5 U.S. 317 107 (1803).
67. *National League of Cities v. Usery*, 426 U.S. 833 (1976).
68. 392 U.S. 183 (1968).
69. 421 U.S. 542 (1975).
70. *Yakus v. U.S.* 321 U.S. 414 (1944).
71. *Melbourne Corp. v. Commonwealth*, (1947) 74 C.L.R. 31.
72. *Melbourne Corp. v. Commonwealth*, (1947) 74 C.L.R. 31.
73. *Fairfax v. Commissioner. of Taxation*, (1965) 114 C.L.R. 1(7); and *Huddart Parker & Co.Pty Ltd. v. Moorehead*, (1908) 8 C.L.R. 330 (409–12).
74. *Airlines of New South Wales v.New South Wales*, (1964–65) 113 C.L.R.54 (112, 115, 116–17) F.C.
75. *Attorney-General for Ontario v Attorney-General of Canada (Reference Appeal) (Ontario, Canada) [1912]* A.C. 571.
76. *McKay v. R.*, (1965) S.C.R. 798; *Ross v. Registrar of Motor Vehicle*, [1975] 1 S.C.R. 5; *Munro v. National Capital Commission*, (1966) S.C.R. 663; *Jones v. A.G. of New Brusnwick*, [1975] 2 S.C.R. 182; *Ref. Anti-Inflation Act*, 9 N.R. 541. 68 D.L.R. (3d) 452 (S.C.C. 1976).
77. *Southwest case*, (1951) 1 BVerfGe 14; Murphy & Tanenhaus, pp. 208 *et seq.*
78. Ref under Article 143, AIR. 1965 S.C. 745 (762).
79. *Bengal Immunity Co. v. State of Bihar*, AIR. 1955 S.C. 661; *State of Punjab v. Sansari Mal*, AIR 1968 S.C. 331.
80. *Atiabari Tea Co. v. State of Assam*, AIR. 1961 S.C. 232.
81. These overwhelming powers, together with the financial resources of the Union, thus, account for the fact that until 1961 (see *State of West Bengal v. Union of India*, AIR 1963 S.C. 1241), there was not a single case between the Union and a State under Article 131.
82. Address by Alladi Krishnaswamy Iyer, AIR 1949 Jour.35.
83. *State of West Bengal v. Union of India*, AIR 1963 S.C. 1241.
84. *Automobile Transport (Rajasthan) Ltd. v. State of Rajasthan*, AIR 1962 S.C. 140; *Kesavananda v. State of Kerala*, AIR. 1973 S.C. 1461 (1584, 1535).
85. *Mahmood Khan Achakzai v. Federation of Pakistan* PLD 1997 S.C. 426; *Zafar Ali Shah v. General Pervez Musharraf Chief Executive of Pakistan*, PLD 2000 S.C. 869.
86. PLD 2015 S.C. 401.
87. Ibid, p. 745.

9 Separation of Powers

Introduction

The terms 'separation of powers' and 'checks and balances' are commonly used descriptions of American government. These phrases do not, however, have a precise and unambiguous meaning.

From the very beginning the concept of 'separation of powers' has been somewhat ambiguous. The importance of a division of governmental powers to prevent tyranny and guarantee political stability dates to Plato's *Laws*. From Plato (c. 427–347 BCE) onward numerous political theorists have seen mixed government as essential for the ideal polity. But ancient political theory did not particularly concentrate upon the importance of a constitutional division of authority among the branches of government as the essential ingredient in a mixed government.

Before the 18th century, political theorists concentrated on the idea of balancing social, economic, and class interests to prevent centralization and create a sound government. The nature of the 'mixture' of interests and how they were to be represented in government was neither clearly articulated by any theorist, nor was it a subject of agreement among them. This confusion in political theory about the proper form that mixed governments should take was caused by the divergent political practices and experiences that theorists drew upon.

In 17th century England, the struggles that culminated in the Glorious Revolution of 1688 reflected in part the struggle to establish a separation of powers between the King and the common law courts. At the same time, a judicial-executive separation of powers was developing, the Glorious Revolution established in practice the principle of parliamentary supremacy. As England entered the 18th century, its government had a separation of powers only in the sense that the common law courts exercised a judicial power independently of Parliament and the Cabinet. There was no separation of powers between the executive and legislative branches, for the executive authority of the King had been taken over by the Cabinet, which was elected by a majority in Parliament.

The origins of the modern theory of separation of powers is customarily traced to Montesquieu's *Esprit des Lois* published in 1748. Montesquieu's theory of the 'separation of powers' was widely read and quoted by literate American colonists. It found its way into James Madison's[1] exegesis on the subject in *The Federalist Papers*.[2]

While Madison went along with the tenor of the times by citing Montesquieu, in fact, the American practice of the 'separation of powers' both in colonial charters and in state constitutions went beyond the British constitution by establishing the principle of 'separation of power' between the legislative and executive branches of the government.

Although, Montesquieu misunderstood the British constitution, proclaiming that it in fact created a separation of powers among the legislative, executive, and judicial branches, his theory was nonetheless an important milestone. He was the first to emphasize the importance of legal divisions of authority among the branches of government. According to him each branch would have its own preserve of power, delegated to it by the constitution, and at the same time would be given sufficient powers to check coordinate branches.

Montesquieu's theory provided a basis for James Madison's discussion of the 'separation of powers' in *The Federalist Papers*. A constitutional system of the separation of powers has come to be known as the Madisonian model of government. An underlying premise of the model is that there is a natural division of governmental power into the legislative, executive, and judicial categories. These functions are separate and distinct and are appropriately exercised by separate branches of government. The functions of government should be commingled through the checks and balances system only insofar as a necessary to preserve the integrity of each branch. The primary thrust of the assumption of a natural division of governmental authority is that the separation of powers is necessary for efficient governmental performance.

In *The Federalist Papers*, however, James Madison did not emphasize the efficiency of government that would be created by the new constitution. He concentrated upon the idea how the 'separation of powers' would prevent arbitrary and capricious government. Madison stated the premise of this negative aspect of the 'separation of powers' in *The Federalist 47,* that

> 'the accumulation of all powers, legislation, executive, and judiciary, in the same hands, whether of one, a few, or many, and whether hereditary, self-appointed, or elected may justly be pronounced the very definition of tyranny.'

Madison's presentation of the separation of powers in this way has always resulted in identifying the Madisonian model with a system that emphasizes the need to control and inhibit government action, rather than the importance of insuring effective performance of legislative, executive, and judicial functions.[3]

Alexander Hamilton's (1755/57–1804)[4] views of the separation of powers in *The Federalist* are in sharp contrast to those of Madison. In *The Federalist 70,* Hamilton proclaimed that –

> 'Energy in the executive is a leading character in the definition of good government. It is essential to the protection of a community against foreign attacks; it is not less essential to the steady administration of the laws, to the protection of property against those irregular and high-handed combinations, which sometimes interrupt the ordinary course of justice, to the security of liberty against the enterprises and assaults of ambition, of faction, and of anarchy.'

Effective, not limited, government was Hamilton's goal. He stated that:

> 'A feeble executive implies a feeble execution of the government, a feeble execution is but another phrase for a bad execution; and a government ill executed, whatever it may be in theory, must be in practice, a bad government.'

The Hamiltonian model conflicts with the Madisonian model in its premises that efficiency and effectiveness are the desired ends of government and that the separation of powers through its creation of an independent executive makes a major contribution to this end.

The Madisonian and Hamiltonian models contrasted not only in their approaches to the goals of the separation of legislative and executive power but in their explanations of the role of the judiciary. Madison was more inclined towards the Jeffersonian view that although the judiciary should be independent, its powers should be limited, Hamilton, by contrast, boldly proclaimed in *The Federalist 78* that an independent judiciary with the authority to overturn unconstitutional acts of Congress was essential to effective constitutional government.

The fact that Madison and Hamilton could view the same constitution in contrasting ways, reflected inherent constitutional ambiguities that, under the doctrine of *Marbury v. Madison*[5] would ultimately had to be resolved by the Court. John Marshall (1755–1835) in the *Marbury* opinion said,

> 'It is emphatically the province and duty of the judicial department to say what the law is,'

It would be up to the Court to resolve any constitutional ambiguities over the legal boundaries of the separation of powers. In resolving these constitutional questions judges supporting the Madisonian model would tend to declare unconstitutional bold exercises of executive discretion, such as those which occurred in *Youngstown Sheet and Tube Company v. Sawyer*[6] in 1952. Madison would have looked favourably upon the majority's decision, whereas Hamilton would have endorsed the vigorous dissent of Chief Justice Fred M. Vinson (1890–1953)[7] who supported the constitutionality of independent executive action to meet national emergencies.

According to Hans Kelsen (1881–1973)[8], the concept of separation of powers designates a principle of political organization

> It presupposes that the three so-called powers can be determined as three distinct coordinated functions of the State, and that it is possible to define boundary lines separating each of these three functions from the others. But this presupposition is not borne out by the facts. ---- there are not three but two basic functions of the State: creation and application (execution) of law, and these functions are not coordinated but sub- and supra-ordinated. Further, it is not possible to define boundary lines separating these functions from each other, since the distinction between creation and application of law - underlying the dualism of legislative and executive power (in the broadest sense) - has only relative character, most acts of State being at the

> same time law-creating and law-applying acts. It is impossible to assign the creation of law to one organ and the application (execution) of law to another so exclusively that no organ would fulfill both functions. Simultaneously, it is hardly possible, and at any rate not desirable to reserve even legislation - which is only a certain kind of law-creation – to a separate body of public servants, to exclude all the other function.[9]

Hans Kelsen after reviewing the whole concept comes to the following conclusion:

> 'Thus, one can hardly speak of any separation of legislation from other functions of the State in the sense that the so called "legislative" organ to the exclusion of so-called "executive" and "judicial" organs would alone be competent to exercise this function. The appearance of such a separation exists because only those general norms that are created by the "legislative" organs are designated as "laws" (*leges*). Even when the Constitution exclusively maintains the principle of the separation of powers, the legislative function is distributed among several organs, but only one of them is given the name of "legislative" organ. This organ never has a monopoly on the creation of general norms, but at most a certain favoured positions such as was previously characterized. Its designation as legislative organ is the more justified the greater the part it has in the creation of general norms.'[10]

In view of the above statement, it may be correct to state that the concept actually boils down to distribution of the power rather than the separation of the power.

Constitutional Background and US Constitution

The Madisonian model of the separation of powers is set forth in *The Federalist papers 47, 48,* and *51*. Madison was careful to point out that although liberty requires the separation of the three branches, neither the theory nor the practice of the 'separation of powers' requires an absolute separation among the branches. Citing Montesquieu, Madison notes that:

> "his meaning ... can amount to no more than this, that where the whole power of one department is exercised by the same hands which possessed the whole power of another department, the fundamental principles of a free constitution are subverted....'

Moreover, Madison said,

> 'If we look into the constitutions of the several states, we find that notwithstanding the emphatical and, in some instances, the unqualified terms in which this axiom has been laid down, there is not a single instance in which the several departments of power have been kept absolutely separate and distinct ....' (*Federalist* 47).

Madison cites theory and practice to support his conclusion that the separation of powers can only be maintained if there is a blend of power among the branches, so that each has a constitutional check upon the other, and each has the means to defend itself against encroachments by coordinate branches.

The 'separation of powers' is to be maintained not only through checks and balances but also by the creation of contrasting motivations for each branch of the government. This was accomplished by giving each branch a separate constituency – Congress being responsible to the people and the states respectively in the House and the Senate, and the President accountable to the Electoral College. The Supreme Court and the judiciary, although nominated by the President and with the advice and consent of the Senate, were to be approved independent of the other branches. Each branch 'should have a will of its own,' wrote Madison in *Federalist* 51. He continued:

> 'The great security against a gradual concentration of the several powers in the same department [branch] consists in giving to those who administer each department, the necessary constitutional means, and personal motives to resist encroachments of the others.'

The personal motives to resist encroachments were supplied by the separate constituencies.

Regardless of how elaborate the constitutional system to prevent the arbitrary exercise of political power was, Madison warned against the possibility of a dominant legislative branch. The future development of the Republic was to see the rise of the 'imperial presidency,' at least in part due to liberal Supreme Court interpretations of the scope of executive authority under the Constitution. But executive power was the least of the expressed concerns of Madison in *The Federalist*. It is not possible, he wrote,

> 'to give to each department an equal power of self-defense. In republican government, the legislative authority [branch] necessarily predominates. The remedy for this inconvenience is to divide the government into different branches; and to render them by different modes of election and different principles of action, as little connected with each other, as the nature of their common functions, and their common dependence on the society will admit' (*Federalist* 51).

By contrast, the inherent weakness of the executive requires that it be fortified, by giving it such powers as the veto over legislative actions. Madison found the source of legislative superiority in the connection between the legislative branch and the people, which inspires the legislative branch 'with an intrepid confidence in its own strength.

> ' The legislature is 'sufficiently numerous to feel all the passions which actuate a multitude; yet not so numerous as to be incapable of pursuing the objects of its passions, by means which reason prescribes; it is against the enterprising ambition of this department, that the people ought to indulge all their jealousy and exhaust all their precautions.'[11]

Madison wrote that another reason for the superiority of the legislature was that

> 'its constitutional powers being at once more extensive, and less susceptible of precise limits, it can, with the greater facility [than other branches] mask, under complicated and indirect measures, the encroachment which it makes on the coordinate departments. It is not infrequently a question of real nicety in legislative bodies, whether the operation of a particular measure will, or will not extend beyond the legislative sphere' (*Federalist 48*).

There are many implications of the Madisonian model to the interpretation of the 'separation of powers'. Acceptance of Madison's premises would lead to a wary view of the motivations and powers of Congress that would strike down legislative action that appeared to intrude upon the executive or judiciary. On the other hand, since Madison's assumption was that executive power is

> 'restrained within a narrower compass, and... [is] simpler in its nature [than legislative power],'

a more lenient view would be taken to executive prerogative actions that would allow an expansion of presidential discretion. The relatively simple and constricted nature of both executive and judicial power led Madison to the conclusion that –

> 'projects of usurpation by either of these departments would immediately betray and defeat themselves' (*Federalist 48*).

Neither the theory of the constitutional separation of powers as stated by Madison in the *The Federalist Papers 47, 48* and *51* nor the provisions of the constitution that implement the separation of powers create clear and unequivocal divisions of power that are to prevail among the three branches. Articles I, II, and III of the Constitution, called the distributing clauses, respectively delegate legislative, executive, and judicial powers to Congress, the President, and the Supreme Court. Article I provides that –

> 'All legislative powers herein granted shall be vested in a Congress of the United Sates, which shall consist of a Senate and House of Representatives.'

Article II states:

> — 'The executive power shall be vested in a President of the United States of America'.

And Article III provides:

> — 'The Judicial power of the United States shall be vested in one Supreme Court, and in such inferior courts as the Congress may from time to time ordain and establish.'

On their face, these articles would seem to imply that no branch can exercise the general powers of coordinate branches. However, the distributing clauses do not themselves segregate governmental powers but delegate to each branch some of the powers of coordinate branches in the form of checks and balances. Therefore, while 'all legislative power' is to reside in Congress, the president is explicitly given the veto power over Congress, which is a clear grant of legislative authority to the president. Under the doctrine of *Marbury v. Madison*, the Supreme Court can nullify executive and legislative acts. Since congressional action can be vetoed by the president and nullified by the Supreme Court, 'all legislative power' does not reside in Congress. Other constitutional checks and balances, although they do not give any branch the authority to exercise directly the powers of coordinate branches, may impede branches in the exercise of their primary constitutional powers.[12]

The language of the American Constitution in combination with Madison's statement of constitutional premises and principles in *The Federalist* makes it clear that there is not to be a complete 'separation of powers' among the 3 branches. The principle of 'separation of powers' is violated only where all legislative, executive, and judicial powers reside in the same hands. Each branch must maintain control over the exercise of its primary constitutional function and at the same time can exercise powers that intrude upon the spheres of other branches if provided for by the constitutional system of checks and balances or if necessary and incidental to the exercise of its primary responsibility. The President can exercise a legislative veto because it is provided by the Constitution. The President can also be given the responsibility by Congress to exercise legislative functions (although not primary legislative power) that are incidental to executive power.

The constitutional provisions themselves reveal, however, that separation was not intended to be airtight. Repeatedly, powers are blended and inter-mixed: for example, the president participates in the legislative process through the veto power; and in diplomatic and military affairs, the President is Commander-in-Chief, makes treaties and appoints ambassadors, but treaties and ambassadorial appointments requires the consent of the Senate, and the Congress has the power to raise and support the army and navy and to declare war. And repeatedly, restraints by one branch upon another are authorized as aspects of the system of checks and balances, which coexists (and is often in tension with) any pure separation of powers scheme. Beyond the explicit restraints and overlaps, moreover, lie boundary lines indistinct in the original document and blurred by historical practice. These areas of uncertainty have left ample room for competition among the branches – conflicts that have historically most often been resolved by tests of political strength. These conflict-producing ambiguities may themselves have contributed to furthering the framers' purpose of combating excessive concentration of power; yet they also yield an area of constitutional law with unclear lines. In the area of separation of powers, far more than with problems of federalism and individual rights, judicial resolutions have been relatively sparse and political accommodations have predominated. Yet sparsity of Court decisions does not make separation of powers any less important and challenging an area of constitutional interpretation.[13]

The need for judicial resolution of questions concerning the separation of powers arises under several circumstances. Usually questions arise when Congress has passed a statute that delegates to itself, to the President, or to the judiciary non-legislative, non-executive, or non-judicial functions respectively. Sometimes the President by prerogative action invades the spheres of coordinate branches.

The question of 'separation of powers' in *Springer v. Philippine Islands*[14] arose out of actions by the Philippine Legislature that delegated to itself executive powers. Congress, in the organic act of the Philippine Islands, had provided for a separation of powers in the island government analogous to that which prevailed in the Constitution. The Philippine Legislature had amended legislation creating government corporations to deny the governor-general the exclusive authority he had possessed under the original statute to vote the stock in these corporations. The amended laws provided that the voting power of the stock of various government corporations would, henceforth, reside in a committee consisting of the governor-general, the president of the Senate, and Speaker of the House of Representatives. As Justice George Sutherland (1862–1942) noted in his majority opinion in the *Springer* case,

> 'The suggestion of the Solicitor-General [of the United States] that this indicates a systematic plan on the part of the legislature [of the Philippines] to take over through its presiding officers, the direct control generally of nationally organized or controlled stock corporations would seem to be warranted.'

The governor-general immediately challenged the action of the legislature and refused to participate in voting for the directors of the government corporations involved. Directors were subsequently chosen by the President of the Senate and the Speaker of the House, and the governor-general successfully challenged, in a *quo warranto* action in the Supreme Court of the Philippines, their right to hold office. Springer and other directors elected by the legislative officers successfully sought a writ of certiorari from the Supreme Court to review the decision of the Supreme Court of the Philippines Islands that ousted them.

The majority opinion in the *Springer* case, written by Justice Sutherland, made it clear that the court considered the actions of the Philippine Legislature to be a violation of the separation of powers contained in the island's organic act. Legislative power, said the majority, is the authority to make the laws, neither to enforce them nor to appoint agents charged with the responsibility of enforcement. The latter are executive functions. Even though the legislation in question did not give legislative officers the direct responsibility of enforcement. The latter are executive functions. Even though the legislation in question did not give legislative officers the direct responsibility to enforce laws or to appoint officials, this was done by indirection in giving the presiding officers of the legislature the power to vote the stock of government corporations, hence giving them the authority to name the directors of the corporations.

Justice Oliver Wendell Holmes Jr (1841–1935), joined by Justice Louis Brandeis (1856–1941), dissented in the *Springer* case. He pointed out that there are many ambiguous provisions in the constitution, including the 'separation of powers.' The dissenting opinion cited numerous instances in which Congress took action that violated a strict 'separation of powers' among the branches by giving both the executive and the courts lawmaking functions and in which it assumed for itself executive responsibilities. And, said the dissenting justices, the Supreme Court did not overturn these seeming transgressions of the 'separation of powers'.

But in view of the 'checks and balances' connecting the three organs of the government, employed by the US Constitution, separation of powers is by no means complete. The fathers of the US Constitution intended that the balance of powers should be attained by checks and balances between the three organs of the state. The American President may veto measures passed by Congress though his veto may be overridden by a two-thirds vote of both Houses. The president has the power to negotiate treaties, but they must be ratified by a two-thirds vote of the Senate. The Supreme Court, asserting the continued significance of the separation of powers, has held that Congress has no power to veto executive acts of the president. The Senate may refuse to confirm certain appointments made by the president notably that of judges of the Supreme Court and the judges of that court, although appointed for life, may be removed by impeachment. The powers of judicial review of legislation were assumed by the Supreme Court, and were not expressly conferred – although it may perhaps be implied – by the constitution. The three branches of government are therefore inter-related; they act as checks on each other.

In the parliamentary form of government, everything is different. The head of the administration, the prime minister, is selected on the ground that he is best qualified to secure a majority in Parliament. He retains his position so long as the parliamentary support is forthcoming. He must be a member of Parliament. The same persons form part of both the legislature and executive. At one time legislature controlled the executive but now executive controls the legislature because it exercises a decisive voice in regard to the passage of legislation.

Therefore, 'separation of powers' means 3 different things.

- First, that the same persons should not form part of more than one of the three organs of government, for example, ministers should not sit in parliament.
- Second, that one organ of government should not interfere with the exercise of functions of another organ, for example, the judiciary should be independent of the executive or ministers should not be responsible to parliament.
- Third, that one organ of government should not exercise the functions of another, for example, ministers should not have legislative powers.[15]

Separation of powers in Pakistan

After the partition of India in 1947, both India and Pakistan, in their constitution making process, were unable to break away from the lasting spell of the Government of India Act 1935. The Act was a significant development in

India's constitutional and political history, it was an evolutionary process from an absolute absence of the Indians from power to their gradual participation with the ultimate object of self-rule. Due to the peculiar circumstances prevailing at that time, the constitution making process was not a matter of reflection and choice but depended on vicissitudes of time and power politics.

The 1973 Constitution of Pakistan, when adopted was also product of these facts and circumstances particularly the events that unfolded themselves in the aftermath of the Indo-Pakistan war of 1971. The Constitution of Pakistan, though it declared itself a federal state with a parliamentary form of the government at the center, was a result of limited choices. The horizontal and vertical separation/distribution of (state) power was not meant to secure the freedoms of the citizens.

The Constitution (Article 90) provided that

> 'the executive authority of the Federation shall vest in the President and shall be exercised by him, either directly or through officer subordinate to him, in accordance with the Constitution.'

If the language of this Article is compared with section 7 of the Act of 1935 and Article 53 of the Indian Constitution, all these provisions are almost identical. Article 1 of the American Constitution on the other hand refers to the 'Executive Power'.

Similarly, the legislative power of the Parliament (Articles 141–143), extends to the Federal List and also the Concurrent List. These provisions are also identical with the provisions in the Act of 1935 (Section 99) and Indian Constitution's Article 245. However, unlike the American Constitution, judicial power has not been separately recognized and conferred on the courts. The constitution does only provide for the establishment of the Supreme Court and the High Courts and such other court as may be established by law. Here again the provisions in the Act of 1935 (Sections 200 & 219) and the Indian Constitution (Articles 124 and 214) are similar.

The foundation and basis for the exercise of the judicial power were therefore, read into the constitution due to

(1) the very fact that it was a written constitution;
(2) fundamental rights were provided and any law repugnant to fundamental rights was declared void (Article 8);
(3) federal structure of the Constitution provided that there would be distribution of powers (all the three) between the provinces and the Center and if there was inconsistency between the federal law and the provincial law, the latter would be void to the extent of inconsistency (Article 143); and
(4) if the Constitution or any other law was enacted/amended in contravention of the provisions relating to enactment/amendment, the law could be declared unconstitutional. In addition to these implicit powers, the Constitution conferred powers of judicial review in the Constitution under Articles 199 and 184.

In contradistinction of the expression 'judicial power' the constitution uses the expression 'jurisdiction'. But the cumulative effect of all these provisions of the constitution comes to this:

> 'In exercising this power, the judiciary claims no supremacy over to other organs of the Government but acts only as administrator of the public will. Even when it declares a legislative measure unconstitutional and void, it does not do so, because, the judicial power is superior in degree or dignity to the legislative power; but because the Constitution has vested it with the power to declare what the law is in the cases which come before it. It thus merely enforces the Constitution as a paramount law whenever a legislative enactment comes into conflict with it because; it is its duty to see that the Constitution prevails.'[16]

It is noticeable that the Act of 1935 (which is interestingly without a preamble) enacted by the British Parliament, was drafted on the Westminster model where there was no watertight separation of power at least to the extent of two branches of the government namely the executive and the legislature. Historically, the judiciary had accepted the supremacy of the Parliament and therefore, there was no question to have a separation of power in the American sense.

In Pakistan also, the parliamentary form of the government was adopted under the Constitution of 1973. In a parliamentary form of government, particularly owing to the party system, there is no scope for real separation of powers between the executive and the legislative branch. The real struggle therefore, is between the executive on the one hand (elected by the legislature) and the judiciary on the other hand arising out of a struggle for the custodianship of the constitution.

The 1973 Constitution, therefore, has neither separation of powers nor checks and balances. In fact, the Constitution hardly provides any balance of powers between the three organs of the State.

The legislative function involves the enactment of laws of constitutional and sub-constitutional nature determining the structure and powers of public authorities and regulating the conduct of citizens. In Pakistan, legislative authority is vested in Parliament consisting of the National Assembly and the Senate.

A Bill when passed by the House, in which it is originated, is transmitted to the other House and when passed by the other House is presented to the president for assent. Not all legislation is directly made by Parliament. An Act of Parliament may delegate legislative power to governments and local authorities for the purpose of making rules and regulations.

The President of Pakistan has power under Article 89 of the 1973 Constitution to promulgate Ordinances for a period of 4 months. The Parliament does not only legislate, it also debates the policies of the government and scrutinizes the work of the government departments. Almost all the Bills are prepared by the government which is responsible for their presentation and drafting, for supervising their passage through each House and for implementing the Acts after they have received the assent of the president. The executive therefore participates actively, and often decisively, in the process of legislation. When the government has a working majority in the National Assembly, no new legislation can be enacted by Parliament which is not approved by the government.

Once a new law has been enacted by Parliament, the authoritative interpretation of that law is a matter for the courts. The interpretation of statutes is in one sense a vital part of the legislative process as it is only after judicial interpretation that it is known whether the intentions of those who framed the law have actually been carried into effect.

The executive function comprises the whole corpus of authority to govern, other than that which is involved in the legislative functions of Parliament and the judicial functions of the courts. The general direction of policy includes the initiation of legislation, the maintenance of order, the promotion of social and economic welfare, administration of public services, and the conduct of the external relations of the state. The executive function has therefore a residual character and is exercised by techniques ranging from the formation of broad policy to the detailed management of routine services. Executive acts performed by the prime minister, ministers and the civil servants are taken in the name of the president. The armed forces, the police, the local authorities and independent statutory bodies also perform executive functions.

The primary judicial function is the resolution of disputes between citizens and citizens, between citizens and governments and between government and government and the interpretation of the constitution and law. This function is exercised mainly in the civil and criminal courts by professional judges. The courts exercise certain legislative functions, for example, the making of rules of court procedure and administrative functions, for example, the administration of the estates of deceased persons. Some work of the court (for example the granting of an uncontested divorce) involves no dispute or controversy. Other tasks (for example the sentencing of criminals) are arguably not essential judicial functions, although they are traditionally the work of judges.[17]

Although, the concept of 'separation of powers' is not expressly enunciated in the Constitution of Pakistan; like the Constitution of the United States, Australia, etc.,; it is a concept inferred from the principles underlying the Constitution of Pakistan itself. This principle is the basis of decisions in some of the leading constitutional cases (e.g. *State v. Zia-ur-Rehman;*[18] *Registrar v. Wali Muhammad;*[19] *Sharif Faridi v. The Federation;*[20] *Government of Baluchistan v. Azizullah Memon;*[21] and *Al-Jehad Trust v. Federation*[22]). It was held in *Mamukanjan Cotton Factory v. The Punjab Province*[23] that to hold otherwise

> 'would also seek to throw into serious disarray the pivotal arrangement in the Constitution regarding the division of sovereign powers of the State among its principal organs, namely, the Executive, the Legislature and the Judiciary, each being the master in its own assigned field under the Constitution.'

In the case of *Mehram Ali v. Federation of Pakistan*,[24] Chief Justice Ajmal Mian(1934–2017) observed –

> 'our Constitution is founded on the theory of trichotomy of power between the three limbs/organs of the State, namely, the Legislature, the Executive and the Judiciary. It delineates the functions of each of the organs. It envisages that each organ of the State shall function/operate within the bounds specified in the Constitution.'

In *Liaquat Hussain v. Federation of Pakistan*,[25] Chief Justice Ajmal Mian observed

> 'we must look to the scheme of the Constitution which is based on the principle of trichotomy of power, meaning thereby that the power is divided between the Executive, the Legislature and the Judiciary. Each of these three limbs of the State enjoys complete independence in their own sphere,'

In *Liaqaut Hussain's* case, Justice Saeeduzzaman Siddiqui (1939–2017), Observed–

> 'Creation of courts outside the control and supervision of Supreme Court or the High Courts, therefore, not only militates against the independence of Judiciary but it also negates the principle of trichotomy of power which is the basic feature of the Constitution.'

At times, separation of powers can lead to confrontation between two of the organs of the State. In Pakistan, a 3 Judge Bench of the Supreme Court suspended the operation of a Constitutional Amendment viz., 14th Amendment; in another matter, a Bench directed the President not to assent to a Bill, which had been duly passed by the National Assembly and the Senate. There were speeches in and out of the National Assembly in respect of the judges, which gave rise to contempt proceedings[26] leading to unfortunate physical attach on the Supreme Court of Pakistan during the hearing of the contempt matter against the then Prime Minister Mian Muhammad Nawaz Sharif (1949) and others. Disposing of the contempt matter, Chief Justice Ajmal Mian said:

> 'All the three organs have to act within the bounds specified in the Constitution, any transgression or encroachment by one organ over the sphere of the other will result in chaos and uncertainty. It is therefore paramount that an equilibrium is to be maintained *inter se* between the three organs of the State within the limits delineated by the Constitution'

Separation of powers in India

India like Pakistan has a federal parliamentary system. Therefore, the theory of 'separation of powers' does not apply to India as well, particularly in relation to the executive and the legislature. However, separation of power does exist between executive and legislature on the one hand and the judiciary on the other hand.

However, certain Indian cases pertaining to 'separation of powers' would be relevant. One of the cases was *Liyanage v. Reginam*[27] decided by the Privy Council and the other was *Indira Gandhi v. Raj Narain*[28] decided by the Supreme Court of India. In the case of *Indira Gandhi*, Justice K. K. Mathew (1911–92)[29], following *Kesavananda Bharati v. State of Kerala*[30] held that the amending power of the Parliament did not extend to destroying 'the basic structure of the Constitution'. The basic structure of the constitution comprised of—

(a) the separation of power;
(b) the supremacy of the Constitution;
(c) the republican form of government;
(d) the secular character of the Constitution; and
(e) the rule of law.

To arrive at this decision a distinction was drawn between plenary (primary) power of constitution-making having no touchstone outside the constitution to test its *vires* and the constituent power of amending the Constitution derived from the Constitution itself.

In this case, Clause (4) of Article 329-A (inserted by the 29th Amendment) providing that election of the prime minister or speaker held before the Amendment was valid and could not be declared void and any finding or other of any court declaring it void would be of no effect. Clause (4) was held by the Supreme Court as legislative judgment violative of separation of powers. The decision in *Indira Gandhi* was based on *Liyanage* case from Ceylon (now Sri

Lanka) decided by the Privy Council. In this case, the validity of the Criminal Law (Special Provisions) Act, 1962 and the Criminal Law Act 1962 were challenged on the ground that these Acts –

> 'constituted an unjustifiable assumption of judicial power by the Legislature or an interference with judicial power, which was outside the Legislature's competence and was inconsistent with the severance of power between Legislature, executive and judiciary, which the constitution ordains',

as these Acts annulled the acquittals of participants of the *Coup*.

In fact, the decision did not so much turn upon the doctrine of 'separation of powers' as it rested on the violation of the Constitution of Ceylon (the Order in Council 1946 read with the Ceylon Independence Act 1947) relating to the vesting of judicial power in Courts to the exclusion of Parliament and the creation of *ex post facto* punishments against particular individuals. The Privy Council, however, held –

> 'that the character of the Act was not that of an act of attainder or a bill of pains or penalties as it neither condemned the appellant for any action nor the disabilities imposed were of the character of punishment for guilt'.

The result was that it was held that there was no exercise of judicial power in a legislative form.

The reliance placed in *Indira Gandhi* on *Liyanage* was misplaced for the reasons that[31]

(a) the doctrine of separation of power is not applicable to the constitution of India;
(b) the judicial power is not constitutionalized in Courts in India whereas the constitution of Ceylon commits judicial power to the courts to the exclusion of parliament.
(c) In the Ceylon case, the Acts were directed towards participants of a *Coup* and the creation of *ex post facto* punishments by annulling acquittals.
(d) In the Indian Constitution, there is no line of demarcation between the legislative and judicial power.
(e) The view taken in *Indira Gandhi* is inconsistent with the view taken in two earlier cases, namely, *Sankri Prasad v. India*,[32] and *Sajjan Singh v. Rajasthan*[33].

In practice, it is only the functional distribution of powers which is operative and the theory of separation of powers is not fully applicable because[34]

(i) All the constitutions including the US Constitution establish 3 branches of government but suggest little as to how and by whom the boundaries among their powers are to be drawn.
(ii) Locke and Montesquieu, the expositors of the doctrine of 'separation of powers' who had the greatest influence on the framers of the US Constitution, offer no insight into the problem of judicial excesses unresolved in the constitution. Nor do the records of the constitutional functions or the debate surrounding consideration of the constitutional question specifically against judicial decision affecting institutions traditionally regulated by executive officials.
(iii) In *Springer v. Philippine Islands*,[35] Justice Oliver Wendell Holmes Jr, said,

> 'we may disguise it by varying words we do not and cannot carry out the distinction between the legislative and executive action with mathematical precision and divide the branches into watertight compartments, were it ever so desirable to do so, which I am far from believing that it is, or that the constitution requires.'

(iv) The inferences drawn from the doctrine of separation of powers in various ways have complicated the delegation of functions by legislative bodies to other agencies. It was considered as an obstacle both to the exercise of rule-making powers of bodies other than legislatures, and also to the exercise of adjudicatory powers by bodies other than courts of law; and the question being debated was as to upon what principle and to what extent the Congress, a repository of many varieties of legislative actions enumerated in the constitution, could delegate its functions in the context of the rigid exercise of power by the legislature alone? But the courts construed the rule against delegation as one that could not be sustained in practice, Chief Justice John Marshall, as early as 1825 in *Wayman v. Southard*,[36] said:

'That the rule was subject to limitation and asserted that Congress may certainly delegate to others power which the Legislature may rightly exercise itself'.

(v) There is a wide gulf between the political doctrine of separation of powers and its application in practice. In the course of time numerous exceptions have been engrafted on the rule. The legislature cannot delegate its power to make a law, but it can make a law to delegate a power to determine some fact or state of things upon which the law makes, or intends to make, its own action depend. To deny this would be to stop the wheels of government.

There was, therefore, an intrusion of the doctrine of agency into constitutional interpretation as a result of which delegation was conceded to the extent of discretion and what was disputed was its scope as it was difficult to draw a line of demarcation between the exercise of two powers, that is, administrative and legislative.

Some Leading Cases on Separation of Powers

1. Congressional power over presidential papers

In *Nixon v. Administrator of General Services,*[37] the court upheld the 'facial validity' of the Presidential Recordings and Materials Preservation Act of 1974, adopted by Congress a few months after President Richard Nixon's (1913–94)[38] resignation. The Act directed the Administrator of General Services, an executive official, to take custody of the Nixon materials, to screen them, and to return to Nixon those materials that are personal and private in nature. Nixon challenged the law on several grounds, including the claimed violation of separation of powers. The 7–2 decision by the court sustained the Act. Justice William Joseph Brennan Jr's (1906–1997)[39] majority opinion stated that only the custody and screening provisions were properly before the court and emphasized the narrowness of the decision, stressing the uniqueness of the Nixon resignation and its aftermath. Nixon's basic contention was that the 'Act encroached upon the Presidential prerogatives to control internal operations of the Presidential office.' Justice Brennan found Nixon's view 'inconsistent with the origins of [the separation of powers] doctrine, recent decisions of the Court, and the contemporary realities of our political system.' In his view, the touchstone for determining whether those principles had been violated was whether one branch's action vis-à-vis another constituted undue 'disruption' on another. The 'disruption' inquiry, he elaborated, 'focuses on the extent to which [the Act] prevents the executive branch from accomplishing its constitutionally assigned functions'; he concluded that there was nothing 'unduly disruptive of the Executive Branch' here. Justice Brennan found adequate justification for the 'limited intrusion into executive confidentiality' here in the 'substantial public interest' reflected in Congress's 'desire to restore public confidence in our political processes by preserving the materials as a source for facilitating a full airing of the events leading to [Nixon's] resignation' and its 'need to understand how those political processes had in fact operated in order to gauge the necessity for remedial legislation.' He emphasized, moreover, that 'control of the material remains in the Executive Branch.' Chief Justice Warren E. Burger's (1907–95)[40] dissent gave three reasons for finding a violation of separation of powers principles: the Act constituted a congressional coercion of the President; the Act was 'an exercise of executive – not legislative – power by the Legislative Branch' and the Act worked 'a sweeping modification of the constitutional privilege and historical practice of confidentiality of every Chief Executive since 1789'. Justice William Rehnquist submitted a separate dissent, largely agreeing with the Chief Justice's separation of powers analysis.

2. Executive Privilege: United States v. Nixon[41]

On 17 June 1972, a burglary occurred at the Democratic National Headquarters in the Watergate building in Washington, D.C. Over the course of the next year, it was discovered that the burglars were connected to the Campaign to Re-elect the President and that high-level White House officials were involved in a cover-up. In the summer of 1973, Senator Sam Ervin (1896–1985) from North Carolina chaired closely watched hearings of the Senate Select Committee on Watergate. One of the dramatic moments occurred when a presidential aide,

Alexander Butterfield (1926)[42], revealed that there was a secret taping system in the Oval Office and that presidential conversations were routinely recorded.

Since top Justice Department officials, including the former attorney general, John Mitchell (1913–88)[43], were suspected of involvement in the cover-up, therefore there was political pressure for an independent investigation. Attorney General Elliot Richardson (1920–99)[44] appointed Harvard law professor Archibald Cox (1912–2004)[45] to serve as a special prosecutor. Cox *subpoenaed* tapes of White House conversations, and the president challenged the *subpoena* in courts. On 12 October 1973, the United States Court of appeals for the District of Columbia sided with the special prosecutor and gave the president one week to file an appeal. On 19 October, the president announced that he would turn over edited transcripts of the tapes and that he would ask Senator John Stennis (1901–95; who was reported to be quite hard of hearing) to listen to the tapes and verify their accuracy. President Nixon also announced that he would comply with no additional subpoenas and turn over no additional tapes.

On 20 October, special prosecutor Archibald Cox declared Nixon's position unacceptable; there was a court order to turn over tapes, not transcripts. More importantly, he would seek whatever tapes he needed. President Nixon ordered Attorney General Elliot Richardson to fire Cox; Richardson refused and resigned. Nixon then asked the Justice Department's number two official to fire Cox; William Ruckelshaus (1932–2019)[46] also refused and resigned. The request was then made to the number three person in the Justice Department, Solicitor General Robert Bork (1927–2019)[47]. Bork then fired Cox in what came to be known as the Saturday Night Massacre.

The first resolutions calling for Richard Nixon's impeachment were introduced into the House of Representatives, and intense political pressure caused the appointment of a new special prosecutor, Leon Jaworski (1905–82)[48]. On 1 March 1974, a grand jury for the United States District Court for the District of Columbia indicted seven top officials of the Nixon administration and the Campaign to Re-elect the President for obstruction of justice and conspiracy to defraud. President Nixon was named an 'unindicted co-conspirator'

On 18 April 1974, a *subpoena* was issued, at the request of the special prosecutor, for the president to turn over tapes and other materials to use as possible evidence in the upcoming criminal trial. On 30 April, President Nixon announced that he was disclosing edited transcripts of 43 conversations, including 20 that were the subject of the *subpoena*. On 1 May, the president moved to quash the *subpoena*. On 20 May, the United States District Court denied the motion to quash and directed the president to provide all of the items that had been *subpoenaed*. The Supreme Court granted review prior to consideration by the court of appeals.

Meanwhile, the House Judiciary Committee was considering Articles of Impeachment against President Nixon. Impeachment hearings were held in July 1974, while the Nixon case was pending before the Supreme Court. The Supreme Court announced its decision on 25 July 1974, and unanimously ruled that Nixon had to comply with the *subpoena*. The House Judiciary Committee voted its first article of impeachment on 25 July for obstruction of justice in connection with the Watergate break-in and cover-up. On 29 and 30 July, the committee voted two additional articles of impeachment for abuse of power and for failure to comply with a Judiciary Committee *subpoena*.

On 6 August 1974, President Nixon complied with the *subpoena* and made the transcripts of the tapes available to the public. The tapes showed that President Nixon clearly had obstructed justice by ordering the Federal Bureau of Investigation not to investigate the Watergate matter. Three days later, on Thursday, 9 August 1974, President Nixon became the only president in history to resign.

Chief Justice Burger wrote the opinion for a unanimous court. The court began by rejecting the president's contention that the case posed a non-justiciable political question because it was an intra-branch dispute and that the president alone had authority to control prosecution. The court said that the president had the authority to delegate this power and that he had done so, through the actions of the attorney general, in creating the office of the special prosecutor. Indeed, the court noted that the regulations creating the office of the special prosecutor, adopted after the Saturday Night Massacre,

> 'give the special prosecutor explicit power to contest the invocation of executive privilege in the process of seeking evidence deemed relevant to the performance of these specially delegated duties.'

Moreover, the court said that there was no doubt that the special prosecutor and the president were adversaries, even though both were executive officials.

After explaining that the *subpoena* followed the procedures and requirements of Federal Rule of Civil Procedure 17(c), the court turned its attention to the issue of executive privilege. The court made 3 major points. First, the court held that it is the role of the court to decide whether the president has executive privilege and, if so, its scope. Nixon claimed that the constitution gave the president executive privilege and that the president alone determined its reach. The court flatly rejected this contention:

> 'The President's counsel, as we have noted, reads the Constitution as providing an absolute privilege of confidentiality for all Presidential communications. Many decisions of this Court, however, have unequivocally reaffirmed the holding of *Marbury v. Madison*, that '[i]t is emphatically the province and duty of the judicial department to say what the law is."

The Supreme Court recognized the existence of executive privilege. The court recognized that the need for candor in communications with advisors justified executive privilege; indeed, the court said that a need for confidentiality was 'too plain to require further discussion.' Although, Article II of the Constitution does not expressly grant this power to the president, the court said that:

> 'the privilege can be said to derive from the supremacy of each branch within its own assigned area of constitutional duties. Certain powers and privileges flow from the nature of enumerated powers; the protection of the confidentiality of Presidential communications has similar constitutional underpinnings.'

United States v. Nixon, thus, recognizes executive privilege as an inherent presidential power. It is in contrast with decisions, such as Justice Hugo Black's (1886–1971)[49] majority opinion in *Youngstown Sheet & Tube Co. v. Sawyer*, which reject any inherent powers.[50] Justice Black concluded that in the absence of statutory authorization, a presidential action must be based on 'some provision of the Constitution.'

The court also held that executive privilege is not absolute, but rather must yield when there are important countervailing interests. The court explained that:

> 'neither the doctrine of separation of powers, nor the need for confidentiality of high-level communications, without more, can sustain an absolute, unqualified presidential privilege of immunity from judicial process under all circumstances.'

More specially, the court said that an absolute privilege would interfere with the ability of the judiciary to perform its constitutional function. The court explained:

> 'The impediment that an absolute, unqualified privilege would place in the way of the primary constitutional duty of the Judicial Branch to do justice in criminal prosecution would plainly conflict with the function of the courts under Article III.'

The court thus concluded that the need for evidence at a criminal trial outweighed executive privilege. The court said that allowing:

> 'the privilege to withhold evidence that is demonstrably relevant in a criminal trial would cut deeply into the guarantee of due process of law and gravely impair the basic function of the courts.'

United States v. Nixon is the definitive case on executive privilege. It recognizes the existence of executive privilege, but refuses to make it absolute. It also is a powerful reaffirmation of the power of judicial review and of the essential principle that no person, not even the president, is above the law.

This case had its critics. It is argued that better course could have been to allow the impeachment process to run its course. The House Judiciary Committee already had voted Articles of Impeachment against Richard Nixon, and some believe that the better course would have been for the judiciary to avoid deciding the issues of the tapes until the congressional proceedings were completed.[51]

3. Piare Dusadh v. Emperor[52]

In 1943, the Federal Court, held that the American rule of separation of powers did not apply to the Government of India Act, 1935. In that case the *vires* of Ordinance (XIX of 1943) was challenged on the ground that it amounted to a legislative judgment. The facts of this case were that the Federal Court earlier set aside the convictions rendered by the courts functioning under the Special Criminal Courts Ordinance (II of 1942); as it held on a construction of sections 5, 10 and 16 of the Ordinance that these provisions did not duly invest the courts with the jurisdiction to try the appellants. Thereupon, the Governor-General promulgated Ordinance (XIX of 1943) which repealed Ordinances (II of 1942) and by section 3 it was provided that the sentences inflicted were to continue subject to appeal or revision. The appellants filed *habeas corpus* petitions in different High Courts of India and as they were not successful they appealed to the Federal Court.

The Federal Court held that as a general proposition it may be correct to say

> 'that legislative function belongs to the legislature and the judicial functions to the judiciary',

but the rigid rule of separation of powers was not applicable to the Constitution Act of 1935. In holding so, the Federal Court relied on the peculiarities of the American Constitution which positively forbade the legislature from exercising judicial power and also for the reason that the 5th and the 14th Amendments limited the legislative power to deprive a person of his life, liberty or property except through due process of law. As no comparable provisions like the 'due process clause' existed in the Constitution Act of 1935, the Federal Court held that the only provisions that existed was in relation to property which provided that its deprivation should only be by authority of law. As for the sanctity of personal freedom the principle of British jurisprudence was held to be a part of the law of British India which was founded on the principle of 'private law' and not as a part of the Constitution. The English rule when compared to the American Amendments only required 'legal justification' and not 'due process of law' and 'such justification could be shown as much by legislation or statutory rules or as by production of an order of Courts. It was next held that it did not follow that the 'Legislature in India' could arbitrarily interfere with the life or liberty of the citizens as only such power could be exercised as was conferred on it by Schedule 7 to the Constitution Act.

Accordingly, the decision turned on the legislative competence of the legislature with regard to the subjects in the legislative lists, and as the impugned Ordinance was covered by the expression 'administration of justice' in Entry No. 1 of List II and the expression 'criminal procedure' in Entry No. 2 of List No. III, it was held to be a valid piece of legislation as the power of validation was ancillary to the power to deal with the particular subjects mentioned in the list.

Lastly, it was held that Ordinance did not attempt to decide the question of guilt or innocence of any of the accused which question was already determined by the tribunals/courts. Therefore, it did not amount to an exercise of judicial power.

4. Hamdan v. Rumsfeld[53]

The Congress enacted the Military Commission Act which provided that noncitizens held as enemy combatants shall not have access to federal courts via a writ of *habeas corpus* or otherwise, except that if there is a military proceeding, the detainee may seek review of its decision in the United States Court of Appeals for the District of Columbia Circuit. In a 5–4 decision, with Justice Anthony Kennedy (1936)[54] writing an opinion joined by Justices John Paul Stevens (1920–2019)[55], David Souter (1939)[56], Ruth Bader Ginsburg (1933–2020)[57], and Stephen Breyer (1938)[58], the Supreme Court held that the preclusion of *habeas corpus* jurisdiction was unconstitutional. Justice Kennedy explained that Article 1 and 9 of the Constitution allows Congress to suspend *habeas corpus* in times of rebellion or invasion. The government did not claim that either of these situations were present.

The Supreme Court concluded that this provision applies to the detainees held in Guantanamo Bay;

> 'We hold that Art. 1, cl. 2, of the Constitution has full effect at Guantanamo Bay. If the privilege of *habeas corpus* is to be denied to the detainees now before us, Congress must act in accordance with the requirements of the Suspension Clause'.

Moreover, the Court decided that the remedy provided review in the D.C. Circuit[59], did not substitute for *habeas corpus*. The Court thus declared:

> 'We hold that petitioners may invoke the fundamental procedural protections of *habeas corpus.* The laws and Constitution are designed to survive and remain in force, in extraordinary times. Liberty and security can be reconciled; and in our system they are reconciled within the framework of the law. The framers decided that *habeas corpus,* a right of first importance, must be a part of that framework, a part of that law'.

Chief Justice John Roberts (1955)[60] dissented, joined by Justices Antonin Scalia (1936–2016)[61], Clarence Thomas (1948)[62], and Samuel Alito (1950)[63], and said that the court should have deferred to the choices made by Congress and the president. He wrote:

> 'Today the Court strikes down as inadequate the most generous set of procedural protections ever afforded aliens detained by this country as enemy combatants. The political branches crafted these procedures amidst an ongoing military conflict, after much careful investigation and thorough debate. The Court rejects them today out of hand, without explaining how the statute fails to vindicate those rights, and before a single petitioner has exhausted the procedures designed by the people's representatives with a set of shapeless procedures to be defined by Federal courts at some future date'.

Chief Justice Roberts argued that the procedures provided in the Military Commission Act were sufficient to avoid there being a suspension of the writ of *habeas corpus.*

Justice Scalia wrote a strong dissenting note, joined by the other dissenting justices, in which he argued that the judiciary has no business being involved in the matter at all. He wrote:

> 'What competence does the Court have to second-guess the judgement of Congress and the President on such a point? None, whatever. But the Court blunders in nonetheless. Henceforth, as today's opinion makes unnervingly clear, how to handle enemy prisoners in this war will ultimately lie with the branch that knows least about the national security concerns that the subject entails'.

The majority and the dissent articulated vastly different views about the role of the federal courts during the war on terrorism. For the majority, the US Constitution and access to the federal courts to enforce it are essential even in times of crisis. From this perspective, the decision was a profound reaffirmation of the rule of law. For the dissent, the decision was dangerous judicial meddling in a realm properly left to the President and Congress. Justice Scalia said that he believed that people would needlessly die because of the majority's opinion. The issue is profoundly important in terms of the appropriate role of the American Constitution, the judiciary and the rule of law in the war on terrorism.

5. Sahib Ram Jawaya Kapur v. Punjab[64]

In the Indian Constitution the system of parliamentary executive is the same as in England and the Council of Ministers, consisting of the members of the Legislature, is like the British Cabinet. It is like a hyphen which joins or a buckle which fastens the legislative part of the State to the executive. The Cabinet enjoying, as it does, a majority in the Legislature, virtually concentrates in, itself the virtual control of both legislative and executive functions and as the Ministers constituting the Cabinet presumably agree on fundamentals and act on the principle of collective responsibility, the most important questions of policy are all formulated by them.

In this case, the Supreme Court held that the impugned legislative ordinance could not be tested on the touchstone of the principle of separation of powers, but on the footing of the competence of the Legislature to legislate on that subject. And as for the character of this ordinance it did not attempt to decide the question of the guilt or innocence of any of the accused as that matter had been decided by tribunals, and all that it did was to validate the sentences. It was therefore, not an exercise of the judicial power.

6. Federation of Pakistan v. United Sugar Mills Ltd[65]

In this case, the *vires* of Clause 4-A of Article 199 of the 1973 Constitution of Pakistan was challenged. The clause provided that an interim order made by a High Court in its writ jurisdiction relating to the

> 'State property or assessment or collection of public revenues shall cease to have effect on the expiration of a period of six months following the day on which it is made'.

The challenge was made on the ground that it violated the 'separation of powers' as the clause amounted to an inroad in the judicial power of the High Court. The Supreme Court held that the vires of the act could not be thrown overboard as this doctrine was not applicable to our constitution. In holding so Justice Muhammad Gul, spoke for the court and observed:

> 'It is also important to observe that our Constitution, like many other modern written Constitutions, does not provide for rigid separation of powers. Indeed, there is no direct provision in that behalf except that the Constitution by various provisions provides for the setting up of the principal institutions for the exercise of the sovereign powers of the State in the appointed field. In actual practice in all modern Governments, separation is only functional to sub serve the practical necessity of an efficient and enlightened Government by providing for checks and balances to avoid abuse of public power. Nowhere so far as I am aware, the principle is pushed to its logical conclusion so as to create watertight compartments.'

7. Fauji Foundation v. Shamim ur Rahman[66]

Muhammad Haleem (1925–2006) Acting C.J. observed:

> '...the absence of clear demarcation of judicial power as a constitutional safeguard in the realm of separation of powers and the difficulty of protecting it from encroachment by the legislature or the executive, and the question does not seem to be resolved by the application of this theory. Accordingly, in the case of every enactment it will be an open question as to whether an enactment is an exercise of judicial power by the legislature where separate powers are constitutionalized'.
>
> '... in theory there is still the constitutionalized principle of separation of powers, but in practice it has suffered a metamorphism so that it is now infected with imprecision's and inconsistencies. One finds that while the judicial power is vested in the Supreme Court and such other Courts as the Congress may establish to decide cases or, controversies yet the Congress possess constitutional authority to enlarge or diminish the Court's appellate jurisdiction. This is not all. Judicial power is also exercised by legislative Courts, namely United States Tax Court and United States Court of Military Appeals, which derive this power from Article 1, section 1. Next there are administrative agencies which not only exercise judicial power but also legislative and executive power. This is because the Congress by law can delegate these functions to such agencies. There are again numerous instances where one branch of the government performs the functions belonging exclusively to the other two branches. It is now the accepted view of the American Courts that the separate powers are not intended to operate with absolute independence and what one finds now is that there are numerous instances of encroachment of the legislative upon the judicial department. The present-day trend is that emphasis is more on the proper balance between the co-ordinate branches rather than on complete division of authority between the three branches.'

Notes

1. James Madison was a Founding Father and the 4th President of the United States of America.
2. *The Federalist Papers* is a collection of articles and essays about the constitution, written by Alexander Hamilton, James Madison and John Jay.
3. Peter Woll, *Constitutional Law*, (New Jersey, U.S.A: Prentice – Hall Inc. 1981)., pp. 102–3.
4. Alexander Hamilton was a Founding Father of the United States, and the first US Secretary of the Treasury.
5. 5 U.S. 137 (1803).
6. 343 U.S. 579 (1952).
7. Fred M. Vinson was the 13th Chief Justice of the United States.
8. Hans Kelsen was an Austrian jurist, legal philosopher and political philosopher.
9. Hans Kelsen, *General Theory of Law and State*, (New York: Russell & Russell, 1961) pp. 269–70.
10. *Ibid*, page 272.
11. Supra Note 3, pp. 105–6.
12. *Ibid*, pp. 106–7.

13. *Kathleen* M. Sullivan, Gerald Gunther, *Constitutional Law*, 15th ed., (New York: Foundation Press, 2004), pp. 343–4.
14. 277 U.S. 189 (1928).
15. A.G. Chaudhry, *Lectures on Constitutional Law*, (Lahore: Irfan Law Book House, 1994), pp. 18–19.
16. *The State v. Zia-ur-Rahman* PLD 1973 SC 49 at page 70; *Fazalul Quader Chowdhary v. Syed Shah Nawaz* PLD 1966 SC 105.
17. Supra Note 15, pp. 20–21.
18. PLD 1973 SC 49.
19. 1997 SC MR 141.
20. PLD 1989 Karachi 404.
21. PLD 1993 S.C. 341.
22. PLD 1996 S.C. 324.
23. PLD 1975 S.C. 50.
24. PLD 1998 S.C. 1445.
25. PLD 1999 S.C. 504.
26. *Masroor Ahsan v. Ardeshir Cowasjee*, PLD 1998 S.C. 823.
27. (1966) 1 All E.R. 650.
28. AIR 1975 S.C. 2299.
29. K. K. Mathew served as a Judge of the Supreme Court of India.
30. AIR 1973 S.C. 1461.
31. Supra Note 15, pp. 23–24.
32. AIR 1951 S.C. 458.
33. AIR 1965 S.C. 845.
34. Supra Note 15, PP. 24–25.
35. 277 U.S. 189 (1928).
36. 23 U.S. 1 (1825).
37. 433 U.S. 425 (1977).
38. Richard Nixon was the 37th President of the United States.
39. William Joseph Brennan Jr was Associate Justice of the US Supreme Court.
40. Warren E. Burger was the 15th Chief Justice of the US Supreme Court.
41. 418 U.S. 683 (1974).
42. Alexander Butterfield served as Deputy Assistant to President Richard Nixon.
43. John Mitchell was the 67th Attorney General of the United States.
44. Elliot Richardson was a lawyer and was a member of the cabinet for both Presidents Richard Nixon and Gerald Ford.
45. Archibald Cox Jr was former Solicitor General of the United States.
46. William Ruckelshaus was US Assistant Attorney General for the Civil Division from 1969 to 1970.
47. Robert Bork was the 35th US Solicitor General, judge, and legal scholar.
48. Leon Jaworski served as the 2nd special prosecutor during the Watergate Scandal.
49. Hugo Black was Associate Justice of the US Supreme Court.
50. 343 U.S. 579 (1952).
51. Erwin Chemerinsky, *Constitutional Law*, (New York: Aspen Law & Business,2002), pp. 349–50.
52. AIR 1944 F.C. 1.
53. 548 U.S. 557 (2006).
54. Anthony Kennedy was Associate Justice of the US Supreme Court.
55. John Paul Stevens was Associate Justice of the US Supreme Court.
56. David Souter is a retired Associate Justice of the US Supreme Court.
57. Ruth Bader Ginsburg was Associate Justice of the US Supreme Court.
58. Stephen Breyer is Associate Justice of the US Supreme Court since 1994.
59. it is the main appellate court for many issues of American administrative law and constitutional law.
60. John Roberts is the 17th Chief Justice of US since 2005.
61. Antonin Scalia was Associate Chief Justice of the US Supreme Court.
62. Clarence Thomas is Associate Justice of the US Supreme Court since 1991.
63. Samuel Alito is Associate Justice of the US Supreme Court since 2006.
64. AIR 1955 S.C. 549.
65. PLD 1977 S.C. 397.
66. PLD 1983 S.C. 457.

10 Presidential Form of Government

Introduction

The US Constitution is regarded as father of the presidential system of government. It has worked well for more than two centuries and is considered one of the main reasons for building United States into a strong nation and eventually, into a World power in the 20th century. The US constitutional model has been followed in the countries that came under American influence in the 19th and 20th century. The Latin American countries in particular, Mexico, Brazil, Argentina, and Venezuela all have the presidential system of government with slight variations. Amongst Asian countries, the Philippines which became a colony of the United States of America from 1898 to 1945, adopted the presidential form of government. For understanding of this system, the US model is discussed in detail below.

The American Constitution devotes more attention to Congress than to the other branches of government. Most of the framers of the constitution expected Congress to be the dominant element of the new national government because, as James Madison[1], recognized in *The Federalist 51*

> "in republican government, the legislative authority necessarily predominates".

Perhaps, Madison's observation was true of a small republic in the late 18th century. It does not, however, apply to the experience of the United States after more than two centuries of constitutional developments. The dominant tendency of American constitutional history has been to concentrate power in the executive branch.

The expansion of presidential power has occurred despite a constitution that provides little to the president by way of specific, enumerated powers. Throughout history, presidents have taken advantage of opportunities to enhance the power of the executive branch, opportunities afforded by crises such as the American Civil War (1861–65), two World Wars (First World War 1914–18; Second World War 1939–45), the Great Depression (1929–33), and, more recently the Cold War (1947–91). The tendency of presidents to seize power to cope with the exigencies of their times is what led noted constitutional scholar Edward S. Corwin (1878–1963) to remark that –

> "the history of the Presidency has been a history of aggrandizement."

In the 1970s, in the wake of the Vietnam War (1955–75) and Watergate scandal (1972), some observers perceived a significant decline in presidential power and prestige. If a decline occurred at all, it was only short-lived. In the 1980s, the administrations of Ronald Reagan (1911–2004)[2] and George H.W. Bush (1924–2018)[3], regained for the presidency a position comparable to the pre-eminence that it held prior to the late 1960s. The allegations of misconduct that plagued Bill Clinton's (1946)[4] two terms had no lasting negative effect on the presidency. George W. Bush (1946)[5] was able to assert effective leadership immediately upon assuming the office of president, in spite of the prolonged and intense battle resulting in his controversial victory in the 2000 election. The devastating terrorist attack on the World Trade Center and the Pentagon on 11 September 2001, instantly enhanced the power and prestige of the presidency, as evidenced by the overwhelming bipartisan congressional and popular support extended to President George W. Bush. While still depending to some extent on the performance and character of the occupant of the office, the power and prestige of the presidency are largely institutionalized.[6]

Structural aspects of the Presidency

During the Constitutional Convention held in 1787, some delegates favored a multiple executive, in which power would be exercised simultaneously by 3 or more individuals. Others insisted on limiting the president to a single term of 7 years or to 2–3year terms. Still others maintained that the president, in concert with the Supreme Court, should function as a 'council of revision,' which would in effect pass on the constitutionality of acts of Congress. The framers, who had recently participated in a successful revolution against the British Crown, were understandably wary of creating an executive institution that could 'degenerate' into a monarchy. The delegates unanimously elected George Washington (1732–99)[7] as the convention president which greatly reduced these fears. In fact, George Washington's daily presence as the presiding officer at the Constitutional Convention (1787) probably contributed to the decision to create a single executive.

Ultimately, the framers not only vested executive power in a single executive, elected for a term of 4 years, but also refused to limit the number of terms the president might serve. George Washington, as the first president of the United States of America, displayed both the leadership and self-restraint that the American people expected. He established an important precedent by refusing to seek a 3rd term, a tradition that survived until Franklin D. Roosevelt (1882–1945) was elected to a 3rd term in 1940, followed by a 4th term in 1944, Roosevelt died in office in 1945. and the Republican Party gained control of both houses of Congress after the elections in 1946. Reacting to Roosevelt's 4 terms of presidency, Congress then proposed the 22nd Amendment, ratified in 1951, prohibiting future presidents from being elected to more than 2 terms. In the aftermath of Ronald Reagan's popular first term and landslide re-election in 1984, some political activists began to urge repeal of the 22nd Amendment. The Iran-Contra affair (1985–87) and other problems effectively diverted attention from this issue during Reagan's second term.[8]

The Electoral College

Contemporary Americans look to the quadrennial presidential elections as symbols of a deep national commitment to democracy. Yet the framers of the Constitution, far less sanguine about democracy, provided for an indirect method of presidential selection. Under Article II, Section 1; which stipulated that each state was authorized to appoint as many electors as it had senators and representatives in Congress. This is known as the Electoral College. It was empowered to choose the president, and the person receiving the second highest number of votes would serve as vice president. The framers assumed that the electors would act independently of the people in making their selections. But, with the advent of the two-party system in the election of 1796, the electors soon lost this independent role.

The controlling influence of party identity was underscored dramatically in the presidential election of 1800. A large majority of the electors supported the Jeffersonian Republican Party and dutifully cast their votes for Thomas Jefferson (1743–1826)[9] and his running mate, Aaron Burr (1756–1836)[10]. The resulting tie vote in the Electoral College threw the election into the House of Representative, which after a contentious political battle ultimately elected Thomas Jefferson.

In the aftermath of this awkward incident, the 12th Amendment was adopted in 1804, placing the offices of president and vice president on separate ballots. The effect of this change was that each party developed its own presidential and vice-president 'tickets,' to which designated slates of electors were pledged. With rare exception, the presidential candidate receiving a plurality of the popular vote in a given state automatically received that state's entire electoral vote. Thus, the Electoral College as a deliberative body became a vestigial organ of American government within less than twenty years after its creation.

Although, the Electoral College has lost its significance as a decision-making body, it retains tremendous importance in that it represents a highly controversial method of electing the president. To win the presidency, a candidate must receive a majority of electoral votes. These votes are allocated among the states based on the size of states' congressional delegations. Thus, each state has 2 electoral votes for its 2 US senators plus a number of electoral votes corresponding to the number of its US representatives. The total number of electoral votes is 538, which equals the total number of US Senators (100), the total number of members of the House of Representatives (435), plus 3 electoral votes assigned to the District of Columbia. Because the candidate who wins a plurality of the popular vote in a given state wins all of that state's electoral votes (except in Maine and Nebraska, which allocate electoral votes by the outcome of popular vote within congressional districts), it is possible for a candidate who receives fewer votes in the aggregated national popular vote to win the presidency.

This in fact occurred in 1876 and 1888, when the winning candidates, Rutherford B. Hayes (1823–93)[11] and Benjamin Harrison (1833–1901)[12], received fewer popular votes than their main rivals, Samuel Tilden (1814–1886)[13] and Grover Cleveland (1837–1908).[14] One does not have to be an historian to know that this same anomaly occurred in the presidential election of 2000, when Republican George W. Bush narrowly defeated Democrat Al Gore (1948) in the electoral vote despite Gore's 'victory' in the national popular vote.

Another glaring example of different results in terms of electoral vote and popular vote was the presidential election of 2016. Donald John Trump[15] (1946) was the election with 306 electoral votes against his opponent Hillary Diane Rodham Clinton[16] (1947) getting 232 electoral votes. In terms of popular votes, Ms Clinton got 65, 853, 514 (48.2% of votes cast). Votes against Trump receiving 62, 984, 828 votes (46.1% of the votes cast). Ms Clinton led Trump by nearly 3 million votes which is clear evidence of the anomaly in the system.

The Electoral College system, for long a subject of academic debate, became a national issue in the wake of the disputed presidential election of 2000. Critics claimed that the system is undemocratic, a vestige of 18th century elitism. But, the Electoral College is not without defenders. Some argue that it is consistent with the federal system and helps to ensure that small states will not be ignored by candidates seeking only to amass individual votes. Abolition of the Electoral College would obviously require a constitutional amendment, which is, of course, difficult to accomplish even when public support is strong. Given that the Electoral College is currently a partisan issue, with Republicans defending the institution and Democrats calling for its abolition, it is unlikely that a proposed amendment could muster the necessary two-thirds majority in either house of Congress. If it did, it would be even more unlikely that three fourths of the states would support ratification. It appears that the Electoral College is destined to remain a controversial feature of the American electoral system for the foreseeable future.[17]

Presidential Succession and Disability

The constitutional problem of presidential succession has troubled generations of Americans. The problem first arose in 1841, when President William Henry Harrison (1773–1841),[18] died after only a month in office. The immediate question was whether Vice President John Tyler (1790–1862)[19] would assume the full duties and powers of the office for the remaining 47 months of Harrison's term or serve merely as an acting president. Unwilling to settle for less than the full measure of presidential authority, John Tyler set an important precedent by successfully assuming full presidential powers. The 8 other individuals who have succeeded to the office because of the death or resignation of an incumbent president have followed this practice.

The related problem of presidential disability has proved more perplexing. Several presidents have been temporarily disabled during their terms of office, with resulting uncertainty and confusion as to the locus of actual decision-making authority. For example, President Woodrow Wilson (1856–1924)[20] was seriously disabled by a stroke in 1919 and for a number of weeks was totally incapable of performing his official duties. No constitutional provision existed at that time for the temporary replacement of a disabled president. The result was that Woodrow Wilson's wife, Edith (1872–1961)[21], took on much of the responsibility of the office, an arrangement that evoked sharp criticism.

The problem of presidential disability is addressed by the 25th Amendment, ratified in 1967. This amendment, proposed in the aftermath of the assassination of President John F. Kennedy (1917–63)[22], establishes, among other things, a procedure under which the vice president may assume the role of acting president during periods of presidential disability. The amendment provides alternative means for determining presidential disability. Section 3 allows the president to transmit to Congress a written declaration that he is unable to discharge the duties of the office, upon which the vice president assumes the role of acting president. The vice president continues in this role unless or until the president is able to transmit a declaration to the contrary. If, however, the president is unable or unwilling to acknowledge the inability to perform the duties of the office, the vice president and a majority of the Cabinet members are authorized to make this determination.[23]

Removal of the President

The ultimate constitutional sanction against the abuse of presidential power is impeachment and removal from office. The American Constitution, in Article II, Section 4, provides:

> 'The President, Vice President and all civil officers of the United States shall be removed from Office on Impeachment for, and Conviction of, Treason, Bribery or other high Crimes and Misdemeanors.'

Only thrice in American history have presidents been impeached and tried, although neither was removed from office. President Andrew Johnson (1808–75)[24] was impeached by the House of Representatives in 1868 but narrowly escaped conviction by the Senate. President Bill Clinton was impeached late in 1998 but was acquitted by the Senate by a fairly comfortable margin.

Andrew Johnson was impeached for overtly political reasons, stemming from his clash with Congress over Reconstruction policy after the American Civil War (1861–65). His ultimate acquittal may have been influenced by the fact that he had not committed indictable offenses, although many in Congress were willing to interpret the 'high crimes and misdemeanors' language in the constitution quite broadly.

Although, there were certainly political motivations behind the impeachment of Bill Clinton, there were serious accusations of misconduct on the president's part. On 11 December 1998, the House Judiciary Committee (voting 21–16) approved four articles of impeachment. These articles alleged that President Clinton:

I. Gave 'perjurious, false and misleading testimony' before a federal grand jury.
II. Obstructed justice by delaying, impeding, covering up, and concealing the existence of evidence in the Paula Jones sexual harassment case.
III. Provided 'perjurious, false and misleading testimony' in the Paula Jones case.
VI. Misused and abused his office by making perjurious statements to Congress in his answers to questions posed by the Judiciary Committee.

On 19 December, the full House, voting basically along party lines, adopted two of these articles. The article accusing the president of 'perjurious, false and misleading testimony' before the federal grand jury was adopted by a vote of 228 to 206. The article alleging obstructing justice in the Paula Jones case was adopted by a vote of 221 to 212.

On 12 February 1999, the Senate voted to acquit President Bill Clinton[25] on both articles of impeachment. The article alleging 'perjurious testimony' garnered 55 votes, well short of the two-third majority necessary for removal. Did the Senate conclude that there was insufficient evidence that the president committed the offences alleged in the articles of impeachment? Or did senators conclude that the offenses were simply not grave enough to warrant the president's removal from office? Senators who voted to acquit were divided between these two perspectives.

The important constitutional question raised by the Clinton impeachment is: What constitutes 'high crimes and misdemeanors'? The prevailing view appears to be that this phrase refers to criminal misconduct alone. But others would argue that a president could be removed from office for abusing power, subverting the Constitution, or even bringing to presidency into disrepute, regardless of whether indictable offenses have been committed.

Although, they were made moot by the president's voluntary departure, similar questions surrounded the possible impeachment of Richard Nixon. Members of the House Judiciary Committee vigorously debated the meaning of 'high crimes and misdemeanors.' A majority of the committee's members seemed to believe Nixon could be impeached for –

> 'undermining the integrity of office, disregard of constitutional duties and oath of office, arrogation of power, abuse of the governmental process, and adverse impact on the system of government'.

On the other hand, Nixon's defenders held that the president could be impeached only for specific offenses against the criminal law, offenses for which he could be indicted by a grand jury (for example, obstruction of justice). In light of information currently available regarding Nixon's role in the Watergate scandal, it seems that he could have been impeached, and convicted, under either of the interpretation of the constitution.[26]

Donald Trump is the first President in American history to be impeached twice. The first impeachment trial of Trump was result of impeachment resolution passed by the House of Representatives by votes of 230 against 197 on the charge of obstruction of Congress. The voting on record charge of abuse of power was 229 to 198. The voting on the impeachment motion was held on 18 December 2019. The two articles for impeachment trial were submitted on 16 January, 2020. The charges of impeachment were put to vote on 5 February 2020. Article I of impeachment (Abuse of Power), the vote was 48 for conviction and 52 for acquittal. On Article II (Obstruction of Congress), the votes were 47 for conviction and 53 for acquittal. In this way, the first impeachment trial of Trump resulted in his acquittal.

The second impeachment trial of Donald Trump began on 9 February 2021 and concluded with his acquittal on 13 February 2021. The House of Representative had adopted impeachment motion against Trump on 13 January 2021. The charge was incitement of insurrection, which meant that he attempted to overturn the 2020 presidential election results (including his false claims of election of fraud and his efforts to pressure election officials in Georgia). He was accused of inciting the attack on the Capital in Washington D.C., on 6 January 2021 while the Congress was convened to count the electoral votes and certify the victory of Joe Biden and Kamala Harris as President and Vice President of the United States respectively. The impeachment motion was passed by the House of Representatives by a vote of 232 to 197. The impeachment trial of Trump was held between 9 February to 13 February 2021. At the conclusion of the trial, the Senate voted 57 to 43 to convict Trump falling 10 votes short of the two-third majority required by the Constitution. Trump was thus acquitted.

Is the question of what constitutes 'high crimes and misdemeanors' solely a matter for the determination of the House and Senate, or is it appropriately a subject for judicial review? The Supreme Court has not been called on to render an authoritative construction of the 'high crimes and misdemeanors' language of Article II of the American Constitution. Should it be asked to do so in the future, the court might well refuse by labeling the issue a 'political question'. It has been suggested, however, that in light of *Powell v. McCormack* (1969)[27], the Court could define 'high crimes and misdemeanors.' In *Powell* case, the court refused to view as 'political' the question of whether Congress could exclude one of its members for reasons other than residency, age, or citizenship.[28] From a formal legal standpoint, this argument is compelling, but the court's decisions reflect more than legal arguments. Realistically, the court could severely jeopardize the delicate balance of its coequal status were it to intervene between president and Congress in an impeachment controversy. Judicial self-restraint would counsel doing otherwise.

The Veto Power

Under Article 1, Section 7:

> '[e]very Bill' and '[e]very Order, Resolution or Vote to which the Concurrence of the Senate and the House of Representatives may be necessary'

must be presented to the president for approval. There are but three exceptions to this presentment requirement:

It is not applicable to actions involving a single house, such as the adoption of procedural rules; it does not apply to concurrent resolutions, such as those establishing joint committees or setting a date for adjournment; finally, it does not apply to constitutional amendments proposed by the Congress.

The alleged legislative veto was a device whereby one or both houses of Congress passed resolutions to veto certain decisions made in the executive branch. In the case of *Immigration and Naturalization Service v. Chadha*,[29] the Supreme Court invalidated the legislative veto partly on the ground that it violated the presentment requirement of Article I.

The president has 10 days (not counting Sundays) to consider legislation presented for approval. The president has several options:

(1) Sign the bill into law, which is what usually occurs;
(2) veto the bill, which can be overridden by a two-thirds majority of both houses of Congress; or
(3) neither sign nor veto the bill, thus allowing it to become law automatically after 10 days.

A major exception applies, however, to the third option:

If Congress adjourns before the 10 days have expired and the president still has not signed the bill, it is said to have been subjected to a pocket veto.

From the president's point of view, the beauty of the pocket veto, is that it deprives Congress of the chance to override a formal veto. This device was first used by President James Madison (1751–1836) in 1812. The pocket veto has been controversial since its inception. The crucial question is: What constitutes an adjournment of Congress?

In the pocket veto case, *Okanogan Indians v. United States*,[30] the Supreme Court upheld President Calvin Coolidge's (1872–1933) authority to pocket veto a bill between sessions of the same Congress. The court held that 'adjournment' means any congressional break that prevents the return of a bill within the requisite 10-day period.

The Power to Grant Pardons

The full and unconditional pardon of former President Richard Nixon following the Watergate affair by President Gerald Ford's (1913–2006) may have been politically unwise, but it was unquestionably constitutional. Article II, Section 2, Clause 1, states that:

> 'the president shall have the power to grant reprieves and pardons for offenses against the United States, except in cases of impeachment'.

Although, impeachment proceedings were initiated against Richard Nixon, his sudden resignation foreclosed any possibility of impeachment, let alone conviction by the Senate. Thus, Ford acted constitutionally in issuing the pardon to Nixon.

Although, President Gerald Ford issued a full pardon to President Nixon, the president may also issue 'conditional' pardons. In *Schick v. Reed*[31], the Supreme Court said:

> 'The plain purpose of the broad [pardoning] power conferred…was to allow…the President to "forgive" the convicted person in part or entirely, to reduce a penalty a specified number of years, or to alter it with conditions which are themselves constitutionally unobjectionable.'

Maurice L. Schick had been convicted of murder and sentenced to death by a military tribunal. Subsequently, President Dwight D. Eisenhower (1890–1969) commuted Schick's sentence to life imprisonment on the condition that he be ineligible for parole.

However, in *Furman v. Georgia*[32], the Supreme Court ruled that the death penalty was in certain instances unconstitutional. Consequently, Schick went back to court arguing in light of the court's capital punishment decision, which had been applied retroactively, that his own original death sentence was unconstitutional and that, accordingly, the no parole provision should likewise be set aside. The court disagreed, holding that the conditional pardon was lawful when issued and that the later decision in *Furman* did not alter its validity.

An unqualified presidential pardon fully restores any civil rights forfeited on conviction of the crime. In *Ex parte Garland*,[33] the court held that a pardon restores an individual's innocence as though a crime had never been committed. In the *Garland* case, this meant that one who had fought for the Confederates in the American Civil War (1861–65), could practice law before the Supreme Court without the need to take an oath that he had not voluntarily borne arms against the United States. The court held that a full pardon by President Andrew Johnson absolved Augustus Hill Garland, the need to take such an oath.

Although, the president has seemingly unlimited authority to grant pardons, it is conceivable that a president might commit an impeachable offense by improperly granting a pardon to a contributor. This issue was raised in January 2001, as President Bill Clinton granted a number of very controversial 'midnight pardons' while he was leaving office. One of them was to a billionaire named Marc Rich, who was living in Switzerland to avoid prosecution for federal tax violations. Rich's ex-wife Denise was a friend and benefactor to President and Mrs Clinton. Critics charged that President Clinton in effect 'sold' a pardon, which would be a violation of federal law. In a subsequent congressional investigation of the matter, Denise Rich asserted her 5th Amendment privilege against self-incrimination. The Bush administration declined to investigate the matter and the controversy subsided. Had the incident taken place prior to the impeachment episode of 1998, there might well have been another article of impeachment adopted against President Clinton.[34]

Appointment and Removal of Officers

The American Constitution provides that the president,

> 'shall nominate and, by and with the advice and consent of the Senate, shall appoint ambassadors ... judges of the Supreme court, and all other officers of the United States, whose appointments are not herein otherwise provided for and which shall be established by law; but the Congress may by law vest the appointment of such inferior officers, as they think proper, in the President alone, in the courts of law, or in the heads of departments' (Article II, Section 2, Clause 2).

Persons appointed in a manner not specified by the Constitution are not 'officers of the United States'; and while no definition of the term 'inferior officers' has ever been made by the courts, it would seem to include all except those in whom the power of appointment might be vested.

The Constitution makes no provision for the removal of officers appointed under Article II, Section 2, Clause 2 While the power of removal is generally regarded as a power derived from the power to appoint, it rests within the sole discretion of the president only when exercised with respect to a purely executive or ministerial office.[35]

Following the decision of *Myers v. United States*,[36] it was generally thought that the power of the president to remove officials appointed by him was plenary, free from any limitations imposed by Congress. The dicta in Chief Justice Willliam Howard Taft's (1857–1930)[37] opinion in the *Myers* case seems to suggest this doctrine. Taft who was a former American President said,

> 'The vesting of the executive power in the President was essentially a grant of the power to execute the laws. But the President alone and unaided could not execute the laws. He must execute them by the assistance of subordinates ......
>
> The power to prevent the removal of an officer who has served under the President is different from the authority to consent to or reject his appointment. When a nomination is made, it may be presumed that the Senate is, or may become, as well advised as to the fitness of the nominee as the President, but in the nature of things the defects in ability or intelligence or loyalty in the administration of the laws of one who has served as an officer under the President are facts as to which the President, or his trusted subordinates, must be better informed than the Senate, and the power to remove him may therefore be regarded as confined for very sound and practical reasons, to the governmental authority which has administrative control. The power of removal is incident to the power of appointment, not to the power of advising and consenting to appointment, and when the grant of the executive power is enforced by the express mandate to take care that the laws be faithfully executed, it emphasizes the necessity for including within the executive power as conferred the exclusive power of removal....'

Justices Louis Brandeis, Oliver Wendell Holmes Jr, and James Clark McReynolds (1862–1946)[38] dissented. All three of them denied that the president either possessed or acquired an unlimited authority to remove inferior officers. Taft stressed efficiency; Brandeis's primary concern was abuse of power.

> 'The doctrine of the separation of powers was adopted by the Conventions of 1787, not to promote efficiency but to preclude the exercise of arbitrary power. The purpose was, not to avoid friction, but by means of the inevitable friction incident to the distribution of governmental powers among three departments, to save the people from autocracy....'

Nine years after the *Myers* decision, the court whittled down the broad rule, holding that the removal of officials from certain independent agencies, such as the Federal Trade Commission, could be limited to causes defined by Congress.[39] The court distinguished positions in the traditional executive departments, for whose administration the president assumed primary responsibility, from those in agencies established by Congress to carry out legislative policy essentially free from any executive influence other than that resulting from appointment.

This distinction was maintained in *Wiener v. U.S.*[40] The case involved President Dwight D. Eisenhower's removal of a member of the War Claims Commission. There were specific statutory limits on the removal of Federal Trade Commissioners, but none in the War Claims Act. Stressing the quasi-judicial nature of the agency, Justice Felix Frankfurter (1883–1965) minimized this distinction:

'Congress did not wish to have hang over the Commission the Damocles' sword of removal by the President for no reason other than he preferred to have on that Commission men of "his own choosing"'.

Presidential Immunity

The US Supreme Court, in addition to a limited power of executive privilege, also, has held that presidents enjoy nearly absolute immunity against private civil suits involving claims stemming from official presidential actions. Not surprisingly, the recent cases in which the court was asked to decide the scope of presidential immunity stemmed from controversies that began during the Nixon administration.

Morton Halperin (1938), a political scientist, was a staff member of the National Security Council during the Nixon administration. After learning that his home telephone had been illegally wire-tapped, Halperin brought suit seeking monetary damages against Nixon, his Secretary of State Henry Kissinger (1923), and the Attorney General, John N. Mitchell (1913–88). In *Kissinger v. Halperin*[41], the Court divided 4–4 (Justice William Rehnquist not participating), thus letting stand a lower federal court decision upholding President Nixon's susceptibility to lawsuit.

In *Nixon v. Fitzgerald*,[42] the court was able to reach majority agreement on the question of presidential immunity. The case involved A. Ernest Fitzgerald (1926–2019), a former management analyst with the Air Force. Fitzgerald had attracted much attention in 1968, when he embarrassed the Department of Defense by revealing huge cost over-runs on the C-5A transport plane. In 1970, Fitzgerald was dismissed, ostensibly as part of a departmental reorganization. Later, the Civil Service Commission found that Fitzgerald had been illegally removed for his whistle blowing on the Pentagon. Following the Commission's decision, Fitzgerald filed suit in federal court. On appeal, the Supreme Court held that the president was entitled to absolute immunity against private civil suits, at least those stemming from the president's official actions during his time in the White House. Writing for the court, Justice Lewis F. Powell Jr (1907–98) opined that:

> '[b]ecause of the singular importance of the President's duties, diversion of his energies by concern with private lawsuits would raise unique risks to the effective functioning of government.'

Justice Byron White (1907–2002)[43] dissented:

> 'Attaching absolute immunity to the office of the President, rather than to particular activities the President might perform, places the President above the law. It is a reversion to the old notion that the King can do no wrong.'

Foreign Policy and International Relations

Scholars have written of the 'two presidencies'. The first form is concerned with domestic affairs, it is severely limited by the American Constitution, the Supreme Court, and the Congress. The second form of presidency involves mainly of foreign affairs and international relations, it is less susceptible to constitutional and political constraints. Although, the thesis may have been overstated, the basic point is valid.

Throughout the American history, Congress, the courts, and the American public have been highly deferential to the president in the conduct of foreign policy. A serious reading of the Constitution indicates to some observers, the framers of the American Constitution intended for the Congress to play a greater role in the foreign policy process; however, the exigencies of history, more than the intentions of the framers, determine the roles played by the institutions of government.

Another factor contributing to presidential dominance of foreign policy is the distinctive structures of Congress and the executive branch. Congress is composed of 535 members, each representing either a state or localized constituency. At the same time, the president represents a national constituency. Is it not reasonable that the president alone should speak for the nation in the international arena.[44]

In foreign affairs, presidential power again is limited by Congress only with great difficulty and on rare occasions. Congressional control of the purse provides a check of growing importance at a time when foreign aid is an important consideration in diplomatic relations. The Court has upheld, the delegation of power by Congress to the president that would have been invalidated if it had been made in domestic legislation. More important to presidential power, however, is the theory of sovereignty set forth in Justice George Sutherland's *Curtiss-Wright* opinion,[45] and the great reservoir of inherent power possessed by the president as representative of the United States in dealing with other nations. Treaties must receive the consent of two-thirds of the Senate. Once it is passed, a treaty may then be the basis of implementing legislation that otherwise would not be within the power of Congress (*Missouri v. Holland*).[46] On the other hand, Congress may by statute alter or negate the effect of a treaty on domestic law.

The tendency of modern presidents to use executive agreements in place of the treaty has freed them from dependency on the Senate. Such agreements have the same legal effect as treaties for e.g., *United States v. Belmont*,[47] *United States v. Pink*.[48] In 1952 and again in 1953 resolutions were introduced in the Senate providing among other things, that

> 'A treaty shall become effective as internal law in the United States only through legislation which would be valid in absence of the treaty.'

These efforts were resisted primarily because of the serious adverse impact such an amendment would inevitably exert on the president's control of foreign relations. With the increasing importance and complexity of foreign policy, the president has found it necessary to play a role unhindered by the ability of one-third-plus-one of the Senate to frustrate his actions.

A case in point was President Jimmy Carter's (1924)[49] notification in December 1978 to terminate this country's Mutual Defense Treaty with Taiwan on 1 January 1980, without congressional approval. Opponents of his efforts framed their objections in constitutional terms. The Senate had ratified the treaty, and even though its terms provided for termination on a year's notice by either signatory, they claimed that the President could not do it alone. So they filed suit. After a defeat in the district court, the court of appeals upheld Carter's unilateral authority. The Senate's authority to ratify does not imply a role in termination, the judges held. The Senate had approved a treaty that provided for terms of a year's notice. It was up to president to give that notice, as the nation's representative in foreign affairs.[50]

In *Goldwater v. Carter*,[51] the court, without hearing oral argument, refused to address the merits of the suit. Six Justices directed the lower court to dismiss the complaint. Two would have assigned the case for full review and decision. Only Justice William Joseph Brennan Jr (1906–97) reached the merits, siding with President Jimmy Carter.

In these circumstances as in numerous others, regarding American constitutional interpretation, the past informs the present and the present sheds light on the past. Bearing on the Taiwan treaty termination is *Myers v. United States*.[52] President Woodrow Wilson (1856–1924) had fired Frank S. Myers, an executive officer, without approval of Senate. Voting 6 to 3, the Supreme Court found the president's power of removal to be incident to his power of appointment, not to the Senate's power of advising and consenting to the appointment. If the removal power is incident to appointment, may not the termination of a treaty be considered incident to negotiation? The fact that the *Myers* case involved internal rather than external affairs; strengthened the constitutional case for President Carter. The President declared Justice George Sutherland in *Curtiss-Wright*,

> 'makes treaties with the advice and consent of the Senate; but he alone negotiates. Into the field of negotiation, the Senate cannot intrude; the Congress itself is powerless to invade it.'

Landmark decisions like *Curtiss-Wright* and *Youngstown*,[53] found renewed application in 1981 when the Court on the last day of its term upheld the legality of President Carter's extraordinary financial actions in the Iranian Hostage Affair (1979–81).[54] This decision upheld certain actions taken by President Carter in January 1981 to settle the controversy resulting from the seizure of American personnel as hostages at the American Embassy in Tehran, Iran, in 1979. To secure the hostages' release, the United States agreed with Iran to terminate legal proceedings in US Courts involving claims by American nationals against Iran, to nullify attachments against Iranian property as entered by US Courts to secure any judgments against Iran, and to transfer such claims from US Courts to newly created arbitration tribunal. These agreements were implemented by executive orders.

The Court upheld these Presidential actions against challenges on the ground that such challenges were unauthorized by law. Agreeing with Justice Felix Frankfurter's words in *Youngstown* that the framers, 'did not make the judiciary the overseer of our government,'

Justice William Rehnquist and all, but, unanimous bench moved to great lengths to justify President Carter's steps in this troubled matter. Strengthened was the constitutional status of executive agreements. Emphasized was the idea that congressional acquiescence or inaction constitutes congressional approval. It demonstrated considerable deference that the court is inclined to show to the executive branch in foreign relations.

The framers made war making a joint enterprise. Congress is authorized to 'declare war'; the President is designated 'commander-in-chief.' Technology has expanded the President's role and correspondingly curtailed the power of Congress. In recognition of vastly changed conditions after World War II (1939–45), Congress itself endorsed executive aggrandizement.

In the face of rising public protest against the undeclared Vietnam War (1955–75), New York Senator Jacob K. Javits (1904–86)[55] sponsored congressional hearings leading to legislation designed to curb presidential power. The result is the controversial War Powers Resolution of 1973, a far cry from the 1964 Gulf of Tonkin Resolution, which declared:

> 'that Congress approves and supports the determination of the President as commander-in-chief, to take all necessary measures to repel any armed attack against the forces of the United States and to prevent further aggression.'

Whether or not the Javits resolution can be effectively enforced remains to be seen.

The President is under a positive obligation 'to take care that the laws be faithfully executed.' His power must be adapted to changed and changing conditions. But, in fulfilling this responsibility, he must also consider those principles and provisions of the Constitution which restrict as well as enhance his powers. As commander-in-chief, he cannot pick and choose the provisions of the Constitution he executes. Congress's share in war making must be adapted to unforeseen developments. Otherwise, technological evolution alone makes emergence of a totalitarian system inevitable.

The framers could not have foreseen conditions as they exist today, but the underlying principles of their handiwork are clear. As to war making, they intended Congress to participate. Early in the Philadelphia Convention debates, James Madison observed:

> 'A rupture with other powers is among the greatest national calamities. It ought therefore to be effectually provided that no part of a nation shall have it in its power to bring them [wars] on the whole'.

Madison was referring to the possibility that individual states might unwittingly involve the country in war, but his conviction that the war-making power should be shared is clear.

The power of Congress in this sensitive area was not meant to cripple and impede; it was designed to produce a wise course of action. It is no less true even today.[56] The war in Iraq (2003–11) is likely to re-open legal controversy yet again.

War Powers

The American Presidency's dominance in international affairs is not limited to or based on the formalities of recognizing and striking agreements with other governments. Integral to the President's foreign policy role is the tremendous power of the US military, over which the Constitution makes the president commander-in-chief. Force is often threatened, and sometimes used, to protect US allies and interests, maintain national security against possible attack, or defend the nation against actual attack.

The success of American foreign policy would be severely limited if the constitution curbed the nation's ability to respond effectively to threats against its interests or security. On the other hand, the constitution was designed as a limitation on the power of US government. Should not such limitations apply (as Justice Hugo Black said in the *Pentagon papers* case)

> 'to prevent the government from deceiving the people and sending them off to distant lands to die of foreign fevers and foreign shot and shell?'

The framers of the Constitution did attempt to provide some limitation on the war making power, as they did with respect to government power generally, by dividing power between the president and Congress. Although, Article II recognizes the president as commander-in-chief, Article I provides Congress with the authority to declare war. Although, the military conflicts in Korea and Vietnam qualify as wars, however, in neither case was there a formal declaration by Congress. Presidential power to commit military forces to combat situations has a long heritage. It was first exercised at the international level in 1801, when President Thomas Jefferson (1743–1826) sent the US Marines to 'the shores of Tripoli' to root out the Barbary pirates. In 1846, President James K. Polk (1795–1849)[57] sent American troops to instigate a war with Mexico that Congress formally approved by declaring war. In 1854, President Franklin Pierce (1804–69)[58] authorized a show of American force that led to the total destruction of an entire city in Central America. In none of these instances, however, did the Supreme Court have the opportunity to decide the scope of the president's power as commander-in-chief.

The court's opportunity came in 1863 in *The Prize Cases*. These cases involved the disposition of vessels captured by the Union Navy during the blockage of Southern ports ordered by President Abraham Lincoln (1809–65) in the absence of a congressional declaration of war. Under existing laws of war, the captured vessels would become the property of the Union Navy only if the conflict were a declared war. In view of the extremely sensitive politics of the day, the court could do nothing but find the seizures to be legal, even though Congress had not formally declared war against the Confederacy. The Court held that:

> 'the President is not only authorized but bound to resist force. He does not initiate the war, but is bound to accept the challenge without waiting for any special legislative authority.'

Additionally, Justice Robert Cooper Grier (1794–1870)[59] noted that the,

> 'President was bound to meet [the Civil War] in the shape it presented itself, without waiting for the Congress to baptize it with a name; and no name given to it by him or them could change the fact,'

In *The Prize Cases*, the Court acknowledged the necessity of deferring to the president's decisions in time of crisis.[60]

The power of the federal government over the armed forces of the nation is divided between the President and the Congress. The legislature has been given the important powers of raising armies and providing a navy under Article I, Section 8, Clause 14; the president, as commander-in-chief of the armed forces under Article II, Section 2 Clause 1, may issue regulations of his own and may take charge of all military operations in time of peace as well as in war.

War does not suspend the guaranties of the Constitution. Speaking for the majority in the *Milligan*[61] case Justice David Davis (1815–86)[62] observed:

> 'No doctrine involving more pernicious consequences was ever invented by the wit of man than that any of its [the Constitution's] provisions can be suspended during any of the great emergencies of the government. Such a doctrine leads directly to anarchy or despotism, but the theory of necessity on which it is based is false; for the government, within the Constitution, has all the powers granted to it, which are necessary to preserve its existence; as has been happily proved by the result of the great effort [secession of the states] to throw off its just authority.'

However, in the case in which this hypocritical pronouncement was made the Constitution was suspended. Echoing one aspect of Justice Davis's observation, Justice Oliver Wendell Holmes Jr remarked in *Frohwerk v. U.S.*[63]

> 'We do not lose our right to condemn either measures or men because the country is at war.'

Nevertheless, under the 'inherent' powers' doctrine Attorney General John N. Mitchell argued in 1971 that:

> 'the President, acting through the Attorney General, may constitutionally authorize the use of electronic surveillance in cases where he had determined that, in order to preserve national security the use of such surveillance is reasonable.'

Countervailing values were asserted in the Court's far-reaching decision in *United States v. United States District Court*.[64]

Two different ways to deal with the issue of waging war successfully can be found in American history. Under President Abraham Lincoln, Congress was ignored or asked to ratify executive actions already accomplished or under way. In World Wars I (1914–11) and II (1939–45), on the other hand, Congress passed a vast number of general statutes of wide scope delegating to the President, or to persons designated by him, vast discretionary powers.

The widest of these delegations was upheld in *Bowles v. Willingham*.[65] When statutory authority is thus added to the President's already expansive powers as commander-in-chief, all constitutional limitations virtually disappear, as seen in the Japanese relocation cases. Even without the support of statute, presidential power in wartime is subject to few limitations. The President can control the movement of the armed forces and prescribe rules, including judicial procedure, for the government of captured territory. He may direct the seizure of former enemy officers and officials after the conclusion of hostilities and set up military commissions to try them in proceedings that are not limited by the Constitution.

Article 1, Section 9 of the Constitution seemingly limits Congress's power of suspending the writ of *habeas corpus* to 'cases of rebellion or invasion.' Nevertheless, President Lincoln, during the Civil War (1861–65), suspended the privilege of the writ without congressional authorization, and ordered his officers to refuse service of a writ of *habeas corpus* issued by Chief Justice Roger B. Taney (1777–1865).[66] Subsequently, Congress authorized the President to suspend the writ in certain cases; the Supreme Court, however, refused to pass on the validity of the President's action in *Ex parte Vallandigham*.[67] President Lincoln provided another extreme example of executive power when he imposed martial law on portions of the Northern states and substituted trial by military commission for the regular processes of law in dealing with traitors and others charged with violations of wartime statutes.

In *Ex parte Milligan*,[68] decided in 1866 after the end of hostilities, the court held that President Lincoln had exceeded his authority, the regular courts of Indiana, where the military commission had convicted Lambdin P. Milligan, being open and prepared to handle the charges against him. Five members of the court went further and stated that martial rule could never exist where the courts were open. Four members thought that Congress could have sanctioned what the executive could not.

During the Second World War (1939–45), a similar result followed, where the Governor-General of Hawaii, pursuant to presidential authorization, invoked martial rule and gave to military commission's jurisdiction over all criminal offenses. In a 6 to 2 decision, the court held such action invalid on the basis of the *Milligan* decision (*Duncan v. Kahanamoku*).[69]

The unique problem was presented at the end of World War II (1939–45), when the court was asked by the Japanese General Tomoyuki Yamashita (1885–1946) and other Japanese war leaders to review their trials by military commissions for violation of the laws of war, claiming serious procedural errors in the trial, as well as innocence of the charge. The court decided that the findings of a military commission are not reviewable, thus in effect permitting these tribunals to follow rules that differ substantially from those required in the regular trial courts. Justices Frank Murphy (1890–1949)[70] and Wiley Blount Rutledge (1894–1949)[71], dissenting, pointed out that the court's decision meant that minimal standards of fairness need not be followed by military commissions, and that such commissions are, thus, effectively placed beyond the 'rule of law' with regard to *In re Yamashita*.[72]

While enemies of the United States of America could not successfully invoke constitutional guarantees, and were, in effect, subjected to the sense of justice of military tribunals, American citizens have been more successful in escaping military control. In *United States ex rel. Toth v. Quarles*,[73] the court held that:

> an honorably discharged serviceman was not subject to court-martial jurisdiction for offenses allegedly committed before discharge, and that a provision of the Uniform Code of Military Justice providing the contrary was invalid.

In 1956, a sharply divided court held that civilians accompanying the armed forces abroad were triable by courts-martial as provided by the Uniform Code of Military Justice (UCMJ). On rehearing, the court made a dramatic about-face and held that Congress could not deprive a civilian citizen of the United States of America, of his constitutional guaranties of trial by jury and other rights in capital cases, regardless of the difficulties in making a civil trial available for instance, *Reid v. Covert*[74] and *Kinsella v. Krueger*.[75] Subsequently, in *Kinsella v. Singleton* case, the rule was extended to non-capital cases.[76]

Although, civilians accompanying the armed forces were thus able to preserve their constitutional rights. In *Wilson v. Girard*,[77] a serviceman in Japan seeking trial by court-martial under the Uniform Code of Military Justice (UCMJ) found that by executive agreement or treaty, the United States could provide for trial in foreign courts of military personnel charged with certain offenses not of a purely military nature

Presidential Power and the War on Terrorism

The tragic events of 11 September 2001 have led to new controversies over the scope of presidential power. For example, President George W. Bush claimed broad authority to detain enemy combatants to protect national security. Those who defended the president's position argued that the Constitution envisioned expansive presidential power to deal with external threats, and that this power especially is needed in dealing with the risk of terrorist attacks on the United States of America.

But, critics argued that the American Constitution rejects such unchecked executive power and that President Bush's actions were unprecedented and unconstitutional. Two of the most important issues thus far have been the power of the president to detain individuals and the constitutionality of the use of military tribunals to try individuals suspected of terrorist activity.[78]

Detentions

The US Supreme Court on 28 June 2004, decided 3 cases where it considered the right of those being detained as part of the war on terrorism to have access to the courts.

In *Hamdi v. Rumsfeld*,[79] the Court, by an 8 to 1 margin, held that an American citizen apprehended in a foreign country and held as an enemy combatant must be accorded due process and a meaningful factual hearing.

In *Padilla v. Rumsfeld*,[80] the Court dismissed on jurisdictional grounds a challenge by an American citizen apprehended in the United States and held as an enemy combatant. The Court ruled that Jose Padilla needed to sue in federal court of South Carolina, where he is being held, rather than in New York where the case was litigated. But, at least, 5 justices clearly signaled that they would rule in favor of Jose Padilla, and held, that the government has no authority to detain an American citizen arrested in the United States as an enemy combatant.

In *Rasul v. Bush*,[81] the Court held that those being detained in Guantanamo Bay detention camp, Cuba have the right to have a *habeas corpus* petition heard in federal court.

Although, only *Hamdi* was a constitutional ruling, all of the decisions are important, especially because they were the Supreme Court's first rulings about the government's actions in the war on terrorism since 11 September 2001.

Four years later, in *Boumediene v. Bush*, the Supreme Court held unconstitutional the denial of *habeas corpus* to non-citizens held as enemy combatants.[82]

These cases are discussed at some length below:

Hamdi v. Rumsfeld[83]

Yaser Esam Hamdi, an American citizen, who was apprehended in Afghanistan and brought to Guantanamo Bay detention camp, Cuba. There it was discovered that he is an American citizen, and later, he was taken to a military prison in South Carolina. He was declared as illegal enemy combatant by the Bush administration and was detained without any charge. His situation is identical to that of John Walker Lindh[84], except that Lindh was indicted and pled guilty to crimes.

The United States Court of Appeals for the Fourth Circuit agreed with the government that an American citizen apprehended in a foreign country and held as an enemy combatant is not entitled to any form of due process or judicial review. The Supreme Court reversed, though without a majority opinion.

There were two issues before the Supreme Court. First, does the federal government have the authority to hold an American citizen apprehended in a foreign country as an enemy combatant? In a 5 to 4 ruling, the court decided in favor of the government. Justice Sandra Day O'Connor wrote the plurality opinion, which was joined by Chief Justice William Rehnquist and Justices Anthony Kennedy and Stephen Breyer. Hamdi contended that his detention violated the Non-Detention Act, which states that:

> '[n]o citizen shall be imprisoned or otherwise detained by the United States except pursuant to an Act of Congress.'

But, the plurality concluded that Hamdi's detention was authorized pursuant to an Act of Congress: the Authorization for Use of Military Force that was passed after 11 September. Justice Sandra Day O'Connor stated that this constituted sufficient congressional authorization to meet the requirements of the Non-Detention Act (1971), and, to permit detaining an American citizen apprehended in a foreign country as an enemy combatant. Justice O'Connor's plurality opinion was joined by Chief Justice William Rehnquist and Justices Anthony Kennedy and Stephen Breyer. Justice Clarence Thomas was the 5th vote for the government on this issue and in a separate opinion he concluded that the president has inherent authority, pursuant to Article II of the Constitution to hold Hamdi as an enemy combatant. Only Justice Clarence Thomas of the 5 justices who composed the majority addressed the president's claim of inherent power as commander-in-chief to detain American citizens as enemy combatants.

The other 4 justices vehemently disagreed. In a powerful dissenting opinion. Justice Antonin Scalia, joined by Justice Paul Stevens, argued that there is no authority to hold an American citizen in the United States as an enemy combatant without charges or trial unless Congress expressly suspends the writ of *habeas corpus*. Justice David Souter, in an opinion joined by Justice Ruth Bader Ginsburg concurring in the judgment in part and dissenting in part, contended that it violates the Non-Detention Act (1971) to hold an American citizen as an enemy combatant. Justice Souter argued that Congress must expressly authorize such detentions and that it had not done so.

The second issue before the US Supreme Court was what, if any, process must be accorded to Hamdi? The Court ruled, with only Justice Thomas dissenting, that Hamdi must be accorded due process. (Justice Scalia, joined by Justice Stevens, did not reach this issue because he believed that there was no authority to detain Hamdi). Justice O'Connor explained that Hamdi is entitled to have his *habeas corpus* petition heard in federal court and that imprisoning a person is obviously the most basic form of deprivation of liberty.

Thus, due process is required, and the procedures required are to be determined by applying the three part balancing test under *Mathews v. Eldridge*,[85] which instructs courts to weigh the importance of the interest to the individual, the ability of additional procedures to reduce the risk of an erroneous deprivation and the government's interests.

Although, the Court did not specify the procedures that must be followed in Hamdi's case, the justices were explicit that Hamdi must be given a meaningful response, and the right to be represented by an attorney. The Court, however, suggested that hearsay evidence might be admissible, and the burden of proof could be placed on Hamdi. The Court remanded the case for the determination of what procedural due process requires, when an American citizen apprehended in a foreign country is detained as an enemy combatant. Only Justice Clarence Thomas rejected this conclusion and accepted the government's argument that the president could detain enemy combatants without any form of due process.

In the fall of 2004, following the Supreme Court's decision, the government and Hamdi reached an agreement. In exchange for Hamdi being released from custody he agreed to leave the country, and, renounce his citizenship, and never to take up arms against the United States of America. Thus, *Hamdi'* case will not be occasion for the Court to spell out the procedures required.

Padilla v. Rumsfeld[86]

In May 2002, Jose Padilla an American citizen, was apprehended at Chicago's O'Hare Airport. He allegedly was planning to build and detonate a 'dirty bomb' in the United States. Although, he was imprisoned in May 2002, he was not indicted or tried for any crime. Instead the government is holding him as an enemy combatant. Padilla's situation is different from Yaser Esam Hamdi's because Padilla was arrested in the United States for a crime allegedly planned to occur in this country.

After his arrest, Padilla was taken to New York. An attorney filed a petition in the Southern District of New York to meet with him. Shortly thereafter, Padilla was transferred to a military prison in South Carolina. But, the litigation over his detention and rights remained in New York, and, ultimately in the Second Circuit. The Supreme Court, in a 5 to 4 decision, with the majority opinion written by Chief Justice William Rehnquist, concluded that the New York court lacked jurisdiction to hear Padilla's *habeas corpus* petition. The Court said that a person must bring a *habeas petition* where he or she is being detained against the person immediately responsible for the detention. Padilla needed to file his *habeas petition* in South Carolina against the head of the military prison there.

Justice John Paul Stevens wrote for the four dissenters and lamented that Jose Padilla, who already had been held for over 2 years, must begin all over again. But, it appears clear that Padilla had 5 votes on the Supreme Court that it is illegal to hold him as an enemy combatant. In a footnote near the end of his dissenting opinion, Justice John Paul Stevens expressly stated that he agreed with the Second Circuit that there was no legal authority to detain Padilla as an enemy combatant. Justice Antonin Scalia was emphatic in his dissent in *Hamdi* that an American citizen cannot be held without trial as an enemy combatant unless Congress suspends the writ of *habeas corpus.*

Subsequently, the United States District Court ruled in Padilla's favor and held that the government either had to criminally charge Padilla or release him from custody. However, the Fourth Circuit reversed and found presidential power to detain an American citizen as an enemy combatant. In November 2005, the United States issued an indictment of Padilla so that he would no longer be held as an enemy combatant and the United States Supreme Court dismissed the matter as moot.[87] In 2007, Jose Padilla was convicted of materially assisting a foreign terrorist organization and sentenced to 17 years, 4 months in prison.

Rasul v. Bush[88]

Beginning January 2002, the United States government has held over 600 individuals as prisoners at a military facility in Guantanamo Bay, Cuba. The first cases before the Supreme Court involved two *habeas corpus* petitions that had been filed on behalf of the Guantanamo detainees. *Rasul v. Bush,* the title under which both cases were decided by the Supreme Court, was brought by the father of an Australian detainee, and the father of a British detainee, and the mother of another British detainee. *Al Odah v. United States* was brought by fathers and brothers of 12 individuals being held at Camp X-Ray in Guantanamo, Cuba.

In both cases, the government moved to dismiss contending that the federal courts lacked authority to hear *habeas corpus* petitions by those being held in Guantanamo Bay detention camp. In March 2003, the United States Courts of Appeals for the District of Columbia Circuit affirmed the dismissal of the case for lack of jurisdiction and ruled that no court in the country could hear the petitions brought by the Guantanamo detainees.

The Court of Appeals based this conclusion on the Supreme Court's decision in *Johnson v. Eisentrager.*[89] In *Johnson's* case, 21 German nationals sought *habeas corpus* after they were arrested in China for working in Japan on behalf of the German government before Germany surrendered. They were taken into custody by the United States Army and convicted by a United States Military Commission, of violating laws of war by engaging in continued military activity in Japan after Germany's surrender, but before Japan had surrendered. The defendants were convicted and repatriated to Germany to serve their sentences in a prison whose custodian was an American army officer. The prisoners sought *habeas corpus* in federal court and the Supreme Court found that there was no jurisdiction in a federal district to hear the petition. The District of Columbia Circuit Court of Appeals found that the Guantanamo detainees are like the petitioners in *Johnson,* and thus, held that the petition in this case be dismissed.

The Supreme Court in a 6 to 3 decision reversed the decision of the Court of Appeals and held that a federal court may hear the *habeas corpus* petition of those being held in Guantanamo Bay detention camp. Justice John

Paul Stevens wrote the opinion for the Court. He emphasized that *Johnson v. Eisentrager* is distinguishable in many important respects. In *Johnson*, those detained were accorded a trial in military tribunals; but those being held in Guantanamo detention camp have never had any form of trial or due process. Also, the Court stressed that unlike the situation in *Johnson*, Guantanamo is functionally under the control and sovereignty of the United States government.

The Court in *Rasul v. Bush* did not address what type of hearing ultimately must be accorded to those in Guantanamo. Rather, the case was limited to the issue of whether a federal court could hear their *habeas corpus* petition.

Boumediene v. Bush[90]

On remand, the government argued that the Guantanamo detainees failed to state a claim upon which relief could be granted. Two judges in the United States District Court for the District of Columbia came to opposite conclusions.[91] One judge found that those in Guantanamo Bay detention camp, stated claims under the US Constitution and under the Geneva Accords, the other judge disagreed and found no cause of action for those being detained in Guantanamo.

The cases were initially argued in the United States Court of Appeals for the District of Columbia Circuit in September 2005, but, it was not until June 2008 in *Boumediene v. Bush* that the court returned to the issue of the Guantanamo detainees and their access to *habeas corpus.*

After the Supreme Court rejected this argument in *Rasul v. Bush*,[92] Congress adopted the Detainee Treatment Act 2005 (DTA), which provided that federal courts could not hear writs of *habeas corpus* by 'enemy combatants'. However, the court held unconstitutional the denial of *habeas corpus* to citizens held as enemy combatants.

Conclusion

American constitutional development has witnessed the transformation of the presidency into the most powerful executive position in the world. The American President possesses awesome powers, most notably the authority to command the world's most formidable military. Nevertheless, the presidency is not without constitutional and statutory constraints, as dictated by the principle of checks and balances. Ultimately, though, the power of the presidency is less determined by congressional or judicial action than by public opinion and world events.

Although the presidency occasionally experiences setbacks—as in the aftermath of the Iran-Contra scandal of 1986 and 1987—such reverses tend to be short-lived. The American people simply demand too much from the presidency to allow it to sink to a position of institutional inferiority.

The Hamiltonian conception of the presidency has become institutionalized to the extent that neither the personality of the occupant nor the occasional crisis of credibility can produce any significant dismantling of the office.

As America wages war on terrorism, the presidency emerges once again as the pre-eminent branch of American government. Whether this pre-eminence is maintained will depend more on the vicissitudes of world events and the tides of American public opinion than on the decisions of courts of law.

Presidential System in Pakistan

General Ayub Khan (1907–74), Pakistan's first military ruler, experimented with the presidential form of government. He imposed a Constitution in 1962 which gave a version of the 'presidential form of government'.

The basic institution under the 1962 Constitution was the Electoral College, consisting of 80000 Electors. Each Province was divided into 40000 Electoral Units and the residents of each Unit elected for a period of five years from amongst themselves an Elector, on the principle of adult franchise. The Electors so chosen constituted the Electoral College and elected the President, members of the National Assembly and members of the Provincial Assemblies of their respective provinces. They also had the exclusive right to vote at any referendum that might be held under the constitution.

- The president, had to be a Muslim, was elected for a period of five years and was eligible for re-election.
- The president was the Supreme Commander of the Defence Services and the executive authority of the Republic vested in him.
- The president had a Council of Ministers, composed of persons who were not members of the National Assembly, to assist him in the discharge of his functions. He could seek the advice of all or any of his Ministers but was not bound to accept it.
- When the National Assembly was not in session, the president could promulgate Ordinances and in a state of emergency, to be formally proclaimed by him, he acquired the power to promulgate Ordinances whether the National Assembly was in session or not.
- The president could dissolve the National Assembly before the expiry of its term but in that event he himself would cease to hold office and must seek re-election.
- Appointments to civil services of the Centre were made by the president and the persons appointed, subject to certain safeguards against dismissal, removal and reduction, hold office during his pleasure.
- As Supreme commander of the Defence Services, he granted Commission in and appointed chief commanders of those Armed Services.

The president's assent was necessary to the Bills passed by the National Assembly and he could, if a Bill be not readily acceptable to him, require a majority of two-thirds of the total number of members of the Assembly before he gave his assent to it or directed a referendum about it. On notice, given to the Speaker by one-third members of the National Assembly, the President was liable to be removed for any glaring breach of the Constitution, misconduct, or infirmity.

- If the resolution for his removal was supported by three-fourths of the total number of members of the Assembly, but if the resolution did not carry at least one-half of such members, those voting for it would lose their seats in the Assembly.

In the provinces, the executive authority vested in the Governor who was appointed by and holds office during the pleasure of the President. He functioned under the directions of the President. Each governor also had a Council of Ministers composed of persons not members of the Provincial Assembly, whose appointment was approved by the President and who could hold office during the pleasure of the Governor, subject to the concurrence of the President. The Governor's assent, like that of the President to Central Bills, was necessary to Bills passed by the Provincial Assembly. In financial and other matters, a Governor's position was generally similar to that of the President at the centre.

The executive authority of the Republic extended to all matters in respect of which the Central Legislature had power to make laws. In the same manner the executive authority of a Province extended to all matters in respect of which the Provincial Legislature was competent to legislate.

There were two provinces, East Pakistan and West Pakistan. The central legislature, called the National Assembly, consisted of 156 members, of whom 150 were elected, half and half, from the two provinces, by the Electoral College. The remaining 6 seats, 3 from each Province, were reserved for women who were elected by members of the National Assembly of their respective provinces. The term of the Assembly was 5 years, but it could be dissolved earlier. Only a part of the Annual Budget was subject to its vote.

Each Provincial Assembly consisted of 155 members, of whom 150 were elected by the members of the Electoral College of the province and 5 seats were reserved for women who were elected by members of its Provincial Assembly. Each Assembly elected a Speaker and its members enjoyed the usual privileges of members of Parliament. A governor could not dissolve the provincial assembly before the expiry of its term, except with the approval of the majority of the National Assembly and the concurrence of the president.

Legislative powers were distributed between the centre and the provinces. The central legislature had the power to legislate on matters specified in the Third Schedule and the provincial legislatures on all other matters; but no court could question the competency of a legislature to legislate on any particular matter, and in case of conflict between a central law and a provincial law, the former prevailed over the latter.

The Supreme Court, with a Chief Justice and as many judges as could be determined by law, and in the absence of any such law, by the president, was the court of ultimate jurisdiction in the country. Besides, being a court of appeal in a limited class of cases, it had advisory and constitutional jurisdiction. It also had original jurisdiction which was confined to inter-governmental disputes. Its special jurisdiction to give leave to appeal was restricted to petitions for leave to appeal against the judgments of the High Courts. The High Courts were regular courts of appeal and revision in the Provinces and also exercised what might be called writ jurisdiction in defined circumstances. The Judges of the Supreme Court and the High courts were appointed by the president and they hold office during good behaviour, until they attained the ages of 65 and 60 years respectively. They could not be removed unless the Supreme Judicial Council, composed of the 3 Chief Justices and 2 senior-most judges of the Supreme Court, after enquiry recommend their removal on the ground of misconduct or infirmity.[93]

The leading judgment of the Supreme Court during this period on presidential system was *Fazlul Qadir Chowdhry v. Muhammad Abdul Haque.*[94] The original Constitution provided that President could not appoint ministers from amongst members of the National Assembly. In case a member of the National Assembly accepted the office of Central Minister, he would cease to be a member of the National Assembly. Some of the Central Ministers chosen by Ayub were members of the National Assembly who did not want to vacate their seats in the Assembly. In order to meet this situation, President Ayub promulgated a law called 'Removal of Difficulties/ Appointment of Ministers) Order, 1962' enabling Ministers appointed from amongst members of the Assembly to retain their seats in the Assembly after such appointment. This law was challenged as unconstitutional and repugnant to the Presidential form of Government. The Supreme Court upheld the challenge and declared the said Order of 1962 as void and *ultra vires* of the Constitution. It was held that responsibility given to the President under the Constitution for removal of difficulties was a limited one and could not be exercised to change the very Presidential system under the Constitution. The Supreme Court expressed itself in the following words:

> "This responsibility at the highest level, was given to vary provisions in the Constitution, not for the purpose of *altering the Constitution itself*, but in order that that Constitution as a whole should be brought into force. Viewed in that light, the provisions to be applied were: (1) that Minisers, and (2) the further provision that Ministers should be included among holders of office of profit in the service of Pakistan, and as such subject to a disability, namely, that they could not be members of any Assembly at the same time. These provisions had a very important purpose, namely, to bring into operation a Presidential form of Government, in which the Executive was to be completely separated from the Legislature. The major duty upon all concerned including the President was to bring these fundamental provisions into operation. What has actually been done in that instead of implementing these basic provisions, they have been altered in a fundamental way so as to change the form of Government from the pure Presidential form to an anomalous Parliamentary form.

The 1962 Constitution did not last for more than 7 years, and, was abrogated by General Yahya Khan (1917–80) in March 1969, when he imposed Martial Law throughout Pakistan. The Constitution could hardly be regarded as a model of presidential democracy. It was dictatorial constitution imposed by a military ruler who had designed it according to his own requirements to perpetuate himself in power. All powers were vested in the president and all other institutions were disempowered and marginalized. The governors were his appointees and had no elected capacity. The people all over Pakistan and particularly in East Pakistan felt alienated and the Constitution was regarded as a symbol of tyranny. In 1968–69, there was widespread political agitation in Pakistan and all political parties demanded its abrogation which came about but at the hands of another military ruler.

NOTES

1. James Madison was a Founding Father who served as the 4th President of the United States.
2. Ronald Reagan was the 40th President of the United States.
3. George H.W. Bush was the 41st President of the United States.
4. Bill Clinton was the 42nd President of the United States.
5. George Walker Bush (1946) was the 43rd President of the United States.
6. Otis H. Stephens Jr, John M. Scheb II, *American Constitutional Law* (California, Belmont: Thomson West, 2003), pp. 164.
7. George Washington was the Founding Father who served as the first President of the United States.
8. Supra Note 6, 164–5.
9. Thomas Jefferson was a Founding Father who served as the 3rd President of the United States.

10. Aaron Burr was a Founding Father, and the 3rd Vice President of the United States during President Thomas Jefferson's first term in office.
11. Rutherford B. Hayes was the 19th President of the United States.
12. Benjamin Harrison served as the 23rd President of the United States.
13. Samuel Tilden served as the 25th Governor of New York.
14. Grover Cleveland served twice as the 22nd and 24th President of the United States. The only President in US history to serve two non-consecutive terms in office.
15. Donald John Trump served as 45th President of the United States (2017–2021).
16. Hillary Diane Rodham Clinton served as 67th US Secretary of State from 2009 to 2013. She is wife of William Jefferson Clinton (1946) who served as the 42nd President of the United States from 1993 to 2001.
17. Supra Note 6, pp. 165–6.
18. William Henry Harrison was the 9th President of the United States in 1841.
19. John Tyler after briefly serving as the 10th vice president in 1841 became the 10th President of the United States serving from 1841 to 1845.
20. Woodrow Wilson was the 28th President of the United States.
21. Edith was first lady and the second wife of Woodrow Wilson the 28th President of the United States.
22. John F. Kennedy was the 35th president of the United States.
23. Supra Note 6, pp. 166–7.
24. Andrew Johnson was the 17th President of the United States.
25. Bill Clinton served as the 42nd President of the United States.
26. Ibid, pp. 167–8.
27. 395 U.S. 486 (1969).
28. Ibid.
29. 462 U.S. 919 (1983).
30. 279 U.S. 655 (1929).
31. 419 U.S. 256 (1974).
32. 408 U.S. 238 (1972).
33. 71 U.S. 333 (1866).
34. Supra Note 6, pp. 178–9.
35. Alpheus Thomas Mason, William Merritt Beaney, Donald Grier Jr Stéphenson, *American Constitutional Law*, (New Jersey: Prentice Hall, Inc., 1983), p. 86.
36. 272 U.S. 52 (1926).
37. William Howard Taft was the 27th President of the United States and the 10th Chief Justice of the United States, the only person to have held both offices.
38. James Clark McReynolds was Associate Justice of the Supreme Court of the United States.
39. *Humphrey's Executor v. United States*, 295 U.S. 602 (1934).
40. 357 U.S. 349 (1958).
41. 452 U.S. 713 (1981).
42. 457 U.S. 731 (1982).
43. Byron White served as Associate Justice of the Supreme Court of the United States.
44. Supra Note 6, p. 182.
45. *Curtiss-Wright Export Corporation v. United States*, 299 U.S. 304 (1936).
46. 252 U.S. 416 (1920).
47. 301 U.S. 324(1937).
48. 315 U.S. 203 (1942).
49. Jimmy Carter served as the 39th President of the United States.
50. Supra Note 35, p. 91.
51. 444 U.S. 996 (1979).
52. 272 U.S. 52 (1926).
53. *Youngstown Sheet & Tube Company v. Sawyer*, 343 U.S. 579 (1952).
54. *Dames & Moore v. Regan*, 453 U.S. 654 (1981).
55. Jacob K. Javits was a Republican Senator from New York.
56. Supra Note 35, pp. 91–92.
57. James K. Polk was the 11th President of the United States.
58. Franklin Pierce was the 14th President of the United States.
59. Robert Cooper Grier served as Associate Justice of the US Supreme Court.

60. Supra Note 6, pp. 186–7.
61. 71 U.S. 2 (1866).
62. David Davis was a United States Senator from Illinois and Associate Justice of the US Supreme Court.
63. 249 U.S. 204 (1919).
64. 407 U.S. 297 (1972).
65. 321 U.S. 503 (1944).
66. Roger B. Taney was the 5th Chief Justice of the US Supreme Court.
67. 68 U.S. 243 (1864).
68. 71 U.S. 2 (1866).
69. 327 U.S. 304 (1946).
70. Frank Murphy served as Associate Justice of the US Supreme Court.
71. Wiley Blount Rutledge served as Associate Justice of the US Supreme Court.
72. 327 U.S. 1 (1946).
73. 350 U.S. 11 (1955).
74. 351 U.S. 487 (1956).
75. 354 U.S. 1 (1957).
76. 361 U.S. 234 (1960).
77. 354 U.S. 524 (1957).
78. Erwin Chemerinsky, *Constitutional Law: Principles and Policies*, 5th ed., (New York: Wolters Kluwer Law and Business, 2015), p. 384.
79. 542 U.S. 507 (2004).
80. 542 U.S. 426 (2004).
81. 542 U.S. 466 (2004).
82. 553 U.S. 723 (2008).
83. 542 U.S. 507 (2004).
84. John Walker Lindh an American was captured as an enemy combatant during the United States' invasion of Afghanistan in November 2001.
85. 424 U.S. 319 (1976).
86. 542 U.S. 426 (2004).
87. *Padilla v. Hanft,* 547 U.S. 1062 (2006), Justices Stevens and Souter dissented from the denial of *certiorari.*
88. 542 U.S. 466 (2004).
89. 339 U.S. 763 (1950).
90. 553 U.S. 723 (2008).
91. *In re Guantanamo Detainee* Cases, 355 F.Supp.2d 443 (D.D.C. 2005) (holding cause of action exists for those being held in Guantanamo); *Khalid v. Bush* 355 F. Supp. 2d 311 (D.D.C. 2005) (holding no cause of action exists for those being held in Guantanamo).
92. 542 U.S. 466 (2004).
93. Muhammad Munir, *Constitution of Islamic Republic of Pakistan: Being a Commentary on the Constitution of Pakistan, 1973*(Lahore: Law Pub. Co., 1976), pp. 54–7.
94. PLD 1963 S.C. 486.

Part IV

Judiciary as Guardian of Constitution

11 Independence of Judiciary

Introduction

The 'independence of judiciary', in any system of government, is of great importance. Constitutional theorists treat it as one of the fundamental concepts. With the advent of liberal democracies and the era of written constitutions, almost all written constitutions ensure the inclusion of provisions that secure judicial independence. However, it remains an essentially contested concept[1] i.e. there is an ongoing debate about its content. In this chapter, it will be explained

— what is meant by 'independence of judiciary',
— what are its main content and how different constitutions have incorporated provisions to secure the independence of the judiciary?

One of the earliest constitutional concepts in the constitutional development was the separate status of the judiciary.

The Separation of Judicial Power

'Judicial independence' is a significant component of a governmental culture in every country. It is shaped by the relation between the branches of government and is one of the basic values which lie at the foundation of administration of justice. 'Judicial independence' must be supported by political climate and social consensus.[2] The culture of 'judicial independence' can only exists in a system, which is based on the doctrine of separation of powers[3]

Alexander Hamilton (1755/57–1804), in *Federalist 78*, described the judiciary as the 'least dangerous' branch of the Government. What he meant by that pithy statement was that it cannot significantly damage the rights of citizens. Courts do not enjoy any law-making power like the legislature or the capacity of the executive to implement political policies. Naturally, courts have the power to interpret the constitution and the laws of the land. Courts are dependent on other branches of the government for financial support. The purse is held by the legislature; while the executive holds the sword which symbolizes power.

Furthermore, courts may not be able to enforce their judgments without the assistance of bailiffs and other executive officials. Hamilton shared Montesquieu's (1689–1755) view that judges are relatively weak. It is, however interesting to note that he also agreed with the French jurist's opinion that:

> 'there is no liberty, if the judiciary's power be not separated from the legislative and executive'.

Otherwise, there might be arbitrary government. Parliament or the Executive would be able to determine when its laws had been broken. Hamilton concluded that an independent judiciary, under a duty to declare the nullity of unconstitutional laws, was 'essential in a limited Constitution', so anticipating the conclusion reached by the Supreme Court in *Marbury v. Madison*[4]. There is general agreement in the United Kingdom on the importance of the 'independence of the judiciary', if not over the wisdom of constitutional review of legislation. But it is unclear what independence of the judiciary really means.[5]

Previously, it has been discussed that the United Kingdom Constitution follows the principle of 'separation of powers', especiallyin the context of judicial powers more diligently than it does for the legislative and executive branches. For example, a full-time judge, either from the High Court or Circuit Court, cannot sit in the House of Commons.[6] The Rules of the House significantly limit the freedom of MPs to criticize the judiciary or to discuss cases pending before the courts, and thus influence their decisions. The most important guarantee of 'judicial independence' is that senior judges hold their position

> 'during good behaviour, subject to a power of removal [by the crown] on an address...presently by both Houses of Parliament.'

Since 1830, no judge has been removed under this procedure; in practice it is inconceivable that the government and the majority of both Houses would agree to the dismissal of a judge because they disliked his decisions in politically controversial cases.

The major concern of the separation of powers principle is to prevent the concentration of authority in the hands of one person or body. The separation of judicial power from two other branches of government is particularly crucial in a constitution such as that of the United Kingdom; where the legislative and executive powers are fused, in the sense that members of the government sit in Parliament and, through the governing political party, are effectively able to control the legislature. There is no system of 'checks and balances' like under the American Constitution, or as in France where the President and National Assembly represent different political parties. English and Scottish judges retain a capacity to challenge the government which the legislature has largely lost. (They may be more inclined to exercise it during a period when one party is in power for a sustained period. This happened under the long period of Conservative government from 1979 to 1997. Lord Phillips of Worth Matravers (1938)[7], President of the Supreme Court, said:

> 'For the first time, we have a clear separation of powers between the legislature, the judiciary and the executive in the United Kingdom. This is important. It emphasizes the independence of the judiciary, clearly separating those who make the law from those who administer it.'[8]

It is crucial, therefore, that the judiciary is independent of control by the legislature or by the executive for the reasons identified by Montesquieu and Hamilton.

The ethos of judicial independence is based on a number of levels; institutional level, which regulates the matters relative to the status of judges and the jurisdiction of courts, the constitutional level which embodies in a constitution the institutional aspects and ensures that the independence of the judiciary shall not be adversely affected by legislation or executive action. An additional level is the legislation level, which regulates in detail the constitutional principles and lastly—the adjudicative level which is the jurisdiction of the court which provides for the interpretation and additional levels in all respects.[9]

The 'independence of the judiciary', therefore, requires constitutional provisions for the appointment and dismissal of judges, appropriate to insulate them from political influence. But a liberal constitution should also provide in broad terms about the functions or, to use a common legal term, the jurisdiction of the courts. Otherwise, a government, through legislation or executive order, would be able, for example, to set up specialist tribunals to decide certain types of cases, for instance, criminal prosecutions which traditionally have been decided by the ordinary courts. Such a move would surely amount to an infringement of judicial power. This would be particularly clear if members of the new specialist tribunals were appointed or elected on political grounds. It would then be immaterial that the judges in the ordinary courts, deprived of their jurisdiction over criminal cases, were wholly independent and performed their remaining functions impartially.

The doctrine of separation of powers also secures the 'independence of the judiciary', therefore, constitutions should allocate judicial functions to independent courts. It is not enough for them simply to guarantee judicial independence. Once the judicial functions are constitutionally valid then the courts by exercising this power can secure their independence. The Privy Council took this point in *Liyanage v. The Queen*.[10] The Parliament of Ceylon (now Sri Lanka) had enacted legislation specifically to deal with the leaders of an unsuccessful insurrection. It widened the scope of the criminal law, prescribed minimum sentences, and set up a special court and rules of procedure for the trial of the 'offenders', who had even been named in a government White Paper. The legislation did not apply for the trial. The Privy Council held that it was invalid, as it eroded judicial power. It was, in the words of Lord Edward Pearce (1901–90)[11], 'it was a grave and deliberate incursion into the judicial sphere'. What really troubled the Privy Council was that Parliament was more or less taking over characteristic functions of the courts, determining guilt or innocence and prescribing the offenders' sentence. It is worth noting that the judges remained independent, and indeed acquitted some of the defendants. But independence of the judiciary diminishes if the courts lose some of their significant functions.

What are judicial functions? There are no easy answers to this question. In the United Kingdom, as in other countries, many decisions which could be left to the courts are allocated by statutes to tribunals/courts and administrative authorities. For example, this is the position with regard to the award of social and other welfare benefits, the grant of planning permission, and the issue of a wide range of licenses and permits. There are good reasons for allocating such decisions to specialist institutions; they are more able than the ordinary courts to handle a large number of applications informally, speedily, and cheaply. However, the High Court ensures that tribunals/courts and administrative authorities work within the scope of their powers and act fairly, in some cases requiring them to follow procedures similar to those that the courts have developed in criminal and civil cases. In particular, they are unwilling to hold that Parliament has excluded their power of judicial review even when that seems to be what the statute intended.

In the *Anisminic* case, a landmark decisions in modern administrative law, the House of Lords ruled that it was entitled to review the legality of decisions of the Foreign Compensation Commission 1950, even though the legislation which set-up the Commission had expressly provided that decisions 'shall not be called in question in any court of law.'[12] Yet, on a literal interpretation of these words in the statute the judges had no business reviewing the Commission's decision.

Although, the ground of judicial review at issue in the *Anisminic* case, constitutes a part of administrative law, the right of the courts to intervene is fundamentally based on constitutional principles, among them the separation of powers. That doctrine requires that independent courts have the final power to resolve decisions on questions of law especially in particular cases, even when, as frequently happens, Parliament provides that the initial decision is taken by an administrative tribunal, such as the Foreign Compensation Commission 1950, or by some other authority.

Moreover, traditionally some types of cases, for example, criminal prosecutions and civil actions for damages, are determined by the courts. It would make no sense of having a separate independent judicial power for these cases to be allocated to administrative authorities or tribunals, closely linked with the executive. In the United Kingdom, the 'separation of power' doctrine gives way to the principle of parliamentary legislative supremacy thus, a statute could confer these powers on other institutions and provide that they could not be reviewed by the ordinary courts. But even then, in the United Kingdom, access to the courts is regarded as a constitutional right.

The *Anisminic* case and many others show that judges in the United Kingdom would disregard a statute which, on its plain meaning, would appear to exclude such access. The courts give prominence to this right for a sound constitutional reason, the crucial importance of preserving judicial power as a check on the other branches of government.[13]

Comparative Analysis of Judicial Independence

As stated earlier, all written Constitutions invariably contain provisions to guarantee judicial independence in a variety of ways. These provisions provide for:

(a) The appointment procedure;
(b) Security of tenures and other related issues like salary etc.;
(c) Removal procedure.

The German Basic Law (*Grundgesetz*) states the appointment stage principle quite explicitly:

> '[t]he judges shall be independent and subject only to the law.'[14]

However, it is probably of more value to ensure, in so far as this is possible, that the appointments process does not give rise to a politically biased bench of judges, and that they are free from political pressure. A number of different procedures can be adopted to neutralize the part inevitably played by political pressure in the appointment stage. In order to deal with this particular stage different procedures have been adopted:

(a) The power of appointment is vested in the Executive;
(b) The power of appointment is vested both in Executive and Legislature;

(c) The power of appointment is vested in a shared Commission comprising all three branches of the government i.e. Executive, Legislature, and Judiciary.

In the United States, the President nominates the judges of the Supreme Court and other federal judges, but their appointment may be blocked by the Senate. This procedure gives senators the opportunity to examine whether the candidate has the right qualifications to sit on the Court, or have the judges been nominated by the President to carry out his political agenda. In 1987, President Ronald Reagan's[15] nomination of Judge Robert Bork (1927–2012)[16], was blocked by the Senate, because of fears that Judge Bork was committed to a conservative political programme, which he intended to discharge on the Supreme Court.

In contrast, European constitutions usually attempt to ensure a balanced court by provisions excluding monopoly rights to nominate its members. For example, the French constitution provides that three members of the Constitutional Council[17] are to be appointed by the President of the Republic, three by the President of the National Assembly, and three by the President of the Senate. Furthermore, a third of the Council's membership is to be replaced every three years. Unless, one party gains controls both the Presidency and the legislature over a sustained period, there is little chance that all members of the Council will be chosen by representatives of one party.

It is obvious that political factors have influenced the nomination procedure, most notoriously when President François Mitterrand (1919–96)[18] chose the Minister of Justice, Robert Badinter (1928)[19], as President of the Council, shortly before the expected Socialist defeat in the 1986 Elections, after which, it was rightly anticipated that the majority of new appointments would be made by Gaullists.

Also, in Germany, appointments to the *Bundesverfassungsgericht* (Federal Constitutional Court)[20] are highly political. But, balance is ensured to some extent by the provision that half its members are elected by a committee of the *Bundestag* (Federal Assembly),[21] and half by the *Bundesrat* (Federal Council)[22] composed of representatives of the *Lander* (State).[23] The Federal Constitutional Court Statute requires a judge to be elected by either two-thirds of the *Bundesrat* Committee or two-thirds of the votes in the *Bundestag*. Apparently, a rule which in effect enables the opposition to bargain with the government, since it can always block the latter's favoured candidate.

There were no provisions of this character in the United Kingdom. The English High Court and Circuit judges were appointed by the Lord Chancellor, a member of the Cabinet, while the Lords Justice of Appeal who sat in the Court of Appeal, and the judges in the House of Lords were chosen by the Prime Minister. (In practice the Lord Chancellor also used to exercise great influence in their appointment as well.) It is difficult to mount a principled defense of the government's monopoly power of appointment, which was exercised in private, without public scrutiny. This situation has changed drastically under the Constitutional Reforms of 2005 in the United Kingdom.

Under the doctrine of separation of powers, no person should exercise more than one of the three functions of government, also called the separation of person's principle. Viscount Gavin Simonds (1881–1971)[24] said in a Privy Council ruling on the separation of powers in Australia,

> '[t]o vest in the same body executive and judicial power is to remove a vital constitutional safeguard'.[25]

Obviously, it would be wrong for a minister or MP to sit as a judge. This is a standard constitutional rule, sometimes described as the 'incompatibility principle'. But there are awkward questions about the scope: is it, for example, a breach of the principle for a judge to preside over a commission of inquiry into a major accident or industrial dispute, as frequently occurs in the United Kingdom?

In Germany, the principle is taken to extreme lengths. Constitutional Court judges are precluded from doing any other work, apart from teaching at a German university. In this respect the British arrangements are less restrictive. For a start, the position of the Lord Chancellor is a constitutional anomaly. He is a member of the Cabinet, has responsibility for appointing senior judges, is Speaker of the House of Lords as a legislative body, and would sit as a member of the Lords in its role as final appeal court. In short, he could participate in all three branches of government, a flagrant breach of the incompatibility principle. Admittedly, in practice most Lord Chancellors rarely sat as judges. It would certainly be regarded as shocking for him to do this in a politically sensitive case as distinct from one involving points of private law. But it was not clear that there was a convention forbidding him to sit as a judge in an appeal to the House of Lords on a question of constitutional law.[26]

It is a common practice, that judges preside over Royal Commissions or commissions of inquiry... The obvious reason for such an appointment is the reputation of impartiality of English judges. The majority of the public and politicians, however, are happy to accept the myth, more so because there is a strong element of truth in the concept, even if it is not easily defined.[27] In such circumstances, they are performing broadly executive, policy-making functions, albeit in an advisory capacity.

Another difficulty arose when Law Lords exercised their freedom to speak in debates in the House of Lords on topics such as sentencing, reform of the legal profession, or the desirability of incorporating the European Convention on Human Rights (ECHR) into British law. On certain occasions, the Law Lords had spoken on political issues, most notoriously when in 1922, Lord Edward Carson (1854–1935)[28] campaigned both in and outside the House of Lords against the Irish Free State Bill. These practices were contrary to the principle of 'separation of powers'. They are in conflict with a strict, incompatibility rule, and would be unconstitutional in Germany. They infringe 'separation of powers' doctrine which asserts that each branch of government has only one function and must stick rigidly to its discharge.

In contrast, arrangements for the payment of judicial salaries do raise questions about judicial independence and the balance of powers between the branches of government. The question was raised with commendable frankness by Alexander Hamilton in the *Federalist Papers*.

> 'Next to permanency in office, nothing can contribute more to the independence of the judges than a fixed provision for their support. In the general course of human nature, a power over a man's subsistence amounts to a power over his will'.[29]

So, he argued that the United States Constitution prohibits the diminishing of judicial salaries.

It is difficult to present the history of this topic in the United Kingdom in a sympathetic light. The salaries were fixed by an Act of Parliament, but were not increased from 1832 until 1954. In the early 1930s, the judges were briefly required to take a cut in their salaries under the National Economy Act, 1933. Whatever the merits of this reduction during economic crises, there is a clear constitutional objection to the ability of the legislature, in effect the government, to lower judicial salaries.

However, salary arrangements are less crucial to the independence of the judiciary than its security of tenure. Judges should be appointed for a reasonable length of time and be protected against arbitrary removal by a government. At one extreme is the position in the United States, where judges hold office 'during good behaviour' without any retirement age. Life tenancy certainly gives security, but it also creates the risk that judges may stay in post when their best years are over.

Some US Supreme Court judges, notably Chief Justice William Howard Taft (1857–1930) and later William J. Brennan Jr. (1906–97) and Thurgood Marshall (1903–93) remained on the Supreme Court, largely to prevent the President replacing them with judges of a different constitutional perspective. This was a factor in the notorious Court-packing controversy in the United States in the 1930s. President Roosevelt was confronted by a Supreme Court dominated by conservative judges, most of them over 70 years old who had in a series of cases held much of the New Deal welfare legislation unconstitutional. The President introduced a Bill which would have increased the size of the Court from nine to fifteen judges. This was considered a threat to the Court's independence, and the crisis only abated when the US Supreme Court began to adopt a more sympathetic attitude to New Deal legislation, which was famously referred to as 'switch-in-time that saved nine'.

In Germany, the arrangements for security of tenure are quite different. The Federal Constitutional Court judges are appointed for a term of 12 years, without any possibility of renewal. This has the disadvantage of limiting the contribution that a great judge may be able to make to the development of constitutional law, but it is certainly a long enough period to establish judicial independence. In contrast to the United States Constitution, the judges may only be dismissed, suspended, or given a different position by a judicial decision.[30] It is hard to imagine a more secure guarantee of their independence than that.

In the United Kingdom, the senior judiciary hold office 'during good behaviour', as in the United States, but could be removed by the Crown upon an address of both House of Parliament. That is the situation since the Act of Settlement 1701. The general view is that by constitutional convention an address of both Houses is necessary for a High Court (or other senior) judges to be dismissed, and it is only appropriate to take this step for gross misconduct in office. Once an address has been passed, it is doubtful that the Crown could constitutionally refuse to act on it. It is also unlikely that the courts would be prepared to intervene by judicial review. However, the government is most unlikely to allow time in Parliament for an address to be debated unless it favours dismissal.

A motion in 1973, supported by 187 Labour Members of Parliament for an address to remove Sir John Donaldson (1920–2005), the first President of the National Industrial Relation Court (NIRC)[31], was never debated. The Speaker was reluctant to allow criticism of individual judges outside a formal motion and became difficult for Members of Parliament to criticize judges in the House of Commons itself. Donaldson eventually became Master of the Rolls.

The independence of the judiciary in the United Kingdom, as in other genuine constitutional democracies, is not much of a problem. But in the United Kingdom this is largely due to convention and practice, rather than a requirement of constitutional law, which exists in Germany and the United States.[32]

Independence of Judiciary in USA

The principle of 'judicial independence' appears in several sections of the Declaration of Independence of 1776. Following the War of Independence (1775–83), several American colonies included tenure and salary provisions in their Constitutions to secure judicial independence.[33]

Article III of the American Constitution created a separate judicial branch. It required that

> The judges, both of the Supreme Court and the inferior courts, Shall hold their offices during good behavior, and shall, at stated Times, receive for their Services, a Compensation, which shall not be diminished during their Continuance in Office.

The Constitution vests the judicial power of the United States

> 'in one Supreme Court, and in such inferior Courts as the Congress may from time to time ordain and establish'.

The Judiciary Act of 1789 provided for a Chief Justice and 5 Associate Judges for the Supreme Court. It divided the United States into 13 districts, with a federal judge for each district, and created 3 Circuits to handle appellate cases; the eastern, middle and southern Circuits. The Judiciary Act of 1801 divided the country into 6 Circuits and reduced the number of Supreme Court Justices from 6 to 5.[34] In 1802, the Congress passed legislation to repeal the Judiciary Act of 1801 abolishing, in effect, 16 Circuit judges and their salaries.

In 1803, *Stuart v. Laird* was a case challenging the right of Congress to abolish the Circuit Courts, but the US Supreme Court, declined to overturn the statute.[35] The US Supreme Court held that the Congress had constitutional authority to establish, from time to time, such inferior tribunals as they may think proper; and to transfer a case from one such tribunal to another and therefore there are no words in the Constitution to prohibit or restrain the exercise of legislative power.

The size of the Supreme Court fluctuated throughout the 19th century, keeping pace with the addition of new circuits. A 7th Justice was added in 1807, after creation of a new judicial circuit. In 1837, the strength of the Supreme Court rose to 9 reflecting the westward expansion, and to 10 by 1863. Three years later in 1866, the Congress lowered the permanent number of judges of the Court to 7, although the membership was never below 8. In 1869, legislation brought the Court's back to its present strength of 9 members.[36]

The Appointment Process

The delegates at the Constitutional Convention in Philadelphia, condemned the British system of executive appointment, associating it with official corruption and debasement of judiciary. At first, they placed the power to select judges with Congress. Next, they considered vesting that responsibility solely in the Senate. Only late in the convention did they settle on joint action by the President and the United States Senate.[37] Under Article II, Section 2 of the US Constitution,

> 'and the [the President] shall nominate, and by and with the Advice and Consent of the Senate, shall appoint......... judges of the Supreme Court'.

The nomination by the President and confirmation of the Senate has created an intensely political process. Senators have throughout wielded considerable power in choosing nominees for federal judgeships. Other sectors of the government have been active and even private organizations have participated. The American Bar Association (ABA) plays a key role and has established a special committee to judge the professional qualifications of candidates nominated. The US Senate Committee on the Judiciary, which holds the hearing of the nominees before vote of confirmation, relies heavily on the American Bar Association evaluation.

The Senate has refused to confirm almost one out of every five presidential nominations to the Supreme Court. 25 nominees have either been rejected, had their names submitted without Senate action, or been forced to withdraw.[38] Most of these actions (18) occurred before 1900. After 1900, the rejection of nominees has been less frequent. In 1930, John J. Parker (1885–1958)[39] was rejected. In 1968, President Lyndon Johnson (1908–73)[40] was forced to withdraw the nomination of Abe Fortas (1910–82)[41] for the position of Chief Justice to succeed Earl Warren (1891–1974)[42]. In 1969, the Senate, rejected two Supreme Court nominees of President Richard Nixon, namely Clement F. Haynsworth Jr (1912–89)[43], and George Harrold Carswell (1919–92)[44]. In 1987, two nominees of President Ronald Reagan (1911-2004)[45], namely Robert H. Bork (1927–2012) was rejected by the Senate, and Douglas H. Ginsburg (1946)[46] was forced to be withdrawn. The nomination of Clarence Thomas (1948), an Afro American, was barely approved by the Senate by close vote of 52 to 48. However, President Bill Clinton's nominees encountered little opposition. Ruth Bader Ginsburg (1933–2020) was confirmed by a vote of 96 to 3; and Stephen Breyer (1938) by a vote of 87 to 9.[47] The latest appointees of the Donald Trump (1946)[48], Neil Gorsuch (1967)[49], Brett Kavanaugh (1965)[50] and Amy Coney Barrett (1972)[51] were voted for confirmation with a thin margin of 54–45, 50–48, and 52–48 respectively.

Tenure and Removal

Under Article III of the US Constitution, judges 'both of the Supreme and inferior Courts, shall hold their offices during good behaviour'. Article I gives the House of Representatives the sole power of impeachment and the Senate has the sole power to try all impeachments. A two-third majority of the Senate is required for conviction. Judges may be removed from office 'on impeachment for, and conviction of, treason, bribery, or other high crimes and misdemeanors.' Thus, the federal judges serve for life unless impeached and removed.

The impeachment process is cumbersome and suitable only for grave offenses. There are therefore, very few examples of removal of judges. The first example of a federal judge impeached and removed from office occurred in 1803 in the case of Judge John Pickering.[52] He was charged with misconduct in a trial and for being on the bench while intoxicated. Actions were brought against a number of other federal judges, many of whom preferred to resign from office rather than defend themselves against the charges.[53]

In 1973, Judge Otto Kerner Jr (1908–76)[54], of the Seventh Circuit was found guilty of bribery, perjury, tax evasion, and other crimes, most of which occurred during his previous service as Governor of Illinois. On appeal, Kerner argued that the Constitution provides only one way to remove a judge; impeachment. The Seventh Circuit decided that judicial immunity does not exempt judges from the operation of criminal laws and affirmed his conviction. In 1984, US District Judge Harry Claiborne (1917–2004)[55] was found guilty of income tax evasion. Two years later, he was impeached and removed. In 1986, US District Judge Walter L. Nixon Jr (1928)[56] of Mississippi was convicted of lying to a federal jury; in 1989 he was impeached and removed.[57] Walter L. Nixon Jr brought an action claiming that his conviction in the Senate was void because he was not granted a trial before full Senate. Instead, he was examined by a 12 member Senate Committee. In 1993, the Supreme Court held that the Senate had sole discretion to choose the procedure to be used for impeachment, including the use of a Committee to take testimony and gather evidence.[58]

There is no instance of a Supreme Court Justice being removed from office. Samuel Chase (1741–1811)[59] was impeached in 1804, but, was acquitted. In 1969, with impeachment proceedings gearing up against him amidst charges of financial and personal improprieties, Judge Abe Fortas resigned as Judge of the Supreme Court.[60]

Independence of Judiciary in the United Kingdom

For proper exercise of judicial power, 'independence of judiciary' is a pre-requisite and no meaningful exercise of judicial power can occur, unless judges feel secure to exercise their judicial functions.

One of the most significant principles of British constitutional law is the independence of the judiciary from the interference by the executive. In order to secure personal, substantive and institutional independence, following factors may be taken into consideration:

(i) the tenure of the judicial office,
(ii) the manner in which judges may be removed,
(iii) Judicial impartiality, and
(iv) Judicial immunity.

(i) *Tenure of judicial office*

A compulsory retiring age of 75 was fixed for Lords of Appeal in Ordinary, and judges of the Supreme Court appointed after 1959.[61] Beyond that age, retired judges, may, however be asked to sit from time to time under the Supreme Court Act, 1981. Circuit judges were judges of the superior court because they sat in the Crown Court of England and Wales, which was a superior court of record.[62] They also sat in the County Court (England and Wales), which was not a superior court. They could be removed by the Lord Chancellor 'on the ground of incapacity or misbehaviour'.[63] They were subject to retiring at the age of 72; except that the Lord Chancellor could in the public interest let them continue in office up to the age of 75.[64] The Lord Chancellor could terminate the appointment of a Recorder on the ground of incapacity or misbehavior or for failure to comply with the terms of his appointment.[65]

(ii) *Procedure for removal*

Judges of the High Court and the Court of Appeal held their offices 'during good behaviour' subject to a power of removal by the King, on an address presented to him by both Houses of Parliament. And under the Appellate Jurisdiction Act 1876,

> 'every Lord of Appeal in Ordinary shall hold his office during good behaviour ... but he may be removed from such office on the address of both Houses of Parliament.'

Such an address must be introduced in the House of Commons. Many Commonwealth countries prescribed a more judicial procedure for the removal of judges, in some cases involving a reference to the Judicial Committee of the Privy Council.

The words 'during good behaviour', used in the British Act 1876, implies that, if, in consequence of misbehavior in respect of his office or from any other cause, an officer of state holding on this tenure has forfeited the confidence of the two Houses, he may be removed, although the Crown would not otherwise have been disposed or entitled to remove him. Such officer's hold as regards the Crown, during good behaviour, as regards Parliament, also during good behaviour through the two Houses could extend the term so as to cover any form of misconduct which would destroy public confidence in the holder of the office. The Crown could remove without an address for official misconduct, neglect of official duties, or (probably) conviction for a serious offence. The Queen would be bound by convention to act on an address from both Houses.[66]

The judges are not 'servants' of the Crown because they are not subject to the orders of the Crown as to the manner in which they shall discharge their duties. One of the hallmarks of the independence of the English judiciary is that they have no duty to advise the executive on cases that do not come before the courts in ordinary course of litigation. But such a duty does not necessarily impair the independence of the court is shown by the fact that it exists in many constitutions, including some in the Commonwealth, and also in the case of the Judicial Committee.

Under Article 186 of the 1973 Constitution of Pakistan, the President may refer any question of law to the Supreme Court for obtaining its opinion. The Supreme Court has to consider the question so referred and report its opinion to the President.

(iii) *Judicial impartiality*

In the administration of justice, the impartiality of the judiciary is considered as the most important element of the 'independence of judiciary'. The impartiality can be achieved by the following factors:—

(a) The judges should not take part in political controversy. For this, the rules have been adopted governing activities of judges outside their courts not only in England but also in other countries.
(b) The judges should be free from personal interest or bias in the cases before them.
(c) The judges should hear both parties to the dispute.
(d) As held in *Scott v. Scott*[67] it is not sufficient that justice be done, but it must be seen to be done and as held in *Home Office v. Harman*[68] 'proceedings in open court ensure that justice is done and is seen to be done and that the public may not be able to ponder whether justice has been done'. Therefore, one of the chief safeguards of the impartial administration of justice lies in the right of the public and the press to be present in the Court.

(iv) *Judicial Immunity*

The absolute privilege accorded by the law of defamation to those taking part in judicial proceedings extends to magistrates as well as judges. Judges are exempt from civil or criminal liability for things done or said while acting within their jurisdiction, even if done maliciously and without reasonable or probable cause.[69] Judges of superior courts are apparently not liable for judicial acts done outside their jurisdiction.[70]

Constitutional Reforms in the United Kingdom

Introduction

Change is a permanent phenomenon and even the most conservative societies are bound to change to keep up with the world. The United Kingdom is considered one of the most conservative societies. When the time for change came, its policy makers abided by the rules of change. The United Kingdom did not have a written constitution, there being no single document that could be called the United Kingdom Constitution.[71] The United Kingdom has recently introduced radical changes in its existing constitutional system in respect of the Judiciary through a written document called the Constitutional Reform Act, 2005. It received the Royal Assent on 24 March 2005. These Reforms became operative from October 2009. These reforms have been introduced due to the integration of the UK with the European Union, and partly due to the reasons of constitutional practices and working of the UK Constitution during the past several decades which required reforms for the smooth working of the constitution. Some of the constitutional practices introduced through the Act of 2005 were already part of the United Kingdom Constitution, in the form of conventions but they were not enforceable being only conventions.

Overview

In order to understand the true scope of United Kingdom Judicial Reforms, it is necessary to review the judicial system. Under the pre-reform constitutional scheme, the office of the Lord Chancellor was the most central office in the Judicial hierarchy. The office of the Lord Chancellor had its origin from the time of Norman Conquest (1066), when the King's secretary became known as the royal 'chancellor'. The first Chancellor is recorded in 1068. In the Middle Ages, the primary role of the Chancellor was to preside over Parliament. From the 14th century, his functions became both parliamentary and judicial and in the latter role presiding over the Court of Chancery until 1875.

Prior to the Constitutional Reforms Act 2005, the office of the Lord Chancellor spanned all three institutions of the state—executive, legislature and judiciary. The Lord Chancellor was a politically appointed member of the Cabinet, the Speaker of the House of Lords and head of the judiciary. Furthermore, as senior judge, the Lord Chancellor was entitled to participate in judicial proceedings, although by convention he would not adjudicate cases, which involved the government or were overtly political in nature. As a head of the judiciary, with wide-ranging powers relating to the appointment of judges, the Lord Chancellor acted as the spokesperson for the judges and defended their independence from the executive.[72]

At the apex of the UK Judicial system was the House of Lords which was the highest court of appeal. In this capacity, it exercised the ancient jurisdiction of High Court of Parliament. The Appellate Jurisdiction Act 1876, provided for the appointments of 2 (which was increased to t12) Lords of Appeal in Ordinary, life peers who have right of audience in all proceedings in the Supreme Court. They retired at the age of 75.[73] The House used to entertain civil and criminal appeals, with leave of itself or the court below, from the Court of Appeal. It also heard appeals from the Court-Martial Appeal Court in certain cases direct from the Divisional Court of the Queen Bench's Division and individual High Court judges under restrictive conditions. It also exercised civil but not criminal appellate jurisdiction in respect of the Scottish courts and heard both civil and criminal appeals from Northern Ireland.[74]

The Supreme Court of Judicature consisted of the Court of Appeal, the High Court and the Crown Court. The Court of Appeal had 2 divisions, civil and criminal: It was presided over by Master of Rolls, and had up to 35 Lord Justices of Appeal who sat in a bench of 2 or 3. The Lord Chief Justice presided in one court of Criminal Division; other High Court judges are often called to hear criminal appeals, but, less frequently to hear civil appeals. Civil Appeals on the civil side mostly lie from the county courts and the High Court; the court could be leapfrogged and an appeal raising a point of law of exceptional difficulty or importance calling for reconsideration of a binding precedent might with the leave of the House of Lords, lie direct from the High Court to the Lords.

The High Court sat in 3 divisions:

(1) Queen's Bench Division,
(2) the Chancery;
(3) and the Family Divisions.

In 1971, the Family Division replaced the Probate, Divorce and Admiralty Division. On appointment a judge was assigned to one of the 3 divisions. The Lord Chief Justice presided in the Queen's Bench Division. The Lord Chancellor, who never sat, was nominally, President of the Chancery Division; and there was Vice-Chancellor, who was also a Chancery judge; and there was a President of the Family Division. The maximum number of other High Court judges (called puisne judges) were around 100. The original civil jurisdiction of the High Courts was unlimited as to amount and persons but subject to the territorial jurisdiction. The High Court also had appellate and supervisory jurisdiction in relation to inferior tribunals.

The Constitutional Reform Act 2005, (hereinafter called the Act), modified the office of Lord Chancellor. It also introduced changes to the way in which some of the functions vested in Lord Chancellor's office are to be exercised. The Act also creates the Supreme Court of the United Kingdom and abolishes the appellate jurisdiction of the House of Lords. It established the Judicial Appointments Commission to select persons for judicial appointments in England and Wales, and provides for judicial discipline in England and Wales. The Act modifies the jurisdiction of the Judicial Committee of the Privy Council and removes the right of the Lord President of the Council to sit judicially.

The main focus of these constitutional reforms in the Judicial branch, relates particularly to the reforms introduced in the process of appointment of Judges. The selection process has traditionally been shrouded in mystery, with records of eligible candidates, who in practice would be successful practitioners, being maintained by the Lord Chancellor's Department. It had long been argued that the appointment of judges should be made by an independent Judicial Appointment Commission rather than on the recommendation of the Lord Chancellor.

The Act has finally brought about reforms and for the first time, an Appointment Commission has been introduced for the selection of judges of the Superior Courts. It may be mentioned here that the idea of judicial appointment commission was introduced by the South African Constitution.[75] The following are some of the significant reforms introduced by the Act.

Part of the Act provides that the Act does not adversely affect the 'Rule of Law' or the Lord Chancellor's role in relation to that principle.

It has been guaranteed that there would be continued judicial independence in the United Kingdom.[76] The Ministers of the Crown (including the Lord Chancellor) have been made responsible to uphold the continued independence of judiciary. A duty has been cast on Ministers of the Crown not to seek the influence particular judicial decisions through any special access to the judiciary. The Lord Chancellor is required to have regard to the need to defend continued independence of the judiciary, the need for the judiciary to have proper support necessary to enable them to exercise their functions, and the need for the public interest in matters relating to the judiciary or otherwise to the administration of justice to be properly represented in decisions affecting those matters.

The Act establishes the Supreme Court of United Kingdom and sets out the composition of the Supreme Court.[77] It also sets out the method of appointing judges, including the president and deputy president. It also provides for the title of the judges of the Supreme Court other than the president and deputy president. The court comprises of 12 judges, who are to be appointed by Her Majesty by letters patent. Her Majesty may, also by letters patent, appoint one of the judges to be president and one to be deputy president. It will be possible for a person to be appointed as president or deputy president without having first served as a judge of the Supreme Court. Her Majesty has power to increase or further increase the number of judges of the Supreme Court by an Order in Council. This may only be done, however, if a draft of the Order has been laid before and approved by each House of Parliament (that is, by affirmative resolution procedure). The judges of the Supreme Court other than the President of the Supreme Court and the Deputy President of the Supreme Court (who will have those titles) are styled 'Justices of the Supreme Court'. The court will still be properly constituted even if there is a vacancy among the judges of the court or in the office of president or deputy president.

The Act provides for eligibility for appointment as a judge of the Supreme Court which would be the same as eligibility for appointment as a Lord of Appeal in ordinary.[78] There are 2 separate modes of qualifications for appointment as a judge of the Supreme Court. In the first place a person is eligible if he has held high judicial office for at least two years. Alternatively, for appointment as a Supreme Court judge a person would have to have been a qualified legal practitioner for at least 15 years.

The Act has provided for a Selection Commission for appointment of judges to the Supreme Court. The Selection Commission consists of the President of the Supreme Court (who chairs the Commission), the Deputy President of the Supreme Court and one member from each of the territorial appointing Commission, one of whom must be a person who is not legally qualified.[79] The Commission would stand dissolved when the Lord Chancellor notifies the selection made by the Commission. This means that when selection of a person by the Commission is accepted by the Lord Chancellor and the Lord Chancellor notifies the Prime Minister for recommendation of that person for appointment the Commission is resolved being *functus officio*.[80]

It is provided that the selection of judges must be made solely on merit. However, the task of setting out the criteria against which merit will be tested lies with the Selection Commission. A member of the commission cannot be selected. During the selection process, the Commission has to consult the senior judges who are not on the Commission or willing to be considered for selection, the Lord Chancellor, the First Minister in Scotland, the Assembly's First Secretary in Wales, the Secretary of State for Northern Island.[81] The Lord Chancellor has the option to either accept the recommendation or ask the Commission to reconsider or reject the recommendation.[82] If the Lord Chancellor asks the Selection Commission to reconsider and after reconsideration the Commission can still put forward the same name with further reasons or recommend an alternative and the Lord Chancellor can then put forward either of the recommended candidates for appointment to the Prime Minister.

The judges of the Supreme Court held office while they are of good behaviour. They can only be removed from office following resolutions passed by both the Houses of the Parliament. The judges can resign from their office or they would be retired at the age of 70 provided under the Judicial Pensions and Retirement Act 1993.[83]

The Supreme Court sits in panels. The basic rule for composition of panels is that an odd number of judges equal to or greater than 3 must be designated to hear any proceedings—there is no flexibility to designate an even number of judges.[84] Given that an odd number must be designated, permanent judges have to be in the majority in order to ensure that the composition is never wholly or predominantly of non-permanent judges. In case, a panel is reduced in number (for example due to death or illness) before the end of proceedings, the presiding judge may direct that the court is still duly constituted. In the event, the court may continue with an even number of judges;

and if it does, and the judges are divided evenly in their decisions, the case must then be re-argued before a court constituted with odd number of judges.[85]

The Lord Chancellor to have a power, by order to prescribe the fees payable in respect of any matter dealt with by the Supreme Court. This includes a power to exempt, remit or reduce fees, and to specify the criteria by which exemptions, reductions and remissions are to operate. The exercise of the power to prescribe fees is, subject to a duty on the Lord Chancellor to have regard to the principle that access to the courts should not be denied. The exercise of the power is also subject to a requirement of prior consultation with the president and deputy president of the new Supreme Court and the senior judiciary in each of the three jurisdictions of the United Kingdom, and the principal legal professional bodies in those jurisdictions.

The Act creates a new independent Judicial Appointments Commission, which has assumed responsibility for the process of selecting people for judicial appointments in England and Wales and for those appointments to tribunals across UK made by the Lord Chancellor. The Judicial Appointments Commission will select one candidate for each vacancy and report that selection to the Lord Chancellor. The Lord Chancellor will either appoint or recommend for appointment the selected candidate, or will have the option to reject a candidate, once, and to ask the Commission to reconsider, once. Having exhausted these options, the Lord Chancellor must appoint or recommend for appointment the selected candidate. The Act makes special provision for the appointment of the Lord Chief Justice and Heads of Division and of Lords Justices of Appeal; in these cases, the Commission will establish a selection panel of 4 members, consisting of 2 senior judges (normally including the Lord Chief Justice) and 2 lay members of the Commission.

Schedule 12 sets out the membership of the Judicial Appointments Commission, and its powers and responsibilities, which will reflect its status as an Executive Non-Departmental Public Body. There will be a lay Chairman and 5 other lay members, 5 judicial members, 2 legal professionals, a tribunal member and a lay magistrate. They will be supported by a Chief Executive and staff. The Act requires that selections for judicial appointment shall be made solely on merit. In addition, the Commission has a statutory duty to have regard to the need to encourage diversity in the range of persons available for selection. The Lord Chancellor will be able to issue guidance to the Selection Commission, which they must have regard for, but the detailed appointments procedures they will follow are a matter for them, and not prescribed in the Act. Guidance can only be issued after consultation with the Lord Chief Justice and after being approved in draft by both Houses of Parliament.

- That judges of the High Court and above can only be removed by the Queen on an Address from both Houses of Parliament.
- Schedule 12 of the Act sets out the size and balance of the Judicial Appointments Commission. The Commission consists of a chairman and 14 other Commissioners, to be appointed by The Queen on the recommendation of the Lord Chancellor. Paragraph 2 provides for the chairman to be a lay member. Of the other Commissioners, 5 must be judicial members, 2 must be professional members, 5 must be lay members, 1 other must be the holder of an office listed in Part 3 of Schedule 12 (which lists members of tribunals and other similar office holders who will be appointed by the Lord Chancellor), and 1 other must be a lay justice member. The judicial members must be made up of one Lord Justice of Appeal, one puisne judge of the High Court, one judge who is either a Lord Justice of Appeal or a puisne judge of the High Court, one Circuit Judge and one District Judge or a person appointed to an office under section 89 of the Supreme Court Act 1981 The two professional members must be a practising barrister and a practising solicitor. A Commissioner only counts towards the total in the category to which he was appointed, so that a lay member, for example, does not become a professional member if he qualifies as a practitioner. Paragraph 3 specifies that a person cannot be appointed as a Commissioner if he is a civil servant. This is to ensure that the Commission is not subject to any covert or improper Governmental influence. Paragraph 4 details what is meant by judicial, professional, lay and lay justice member. A judicial member holds one of the offices specified in paragraph 2(3) (set out above) and is not a practising lawyer (defined in paragraph 6 as a practising solicitor or barrister in England and Wales, a solicitor or advocate in Scotland and a Solicitor or member of the Bar in Northern Ireland which includes those employed to give legal advice or providing legal advice under a contract for services). A professional member is a barrister or solicitor practising in England and Wales (again further defined in paragraph 6 to include employed lawyers and those who give legal advice under a contract for

services). A lay member is an England and Wales resident who has never been a holder of a listed judicial office or a practising lawyer. The Lord Chancellor to increase the size of the Commission, by increasing the size of any or all of the different categories of Commissioner. He can do this by order, but only with the agreement of the Lord Chief Justice, and subject to affirmative resolution in both Houses of Parliament This is to prevent a Lord Chancellor seeking improperly to influence selections by altering the balance of the Commission in one direction or another at his own unchecked discretion.

Independence of Judiciary in India

Introduction

Modern Indian judiciary was structured by the British between the end of the 18th and the middle of the 20th century. Various branches of Indian law, apart from modern constitutional law, were developed and defined on the basis of the British model. This transformation of the traditional normative system emerges as one of the most remarkable achievements of the history of inter-cultural relations, comparable to the revolutionary legal structures devised by the Romans to administer the regions they had conquered.

Adapting the British system of law to one suitable for India presented several difficulties. The cultural traditions were different as were the different ways of thinking. An Indian was primarily a member of a particular caste or religion, and, could therefore be scarcely regarded as an autonomous being, while the British legal system was generally premised on the individual. Added to this problem was India's size, which often led to difficulties of various kinds, because it was not conducive to a unified, inflexible legal structure.

In spite of these and several similar problems, it is remarkable how the Indian legal elite have not only succeeded in preserving an admirable judicial system, as the most anglicized of Indian institutions, but at the same time, it had been developed and revitalized, to play a crucial role in developing social and political life of the country. Several judges who served the judiciary contributed immeasurably to its achievements.

The Indian judicial journey initially commenced with the Letters Patent High Courts, at the Presidency towns[86] of Calcutta, Madras and Bombay, and, then at other places like Allahabad and Lahore. Appeals would lie to the Privy Council against the decisions of the said High Courts under the Privy Council Act 1833. After the Government of India Act 1935 came into force, a Federal Court was created, and the Privy Council was granted Appellate jurisdiction. The Federal Court of India, supervised by the Privy Council, continued till 1950, and was succeeded by the Supreme Court of India, after India adopted its constitution in January 1950.

The US Supreme Court and Britain's House of Lords served as models for the Supreme Court of India. Various principles and concepts that had been developed by the English and American Courts, served as a point of reference for the Indian Supreme Court and furnished the jurisprudential basis for ruling on cases in India, necessarily tempered and adapted to the prevalent conditions.

After Independence, India was intensely political, with economic development high on the national agenda, with diverse ideas as to the direction and form of such development. The Indian Constitution conferred vital responsibility on the Indian Supreme Court to act as the apex adjudicator of disputes and the fountain-head of jurisprudence. In the judicial sphere it was accountable to none, except for the limitations it imposed on itself.

The judiciary in India has throughout sought to be a defender of the rights of the people against excesses of the executive. When the executive was weak or negligent, the courts were obliged to step in to ensure that the urgent needs of the people were met.[87]

Appointment process in India

The Supreme Court of India is the apex court in India established under the Constitution. It consists of the Chief Justice of India, and, as many judges prescribed by law passed by the Indian Parliament.[88] The Chief Justice is appointed by the President of India. While other judges of the Supreme Court are appointed by the Indian President; after consultation with the Chief Justice and such other judges of the Supreme Court as the President may deem necessary for the purpose.[89] The Supreme Court has original jurisdiction in the cases of enforcement of fundamental rights.[90]

There is provision of High Courts for each state or group of states in the Union of India. They are highest courts of appeal in the states and appeal against their decisions lies to the Supreme Court of India. It has original Constitutional jurisdiction in the matter of prerogative writs and enforcement of fundamental rights.[91] High Courts are courts of record. Each High Court consists of a Chief Justice and as many other judges which the President may deem necessary to appoint.[92] Every judge of a High Court is appointed by the President; after consultation with the Chief Justice of India and the State Governor, and, in case of appointment of a judge other than the Chief Justice, the Chief Justice of the High Court.[93]

The Supreme Court of India, while interpreting the provisions of the Constitution regarding appointment of judges, held that the consultation/opinion of the Chief Justice of India and the Chief Justice of the High Court concerned would have primacy over that of other constitutional consultees and that such consultation/opinion would be binding on the President/Executive. In case, the President differs or ignores such consultation/opinion, he would have to give reason for the same which would then be justiciable.[94]

The Government of India was not happy with judgment in *Advocates-on-Record* case, which gave primacy to the opinion of the Chief Justice of India (CJI) in the matter of appointment of judges. Consequently, a presidential reference was sent to the Supreme Court in 1998 seeking its opinion as to whether sole individual opinion of CJI would constitute 'Consultation' for appointment of judges under the Constitution. A 9-member bench of the Indian Supreme Court answered the reference by holding that the opinion of CJI should be expressed in consultation with collegium of judges. It was, however, held that the collegium should consist of the Chief Justice of India and the 4 senior-most judges of the Supreme Court. It was also held that in case of appointment of a High Court Judge, the consultation process should include senior-most judge of the Supreme Court who hails from such High Court. Opinion of all members of the collegium should be in writing to be conveyed by CJI to Government with recommendation. It was also stated in the judgment that if the majority of collegium were not in favour the appointment of a person, then they should not be appointed.[95]

In the aftermath of Constitutional Reforms Act 2005, and partly impressed by the South African Constitution and due to the criticism of the existing procedure of appointments, India introduced a Judicial Commission through the 99th Amendment in 2014. The Supreme Court of India, however, struck down the Amendment mainly on the ground of independence of the judiciary, being a basic feature of the Indian Constitution.[96]

Tenure and Removal

A judge of the Supreme Court serves until he attains the age of 65 years.[97] A High Court judge retires at the age of 62.[98] A judge of the Supreme Court cannot be removed from office except by an order of the President passed after an address by each House of Parliament supported by a majority of the total membership of that House and by a majority of not less than two-thirds of the membership of that House present and voting has been presented to the President in the same session for such removal on the ground of proved misbehavior or incapacity.[99] The same procedure is provided for removal of a judge of a High Court as provided in the removal of a judge of the Supreme Court.[100]

The removal process of the judges is difficult and cumbersome. However, 2 important cases involving misconduct of judges are discussed below:

The Ramaswamy case

Veeraswamy Ramaswamy (1929), was functioning as the Chief Justice of the Punjab and Haryana High Court and was later elevated to the Supreme Court. While functioning as Chief Justice, it was alleged by the Comptroller and Auditor General of the state that, he had committed several financial irregularities.

The Supreme Court, the Bar Association, and the media took notice of the allegations. Notice was served by 108 members of the *Lok Sabha* for his impeachment. The Speaker admitted the motion and constituted a committee of inquiry. Minutes after the admission of the motion and the constitution of the committee by, the speaker, the *Lok Sabha* was dissolved. The Congress party came to power and treated the motion admitted by the Speaker as having lapsed after the dissolution of Parliament and deemed the inquiry committee to have ceased with it. It was believed that Ramaswamy had the support and confidence of the Congress party.

A section of the Supreme Court Bar Association took up the cause against Ramaswamy and demanded that the inquiry committee complete its inquiry. Before the Constitution Bench, several questions relating to the power, jurisdiction, propriety, and *bonafides* of the Speaker in passing the order in the circumstances and its validity after the dissolution of the House were raised. Further questions relating to the *locus standi* of the petitioners and interpretation of Judges Enquiry Act 1966, and its validity were the subject matter for decision before the Court.

The majority held that the doctrine of lapse did not apply in these cases. Judicial review lies against the first part of the proceedings from initiation of investigation ending in proof of the Speaker's action which is statutory and not in relation to the second part of the proceedings which is a parliamentary process. The purview of judicial review is in relation to the first part of the processing from initiation of the investigation ending in proof of the Speaker's action which is statutory and not in relation to the second part of the proceedings which is a parliamentary process. The judge concerned was held to be not entitled to any notice of hearing. The doctrine of necessity protects the Speaker from any allegations of acting *malafide*. Though the petitioners had *locus standi*, but the judgement was merely declaratory. The dissenting judge held the entire process to have been parliamentary and that therefore, the matter was not justiciable.[101]

In the meantime, Ramaswamy's wife had filed a writ petition seeking that a copy of the inquiry report of the committee be furnished to her husband before it was forwarded to the Speaker. It was held by the majority that judicial review is not available against the findings of the committee.[102] The same cannot be made available before its submission to the Speaker, but, that the Speaker is obliged to supply a copy of the report to the judge concerned when causing it to be laid before Parliament under Section 4(3) of the Act for consideration of the motion against the judge. Parliament's decision to adopt the motion or reject it has to be on merits on the basis of the entire material, including the dissenting opinion of any member of the committee, if any, as well as the comments of the judge concerned. Prior to the decision the judge should be afforded an opportunity to show cause. The motion to impeach Ramaswamy was defeated in Parliament because the members of the Congress and AiADMK (All India Anna Dravida Munnetra Kazhagam) parties abstained from voting.

The Veerasamy Case.

Kuppuswami Naidu Veeraswamy (1914–2010), was Chief Justice of the Madras High Court. The Central Bureau of Investigation (CBI) had registered a case against him alleging possession of assets disproportionate to his known sources of income and for committing an offence under the Prevention of Corruption Act.

After investigation, a charge sheet was filed. The special judge issued notice for his appearance. He challenged the trial as whole being without jurisdiction and therefore illegal and void. His contention was that he was not a public servant and that the Prevention of Corruption Act did not apply to judges of High Courts and the Supreme Court. Dismissing the appeal, the majority held that High Court judges and those of the Supreme Court are public servants. The President of India is the sanctioning and removing authority but in the interest of the independence of the judiciary, the sanctioning authority must act in accordance with the advice of the Chief Justice of India. There is no law protecting the judges from criminal prosecution.[103]

Conclusion

The Indian judiciary has asserted its independence throughout its history. There have been periods of tensions between the judiciary and the legislature on the one hand; and the judiciary and the executive on the other. During the 1970s, the tension between the judiciary and the Parliament was at its highest point, when the Supreme Court in a number of cases struck down the constitutional amendments passed by the Parliament on the basis of the theory of basic structure and features of the Constitution.[104]

From 1973 to 1977, the tension with the executive has also been at its highest when the courts declared the election of Indira Gandhi (1917–84)[105], the then Prime Minister of India, as void on the ground of malpractices during the elections. The tension further intensified during the period of emergency imposed by Mrs Gandhi from

1975 to 1977. She struck back by trying to weaken the judiciary. It had been a consistent practice that the senior most judge of the Supreme Court was appointed as the Chief Justice of India.

However, in 1973, Indira Gandhi appointed a junior judge of the Supreme Court, Justice Ajit Nath Ray (1912–2009),[106] as the Chief Justice of India superseding 3 senior judges of the Supreme Court who all resigned in protest.[107] In 1977, Justice Mirza Hameedullah Beg (1913–88)[108] was appointed the Chief Justice of India, superseding Justice Hans Raj Khanna (1912–2008)[109] of the Supreme Court who also resigned in protest.[110]

However, the judiciary in India has been very jealous of its independence and after these events, there has been a consistent practice of appointment of senior most judges as the Chief Justice of India. The Supreme Court of India has been an activist court and has played a key role in defending the Constitution and interpreting it in favour of the common citizen. It has played a significant role in the socio-political and economic development of society and is a watchdog against the highhandedness of the executive. It has asserted itself forcefully as the ultimate arbiter of the Constitution, while dealing with the Parliament at the centre and the legislatures in the States.

Independence of Judiciary in Pakistan

Introduction

Upon Independence in August 1947, Pakistan inherited a healthy judicial system from the colonial period. This was mainly attributable to a fair system of appointment of judges wherein such appointments were made generally on merit. There were, however, two channels of appointments to the High Courts – one from the Indian Civil Service and the other from among the leading lawyers. Barring few exceptions, the judges of High Courts in British India had a reputation for integrity and competence. If anyone faltered, it was due to his innate weakness and shortcomings and not because of his lack of qualifications at the time of his appointment. The quality of the judgments rendered was generally high.

In 1949, the Federal Court of Pakistan was established which became the apex court in Pakistan. In 1950, the jurisdiction of the Privy Council *l* was abolished, shortly after India had done so. Thus, in 1949 the superior judiciary of Pakistan, consisted of:

- Federal Court of Pakistan,
- Lahore High Court,
- High Court of East Bengal,
- Sindh Chief Court
- Court of Judicial Commissioners Peshawar
- Court of Judicial Commissioners Quetta.

Justice Mian Abdul Rashid (1889–1981) took office in June 1949 as the first Chief Justice of Pakistan.

The Constituent Assembly formed in 1947 was entrusted the task of giving a Constitution to Pakistan. It also served as the central legislature for making ordinary laws. It also had the responsibility of forming government at the center. Unprecedented problems faced by the new central government in Karachi, and new provincial governments throughout Pakistan, absorbed the time of the Constituent Assembly in the first couple of years of independence. Similarly, the massacre and blood bath that accompanied the partition of Punjab in August/September 1947, resulting in the death of more than a million people and exchange of population between the two parts of partitioned Punjab, created the urgency of rehabilitation and settlement of the refugees that crossed over from the districts in East Punjab and other parts of India to West Punjab, and also, refugees from other parts of India to Pakistan in general. This was a colossal task for a new nation and for a government in its infancy. Naturally, the main focus of Constituent Assembly for the first 2 years was not the Constitution making.

When the Constituent Assembly started working on the draft of the constitution, it was mired in a number of controversies arising out of the peculiarity of geographical separation between East and West Pakistan and various political, social, economic, ethnic, and linguistic issues. Finally, in October 1954, a draft of the constitution was finalized by the Constitutional Assembly. By this time the bureaucracy in Pakistan had been deeply politicized and was dominating the power structure of the state. Ghulam Muhammad (1895–1956)[111], a career bureaucrat had managed to become Governor General of Pakistan on the assassination of the first Prime Minister of Pakistan, Liaquat Ali Khan (1895–1951)[112] on 16 October 1951. On 29 June 1954, Mian Abdul Rashid retired as the first Chief Justice of the Federal Court and was succeeded by Justice Muhammad Munir (1895–1979).[113] On 24 October 1954, Governor General Ghulam Muhammad dissolved the Constituent Assembly, and this action was challenged by the Speaker of the Assembly, Maulvi Tamizuddin Khan (1889–1963),[114] before the Sindh Chief Court. The Sindh Chief Court struck down the action of the Governor General as invalid. However, on appeal, the Federal Court reversed the judgment of the Sindh Chief Court on a highly technical ground that law conferring writ jurisdiction was itself invalid because it had not received the assent of the ...... Governor General.[115]

This case and other such cases during the early period adversely affected the prestige and reputation of the Federal Court. The Court was seen as lacking independence and inclined towards supporting the government in power. Chief Justice Muhammad Munir's, reputation and prestige suffered the most. He was seen as a judge who was inclined to decide in favour of the establishment, and for leading the Federal Court on an uncertain path in its infancy.

Process of appointment of judges

The first Constitution of Pakistan was adopted in March 1956. The Constitution provided for the Supreme Court as the apex court in the country and 2 High Courts, one for the province of East Pakistan and the other for West Pakistan. The Chief Justice of Pakistan would be appointed by the President and other judges of the Supreme Court would be appointed by the President after consultation with the Chief Justice.[116] Each judge of the High Court would be appointed by the President after consultation with the Chief Justice of Pakistan, the Governor of the Province to which the appointment would relate and, if the appointment was not that of the Chief Justice, the Chief Justice of the High Court of that Province.[117]

The Constitutions of 1962 and 1973, had similar provisions for appointment of judges of the Supreme Court and the High Courts.[118] Over the years, the system of appointment of judges became increasingly politicized. The Supreme Court was ultimately called upon to give its judgment based on the interpretation of the provisions relating to appointment of judges in the Constitution.

The judgment in *Judges'* case deserve a special mention. The Supreme Court of Pakistan granted leave to appeal against the appointment of 20 judges in the Lahore High Court, in order to consider the constitutionality of such appointments. After considerable arguments spread over several months, a bench of the Supreme Court comprising of 5 judges gave a majority judgment of 4 to 1 holding as under:[119]

1. Appointment of *ad hoc* judges against permanent vacancies of the Supreme Court violates the Constitution.
2. Appointment of Acting Chief Justices can only be a stop-gap arrangement for a short period and not, in any case, exceed a period of 90 days.
3. An Acting Chief Justice cannot be a consultee for the purposes of appointment of judges, and the appointments made on the recommendation of an Acting Chief Justice were invalid and unconstitutional.
4. All permanent vacancies in the judiciary, particularly those of the Chief Justices, should be filled in advance if they are normal ones (like arising out of retirement) and in any case, not later than 30 days after their occurrence.
5. The senior most judge of a High Court has a legitimate expectancy to be considered for appointment as Chief Justice. He is entitled to be appointed as Chief Justice of that Court in the absence of strong reasons to the contrary to be recorded by the President/Executive.
6. The words 'after consultation' occurring in Articles 177 and 193 of the Constitution involve a participatory consultative process between the consultees and the Executive. It should be effective, meaningful, purposive, and consensus oriented, leaving no room for complaint of arbitrariness or unfair play. The court found it to be a consistent practice that has acquired the status of convention during the pre-partition days of India as well as the post-partition period, that the recommendations of the Chief Justice of a High Court and the Chief Justice of the Supreme Court, in India as well as in Pakistan, have been consistently accepted and acted upon except in very rare cases.

This judgment was subsequently followed by *Asad Ali's* case. In 1997, strong differences had arisen between the then Chief Justice, Justice Sajjad Ali Shah (1933–2017)[120] and the majority of the judges of the Supreme Court. Consequently, 10 judges (out of the total of 17) headed by Justice Saeeduzzaman Siddiqui (1937–2017)[121] formed a Bench and held that the senior most judge of the Supreme Court of Pakistan, in the absence of any concrete or valid reason, has to be appointed the Chief Justice on the basis of convention. Since the appointment of Justice Sajjad Ali Shah as Chief Justice, superseding 3 senior judges of the court, was made without any concrete or valid reason, therefore, such an appointment was held unconstitutional, illegal and contrary to the decision of the court in the judges' case. The court further ruled that Justice Sajjad Ali Shah had ceased to hold the office of Chief Justice of Pakistan and ordered his reversion to the position of a judge of the Supreme Court in accordance with his seniority among the judges of the Supreme Court.[122]

The Constitution (18th Amendment Act 2010), radically changed the process and procedure for appointment of judges of the Supreme Court and the High Courts. Article 175A was introduced in the Constitution which provided for 2 bodies to deal with the matter of appointment of judges, namely, Judicial Commission of Pakistan and Parliamentary Committee.

The Judicial Commission consists of the Chief Justice of Pakistan as its chairman, 2 senior most judges of the Supreme Court, a former judge of the Supreme Court (for 2 years), Federal Law Minister, Attorney General for Pakistan and a Senior Advocate of the Supreme court nominated by the Pakistan Bar Council (for 2 years) as its members. For appointment of judges of the High Courts, the Judicial Commission would also include the Chief Justice of the High Court concerned and its most senior judge, Provincial Law Minister and a senior advocate nominated by the concerned Provincial Bar Council.

The Parliamentary Committee consists of 8 members, 4 each from the Senate and the National Assembly. Out of these 8 members, 4 are to be from Treasury Benches (2 from each House) and 4 from the Opposition Benches (2 from each House). The Judicial Commission, after selecting the names for appointment as judges, sends the nominees to the Parliamentary Committee which can only reject any of the nominees by three-fourth majority of its total membership. Otherwise the nominees would be deemed to have been approved for appointment.

This provision (Article 175A) was challenged before the Supreme Court on the touchstone of theory of basic structure of Constitution particularly the basic features of independence of judiciary and separation of powers. This case was argued for months during the Summer of 2010, but, has remained undecided. However, an interim order was passed by the Supreme Court in October 2010, in which certain recommendations were made to the Parliament which included increase in the number of senior most judges of the Supreme court from 2 to 4 as members of the Judicial Commission and empowering the Chief Justice of Pakistan, to initiate the names of the candidates for appointment to the Supreme Court and Chief Justices of the High Courts and Federal *Shariat* Court to initiate the names of the candidates for appointment to their respective courts.[123]

The recommendations of increasing the members of senior most Supreme Court judges was adopted by the Parliament under the Constitution (19th Amendment) Act 2010. The matter of initiating the names of the candidates for appointment as judges has been incorporated in the Rules for Judicial Commission framed by the Commission.

The differences between the Judicial Commission and the Parliamentary Committee did not take too long to occur. The rejection by the Parliamentary Committee of the recommendees of the Judicial Commission were challenged before the Supreme Court, which assumed jurisdiction in the matter and held the opinion/decision of the Parliamentary Committee as justiciable. The Supreme Court held that the Judicial Commission, comprised of 5 judges of the Supreme Court and 2 judges of the High Court (in case of appointment of High Court) who were in a better position to evaluate professional calibre, legal acumen, judicial skill and other related criteria for appointment as judges. The Parliamentary Committee could only reject the nominations on grounds falling within its domain for very strong reason which would be justiciable. The Supreme Court issued direction to the Federation to notify the appointments on the recommendation received from Judicial Commission regardless of the opinion of the Parliamentary Committee.[124]

However, in the year 2015, the cases challenging the 18th Amendment to the extent of Article 175A, came up for hearing before the full court of 17 judges. These cases were heard along with the cases challenging 21st Amendment to the Constitution introducing military courts for a period of 2 years. By a majority of 13 to 04, all the Constitution Petitions (challenging 18th and 21st Amendments) were held to be maintainable. However, by a majority of 14 to 03, the Constitution Petitions challenging the 18th Amendment were dismissed, while by a majority of 11 to 06, the Constitution Petitions challenging 21st Amendment were dismissed.[125]

Tenure of Judges and their Removal

Under the Constitutions of 1956 and 1962, there was no lower age limit for appointment of judges. So, any lawyer of 10 years practice at the High Court or judicial officer with 10 years' service could be appointed as judge of the High Court. However, the retirement age for the judges of the Supreme Court was 65 years and for the judges of the High Court 60 years.[126] The retirement age of the judges of the Supreme Court, under 1973 Constitution remained the same as 65 by that of the High Courts, it was increased to 62.[127]

The judges under all the Constitutions of Pakistan, had the security of tenure to serve as such till they attain the age of retirement. The procedure of their removal has always been rigid and cumbersome. The 1956 Constitution, provided that judge of the Supreme Court could not be removed from his office except by the order of the President made after an address by the National Assembly; supported by the majority of total number of members of the Assembly, and by the votes of not less than two-thirds of the members present and voting, had been presented to the president for the removal of the judge on the ground of proved misbehavior or infirmity of mind or body.[128] A judge of a High Court could not be removed from office except by an order of the President made on the ground of misbehavior or infirmity of mind or body, if the Supreme Court on reference being made to it by the president reports that the judge ought to be removed on any of these grounds.[129] During General Ayub Khan (1907–74)[130] rule, a judge of the West Pakistan High Court namely Justice Ikhlaq Husain was removed under this provision.

However, the procedure for removal of a judge was completely changed under the 1962 Constitution. A Supreme Judicial Council consisting of the Chief Justice of the Supreme Court, 2 next senior most judges of the Supreme Court and 2 Chief Justices of the High Courts, would be constituted to whom the President could send reference to enquire into alleged gross misconduct or alleged physical or mental incapacity of a judge. If, after such enquiry, the Supreme Judicial Council reported to the President that such misconduct or incapacity has been proved, then the President might remove that judge from office.[131] The safeguard provided to the judges was that they could not be removed from office by the President unless enquiry is held by the Supreme Judicial Council and there is report of misconduct or incapacity. In 1971, during General Yahya Khan (1917–80)[132] rule, a judge of the Lahore High Court, Justice Shaukat Ali was removed from office under this procedure.[133]

The 1973 Constitution retained the procedure provided under the 1962 Constitution.[134] Under this provision, a reference was sent by the President Pervez Musharraf (1943) against Chief Justice Iftikhar Muhammad Chaudhry (1948)[135] to the Supreme Judicial Council for alleged misconduct. This reference was challenged before th Supreme Court and a bench of 13 judges of the Supreme Court held the reference as *malafide* and invalid.[136]

Conclusion

The judiciary in Pakistan has a chequered history. Its image of being weak and pliable particularly towards the military regimes and has been bending backward to justify violations and subversions of the Constitution at the hands of the military rulers. It has been legitimizing the military regimes and in the process enjoying the fruits of powers. It has therefore politicized the judicial organ of the State with irreparable damage to its reputation and credibility. A few good judgments here and there are an exception rather than the rule.

There are certain instances of public interest litigation which is not seen with favour by the undemocratic regimes and the impeachment process against the Chief Justice of Pakistan, Justice Iftikhar Muhammad Chaudhry appears to be reaction of Musharraf regime[137] to his judicial activism. After the introduction of a new system of appointment of judges to the High Courts and Supreme Court the dream of judicial independence ensuring institutional and personal independence remains elusive.

Notes

1. Michel Rosenfeld, Andras Sajo, *The Oxford Handbook of Comparative Constitutional Law* (Oxford: OUP, 2012), page 83.
2. Shimon Shetreet, Christopher Forsyth, *The Culture of Judicial Independence* (Leiden: Martinus Nijhoff Publishers, 2011), p. 18.
3. Ibid page 19.
4. 5 U.S. 137 (1803).
5. Eric Barendt, *An Introduction to Constitutional Law*, (New York: Oxford University Press, 1998), p. 129.p. 129.
6. House of Commons Disqualification Act, 1975.
7. Lord Phillips of Worth Matravers served as the President of the Supreme Court of the United Kingdom.
8. https://assets.cambridge.org/97805214/93376/excerpt/9780521493376_excerpt.pdf cited in the Roger Masterman, *Separation of Powers in the Contemporary Constitution* (Cambridge University Press, 2011).
9. Supra Note 2, page 20.
10. (1967) 1 AC 259.
11. Lord Edward Pearce served as a Lord of Appeal in Ordinary. In 1972, he presided as Chairman of Rhodesia Inquiry.
12. *Anisminic Ltd. v. Foreign Compensation Commission*, (1969) 2 AC 147.
13. Supra Note 1, pp. 130–3.
14. Art. 97(1) GG.
15. Ronald Reagan was the 40th President of the United States.
16. Robert Bork served as Solicitor General and Federal Judge.
17. Constitutional Council of France was established by the Constitution of the Fifth Republic on 4 October 1958 to ensure that constitutional principles and rules are upheld.
18. François Mitterrand was the first socialist President of France from 1981–95.
19. Robert Badinter served as Miniter of Justice under President François Mitterrand.
20. *Bundesverfassungsgericht* (Federal Constitutional Court) is the supreme constitutional court for the Federal Republic of Germany.
21. *Bundestag* is the German federal parliament. It is the only body that is directly elected by the German people on the Federal level.
22. *Bundesrat*, (Federal Council) is the Upper House and acts mainly in an advisory capacity, since political power resides in the popularly elected Bundestag.
23. Art. 56. Basic Law, Art. 94(1).
24. Viscount Gavin Simonds was a British judge, politician and Lord High Chancellor of Great Britain.
25. *Att: Gen. For Australia v. The Queen & the Boilermaker's Society of Australia*, (1957) AC 288.
26. *Duncan v. Cammell, Laird & Co. Ltd.* (1942) AC 624.
27. Robert Steven, *The English Judges* (Oxford: Hart Publishing 2002), p. 83.
28. Lord Edward Carson was an Irish unionist politician, barrister and judge.
29. Louis Fisher, *American Constitutional Law*, 6th ed. (North Carolina, Durham: Carolina Academic Press, 2005), p. 132.
30. German Basic Law (*Grundgestz*), Art 97(2).
31. National Industrial Relations Court (NIRC), also known as the Industrial Relations Tribunal, was a way to limit the power of trades union in the United Kingdom.
32. Supra Note 1, pp. 137–8.
33. Supra Note 29, p. 115.
34. Ibid, pp. 116–7.
35. 5 U.S. 298 (1803).
36. Supra Note 29, pp. 117–8.
37. Ibid, p. 123.
38. Ibid, P. 124.
39. John J. Parker was a United States Circuit Judge of the United States Court of Appeals for the Fourth Circuit.
40. Lyndon Johnson was the 36th President of the United States.
41. Abe Fortas was an Associate Justice of the Supreme Court of the United States from 1965 to 1969.
42. Earl Warren was the 14th Chief Justice of the US Supreme Court from 1953 to 1969.
43. Clement F. Haynsworth Jr was a United States Circuit Judge of the United States Court of Appeals for the Fourth Circuit.
44. George Harrold Carswell was a United States Circuit Judge of the United States Court of Appeals for the Fifth Circuit.
45. Ronald Reagan was the 40th President of the United States.
46. Douglas H. Ginsburg serves as a judge on the United States Court of Appeals for the District of Columbia Circuit.

47. Supra Note 29, pp. 124–6. In the matter of confirmation of nominees to the Supreme Court, there is clear and visible large influence of a Jewish lobby in the Senate. Both Ginsburg and Breyer had were confirmed by the Senate in 1990s. It was not so in the 1960s. Abe Fortas faced stiff opposition in the Senate and his nomination as Chief Justice had to be withdrawn. It is doubtful that he would have faced such opposition in 1990s or afterwards with the Senate so deeply predisposed towards the Jewish lobby.
48. Donald Trump served as the 45th President of the United States.
49. Neil Gorsuch is an Associate Justice of the US Supreme Court.
50. Brett Kavanaugh is an Associate Justice of the US Supreme Court.
51. Amy Coney Barrett is an Associate Justice of the US Supreme Court.
52. John Pickering (1737–1805) was a federal judge for the United States District Court for the District of New Hampshire.
53. Supra Note 29, P. 129.
54. Otto Kerner Jr served as a US Circuit Judge of the US Court of Appeals for the Seventh Circuit.
55. Harry Claiborne was a US District Judge of the US District Court for the District of Nevada.
56. Walter L. Nixon Jr is a former US District Judge of the US District Court for the Southern District of Mississippi.
57. Supra Note 29, pp. 129–130.
58. *Nixon v. United States*, 506 U.S. 224(1993).
59. Samuel Chase was an Associate Justice of the US Supreme Court.
60. Supra Note 29, pp. 124 and 129.
61. Judicial Pensions Act 1959, Supreme Court Act 1981, S. 11(2). *See also* Supreme Court Act 1981, S. 11(8) for the compulsory retirement of judges incapacitated by ill health.
62. Courts Act 1971 S. 17.
63. Courts Act 1971, S. 17(4). A Circuit judge who was convicted on a charge of smuggling was removed from office by the Lord Chancellor in 1983, *The Times London*, 6 December 1983.
64. Courts Act 1971 S. 17.
65. Court Act 1971, S 21(6), Section 21(3); provides that a Recorder's appointment shall specify the frequency and duration of the occasions on which he must be available to perform his duties.
66. A.G. Chaudhry, *Lectures on Constitutional Law* (Lahore: Irfan Law Book House, 1994), pp. 69–70.
67. (1913) A.C. 417.
68. (1981) Q.B. 534.
69. *Anderson v. Gorrie* (1895) 1 Q.B. 668.
70. *Hamond v. Howell* (1677) 2 Mod. 210, quoted by A.G. Chaudhry, Supra Note 35, p. 72.
71. There are about 25 documents (which are called legal sources of the UK Constitution) which include the *Magna Carta* (1215), The Petition of Rights 1628, The Bill of Rights 1689, the Act of Settlement 1700, The Treaty of Union 1706 and the European Communities Act, 1972.
72. Hilaire Barnett, *Constitutional and Administrative Law*, 7th ed. (UK: Routledge-Cavendish, 2009), pp. 81–82.
73. Lords of Appeal appointed after 1993 are subject to a retirement age of 70: Judicial Pensions and Retirement Act 1993.
74. Stanley A. De Smith, Harry Street, Rodney Brazier, *Constitutional and Administrative Law*, 8th ed. (Indiana University: Penguin, 1985).
75. Section 178 of the South African Constitution.
76. 2005 c.4, Section 3.
77. 2005 c.4, Section 23.
78. 2005 c.4, Section 25.
79. Schedule 8 to the Act.
80. Part 2 of Schedule 8, 2005 c.4.
81. 2005 c.4, Section 27.
82. 2005 c.4, Section 29.
83. 2005 c.4, Section 35.
84. 2005 c.4, Section 42.
85. 2005 c.4, Section 42 sub section (5).
86. Presidency towns were provinces and were the administrative divisions of British governance in India.
87. Gobind Das, 'The Supreme Court: An Overview' in B. N. Kirpal, Ashok H. Desai, Gopal Subramaniam, Raju Ramachandran, Rajeev Dhavan, *Supreme But Not Infallible: Essays in Honour of the Supreme Court of India*. (New Delhi: Oxford University Press, 2000), p. 16–7.
88. Indian Const. Art. 124.
89. Ibid.
90. Indian Const. Art. 32.

91. Indian Const. Art. 226.
92. Indian Const. Art. 216.
93. Indian Const. Art. 217.
94. *Advocates-on-Records Association v. Union of India,* AIR 1994 S.C. 268.
95. *In re: Presidential Reference* (Special Reference No. 1 of 1998), AIR 1999 S.C. 1.
96. *Supreme Court Advocates on Record v. Union of India* (2016) 5 SCC 1.
97. Indian Const. Art. 124(2).
98. Indian Const. Art. 217(1).
99. Indian Const. Art. 124(4).
100. Indian Const. Art. 218.
101. *Sub Committee of Judicial Accountability v. Union of India,* AIR 1992 S.C. 320.
102. *Sarojini Ramaswamy v. Union of India,* AIR 1992 S.C. 2219.
103. *K. Veeraswami v. Union of India,* (1991) 3 SCC 655.
104. *Kesavananada Bharati v. State of Kerala,* AIR 1973. S.C. 1461; *Indira Nehru Gandhi v. Raj Nariane,* AIR 1975 S.C. 2299; *Minerva Mills Ltd. v. Union of India,* AIR 1980 S.C. 1789. These cases and other similar cases have been discussed in detail in the Chapter on 'The theory of Basic Structure of the Constitution'.
105. Indira Gandhi was the daughter of Jawaharlal Nehru and the first female Prime Minister of India from 1966–77.
106. Justice Ajit Nath Ray was 14th Chief Justice of the Supreme Court of India.
107. The names of the superseded judges were Justices Jaishankar Manilal Shelat, Kowdoor Sadananda Hegde and Anand Grover.
108. Justice Mirza Hameedullah Beg was the 15th Chief Justice of India.
109. Justice Hans Raj Khanna was a judge of the Supreme Court of India in 1971 where he continued till his resignation in 1977.
110. The appointments of Chief Justices Ajit Nath Ray and Mirza Hameedullah Beg were both made by the Indira Gandhi government.
111. Ghulam Muhammad was a politician and financier who served as the 3rd Governor-General of Pakistan.
112. Liaquat Ali Khan was one of the leading founding fathers and first Prime Minister of Pakistan.
113. Muhammad Munir served as the 2nd Chief Justice of Pakistan.
114. Maulvi Tamizuddin Khan served as the Speaker of Pakistan's Constituent Assembly from 1948 to 1954 and in the same capacity also served in the National Assembly of Pakistan between 1962–63.
115. *Moulvi Tamizuddin Khan v. Federation of Pakistan,* PLD 1955 Sindh 96 and *Federation of Pakistan v. Moulvi Tamizuddin Khan,* PLD 1955 F.C. 240.
116. 1956 Pakistan Const. Art. 149.
117. Pakistan Const. Art. 166.
118. 1962 Pakistan Const. Art. 50 and 92; similarly, 1973 Pakistan Const. Art. 177 and 193.
119. *Al-Jehad Trust v. Federation of Pakistan,* PLD 1996 S.C. 324.
120. Sajjad Ali Shah was the 13th Chief Justice of Pakistan from 4 June 1994 to 2 December 1997.
121. Saeed uz Zaman Siddiqui served as the 15th Chief Justice of Pakistan.
122. *Asad Ali v. Federation of Pakistan,* PLD 1998 S.C. 161.
123. *Nadeem Ahmed v. Federation of Pakistan,* PLD 2010 S.C. 1165.
124. *Munir Hussain Bhatti v. Federation of Pakistan.* PLD 2011 S.C. 407.
125. *District Bar Association, Rawalpindi v. Federation of Pakistan,* PLD 2015 SC. 401.
126. Articles 150 and 166 of the 1956 Constitution. Articles 52 and 94 of the 1962 Constitution.
127. Articles 179 and 195 of the 1973 Constitution.
128. Article 151.
129. Article 169.
130. Ayub Khan served as a General in Pakistani Army and the 2nd President of Pakistan.
131. Article 128 of the 1962 Constitution.
132. Yahya Khan was a General of the Pakistan Army who also served as the 3rd President of Pakistan.
133. *State v. Justice Sheikh Shaukat Ali.* PLD 1971 S.C. 585.
134. Article 209 of the Constitution.
135. Iftikhar Muhammad Chaudhry was the 20th Chief Justice of Pakistan.
136. Short order is reported as *Chief Justice of Pakistan Iftikhar Muhammad Chaudhry v. President of Pakistan* as PLJ 2007 S.C. 814 and the detailed judgment with detailed reasoning is reported as PLD 2010 S.C. 61.
137. Musharraf regime duration was from October 1999 to August 2008.

12 Judicial Power and the Doctrine of Judicial Review

Introduction

'Judicial Review' is a doctrine according to which the courts are entitled, in the exercise of the judicial power of the state, to examine and decide—

(a) the constitutional validity of any law, be it the result of primary or subordinate legislation, and
(b) the constitutional validity or lawfulness of a decision, action or inaction of a person or body in relation to the exercise of a public function.[1]

Alexander Hamilton (1755/57–1804) described the judiciary as the weakest of the 3 organs of the state. What transformed the weakest organ into the most powerful one was none other than the doctrine of 'judicial review'.

The American Contribution for Judicial Review

Edward Samuel Corwin (1878–1963) delineated 4 periods of constitutional interpretation in the US.[2]

The first period was until the end of Chief Justice John Marshall's (1755–1835) long tenure from 1801 to 1835, features 'the dominance of the Constitutional Document.' To support his nationalist bias, Marshall frequently cited theories of the Constitution. The second period, stretching from 1835 to about 1895, is marked by 'the *par excellence* of the constitutional theory.' Using dual 'federalism', 'due process of law', the conception of liberty as 'freedom of contract,' and other judicial penumbra. The Justices put,

> 'the national law-making power into a straitjacket so far as the regulation of business was concerned'.

Corwin calls the third period, 1895–1937, 'judicial review pure and simple.' By this time, the US Supreme Court found itself heir to such,

> 'a variety of instruments of constitutional exegesis that it was often able to achieve almost any result ... it considered desirable and that without flagrant departure from good form.'

During the 4th period, 1937–1969, the Supreme Court justices led a revolution. A new Constitution emerged. After 1937, the Court stopped vetoing social and economic legislation, apparently content to leave protection of property rights to the mercy of the political controls. Justification for acquiescence in vastly increased government power over the economy was found in the slogan 'back to the Constitution' (the Constitution as it was before 1890). Having abandoned guardianship of property, the Court became increasingly preoccupied with human beings and their rights as people; such as freedom of speech and press, rights of the accused and of the poor, freedom from racial discrimination, and the right to political equality in legislative districting.

The new Constitution emerged gradually. Vigorous protests marked every step, particularly, in relation to those dramatic shifts made after the appointment of Earl Warren (1891–1974) as Chief Justice in 1953. The new Constitution protects civil liberties against bigots, defends the right to a fair trial of indigent and ignorant persons accused of crime, guarantees the right of a majority to prevail over entrenched minorities in an election.

The court's work load reflected this change of the 160 decisions in which opinions were written during the 1935–36 term, only 2 were in the area of civil rights. In 1960–61, 54 of the 120 decisions in which opinions were prepared concerned civil liberties. Even today, disproportionate judicial concern for civil liberties continues.

The constitution was not intended to be a straitjacket, but in practice it proved to be one. Constitutional interpretation has been definitely variable. Since judges do not live in a vacuum, their decisions are influenced by inheritance, education, and the pressures of economic and social forces. During the years 1890–1936, the US

Supreme Court showed restraint, as well as initiative in cases such as *Brown v. Board of Education of Topeka*[3] and *Baker v. Carr*.[4] The innovations that marked the regime of Chief Justice Earl Warren, although diminished, have not disappeared. It would be difficult to find ultimate and thoroughly satisfactory justification for some of them in constitutional terms.

In *Reynolds v. Sims*[5] the court plainly reached out for a desired result. This attempt to reach out was even more obvious in the decision on abortion. Nevertheless, over the years a majority of the justices have felt authorized to intervene where injustices exist, for which there is no perceived and probable remedy by other institutions. Debate on the nature and scope of judicial power continues not only within the confines of the court, but, in the give-and-take of the political system. American constitutional law has been shaped by the US Supreme Court. Sometimes, the role of the people and the substance of decisions they will accept is forgotten.

The pervasiveness of judicial power is now one of the most conspicuous aspects of the Supreme Court. The court decrees have touched every aspect of the American life. Its docket reads like a policy agenda for the nation. This development is all the more extraordinary, in light of the fact that it is the work of a Court, in which 4 members were appointed by President Richard Nixon, who pledged himself to curb judicial activism, taking as his model the apostle of 'judicial self-restraint', Justice Felix Frankfurter (1882–1965)[6]. Robert Yates's (1738–1801)[7] prediction of 1788, that –

> the US Supreme Court would finally expand its power so as to be able to 'mould' the American Constitution into any shape it pleased, has been fulfilled.

The effect of judicial decisions has been to expand and enlarge the sphere of government, rather than to qualify and restrict it. 'The restraining power of the judiciary does not manifest its chief worth,' Judge Benjamin Nathan Cardozo (1870–1938)[8] observed,

> 'in the few cases in which the legislature has gone beyond the lines that mark the limits of discretion.' Its primary value has been in 'making vocal and audible the ideals that might otherwise be silenced....'

Had this not been so, a document framed in the context of agrarianism, and largely unamended except by constitutional interpretation, could not serve the expanding needs of government in a complex industrialized society.[9]

Early Establishment of Judicial Review

In 1803, it was John Marshall's opinion in *Marbury v. Madison*[10], that unequivocally proclaimed the authority of the Supreme Court to declare Acts of Congress unconstitutional, the issue had been raised before the Court in several previous cases. By the time of the *Marbury* decision, John Marshall's dictum was generally accepted by Supreme Court justices and federal judges.[11]

In 1792, *Hayburn's* case[12] and related cases, 5 of the 6 justices of the Supreme Court, acting as Circuit Court judges, agreed that they could not execute an Act of Congress in their capacity as judges because the Act delegated non-judicial functions to the circuit courts. It delegated to the courts the power to pass upon pension claims for widows, orphans, and disabled veterans of the American Revolution War (1775–83). And made the decision of the circuit courts subject to review by the Secretary of War and ultimately the legislature. The Act essentially, delegated to the circuit courts what today would be called administrative functions, subject to review not by higher courts but by the executive and legislative branches.

Five Supreme Court justices, Chief Justice John Jay (1745–1829); and justices William Cushing (1732–1810), John Blair (1732–1800), James Wilson (1742–98), James Iredell (1751–99), sitting as circuit court judges, refused to carry out the act, the 6th Justice Thomas Johnson (1732–1819) was not involved. Chief Justice John Jay and Justice William Cushing, sitting on the Circuit Court of the District of New York, issued a formal opinion in the case, while Justices John Blair, James Wilson, and James Iredell expressed their objection in letters written to President George Washington (1732–99).

Jay's opinion from the circuit court bench in the first case under the Act, emphasized the importance of preserving the 'separation of powers' among the legislative, executive, and judicial branches, which, he said, meant that no non-judicial functions can be given to the courts, nor can their opinions be subject to further review by coordinate branches.

Marbury v. Madison: The Authority for Judicial Review of Congressional and Presidential Actions.

Marbury v. Madison[13] is the single most important decision in American constitutional law. It established the authority for the judiciary to review the constitutionality of executive and legislative acts. Although, the American Constitution is silent as to whether federal courts have this authority, the power has existed ever since *Marbury*.

Facts

The American presidential election of 1800, was fiercely contested among 3 candidates: the incumbent President John Adams (1735–1826)[14], Thomas Jefferson (1743–1823)[15], and Aaron Burr (1756–1836)[16]. Jefferson received a majority of the popular vote but tied in the Electoral College vote with Burr. The clear loser was President Adams.

In January 1801, John Adams's Secretary of State, John Marshall (1755–1835), was selected to serve as the fourth Chief Justice of the United States Supreme Court. Throughout the remainder of Adams's presidency, Marshall served as both Secretary of State and Chief Justice. John Adams was a Federalist; and the Federalists were determined to exercise their influence before the Republican Thomas Jefferson took office as US President.

On 13 February 1801, the US Congress enacted the Judiciary Act, 1801, which reduced the number of Supreme Court justices from 6 to 5, and decreasing the opportunity for Republican control of the court. The Act also eliminated the Supreme Court justices' duty to serve as circuit judges and created 16 new judgeships on the circuit courts. However, this change was short-lived. In 1802, Congress repealed this statute, restoring the practice of circuit riding by Supreme Court justices and eliminating the newly created circuit court judgeships. The constitutionality of congressional abolition of judgeships was not tested in the courts.[17]

On 27 February 1801, less than a week before the end of President John Adams's term, Congress adopted the Organic Act of the District of Columbia, which authorized the President to appoint 42 justices of the peace. John Adams announced these nominations on 2 March, and on 3 March; the day before Thomas Jefferson's inauguration, the Senate confirmed these nominees. Immediately, Secretary of State (and Chief Justice) John Marshall signed the commissions for these individuals and dispatched his brother, James Marshall, to deliver them. A few commissions, including one for William Marbury (1762–1835), were not delivered before Jefferson's inauguration. President Thomas Jefferson instructed his Secretary of State, James Madison (1751–1836), to withhold the undelivered commissions.

William Marbury filed suit in the United States Supreme Court seeking a writ of *mandamus* to compel James Madison, as Secretary of State, to deliver the commission. Marbury claimed that the Judiciary Act 1789; authorized the US Supreme Court to grant *mandamus* in a proceeding filed in the Supreme Court. Although, Marbury's petition was filed in December 1801, the Supreme Court did not hear the case until 1803, because Congress by statute, abolished the June and December 1802 Terms of the Supreme Court.

Finding

The US Supreme Court ruled against William Marbury and held that it could not constitutionally hear the case as a matter of original jurisdiction. The Court held that although the Judiciary Act 1789, authorized such jurisdiction, this provision of the statute was unconstitutional because Congress cannot allow original jurisdiction beyond the situations enumerated in the Constitution.

Before examining the Court's reasoning, the question is whether the Court acted improperly in considering any of the issues presented besides the jurisdictional question. It, of course, a long-standing principle that 'the first question necessarily is that of jurisdiction'.[18] Because the Court held that it lacked jurisdiction, all of the other parts of the opinion—such as considering whether the commission had vested and the ability of the judiciary to review the executive's action—were arguably improper.

Perhaps, these parts of the opinion were meant to show that the Court saw no way to decide the case without considering the constitutionality of the statute. Or perhaps these parts of the opinion were simply Chief Justice John Marshall's way of chastising the Thomas Jefferson administration for its refusal to deliver the commissions. Politically, Marshall knew that a ruling in favour of Marbury would be futile. The Jefferson administration would ignore it, and that would undermine the Court's authority at the beginning of its history. Therefore, Marshall may have included the initial parts of the opinion to show that the Jefferson administration improperly denied William Marbury his commission, knowing that it was the most Marshall could do for Marbury.

Indeed, it is questionable, whether John Marshall should have participated in deciding the case at all because of his conflict of interest. He was the Secretary of State who signed William Marbury's commission and who was responsible for its delivery. In light of his participation in the events that gave rise to the litigation, there were strong grounds for Marshall to have withdrawn from the Court.

John Marshall is likely to have perceived that the case presented a unique opportunity: the chance to claim the power of judicial review, but in a context least likely to draw opposition. The statutory provision being declared unconstitutional was one that enlarges the judiciary's power, and the Thomas Jefferson administration obviously welcomed the result.[19]

ISSUE 1: *DOES MARBURY HAVE A RIGHT TO THE COMMISSION?*

Chief Justice John Marshall structured the opinion around three questions;

— First does William Marbury have a right to the commission?
— Second, if so, do the laws of his country afford him a remedy?
— Third, if so, can the US Supreme Court issue this remedy?

Chief Justice Marshall then answers each question in turn.

As to the first question, the court concluded that Marbury had a right to the commission because all appropriate procedures were followed. Chief Justice Marshall concluded:

> 'It is .... decidedly the opinion of the court, that when a commission has been signed by the President, the appointment is made; and that the commission is complete, when the seal of the United States has been affixed to it by the Secretary of State.'

The Court might have decided this issue differently. President Thomas Jefferson took the position that,

> 'if there is any principle of law never yet contradicted, it is that delivery is one of the essentials to the validity of the deed.'

But the Court rejected this view and ruled that delivery was merely a custom and that therefore, withholding Marbury's commission was 'violative of a vested legal right.'

ISSUE 2: *DO THE LAWS AFFORD MARBURY A REMEDY?*

Chief Justice Marshall's initial answer to this question was that:

> '[t]he very essence of civil liberty certainly consists in the right of every individual to claim the protection of the laws, whenever he receives an injury.'

The specific issue was whether the Court could give Marbury a remedy against the executive branch of government. The Court answered this by declaring that:

> '[t]he government of the United States has been emphatically termed a government of laws, and not of men.'

In other words, no person—not even the President- is above the law.

The Court then drew a distinction as to when the judiciary could afford relief. The judiciary could provide remedies against the executive when there is a specific duty to a particular person, but not when it is a political matter left to executive discretion. Chief Justice Marshall wrote:

> '[W]here the heads of departments are the political or confidential agents of the executive, merely to execute the will of the President, or rather to act in cases in which the executive possesses a constitutional or legal discretion, nothing can be more perfectly clear than that their acts are only politically examinable. But where a specific duty is assigned by law, and individual rights depend upon the performance of that duty, it seems equally clear that the individual, who considers himself injured, has a right to resort to the laws of his country for a remedy.'

The Court returned to this distinction in considering the next issue; whether *mandamus* was an appropriate remedy.

Issue 3: *Can the Supreme Court Issue this Remedy? Is Mandamus an Appropriate Remedy?*

In considering the former question, the Court again used the distinction between ministerial acts, where the executive had a duty to perform, and political acts, within the discretion of the executive. Judicial review, including *mandamus*, was deemed appropriate only in the former realm. Chief Justice John Marshall said:

> 'Questions, in their nature political, or which are, by the constitution and laws, submitted to the executive, can never be made in this court.... [But where the head of department] is directed by law to do a certain act affecting the absolute rights of individuals....it is not perceived on what ground the courts of the country are further excused from the duty of giving judgment that right be done to an injured individual.'

Marbury case, then establishes the power of the judiciary to review the constitutionality of executive actions. Some matters-such as whether to veto a bill or who to appoint for an office are entirely within the president's discretion and cannot be judicially reviewed. But where the executive has a legal duty to act or refrain from acting, the federal judiciary can provide a remedy, including a writ of *mandamus*.

The Court's claimed authority to review executive actions drew the most criticism. But, because the Court announced this power in a case in which it ruled in favour of the President, there was neither a confrontation nor disregard of a judicial order.

The power of the federal courts to review presidential actions is the basis for many important Supreme Court decisions throughout American history. Perhaps, most notably, in *United States v. Nixon*, the Court's holding that the president had to comply with a subpoena to provide tapes of conversations for use in a criminal trial led to the resignation of President Richard Nixon.[20]

Does the Law Authorize Mandamus on Original Jurisdiction?

Having concluded that William Marbury had a right to the commission and that the US Supreme Court had the authority to issue *mandamus* as a remedy; the court then turned its attention to the issue of jurisdiction. As mentioned above, there is a strong argument that the Court should have begun with the jurisdictional question and discussed nothing else once it concluded that jurisdiction was absent.

Marbury argued that the US Supreme Court had original jurisdiction to hear his suit for *mandamus* pursuant to Section 13 of the Judiciary Act 1789. The Court agreed. Nevertheless, a close reading of Section 13 of the Judiciary Act raises doubts as to the Court's conclusion. Section 13 stated, in part:

> 'The Supreme Court shall also have appellate jurisdiction from the circuit courts and courts of the several states, in the cases herein after specially provided for; .... and shall have power to issue writs of prohibition .... to the district courts, when proceeding as courts of admiralty and maritime jurisdiction, and writs of mandamus, in cases warranted by the principles and usages of law, to any court appointed, or persons holding office, under the authority of the United States.[21]

Although, the Court read this statute as granting it original jurisdiction over requests for *mandamus*, alternative readings seem even more plausible. For example, the statute might be read as pertaining only to the Court's appellate jurisdiction because that is the only type of jurisdiction mentioned. Alternatively, the statute might be understood as according the Court the authority to issue *mandamus* where appropriate, in cases properly within its jurisdiction.

By this reading, the statute does not create original jurisdiction, but simply grants the Court the remedial powers when it has jurisdiction. Under either of these approaches, Marbury still would have lost, but the Court would have avoided the question as to whether the statute was constitutional, and thus, would have lost the opportunity to announce its power to declare statutes unconstitutional.

Does Mandamus on Original Jurisdiction Violate Article III?

Once it concluded that Section 13 of the Judiciary Act 1789, authorized *mandamus* on original jurisdiction, the Court then considered whether this violated Article III. The Court concluded that Article III enumerated its original jurisdiction and that US Congress could not enlarge it. Article III authorizes original jurisdiction for suits,

> 'affecting Ambassadors, other public Ministers and Consuls, and those in which a State shall be party'.

The Court said that Congress could not add to this list cases seeking a writ of *mandamus*.

Chief Justice John Marshall stated:

> 'If it had been intended to leave it in the discretion of the legislature to apportion the judicial power between the supreme and inferior courts according to the will of that body, it would certainly have been useless to have proceeded further than to have defined the judicial power, and the tribunals in which it should be vested.'

In other words, Marshall said that Article III's enumeration of original jurisdiction would be 'mere surplusage, entirely without meaning,' if Congress could add more areas of original jurisdiction.

Justice Marshall's analysis again is open to question. Article III's enumeration of the Court's original jurisdiction still has meaning even if Congress can increase it. Article III might be viewed as the floor, the minimum grant of jurisdiction that cannot be reduced by Congress.

Irrespective of possible alternative interpretations, the Court's holding that Congress cannot increase the US Supreme Court's original jurisdiction remains the law to this day. However, the Court's statement that the categories of original and appellate jurisdiction are mutually exclusive has not been followed. The Supreme Court subsequently held that Congress could grant the district courts concurrent jurisdiction over matters within the court's original jurisdiction.[22]

Generally, Article III is seen as the ceiling of federal jurisdiction, William Marbury helped establish the principle that federal courts are courts of limited jurisdiction, and that US Congress may not expand the jurisdiction granted in Article III of the US Constitution.

Can the Supreme Court Declare Laws Unconstitutional?

Having decided that the provision of the Judiciary Act 1789 was unconstitutional, the Court then considered the final question: Did it nonetheless have to follow that provision, or could the Court declare it unconstitutional? The Court began by stating:

> 'The question, whether an act, repugnant to the Constitution, can become the law of the land, is a question deeply interesting to the United States; but, happily, not of an intricacy proportioned to its interest.'

Marshall then offered several reasons why the Court could declare federal laws unconstitutional. Interestingly, although they are persuasive arguments, for each there is a reasonable answer.

Marshall argued, for example, that the US Constitution imposes limits on government powers and that these limits are meaningless unless subject to judicial enforcement. Borrowing from Alexander Hamilton's (1755/57–1804) *Federalist 78*, the Court stated:

> 'The powers of the legislature are defined and limited; and that those limits may not be mistaken or forgotten, the constitution is written.'

This is a powerful argument for 'judicial review', but it must be remembered that many other nations with written constitutions exist without according the judiciary the power to invalidate conflicting statutes.

Marshall also argued that it is inherent to the judicial role to decide the constitutionality of the laws that it applies. In perhaps the most frequently quoted words of the opinion, Marshall wrote:

> 'It is emphatically the province and duty of the judicial department to say what the law is.'

However, the Court could interpret and apply a law without deciding its constitutionality. As mentioned above, there are other countries with judiciaries and constitutions, but without the power of the courts to declare laws unconstitutional.

Marshall then argued that the Court's authority to decide 'cases' arising under the US Constitution implied the power to declare unconstitutional laws conflicting with the basic legal charter. But as Professor David P. Currie (1936–2007)[23] explains,

> 'jurisdiction over 'cases arising under this Constitution need not mean that the Constitution is supreme over federal laws as well as over executive or state action'.

In other words, the Court's power to decide cases under the Constitution still could have significant content even if the judiciary lacked the power to invalidate federal statutes. The Court would apply federal statutes to decide cases and could evaluate the constitutionality of state enactments.

Chief Justice John Marshall also defended 'judicial review' on the ground that judges take an oath of office and that they would violate this oath if they enforced unconstitutional laws. But this argument begs a question: Judges would not violate their oath by enforcing unconstitutional laws if they did not have the power to strike down such statutes. In a famous state court's dissenting opinion argued against judicial review, Justice John Bannister Gibson (1780–1853)[24] stated:

> '[The] oath to support the constitution is not peculiar to the judges, but is taken indiscriminately by every officer of the government, and is designed rather as a test of the political principles of the man, than to bind the officer in the discharge of his duty.'[25]

Finally, Chief Justice Marshall argued that judicial review is appropriate because Article VI makes the Constitution 'the supreme law of the land';

> 'the constitution itself is first mentioned; and not the laws of the United States generally, but those only which shall be made in pursuance of the constitution, have that rank.'

Again, though, to say that the constitution should control over all other laws does not necessarily mean that the judiciary has the power to invalidate laws. The supremacy clause in Article VI could be viewed as a declaration that Congress only should enact laws if they are authorized by the American Constitution.[26]

Reaction to *Marbury v. Madison*

Chief Justice John Marshall's in *Marbury v. Madison* contained lengthy *dicta* discoursing on the authority of the judiciary to say what the law is and to void unconstitutional statutes. The decision itself, in practical application, voided a section of the Judiciary Act 1789 that granted the Supreme Court the authority to issue writs of *mandamus* in its original jurisdiction. But neither the *obiter dictum* announcing the power of judicial review, nor the overturning of a section of the Judiciary Act 1789, caused any significant comment in the press after the decision was announced.

The doctrine of 'judicial review' was well accepted and it had been applied in a number of cases before *Marbury* and, as pointed out above, was not really a matter of debate except as it was raised in reference to the Repeal Act

1802. It was Marshall's lengthy, and in Jefferson's words, 'gratuitous', discussion of the right of the defendants to their commissions, and the responsibility of the executive to deliver them, that raised a storm of criticism from Jefferson and the Republicans on the one hand, and praise from the Federalists on the other.

Marshall's dicta in support of William Marbury's legal right to the commission, and his direct statement that the President should carry out the laws of Congress and be 'amenable to the laws for his conduct,' was considered by the Republicans to be a gratuitous and unjustified intrusion upon the authority of the executive. Charles Warren (1868–1954)[27] reports Jefferson's reaction,

> '..[Jefferson's] indignation over Marshall's opinion continued hot up to the day of his death. Writing four years later, at the time of the Burr trial, he stated that he had "long wished for a proper occasion to have the gratuitous opinion in *Marbury v. Madison* brought before the public and denounced as not law," and as late as 1823, he wrote to Judge William Johnson that "the practice of Judge Marshall in traveling out of his case to prescribe what law would be in a moot case not before the Court" was "very irregular and very censurable," and that in the *Marbury* Case' the Court determined at once that, being an original process, it had no cognizance of it; and therefore, the question before them was ended. But the Chief Justice went on to lay down what the law would be, had they jurisdiction of the case, to wit: that they should command the delivery [of the commissions]. The object was clearly to instruct any other Court having the jurisdiction what they should do if *Marbury* should apply to them. Besides the impropriety of this gratuitous interference [with the executive] could anything exceed the perversion of the law? Yet, this case of *Marbury v. Madison* is continually cited by Bench and Bar as if it were settled law, without any animadversion on its being merely an *obiter* dissertation of the Chief Justice.' (Warren, The Supreme Court, 1:244–245).

Although, Marshall's explicit elaboration of the authority of the Court to exercise 'judicial review' went virtually unnoticed at that time, the case has historical importance because of the numerous occasions on which this *dicta* has been cited, not as an original justification of the power of judicial review, but as an affirmation of the authority of the Court to interpret and apply the constitution to congressional and executive actions, even though the part of the *Marbury v. Madison* decision which discusses 'judicial review' is limited to an affirmation of the power in reference to congressional laws.

'Judicial review' of executive action, however, does come into the picture in *Marbury v. Madison* because of Marshall's assertion that; if the court had the power to issue a *mandamus* it would have done so, thus, directly interfering in the internal affairs of the executive branch.

President Thomas Jefferson had directed his Secretary of State James Madison, to withhold the commission. The inference of Marshall's *opinion* was that if a proper action had been brought before the lower court, a *mandamus* appropriately could have been issued to direct Madison to deliver William Marbury's commission. Marshall was not basing this part of his decision upon the Constitution, but upon the Organic Act of the District of Columbia that had been passed by Congress that authorized the President to appoint justices of the peace.

In refusing to deliver the commissions that had been executed under President John Adams' administration, President Thomas Jefferson had, although not mentioned by name in Marshall's opinion, violated statutory and not constitutional law.[28]

Judicial Activism and Restraint: Differing Exercise of Judicial Review

The terms 'activism' and 'restraint' sometimes referred to as maximalism and minimalism; to describe particular decisions, doctrines, or justices' approaches are commonly used throughout the world at present. These terms denote opposing philosophies regarding the exercise of judicial power and commonly used throughout the world at present.

Under the philosophy of 'judicial restraint', the courts are viewed as performing a circumscribed role in the political system. They are not seen as 'Platonic guardians' or 'philosopher kings'. They are not the primary custodians of the general welfare, since that role belongs to Congress and the state legislatures. Doctrines like 'standing', 'mootness', 'ripeness', and the like are reflections of 'judicial restraint', in that they serve to limit judicial inquiry into constitutional matters.[29]

The countervailing philosophy to judicial restraint is judicial activism. Activist judges tend to see the courts as coequal participants, along with the legislative and executive branches, in the process of public policy making. Activists are thus impatient with self-imposed limitations on judicial review and tend to brush aside doctrinal restraints. A jurist of activist views, Justice William O. Douglas (1898–1980)[30] once remarked that:

> '[i]t is far more important to be respectful to the Constitution than to a coordinate branch of government' (*Massachusetts v. Laird*,[31] dissenting opinion).

Dissenting in *Paul v. Davis*,[32] Justice William J. Brennan Jr[33] expressed similar views regarding the role of the Supreme Court.

> 'I had always thought that one of this court's most important roles was to provide a bulwark against governmental violation of the constitutional safeguards securing in our free society the legitimate expectations of every person to innate human dignity and a sense of worth.'

The judicial power has been used for liberal or conservative policy goals. The debate over 'judicial activism' is a long-standing one and can be traced to decisions like *Dred Scott v. Sandford*,[34] in which a conservative Supreme Court actively defended the institution of slavery on dubious constitutional grounds.

Along the same lines, in *Lochner v. New York*,[35] a conservative court used its power without restraint to frustrate the implementation of progressive economic legislation. 'Judicial activism' when it transcends limits can cause anxiety amongst judges, lawyers and even litigants. Justice Oliver Wendell Holmes Jr[36], expressed his anxiety saying 'I see hardly any limit but the sky....'[37]

Much of American constitutional law can be seen as an ongoing debate between 'judicial activism' and 'judicial restraint'. In a system committed both to representative democracy and avoiding the tyranny of the majority, it is inevitable that the courts will wrestle with the problem of defining the proper judicial role. This dynamic tension is most visible in the Supreme Court's exercise of the power of 'judicial review'.

Limiting Doctrines

The philosophy of 'judicial restraint' counsels judges to avoid broad or dramatic constitutional pronouncements. Accordingly, various doctrines limit the exercise of 'judicial review', even after a federal court has reached the merits of a case. Some of these rules are codified in Justice Louis Brandeis's (1856–1941)[38] oft-cited concurring opinion in *Ashwander v. Tennessee Valley Authority*.[39]

In *Ashwander* case, the US Supreme Court upheld the federal government's program of building dams to generate electrical power in the Tennessee Valley region. Justice Brandeis's concurring opinion has become a classic statement of the principles of 'judicial restraint'. The *Ashwander* rules, as they have come to be known, seek to protect judicial power not only by deflecting constitutional questions but by rendering narrow rulings when constitutional pronouncements cannot be avoided.

(i) The Doctrine of Strict Necessity

Under the doctrine of 'strict necessity', federal courts would attempt to avoid a constitutional question; if a case can be decided on non-constitutional grounds. For example, in *Communist Party of the United States v. Subversive Activities Control Board*,[40] the US Supreme Court remanded a case to a government agency for further proceedings rather than reach the sensitive political issue of whether the Communist Party enjoyed constitutional protection.

Similarly, in *Hurd v. Hodge*,[41] the Court addressed the issue of 'restrictive covenants', private agreements prohibiting the sale and rental of housing to blacks and other minorities. The Court held that enforcement of 'restrictive covenants' by federal courts in the District of Columbia would violate national public policy, but it did not reach the question of whether such enforcement would violate the Constitution. The Court said:

> 'It is a well settled principle that this court will not decide constitutional questions where other grounds are available and dispositive of the issues of the case.'

The Court chose not to avoid this constitutional issue in a similar case arising in a state court, however, ruling that state judicial enforcement violates the Equal Protection Clause of the 14th Amendment.

(ii) The Doctrine of Saving Construction

In order for a court to determine the constitutionality of a statute, it must first determine its exact meaning. This is known as 'statutory construction'. In construing statutes, courts often look beyond the language of the law to the intent of the legislature. Sometimes, the intent is clearly revealed in the legislative debate surrounding the adoption of the law. Often, however, legislative intent is not clear, and courts must exercise discretion in deciding what the law means.

The judicial interpretation of the statute may determine its constitutionality. Where a challenged law is subject to different interpretations, judicial restraint demands that the court choose an interpretation that preserves the constitutionality of the law. This is known as the doctrine of saving construction.

In *National Labor Relations Board v. Jones & Laughlin Steel Corporation*,[42] the Supreme Court upheld the Wagner Act 1935, a controversial federal statute regulating labour management relations in major industries. The Jones & Laughlin Steel Corporation argued that the Act was a thinly disguised attempt to regulate all industries, rather than merely those that affected interstate commerce. This point was crucial, because Congress' power in this field is limited to the regulation of interstate commerce. Given the choice between two interpretations of the Act, the Court chose the narrower one, leading to the conclusion that the Act was valid. Writing for the majority, Chief Justice Charles Evan Hughes Sr (1862–1948)[43] observed:

> "The cardinal principle of statutory construction is to save and not to destroy. We have repeatedly held that as between two possible interpretations of a statute, by one of which it would be unconstitutional and by the other valid, our plain duty is to adopt that which will save the Act.'

On 24 April 1996, President Bill Clinton (1946) signed into law the Anti-terrorism and Effective Death Penalty Act 1996. One of the provisions of this statute curtails second *habeas corpus* petitions by state prisoners who have already filed such petitions in federal court. Under the new statute, any second or subsequent *habeas* petition must meet a particularly high standard and must pass through a gate keeping function exercised by the US Courts of Appeals. A Circuit Court must grant a motion giving the inmate permission to file the petition in a district court; denial of this motion is not appealable to the Supreme Court. A prisoner on death row in the state of Georgia challenged the constitutionality of this provision, posing two constitutional objections:

(1) that the new law amounted to an unconstitutional suspension of the writ of *habeas corpus*; and
(2) that the prohibition against Supreme Court review of a circuit court's denial of permission to file a subsequent *habeas* petition is an unconstitutional interference with the Supreme Court's jurisdiction as defined in Article III of the Constitution.

In *Felker v. Turpin*,[44] the US Supreme Court unanimously rejected these challenges to the statute. In a 'saving construction', the Court interpreted the statute in such a way as to preserve the right of state prisoners to file *habeas* petitions directly in the Supreme Court. The Court stated, however, that it would exercise this jurisdiction only in 'exceptional circumstances'.

(iii) The Presumption of Constitutionality

'Presumption of constitutionality' is perhaps the most fundamental self-imposed limitation on the exercise of 'judicial review'. Under this doctrine, the courts will presume that the disputed statute is valid, until it is demonstrated otherwise.

In other words, the party attacking the validity of the law carries the burden of persuasion. This doctrine is based on an appreciation for the counter-majoritarian character of 'judicial review' and a fundamental respect for the legislative bodies in a democratic system.

The modern US Supreme Court has modified the doctrine of 'presumptive constitutionality' with respect to laws discriminating against citizens on grounds such as race, religion, and national origin. Such laws are now seen as inherently suspect and are subjected to strict scrutiny. Similarly, laws abridging fundamental rights are not afforded the traditional presumption of validity.

(iv) The Narrowness Doctrine

When a federal court invalidates a statute, it usually does so on fairly narrow grounds. The 'narrowness doctrine' counsels courts to avoid broad pronouncements that might carry unforeseen implications for future cases. The federal court's narrowly grounded decision accomplishes the desired result, striking down an unconstitutional statute, while preserving future judicial and legislative options.

In *Browsher v. Synar*,[45] the US Supreme Court struck down a provision of the Gramm-Rudman-Hollings Act, a law designed to reduce the federal deficit through automatic spending cuts. The plaintiff, Congressman Mike Synar (1950–96),[46] asked the Court to invalidate the statute on the grounds that it delegated Congress' lawmaking power to the comptroller general, an appointed official.

Instead, the Court held that Congress could not exercise removal powers over the comptroller general since he performed executive functions under the Act. Thus, the Court avoided the issue of congressional delegation of legislative power altogether. The delegation issue is potentially explosive because so many of the regulations promulgated by the federal bureaucracy are based on authority delegated by Congress to the executive branch.

(v) Avoiding the Creation of New Principles

A variation on the 'narrowness doctrine' is that courts should not create a new principle if a case may be decided on the basis of an existing one. Thus, in *Stanley v. Georgia*,[47] the US Supreme Court struck down a state law, making it a crime to possess obscene material in the home. Stretching the boundaries of the First Amendment, the Court held that this law was a violation of the freedom of expression.

Alternatively, the Court could have created a right of privacy to engage in certain activities in the home that might be subject to arrest outside the home. This, however, would have required the Court to consider the constitutionality of numerous criminal prohibitions, including laws governing possession and use of 'recreational' drugs.

The federal appellate courts are not bound to address constitutional issues precisely as they have been framed by the litigants. In its grant of *certiorari*, the Supreme Court may direct the parties to address certain issues, and then refuse to decide these issues.

For example, in *Illinois v. Gates*,[48] the Supreme Court directed the parties to argue the so-called 'good faith exception' to the 4th Amendment exclusionary rule. In its final decision in *Gates*, the Court did not address the highly controversial 'good faith exception', but, decided the case on other grounds, thus postponing for one year the creation of a new principle of constitutional law.

(vi) Stare Decisis

The term '*stare decisis*' (stand by decided matters) refers to the doctrine of precedent. It is axiomatic that American courts of law should follow precedent whenever possible, thus maintaining stability and continuity in the law. As Justice Louis Brandeis (1856–1941) once remarked,

> '*Stare decisis* is usually the wise policy, because in most matters it is more important that the applicable rule of law be settled than that it be settled right' (*Burnett v. Coronado Oil Company*[49], dissenting opinion).

Devotion to precedent is considered a hallmark of judicial restraint. Obviously, following precedent limits a judge's ability to determine the outcome of a case in a way that he or she might choose if it were a matter of first impression. The decision in *Roe v. Wade*[50] poses an interesting problem for the new US Supreme Court justices, who believe that the decision legalizing abortion was incorrect. Should a new justice who believes *Roe* was wrongly decided vote to overrule it, or should '*stare decisis*' be observed?

Although, the doctrine of '*stare decisis*' applies to American constitutional law, it is not uncommon for the Court to depart from precedent. Perhaps, the most famous reversal is *Brown v. Board of Education of Topeka*,[51] in which the Supreme Court repudiated the 'separate but equal' doctrine of *Plessy v. Ferguson*.[52] The 'separate but equal' doctrine had legitimized racial segregation in United States of America, for nearly 6 decades. Beginning with the *Brown* decision, official segregation was invalidated as a denial of the equal protection of the laws.

(vii) The Severability Doctrine

Under the doctrine of 'severability', the federal courts would generally attempt to excise the unconstitutional elements of a statute while leaving the rest of the law intact. In *Champlin Refining Company v. Corporation Commission of Oklahoma*,[53] the US Supreme Court said that

> invalid provisions of a law are to be severed 'unless it is evident that the Legislature would not have enacted those provisions which are within its power, independently of that which is not.'

The 'severability' doctrine is consistent with the philosophy of 'judicial restraint', in that 'judicial review' is employed with a minimum of 'damage' to the work of the legislature.

In *Immigration and Naturalization Service v. Chadha*,[54] for example, the US Supreme Court invalidated Section 244(c)(2) of the Immigration and Nationality Act. This specific provision permitted one House of Congress to veto decisions of the executive branch regarding deportation of aliens. The Court found this 'legislative veto' to be an unconstitutional exercise of power by Congress. The remainder of the Immigration and Nationality Act, a very important statute from the standpoint of immigration policy, was left intact.

Frequently, Congress will attach a severability clause to a piece of legislation, indicating its desire that any unconstitutional provisions be severed from the rest of the statute. In the absence of 'severability' doctrine, federal courts might presume an enactment was intended to be judged as a whole.

Related to the concept of 'severability' is the inclusion of a saving clause in many statutes. In attempting to keep pace with social change and current demands on government, Congress routinely enacts legislation repealing earlier statutes. Logically, a repeal would set aside or bring to an end all pending matters governed by the repealed statute. The saving clause simply indicates that repeal of the earlier statute is subject to certain exceptions. For example, in repealing criminal statutes, Congress often provides that prosecutions initiated prior to repeal may be pursued under repealed provisions. Although, serious constitutional questions may be raised with respect to such clauses, the Supreme Court generally recognizes their validity.

The point is well illustrated by the decision in *Bradley v. United States*.[55] Bradley was convicted in 1971; of conspiring to sell cocaine in violation of a federal statute that imposed a mandatory 5year prison term on offenders. The statute under which he was prosecuted was repealed 5 days before his conviction and sentencing. The new law contained less punitive sentencing requirements. Nevertheless, Bradley was sentenced to mandatory 5-year term under the original statute. The Supreme Court affirmed his conviction and sentence, upholding the validity of the saving clause contained in the act of repeal.

(viii) Unconstitutional as Applied

Under the Immigration and Nationality Act, the 'severability' clause distinguishes between judicial invalidation of a law as inherently unconstitutional, and, invalidation of a law as applied to particular persons or circumstances.

The philosophy of 'judicial restraint' suggests that, if possible, courts should refrain from making declarations that a challenged statute is invalid 'on its face'. Whether a federal court will invalidate a statute on its face or as applied depends on the language of the law and the facts of the case in which the law is challenged.

In *Cohen v. California*,[56] the US Supreme Court held that Section 415 of the California Penal Code concerning 'offensive conduct' law was unconstitutional. As applied in the case, where Paul Robert Cohen, was prosecuted for wearing a jacket bearing the slogan 'Fuck the Draft'. The Court held that to punish Cohen's 'immature antic' as offensive conduct would be to deny his right of free speech guaranteed by the First Amendment.

On the other hand, in *Brandenburg v. Ohio*,[57] the Court struck down Ohio state criminal syndicalism law, as inherently unconstitutional under the First Amendment, because the law prohibited the 'mere advocacy' of violence.

It should be noted that all of the limiting doctrines are subject to a degree of manipulation in order to achieve the desired outcomes. Doctrines are sufficiently complex and imprecise; to permit 2 judges to reach opposite conclusions about their application to a given case. Nevertheless, the creation and continuance of these doctrines suggest sensitivity on the part of the federal judiciary to the inherent tensions surrounding the exercise of judicial review in a democratic polity.

Principles of Judicial Restraint

The principles of 'judicial restraint' were stated concisely by Justice Louis Brandeis in *Ashwander v. Tennessee Valley Authority*[58] decided by the US Supreme Court which are now known to be *Ashwander* Rules. These are:—

1. The court will not pass on the constitutionality of legislation in a friendly, non-adversary proceeding, declining because to decide such questions is legitimate only in the last resort, and as a necessity in the determination of a real, earnest, and vital controversy between individuals.
2. The Court will not anticipate a question of constitutional law in advance of the necessity of deciding it.
3. It is not the habit of the Court to decide questions of a constitutional nature unless absolutely necessary to a decision of the case.
4. The Court will not formulate a rule of constitutional law broader than is required by the precise facts to which it is to be applied.
5. The Court will not pass upon a constitutional question although properly presented by the record, if there is also present some other ground upon which the case may be disposed of.
6. The Court will not pass upon the validity of a statute upon complaint of one who fails to show that he is injured by its operation.
7. The Court will not pass upon the constitutionality of a statute at the instance of one who has availed himself of its benefits.
8. When the validity of an act of the Congress is drawn in question, and even if a serious doubt of constitutionality is raised, it is a cardinal principle that this court will first ascertain whether a construction of the statute is fairly possible by which the question may be avoided.

The Political Question Doctrine.

(i) Definition

The US Supreme Court has been of the view that certain allegations of unconstitutional government conduct should not be ruled on by the federal courts even though all of the jurisdictional and other justiciability requirements are met. The Court has said that constitutional interpretation in these areas should be left to the politically accountable branches of government, the President and US Congress.

In other words, the 'political question' doctrine refers to subject matter that the Court believes to be inappropriate for 'judicial review'. Although, there is an allegation that the US Constitution has been violated, the federal courts refuse to rule and instead dismiss the case, leaving the constitutional question to be resolved in the political process.[59]

(ii) Why Is the Political Question Doctrine Confusing?

In many ways, the 'political question' doctrine is the most confusing of the justiciability doctrines.

Firstly, the confusion stems from the fact that the 'political question' doctrine is a misnomer; the federal courts deal with political issues all the time. For example, in *United States v. Nixon*,[60] the Court decided that President Richard Nixon had to comply with a *subpoena*; to produce tapes of presidential conversations that were needed as evidence in a criminal trial—a decision with the ultimate political effect of causing a President to resign. The Supreme Court's direct involvement in the long political process has included ending racial discrimination in political primaries and elections.[61] Secondly, the 'political question' doctrine is particularly confusing; because the Court has defined it very differently over the course of American history.

The Court first spoke of political questions in *Marbury v. Madison*.[62] Chief Justice John Marshall wrote:

> 'By the Constitution of the United States, the President is invested with certain important political powers, in the exercise of which he is to use his own discretion and is accountable only to his country in his political character and to his own conscience...The subjects are political. [B]eing entrusted to the executive, the decision of the executive is conclusive. Questions, in their nature political, or which are by the constitution and laws, submitted to the executive can never be made in this court'.

Chief Justice Marshall contrasted political questions with instances where individual rights were at stake; the latter, according to the Court, never could be political questions.

The Court's definition of 'political questions' in *Marbury v. Madison* was quite narrow. It included only matters where the president had unlimited discretion, and there was thus no allegation of a constitutional violation. For example, presidents have the choice of whether to sign or veto a bill or who to appoint for a vacancy on the federal judiciary. Because the Constitution vests the president with plenary authority in these areas, there is no basis for a claim of a constitutional violation regardless of how the president acts. But, if there is a claim of an infringement of an individual right, in other words, if the plaintiff has standing, there is not a political question under the formulation presented in *Marbury v. Madison*.In sharp contrast, the 'political question' doctrine now includes instances where individuals allege that specific constitutional provisions have been violated and that they have suffered a concrete injury.[63] The 'political question' doctrine definitely is not limited to instances in which the president is exercising discretion and there is no claim of unconstitutional conduct. But, the Court has never explained the differing content given to the term 'political question'; in fact, the Court even invokes *Marbury* in its modern different cases.

(iii) The Baker Criteria

Finally, and perhaps most importantly, the 'political question' doctrine is confusing because of the court's failure to articulate useful criteria for deciding what subject matter presents a non-justiciable political question. The classic, oft-quoted statement of the 'political question' doctrine was provided in *Baker v. Carr*.[64] The US Supreme Court stated:

> 'Prominent on the surface of any case held to involve a political question is found a textually demonstrable commitment of the issue to a coordinate political department; or a lack of judicially discoverable and manageable standards for resolving it; or the impossibility of deciding without an initial policy determination of a kind clearly for non-judicial discretion; or the impossibility of a court's undertaking independent resolution without expressing lack of the respect due coordinate branches of government; or an unusual need for unquestioning adherence to a political decision already made; or the potentiality of embarrassment from multifarious pronouncements by various departments on one question.'

Virtually, every case considering the 'political question' doctrine quotes this language. But, these criteria seem useless in identifying what constitutes a political question. For example, there is no place in the Constitution where the text states, that the legislature or executive should decide whether a particular action constitutes a constitutional violation.

The Constitution does not mention 'judicial review', much less limit it by creating 'textually demonstrable commitments' to other branches of government. Similarly, most important constitutional provisions are written in broad, open-textured language and certainly do not include 'judicially discoverable and manageable standards'.

The Court also speaks of determinations of a kind 'clearly for a nonjudicial discretion', but that hardly is a criterion that can be used to separate 'political questions' from justiciable cases.

In other words, it may be impossible for a court or a commentator to apply the *Baker v. Carr* criteria to identify what cases are 'political questions'. As such, it is hardly surprising that the doctrine is described as confusing and unsatisfactory.

The 'political question' doctrine can be understood only by examining the specific areas where the Supreme Court has invoked it. Specifically, the Court has considered the 'political question' doctrine in the following areas: the republican form of government clause and the electoral process, foreign affairs, Congress's ability to regulate its internal processes, the process for ratifying constitutional amendments; instances where the federal court cannot shape effective equitable relief, and the impeachment process.

(iv) Justifications for the Political Question Doctrine

The underlying issue is whether the 'political question' doctrine should exist at all. Defenders of the doctrine make several arguments. First, and most commonly, it is argued that the 'political question' doctrine accords the federal judiciary the ability to avoid controversial constitutional questions and limits the courts' role in a democratic society.

Professor Alexander Bickel (1924–74)[65] was the foremost advocate of this position. He wrote:

> 'Such is the foundation, in both intellect and instinct, of the political question doctrine: the Court's sense of lack of capacity, compounded in unequal part of—
> (a) the strangeness of the issue and its intractability to principled resolution;
> (b) the sheer momentousness of it, which tends to unbalance judicial judgment;
> (c) the anxiety, not so much that the judicial judgment will be ignored, as that perhaps it should but will not be;
> (d) finally ('in a mature democracy'), the inner vulnerability, the self-doubt of an institution which is electorally irresponsible and has no earth to draw strength from.'[66]

Professor Bickel contended that it was simply better for the federal courts to avoid deciding certain cases, especially, so as to preserve what he perceived as the judiciary's fragile political legitimacy. Justice Felix Frankfurter (1882–1965) argued, on this basis, the court should not have decided whether malapportionment violates the Constitution,[67] and many commentators have suggested that the federal courts should not review impeachment proceedings conducted by Congress because any ruling would jeopardize the court's credibility and prestige.

A second argument for the 'political question' doctrine is that; it allocates decisions to the branches of government that have superior expertise in particular areas. For example, some argue that the Court rightly has treated many constitutional issues concerning foreign policy to be 'political questions' because of the greater information and expertise of the other branches of government.

Third, the 'political question' doctrine is defended on the ground that the federal courts' self-interest disqualifies them from ruling on certain matters. Specifically, it is argued that the courts should not become involved in reviewing the process for ratifying constitutional amendments because amendments are the only way to overturn the Supreme Court's constitutional interpretations. Justice Lewis Franklin Powell Jr (1907–98), for example, spoke of the dangers 'of having the Supreme Court oversee the very constitutional process used to reverse [its] decisions.'[68]

Finally, the 'political question' doctrine is justified on 'separation of powers' grounds; as minimizing judicial intrusion into the operations of the other branches of government. The argument is that in certain cases an effective remedy would require judicial oversight of day-to-day executive or legislative conduct. For example, a lawsuit contending that there were constitutional deficiencies in training the Ohio National Guard, was deemed to be a 'political question' because a remedy would involve judicial control and supervision over the National Guard's activities.[69]

(v) Justiciability of *Bush v. Gore*

The case of *Bush v. Gore* and its justiciability has great relevance to the doctrine of political question. On 12 December 2000, the US Supreme Court for the first time in American history, effectively, decided a presidential election with its ruling in *Bush v. Gore*.[70]

In a *per curiam* opinion joined by 5 of the justices, the Supreme Court ruled 5 to 4; that counting the uncounted ballots without standards denies equal protection and that counting could not continue because the state of Florida wished to choose its electors by the 12 December 'safe harbor' date set by federal law.

The *per curiam* opinion was joined by Chief Justice William Rehnquist and Justices Sandra Day O'Connor, Antonin Scalia, Anthony Kennedy, and Clarence Thomas. Additionally, Chief Justice Rehnquist wrote an opinion concurring in the judgment, which was joined by Justices Scalia and Thomas, arguing that the Florida Supreme Court had impermissibly changed Florida's election law in a manner that violates federal law. Each of the other 4 Justices wrote dissenting opinions.

The *per curiam* opinion began its analysis by reiterating that the right to vote is a fundamental right and that

> '[w]hen the state legislature vests the right to vote for President in its people, the right to vote as the legislature has prescribed is fundamental and one source of its fundamental nature lies in the equal weight accorded to each vote and the equal dignity owed to each voter.

The US Supreme Court said that the central problem was that the Florida Supreme Court ordered the counting of the uncounted ballots, but failed to prescribe standards. The *per curiam* opinion stated:

> 'The problem inheres in the absence of specific standards to ensure its equal application. The formulation of uniform rules to determine intent based on these recurring circumstances is practicable and, we conclude, necessary.'

The Court said that this results in similar ballots being treated differently. The Court also objected to the procedures being followed in the recount:

> 'In addition to these difficulties the actual process by which the votes were to be counted under the Florida Supreme Court's decision raises further concerns. That order did not specify who would recount the ballots. The county canvassing boards were forced to pull together ad hoc teams comprised of judges from various Circuits who had no previous training in handling and interpreting ballots. Furthermore, while others were permitted to observe, they were prohibited from objecting during the recount.'

The Court thus concluded that counting the uncounted ballots pursuant to the order of the Florida Supreme Court would deny equal protection:

> 'The recount process, in its features here described, is inconsistent with the minimum procedures necessary to protect the fundamental right of each voter in the special instance of a statewide recount under the authority of a single state judicial officer.'

The Court was explicit that it was deciding just the matter before it and was not setting a general precedent. The *per curiam* opinion declared:

> 'Our consideration is limited to the present circumstances, for the problem of equal protection in election processes generally presents many complexities.'

The Court then confronted the key question: Should the case be remanded to the Florida Supreme Court for it to set standards for the counting or should the US Supreme Court order an end to the counting process? The Court, in its *per curiam* opinion, said that Florida indicated that it wished to observe the 12 December date set by federal law, which created a conclusive presumption that a state's electors chosen by that date would be recognized by Congress. The Court thus ordered an end to the counting, stating:

> The Supreme Court of Florida has said that the legislature intended the State's electors to "participat[e] fully in the federal electoral process," as provided in 3 U.S.C. § 5. That statute, in turn, requires that any controversy or contest that is designed to lead to a conclusive selection of electors be completed by December 12. That date is upon us, and there is no recount procedure in place under the State Supreme Court's order that comports with minimal constitutional standards. Because it is evident that any recount seeking to meet the December 12 date will be unconstitutional for the reasons we have discussed, we reverse the judgment of the Supreme Court of Florida ordering a recount to proceed.
>
> Seven Justices of the Court agree that there are constitutional problems with the recount ordered by the Florida Supreme Court that demand a remedy. The only disagreement is as to the remedy. Because the Florida Supreme Court has said that the Florida Legislature intended to obtain the safe-harbor benefits of 3 U.S.C. § 5, Justice Breyer's proposed remedy – remanding to the Florida Supreme Court for its ordering of a constitutionally proper contest until December 18 – contemplates action in violation of the Florida election code, and hence could not be part of an "appropriate" order authorized by Fla. Stat. §s 102. 168(8) (2000).

Thus, the *per curiam* order put an end to the counting of votes in the state of Florida based on its interpretation of the Florida election law.

Chief Justice William Rehnquist wrote a separate opinion concurring in the judgment, which was joined by Justices Antonin Scalia and Clarence Thomas. Justice Rehnquist opinion focused on 3 U.S.C. § 5, which provides that the state's selection of electors

> 'shall be conclusive, and shall govern in the counting of the electoral votes as provided in the Constitution, and as hereinafter regulated, so far as the ascertainment of the electors appointed by such State is concerned.'

If the electors are chosen under laws enacted prior to election day, and if the selection process is completed 6 days prior to the meeting of the electoral college. Chief Justice Rehnquist said that this prevents a state from changing its electoral process after the election, and that, Florida Supreme Court had done this by usurping the authority of Florida law, vested in the Florida Secretary of State and the Florida Circuit Courts. Chief Justice Rehnquist concluded that the Florida Supreme Court:

> 'significantly departed from the statutory framework in place on November 7, and authorized open-ended further proceedings which could not be completed by December 12, thereby preventing a final determination by that date.

Each of the other 4 Justices wrote dissenting opinions. Justice John Paul Stevens, joined by Justices Ruth Bader Ginsburg and Stephen Breyer, challenged the *per curiam*'s premise that there was a denial of equal protection. He argued that the procedure created by the Florida Supreme Court, with a trial judge resolving disputes, could prevent unequal treatment of like ballots. He explained:

> 'Admittedly, the use of differing substandard for determining voter intent in different counties employing similar voting systems may raise serious concerns. Those concerns are alleviated – if not eliminated – by the fact that a single impartial magistrate will ultimately adjudicate all objections arising from the recount process.'

Justice Stevens said that if the lack of standards for counting is the problem, the solution is to send the case back to Florida for the creating of standards and the subsequent counting. He concluded his dissent with powerful language:

> 'The endorsement of that position by the majority of this Court can only lend credence to the most cynical appraisal of the work of judges throughout the land. It is confidence in the men and women who administer the judicial system that is the true backbone of the rule of law. Time will one day heal the wound to that confidence that will be inflicted by today's decision. One thing, however, is certain. Although we may never know with complete certainty the identity of the winner of this year's Presidential election, the identity of the loser is perfectly clear. It is the Nation's confidence in the judge as an impartial guardian of the rule of law.'

Justice Souter's dissenting opinion, joined by the other 3 dissenting Justices, objected to the Court hearing the case at all. Justice Souter argued that there were no significant federal issues raised and that the case should have been left to the Florida courts to resolve. Justice Ginsburg's dissent argued that there was no denial of equal protection and that, in any event, the appropriate solution was to have the case sent back to Florida for the counting to continue.

Finally, Justice Breyer acknowledged that there were 'equal protection' problems with counting votes without standards but argued that the Court was wrong in ending the counting rather than remanding the case for counting with standards. He stressed that there is nothing magical about the 12 December deadline; states could still choose their electors after that date and could be confident that Congress would recognize them. He ended his opinion forcefully:

> 'I fear that in order to bring this agonizingly long election process to a definitive conclusion, we have not adequately attended to that necessary "check upon, our own exercise of power", "our own sense of self-restraint." Justice Brandeis once said of the Court, "The most important thing we do is not doing." What it does today, the Court should have left undone, I would repair the damage done as best we now can, by permitting the Florida recount to continue under uniform standards.'

(vi) Issues to Consider concerning *Bush v. Gore*

There are many issues to consider regarding *Bush v. Gore.* First, was the case justiciable? Gore did not raise justiciability issues in his briefs or at oral argument. Yet, justiciability is jurisdictional; the Court must raise it on its own. The question is whether Bush had standing to raise the equal protection claims of the Florida voters. Also, was the case ripe for review at the time it was decided by the United States Supreme Court? Should the Court have found that the matter was a 'political question' and left it to Congress to ultimately resolve?

Second, was the Court correct in finding a denial of equal protection? 7 of the Justices expressed concern over a denial of equal protection from counting votes without uniform standards. However, it is notable that Justices Souter and Breyer, who shared this concern with the majority, did not file opinions 'concurring in part and dissenting in part,' but rather just dissented. How, exactly, was equal protection denied? Also, there will be the issue of whether the Court has created a new principle of equality in voting that will be the basis for future successful challenges to variations within a state in election practices. Several such suits have already been filed. The Court said that it was deciding only the issue before it, but its ruling already has led to lawsuits across United States arguing that variations within a state in conducting elections violate equal protection.[71]

Third, was the Court justified in ending the counting in Florida? The Court, in its *per curiam* opinion, said that the Florida Supreme Court had indicated that it wanted to follow the 12 December deadline set by the federal 'safe harbor' statute. Since it was 12 December, the Supreme Court ordered an end to the counting. But, because it was an issue of Florida state law, should the Supreme Court have remanded the case for the Florida Supreme Court to decide the content of Florida law under the unprecedented circumstances?

Racial Discrimination in Voting Rights.

The 15th Amendment precludes denial of the right to vote on account of race or previous condition of servitude. Race discrimination with regard to voting also receives strict scrutiny under the 'equal protection' clause of the 14th Amendment as a racial classification and as an infringement of the fundamental right to vote.

For example, any laws that would exclude a racial minority from voting are sure to be declared unconstitutional as denying 'equal protection'. In *Nixon v. Herndon*, the Supreme Court invalidated a Texas law that excluded blacks from voting in political primary elections.[72] Subsequently, when the state attempted to stop holding political primary elections, the state delegated this task to private entities, the parties themselves. The US Supreme Court concluded that this, too was unconstitutional and ruled that because the parties were performing public function they had to meet the requirements of equal protection.[73]

Even laws that are facially neutral would be declared unconstitutional when they were motivated by a discriminatory purpose and have a discriminatory impact. For instance, in 1865, in *Guinn v. United States*; the Supreme Court declared unconstitutional a literacy test for voting that contained a 'grandfather clause' that exempted from the requirement all who could vote, and their descendants.[74] The obvious motivation was to exclude blacks from voting while providing an exception that benefited solely whites.

In *Gomillion v. Lightfoot*, the Court found a denial of equal protection when city borders were redrawn to exclude black voters.[75] Tuskegee, Alabama, redrew its boundaries in a manner that changed its shape from a square to a 28 sided figure. Virtually, all of the African American voters were placed outside the city. The racial discrimination was obvious and thus, so was the unconstitutionality of the districting.[76]

Two difficult questions concern whether at large elections are unconstitutional where they have a discriminatory effect and whether the government may use race in drawing election districts to help racial minorities.

Doctrine of Political Question in Pakistan

On the doctrine of political question, the Supreme Court of Pakistan has held that any question being on a political issue would not deter the Court from determining it on the touchstone of the Constitution. The courts should not adopt a 'political question' doctrine for refusing to determine difficult and knotty problems barring political overtones. It would amount to abdication of judicial power which neither the Constitution permits, nor the law allows. The crucial factor is that the action impugned is shown to be violative of the Constitution.[77] In another case, it was held that, if the question before it is political in nature and involves interpretation of Constitutional provisions, the Court would be entitled to resolve the controversy.[78]

Judicial Review in the United Kingdom, Pakistan, India and other countries

Since the Constitution is the supreme law, the courts have the power to judicially review the legislative enactments and executive actions and declare them *ultra vires* of the constitution and therefore void and of no legal effect if they are found in conflict with constitutional provisions or not supported by them.

The power of 'judicial review' is of necessity; to be exercised by the courts as it has the final say in the construction of the constitution and interpretation of law while acting as arbiters of legal disputes. The Supreme Court India in interpreting the words of the constitution, held in *Navinchandra Mafatlal v. Commissioner of Income Tax, Bombay*,[79] that the same principles apply which are applicable in interpreting statutes. Constitutional provisions must be construed liberally and broadly and not in any narrow or pedantic sense because as observed by the Privy Council in *Henrietta Muir Edward v. Attorney-General for Canada*,[80] a constitution is a living tree capable of growth and expansion within its natural limits.

> 'So, while construing a constitutional provision, the approach of the court should be dynamic, progressive and liberal keeping in view the changed situation, which is intended to be catered for by an existing provision of the constitution or by a new legislation within the compass of the Constitution'

as observed by Chief Justice Ajmal Mian[81] in *Sabir Shah v. Shad Muhammad Khan*.[82]

There have been in the past, two approaches to the interpretation of constitutional instruments, namely, the progressive approach originally adopted by the United States Supreme Court and the literal approach followed by the British Courts. The British Courts have invariably used the phrase of 'Interpretation of Constitution', according to which the Courts are concerned with the meaning of the words employed in the organic laws. The term has been employed in countries whose constitutions are legislative Acts given by British Parliament.

The Privy Council in entertaining appeals from Commonwealth countries on constitutional questions, regularly said in the past that since these constitutions were Acts of the British Parliament, the judicial role was the traditionally limited one of interpreting legislative language. Viscount Richard Haldane L.C. (1856–1928)[83], was representative of this view when he said in 1913 in *Attorney General for Commonwealth of Australia v. Colonial Sugar Refining Co. Ltd.*,[84] a case involving the Australian Constitution:

> 'The question (their Lordships) have to decide depends simply on the interpretation of the language of an Act of Parliament'.

The Privy Council, accordingly resolved constitutional issues by utilizing the ordinary rules of statutory interpretation and generally refused to consider anything other than the parliamentary language. Such interpretation was in fact tantamount to finding the intent of those responsible for the use of such language. Courts concerned with constitutional adjudication and construction in countries of the British Commonwealth having written constitutions have been said to be unduly literalistic and legalistic, to apply statutory rules of interpretation to constitutions, to generally refuse to appreciate the importance of facts in constitutional construction, to be unreceptive to materials outside the constitution, to be disinclined to explore openly the alternatives open to them and social consequences of possible rulings, and had not generally understood the proprieties of the methodology of a jurisprudence of interests.

(i) Purposive approach

In England, the general rule has been the 'exclusionary rule' according to which, for example, reference to external sources or materials was not permissible for parliamentary material as an aid to statutory construction.

The rule was probably first stated by Justice Willes, in *Millar v. Taylor*[85] and re-affirmed in *Davis v. Johnson*[86] and *Hadmor Production Ltd. v. Hamilton.*[87] The rule was first extended in *Salkeld v. Johnson,*[88] so as to prohibit the court from looking even at reports made by commissioners on which legislation was based. It was however later relaxed so as to permit reports of commissioners and white papers to be looked at for the purpose solely of ascertaining the mischief which the statute is intended to cure, but not for the purpose of ascertaining the meaning of the words used by parliament to affect such cure.

For instance the *Eastman Photographic Materials Co. Ltd. v. Comptroller-General of Patents, Designs and Trademarks,*[89] *Assam Railway and Trading Co. Ltd. v. Commissioner of Inland Revenue,*[90] *Reg. v. Secretary of State for Transport, Ex parte Factortame Ltd.*[91] The House of Lords went further than this and took into consideration a Law Commission Report not only for the purpose of ascertaining the mischief but also for the purpose of drawing an inference as to parliamentary intention from the fact that Parliament had not expressly implemented one of the Law Commissioner's recommendations.

In *Pickstone v. Freemans,*[92] the House of Lords in construing a statutory instrument, did have regard to what was said by the Minister who initiated the debate on the regulations. Lord Keith of Kinkel (1920–2002)[93] after pointing out that the –

> 'draft Regulations were not capable of being amended when presented to Parliament,' said that it was 'entirely legitimate for the purpose of ascertaining the intention of Parliament to take into account the terms in which the draft was presented by the responsible Minister and which formed the basis of its acceptance'.

Further, in *Fothergill v. Monarch Airlines Ltd.*[94] Lord Kenneth Diplock (1907–85)[95] said:

> 'Elementary justice or .... the need for legal certainly demands that the rules of which the citizen is to be bound should be ascertainable by him (or, more realistically, by a competent lawyer advising him) by reference to identifiable sources that are publicly accessible'.

The Law Commission Act, 1965 of England and Scotland; in their joint Report on the Interpretation of Statutes in 1969; and, also the Renton Committee on the Preparation of Legislation, in 1975; both recognized that there was much to be said in principle for relaxing the rule, but, advised against a relaxation at present on practical grounds. However, both bodies recommended changes in the form of legislation which would, if implemented, would assist the court in its search for the true parliamentary intention in using the statutory words.

But in the same year, Lord Reid (1890–1975)[96] in *Reg. v. Warner,*[97] recognized the necessity of referring to parliamentary proceedings. He said:

> '.... fees which would otherwise have been paid by members of the public for the places which the taxpayers' children occupied. The education of the children at reduced fee was treated as emoluments of the employment and accordingly chargeable to income tax. The question for decision arose as to what is "the cash equivalent of the benefit". The taxpayers contended that the admission of the taxpayers' children did not increase these basic expenses in any way. The only expenses attributable to the education of the taxpayer's children (additional food, laundry, stationary etc., was fully covered by the one-fifth concessionary fee paid by the taxpayers. Therefore, "the cash equivalent of the benefit" was nil.

The revenue on the other hand contended that the 'expense incurred in or in connection with' the provision of education for the children of the taxpayers was exactly the same as the expense incurred in or in connection with the education of all other pupils at the school and accordingly, the expense of education of any one child is a proportionate part of the cost of running the whole school. The special commissioner held in favour of taxpayers. That decision was reversed by Justice John Vinelott (1923–2006)[98], whose decision was affirmed by the Court of Appeal. The taxpayers' appeal to the House of Lords was allowed with costs.

In order to decide which of the two rival contentions represented the intention of Parliament in using the statutory words, the House of Lord invited the parties to consider whether they wished to present argument on the question; whether it was appropriate for the House (under Practice Statement ([Judicial Precedent] [1966] 1. W.L.R. 1234) to depart from previous authority of this House, which forbids reference to such material provided in deciding the present appeal.

Two question arose before the House.

- First was whether in construing ambiguous or obscure statutory provisions the House of Lords should relax the historic rule that the courts must not look at the parliamentary history of legislation or *Hansard*[99] for the purpose of construing such legislation.
- Second was whether, if reference to such materials would otherwise be appropriate, it would contravene Article 9 of the Bill of Rights 1688 or parliamentary privilege so to do. Article 9 of the Bill of Rights 1688 provides:

> 'that the freedom of speech and debates or proceedings in parliament ought not to be impeached or questioned in any Court or place out of Parliament'.

Lord William Hugh Griffiths (1923–2015)[100] held–

> 'The ever-increasing volume of legislation must inevitably result in ambiguities of statutory language which are not perceived at the time the legislation is enacted. The object of the Court in interpreting legislation is to give effect, so far as the language permits, to the intention of the legislature. If the language proves to be ambiguous there is no sound reason not to consult *Hansard* (official record of parliamentary debates in UK) to see if there is a clear statement of the meaning that the words are intended to carry. The days have long passed when the Courts adopted a strict constructionist view of interpretation which required them to adopt the literal meaning of the language. The Courts now adopt a purposive approach which seeks to give effect to the true purpose of legislation and are prepared to look at much extraneous material that bears upon the background against which the legislation was enacted. Why then cut ourselves off from the one source in which may be found an authoritative statement of the intention with which the legislation is placed before Parliament.'

Lord Browne-Wilkinson (1913–2018)[101] held:

> 'Statute law consists of the words that Parliament has enacted. It is for the Courts to construe those words and it is the Court's duty in so doing to give effect to the intention of Parliament in using those words. It is an inescapable fact that, despite all the care taken in passing legislation some statutory provisions when applied to the circumstances under consideration in any specific case are found to be ambiguous. Why in such a case should the Courts blind themselves to a clear indication of what Parliament intended in using those words? The Court cannot attach a meaning to words which they cannot bear, but if the words are capable of bearing more than one meaning why should Parliament's true intention not be enforced rather than thwarted. The Courts can now look at white papers and official reports for the purpose of finding the "mischief" sought to be corrected, although not at draft clause or proposals for the remedying of such mischief. A ministerial statement made in Parliament is an equally authoritative source of such information: why should the Courts be cut off from this source of information as to the mischief aimed at? In any event, the distinction between looking at reports to identity the mischief aimed at but not to find the intention of Parliament in enacting the legislation is highly artificial. The conclusion, therefore, is that parliamentary material can be used as an aid to the construction of statute where:
>
> (i) legislation is ambiguous or obscure, or leads to an absurdity;

(ii) the material relied upon consists of one or more statements by a Minister or other prompter of the Bill together if necessary with such other parliamentary material as is necessary to understand such statements and their effect;

(iii) the statements relied upon are clear'.

In *Regina v. Warwickshire County Council, ex parte Johnson*,[102] the House of Lords had to consider Section 20(1) of the Consumer Protection Act 1987. In allowing the appeal, the House referred to and found decisive an explanation of a clause by the Minister of Committee in the House of Lords, when an amendment to clarify the clause was made but withdrawn. Six days later, in *Stubbings v. Webb*,[103] the House allowed the appeal after referring to and finding persuasive what the prompter of the Bill which became the Law Reform (Limitation of Actions) Act 1954 had said, in the debate on the Second Reading in 1953.

Finally, in *Foster v. Chief Adjudication Officer*[104] the House again referred to *Hansard*, this time to the consideration by the House of Commons; of the amendments made in the House of Lords, to the Bill which became the Social Security Act 1936. Lord Bridge of Harwich (1917–2007)[105] said, that he doubted whether those who had sat in *Pepper v. Hart*[106] anticipated that within so short a time, *Hansard* would have been found to provide the answer in 3 other cases before the House.[107]

(ii) Progressive approach

A written constitution like that of Pakistan, India and the US can only be construed and not interpreted. It has to be given not only meaning to its clauses and words but also their significances have to be found. The reason is, as observed in *McCulloch v. Maryland*,[108] Chief Justice John Marshal,

> 'The Constitution [is] intended to endorse for ages to come, and, consequently, to be adapted to the various crises of human affairs.

Further, as observed by Justice Saeeduzzaman Siddiqui (1939–2013)[109] in *Sabir Shah v. Shad Muhammad Khan*,[110]

> 'The Constitution of a country is an organic document which reflects the will and aspiration of the nation and provides for the system of governance not only in the present but also for future. The Constitution of the country is rarely changed, and it is intended to remain operative for centuries. A document of such basic nature, therefore, has to be interpreted in a manner which promotes and preserves its organic characteristics and does not make it an imprisonment of the past alone'.

Chief Justice Marshall in a *locus classicus* on constitutional construction, namely, *McCulloch v. Maryland* applying the progressive approach, ruled on the relations between the Federal Union and its Constituent States. Chief Justice Sir Samuel Walker Griffith (1845–1920)[111] of the Australian High Court in *D'Emden v. Pedder* (1904)[112] followed the approach and reasoning of Chief Justice John Marshall and remarked:[113]

> 'We are not, of course, bound by the decision of the Supreme Court of United States. But we all think that it would need some courage for any Judge at the present day to decline to accept the interpretation placed upon the United States Constitution by the succession of great jurists who have since adorned the Bench of the Supreme Court at Washington. So far, therefore, as the United States Constitution and the Constitution of the Commonwealth are similar, the construction put upon the former by the Supreme Court of the United States may well be regarded by us in construing the Constitution of the Commonwealth, not as an infallible guide, but as a most welcome aid and assistance.'

(iii) Sociological construction

The approaches of the courts to constitutional construction have been historical, philosophical, and sociological. Today, constitutional construction is increasingly considered as sociological in the sense that courts openly investigate the social utility of proposed rulings and consciously weigh competing societal interests and balance the same to accord with the community consensus of values.

Sociological jurisprudence minimizes framers' interests, literalism of language, the uses of history and judicial precedents. It stresses an awareness of the importance of facts in constitutional litigation, the need to consider the social consequences of alternative ruling open to a court, and the obligation to identify, balance and adjust the opposed social interests or values involved in a particular case. Roscoe Pound (1870–1964)[114] in his famous book *Law Finding Through Experience and Reason* (1960) at page 63 wrote:[115]

> 'The Constitution is not a glorified police manual. Constitutional provisions lay down great principles to be applied as starting points for legal and political reasoning in the progress of society. A constitution may lay down hard and fast rules such as, for example, those fixing the exact terms of office and apportioning duties among public functionaries. But the principles established by the Constitution are not to be interpreted and applied strictly according to the literal meaning of words used by the framers as if they laid down rules. Interpretation of constitutional principles is a matter of reasoned application of rational precepts to conditions of time and place'.

(iv) Change in approach by Commonwealth Courts

There are now sufficient authorities and utterances from those courts to suggest their own serious doubts about the wisdom of their ways. The Australian High Court was certainly neither literalistic nor legalistic when in *R. v. Brislan; Ex parte Williams*,[116] it held the Commonwealth Parliament had legislative power over radio broadcasting although the Australian Constitution conferred upon it only power over 'postal, telegraphic, telephonic and other like services.' In 1964, the Australian High Court further held in *R. v. Public Vehicles Appeal Tribunal*,[117]

> 'We must remember that it is a Constitution we are construing, and it should be construed with all the generality which the words admit.'

Similarly, Burma Supreme Court in *U Htwe (a) A. E. Madari v. U Tun Ohn & One*;[118] Chief Justice Sir Ba U (1887–1963)[119] said:

> 'The sections of the Constitution should not be interpreted in a narrow and technical manner but should on all occasions be interpreted in a large, liberal and comprehensive spirit. The time has surely come for the Privy Council and the High Courts of Commonwealth countries to commit themselves openly to the methodologies of a jurisprudence of interests in constitutional adjudication.'

(v) Approach of Pakistan Supreme Court

In Pakistan, the earlier judgment of the Supreme Court borrowed the rules of literal interpretation from the judgments of the British Courts, giving least thought to the consequences of such interpretation.

In fact, the Supreme Court, in *Special Reference*,[120] observed that:

> 'the rule of construction is to intend the legislature to have meant what they actually expressed', and 'it matters not, in such a case, what the consequences may be'.

Chief Justice Muhammad Munir (1895–1979), in this case also said that,

> 'it is wrong to start with some a *priori* ideas of that intention and to try by construction to wedge it into the words of the statute.'

However, in the same year Chief Justice Muhammad Munir in *Jibendra Kishore v. East Pakistan*,[121] stated:

> 'Consistently with the language used, constitutional instruments should receive a broader and more liberal construction than statutes.

Later, in *Abul A'la Maudoodi v. Govt. of West Pakistan*,[122] there is an inclination of the Supreme Court in favour of progressive approach. Here, the Supreme Court while interpreting the fundamental right of freedom to form associations held that

> 'forming of associations necessarily implies carrying on the activities of an association, for the mere forming of association would be of no avail.'

It was further held that:

> 'the ordinary conception of a political party includes a right within the framework of the Constitution to exert itself through its following and organization, and using all available channels of mass communication, to propagate its view in relation to the whole complex of the administrative machine, including the Legislatures, in respect of matters which appear to it to require attention for the amelioration of conditions generally throughout the nation, for improvements particularly in administrative procedures and policies as well as in the legislative field, even to the extent of proposing and pressing for amendment of the Constitution itself.'

Further, in *Benazir Bhutto v. Federation of Pakistan*,[123] Chief Justice Muhammad Haleem (1925–2006) held that the progressive approach,

> 'is meant to establish that the Constitution is not merely an imprisonment of the past, but is also alive to the unfolding of the future,'

and ruled that:

> 'The liberties, in this context, if purposefully defined, will serve to guarantee genuine freedom; freedom not only from arbitrary restraint of authority, but also freedom from want, from poverty and destitution and from ignorance and illiteracy.'

Benazir Bhutto (1953–2007) had challenged the compulsory registration of political parties and the rendition of accounts by such parties as violative of the right to form and be member of a political party contained in Article 17(2) of the Constitution. The Supreme Court held that the right conferred by Article 17(2), includes not merely the right to form a political party but comprised, also, other consequential rights. Similarly, in *Benazir Bhutto v. Federation of Pakistan*,[124] it was held that:

> 'the right to form or to be a member of a political party comprises the right to participate in and contest an election'.

Lastly, in *Muhammad Nawaz Sharif v. Federation of Pakistan*,[125] Chief Justice Dr Nasim Hasan Shah (1929–2015) made a formal declaration in favour of the progressive approach by observing:

> 'With the passage of time and the evolution of civil society great changes occur in the political, social and economic conditions or society. There is, therefore, the corresponding need to re-evaluate the essence and soul of the fundamental rights as originally provided in the Constitution. They require to be construed in consonance with the changed conditions of the society and must be viewed and interpreted with a vision to the future… It is on this principle of interpretation that the import of the rights given in the US Constitution such as the "right of assembly" and the "right of association", has been so expanded and so enlarged by the US Supreme Court that even peripheral rights (or rights of penumbra as described in some judgments, i.e., rights so closely associated to the basic right which is specifically given in the Constitution) are now being also enforced as basic rights.'

Justice Shafiur Rahman (1929) in this case observed that:

> 'while the language of the Constitution does not change, the changing circumstances of a progressive society for which it was designed yield new and fuller import to its meaning.'

Applying the progressive approach, the Supreme Court in *Nawaz Sharif*, held that the fundamental 'right to form or be a member of a political party' includes the peripheral right to form the government, and, continue in government for its normal tenure, and, not to be dismissed by the head of the state if the political party possesses the requisite majority in the National Assembly.

The following special rules of constitutional interpretation were enunciated by Chief Justice Muhammad Munir, in the *Special Reference*,[126]—

(i) The duty imposed upon the judiciary, however, of discovering the intention of the framers of the Constitution and true meanings of the constitutional instrument is equally imperative, and the fundamental principle of constitutional construction has always been to give effect to the intent of the framers of the organic law and of the people adopting it.
(ii) Another elementary rule of construction of constitutional instruments is that effect should be given to every part and every word of the Constitution. Hence, as a general rule, the Courts should avoid a construction which renders any provision meaningless or inoperative and must lean in favour of a construction which will render every word operative rather than one which may make some words idle and nugatory.
(iii) The next rule in construing constitutional provision is that it is the duty of the Courts to have recourse to the whole instrument, if necessary, to ascertain the true intent and meaning of any particular provision. The best mode of ascertaining the meaning affixed to any word or sentence by a deliberative body is by comparing it with the words and sentences with which it stands connected, and a constitutional provision or a 'phrase in a constitutional provision must be read in connection with the context.' Therefore, particular phrases of a Constitution must be construed with regard to the remainder of the instrument and to the express intent of the constitutional convention in adopting it.'
(iv) And the last rule... is that if there be any apparent repugnancy between different provisions, the Court should harmonize them if possible. The rules of construction of constitutional law require that two sections be so construed, if possible, as not to create a repugnancy, but that both be allowed by stand, and that effect given to each. Cases may, however, arise where it is impossible to harmonize or reconcile portions of a Constitution. In such a case, if there is a conflict between a general and a special provision, the special provision must prevail in respect of its subject-matter, as it will be regarded as a limitation on the general grant'.

The rules of construction, enunciated in *Special Reference*, were affirmed and reiterated by Justice Hamoodur Rahman (1910–81), (later the 7th Chief Justice of Pakistan) in *Fazlul Quader Chowdhry v. Muhammad Abdul Haque*,[127] and *State v. Zia-ur-Rahman*,[128] Justice Shafiur Rahman, in *Muhammad Nawaz Sharif* said that:

> 'There are three rules of interpretation peculiar to the Constitution distinguishing it from every other instrument. These principles stand recognized in all countries having written Constitution. While the language of the Constitution does not change, the changing circumstances of a progressive society for which it was designed yield new and fuller import to its meaning. The entire Constitution has to be read as an integrated whole, and no one particular provision destroying the other but each sustaining the other. This is the rule of harmony, rule of completeness and exhaustiveness and the rule of paramountcy of the written Constitution. The words of the written Constitution prevail over all unwritten Conventions, Precedents and Practices.'

In *Shirin Munir v. Government of the Punjab*,[129] Justice Shafiur Rahman, after reproducing the rules of Interpretation of Constitution enunciated by Chief Justice Muhammad Munir, in *Special Reference No. 1 of 1957*,[130] re-stated some other special rules enunciated by Chief Justice Hamoodur Rahman, in *Zia-ur-Rahman* case, and summarized in *Federation of Pakistan v. Saeed Ahmad Khan*,[131] as follows:

(i) The Constitution is a fundamental or organic supreme law standing on a somewhat higher position than the other laws of the country.
(ii) The Constitution is the source from which all governmental power emanates and it defines its scope and ambit so that each functionary should act within his respective sphere.
(iii) The Courts are creatures of the Constitution; they derive their powers and jurisdictions from the Constitution and must confine themselves within the limits set by the Constitution.
(iv) Under a Constitution prescribing system where there is a trichotomy of sovereign powers, the judicial power must from the very nature of things be vested in the judiciary.

(v) The judiciary does claim and has always claimed that it has the right to interpret the Constitution and to say as to what a particular provision of the Constitution means or does not mean even if it is a provision seeking to oust its own jurisdiction.

(vi) That ouster of jurisdiction is not to be readily inferred, because the consistent rule is that provisions seeking to oust the jurisdiction of superior Courts, even by a constitutional provision, are to be construed strictly with pronounced leaning against ouster.

(vii) It is not, however, the function of the judiciary to legislate or to question the wisdom of the law-giver if the law has been competently made without transgressing the limitations of the Constitution. If a law has been competently made the judiciary cannot refuse to enforce it even if the result be to nullify its own decisions.

(viii) The law-giver has also every right to change, amend or clarify the law if the judiciary has found that the language used conveys an intent different from that which was sought to be conveyed by the law giver.

(ix) The Constitution has to be construed like any other document reading it as a whole and giving to every part thereof a meaning consistent with the other provisions of the Constitution.

(x) As far as possible each provision of the Constitution should be construed so as to harmonize it with all the others.

To sum up, the Supreme Court of Pakistan, if and when the opportunity arises, has to amend the principles of interpretation in their application to the constitutional provisions owing to the changing conditions of the society, for the reason, that the words of the permanent document never change, but, the conditions of the society are subject to continuous change. The constitution has to be treated as a progressive and not static document.

(vi) Approach of Indian Supreme Court

In India, the following American principles relating to judicial deference to determinations of fact by the legislature or the executive, have been followed in numerous cases. It was held in *State of Madras v. V.G. Row*:[132]

> 'While the Court naturally attaches great weight to the legislative judgment, it cannot desert its own duty to determine finally the constitutionality of an impugned statute.'

In *Hanif Quareshi v. State of Bihar* case,[133] it was held:

> 'The legislature is the best judge of what is good for the community, by whose suffrage it comes into existence. This should be the proper approach for the Court but the ultimate responsibility for determining whether a restriction upon a fundamental right is in the interests of the public must rest with the Court and the Court must not shirk that solemn duty cast on it by the Constitution.'

Thus, the Indian Supreme Court starts with the proposition that:

> 'The legislature is the best judge of what is good for the community,'[134] But, the final power and duty to determine the constitutional validity of the law rests with the court.[135]

As regards the executive, under the system of parliamentary government, the executive is responsible to the legislature regarding the administration of the country and matters of administration are beyond the reach of the judiciary.[136] The broad principle is that the courts would not interfere in matters involving administrative policy[137] or relating to the day-to-day administration, unless—

(a) some constitutional provision is violated by such administrative action[138]; or
(b) where the administrative policy, action or instruction is arbitrary, irrational or *malafide*.[139]
(c) where the administrative policy, action or instruction is arbitrary, irrational or *malafide*.[140]
(d) where the administrative power is conferred or regulated by statute, the impugned action is *ultra vires*.

Therefore, whenever the government has the power to determine facts or to form an opinion on the basis of certain facts or a matter of policy, the court would start with the presumption that the executive determination is proper, unless *ultra vires* or *mala fides* is established.

The presumption in favour of the executive determination enhances where the power is vested in some expert body or authority,[141] or the matter involves what is called 'expertise' for e.g., as to what is needed for the maintenance of integrity and efficiency in the public services.[142]

Subject to the foregoing exceptions, the general proposition remains, that the court cannot pronounce upon the wisdom of executive policy because it does not appeal to the court;[143] or to substitute its own judgment or wisdom for that of the executive.[144]

In *Marbury's* case, Chief Justice John Marshall placed the doctrine on a sure footing by saying that, since the judges, as directed by the US Constitution, took oath to support the Constitution, which is paramount law of the nation, it was the duty of the judges to annul any law made by the legislature which violated the Constitution or was repugnant to it.

In India, this proposition has been embodied in Article 13 of the Indian Constitution itself, so far as the provisions guaranteeing the Fundamental Rights (in Part III) are concerned. Clauses (1) and (2) of this Article lay down that,

> 'any law made by any legislature in India, whether before or after the commencement of the Constitution, shall be void if and in so far as it offends against any of the Fundamental Rights included in Part III.'[145]

But, as Chief Justice Sir Harilal Jekisundas Kania (1890–1951),[146] observed, in the early case of *Gopalan*,[147]

> 'The inclusion of Article 13(1) and (2) in the Constitution appears to be a matter of abundant caution. Even in their absence, if any of the fundamental rights was infringed by any legislative enactment, the Court has always the power to declare the enactment, to the extent it transgresses the limits, invalid.'

Of coursc, in *Gopalan's* case, the Supreme Court of India did not, in the foregoing context, explain why, even without any express provision such as Article 13; a statute offending against a constitutional guarantee of fundamental right would have been declared by the court as 'void'. But, that was because the Indian Supreme Court acknowledged the Marshallian doctrine of the constitution being the higher or 'paramount' or fundamental law of the land. As Chief Justice Kania, observed later—

> 'It is difficult upon any general principles, to limit the omnipotence of the sovereign legislative power by judicial interposition, except so far as the express words of a written Constitution give that authority ... [But] it is only in express constitutional provisions limiting legislative power and controlling the temporary will of a majority by a permanent and paramount law settled by the deliberate wisdom of the nation that one can find a safe and solid ground for the authority of Courts of Justice to declare void any legislative enactment.'

As the paramount law, the constitution creates the legislature itself, and confers upon it the power to make laws subject to certain limitations, without which, of course, the power of the legislature to make laws would have been plenary. It is because the limitations contained in Part III, and, other Articles[148] of the Indian Constitution are imposed by a paramount or fundamental law, that a law made by the legislature must give way whenever it transgresses the limitations imposed by the constitution, and out of that arises the function of the judiciary, to invalidate such unconstitutional law, as Justice Sudhi Ranjan Das (1894–1987),[149] explained in *Gopalan*'s case.

> 'While in the main leaving our Parliament and the State Legislatures supreme in their respective legislative fields, our Constitution has, by some of the Articles put upon the legislatures certain specified limitations some of which will have to be discussed hereafter. The point to be noted, however is that in so far as there is any limitation on the legislative power, the Court must, on a complaint being made to it, scrutinize and ascertain whether such limitation has been transgressed and if there has been any transgression the Court will courageously declare the law unconstitutional, for the Court is bound by its oath to uphold the Constitution.'

More explicit was Chief Justice P.B. Gajendragadkar (1901–81),[150] in *the Reference* case[151]—

> '...though our Legislatures have plenary powers, they function within the limits prescribed by the material and relevant provisions of the Constitution.'
>
> 'In a democratic country governed by a written Constitution, it is the Constitution which is supreme and sovereign. It is no doubt true that the Constitution itself can be amended by the Parliament, but that is possible because Article 368 of the Constitution itself makes a provision in that behalf, and the amendment of the Constitution can be validly made only by following the procedure prescribed by the said article ......'
>
> 'When a statue is challenged on the ground that it has been passed by a legislature without authority, or has otherwise unconstitutionally trespassed on fundamental rights, it is for the courts to determine the dispute and decide whether the law passed by the legislature is valid or not... so, we feel no difficulty in holding that the decision about the construction of Article 194(3) must ultimately rest exclusively with the Judicature of this country'.

It would be evident that the doctrine of 'higher law' has since been firmly established in India, if the mandatory provisions of the constitution are considered outside the Fundamental Rights in Part III. In that wide realm, there is only one provision in Article 254(1) which enjoins the courts to annul a State law which is repugnant to a Union law in the Concurrent sphere. But, even though there is no provision corresponding to Article 13 or 254(1), to invalidate a Union or State law which violates any of the other provisions of the constitution, it is now settled that the same result would happen if the provision which has been violated is 'justiciable' and 'mandatory' in nature. The instances are numerous and can hardly be exhausted.[152]

Judicial Activism in India and Pakistan

In India and Pakistan, there have been various phases of 'judicial activism' and 'judicial restraint'; in the exercise of the doctrine of 'judicial review'. Since Britain does not have a written constitution, the 'judicial review' is restricted to subordinate legislation or the executive actions.

Nevertheless, Lord Tom Denning (1899–1999)[153] is known for activism in the recent judicial history of UK. He is credited for introducing doctrines of 'promissory estoppel' and 'legitimate expectations' in the English law. These doctrines have been sources of judicial activism in UK.

The case of *Kesavananda Bharati v. State of Kerala*,[154] was one of the earliest examples of 'judicial activism' on the part of the Supreme Court of India; where it was held that the Supreme Court could strike down even a constitutional amendment if it is inconsistent with the basic structure of the Constitution. The concept of 'basic structure/features' of the Constitution is now fully established in Indian jurisprudence, the latest example being the striking down of the 99th Constitutional Amendment introducing, a Judicial Commission for selection of judges, the same being held as it violates one of the basic features of the Constitution namely '*independence of judiciary*'.[155]

The Supreme Courts of India and Pakistan have frequently engaged in 'judicial activism' with regard to the appointment of judges. It began with the case of *Supreme Court Advocates-on-Record Association v. Union of India*,[156] in which, word 'consultation' with the Chief Justice of India was interpreted not to mean ordinary consultation but, meaningful and binding consultation, in the context of independence of judiciary. The Supreme Court of Pakistan followed this interpretation soon thereafter, in what is known as *judges'* case.[157]

The Supreme Court of India, in its opinion given in Presidential Reference for advisory jurisdiction, virtually created a new body of judges by the name of Collegium of Judges of the Supreme Court, which is composed of a 4 senior most judges, who assist and advise the Chief Justice of India in the process of consultation, for selection and appointment of judges of the Supreme Court and the High Courts. The Constitution of India makes no mention of Collegium of Judges anywhere in its provision. However, this body is purely a product of 'judicial activism' of the Supreme Court of India.

In Pakistan, the Supreme Court has been resisting the acceptance of the theory of 'basic structure/features' of the Constitution. In the case of *Mahmood Khan Achakzai v. Federation of Pakistan*,[158] the Supreme Court for the first time tried to identify certain 'basic structure/features' guiding principles of the Constitution, as based on Islamic principles of democracy, equality, freedom, justice and fair play. In the case of *Zafar Ali Shah v. Pervez Musharraf*,[159] the Supreme Court further elaborated the concept by describing the independence of judiciary, federalism, parliamentary form of government blended with Islamic provisions as the salient features of the Constitution. Finally, in *District Bar Association, Rawalpindi v. Federation of Pakistan*,[160] 17 judges of the Supreme Court, sitting as a full Court, deciding the constitutionality of the 21st Constitutional Amendment and by a majority of 13 to 4 held, among others, that the salient features of the Constitution of Pakistan include democracy, parliamentary form of government and the independence of judiciary.

From the above review of cases from India and Pakistan, it is evident that the Supreme Courts of both, India and Pakistan have followed the course of 'judicial activism' particularly in the matter of interpretation of the provisions of the Constitution of Pakistan.

NOTES

1. Justice Fazal Karim, *Judicial Review of Public Action*, 2nd ed, (Karachi: Pakistan Law House, 2018), pp. 7–8.
2. Alpheus Thomas Mason, William Merritt Beaney, Donald Grier Jr. Stéphenson, *American Constitutional Law*, 7th ed. (New Jersey: Prentice-Hall Inc., 1983), p. 37.
3. 347 U.S. 483 (1954).
4. 369 U.S. 186 (1962).
5. 377 U.S. 533 (1964).
6. Felix Frankfurter served as an Associate Justice of the US Supreme Court.
7. Robert Yates was a politician and a judge, best known for his anti-federalist stances.
8. Benjamin Nathan Cardozo served as an Associate Justice of the US Supreme Court.
9. Supra Note 2, p. 38.
10. 5 U.S. 137 (1803).
11. Peter Woll, *Constitutional Law: Cases and Comments* (N.J.: Prentice-Hall, Inc., 1981), p. 8.
12. *Hayburn's Case*, 2 U.S. 409 (1792).
13. 5 U.S. 137 (1803).
14. John Adams was a founding father and served as 2nd US President.
15. Thomas Jefferson was a founding father and served as 3rd US President.
16. Aaron Burr served as the 3rd vice president of the United States during President Thomas Jefferson's first term.
17. Erwin Chemerinsky, *Constitutional Law: Principles and Policies*, 2nd ed. (N.Y.: Aspen Law & Business, 2002), pp. 39–40.
18. *Ex part McCardle*, 74 U.S. 506 (1869).
19. Supra Note 17, p. 41.
20. 418 U.S. 683 (1974).
21. The Judiciary Act 1789, 1 Statute 73 at 81.
22. *Ames V Kansas*. 111 U.S. 449 (1884).
23. David P. Currie was the Edward H. Levi Distinguished Professor of Law at the University of Chicago. Chronicler of the US Supreme Court.
24. John Bannister Gibson served as Chief Justice of the Supreme Court of Pennsylvania.
25. *Eakin v. Raub*, 12 Sergeant & Rawle 330 (Pa 1825) (Justice Bannister Gibson Dissenting), reprinted in Gerald Gunther, Kathleen M. Sullivan, *Constitutional Law*, 13th ed. (Foundation Press, 1997).
26. Supra Note 17, pp. 45–6.
27. Charles Warren was an American lawyer and legal scholar.
28. Peter Woll, Supra note 7, pp. 21–2.
29. Otis H. Stephens Jr, John M Schebs, *American Constitutional Law*, 3rd ed. (Belmont, California: Thomson West, 2003), pp. 44.
30. William O. Douglas served as an Associate Justice of the US Supreme Court.
31. 400 U.S. 886 (1970).
32. 424 U.S. 693 (1976).
33. William J. Brennan Jr. was an Associate Justice of the US Supreme Court.
34. 604 U.S. 393 (1857).
35. 198 U.S. 45 (1905).
36. Oliver Wendell Holmes Jr. was an Associate Justice of the US Supreme Court.
37. *Baldwin v. Missouri*, 281 U.S. 586 (1930).
38. Louis Brandeis was an Associate Justice of the US Supreme Court.
39. 297 U.S. 288 (1936).
40. 351 U.S. 115 (1956).
41. 334 U.S. 24 (1948).

42. 301 U.S. 1 (1937).
43. Charles Evan Hughes Sr. was the 11th Chief Justice of the United States (1930–41).
44. 518 U.S. 105 (1996).
45. 478 U.S. 714 (1986).
46. Mike Synar was a Democrat who represented Oklahoma.
47. 394 U.S. 557 (1969).
48. 462 U.S. 213 (1983).
49. 285 U.S. 393 (1932).
50. 410 U.S. 113 (1973).
51. 347 U.S. 483 (1954).
52. 163 U.S. 537 (1896).
53. 286 U.S. 210 (1932).
54. 462 U.S. 919 (1983).
55. 410 U.S. 605 (1973).
56. 403 U.S. 15 (1971).
57. 396 U.S. 444 (1969).
58. 297 U.S. 288 (1936).
59. Supra Note 17, pp. 127–8.
60. 418 U.S. 683 (1974).
61. *Nixon v. Herndon*, 273 U.S. 536 (1972) (declaring unconstitutional racial discrimination in the Democratic political primary in Texas). The Court said that a claim that the matter was a political question because it involved the political process was 'little more than a play upon words'.
62. 5 U.S. 137 (1803).
63. *Luther v. Borden*, 48 U.S 1 (1849) (declaring non-justiciable a suit brought under the republican form of government clause even though the effect was to leave people in jail who contested the constitutionality of their conviction).
64. 369 U.S. 186 (1962).
65. Alexander Bickel was an American legal scholar and an expert on the United States Constitution.
66. Alexander Bickel. *The Supreme Court 1960 Term Foreword: The Passive Virtues*, 75 Harv. L. Rev. 40, 46 (1961).
67. *Baker v. Carr*, 369 U.S. 186 (1962) p. 267.
68. Supra Note 17, pp. 130–1.
69. *Gilligan v. Morgan*, 413 U.S. 1 (1973).
70. 531 U.S. 98 (2000).
71. Supra Note 17, pp. 866–7.
72. 273 U.S. 536 (1927).
73. *Terry v. Adams* 345 U.S. 461 (1953); *Smith v. Allwright*, 321 U.S. 649 (1944); *Nixon v. Condon*, 286 U.S. 73 (1932), (discussing holding elections for public office as a public function).
74. 238 U.S. 347 (1915).
75. 364 U.S. 339 (1960).
76. *Hunter v. Underwood*, 471 U.S. 222 (1985) (declaring unconstitutional a state law denying the right to vote to those convicted of crimes involving moral turpitude because the law was motivated by a discriminatory purpose).
77. *Mahmood Khan Achakzai v. Federation of Pakistan*, PLD 1997 S.C. 426.
78. *Manzoor Ahmad Wattoo v. Federation of Pakistan*, PLD 1997 Lahore 38.
79. AIR 1955 S.C. 58.
80. 1930 AC 124.
81. Ajmal Mian was the 14th Chief Justice of Pakistan.
82. PLD 1995 S.C. 66.
83. Viscount Richard Haldane was an influential British Liberal and later Labour politician, lawyer and philosopher.
84. (1913) UKPC 76.
85. (1769) 4 Burr. 2303.
86. (1979) A.C. 264.
87. (1983) 1 A.C. 191.
88. (1848) 2 Exch. 256.
89. (1898) A.C. 571.
90. (1935) A.C. 445.
91. (1990) 2 A.C. 85.
92. (1989) A.C. 66.

93. Lord Keith of Kinkel a Scottish judge, was appointed as Lord of Appeal in Ordinary.
94. (1981) A.C. 251.
95. Lord Kenneth Diplock was Justice of the High Court in England and Wales and Lord Justice of Appeal before being created a Law Lord.
96. Lord James Reid was a Scottish Unionist politician and one of the most outstanding judges of the 20th century.
97. (1969) 2 A.C. 256.
98. Sir John Vinelott was a leading barrister at the Chancery bar and an English High Court judge in the Chancery Division.
99. *Hansard* is the traditional name of the transcripts of parliamentary debates in Britain and many Commonwealth countries.
100. Lord William Hugh Griffiths was a Lord Justice of Appeal, and was also Lord of Appeal in Ordinary, a life peer with the title Baron Griffiths.
101. Lord Browne-Wilkinson was a British judge who served as a Lord of Appeal in Ordinary, and also as Senior Lord of Appeal in Ordinary.
102. (1993) 2 W.L.R. 1, (1993) 1 All E.R. 299.
103. (1993) 2 W.L.R. 120, (1993) 1 All E.R. 322.
104. (1993) 2 W.L.R. 292, (1993) 1 All E.R. 705.
105. Lord Bridge of Harwich was a British judge who served as Lord of Appeal in Ordinary.
106. [1992] UKHL 3; [1993] AC 593.
107. A.G. Chaudhry, *Lectures on Constitutional Law* (Lahore: Irfan Law Book House, 1994), pp. 297–9.
108. 17 U.S. 316 (1819).
109. Saeeduzzaman Siddiqui was the 15th Chief Justice of Pakistan.
110. PLD 1995 S.C. 66 at 225.
111. Sir Samuel Walker Griffith was the 1st Chief Justice of Australia.
112. [1904] HCA 1; (1904) 1 CLR 91.
113. Supra Note 107, pp. 300–1.
114. Roscoe Pound was an American legal scholar and educator.
115. Ibid, p. 301.
116. (1935) 54 CLR 262.
117. (1964) 113 CLR 225.
118. (1948) BLR 541.
119. Sir Ba U served as Chief Justice of the Supreme Court of Burma from 1948–52, and President of the Union of Burma.
120. PLD 1957 S.C. 219.
121. PLD 1957 S.C. 9.
122. PLD 1964 S.C. 673.
123. PLD 1988 S.C. 416.
124. PLD 1989 S.C. 66.
125. PLD 1993 S.C. 473.
126. PLD 1957 S.C. 219.
127. PLD 1963 S.C. 486.
128. PLD 1973 S.C. 49.
129. PLJ 1990 S.C. 159.
130. PLD 1957 S.C. 219.
131. PLD 1974 S.C. 151.
132. (1952) S.C.R. 597.
133. *Hanif Quareshi v. State of Bihar,* AIR 1958 S.C. 731.
134. *State Of Bihar vs Maharajadhiraja Sir Kameshwar,* 1952 1 SCR 889.
135. *Abdul Hakim Quareshi v. State of Bihar,* AIR 1961 S.C. 448.
136. *Virendra v. State of Punjab,* AIR 1957 S.C. 896, 1958 SCR 308.
137. *Tamil Nadu Education Dept. v. State of Tamil Nadu,* AIR 1980 S.C. 379.
138. *State of Madras v. V.G. Row,* AIR 1952 S.C. 597; *Joseph Kuruvilla Vellukunnel v. Reserve Bank of India,* AIR 1962 S.C. 1371.
139. *Barium Chemicals v. Company Law Bd.,* AIR 1967 S.C. 295; *Iswarlal Girdharlal Joshi v. State of Gujarat,* AIR 1968 S.C. 870; *Swadeshi Cotton Mills v. State of U.P.,* AIR 1961 S.C. 1381; *Matajog Dobey v. H.C. Bhari,* (1955) 2 S.C.R. 925; *Ram Krishna Dalmia v. Justice S.R. Tendolkar,* AIR 1958 S.C. 538; *Union of India v. Jyoti Prakash Mitter,* AIR 1971 S.C. 1093; *Union of India v. Sankal Chand Himatlal,* AIR 1977 S.C. 2328; *S.P. Gupta v. Union of India,* AIR 1982 S.C. 149.

140. *Barium Chemicals v. Company Law Bd.*, AIR 1967 S.C. 295; *Iswarlal Girdharlal Joshi v. State of Gujarat*, AIR 1968 S.C. 870; *Swadeshi Cotton Mills v. State of U.P.*, AIR 1961 S.C. 1381; *Matajog Dobey v. H.C. Bhari*, (1955) 2 S.C.R. 925; *Ram Krishna Dalmia v. Justice S.R. Tendolkar*, AIR 1958 S.C. 538; *Union of India v. Jyoti Prakash Mitter*, AIR 1971 S.C. 1093; *Union of India v. Sankal Chand Himatlal*, AIR 1977 S.C. 2328; *S.P. Gupta v. Union of India*, AIR 1982 S.C. 149.
141. *Joseph v. Reserve Bank of India*, AIR 1962 S.C. 1371; *Prag Oil Mill v. Union of India*, AIR 1978 S.C. 1296.
142. *Cf. Kameshwar v. State of Bihar*, AIR 1962 S.C. 1166.
143. *Gupta v. Union of India*, AIR 1982 S.C. 149.
144. *Nagarajan v. State of Karnataka*, AIR 1976 S.C. 1976, *Makashi v. Menon*, AIR 1982 S.C. 101.
145. *Mahendra v. State of U.P.*, AIR 1963 S.C. 1019.
146. Sir Harilal Jekisundas Kania was the first Chief Justice of India.
147. *Gopalan v. State of Mahas* (1950) S.C.R. 88.
148. *In re: Delhi Laws Act*, (1951) S.C.R. 747.
149. Sudhi Ranjan Das was the 5th Chief Justice of India.
150. P. B. Gajendragadkar was the 7th Chief Justice of India.
151. *In re: Article 143, Constitution of India*, AIR 1965 S.C. 745.
152. Durga Das Basu, *Comparative Constitutional Law*, (New Delhi: Prentice Hall of India (Pvt) Ltd. 1984), pp. 466–8.
153. Lord Tom Denning was a British judge and was appointed Master of the Rolls in Court of Appeals.
154. AIR 1973 SC 1460.
155. *Supreme Court Advocates- on- Record Association v. Union of India* (2016) 5 SCC 1.
156. AIR 1994 SC 268.
157. *Al Jehad Trust v. Federation of Pakistan*, PLD 1996 S.C. 324.
158. PLD 1997 S.C. 426.
159. PLD 2000 S.C. 869.
160. PLD 2015 S.C. 401.

13 Theories of Constitutional Interpretation

Judicial Interpretation of the Constitution

The remarkable adaptability of the US Constitution is, to a very considerable degree, a function of the power of the courts, and especially of the US Supreme Court, to interpret the provisions of the document in an authoritative manner. In *Marbury v. Madison*,[1] the US Supreme Court asserted that:

> "[i]t is, emphatically, the province and duty of the judicial department to say what the law is."

In *Marbury*, Chief Justice John Marshall (1755–1835), was referring not only to the interpretation of ordinary legislation, but to the interpretation of the US Constitution. Although, the courts do not have a monopoly on constitutional interpretation, it has been widely recognized and generally accepted since *Marbury v. Madison* that the court's interpretations are authoritative.

Judges, lawyers, politicians, and scholars have long debated theories of how to understand and apply the constitution of the 18th century to the issues of the day. The debate over 'constitutional interpretation' has become more heated and more public as the federal courts have assumed a more central role in the public policy making process.

On one side of the debate are those who subscribe to the doctrine of original intent, which holds that, in applying the provision of the US Constitution to a contemporary question, judges should try determining what the framers intended to mean by that provision. On the other side, there are those who advocate the idea of a 'living Constitution,' whose meaning must change to reflect the spirit of the age. This debate is often lurking behind disagreements over particular constitutional questions ranging from abortion to women's rights. It's being constantly reargued and rekindled by the decisions of the US Supreme Court.

In some instances, the language of the Constitution leaves little room for varying judicial interpretation. For example, Article I, Section 3, provides unequivocally that—

> '[t]he Senate of the United States shall be composed of two Senators from each State.'

But, not all of the provisions in the Constitution are as clear in their meaning. Perhaps, the best example is the 'necessary and proper' Clause of Article I, Section 8. It is through this clause that the Supreme Court, granted Congress a deep reservoir of implied powers in what can undoubtedly be called the second most important case in US constitutional law, *McCulloch v. Maryland*.[2]

Another example is, Article I, Section 8, Clause 3, giving Congress the authority to 'regulate Commerce ... among the several States.' The Supreme Court under this clause, has upheld sweeping congressional action in the fields of labor relations, antitrust policy, highway construction, airline safety, environmental protection, criminal justice, and civil rights, to name just a few of the more prominent examples.[3]

The Doctrine of 'Implied Powers'

Article I, Section 8 of the US Constitution enumerates the powers of Congress. It also grants Congress the authority:

> 'to make all laws which shall be necessary and proper for carrying into execution the foregoing (enumerated) powers, and all powers vested by this Constitution in the government of the United States, or in any department or officer thereof.'

In the first decade of the Republic, the US Supreme Court faced the issue of the constitutional scope of congressional powers. Would the Congress be limited to the exercise of those powers explicitly enumerated, with the necessary and proper clause being narrowly interpreted to encompass only the means of execution of the enumerated powers? Or would the Congress be granted wide latitude in exercising powers that could be broadly implied from the enumerated provisions of Article I?

The early debate on what constituted legitimate congressional authority arose in context to federalism, reflecting on the underlying political controversy over the boundaries of national power in relation to the states. In 1791, Alexander Hamilton's (1755/57–1804) successful attempt to establish a national bank, known as First Bank of the United States (1791–1811)[4], focused on this debate between the Federalists (now a political party) and the anti-Federalists (now the Republican Party), over the proper scope of national power in relation to the states. Hamilton's arguments in favor of the bank essentially repeated those he had made in *The Federalist*, that supported expanded national powers, which went far beyond Article I's specifically enumerated powers.[5]

After the Congress passed its first legislation creating a national bank in 1791; President George Washington (1732–99), requested the views of Alexander Hamilton and Thomas Jefferson (1743–1826), regarding the bank's constitutionality. Hamilton wrote to the President,

> '... It is conceded that implied powers are to be considered as delegated equally with expressed ones. Then it follows, that as a power of erecting a corporation may as well be implied as any other thing, it may as well be employed as an instrument or means of carrying into execution any of the specified powers, as any other instrument or means whatever. The only question must be in this, as in every other case, whether the means to be employed, or, in this instance the corporation to be erected, has a natural relation to any of the acknowledged objects or lawful ends of the government. Thus, a corporation may not be directed by Congress for superintending the police of the city of Philadelphia, because they are not authorized to regulate the police of that city. But one may be erected in relation to the collection of taxes, or to the trade with foreign nations, or to the trade between the states, or with the Indian tribes; because it is the province of the federal government to regulate those objects, and because it is incident to a general sovereign or legislative power to regulate a thing, to employ all the means which relate to its regulation to the best and greatest advantage.'[6]

Jefferson countered Hamilton's views with the following statement:

> 'I considered the foundation of the Constitution as laid on this ground: That all powers not delegated to the United States, by the Constitution, nor prohibited it to the states, are reserved to the states or to the people.' ... To take a single step beyond the boundaries thus specially drawn around the powers of Congress is to take possession of a boundless field of power, no longer susceptible of any definition. The incorporation of a bank, and the powers assumed by this bill, has not, in my opinion, been delegated to the United States by the Constitution.'

Jefferson went on to point out that the power to incorporate a bank is not specifically enumerated, nor can it be implied by the enumerated powers. Therefore, a bank, is not a means of executing any of the enumerated powers, nor, Jefferson added, is it necessary for such powers to be executed. In February 1791, the Hamiltonian opinion, won the day, when President George Washington signed the 'bank bill' creating the First Bank of the United States.

By 1811, the Republican Party controlled the Congress with a Jeffersonian cast, and refused to grant a new charter to the bank, which was dissolved then. The ensuing financial chaos caused by the burgeoning of state banks issuing paper money, aggravated by the financial crisis created by the War of 1812,[7] convinced a Republican Congress and President James Madison (1751–1836), to re-establish the bank in 1816. Madison and many of his Republican colleagues in Congress, including the great states-rights advocate, John C. Calhoun (1782–1850),[8] of South Carolina, agreed that a national bank was both constitutional and necessary. But, opponents of the bank repeated the strict constructionist arguments, that had been advanced by Thomas Jefferson in 1790 against the first bank act.

In 1819, the question of the constitutional validity of the bank, was faced by the Supreme Court in *McCulloch v. Maryland*. The state of Maryland had passed a law that in effect levied a tax upon a branch of the national bank operating in the state. In contravention of the state law, the bank had issued notes without paying the requisite fee under state legislation. In Baltimore County Court, the state sued James William McCulloch, a cashier of the Second Bank of the United States,[9] of Baltimore branch; and McCulloch lost the case. The case was then appealed to the Maryland Court of Appeals; the judgment was upheld by the Court, it was later appealed to the United States Supreme Court by a writ of error.[10]

McCulloch v. Maryland and The Scope of Congressional Powers

Factual Background of *McCulloch*

McCulloch v. Maryland is the seminal case defining the scope of the federal legislative power and its relationship to state government authority. The specific issue posed in *McCulloch*, is whether the state of Maryland could collect a tax from the Bank of the United States. Chief Justice John Marshall (1755–1835) used the case as an opportunity to broadly define Congress's powers and narrowly restrict the authority of state governments to impede the federal government.

The controversy over the First Bank of the United States began almost 30 years before *McCulloch*, in 1790, when there was a major dispute in both Congress and the executive branch, as to whether Congress had the authority to create such a bank.[11] The Secretary of the Treasury, Alexander Hamilton, strongly favored creating a Bank of the United States, but was opposed by the Secretary of State, Thomas Jefferson and Attorney General, Edmund Randolph (1753–1813)[12]. Both Jefferson and Randolph argued that Congress lacked the authority under the US Constitution to create such a bank, and that, by doing so would usurp state government prerogatives. Ultimately, Alexander Hamilton convinced President George Washington to support establishing the bank, but the debate persisted in Congress. James Madison, then in the House of Representatives, echoed the views of Jefferson and Randolph, and opposed the bank. Despite this opposition, the Federalists (political party), who by then solidly controlled Congress, successfully enacted legislation to create the First Bank of the United States.

The bank existed for 21 years, until its charter expired in 1811. However, after the War of 1812, the country experienced serious economic problems and, evidently, the Second Bank of the United States[13] was re-created in 1816. Although, James Madison had opposed such a bank, a quarter of a century earlier, but, as President of the United States, he endorsed its re-creation. The United States government actually owned only 20 percent of the new bank.

The Second Bank of the United States (1813–36), did not solve the country's economic problems and, indeed, many blamed the bank's monetary policies for aggravating a serious depression. State governments were particularly angry at the bank, especially, because the bank called in loans owned by the states. Thus, many states adopted laws designed to limit the operation of the bank. Some states, adopted laws prohibiting its operation within their borders; others, such as state of Maryland, taxed it. The state of Maryland law required that any bank, not chartered by the state, pay either an annual tax of $15000 or a tax of 2 percent on all of its notes, which needed to be on special stamped paper.

The bank refused to pay the Maryland tax, and John James, sued for himself and the State of Maryland, in the Baltimore County Court, to recover the money owed under the tax. The defendant, James McCulloch, was the cashier of that branch of the Bank of the United States. The trial court rendered judgment in favor of the plaintiff, and the Maryland Court of Appeals affirmed.

The Supreme Court, in a famous opinion by Chief Justice John Marshall, reversed the judgment. Marshall's opinion considered two major questions:

— First, does Congress have the authority to create the Bank of the United States; and
— second, is the state tax on the bank constitutional?

Chief Justice John Marshall posed the first question, because technically the sole issue before the US Supreme Court was whether, Maryland constitutionally could collect its tax. There are probably several reasons why Marshall began by considering Congress's power. Once, it is established that Congress has the power to create the bank, it is easier then to explain why the states cannot tax or regulate it. Also, undoubtedly, John Marshall recognized this case as an ideal opportunity to articulate a broad vision of federal power, as he used *Marbury v. Madison* to establish the power of 'judicial review'.

Congress's Authority to Create the Bank of the United States

As to the first question, whether Congress has the authority to create the First Bank of the United States, Chief Justice Marshall put forth 4 arguments. First, historical practice established the power of Congress to establish the bank. Marshall began his opinion by declaring:

> 'It has been truly said, that this can scarcely be considered as an open question, entirely unprejudiced by the former proceedings of the nation respecting it. The principle now contested was introduced at a very early period of our history, has been recognized by many successive legislatures, and has been acted upon by the judicial department, in cases of peculiar delicacy, as a law of undoubted obligation.'

In other words, Marshall invoked the history of the First Bank of the United States, as authority for the constitutionality of the Second Bank of the United States. Marshall expressly noted that, the First Congress enacted the bank after great debate and that it was approved by an executive–

> 'with as much persevering talent as any measure has ever experienced and being supported by arguments which convinced minds as pure and as intelligent as this country can boast ....'

Although, Marshall did not mention James Madison by name, Marshall remarked on how even those who opposed the first bank endorsed creating the second bank. Marshall concluded that:

> '[i]t would require no ordinary share of intrepidity, to assert that a measure adopted under these circumstances, was a bold and plain usurpation, to which the Constitution gave no countenance.'

Marshall's second major point in considering the constitutionality of the Bank of the United States, was to refute the argument that states retain ultimate sovereignty because they ratified the Constitution. This view, sometimes called 'compact federalism,' which sees the states as sovereign, because they created the United States, by ceding some of their power, and by ratifying the US Constitution. Chief Justice Marshall described this view when he stated:

> 'The powers of the general government, it has been said, are delegated by the states, which alone are truly sovereign; and must be exercised in subordination to the states, which alone possess supreme dominion. The implication is that if the states are sovereign, then they would have the authority to veto a federal action, such as the creation of the Bank of the United States.'

Marshall emphatically rejected this view, and, contended that it was the people who ratified the Constitution, and thus, the people are sovereign, not the states. Marshall wrote:

> 'The government proceeds directly from the people; is "ordained and established" in the name of the people... The assent of the States, in their sovereign capacity, is implied, in calling a convention, and thus submitting that instrument to the people. But the people were at perfect liberty to accept or reject it; and their act was final. It required not the affirmance, and could not be negatived, by the state governments.'

Marshall's argument is rhetorically powerful; it concludes that:

> '[t]he government of the Union ... is, emphatically, and truly, a government of the people. The Court thus rejected the view that the Constitution should be regarded as a compact of the states and that the states retain ultimate sovereignty under the Constitution.'

The third major point of the US Supreme Court's, discussion was to address the scope of congressional powers, under Article I. It is important to note that the Court broadly described Congress's authority even before addressing the necessary and proper clause. Chief Justice John Marshall admitted, that the Constitution does not enumerate, a power to create a Second Bank of the United States, but, said that this is not dispositive as to Congress's power to establish such an institution. Marshall explained that

> '[a] constitution, to contain an accurate detail of all the subdivisions of which its great powers will admit, and of all the means by which they may be carried into execution, would partake of the prolixity of a legal code, and could scarcely be embraced by the human mind.'

Marshall, then uttered some of the most famous words in all of the United States Reports:

> 'In considering this question, then, we must never forget that it is a constitution we are expounding.'

The fourth and final point, that Marshall made in explaining the constitutionality of the creation of the Second Bank of the United States, concerns the meaning of the 'necessary and proper' clause. Article I, Section 8, concludes by granting Congress the power:

> '[t]o make all Laws which shall be necessary and proper for carrying into Execution the foregoing Powers, and all other Powers vested by this Constitution in the Government of the United States, or in any Department or Officer thereof.'

Chief Justice Marshall said that, this provision makes it clear that Congress may choose any means, not prohibited by the US Constitution, to carry out its express authority. In some of the most important words of the opinion, Marshall writes:

> 'Let the end be legitimate, let it be within the scope of the constitution, and all means which are appropriate, which are plain adapted to that end, which are not prohibited, but consistent with the letter and spirit of the constitution, are constitutional.'

Marshall rejects that restrictive interpretation of the 'necessary and proper' clause. Necessary here means useful or desirable, not indispensable or essential. In part, Marshall again explains that this is because of the nature of a constitution. Marshall observed that the

> 'provision is made in a constitution, intended to endure for ages to come, and consequently, to be adapted to the various crises of human affairs.'

Furthermore, Marshall noted that the 'necessary and proper' clause is placed in Article I, Section 8, which expands Congress's powers, and not in Article I, Section 9, which limits them. Furthermore, it's

> 'terms purport to enlarge, not to diminish the powers vested in the government.'

The court, however, rejected any contention that this gives Congress limitless authority. Marshall stated that:

> '[s]hould congress, in the execution of its powers, adopt measures which are prohibited by the constitution; or should congress, under the pretext of executing its powers, pass laws for the accomplishment of objects not entrusted to the government; it would become the painful duty of this tribunal … to say, that such an act was not the law of the land.'

Marshall thus, reaffirmed *Marbury v. Madison* and the power of the judiciary to review the constitutionality of federal laws.

The Constitutionality of Maryland's Tax

Chief Justice Marshall then addressed the second major issue posed by the case, having concluded that Congress had the authority to create the Second Bank of the United States: Did Maryland have the authority to tax the bank? This question required a much less detailed answer. Marshall explained that, the power to create the bank includes a power to preserve its existence. However, he pointed out, that:

> 'the power to tax involves the power to destroy; [and] that the power to destroy may defeat and render useless the power to create ….'

Thus, the Court concluded, that the state may not tax the Second Bank of the United States, because such exactions could greatly impede its operation, and potentially even tax it out of existence. An alternate approach would have been for the Court to allow state taxation up to the point of its interfering with or endangering the bank. But the Court rejected this argument, in part, because it did not want to embark on assessing the impact of each and every tax. Also, the court noted, that a state tax on the Second Bank of the United States, essentially, was a state tax on those in other states. Those who were being taxed therefore, were not represented in the state imposing the tax, and the tax was thus, illegitimate. As described below, this is an essential aspect of limits on the ability of states to put a burden on commerce from other states: It is unfair to allow a state to regulate those who have no representation in the state.

Comments

McCulloch v. Maryland thus establishes several crucial aspects of constitutional law. First, by rejecting 'compact federalism,' *McCulloch* emphatically, declared that, the federal government is supreme over the states, and that, the states have no authority to negate federal actions. Second, the Court expansively defines the scope of Congress's powers. Finally, the Court limits the ability of the states to interfere with federal activities, such as by imposing taxes or regulations on the federal government. This framework for government articulated in *McCulloch* continues to this day.

But, Marshall's reasoning can be questioned. Article VII of the US Constitution states:

> 'The Ratification of the Conventions of nine States shall be sufficient for the Establishment of this Constitution between the States so ratifying the same.'

The Constitution was not approved by a national plebiscite; it was ratified by the states. Marshall explains, that it was natural that people would act within states, but this does not address the language of Article VII, which clearly indicates that the states themselves had to ratify the Constitution, not the people.

Nonetheless, Marshall's view has dominated American history throughout. There, however, have been challenges, and reassertions, of the theory of 'compact federalism'. During the early part of the 19th century, John C. Calhoun, defended slavery by claiming that, states could interpose their sovereignty between Congress and the people, and nullify federal actions.

During the 1950s and 1960s, opponents of federal civil rights initiatives, again raised claims of state sovereignty. More recently, in 1995, in *United States Term Limits, Inc. v. Thornton*,[14] Justice Clarence Thomas (1948), in dissent, expressed the view that, states retain ultimate sovereignty except in those areas where the US Constitution expressly delegates power to the federal government. Although, it was not surprising to see the justices in the majority respond by quoting John Marshall's opinion in *McCulloch v. Maryland.*

However, if the power of Congress had been strictly restricted to those enumerated in the constitution, it is doubtful, that the constitution could have survived, at least without extensive amendments. The problems of the 20th century, and the range of laws needed to deal with them, can only be dealt with under an 18th century US Constitution; because of the broad construction of congressional powers found in *McCulloch*. What is notable, and often overlooked, is that the court adopted this expansive view even before it considered the 'necessary and proper clause.'[15]

The doctrine may be illustrated by the *United States v. South-Eastern Underwriters Association*,[16] where the United States had obtained, an indictment against South-Eastern Underwriters Association on the basis of the allegation, that the Association had violated the provision of the Sherman Antitrust Act 1890[17]. In the United States District Court[18], the defence –

> 'that business of the insurance is not commerce either intra-state or inter-state,'

was accepted. The United States appealed from this decision to the Supreme Court. Justice Hugo Black (1886–1971), began his judgment by acknowledging that for 75 years, whenever, the question has been presented, it has been held by the Supreme Court that the 'Commerce Clause' of the US Constitution, does not deprive the individual states of power to regulate and tax specific activities of foreign insurance companies which sell policies within their territories. But, he proceeded to draw distinction between all prior determinations, and, the case before him upon the ground that:

> 'not one of all these cases, however, has involved an Act of Congress which required the Court to decide the issue of whether the Commerce Clause grants to Congress the power to regulate insurance transactions stretching across state lines. To-day for the first time in the history of the Court that issue is squarely presented and must be decided.'

He then observed:

> 'Ordinarily courts do not construe words used in the Constitution so as to give them a meaning more narrow than one which they had in the common parlance of the times in which the constitution was written. To hold that the word "commerce" as used in the Commerce Clause does not include a business such as insurance would do just that. Whatever other meanings "commerce" may have included in 1787, the dictionaries, encyclopedia, and other books of the period show that it included trade: business in which persons bought and sold, bargained and contracted. And this meaning has persisted to modern times. Surely, therefore, a heavy burden is on him who asserts that the plenary power which the Commerce Clause grants to Congress to regulate "Commerce among the several States" does not include the power to regulate trading in insurance to the same extent that it includes power to regulate other trades or business conducted across state lines.'
>
> 'Our basic responsibility in interpreting the Commerce Clause is to make certain that the power to govern intercourse among the states remains where the Constitution placed it. That power, as held by this Court from the beginning, is vested in the Congress, available to be exercised for the national welfare as Congress shall deem necessary. No commercial enterprise of any kind which conducts its activities across State lines has been held to be wholly beyond the regulatory power of Congress under the Commerce Clause. We cannot make exception of the business of insurance.'

Problems relating to Constitutional Interpretation

'How should the constitution be interpreted'? is a constant theme concerning constitutional law In applying any law – be it a statute, regulation, or constitution – judges must decide what it means. Three factors make 'constitutional interpretation' uniquely complicated, and produce a great many of the interpretive questions before the Supreme Court.[19]

Firstly, countless problems arise, that the American Constitution does not expressly consider. These problems are less a matter of deciding the meaning of a particular phase in the constitution, and more a reflection of the reality, that countless issues of governance are not dealt within any of the language of the constitution. Chief Justice John Marshall expressed this when he explained that the US Constitution was not meant to have the 'prolixity of a legal code,' but instead,

> '[i]ts nature ... requires, that only its great outlines should be marked, its important objects designated..... [W]e must never forget that it is a constitution we are expounding.... [A]constitution, intended to endure for ages to come, and consequently, to be adapted to the various crises of human affairs.'[20]

Secondly, even where there are constitutional provisions, much of the constitution is written in open-textured language using phrases such as 'commerce among the states,' 'necessary and proper,' 'freedom of speech,' 'due process of law,' 'liberty,' 'taking,' 'equal protection,' and 'cruel and unusual punishment.' How should the court decide the content and meaning of these and other similar clauses that are found throughout the American Constitution? There is no doubt that this open-textured language is what has allowed the constitution to survive for over 200 years and to govern a world radically different from the one that existed when it was drafted. But, it is this very nature of the constitution that requires that courts interpret it and decide its meaning.

Thirdly, inevitably in constitutional law, courts must face the question of what, if any, government justifications are sufficient to permit the government to interfere with a fundamental right or to discriminate. Even though the First Amendment says that Congress shall make 'no law' abridging freedom of speech; that provision never has been regarded as an absolute. Although, the 14th Amendment says that, states shall not deny any person equal protection of the laws, inevitably states must draw distinctions among people. For instance, every state requires that people be 16 years of age in order to get a driver's license, and that they have a low income in order to receive welfare benefits. These, and an infinite variety of other laws, can be challenged as treating benefits.

These, and an infinite number of other laws, maybe questioned as treating individuals unequally, and courts must decide when disparities in treatment are justified and when equal protection is denied. The point is that in interpreting and applying the constitution, courts must decide what, if any, justifications permit deviating from the text, or interfering with a right for discriminating.

Doctrine of Originalism and Non-originalism

The debate frequently has been characterized as one between 'originalism', sometimes synonymously called 'interpretivism', and 'non-originalism', sometimes, termed 'non-interpretivism'. 'Originalism' is the view that,

> 'judges deciding constitutional issues should confine themselves to enforcing norms that are stated or clearly implicit in the written Constitution.'

In contrast, non-originalism is the,

> 'contrary view that courts should go beyond that set of references and enforce norms that cannot be discovered within the four corners of the document.'[21]

Originalists believe that, the courts should find a right to exist in the constitution, only if it is expressly stated in the text or was clearly intended by its framers. If the constitution is silent, originalists say it is for the legislature, unconstrained by the courts, to decide the law. Non-originalists think that, it is permissible for the court to interpret the constitution, to protect rights that are not expressly stated or clearly intended. Originalists believe that, the meaning of a constitutional provision was set when it was adopted and that it can be changed solely by amendment; non-originalists believe that the constitution's meaning can evolve by amendment and by interpretation.[22]

The disagreement between originalists and non-originalists, is not only about whether the court should recognize unenumerated rights. Originalists and non-originalists also disagree over how the court should decide the meaning of particular constitutional provisions. For example, an issue arose before the Supreme Court as to whether the 4th Amendment requires that, police officers 'knock and announce' before searching a residence.[23] Justice Clarence Thomas (1948), following his originalist philosophy, decided the issue by considering the law as of 1791, when the 4th Amendment was adopted, and concluded that knock and announce is generally required because at this time it was part of the law. For a non-originalist, such historical practice might be of interest, but is not necessarily decisive because the meaning of the constitution is not limited to what the framers experienced or intended.

Thus, the disagreement between originalists and non-originalists, is basically over how the American Constitution should evolve. Originalists explicitly state that, amendment is the only legitimate means for constitutional evolution. If there is to be a right to use contraceptives or a right to abortion, originalists would say that the constitution must be amended.

In contrast, non-originalists believe that, the constitution's meaning is not limited to what the framers intended; rather, the meaning and application of constitutional provisions should evolve by interpretation.[24] The fact that the framers of the 14th Amendment did not intend to prohibit gender discrimination or to apply the Bill of Rights to the states is not decisive for the non-originalist in deciding what the constitution means. In recent years, this discussion has been expressed as a debate over whether the document is a 'living Constitution.'

Other theories of Constitutional interpretation

As the above historical development indicates, the Supreme Court's power of 'judicial review', may be used boldly or with caution. To some extent, the approach the court adopts, in a given case, depends on the nature of the issue and the complexion of political forces surrounding the case.

It also depends, however, on the philosophies of the judges who happen to be on the court at a given time. The judges have varying views about the role of the court in the political system, and the conditions under which 'judicial review' ought to be exercised. They also differ in their understandings of the constitution, and their theories as to how the constitution should be interpreted.

Doctrine of Original Intent

Interpretivism is known as the most orthodox judicial philosophy, because of its insistence that the proper judicial function is interpretation, so opposed to lawmaking.

Interpretivism holds that, judicial review is legitimate only insofar, as judges base their decisions squarely on the constitution. In interpreting the constitution, judges must be guided by the plain meaning of the text, when it is clear. In the absence of plain textual meaning, judges should attempt to determine the original intentions of the framers. This element of the interpretivist perspective is often referred to as originalism or the doctrine of 'original intent'.

The doctrine of 'original intent' took on a distinctly political aspect during the 1980s. It was very much a part of the Reagan administration's judicial philosophy. US Attorney General Edwin Meese (1931)[25] made a series of public speeches in 1985; in which he castigated the modern court for allegedly ignoring 'original intent'. In a highly publicized speech at Georgetown University, Justice William Brennan (1906–97) rebutted Meese, saying,

> 'It is arrogant to pretend that from our vantage point we can gauge accurately the intent of the Framers on application of principle to specific, contemporary questions.'

Brennan argued that judges must:

> 'read the Constitution the only way we can as twentieth century Americans'

The doctrine of 'original intent' also played an important role in the Reagan administration's attempt to reshape the federal judiciary. It was largely because his adherence to this doctrine that Robert Bork (1927–2012), was nominated to the Supreme Court when Justice Lewis F. Powell Jr (1907–98) retired in 1987. Bork's defense of strict originalism was one of several factors contributing to his rejection by the Senate following a heated confirmation battle. In addition to its emphasis on 'original intent', 'interpretivism' stresses the need for judges to respect history and tradition and, in particular, legal precedent. Essentially, 'interpretivism' calls for judges to maintain as best they can the original US Constitution, with a minimum of judicial modification.[26]

Many judges and constitutional scholars do not accept the interpretivist view. They raise serious questions about the practicability and desirability of 'interpretivism', especially on the issue of 'original intent'. It is often argued that the 'intent of the framers' is impossible to discern on many issues. Many would argue that 'original intent', even if knowable, should not control contemporary constitutional decision making. These commentators tend to view the American Constitution as a living document, the meaning of which evolves according to what Justice Oliver Wendell Holmes Jr (1841–1935) called 'felt necessities' of the times.

Numerous non-interpretive theories have been developed, drawing on a number of schools of legal thought. Some have suggested that the court should strive to reflect societal consensus. Others have recommended that an explicit role of moral leadership should be assumed by the court, aiming to elevate and enlighten society rather than simply representing prevailing norms. Non-interpretivists, whatever their particular philosophies, are united in their rejection of the idea that the meaning of the constitution is rigid and static.

Another perspective, not easily identified with either interpretivism or non-interpretivism, is one that argues for judicial reliance on 'natural law. 'Natural law' is a complex term with many connotations, but, it generally refers to a set of principles transcending human authority that may be discovered through reason. 'Natural law' is often associated with religion and, in particular, the moral and ethical values of the Judeo-Christian tradition. Although, occasionally invoked by individual judges, the 'natural law' perspective has, for the most part, been eschewed by the modern Supreme Court.[27]

The Doctrine of Strict Necessity

Under the doctrine of 'strict necessity', US federal courts would seek to avoid a constitutional question if a case could be resolved on non-constitutional grounds. For example, in *Communist Party of the United States v. Subversive Activities Control Board*,[28] the US Supreme Court remanded a case to a government agency, for further proceedings rather than reach the sensitive political issue of whether, the Communist Party enjoyed constitutional protection.

Similarly, in *Hurd v. Hodge*,[29] the Court addressed the issue of 'restrictive covenants,' private agreements prohibiting the sale and rental of housing to blacks and other minorities. The Court held that, enforcement of restrictive covenants by federal courts in the District of Columbia would violate national public policy, but, it did not reach the question of whether such enforcement would violate the constitution. The Court said:

> 'It is a well settled principle that this court will not decide constitutional questions where other grounds are available and dispositive of the issues of the case.'

The Court chose not to avoid this constitutional issue; in a similar case arising in a state court, however, ruling that state judicial enforcement violates the 'Equal Protection Clause' of the 14th Amendment in *Shelley v. Kraemer*.[30]

The Doctrine of Saving Construction

Before a court can determine the constitutionality of a statute, it must first determine its exact meaning. This is known as statutory construction. In construing statutes, courts often look beyond the language of the law and to the intent of the legislature. Sometimes, the intent is clearly revealed in the legislative debate surrounding the adoption of the law. Often, however, legislative intent is not clear, and courts must exercise discretion in deciding what the law means.

Sometimes, the judicial interpretation of the statute may determine its constitutionality. Where a challenged law is subject to different interpretations, judicial restraint demands that a court choose an interpretation that preserves the constitutionality of the law. This is known as the 'doctrine of saving construction'.

In *National Labor Relations Board v. Jones & Laughlin Steel Corporation*,[31] the US Supreme Court upheld the Wagner Act 1935, a controversial federal statute regulating labor-management relations in major industries. The Jones & Laughlin Steel Corporation argued that the Act was a thinly disguised attempt to regulate all industries, rather than merely those that affected interstate commerce. This point was crucial, because Congress's power in this field is limited to the regulation of interstate commerce. Given the choice between two interpretations of the Act, the Court chose the narrower one, leading to a conclusion that the Act was valid. Writing for the majority, Chief Justice Charles Evans Hughes (1862–1948) observed:

> 'The cardinal principle of statutory construction is to save and not to destroy. We have repeatedly held that as between two possible interpretations of a statute, by one of which it would be unconstitutional and by the other valid, our plain duty is to adopt that which will save the act.'

On 24 April 1996, President Bill Clinton (1946) signed into law the Antiterrorism and Effective Death Penalty Act of 1996 (AEDPA). One of the provisions of this statute curtails second *habeas corpus* petitions by state prisoners, who have already filed such petitions in federal court. Under the new statute, any second or subsequent *habeas* petition must meet a particularly high standard and must pass through a gate keeping function exercised by the US Courts of Appeals. A circuit court must grant a motion giving the inmate permission to file the petition in a district court; denial of this motion is not appealable to the Supreme Court. Ellis Felker, a prisoner on death row in Georgia challenged the constitutionality of this provision, posing two constitutional objections:

(1) that the new law amounted to an unconstitutional suspension of the writ of *habeas corpus*; and
(2) that the prohibition against Supreme Court review of a circuit court's denial of permission to file a subsequent *habeas* petition is an unconstitutional interference with the Supreme Court's jurisdiction as defined in article III of the Constitution.

In *Felker v. Turpin*,[32] the Supreme Court unanimously rejected these challenges to the statute. In a saving construction, the Court interpreted the statute in such a way as to preserve the right of state prisoners to file *habeas petitions* directly in the Supreme Court. The Court stated, however, that it would exercise this jurisdiction only in 'exceptional circumstances.'

The Presumption of Constitutionality

Presumption of constitutionality is perhaps the most fundamental self-imposed limitation on the exercise of 'judicial review'. Under this doctrine, courts will presume that a challenged statute is valid, until it is demonstrated otherwise. In other words, the party attacking the validity of the law carries the burden of persuasion. This doctrine is based on an appreciation for the counter-majoritarian character of 'judicial review' and a fundamental respect for the legislative bodies in a democratic system.

The modern US Supreme Court has modified the doctrine of 'presumptive constitutionality', with respect to laws discriminating against citizens on grounds such as race, religion, and national origin. Such laws are now seen as inherently suspect and are subject to strict scrutiny. Similarly, laws abridging fundamental rights are not afforded the traditional presumption of validity.[33]

Doctrine of Original Package

The Doctrine of Original Package was stated by Chief Justice John Marshall (1755–1835) in *Brown v. Maryland*,[34] whilst interpreting the constitutional clause providing:

> 'No State shall without the consent of the Congress lay any imposts, or duties on imports, or exports except what may be absolutely necessary for executing its inspection laws.'

In this case, the state of Maryland required that importers of foreign goods by bale or package, and, sellers of such goods take out a licence for 50 dollars or pay a penalty. And the point that arose for consideration was whether, the legislature of a state could constitutionally require the importer of foreign articles to take out a licence from the state before he should be permitted to sell a bale or package so imported. Chief Justice Marshall observed:

> 'Whether the prohibition to lay imposts, or duties on imports or exports, proceeded from an apprehension that the power might be so exercised as to disturb that equality among the States which was generally advantageous, or that harmony between them which it was desirable to preserve, or to maintain unimpaired our commercial connections with foreign nations, or to confer this source of revenue on the government of the Union, or whatever other motive might have inducted the prohibition, it is plain that the object would be as completely defeated by a power to tax the article in the hands of the importer the instant it was landed as by a power to tax it while entering the port. There is no difference, in effect, between a power to prohibit the sale of an article and a power to prohibit its introduction into the country. The one would be a necessary consequence of the other. No goods would be imported if none could be sold. No object of any description can be accomplished by laying a duty on importation, which may not be accomplished with equal certainty by laying a duty on the thing imported in the hands of the importer. It is obvious that the same power which imposes a light duty can impose a very heavy one, one which amounts to a prohibition. Questions of power do not depend on the degree to which it may be exercised. If it may be exercised at all, it must be exercised at the will of those in whose hands it is placed.'
>
> 'The constitutional prohibition on the States to lay a duty on imports – prohibition which a vast majority of them must feel an interest in preserving – may certainly come in conflict with their acknowledged power to tax persons and property within their territory. The power, and the restriction on it, though quietly distinguishable when they do not approach each other, may yet, like the intervening colours between white and black, approach so nearly as to perplex the understanding, as colours perplex the vision in marking the distinction between them. Yet the distinction exists and must be marked as the cases arise. Till they do arise, it might be premature to state any rule as being universal in its application. It is sufficient for the present to say, generally, that when the importer has so acted upon the thing imported that it has become incorporated and mixed up with the mass of property in the country, it has, perhaps, lost its distinctive character as an import, and has become subject to the taxing power of the State; but while remaining the property of the importer,

> in his warehouse, in the original form or package in which it was imported, a tax upon it is too plainly a duty on imports to escape the prohibition in the Constitutions.'

The Rise and Fall of the Doctrine of Original Package

In 1872, the 'original package' dictum was accorded formal constitutional status, providing the basis for invalidating a nondiscriminatory property tax on imported goods that, although, no longer in the 'stream of commerce,' remained in their original packages (*Low v. Austin*).[35]

The 'original package' doctrine had the appeal of apparent simplicity, and over time it acquired the aura accorded to many of the pronouncements of Chief Justice Marshall. But, as many scholars pointed out, the doctrine was both mechanical and inconsistent with the purpose of the Imports-Exports Clause, which was simply to prevent discriminatory state taxation on goods moving from or to foreign markets.

Generally speaking, the development of American law relies heavily on precedent. Although, less pronounced in constitutional law than in most other legal subfields, 'stare decisis' is a powerful factor in the decision-making process. Perhaps, this explains the durability of the 'original package' doctrine. However, with advances in technology and great increases in the volume of foreign trade, the doctrine became untenable.

By the 1940s, legal scholars were calling for its abandonment. They urged the substitution of a simple test focusing on the question of whether a given state tax is discriminatory. Finally, in the 1976 case of *Michelin Tire Corporation v. Wages*,[36] the Supreme Court adopted this position. It overruled *Low v. Austin* and upheld a nondiscriminatory Georgia tax on tires and tubes imported from France and Canada. Writing for the majority, Justice William Brennan Jr (1906–97) took note of the extensive criticism of the 'original package' doctrine and of its departure from the intent of the framers. He then concluded:

> 'Our independent study persuades us that a nondiscriminatory *ad valorem* property tax is not the type of state exaction which the Framers of the Constitution or the Court in *Brown* [*v. Maryland*] had in mind as being an 'impost' or duty and the *Low v. Austin's* reliance upon the *Brown* dictum to reach the contrary conclusion was misplaced.'

In this way, the Court managed to nullify the original package doctrine without challenging John Marshall's initial statement of the formula, thus, according deference to judicial tradition while at the same time overruling a troublesome constitutional precedent.

The Indian Supreme Court in *State of Bombay v. Balsora*[37] said that, this doctrine has no place in India having regard to the scheme of the constitution in which entries in the legislative lists have been expressed in clear and precise language.

Doctrine of Pith and Substance and Incidental Trespass

It is well established that the validity of an Act is not affected if it incidentally trenches on matters outside the authorized field, and therefore, it is necessary to enquire in each case, what is the 'pith and substance' of the Act impugned.

If the Act, when so viewed, substantially falls within the powers expressly conferred upon the legislature which enacted it, then it cannot be held to be invalid merely because it incidentally encroaches on matters which have been assigned to another legislature. In determining what are the 'pith and substance' of an impugned Act, we have to look at the essential burden of legislation and not merely the form of legislation much less the name given to it by the legislature. This can only be done by examining the provisions of the impugned Act in an effort to see what it is that the legislature has attempted to achieve.[38]

Closely allied to the rule of 'pith and substance' is the doctrine of what is called 'incidental trespass'. If viewing the statute as a whole you find that the substance of the legislation is within the express powers, then it is not invalidated, if incidentally it affects matters which are outside the authorized field. Limitation upon the application of this rule is that legislation must not, under the guise of dealing with one matter, in fact be designed to encroach upon the forbidden field. The true nature and character of the legislation in each particular case must always be determined in order to ascertain the class of subjects to which it really belongs.[39]

The problem posed by the doctrine of 'incidental trespass', was lucidly and comprehensively stated by the Privy Council in *Prafulla Kumar Mukherjee v. Bank of Commerce Ltd., Khulna.*[40] The facts in this case were that a Provincial Act, namely, Bengal Money Lenders Act 1940, limited the amount recoverable by a money lender on his loans for principal and interest and prohibited the payment of sums larger than those permitted by the Act. The Provincial Legislative List, item 27 of the Government of India Act 1935, enabled the Provincial Legislature to make laws with respect to –

> 'Trade and Commerce within the Province ...... money lending and money lenders.'

It was contended that, this Act was in conflict with the exclusive jurisdiction of the Federal Legislature in that Items 28, 33 and 38, provided for –

> 'cheques, bills of exchange, promissory notes and other like instruments, Corporations; banking and the conduct of banking business.'

The courts in India found that, the Bengal Money Lenders Act 1940, dealt in 'pith and substance', with the money lenders and money lending, a view with which the Privy Council agreed, but, as this was not sufficient in the opinion of the judges to dispose of the controversy before them, they proceeded to deal with the following two questions:

1. If the Act deals in pith and substance with money lending, is it valid though it incidentally trenches upon matters reserved for the Federal Legislature?
2. If it is determined that the Act deals in pith and substance with money lending, is the extent to which the Federal field is invaded material matter?

The Privy Council approved the holding of Chief Justice Sir Maurice Gwyer (1878–1952)[41] of the Federal Court of India which was as follows:

> 'It must inevitably happen from time to time that legislation though purporting to deal with a subject in one list, touches also upon a subject in another list, and the different provisions of the enactment may be so closely intertwined that adherence to a strictly verbal interpretation would result in a large number of statutes being declared invalid because the Legislature enacting them may appear to have legislated in a forbidden sphere. Hence the rule where has been evolved by the Judicial Committee, whereby the impugned statute is examined to ascertain its pith and substance, or its true nature and character for the purpose of determining whether it is legislation with respect to matters in this list or in that.'[42]

The Privy Council observed as follows:

> 'Their Lordships agree that this passage correctly describes the grounds upon which the rule is founded, and that it applies to Indian as well as to Dominion Legislation. No doubt experience of past difficulties has made the provisions of the Indian Act more exact in some particulars and the existence of the Concurrent List has made it easier to distinguish between those matters which are essential in determining to which list particular provisions should be attributed and those which are merely incidental. But the overlapping of subject-matter is not avoided by substituting three lists for two or even by arranging for a hierarchy of jurisdiction.
>
> 'Subjects must still overlap and where they do the question must be asked what in pith and substance is the effect of the enactment of which complaint is made and in what list is its true nature and character to be found. If these questions could not be asked, much beneficent legislation would be stilled at birth, and many of the subjects entrusted to Provincial Legislation could never effectively be dealt with.
>
> 'No doubt it is an important matter, not, as their Lordships think, because the validity of an Act can be determined by discriminating between degrees of invasion, but for the purpose of determining what is the pith and substance of the impugned Act. Its provisions may advance so far into Federal territory as to show that its true nature is not concerned with Provincial matters, but is the trespass, whatever it be, such as to show question is not, has it trespassed more or less, but that the pith and substance of the impugned Act is

> not money-lending but promissory notes or banking? Once that question is determined the Act falls on one or the other side of the line and can be seen as valid or invalid according to its true content.
>
> 'This view places the precedence accorded to the three lists in its proper perspective. No doubt where they come in conflict List I has priority over Lists III and II and List III has priority over List II, but, the question still remains, priority in what respect? Does the priority of the Federal Legislature prevent the Provincial Legislature from dealing with any matter which may incidentally affect any item in its list or in each case has one to consider what the substance of an Act is and, whatever its ancillary effect, attribute it to the appropriate list according to its true character? In their Lordships opinion the latter is the true view.'[43]

It would be noticed that the judges of the Privy Council looked at the problem of 'incidental trespass' or invasion of the forbidden field, not as primary consideration relevant for determining the validity or otherwise of an impugned Act, but merely, for the purpose of determining the 'pith and substance' of the impugned Act. The crucial question in their words is not,

> 'Has the Provincial Legislature trespassed more or less, but is the trespass, whatever it be, such as to show that the pith and substance of the impugned Act is not money lending but promissory notes or banking.'

Doctrine of Occupied Field

This doctrine is stated in *The Attorney-General of Saskatchewan v. The Attorney General of Canada,*[44] where the Privy Council held that –

> 'regard must be had to the substance and not to the mere form of the enactment, so that you cannot do that indirectly which you are prohibited from doing directly. If, under colour of an arrangement which purports to deal only with the principal of a debt, it is really the contractual obligation to pay interest on the principal which is modified, the enactment should be regarded as dealing with interest.'

It further held that:

> 'the doctrine of the occupied field applies only where there is a clash between the Dominion Legislation and Provincial Legislation within an area common to both.'

The doctrine of 'occupied field', like the doctrine of 'incidental encroachment', is only another way of discovering what is the 'pith and substance' of an impugned Act. The law would be valid, if in 'pith and substance', it falls in the provincial field but, incidentally encroaches upon the forbidden field with the limitation that only to the extent of repugnancy, those incidental provisions will be knocked out if they come in clash with the previously enacted law which occupies the forbidden field. The provincial law, will however, be fully valid if, in relation to the incidental encroachment upon the forbidden field, it could be said that it has only trenched upon the unoccupied portion of that field.[45]

Notes

1. 5 U.S. 137 (1803).
2. 17 U.S. 316 (1819).
3. Otis H. Stephens, John M. Scheb, *American Constitutional Law,* (California, Belmont: Thomson/West, 2003), p. 12.
4. The First Bank of the United States was a national Bank, chartered for a term of 20 years by the US Congress on 25 February 1791.
5. Peter Woll, *Constitutional Law: Cases and Comments,* (New Jersey: Prentice-Hall Inc., 1981), p. 164.
6. Ibid.
7. War of 1812 was a war between United States and Great Britain over British violation of US Maritime rights.
8. John C. Calhoun was the 7th Vice President of the United States.
9. The Second Bank of the United States, located in Philadelphia, Pennsylvania, was the second federally authorized Hamiltonian national bank.
10. Ibid, p. 165.

11. Erwin Chemerinsky, *Constitutional Law: Principles and Policies*, 2nd ed. (New York: Aspen Law & Business, 2002), p. 232.
12. Edmund Randolph was the First Attorney General of the United States.
13. The Second Bank of the United States was chartered in 1816 with the same responsibilities and powers as the First Bank of the United States.
14. 514 U.S. 779 (1995).
15. Supra Note 11, pp. 233–8.
16. 322 U.S. 533 (1944).
17. The Sherman Antitrust Act 1890, Congress passed a United States antitrust law, the purpose was to promote the rule of free competition, and economic fairness, to regulate interstate commerce.
18. United States District Courts are the general trial courts of the United States federal judiciary, where both civil and criminal cases are filed.
19. Erwin Chemerinsky, *Constitutional Law, Principles and Policies*, 4th ed. (New York: Wolters Kluwer Law & Business, 2011), pp. 15–16.
20. *McCulloch v. Maryland*, 17 U.S. 316 (1819).
21. Supra Note 11, p. 17.
22. Ibid.
23. *Wilson v. Arkansas*, 514 U.S. 927 (1995).
24. *See also, e.g., Gregg v. Georgia*, 428 U.S. 153 (1975); (Justice Brennan, dissenting) (arguing that the cruel and unusual punishment clause should be interpreted according to contemporary norms).
25. Edwin Meese was the 75th United States Attorney General and is an American attorney, law professor, author and member of the Republican Party.
26. Supra Note 3, pp. 42–3.
27. Ibid, pp. 43–4.
28. 351 US. 115 (1956).
29. 334 U.S. 24 (1948).
30. 334 U.S. 1 (1948).
31. 301 U.S. 1 (1937).
32. 518 U.S. 651 (1996).
33. Supra Note 3, pp. 46–7.
34. 25 U.S. 419 (1827).
35. 80 U.S. 29 (1871).
36. 423 U.S. 276 (1976).
37. AIR 1951 SC 318.
38. A.G. Chaudhry, *Lectures on Constitutional Law*, (Lahore: Irfan Law Book House, 1996), p. 46.
39. *Russell v. Queen*, 46. L.T. 889.
40. AIR 1947 P.C. 60. See also *Muhammad Nurullah v. M.C. Karachi*, PLD 1960 S.C. 24; *Ghulam Ali Shah v. State* PLD 1990 S.C. 253; *F.B. Ali v. The State* PLD 1975 S.C. 506.
41. Sir Maurice Gwyer was a British judge, lawyer, and academic administrator.
42. AIR 1940 F.C. 188.
43. These extracts of Privy Council judgment are taken from the book of A.K. Brohi, *Fundamental Law of Pakistan*, (Karachi: Din Muhammadi Press, 1958), pp. 239–40.
44. *Attorney-General of Saskatchewan v. The Attorney-General of Canada*, https://www.legitquest.com/case/the-attorney-general-of-saskatchewan-v-the-attorney-general-of-canada-and-others/11EE48
45. Supra Note 38, pp. 48–50.

14 Precedents

The law of England would be a strange science if indeed it were decided by precedent only. 'Precedents' serve to illustrate principles and to give them a fixed certainty. But the law of England, which is exclusive of positive law, enacted by statute, depends upon principles and these principles run through all the cases according as the particular circumstances of each have been found to fall within the one or the other of them.[1]

Disputes resolution in the exercise of judicial power of the state involves three aspects:

— determination of facts,
— knowing the law applicable to those facts, and
— knowing the right way of applying law to them.

Knowing the law means knowing how to find it in judicial precedents, statutes, and customs and usages having the force of law.

The doctrine of 'judicial precedents' used to be the exclusive feature of English common law where judges are the central figures in the common law system. It is relatively easy to define the precedents with reference to the English legal system. *Stare decisis*, which literally means 'to stand by things decided' has its origin in the Latin phrase '*stare decisis et non quieta movere*' 'to stand by decisions and not to disturb settled matters.' It is the basis of the modern doctrine of binding precedent, the effect of which is that judicial decisions have binding force and enjoy the status of law *per se*.

This doctrine in its present form developed in the 19th century from the looser *stare decisis*, and took on more of character of binding set of rules, whereby the decision of a higher court with the same national or province, state or district jurisdiction acts as a binding authority depending on the hierarchy of courts; higher courts bind the lower courts but not *vice versa*. The status of binding law applies to a legal principle enunciated in a decision, its *ratio decidendi* as stated by Sir George Jessel (1824–83)[2] Master of Rolls:

> the only thing in a judicial decision binding as an authority upon a subsequent judge is the principle behind a decision upon which the case was decided.[3]

A decision of the High Court, for example is 'law' although it is not binding on any court superior to itself. Two conditions had to be satisfied before *stare decisis* could become established.

(1) There had to be a settled judicial hierarchy before there could be any clear-cut doctrine of binding authority, for until then it could not be known whose decisions bound whom.
(2) There had also to be reliable reports of cases. If cases are to be authoritative as law, there should be precise records of what they lay down.

Stare decisis should also be distinguished from another doctrine known as *res judicata*, which means that the final judgement of a court of competent jurisdiction may not be disputed by the parties or their successors or any parties in any subsequent legal proceeding. The main differences between the two doctrines are:

(1) *Res judicata* applies to the decision in question, while *stare decisis* operates as to the ruling of law involved.
(2) *Res judicata* normally binds only the parties and their successors, *stare decisis*, relating as it does to the ruling law, binds everyone including those who come before the courts in other cases.
(3) *Res judicata* applies to all courts. *Stare decisis* is brought into operation only by decisions of the superior courts.
(4) *Res judicata* takes effect only after the time for appeal against a decision is over and it has attained finality. *Stare decisis* operates at once.

So long as the hierarchy of courts remained unsettled, the modern doctrine of 'bindingness' of decisions could not come into existence. It assumed substantially its present shape in the Judicature Act of 1873 and is now modified by the Courts Act 1971. As a result of these enactments, the pyramid of courts stands established.

Only decisions of the High Court and above in theUK are quotable as law. With regard to the binding force of decisions, the rule is that higher courts bind lower courts and the courts of co-ordinate authority do not bind each other. The High Court does not bind itself. Where two High Court decisions are found to be in conflict, the judge hearing a subsequent case should follow the later decision unless he is convinced that the judge in the latter case was wrong in not following the law laid down in the earlier case.[4]

The Court of Appeal and possibly Divisional Courts still consider themselves bound by their decisions. In *Young v Bristol Aeroplane Co*[5] the Court of Appeal laid down certain rules in this respect, which may be summarized below:

(1) If two decisions are in conflict, the Court of Appeal must choose between them.
(2) If a decision, although not over-ruled, is inconsistent with a decision of the House of Lords or of the Privy Council, the Court of Appeal is not bound by it.
(3) If a decision was give *per incurium* i.e. in ignorance of a statute or other binding authority, the Court of Appeal is not bound by it; nor may it be bound where the previous court had followed an incomplete report of a still earlier case.[6] The *in curia* rule does not apply where the previous court, which is alleged to have over-looked an earlier case, had in fact alluded to it, nor does it apply where the earlier of the conflicting cases exerted only persuasive authority.[7]

The House of Lords, the highest court in UK, which for a long time used to be bound by its own decisions, subject to some exceptions, altered this practice in 1966, and now it considers itself free to depart from its previous decisions.[8] Similarly, the Judicial Committee of the Privy Council, as the highest appellate court from different parts of the Commonwealth sometime used to hear appeals from jurisdictions where different set of laws prevailed. Clearly, a decision given in one system could not be binding in a case coming from a different system. With regard to any one particular system, the Privy Council laid down that as long as there is higher court of appeal such as itself, a lower appellate court is right to consider itself bound by its own previous decision. However, it has also observed that whether such lower appellate court should or should not follow a decision previously given by itself, which it now considers to be wrong, is a matter of policy of which the local court is a better judge than the Privy Council.[9] The House of Lords is not bound by the decisions of the Privy Council and the *vice versa*.

It has been stated above that knowing the law is one of the conditions for precedents in deciding disputes judiciously. What precedent is law is its *ratio decidendi*, which concerns future litigants as well as those involved in the instant dispute. Knowing the law in this context means how to extract the *ratio decidendi* from cases. Statements that are not part of the *ratio decidendi* are distinguished as *obiter dicta* and are not authoritative. There are three shades of meanings that are attached to the expression *ratio decidendi.* The first is the translation of ratio decidendi. It is the 'the reason (or of) deciding'. Even finding of fact may in this sense be the *ratio decidendi.* Thus, a judge may state a rule, but he may decide that the facts do not fall within its scope. Secondly, it may mean 'the rule of law proffered by the judge as the basis of his decision'. Thirdly, it may mean 'the rule of law which others regard as being binding authority'.

There is a temptation to suppose that a case has given one fixed ruling which is there and discoverable, here and now and once and for all. This is not so, for the *ratio* is not only the ruling given by the deciding judge for his decision but any one of series of rulings that are elucidated by subsequent interpretations. The pronouncement of the judge who decided the case is a necessary step towards ascertaining the *ratio* but the process ratio decidendi by no means ends there. Subsequent interpretations are at least as significant, sometimes more so. Cases of overruling and reversal by superior authority are obvious instances of subsequent correction. For, apart from these, the judge may restrict or enlarge the ruling as stated by the deciding judge, or he may reinterpret it in such a way to relegate it to the level of *obiter dictum.* Accordingly, *ratio* is best regarded as a pointer towards the direction, which subsequent decisions should take within a broad spectrum of variations. It is not something identifiable, once and for all, but a continuing process, and as such it has to be viewed in a continuity of time.

The following points may be taken into consideration:

1. Although the task of finding the *ratio* is a difficult one, yet there would be a measure of agreement in propounding that no rule should be treated as *ratio* which would not support the ultimate order.[10] Where a stated rule obviously bears no relation to the facts of the case, it is no more than a *dictum*.
2. Even when the deciding judge has given no reason for his decision, it may be possible for a subsequent judge to extract one from it. Howsoever, no judge is required to accomplish the impossible. 'If it is not clear' said Viscount Dunedin (1849–1942)[11], 'then I do not think it is part of the tribunal's duty to spell out with great difficulty a *ratio decidendi* in order to be bound by it'.[12]
3. It follows from what is stated above that different *rationes decidendi* may be extracted from a case depending on different ways of stating facts.
4. More rarely, a judge may demote a proposition in a previous case from its status of ratio to that of dictum
5. Certain types of cases do not deserve to be authorities. One type, already alluded to, is that in which is there is no discoverable *ratio decidendi*. Others are cases purely turning on facts, those involving the exercise of discretion,[13] and those which judges themselves do not think worthy of being precedents. Decisions on interpretation of documents are sometime used as precedents, which is regrettable since a court may find itself construing, not the document before it, but judicial interpretations of similar wording in other, slightly different documents. 'I do not think right' said Lord Denning (1899–1999)[14] Master of Rolls, 'to look at previous cases in this way. The only legitimate purpose is to use them as guide towards the meanings of the words, so as to help in the search for the testator's intention. They should never be used so as to defeat his intention.'[15]

Before proceeding further, it would be appropriate to explain little more about the *obiter dicta*. There is a distinction between the holding and *dicta* of a case. The holding of an appellate court constitutes the precedent, as a point necessarily decided. *Dicta* do not: they are merely remarks made in the course of a decision but not essential to the reasoning behind that decision. A holding consists of

> 'Court's determination of a matter of law pivotal to its decision. Everything else amounts to dicta.'[16]

Remarks by a court which are not part of the *ratio decidendi* are classed as *obiter dicta*. They are not authoritative *rationes* and *dicta* tend to shade into each other. The former has the status of law and are binding on law courts, *dicta* too have status of law but they are not binding at all *vis à vis* a lower court. Even the *ratio decidendi* of a lower court's decision has only persuasive force like the *dictum*. It has been pointed out that, some *dicta* are so authoritative that distinction between *ratio* and *dicta* is reduced to a vanishing point. *Dicta* which have no force, are propositions stated by way of illustration or being based on hypothetical facts.[17]

The weight accorded to *dicta* varies with the type of *dictum*. Mere casual observations carry no weight at all. Not every passing expression of judge, however eminent, can be treated as an *ex cathedra* statement.[18] On the other hand, *dicta* which have been acted upon over the years may acquire increasing respect. It may further be stated that a *dictum* may also be adopted as the *ratio decidendi* of a subsequent decision and will then acquire the authority of law.

It is abundantly clear from all this that, the *ratio decidendi* of a case depends on the interpretation placed upon it by a subsequent court and is no less important than what the deciding judge himself propounded. Later history is thus, an indispensable and continuing part of the *ratio*. It also shows the limits of 'bindingness'.

While dealing with the precedents, following aspects are very important:

1. A case may be reversed on appeal. The effect of reversal is normally that the earlier judgement ceases to have any effect at all. The situation is different if the case is affirmed or reversed by an appellate court on a point different from that on which the decision of the lower court was based. In one case, a Master of the Rolls said that in such a situation, the previous decision will be 'of no effect at all'.[19] This probably goes too far, and in another case it was said that the first judgement remains binding.[20] The truth seems that in such a situation a later court has the freedom to deal with the earlier decision as it pleases.

2. Before the doctrine of *stare decisis* came into being, judges freely refused to follow the cases which they considered contrary to some principle of law. A judge may even now refuse to follow a decision of co-ordinate authority, in which event the conflict awaits resolution by a superior tribunal. Repeated refusals to follow will weaken the authority of a case; as also the refusal by higher court to adopt the rule enunciated by a lower court, but only if such refusal implies disapproval of it.[21]
3. Repeated distinguishing of a case is evidence that the decision is not approved, and the effect may also be to confine it more and more closely to its own special facts. It is thus evident that the 'bindingness' in *stare decisis* is not rigid because judges should have some latitude in evading unwelcome authorities. All that the doctrine means is that a judge must follow a precedent except where he can reasonably distinguish it; but possibilities of the latter are such that they reduce 'bindingness' to the semblance of a cloud, solid looking and clear-cut viewed from afar, but less so when one actually gets into it. A case is only an authority for what it actually decides. 'l entirely deny that it can be quoted for proposition that—may seem to follow logically from it': so said Lord Halsbury (1823–1921)[22].[23]
4. Overruling of an authority is another important aspect of an authority. This refers to the action of a superior court in upsetting the *ratio* laid down by a lower court in some other case. Reversal, which is the overthrow of a decision on an appeal in the same case may involve disapproval of the *ratio* as stated by the lower court; but it need not be, as where the decision is reversed on some other point. Overruling necessarily involves disapproval of the *ratio* but never affects the previous decision so that the parties in the overruled case continue to be bound by the doctrine of *res judicata*; and the accounts that have been settled are not affected.[24]

Doctrine of Precedents in USA

> 'To avoid an arbitrary discretion in the courts, it is indispensable that they should be bound down by strict rules and precedents, which serve to define and point out their duty in every particular case that comes before them.'[25]

If a group of cases involves the same point, the parties expect the same decision. It would be a gross injustice to decide alternate cases on opposite principles. If a case was decided against me yesterday when I was defendant, I shall look for the same judgement today if I am plaintiff. To decide differently would raise a feeling of resentment and wrong in my breast; it would be infringement, material and moral, of my rights... Adherence to precedent must then be the rule rather than exception if the litigants are to have faith in the even-handed administration of justice in the courts.[26]

The US Constitution does not contain any specific provision with regard to giving the binding effect to the decisions of the US Supreme Court. But, it is clear from the statement of Alexander Hamilton (1755/57–1804) that, the founding fathers were familiar with the doctrine. Later on, the Supreme Court had to give a decision to explain the basis of the supremacy of the Supreme Court when not only the executive but judiciary in certain states refused to comply with the decision of the Supreme Court with respect to the decisions on segregation.[27] The Supreme Court had to derive its authority from Article VI of the Constitution which lays down:

> 'This Constitution ...shall be the supreme law of the Land; and the Judges in every State shall be bound thereby, anything in the Constitution or Laws of any State to the Contrary notwithstanding.'
>
> 'all executive and judicial officers ... of several States shall be bound by Oath or Affirmation, to support this Constitution...'

So far as the authority of the US Constitution is concerned, it will be seen that the above sanction is express. But, to add the authority of the Supreme Court to it, the Court had to rely on the doctrine laid down by the Supreme Court in *Marbury's* case (1803), by quoting that–

> 'it is empathically the province and duty of the judicial department to say what the law is'

and that,

> 'the Constitution was nothing but the fundamental and paramount law of the nation.'[28]

The federal judiciary being the ultimate authority on the exposition of the Federal Constitution, it logically followed that the State Executive and the judiciary were bound by their oaths, to support not only the constitution, but, the interpretation placed thereon by the Supreme Court.

Not only in the matters of the constitution, but, also in other branches of law, the American legal system is based on common law, which essentially requires that the decisions of the highest court should be followed. But, in American law, the realist movement started by Oliver Wendell Holmes Jr (1841–1935) and continued by Louis Brandeis (1846–1941) has maintained the tradition of common law without compromising on the fundamental and famous quotation that–

> 'the life of the law has not been the logic: it has been the experience.'

Doctrine of Precedent in India

The Indian legal system in its present form is based on the English legal system. Before the Government of India Act 1935, came into effect,[29] various High Courts in India were established under the Letters Patents issued by His Majesty's Government in England. Appeals against the decisions of the High Courts would go to the Judicial Committee of the Privy Council. A decision of the Privy Council was binding on the High Courts and subordinate courts in India although it might be in conflict with a decision of the House of Lords.[30] It was not open to the courts in India to question any principle enunciated by the Privy Council, which must, therefore, be followed irrespective of the inconvenient and embarrassing results, which might attend the application of that principle.[31]

After the Government of India Act 1935, came into force, a Federal Court was established in India. The inaugural sitting of the Federal Court took place in the Princes' Chamber in New Delhi on 6 December 1937. The first Chief Justice of the Federal Court, Sir Maurice Gwyer (1878–1952) declared:

> 'the Federal Court will declare and interpret the law and that, I am convinced, in no spirit of formal and barren legalism.'[32]

Section 212 of the Act of 1935 provided the law declared by the Federal Court and by any judgement of the Privy Council shall, so far as applicable, be recognized as binding on, and shall be followed by, all courts in any Governor's province or Chief Commissioner's province, and, so far as respects the application and interpretation of this Act or any Order in Council, or order there under or any matter with respect to which the Federal Legislature has power to make law in relation to the state, in any Federal States.' Thus, as a result of this provision in the Act, the doctrine of 'precedent' was formally accorded sanctity.

In Section 212, the word 'all courts' did not include the Federal Court and therefore, the Federal Court was no longer bound by the Privy Council practice and 'precedents'. There was no reason for it to deviate from the principles which had been laid down by the Privy Council, defining the limits within which interference with the course of criminal justice dispensed in the subordinate courts warranted.[33] However, a decision of the House of Lords is of the highest authority binding on the Courts and Dominions, and might therefore be preferred on question of common law to an earlier view of the of the Privy Council.[34]

On becoming a Republic under the Constitution of 1950, a Supreme Court was established that was the final Court in India.[35] Article 141 of the Indian Constitution provided that–

> 'the law declared by the Supreme Court shall be binding on all courts within the territory of India.'

As a result of this provision, all courts in India were bound to follow the decisions of the Supreme Court of India, even though they were contrary to decisions of the House of Lords[36] or of the Privy Council.[37] The law laid down by the Supreme Court is binding on all courts and tribunals, and, where the Supreme Court has stated that the law laid down in a particular case is the applicable law, the High Court cannot consider or rely on any supposedly conflicting decision, and, where the Supreme Court contradicts the law declared in another case, the law stands over-ruled.[38]

The doctrine of *stare decisis* has always been strictly adhered to by the courts of law in order to avoid confusion and uncertainty, and to serve the ends of justice. A case decided as early as 1970 and having been followed for the last three decades and in innumerable matters having been dealt with on the basis thereof, a different view would unsettle the situation.[39] A decision which is not express and is not founded on reasons nor proceeds on a consideration of the issue cannot be deemed be to a law declared to have binding effect as is contemplated by Article 141.[40] An earlier decision of the Supreme Court cannot be overruled by its co-equal Bench, and a different view taken by the Division Bench of the High Court was in total misunderstanding of the law of precedents and the Article 141.[41]

To the general law of 'precedents', the rules of *per incuriam* and *sub-silentio* operate as exceptions. '*Incuria*' literally means 'carelessness'. In practice, *per incuriam* appear to mean per *ignornatium.* The 'quotable in law' is avoided and ignored, if it is rendered in *ignorntium* of a statue or binding authority. The other exception to the rule of 'precedents' is the rule of *sub-silentio.* A decision is passed *sub silentio,* when the particular point of law involved in the decision is not perceived by the court or not present to its mind or is not consciously determined by the court and it does not form part of the *ratio decidendi* and is not binding.[42] A decision is available as a 'precedent' only if it decides a question of law.[43] The judgment must be read, as a whole and the observations from the judgement have to be considered in the light of the questions, which were before the court.[44]

The language of Article 141 postulates that it is the Supreme Court which declares the law. According to Chief Justice Sabyasachi Mukharji (1927–90), in the *Dehli Transport Corporation* case–

> 'the Court must do away with the childish fictions that law is not made by the Judiciary.[45] The Court under Article 141 of the Constitution is enjoined upon to declare law. The expression "declared"[46] is wider than the words "found or made". Indeed, the latter involves the process, while former expresses result. The law declared by the Supreme Court is the law of the land. To deny this power to the Supreme Court on the basis of some out-moded theory that the Court only finds law but does not make it, is to make ineffective the powerful instrument of justice placed in the hands of the highest judiciary of the country.'

Indian Courts do recognize their sub-ordinate position to the legislature in making laws but even to achieve this purpose, interpretation of law by the courts is essential. But, in the effort to interpret law creativity is essential.[47] No doubt, a statute is binding; but it is the statute as, interpreted by the highest court, which is binding on all other courts.[48] In this way, the Indian Supreme Court has always been a lawmaker and its role traveled beyond being a mere dispute-settler. It is a problem-solver in the 'nebulous areas' without ignoring statutory provisions.

By making the foregoing observations, Justice Mukharji pleaded for judicial activism in the matter of interpretation of statutes by rising above the doctrine of 'literal interpretation'. Since then other judges have followed this line and the doctrines of purposive and progressive interpretation have come to prevail in the matter of statutory as well as constitutional interpretation, subject to the limitation that the court cannot re-write the provisions, in the guise of interpretation.[49]

Doctrine of Precedents in Pakistan

The Government of India Act 1935, with necessary modifications, was adopted as the interim Constitution of Pakistan after its independence on 14 August 1947. In 1949, after the Federal Court was established, it made judicial pronouncements that were binding on the High Courts and other subordinate courts in Pakistan. Chief Justice Muhammad Munir (of the Lahore High Court) speaking for the Court held and declared:

> 'the obligation of a judge to follow the judgement of a superior Court does not disappear merely because his own view of the law is different or because the judgment by the superior Court was given *per incuriam* e.g., in ignorance of a statutory provision. The application of the doctrine of *per incuriam* to the precedent decisions is limited to the precedents of the same Court or a Court of co-ordinate jurisdiction and with the exception of *Drummond v. Drummond*[50] which holds that "what has a statutory force and effect must prevail against most authoritative decision of even the Supreme Judge in the Court of the Chancery, I am not aware of any decision where the doctrine might have been applied to decisions of a superior Court to the precedent

> decisions." Apart from the English Common Law rule governing authority precedents which were not strictly applicable in Pakistan, there was no provision whereby the law declared in the judgment of Federal Court was given binding effects.'[51]

Another important issue that came up for determination before the Federal Court was: whether it was bound by its own previous judgment? The Federal Court by majority held that the Federal Court was entitled to change its earlier view. Chief Justice Muhammad Munir (now of the Federal Court) speaking for the majority declared and held:

> 'I am strongly of the view that the rule laid down in *Khairdi Khan's* case that bias itself vitiates all proceedings and order made therein is not correct, and there can be no doubt that this Court on whom rests the ultimate responsibility of interpreting the law of the land is entitled to change its opinion and take a view different from the one it has hitherto held.'[52]

In 1956, the first Constitution of Pakistan came into force. It contained a provision similar to that of the Indian Constitution, in the form of Article 163, which stated that:

> 'The Law declared by the Supreme Court shall be binding on all courts in Pakistan.'

There is no reported judgement on the said Article 163(1) of the Constitution, but one can safely assume that the interpretation given to the provision of the Indian Constitution (Article 141) would also be applicable in the interpretation of Article 163.

The 1956 Constitution was abrogated on 7 October 1958. In 1962, a new Constitution came into force. As the doctrine of 'judicial precedents' was essential to the working of the judicial system based on the Common Law principles, a similar provision was kept in this Constitution by way of Article 63. Article 63 was essentially different in content from Article 163 of the last Constitution which was based on the pattern of Indian Constitution. The new Article 63 provided that–

> 'Any decision of the Supreme Court shall, to the extent it decides a question of law or is based upon or enunciates a principle of law,[53] be binding on all other Courts in Pakistan.'.

No one can doubt that a decision given by the Supreme Court of Pakistan is binding precedent on all courts in this country to the extent that the decision decides a question of law or is based upon or enunciates a principle of law. It was held by the Supreme Court while interpreting Article 63 that–

> 'We do not want to lay more stress on this point except to point out to the learned judge the constitutional duty that any decision of the Supreme Court shall to the extent that it decides a question of law or is based upon or enunciates a principle of law is binding on all other Courts in Pakistan and that all judicial authorities throughout Pakistan shall act in aid of the Supreme Court.'[54]

A similar provision was included in the 1973 Constitution in the form of Article 189. There is a similar Article (Article 201) for the High Courts in the Constitution. Therefore, the law declared by the Supreme Court is applicable from the date when such law being interpreted was enacted. Although, as under the Constitution, only the decision of the Supreme Court on a question of law or insofar as it enunciates a principle of law is binding on all courts and authorities in the country, yet the possibility that the same provision of law or Constitution before it came up for interpretation before the Supreme Court, was interpreted or understood differently could not be ruled out.

Therefore, as a result of interpretation of a law or a constitutional provision by the Supreme Court, the existing interpretation or meaning of the law is changed, then it is more of a matter of public policy based on justice, equity and good conscience than a rule of law, that an innocent person who acting *bonafide* on the prevailing interpretation or meaning of law created a liability or acquired a right, be protected against the change brought about in the existing state of law as a result of its interpretation by the court.

However, where a person or authority acts in defiance of a clear provision of law or constitution or interpretation by the Supreme Court, which does not have the effect of changing the prevailing understanding or the meaning of the provision of law or the constitution, the question of protecting anyone against the effect of such interpretation by the court on the principle that the effect of interpretation by giving prospective operation, does not arise. For example, if a particular provision of law or the constitution has not come up for interpretation before any court and the functionaries responsible for giving effect to it, have consistently interpreted the said provision and administered it in a particular manner, and, acted upon it accordingly over length of time, then, all of a sudden, such functionaries may not follow a different practice according to new interpretation of that provision. If in such a case the matter is brought before the court, the court may strike down deviation by the functionaries in the light of changed interpretation as illegal and unconstitutional. In this situation, neither the functionaries nor the persons deriving any benefit on the basis of previous practice could defend the illegality or unconstitutionality of the action on the principle that the interpretation given by the courts be applied prospectively and not retrospectively.

The principle that the change in the state of law as a result of interpretation by this court is to be given effect to from the date, the court interpreted the law is also not applicable in those cases which could be brought under challenge in accordance with the law before or after the interpretation of the provision by the court. Even otherwise, the Supreme Court, while adopting an interpretation of the provision of the law or the Constitution which is at variance from the existing view, is only declaring the correct law as an apex court. By doing so, it neither legislates any new law, nor amends the existing law. Therefore, while interpreting a provision of law or the Constitution, Supreme Court can also provide the date from which the interpretation given by it is to come into effect, keeping in view the nature of the provision it is interpreting, the likelihood of possible prejudice which may be caused to an individual or a body of individuals and the requirement of justice in the cases.[55]

It is noticeable that the binding nature of the pronouncement of the superior courts is constitutionally limited to the courts functioning in Pakistan and to the extent visualized by Articles 189 and 201. The reason is not far to seek namely, that for the concerned courts it is impermissible to travel beyond or cut across the enunciations of law recorded by the Supreme Court or, where applicable, the concerned High Court. This, however, does not imply that the pronouncements of the superior courts are not entitled to the highest respect, if and when, such are referred to or relied upon by authorities, whether executive, quasi-judicial or judicial, though not covered by the constitutional provisions above-referred.

It has, therefore, evolved that when a precedent of one High Court is cited even before another High Court, the same has considerable persuasive force.[56] It has been held that the Supreme Court is not a slave of the precedent and where justice demanded, the Court could deviate from its past decisions.[57] The safe course however, is that, if a present bench of the Supreme Court consisting of equal number of judges does not agree with an earlier decision then the matter should be referred to the Chief Justice for forming a larger bench.[58]

It is a settled law that–

> 'every judgment must be read as applicable to the particular facts proved or presumed to be proved since the generality of the impressions which may be found there are not intended to be expositions of the whole law, but governed and qualified by the particular facts of the case in which such expressions are to be found.'[59]

It will be noticed that the courts in Pakistan, while dealing with cases of civil nature extends deference to the earlier judgments. But, in criminal matters, the effectiveness of the earlier ruling is sometimes whittled down. The reason seems to be that in criminal cases, the matter is mostly based on facts and discretion.

Similarly, the provision of Article 189 lays down that the 'decides a question of law'. The question would arise that:

— what would be the effect of the interpretation on the cases already decided but yet not implemented.
— And also the effect of a decision on pending proceedings?

There is ample authority on this point that a case is to be decided on the basis of the law in force at the time of filing of the suit or case. The ordinary rule is that rights of the parties must be determined as on the date of the filing of the suit and not on the basis of rights, which accrued to them after the institution of the suit.[60] It is equally well settled that the decision of the Supreme Court is prospective and not retrospective, and, the earlier decisions are protected under the principle of past and closed transaction,[61] and, executive act would not negate such judgements.

But in a recent judgment,[62] after the pronouncement of the judgment by the Supreme Court, the Federal Government passed two ordinances whereby the Customs Act 1969, and the Sales Tax Act 1990, were amended, and as a result of those amendments, the Federal Government, a party to the proceedings, succeeded in negating the judgment of the Supreme Court. The Supreme Court held as under:

> 'A perusal of the above principles tends to hold that there can be no cavil with the proposition. As far as the later principle is concerned, it may be observed that unless the basis for judgment in favour of party is not removed, it could not affect the rights of the party in whose favour the same was passed, in the instant case, as discussed above, the Legislature had promulgated two Ordinances, in order to remove the basis on which the judgement dated 19 February 2001 was founded, therefore this judgement has no bearing on the instant case.'

The reasoning given in this judgment is erroneous. In the first place, those ordinances had not been promulgated by the Legislature. Secondly, giving such a power to the executive, to promulgate ordinances to annul a judgment is against the principle of 'separation of power',[63] and fundamental rights of the people. The very conception of the fundamental right is that, it being a right guaranteed by the Constitution cannot be taken away by the law. In such a situation, in an earlier case, the Supreme Court held that it is not only technically inartistic, but, a fraud on the citizens for the makers of a constitution to say that a right is fundamental, but, that may be taken away by the law.[64] The Court also failed to notice, that, here ordinances were issued by the Executive which, was only indemnified under the doctrine of necessity. Imputing such a high deference to the decisions of the 'executive' and 'legislation' by the executive is totally unjustified.

Notes

1. *Lord Mansfield Jones v. Randle,* (1774) 1 Cowp, 37; cited in Adam Gearey, Wayne Morrison, Robert Jago, *The Politics of the Common Law Perspectives, Rights, Processes, Institutions*, 2nd ed., (UK: Routledge-Cavendish, 2013).
2. George Jessel, was one of the most influential commercial law and equity judges of his time, and served as the Master of the Rolls.
3. *Osborne v. Rowlett,* (1880) 13 Ch D 774 at 785.
4. *Colchester Estates (Cardiff) v. Carlton Industries,* (1984) 2 All ER 601; and *Young v. Bristol Aeroplane Co Ltd.*, (1944) 2 All ER 293.
5. (1944) 2 All ER 293.
6. *Industrial Properties (Barton Hill) Ltd. v. Associated Electrical Industries,* (1977) 2 All ER 293.
7. *Johnson v. Agnew,* (1978) 1 All ER 883.
8. *Conway v. Rimmer,* (1968) 1 All ER 874.
9. *Geelong Harbour Trust Commissioners v. Gibbs Bright & Co.*, (1974) 2 WLR 507.
10. *The Wagon Mound (No. 2)*, (1967) 2 All ER 709.
11. The Viscount Dunedin was a Scottish politician and judge. He served as Lord Justice General, and Lord President of the Court of Session; and as a Lord of Appeal in Ordinary.
12. *Great Western Railway Co v. Mostyn (Owners)*, (1928) AC 57 at 73.
13. *Bragg v. Crosville Motor Services,* (1959) 1 All ER 613.
14. Lord Denning served as a judge for nearly 40 years, from 1944 to 1982, and also as Master of the Rolls.
15. *Ward-Smith v. Jebb,* (1965) 3 All ER 358.
16. Bryan A Garner, Carlos T Bea, Rebecca White Berch, Neil M Gorsuch, Harris L Hartz, and more, *The Law of Judicial Precedent*, (St. Paul, MN: Thomson Reuters, 2016), p. 44.
17. *Donoghue v. Stevenson,* (1932) AC 562.
18. *Lord Porter in London Graving Dock Co ltd v. Horton,* (1951) 2 All ER 1.
19. *Hack v. London Provident Building Society,* (1883) 23 Ch D 103 at 112.
20. *Curtis Moffat v. Wheeler,* (1929) 2 Ch. 224.
21. *Dutton v. Bognor Regis UDC,* (1972) 1 All ER 462.
22. Lord Halsbury was a British lawyer and Conservative politician. He served 3 times as Lord High Chancellor of Great Britain, for a total of 17 years.
23. *Quinn v. Leathem,* (1901) A C 495.
24. *Thomson v Catharine's College, Cambridge,* (1919) AC 468.
25. Alexander Hamilton, *Federalist 78*, Federalist Papers. https://constitution.org/fed/federa00.htm
26. Benjamin N. Cardozo, *The Nature of the Judicial Process* (New Haven, Connecticut: Yale University Press, 1921), pp. 33–34.
27. *Cooper v. Aaron,* 358 US 1 (1958).
28. *Marbury v. Madison,* 5 U.S. 137 (1803).
29. The commencement date is 1 April 1937.

30. *Firm Karam Narain Daulat Ram v. Messrs. Volkart Bros.*, AIR 1946 Lahore 116 (F.B.).
31. AIR 1938 Nagpur 423.
32. Federal Court Reports Vol. 1 page 9.
33. *Kapildeo Singh v. The King*, AIR 1950 FC 80.
34. AIR 1947 Sind 154.
35. Date of coming into force of the India Constitution is 26 January 1950. See Article 124.
36. *I.T. Commissioner v. Shrinibbai*, AIR 1965 Bombay 586.
37. *Dwarkadas Shrinivas v. Shohlapur Spinning Mills*, AIR 1954 SC 119; *Indra Sawhney v. Union of India*, AIR 2000 SC 498.
38. *C.N. Rudramurthy v. K. Barkatullah Khan*, (1999) 8 SCC 275.
39. *Mishri Lal v. Dhirendra Nath*, (1999) 4 SCC 11.
40. *State of U.P. And Anr v. M/S Synthetics and Chemicals Ltd.*, (1991) 4 SCC 139.
41. *Indian Oil Corporation Limited v. Municipal Corporation*, AIR 1995 SC 1480.
42. *Arnit Das v. State of Bihar*, (2000) 5 SCC 488.
43. *State of Punjab v. Surrender Kumar*, AIR 1992 SC 1593.
44. *Commissioner of Income Tax v. Sun Egineering Works Ltd.*, AIR 1993 SC 43.
45. *Delhi Transport Corporation v. DTC Mazdoor Union*, AIR 1991 SC 101.
46. To 'declare' means to announce opinion.
47. Supra Note 42.
48. *Bengal Iron Corporation v. Commercial Tax Officer*, AIR 1993 SC 2414.
49. *Supreme Court Advocates on Record Association v. Union of India*, AIR 1994 SC 268.
50. *LR 2 Equity cases* 335.
51. *Qadir Bakhsh v. The Crown*, PLD 1953 Lahore 588 at 591.
52. *Anwar v. Crown*, PLD 1955 F.C. 185.
53. *Hashim Ali v. State*, PLD 1963 SC 82.
54. *Mohammad Khan v. Sanaullah*, PLD 1971 SC 324 at 329.
55. *Asad Ali v. Federation of Pakistan*, PLD 1998 S.C. 161 at 344.
56. *Syed Ali Gul Shah v. Government of Sindh*, 1999 SCMR 988 at 994.
57. *Shahid Pervez v. Ejaz Ahmed*, 2017 SCMR 206.
58. *Shafqat @ Shafaat v. the State*, 2019 SCMR 43.
59. *Hidayatullah v. the State*, 2006 SCMR 1920 at 1926.
60. *Province of East Pakistan v. Major Nawab KhawajaHasan Askari*, PLD 1971 SC 82 at 90.
61. *Molasses Trading & Export (Pvt.) Ltd. v. Federation of Pakistan*, 1993 SCMR 1905. *Pakistan Medical and Dental Council v. Muhammad Fahad Malik*, 2018 SCMR 1956.
62. *Fecto Belarus Tractor Ltd. v. Government of Pakistan through Finance Economic Affairs*, PLD 2005 SC 605, at p. 654.
63. *Zafar Ali Shah v. Pervez Musharraf*, PLD 2000 SC 869.
64. *Jibendra Kishore Achharyya Chowdhury and 58 others v. The Province of East Pakistan*, PLD 1957 SC 9 at 41.

Part V

Fundamental Human Rights

15 Right to Life and Liberty

In the US, the concept of right to life, liberty, and property is closely connected with due process of law. In any case of deprivation of life, liberty, and property, the person in jeopardy, has a right to invoke 'Due Process Clause' of the US Constitution and is entitled to the protection of both; substantive and the procedural due process of law. In the 5th Amendment to the Constitution, it is clearly laid down that–

> 'nor (a person) be deprived of life, liberty, or property, without due process of law.'

This protection was extended to the citizens of the states as well by the 14th Amendment passed after the American Civil War in 1868 which read,

> 'nor shall any State deprive any person of life, liberty, or property, without due process of law.'

Thus, the right to life, liberty or property is best understood in its denial or deprivation. The US Supreme Court in a number of cases has tried to articulate as to what constitutes deprivation. It is in this context that these rights are discussed below:

Deprivations of 'Life'

Unlike the terms 'property' and 'liberty', which have produced a great deal of litigation over their meaning in the United States, the term 'life' in the 'due process clause' is rarely the subject of controversy. In part, this is because there are fewer instances in which it is alleged that the state impermissibly took a person's life without due process, than there are claims of state wrongful deprivations of liberty or property. In part, too, it is because when such cases arise, they are not over the meaning of 'life'.

In the substantive due process context, issues over life have arisen in two areas. Once is the controversy over abortion rights. Even here, however, the debate is rarely couched in terms of the meaning of the word 'life' in the 'due process clause' but, instead, is usually about whether women have a right to terminate their pregnancies and whether fetuses should be considered persons under the Constitution.[1] The other area of controversy is over whether there is a right of individuals to refuse life-saving, medical treatment. This, too, is not about the meaning of the word 'life' in the 'due process clause', but, rather about whether individuals have a liberty interest in refusing treatment and the circumstances under which the state can interfere with such choices.[2]

Otherwise, claims concerning state deprivations of life are litigated under constitutional provisions other than due process. For example, challenges to the constitutionality of the death penalty usually involve the 8th Amendment, and if they do involve due process, they concern the requirements of due process in capital cases rather than the definition of life.

Also, the US Supreme Court has ruled that claims against the police for excessive force or impermissible use of deadly force cannot be brought under the due process clause. The Court has said that they are properly brought under the 4th Amendment as impermissible seizures or perhaps under the 8th Amendment as cruel and unusual punishment, but not under due process.[3]

Deprivations of 'Liberty'

In *Roth v. Board of Regents*, the Court also attempted to clarify the meaning of 'liberty.' The Court said:

> While this Court has not attempted to define with exactness the liberty....guaranteed [by the 5th and 14th Amendments], the term denotes not merely freedom from bodily restraint but also the right of the individual to contract, to engage in any of the common occupations of life, to acquire useful knowledge, to marry, establish

> a home and bring up children, to worship God according to the dictates of his own conscience, and generally to enjoy those privileges long recognized....as essential to the orderly pursuit of happiness by free men. In a Constitution for a free people, there can be no doubt that the meaning of 'liberty' must be broad indeed.[4]

Roth, thus, includes in its definition of liberty rights that are expressly stated in the text, such as free exercise of religion, and rights that are not enumerated, such as the right to marry.

There, of course, is no doubt that constitutional rights are in the interest of liberty. The difficult question that arises as to what other interests fit under the rubric of liberty and require due process. Again, there are two different ways for the court to approach this and define liberty. One would be for the court to determine what is 'liberty' based on the importance of the interest at stake. Another way would be to determine whether there is a liberty interest based on the expectations engendered by state law. Again, both are present in the case law. Specifically, considered below are cases involving freedom from physical restraint, parental rights, deportation proceedings, prisoners' rights, and reputation as a liberty interest. Although, this is by no means an exhaustive list of what is considered to be a liberty interest, it does encompass the vast majority of Supreme Court cases pertaining to the meaning of liberty in the context of procedural due process.[5]

Freedom from Physical Restraint

The most obvious and most basic aspect of liberty is 'freedom from physical restraint'. Institutionalizing a person, by definition, takes away that individual's liberty. Indeed, attempts to define liberty throughout this century usually begin by saying that liberty is more than 'merely freedom from bodily restraint.'[6] The Supreme Court held that, an American citizen detained as an enemy combatant was entitled to due process. Justice Sandra Day O'Connor (1930), in her plurality opinion, noted that *Hamdi* case presented –

> 'the most elemental of liberty interests – the interest in being free from physical detention by one's own government.'[7]

Obviously, many provisions of the Bill of Rights concern the procedures that the government must follow, before it deprives a person of liberty in criminal proceedings. These include the prohibition of excessive bail found in the 8th Amendment, and the many procedural safeguards at trial including the 6th Amendment's rights, to a speedy and public trial before an impartial jury, with the assistance of counsel and the right to confront adverse witnesses. The Court has also found that 'due process' requires basic protections such as the 'presumption of innocence'[8] and the requirement for proof beyond a reasonable doubt.[9]

A person's freedom from bodily restraint also can be taken away by civil proceedings, most notably through 'civil commitment'. The US Supreme Court–

> 'repeatedly has recognized that civil commitment for any purpose constitutes a significant deprivation of liberty that requires due process protection.'[10]

Thus, in *O'Connor v. Donaldson*, the Supreme Court rules that–

> 'a State cannot constitutionally confine a non-dangerous individual who is capable of surviving safely in freedom by himself or with the help of willing and responsible family members or friends.'[11]

The Court, however, rejected the argument that, there must be proof beyond a reasonable doubt—the standard in criminal cases—in civil commitment proceedings. The Court declared'–

> 'We have concluded that the reasonable doubt standard is inappropriate in civil commitment proceedings because, given the uncertainties of psychiatric diagnosis, it may impose a burden that the state cannot meet and thereby erect an unreasonable barrier to needed medical treatment.'

Thus, the Court concluded that a state may institutionalize a person through 'civil commitment' only if there is 'clear and convincing evidence' of the need for commitment.

The procedural protections accorded to adults in civil commitment proceedings are not required for children who are being institutionalized by their parents.[12] In *Parham v. J.R.*, the Supreme Court held that, it generally assumes that parents act in the best interests of their children, so that all a child is entitled to before commitment is a screening proceeding by a doctor or other neutral fact-finder.[13] In other words, a child institutionalized by a parent need not be accorded an adversarial hearing, but only review by a neutral individual who approves the commitment.[14]

Parham is based on a long line of cases that hold that parents generally have the right to make decisions concerning the upbringing of their children. The Court followed this authority and ruled that, the deference to parents extends even to situations where children are being civilly committed. But it can be questioned whether, this deference is appropriate when there is such a dramatic restriction of a child's freedom, with such long-term consequences, as occurs with civil commitment. Although, it may be the exception, rather than the rule, there is the danger that a parent, together with a cooperative doctor, could institutionalize a child under inappropriate circumstances.

Deportation and Exclusion Proceedings

The Supreme Court, has recognized that deportation involves a loss of liberty, and that therefore, 'due process' must be provided before an alien is deported.[15] For example, notice must be given before a deportation proceeding.[16] Individuals facing possible deportation have a right to a hearing and have a right to representation by an attorney at the hearing.[17] The Supreme Court has held that, there must be 'clear, unequivocal, and convincing' proof before a person can be deported.[18]

On the other hand, the Court has refused to recognize a liberty interest in entering the country and has allowed exclusion without any due process.[19] In *Shaughnessy v. Mezei*, the Supreme Court held that–

> '[w]hatever the procedure authorized by Congress is, it is due process as far as an alien denied entry is concerned.'[20]

However, the Supreme Court recently distinguished *Shaughnessy*, and held that the indefinite detention of those who are legally present in the country violates federal law. In *Zadvydas v. Davis*,[21] the Court considered the permissibility of the government's policy of indefinitely detaining non-deportable aliens. Kestutis Zadvydas, for example, who was an alien and lawfully in the United States, committed a crime and served a prison sentence. Under federal law, the Immigration and Naturalization Service (INS) sought to deport him after the completion of his sentence. Because he was born in a displaced person's camp in Lithuania after the Second World War, no country would recognize him as a citizen or accept him. The United States simply kept him—and thousands of others in a similar situation—locked up indefinitely.

The Supreme Court, in a 5 to 4 decision, held that the indefinite detention of non-deportable aliens is not authorized by federal law. Justice Stephen Breyer (1938), writing for the Court, emphasized that all who enter the United States lawfully are protected under the 'due process clause' and, that freedom from incarceration is obviously one of the most basics aspects of liberty. Justice Breyer explained that if federal law were interpreted to allow indefinite detention, there would be serious constitutional doubts about the statute. To avoid the constitutional doubts, the Court construed the law to not authorize indefinite detention. Justice Antonin Scalia (1936–2016), dissented and disagreed with the majority's premise that non-deportable aliens have a liberty interest in being free from incarceration.[22] He argued that under federal law, aliens who commit crimes have no right to remain in the country at all, and they should not gain that right because another nation will not accept them in a deportation proceeding. Justice Anthony Kennedy (1936), dissented and maintained that due process required only that non-deportable aliens be given procedural due process, notice and a hearing, before being held, and that this was provided.[23]

Liberty Interests for Prisoners

In defining 'liberty', the US Supreme Court has struggled most with cases involving prisoners. At the end of 20th century, the Court has shifted its approach several times. Initially, the Court indicated that prisoners have a liberty interest when an important matter is at stake. The Court, however, later moved away from this approach and repeatedly held that, liberty interests for prisoners are a function of statutes and regulations; prisoners have liberty interests when the relevant statutes and regulations create them. However, in *Sandin v. Conner*, the Supreme Court backed away from this approach and held that, regardless of the content of statutes and regulations, there is a liberty interest only if there is a significant deprivation of freedom which is atypical to the usual conditions of confinement.[24]

In *Morrissey v. Brewer*, the Supreme Court held that revocation of parole is a deprivation of liberty that requires the provision of due process.[25] The Court emphasized the importance of the interest to the individual. When out on parole an individual can be–

> 'gainfully employed and is free to be with family and friends and to form the other enduring attachments of normal life.'

This, of course, is taken away if parole is revoked, and the Supreme Court found that there was a liberty interest in remaining on parole because ending parole–

> 'inflicts a grievous loss on the parole and often on others.'

In other words, *Morrissey* found a liberty interest based on the significance of the interest to the parole, rather than focusing on the specifics of the state law involved.

Likewise, a year later, in *Gagnon v. Scarpelli*, the Supreme Court ruled that the revocation of probation is a deprivation of liberty requiring due process.[26] The Court explained that–

> 'revocation of probation .... is constitutionally indistinguishable from the revocation of parole.'

Soon after these cases, however, the Court shifted its approach and based its determination of whether there is a liberty interest on the content of the statutes or rules, rather than on the importance of the interest to the individual. For example, in *Wolff v. McDonnell*, the Supreme Court held that prisoners have a liberty interest in 'good time credits' awarded under state law.[27] The Court explained that although, a state need not give prisoners good time credits,

> 'the State having created the right to good time...., the prisoner's interest has real substance and is sufficiently embraced within 14th Amendment liberty to entitle him to those minimum procedures...required by the Due Process Clause to ensure that the state-created right is not arbitrarily abrogated.'

The Court said that a –

> 'person's liberty is equally protected, even when the liberty itself is a statutory creation of the state.'

In other words, *Wolff* found a liberty interest based on the expectations created by state law, rather than based on the significance of the credits for the individual prisoner.

The Court applied *Wolff* in *Meachum v. Fano*, where the Supreme Court held that, prisoners do not have a liberty interest in remaining in a minimum, as opposed to a maximum, security facility, unless the state or federal law clearly creates such an expectation.[28] A prisoner argued that a transfer from a minimum to a maximum security facility obviously meant that he had less liberty. The Court disagreed and declared:

> 'We reject at the outset the notion that any grievous loss visited upon a person by the State is sufficient to invoke the procedural protections of the Due Process Clause...That life in one prison is much more disagreeable than in another does not in itself signify that a 14th Amendment liberty interest is implicated.'

In dissenting, Justice Paul Stevens (1920–2019), joined by Justices William J. Brennan Jr (1906–97) and Thurgood Marshall (1908–93), disagreed and held that–

> 'neither the Bill of Rights nor the laws of sovereign States create the liberty which the Due Process Clause protects...It is...basic freedom which the Due Process Clause protects, rather than the particular rights or privileges conferred by specific laws or regulations.'

The conflict between the dissent and the majority was over how to determine when a prisoner has a liberty interest. For the dissent, a deprivation of liberty occurs where a prisoner is denied important freedoms regardless of the content of statutes or regulations. For the majority, a deprivation of liberty occurs if there is the removal of a freedom created by a statute or regulation.[29]

After *Wolff* and *Meachum*, the question becomes, what statutes and rules create liberty interests? The Supreme Court focused on whether a law or rule was sufficiently mandatory, so as to create a reasonable expectation on the part of the prisoner. For example, in *Greenholtz v. Inmates of Nebraska Penal and Correctional Complex*, the Supreme Court held that, the existence of a parole system is not enough to create a liberty interest in parole; rather, there must be specific requirements in the law that transform parole from a mere hope to an entitlement under particular circumstances.[30] The Court found that Nebraska created a liberty interest in parole because state law allowed the denial of parole only under specific statutorily defined reasons and because the law allowed denial only if there were specific findings to support the decision. The Court emphasized that the word 'shall' in the state law created a legitimate expectation to release on parole unless one of the statute's exception was met.[31]

The difference in approach between *Morrissey* and *Greenholtz* is striking. *Morrissey* found a liberty interest in parole because it determines a person's freedom. *Greenholtz* held that, there is a liberty interest in parole only if the state law makes it one by its mandatory language.

The *Greenholtz* approach, was followed in a series of cases spanning over two decades. In *Hewitt v. Helms*, the Supreme Court found that a prison had to provide due process before placing a prisoner in administrative segregation because state law had created such a liberty interest.[32] The Court explained that generally prisoners have no liberty interest in being confined in one place as opposed to another. But the Court said that, the state had done more than issue procedural guidelines; it had used 'language of an unmistakably mandatory character' and, made it clear that a prisoner would not be placed in administrative segregation 'absent specific substantive predicates.'

In contrast in *Olim v. Wakinekona*, the Court refused to find a liberty interest for a prisoner in not being transferred from a prison in Hawaii to maximum security prison in California.[33] The Court focused on the discretionary nature of the transfer decision and the absence of any mandatory language in the regulation in concluding that there was not a deprivation of liberty. The Court explained that–

> 'a State creates a protected liberty interest by placing substantive limitations on official discretion.'

Similarly, in *Connecticut Board of Pardons v. Dumschat*, the Supreme Court found that a prisoner did not have a liberty interest in having a review of a request for commutation of a life sentence.[34] The Court explained that state law did not create an expectation that sentences would be commuted, even though in practice the review board commuted most of the life sentences in the cases it considered. The Court said that the Connecticut law governing commutation of sentences did not provide 'particularized standards or criteria [to] guide the State's decision makers.'

In other words, in deciding whether a prisoner has a liberty interest, the Court would examine the statutes and regulations governing the prison. If they were written in mandatory language and created a legitimate expectation of a benefit, then the Court would find a liberty interest. The Court expressly stated this in *Kentucky Department of Corrections v. Thompson*, where it declared–

> 'We have ......articulated a requirement...that the regulations contain explicitly mandatory language, i.e., specific directives to the decision maker that if the regulations' substantive predicates are present, a particular outcome must follow in order to create a liberty interest.'[35]

In *Thompson*, the Supreme Court held that, prisoners in Kentucky did not have a liberty interest in visitation, even visitation from family members, because the regulations 'lack the requisite relevant mandatory language.'

Although, in all of these cases the Court emphasized the content of the laws and regulations, there were some cases that did not fit this pattern and where the Court found a liberty interest primarily based on the importance of the interest to the prisoner. For example, in *Vitek v. Jones,* the Court held that a prisoner is deprived of liberty when transferred from a prison to a mental hospital.[36] The Court, in part, focused on the content of the state's prison regulations and concluded that they created an expectation that the inmate would be kept in prison facilities and not moved to a mental hospital without a proven need for treatment. But the Court also emphasized that there was a loss of liberty because confinement to a mental hospital likely would mean the imposition of mandatory treatment and also a realistic possibility of stigma. The clear implication of *Vitek* is that prisoners have a liberty interest in not being transferred to a mental hospital regardless of the content of the specific laws or regulations for that prison.

Also, in *Washington v. Harper,* the Supreme Court recognized that prisoners have a liberty interest in avoiding the involuntary administration of antipsychotic medications.[37] The Court made it clear that independent of any state law or regulation, prisoners have a liberty interest in being free from the involuntary administration of psychotropic drugs. The Court found that the state's law met the requirements for procedural and substantive due process before the administration of these drugs. Prison regulations required that the prisoner be given at least 24 hours' notice before the administration of this medication, and it provided the opportunity for a hearing before health professionals and prison officials. The Court found that this was procedurally adequate to meet the requirements of due process.

Thus, up until June 1995, a liberty interest for prisoners could be found either if the prison statutes and regulations were written in mandatory language and created such an interest, or if the interest was so important that the Court would deem it to be a part of liberty regardless of the content of the statutes or regulations. In *Sandin v. Conner,* however, the Court called into question the approach of finding liberty interests based on the content of statutes and regulations.[38]

Sandin, involved a Hawaii prisoner who was placed in disciplinary segregation for vocally objecting to a body cavity search. The United States Court of Appeals for the Ninth Circuit, had found that there was a liberty interest based on Hawaii prison regulations that provided that an individual only would be placed in disciplinary segregation if there was 'substantial evidence' of misconduct.[39] The Supreme Court reversed and strongly criticized the approach of finding liberty interests based on the language of statutes and regulations. The Court said that this approach had produced two undesirable consequences. First,

> 'it creates disincentives for States to codify prison management procedures in the interest of uniform treatment.'[40]

The Court explained that rather than create a judicially enforceable liberty interest requiring due process, a state might choose not to place matters in regulations. This, the Court said, is undesirable because it does not provide standards to guide prison employees in how to exercise their discretion. Second, the Court said that the–

> 'approach has led to the involvement of federal courts in the day-to-day management of prisons, often squandering judicial resources with little offsetting benefit to anyone.'

Chief Justice William Rehnquist (1924–2005), writing for the Court, listed a series of cases where prisoners sued objecting to such matters as being given a sack lunch rather than a tray lunch or receiving a paperback dictionary. Rehnquist said that the federal courts' actions have run counter to the Court's view–

> 'that federal courts ought to afford appropriate deference and flexibility to state officials trying to manage a volatile environment.'

The Court thus concluded

> 'that the search for a negative implication from mandatory language in prisoner regulations has strayed from the real concerns regarding the liberty protected by the Due Process Clause.'

The Court then sought to clarify when a prisoner has a liberty interest. The Court stated:

> Following *Wolff*, we recognize that States may under certain circumstances create liberty interests which are protected by the Due Process Clause. But these interests will be generally limited to freedom from restraint which, while not exceeding the sentence in such an unexpected manner as to give rise to the Due Process Clause of its own force, nonetheless imposes atypical and significant hardship on the inmate in relation to the ordinary incidents of prison life.

As examples, the Court cited *Vitek v. Jones* and *Washington v. Harper.*

After *Sandin v. Conner*, a statute or regulation creates a liberty interest for prisoners only if it

> 'imposes atypical and significant hardship....in relation to the ordinary incidents of prison life.'

Sandin raises many questions, First, what is such a hardship? There is every reason to believe that the Court will be narrow in defining this. Certainly, any decision that affects the length of confinement—such as revoking parole or good time credits when created by mandatory language in state law—should be regarded as a deprivation of liberty. But *Sandin*, holds that being placed in disciplinary segregation is not such an interest. This seems to mean that absent a claim that a sanction is cruel and unusual punishment, prisoners will not succeed in seeking judicial review of prison discipline.

In other words, if the prisoner is claiming that the government's action is causing or increasing incarceration, then courts are likely to recognize a deprivation of liberty; but if the prisoner is challenging conditions of confinement, then a due process challenge is much less likely to succeed. For example, in *Young v. Harper*, the Supreme Court unanimously found that the revocation of pre-parole release was a deprivation of liberty.[41] Oklahoma, because of prison over-crowding, released a prisoner before he was eligible for parole. When space became available in the prison, it demanded the re-incarceration of the individual claiming that he always had been in government custody, even while on pre-parole release. The Supreme Court, however, disagreed and found that the release from custody gave the individual obvious freedom, which was a liberty interest requiring due process before re-incarceration.

In *Wilkinson v. Austin*, the Court applied *Sandin* to find that placing a prisoner in a 'super-max' facility in a deprivation of liberty requiring due process.[42] Justice Anthony Kennedy explained that prisoners in such facilities spend 23 hours a day in their cell without contact with other human beings. All meals are taken alone in the inmate's cell. A light is on 24 hours a day. He noted that inmates suffer–

> 'severe limitations on all human contact for a prolonged period of time, placement is indefinite, with only annual review.'

Thus, the Court found, that under *Sandin*, super-max facilities–

> 'impose an atypical and significant hardship within the correctional context.'

The Court, however found that the procedures provided, including the ability to contest placement in a super-max facility and several levels of administrative review was sufficient to meet due process.

Second, from a normative perspective, it can be questioned whether *Sandin* provides sufficient protection for prisoners from arbitrary treatment. Prisons obviously have enormous power over every aspect of a prisoner's life. *Sandin* holds that this authority does not have to be accompanied by due process unless both there is mandatory language in the relevant law and it is a significant, atypical deprivation of freedom. The Court defends this based on a need to encourage prisons to write regulations and based on a desire to minimize federal court oversight of prisons. Yet, the issue is whether this leaves prisoners, who have no way to protect themselves, sufficient safeguards against arbitrary and capricious treatment.

The transformation of the law with regard to defining liberty interest for prisoners is revealing. Initially, the Court found a liberty interest when prisoners suffered a 'grievous loss.' In an effort to narrow the scope of liberty interest, the Court ruled that liberty interests exist when there is a statute or regulation that in mandatory language limits the government's discretion over the prisoner. The liberal judges on the Court repeatedly objected to this approach and argued that a liberty interest should be found when there is a significant deprivation of freedom, regardless of the content of the statutes or regulations.

However, it is the conservatives on the Court—the majority in *Sandin* was William Rehnquisit, Sandra Day O'Connor, Antonin Scalia, Anthony Kennedy, and Clarence Thomas—who have abandoned finding liberty interests based on mandatory language. They seek to narrow greatly the circumstances where liberty interests will be found.

The Supreme Court extended the protections of the 5th and 14th Amendments by holding that a suspect in the hands of police authorities must be clearly informed prior to any questioning that he has the right to remain silent, and that, anything he says can be used against him in a court of law; that he has the right to the presence of an attorney; and that if he cannot afford an attorney, one must be appointed for him.[43]

The Freedom of a Person in the UK

A. Personal Freedom

No Constitutional Guarantees

The UK Constitution provides no formal guarantees of liberty apart from the declarations of rights, contained in the ancient charters and the restrictions on the arbitrary power of the Crown imposed by the Revolution Settlement of 1688. The citizen may go where he pleases and do or say what he pleases, provided that he does not commit an offence under the criminal law or infringe the rights of others. If his legal rights are infringed by others, e.g. by trespassing upon his property or defaming his reputation, he may protect himself by the remedies provided by the law. It is in the law of crimes and of tort and contract, part of the ordinary law of the land, and not in any fundamental constitutional law, that the citizen finds protection for his political liberty, whether it is infringed by officials or by fellow-citizens. In times of emergency the Executive is accorded special powers by Parliament, but there are no formal guarantees—such as are to be found in a constitutional code formally enacted.[44]

Trial by Jury

The right to 'trial by jury', which is the right of everyone accused of an indictable offence, may be regarded as a substitute for a formal constitutional guarantee that no person can be deprived of his liberty unless the prosecution has satisfied a jury of his fellow citizens of his guilt. Although, the jury system has come under much criticism, and no one would claim that the institution is infallible, it is nevertheless an important safeguard against arbitrary imprisonment at the instance of the executive, including the police. As a forum for the determination of civil liability the jury has ceased to be of much practical importance except in cases of defamation and wrongful arrest. It is not without significance that the right to a jury in actions for false imprisonment ranks it with the absolute right to such trial in prosecutions for indictable offences

International Aspect

There is an international aspect of civil liberty ever since the United Kingdom ratified in 1951 the European Convention for the Protection of Human Rights and Fundamental Freedoms. Article 5, provides that everyone has the right to liberty and security of person; that no one shall be deprived of his liberty save in specified cases, such as after conviction by a competent court; and that everyone deprived of his liberty by arrest or detention shall be entitled to take proceedings by which the lawfulness of the arrest shall be decided. Provision is made for the legality of measures conflicting with these obligations in time of war or other emergency which threatens the life of the nation.

When Archbishop Makarios III (1913–77)[45] a leading political figure was deported from Cyprus, the legality of his arrest and detention could not be successfully challenged either in Cyprus, where emergency regulations were in force, or in the Seychelles, where special legislation operated. There was some doubt, whether the deportation was not in breach of the Convention, and therefore, a matter which could come before the European Court of

Human Rights (ECHR). In this situation, where an individual seeks to protect his rights in an extra-national court, when he has no remedy in the courts in his own country is sufficient commentary on the importance which is attached to the right to liberty in the Western World. The United Kingdom has not yet accepted the jurisdiction of the European Court of Human Rights, where private citizens could seek redress against their own government.[46]

Justification for Imprisonment

A British subject cannot claim his freedom to be guaranteed, but he can, nevertheless, protect himself by proceedings in the civil and criminal courts against those who interfere with his liberty. A privilege is of little use unless it is protected and enforced. Under English law interference with freedom, i.e. physical coercion and restraint, can only be justified on certain grounds. If none of these are present, the person detained has a cause of action for damages for false imprisonment against his gaoler, or he can prosecute him for assault. The principal grounds for lawful detention are:

(1) Arrest and detention pending trial, when permitted by law, on a criminal charge.
(2) Sentence of imprisonment or detention imposed after due trial by a court, e.g. in a Borstal Institution after conviction on a criminal charge, or committal to an approved school.
(3) Imprisonment for civil debt[47] and for contempt of court, including imprisonment for contempt of either House of Parliament.
(4) Detention under the law relating to mental treatment under the Mental Health Act 1959 or detention of a child in need of care or protection under the Children and Young Persons Acts 1933 to 1963.
(5) The exercise of parental authority over an infant. A husband has no such authority over his wife.[48]

Arrest with Warrant

The extent of the power of arrest, and the kindred power of search has been discussed in many leading cases of constitutional importance. An arrest may lawfully be effected by a police officer who acts on a written warrant for arrest granted by a justice of the peace or other judicial authority who is empowered to issue warrants after application (an information) supported by a statement on oath outlining the alleged offence. The warrant must indicate specifically the person whose arrest is to be affected. There is no power to issue a general warrant to search for and to arrest an unnamed person.

Arrest without Warrant

More complicated is the extent of the power and duty of police officers and private citizens to arrest without warrant, where they suspect that a crime has been committed or to prevent the commission of a crime. The Executive has no power to interfere, through the police or otherwise, with the personal freedom of the subject by means of arbitrary arrest; for the plea of an act of state is no defence to an action brought by a subject in defence of his private rights.[49]

There are, however, numerous occasions where arrest without warrant is justified either by common law or statute. The powers of a police officer are somewhat wider than those of a private citizen. Anyone, whether police officer or private citizen, is required by law to arrest any person who in his presence commits a treason or felony or dangerous wounding. It has for a long time, not been the practice to prosecute a private person for failure to arrest a felon, unless he has been called upon by a police officer for assistance. The duty, however, exists. A police officer must, and a private person may, also prevent such crimes, and indeed any breach of the peace, by detaining temporarily any person plainly about to commit such an offence.[50]

There is also a power to arrest without warrant any person reasonably suspected of having committed treason or a felony or dangerous wounding. In such a case, however, a private citizen would have no defence to an action for false imprisonment, if the crime in question had not in fact been committed by anyone.[51] An illegal arrest without a warrant for a petty offence cannot be subsequently justified on the grounds that there was a reasonable suspicion that the person arrested had, in fact, committed a felony. A person on being arrested without a warrant, is entitled to be told, then and there on what grounds he has been detained unless he is caught in the actual commission of an offence, such as burglary.[52] Any passer-by may be called upon to assist a constable, who has seen a breach of the peace committed by more than one person or who has been assaulted or obstructed in the arrest of a felon and has had reasonable necessity for calling upon others to assist him. To refuse assistance in such circumstances is a misdemeanor.[53] It has been held that, a police officer, may enter private premises to prevent a breach of the peace, and per Lord Chief Justice Gordon Hewart (1873–1973),[54] to prevent the commission of any offence that he reasonably believes is imminent or is likely to be committed.

In *Thomas v. Sawkins*,[55] police officers successfully maintained their right to be present, though not invited by the organizers, at a meeting held on private premises which the general public had been invited by advertisement to attend. Numerous statutory provisions authorize a police officer to arrest without warrant in particular cases.

Questioning of Suspected Persons

In 1912, the judges of the King's Bench Division, drew up certain rules to govern the taking of statements from persons who may subsequently be put on trial after questioning conducted by the police. The rules, which are known as the Judges' Rules, have not the force of law, but statements obtained contrary to the rules may, and normally will, be rejected by the judge at the trial.[56]

These Rules were amended in 1964. The constitutional importance of the rules lies in the protection which they afford against a confession being made by an accused person under duress or without being aware that any statement he may make after being taken into custody can be used in evidence against him, as well as in his favour, at his trial. These rules are not the least important of the safeguards contained in the rules of evidence relating to criminal cases, which secure a fair trial, and thus, they are an important part of the protection afforded to the citizen against an abuse of power by the police. The rules in their recently revised form require that a caution shall be administered to any person who is being questioned by the police, whenever, there is evidence which would afford reasonable grounds for suspecting that the person has committed an offence. Once a person has been charged or told that he may be prosecuted for an offence, he must again be cautioned.[57]

In the Introduction to the 1964 amended Judges Rules, the judges emphasize that the rules are not to affect certain principles:

(a) that the citizen is under a duty to help a police officer to discover and apprehend offenders;
(b) that a police officer otherwise than by arrest cannot compel any person against his will to come to or remain in any police station;
(c) that every person at any stage of an investigation should be able to communicate and consult privately with a solicitor; and
(d) generally, that a person should be charged with an offence as soon as there is enough evidence to prefer the charge, and that no evidence should be admitted against him unless it is voluntary in the sense that it has not been obtained from him by fear of prejudice or hope of advantage exercised or held out by a person in authority or by oppression.

General Warrant Cases

The principle that a plea of the public interest does not justify a wrongful act was established by the 18th century cases, known as the General Warrant Cases. The practice of issuing general warrants to arrest unspecified persons, and, to search property is said to have originated with the Court of Star Chamber.[58] It is obviously a powerful weapon, to assist an embarrassed Executive to obtain material upon which to formulate charges against persons suspected of hostility towards the government.

At a later stage, the practice was authorized by the Licensing Act 1662, for use by a Secretary of State, to prevent publication of unlicensed material, and such warrants continued after the lapse of that Act in 1695. The General Warrant Cases, arose out of the attempt of King George III's Government, to stifle the political activities of John

Wilkes and others, and publications, such as the *North Briton*.[59] Even at a later date, the severity of the law against seditious publications was maintained largely by executive action, but the cases decided once and for all the illegality of general warrants, and thus, deprived the Executive of a formidable instrument of oppression.

Of these three cases, *Leach v. Money*,[60] decided that a general warrant to arrest unnamed persons (the printers and publishers of the North Briton), against whom a charge had not yet been formulated, was illegal. *Wilkes v. Wood*,[61] that the papers of an unnamed person could not be seized on a warrant of this description. *Entick v. Carrington*,[62] that there was no inherent power in the Secretary of State as a Privy Councillor,[63] to order an arrest except in cases of treason, and that a general warrant as to the papers of a named person was illegal. The warrant had specified the name of the person against whom it was directed, but, as regards to the papers it was a general search warrant giving authority to the messengers to take all Entick's books and papers.

The sequel to these cases was a successful action against Lord Halifax (1881–1959)[64] as the Secretary of State who had issued the warrants. A later decision has, however, seriously diminished the protection afforded by *Entick v. Carrington*, in cases where the police have affected the lawful arrest of one man but are in search of evidence of the commission by a different person of another offence. The police have a right by common law, to search the person of anyone who is arrested on a warrant, and, in practice the search extends to anything in the possession and control of arrested persons, which may be relevant to the charge brought against them. It is also customary to search all persons taken into custody on a serious charge, whether arrested on a warrant or not. In *Elias v. Pasmore*,[65] it was held that upon the arrest by lawful process of an accused person the police can search the premises, where the prisoner is arrested and seize material, which is relevant to the prosecution for any crime committed by any person, not merely by the prisoner himself.[66] The decision does not, however, justify the wholesale seizure of the contents of the premises, except, in so far as any of the contents are evidence of the commission of an offence by someone.

Search Warrants

There are a number of cases where search warrants may lawfully be issued under the authority of a statute. Such cases in effect form exceptions to the rule that general warrants are illegal. The oldest and, indeed, one which was admitted in *Entick v. Carrington* (ante) to exist at common law, permits the issue of a warrant for the search of premises which are suspected of being made a receptacle for goods where there is a reasonable suspicion of a theft.[67]

The more important from the constitutional point of view are those conferred by the Official Secrets Act 1911, Section 9; and the Incitement to Disaffection Act 1934, Section 2(2); the former provisions reads as follows:

> (1) If a justice of the peace is satisfied by information on oath that there is reasonable ground for suspecting that an offence under this Act has been, or is about to be committed, he may grant a search warrant authorizing any constable named therein to enter at any time any premises or place named in the warrant, if necessary, by force, and to search the premises or place and every person found therein and to seize...anything which is evidence of an offence under this Act having been or being about to be committed...
>
> (2) Where it appears to a superintendent of police that the case is one of great emergency and that in the interests of the State immediate action is necessary, he may by a written order....give to any constable the like authority ....

In the Incitement to Disaffection Act 1934, a High Court Judge is substituted for a justice of the peace, and elaborate restrictions are imposed upon the right to search (Section 2(2)-(4)).

Under the authority of various statutes search warrants related to an alleged offence may be issued, e.g.

- for explosive substances intended to be used for felonious purposes;
- for unlicensed firearms;
- for forged documents and instruments of forgery;
- for counterfeit coins and coinage tools;
- for goods which infringe the provisions of the Merchandise Marks Act 1887.
- Search for a woman or girl detained for immoral purposes, or
- for ill-treated or neglected children, may also be authorized by warrant.

In certain special cases under the Larceny Act 1916, Section 42(2), any constable may be authorized in writing by a chief police officer without a justice's warrant to search premises for stolen property. Sometimes a warrant is dependent on a belief that a breach of the law has occurred; in other cases the warrant may be issued by a justice on complaint that there is reason to suspect an offence. In the former category come offences under the licensing Act 1964, relating to clubs, the holding of parties for gain on premises where intoxicants are supplied or consumed outside permitted hours, and the sale of intoxicants by retail on unlicensed premises. Examples of the latter type may be found in the Gaming Act 1845 (use a house for unlawful gaming), and similarly the Betting Act 1853[68] (suspicion of using a house as a betting house), under the Dangerous Drugs Act 1951 (suspicion of drugs being in possession), and the Children and Young Persons (Harmful Publications) Act 1955 (suspicion of possession of works to which the Act applies).

In the case of obscene articles before the Obscene Publications Act 1959 it was necessary to swear to a belief that obscene articles were kept on the premises and that there had been a sale.[69] Under Section 3 of the 1959 Act, it is only necessary to satisfy a justice by information on oath that there is reasonable ground for suspecting that obscene articles are kept for publication for gain on the premises. There is no longer any need to prove a sale of the offending articles.

Civil Detention

Compulsory admission to hospital in the case of mental patients formerly required judicial authority in addition to medical advice. Under the Mental health Act 1959, Part IV, compulsory admission for observation or for treatment is founded on the written recommendations of two medical practitioners, one of whom must have had special experience in the diagnosis or treatment of mental disorders; judicial sanction, a power which was formerly given to justices of the peace, is no longer required. But, courts of criminal jurisdiction have the power to make orders for compulsory detention of persons suffering from mental disorder who come before them. In certain circumstances hospital admission can be ordered without recording a conviction.

The provisions of Part IV of the Mental Health Act, thus, enable a patient to be deprived of his liberty simply on medical recommendations without the normal safeguard of an order of a court, judge or magistrate. This innovation is doubtless justifiable in the interests of equating the treatment of mental illness to that of other diseases. But, this is the only instance known to English law, apart from the powers of parents over their children, where liberty can be taken away without judicial sanction. Provision is, however, made for appeals to mental health review tribunals, one for each area for which a regional hospital board is constituted. The members of the tribunal are appointed by the Lord Chancellor, who must appoint a legal member to be chairman.

Protection of Life and Personal Liberty in India

Article 21 of the Indian Constitution

Introduction

Article 21 of the Indian Constitution states that:

> 'No person shall be deprived of his life or personal liberty except according to procedure established by law.'

Prior to *Maneka Gandhi's* decision, Article 21 guaranteed the right to life and personal liberty to citizens only against the arbitrary action of the executive, and not from legislative action. The state could interfere with the liberty of citizens if it could support its action by a valid law. But, after the *Maneka Gandhi*'s decision, Article 21 now protects the right of life and personal liberty of citizen not only from the Executive action but from the Legislative action also. A person can be deprived of his life and personal liberty, if two conditions are complied with, first, there must be a law; and, secondly, there must be a procedure prescribed by that law, provided that the procedure is just, fair and reasonable.[70]

RIGHT TO EDUCATION A FUNDAMENTAL RIGHT

By the Indian Constitution (86th Amendment) Act 2002 Article 21A, has been added which provides –

> 'The State shall provide free and compulsory education to all children of the age of six to fourteen years in such manner as the State may, by law, determine.'

However, the right guaranteed in Article 21 is available to 'citizens' as well as 'non-citizens.'

PRIOR TO *MANEKA GANDHI'S* DECISION

The words 'personal liberty' under Article 21, if interpreted widely is capable of including the rights mentioned in Article 19. But in *Gopalan's* case,[71] the Indian Supreme Court took a very restricted view and interpreted these words very narrowly. The Court took the view that since the word 'liberty' is qualified by the word 'personal' which is of narrower concept, and therefore, it does not include all that is implied in the term 'liberty'. So interpreted, it means nothing more than the liberty of the physical body – freedom from arrest and detention from false imprisonment or wrongful confinement.

The meaning of the words 'personal liberty' came up for consideration in the Supreme Court for the first time in *A.K. Gopalan v. Union of India.* In that case the petitioner, A.K. Gopalan (1904–77), a communist leader was detained under the Preventive Detention Act 1950. The petitioner challenged the validity of his detention under the Act on the ground, that it was violative of his right to freedom of movement under Article 19(1)(d), which is the very essence of personally liberty guaranteed by Article 21 of the Indian Constitution. He argued that the words 'personal liberty' include the freedom of movement also, and therefore, the Preventive Detection Act 1950, must also satisfy the requirement of Article 19(5). In other words, the restrictions imposed by the detention law on the freedom of movement must be reasonable under Article 19(5) of the Indian Constitution.

Rejecting both the contentions, the Indian Supreme Court held that the 'personal liberty' in Article 21, means nothing more than the liberty of the physical body, that is, freedom from arrest and detention without the authority of law. This was the definition of the phrase 'personal liberty' given by Professor A.V. Dicey (1835–1922), according to whom personal liberty means freedom from physical restraint and coercion which is not authorized by law. The word 'liberty' is a very comprehensive word and, if properly interpreted it is capable of including the rights mentioned in Article 19. But by qualifying the word 'liberty' the court said, the import of the word 'personal liberty' is narrowed down to the meaning given in English law to the expression 'liberty of the person'. The majority took the view that Articles 19 and 21 deal with different aspects of 'liberty'; Article 21 is, guarantee against deprivation (total loss) of personal liberty, while Article 19, affords protection against unreasonable restrictions (which is only partial control) on the right of movement. Freedom guaranteed by Article 19 can be enjoyed by a citizen, only when he is a freeman and not if his personal liberty is deprived under a valid law.

In *Gopalan*, the Supreme Court of India interpreted the 'law' as 'state made law' and rejected the plea that by the term 'law' in Article 21 should include natural law. Justice Saiyid Fazal Ali (1886–1959), however, in his dissenting judgment held, that the Act was liable to be challenged as violating the provisions of Article 19. He gave a wide and comprehensive meaning to the words 'personal liberty' as consisting of freedom of movement and locomotion. Therefore, any law which deprives a person of his personal liberty must satisfy the requirements of both Articles 19 and 21.

But, this restrictive interpretation of the expression 'personal liberty' in *Gopalan*'s case, has not been followed by the Supreme Court in its later decisions. In *Kharak Singh*'s case,[72] it was held that 'personal liberty' was not only limited to bodily restraint or confinement to prisons only but was used as a compendious term including within itself all the varieties of rights which go to make up the personal liberty of a man other than those dealt within Article 19(1). In other words, while Article 19(1) deals with particular species or attributes of that freedom, 'personal liberty' in Article 21 – takes in and comprises the residue.

Finally, in *Maneka Gandhi*, the Supreme Court of India, has not only overruled *Gopalan's* case but has widened the scope of the words 'personal liberty' considerably. Justice P. N. Bhagwati (1921–2017), (as he then was) observed:

> 'The expression "personal liberty" in Article 21 is of widest amplitude and it covers a variety of rights which go to constitute the personal liberty of man and some of them have raised to the status of distinct fundamental rights and given additional protection under Article 19.'

The Court said that the provision relating to fundamental rights should be interpreted widely; Justice Bhagwati, said:

> 'The attempt of the Court should be to expand the reach and ambit of the Fundamental Rights rather than to attenuate their meaning and content by a process of judicial construction'.

The Court lays down great stress on the procedural safeguards. The procedure must satisfy the requirement of natural justice, i.e. it must be just, fair and reasonable.

In *Kharak Singh v. State of Uttar Pradesh*, it was held that the expression' life' was not limited to bodily restraint or confinement to prison only but something more than mere animal existence. In that case the petitioner, Kharak Singh, had been charged in a dacoity case but, was released as there was no evidence against him. Under the Uttar Pradesh Police Regulations, the police opened a history-sheet for him and, he was kept under police surveillance, which included secret picketing of his house by the police, domiciliary visits at nights and verification of his movements and activities.

'Domiciliary visits' mean visits by the police in the night to the private house for the purpose of making sure that the suspect is staying home or whether he has gone out. The Supreme Court held that the domiciliary visits of the policemen were an invasion on the petitioner's personal liberty. By the term 'life' as used here something more is meant than mere animal existence. The inhibition against its deprivation extends to all those limits and faculties by which life is enjoyed. It is true that in Article 21 the word 'liberty' is qualified by a word 'personal' but this qualification is employed in order to avoid overlapping between those incidents of liberty which are mentioned in Article 19. An unauthorized intrusion into a person's home and the disturbance caused to him is the violation of the personal liberty of the individual. Hence, the Police Regulation authorizing domiciliary visits were plainly violative of Article 21, as there was no law under which it could be justified, and it must be struck down as unconstitutional.

But in *Govind v. State of Madhya Pradesh*,[73] the Supreme Court held that Madhya Pradesh Police Regulations 855 and 856, authoring domiciliary visits were constitutional as they have the force of law. These Regulations were framed by the Government under Section 46(2)(e) of the Police Act. The petitioner challenged the validity of those Regulations, on the ground that they were violative of his fundamental right guaranteed in Article 21, which also includes the 'right of privacy.' The Supreme Court held that these Regulations have the force of law and, therefore, they were valid. With regard to the 'right of privacy', the Court said, that the right to privacy would necessarily have to go through a process of case by case development.

Therefore, assuming that the right to personal liberty, the right to move freely throughout the territory of India, and the freedom of speech, create an independent right of privacy, which can be characterized as a fundamental right, the right is not absolute. Depending upon the character, and, antecedents of the person subject to surveillance, and, the object and limitations under which surveillance is made, it cannot be said that surveillance by 'domiciliary visits' would always be unreasonable restriction upon the right of privacy. The impugned Regulation 855 empowers surveillance only of persons against whom reasonable material exists to include the opinion that they show 'a determination to lead a criminal life'. The petitioner was shown to be a dangerous criminal whose conduct showed that he was determined to lead a criminal life. The Regulations imposed reasonable restrictions on the fundamental right of petitioner guaranteed in Article 21 and therefore, they are valid.

It is to be noted that in *Kharak Singh*'s case, the validity of a similar Police Regulation was challenged. In that case, the Regulations were declared unconstitutional, because they did not have the force of law. On the other hand, in *Govind*'s case the validity of a similar Police Regulation was upheld as they had the force of law.

Right to Travel Abroad

In *Satwant Singh Sawhney v. D. Ramarathnam, Assistant Passport Officer, Government of India, New Delhi*,[74] the Supreme Court of India further extended the scope of this Article and held that the 'right to travel abroad' was part of a person's 'personal liberty' within the meaning of Article 21 of the Indian Constitution. In that case the petitioner, who was a citizen of India, had to travel abroad frequently for business purposes. The government ordered him to surrender his passport. He challenged the action of the government on the ground, that it was violative of his fundamental rights under Article 21. His contention was, that right to leave India or travel abroad and return to India was part of his personal liberty, which could be restricted only by authority of law. The government cannot deny him a passport in the exercise of its executive power.

The contention of the Union Government was that the right to travel abroad was not included in the expression 'personal liberty,' and that, a passport was a political document to which no one had a legal, much less a constitutional right. The Supreme Court accepted the contention of the petitioner and held, that the right to travel abroad was part of a person's 'personal liberty' within the meaning of Article 21 and, therefore, no person could be deprived of his right to travel abroad except, according to procedure established by law.

In fact, there was no such law on which the government could justify its action. The Court observed that the expression 'liberty' in Article 21 is a comprehensive term. 'Personal liberty' in Article 21 takes in the right of locomotion – to go where and when one pleases, and the right to travel abroad is included in it. It only excludes the ingredients of liberty mentioned in Article 19.[75]

Maneka Gandhi's Case – A New Dimension

In *Maneka Gandhi v. Union of India*, the meaning and content of the words 'personal liberty' again came up for the consideration of the Supreme Court. The Court, in that case, has given the widest possible interpretation to the words 'personal liberty.' The petitioner's passport was impounded by the Central Government under Section 10(3)(c) of the Passport Act 1967.

The Act authorized the government to do so, if it was necessary 'in the interest of the general public.' The Government of India declined 'in the interest of the general public' to furnish the reasons for its decision. The petitioner challenged the validity of the said order on the following grounds that –

(1). – Section 10(3)(c) was violative of Article 14 as conferring an arbitrary power since it did not provide for a hearing of the holder of the passport before the passport was impounded.

(2). – Section 10(3)(c) was violative of Article 21, since it did not prescribe 'procedure' within the meaning of that Article 21.

(3). – Section 10(3)(c) was violative of Article 19(1)(a) and (g) since it permitted imposition of restrictions not provided in Clause (2) or (6) of Article 19.

The reasons for the order were, however, disclosed in the affidavit filed on behalf of the Indian Government, which stated, that the petitioner's presence was likely to be required in connection with the proceedings before a commission of inquiry. Regarding the opportunity to be heard; the Attorney-General filed a statement, that the petitioner could make a representation in respect of impounding passport and that the representation would be dealt with expeditiously in accordance with law.

The Supreme Court held, that the government was not justified in withholding the reasons for impounding the passport from the petitioner. Delivering the majority judgment, Justice P.N. Bhagwati, asked – Is the prescription of some sort of procedure enough or must the procedure comply with any particular requirement? He then held, that the procedure contemplated in Article 21 could not be unfair or unreasonable. And this principle of reasonableness which was an essential element of equality or non-arbitrariness, pervaded Article 14 like a brooding omnipresence, and, the procedure contemplated in Article 21 must answer the test of reasonableness, in order to be in conformity with Article 14.

Hence, any procedure which permitted impairment of individual's right to go abroad without giving him a reasonable opportunity to be heard could not, but, be condemned as unfair and unjust. The order withholding reasons for impounding the passport was therefore, not only in breach of statutory provisions (Passport Act) but also in violation of the rule of natural justice embodied in the maxim '*audi alteram partem*.' Although, there were no positive words in the statute (Passport Act) requiring, that the party should be heard, yet the justice of the common law would supply this omission of legislature. The power conferred under the Act on the passport authority to impound a passport is a quasi-judicial power. The rules of natural justice would, therefore, be applicable in the exercise of this power. Natural justice is a great humanizing principle intended to invest law with fairness and to secure justice. Fairness in action, therefore, demands that an opportunity to be heard should be given to the person affected. A provision requiring of such opportunity to the affected person can and should be read by implication in the Passport Act 1967. If such provisions were held to be incorporated in the Act by necessary implication, the procedure prescribed for impounding passport would be right, fair and just and would not suffer from the vice of arbitrariness or unreasonableness. It must, therefore, be held that the procedure 'established' by the Act for impounding a passport is in conformity with the requirement of Article 21 and is not violative of that Article.

Thus, Article 21 requires the following conditions to be fulfilled before a person is deprived of his personal liberty:—

1. There must be a valid law.
2. The law must provide a procedure.
3. The procedure must be just, fair and reasonable.
4. The law must satisfy the requirements of Articles 14 and 19 i.e., it must be reasonable.

However, in view of the statement of the Attorney-General, that the government was agreeable to consider the representation of the petitioner, it was held by the majority of the Supreme Court (Chief Justice Mirza Hamedullah Beg,[76] dissenting), that the defect of the order was removed and the order was, therefore, passed by the passport authority in accordance with the procedure established by law.

In *Nand Lal v. State of Punjab*,[77] the validity of an order of detention made under Section 3 of the Prevention of Blackmarketing and Maintenance of Supplies of Essential Commodities Act 1980, was challenged on the ground that procedure adopted by Advisory Board in allowing legal assistance to the state, but, denying such assistance to the detenue, was both arbitrary and unreasonable, and thus, violative of Article 21 read with Article 14 of the Constitution. The Court applying the *Maneka Gandhi*'s principle, held that the procedure adopted by the Advisory Board was arbitrary and illegal and consequently, the detention order was liable to be quashed. Although, under the above Act the detenue had no right to legal assistance in the proceedings before the Advisory Board, but it did not preclude the Board to allow such assistance to the detenue when it allows the same to the state.

Natural Justice

In *Gopalan's* case it was argued, that the word 'law' in Article 21 did not merely mean an enacted piece of law but, it incorporated the principles of natural justice, and a law which deprived a person of his personal liberty without complying with the rules of natural justice could not be held to be valid under Article 21. Rejecting the argument, the Supreme Court of India held, that the 'law' in Article 21 must mean a law enacted by the legislature, and, not the law in the abstract or general sense embodying the principles of natural justice as interpreted by the US Supreme Court.

In *Maneka Gandhi's* case, the Supreme Court has held that the word 'law' in Article 21 does not mean merely an enacted piece of law, but must be just, fair and reasonable law, i.e. which embodies the principles of natural justice. It is true that Article 21 is worded in negative terms, but, it is now well settled that Article 21 has both negative and affirmative dimension. 'Positive rights' are very well conferred under Article 21 of the Indian Constitution.

The following rights are held to be covered under Article 21:—

(i) *Right to live with human dignity* Thus in *Maneka Gandhi's* case, the Supreme Court of India gave a new dimension to Article 21. It held that the right to 'live' is not merely confined to physical existence, but, it includes within its ambit the right to live with human dignity. Elaborating the same view, the Court in *Francis Coralie Mullin v. The Administrator, Union Territory of Delhi*,[78] said that, the right to live is not restricted to mere animal existence. It means something more than just physical survival. The right to 'live' is not confined to the protection of any faculty or limb through which life is enjoyed or the soul communicates with the outside world but it also includes 'the right to live with human dignity,' and all that goes along with it, namely, the bare necessities of life such as, adequate nutrition, clothing and shelter and facilities for reading, writing and expressing ourselves in diverse forms, freely moving about and mixing and commingling with fellow human being.

Following *Maneka Gandhi* and *Francis Coralie* cases, the Indian Supreme Court in *People's Union for Democratic Rights v. Union of India*,[79] held that non-payment of minimum wages to the workers employed in various ASIAD-82 Projects in Delhi was a denial to them of their right to live with basic human dignity and violative of Article 21 of the Indian Constitution. Justice P.N. Bhagwati, speaking for the majority held, that the rights and benefits conferred on the workmen employed by a contractor under various labour laws are–

> 'clearly intended to ensure basic human dignity to workmen and if the workmen are deprived of any of these rights and benefits, that would clearly be a violation of Article 21'.

He held that the non-implementation by the private contractors and non-enforcement by the State Authorities of the provisions of various labour laws violated the fundamental right of workers 'to live with human dignity.'

This decision has heralded a new legal revolution. It has clothed millions of workers in factories, fields, mines and projects sites with human dignity. They had fundamental right to maximum wages, drinking water, shelter crèches, medical aid and safety in the respective occupation covered by the various welfare legislations.

In *Chandra Raja Kumari v. Police Commissioner Hyderabad*,[80] it has been held, that the right to live includes right to live with human dignity or decency and therefore, holding of beauty contest is repugnant to dignity or decency of women and offends Article 21 of the Constitution. The government is empowered to prohibit the contest as objectionable performance under Section 3 of the Andhra Pradesh Objectionable Performances Prohibition Act 1956. If it is grossly indecent, scurrilous or obscene or intended for blackmailing.

In state of *State of Maharashtra v. Chandrabhan Tale*,[81] the Court struck down a provision of Bombay Civil Service Rules 1959, which provided for payment of only a nominal subsistence allowance of one rupee per month to a suspended Government Servant upon his conviction during the pendency of his appeal as unconstitutional on the ground that it was violative of Article 21 of the Constitution.

Right to life embodies several aspects of life and it includes 'opportunity.'[82] Hence, before a person's reputation is likely to be affected, he must be heard even if the same is passed by the High Court.[83]

In *Chameli Singh v. State of U.P.*,[84] it was held, that in an organized society, the right to live as a human being is not ensured by meeting only the animals needs of man. It is secured only when he is assured of all facilities to develop himself and is freed from restrictions, which inhibits the growth. All human beings are designed to achieve this object. Right to live guaranteed in any civilized society implies the right to food, water, decent environment, education, medical care, and shelter. These are basic human rights known to any civilized society. Shelter for human being is not a mere protection of his life and limb. It is house where he has opportunities to grow physically, mentally, intellectually, and spiritually. Right to shelter includes adequate living space, safe and decent structure, clean and decent surroundings, sufficient light, pure air and water, electricity, sanitation and other civic amenities like roads etc., so as to have easy access to his daily avocation...... want of decent residence, frustrates this very object of constitutional animation of right to equality, economic justices, fundamental right to residence, dignity of person and right to live itself.[85]

(ii) *Right to livelihood*—In *Olga Tellis v. Bombay Municipal Corporation*,[86] popularly known as the 'pavement dwellers case' a five-judge bench of the Court has finally ruled that the word 'life' in Article 21 includes the 'right to livelihood' also. The court said:

> 'It does not mean merely that life cannot be extinguished or taken away as, for example, by the imposition and execution of death sentence, except according to procedure established by law. That is but one aspect of the right to life. An equally important facet of that right is the right to livelihood because no person can live without the means of livelihood. If the right to livelihood is not treated as a part of the constitutional right to life, the easiest ways of depriving a person of his right to life would be to deprive him of his means of livelihood. In view of the fact that Articles 39(a) and 41 require the State to secure to the citizen an adequate means of livelihood and the right to work, it would be sheer pedantry to exclude the right to livelihood from the content of the right to life.'

The petitioners, in that case had challenged the validity of certain Sections of the Bombay Municipal Corporation Act 1888, which empowered the Municipal Authorities to remove their huts from pavement and public places on the ground, that their removal amounted to depriving them of their right to livelihood and hence it was violative of Article 21.

While agreeing that the right to livelihood is included in Article 21 the Court held, that it can be curbed or curtailed by following just and fair procedure. It was held that the above Sections of the Bombay Municipal Corporation Act were constitutional, since they imposed reasonable restrictions on the right of livelihood of pavement and slum dwellers in the interest of the general public humanistic view and in order to minimize their hardships involved in the eviction, it directed the Municipal Authorities to remove them only after the end of the current monsoon season. The court also directed the corporation, to frame scheme for demarcating hawking and non-hawking zones and give them licences for selling their goods in hawking zones; hawking cannot be refused except for good reasons.

But, in *Sodan Singh Etc. Etc. v. New Delhi Municipal Committee*,[87] a five-judge bench of the Supreme Court has held, the right to carry on any trade or business is not included in the concept of life and personal liberty. Article 21 is not attracted in a case of trade and business. The petitioners, hawkers doing business on the pavement of roads in Delhi, had claimed, that the refusal by the Municipal Authorities to them, to carry on business of their livelihood amounted to violation of their right under Article 21 of the Constitution. The Court distinguished the ruling of the court in *Olga Tellis* case and held that it is not applicable in this case.

In a land mark judgment, in *Delhi Development Horticulture Employees' Union v. Delhi Administration*,[88] the Indian Supreme Court has held, that daily wages workmen employed under the *Jawahar Rozgar Yojna*, has no right of automatic regularization even though they have put in work for 240 or more days. The petitioners who were employed on daily wages in the *Jawahar Yojna* filed a petition for their regular absorption as a regular employees in the Development Department of the Delhi Administration. They contended that right to life, includes the right to livelihood and therefore, right to work. The Court held, that although broadly interpreted and as a necessary logical corollary, the right to life would include the right to livelihood, and therefore, right to work, but this country has so far not found it feasible to incorporate the right to livelihood as a fundamental right in the Constitution. This is because the country has so far not attained the capacity to guarantee it, and not because it considers it any the less fundamental to life. Advisedly, therefore, it has been placed in the chapter on Directive Principles, Article 41 of which enjoins upon the state to make effective provision for securing the same, 'within the limits of its economic capacity and development.' The ruling of the court is helped in preventing back door entry in government departments and public sector undertakings.

In a significant judgment in *D.K. Yadav v. J.M.A. Industries*,[89] the Supreme Court held, that the right to life enshrined under Article 21 includes the right to livelihood, and therefore, termination of the service of a worker without giving him reasonable opportunity of hearing, is unjust, arbitrary and illegal. The procedure prescribed for depriving a person of livelihood must meet the challenge of Article 14 and so it must be right, just and fair and not arbitrary, fanciful or oppressive. In the instant case, the appellant was removed from service by the management of the M/s. J.M.A. Industries Ltd.; on the ground that he had willfully absented from duty continuously for more than 8 days without leave or prior permission from the management and, therefore, 'deemed to have left the service of the company under Clause 12(2)(iv) of the Certified Standing Order.' But the appellant contended that despite his reporting to duty every day he was not allowed to join duty without assigning any reason.

The Labour Court upheld the termination of the appellant from service as legal. The Supreme Court held that the right to life enshrined under Article 21 includes right to livelihood and 'therefore' before terminating the service of an employee or workman fair play requires that a reasonable opportunity should be given to him to explain his case. The procedure prescribed for depriving a person of livelihood must meet the requirement of Article 14, that is, it must be right, just and fair and not arbitrary, fanciful or oppressive. In short, it must be in conformity of the rules of natural justice, Article 21 clubs together life with liberty, dignity of person with means of livelihood without which the glorious content of dignity of person would be reduced to animal existence. The Supreme Court of India set aside the Labour Court award and ordered his reinstatement with 50 per cent back wages.

However, the Supreme Court has been careful to point out that individual rights cannot be absolute in a welfare state. It has to be subservient to the rights of the public at large.[90] Hence, financial constraints of the state have also to be considered and recognized when demands of medical and health facilities arise in a welfare state.[91]

(iii) *Right to members of protective homes*—In *Vikram Deo Singh Tomar v. State of Bihar,*[92] through a public interest litigation, it was brought to the notice of the Supreme Court, that the female inmates of the 'Care Home Patna' were compelled to live in inhuman conditions in an old ruined building. They were illiterate and provided insufficient and poor quality of food, and no medical attention was afforded to them.

The Supreme Court held that 'the right to live with human dignity' is the fundamental right of every citizen, and, the state is under duty to provide at least the minimum conditions ensuring human dignity. Accordingly, the Court directed the state to take immediate steps for the welfare of inmates of 'Care Home Patna.' Pending construction of new building, the Court directed that the existing building must be renovated and sufficient amenities by way of living rooms, bath rooms and toilets within the building and adequate water and electricity etc., must be provided. The Court also directed the state to appoint a full-time superintendent to take care of the home and to ensure that a doctor visits the home daily.

In *B.R. Kapoor v. Union of India,*[93] where through a public interest litigation, mismanagement of Hospital for Mental Diseases, located at Shahdara, an institute maintained and run by Delhi Administration; was brought to the notice of the Court, the Court directed that the Government of India to take over its management from Delhi Administration and to take steps to improve its working conditions.

(iv) *Right to die - Constitutional or Unconstitutional*—The question of whether the right to die is included by Article 21 of the Indian Constitution, came before the Bombay High Court for consideration for the first time in *State of Maharashtra v. Maruti Shripati Dubal.*[94]

The Bombay High Court held that the 'right to life' is guaranteed by Article 21 includes a right to die, and consequently the Court struck down Section 309 of the Indian Penal Code (I.P.C); which provides punishment for attempt to commit suicide by a person as unconstitutional. The judges felt that the desire to die is not unnatural, but, merely abnormal and uncommon. They listed several circumstances in which people may wish to end their lives, including disease, cruel or unbearable condition of life, a sense of shame or disenchantment with life. They held that everyone should have the freedom to dispose of his life as and when he desires.

On the other hand, the Andhra Pradesh High court in *Chenna Jagadeeswar v. State of Andhra Pradesh,*[95] held that the right to die is not a fundamental right within the meaning of Article 21 and hence, Section 309 in the I.P.C (Indian Penal Code) is not unconstitutional.

In *P. Rathinam v. Union of India,*[96] a Division Bench of the Supreme Court agreed with the view of the Bombay High Court in *Maruti Shripati Dubal* case and held that a person has a 'right to die' and declared unconstitutional, Section 309 of the Indian Penal Code (I.P.C), which makes 'attempt to commit suicide' a penal offence. The 'right to live' in Article 21 of the Indian Constitution includes the 'right not to live', i.e. right to die or to terminate one's life. In the present case the petitioners had challenged the validity of Section 309 on the ground that it was violative of Articles 14 and 21 of the Constitution, and, prayed for quashing the proceedings initiated against the petitioner under Section 309; pending in the Court of Sub-Judge, Gunpur in the District of Koraput, Orissa for attempting to commit suicide. The Court held, that Section 309 of the I.P.C. was violative of Article 21 and hence void. A person cannot be forced to enjoy right to life to his detriment, disadvantage or disliking. The court held, that Section 309 of the I.P.C was 'a cruel and irrational provision.' The court held that–

> 'right to life of which Article 21 of the Constitution speaks of can be said to bring in its trial the right not to live a forced life.'

Explaining the reason for its decision the Court said that:

> 'Section 309 I.P.C deserves to be effaced from the Statute Book to humanize our penal laws. It is a cruel and irrational provision and may result in punishing a person again (Doubly) who has suffered agony and would be undergoing ignominy because of his failure to commit suicide.'

However, the court rejected the plea that 'euthanasia' (mercy killing), should be permitted by law. The judges said that they would not decide this point, because in euthanasia a third person is either actively or passively involved about whom it may be said that he aids or abets the killing of another person. There is a distinction between an attempt of a person to take his own life and action of some others to bring to an end the life of a third person such a distinction can be made on principle and is conceptually permissible.

In *Smt. Gian Kaur v. State of Punjab,*[97] a five-judge Constitution Bench of the Supreme Court overruled the *P. Rathinam's* case and held that 'right to life' under Article 21 of the Constitution does not include 'right to die' or 'right to be killed.' 'The right to die,' is inherently inconsistent with the 'right to life' as is 'death with life'.

Delivering the unanimous judgment of the Court, Mr Justice Jagdish Sharan Verma (1933–2013)[98], observed:

> 'Any aspect of life which makes it dignified may be read into Article 21 of the Constitution but not that which extinguishes it and is, therefore, inconsistent with the continued existence of life resulting in effacing the right itself'.
>
> 'Right to life' is a natural right embodied in Article 21 but suicide is an unnatural termination or extinction of life and, incompatible and inconsistent with the concept of 'right to life'.

Referring to protagonists of euthanasia's view that existence in persistent vegetative state was not a benefit to the patient to terminal illness being unrelated to principle of 'sanctity of life' or the 'right to live with dignity' the Court said, that this argument was no assistance to determine the scope of Article 21 of the Constitution for deciding whether the guarantee of 'right to life' therein includes the 'right to die'.

The Court made it clear, that the 'right to life' including the right to live with human dignity would mean the existence of such a right up to the end of natural life. This also includes the right to a dignified life up to the point of death including a dignified procedure of death.

This may include the right of a dying man to also die with dignity when his life is ebbing out. But the 'right to die', with dignity at the end of life is not to be confused with the 'right to die' an unnatural death curtailing the natural span of life.' The Court reiterated, that the argument to support the views of permitting termination of life in such cases (dying man who is terminally ill or in a vegetative state) by accelerating the process of natural death when it was certain and imminent was not available to interpret Article 21 to include therein the right to curtail the natural span of life. The Court, accordingly held, that Section 309 of I.P.C is not violative of Article 21 of the Indian Constitution.

The Indian Supreme Court also rejected the contention that Section 309 of I.P.C is unconstitutional being violative of Article 14. The Court said that the desirability of bringing about such a change is the function of the legislature, which may be enacting suitable law providing adequate safeguards to prevent any possible abuse.

The Court, thus, set aside the judgment of the Bombay High Court in *Maruti Shripati Dubal v. State of Maharashtra*, and the decision of the Supreme Court in *P. Rathinam v. Union of India* cases; wherein Section 309 I.P.C was held to be unconstitutional and upheld the judgment of the Andhra Pradesh High Court holding that Section 309 of the I.P.C was not violative of Articles 14 and 21 of the Indian Constitution.

(v) *Right to pollution free water and air*—In *Subhash Kumar v. State of Bihar,*[99] it has been held that, public interest litigation is maintainable for ensuring enjoyment of pollution free water and air which is included in the 'right to live' under Article 21 of the Constitution.

(vi) *Protection of Ecology and Environmental Pollution*—In *Rural Litigation and Entitlement Kendra, Dehradun v. State* of U.P.,[100] the Supreme Court ordered the closure of certain limestone quarries on the ground that there were serious deficiencies regarding safety hazards in them. The Court had appointed a committee for the purpose of inspecting certain limestone quarries. The committee had suggested the closure of certain categories of stone quarries having regard to adverse impact of mining operations therein. A large-scale pollution was caused by limestone quarries adversely affecting the safety and health of the people living in the area.

In *Shriram Food and Fertilizer case,*[101] the Supreme Court directed the company manufacturing hazardous and lethal chemicals and gases posing danger to health and life of workmen and people living in its neighbourhood, to take all necessary safety measures before reopening the plant. There was a leakage of chlorine gas from the plant resulting in death of one person and causing hardships to workers and residents of the locality. This was due to the negligence of the management in maintenance and operation of the caustic chlorine plant of the company. The matter was brought before the court through a public interest litigation. The management was directed to deposit a sum of Rs 20 lacs by way of security for payment of compensation claims of the victims of gas leak with the Registrar of the Supreme Court. In addition, a bank guarantee for a sum of 15 lacs was also directed to be deposited, which would be encashed, in case of any escape of chlorine gas within a period of 3 years from the date of the judgment, resulting in death or injury to any workman or any person living in the vicinity. Subject to these conditions the Court allowed the partial reopening of the plant.

In *M.C. Mehta v. Union of India*,[102] the Supreme Court ordered the closure of tanneries at Jajman near Kanpur, polluting the river *Ganga*. The matter was brought to the notice of the Court by the petitioner M.C. Mehta (1946),[103] a social worker, through a public interest litigation. The Court said, that notwithstanding the comprehensive provisions contained in the Water (Prevention and Control of Pollution) Act and the Environmental (Protection) Act, no effective steps were taken by the Indian Government to stop the grave public nuisance caused by the tanneries at Jajman, Kanpur. In these circumstances, it was held that the court was entitled to order the closure of tanneries unless they took steps to set up treatment plants.

In *M.C. Mehta v. Union of India (No. 2)*,[104] the petitioner M.C. Mehta, brought a public interest litigation against *Ganga* water pollution requiring the court to issue appropriate directions for the prevention of *Ganga* water pollution. He claimed that although, Parliament and the State Legislatures have passed several laws imposing duties on the Central and State Boards constituted under various statutes, they have just remained on paper and no proper action had been taken pursuant thereto. The Supreme Court held, that the petitioner although not a riparian owner (living on the river side) was entitled to move the court for the enforcement of various statutory provisions which impose duties on the municipal and other authorities. He is a person interested in protecting the lives of the people who make use of the *Ganga* water. The nuisance caused by the pollution of the river *Ganga* is a public nuisance, which is widespread and affecting the lives of large number of persons and, therefore, any particular person can take proceedings to stop it as distinct from the community at large.

Accordingly, the Court directed the Kanpur Municipality to submit its proposals for effective prevention and control of water pollution within 6 months to the Board constituted under the Water Act. It also directed the Kanpur Nagar Mahapalika (municipal corporation), to get the dairies shifted to a place outside the city, and, arrange for removal of wastes accumulated at the dairies so that it may not reach the river *Ganga*, to lay sewerage line wherever it is not constructed, to construct public latrines and urinals, for the use of poor people free of charge, to ensure that dead bodies or half burnt bodies are not thrown into the river *Ganga* and to take action against the industries responsible for pollution, licences to establish new industries should be granted only to those who make adequate provisions for the treatment of trade effluent flowing out of the factories.

The above directions would apply *mutatis mutandis* to all other municipalities, which have the jurisdiction over the areas through which the river Ganga flows.

The Indian Supreme Court, in a significant judgement in *Indian Council for Enviro-Legal Action v. Union of India*,[105] has held, that if by the action of private corporate bodies a person's fundamental right is violated the Court would not accept the argument that it is not 'State' within the meaning of Article 12 and, therefore, action cannot be taken against it. If the Court finds that the government or authorities concerned have not taken the action required of them by law and this has resulted in violation of the right to life of the citizens, it will be the duty of the Court to intervene.

In this case an environmentalist organization filed a writ petition under Article 32 before the Supreme Court, complaining the plight of people living in the vicinity of chemical industrial plants in India and requesting for appropriate remedial measures. The fact was that, near a small village Bichhri in Udaipur district of Rajasthan; a major industrial complex had developed, and respondents had established their chemical industries therein. Some of the industries were producing chemicals like Oleum and single super Phosphate. The respondent had not obtained the requisite licences and, nor did they install any equipment for treatment of highly toxic effluents discharged by them. As a result, the water in the wells became unfit for human consumption. It spread diseases, death and disaster in the village and surrounding areas. The villagers revolted against all this resulting in stoppage of manufacturing 'H' acid and ultimately these industries were closed. But, the consequences of their action remain in existence causing damage to the village. The court requested the National Environmental Engineering Research Institute (NEERI), to study the situation and to submit their report. In the technical report, it was found that out of 2440 tonnes of sludge, about 720 tonnes was still there. With a view to conceal it from the eyes of the inspection teams the respondents had dispersed it all over the area and covered it with earth. In spite of the Court's order they did not remove the sludge.

The Supreme Court directed the government and the authorities concerned to perform their statutory duties under various environmental laws. The court held, that the respondents were responsible for all the damages to the soil, to the underground water and to the village in general. Regarding, the determination of cost of remedial measures, the court held the Central Government had power to decide it. The principle on which the liability of the respondents so defray the costs of remedial measures would be determined is, the 'Polluter Pays,' that is, the responsibility for 'repairing damages is that of the offending industry'.

In another case in *M.C. Mehta v. Union of India,*[106] the Supreme Court of India, ordered the shifting of 168 hazardous industries operating in Delhi, as they were causing danger to the ecology and directed that they be reallocated. The court directed these industries to close down w.e.f. (with effect from) 30 November 1996. The Court gave necessary specific directions for the protection of the rights and benefits of the workmen employed in these industries. Likewise, in *Council for Enviro-legal Action v. Union of India*[107] the Court issued appropriate orders and directions for implementing and enforcing the laws to protect ecology.

In *Vellore Citizens Welfare Forum v. Union of India,*[108] the petitioner Vellore Citizens Welfare Forum, filed a writ petition by way of public interest litigation drawing the attention of the court towards the pollution caused by enormous discharge of untreated effluent by the tanneries and other industries in the State of Tamil Nadu. It was argued, that the tanneries were discharging untreated effluent into agricultural fields. Waterways, open lands, and rivers rendering the river water unfit for human consumption, contaminating the subsoil water and, had spoiled the physico-chemical properties of the soil making it unfit for agricultural purposes.

The Supreme Court held that such industries though are of vital importance to the country's development, but, they cannot be allowed to destroy the ecology, degrade the environment and pose a health hazard and cannot be permitted to continue their operation unless they set up pollution control devices. The principle of 'sustainable development' must be adopted by these industries as a balancing concept between ecology and development. It was held that the 'precautionary principle' and the 'Polluter Pays' principle, are essential feature of 'sustainable development' and must be adopted. Remediation of the damaged environment is part of the process of sustainable development, and, as such the polluter is liable to pay the cost to the individual who suffers, as well as the cost of reversing the damaged ecology.

'The Precautionary Principle' and the 'Polluter Pays' principle, the Court held, have been accepted as part of the law of the land. Article 21 of the Indian Constitution guarantee protection of life and personal liberty. Articles 47, 48A and 51A(g) form the Constitutional mandate to protect and improve the environment. Apart from the constitutional mandate there are number of legislations on the subject which impose duty on the governments to protect ecology and environment from pollution. The Court directed the closure of these industries unless they install pollution control devices. All the tanneries were required to obtain the consent of the concerned Board for further operation with effect from 15 December 1996. The Court imposed pollution fine of Rs 10000 on each industry. The money was to be deposited in the 'Environmental Protection Fund' and should be utilised for compensating the affected persons and also for restoring the damaged environment.

In *S. Jagannath v. Union of India,*[109] the petitioner, Chairman of a voluntary organization, *Gram Swaraj* Movement, for uplift of weaker sections of society, filed a petition by way of a public interest litigation, seeking the enforcement of Coastal Zone Regulation (CRZ) Notification 1991, issued by the Government of India, stopping of intensive and semi-intensive type of prawn farming in the ecological fragile coastal areas, prohibition from using the wet lands for prawn farming and the constitution of a National Coastal Management Authority to safeguard the marine life and coastal areas. It was contended that a large number of private and multinational companies have started setting up shrimp farms in the coastal areas of the country causing serious threat to the environment and ecology of these areas.

The Indian Supreme Court held that setting up of shrimp culture farms within the prohibited areas and in ecology fragile coastal areas have adverse effect on environment and coastal ecology and economics and, therefore, they cannot be permitted to operate. Shrimp culture industry is neither 'directly related to water front' nor 'directly needing foreshore facilities' and cannot be allowed to be set up anywhere in the Coastal Regulation Zone.

The Court further held, that the traditional type of shrimp farming are environmentally benign and pollution free. But, the modern technological type of farming using chemical to create more produce, create pollution and degrading effect on the environment and ecology, and therefore, such type of shrimp farming cannot be permitted. The Court issued comprehensive direction for the regulation and control of shrimp industries in the coastal areas.

(vii) *Right to education*—In a landmark judgement in *Mohini Jain v. State of Karnataka*,[110] popularly known as the 'Captivation Fee Case' the Supreme Court of India held that the right to education is a fundamental right under Article 21 of the Indian Constitution, which cannot be denied to a citizen by charging higher fee known as the captivation fee. The right to education flows directly from 'right to life'. The 'right to life' under Article 21 and the dignity of an individual cannot be assured unless it is accompanied by the right to education.

In this case, the petitioner Miss Mohini Jain of Meerut, Uttar Pradesh, had challenged the validity of a notification issued by the State of Karnataka Government, under the Karnataka Educational Institutions (Prohibition of Capitation Fee) Act 1984, which was passed to regulate tuition fee to be charged by the private medical colleges in the state. Under the Notification the tuition fee to be charged from students was as follows:

— Candidates admitted against Government seats Rs 2000 per year,
— the Karnataka Students Rs 25000 per annum and
— students from outside Karnataka Rs 60000 per annum.

The petitioner Miss Mohini Jain was denied admission on the ground that she was unable to pay the exorbitant tuition fee of Rs 60000 per annum. The 2 judge Division Bench, held that the right to education at all level is a fundamental right of citizen under Article 21 of the Indian Constitution, and charging captivation fee for admission to education institutions is illegal and amounted to denial of citizen's right to education and also violative of Article 14 being arbitrary, unfair and unjust. Captivation fee makes the availability of education beyond the reach of poor. The right to education is concomitant to the fundamental rights enshrined under Part III of the Constitution of India. The fundamental right to speech and expression cannot be fully enjoyed unless a citizen is educated and conscious of his individualistic dignity. The education in India has never been a commodity for sale.

In *Unni Krishnan, J.P. v. State of Andhra Pardesh*,[111] the Supreme Court of India, was asked to examine the correctness of the decision given by the Court in *Mohini Jain*'s case. The petitioners running medical and engineering colleges contended that, if *Mohini Jain* decision is correct and is followed and implemented by the respective State Government, they would have to close down their colleges. The 5 Judge bench by 3to 2 majority partly agreed with the *Mohini Jain* decision and held that right to education is a fundamental right under Article 21 of the constitution as 'it directly flows' from right to life. But, as regards to its content the court partly overruled the *Mohini Jain*'s case and held that the right to free education is available only to children until they complete the age of 14 years, but after that the obligation of the state to provide education is subject to the limits of its economic capacity and development. The obligations created by Articles 41, 45 and 46; can be discharged by the state either establishing its own institutions or by aiding, recognizing or granting affiliation to private institutions. Private education institutions are necessity in the present-day context. *Mohini Jain*'s case was not correct in holding that any amount charged must be described as captivation fee. To say so amounts to imposing an impossible condition. It is not possible for the private educational institutions to survive if they charge fee prescribed by government institutions. The private sector should be involved and encouraged in the field of education. But they must be allowed to do so under strict regulatory controls, in order to present private educational institutions from commercializing education. The charging of the permitted fees by the private educational institutions which is bound to be higher than charged by similar government institutions cannot itself be characterized as captivation fee.

In *Unni Krishnan, J.P. v. State of Andhra Pardesh*,[112] the Indian Supreme Court modified the scheme laid down in *Mohini Jain*'s case in relation to (NRI) Non-Resident Indian students and held that out of the seats only 5 per cent seats can be filled up by NRI students on the basis of merit to be judged by the management of the college concerned and not on the basis of entrance examination.

In *Shahal H. Musaliar v. State of Kerala*,[113] the court extended the application of the scheme framed by it, in *Unni Krishnan, J.P. v. State of Andhra Pardesh*, to minority educational institutions with certain modifications. The court held that:

— Firstly, it is for the government to decide whether an institution is a minority institution.
— Secondly, 50% seats would be filled up by agencies of the State Government on the basis of competitive examinations and selected candidates would pay fees as applicable to this class of students determined by the government.

— Thirdly, the remaining 50 per cent seats would be filled up by the management of the institution belonging to the particular religions or linguistic minority strictly on the basis of merit and candidates so selected would abide by such conditions of payment of fee as prescribed by the government.

Thus, out of the 50 per cent seats to be filled up by government; half would be 'payment seats' and half would be 'free seats'. Similarly, out of the 50 per cent seats to be filled up by the management half would be 'payment seats' and half 'free seats', out of the payment seats to be filled by the management. However, 5% seats could be filled up by Non-Resident Indian students (NRI). The court held that this modified scheme will not apply to the specified minority institutions.

The judgement of the court did go a long way in preventing the commercialization of professional education. It made amply clear that merit alone should be the basis of access to higher education.

In *All India Imam Organization v. Union of India*,[114] the Supreme Court held that Imams who are in charge of religious activities of mosques, are entitled to emoluments even in absence of statutory provisions in the Wakf Act 1954. It has been considered in number of cases that the right, if enshrined in Article 21, means right to live with human dignity. The court did not accept the contention of the Wakf Board, that since Imams performed religious duties they were not entitled to any emoluments. Whatever might have been the ancient concept, it has undergone a change and even in the Muslim countries mosques are subsidized and the Imams are paid their remuneration. Therefore, the submission, that in Indian set up or in absence of any statutory provision in the Wakf Act they were not entitled to any remuneration cannot be accepted. Financial difficulties of the institution cannot be above fundamental rights of a citizen. If the Boards have been vested with responsibility of supervising and administering the Wakf, then it is their duty to arrange resources to pay Imams. The court gave detailed directions to the Government of India and the Central Wakf Board to prepare a scheme for determining the remuneration of Imams.

Right to Liberty

Prisoner's right and Article 21—The protection of Article 21 is available even to convicts in jails. The convicts are not by mere reason of their conviction deprived of all the fundamental rights which they otherwise possess. Following the conviction, a convict is put into the jail. He may be deprived of fundamental freedoms like the right to move freely throughout the territory of India or the right to 'practice' a profession. But the Constitution guarantees to them other freedom like the right to acquire, hold and dispose of property for the existence of which detention can be no impediment. Likewise, even a convict is entitled to the precious right guaranteed by Article 21, and, he should not be deprived of his life or personal liberty except according to procedure established by law.

In *D. Bhuvan Mohan Patnaik v. State of Andhra Pardesh*,[115] the petitioners, who were Naxalite, were undergoing the sentence in the Central Jail at Visakhapatnam. They contended that the armed police guards posted around the jail and the live-wire electrical mechanism fixed on the top of the jail was an infringement of their right to 'life' and 'personal liberty' guaranteed by Article 21 of the Indian Constitution. The Court said,

> 'A convict has no right, more than any one else, to dictate, where guards were to be posted to prevent the escape of prisoners. The installation of live wire mechanism did not offend their right. It was a preventive measure intended to act as a deterrent and to cause death only if a prisoner invite death by scaling the wall while attempting to escape from lawful custody. The installation of live-wire would not by itself cause the death of the prisoner.'

In *Babu Singh v. State of U.P.*,[116] it was held that 'refusal to grant bail' in a murder case without reasonable ground would amount to deprivation of personal liberty under Article 21. In that case 6 appellants were not convicted by the Sessions Judge in a murder case. In appeal by the state, the High Court convicted the appellants and sentenced them to life imprisonment. Five appellants were given sentences of 20 months and the 6th was granted bail. These appellants were the entire male members of their families and all of them were in jail. The appellants applied for bail during pendency of their appeal before the Supreme Court. The Supreme Court held, that refusal to grant bail amounted to deprivation of personal liberty of accused persons. Personal liberty of an accused or convict is fundamental and can be taken away only in accordance with procedure established by law.

Right against solitary confinement

In *Sunil Batra v. Delhi Administration (No. 1)*,[117] the key question raised before the Supreme Court was whether 'solitary confinement' imposed upon prisoners who were under sentence of death was violative of Articles 14, 19, 20 and 21 of the Indian Constitution.

Sunil Batra was sentenced to death by the District and Sessions Judge, and his sentence was subject to confirmation by the High Court, and a possible appeal to the Supreme Court. Batra complained, that from the date of his conviction by the Sessions Judge, he was kept in solitary confinement till the Supreme Court intervened on 24 February 1978. It was contended that Section 30(2) did not authorize prison authorities to impose the punishment of solitary confinement. The Supreme Court accepted the argument of the petitioners and held that Section 30(2) of the Prisons Act 1894, did not empower the prison authorities to impose solitary confinement on a prisoner under sentence of death. Under Section 73 and Section 74, of I.P.C (Indian Penal Code), solitary confinement is itself a substantive punishment which can be imposed by a court of law. It cannot be left to the whims of prison authorities. The Court held that the expression 'prisoner under sentence of death' in the context of Section 30(2) could only mean the prisoner whose sentence of death had become final and could not be annulled or violated by any judicial or constitutional procedure. Thus, a prisoner was not under sentence of death till he had the right to appeal against his sentence or to appeal for mercy.

Charles Sobhraj, a foreigner, and an under-trial prisoner challenged the action of the Superintendent of Tihar Central Jail, New Delhi, for putting him into bar fetters. He was arrested on 6 July 1976 and detained. From the time he was lodged in jail he was put in bar fetters notwithstanding the recommendation of the jail doctor that bar fetters be removed. Sobhraj contended that Section 56 of the Prisons Act justified putting him into bar fetters. The petitioner, Charles Sobhraj, contended that Section 56 was violative of Articles 14 and 21 as conferred unguided and arbitrary powers on the superintendent to confine a prisoner in irons. The Court held that continuously keeping a prisoner in fetters, day and night, reduces the prisoner from a human being to an animal and that this treatment was cruel and unusual and that the use of bar fetters was against the spirit of the Constitution.[118]

Right to speedy trial

In *Hussainara Khatoon v. Home Secretary, State of Bihar (No. 1)*,[119] a petition for a writ of *habeas corpus* was filed by number of under-trial prisoners who were in prisons in the State of Bihar for years awaiting their trial. The Supreme Court held that 'right to a speedy trial' is a fundamental right which is implicit in the guarantee of life and personal liberty enshrined in Article 21 of the Indian Constitution. Speedy trial is the essence of criminal justice. It is implicit in the broad sweep and content of Article 21 as interpreted in *Maneka Gandhi's* case. No procedure which does not ensure a reasonable quick trial can be regarded as 'reasonable, fair or just'. For this reason the Court ordered the State of Bihar Government to release forthwith the under-trial prisoners on their personal bonds.

In *Hussainara Khatoon (No. 2)*[120] and *Hussainara Khatoon (No. 3)*[121] cases, the Indian Supreme Court reiterated the same view. In a signification judgement in *Abdul Rehman Antulay v. R.S. Nayak*,[122] the Supreme Court laid down detailed guidelines for speedy trial of an accused in a criminal case, but, it declined to fix any time limit for trial of offences. The burden lies on the prosecution to justify and explain the delay. The court held that the right to speedy trial flowing from Article 21 is available to accused at all stages, namely, the stage of investigation, inquiry, trial, appeal, revision and retrial.

The concerns underlying the right to speedy trial from the point of view of the accused are:—

(a) the period of remand and pre-conviction detention should be as short as possible;
(b) the worry, anxiety, expense and disturbance to his vocation and peace resulting from an unduly prolonged investigation, inquiry or trial should be minimal; and
(c) undue delay may result in impairment of the ability of the accused to defend himself whether on account of death, disappearance or non-availability of witnesses or otherwise.

The court said, that the accused cannot be denied the right of speedy trial merely on the ground that he had failed to demand a speedy trial. As regards to the time limit the court said, that it has to be decided by balancing the attendant circumstances and relevant factors, including nature of offence, number of accused and witnesses, the workload of the court etc. No time limit can be fixed for speedy trial.

In *Raghubir Singh v. State of Bihar,*[123] the accused persons who were being tried for waging war against the state, filed writ petitions before the Supreme Court for quashing the proceedings before the Special Judge on the ground of violation of their right to speedy trial under Article 21 of the Constitution. The Court held that there was no delay in investigating and trial of their cases warranting quashing of proceeding against them. The Court held that the right of a speedy trial is one of the dimensions of the fundamental right to life and liberty guaranteed by Article 21. But the question whether the right to speedy trial was infringed depends upon various factors.

— Was the delay owing to the nature of the case?
— Was the delay caused by the prosecuting agency?
— Was it due to the tactics of the defence?

In the instance case, it was found that the delay was caused due to the tactics of the accused, as they did assert their rights which were evident from the number of petitions filed before the Magistrate, and the Special Judge from time to time. The delay in investigation and trial was the outcome of the nature of the case and the general situation prevailing in the country.

In *Sunil Batra v. Delhi Administration (No. 2),*[124] it was held that the practice of keeping under-trials prisoners with convicts in jails offended the test of reasonableness in Article 19 and fairness in Article 21. The under-trials prisoners are presumably innocent until convicted and if they are kept with criminals in jail it violates the test of fairness of Article 21. Justice V. R. Krishna Iyer (1915–2014), delivering the majority judgement, held that integrity of physical person and his mental personality is an important right of a prisoner, and must be protected from all kinds of atrocities. The Supreme Court gave the following directions to the Central and State Governments and the Jail authorities:—

(1) that the petitioner's torture was illegal and he should not be subjected to any such torture until fair procedure is complied with.
(2) No corporal punishment or personal violence shall be inflicted.
(3) Lawyers nominated by the D.M. Session Judge, High Court and the Supreme Court would be given all facilities to interview, right to confidential communications with prisoners, subject to discipline and security considerations.
(4) Grievance deposit boxes should be maintained in jails which should be opened by D.M. and the Session Judges frequently. Prisoners should have access to such boxes.
(5) D.M. and Sessions Judges should inspect jails once every week, should make enquiries into grievances, and take suitable actions.
(6) No solitary or punitive cell, no hard labour or dilatory charge, denial of privileges and amenities, no transfer to other prison as punishment should be imposed without judicial approval of the session Judge.

Right against handcuffing—In *Prem Shankar Shukla v. Delhi Administration,*[125] the Supreme Court made another move for prison reform and prisoners' rights. As a result, the validity of certain Clauses of Punjab Police Rules were challenged as violation of Article 14, 19 and 21 of the Constitution. Justice V. R. Krishna Iyer, delivering the majority judgement held that provisions that every under-trial prisoner, who was accused of a non-bailable offence punishable with more than 3 years jail-term would be handcuffed, were violative of Articles. 14, 19 and 21 of the constitution. Handcuffing should be resorted to only when there is *'clear and present danger of escape'* of breaking out of the police control and for this there must be clear material, not merely an assumption. The Supreme Court said:–

> 'Handcuffing is *prima facie* inhuman and, therefore, unreasonable, is over harsh and at the first flush, arbitrary. Absent fair procedure and objective monitoring, to inflict 'irons' is to resort to zoological strategies repugnant to Article 21....'

In *Sunil Gupta v. State of Madhya Pradesh*,[126] the petitioners were educated persons, social workers and members of *Kisan Adivasi Sangathan*, Kerala, who were remanded in judicial custody, were taken to court from jail and back from court to the prison by the escort partly handcuffed. They had staged a '*dharna*' for a public cause and voluntarily submitted themselves for arrest. They had no tendency to escape from the jail. In fact, they even refused to come out on bail, but chose to continue in prison for the public cause. It was held that this act of the escort party was violative of Article 21 of the Constitution. There was no reason recorded by the escort party in writing for this inhuman act. The Supreme Court directed the Madhya Pradesh Government to take appropriate action against the erring escort party for having unjustly and unreasonably hand-cuffing the petitioner.

In *Citizen For Democracy v. State of Assam*,[127] the Supreme Court expressed serious concern over the violation of the law laid down by that court in *Prem Shankar Shukla*'s case against handcuffing of under-trial or convicted prisoners by the police authorities. In the instance case, Mr Kuldip Nayar (1923–2018), an eminent journalist in his capacity as President of 'Citizen for Democracy' (CFD), by letter, brought to the Supreme Court's attention, that the seven TADA detainees lodged in the hospital in the State of Assam were handcuffed and tied with a long rope to check their movement. Security guards were also posted outside the hospital. The Court treated the letter as a petition under Article 32 of the Indian Constitution and held, that handcuffing and in addition tying with ropes of the prisoners who were lodged in the hospital is inhuman and in violation of human rights guaranteed to an individual under international law and the law of the land.

Right against inhuman treatment—In *Kishore Singh Ravinder Dev Etc. v. State of Rajasthan*,[128] the Supreme Court held that the use of 'third degree' method by police is violative of Article 21 and directed the government to take necessary steps to educate the police so as to inculcate a respect for the human person. The court also held that the punishment of solitary confinement for a long period from 8 to 11 months and putting bar fetters on the prisoner in jail for several days on flimsy ground must be regarded as barbarous and against human dignity and hence violative of Articles. 21, 19 and 14 of the Indian Constitution.

Similarly, torture and ill-treatment of women suspects in police lockups has been held to be violative of Article 21 of the Constitution. The Court gave detailed instruction to concerned authorities for providing security and safety in police lockup and particularly to women suspects. Female suspects should be kept in separate police lockups and not in the same in which male accused are detained and should be guarded by female constables. The Court directed the Inspector General of Prisons and State Board of Legal Aid Advice Committee to provide legal assistance to the poor and indigent accused (male and female) whether they are under-trial or convicted prisoners.[129]

The Supreme Court held that torture, assault and death in custody, raises serious questions about the credibility of the rule of law and administration of the criminal justice system. It was observed that there has been increase in instances of custodial violence/torture attributed to misuse of police machinery by those at the helm of affairs to settle personal scores.[130]

Right against delayed execution—In *T.V. Vatheeswaran v. State of Tamil Nadu*,[131] a 2 judge Bench of the Supreme Court held, that delay in execution of death sentence exceeding 2 years would be sufficient ground to invoke the protection of Article 21 and the death sentence would be commuted to life imprisonment.

In *Sher Singh v. State of Punjab*,[132] the 3 Judge Bench of the Supreme Court agreed with this view, that prolonged delay in the execution of a death sentence was an important consideration for invoking Article 21 for judging whether the sentence should be allowed to be executed or should be converted into sentence of imprisonment. Prolonged detention to await the execution of a sentence of death is an unjust, unfair and unreasonable procedure and the only way to undo the wrong is to quash the death sentence.

However, the Court held that this cannot be applied as a rule in every case and each case should be decided on its own facts. The Court should consider whether the delay was due to the conduct of the convict (where he pursues series of legal remedies), the nature of offence, its impact on the society, its likelihood of repetition, before deciding to commute the death penalty into a sentence of life imprisonment. In the instant case, the delay was found to be due to the conduct of the convict, and therefore, it was held that the death sentence was not liable to be quashed. Accordingly, the Court overruled the decision in *T.V. Vatheeswaran v. State of Tamil Nadu*.

But, where there is delay in execution of death sentence of more than 2 years and the conduct and behaviour of the accused in the jail, evident from the report of the jail authorities show that he was showing genuine repentance, it was held that the death sentence could be commuted to life imprisonment.[133]

Finally, in *Smt. Triveniben v. State of Gujarat,*[134] a 5 judge Bench of the Supreme Court has set the matter at rest and held that undue long delay in execution of the death sentence will entitle the condemned person to approach the Court for conversion of death sentence into life imprisonment, but before doing so the Court will examine the nature of delay and circumstances of the case.

In *Francis Coralie Mullin v. The Administrator, Union Territory of Delhi,*[135] the Supreme Court held that the detenue's right to have interview with his lawyer and family member is part of his 'personal liberty' guaranteed by Article 21 of the Indian Constitution and cannot be interfered with except in accordance with reasonable, fair and just procedure established by law. Consequently, the validity of the provisions of the law which provided, that a detenue can have interview with his lawyer only after obtaining prior permission of the District Magistrate, and that too, in the presence of an officer, and, permitted interview of the family members only once in the month, were challenged on the ground that they were arbitrary and unreasonable and violative of Articles 14 and 21.

The Supreme Court of India, held that the provisions of the law which permitted only one interview in a month to detenue with members of his family were violative of Articles 14 and 21 and unconstitutional and void.

> The expression 'personal liberty' in Article 21 is of the widest amplitude and it includes the 'right to socialize' with members of family and friends, subject of course, to any valid prison regulations which must be reasonable and non-arbitrary.

The provision which restricts the interview only to once in a month is unreasonable and arbitrary, particularly, when a detenue stands on a higher footing than an under-trial prisoner or a convict. On the same reasoning, the provisions regarding permission to have interview with a lawyer was also held to be unconstitutional because it would cause great hardship and inconvenience to the lawyer, who would have to apply to the District Magistrate well in advance and the time fixed by the District Magistrate might not be suitable to the lawyer.

In *Vincent Panikurlangara v. Union of India,*[136] the Supreme Court held, that the right to maintenance and improvement of public health is included in the right to live with human dignity enshrined in Article 21. A healthy body is the very foundation of all human activities. In a welfare state this is the obligation of the state to ensure the creation and sustaining of conditions, congenial to good health.

Protection against illegal arrest, detentions, and custodial death—In *Jogindar Kumar v. State of U.P.,*[137] the Supreme Court has laid down guidelines governing arrest of a person during investigation. This has been done with a view to strike a balance between the needs of the police on the one hand and the protection of human rights of citizens from oppression and injustice at the hands of law enforcing agencies. On the other hand, the Court has held that a person is not liable to arrest merely on the suspicion of complicity in an offence. There must be some reasonable justification in the opinion of the police officer effecting the arrest that such arrest was necessary and justified.

In the instant case, a practicing lawyer Joginder Kumar, had been called to the police station in connection with a case under inquiry on 7 January 1994. On not receiving any satisfactory account of his whereabouts the family member of the detained lawyer filed a *habeas corpus* petition before the Supreme Court and in compliance with the notice, the lawyer was produced before the court. The police contended that the lawyer was not in detention but was only assisting the police to detect some cases. The Court held that though at this stage the relief in *habeas corpus* could not be granted yet the Supreme Court laid down certain requirements to be followed by the police before arresting a person such as the following:

(1) An arrested person being held in custody is entitled, if he so requests to have one friend, relative or other person who is known to him or likely to have an interest in his welfare told as far as is practicable that he has been arrested and where is being detained.
(2) Police officer shall inform the arrested person of this right when he is brought to the police station.
(3) An entry shall be required to be made in the Diary as to who was informed of the arrest.

These protections have been provided in compliance withArticle 21 and Article 22 of the Constitution and therefore, they must be strictly enforced. In *Smt. Nilabati Behera (alias Lalit Behera) v. State of Orissa*[138] the Supreme Court awarded compensation of Rs 150000 to the mother of the deceased who died in police custody due to beating.

In a landmark judgement in *D.K. Basu v. State of WestBengal*,[139] the Supreme Court has laid down detailed guidelines to be followed by the Central and the State, investigating and security agencies in all cases of arrest and detention.

> 'Custodial death is perhaps one of the worst crimes in a civilized society governed by the rule of law'.

The Court held that, any form of torture or cruel, inhuman or degrading treatment, would fall within the inhibition of Article 21 of the Constitution, whether it occurs during investigation, interrogation or otherwise.

The Supreme Court of India laid down guidelines to be followed in all cases of arrest or detention until legislative measures are taken:–

1. The police personnel carrying out the arrest and handling the interrogation of the arrest should bear accurate, visible and clear identification and name-tags with their designation.
2. The police officer carrying out arrest of a person shall prepare a memo of arrest at the time of arrest and such memo must be attested by at least one witness, who may be either a member of the family of the arrestee or a respectable person of the locality from where the arrest is made.
3. A person who has been arrested or detained shall be entitled to have one friend or relative or other person known to him or having interest in his welfare informed as early as possible.
4. The time, place of arrest and venue of custody of an arrestee must be notified by the police where the next friend or relative of the arrestee lives outside the district or town through the legal aid organization in the district and the police station of the area concerned telegraphically within a period of 8 to 12 hours after the arrest.
5. The person arrested must be aware of this right to have someone informed of his arrest or detention as soon as he is put under arrest or is detained.
6. An entry must be made in the diary at the place of detention regarding the arrest of the person which shall also disclose the name of next friend of the person who has been informed of the arrest and the names and particulars of the police officials in whose custody the arrestee is.
7. The arrestee should, where he so requests, be also examined at the time of his arrest and major and minor injuries, if any, present on his or her body, must be recorded at that time. The 'inspection memo' must be signed both by the arrestee and the police officer affecting the arrest and its copy provided to the arrestee.
8. The person should be subjected to medical examination by a trained doctor within 48 hours during his detention or by a doctor on panel of approved doctors appointed by Director, Health Services of the concerned State or Union Territory.
9. Copies of all the documents including the memo of arrest should be sent to the area Magistrate for his record.
10. The arrestee may be permitted to meet his lawyer during interrogation, though not throughout the interrogation.
11. A police control room should be provided at all district and State headquarters where information regarding the arrest and place of custody of the arrestee shall be communicated by the officer causing the arrest within 12 hours of effecting the arrest and it should be displayed conspicuously on the notice-board of the police control room.

The Supreme Court made it clear, that failure to comply with the guidelines should apart from rendering the official concerned liable for departmental action, also, render him liable to contempt of court and the proceedings for contempt may be instituted in any High Court of the country, having territorial jurisdiction over the matter. The requirements referred to in the guidelines flow from Articles 21 and 22(1) of the Indian Constitution and need to be strictly followed. These would apply with equal force to the other governmental agencies. These requirements are in addition to the constitutional and statutory safeguards and do not detract from various other directions given by courts from time to time in connection with the safeguarding of the right and dignity of the arrestee.

Compensation for violation of Article 21

The Supreme Court of India in a judgement of far reaching importance in *Rudal Sah v. State of Bihar,*[140] has held that the Courts have the power to award monetary compensation in appropriate cases, where there has been violation of the constitutional rights of citizens. The Supreme Court directed Bihar Government to pay 'Compensation of Rs 30000' to Rudal Sah who had to remain in the jail for 14 years because of the irresponsible behaviour of the State Government Officers, even after his acquittal. Thus, it is clear from this ruling, that the Court can order payment of compensation to victims of state violence.

Similarly, in *Bhim Singh, MLA v. State of J & K,*[141] the court awarded a sum of Rs 50,000 to the petitioner as compensation for the violation of his constitutional right of personal liberty under Article 21 of the Constitution. The petitioner, Bhim Singh, a Member of Legislative Assembly, was arrested and detained in police custody and deliberately prevented from attending a Session of the Legislative Assembly. The police officers acted deliberately and *mala fide*, and the Magistrate and the Sub Judge, aided them either by colluding with them or by their casual attitude.

When the constitutional right of personal liberty is invaded, the invasion is not washed away by his being set free. In appropriate cases, the Supreme Court has jurisdiction to award monetary compensation by way of exemplary costs or otherwise. In *Peoples' Union for Democratic Rights v. Police Commissioner, Delhi Headquarters,*[142] a labourer was taken to the police station for carrying out some work. He was severely beaten when he demanded wages and ultimately succumbed to the injuries. It was held that the state was liable to pay compensation, and accordingly, directed the government to pay Rs 75,000 as compensation to the family of the deceased.

Similarly, in *Saheli, a Women's Resources Centre v. Commissionerof Police,*[143] the Supreme Court directed the Delhi Administration to pay Rs 75,000 as exemplary compensation to the mother of a 9 year old child who died due to beating by the police officer.

In *Smt. Kewal Pati v. State of Uttar Pradesh,*[144] the Court awarded compensation to the widow of a convict, who was killed in jail by a co-accused while serving his sentence under Section 302 I.P.C, as it resulted in deprivation of his life, contrary to law and in violation of Article 21. A prisoner does not cease to have constitutional right except to the extent he has been deprived of it in accordance with law. His death was caused due to the failure of the jail authorities to protect him. Accordingly, the Court directed the government to pay a compensation of Rs 100000 to the widow and children of the deceased.

Compensation to persons killed in 'Fake Encounter'—In *Peoples' Union for Civil Liberties (PUCL) v. Union of India,*[145] the Supreme Court held, that killing of 2 persons in fake encounter by the police was clear violation of the right to life guaranteed in Article 21 of the Constitution and the defence of sovereign immunity does not apply in such case. The Court awarded Rs 100,000 as compensation for each deceased.

Safeguards against Arbitrary Arrest and Detention

(Article 22)

Introduction

According to Article 21, no person can be deprived of his life or personal liberty except according to procedure established by law. This means that a person can be deprived of his life or personal liberty provided his deprivation was brought about in accordance with the procedure prescribed by law. Article 22 provides those procedural requirements which must be adopted and included in any procedure enacted by the legislature. If these procedural requirements are not complied with, it would then be deprivation of personal liberty which is not in accordance with the procedure established by law.

Therefore, Article 22 prescribes the minimum procedural requirements that must be included in any law enacted by the legislature in accordance with which a person may be deprived of his life and personal liberty. Article 22 deals with two separate matters;

(1) persons arrested under the ordinary law of crimes; and
(2) persons detained under the law of 'Preventive Detention'.

The first two Clauses of Article 22 deal with detention under the ordinary law of crime and lay down the procedure which has to be followed when a man is arrested and the remaining Clauses (3), (4), (5), and (6) deal with persons detained under a preventive detention law and lay down the procedure, which is to be followed when a person is detained under that law.

PREVENTIVE DETENTION

Article 22 mainly deals with safeguards against 'preventive detention'. 'Preventive detention' is not to punish a person for any wrong done by him, but at curtailing his liberty, with a view to preventing him from committing certain injurious activities in future. The Indian Supreme Court observed:[146]

> 'Whereas punitive incarceration is after trial on the allegations made against a person, punitive detention is without trial into the allegations made against him.'

Article 22 is not a complete code—At one time, it was considered that Article 22 was a complete code with regard to the laws providing for preventive detention, and, that the validity of an order of detention should be determined strictly according to the terms within the four corners of Article 22.

It was held in *Gopalan*'s case,[147] that a detenue cannot claim the freedoms guaranteed by Article 19(1)(d), if it was infringed by his detention, and that the validity of the preventive detention law was not to be tested in the light of the reasonableness of the restrictions imposed thereby on the freedom of movement, nor on the ground that his right to personal liberty was infringed under Article 21, otherwise, than, according to the procedure established by law. This view has now been shown to be wrong in *Rustom Cavasjee Cooper v. Union of India*.[148] Although, this case is concerned with Article 31(2) but, in *Maneka Gandhi*'s case,[149] the Court has applied it in relation to Article 21 also. According, to this view a law relating to 'preventive detention' must now satisfy not only the requirements of Article 22, but also the requirements of Article 21 of the Indian Constitution. In other words, the procedure prescribed under the 'preventive detention' law must be reasonable and just and fair under Articles 14, 19 and 21 of the Constitution.

RIGHTS OF ARRESTED PERSONS UNDER ORDINARY LAWS

Clauses (1) and (2)—Clauses (1) and (2) of Article 22 guarantee four rights on a person who is arrested for any offence under an ordinary law.

(a) the right to be informed' as soon as may be' of ground of arrest,
(b) the right to consult and to be represented by a lawyer of his own choice,
(c) the right to be produced before a Magistrate within 24 hours, and
(d) the freedom from detention beyond the said period except by the order of the Magistrate.

The above fundamental rights guaranteed to arrested persons by Clauses (1) and (2) of Article 22 are available to both citizens and non-citizens, and not to persons arrested and detained under any law providing for 'preventive detention.'

(a) *The rights to be informed of grounds of arrest*—This is necessary to enable the arrested person to know the grounds of his arrest and to prepare for his defence. Article 22 is, in the nature of the directive, intended for the arresting authorities to immediately disclose the grounds for the arrest of a person. The words used in Article 22(1) are 'as soon as may be' which means as nearly as is reasonable in the circumstances of a particular case.[150] If the grounds of arrest is delayed it must be justified by 'reasonable circumstances.' This right of being informed of the grounds of arrest, is not dispensed with by offering to make bail to the arrested person.[151]

In *Joginder Kumar v. State of U.P.*,[152] the Supreme Court has laid down guidelines, governing arrest of a person during the investigation. This is intended to strike a balance between the needs of police on one hand and the protection of human rights of citizens from oppression and injustice at the hands of law enforcing agencies. The Court has held that a person is not liable to arrest merely on the suspicion of complicity in an offence. There must be some reasonable justification in the opinion of the police officer effecting the arrest that such arrest was necessary and justified.

The National Police Commission of India (NPC), in its third report has pointed out that power of arrest is one of the chief source of corruption in the police. According, to the report, nearly 60 per cent of the arrests are either unnecessary or unjustified.[153]

(b) *Right to be defended by a lawyer of his choice*—In USA, if a person is arrested, he must be afforded the opportunity to consult with a lawyer of his choice and if he is unable to employ a counsel, it is the duty of court to engage a lawyer for him.[154] Prior to the *Maneka Gandhi*'s decision, in India the view of the Court was, that it was not bound to provide the help of a lawyer unless a request was made by him. But, as a result of the ruling of the Indian Supreme Court in *Maneka Gandhi*'s case and a series of cases following that case, it is clear that the courts will be bound to provide the assistance of a lawyer to a person arrested under an ordinary law also.

In *Hussainara Khatoon v. Home Secretary, Bihar*,[155] the Supreme Court held, that it is the constitutional right of every accused person, who is unable to engage a lawyer and secure legal services on account of reasons such as poverty, indigence or incommunicado situation, to have free legal services provided to him by the state, and the state is under constitutional duty to provide a lawyer to such persons, if the needs of justice so require. If free legal services are not provided the trial itself may be vitiated as contravening Article 21.

(c) *Right to be produced before a Magistrate*—In addition to the furnishing of the grounds of arrest, the arrested person must be produced before the magistrate within 24 hours of his arrest. It can be extended beyond 24 hours, only under the judicial custody. It affords a possibility, if not an opportunity, for immediate release in case the arrest is not justified.

This has been held as mandatory provision.[156] The Indian Supreme Court, criticized in very strong terms the conduct of a magistrate, who passed an order remanding the accused to police custody without the accused having been produced before him personally. The police officer, it was held, acted deliberately and *mala fide* and the magistrate, aided him either by colluding with him or by his casual attitude, which was a gross violation of the constitutional rights of the accused under Articles 21 and 22; and monetary compensation was awarded to the accused.[157]

(d) *No detention beyond 24 hours except by order of the Magistrate*—This means that if there is necessity of detention beyond 24 hours, it is only possible under judicial orders. The expression 'arrest and detention' in Articles 22(1) and (2), was held not to apply to a person arrested under a warrant issued by the court, on a criminal or quasi-criminal complaint or under security proceedings. Article 22 is designed to give protection against the act of the executive or order of non-judicial authorities and, applies to a person who has been accused of a crime or of offence of criminal or quasi-criminal nature or some act prejudicial to the state or public interest. Therefore, under Article 22(1) and (2); the arrested person has a right to be produced before the nearest magistrate within period of 24 hours. This would enable the arrested person to get a speedy trial. This means that if the person arrested is not produce before the nearest magistrate within 24 hours, the arrest would be made illegal. This is also available to a person arrested under a warrant issued, by the speaker of a Legislative Assembly of Uttar Pradesh for committing contempt of the House; as it was in violation of his right guaranteed by Clause (2) of Article 22 of the Constitution.[158]

In *State of Punjab v. Ajaib Singh*,[159] the Supreme Court held valid the Abducted Person (Recovery and Restoration) Act 1949, under which an abducted person could be arrested and delivered to the officer-in-charge of the nearest camp. The arrest of an abducted person under the Act was held not to constitute 'arrest and detention' because the person was not accused of any offence of a criminal or quasi-criminal nature. Likewise, the removal of a minor girl from a brothel under the Bengal Suppression of immoral Traffic Act 1923, was held not to constitute 'arrest and detention' under Article 22.[160] The reason is, that person who is arrested under a warrant of a court is informed of the grounds of his arrest.

In a significant judgment, in *Central Bureau of Investigation v. Anupam J. Kulkarni*,[161] the Supreme Court laid down detailed guidelines governing arrest of an accused when investigations cannot be completed within 24 hours. The Court has held, that when a person is arrested under Section 57 of Cr.P.C., he should be produced before the nearest Magistrate within 24 hours. The Judicial Magistrate can authorize the detention of the accused in such custody, i.e. either police or judicial from time to time, but, the total period of detention cannot exceed 15 days in the whole. After the expiry of the first period of 15 days, the further remand can only be in judicial custody. There cannot be any detention in the police custody after the expiry of first 15 days. If the investigation is not completed within the 90 days or 60 days, then the accused has to be released on bail as provided under Section 167(2) of the Cr.P.C. The period of 90 days or 60 days has to be computed from the date of detention as per the orders of the Magistrate and not from the date of arrest by the police.

The Supreme Court observed that the constitutional requirement to produce an arrested person before a Judicial Magistrate within 24 hours of his arrest must be strictly and scrupulously observed.[162]

Exceptions—Clause (3) of Article 22, provides two exceptions to the rule contained in Clauses (1) and (2). It says that the rights given to arrested person under Clause (1) and (2) are not available to following persons:

(1) an enemy alien, and
(2) a person arrested and detained under a Preventive Detention law.

An enemy alien may, however, seek the protection under Clause (4) and (5) of Article 22; if arrested under a law of 'preventive detention,' but subject to the law passed by the Parliament.

Preventive Detention Laws

Clauses (4) to (7) of Article 22, provide the procedure which is to be followed, if a person is arrested under the law of 'preventive detention'. In Indian law, there is no authoritative definition of the term 'preventive detention'. The word 'preventive' is used in contra-distinction to the word 'punitive'. It is not a punitive but a preventive measure. While the purpose of the punitive detention is to punish a person for what he has already done; the purpose of preventive detention is not to punish a man for having done something, but, to intercept him before he does it and to prevent him from doing it. No offence is proved nor any charge is formulated.

The sole justification of such detention is suspicion or reasonable probability of the detenue committing some act likely to cause harm to the society or endanger the security of the government, and not criminal conviction which can only be warranted by legal evidence.[163]

Necessity of such provision—Preventive detention laws are repugnant to democratic constitution, and, they are not found in any of the democratic countries of the world. No country in the world has made these laws an integral part of their constitution, as has been done in India and Pakistan. There is no such law in USA. It was resorted to in England during the First World War, certain regulations framed under the Defence of the Realm Act 1914 (DORA), provided for preventive detention at the satisfaction of the Home Secretary, as a war measure, and, they ceased to have effect at the conclusion of hostilities. The same thing happened during the Second World War. These regulations were upheld by a British Court.[164]

The Indian Constitution, however, recognizes preventive detention in normal times as well. In *A.K. Gopalan v. State of Madras*[165] Justice M. Patanjali Shastri (1889–1963),[166] explaining the necessity of this provision said:

> 'The sinister looking feature, so strangely out of place in democratic Constitution, which invests personal liberty with the sacrosanctity of a fundamental right, and so incompatible with the promises of its preamble, is doubtless designed to prevent the abuse of freedom by anti-social and subversive elements which might imperil the national welfare of the infant republic.'

The Preventive Detention Acts—The first Preventive Detention Act was enacted by the Parliament on 26 February 1950. The object of the Act was to provide for detention with a view to preventing any person from acting in a manner prejudicial to the defence of India, the relation of India with foreign powers, the Security of India or a state or the maintenance of public order, the maintenance of supplies and services essential to the community. Section 3 empowered the Central and the State Governments and certain officers, under them to make orders of detention if they were satisfied, that it was necessary to detain a person with a view to prevent him from acting in any manner prejudicial to the things mentioned above.

The Act was purely a temporary measure and was to cease to have effect on 1 April 1951. But its life was extended from time to time till it lapsed on 31 December 1969. But, the Preventive Detention Law was revived in the form of Maintenance of Internal Security Act 1971 (MISA), in less than 2 years' time, after the lapse of the first Preventive Detention Act 1950. This Act continued to be in operation until the year 1977. The Act was repealed by the Janata Party Government in 1978, which came to power after the defeat of the Congress Ministry headed by Indira Gandhi (1917–84).[167] But, in less than 2 years' time after the repeal of the MISA, the caretaker Government headed by Charan Singh (1902–87),[168] again revived the Preventive Detention Law in the form of Prevention of Blackmarketing and Maintenance of Supplies of Essential Commodities Act 1980. Its objective was to prevent blackmarketing, hoarding of essential commodities. It requires the detaining authority to furnish grounds of detention within a period of 5 days from the date of detention, extendible to 10 days in exceptional cases. Within 3 weeks, the government is required to place grounds of detention along with detenu's representation before the Advisory Board. The Board must submit its report to the government within 7 weeks from the date of detention. The maximum period for which a person could be detained after the confirmation by the Advisory Board, has been restricted to 6 months from the date of detention. The aggrieved person has right to move the courts under Articles 32 and 226 of the Indian Constitution.

Again in, 1980 the President of India, issued the National Security Ordinance providing for preventive detention of persons responsible for communal and caste riots and other activities prejudicial to the country's security. The Ordinance has now become the National Security Act (NSA). It provides for detention up to a maximum period of 12 months, but does not bar the detenue from challenging his detention in a court of law on grounds, amongst others, of infringement of his fundamental rights. The detenue would be conveyed the grounds of detention within 10 days of his detention. He shall have rights to represent to the Advisory Board against his detention. It also provides for detention of a person, with a view to preventing him from acting in any manner prejudicial to the security of the state or the maintenance of public order or supplies and services essential to the life of the community.

The NSA was amended by an Ordinance in 1984 in order to make it more effective. The amended Act 1984, separates each of the grounds for detention and, allows further detention of a person whose earlier detention had either expired or had been removed. Prior to this amendment, grounds on which the detention was based was held to be infirm, the entire detention order was considered bad in law by the court. The new Section 5 which has been inserted in the Act, provides that a detention order under Section 3 of the Act for which two or more grounds have been mentioned, would not be deemed to be invalid or inoperative merely because one, or some of the grounds are considered vague, non-existent, non-relevant, unconnected or invalid. The amendment to Section 14 has been made to remove any bar on another detention order being issued under Section 3 against the same person. Section 14-A has been amended to substitute the words, '2 years' in place of '12 months' for Punjab and Chandigarh. The amendment was necessitated by the extraordinary situations prevailing in the State of Punjab due to Akali agitation.

The amendment limits the scope of judicial review of preventive detention laws considerably. It thus nullifies the effect of numerous decisions of the courts, in which the detention orders have been struck down on the ground, that one of the several grounds of detention was found to be vague, non-existent or unconnected with the grounds of detention supplied to detenue. The only difference between the earlier preventive laws and the present one is that the present laws give the detenue a right to go to the court and challenge the validity of his detention.

In *A.K. Roy v. Union of India*,[169] popularly known as the NSA case, the Supreme Court by 4 to 1 majority upheld the constitutional validity of the NSA and the Ordinance which preceded the Act. The Court held, that Act was neither vague nor arbitrary in its provisions providing for detention of persons on certain grounds, as acting in a manner prejudicial to the 'defence of India', 'security of India', 'security of the State', and to 'relations with foreign power'. While upholding the validity of the NSA and Ordinance preceding it, the Supreme Court issued a number of directions with a view to safeguarding the interests of detenues detained under the NSA. The Court directed:

(1) that immediately after detention his kith and kin must be informed in writing about his detention and his place of detention;
(2) the detenue must be detained in a place where he habitually resides unless exceptional circumstances require detention at some other place;
(3) that detenue is entitled to his book and writing materials, his own food, visits from friends and relatives;
(4) he must be kept separate from those convicted; and
(5) no treatment of a punitive character should be meted out to him and he should be treated according to the civilized norms of human dignity.

Terrorist and Disruptive Activities (Prevention) Act, 1987 (TADA)—TADA was primarily passed with a view to dealing with specific situations of terrorism in Punjab, Kashmir and even parts of the north-east. The Act vests sweeping powers in the State Governments, which are likely to be misused and have actually been misused.

In *Kartar Singh v. State of Punjab*,[170] the Supreme Court has considerably narrowed down the scope and ambit of the TADA, and held, that unless the crime alleged against an accused could be classified as a 'terrorist act' in letter and spirit, he should not be charged under the Act and should be tried under ordinary penal laws by the regular courts. The Court held that Section 3 of the Act operates, when a person not only intends to overawe the government or create a terror in people etc., but also, when he uses the arms and ammunition which results in death or likely to cause deaths and damages the property. In other words, the Court held that–

> 'a person becomes a terrorist or is guilty of terrorist activity when his intention, action and consequence all the three ingredients are found to exist together'.

Thus, an activity which is sought to be punished under Section 3(1) of TADA has to be such which cannot be classified as a mere law and order problem and cannot be tackled under the ordinary penal law.

Another safeguard laid down by the court against the misuse of the Act, was that of speedy trial of accused which is an essential part of the fundamental right to life and liberty under Article 21 of the constitution. The Court also struck down Section 22 of the Act as violative of Article 21 of the Indian Constitution. Section 22 permitted identification of an accused on the basis of his photograph. Referring to violation of human rights by the state law enforcing agencies, the court said, that these acts were in utter disregard and in all breaches of humanitarian law and universal human rights as well as in total negation of the constitutional guarantee and human decency. The Supreme Court held, that the Act did not provide a blanket power of unlimited detention without trial and a citizen should be entitled to bail in case the police fail to complete the investigation within 6 months, extendable to maximum of 1 year with the permission of designated court.

Constitutional safeguards against Preventive Detention Laws—although the Constitution of India has recognized the necessity of laws like Preventive Detention, it has also provided safeguards to mitigate their harshness by placing fetters on legislative power conferred on the legislature. It is for this reason that Article 22 has been given a place in the Chapter on 'guaranteed rights.'[171] Clauses (4) to (7) guarantee the following safeguards to a person arrested under Preventive Detention Law:—

(a) Review by Advisory Board.
(b) Communication of grounds of detention to detenue.
(c) Detenue's right of representation.
(a) Review by Advisory Board

(a) *Review by the Advisory Board*—Clause (4) provided, that no law providing for preventive detention shall authorize the detention of a person for a longer period than '3 months' unless an Advisory Board constituted of person, who are or have been qualified to be High Court Judge has reported before the expiration of the said period of 3 months, that there is in its opinion sufficient cause for such detention. If in the opinion of Advisory Board the detention was not justified the Government was bound to revoke the detention order.[172] If the Advisory Board reported that the detention was justified then the detaining authority would determine the period of detention.

However, the period of detention could not be indefinite. The detention could not exceed in any case beyond the maximum period prescribed by any law made by the Parliament for that class of detenue under Sub-Clause (b) of Clause (7). Any law providing for detention for a period longer than 3 months without obtaining the opinion of the Advisory Board must provide the class or classes of cases and also the circumstances under which a person may be detained for more than 3 months. It means that the Parliament must provide both (a) the classes or cases, and (b) the circumstances under which detention for a longer period of 3 months could be made.[173] Clause 7 of Article 22 contained an exception to Clause (4). It empowered Parliament to enact a law and provide for a detention for more than 3 months without the opinion of the Advisory Board. Therefore, the opinion of the Advisory Board was not necessary in the cases:–

(1) when period of detention did not exceed 3 months, and
(2) when Parliament by law prescribed the maximum period for which a person may be detained under Clause (4) (b) and Clause (7) (a).

After the 44th (Amendment) Act 1978, Clause (4) has been substituted, this reduces the period of detention from 3 to 2 months without obtaining the opinion of the Advisory Board.

(b) *Grounds of detention must be communicated to the detenue*—Article 22(5) gives 2 rights to the detenue:

(a) the authority making the order of detention must 'as soon as may be' communicate to the person detained the grounds of his arrest, that is, the grounds which led to the subjective satisfaction of the detaining authority, and
(b) to give the detenue 'the earliest opportunity' of making a representation against the order of detention, that is, to be furnished with sufficient particulars to enable him to make a representation.

Clause (5) imposes an obligation on the detaining authority to furnish to the detenue the grounds for detention 'as soon as possible'. The grounds of detention should be very clear and easily understandable by the detenue. The sufficiency of the particulars conveyed to a detenue is a justiciable issue, the test being whether they are sufficient to enable the detenue to make an effective representation. 'communicate' is strong word. It requires that sufficient knowledge of the basic facts constituting the grounds, should be imparted effectively and fully, to the detenue in writing in a language which he understands, so as to enable him to make a purposeful and effective representation. If the grounds are only verbally explained to the detenue and nothing in writing is left with him in a language which he understands then that purpose is not served, and the constitutional mandate in Article 22(5) is infringed.[174] Consequently, where the detenue did not know sufficient English to understand the grounds communicated to him; it was held that there was no sufficient compliance with the requirements laid down in the Constitution.

Similarly, in *Lallubhai Jogibhai Patel v. Union of India*,[175] the detenue did not know English but the grounds of detention were drawn in English and the detaining order stated, that the Police Inspector while serving the grounds of detention fully explained the grounds in Gujarati to the detenue; but no translation of the grounds of detention into Gujarati was given to the detenue. It was held that there was no sufficient compliance of Article 22(5), and hence, the order of detention was invalid.

In *Kubic Dariusz v. Union of India*,[176] the grounds of detention were served to the detenue in English, and he acknowledged the receipt thereof putting his signature in English. After 1 month thereafter, he made a representation that he knew only Polish language and not English. It was held that there was no violation of Article 22(5), as the detune had working knowledge of English, but he was showing ignorance. Where the document supplied was in Tamil, a language which was not known to the detenue, he was held to have been deprived of the right to make an effective representation.[177]

The grounds of detention must be in existence at the time of making the order. No part of such ground can be held back nor can new ground be added thereto.[178]

In *Shibban Lal Saksena v. State of Uttar Pradesh*,[179] the petitioner was supplied with 2 grounds of his detention. But, later on, the detaining authority revoked one of the grounds communicated to him earlier. The detenue challenged the detention as illegal. The State of Uttar Pradesh, contended that the remaining ground was sufficient to sustain the detention. The Supreme Court held the detention illegal and observed,

> 'To say that the other ground, which still remains, is quite sufficient to sustain the order, would be to substitute on objective judicial test for the subjective decision of the executive authority which is against the legislative policy underlying the statute. In such cases, we think, the position would be the same as if one of these grounds was irrelevant for purposes of the Act, or was wholly illusory and this would vitiate the detention order "as a whole".'

In *Ram Bahadur Rai v. State of Bihar*,[180] it was held that where the order of detention was based on distinct and separate grounds and if any of the grounds was vague, or irrelevant the entire order would fail. In *Fogla & Anr v. State of West Bengal*,[181] where one of the reasons for detention was not communicated to the detenue, it was held that the detenue had no opportunity to make an effective representation to the Government and therefore the detention was violative of Article 22(5) and must be set aside.

Amendment in National Security Act—In view of the amendments in the National Security Act (NSA), the scope of judicial review of 'preventive detention' laws has been considerably reduced. The 2nd amendment in NSA, provides that a detention order made under the Act for which two or more grounds had been mentioned would not be deemed to be invalid or inoperative, merely, because some of the grounds were considered vague, non-existent, non-relevant, unconnected or invalid. The grounds of detention is separable and a person can be detained again and again on the same ground. The amendment has nullified the effect of several decisions of the Court in which detention orders were struck down on one or the other grounds mentioned therein.

In *Shafiq Ahmad v. District Magistrate, Meerut*,[182] it has been held that even where one of the grounds was found to be bad and unsustainable, the detention under NSA, would not be vitiated if remaining grounds are valid.

(c) *Right of Representation*—The other right granted to the detenue is that he should be given the earliest opportunity of making a representation against detention order. It means that the detenue must be furnished with sufficient particular of ground of his detention to enable him to make a representation which on being considered may give him relief.[183]

The 'grounds' under Article 22(5) means all the 'basic facts' and materials, which have been taken into account by the detaining authority in making the order of detention and on which, therefore, the order of detention is based. Nothing less than all the basic facts and materials which influenced the detaining authority in making the order of detention must be communicated to the detenue. This is the plain requirement of the first safeguard in Article 22(5).

The second safeguard in Article 22(5) requires, that the detenue shall be afforded the earliest opportunity of making representation against the order of detention. No available delay, no shortfall in the materials communicated shall stand in the way of the detenue in making an earlier, yet comprehensive and effective representation in regard to all basic facts and materials which may have influenced the detaining authority in making the order of detention depriving him of his freedom. These are the legal safeguards enacted by the Constitution-makers against arbitrary or improper exercise of the vast power of 'preventive detention' which may be vested in the executive by a law of 'preventive detention.'[184]

The reason why grounds are required to be communicated 'as soon as possible' is two-fold; Firstly, it acts as a check against arbitrary and capricious exercise of power. The detaining authority cannot whisk away a person and put him behind bars at its own sweet will. It must have grounds for doing so. Secondly, the detenue has to be afforded an opportunity of making a representation against the order of detention. But, if the grounds are not supplied to him, it is not possible for him to make effective representation, and, in fact the right to make representation would become illusory.

The 'materials and documents' relied on in the order of detention must be supplied to the detenue along with 'grounds'. The supply of 'grounds' simpliciter would give him not a real but merely an illusory opportunity to make a representation and would thus make the procedure unjust and unreasonable which would be liable to be struck down.[185] Inordinate delay in considering the representation under Section 8 of NSA, by the detaining authority will make detention order invalid.[186] Similarly, the non-supply of the copies of documents relied on by detaining authority will make the detention illegal.[187]

The word 'and shall afford' in Article 22(5), put an obligation on detaining authority to inform the detenue while serving the detention order, that he has a right to make representation against the detention order, and, also a right to be heard by the Advisory Board. This procedural safeguard must be observed strictly and the failure to comply with this requirement would vitiate the detention order. But, where a detenue who was an enlightened person and had been in active politics and was therefore, fully cognizant of his right to make representation under Article 22(5) and Section 8 of the NSA, and he, in fact, appeared before the Advisory Board, and was personally heard by the Board, it was held that failure to comply with the above requirement would not have the effect of vitiating the order of detention.[188]

But, merely because the detenue was not 'simultaneously furnished with the grounds of detention along with the order of detention' it cannot be said that the detenue was thereby deprived of the right of being afforded the earliest opportunity of making a representation against the order of detention. Thus, when the detenue did not allege that the detention was for non-existent grounds, nor did he attribute any *mala fide* on the part of the detaining authority the order of detention could not become invalid, merely because the grounds were furnished 2 days later. The law is that the detaining authority must communicate to the detenue the grounds of detention which is specified under Section 48 of the NSA i.e., within 5 to 10 days, depending upon the circumstances of each case.[189]

Under Article 22(5) the government is bound to consider the petitioner's representation as expeditiously as possible. Delay in deciding detenue's representation will make the detention illegal.[190] Delay in considering the representation of the detenue must be properly explained otherwise it will make the detention illegal.

Similarly, it has been held that refusal on the part of the detaining authority to send the representation of the detenue to the Central Government amounts to denial of the right conferred on him under Article 22(5) of the Indian Constitution and hence, the order of detention made under Section 14 of the National Security Act 1980, would become illegal and was liable to be struck down. When the representation was addressed to the Central Government it was incumbent on the part of the detaining authority to forward the same to the Central Government and not to take pre-emptive action thereupon of its own.[191]

Similarly, it has been held that where there is an unexplained long delay in disposal of representation the order of detention will be invalid. In *T.D. Abdul Rahman v. State of Kerala,*[192] the court held that the delay of 72 days in the absence of satisfactory explanation was too long a period for ignoring the indolence on the part of the concerned authority and, hence, the order of detention was invalid. The explanation given that delay had occurred in seeking the comment of the Collector of Customs etc., was held to be not at all convincing and acceptable.

Thus, there is dual obligation on the appropriate government and the dual right in favour of the detenue, namely,

(1) to have his representation considered by the appropriate authority, and
(2) to have once again the representation considered by the Advisory Board.[193]

If in the light of that representation the Advisory Board finds that there is no sufficient cause for detention, the government has to revoke the order of detention and set the detenue at liberty. Thus, whereas the government considers the representation to ascertain whether the order is in conformity with its power under the relevant law, the Board considers such representation from the point of view of arriving at its opinion whether there is sufficient cause for detention. The obligation of the appropriate government to afford to the detenue the opportunity to make representation and to consider that representation is distinct from the government's obligation to constitute a Advisory Board and to communicate the representation amongst other materials to the Board to enable it to form its opinion. The above conclusion is strengthened by the provisions of the Preventive Detention Act 1950, made in conformity with Clauses (4) and (5) of Article 22. Consequently, the detenue has a constitutional right and there is, on the government, corresponding constitutional obligation to consider his representation irrespective of whether it is made before or after his case is referred to the Advisory Board.

Thus, where the State Government waited till the receipt of the Advisory Board's opinion and there was an unexplained period of 24 days of non-consideration of the representation and there was no independent consideration of the representation by the State Government, it was held that there was clear non-compliance of Article 22(5) and consequently, the detention was liable to be quashed.[194]

In *Jayanarayan Sukul v. State of West Bengal,*[195] the Court held that the language of Article 22(5) of the Constitution makes it obligatory for the State Government to consider the representation of the detenue as soon as it is received by it. The opinion of Advisory Board is no substitute for the consideration of the representation by the Government. The Court has enunciated the following 4 principles to be followed in regard to the representation of the detenue:

(1) The appropriate authority is bound to give an opportunity to the detenue to make representation and to consider the representation as early as possible.
(2) The consideration of the representation of the detenue by the appropriate authority is entirely independent of any action by the Advisory Board, including the consideration of the representation by the Board.
(3) There should not be any delay in the matter of consideration.
(4) The appropriate Government is to exercise its opinion and judgment on the representation before sending the case along with the detenue's representation to the Advisory Board. If the appropriate Government will release the detenue it will not send the matter to the Advisory Board. If the Government will not release, it will send the case along with detenue's representation to the Board. If the Board reports in favour of release the Government will release. If the Board expresses its opinion against the representation the Government may still exercise the power to release the detenue.

Thus, where the detenue made a representation against the order of his detention, and the State Government without considering the representation confirmed the order of detention it was held that the State Government failed in its obligation and that the confirmation of detention was in violation of Section 7 of the MISA (Maintenance of Internal Security Act), and Article 22(5) of the Constitution and therefore, invalid. The subsequent consideration and rejection of the representation could not cure such invalidity of the confirmation of the order of detention and consequently the detention was illegal and void.[196]

In *Balchand Choraria v. Union of India*,[197] the representation was filed by the detenue through his counsel. The government did not consider the representation and approved the detention on the ground that it was not filed by the detenue. The Supreme Court held, that the High Court was wrong in construing that the representation was not made by the detenue himself but by his counsel. The lawyer had filed the representation on the instruction of the detenue. The Supreme Court said that in matters where the liberty of the individual is concerned and a highly cherished right is involved the representation should be construed liberally, and, not technically so as to frustrate or defeat the concept of liberty which is guaranteed by Article 21 of the Constitution. As the representation was not considered at all by the government which it was duty bound to consider the detention order was vitiated and detenue is to be released forthwith.

In *Kamla Kanahiyalal Khushalani v. State of Maharashtra*,[198] the Supreme Court has expressed great concern about the non-compliance of the constitutional safeguards contained in Article 22(5) by the detaining authorities. Despite repeated warnings of the court in a series of decisions, the detaining authorities do not take care to comply these requirements. When the detaining authority applies its mind to the documents and materials which form basis of the detention, there could be no difficulty in getting photostat copies of the same and attached the same along with the grounds of detention, if he is really serious in passing a valid order of detention. Unfortunately, these requirements are not complied with resulting in the orders of detention being set aside by the court, even though on merits they might have been justified in suitable cases. The Supreme Court suggested, that whenever a detention is struck down by the courts, the detaining authority or officer concerned who are associated with the preparation of the grounds of detention must be held personally responsible and action should be taken against them for not complying with the constitutional requirements contained in Article 22(5).

It is high time, the Supreme Court suggested, that the government should impress on the detaining authority the desirability of complying with above constitutional safeguard. In the instant case, the order of detention was declared void on the ground that the documents and materials were not supplied along with the detention order and also there was an unexplained delay of 25 days in disposing of the representation of the detenue. Similarly, the detention was declared to be void on the ground that there was undue delay of 75 days in disposal of the representation by the Central Government.[199]

Even when detenue's representation is received after the Advisory Board has considered his case and held his detention to be justified, the government is still obligated to consider the representation, for it is not bound to accept the Board's opinion automatically and may still take the view, after considering the representation, that it was no longer necessary to detain him.[200]

In *Sheela Devi v. Mohan Sarup*,[201] the grounds of detention communicated to the detenue were not legible. The legible copies of documents were supplied to him later on. The detention order was confirmed before the supply of legible copies of document. The court held that this was violative of Article 22, as he was denied the opportunity of making representation and hence, entitled to be released.

Subjective satisfaction of detaining authority—The language used in the 'preventive detention' laws make it clear that the power of detention was to be exercised on the 'subjective satisfaction' of the detaining authority. The court will not normally interfere with the decision of the detaining authority whether the grounds given in the detaining order are sufficient or not.[202]

However, the 'subjective satisfaction' of the detaining authority is not wholly immune from judicial scrutiny. The courts have by judicial decision, carved out an area, limited though it be, within which the validity of the 'subjective satisfaction' can yet be subject to judicial scrutiny. The basic postulate on which the courts have proceeded is that 'subjective satisfaction' begin a condition precedent for the exercise of the power conferred on the Executive the courts can always examine whether the requisite satisfaction is arrived at by the authority, if it is not the condition precedent to the exercise of the power would not be fulfilled and the exercise of power would be bad.[203]

The 'subjective satisfaction' of the detaining authority can be challenged on the following grounds, namely, *mala fide* or vagueness, and irrelevant or non-existent grounds or mechanical application of mind of detaining authority.

However, the amendments in the NSA (National Security Act) have considerably limited the scope of judicial review of the subjective decision of the detaining authority. The amendments provide that the validity of the preventive detention order cannot be challenged on the ground that one of the several grounds of detention is vague, or non-existent or unconnected or invalid. The Act, thus, gives an extraordinary power of high potency to the executive. If these powers are exercised with due discretion and care it may prove to be an effective weapon for fighting social evils, encompassed by the statute that are eating into the vitals of the nation and pose a threat to its stability. But, if wielded casually and capriciously, the power may turn into an engine of oppression posing a threat to the democratic way of life itself. The need for utmost good faith and caution in exercise of this power, therefore, cannot be over-emphasized.[204]

In *Srilal Shaw v. State of West Bengal*,[205] the petitioner was detained under the provisions of the Maintenance of Internal Security Act 1975 (MISA), for unlawful possession of railway property. The detenue was prosecuted under the Railway Property (Unlawful Possession) Act 1966. But, the case was not proceeded with, because according to District Magistrate, the witnesses did not dare to give witness against detenue for fear of their lives and, therefore, the case was dropped. The Supreme Court held the detention invalid. However, the Court made an important observation. It said,

> 'this is typical case in which for no apparent reason a person who could easily be prosecuted and punished under the punitive law is being preventively detained. The Railway Property (Unlawful Possession) Act 1966, confers extensive powers to bring to book persons who are found in unlawful possession of railway property.'

But, the courts will uphold the detention valid even on isolated grounds if they are so serious to effect the whole community. In *Babulal v. State of West Bengal*,[206] the Court upheld the detention of detenues under MISA (Maintenance of Internal Security Act), valid on the ground that they were member of a gang which committed an organized dacoity in a running train equipped with firearms and putting innocent passengers to peril of life and property.

In *Habeas Corpus* case,[207] the constitutional validity of Section 16-A of the MISA (now repealed) was challenged. It was contended on behalf of the detenue that it was violative of Article 226, inasmuch, as it prevented the High Court from exercising the jurisdiction under the Article to issue writ of *habeas corpus* and examining whether the detention under the Act was based on proper satisfaction of executive authority or not. The Supreme Court by 4 to 1 majority, (Justice Hans Raj Khanna [1912–2008][208], not expressing any opinion on the question) held, that Section 16-A, was constitutionally valid. The Court held, 'that it was a rule of evidence and it was not open either to the detenue or to the Court to ask for grounds of detention.' Section 16-A did not affect the jurisdiction of High Court under Article 226.

The jurisdiction to issue writs was neither abrogated nor abridged. It is a rule of evidence. Therefore, the detaining authority was bound by Section 16-A and forbidden absolutely from disclosing grounds of arrests, no question could arise for adverse inference against the authority that the power was exercised *mala fide* or not on subjective satisfaction. Even if a detenue makes out a prima facie case that the detention was *mala fide* the affidavit of the authority will be the answer and judicial inquiry will be closed. The courts cannot insist on the production of the file or hold that the case of detenue stands un-rebutted by reason of non-disclosure of grounds of arrest.

The effect of the decision in *Habeas Corpus* case was that, courts were barred from examining the question of *mala fide* of the detention order or *ultra vires* character of the detention orders or that the order was not passed on the 'subjective satisfaction' of the detaining authority. The Supreme Court decision overrules impliedly a number of earlier decisions in which it had claimed that it could examine the validity of the detention order on the ground, either, that the order was not passed on the 'subjective satisfaction' of the detaining authority or the detention was made *mala fide* or the detention was made not for the purposes of the 'preventive detention' laws.[209]

It is interesting to note that Section 14 of the Preventive Detention Act 1951, which was similar to the present Section 16-A of the MISA (Maintenance of Internal Security Act), was struck down as unconstitutional by the Supreme Court, in the case of *A.K. Gopalan v. State of Madras,*[210] on the ground, that it foreclosed the judicial inquiry of the legality of the detention under the said Act. In view of the 42nd Amendment the decision of the *Habeas Corpus* case is no longer a good law.

Right to life and liberty under Pakistan's Constitution

Article 9 of the 1973 Pakistan Constitution, provides that:–

> 'no person shall be deprived of life or liberty save in accordance with law.'

This is the first fundamental right which finds its place in Chapter 1, Part II of the Pakistan Constitution, in which 20 fundamental rights are enumerated. The language of Article 21 of the Indian Constitution which corresponds to Article 9 of the Pakistan Constitution is somewhat different. It says that:–

> 'no person shall be deprived of his life or personal liberty except according to procedure established by law'.

The principal difference is that in Article 9 of the Pakistan Constitution the words used are 'save in accordance with law' whereas Article 21 of the Indian Constitution uses the words 'except according to procedure established by law'.

The provisions of Articles 9 and 21 of the Constitution of Pakistan and India, respectively amount to a declaration, that no person is to take life or liberty of another person except under a law authorizing him to do so. The persons whose life and liberty is threatened is therefore entitled to require the person seeking to deprive him of the right to live or more freely to show the legal authority under which he is purporting to act.

In *Sakhi Daler Khan v. Superintendent-in-Charge, Recovery of Abducted women,*[211] the Lahore High Court set the petitioner at liberty, as it found that the respondent had arrested and detained him in flagrant violation of the provisions of the Pakistan (Recovery of Abducted Persons) Act 1949. The High Court held, that no authority can deprive a person whether citizen or not, of his liberty in violation of law, and the deprivation of liberty of the petitioner had to be declared without lawful authority and of no legal effect because it was not in accordance with law.

Right to life

The 'right to life' includes the right to live with human dignity, and everything that goes with it, namely, the bare necessities of life, such as adequate nutrition, clothing and shelter and other facilities required for life.

With reference to a corresponding provisions in the 5th and 14th Amendments of the US Constitution, which says that no person shall be deprived of his 'life, liberty or property without due process of law', in *Munn v. Illinois,*[212] the US Supreme Court spoke of the right to life in the following words:—

> 'By the term "life" as here used something more is meant than mere animal existence. The inhibition against its deprivation extends to all those limbs and faculties by which life is enjoyed. The provision equally prohibits the mutilation of the body by the amputation of an arm or leg, or the putting out of any eye, or the destruction of any other organ of the body through which the soul communicates with the outer world.'

The Supreme Court of Pakistan in *Ms Shehla Zia v. Wapda,*[213] held that environmental pollution caused by

> 'electromagnetic radiation of high voltage transmission lines of electricity posed a serious health hazard to the quality of life and was therefore violative of the right to life guaranteed by Article 9 of the Constitution.'

Similarly, the Supreme Court of Pakistan in *Employees of Pakistan Law Commission, Islamabad v. Ministry of Works,*[214] ruled that the right to life includes the right of enjoyment of life and maintaining adequate level of living. Therefore, the provisions of accommodation by the Government to its servants, during the tenure of service of its employees being necessary for maintaining adequate level of living, is covered by the 'right to life' guaranteed by Article 9 of the Constitution. In *Suo Moto Case No. 7 of 2017,* it was held that preventing the sick from reaching hospitals and doctors infringes their right to life which would require enforcement.[215]

In Article 9 of the Constitution of Pakistan, deprivation of liberty means deprivation of the right to eat and sleep when one likes or to work or not to work as and when pleases etc. Any assault on the body of a person, for example, whipping, torture, blind-folding, fettering, house arrest, solitary confinement, preventing a person from reading a book, religious or non-religious, is an invasion of liberty, and in the absence of a law or rule having the force of law authorizing it, such act of invasion would be violative of Article 9, in *Begum Shamim Afridi v. Province of the Punjab,*[216] The Lahore High Court held that solitary confinement and similar other restraints fall within the meaning of torture and are prohibited by the Constitution.

> Word 'life' used in Art. 9 of the Constitution, includes all such amenities and facilities, which a person born in a free country is entitled to enjoy with dignity, legally and constitutionally. Word 'life' in the Constitution has not been used in a limited manner; a wide meaning should be given to enable a man not only to sustain life but to enjoy it.... Legislature, under the Objectives Resolution, which is part of the Constitution, has to ensure an egalitarian society, based on Islamic concept of fair play and social justice.[217]

The Supreme Court, held the high rate of population growth in Pakistan as a threat to the right of life because it causes poverty, high maternal and child mortality rate, low literacy, lack of access to clean water and adequate food.[218] In another case it was held that inhibition against deprivation of 'right to life' extends to all those limbs and faculties by which life is enjoyed. The term 'life' includes 'reputation', 'status' and all other ancillary privileges which the law confers on the citizen. A civil servant is fully protected under Article 9 and cannot be deprived of his right of reputation and status.[219] Under Article 9, a person is entitled to have an impartial Court and tribunal. It was also held that 'right to life' includes requirement of separation of the 'Executive' from the 'Judiciary' under Article 175(3) of the Constitution.[220] Even a transaction, which is not transparent, and goes against the interests of the general public constitutes violation of Article 9 of the Constitution.[221]

Arrest and Detention under Pakistan's Constitution

Article 10 of the Constitution of Pakistan, 1973, provides that–

(1) no person who is arrested shall be detained in custody without being informed, as soon as may be, of the grounds for such arrest, nor shall he be denied the right to consult, and be defended by a legal practitioner of his choice.

(2) Every person who is arrested and detained in custody shall be produced before a magistrate within a period of twenty-four hours of such arrest, excluding the time necessary for the journey from the place of arrest to the court of the nearest magistrate, and no such person shall be detained in custody beyond the said period without the authority of a magistrate.

By virtue of Clause (3) of Article 10, the conditions contained in Clauses (1) and (2) of Article 10, do not apply to any person who is arrested 'or detained under any law providing for preventive detention. Clause (4) of Article 10 provides that–

> No law providing for preventive detention shall be made except to deal with persons acting in a manner prejudicial to the integrity, security or defence of Pakistan or any part thereof, external affairs of Pakistan,

> or public order, or the maintenance of supplies or services, and no such law shall authorize the detention of a person for a period exceeding [three months] unless the appropriate Review Board has, after affording him an opportunity of being heard in person, reviewed his case and reported, before the expiration of the said period, that there is, in its opinion, sufficient cause for such detention, and, if the detention is continued after the said period of [three months], unless the appropriate Review Board has reviewed his case and reported, before the expiration of each period of three months, that there is, in its opinion, sufficient cause for such detention.

In this Article the appropriate Review Board has been defined,

(1) in the case of a person detained under a Federal Law, a Board appointed by the Chief Justice of Pakistan and consisting of a Chairman and two other persons, each of whom is or has been a Judge of the Supreme Court or a High Court;
(2) and in the case of a person detained under a Provincial Law, a Board appointed by the Chief Justice of the High Court concerned and consisting of a Chairman and two other persons, each of whom is or has been a Judge of a High Court.
(3) The opinion of Review Board shall be expressed in terms of the views of the majority of its members.

Under Clause (5) of Article 10,

> When any person is detained in pursuance of an order made under any law providing for preventive detention, the authority making the order shall, [within fifteen days] from such detention, communicate to such person the grounds on which the order has been made, and shall afford him the earliest opportunity of making a representation against the order; Provided that the authority making any such order may refuse to disclose facts which such authority considers it to be against the public interest to disclose.

Under Clause (6) of the Article, it is incumbent on –

> the authority making the order to furnish to the appropriate Review Board all documents relevant to the case unless a certificate, signed by a Secretary to the Government concerned, to the effect that it is not in the public interest to furnish any documents, is produced.

Clause (7) of the Article provides that–

> within a period of twenty-four months commencing on the day of his first detention in pursuance of an order made under a law providing for preventive detention, no person shall be detained in pursuance of any such order for more than a total period of eight months in the case of a person detained for acting in a manner prejudicial to public order and twelve months in any other case.

However, this condition does

> not apply to any person who is employed by, or works for, or acts on instructions received from, the enemy or who is acting or attempting to act in a manner prejudicial to the integrity, security or defence of Pakistan or any part thereof or who commits or attempts to commit any act which amounts to an anti-national activity as defined in a Federal law or is a member of any association which has for its objects, or which indulges, in any such anti-national activity.

Clause (9) of Article 10 denies the right and protection guaranteed by this Article 'to any person who for the time being is an enemy alien'.

Nature of provisions of Article 10

The constitutional provisions of Article 10 relating to safeguards as to arrest and detention are of the nature of inorganic provisions, that is, provisions of the nature of statute law which lay down conditions governing all persons arrested or detained under all sub-constitutional laws. The Supreme Court of Pakistan in *Abdul Aziz v. Province of West Pakistan*,[222] held that–

> 'when Article 7 proceeds to make detailed provisions regarding particular aspects of arrest and detention, it is clearly laying down law in a field which is included in the larger subject of the liberty of persons under the law. While constitutions are largely concerned with laying down principles which shall be followed in the making of laws, there is nothing to prevent a constitution-making body from making law of a special nature dealing with a special subject in the course of making a Constitution. In Article 10 there are included general statements of conditions affecting the questions of arrest and detention of persons, under all sub-constitutional laws relating to that subject. In so doing, the Article makes fresh law, of a detailed character, belonging to the category of statute law, albeit enacted in the Constitution'.

The Supreme Court further held, that the Article contains, nothing in the way of a direction obliging the insertion of its provisions in every statute of the relevant kind. The clause imposes a condition upon the power of detention without trial vested in authorities under existing law, viz., that the satisfaction of the detaining authority regarding the need for detaining a particular person shall not by itself be sufficient for continuing that detention beyond an initial period of three months, unless an Advisory Board, as prescribed, has concurred in the opinion held by the detaining authority in that respect.

This case was followed in *Govt. of East Pakistan v. Mrs Rowshan Bijaya Shaukat*[223] and *Habiba Jilani v. Federation of Pakistan.*[224] Though in *State v. Zia-ur-Rahman,*[225] it has been held that even non-constitutional provisions, if incorporated in the constitution, acquire the status of constitutional provisions, it does not mean that the provisions of a statute may be struck down if they are not in full conformity with constitutional provisions of inorganic nature. In such a situation, the provisions of the statute have simply to be ignored and the provisions of the constitution applied instead.

The Supreme Court of Pakistan in *Government of East Pakistan v. Rowshan Bijaya Shaukat* made very important observation. It said that preventive detention makes an inroad on the personal liberty of a citizen without the safeguard inherent in a formal trial before a judicial tribunal and it must therefore, be jealously kept within the bounds fixed by the Constitution.

Rights of arrested persons

Clauses (1) and (2) of Article 10 of the Pakistan Constitution confer four rights on an arrested person, namely—

(i) He shall not be detained in custody without being informed, as soon as may be, of the grounds of his arrest.
(ii) He shall have the right to consult and to be represented by a lawyer of his own choice.
(iii) He has the right to be produced before the nearest magistrate within 24 hours of his arrest and in computing this period, the time spent on the journey from the place of arrest to the court of the magistrate is to be excluded.
(iv) He is not to be detained in custody beyond the said period of 24 hours without the authority of the Court.

The first two requirements are meant to afford the earliest opportunity to the arrested person to remove any mistake, misapprehension or misunderstanding in the mind of the arresting authority and also to know exactly what the accusation against him is, so that he can exercise the second right, namely, of consulting a legal practitioner of his choice and to be defended by him. The third requirement is that the arrested person must be produced before a magistrate within 24 hours of such arrest, so that an independent authority exercising judicial powers may without delay apply its mind to his case. The Code of Criminal Procedure 1898, contains analogous provision in Section 61. Failure to comply with these provisions would render, as held in *Sakhi Daler Khan v. Superintendent in Charge, Recovery of Abducted women,*[226] further detention illegal.

Arrest under a warrant

There seems to be unanimity of opinion between the Pakistan and Indian Courts on the legality of arrest effected under a warrant of arrest. Both *Sakhi Daler Khan* of the Lahore High Court, and, *State of Punjab v. Ajaib Singh,*[227] of the Indian Supreme Court held that

> the fundamental rights conferred by Article 22, gives protection, against such arrests as are effected otherwise than under a warrant issued by a court on the allegation or accusation that the arrested person has or is suspected to have committed or is about or likely to commit an act of criminal or quasi-criminal nature of some activity prejudicial to the public or the State interest.

Firstly, the reason that a person who is arrested under a warrant of a court, is made acquainted with the grounds of his arrest before the arrest is actually effected. Secondly, the person must have been taken into custody on the allegation or accusation of an actual or suspected or apprehended commission, by that person of any offence of a criminal or quasi-criminal nature or some act prejudicial to the state or public interest.

Therefore, in *State of Punjab v. Ajaib Singh*,[228] the detention of an abducted person by a police officer and the delivery of such person by him into the custody of the officer in charge of the nearest camp under Section 4 of the Abducted Persons (Recovery and Restoration) Act 1949, was held not to constitute 'arrest and detention' within the meaning of the Article because there was no allegation or accusation of any actual or apprehended commission by that person of any offence of a criminal or quasi-criminal nature.

Right to counsel

The constitutional provisions that gives to an accused person the right to be defended by counsel must be read as part of the law, irrespective of whether the law gives or denies such right. This was held by the Dacca High Court in *Mrs Rowshan Bijaya Shaukat v. Govt. of East Pakistan*,[229] and by the Lahore High Court in *Muhammad Usman v. The State*,[230] which held that the provision of the law which deny to such person the right to be defended by a legal practitioner are void, unless the arrest is under a law relating to 'preventive detention'. The person arrested must be given, as held in *Moslemuddin Sikdar v. Chief Secretary*,[231] a reasonable opportunity to engage a counsel and the counsel engaged must be given reasonable opportunity to defend the arrested person.

Appraisal of procedure adopted by Trial Court

The accused after having been declared as an absconder had been tried 'in absentia' by the Trial Court. No charge was framed against the accused under Section 21-L of the Anti-Terrorism Act 1997. No evidence was recorded to prove the ingredients of the said Section 21-L. No point for determination concerning the said offence was framed. No discussion was made by the Trial Court in the judgment with regard to any evidence available on record. The accused had been convicted and sentenced under Section 21-L of the said Act in a cursory manner. The procedure adopted by Trial Court was illegal and not warranted by law. Even otherwise, the trial of the accused 'in absentia' was violative of Articles 9 & 10 (1) of the Constitution of Pakistan and Section 10 (11-A) of Anti-Terrorism Act 1997. The accused was acquitted under these circumstances.[232]

Trial in absentia

Trial in absentia, is a criminal proceeding in which the accused is not physically present at the proceedings, it is held to be violation of fundamental rights and principles of natural justice. Trail of accused 'in absentia' is violative of Articles 9 & 10(1) of the Pakistan Constitution and Section 10(11-A) of the Anti-Terrorisms Act 1997. Condemning of accused without affording an opportunity of hearing is also contrary to the principles of natural justice.[233]

Preventive detention

There is no authoritative definition of the term 'preventive detention' in law. The expression had its origin in the language used by the Law Lords in England, while explaining the nature of detention under Regulation 14-B, Defence of the Realm Act 1914, passed on the outbreak of the First World War (1914–18), and the same language was repeated in connection with emergency regulations made during the Second World War (1939–45). The word 'preventive' is used in contradistinction to the word 'punitive'. Lord Robert Finlay (1842–1949)[234] in *Rex v. Halliday,*[235] said, 'It is not punitive but precautionary measure'.

'Preventive detention' differs from the ordinary or punitive detention both in respect of its purpose and its justification. The object of 'preventive detention' is not to punish a man for having done something but to intercept him before he does it and to prevent him from doing it. No offence is proved nor any charge formulated. The justification of such detention is suspicion or reasonable probability of the impending commission of the prejudicial act and not criminal convict on which can only be warranted by legal evidence. During the First and Second World Wars, the British Parliament empowered the government to pass orders of 'preventive detention' and the courts upheld the power on the ground of necessity.

No power of 'preventive detention' has ever been exercised by the British Parliament during peace time. The Constitution of Pakistan, however, recognizes 'preventive detention' in normal times also. Although, the constitution-makers recognized the necessity of 'preventive detention', they considered it necessary to provide in Clauses (4) to (7) of Article 10 of the 1973 Constitution, a number of safeguards to mitigate its harshness, to place certain limitations on legislative power and to prevent misuse of the power by the executive.

JUSTIFICATION FOR DETENTION

Reasonableness of the grounds of detention can be examined while exercising constitutional jurisdiction which could not have been done in vacuum and the material/evidence which could not be produced in Court should have been made available in chamber.

The order of detention must show on the face of it, that the detaining authority is satisfied to the effect specified under the relevant detention law and if there is no record of satisfaction of the detaining authority the order of detention can be declared to have been passed without lawful authority and ab initio void. It is not the 'subjective satisfaction' of the detaining authority alone which is sufficient, but, it is also his duty to satisfy the Court that there existed material on which any reasonable person could have formulated the opinion as to the necessity of the detention. Court can see whether the satisfaction of the detaining authority about the existence of the requisite condition is a 'satisfaction really and truly' existing in the mind of detaining authority or 'one merely professed by the detaining authority'. Detention order which is really passed for an ulterior purpose and not because the detaining authority is really satisfied that it is necessary to detain the intended detenue with a view to preventing him from acting prejudicially to certain objects will be void.[236]

An order of 'preventive detention' has to satisfy the following requirements:

(i) The Court must be satisfied that the material before the detaining authority was such that a reasonable person would be satisfied as to the necessity for making the order of preventive detention;
(ii) that satisfaction should be established with regard to each of the grounds of detention, and, if one of the grounds is shown to be bad, non-existent or irrelevant, the whole order of detention would be rendered invalid;
(iii) that initial burden lies on the detaining authority to show the legality of the preventive detention, and
(iv) that the detaining authority must place the whole material, upon which the order of detention is based, before the Court notwithstanding its claim of privilege with respect to any document, the validity of which claim shall be within the competence of the Court to decide.

In addition to these requirements, the Court has further to be satisfied, in cases of 'preventive detention', that the detention order was made by the authority prescribed in the law relating to 'preventive detention'; that each of the requirements of the law relating to 'preventive detention' should be strictly complied with; that 'satisfaction' in fact existed with regard to the necessity of 'preventive detention' of the detenue; that the grounds of detention had been furnished within the period prescribed by law, and if no such period is prescribed, then 'as soon as may be'; that the grounds of detention should not be vague and indefinite and should be comprehensive enough to enable the detenue to make representation against his detention to the authority prescribed by law; that the grounds of detention, that is, they are not irrelevant to the aim and object of this law and that the detention should not be for extraneous considerations or for purposes which may be attacked on the ground of malice.[237]

Basic Principles Governing Preventive Detention

The Sindh High Court in *Muhammad Younus v. Province of Sindh*,[238] per Justice Noorul Arfin, laid down the following principles relating to preventive detention:—

(i) It is the inalienable right of every citizen to be treated in accordance with law and only in accordance with law that is, according to the accepted norms of legal process and in strict compliance with all the functions and duties laid down by law.

(ii) The superior Courts are expressly empowered to probe into the exercise of public power by executive authorities to determine whether they have acted with lawful authority and in lawful manner.

(iii) The burden lies on the detaining authority to show the legality of the preventive detention, for which purpose the authority must place the whole material, upon which the order of detention is based, before the Court, the validity of the claim of privilege with respect to any document being within the competence of the Court alone to decide.

(iv) The exercise of power by the detaining authority is subject to ascertainment of reasonable grounds, which is a judicial or quasi-judicial function.

(v) Action taken without proper application of the mind by the detaining authority would not qualify as action in accordance with law because the power to order detention of a particular person is coupled with the duty to apply mind as to the necessity of such person's detention on the material available to the authority.

(vi) The superior Courts are empowered to examine the reasonableness of the action of the detaining authority, that is to say, to see whether a reasonable person would have formed, on the material available to the detaining authority the same opinion as formed by the authority with regard to the detention of the detenue, and in doing so it would be competent to also consider whether the grounds are within the law-making power of the legislature and within the ambit of the statute relating to preventive detention and are not non-existent or otherwise bad.

(vii) 'Satisfaction' of the detaining authority means a state of mind which has been induced by the existence of reasonable grounds for such satisfaction. The word 'satisfaction' connotes a state of mind bordering on conviction induced by the existence of facts which have removed the doubts, if any, from the mind and taken it out of the stage of suspicion.

(viii) The superior courts are empowered to make an enquiry into the *bonafides* or good faith of the action taken by the detaining authority.

(ix) If there are several grounds of detention, then each ground contributes to the satisfaction of the detaining authority and no ground can be excluded from consideration in judging the legality of the order of detention and wrongful inclusion of any ground would render the orders of arrest and detention illegal.

There are two principal safeguards which have been made available to a person arrested under a detention law:

(1) That no person detained under any such law can be detained for a period exceeding three months unless, before the expiration of that period, the Government obtains from the Review Board the opinion that there is enough cause for such detention;

(2) That the authority ordering the detention must, within fifteen days, communicate to the arrested person the grounds for his detention, unless the disclosure of any particular ground be against the public interest, and afford him the earliest opportunity of making a representation against his detention.

The cases of *Sirajuddin v. State*[239] and *Rahmat Ellahi v. Government of West Pakistan*,[240] took the view, that the provisions of a statute which impose restrictions on the personal liberty of a subject must be strictly and rigorously complied with, and unless such order is passed in strict conformity with the provisions of the detention law, however formal in character they may appear to be, and all the statutory obligations enjoined on the detaining authority are carried out to the letter, the order will not be upheld. Restricting a person's movement to his dwelling/house is detention. This was so held in *Ch. Muhammad Anwar v. Government of Pakistan*.[241]

Review Boards

Where a person has been ordered to be detained for 2 months but before the expiry of that time, the Review Board, by reference to him, has reported that there have been sufficient grounds for detention for more than 2 months.

A Bench of 5 Judges of the Lahore High Court in *Rahmat Ellahi v. Government of West Pakistan*,[242] held that detention beyond 3 months was illegal, the ground of the decision being that to justify further detention the Review Board must report not only that there were sufficient reasons for detention but also that the reasons justified detention for a period exceeding 3 months.

In so holding, the Lahore High Court differed from the view taken by the Supreme Court of India in *Puranlal Lakhanpal v. Union of India*,[243] that what the Advisory Board is concerned with is whether the grounds for detention were sufficient and that, on that finding, it is for the government to determine the period of detention. The answer to the question depended on whether the words such as detention' referred to the words 'preventive detention' or to the words 'detention of a person for a period exceeding 3 months' in Article 22 Clause (4) of the Indian Constitution 1949. The Indian view is founded on the principle that the government is the judge of the period for which a person should be detained and not the Advisory Board, for the reason that at the stage it functions, the Board does not have sufficient material for the performance of what is essentially an executive function.

The Indian Supreme Court held, that the expression 'such detention' occurring in the comparative Clause (4) of Article 10 of Pakistan Constitution, refers to the expression 'preventive detention' occurring in the beginning of the clause and not to the words 'detention of a person for a period exceeding 3 months'. The expression 'preventive detention' only pertains to the making of laws to deal with 'persons acting in a manner....'etc., and has no connection with whatever the expression 'such detention' and the words 'detention of a person for a period exceeding 3 months' fall within the domain of Review Board as the expression 'such detention' is clearly relatable to these words.

Where the case is not placed before the Review Board within the prescribed time, the detention would be illegal as held in *Rowshan Bijaya*[244] by the Dacca High Court. But, as held in *Muhammad Ghafoor v. N.W.F.P.*,[245] where a person is specifically ordered to be detained for a period of 30 days, no reference to the Review Board is necessary and the detenue can apply to the High Court under Article 199 of the 1973 Constitution, if he alleges *mala fides*. In case, the opinion of the Board is not obtained within 3 months of detention, the detention becomes illegal and the detenue is entitled to be released even though, the opinion of the Board has been obtained within 3 months of a second order of detention revoking the first and authorizing the continuation of detention on the same ground on which the original detention was made. This was so held in *Abdul Latif Abdul Wahab Sheikh v. B.K. Jha*[246] by the Indian Supreme Court.

Grounds of detention and representation

The grounds for detention must be communicated to the person detained within 15 days of the order of detention, to enable him to make a representation against the action taken, and the detention would be illegal, if the grounds are not communicated to him at all or not within the specified time. It was so held by the Lahore High Court in *Ghulam Muhammad Khan Lundkhwar v. Crown*,[247] that communication means imparting to the detenue sufficient knowledge of all the grounds of detention which are in the nature of charges against him.

Objective or subjective satisfaction of detaining authority

The Supreme Court of Pakistan, however, in *Ghulam Jilani v. Government of West Pakistan*,[248] departed from the British, Indian, and its own previous decisions and held, that the Court must itself be satisfied of the reasonableness and sufficiency of the grounds of detention.

The laws authorizing 'preventive detention' normally use such expression as, if the authority has 'reasonable cause to believe', 'being satisfied'; 'suspecting upon reasonable grounds', 'if he shall feel fit'; 'if he is of the opinion' etc.

The leading case on the point is that of the House of Lords in *Liversidge v. Anderson*,[249] where the words used were 'if the Secretary of State has reasonable cause to believe any person to be of hostile origin'. Construing this expression Lord Frederic Maugham (1866–1958),[250] with whom 3 other Law Lords agreed, observed:

> I am not disposed to deny that, in the absence of a context, the *prima facie* meaning of such a phase as 'If A.B. has a reasonable cause to believe' a certain circumstances or thing, should be construed as 'if there is in fact reasonable cause for believing' that thing, and that A.B. believes it. However, I am quite unable to take the view that the words can have only that meaning. It seems to me reasonably clear that, if the thing to be believed is something which is essentially one within the knowledge of A.B., one for the exercise of his exclusive discretion, the words may well mean If A.B. acting on what he thinks is reasonable cause, and of course acting in good faith, believes the thing in question.

For some time after *Liversidge*, it continued to be held that mere production of the detention order reciting, that the relevant authority was satisfied, was a good answer to an application for a writ until in *Ghulam Jilani v. The Government of West Pakistan*,[251] the Supreme Court held, that mere production of the order reciting to the satisfaction of the authority was not sufficient and, that the authority must also place before the Court, the material on which it claims to have been satisfied, so that the Court may discharge its duty satisfied, that the detenue is not being held without lawful authority. The difference between 'being satisfied' and 'suspecting on reasonable grounds' was also brought out in this case.

This view was reiterated in the subsequent case of *Abdul Baqi Baloch v. Government of Pakistan*.[252] Also, in *Government of West Pakistan v. Begum Agha Abdul Karim Shorish Kashmiri*,[253] in spite of the change in the language of the statute, the Supreme Court of Pakistan arrived at the same conclusion. In this case, in a writ petition filed on behalf of a detenue who had been detained under the Defence of Pakistan Ordinance 1965, and the Rules there-under, the state had taken a preliminary objection against the jurisdiction of the High Court to examine the grounds of detention of the detenue upon the basis of the rule laid down in *Ghulam Jilani*.

The ground of the objection was that Clause (x) of Subsection (2) of Section 3 of the Defence of Pakistan Ordinance 1965, had been amended by the Defence of Pakistan (Amendment) Ordinance 1968, after the decision in *Ghulam Jilani's* case, with the specific object of making a provision that the High Court should not examine either the sufficiency or the reasonableness of the grounds of detention under the said Ordinance. Aggrieved by the decision of the Division Bench of the High Court on that objection, the state filed an appeal before the Supreme Court and urged that although the High Court has undoubtedly under Article 98 of the 1962 Constitution, the power of judicial review of executive actions yet unless the statute under which an action is taken by the executive authority itself requires the authority to act honestly or reasonably or upon reasonable grounds, the satisfaction or the opinion or belief of the authority concerned is his subjective satisfaction and it is enough for him to state that he is so satisfied. It must then be presumed that he had acted *bonafide* in the lawful exercise of his powers and unless the party challenging his action is able to substantiate, that he had acted *mala fide* or without any ground whatsoever, the courts cannot call upon the authority or the officer concerned to disclose the material upon which he had based his opinion, belief or satisfaction. It was further contended that even if it was possible to say that 'satisfaction' being firmer state of mind' than mere 'belief' or 'opinion' or 'suspicion' had of necessity to be grounded upon some facts then the amendments have even taken care of that by not using the word 'satisfied' but merely saying that it would be enough if the authority concerned 'is of the opinion' that the apprehension of detention is necessary.

The Supreme Court repelled the objection and held that –

> 'this argument does not of course take into account the difference that has been made to the jurisdiction of the Court by the language of Article 98 of the 1962 Constitution itself.'

It was observed that Article 98 of the 1962 Constitution, is radically different from the old Article 170 of the abrogated Constitution of 1956 or Article 226 of the Indian Constitution. Article 98 has given to the courts the power to give directions to person performing certain functions in connection with the affairs of the government or local authority; to do or to refrain from doing that which the law requires them to do or which it does not permit them to do or to refrain from doing that which the law requires them to do or which it does not permit them to do and to

> 'declare acts done by such persons to 'have been done or taken without lawful authority and as being of no legal effect.'

In the case of persons detained in custody, however, the power given is to issue a direction to have such a person brought before the High Court so that the court may –

> 'satisfy itself that he is not being held in custody without lawful authority or in an unlawful manner'.

The difference in the language of the provisions of Sub-Clauses (a) and (b) of Clause (2) of Article 98 is worth noting. Whilst in the first case the direction is limited to the making of an order for doing or refraining from doing that which the law permits or does not permit, as the case may be. In the case of detention, the High Court is enjoined upon to 'satisfy itself' that the person is not being held in custody

(a) without lawful authority or
(b) in an unlawful manner.

This distinction in the terminology of the two clauses of Article 98, was pointed out by this court in the case of *Abdul Baqi Baluch*,[254] for the first time. The expression 'without lawful authority' and 'in an unlawful manner' occurring in Sub-Clause (b) were not merely abstract expressions. A definite meaning had, therefore, to be given to each of them. The Constitution, it appears, casts a heavy responsibility upon the Court to satisfy itself with regard to both these two matters.

The words 'in an unlawful manner' in Sub-Clause (b) of Article 98(2) have been used deliberately to give meaning and content to the solemn declaration under Article 2 of the Constitution itself that it is the inalienable right of every citizen to be treated in accordance with law and only in accordance with law. Therefore, in determining as to how and in what circumstances a detention would be detention in an unlawful manner one would inevitably have first to see whether the action is in accordance with law, if not, then it is action in an unlawful manner. Law is here not confined to statute law alone but is used in its generic sense as connoting all that is treated, as law in this country including even the judicial principles laid down from time to time by the superior courts. It means according to the accepted forms of legal process and postulates a strict performance of all the functions and duties laid down by law. It may well be, that in this sense it is as comprehensive as the American 'due process' clause. It is in this sense that an action which is *mala fide* or colourable is not regarded as action in accordance with law. Similarly, action taken upon extraneous or irrelevant considerations is also not action in accordance with law. Action taken upon no ground at all or without proper application of the mind of the detaining authority would also not qualify as action in accordance with law and would, therefore, have to be struck down as being action taken in an unlawful manner.[255]

Vague grounds

The detaining authority is under obligation to furnish the grounds on which the detention order is based. This constitutional obligation is not discharged if the grounds communicated to the detenue are vague. A ground will be vague when it does not enable the detenue to make an effective representation against the order of detention.

Now the question of whether or not the reasons given are vague is ultimately a question to be determined on the basis of circumstances of each case, as was pointed out by the Supreme Court of India in *The State of Bombay v. Atma Ram Sridhar Vaidya*[256] and *Dhananjoy Das v. District Magistrate*.[257] It has been further held by the Indian Supreme Court in *Lawrence Joachim Joseph D'Souza v. The State of Bombay*,[258] that the constitutional right of the detenue would be infringed if he is not supplied with reasonable definite grounds. If the grounds are vague, the order would be set aside, and this would happen even if only one of the several grounds is vague, as held in *Dr Ram Krishan Bhardwaj v. The State of Delhi*,[259] and *Pushkar Mukherjee v. State of West Bengal*.[260]

Similarly, the Dacca High Court has held in *Mrs Rowshan Bijaya v. Government of East Pakistan*,[261] the grounds must be sufficiently particularized with facts and information to enable the detenue to understand the alleged reason for his arrest and make an effective representation.

Maximum period of detention

The 1962 Constitution of Pakistan, had not specified the maximum period of detention but the 1973 Constitution of Pakistan, removes that ambiguity and fixes the maximum period of detention as 8 months, in the case of a person detained for acting in manner prejudicial to public order and 12 months in other cases. This period must fall within a period of 24 months commencing from the date of first detention. This safeguard provided by Clause (7) of Article 10 of the Pakistan Constitution 1973, however, is not available–

> 'to any person who is employed by, or works for, or acts on instructions received from, the enemy or who is acting or attempting to act in a manner prejudicial to the integrity, security or defence of Pakistan or any part thereof or who commits or attempts to commit any act which amounts to an antinational activity as defined in a Federal Law or is a member of any association which has for its objects, or which indulges in, any such anti-national activity.'

Notes

1. *Roe v. Wade*, 410 U.S. 113 (1973).
2. *Washington v. Glucksberg*, 521 U.S. 702 (1997) (no liberty interest in a right to physician-assisted suicide); *Cruzan v. Director, Mo. Dept. of Health*, 497 U.S. 261 (1990) (a liberty interest exists in refusing unwanted medical treatment).
3. *Graham v. Connor*, 490 U.S. 386 (1989); *Tennessee v. Garner*, 471 U.S. 1 (1985).
4. *Roth v. Board of Regents*, 408 U.S. 564 (1972).
5. Erwin Chemerinsky, *Constitutional Law: Principles and Policies*, 4th ed. (New York: Wolters Kluwer Law & Business, 2011), pp. 578.
6. *Meyer v. Nebraska*, 262 U.S. 390 (1923); *Roth v. Board of Regents*, 408 U.S. 564 (1972).
7. *Hamdi v. Rumsfeld*, 542 U.S. 507 (2004).
8. *Taylor v. Kentucky*, 436 U.S. 478 (1978).
9. *In re Winship*, 397 U.S. 358 (1970).
10. *Addington v. Texas*, 441 U.S. 418, (1979); also *Jones v. United States*, 463 U.S. 354, (1983).
11. *O'Connor v. Donaldson*, 422 U.S. 563, (1975); *see also Specht v. Patterson*, 386 U.S. 605 (1967) (due process denied to an indefinite commitment to a mental institution for a person convicted of a sex crime for which there was a mandatory 10 year punishment).
12. Children are entitled to basic procedural protections in criminal proceedings, such as proof beyond a reasonable doubt (*In re Winship*, 397 U.S. 358 (1970) and the assistance of an attorney (*In re Gault*, 387 U.S. 1 (1967).
13. 442 U.S. 584 (1979).
14. The child, of course, has a liberty interest in not being institutionalized, even by a parent. Therefore, *Parham* really is about the procedures required, rather than the issue of whether there is a liberty interest.
15. *Chew v. Colding*, 344 U.S. 590 (1953); *Sung v. McGrath*, 339 U.S. 33 (1950).
16. *Hirsh v. INS*, 308 F. 2d 562 (9th Cir.1962).
17. *Snajder v. INS*, 29 F.3d 1203 (7th Cir.1994).
18. *Woodby v. INS*, 385 U.S. 276, 285 (1966).
19. *Shaughnessy v. United States ex rel. Mezei*, 345 U.S. 206 (1953); *United States ex rel. knauff v. Shaughnessy*, 338 U.S. 537 (1950); *see* Charles D. Weisselberg, *The Exclusion and detention Aliens; Lessons from the Lives of Ellen Knauff and Ignatz Mezei*, 143 U. Pa. L. Rev. 933 (1995).
20. 345 U.S. 206, 212 (1953).
21. 533 U.S. 678 (2001).
22. Ibid at 2504 (Scalia, J., dissenting).
23. Ibid at 2514–2517 (Kennedy, J., dissenting).
24. 515 U.S. 472 (1995).
25. 408 U.S. 471 (1972).
26. 411 U.S. 778 (1973).
27. 418 U.S. 539 (1974).
28. 427 U.S. 215 (1976).
29. *Montanye v. Haymes*, 427 U.S. 236 (1976) (no loss of liberty when a prisoner is transferred from one prison to another).
30. 442 U.S. 1 (1979).
31. *Board of Pardons v. Allen*, 482 U.S. 369 (1987).

32. 459 U.S. 460 (1983).
33. 461 U.S. 238 (1983).
34. 452 U.S. 458 (1981).
35. 490 U.S. 454 (1989).
36. 445 U.S. 480 (1980).
37. 494 U.S. 210 (1990).
38. 515 U.S. 472 (1995).
39. Erwin Chemerinsky, *Constitutional Law: Principles and Policies*, 2nd ed. (New York: Aspen Law & Business, 2002), pp. 542–4, 645–51.
40. 515 U.S. 472 (1995).
41. 520 U.S. 143 (1997).
42. 545 U.S. 209 (2005).
43. *Miranda v. Arizona*, 384 U.S. 436 (1966).
44. E. C. S. Wade, A.W. Bradley, *Constitutional Law*, 7th ed, (London: Longmans, 1965), pp. 488–9.
45. Archbishop Makarios III was Primate of the Orthodox Church of Cyprus and was also the President of independent Cyprus.
46. Supra Note 44, pp. 489–90.
47. Since the Debtors Act 1869, imprisonment for debt is confined to the case of persons of proved capacity to pay who decline to obey the order of the court; to satisfy a judgement debt or other order of a court for payment.
48. *The Queen v. Jackson*, (1891) 1 Q.B. 671.
49. *Leach v. Money* (1763) 19 State Trials 981; *Entick v. Carrington* (1765), 19 State Trials 1030; K. & L. 174.
50. Supra Note, p. 491.
51. *Walters v. W.H. Smith & Son, Ltd.*, (1914) 1 K.B. 595.
52. *Christie v. Leachinsky*, (1947) A.C. 573.
53. *The Queen v. Brown*, (1841) Car. & M. 314; K. & L. 428.
54. Gordon Hewart was a politician and Lord Chief Justice of England from 8 March 1922 - 12 October 1940.
55. (1935) 2 K.B. 249.
56. Supra Note 44, p. 492.
57. For the text of the Judges' Rules, *see* (1964) 1 All E.R. 237.
58. The Court of Star Chamber was created by King Henry VII in 1487, in the royal Palace of Westminster. The Star Chamber was a Court of the monarch and consisted of privy councillors and two royal judges.
59. *North Briton* was a radical newspaper published in 18th century London.
60. (1765), 19 St. Tr. 1026.
61. (1763), 19 St. Tr. 1153.
62. (1765), 19 St. Tr. 1030; K. & L. 174.
63. All Privy Councillors are by custom Justices of the Peace and can therefore, commit for any indictable offence.
64. Lord Halifax was a senior British Conservative politician and diplomat of the 1930s.
65. (1934) 2 K.B. 164.
66. Supra Note 43, p. 494.
67. *Jones v. German* (1896) 2 Q.B. 418; extended to goods obtained by other fraudulent practices by the Larceny Act 1916, Section 42(1).
68. *See also* Betting, Gaming and Lotteries Act 1963, Section 51.
69. Obscene Publications Act 1857, Section 1.
70. *Maneka Gandhi v. Union of India*, AIR 1978 SC 597.
71. *A.K. Gopalan v. State of Madras*. AIR 1950 SC 27.
72. *Kharak Singh v. State of U.P.*, AIR 1963 SC 1295.
73. AIR 1975 SC 1379.
74. AIR 1967 SC 1836.
75. J.N. Pandey, *Constitutional Law of India*, 38th ed. (Allahabad: Central Law Agency, 2002), pp. 202–5.
76. Mirza Hameedullah Beg (1913–88) was the 15th Chief Justice of India, serving from January 1977 to February 1978.
77. AIR 1981 SC 2041.
78. AIR 1981 SC 746.
79. AIR 1982 SC 1473.
80. AIR 1998 AP 302.
81. (1983) 3 SCC 387.
82. *Reliance Energy Ltd. v. Maharashtra State Road Transport Corporation. Ltd.*, (2007) 8 SCC 1.

83. Durga Das Basu, *Commentary on the Constitution of India*, 8th ed., Vol. 3 (Nagpur: Lexis Nexis Butterworth Wadhwa & Co., 2008), p. 3111.
84. AIR 1996 SC 1051, (1996) 2 SCC 549. See also *Consumer Education and Research Centre v. Union of India.*, AIR 1995 SC 922; *P.A. Jacob v. Supt. Of Police, Kotta-yams*, AIR 1993 Ker 1; *D.D. Vyas v. Ghaziabad Development Authority*, AIR 1993 All 57; *Subhash Kumar v. State of Bihar*, AIR 1991 SC 420; *Bijayalakshmi Tripathy v. Managing Committee of Working Women Hostel*, AIR 1992 Ori 242; *Air India Statutory Corporation. V. United Labour Union*, AIR 1997 SC 645; *U.P. Avas Evam Wikas Parishad v. Friends Co-operative Housing Society Ltd.*, AIR 1996 SC 114.
85. *U.P. Avas Evam Vikas Parishad v. Friends Co-operative Housing Society ltd.*, AIR 1996 SC 114, 1995 (Supp-3) SCC 456.
86. AIR 1986 SC 180, (1985) 3 SCC 545.
87. AIR 1989 SC 1988.
88. AIR 1992 SC 789.
89. (1993) 3 SCC 258.
90. M.P Jain, *Indian Constitutional Law*, 6th ed. (Nagpur: Lexis Nexis Butterworth Wadhwa & Co.,2010), p. 1226.
91. *Confederation of Ex-servicemen Association v. Union of India*; AIR 2006 S.C. 2945, (2006) 8 SCC 399.
92. AIR 1988 SC 1782.
93. AIR 1990 SC 752.
94. 1986 Mah LJ 913.
95. 1988 Cr. LJ 549.
96. 1994 SCC (3) 394, 1994 AIR 1844.
97. 1996 SCC (2) 648.
98. Jagdish Sharan Verma served as the 27th Chief Justice of India from 25 March 1997 to 18 January 1998.
99. AIR 1991 SC 420.
100. (1985) 2 SCC 431.
101. *M.C. Mehta v. Union of India*, (1986) 2 SCC 176.
102. (1987) 4 SCC 463.
103. Mahesh Chandra Mehta is a public interest attorney. Government of India awarded him the civilian honour of the Padma Shri in 2016.
104. (1988) 1 SCC 471.
105. 1966 (3) SCC 212; also *Vellore Citizens Welfare Forum v. Union of India*, 1966 (5) SCC 647.
106. 1996 (4) SCC 750.
107. (1996) 5 SCC 281.
108. (1996) 5 SCC 647.
109. AIR 1997 SC 811.
110. (1992) 3 SCC 666.
111. (1993) 1 SCC 594.
112. AIR 1993 S.C. 2178, 1993 SCR (1) 594.
113. (1993) 4 SCC 112.
114. AIR 1993 SC 2086.
115. AIR 1974 SC 2092. Also *Sunil Batra v. Delhi Administration*. AIR 1978 SC 1675 where instead of a release order the court gave certain directions to the government and jail authorities to be complied with regarding the rights of a prisoner.
116. AIR 1978 S.C 527.
117. AIR 1978 S.C. 1675. See also *Sunil Batra v. Delhi Administration (No. 2)*, AIR 1980 S.C. 1579.
118. *Charles Sobhraj v. Superintendent Jail, Tihar, New Delhi*, AIR 1978 S.C. 1514; (1978) 4 SCC 104.
119. AIR 1979 SC 1360; followed in *Kadra Pehadiya v. State of Bihar*, (1981) 3 SCC 671.
120. AIR 1979 SC 1369.
121. AIR 1979 SC 1377.
122. AIR 1988 SC 1531.
123. (1986) 4 SCC 481.
124. AIR 1980 SC 1579.
125. AIR 1980 SC 1535.
126. (1990)3 SCC 119.
127. (1995) 3 SCC 743.
128. AIR 1981 SC 625.
129. *Sheela Barse v. State of Maharashtra*, (1983) 2 SCC 96.
130. *Munshi Singh Gautam (D) v. State of Madhya Pradesh*, AIR 2005 S.C. 402; (2005) 9 SCC 631.
131. AIR 1983 SC 361.

132. AIR 1983 SC 465.
133. *Javed Ahmed Abdul Hamid Pawala v. State of Maharashtra.* AIR 1985 231.
134. AIR (1989) SC 142.
135. AIR 1981 SC 746.
136. (1987) 2 SCC 165.
137. (1994) 4 SCC 260.
138. (1993) 2 SCC 746; *Sheela Barse v. State of Maharashtra*, AIR 1983 SC 378.
139. AIR 1997 SC 610.
140. (1983) 4 SCC 141. See also *Sebastian M. Hongray v. Union of India*, AIR 1984 SC 1026.
141. (1985) 4 SCC 677.
142. (1989) 4 SCC 730.
143. AIR 1990 SC 513.
144. (1995) 3 SCC 600.
145. AIR 1997 S.C. 1203.
146. *State of Tamil Nadu v. Senthil Kumar*, AIR 1999 S.C. 971: (1999) 2 SCC 646.
147. 1950 AIR 27, 1950 SCR 88.
148. 1970 AIR 564, 1970 SCR (3) 530.
149. 1978 AIR 597, 1978 SCR (2) 621.
150. *Tarapada De v. State of West Bengal*, AIR 1951 174.
151. *State of Madhya Pradesh v. Shobharam*, AIR 1966 SC 1910.
152. AIR 1994 S.C. 1349; (1994) 4 SCC 260.
153. J. N. Pandey, Supra Note 69, p. 240.
154. *Powell v. Alabama*, 287 US 45 (1932).
155. AIR 1979 SC 1369.
156. *State of Uttar Pradesh v. Abdul Samad*, AIR 1962 S.C. 1506.
157. *Bhim Singh, MLA v. State of Jammu and Kashmir*, AIR 1986 S.C. 494; (1985) 4 SCC 677.
158. *Gunupati Keshavram Reddy v. Nafisul Hasan & State Of U.P*, AIR 1954 SC 636.
159. AIR 1953 SC 10.
160. *Raj Bahadur Singh v. Legal Remembrancer*, AIR 1955 Cal 522.
161. (1992) 3 SCC 141.
162. *Khatri and Others v. State of Bihar*, 1981 SCR (2) 408, 1981 SCC (1) 627.
163. *Liversidge v. Anderson*, (1942) AC 206; *A.K. Gopalan v. State of Madras*, AIR 1950 SC 27.
164. *Liversidge v. Anderson*, (1942) AC 206; *Rex v. Halliday*, (1917) AC 263 (Held, personal liberty can be sacrificed for the national success in war).
165. AIR 1950 SC 27.
166. M. Patanjali Shastri was the 2nd Chief Justice of India, serving in the post from 7 November 1951 to 3 January 1954.
167. Indira Gandhi was daughter of Jawaharlal Nehru. She was the first and, to date, only female Prime Minister of India.
168. Charan Singh served as the 5th Prime Minister of India.
169. AIR 1982 SC 710.
170. (1994) 3 SCC 569.
171. *Pankaj Kumar Chakrabarty v. State of Bengal*, AIR 1970 SC 97.
172. *Shibban Lal Saksena v. State of U.P.*, AIR 1954 S.C. 179.
173. *Sambhu Nath Sarkar v. The State Of West Bengal*, AIR 1973 SC 1425.
174. *Kubic Dariusz v. Union of India*, (1990) 1 SCC 568; *Harikisan v. State of Maharashtra*, 1962 AIR 911; *Surjeet Singh v. Union of India* AIR 1981 1153.
175. (1981) 2 SCC 427; *Nainmal Pratap Mal Shah v. Union of India*, AIR 1980 SC 2129.
176. (1990) 1 SCC 568.
177. *Nandoli Mohamed Rafeeq v. Union of India*, 2004 (12) SCC 218.
178. *State of Bombay v. Atma Ram Sridhar Vaidya*, AIR 1954 SC 157.
179. AIR 1954 SC 179; see also *Kamalakar Prasad Chaturvedi v. State of M.P.*, 1984 AIR 211, 1984 SCR (1) 317.
180. AIR 1975 SC 223.
181. AIR 1975 SC 245.
182. 1990 AIR 220, 1989 SCR Supl. (1) 56.
183. *Lawrence Joachim Joseph D. Souza v. State of Bombay*, AIR 1956 SC 531, see also *Mohammad Yousuf Ratherv. State of Jammu & Kashmir*, AIR 1979 SC 1925.
184. *Hansmukh v. State of Gujarat*, AIR 1981 SC 28; *Khudiram Das v. State of West Bengal*, AIR 1975 SC 550.

185. *Kamla Kanahiyalal Khushalani v. State of Maharashtra*, (1981) 1 SCC 748.
186. *Raj Kishore Prasad v. State of Bihar*, AIR 1983 SC 320.
187. *Yumnam Mangibabu Singh v. State of Manipur*, AIR 1983 SC 300. See also *Abdul Aziz v. Delhi Administration*, AIR 1981 SC 1389.
188. *Wasiuddin Ahmad v. District Magistrate, Aligarh*, AIR 1981 SC 2166.
189. *Ashok Kumar v. Delhi Administration*, AIR 1982 SC 1143.
190. *Satya Deo Prasad v. State of Bihar*, AIR 1975 SC 367.
191. *Prem Lala Sharma v. District Magistrate Mathura*, AIR 1998 SC 2212.
192. AIR 1990 SC 225.
193. *Pankaj Kumar Chakrabarty v. State of West Bengal* AIR 1970 SC 97.
194. *Rahmatullah v. State of Bihar*, AIR 1981 SC 2069.
195. AIR 1979 SC 675.
196. *S Sekawat v. State of West Bengal*, AIR 1975 SC 64.
197. AIR 1978 SC 297.
198. AIR 1981 SC 814, (1981) 1 SCC 748.
199. *Raghavendra Singh v. Superintendent District Jail, Kanpur*, AIR 1986 SC 356.
200. *Vimal Chand Jawantraj Jain v. Shri Pradhan*, AIR 1979 S.C. 1501, 1979 SCR (3)1007; *Usha Agarwal v. Union of India*, 2006 CriLJ 2934.
201. (1987) 2 SCC 235.
202. *Saraswathi Seshagiri v. State of Kerala*, AIR 1982 SC 1165; *Khudiram Das v. State of West Bengal*, AIR 1975 SC 550.
203. *Sambhu Nath Sarkar v. Union of India*, AIR 1973 SC 1425.
204. *Bankatlal v. State of Rajasthan*, AIR 1975 SC 522.
205. AIR 1975 SC 393; see also *Abdul Gaffar v. State of West Bengal*, AIR 1975 SC 1496.
206. AIR 1975 SC 606; see also *Abdul Sathar Ibrahim Manik v. Union of India*, AIR 1991 SC 2261.
207. *Additional District Magistrate, Jabalpur v. Shukla*, AIR 1976 SC 1207.
208. Hans Raj Khanna served as the Chief Justice of Delhi High Court from 1969–1971.
209. *Makhan Singh v. State of Punjab*, AIR 1964 SC 381.
210. AIR 1950 SC 27.
211. PLD 1957 Lahore 813.
212. 94 U.S. 113 (1877).
213. PLD 1994 SC 693. *Arshad Mahmood v. Government of Punjab*, PLD 2005 S.C. 193; *Watan Party v. Federation of Pakistan*, PLD 2011 S.C. 997.
214. 1994 SCMR 1548. *NESPAK v. Kamil Khan Mumtaz*, 2018 SCMR 211.
215. PLD 2019 S.C. 318.
216. PLD 1974 Lahore 120.
217. *Arshad Mahmood v. Government of Punjab*, PLD 2005 S.C. 193.
218. *Human Rights Case No. 17599 of 2018*, 2019 SCMR 247.
219. *In Re: Contempt Proceedings Against Chief Secretary, Sindh*, 2013 SCMR 1752.
220. *Sh. Riaz-ul-Haq v. Federation of Pakistan*, PLD 2013 SC 501.
221. *Suo Moto Case No. 13 of 2009*, PLD 2011 S.C. 619.
222. PLD 1958 SC 499.
223. PLD 1966 SC 286.
224. PLD 1974 Lahore 153.
225. PLD 1973 SC 49.
226. PLD 1957 Lahore 813.
227. AIR 1953 SC 10.
228. AIR 1952 SC 10.
229. PLD 1965 Dacca 241.
230. 1975 SCMR 391.
231. PLD 1957 Dacca 101.
232. *Arbab Khan v. The State*, 2010 SCMR 755; *Mir Ikhlaq Khan v. The State*, 2008 SCMR 951.
233. Ibid.
234. Sir Robert Finlay was a British lawyer, doctor and politician who became Lord High Chancellor of Great Britain.
235. (1917) A.C. 260.
236. *Federation of Pakistan v. Mrs Amatul Jalil Khawaja*, PLD 2003 S.C. 442.
237. Ibid.

238. PLD 1973 Karachi 694.
239. PLD 1957 Lahore 962.
240. PLD 1965 Lahore 112.
241. PLD 1963 Lahore 109.
242. PLD 1965 Lahore 112.
243. AIR 1958 S.C. 163.
244. PLD 1965 Dacca 241.
245. PLD 1974 Peshawar 28.
246. AIR 1987 S.C. 725.
247. PLD 1955 Peshawar 45.
248. PLD 1967 S.C. 373.
249. [1941] UKHL 1.
250. Lord Frederic Maugham was a British barrister and judge who was Lord Chancellor from March 1938 until September 1939.
251. PLD 1967 S.C. 373.
252. PLD 1968 S.C. 313.
253. PLD 1969 S.C. 14.
254. PLD 1968 SC 313.
255. A.G., Chaudhry, *Lectures on Constitutional Law* (Lahore: Irfan Law Book House, 1996), pp. 109–21.
256. AIR 1951 SC 157.
257. AIR 1982 S.C. 1315.
258. AIR 1956 S.C. 531. 1956 SCR 382.
259. AIR 1953 S.C. 318.
260. AIR 1970 S.C. 852. 1969 SCR (2) 635.
261. PLD 1965 Dacca 241.

16 Right to Property

Property as an 'Entitlement' in the USA

There has never been any doubt that the government must provide 'due process' before it deprives a person of real or personal property. After the demise of the rights-privileges distinction, the question would be: When are government benefits, such as jobs or payments, to be considered 'property'?

In *Roth v. Board of Regents*,[1] the US Supreme Court attempted to define property. The Court said that –

> '[t]o have a property interest in a benefit, a person clearly must have more than an abstract need or desire for it. He must have more than a unilateral expectation of it. He must, instead, have a legitimate claim of entitlement to it. It is a purpose of the ancient institution of property to protect those claims upon which people rely in their daily lives, reliance that must not be arbitrarily undermined.'

The Court explained that –

> '[p]roperty interests, of course, are not created by the Constitution. Rather, they are created and their dimensions are defined by existing rules or understandings that stem from an independent source such as state law- rules or understandings that secure benefits and that support claims of entitlement to those benefits.'

In other words, *Roth* defines 'property' as an 'entitlement.' The problem is that in defining entitlement, the above-quoted language from *Roth* offers two inconsistent approaches. One approach is that an 'entitlement' is defined by the importance of the interest to the individual. If people rely on a government benefit in 'their daily lives,' then it should be regarded as a property interest that 'must not be arbitrarily undermined.' But the Court then goes on to say that the existence of an 'entitlement' is determined by an 'independent source such as state law' and the 'rules or understandings' that it creates.

By this view, an 'entitlement' exists if there is a reasonable expectation to continued receipt of a benefit. In other words, the former approach to defining 'entitlement' would find a property interest if there is an important benefit regardless of the content of the state law. The latter definition, however, would find a property interest only if the state law creates a reasonable expectation to receipt of a benefit, regardless of the importance of the interest.

Each definition has its own problems. If the existence of property is determined solely by the importance of the benefit, there seems no principled way to decide which government benefits are sufficiently significant to constitute property. The government provides a vast array of services and programs that people rely upon. How is the Court to decide which are important enough to constitute property and require due process when they are ended?

Defining 'property' based on whether the law creates a reasonable expectation to continued receipt of a benefit solves this problem because it provides a basis for deciding what constitutes 'property' apart from the importance of the interest. But it creates a different major difficulty: could the state simply deny the existence of property by expressly stating that individuals should have no expectation to continued receipt? In other words, if property is defined by expectations, the state can defeat property interests by making it clear that people should have no expectations. In essence, the rights-privileges distinction is re-created under a different label; the state could deny a property interest merely by making it clear that the benefit or program was something that the government could terminate at any point. Indeed, the more arbitrary the government is, the less there can be reasonable expectations to continued receipt of the benefit, the less likely there will be a requirement for due process.

To this day, the US Supreme Court has not resolved this predicament. The Court generally has adopted the second approach to defining 'property'- that is, as a reasonable expectation to continued receipt of a benefit. However, the Court has been inconsistent in its willingness to accept the consequence, that the government then can deny a property interest merely by informing people that they should not expect the benefit to continue.

Government Benefits

The same equivocation between the two definitions of 'entitlement' described above is also present in cases concerning when government benefits are property. In *Goldberg v. Kelly*[2], it was held that welfare benefits were property because of the importance of these benefits in the lives of the recipients. Likewise, in *Bell v. Burson*[3], the US Supreme Court held, that the government had to provide a hearing before suspending a person's driver's license based on the person's alleged responsibility for an accident The Court explained that –

> '[o]nce licenses are issued ....continued possession may become essential in the pursuit of a livelihood. Suspension of issued licenses thus involves state action that adjudicates important interests of the licensees.'

Similarly, in *Goss v. Lopez*[4], the Supreme Court found that there was a property interest in continued receipt of an education when the government creates a public school system and requires children to attend. The Court explained that –

> 'on the basis of state law, appellees plainly had legitimate claims of entitlement to a public education.'

Even though the government had no constitutional duty to provide a public education, the Court found that there was a property interest in continued schooling created by state laws and a liberty interest in not being stigmatized by suspension. The Court emphasized the importance of education, terming it 'perhaps the most important function of state and local governments,' and concluding that 'the total exclusion from the educational process for more than a trivial period' is a deprivation of property and liberty requiring due process.

In subsequent cases, the Court has defined 'property' less on the basis of the importance of the interest and more on the content of the expectations created by the laws. For instance, in *Memphis Light, Gas & Water Division v. Craft,* the Supreme Court held, that a public utility company could not terminate a customer's service without due process because state law provided that utility service could be cut off only 'for cause.'[5] Also, in *O'Bannon v. Town Court Nursing Center,*[6] the Supreme Court held, that residents in a nursing home had no property interest and thus, no right to 'due process' before a government agency revoked their home's certification to receive payments from the government. Although, the ability to remain in the home of their choice was obviously quite important to the patients, the Court found that the patient did not have a property interest in remaining in a particular home. The Court said, that the patients have no –

> 'interest in receiving benefits for care in a particular facility that entitles them...to a hearing before the Government can decertify the facility.'

In its most recent case, *American Manufacturers' Mutual Insurance Company v. Sullivan,*[7] determining whether there is a property interest in benefits, the Court also examined whether state law creates an 'entitlement.' *Sullivan* addressed whether a Pennsylvania law, authorizing insurance companies to withhold medical care payments pending a study of usage that violated due process. The Court found, that the decisions of the insurance companies was not attributable to the state. Additionally, the Court went on and said, that there was not a property interest. Chief Justice William Rehnquist (1924–2005), writing for the Court, said that

> 'for an employee's property interest in the payment of medical benefits to attach under state law, the employee must clear two hurdles. First, he must prove that an employer is liable for a work-related injury, and second, he must establish that the particular medical treatment at issue is reasonable and necessary. Only then does the employee's interest parallel that of the beneficiary of welfare assistance in *Goldberg v. Kelly* and the recipient of disability benefits in *Mathews*.'

Chief Justice Rehnquist said, that the beneficiaries did not have a property interest because they

> 'have yet to make good on their claim that the particular medical treatment was reasonable and necessary.'[8]

Although, the plaintiffs claimed that they should have a hearing before the insurance company could withhold payments on the ground that they were not reasonable and necessary. Chief Justice Rehnquist, however, said that there is no property interest until the plaintiffs proved that the payments were reasonable and necessary. In other words, in order to claim a property interest, the plaintiffs would somehow need to prove the very matter in dispute before being granted a hearing. The Court based this conclusion on its reading of the state statutes, thus, clearly indicating that the Court is defining what constitutes property based on the entitlement approach and not on the importance of the interest to the individual.

The word 'property' has been held to include 'chose in action' in such airspace: a land owner, it has been held, owns at least as much of the space above the ground as he can occupy or use in connection with the land and the fact that the owner did not occupy it in a physical sense – by the erection of buildings and the like – was not material;[9] contracts or agreements;[10] easement rights and rights of way;[11] interest or other earnings on funds or money.

It was held in *Webb's Fabulous Pharmacies Inc. v. Beckwith*,[12] that the earnings on a fund were incidents of ownership of the fund itself, and were property just as the fund itself was property. Leaseholds: in *US v. General Motors*,[13] the federal government occupied temporarily a portion of a building held by a tenant under a long-term lease, it was held that the term 'property' dealt with what lawyers termed the individual's 'interest' in the thing in question. That interest could comprise a group of rights for which the shorthand term was 'a fee simple' or it may be the interest known as an 'estate or tenancy for years'; security interest, such as mortgagee's rights.[14] It was held in *James v. Campbell*,[15] that when the government granted letters patent for a new invention or discovery, it conferred upon the patentee an exclusive property in the patented invention and the right was protected as right to property.[16]

B. Enjoyment of Property Rights in the United Kingdom

Public Control of Land

The right freely to enjoy property is conditioned by the obligations which the law imposes upon the owner or occupier. The common law recognizes obligations to neighbours and others and these have been supplemented by statutory duties relating to the use of land and other forms of property. In the twentieth century, the conception of ownership of land and buildings, so far, as the relationship between the individual owner and the state is concerned, has been radically changed, without, however, altering the obligations which occupation of land imposes towards neighbouring owners. Although, the content of proprietary rights has been modified by statute, the common law with regard to nuisance, negligence and trespass, so far as it concerns land, has not been changed, nor has the private control over the use of land that is exercised through restrictive covenants.

The universal system of 'planning control' contained in the Town and Country Planning Act 1962 (UK), means that before an owner can develop his land, e.g. erect new buildings on it, or change the use of existing buildings from flats to offices, he needs planning permission from the local planning authority. From the local authority's decision there is a right of appeal to the minister, but, at both levels the decision is based on considerations of planning policy and no owner can rely on the principle that he should be free to do what he likes with his own land. Moreover, where planning permission is refused, there is, in general, no right to compensation, although limited compensation is payable in certain situations.[17]

Compulsory Purchase; Powers and Procedure

The Parliament's sanction, subject to compensation, of the compulsory acquisition of land for stated public purposes was another necessity for modern society. Even an individual who claims nothing more than the freedom to continue using his land in the way, in which it has always been used may be compelled to transfer his ownership to a government department or local authority. Most public authorities have powers of compulsory purchase of land for their statutory functions and, even where general powers of this kind are not relied on, an authority may promote a private Bill in Parliament for the acquisition of specified land.

In some instances, powers of acquisition are available to commercial undertakings; thus, by the Pipe-lines Act 1962 (UK), an oil company may be authorized to acquire land compulsorily for the construction of a pipe-line. Public authorities enjoy wide powers of compulsory purchase of land under town planning legislation, in particular for the implementation of approved development plans. Therefore, one cannot today discuss freedom of enjoyment of property without taking account of the possibility of compulsory purchase, the system of town planning control, as well as other social legislation affecting land, such as the Housing Acts and the Public Health Acts.

Property may be acquired compulsorily for public purposes if a statute so authorizes. Without statutory authority, the central government has no power to acquire land except by agreement with the owner, while a local authority requires statutory authority even for acquisition by agreement, since it is only for the purpose of its statutory services that acquisition by a local authority is lawful. The same is true of the public corporations like the transport boards. Powers of compulsory purchase may be given either by an Act of Parliament, authorizing the acquisition of specific property for a specific purpose or by orders made under an Act, conferring general powers to be exercised for purposes and under conditions laid down in the Act. In the latter case, land can be acquired by a public utility undertaking (statutory undertaker, such as a waterworks company) or a local authority on an order made by a minister, or sometimes under a scheme confirmed by him. Thus, in all such cases the authority of a central government department is required.

Formerly, compulsory purchase was authorized by private legislation or by the provisional order procedure.[18] Now the standard procedure is by compulsory purchase order confirmed by the minister under the Acquisition of Land (Authorization Procedure) Act 1946. Parliamentary approval is needed only when special classes of land e.g. common land, National Trust property, are affected.

The details of the authorization procedure must be looked at to figure out to what extent the right of ownership is protected; the constitutional importance of this procedure in settling the dispute between the individual's rights, and the public interest. Although, the courts can help to ensure that a fair procedure is observed, the decision whether particular land should be acquired compulsorily is essentially a governmental decision, for which there is political responsibility to the Parliament. Once acquisition has been authorized, the technical machinery for taking over the land is contained in the Lands Clauses Acts;[19] these Acts are, unless expressly excluded or varied, included in all Acts which authorize the compulsory purchase of land.

Compensation

Where a statute authorizes the compulsory acquisition of property, it is an invariable practice to arrange for the payment of compensation. It is an established rule of construction that express words are required to authorize the taking of property without payment.[20] It is important that the statute should provide rules by which compensation may be assessed and, that there should be machinery for securing an impartial assessment of compensation in accordance with the rules. The amount of compensation should not be left to the discretion of the acquiring authority, nor should an owner be able to require payment of an exorbitant sum.

The Lands Clauses Acts provided procedures for the independent adjudication of compensation but without any rules for assessment, with the result that awards of compensation heavily favoured the owner by the inclusion of an almost punitive element as if for damages in trespass. Since 1919, acquisition by public authorities has been subject to detailed rules of compensation, the basic rule being that compensation should be the amount which the land might be expected to realize if sold in the open market by a willing seller.[21] This rule envisages a free market in land, but the advent of strict planning control after the Second World War (1939–45) meant that the value of land, particularly where it was undeveloped, might depend almost entirely on the decisions of the local planning authority and the minister in granting or refusing permission for development.

The Town and Country Planning Act 1947 attempted a lasting solution of this problem by which, in effect, the state acquired once and for all the development value of all land in return for statutory compensation, leaving the owner simply with the value of the land for its existing use. As part of this general solution, on the compulsory purchase of land the owner was compensated only for the existing use value of the land. Although, there were good reasons for the introduction of the scheme, in practice it proved difficult to operate and unpopular; in that owners who were forced to sell to a public authority might receive appreciably less than on a sale by agreement to another private owner; this discrepancy led to discontent not only with the rules of compensation but also with the powers and procedures of compulsory acquisition.[22]

Since 1959, there has been a return to the basis of open market value, including the element of development value, but subject to complex rules for taking account of town planning control.[23] The general rules of compensation may be modified by statute for special purposes; thus the owner of a dwelling-house, which is condemned as unfit for human habitation usually receives only the site value of his property and nothing in respect of the house itself.[24] Where the owner and the acquiring authority cannot agree as to the amount of compensation payable, the dispute is referred to the Lands Tribunal,[25] which in effect is a specialized court for the valuation of land. In its operation it is completely independent of ministerial pressure and is subject only to the statutory rules of compensation and to the right of appeal on a point of law from its decisions to the Court of Appeal.

Acquisition for Defence

According to the prerogative, the Crown has the power to deprive the subject of possession of his property in order to defend the realm in times of national danger.[26] Various precedents extending back to the 17th century point to a usage of payment, but, Lord Dunedin (1849–1942)[27], in the case cited, did not consider that such usage imposed an obligation upon the Crown to pay compensation.

But in *Burmah Oil Company, Ltd. v. Lord Advocate,*[28] the House of Lords by a bare majority held that if, in the exercise by the Crown of the royal prerogative in relation to war, a subject was deprived of property for the benefit of the state, the subject was entitled to compensation at the public expense, except where damage was done to the subject's property in the actual course of battle. There are permanent Acts which govern the 'acquisition' or 'requisition'[29] of land for defence purposes (Defence Acts 1842 to 1873; and the Land Powers (Defence) Act 1958), and under these Acts compensation is payable.

During both the First (1914–18) and Second (1939–45) World Wars additional powers were taken. The Defence of the Realm Act 1914, provided for the suspension by regulation of any restrictions on the acquisition of land contained in the Defence Acts, though the Crown was not thereby relieved by the obligation to pay compensation. The specific purposes for which regulations could be made under the Emergency Powers (Defence) Act 1939 included

> (a) the taking possession or control on behalf of His Majesty.

No regulations were, however, made under this Act authorizing the acquisition as distinct from the requisition of land. The acquisition by the Crown of land requisitioned for war purposes is governed by the Requisitioned Land and War Works Acts 1945 and 1948. The assessment of compensation for the use of land and the acquisition of other property during the Second World War (1939–45) was regulated by the Compensation (Defence) Act 1939.[30] During the First World War (1914–18), it was held that the Crown could not compel an owner of requisitioned property to accept a rent assessed on an *ex gratia* basis by a non-statutory tribunal, the Defence of the Realm Losses Commission.

Under the Compensation (Defence) Act 1939, two specialized tribunals were established – a General Claims Tribunal, and a Shipping Claims Tribunal. Both tribunals could be compelled by the High Court to state a special case for the opinion of the court on a point of law.

General Restrictions on Use of Property and Freedom of Contract

The law does not allow a private owner unlimited and unlicensed use of his property. The old writ of trespass and its extensions by means of actions on the case provided the common law with the means of resisting invasion of proprietary rights. Trespass to land and conversion of goods are civil wrongs and, if malicious injury be inflicted, are also statutory criminal offences. The owner or occupier may not use his land so as to constitute a nuisance either to the public at large or to his neighbour in particular. Adjoining owners are liable for the support of adjacent land, but not buildings thereon, in the absence of a right of support being acquired. There is a liability accruing from the escape of dangerous things. Both as to land and other forms of property there are numbers of statutory restrictions on use or disposition, which are imposed by such statutes as Public Health Acts 1875–1936; Petroleum (Production) Act 1934; Coal Industry Nationalization Act 1946, and the Town and Country Planning Act 1962. No building can be erected without approval of the plans by the appropriate authority.

The relationship of landlord and tenant is for the most part controlled by statutes which restrict freedom of contract with the object of protecting the tenant. Freedom of contract in other spheres is often restricted; employers are required to contribute for the benefit of their employees, as well as on account of themselves and their families to the national insurance scheme and, also to contribute to the insurance of their employees against industrial injuries received in the course of employment. Under war conditions all production and manufacture were under the control of agencies of the Central Government and many of these controls were continued into the post-war economy, though the majority have now been abandoned or relaxed.

The catalogue of restrictions which are now a permanent part of the welfare state must not lead to the inference that similar restraints exist in the sphere of political, as compared with economic, liberty, freedom of the person from arrest, freedom of speech in all its aspects could be made subject to restrictions in the same way as restraint has been imposed upon freedom of contract in the economic sphere, namely by Parliament. But the climate of political opinion is the constitutional safeguard against an abuse of the legal power of Parliament to destroy what has been built up over centuries by Parliament itself and no less by the judiciary in restraining the powers of the executive.[31]

Right to Property in India

The Janata Party passed the 44th (Amendment) to the Constitution of India officially known as the Constitution (44th Amendment) Act 1978, has taken away the right to property as a fundamental right under the Indian Constitution, and makes it only a constitutional right which would be regulated by ordinary law. Consequently, Articles 19(f) and 31 have been deleted. However, Article 31 has re-appeared, though in part, as a new Article 300-A which provides that –

> 'no person shall be deprived of his property save by authority of law'.

Thus, the only condition to be complied with for the acquisition of private property under the new Article 300-A is a law of the legislature. The purpose for which property would be taken away or whether any compensation would be paid (both these conditions were necessary under repealed Article 31) would be determined by the legislature.

The effect of the amendment is, that for violation of his right to property under Article 300-A, a person will not be entitled to invoke the writ jurisdiction of the Supreme Court under Article 32. He will, however, be entitled to invoke the jurisdiction of High Courts under Article 226. In *Jilubhai Nanbhai Khachar v. State of Gujarat*,[32] it has been held that the right to property guaranteed by Article 300-A is not a basic feature of the Indian Constitution. It is only a constitutional right.

The Janata Government which won the 1977 General Elections campaigned on the promise that they were committed to the electorate for the abolition of the right to property as a fundamental right. Abolition of the right to property as a fundamental right has, however, been criticized by certain constitutional jurists. H. M. Seervai (1906–96)[33], an eminent constitutional jurist was of opinion that the abolition of the right to property as fundamental right would destroy other fundamental rights which were embodied in the Indian Constitution. A party pledged to restore fundamental rights to the people cannot derogate a right which is essential for the existence of other valuable rights. It is enough to say, he stated,

> that the fundamental right to the freedom of speech and expression (which includes the freedom of the press and freedom of association, the freedom to move freely throughout the territory of India, to settle in any part of India, to carry on business, profession or vocation in any part of India) would be destroyed if the right to property is not guaranteed as a fundamental right and the obligation to pay compensation for private property, acquired for public purpose is not provided for.[34]

Dr P.K. Tripathi (1924–2001)[35], however, said that now the right to property of both, the citizens as well as the non-citizens, was more firmly and comprehensively secured under the Indian Constitution, than ever before because an amendment in the existing position would require not only the procedure laid down in Article 368, but also the consent of the states as prescribed in the proviso to Article 368. He said that the state would not be able to acquire private property without showing public purpose and without paying full compensation or the market value of the property.

Under Entry 42 of the Concurrent list (7th Schedule), the Parliament and the State Legislatures have power to legislate on 'acquisition or requisition of property.' The condition inherent in this power is that it cannot be used arbitrarily, that is, it must be used for public purpose, and after paying full compensation to the person deprived of his property. As long as these conditions were expressly laid down in Article 31, they could not be read impliedly. Since Article was deleted the implication would become operative. Under new Article 300-A, the only requirement is that there must be a law for depriving a person of his property. This law must be a valid law, and no law of acquiring a private property can be valid unless it provides for acquisition or requisition of property for a public purpose and unless there is a provision in such a law for paying compensation.[36]

In view of the decision of the Supreme Court in *Maneka Gandhi's* case[37] and a series of cases following that case, it can be said that the validity of a law passed under the new Article 300-A; for depriving a citizen of his property can be challenged on the ground that it does not provide for payment of compensation and is not for 'public purpose'. It has been held, that the 'law' and procedure enacted and prescribed for the deprivation of personal liberty must be just, fair and reasonable. So, if a law under Article 300-A does not provide for taking away private property of an individual for public purpose and for payment of compensation it will be an unjust, unfair and unreasonable law and hence can be declared unconstitutional and void.

Eminent Domain—Every Government has an inherent right to take, and appropriate, the private property belonging to individual citizen for public use.[38] This power is known as 'eminent domain'. It is an offspring of political necessity. The right rests upon the famous maxim – *Salus populi est suprema lex* – which means that the welfare of the people or the public is the paramount law; and also, on the maxim *necessitas publica major est quam,* which means public necessity is greater than private'.[39]

Therefore, property may be needed and acquired under this power for government office, libraries, slum clearance projects, public schools, colleges and universities, public highways, public parks, railways, telephone lines, dams, drainages, sewer and water systems and many other projects of public interest, convenience and welfare.[40] The exercise of such power (compulsory acquisition by state) has been recognized in the jurisprudence of all civilized countries as conditioned by public necessity and payment of compensation.[41] But the power is subject to restrictions provided in the Constitution. In USA, there are limitations on the power of 'eminent domain' –

(1) there must be a law authorizing the taking of property,
(2) property must be taken for public purpose, and
(3) just compensation should be paid.

However, the Indian Supreme Court rejected the argument that a law relating to acquisition of property must satisfy Article 21 (Right to Life and Liberty). It was held that the State's power of 'eminent domain' or to acquire property is not subject to the right of livelihood under Article 21 and that the state may acquire a property notwithstanding the impact of acquisition on the livelihood of the owner of the property.[42] The Court admitted that the exercise of power of 'eminent domain' recognized in Article 300-A requires existence of public purpose, and payment of money for acquisition of property, but the payment need not be just equivalent of the market value of the property so acquired.[43]

In India, Article 31 imposed similar limitation on this power of 'eminent domain'. The new Article 300-A imposes only one limitation on the power of 'eminent domain' i.e. authority of law.

'Property' – Meaning of—The word 'property' as used in Article 31 the Supreme Court has said

'should be given a liberal meaning and should be extended to all those well recognized types of interests which have the insignia or characteristic of property right.'[44] It includes both corporeal and incorporeal right.[45] In includes money,[46] contract, interest in property, e.g., interest of an allottee, licensee, mortgagee or lessee of a property. The Mahantship of a Hindu Temple, and shareholders' interests in the company are recognizable interest in property. The right to receive pension is property.[47]

Pension and gratuity are not bounty to be distributed by the government to its employees on their retirement, but are valuable right and property and any delay in settlement and payment thereof must be visited with the penalty of payment of interest at the current market rate. The liability to pay penal interest on these dues commences at the expiry of 2 months from the date of retirement. In a case, where the delay in payment of the above retirement benefits was due to the non-production of last pay certificate by the issuing authority it was held that the government was liable to pay interest.[48]

No deprivation of property except by authority of law—Article 31(1) provided that no person shall be deprived of his property except by authority of law. This means that the state has authority to take away the property of an individual, but, it can do so only by authority of law. The word 'law' as used in Article 300-A makes it clear that the deprivation of the property can only be made by the authority of law, be it an Act of Parliament or State Legislature or a rule or statutory order having force of law, and not by an executive fiat or an order.[49] In *Wazir Chand v. State of Himachal Pradesh*,[50] it was held that illegal seizure of goods in possession of the petitioner in India under no authority of law at the instance of the Jammu and Kashmir police was clearly an infringement of the fundamental right under Article 13(1).

The protection of Article 31(1) extends to citizens as well as aliens. But Article 31(1) is not attracted where a person is deprived of his property by action of another private person.[51] The new Article 300-A lays down similar condition for taking away the private property of an individual. A person can be deprived of his property only by the authority of law.

Right to Acquire and Dispose of Property in Pakistan

Article 23 of the 1973 Pakistan Constitution makes provisions as to property by laying down that –

> 'every citizen shall have the right to acquire, hold and dispose of property in any part of Pakistan, subject to the Constitution and any reasonable restrictions imposed by law in the public interest'.

The right guaranteed in this Article is of a general nature which gives to every citizen the right to acquire, hold and dispose of property 'subject to the constitution and any reasonable restrictions imposed by law in the public interest'.

Subject to the Constitution

The right to acquire, hold and dispose of property guaranteed to the citizens of Pakistan is subject to other provisions of the Constitution. First, the right is subject to Article 24 which authorizes—

1. compulsory acquisition of land with compensation by clause (2) of Article 24;
2. the compulsory acquisition of land without compensation for preventing danger to life, property or public health or enemy property or evacuee property and the taking over of property acquired by unfair means, and the management of property for a limited period in public interest provided by clause (3) of Article 24.
3. Compulsory acquisition of property without compensation for the purpose of—

   (i). Providing education and medical aid to all or any specified class of citizens; or
   (ii). Providing housing and public facilities and services such as roads, water supply, sewerage, gas and electric power to all or any specified class of citizens; or
   (iii). Providing maintenance to those who, on account of unemployment, sickness, infirmity or old-age, are unable to maintain themselves, or provided by Article 24(3)(e)(i) t(iii).
   (iv). The determination of compensation the adequacy or otherwise whereby is beyond the jurisdiction of any Court, provided by Article 24(4).

Second, the right guaranteed in this Article is subject to Article 253, which authorizes the making of law for placing maximum limits on the holding of property and empowers the Parliament by law to declare that any trade, business, industry or service shall be owned exclusively by the government.

Third, the right is subject to Article 18(c) which authorizes the government to carry on any trade, business, industry or service to the exclusion of citizens.

Fourth, the Article is subject to the provisions of Articles 37 and 38, which lay down principles of policy for

(i) promotion of social justice and eradication of social evils, and
(ii) promotion of social and economic well-being of the people.

Fifth, the Article is subject to Article 3 which lays down that –

> 'the State shall ensure the elimination of all forms of exploitation and the gradual fulfillment of fundamental principle, from each according to his ability to each according to his work'.

Sixth, the Article is subject to the provisions of the preamble (which is reproduction of the Objectives Resolution) which provide for dispensation of social justice and establishment of egalitarian society.

Property rights under Pakistan's Constitution

The right to acquire, hold and dispose of property, recognized by Article 23 extends to every species of property, tangible or intangible, movable or immovable and to all interests in property. Property includes every species of concrete as well as abstract rights to property, in other words, anything that may, under the law, be acquired, held and disposed of, e.g., an interest in property, like that of a mortgage or lessee, patents, copyrights and every other thing of exchangeable value.

In the absence of a specific provision, the right of an individual to engage in a lawful occupation is included in the constitutional guarantee to the right to acquire, hold and dispose of property and so is the liberty to contract within the guarantee of property. Furthermore, the right to terminate a contract, subject to civil liability for damages in case of breach, is likewise a right protected by the guarantee of property. The right of a labourer to bargain for wages or to recover wages already earned, is a right to acquire property which can be subjected to reasonable restriction in the public interest; and so is the right of an advocate to gain a livelihood by legal practice. A contract relating to property may be a contract to acquire or dispose of property, in which case it can be subjected to reasonable restrictions, but it is doubtful whether a mere personal contract having no direct reference to acquisition of property will be treated as property.

The right to possession, enjoyment and disposal is only granted to the owner of the property, i.e., to the person who has the legal title to the property, and no one has the right to acquire property in anything that is not the object of private property by law, or the right of disposing of property that has not been duly acquired under the law of the land.[52]

Restrictions on Property Rights

The right to acquire, hold and dispose of property is subject to reasonable restrictions in the public interest and the question whether a restriction imposed by law is or is not reasonable or in the public interest is for the court to determine. Instances of such restrictions in the existing law are those imposed by laws prohibiting or regulating by licences the possession and sale of dangerous drugs, e.g., poisons, narcotics, explosives, firearms and intoxicating liquors. Law prohibiting or restricting exports and imports; laws regulating, in the interest of public health, sanitation and planning, the owner's right to build on land, e.g., Municipal, Town Planning and Cantonment Acts; Rent restriction and Control Laws;

- restricting the owner's powers to let, eject or enhance rent;
- laws regulating the supply and distribution of commodities essential to the life of the community;
- laws fixing maximum limit of agricultural holdings, regulating rent or prohibiting ejectment; and
- laws regulating private banking and money-lending and granting relief against indebtedness.

Any future laws made with a view to giving effect to principles of policy, as, for instance, laws enacted to promote the interests of backward peoples and well being of the people in general, to advance the interests and raise the status of underprivileged classes, by providing basic necessities.

Taxation

In the United States, the constitutional right to property is subject to the power of the government to tax. In India, it has been held by the Supreme Court, that a tax law must not contravene Article 13 of the Indian Constitution and, therefore, a tax law may be questioned on the ground that it violates a fundamental right, as for, instance, the right to the equal protection of the laws. Under the 1973 Pakistan Constitution, the position is substantially the same. Tax can only be levied under an Act of Parliament.

Protection of property rights

Article 24 of the Pakistan Constitution provides that –

(1) No person shall be compulsorily deprived of his property save in accordance with law.
(2) No property shall be compulsorily acquired or taken possession of save for a public purpose, and save by the authority of law which provides for compensation therefore and either fixes the amount of compensation or specifies the principles on and the manner in which compensation is to be determined and given.
(1) Nothing in this Article shall affect the validity of—

 (a) any law permitting the compulsory acquisition or taking possession of any property for preventing danger to life, property or public health; or
 (b) any law permitting the taking over of any property which has been acquired by, or come into the possession of, any person by any unfair means, or in any manner, contrary to law; or
 (c) any law relating the acquisition, administration or disposal of any property which is or is deemed to be enemy property or evacuee property under any law (not being property which has ceased to be evacuee property under any law); or
 (d) any law providing for the taking over of the management of any property by the State for a limited period, either in the public interest or in order to secure the proper management of the property, or for the benefit of its owner; or
 (e) any law providing for the acquisition of any class of property for the purpose of—

  (i) providing education and medical aid to all or any specified class of citizens; or
  (ii) providing housing and public facilities and services such as roads, water supply, sewerage gas and electric power to all or any specified class of citizens; or
  (iii) providing maintenance to those who, on account of unemployment, sickness, infirmity or old-age, are unable to maintain themselves, or any existing law or any law made in pursuance of Article 253.

(2) The adequacy or otherwise of any compensation provided for by any such law as is referred to in this Article, or determined in pursuance thereof, shall not be called in question in any Court.

Act of State

A sovereign state cannot exercise, as held in *Virendra Singh v. State of Uttar Pradesh*,[53] an act of state against its own citizens. A plea of act of state cannot be taken even against a friendly alien. But, it may be taken, as held in *Johnstone v. Pedlar*,[54] against a resident enemy alien. Similarly it has been held in *United States v. Chemical Foundation, Inc.*,[55] that the state can confiscate the property of an alien enemy without compensation. A Martial Law Court had no power to order confiscation of property when convicting a person and that order was declared to be without lawful authority.[56]

Eminent domain

Article 24(2) of the 1973 Pakistan Constitution, imposes restrictions on the law of 'eminent domain'. Article 24(2) applies only where property is acquired or taken possession of, and in any such case the constitutional requirements are that the acquisition or dispossession:

(1) must be for a public purpose;
(2) should be authorized by law; and
(3) that the law under which the property is acquired or possessed should either itself provide for compensation or specify the principles on which and the manner in which compensation is to be determined and given.

The power of 'eminent domain' is an essential attribute of sovereignty. This power connotes the legal capacity of the state to take the private property of individuals for public purpose.

Since the power of 'eminent domain' is an inseparable incidence of sovereignty, there is no need to confer this authority expressly by the Constitution. It exists without any declaration to that effect. While the existence of the power is recognized, constitutional provisions provide safeguards subject to which the right may be exercised. For instance, in USA three limitations, as noted by Thomas McIntyre Cooley (1824–69)[57] in *Constitutional Limitations*[58], exist;

(i) there must be a law authorizing the taking of property;
(ii) the property must be taken for some public use; and
(iii) just compensation should be paid.

The importance of the power of 'eminent domain' to the life of the state need hardly be emphasized. It is necessary for the property performance of governmental functions to take private property for public use. The power of 'eminent domain' is the offspring of political necessity. The power is inalienable for it is founded upon the common necessity and interest of appropriating the property of the individual members of the community to the greater interests of the whole community.

Therefore, property may be needed and acquired under this power for government offices, libraries, slum clearance projects, public schools, colleges and universities, public highways, public parks, railways, telephone and telegraph lines, dams, drainage, sewers and water system and many other projects or public interest, convenience and welfare.

It was held in *Fauji Foundation v. Shamimur Rehman*,[59]

> 'the power of eminent domain is a proprietary aspect of sovereignty and is inseparable from it and the justification for acquisition of property for public purpose is on the principle that the interests of the public are paramount and that private interests have to be subordinated to public interests and necessities of government'.

Exceptions

Article 24(3) of the Pakistan Constitution provides that the rule of acquisition of property for public purpose and on payment of compensation does not apply to any law under which a person may be deprived of property with a view to preventing danger to life, property or public health.

Nor is the rule applicable to the acquisition, administration or disposal of property under any law relating to enemy or evacuee property, or to any law where the property of another person may be taken in management for his benefit, for example, under the Guardians and Wards Act (1890), and the Court of Wards Act, or to any existing law, for example, the Land Acquisition Act (1894), and the Capital Development Authority Ordinance 1960, or any law made in pursuance of Article 253. Property acquired by unfair means or in contravention of the law is also not protected.

Notes

1. *Roth v. Board of Regents*, 408 U.S. 564 (1972).
2. 397 US 254 (1970).
3. 402 U.S. 535 (1971).
4. 419 U.S. 565 (1975).
5. 436 U.S. 1 (1978). Earlier, the Supreme Court had held that a private utility company does not have to provide due process before terminating a customer's service because there is no state action. *Jackson v. Metropolitan Edison Co.*, 419 U.S. 345 (1974).
6. 447 U.S. 773 (1980).
7. 526 U.S. 40 (1999).
8. Erwin Chemerinsky, *Constitutional Law: Principles and Policies*, 2nd ed. (New York: Aspen Law & Business, 2002), pp. 536–8, 540–1.
9. *US v. Causby*, 328 US 256 (1946).
10. *Omnia Commercial Co. v. US*, 261 US 502 (1923).
11. *Western Union Tel. Co v. Pennsylvania R. Co.*, 195 US 540 (1904).
12. 449 US 155 (1980).
13. 323 US 373 (1950).
14. *Louisville Joint Stock Land Bank v. Radford*, 295 US 555 (1935).
15. 104 US 356 (1881).
16. Justice Fazal Karim, *Judicial Review of Public Actions*, 2nd ed., vol.2 (Karachi: Pakistan Law House, 2018), pp. 1294–5.
17. *See* Town and Country Planning Act 1962, Parts VI and VII, section 43.
18. E.C.S. Wade, A.W. Bradley, *Constitutional Law*, 7th ed. (London: Longmans, 1965), pp. 507–8.
19. Lands Clauses Consolidation Act 1845, and subsequent amending Acts. Other codes regulate acquisition for particular purposes, *e.g.* Railways Clauses Consolidation Act 1845.
20. *Newcastle Breweries v. The King*, (1920) 1 K.B. 854. The decision, though not the principle mentioned, was disapproved in *Hudson Bay Co. v. Maclay* (1920), 36 T.L.R. 469, and *Robinson v. The King*, (1921) 3 K.B. 183. The question of what constitutes the taking of property for this purpose was considered in *France Fenwick and Co. v. The King*, (1927) 1 K.B. 458; also, in relation to town planning control, *Belfast Corporation v. O.D. Cars Ltd.*, (1960) A.C. 490.
21. Land Compensation Act, Section 5.
22. Report of the Franks Committee on Administrative Tribunals and Enquiries 1957, Cmnd. 218, p. 61.
23. Land Compensation Act 1961, Parts II-IV.
24. Land Compensation Act 1961, section. 10 and Second Schedule.
25. The Lands Tribunal is an expert tribunal established by the Lands Tribunal & Compensation Act (NI) 1964. Although it is a court, it includes valuer as well as legal members.
26. *Attorney-General v. De Keyser's Royal Hotel Ltd.*, (1920) A.C. 508.
27. Lord Dunedin served as Secretary for Scotland between 1903–05 as Lord Justice General, and Lord President of the Court of Session between 1905–13, and as a Lord of Appeal in Ordinary between 1913–32.
28. (1965) A.C. 75.
29. Requisition, as opposed to acquisition, implies temporary occupation.
30. This Act gave rise to a good example of administrative quasi-legislation (p. 622, post). The Act excluded fair wear and tear from the Crown's liability to make good damage done. The Treasury ruled that fair wear and tear might be taken into account. It may be suggested that the proper course would have been to amend the Act by deleting the exclusion. As it was, the subject had no right enforceable by law to claim for fair wear and tear.
31. Supra Note 18, pp. 511–2.
32. AIR 1995 SC 142.
33. H. M. Seervai was an eminent Indian jurist, lawyer and author. He is also considered to be a renowned constitutional expert.
34. H.M.Seervai, *The Emergency, Future Safeguards and the Habeas Corpus Case: a criticism*. The Cambridge Law Journal, vol. 37, issue 2, November 1978, pp. 368–369.
35. Dr P.K. Tripathi was a pioneering modernizer of Indian legal education and research, and a constitutional law scholar.
36. P.K. Tripathi – *Right of Property after 44th Amendment Better Prosecuted Than Ever Before*. AIR 1980 Journal (51).
37. AIR 1978 SC 597.
38. *Chiranjit Lal Chowdhuriv. Union of India*, AIR 1951 SC 41.
39. Quoted in Om Prakash Aggarwal's, *Fundamental Rights and Constitutional Remedies*, p. 584 (Vol. 1, 1st ed.).

40. V.N. Shukla, *The Constitution of India*, 5th ed. (Lucknow: Eastern Book Company, 1969), p. 144.
41. *State of Bihar v. Kameshwar Singh*. AIR 1952 SC 252.
42. *New Reviera Coop. Housing Society v. Special Land Acquisition Officer*, (1996) 1 SCC 731; *Chameli Singh v. State of U.P*, (1996) 2 SCC 549, AIR 1996 SC 1051.
43. *Jilubhai Nanbhai Khachar v. State of Gujrat*; 1995 Supp (1) SCC 596; AIR 1995 SC 142.
44. *The Commissioner, Hindu Religious Endowment, Madras v. Sri Lakshmindra Thirtha Swamiar*, AIR 1954 SC 282.
45. *Dwarkadas Srinivas of Bombay v. Sholapur Spinning and Weaving Co. Ltd*. 1954 AIR 119, 1954 SCR 674.
46. *Bombay Dyeing & Manufacturing Co. v. State of Bombay*, AIR 1958 SC 328.
47. *Bharat Petroleum Management Staff v. Bharat Petroleum Corp. Ltd*., (1988) 3 SCC 32, 1988 AIR 1407; *Deokinandan Prasad v. State of Bihar*, AIR 1971 SC 1409.
48. *State of Kerala v. M. Padmanabhan Nair*, (1985) 1 SCC 429.
49. *Jilubhai Nanbhai Khachar v. State of Gujarat*, AIR 1995 SC 142.
50. AIR 1954 SC 415.
51. *P.D. Shamdasani v. Central Bank of India*, AIR 1952 SC 59.
52. A.G. Chaudhry, *Lectures on Constitutional Law*,(Lahore: Irfan Law Book House, 1994)., pp. 216–8.
53. AIR 1954 S.C. 447.
54. (1921) AC 262.
55. 272 U.S. 1 (1926).
56. *Saeed Ahmad v. The Province*, PLD 1993 Lahore 218.
57. Thomas McIntyre Cooley served as the 25th Justice and a Chief Justice of the Michigan Supreme Court, between 1864 and 1885.
58. In 1868 Cooley published this treatise, probably considered as the best-known legal treatise of its time.
59. PLD 1983 S.C. 457 at 670.

17 Freedom of Conscience and Religion

Freedom of Religion under the US Constitution

Introduction

The First Amendment provides that –

> "Congress shall make no law respecting an establishment of religion, or prohibiting the free exercise thereof."

The two clauses have given rise to separate bodies of case law. But this should not obscure the fact that the two clauses are interrelated. They protect overlapping values, but they often exert conflicting pressures. Consider the common practice of exempting church property from taxation.

— Does the benefit conveyed by the government to religion via that exemption constitute an 'establishment'?
— Would the 'free exercise' of religion be unduly burdened if church property were not exempted from taxation?

Articulating satisfactory criteria to accommodate conflicting emanations of the two religion clauses has always been a recurrent challenge.

It has never been easy to define religion. Then it has to be understood how a government may be said to abridge the 'free exercise' of religion. The most direct way is by deliberately prohibiting or disadvantaging a religious sect or it's central practices. While such laws are rare in contemporary society, the Court has subjected them to strictest scrutiny. A harder case is presented when religious objections are raised to the application of general regulations. For example, may the Amish claim constitutional exemption from compulsory education laws? Such claims raise one of the tensions arising from the coexistence of the two religion clauses:

— If a state must grant an exemption because of the 'free exercise' command, is it thereby granting a preference to religion in violation of the 'establishment' provision?

The US Supreme Court has held 'free exercise' to require some religious exemptions from generally applicable laws but has narrowed the scope of such compelled exemptions in recent cases. Congress sought to reverse that trend in by providing for statutory religious exemption claims under the Religious Freedom Restoration Act (RFRA) of 1993

The 'Establishment' Clause raises the following issues:

— the use or apparent endorsement of religious teachings or symbols by governmental bodies;
— the rendering of government financial aid to activities conducted by religious organizations; and
— the grant by government of exemptions from general laws or other accommodation of religion.

The third issue is related to the question of compelled exemptions under the Free Exercise Clause; it asks

— whether government is permitted to exempt religiously motivated practices from general laws, even if it is not compelled to do so.[1]

The principal tension in the Establishment Clause cases is the concept of government neutrality under the Establishment Clause:

— Does it require a 'wall of separation' between church and state?

- Does it require formal neutrality, whereby the government never adverts to religion, for advantage or for disadvantage? Or
- does it require simply that government treat religious organizations and activities equally, including them in any benefit schemes generally enjoyed by others?

What Constitutes Religion for First Amendment Purposes?

Before one can define 'establishment of religion' or 'the free exercise thereof,' one must understand what is meant by the term 'religion'. It comes from the Latin word *religare*, which means 'to tie down' or 'to restrain.' The term 'religion' has had a distinctly theological connotation since its introduction in the English language at the beginning of the 13th century. Dictionaries offer several definitions of the term.[2] The first is:

> 'the personal commitment to and serving of God or a god with worshipful devotion....'

Another definition of 'religion' is –

> 'a personal awareness or conviction of the existence of a supreme being or of supernatural powers or influences controlling one's own, humanity's, or all nature's destiny....'

In the 1890 case of *Davis v. Beason*,[3] the Supreme Court first had occasion to define 'religion'. In a majority opinion authored by Justice Stephen Johnson Field (1816–99)[4], the Court stated that –

> 'the term "religion" has reference to one's view of his relations to his Creator, and to the obligations they impose of reverence for His being and character, and obedience to His will.'

This conception of 'religion' was strictly theistic, which no doubt mirrored popular attitudes circa 1890. By the 1960s, however, American society had become much more religiously diverse, and non-theistic creeds from Asia, such as Buddhism and Taoism, were beginning to find adherents in this country.[5]

Religion Broadly Defined

In 1965, the US Supreme Court attempted to define 'religion' in a manner broad enough to respect the diversity of creeds that coexist in modern America. The definitional problem arose in *United States v. Seeger*,[6] a case involving four men who claimed 'conscientious objector status' in refusing to serve in the Vietnam War following America's involvement in 1965. In the Universal Military Training and Service Act 1940, Congress exempted from combat duty anyone –

> 'who, by reason of religious training and belief, is conscientiously opposed to participation in war in any form.'

The Act defined 'religious training and belief' as training or belief 'in a relation to a Supreme Being involving duties superior to those arising from any human relation.'

Although, some organized religions (such as the Quakers) do not approve of participation in war, Daniel Seeger was not a member of any such group. Nevertheless, they sought 'conscientious objector status' on religious grounds. When specifically asked about his belief in a Supreme Being, Seeger stated that –

> 'you could call [it] a belief in the Supreme Being or God. These just do not happen to be the words that I use.'

Forest Britt Peter, another man whose refusal to serve in Vietnam was before the Supreme Court in *Seeger* case, claimed that after considerable meditation and reflection –

> 'on values derived from the Western religious and philosophical tradition,'

he determined that it would be –

> 'a violation of his moral code to take human life and that he considered this belief superior to any obligation to the state.'

In deciding the *Seeger* case, the US Supreme Court avoided a constitutional question by interpreting the statutory definition of religion broadly. Writing for the Court, Justice Tom C. Clark (1899–1977)[7] held that:

> 'Congress, in using the expression "Supreme Being" rather than the designation "God", was merely clarifying the meaning of religious tradition and belief so as to embrace all religions and to exclude essentially political, sociological, or philosophical views [and] the test of belief "in a relation to a Supreme Being" is whether a given belief that is sincere and meaningful occupies a place in the life of its possessor parallel to the orthodox belief in God.'

Apparently, the Court was persuaded that Daniel Seeger, Forest Britt Peter, and the others whose refusal to serve in Vietnam was before the Court possessed such a belief and recognized them as conscientious objectors on religious grounds.

(i) *A Working Definition of Religion*

Subsequent decisions in both federal and state tribunals/courts have expanded the definition of 'religion' adopted by the Supreme Court in the *Seeger* case. Essentially, a creed must meet four criteria to qualify as a religion as this term is used in the First Amendment. First, as noted earlier, there must be a belief in God or some parallel belief that occupies a central place in the believer's life. Second, the religion must involve a moral code that transcends individual belief – it cannot be purely subjective. Third, some associational ties must be involved. That is, there must be some community of people united by common beliefs. Fourth, there must be a demonstrable sincerity of belief.

Under these criteria, even the non-theistic creeds, such as Taoism or Zen Buddhism, qualify as religions. But frivolous or ridiculous beliefs, such as Stanley Oscar Brown's professed 'faith' in 'Kozy Kitten Cat Food' fail to meet any of the four criteria in *Brown v. Pena*.[8] Of course, there is a long continuum between ludicrous beliefs such as Brown's and conventional religions.[9]

The Establishment Clause

Introduction

The Establishment Clause, according to all interpretations, prohibits the creation of an official church. Thus, requiring oaths of fidelity to a faith or tithes or other financial support for a church would be paradigmatic violations of the clause. There, however, the agreement comes to an end. Modern debates over the scope of the Establishment Clause have centered on what the clause might prohibit beyond official oaths or tithes.[10]

- Does the Establishment Clause bar official sponsorship of religious tenets or symbols, even if no citizen is coerced to support them?
- Should psychological 'coercion' count?
- Is government 'endorsement' of religion troubling even in the absence of coercion?
- Must religious entities be excluded from all forms of public financial support?
- May they be included on an equal footing with other recipients of government largesse?
- Or should there be an absolute bar on government aid to religious evangelism?

The case that follows explore these questions which include cases involving claims that government has impermissibly sponsored religious doctrines or symbols, when, if ever, government financial aid to religion might be permissible, or what are possible establishment clause objections to government's deliberate efforts to accommodate religion, for example by legislative exemptions from general laws.

In *Lemon v. Kurtzman*,[11] it must be noted that the US Supreme Court set forth an influential test for the Establishment Clause violations., *Lemon* case, struck down certain types of financial aid to public schools. Summarizing past decisions, the Court held that a statute must meet three criteria in order to avoid violating the Establishment Clause:

> First, the statute must have a secular legislative purpose; second, it's principal or primary effect must be one that neither advances nor inhibits religion; finally, the statute must not foster "an excessive government entanglement with religion".

The wall of separation

The Establishment Clause of the First Amendment was adopted in contradiction to the practice, prevalent not only in Europe but among the American colonies, of having official churches supported by taxation. Indeed, as previously noted, some states maintained their established churches well into the 19th century. Thus, the concept of 'a wall of separation between church and state,' as Thomas Jefferson (1743–1826)[12] referred to it, was an American invention whose application remained to be worked out in practice. In *Everson v. Board of Education*[13], the Supreme Court adopted Jefferson's metaphor as encapsulating the meaning of the Establishment Clause.

(i) *Competing Interpretations of the Establishment Clause*

Since it's ratification more than two centuries ago, Americans both on and off the Supreme Court have disagreed sharply over the meaning of the Establishment Clause. One view is that it merely forbids the establishment of an official, state-supported religion. According, to this restrictive interpretation, Congress does not run afoul of the First Amendment as long as it refrains from selecting one denomination as the official or preferred religion. However, even the literal language of the First Amendment suggests a broader prohibition. It does not state that Congress shall make no law establishing an official religion; rather, it states that –

> 'Congress shall make no law respecting an establishment of religion'.

This general language indicates a broader restriction than mere prohibition of an established church. For the most part, the Supreme Court has opted for this broader interpretation.

When surveyed, most Americans responded positively to the abstract concept of the separation of church and state. Yet, there is no consensus on how high or how thick the wall of separation should be. Therefore, the Supreme Court's decisions applying this concept to a particular situation has been even more controversial than its decisions under the Free Exercise Clause. Many of these controversial decisions involve education, notably prayer in public schools and state aid to private religious schools.[14]

(ii) *Traditional Government Practices*

Potential Establishment Clause questions are implicit in many traditional government practices. For example, in *Marsh v. Chambers*,[15] consider the practice of Congress and every state legislature of paying a chaplain, usually of a particular Protestant denomination, to lead US representatives in public prayer. What about the inscription 'In God We Trust' on American currency? Or the Supreme Court's time-honored practice of opening oral argument with the invocation 'God save the United States and this honorable Court?' Or the recognition of America as 'one nation under God' in the official pledge of allegiance to the flag? These and other common practices indicate the degree to which religion figures prominently in the public life of the United States.

Although, many Americans no doubt approve of such official endorsement and invocation of religion, what about the rights of non-believers? How far does the First Amendment allow the government to go in recognizing, endorsing or accommodating religious beliefs? As the controversial Supreme Court decisions interpreting the Establishment Clause demonstrate, the answer to this question is far from clear.

(iii) *The Lemon Test*

In 1971, the US Supreme Court laid down a three-pronged test for determining the constitutionality of policies challenged under the Establishment Clause (*Lemon v. Kurtzman*).[16] The so-called *Lemon* test synthesized various elements of the Court's Establishment Clause jurisprudence as it had evolved during the 1940s, 1950s, and 1960s.

Although, controversial from its inception, the *Lemon* test has been applied to a broad range of issues involving separation of church and state. Under the *Lemon* test, a challenged policy must meet the following criteria in order to be valid under the Establishment Clause:

(1) it must have a 'secular purpose';
(2) it must not have the principal or primary effect of 'inhibiting or advancing religion'; and
(3) it must avoid an 'excessive government entanglement with religion.'

The *Lemon* test, has been sharply criticized, and several justices have called for its express repudiation. The principal criticisms are:

(1) that the 'purpose' requirement, taken literally, would invalidate all deliberate government accommodation of religion, even though such accommodation is sometimes required by the Free Exercise' Clause, and has sometimes been held permissible under the 'establishment' clause even if not constitutionally compelled;
(2) that legislative 'purpose' is in any case difficult to ascertain in a multi-member body, and
(3) that the 'entanglement' is essential to ensure that government aid does not excessively promote religious purposes.

Faced with these criticisms, the Court has not formally renounced the *Lemon* test, but has relied on it less and less in recent cases. The Court's decisions recently increasingly employ entirely different sets of analytical devices for distinguishing establishments.

It should go without saying that the *Lemon* test does not contain hard and fast criteria for judicial decision making. Rather, like all judicial doctrines, it is subject to some degree of manipulation by those who are predisposed to a particular result. For example, how can the 'purpose' of a challenged law be determined with certainty by the courts? How does one distinguish the 'principal' or 'primary' effects of a law from its secondary or tertiary effects?

Finally, how much entanglement between religion and government is 'excessive'? During the 1970s and 1980s, the Court was often criticized for inconsistency in its application of the *Lemon* test, leading some scholars to question the value of the test altogether. Since the 1990s, the Court has moved away from a strict application of the *Lemon* test but has stopped short of repudiating it altogether (for example, *Agostini v. Felton*[17]). The test has not been overruled or discarded and has been invoked in recent years. The Court declared unconstitutional a county's effort to post Ten Commandments in county buildings.[18]

Religion and Public Education

In *Everson v. Board of Education* (1947),[19] the first case in which the US Supreme Court applied the Establishment Clause to the states through the 14th Amendment. The issue was whether a local school board could reimburse parents for expenses they incurred in transporting their children to and from Catholic schools. The payments to parents of children in parochial schools were part of a general program under which all parents of children in public schools and non-profit private schools, regardless of religious affiliation, were entitled to reimbursement for transportation costs.

However, it is worth noting that the overwhelming numbers of children attending non-profit private schools in this New Jersey school district were enrolled in Catholic schools. Writing for a sharply divided Court, Justice Hugo Black (1886–1971)[20] justified the challenged payments on the theory that the school board was merely furthering the state's legitimate interest in getting children, –

> 'regardless of their religion, safely and expeditiously to and from accredited schools.'

Justice Wiley Blount Rutledge (1894–1949),[21] joined by Justices Felix Frankfurter (1882–1965),[22] Robert H. Jackson (1892–1954),[23] and Harold Hitz Burton (1888–1964),[24] dissented vigorously. Professing sympathy for the economic hardships involved in sending one's children to private, religious schools. Justice Rutledge nevertheless asserted:

> 'Like St. Paul's freedom, religious liberty with a great price must be bought. And for those who exercise it most fully, by insisting upon religious education for their children mixed with secular, by the terms of our Constitution the price is greater than for others.'

The child benefit theory articulated in *Everson* has for the most part been maintained. Thus, for example, in *Board of Education v. Allen*,[25] the Supreme Court upheld a New York statute requiring local public school districts to lend textbooks on secular subjects to students in private and parochial schools.

Release Time Programs and Equal Access Policies

To accommodate the religious beliefs of public-school students, the Court has upheld release time programs, which allow students to leave campus early to attend religious classes Distinguishing a 1948 decision in *McCollum v. Board of Education*, which struck down an on-campus release time program.[26] The Supreme Court in *Zorach v. Clauson*,[27] upheld a New York policy under which public school students who received parental permission left campus to attend religious services while other students attended study hall. Writing for the Court, Justice William O. Douglas (1898–1980),[28] stressed the need for governmental accommodation of religious practices, a position from which he would later retract.

Release time programs, although, constitutionally permissible under *Zorach v. Clauson*, are not widely in use in public schools today. More common today are policies under which religiously oriented student groups are permitted equal access to school facilities. In *Widmar v. Vincent*,[29] the Supreme Court said, that public school facilities that have been designated an open forum may not be placed off-limits to religious groups. In *Board of Education v. Mergens*,[30] the Court upheld the Equal Access Act 1984, in which Congress prohibited public secondary schools that receive federal funds from disallowing meetings of student groups on the basis of –

> 'religious, political, philosophical or other content of the speech at such meetings.'

Three years later, in *Lamb's Chapel v. Center Moriches Union Free School District*,[31] the US Supreme Court held, that the limited public forum approach could not be used to bar a religious organization from a showing a film after school hours dealing with family planning and child-rearing issues, while permitting discussion of these issues by non-religious groups. According to the Court, the school district rule at issue in this case amounted to viewpoint discrimination in violation of the First Amendment's free speech guarantee. The Supreme Court rejected the argument that *Lamb's Chapel's* after-hours use of school property violated the *Lemon* test.

In *Good News Club v. Milford Central School* (2001),[32] the Court went one step further by holding that if a school permits after-hours activities concerning moral or character development, it cannot prohibit activities even if they involve religious instruction of elementary school students.

Government Efforts to assist Religious Schools

In *Lemon v. Kurtzman* (1971), the Supreme Court struck down Pennsylvania and Rhode Island policies, providing publicly funded salary supplements to teachers in parochial schools as fostering 'excessive entanglement.' Similarly, in *Committee for Public Education v. Nyquist*,[33] the Court used the three-pronged test in striking down a New York law that provided various forms of economic aid to parochial schools. Although, the release time programs approved in the *Zorach* case, have not been recently litigated before the Supreme Court, it is highly unlikely such programs could survive a rigorous application of the *Lemon* test.

The US Supreme Court reinforced its holdings in *Lemon* and *Nyquist* in two significant decisions of the mid-1980s. In *Aguilar v. Felton*, 473 U.S. 402 (1985), the Court struck down a New York City program, that used federal funds to supplement the salaries of public school teachers who taught remedial courses on the premises of religious schools. Similarly, in *Grand Rapids School District v. Ball*,[34] the Court invalidated a program in which supplementary classes for students in sectarian schools were taught by public school teachers at public expense. Writing for the Court in the *Grand Rapids* case, Justice William J. Brennan Jr (1906–97)[35] observed that –

> 'the symbolic union of church and state inherent in the provision of secular, state-provided instruction in the religious school buildings threatens to convey a message of state support for religion to students and to the general public.'

Justice Byron White (1917–2002),[36] used the occasion to dissent not only from the Court's *Grand Rapids* case, holding but from the entire thrust of the court's decisions in the area of state aid to religious schools:

> 'I am firmly of the belief that the Court's decision in these cases, like it's decisions in *Lemon* and *Nyquist*, are not required by the First Amendment and [are] contrary to the long-range interest of the country.... I am satisfied that what the States have sought to do in these cases is well within their authority and is not forbidden by the Establishment Clause.'

In 1994 the Court, reaffirmed its decisions in *Aguilar v. Felton* and *Grand Rapids School District v. Ball*, by striking down a New York law that created a new special school district in a community occupied exclusively by Hassidic Jews. Virtually all of the community's children were being educated in private schools. The new district was established for the purpose of enabling the community to avail itself of public funds for the education of children with disabilities. Under *Aguilar* and *Grand Rapids* cases, this kind of assistance could not be provided directly to the community's private schools, thus, explaining the creation of a new public school district.

In *Board of Education of Kiryas Joel School District v. Grumet*,[37] the Court found this arrangement to be an unconstitutional establishment of religion. In this case, the Court conspicuously avoided relying on the *Lemon* test, encouraging commentators to wonder whether this three-pronged formulation was being phased out. Recalling Justice Byron White's dissent in *Grand Rapids*, Justice Antonin Scalia (1936–2016), joined by Chief Justice William Rehnquist (1924–2005) and Justice Clarence Thomas (1948), was sharply critical of the Court's decision and indeed of it's general approach in this area.

By 1997, a Court majority was willing to give ground in the area of aid to parochial schools. Thus, in *Agostini v. Felton*,[38] a bare majority of justices voted to overturn *Aguilar v. Felton*,[39] and corresponding portions of *Grand Rapids School District v. Ball*. In her majority opinion, Justice Sandra Day O'Connor (1930), maintained that *Aguilar* was inconsistent with the Court's later Establishment Clause decisions. Justice Sandra Day O'Connor stressed the neutrality of the federally funded remedial instruction and the procedural safeguards surrounding the program. She also noted that this program could not 'reasonably be viewed as an endorsement of religion.' With the concurrence of Chief Justice William Rehnquist (1924–2005) and Justices Antonin Scalia (1936–2016), Anthony Kennedy (1936), and Clarence Thomas (1948), Justice Sandra Day O'Connor therefore concluded that

> '*Aguilar*, as well as the portion of Ball addressing *Grand Rapids* 'shared time' program, are no longer good law.'

In dissent, Justices John Paul Stevens (1920–2019)[40], David Souter (1939)[41], Ruth Bader Ginsburg (1933–2020)[42], and Stephen Breyer (1938)[43] continued to express concern about the difficulty of limiting government assistance in this area to purely secular objectives.

In *Mitchell v. Helms*,[44] the Court, by a 6 to 3 vote, expanded the types of public aid, that government may provide to parochial schools. Relying heavily on the *Agostini v. Felton* precedent, the Court upheld a Louisiana statute permitting state and local governments to lend library books, projectors, televisions, computers, software, and similar equipment to parochial and other private not-for-profit elementary and secondary schools. The 6 members of the majority could not agree on a single opinion, however, Justice Clarence Thomas, in a plurality opinion joined by Chief Justice William Rehnquist and Justices Antonin Scalia and Anthony Kennedy, indicated his willingness to go further than the Court's holding, suggesting that he and his three colleagues in the plurality would be willing to support even broader public assistance to religious schools. His position is summarized in the following statement:

> 'If religious, irreligious and areligious are all eligible for governmental aid, no one would conclude that any indoctrination that any particular recipient conducts has been done at the behest of the government.'

In a separate opinion concurring in the judgment only, Justice Sandra Day O'Connor, joined by Justice Stephen Breyer, criticized what she viewed as the 'unprecedented breadth' of the rule announced by the plurality. She contended that considerations of neutrality alone are not sufficient in determining whether governmental aid to religious schools violates the Establishment Clause. Such factors as 'endorsement' of religion should also be taken into account. Clarence Thomas's opinion, she maintained, foreshadowed –

> 'the approval of direct monetary subsidies to religious organizations, even when they use the money to advance their religious objectives.'

In dissent, Justice David Souter, supported by Justices John Paul Stevens and Ruth Bader Ginsburg, expressed alarm at the scope of the plurality opinion:

> As a break with consistent doctrine the plurality's new criterion is unequaled in the history of Establishment Clause interpretation. Apparently, it appears to take even-handedness neutrality and in practical terms promote it to a single and sufficient test for the establishment [sic] constitutionality of school aid.

If evenhanded neutrality were the sole standard for determining the constitutionality of public aid, Justice Souter reasoned,

> 'religious schools could be blessed with government funding as massive as expenditures made for the benefit of their public school counterparts and religious missions would thrive on public money.'

Mitchell v. Helms, could have the effect of giving virtually all schoolchildren access to the Internet. Some critics have noted that computers, by contrast with textbooks loaned to parochial schools at public expense, can be used in an endless variety of ways, both secular and religious. Barry W. Lynn (1948), executive director of Americans United for Separation of Church and State (AU)[45], observed that as a result of this decision,

> 'religious schools can now have students surf the Internet to read the Bible in religion classes, learn theology from Jerry Falwell, or download crucifixes as screen savers.'

On the other hand, children in religious schools might well use the Internet to access ideas that run counter to the religious views of their teachers and parents.

The Supreme Court has drawn a distinction between programs that benefit all students and those just available for non-public school students. An assistance program benefiting only non-public school students violates the Establishment Clause. However, a program that is available to all students is permissible unless it violates any other criteria.

This distinction was made clear in the Court's important decision concerning aid/vouchers, *Zelman v. Simmons-Harris.*[46] State of Ohio created Pilot Project Scholarship Program in the Cleveland City School District, the program provides tuition aid/vouchers to qualified students to attend participating public or private schools of their parent's choosing. Both religious and non-religious schools in the district may participate. Tuition aid/voucher was distributed to parents according to financial need, and where the aid/voucher was spent depends solely upon where parents choose to enrol their children.

Tuition aid/vouchers was distributed by the government paying a greater amount for poorer students. Vouchers/aid were for $2250 and was for the poorest students, the government paid 90 percent of that amount. Almost all of the vouchers/aid were used in religious schools. 96 percent were used in parochial schools and 82 percent of the schools receiving aid/vouchers were religiously affiliated. Nonetheless, the Supreme Court upheld the program as constitutional. Chief Justice William Rehnquist, writing for the Court in a 5 to 4 decision, said that prior decisions –

> 'make clear that where a government aid program is neutral with respect to religion, and provides assistance directly to a broad class of citizens who, in turn, direct government aid to religious schools wholly as a result of their own genuine and independent private choice, the program is not readily subject to challenge under the Establishment Clause.'

The United States Court of Appeals for the Sixth Circuit had invalidated the program as having been structured in a manner that encouraged parents to send their children to parochial schools and, thus, having the impermissible effect of advancing religion. The Supreme Court reversed and disagreed. Chief Justice William Rehnquist stressed the program's neutrality:

> 'Program benefits are available to participating families on neutral terms, with no reference to religion. The only preference stated anywhere in the program is a preference for low-income families, who receive greater assistance and are given priority for admission at participating schools.
>
> There are no 'financial incentive[s]' that 'ske[w]' the program toward religious schools. Such incentives [are] not present… where the aid is allocated on the basis of neutral, secular criteria that neither favour nor disfavour religion, and is made available to both religious and secular beneficiaries on a non-discriminatory basis.'

The Court explained that the government was acting out of the important secular purpose of improving education for children in Cleveland, and, that if the aid ends up being spent in religious schools, it is because of parent choices not government decisions.

Justice Sandra Day O'Connor wrote a concurring opinion to emphasize, that she did not see the decision as departing from precedent and to explain that parents had a range of choices in Cleveland that made the voucher/aid program acceptable. Justice Clarence Thomas wrote a concurring opinion in which he discussed the need to improve education for inner-city children from minority races. He also questioned whether the Establishment Clause should apply to the states at all.

There were 4 dissenters and 3 dissenting opinions. Justice John Paul Stevens wrote a brief dissent in which he argued, that none of the characteristics of the program, such as the educational need of the students or the range of choices available, excused the government in providing such aid to parochial schools. Justice David Souter in a lengthy dissent criticized what he saw as an unprecedented transfer of government funds to religious coffers. Justice Stephen Breyer's dissent emphasized the inherent divisiveness of the government giving such aid to religion.

The 5 to 4 decision in *Zelman*, reflects very different views between the majority and the dissent over the need for restrictions on government aid to religious schools. As a descriptive matter, *Zelman* case largely resolves the constitutional issues concerning vouchers/aid under the 1st Amendment. There still might be litigation, for example, over a types of choices must be available for voucher/aid programs to be constitutional.[47]

The School Prayer Controversy

Few decisions of the modern US Supreme Court have been criticized more intensely than the school prayer decisions of the early 1960s. In *Engel v. Vitale*,[48] the Court invalidated a New York Board of Regents policy, that established the voluntary recitation of a brief generic prayer by children in the public schools at the start of each school day. Justice Hugo Black (1886–1971), wrote the opinion for the majority, saying that

> 'in this country it is no part of the business of government to compose official prayers for any group of the American people to recite as part of a religious program carried on by government.'

Justice Potter Stewart (1915–85),[49] the lone dissenter in *Engel v. Vitale*, compared the recitation of the regents' prayer to other official recognitions of God and religion, such as the pledge of allegiance to the flag, the president's oath of office, and the invocation said prior to oral argument in the Supreme Court in the following words:

> I do not believe that this Court, or the Congress, or the President has by the actions and practices I have described established an 'official religion' in violation of the Constitution. And I do not believe the State of New York has done so in this case. What each has done has been to recognize and to follow the deeply entrenched and highly cherished spiritual traditions of our Nation.

In 1963, the US Supreme Court reinforced the *Engel* decision in the companion cases of *Abington School District v. Schempp*[50] and *Murray v. Curlett*,[51] by striking down the practice of Bible reading and the recitation of the Lord's Prayer in the Pennsylvania and Maryland public schools. Again, only Justice Potter Stewart dissented.

The reaction to the Court's school prayer decisions came fast and furious and, indeed, has still not disappeared. The Court was roundly condemned by religious leaders and conservative members of Congress and, through resolutions passed by several state legislatures. Polls have consistently shown that a majority of Americans oppose the Court's ban on school prayer. Even today, the public has lower regard for the Court's work in this area than in other policy areas.

On several occasions, constitutional amendments have been introduced in Congress aimed specifically at overturning the school prayer decisions. In November 1971, one such proposal in the House of Representatives fell only 28 votes short of the two-thirds majority required for constitutional amendments. In the 1980 US presidential election, Ronald Reagan (1911–2004)[52] capitalized on public sentiment about school prayer by advocating a 'school prayer amendment.' However, once in office, President Reagan was either unwilling or unable to push this proposal through Congress.

Negative public reaction and widespread noncompliance notwithstanding, the US Supreme Court has maintained, although, by a shrinking majority, the position articulated in the school prayer cases. For example, in *Stone v. Graham*,[53] the Court invalidated a Kentucky law requiring that the Ten Commandments be posted in all public school classrooms. In *Wallace v. Jaffree*,[54] the Court struck down an Alabama law that required public school students to observe a moment of silence 'for the purpose of meditation or voluntary prayer' at the start of each school day. In *Lee v. Weisman*,[55] the Court held unconstitutional the practice of inviting a member of the clergy to deliver a nonsectarian prayer at a public school graduation ceremony. In *Santa Fe Independent School District v. Doe*,[56] the Court split 5 to 4 in striking down a public high school's policy of allowing students to elect a chaplain to deliver invocations before football games. In *Mitchell v. Helms*,[57] the Court emphasized the need for the government to treat religious beliefs and groups equally with non-religious ones with Justice Clarence Thomas refers to this as the government being neutral in its treatment of religion.

The reaction to the US Supreme Court's decisions, in this area have been predictable. Conservative organizations and religious activists have been harshly critical. In the wake of the *Santa Fe* decision, conservative activist and Republican presidential candidate Gary Bauer (1946)[58] said the decision 'proves that a majority of the Court is at war with the religious tradition of America.' On the other hand, civil liberties groups have applauded the Court for these decisions.

Note that in no case has the US Supreme Court held that it is unconstitutional for a student to pray voluntarily in the public school classrooms, although some school officials have interpreted the court's position this way. What the Court has said, is that it is unconstitutional for the state schools to require, endorse, or sanction prayer, either directly or indirectly. One might think that if this were better understood, some of the public hostility toward the Court's decisions would abate. On the other hand, given the nature and intensity of feelings on this issue, it is unlikely that an accurate public perception of the court's holdings would diminish the public opprobrium.

The Evolution-Creationism Conflict

With the rapid expansion of public education in the early 20th century, especially in rural areas dominated by fundamentalist Protestantism, a controversy erupted over the teaching of evolution in the public schools.

The controversy achieved national prominence in 1925 when John T. Scopes (1900–70), a high school biology teacher in Dayton, Tennessee, was prosecuted for teaching evolution in violation of a state law that had been passed earlier that year. Amid a carnival-like atmosphere, the *Scopes* trial – or the 'Monkey Trial,' as it was caricatured in the press—pitted famous politician and orator William Jennings Bryan (1860–1925)[59] against celebrated lawyer Clarence Darrow (1857–1938),[60] in a battle royal in the courtroom. Although, Darrow outsmarted Bryan in a much-publicized debate over biblical literalism, Scopes was nevertheless convicted of violating the state statute. The Tennessee Supreme Court reversed the conviction on technical grounds, however, preventing the US Supreme Court from having to consider what was potentially the most explosive constitutional question of that decade.

In the wake of the *Scopes* trial, two states, Arkansas and Mississippi, enacted legislation similar to the Tennessee 'anti-evolution' law. However, it was not until 1968, that one of these laws was challenged in Court. Susan Epperson, a high school biology teacher in Little Rock, filed a lawsuit challenging the Arkansas 'anti-evolution' statute. Although, the Arkansas Chancery Court ruled in favor of Epperson, and struck down the 'anti-evolution' law. But the State of Arkansas repealed in the Arkansas Supreme Court which reversed and reinstated the statute. On *certiorari*, the US Supreme Court reversed the judgement in *Epperson v. Arkansas*.[61] Writing for the Court, Justice Abe Fortas (1910–82)[62] asserted that Arkansas could not–

> 'prevent it's teachers from discussing the theory of evolution because it is contrary to the belief of some that the Book of Genesis must be the exclusive source of doctrine as to the origins of man.'

The *Epperson* decision put to rest the issue of whether states could prohibit the teaching of evolution in their public schools. But, two decades later, the 'evolution-creationism' conflict resurfaced in Louisiana. This time, the question was whether the state could mandate that 'creationism', or creation science, be given equal time in the classroom along with the theory of evolution.

In *Edwards v. Aguillard*,[63] the US Supreme Court answered this question in the negative. Writing for a majority of 7, Justice William J. Brennan Jr (1906–97), averred that 'the primary purpose' of the Louisiana Creationism Act, was 'to endorse a particular religious doctrine,' rather than further the legitimate interests of the state in fostering different points of view in the classroom.

In the wake of such decisions as *Edwards v. Aguillard* and *Epperson v. Arkansas*, as well as the previously discussed school prayer decisions, fundamentalist Christians began to argue that, in it's attempt to expunge religious teaching and symbols from the public schools, the Supreme Court had fostered a 'religion' of 'secular humanism.' According to its detractors, 'secular humanism' is a philosophy emphasizing the view that morality is a human invention and that moral choices are largely matters of personal values. In the view of some fundamentalists, the pervasiveness of 'secular humanism' in public school curricula was highly corrosive to traditional values and institutions.

In 1987, *Smith v. Board of School Commissioners of Mobile County* was the lawsuit in which a federal district court barred the use of certain widely used history, social studies, and home economics textbooks in the public schools of Mobile County, Alabama. In essence, the district judge held that these books advanced the religion of 'secular humanism'. In embracing this philosophy, the textbooks allegedly ignored or understated the historical and contemporary significance of traditional religion in American life, thus, abridging the Free Exercise rights of students holding theistic beliefs. The teaching of 'secular humanism' amounted to 'a sweeping fundamental belief that must not be promoted by the public schools.' Such promotion, the district court concluded, was a violation of the Establishment Clause of the First Amendment. The Court of Appeals for the Eleventh Circuit promptly overruled this novel decision, finding that the 'purpose' for using the textbooks in question was 'purely secular'.[64]

Another similar case, *Mozert v. Hawkins County Public Schools* initiated in 1986, by fundamentalist parents in Hawkins Country, Tennessee; sued their country school board over the reading curriculum in the local public schools, complaining of the humanist perspective embodied in the curriculum. Although, the plaintiffs won at trial, the judgment was overruled on appeal by the Court of Appeals for the Sixth Circuit. The US Supreme Court declined to review the case, thus letting the Appeals Court's decision stand.[65]

Discrimination against Religious Expression in the Public Educational Arena

If a public school or university subsidizes a variety of student newspapers, can it withhold funds from a particular paper solely because it 'promotes or manifests a particular belief in or about a deity or an ultimate reality?'

This issue was brought before the US Supreme Court in *Rosenberger v. University of Virginia*.[66] The university denied a subsidy to '*Wide Awake*', a Christian perspective at the University of Virginia (UVA). The student-publisher of the paper went to court. The Supreme Court found the denial of support violative of free speech, in that the university was discriminating against the paper based on its content. Moreover, the Court rejected the argument that to subsidize the paper, the university would be breaching the wall of separation between church and state. Four justices, David Souter, John Paul Stevens, Ruth Bader Ginsburg, and Stephen Breyer dissented, claiming that for the university to provide the subsidy in question would constitute a clear violation of the Establishment Clause. Some observers regarded Justice Sandra Day O'Connor's concurring opinion as somewhat equivocal, leading them to speculate that in a similar case O'Connor might be persuaded to go the other way. It is possible that the *Rosenberger* decision will be limited to its rather unique facts.

Government affirmations of religious belief

In a religious society such as America, it is inevitable (and, many would say, desirable) for there to be numerous public affirmations of belief. The court's decision in *Abington School District v. Schempp* suggests, however, that government sponsorship of such affirmations may be unconstitutional.

Nevertheless, the Supreme Court has been unwilling to hold government-sponsored displays or affirmations of belief to the same standard of strict neutrality that underlines the school prayer decisions. For example, in *McGowan v. Maryland*,[67] the Court upheld laws that prohibited certain business from operating on Sunday, despite the obvious religious underpinnings of such restrictions. In the Court's view, these Sunday closing laws had a secular purpose in that they represented the community's desire for a day of rest and relaxation, independent of any religious significance. The fact that this day of rest happened to be the day of worship for most Christians was merely incidental. Writing for the Court in *McGowan*, Chief Justice Earl Warren (1891–1974)[68] noted that:

> It is common knowledge that the first day of the week has come to have special significance as a rest day in this country. People of all religions and people with no religion regard Sunday as a time for family activity, for visiting friends and relatives, for late sleeping, for passive and active entertainments, for dining out, and the like.

Perhaps, the best example of the Court's unwillingness to extend the holding of *Abington School District v. Schempp*, came to its logical conclusion in *Marsh v. Chambers*.[69] Here, the Court refused to invalidate Nebraska's policy of beginning legislative sessions with prayers offered by a Protestant chaplain retained at the taxpayers' expense.

Writing for the Court, Chief Justice Warren E. Burger (1907–95),[70] made no pretense of applying the strict three-part test laid down in his own majority opinion in *Lemon v. Kurtzman*.[71] Instead, Burger's opinion relied heavily on history and the need for accommodation of popular religious beliefs. In a caustic dissent, Justice William J. Brennan Jr (1906–97) observed that –

> 'if any group of law students were asked to apply the principles of *Lemon* to the question of legislative prayer, they would nearly unanimously find the practice to be unconstitutional.'

The Supreme Court decision in *Marsh v. Chambers*, suggested to some observers that the Court was prepared to abandon the strict three-prongs of the *Lemon* test for determining establishment of religion. To others, *Marsh* was a mere aberration, based on the pragmatic realization that the Court would inevitably be embarrassed, if it were to attempt to strike down a practice that occurs in nearly every legislature in the United States, including the US Congress. This case provides a good illustration of the practical limits of judicial power.

Religious Displays on Public Property

The decision in *Lynch v. Donnelly*,[72] suggests that *Marsh v. Chambers*, was more than a mere aberration. In the *Lynch* case, the Court upheld a city-sponsored nativity scene in Pawtucket, Rhode Island. Chief Justice Warren E. Burger's majority opinion barely mentioned the *Lemon* test. Again, Justice Burger relied on history and the fact that the crèche had become for many a 'neutral harbinger of the holiday season,' rather than a symbol of Christianity.

Five years later, in the Pennsylvania case of *County of Allegheny v. American Civil Liberties Union*,[73] the Court reexamined the constitutional question posed by traditional holiday displays on public property. Here, the justices considered two separate displays; a crèche prominently situated on the grand staircase inside the country courthouse and, an arrangement featuring a Christmas tree and a Hanukkah menorah placed just outside the nearby city–county building. A sign bearing the mayor's name and entitled the slogan 'Salute to Liberty' was placed at the foot of the Christmas tree.

Justice Harry Blackmun (1908–99)[74], for a majority of the Court, maintained that the display of the crèche inside the courthouse, with the accompanying words 'Gloria in Excelsis Deo,' clearly conveyed a religious message. By authorizing the display, the country had, in Blackmun's view, indicated its endorsement of that message. Such endorsement, he concluded, was a violation of the Establishment Clause. By contrast, the Christmas tree and Menorah display, in tandem with the mayor's message, was not in the Court's view

> 'an endorsement of religious faith, but simply recognition of cultural diversity.'

The overall display conveyed a predominantly secular message and thus, did not violate the Establishment Clause.

The Supreme Court's decisions in *Marsh* and *Lynch*, indicate that the Burger Court retreated from the strict neutrality of the Warren Court, in favor of an approach that might be labeled accommodation or benevolent neutrality. The *Allegheny County* decision suggested, however, that the Rehnquist Court was seeking a middle ground in this area.

In *Van Orden v. Perry,* the Court considered the constitutionality of a 6 foot high, 3 foot wide Ten Commandments monument between the Texas State Capitol and Texas Supreme Court.[75] Justices John Paul Stevens, Sandra Day O' Connor, David Souter, and Ruth Bader Ginsburg dissented, and, would have found the monument unconstitutional as an impermissible symbolic endorsement. Justice Stephen Breyer, though, concurred in the judgment and voted to uphold the monument's constitutionality. He expressly said, that he agreed with the symbolic endorsement test, but concluded, that there was not symbolic endorsement in this case because of the presence of many other secular monuments on the Texas State Capital grounds and, because the monument had been there without challenge for over 40 years.

The Free Exercise of Religion

Introduction

To some extent, claims based on the 'free exercise' of religion overlap with 'free speech' claims. For example, there were free speech objections raised by members of Jehovah's Witnesses; in cases such as *Cantwell v. Connecticut,*[76] *Lovell v. City of Griffin,*[77] *Martin v. City of Struthers,*[78] and *Wooley v. Maynard.*[79] But the 'free exercise' guarantee raises distinctive problems. First, 'exercise' implies more than belief or expression; it often implies conduct or action. In many of the cases that follow, the 'free exercise' claimant argues, that a general law resting on state interests not related to religion either interferes with behavior dictated by religious belief or compels conduct forbidden by religious belief. Should government have more leeway to regulate conduct than belief? Second, the Establishment Clause has no parallel in the speech clause. In the religion context, however, it places limits on how far either legislatures or courts can go in exempting religious believers from general regulations, or otherwise accommodating 'free exercise' values.

The 'free exercise' cases which follow first look at the question whether government may deliberately disadvantage religion or a particular religion, and second at whether religious practitioners are entitled to exemptions from generally applicable laws which conflict with dictates of their faith.[80]

Religious belief and the right to proselytize

The First Amendment provides virtually absolute protection with respect to individual religious convictions and beliefs. The government may never question a person's beliefs or impose penalties or disabilities based solely on those beliefs. Thus, in *Torcaso v. Watkins,*[81] the US Supreme Court unanimously struck down a Maryland constitutional provision, requiring persons seeking public office to take an oath declaring their belief in God. Likewise, in *McDaniel v. Paty,*[82] the Court was unanimous in holding, that states may not bar priests and ministers from serving as delegates to state constitutional conventions.

> The Free Exercise Clause obviously protects more than belief – it carries over into the realm of action. But here the protections are somewhat attenuated. Whether specific actions are protected by the First Amendment depends on the character of those actions and the government's rationale for trying to regulate them.

(i) *Religious Solicitation*

The highest degree of protection is accorded to religious speech and other expressive religious conduct. In *Cantwell v. Connecticut*,[83] the US Supreme Court struck down a state law, that prohibited door to door solicitation for any religious or charitable cause without prior approval of a state agency.

The law was challenged by Newton Cantwell, a member of the Jehovah's Witnesses, a sect committed to active proselytizing. Cantwell and his 2 sons routinely went from door to door or stopped people on the street in order to communicate a message that was highly critical of the Roman Catholic Church and other organized religions. Eventually, they were arrested and charged with failure to obtain approval for solicitation under the state law, as well as with 'common law breach of the peace.' The Court reversed the 'breach of the peace' conviction and invalidated the state statute, saying in part:

> In the realm of religious faith, and in that of political belief, sharp differences arise. In both fields the tenets of one man may seem the rankest error to his neighbor. To persuade others to his point of view, the pleader, as we know, resorts to exaggeration, to vilification of men who have been, or are, prominent in church or state, and even to false statement. But the people of this nation have ordained in the light of history, that, in spite of the probability of excesses and abuses, these liberties are, in the long view, essential to enlightened opinion and right conduct on the part of citizens of a democracy.

Three years later, the US Supreme Court in *Douglas v. City of Jeanette*[84] held, that police could not prohibit members of the Jehovah's Witnesses from peaceable and orderly proselytizing on Sundays, merely because other citizens complained. In 1943, another case involving the Jehovah's Witnesses, *Murdock v. Pennsylvania*,[85] the Court held that a state law requiring the payment of a tax for the privilege of solicitation could not be constitutionally applied to religious solicitation. Writing for the Court, Justice William O. Douglas (1898–1980),[86] observed that –

> 'a person cannot be compelled to purchase…a privilege freely granted by the Constitution.

In *Niemotko v. Maryland*, another case involving members of the Jehovah's Witnesses,[87] the Supreme Court held unconstitutional a city council's denial of a permit to the Jehovah's Witnesses to use the city park for a public meeting. The city council had refused to grant the permit because the Jehovah's Witnesses' answers to questions about Catholicism, military service, and other issues were 'unsatisfactory.' A unanimous Supreme Court regarded this denial of the public forum to an unpopular religious group as blatant censorship.

(ii) *Time, Place, and Manner Regulations*

Like freedom of speech, wherein it provided, that the First Amendment does not guarantee the right to communicate one's views at all times and places or in any manner that may be desired, religious expression in the public forum is subject to reasonable time, place and manner regulations.

Airports, courthouses, and other public buildings may be declared off limits to all First Amendment activities, as long as particular groups are not singled out. Similarly, religious proselytizing in congested areas may be limited to certain areas so as to maintain the safe and orderly flow of pedestrian and vehicular traffic (see, for example, *Heffron v. International Society for Krishna Consciousness*[88]).

Unconventional Religious Practices

Although, the Supreme Court has consistently defended the right of unpopular religious groups to meet, canvass, solicit, and proselytize in the public forum, it has generally rejected arguments that the Free Exercise Clause allows religious groups to engage in activities that are proscribed as detrimental to public health, safety, or morality.

Thus, in 1975, the Court refused to review a lower court decision upholding Tennessee's law prohibiting the handling of poisonous snakes in religious ceremonies. In *Employment Division v. Smith*,[89] the Supreme Court rejected a claim made by members of the Native American Church that their ritualistic use of peyote[90] constituted free exercise of religion.

(i) *The Mormon Polygamy Case*

In *Reynolds v. United States*, the US Supreme Court made first major pronouncement on the subject of unconventional religious practices.[91] In this landmark case, the Court upheld application of the federal anti-polygamy statute to a Mormon, who claimed it was his religious duty to have several wives.

The Morrill Anti-Bigamy Act,[92] a federal law in question had merely adopted the long-standing common law prohibition against bigamy (the crime of having more than one spouse). Although, the law applied to everyone regardless of religion, it is clear from the congressional debates surrounding this legislation, that the law was aimed at the Mormons, a highly controversial sect in 19th century America.

The *Reynolds* decision was based on a sharp distinction between belief and conduct. According to Chief Justice Morrison Waite (1816–88),[93]

> 'Congress was deprived of all legislative power over mere opinion, but was left free to reach actions which were in violation of social duties or subversive of good order.'

Although, the US Supreme Court has occasionally reiterated the distinction between religious belief and conduct, it has largely repudiated the position taken in *Reynolds* case, that religious conduct is beyond the pale of the Free Exercise Clause. After all, few if any government policies infringe religious belief *per se*; rather, they are aimed at particular kinds of actions deemed socially undesirable.

(ii) *The Warren Court Establishes the Compelling Interest Test*

In its post-New Deal expansion of civil liberties, the US Supreme Court markedly increased the degree of judicial protection of religiously motivated conduct, but this did not mean that religious activity received absolute immunity from government regulation. The Court remained willing to uphold public policies, that infringed on religious practices, if the government could point to an important secular justification for such infringement.

In *Sherbert v. Verner*,[94] the Court said, that freedom of religion is a fundamental right that could be abridged only if necessary to protect compelling government interests. Although, the justices often disagreed over precisely which government interests should be viewed as compelling, this general standard established a strong presumption in favor of the free exercise of religion.

(iii) *The Oregon Peyote Case*

The US Supreme Court throughout the 1970s and 1980s, continued to apply the rationale established in *Sherbert v. Verner*, for example, *Thomas v. Review Board of the Indiana Employment Security Division*[95] and *Hobbie v. Unemployment Appeals Commission of Florida*.[96]

These cases stood for the proposition, that, in the absence of a compelling justification, a state could not withhold unemployment compensation from an employee who resigned or was discharged due to unwillingness to depart from religious practices or beliefs that conflicted with job requirements.

In 1990, however, a sharply divided US Supreme Court, in *Employment Division v. Smith*,[97] departed dramatically from this approach and imposed potentially serious limits on the scope of religious freedom protected by the First Amendment.

In *Smith* case, a state's interest in prohibiting the use of illicit drugs came into conflict with well-established practices of the Native American Church,[98] a sect outside the Judeo-Christian[99] mainstream of American religion. Alfred Leo Smith and Galen Black, members of this church, worked as drug rehabilitation counselors for a private social service agency in Oregon State. Along with other church members, Smith and Black ingested peyote, a hallucinogenic drug, at a sacramental ceremony practiced by Native Americans for hundreds of years. Citing their use of peyote as 'job-related misconduct,' the social service agency fired Smith and Black. Recognizing no exception, even for sacramental purposes, Oregon's controlled substances statute made the possession of peyote a criminal offense. Although, Smith and Black were not charged with violation of this law, it's existence figured prominently in the Supreme Court's ultimate resolution of the free exercise issue.

Shortly, after they were fired, Smith and Black applied for unemployment compensation. The Oregon Employment Appeals Board denied their applications, accepting the employer's explanation that Smith and Black had been discharged for job-related misconduct. The former counselors successfully challenged this administrative ruling in the Oregon Court of Appeals, thus, initiating a lengthy and complex judicial struggle that generated several state court decisions and two rulings by the US Supreme Court. On remand from the first of these rulings, the Oregon Supreme Court held, that the controlled substance law, as applied in this case, violated the Free Exercise Clause of the 1st Amendment and that Smith and Black were therefore, entitled to unemployment compensation.

Reviewing the case for a second time and finally reaching the basic constitutional issue, the US Supreme Court reversed. Justice Antonin Scalia (1936–2016), writing for the majority, ruled that

> 'if prohibiting the exercise of religion ... is ... merely the incidental effect of a generally applicable and otherwise valid [criminal] law, the First Amendment has not been offended.'

According to this reasoning, the Free Exercise Clause would be violated only if a particular religious practice were singled out for proscription. In supporting this holding, Justice Scalia, relied heavily on *Reynolds v. United States*,[100] in effect equating Oregon's drug prohibition with the federal anti-polygamy statute. He contended that –

> '[t]o make an individual's obligation to obey such a law contingent upon the law's coincidence with his religious beliefs except where the state's interest is compelling ... contradicts both constitutional tradition and common sense.'

The legislature, Justice Scalia maintained, is free to make accommodations for religious practices. Such accommodation, however, are not required, no matter how 'central' a particular practice might be to one's religious beliefs.

As Justice Sandra Day O'Connor's concurring opinion indicates, Justice Scalia's rejection of the compelling governmental interest test was the most controversial aspect of this decision. Although, she supported the Court's judgment, that the Free Exercise Clause had not been violated, Justice O'Connor sharply criticized the majority opinion as a dramatic departure –

> 'from well-settled First Amendment jurisprudence ... and ... [as] incompatible with our Nation's fundamental commitment to individual religious liberty.'

This part of Justice O'Connor's opinion was supported by Justices William J. Brennan Jr, Thurgood Marshall, and Harry Blackmun, who dissented from the Court's decision. 'The compelling interest test', Justice O'Connor asserted,

> 'effectuates the First Amendment's command that religious liberty is an independent liberty, that it occupies a preferred position, and that the Court will not permit encroachments upon this liberty, whether direct or indirect, unless required by clear and compelling governmental interests "of the highest order".'

In a separate dissenting opinion, Justice Harry Blackmun, joined by Justices Brennan and Marshall, charged the majority with 'mischaracterizing' court precedents and

> 'overturning ... settled law concerning the Religion Clauses of our Constitution.'

With evident sarcasm, Justice Blackmun expressed –

> the hope that the Court was 'aware of the consequences' and that the result was not a 'product of overreaction to the serious problems the country's drug crisis [had] generated.'

He pointed out that the Native American Church restricted and supervised the sacramental use of peyote. The state, thus, had no significant health or safety justification for regulating this form of drug use. Justice Blackmun also noted that Oregon had not attempted to prosecute Smith and Black or, for that matter, any other Native American for the sacramental use of peyote. He concluded that –

> 'Oregon's interest in enforcing is drug laws against religious use of peyote [was] not sufficiently compelling to outweigh respondents' right to the free exercise of their religion.'[101]

(iv) *Is the Denial of Funding a Violation of the Free Exercise Clause?*

The US Supreme Court has confronted one other important free exercise issue since *Employment Division v. Smith*:

— Whether the refusal to allow aid to be used for religious education impermissibly violates free exercise of religion.

Locke v. Davey[102] held, that a state government can restrict its college scholarships so as to prevent them from being used by those studying for the ministry. The Court emphasized, that while the government may constitutionally allow such use of its scholarships, it is not constitutionally required to do so.

Locke v. Davey arose from State of Washington's program of giving scholarships to students who qualify academically and financially and who attend college in the state. Students can attend any public or private college, including a religiously affiliated college, and may study whatever they choose. But, there is one limit:

— students must not be pursuing a degree that is 'devotional'; that is, the student cannot use the scholarship to study for training to become a minister.

State of Washington justified this restriction based on a provision in its state constitution which provides that –

> '[n}o public money or property shall be appropriated for or applied to any religious worship, exercise or instruction, or the support of any religious establishment'.

Joshua Davey, a recipient of a Promise Scholarship, chose to attend Northwest College, a private Christian college affiliated with the Assemblies of God (AG, USA)[103] denomination. Davey sought to become a minister and had a double major in pastoral ministries and business management/administration. Davey was informed that he could not receive the Promise Scholarship, if he pursued training to become a minister, he refused the aid and filed a lawsuit challenging the restriction. Davey argued that, State of Washington violated the free exercise clause of the First Amendment by allowing students to receive scholarship assistance, if they pursued secular but not religious studies.

In a 7 to 2 decision, with the majority opinion written by Chief Justice William Rehnquist (1924–2005), the US Supreme Court rejected that contention and ruled in favor of the State of Washington. At the outset, the Court emphasized that Washington could, if it wanted, allow its scholarships to be used by students studying to be clergy members.

In *Witters v. Washington Department of Services for the Blind*,[104] the Supreme Court unanimously ruled, that it did not violate the Establishment Clause of the First Amendment for the government to permit students receiving scholarship assistance to study for the ministry.

But, the court explained that denying Joshua Davey scholarship money to study to be a minister does not interfere with his free exercise of religion in any way. He still can receive training to be a pastor, just without it being subsidized by the government. The Court stressed, that many states historically have sought to limit use of their taxpayers' money to subsidize religious institutions.

A different ruling would have drastically altered the law, requiring the government to provide the same assistance to religious institutions whenever it provides assistance to private secular.

Ultimately, *Locke v. Davey* meant, that government at all levels can choose how it wants to spend taxpayers' money and the extent, if any, it wants to financially support religion. The Court recognized, that the case posed an issue where there is some tension between the Establishment Clause and the Free Exercise Clause, but it concluded that it is a choice to be made by the political process and not the courts.

(v) *The Religious Freedom Restoration Act*

Negative public reaction to the US Supreme Court's decision in *Employment Division v. Smith*, especially from the religious community, convinced a majority in Congress to pass the 1993 Religious Freedom Restoration Act (RFRA). The RFRA (Religious Freedom Restoration Act) prohibited government at all levels from substantially burdening a person's free exercise of religion, even if such burden resulted from a generally applicable rule, unless the government could demonstrate a compelling interest and that the rule constituted the least restrictive means of furthering that interest.

In passing the RFRA (Religious Freedom Restoration Act), Congress sought to restore the *status quo ante* – to return the law in this area to what it was prior to the *Smith* decision. In adopting this statute, Congress relied on its broad powers under Section 5 of the 14th Amendment.

In *City of Boerne v. Flores*,[105] the US Supreme Court, dividing 6 to 3, declared, that the RFRA(Religious Freedom Restoration Act) is unconstitutional. While conceding, that Congress has broad power to enforce the provisions of the 14th Amendment, Justice Anthony Kennedy (1936), writing for the majority, concluded that –

> 'RFRA contradicts vital principles necessary to maintain separation of powers and the federal balance.'

In this decision the Court stressed the primacy of it's role as interpreter of the American Constitution. It was firm and unequivocal in rejecting, on broad institutional grounds, a direct congressional challenge of final judicial authority on a question of constitutional interpretation.

In *Gonzales v. O Centro Espírita Beneficente União do Vegetal*[106], the US Supreme Court used the Religious Restoration Act (RFRA), to rule in favour of religion that wanted to use a controlled substance in its religious rituals, though the Court did not expressly consider whether RFRA is constitutional as applied to the federal government.

(v) *Is Animal Sacrifice 'Free Exercise of Religion'?*

In 1987, the city of Hialeah, a Miami suburb, passed an ordinance making it a crime to –

> 'unnecessarily kill, torment, torture, or mutilate an animal in a public or private ritual or ceremony not for the primary purpose of food consumption.'

The ordinance came in response to local concern over the sacrificial practices associated with Santeria, a blend of Roman Catholicism and West African religions brought to the Caribbean by East African slaves. Santeria, which literally means 'worship of the saints,' involves occasional sacrifices of live animals, usually goats or chickens. According to some estimates, there are as many as 70000 devotees of Santeria in Miami area, and perhaps, as many as one million nationwide. Ernesto Pichardo, a Santeria priest, challenged the Hialeah law as a violation of the 1st Amendment.

In *Church of the Lukumi Babalu Aye, Inc. v. City of Hialeah*,[107] the justices unanimously invalidated the Hialeah ordinance. Writing for the Supreme Court, Justice Anthony Kennedy (1936), observed that –

> 'the laws in question were enacted by officials who did not understand, failed to perceive, or chose to ignore the fact that their official actions violated the Nation's essential commitment to religious freedom.'

Justice Kennedy was careful to point out that the ordinance in question was not a generally applicable criminal prohibition, but rather singled out practitioners of Santeria in that it forbade animal slaughter only insofar as it took place within the context of religious rituals.

Freedom of Religion in India

Article 25 of the Indian Constitution

Article 25 of the 1949 Indian Constitution provides that –

Freedom of conscience and free profession, practice and propagation of religion

(1) 'Subject to public order, morality and health and to the other provisions of this part, all persons are equally entitled to freedom of conscience and the right to freely profess, practice and propagate religion.'
(2) Nothing in this article shall affect the operation of any existing law or prevent the State from making any law—

 (a) regulating or restricting any economic, financial, political or other secular activity which may be associated with religious practice,
 (b) providing for social welfare and reform or the throwing open of Hindu religious institutions of a public character to all classes and sections of Hindus.

Explanation I—. The wearing and carrying of *kirpans* shall be deemed to be included in the profession of the Sikh religion.

Explanation II—. In Sub-clause (b) of clause (2), the reference to Hindus shall be construed as including a reference to persons professing the Sikh, Jain or Buddhist religion, and the reference to Hindu religious institutions shall be construed accordingly.

Article 26 of the Indian Constitution

Article 26 of the Indian Constitution provides that -

Subject to public order, morality and health, every religious denomination or any section thereof shall have the right—

(a) to establish and maintain institutions for religious and charitable purposes;
(b) to manage it's own affairs in matter of religion;
(c) to own and acquire movable and immovable property; and
(d) to administer such property in accordance with law.

Articles 25 and 26 should be read together. The right guaranteed by Article 25 is an individual right as distinguished from the right of an organized body like the religious denomination or any section thereof dealt with by Article 26. Both these articles protect matters of religious doctrine or belief as well as acts done in pursuance of religion-rituals, observances, ceremonies and modes of worship. These articles embody the principles of religious tolerance.

India is a Secular State—The concept of 'secularism' is implicit in the Preamble to the Constitution of India, which declares -

> the resolve of the people to secure to all its citizens 'liberty of thought, belief, faith, and worship'.

The 42nd Amendment Act 1976, has inserted the word 'Secular' in the Preamble. This amendment is intended merely to spell out clearly the concept of 'secularism' in the constitution. There is no mysticism in the secular character of the state. In India, a secular state was never considered as an irreligious or atheistic state. It only means that in matters of religion it is neutral. It is the ancient doctrine in India, that the state protects all religions but interferes with none.[108] Explaining the secular character of the Indian Constitution the Supreme Court said,

> 'There is no mysticism in the secular character of the State. Secularism is neither anti-God nor pro-God, it treats alike the devout, the antagonistic and the atheist. It eliminates God from the matters of the State and ensures that no one shall be discriminated against on the ground of religion.'[109]

The state can have no religion of its own. It should treat all religions equally. The state must extend similar treatment to the church, the mosque and the temple. In a 'secular state', the state is only concerned with the relation between man and man. It is not concerned with the relation of man with God. It is left to the individual's conscience. Every man should be allowed to go to Heaven in his own way. Worshipping God should be according to the dictates of one's own conscience. Man is not answerable to the state for the variety of his religious views. The right of worship was granted by God for man to worship as he pleased. There can be no compulsion in law of any creed or practice of any form of worship.

In *S.R. Bommai v. Union of India*[110] the Supreme Court has held that –

> 'secularism is a basic feature of the constitution.'

The state treats equally all religions and religious denominations. Religion is a matter of individual faith and cannot be mixed with secular activities. Secular activities can be regulated by the state by enacting law. Justice Katikithala Ramaswamy (1932–2019) observed that 'secularism' is not anti-God. In the Indian context 'secularism' has a positive content. The Indian Constitution embodies the positive concept of 'secularism' and has not accepted the American doctrine of 'secularism' i.e., the concept of erecting 'a wall of separation between Religion and State.' The concept of 'positive secularism' separates spiritualism with individual faith. The state is neither anti-religion nor pro-religion. In the matter of religion, the state is neutral and treats every religion equally.

Sanskrit language not anti-secular

In a landmark judgment in *Santosh Kumar v. Secretary Ministry of Human Resources Development*,[111] the Supreme Court of India held, that introduction of Sanskrit language as a subject in the Central Board of Secondary Education (CBSE) is not against 'secularism' as it is the 'mother of all Indo-Aryan language.'

The Court directed the CBSE (Central Board of Secondary Education), to make necessary amendments in the syllabus within 3 months to make Sanskrit an elective subject for nurturing Indian cultural heritage. The Court rejected the government's contention that 'by conceding to Sanskrit alone as an elective subject it would act against secularism.' It also rejected the argument that if Sanskrit was introduced then Arabic and Persian would also have to be given similar status. The Court said, that

> without the learning of Sanskrit language, it is not possible to 'decipher' Indian philosophy, culture and heritage. All the classics of Hindu religion such as Vedas, Puranas and Upanishads are written in Sanskrit. The teachings of Shankaracharya, Ramanuja, Madhawacharya, etc., would not have been possible without this language. This is the historical relevance of the ancient language.

The Court said that –

> 'State tolerance of religion does not make it either a religious or a theoretical State'.

Secularism represents faith born out of the rational faculties and it enables to see the imperative requirements for human progress in all aspects. Secularism is neither anti-God nor pro-God, as it treats alike the devout, agnostic and the atheist.

What is Religion?—The term 'religion' is not defined in the Indian Constitution and indeed it is a term which is hardly susceptible to any rigid definition. The Indian Supreme Court has defined it broadly.

> 'Religion is a matter of faith with individuals or communities and it is not necessarily theistic. A religion has it's basis in "a system of beliefs or doctrines which are regarded by those who profess that religion as conducive to their spiritual wellbeing," "but it will not be correct to say that religion is nothing else but a doctrine of belief." A religion may only lay down a Code of ethical rules for its followers to accept, it might prescribe rituals and observances, ceremonies and modes of worship which are regarded as integral parts of religion, and those forms and observances might extend even to matters of food and dress.'[112]

Religion is thus, essentially a matter of personal faith and belief. Every person has the right not only to entertain such religious belief and ideas as may be approved by this judgment or conscience but also exhibit his belief and ideas by such overt acts which are sanctioned by his religion. Freedom of Conscience and Religion under the Indian Constitution.

Article 25 merely protects the freedom to practice rituals and ceremonies etc., which are only the integral part of the religion. A disposition towards making gift for charitable or religious purposes may be a pious act of a person but the same cannot be said to be an integral part of any religion.[113]

Freedom of Conscience and Religion under the Indian Constitution

Under Article 25 (1) a person has a two-fold freedom:—

(a) freedom of conscience;
(b) freedom to profess, practice and propagate religion.

The freedom of 'conscience' is absolute inner freedom of the citizen to mould his own relation with God in whatever manner he likes. When this freedom becomes articulate and expressed in outward form it is 'to profess and practice religion.' To 'profess' a religion means to declare freely and openly one's faith and belief. He has right to practice his belief by practical expression in any manner he likes. To 'practice' religion is to perform the prescribed religious duties, rites and rituals, and to exhibit his religious beliefs and ideas by such acts as prescribed by religious order in which he believes. To 'propagate' means to spread and publicize his religious view for the edification of others. But the word 'propagation' only indicates persuasion and exposition without any element of coercion. The right to propagate one's religion does not give a right to convert any person to one's own religion. There is no fundamental right to convert any person to one's own religion.

What Article 25(1) guarantees is not right to convert another person to one's own religion, but to transmit or spread one's religion by an exposition of its tenets. Article 25 guarantees 'freedom of conscience' to every citizen, and not merely to the followers of one particular religion. It, therefore, postulates, that there is no fundamental right to convert another person to one's own religion because if a person purposely undertakes the conversion of another person to his religion, as distinguished from his effort to transmit or spread the tenets of his religion that would impinge on the 'freedom of conscience', guaranteed to all the citizens of country alike.[114]

The protection of Articles 25 and 26 is thus not, limited to matters of doctrine of belief. It extends also to acts done in pursuance of 'religion' and, therefore, contain a guarantee for rituals and observances, ceremonies and modes of worship which are integral parts of religion. What constitutes an essential part of religions or religious practice has to be decided by the courts with reference to a doctrine of a particular religion and include practices which are regarded by the community as a part of its religion.[115]

In a judgment of far reaching importance in the *National Anthem* case,[116] the Supreme Court has held, that no person can be compelled to sing the National Anthem: '*Jana Gana Mana*',[117] 'if he has genuine, conscientious religious objection.' In the instant case, three children belonging to the 'Jehovah's witnesses' of the Christian community were expelled from the school for refusing to sing the national anthem. They challenged the validity of their expulsion on the ground that it was violative of their fundamental right under Article 25(1). A circular issued by the Director of Public Instructions had made it compulsory for all children in schools to sing the national anthem. They had stood up respectfully when the national anthem was being sung every morning at their school, but they did not join in the singing of it. They refused to sing the national anthem as according to them it was against the tenets of their religious faith, which did not permit them to join in any rituals except if it be in their prayer to Jehovah, their God.

The Kerala High Court held, that was their fundamental duty under the Constitution to sing the national anthem. It held that if the pupil belonging to the religious group refused to participate in the singing of the national anthem it would have a very bad influence on the other pupils and the headmistress, was therefore, within her right not to permit them to attend the class until they gave in writing that they will participate in the singing of the national anthem in the school. The conduct of the children is not showing unqualified respect to the national anthem, the High Court said, would endanger the security of the nation in that the same will develop among the citizens a tendency to ignore the mandates of the constitution, thereby, defeating the object (discernible from the Preamble and other provisions) to accomplish which the people gave the constitution themselves. If religious practices run counter to public order, morality, health or a policy of the government, to uphold the sovereignty, integrity, and unity, of the nation then, the said religious practices must be abandoned for the benefit of the people and the nation as a whole.

On appeal, however, the Indian Supreme Court reversed the High Court decision and held, that there is no legal obligation in India for a citizen to sing the national anthem. The right under Article 25(1), cannot be regulated by executive instructions which had no force of law. The court said, that by standing up while the national anthem was being sung the children had shown proper respect to the national anthem, and, had thus, not violated the fundamental duties laid down in Article 51-A of the Indian Constitution. Their conduct did not amount to an offence under the Prevention of Insults of National Honour Act 1971, as they did not prevent the singing of the national anthem nor caused disturbance to the assembly in the singing of the national anthem. Accordingly, the Supreme Court directed the authorities to re-admit the children in the school and to allow them to pursue their study. The Supreme Court judgment would have far-reaching consequences. In ruling so, the Supreme Court relied heavily on the decisions of the American Supreme Court.

In *Ramesh v. Union of India*,[118] the petitioner, a practicing advocate of High Court filed a public interest litigation under Article 32, for issue of a writ in the nature of prohibition restraining the respondents, namely, the Union of India, the Director-General of Doordarshan,[119] New Delhi, and the producer from telecasting or screening the serial titled '*Tamas*' and to enforce petitioner's fundamental right under Article 25 of the Indian Constitution. The serial '*Tamas*' is based on a novel written by Shri Bhisham Sahni (1915–2003).[120] It depicts how during partition of India communal violence was generated by fundamentalists in both the communities. It was held that although, in this case there was no violation of Article 25 but accepted, that the petitioner has a right to draw attention of the Court to ensure that the communal atmosphere is kept clean and unpolluted. In this case, the Court held, that there was no such danger as the respondents had not acted with malice or bad motive in screening the serial. Instead it gives lesson to the people that such things should not be repeated.

In *Dr M. Ismail Faruqui v. Union of India*,[121] the Indian Supreme Court by a majority has held, that the state can, in exercise of its sovereign power acquire places of worship like mosques, churches, temples etc., which is independent of Article 300-A of the Indian Constitution, if it is necessary for maintenance of law and order. Such acquisition *per se* does not violate Articles 25 and 26 of the Constitution. What is protected under Articles 25 and 26 is a religious practice which forms an essential and integral part of religion. A practice may be a religious practice but not an essential part of religious practice. While offer of prayer or worship is a religious practice, it's offering at every location where such prayers can be offered would not be an essential religious practice. Status of mosque in secular India is same as and not higher than that of places of worship of other religion such as temple, church etc. A mosque is not an essential part of the practice of the religion of Islam and *Namaz* (prayer) by Muslims may be offered anywhere, even in open. The right to worship, does not include the right of worship at any and every place, so long as it can be practiced effectively, unless the right to worship at a particular place is itself an integral part of that right.

Under the Muslim law applicable to India, title of a mosque may be lost by adverse possession. The matter in this case was referred to the Supreme Court for its advisory opinion by the President Shankar Dayal Sharma (1918–99)[122] on 6 December 1992, because due to the demolition of Babari Mosque at Ayodhya, law and order in the country was disturbed. In order to defuse the crises, the Central Government acquired the whole property surrounding the mosque under The Acquisition of Certain Area at Ayodhya Act 1993 ('Act No. 33 of 1993'). This was challenged by the petitioners on the ground that it was violative of Articles 25 and 26 of the Constitution; as they were deprived of their right to worship in the mosque, but Hindus were allowed to worship. Therein, the Court held, the Act valid as it does not interfere with the essential element of religion. While the right to worship is an essential part of a religion, but, it does not include the right to worship at any place and every place.

The demolition of Babri Masjid in December 1992 was challenged before the Allahabad High Court which announced the verdict on 30 September 2010. The 3 judge bench of Allahabad High Court held that 2.77 acres of Ayodhya land (over which the mosque stood) be divided into three parts, with 1/3rd going to Ram Lilla of Birpant Rama represented by the Hindu Mahasbha, 1/3rd going to Uttar Paradesh Sunni Central Waqf Board, and the remaining going to Nirmohi Akhara. The judgment affirmed that the disputed land was birthplace of Rama as per the faith and belief of Hindus and that the Babri Masjid was built after the demolition of a Hindu temple.[123] The appeal against the verdict of Allahabad High Court was heard by 5-member bench of the Supreme Court which announced its unanimous verdict on 9 November 2019 overruling the verdict of the High Court.[124] It was held: -

- the Government of India was ordered to create a trust to build the Ram Mandar temple and form a Board of Trustees within three months. The ownership of the land would vest in Government of India which would be transferred to the Trust after its formation.
- the entire disputed land measuring 2.77 acres would be allocated for construction of a temple while an alternative piece of land measuring 5 acres would be allocated to Uttar Pradesh Sunni Central Waqf Board for the construction of a mosque at a suitable place within Ayodhya.
- it was ruled that the demolition of the Babri Masjid and the 1949 desecration of the Babri Masjid was in violation of law.
- it was observed that the Muslim parties including Uttar Pradesh Sunni Central Waqf Board, failed to establish exclusive possession of disputed land while the Hindu parties furnished better evidence to prove that Hindus had worshipped continuously inside the mosque, believing it to be the birth-place of the Hindu deity Rama.

The Supreme Court in this judgment has travelled far beyond its secular stance that it had consistently maintained since its judgments based on the theory of basic structure of Constitution in 1970s onwards. It appears to have been influenced and overawed by the environment created by the BJP (Bharati Janata Party) government of Narendra Modi since 2014. The religio-political tendencies towards the philosophy of Hindutva appear to have bearing on the minds and thoughts of the Judges.

In *Gulam Kadar Ahmadbhai Memon v. Surat Municipal Corporation*,[125] the Gujarat High Court has held, that the right to religion guaranteed to citizens under Articles 25 and 26 of the Constitution does not prohibit the state to acquire any place of worship for public purpose. In this case the petitioners had challenged the validity of Section 212 of the Bombay Provincial Municipal Corporation Act 1949. Under the Act, the Municipal Corporation had ordered the demolition of some parts of the two mosques situated in main road of Surat district in the State of Gujarat. The Court held, that the acquisition of a religious place or a part thereof is not prohibited by the constitution, and therefore, can be acquired in the public interest for widening the road. Accordingly, it was held that the order for the demolition of certain portions of the two mosques for widening the road was valid.

In *Moulana Mufti Syed Mohd. Noorur Rehman Barkariq v. State of West Bengal*,[126] the Calcutta High Court has held, that the restrictions imposed by the state on the use of microphones and loudspeakers at the time of *Azan* is not violative of right under Article 25 of the Indian Constitution. *Azan* is certainly an essential and integral part of Islam but use of microphone and loudspeakers are not an essential and integral part. Microphones are a technological gift, but their negative impact can be felt all over the world. It is not only a source of pollution, but also one that poses a number of health risk. Traditionally and according to the religious order, *Azan* has to be given by the *Imam* or the person in charge of the mosques in their own voices.

In *A.S. Narayan Deekshitulu v. State of Andhra Pradesh*,[127] it has been held that the word 'religion' used in Articles 25 and 26 of the Indian Constitution is personal to the person having faith and belief in the religion. Religion is that which binds a man with cosmos, his Creator or super power. The petitioner, the Chief Priest (*archaka*) Shri A.S. Narayan Deekshitulu, in the ancient and renowned Hindu Temple at Thirumala Thirupati and known in North India as Balaji Temple, had challenged the validity of the Andhra Pradesh Charitable and Hindu Religious and Endowments Act 1987; abolishing hereditary rights of *archaka* (Chief Priest), and other office holders, prescribing regulations for appointment of *archakas* (Chief Priest) and taking away their right to a share of offerings made to the deity, it infringed his right to freedom of religion under Articles 25 and 26 of the Constitution of India. It was contended that abolition of hereditary rights created by the founders in rendering services to the temple by *archaka* (Chief Priest) etc., in charitable and religion institutions and endowments interfered with religious practices and customs which were essential part of religion. The Supreme Court of India held, that the Act is not violative of Articles 25 and 26 of the Constitution and is valid. The hereditary right to appointment of priests is not an essential of religion or matter of religion or religious practice. The right to religion guaranteed under Articles 25 and 26 is not an absolute or unfettered right but subject to regulation by the state of any activity – economic, financial, or secular. The appointment of *archaka* (Chief Priest), is a secular activity which could be regulated by law. The Act regulates only secular part of the religious institutions or endowments. The Act does not interfere with the performance of any religion's worship or ceremony.

In *Lily Thomas v. Union of India*,[128] a question arose as to whether the second marriage of a Hindu husband after conversion to Islam, without having his first marriage dissolved under law, would be invalid in view of Section 494 of Indian Penal Code (I.P.C)[129]. The second question would be, if he was punishable under Section 494 I.P.C. The Court held that under the Hindu Marriage Act 1955, any marriage with a person whose previous marriage was subsisting on the date of marriage would be *void ab initio* and was punishable for bigamy under Sections 494 and 495 I.P.C. Any marriage does not automatically dissolve due to conversion or apostasy if it is solemnized under the Act. Only on a petition under Section 18 of Hindu Marriage Act 1955, presented by either husband or the wife, a marriage can be dissolved by a decree of divorce on the ground, that he or she has ceased to be Hindu by conversion to another religion

Restrictions on freedom of religion

(1) *Religious liberty subject to public order, morality and health*

The right under Clause (a) of Article 26 is a group right and is available to every religious denomination or any section thereof, be it of majority or any section thereof. It is evident from the opening words of Article 26 that this right is subject to public order, morality and health.[130]

In the name of religion, no act can be done against public order, morality and health of the public. Thus, Section 34 of the Police Act 1861, prohibits the slaughter of cattle or indecent exposure one's person in a public place. These acts cannot be justified on plea of practice of religious rites. Likewise, in the name of religion 'untouchability or traffic in human beings' e.g. system of *devadasis* (as prevalent in South India) cannot be tolerated. This freedom is also subject to the 'other provisions of this Part', e.g. right to freedom of speech and expression, freedom of assembly and association, freedom to carry on a profession, trade and business. The freedom to practice religion cannot affect the exercise of these freedoms by others. These rights are subject to the reasonable restrictions under Clause (2) of Article 19.

The Right to propagate one's religion does not give right to anyone to 'forcibly' convert any person to one's own religion. Forcible conversion of any person to one's own religion might disturb the public order hence could be prohibited by law. In *Rev. Stainislaus v. State of Madhya Pradesh*,[131] the validity of the two Acts–the Madhya Pradesh Dharma Swatantrya Adhiniyam 1968, and the Orissa Freedom of Religion Act, 1967– passed by State Legislatures of Madhya Pradesh and Orissa, respectively was challenged on the ground that they were violative of the fundamental right of the appellant guaranteed under Article 25 (1) of the Constitution of India. These Acts were passed to prohibit forcible conversion of any person to one's own religion. The appellant was prosecuted for the commission of offences under the Madhya Pradesh Act. He contended that right to 'propagate' one's religion meant the right to convert person to one's own religion and was a fundamental right under Article 25(1) of the Indian Constitution. Thus, if an attempt is made to raise communal passions, e.g., on the ground that someone has been 'forcibly' converted to another religion, it would, in all probability, give rise to an apprehension of a breach of the public order, affecting the community at large. Therefore, legislation prohibiting forcible conversion of one's own religion in the interest of public order could be passed and would be valid.

In *Gulam Abbas v. State of Uttar Pradesh*,[132] it has been held that the direction given by the Supreme Court of India, for shifting a property connected with religion to avoid clashes between two religious communities or sects does not affect religious rights being in the interest of public order. In that case the facts were that there had been a long-standing dispute between the Shias and Sunnis of Mohalla Doshipura, Varanasi; regarding the performance of religious rites by members of Shia sect on certain plots and properties situated in the Mohalla. There had been violent clashes between the two religious communities leading to proceeding and several petitions before the Indian Supreme Court. To find a permanent solution to the problem the Supreme Court appointed a committee of 7 persons consisting of 3 nominees of Shias, and 3 nominees of Sunnis, and the Divisional Commissioner as Chairman. The committee recommended, that the shifting of two graves of Sunnies, so as to separate the places of worship of Shias and Sunnis was feasible. The Sunnis challenged the implementation of the recommendation on the ground, that it was violative of their rights under Articles 25 and 26 of the Constitution of India. The

Supreme Court, however, rejected their contentions and held, that the order of the court for implementing the Committee's recommendations was not violative of the rights of the petitioners under Articles 25 and 26. The exercise of fundamental rights under Articles 25 and 26 is not absolute but subject to the maintenance of public order and the impugned suggestion for the shifting of graves was in the larger interest of the society, for the purpose of maintaining public order on the occasion of the performance of religious ceremonies and functions by members of both sects. If the Court finds, that the implementation is in the interest of maintenance of public order the consent of parties would be immaterial.

In *Acharya Jagdishwaranand Avadhuta v. Commissioner of Police, Calcutta,*[133] (popularly known as *Ananda Marga* case) the Supreme Court held, that the '*Tandava*'[134] dance in procession or at public places by *Ananda Marga,*[135] carrying lethal weapons and human skulls was not an essential religious rite of the followers of *Ananda Marga*, and hence, the order under Section 144, Cr.P.C. prohibiting such procession in the interest of public 'order' and 'morality' was not violative of the rights of petitioners under Articles 25 and 26 of the Constitution. *Ananda Marga* is not a separate religion, but basically subscribe to the fundamental notions of Hindu religion and philosophy. But, it is certainly a religious denomination within the meaning of Article 26. *Ananda Marga* as a religious order is of recent origin and *Tandava* dance as a part of religious rites of that order is still more recent. Even accepting that *Tandava* dance is prescribed as a religious ceremony for every follower of *Ananda Marga*, it does not necessary imply, that they have the right to perform it in public places. The order under Section 144 did not ban procession or gatherings at public places even by *Ananda Marga*. It only prohibits carrying of daggers, *trishuls* and skulls which poses danger to public order and is also against morality.

(2) *Regulation of economic, financial, political, and secular activities associated with religious practices – Clause (2)(a)*

The freedom to practice extends only to those activities which are the essence of religion. It does not cover secular activities which do not form the essence of religion. It is not always easy to say which activities fall under religious practice, or which are of secular, commercial, or political nature associated with religious practice. Each case must be judged by its own facts and circumstances.

In *Mohd. Hanif Quareshi v. State of Bihar,*[136] the petitioner claimed, that the sacrifice of cows on the occasion of *Bakra eid*[137] was an essential part of his religion, and therefore, the state law forbidding cows slaughter of was violative of his right to practice religion. The court rejected this argument and held, that the sacrifice of cow on the *Bakra eid* day was not an essential part of Muslim religion, and hence, could be prohibited by state under Clause (2)(a) of Article 25.

In *Adelaide Co of Jehovah's Witnesses Inc. v. Commonwealth,*[138] it was held, that a person could not be allowed in exercise of his freedom of religious practice and profession to carry on an anti-war propaganda in the guise of religion when the nation is at war. Thus, the political activities though arising out of religious belief by a particular organization were held not to be protected by the Constitution.

In *State of West Bengal v. Ashutosh Lahiri,*[139] the respondents challenged the validity of exemption of cow slaughter of from the operation of the West Bengal Animal Slaughter Control Act 1950, on *Bakra eid* day. The petitioners contended before the High Court that the State of West Bengal had wrongly invoked Section 12 of the Act, when it exempted from the operation of the Act, the slaughter of healthy cows on the occasion of *Bakra eid* on the ground that such exemption was required to be given for the religious purpose Muslim Community. Following its decision in the case of *Mohd. Hanif Quareshi v. State of Bihar*, the High Court held, that the slaughter of cows by members of Muslim Community on *Bakra eid* day was not an essential requirement of Muslim religion and therefore, such exemption was invalid. The respondents, the State of West Bengal and the Muslim Community filed an appeal in the Supreme Court against the judgment of the High Court. The Supreme Court approved the decision of the High Court and dismissed the appeal. The Court held, that before exercising the power of exemption under Section 12, it must be shown that such exemption is necessary to be granted for sub serving an essential, religious, medicinal or research purpose. If granting of such exemption is not essential or necessary for effectuating such a purpose no such exemption can be granted, so as to bypass the thrust of the main provisions of the Act. For such an exercise non-essential religious practices cannot be made basis. The slaughtering of cows on the *Bakra eid* day is optional and not obligatory. It is not essential or required for religious purpose of Muslim. Article 25 exempts only the essential religious practices from state regulation.

In *S.P. Mittal v. Union of India*,[140] the petitioners challenged the validity of the Auroville (Emergency Provisions) Act 1980, on the ground that it was violative of their rights to freedom of religion under Articles 25 and 26 of the Indian Constitution. Sri Aurobindo (1872–1950)[141] originated the philosophy of cosmic salvation through spiritual evolution and propagated the theme of integral yoga. He and his disciples formed the Aurobindo Society, which was registered under the West Bengal Societies Registration Act 1961. The Society preaches and propagates the ideas and teachings of Sri Aurobindo and 'the Mother' (1878–1973),[142] through its numerous centers in India and abroad. After his death 'the Mother' proposed a project of setting up an international cultural township at Auroville in Pondicherry. The Society received large funds as grants from the Central and State Governments, and different organizations in India and abroad for development of the township. But, after the death of 'the Mother', the Government received complaints about the mismanagement of the affairs of the Society, and accordingly enacted the Auroville (Emergency Provisions) Act 1980, providing for taking over the management of Auroville for a limited period.

The Supreme Court by a majority of 4 to 1 held, that the Memorandum of Association of Society and repeated uttering of Sri Aurobindo and 'the Mother'; that the Society and Auroville were not religious institutions and other documents make it clear that neither the Society nor Auroville constituted a –

> 'religious denomination and that teachings of Sri Aurobindo did not constitute a 'religion'

and therefore, taking over the Aurobindo Ashram by the Government did not infringe the petitioner's (Society) right under Articles 25 and 26 of the Indian Constitution. The teachings of Sri Aurobindo only represented his philosophy and not a religion.

(3) *Social Welfare and Social Reforms – Clause (2)(b)*

Under Clause (2)(b) of Article 25, the state is empowered to make laws for social welfare and social reform. Thus, under this clause the state can eradicate social practices and dogmas which stand in the path of the country's onwards progress. Such laws do not affect the essence of any religion. This clause declares, that where there is conflict between the need of social welfare and reform and religious practice, religion must yield. Social evils cannot be practised in the name of the religion.

In *State of Bombay v. Varasu Bapamali*,[143] an Act which prohibited bigamy was held valid under Clause (2)(b), saying that polygamy is not an essential part of the Hindu religion, therefore, it can be regulated by law. Prohibition of civil practices such as *sati* or system of *devadasi* has been held to be justified under this clause.[144]

Under this Sub-clause, the state is empowered to throw open all Hindu religious institutions of a public character, to all classes and sections of Hindus. It ensures an individual's legal right to enter into a temple unobstructed irrespective of his caste, untouchability, social inequality or under-privileged class. The Hindu Temples, the Sikh Gurdwara, the Jain Temples and Budh Vihars can be thrown open to all sections of Hindus. The expression, 'Hindu' includes Jain, Sikh and Buddhists. The right protected under this clause is a right to enter into a temple for the purpose of worship. But it does not follow from this that, that right is absolute and unlimited in character. No one can claim that a temple must be kept open for worship at all hours of the day and night or that he should be permitted to perform those services personally which the *Acharya* (religious teacher) alone could perform.[145] The state cannot regulate the manner in which the worship of the deity is performed by the authorized *pujaris* of the temple or the hours and days on which the temple is to be kept open for *darshan* or *puja* for devotees.[146]

(a) *Freedom to manage religious affairs – (Article 26)*

The right guaranteed by Article 25 is an individual right, while right guaranteed by Article 26 is the right of an 'organized body' like the religious denomination or any section thereof. In Webster's Dictionary, the word 'denomination' has been defined as a 'collection of individuals, classed together under the same name' generally a religious sect or body having a common faith and organization and designated by a distinctive value. The words 'religious denomination' in Article 26 must take their colour from the word 'religion' and therefore, it must also satisfy three conditions:

(1) It must be a collection of individuals who have a system of beliefs which they regard as conducive to their spiritual wellbeing, that is, a common faith;
(2) It must have a common organization and
(3) It must be designated by a distinctive name.[147]

Thus, in the larger sense, 'Hinduism' is a denomination in contradistinction to Christianity and Islam. In limited 'sense' the various philosophies governing the Hindu society, such as, *Advaita Vedanta*, *Dvaita Vedanta*, *Vishishtadwaitas* and *Saivites* can also be termed as denomination.[148] Likewise, it has been held that '*Ananda Marga*' is a religious denomination with the Hindu religion.[149]

In *Bramchari Sidheswar Bhai v. State of West Bengal*,[150] popularly known as the *Ramkrishna Mission* case, the Supreme Court has held that the followers of Ramkrishna, who are collection of individuals, and who adhere to a system of beliefs as conducive to their spiritual wellbeing, who have organized themselves collectively and who have an organization with definite name as *Ramkrishna Math* or Mission can be regarded as a religious denomination within Hindu religion as they satisfy the tests regarding a denomination as 'religious denomination', and would 'therefore' be entitled to claim the fundamental rights conferred on them under Article 26 of the Indian Constitution.

Right to establish and maintain – Institutions for religious and charitable purpose—Under Clause (a) of Article 26 every religious denomination has right to establish and maintain institutions for religious and charitable purposes. The words 'establish and maintain' in Article 26(a) must be read together and therefore, it is only those institutions which a religious denomination establishes which it can claim to maintain it. Thus, in *S. Azeez Basha v. Union of India*,[151] the Supreme Court held, that the Aligarh University was established in 1920 by the Aligarh Muslim University Act, No. XL of 1920 (referred to as the 1920-Act); it was not established by the Muslim minority and therefore, it could not claim the right to 'maintain' it. It was established that the Parliament had the right to amend that statute as it thought fit in the interest of education and the amendments made by the Acts of 1951 and 1965 were perfectly valid.

Right to manage 'matters of Religion'—Under Article 26(b) a religious denominations or organization is free to manage its own affairs in 'matters of religion.' The state cannot interfere in the exercise of this unless they run counter to public order, health or morality. Accordingly, every religious denomination or organization enjoys complete freedom in the matters of deciding what rites and ceremonies are essential according to the tenets of the religion they hold. The court has the right to determine whether a particular rite or ceremony is regarded as essential by the tenets of a particular religion.[152]

The right is, it is to be noted, confined to 'matters of religion'. The term 'matters of religion' include religious practices, rites and ceremonies considered essential for practice of religion. The right is, however, subject to the regulatory power of the state under Clause (2)(b) of Article 25. This means that secular activities connected with religious institution can be regulated by the states through law. The places of worship like temples, mosques, *gurudwaras* cannot be used for hiding criminals or carrying on anti-national activities. They cannot be used for political purpose. The state has power under Article 25(1) and Clause (2) to prohibit these activities in the places of worship. The state cannot be a passive spectator when, exercise of right of religion threatens the public order, morality and health of the community. It must play a positive role and ensure maintenance of public order, health and morality in the society. The constitution requires not only that the state will be away from religion but, also imposes a positive duty on the state to free many aspects of our life from the control of religion. The provisions of the constitution are very clear in this respect. This state is not expected to remain a mere passive spectator when the freedom of religion is being used against the interest of society and the nation as a whole.[153]

In *Sardar Syedna Taher Saifuddin Saheb v. State of Bombay*,[154] the petitioner, who was the head of the Dawoodi Bohra community, challenged the constitutionality of the Bombay Prevention of Ex-Communication Act 1949, on the ground that the provisions of the Act infringed his rights guaranteed in Articles 25 and 26. The petitioner claimed that as the head of the Dawoodi Bohra community he had the right to ex-communicate a member and this power was an integral part of the religious faith and belief of the Dawoodi Bohra Community. The Supreme Court struck down the impugned provision as violative of Article 25 and 26 of the Constitution of India. The majority said, that where an ex-communication was itself based on religious grounds such as lapse from the orthodox religious creeds or doctrine or breach of some practices considered as an essential part of religion by a community it formed part of the management of the community, through its religion's head, 'of its own affairs in matters of religion.' The impugned enactment which took away this right of the head of the community to ex-communicate even on religious grounds was violative of Article 26 (b). The position of the *Dai-ul-Mutlaq* is an essential part of the creed of the Dawoodi Bohra sect. Faith in his spiritual mission and in the efficacy of his administration is one of the bonds that hold the community together as a unit. The power of ex-communication is vested in him for the purpose of enforcing discipline and kept the denomination together as an entity. The purity of fellowship is secured by the removal of persons who has rendered themselves unfit and unsuitable for membership of the sect. The majority observed:

> 'The mere fact that certain civil rights which might be lost by members as a result of ex-communication made on religious grounds which the Act protects, does not offer sufficient basis for a conclusion that it is a law 'providing for social welfare and reform' within Article 25(b).'

Chief Justice Bhuvaneshwar Prasad Sinha (1899–1986), however, gave a dissenting judgment. He was of the view, that the right of ex-communication was not a purely religions matter and that it had its social implications in making the ex-communicated person a sort of 'untouchable' in his community, which would be contrary to the injunctions mentioned in Article 17 of the Constitution of India, by which 'untouchability' has been abolished. The decision has been criticized by jurists.[155]

In *Raja Birakishore Dev v. State of Orissa*,[156] the Shri Jagannath Temple Act 1954, took the management of secular activities of temple from the Raja of Puri,[157] and vested it in committee constituted under the Act. The Court held the Act 'valid' as it did not affect the religious aspect.

In *Atheist Society of India v. Government of Andhra Pradesh*,[158] the petitioner, Atheist Society of India, prayed for issuing a writ of *mandamus* directing the Government of Andhra Pradesh to prohibit breaking of coconuts, performing of *poojas*, chanting of *mantras* or *sutras* of different religions at state functions. The Andhra Pradesh High Court rejected their prayer and held, that these activities have been a part of the Indian tradition and are meant to invoke the blessings of Almighty for the success of the project undertaken. Such noble thought cannot be found fault with as offensive to anyone except may be, that the petitioners society who claim to be atheist or do not appreciate the invocation of gods as they do not belief in God. There is no constitutional guarantee to the faith of the athiest who worship barren reason that there is no God. It is not the object of the Constitution of India to turn the country into an irreligious place. A secular state does not prohibit the practices of religion. If, that is prevented it will infringe the rights of crores of Indians, which are granted to them under Article 25 and will run directly contrary to the secular objectives of the Preamble to the Constitution which is one of the basic structures. It would deprive them of their right of thought, expression, belief, faith and would amount to abolition of Indian tradition and religious practices.

Right to administer property owned by denomination—Under Clauses (c) and (d) of Article 26, a religious denomination has the right to acquire and own property and to administer such property in accordance with law. The right to administer property owned by a religious denomination is a limited right, and it is subject to the regulatory power of the state in Clause (2)(a) of Article 25 and also any general property law. Thus, there is a clear distinction between the right to manage its own affairs in 'matters of religion' and the right to 'manage its property' by a religious denomination. The right of a religious denomination to manage its property has thus been placed on a different footing from the right to manage its own affairs in matters of religion. The former is a fundamental right which cannot be taken away except on grounds mentioned in Article 25, while the latter can be regulated by law, that is, it can be abridged or taken away by a valid law.[159]

It is to be noted that the rights under Clauses (c) and (d) of Article 26, are confined to the existing rights to administer it's property where they had already been vested in a religious denomination. Clauses (c) and (d) do not create any new rights, but, they simply protect the continuance of the existing rights. The existing rights to administer it's property by a religious denomination cannot be destroyed or taken away completely. It can only be regulated by law with a view to improve the administration of property for the better utilization of the endowment property. Thus, the law must leave the right of administration of property to the religious denomination itself subject to such restrictions and regulations as it might choose to impose.

In *Ratilal Panachand Gandhi v. State of Bombay*,[160] a law which took away the right of administration altogether from religious denomination and vested it in other secular authority was held to be violative of the right guaranteed by Article 26 (d). However, if the right to administer property had never vested in the denomination or had validly surrendered by it or had otherwise been lost, Article 26 will not create any such right in religious denomination.[161]

Freedom from Taxes for Promotion of Any Particular Religion. – Article 27

Article 27 in the Constitution of India provides, that no person shall be compelled to pay any tax for the promotion or maintenance of any particular religion or religious denomination. This Article emphasizes the secular character of the state. The public money collected by way of tax cannot be spent by the state for the promotion of any particular religion.

The reason underlying this provision is, that India being a secular state and there being freedom of religion guaranteed by the Constitution, both to individual and groups, is against the policy of the Constitution to pay out of public funds any money for the promotion or maintenance of the particular religion of religious denomination.[162] It is to be noted here that what this Article prohibits is the levying of tax and not of fee.

In *Ratilal Panachand Gandhi v. State of Bombay*,[163] the Supreme Court held, that a tax is in the nature of a compulsory exaction of money by a public authority for public purposes. The imposition is made for public purpose to meet the general expenses of the state without reference to any special advantage to be conferred upon the tax payer. Tax is a common burden and the only return which the tax payer gets is a participation in the common benefits of the state. Fees are, on the other hand, payments primarily in public interest but for some special service rendered or some special work done for the benefit of those from whom the payments are demanded. In determining whether a levy is a fee, the true test must be whether it's primary and essential purpose is to render specific services to a specified area or class; it may not be consequence that the state may ultimately and indirectly be benefited by it. The traditional view that there must be actual *quid pro quo* for a fee has undergone a great change. The element of *quid pro quo* in the strict sense is not always a *sine qua non* for a fee. The co-relationship between the levy and the services rendered or expected is one of general character and not of mathematical exactitude. All that is necessary is that there should be 'reasonable relationship' between the levy of the fee and the services rendered.[164]

On the basis of distinction between tax and fee, the Indian Supreme Court in *Mahant Sri Jagannath Ramanuj Das v. State of Orissa*,[165] held that the levy under the Orissa Hindu Religious Endowments Act 1939, was in the nature of a fee and not tax. The payment was demanded only for the purpose of meeting the expenses of the Commissioner of Hindu Religious Endowments and his office, which was the machinery set up for due administration of the affairs of the religious institutions. The object of the contribution was not the fostering or preservation of Hindu religion or of the denomination within it, but to see that religious institutions were property administered.

The prohibition is against giving aid to any particular religion. This means that if state aid is extended to all religious institutions along with secular ones alike without any discrimination, Article 27 will not be applicable.

Prohibition of Religious Instruction in State-aided Institution. – Article 28

According to Article 28(1) in the Constitution of India 1949,

(1) no religious instruction should be imparted in any educational institution wholly maintained out of State funds.

(2) Nothing in Clause (1) shall not apply to an educational institution which is administered by the State but has been established under any endowment or trust which requires that religious instruction shall be imparted in such institution.

(3) No person attending any educational institution recognized by the State or receiving aid out of State funds shall be required to take part in any religious instruction that may be imparted in such institution or to attend any religious worship that may be conducted in such institution or to any premises attached thereto unless such person or, if such person is a minor, his guardian has given his consent thereto.

Thus, Article 28 mentions four types of educational institutions:

(a) Institutions wholly maintained by the state.
(b) Institutions recognized by the state.
(c) Institutions that are receiving aid out of the state fund.
(d) Institutions that are administered by the state but are established under any trust or endowment.

In the institutions of (a) type no religious instructions can be imparted. In (b) and (c) type institutions religious instructions may be imparted only with the consent of the individuals. In the (d) type institutions, there is no restriction on religious instructions.[166]

Freedom of Religion in Pakistan

Article 20 of the 1973 Pakistan Constitution, provides that –
Subject to law, public order and morality,—

(a) every citizen shall have the right to profess, practice and propagate his religion; and
(b) every religious denomination and every sect thereof shall have the right to establish, maintain and manage its religious institutions.

Subject to public order and morality

If a religion is immoral as, for instance, where it allows indecent exposure of human body, or it's practice leads to public disorder, the legislature may step into regulate it's profession, practice and propagation. So long as religious beliefs are held, professed and practiced in private, no question of public disorder can arise, but, when they are practiced and propagated in public, by speeches, processions and placards, and are accompanied by denunciation of other religions, they are bound to clash with the rights of others, and thus lead to breaches of the peace. It is for consideration like these that the practice and propagation of religion is made subject to law.

In *Ch. Abdul Ghani v. The Islamic Republic of Pakistan*,[167] it was held, that if in the performance of a religious ritual, some secular steps are to be taken, as, for instance, procuring foreign exchange for a pilgrimage, the law may make provisions in regard to such matter. While the right to freely practice religion subject to the limitations of public order, health and morality is guaranteed, there is no such protection to activities which are economic, commercial or political in their character, though they are associated with religious practice.

It may not always clear whether a particular matter is essential religious practice or merely a secular, commercial or political activity that has become associated with religion. A few cases from the American and Australian Constitutions may be cited to illustrate the difficulty.

In *Adelaide Co of Jehovah's Witnesses Inc v. Commonwealth*,[168] a religious organization of 'Jehovah's Witnesses' which, among other things, was opposed to all wars, in 1941 started proclaiming and teaching matters, which were prejudicial to war activities and the defence of the Commonwealth. Steps were taken against them under the National Security (Subversive Organisations) Regulations 1940. The legality of government action was raised by means of a writ petition before the High Court of Australia. The High Court sustained the action of the Australian Government and held, that the religious freedom was not in any way infringed by the National Security (Subversive

Organisations) Regulations 1940. This is an instance where political activities, though arising out of religious belief entertained by a particular community, were considered not to be protected by the Constitution.

In *Mrs Arshad Ali Khan v. Govt. of the Punjab*,[169] it was held that the phrase 'public order' is synonymous with public peace, safety, and tranquility and is of local significance as distinguished from national upheavals, 'law and order' and 'security of state'. Law and order represents the largest circle within which is the next circle representing public order and the smallest circle represents security of the state. Hence, an activity which affects law and order may not necessarily affect public order and an activity, which may be prejudicial to public order may not necessarily affect security of the state.

An act prejudicial to public order must affect the public at large. An act which concerns only an individual and does not amount to an activity prejudicial to the public peace and tranquility cannot fall within the ambit of Article 10(4) and (7) of the 1973 Constitution.

SUBJECT TO LAW

The fundamental right in the Pakistan Constitution has been subjected to law. But it does not mean that it can be taken away by law. It was held in *Jibendra Kishore v. The Province of East Pakistan*,[170] that the very conception of a fundamental right is, that it being a right guaranteed by the Pakistan Constitution cannot be taken away by the law. Therefore, in accordance with the principle that a Constitution should receive liberal interpretation in favour of citizen especially with respect to those provisions which were designed to safeguard the freedom of conscience and worship, the words 'subject to law' cannot mean that the right to profess, practice and propagate religion may completely be taken away by the law, they should be interpreted as merely permitting the making of laws by which the manner in which religion is to be professed, practised and propagated and the establishment, management and maintenance of religious institutions, e.g., *waqf alal-aulad*, may be regulated. This view was expressed by Justice Shafiur Rahman (1929–2021)[171], in *Zaheeruddin v. The State*.[172]

In *Zaheer-ur-Din's* case, validity of Sections 298B and 298C of Pakistan Penal Code (PPC) was challenged in the light of Clause (3) of Article 260 of the Pakistan Constitution which defines 'Muslim' and 'Non-Muslim'. The two definitions read together clearly oust persons of Qadiani group or Lahori group (who call themselves 'Ahmadis') from the pale of Islam. The majority of the bench hearing the case upheld the constitutionality of Sections 298B and 298C of PPC (Pakistan Penal Code). The matters before the Supreme Court of Pakistan, were appeals arising out of convictions and sentences recorded in cases registered under Section 298C, the charge being that the appellants were found wearing badges of *'Kalma Tayyaba'* and claiming themselves to be 'Muslims' contrary to that section. Justice Abdul Qadeer Chaudhry (1929),[173] writing for the majority of 4 to 1, held that–

> although religious practices are protected by the term 'freedom of religion', yet only such practices are covered which are integral and essential part of the religion. It is for the courts to determine whether a particular practice constitutes essential and integral part of the religion or not.

The appellants, according to the majority, had failed to explain that the epithets *'Masjid'*, *'Azan'* etc., and various ceremonies which they intended to hold were essential part of their religion. It was held that 'freedom of religion' did not allow interference with the law and order, or public peace and tranquility and the state would be justified not to permit anyone to violate or take away the fundamental rights of others in the enjoyment of his own. No one can be allowed to insult, damage or defy the religion of any other class or outrage their religious feelings so as to give rise to law and order situation. The use of such epithets would be deliberate and calculated act of defiling their holy personages, a threat to the integrity of *Umma* and tranquility of the nation giving rise to a serious law and order situation.

Justice Shafiur Rahman, the lone dissenter, observed that naming of place of worship by the *'Qadianis'* and *'Ahmadis'* as *'Masjid'* and calling *'Azan'* were historically shown to be their tenets or practice not of recent origin and were not adopted with a view to annoy, outrage the feelings and sentiments of Muslims. Being an essential element of their faith and not being offensive *per se*, prohibition on their use and making them offences punishable with imprisonment or fine violates the fundamental right of religious freedom of professing, practicing, and propagating their religion and also fundamental right of equality inasmuch as only *'Qadianis'* or *'Ahmadis'* are prevented from doing so and no other religious minorities. It is not the use of words *'Azan'* or *'Masjid'* which have been made objectionable by law but doing so by *'Ahmadis'* or *'Qadianis'* alone.

The validity of Sections 498B and 498C had earlier been upheld in *Mujib ur Rahman v. The Federal Government of Pakistan*,[174] on the touchstone of the injunctions of Islam and were held valid and 'in implementation of the Constitutional objectives.'[175]

XIV. *Safeguards against taxation for purposes of any particular religion*

Article 21 of the 1973 Pakistan Constitution provides that –

> 'no person shall be compelled to pay any special tax the proceeds of which are to be spent on the propagation or maintenance of any religion other than his own.'

Unlike the Indian Article 27, which imposes a complete ban against a tax, the proceeds of which are appropriated for the purpose of promoting any particular religion, in Pakistan, the safeguard is only against a special tax, i.e. levied for the promotion of a particular religion, and the prohibition is against the collection from the members of a different religious community. Persons belonging to the religion thus benefited may, therefore, be taxed.

Levy must be tax

The levy must be a tax in order to be subject to the provisions of these articles; if it is imposed in the form of a fee, it is not subject to the prohibition of this article. There is no generic difference between a tax and a fee. Both are different forms in which the taxing power of a state manifests itself, as held in *Mahant Sri Jagannath Ramanuj Das v. State of Orissa*.[176]

But, in both the Indian and Pakistan Constitutions, taxes, duties and fees are separately dealt with in the legislative lists. For example, duties are mentioned in items 43 to 46, taxes are mentioned in items 47 to 53, whereas fees are mentioned in item 54 of part I and item 5 in Part II of the Federal Legislative list, and item 44 of the concurrent list contained in the Fourth Schedule of the Pakistan Constitution.

Similarly, the Indian Constitution has also made a distinction between a tax and a fee for legislative purposes and while there are various entries in the lists with regard to various forms of taxation, there is an entry at the end of each one of these lists as regards fees which could be levied in respect of every one of the matters that are included therein.[177]

Distinction between tax and fee

In *Muhammad Ismail & Company v. Chief Cotton Inspector*,[178] Justice S.A. Rahman (1903–90),[179] of the Supreme Court of Pakistan referred to the *The Commissioner, Hindu Religious Endowment, v. Sri Lakshmindra Thirtha Swamiar of Shirur Mutt*,[180] and held that the learned judges of the Indian Supreme Court adopted the definition of 'tax' given in Chief Justice John Latham (1877–1964),[181] of the High Court of Australia, in *Matthews v. Chicory Marketing Board (Vic)*,[182] where the learned Chief Justice Latham, said,

> 'a tax is a compulsory exaction of money by public authority for public purposes enforceable by law and is not payment for services rendered and a fee may be generally defined on as a charge for a special service rendered to individuals by some governmental agency'

The conclusion that Chief Justice S.A. Rahman, drew from the precedents cited at the Bar, mostly the Indian decisions, was that –

> 'no hard and fast rule was laid down, which could serve to distinguish a tax from a fee.'

It would appear that the question has to be decided on the basis of the special facts and circumstances of each case. It was held in this case that imposition of fee for administration of an Act was possible in law.

XV. *Safeguards as to educational institutions in respect of religion etc.*

Article 22 of the 1973 Pakistan Constitution provides that –

(1) No person attending any education institution shall be required to receive religious instruction, or take part in any religious ceremony, or attend religious worship, if such instruction, ceremony or worship relates to a religion other than his own.
(2) In respect of any religious institution, there shall be no discrimination against any community in the granting of exemption or concession in relation to taxation.
(3) Subject to law,
 (a) no religious community or denomination shall be prevented from providing religious instruction for pupils of that community or denomination in any educational institution maintained wholly by that community or denomination, and
 (b) no citizen shall be denied admission to any educational institution receiving aid from public revenues on the ground only of race, religion, caste or place of birth.
(4) Nothing in this Article shall prevent any public authority from making provision for the advancement of any socially or educationally backward class of citizens.

Under this Article every religious community has a constitutional right to provide for its members religious instruction in its educational institutions, provided:

(1) the institution is wholly maintained by such community; and
(2) no pupil belonging to a different community and attending such an institution is required to receive religious instruction or take part in any religious ceremony or attend any religious worship relating to a religion other than his own.

If, for instance, an institution is wholly maintained by the Christian community, it may provide religious education in Christianity for its own Christian pupils, but Muslim pupils cannot be required to receive such education. The institution may, however, make provision for education of Muslim pupils in their own religion.[183]

An institution is maintained or aided by public funds, or private donations by other communities, it may prescribe such courses in religious instruction as its management may deem fit because ex-hypothesis the institution is no maintained wholly by that community. But no student will be required to take a course of instruction in a religion other than his own.

If, an educational institution receives aid from public revenues, it cannot refuse admission to a student merely on the ground of his race, religion, caste or place of birth. It may, however, regulate the admission on the ground of other factors, e.g., merits or residence. This was held in *Naseem Mahmood v. Principal, King Edward Medical College*.[184] It was further held in this case, that the Article is not applicable to socially and educationally backward classes, and a public authority may, by virtue of Clause (4), make special provision for the advancement of any such class of citizens; but that clause does not control any other type of provisions or reservations which a public authority may make in the matter of admission to educational institutions. The Government may, therefore, make a regional classification for admission to an educational institution.

LEADING CASES:

Certain leading cases decided by US Supreme Court on the interpretation of freedom of religion are discussed:

Everson v. Board of Education[185]

In this case, which is the seminal decision in the US Supreme Court's Establishment Clause jurisprudence, the issue is whether the First Amendment prohibits a local school board from reimbursing parents for costs incurred as a result of transporting their children to and from parochial schools.

Justice Hugo Black delivered the opinion of the US Supreme Court

A New Jersey statute authorizes it's local school districts to make rules and contracts for the transportation of children to and from schools. The appellee, a township board of education, acting pursuant to this statute, authorized reimbursement to parents of money expended by them for the bus transportation of their children on regular buses operated by the public transportation system. Part of this money was for the payment of transportation of some children in the community to Catholic parochial schools. These church schools give their students, in addition to secular education, regular religious instruction conforming to the religious tenets and modes of worship of the Catholic Faith. The superintendent of these schools is a Catholic priest.

The appellant, in his capacity as a district taxpayer, filed suit in a state court challenging the right of the Board to reimburse parents of parochial school students. He contended that the statute and the resolution passed pursuant to it violated both the State and the Federal Constitutions. That court held that the legislature was without power to authorize such payment under the State Constitution.... The New Jersey Court of Errors and Appeals reversed, holding that neither the statute nor the resolution passed pursuant to it was in conflict with the State Constitution or the provisions of the Federal Constitution in issue...

Since there has been no attack on the statute on the ground that a part of its language excludes children attending private schools operated for profit from enjoying State payment for their transportation, we need not consider this exclusionary language; it has no relevancy to any constitutional question here presented. Furthermore, if the exclusion clause had been properly challenged, we do not know whether New Jersey's highest court would construe its statutes as precluding payment of the school transportation of any group of pupils, even those of a private school run for profit. Consequently, we put to one side the question as to the validity of the statute against the claim that it does not authorize payment for the transportation generally of school children in New Jersey....

The New Jersey statute is challenged as a

> 'law respecting the establishment of religion.'

The First Amendment, as made applicable to the states by the 14th Amendment commands that a state

> 'shall make no law respecting an establishment of religion, or prohibiting the free exercise thereof... '

These words of the First Amendment reflected in the minds of early Americans a vivid mental picture of conditions and practices which they fervently wished to stamp out in order to preserve liberty for themselves and for their posterity. Doubtless their goal has not been entirely reached; but so far has the Nation moved toward it, that the expression 'law respecting the establishment of religion,' probably does not so vividly remind present-day Americans of the evils, fears, and political problems that caused that expression to be written into our Bill of Rights....

The meaning and scope of the First Amendment, preventing establishment of religion or prohibiting the free exercise thereof, in the light of its history and the evils it was designed forever to suppress, have been several times elaborated by the decisions of this Court prior to the application of the First Amendment to the states by the 14th. The broad meaning given the Amendment by these earlier cases has been accepted by this Court in its decisions concerning an individual's religious freedom rendered since the 14th Amendment was interpreted to make the prohibitions of the First applicable to state action abridging religious freedom. There is every reason to give the same application and broad interpretation to the 'establishment of religion' clause...

> The 'establishment of religion' clause of the First Amendment means at least this: Neither a state nor the Federal Government can set up a church. Neither can pass laws which aid one religion, aid all religions, or

> prefer one religion over another. Neither can force nor influence a person to go to or to remain away from church against his will or force him to profess a belief or disbelief in any religion. No person can be punished for entertaining or professing religious beliefs or disbeliefs, for church attendance or nonattendance. No tax in any amount, large or small, can be levied to support any religious activities or institutions, whatever they may be called, or whatever form they may adopt to teach or practice religion. Neither a state nor the Federal Government can, openly or secretly, participate in the affairs of any religious organizations or groups and vice versa. In the words of Jefferson, the clause against establishment of religion by law was intended to erect 'a wall of separation between church and State.'

We must consider the New Jersey statute in accordance with the foregoing limitations imposed by the First Amendment. But we must not strike that state statute down if it is within the State's constitutional power even though it approaches the verge of that power… New Jersey cannot consistently with the 'establishment of religion' clause of the 1st Amendment contribute tax-raised funds to the support of an institution which teaches the tenets and faith of any church. On the other hand, other language of the amendment commands that New Jersey cannot hamper its citizens in the free exercise of their own religion. Consequently, it cannot exclude individual Catholics, Lutherans, Mohammedans, Baptists, Jews, Methodists, Non-believers, Presbyterians, or the members of any other faith, *because of their faith, or lack of it*, from receiving the benefits of public welfare legislation. While we do not mean to intimate that a state could not provide transportation only to children attending public schools, we must be careful in protecting the citizens of New Jersey against state-established churches, to be sure that we do not inadvertently prohibit New Jersey from extending its general state law benefits to all its citizens without regard to their religious belief.

Measured by these standards, we cannot say that the First Amendment prohibits New Jersey from spending tax-raised funds to pay the bus fares of parochial school pupils as a part of a general program under which it pays the fares of pupils attending public and other schools. It is undoubtedly true that children are helped to get to church schools. There is even a possibility that some of the children might not be sent to the church schools if the parents were compelled to pay their children's bus fares out of their own pockets when transportation to a public school would have been paid for by the State. The same possibility exists where the state requires a local transit company to provide reduced fares to school children including those attending parochial schools, or where a municipally owned transportation system undertakes to carry all school children free of charge. Moreover, state-paid policemen, detailed to protect children going to and from church schools from the very real hazards of traffic, would serve much the same purpose and accomplish much the same result as state provisions intended to guarantee free transportation of a kind which the state deems to be best for the school children's welfare. And parents might refuse to risk their children to the serious danger of traffic accidents going to and from parochial schools, the approaches to which were not protected by policemen. Similarly, parents might be reluctant to permit their children to attend schools which the state had cut off from such general government services as ordinary police and fire protection, connections for sewage disposal, public highways and sidewalks. Of course, cutting off church schools from these services, so separate and so indisputably marked off from the religious function, would make it far more difficult for the schools to operate. But such is obviously not the purpose of the 1st Amendment. That amendment requires the state to be a neutral in its relations with groups of religious believers and non-believers; it does not require the state to be their adversary. State power is no more to be used so as to handicap religions than it is to favor them.

This Court has said that parents may, in the discharge of their duty under state compulsory education laws, send their children to a religious rather than a public school if the school meets the secular educational requirements which the state has power to impose… . It appears that these parochial schools meet New Jersey's requirements. The State contributes no money to the schools. It does not support them. It's legislation, as applied, does no more than provide a general program to help parents get their children, regardless of their religion, safely and expeditiously to and from accredited schools.

The First Amendment has erected a wall between church and state. That wall must be kept high and impregnable. We could not approve the slightest breach. New Jersey has not breached it here… .

Justice Robert H. Jackson (1892–1954),[186] dissenting.

> I find myself, contrary to first impressions, unable to join in this decision. I have sympathy, though it is not ideological, with Catholic citizens who are compelled by law to pay taxes for public schools, and also feel constrained by conscience and discipline to support other schools for their own children. Such relief to them

> as this case involves is not in itself a serious burden to taxpayers and I had assumed it to be as little serious in principle. Study of this case convinces me otherwise. The Court's opinion Marshalls every argument in favor of state aid and puts the case in its most favorable light, but much of its reasoning confirms my conclusions that there are no good grounds upon which to support the present legislation. In fact, the undertones of the opinion, advocating complete and uncompromising separation of Church from State, seem utterly discordant with its conclusion yielding support to their commingling in educational matters. The case which irresistibly comes to mind as the most fitting precedent is that of Julia who, according to Byron's reports, 'whispering 'I will ne'er consent/—consented.'

This policy of our Federal Constitution has never been wholly pleasing to most religious groups. They all are quick to invoke it's protections; they are all irked when they feel it's restraints. This Court has gone a long way, if not an unreasonable way, to hold that public business of such paramount importance as maintenance of public order, protection of the privacy of the home, and taxation may not be pursued by a state in a way that even indirectly will interfere with religious proselytizing.

But we cannot have it both ways. Religious teaching cannot be a private affair when the state seeks to impose regulations which infringe on it indirectly, and a public affair when it comes to taxing citizens of one faith to aid another, or those of no faith to aid all. If these principles seem harsh in prohibiting aid to Catholic education, it must not be forgotten that it is the same Constitution that alone assures Catholics the right to maintain these schools at all when predominant local sentiment would forbid them.... Nor should I think that those who have done so well without this aid would want to see this separation between Church and State broken down. If the state may aid these religious schools, it may therefore regulate them. Many groups have sought aid from tax funds only to find that it carried political controls with it. Indeed this Court has declared that –

> 'It is hardly lack of due process for the Government to regulate that which it subsidizes.' ...

Abington School District v. Schempp[187]

This is one of the controversial 'school prayer decisions' handed down by the Warren Court during the early 1960s. Edward and Sidney Schempp, members of the Unitarian religion and parents of children attending a public high school, brought suit to challenge the official practice of opening the school day with Bible reading recitation or the Lord's Prayer. A three-judge panel of the US District Court for the Eastern District of Pennsylvania held the practice unconstitutional under the Establishment Clause of the First Amendment. The school district appealed.

Justice Tom C. Clark (1899–1977)[188] delivered the opinion of the Court.

> ... On each school day at the Abington Senior High School ... opening exercises are conducted pursuant to [state taw]. The exercises are broadcast into each room in the school building through an intercommunications system and are conducted under the supervision of a teacher by students attending the school's radio and television workshop. Selected students from this course gather each morning in the school's workshop studio for the exercises, which include readings by one of the students of 10 verses of the Holy Bible, broadcast to each room in the building. This is followed by the recitation of the Lord's Prayer, likewise over the intercommunications system, but also by the students in the various classrooms, who are asked to stand and join in repeating the prayer in unison. The exercises are closed with the flag salute and such pertinent announcements as are of interest to the students. Participation in the opening exercises, as directed by the statute, is voluntary. The student reading the verses from the Bible may select the passages and read from any version he chooses, although the only copies furnished by the school are the King James version, copies of which were circulated to each teacher by the school district. During the period in which the exercises have been conducted the King James, the Douay and the Revised Standard versions of the Bible have been used, as well as the Jewish Holy Scriptures. There are no prefatory statements, no questions asked or solicited, no comments or explanations made and no interpretations given at or during the exercises. The students and parents are advised that the student may absent himself from the classroom or, should he elect to remain, not participate in the exercises... .

The wholesome 'neutrality' of which this Court's cases speak ... stems from a recognition of the teachings of history that powerful sects or groups might bring about a fusion of governmental and religious functions or a concert or dependency of one upon the other to the end that official support of the State or Federal Government would be placed behind the tenets of one or of all orthodoxies. This the Establishment Clause prohibits. And a further reason for neutrality is found in the Free Exercise Clause, which recognizes the value of religious training, teaching and observance and, more particularly, the right of every person to freely choose his own course with reference thereto, free of any compulsion from the state. This the Free Exercise Clause guarantees. Thus, the two clauses may overlap...

[T]he Establishment Clause has been directly considered by this Court eight times in the past score of years and, with only one Justice dissenting on the point, it has consistently held that the clause withdrew all legislative power respecting religious belief or the expression thereof. The test may be stated as follows: what are the purpose and the primary effect of the enactment? If either is the advancement or inhibition of religion then the enactment exceeds the scope of legislative power as circumscribed by the Constitution. That is to say that to withstand the strictures of the Establishment Clause there must be a secular legislative purpose and a primary effect that neither advances nor inhibits religion... The Free Exercise Clause, likewise considered many times here, withdraws from legislative power, state and federal, the exertion of any restraint on the free exercise of religion. Its purpose is to secure religious liberty in the individual by prohibiting any invasions thereof by civil authority. Hence, it is necessary in a free exercise case for one to show the coercive effect of the enactment as it operates against him in the practice of his religion. The distinction between the two clauses is apparent—a violation of the Free Exercise Clause is predicated on coercion while the Establishment Clause violation need not be so attended.

Applying the Establishment Clause principles to the cases at bar, we find that the States are requiring the selection and reading at the opening of the school day of verses from the Holy Bible and the recitation of the Lord's Prayer by the students in unison. These exercises are prescribed as part of the curricular activities of students who are required by law to attend school. They are held in the school buildings under the supervision and with the participation of teachers employed in those schools... The trial court ... has found that such an opening exercise is a religious ceremony and was intended by the State to be so. We agree with the trial court's finding as to the religious character of the exercises. Given that finding, the exercises and the law requiring them are in violation of the Establishment Clause... .

The conclusion follows that, the laws require religious exercises, and such exercises are being conducted in direct violation of the rights of the appellees and petitioners. Nor are these required exercises mitigated by the fact that individual students may absent themselves upon parental request, for that fact furnishes no defense to a claim of unconstitutionality under the Establishment Clause. Further, it is no defense to urge that the religious practices here may be relatively minor encroachments on the First Amendment. The breach of neutrality that is today a trickling stream may all too soon become a raging torrent and, in the words of James Madison (1751–1836),[189] 'it is proper to take alarm at the first experiment on our liberties....'[190]

> It is insisted that unless these religious exercises are permitted a 'religion of secularism' is established in the schools. We agree of course that the State may not establish a 'religion of secularism' in the sense of affirmatively opposing or showing hostility to religion, thus 'preferring those who believe in no religion over those who do believe.' ... We do not agree, however, that this decision in any sense has that effect. In addition, it might well be said that one's education is not complete without a study of comparative religion or the history of religion and its relationship to the advancement of civilization. It certainly may be said that the Bible is worthy of study for its literary and historic qualities. Nothing we have said here indicates that such study of the Bible or of religion, when presented objectively as part of a secular program of education, may not be effected consistently with the First Amendment. But the exercises here do not fall into those categories. They are religious exercises, required by the State in violation of the command of the First Amendment that the Government maintain strict neutrality, neither aiding nor opposing religion.

Finally, we cannot accept that the concept of neutrality, which does not permit a State to require a religious exercise even with the consent of the majority of those affected, collides with the majority's right to free exercise of religion. While the Free Exercise Clause clearly prohibits the use of state action to deny the rights of free exercise to anyone, it has never meant that a majority could use the machinery of the State to practice it's beliefs.

The place of religion in our society is an exalted one, achieved through a long tradition of reliance on the home, the church and the inviolable citadel of the individual heart and mind. We have come to recognize through bitter experience that it is not within the power of government to invade that citadel, whether it's purpose or effect be to aid or oppose, to advance or retard. In the relationship between man and religion, the State is firmly committed to a position of neutrality. Though the application of that rule requires interpretation of a delicate sort, the rule itself is clearly and concisely stated in the words of the 1st Amendment. Applying that rule to the facts of these cases, we affirm… .

Justice Potter Stewart (1915–85),[191] dissenting.

> I think the records in the two cases before us are so fundamentally deficient as to make impossible an informed or responsible determination of the constitutional issues presented. Specifically, I cannot agree that on these records we can say that the Establishment Clause has necessarily been violated. But I think there exist serious questions under both that provision and the Free Exercise Clause—insofar as each is Imbedded in the 14th Amendment—which require the remand of these cases for the taking of additional evidence.

What our Constitution indispensably protects is the freedom of each of us, be he Jew or Agnostic, Christian or Atheist, Buddhist or Freethinker, to believe or disbelieve, to worship or not worship, to pray or keep silent, according to his own conscience, uncoerced and unrestrained by government. It is conceivable that these school boards, or even all school boards, might eventually find it impossible to administer a system of religious exercises during school hours in such a way as to meet this constitutional standard—in such a way as completely to free from any kind of official coercion those who do not affirmatively want to participate. But I think we must not assume that school boards so lack the qualities of inventiveness and good will as to make impossible the achievement of that goal.

I would remand both cases for further hearings.

Notes

1. Gerald Gunther, Kathleen M.Sullivan, *Constitutional Law*, 13th ed., (N.Y.: The Foundation Press, 1997), p. 1461.
2. Merriam-Webster's Third New International Dictionary of the English Language (1986).
3. 133 U.S. 333 (1890).
4. Stephen Johnson Field was an Associate Justice of the US Supreme Court from 20 May 1863 to 1 December 1897.
5. Otis, H. Stephens Jr., John M. Scheb II, *American Constitutional Law*, (California, Belmont: Thomson/West, 2003), p. 511.
6. 380 U.S. 163 (1965).
7. Tom C. Clark was Associate Justice of the US Supreme Court from 1949 to 1967.
8. 441 F. Supp. 1382 (1977).
9. Supra Note 4, p. 512.
10. Supra Note 1, p. 1500.
11. 403 U.S. 602 (1971).
12. Thomas Jefferson was a Founding Father who was the 3rd President of the United States from 1801 to 1809.
13. 330 U.S. 1 (1947).
14. Supra Note 3, 519–20.
15. 463 U.S. 783 (1983).
16. 403 U.S. 602 (1971).
17. 521 U.S. 203 (1997).
18. *McCreary County v. American Civil Liberties Union of Kentucky*, 545 U.S. 844 (2005).
19. 330 U.S. 1 (1947).
20. Hugo Black served as a US Senator from 1927 to 1937 and as Associate Justice of the US Supreme Court o 1971.
21. Wiley Blount Rutledge was an American educator and Associate Justice of the US Supreme Court.
22. Felix Frankfurter served as Associate Justice of the US Supreme Court.
23. Robert H. Jackson served as Associate Justice of the US Supreme Court.
24. Harold Hitz Burton served as Associate Justice of the US Supreme Court.
25. 392 U.S. 236 (1968).
26. 333 U.S. 203 (1948).
27. 343 U.S. 306 (1952).
28. William O. Douglas served as Associate Justice of the US Supreme Court.
29. 454 U.S. 263 (1981).
30. 496 U.S. 226 (1990).

31. 508 U.S. 384 (1993).
32. 533 U.S. 98 (2001).
33. 413 U.S. 756 (1973).
34. 473 U.S. 373 (1985).
35. William J. Brennan Jr served as Associate Justice of the US Supreme Court from 1956 to 1990.
36. Byron White served as Associate Justice of the US Supreme Court from 1962 to 1993.
37. 512 U.S. 687 (1994).
38. 521 U.S. 203 (1997).
39. 473 U.S. 402 (1985).
40. John Paul Stevens served as Associate Justice of the US Supreme Court from 1975 until his voluntary retirement in 2010.
41. David Souter served as Associate Justice of the US Supreme Court from October 1990 until his retirement in June 2009.
42. Ruth Bader Ginsburg served as Associate Justice of the US Supreme Court from 1993 until her death in 2020.
43. Stephen Breyer serves as Associate Justice of the US Supreme Court.
44. 530 U.S. 793 (2000).
45. Americans United for Separation of Church and State (AU) is a nonprofit organization that advocates separation of church and state.
46. 536 U.S. 639 (2002).
47. Erwin Chemerinsky, *Constitutional Law: Principles and Policies*, 4th ed., (New York: Wolters Kluwer Law & Business, 2011), pp. 1279–80.
48. 370 U.S. 421 (1962).
49. Potter Stewart served as Associate Justice of the US Supreme Court from 1958 to 1981.
50. 374 U.S. 203 (1963).
51. 179 A.2d 698 (Md. 1962).
52. Ronald Reagan served as the 40th President of the United States from 1981–89.
53. 449 U.S. 39 (1980).
54. 472 U.S. 38 (1985).
55. 505 U.S. 577 (1992).
56. 530 U.S. 290 (2000).
57. 530 U.S. 793 (2000).
58. Gary Bauer is an American civil servant, activist, and former political candidate.
59. William Jennings Bryan served as the 41st US Secretary of State under Woodrow Wilson.
60. Clarence Darrow was an American lawyer and a leading member of the American Civil Liberties Union.
61. 393 U.S. 97 (1968).
62. Abe Fortas served as Associate Justice of the US Supreme Court from 1965 to 1969.
63. 482 U.S. 578 (1987).
64. 827 F.2d 684 (11th Cir. 1987).
65. 647 F. Supp. 1194 (E.D. Tenn. 1986).
66. 515 U.S. 819 (1995).
67. 366 U.S. 420 (1961).
68. Earl Warren was the 14th Chief Justice of the US Supreme Court from 1953–69.
69. 463 U.S. 783 (1983).
70. Warren E. Burger was the 15th Chief Justice of the US Supreme Court from 1969–86.
71. 403 U.S. 602 (1971).
72. 465 U.S. 668 (1984).
73. 492 U.S. 573 (1989).
74. Harry Blackmun served as Associate Justice of the US Supreme Court from 1970–94.
75. 545 U.S. 677 (2005).
76. 310 U.S. 296 (1940).
77. 303 U.S. 444 (1938).
78. 319 U.S. 141 (1943).
79. 430 U.S. 705 (1977).
80. Supra Note 1, p. 1471.
81. 367 U.S. 488 (1961).
82. 435 U.S. 618 (1978).
83. 310 U.S. 296 (1940).
84. 319 U.S. 157 (1943).

85. 319 U.S. 105 (1943).
86. William O. Douglas served as Associate Justice of the US Supreme Court from 1939–75.
87. 340 U.S. 268 (1951).
88. 452 U.S. 640 (1981).
89. 494 U.S. 872 (1990).
90. Peyote is a small, spineless cactus, known for its psychoactive properties when ingested.
91. 98 U.S. 145 (1878).
92. Morrill Anti-Bigamy Act banned bigamy in federal territories such as Utah and limited church and non-profit ownership in any territory of the United States to $50,000.
93. Morrison Waite served as 7th Chief Justice of the US Supreme Court from 1874–88.
94. 374 U.S. 398 (1963).
95. 450 U.S. 707 (1981).
96. 480 U.S. 136 (1987).
97. 494 U.S. 872 (1990).
98. A North American Indian religious organization combining elements of Christianity with indigenous beliefs and practices, especially the ritual use of the drug peyote.
99. Designating a church or community consisting of Jews who have become Christians.
100. 98 US 145 (1879).
101. *Employment Division v. Smith.* 494 U.S. 872(1990).
102. 540 U.S. 712 (2004).
103. is a Pentecostal Christian denomination in the United States founded in 1914 at Hot Springs, Arkansas.
104. 474 U.S. 481 (1986).
105. 521 U.S. 507 (1997).
106. 546 U.S. 418 (2006).
107. 508 U.S. 520 (1993).
108. *Vasudev v. Vamanji*, ILR 1881 Bom. 80.
109. *The Ahmedabad St. Xavier's College v. State of Gujrat*, AIR 1974 SC 1389 at 1414.
110. AIR 1994 S.C. 1918,(1994) 3 SCC 1. *Dr M. Ismail Farooqui v. Union of India*, AIR 1995 S.C. 604, (1994) 6 SCC 360.
111. AIR 1995 S.C. 293.
112. *The Commissioner, Hindu Religious Endowments, Madras v. Sri Lakshmindra Thirtha Swamiar of Shri Shirur Mutt*, AIR 1954 SC 282; *S.P. Mittal v. Union of India*, AIR 1983 SC 1.
113. *John Vallamattom v. Union of India*, AIR 2003 S.C. 2902, (2003) 6 SCC 611.
114. *Rev. Stainislaus v. State of Madhya Pradesh*, AIR 1977 SC 908.
115. *The Commissioner, Hindu Religious Endowments, Madras v. Sri Lakshmindra ThirthaSwamiar of Shri Shirur Mutt.* AIR 1956 SC 282; *F.R.J. Swami v. State of Tamil Nadu*, AIR 1972 SC 1585; *Acharya Jagdishwaranand Avadhuta v. Commissioner of Police, Calcutta*, (1984) 4 SCC 522.
116. *Bijoe Emmanuel v. State of Kerala*, AIR 1987 SC 748, 1986 SCR (3) 518.
117. *Jana Gana Mana* the national anthem of India was composed by Rabindranath Tagore.
118. (1988) 1 SCC 668.
119. Doordarshan is an autonomous public service broadcaster founded by the Government of India.
120. Bhisham Sahni was an Indian writer, playwright in Hindi.
121. (1994) 6 SCC 360.
122. Shankar Dayal Sharma was the 9th President of India, serving from 1992 to 1997.
123. It was heard by three judges bench of the Allahabad High Court consisting of Justice Sibghat Ullah Khan, Justice Sudhir Aggarwal and Justice Dharam Veer Sharma.
124. *M. Siddiq (Ram Jenmabhumi temple case) v. Mahant Sureshi Das & others*, (2020) 1 SCC 1.
125. AIR 1998 Gujarat 234.
126. AIR 1999 Calcutta 15.
127. AIR 1996 S.C. 1765.
128. (2000) 6 SCC 224.
129. Bigamy is a non-cognizable offence. It is bailable and compoundable with the permission of court if the offence is committed under Section 494 of the I.P.C. The punishment for bigamy is imprisonment, which may extend till 7 years or fine or both.
130. *T.M.A. Pai Foundation v. State of Karnataka*, AIR 2003 S.C. 355, (2002) 8 SCC 481.
131. AIR 1977 SC 908.
132. AIR 1981 SC 2198, 1982 SCR (1)1077.

133. (1984) 4 SCC 522.
134. Tandava also known as Taṇḍava natyam, is a divine dance performed by the Hindu gods.
135. Ananda Marga is a world-wide socio-spiritual organisation and movement founded in Jamalpur.
136. AIR 1958 SC 731.
137. Also known as Eid al-Adha.
138. (1943) 67 CLR 116.
139. AIR 1995 SC 464; (1995) 1 SCC 189.
140. AIR 1983 SC 1.
141. Sri Aurobindo was an Indian philosopher, yogi, guru, poet, and nationalist.
142. Mirra Alfassa (referred to as 'The Mother') was his French spiritual guru, an occultist and a collaborator.
143. AIR 1953 Bom. 84.
144. *Sardar Syedna Taher Saifuddin Saheb v. State of Bombay*, AIR 1963 SC 853.
145. *Sri Venkataramana Devaruand v. State of Mysore*, AIR 1958 SC 255.
146. *Sastri Yagnapurushadji v. Muldas Brudardas Vaishya*, AIR 1966 SC 1119.
147. *S.P. Mittal v. Union of India*, AIR 1983 SC 1.
148. *The Commissioner, Hindu Religious Endowments, Madras v. Sri Lakshmindra Thirtha Swamiar of Shri Shirur Mutt*, AIR 1954 SC 282.
149. *Acharya Jagdishwaranand Avadhuta v. Commissioner of Police, Calcutta*, (1982) 4 SCC 522.
150. (1995) 4 SCC 646.
151. AIR 1968 SC 662; also *St. Stephen's College v. University of Delhi*, (1992) 1 SCC 558.
152. *Acharya Jagdiswaranand Avadhuta v. Commr. of Police, Calcutta*, (1984) 4 SCC 522; *Mohd. Hanif Quareshi v. State of Bihar*, AIR 1958 SC 731.
153. J.N. Pandey, *Constitutional Law of India*, 38th ed., (Allahabad: Central Law Agency, 2002), pp. 289–90.
154. AIR 1962 SC 853.
155. Dr P.K. Tripathi – *Secularism: Constitutional Provision and Judicial Review*, Journal of the Indian Law Institute, vol. 8, no. 1 (Jan-March 1966), pp. 1–29 (29 pages).Dr Tripathi supports the minority opinion; J. Duncan M. Derrett, *Freedom of Religion under the India Constitution: Ex-Communication (Based on Sardar S. T. Saifuddin Saheb v. State of Bombay)*, The International and Comparative Law Quarterly, vol. 12, no. 2 (Cambridge University Press, Apr., 1963), pp. 693–697 (5 pages).
156. AIR 1964 SC 1501.
157. Birakisore Deva III (1956–1970) was the Maharaja of Puri of the Bhoi dynasty.
158. AIR 1992 AP 310.
159. *S.P. Mittal v. Union of India*. AIR 1983, SC 1.
160. AIR 1954 SC 388; *The Commissioner, Hindu Religious Endowments, Madras v. Sri Lakshmindra Thirtha Swamiar of Shri Shirur Mutt*, AIR 1956 SC 282.
161. *Dargah Committee, Ajmer v. Hussain Ali*, AIR 1961 SC 1402. Also *S. Azeez Basha v. Union of India*, AIR 1968 SC 662.
162. *The Commissioner, Hindu Religious Endowments, Madras v. Sri Lakshmindra Thirtha Swamiar of Shri Shirur Mutt*, AIR 1961 SC 282.
163. AIR 1954 S.C. 388.
164. *Sreenivasa General Traders v. State of Andhra Pradesh* 1983 SCR (3) 843.
165. AIR 1954 SC 400.
166. Supra Note 152, pp. 292–3.
167. PLD 1958 Lahore 584.
168. (1943) 67 CLR 116.
169. 1994 SCMR 1532.
170. PLD 1957 S.C. (Pak) 9.
171. Shafiur Rahman was one of the longest serving judges of the Supreme Court of Pakistan from 1981 to 1994.
172. 1993 SCMR 1718.
173. Abdul Qadeer Chaudhry served as Justice of the Supreme Court of Pakistan from 13 Dec 1989 to 12 Jul 1994.
174. PLD 1985 FSC 8.
175. Article 2 of the Constitution which declares Islam as the State religion of Pakistan.
176. AIR 1954 SC 400.
177. A.G. Chaudhry, *Lectures on Constitutional Law*, (Lahore: Irfan Law Book House, 1994), pp. 207–11.
178. PLD 1966 S.C. 388.
179. S. A. Rahman was the 5th Chief Justice of Pakistan in 1968.
180. AIR 1954 S.C. 282.

181. John Latham served as the 5th Chief Justice of Australia from 1935 to 1952.
182. 60 CLR 263.
183. Supra Note 106, 214–5.
184. PLD 1965 Lahore 272.
185. 330 U.S. 1. (1947).
186. Robert H. Jackson served as Associate Justice of the US Supreme Court from 1941 to 1954.
187. 374 U.S. 203 (1963).
188. Tom C. Clark served as Associate Justice of the US Supreme Court from 1949 to 1967.
189. James Madison was a Founding Father who served as the 4th President of the United States from 1809 to 1817.
190. '*Memorial and Remonstrance against Religious Assessments, [ca. 20 June] 1785*,' Founders Online, National Archives, https://founders.archives.gov/documents/Madison/01-08-02-0163.
191. Potter Stewart served as Associate Justice of the US Supreme Court from 1958 to 1981.

18 Right to Privacy Including Searches and Seizures

Introduction

US Constitution and Right of Privacy

The 'right of privacy' guaranteed by the American Constitution protects individual from unwarranted government interference, especially in intimate personal relationships or activities. This right has developed since the mid-1960s; the 'right of privacy' includes the freedom of the individual to make fundamental choices involving sex, reproduction, family life, and other intimate personal relationships. Of the various constitutional rights, the 'right of privacy' is one of the most intensely disputed fundamental rights. The controversy stems in part from the absence of any specific reference to privacy in the US Constitution.

Some American scholars and judges still adhere to the view once expressed by Justice Hugo Black (1886–1971),[1] that a right of privacy cannot be reasonably inferred from the language of the original Constitution or any of its amendments. However, this appears to be a minority view these days. Among recent nominees to the Supreme Court, only Judge Robert Bork (1927–2012),[2] rejected the interpretive foundation of the right of privacy. For most Americans, the debate over privacy has less to do with competing theories of constitutional interpretation than with the profound implications of the principle of privacy for determining divisive social and moral questions such as abortion, gay rights, and euthanasia.

In *Roe v. Wade*,[3] the US Supreme Court held that the right of privacy –

> 'is broad enough to encompass a woman's decision whether or not to terminate her pregnancy.'

As the ongoing anti-abortion protests demonstrate, abortion is hardly an ordinary issue of public policy. Nor was *Roe v. Wade* a run-of-the-mill Supreme Court decision. Unlike most constitutional decisions, *Roe* aroused deep philosophical conflict and even deeper political and emotional turmoil. *Roe v. Wade* drew the Supreme Court into a firestorm of political controversy, that continues unabated after three decades. This controversy has dominated public discussion of the court, often eclipsing other important issues, and likewise, influencing the debate surrounding nominations to the Supreme Court.

Although, abortion is the focal point of the debate over the 'right of privacy', the viability of the 'right of privacy' is not based solely on the continued vitality of *Roe v. Wade.* Even if *Roe* were to be overturned, the 'right of privacy' would still exist as an independent constitutional right, *albeit* somewhat circumscribed. The 'right of privacy' is now well established in both federal and state constitutional law and has application to numerous questions of public policy beyond abortion.

Philosophical Foundations of the Right of Privacy

When the US Supreme Court invoked the 'right of privacy' to effectively legalize abortion within stated limits, it was giving expression to a sense of 'moral individualism' that is deeply rooted in American culture. However, countervailing notions of traditional morality are also deeply ingrained in American society, as the relentless and wide-spread attacks on *Roe v. Wade* demonstrate. In no other area of constitutional law are individualism and traditional morality as sharply antagonistic as is in the area of privacy rights.

The 'moral individualism' underlying the constitutional right of privacy was conceived as a concept of 'political liberalism'. The English philosopher John Stuart Mills (1806–73), in his influential essay *On Liberty* (1859), argued that –

> 'there is a sphere of action in which society, as distinguished from the individual, has, if any, only an indirect interest; comprehending all that portion of a person's life and conduct which affects only himself, or if it also affects others, only with their free, voluntary and undeceived consent and participation.'

In the modern era, the idea, that each individual should be considered an autonomous actor with respect to personal matters is associated with the philosophy of 'libertarianism', which consider, that individual freedom is the highest good and, that law should be interpreted to maximize the scope of liberty.

During and after the 1960s, the libertarian perspective became increasingly widespread among Americans, especially younger people. In the late 1960s, and throughout the 1970s, a large number of people began to question the authority of government to regulate the private lives of individuals in the name of traditional morality. In the libertarian view, the legitimate role of government is protection of individuals from one another, not from their own vices. Thus, libertarians often object to laws regulating sexual conduct, living arrangements, and the private use of drugs—and even to laws mandating that motorcycle riders wear helmets. Perhaps, the ultimate libertarian position is opposition to the criminal law against suicide. In the libertarian view, the individual has the right to make basic decisions regarding his or her own life or death.[4]

The countervailing position, which might be dubbed 'classical conservatism,' holds that individuals must often be protected against their own vices. Classical conservatives not only defend traditional morality but the embodiment of that morality in the law. Justice Antonin Scalia (1936–2016) of US Supreme Court has endorsed the classical conservative view of law and morality. In *Barnes v. Glen Theatre, Inc*,[5] Justice Scalia wrote:

> 'Our society prohibits, and all human societies have prohibited, certain activities not because they harm others but because they are considered…immoral. In American society, such prohibitions have included, for example, sadomasochism, cockfighting, bestiality, suicide, drug use, prostitution and sodomy. While there might be a great diversity of views on whether several of these prohibitions should exist, there is no doubt that absent specific constitutional protection for the conduct involved, the Constitution does not prohibit them simply because they regulate "morality".'

The debate over the constitutional right of privacy is ultimately a debate between two sharply divergent views of the law. In the libertarian view, the law exists to protect individuals from one another. In this view, morality is not in and of itself a legitimate basis for law. The classical conservative view, on the other hand, sees law and morality as inseparable and holds that the maintenance of social morality is one of the essential functions of the legal system.

Constitutional foundations of the right of privacy

However, it cannot be said that any of the framers of the US Constitution were libertarians in the modern sense of the term. Certainly, the framers believed in individual freedom, but most of them did not conceive of freedom, as including the right to flout traditional principles of conduct embodied in the common law. The right to privacy, which is essentially the constitutionalization of libertarianism, has been 'found' by the US Supreme Court to derive from various provisions of the Bill of Rights (see *Griswold v. Connecticut*).[6]

Several provisions of the Bill of Rights (first 10 Amendments to the US Constitution) were adopted to protect individuals from unreasonable invasions of privacy. The 3rd Amendment explicitly protects the privacy of the home in peacetime from soldiers seeking quarters. The 4th Amendment protects individuals from unreasonable searches and seizures where they have a 'reasonable expectation of privacy' (*Katz v. United States*).[7] The 5th Amendment prohibits compulsory self-incrimination, thus, protecting the privacy of an accused individual's thoughts. The First Amendment ensures freedom of conscience in both political and religious matters, again recognizing the autonomy of the individual. Finally, the First Amendment's implicit guarantee of freedom of association protects one's right to choose one's friends, one's spouse, one's business partners, and so on. In *Griswold v. Connecticut*, the Supreme Court interpreted these protections as embodying a right to be free of those government intrusions into the realm of intimate personal decisions.

The proponents of constitutional 'right of privacy' often cite the 9th Amendment, which guarantees rights 'retained by the people' even though they are not enumerated in the Constitution. Historically, the courts have always recognized a variety of unenumerated constitutional rights. The right to marry, to choose one's spouse, to select an occupation, to travel freely within the country, and to enter into contracts are all examples of long-standing rights retained by the people and recognized by the courts, though, they are not explicitly provided for in the constitution. They have achieved constitutional status by virtue of the fact, that they are elements of the 'liberty' protected by the 'Due Process clauses' of the 5th and 14th Amendments.

Dissenting in *Olmstead v. United States*,[8] Justice Louis Brandeis (1846–1941)[9] wrote:

> 'The makers of our Constitution undertook to secure conditions favourable to the pursuit of happiness. They recognized the significance of man's spiritual nature, of his feelings and his intellect. They knew that only a part of his pain, pleasure, and satisfactions of life are to be found in material things. They sought to protect Americans in their beliefs, their thoughts, their emotions and their sensations. They conferred, as against the Government, the right to be let alone–the most comprehensive of rights and the right most valued by civilized men.'

These words were written by way of dissent in a case dealing with the scope of the 4th Amendment's protection against wiretapping. Yet, they may be interpreted as foreshadowing the modern right of privacy, which is, in essence, the right to be let alone.

THE ABORTION CONTROVERSY: *ROE V. WADE*

Norma McCorvey (1947–2017), also known as Jane Roe, was a 25 years-old unmarried Texas woman who was faced with an unwanted pregnancy resulting from an alleged gang rape, that she later admitted had never occurred. After her doctor informed her that abortion was illegal in Texas, she went to see an attorney. That attorney, Linda Coffee (1942), introduced McCorvey to Sarah Weddington (1945),[10] a young woman just out of law school, who would ultimately argue the case before the US Supreme Court. Weddington expressed her view, that the American Constitution allows a woman to control her own body, including the decision to terminate an unwanted pregnancy. Shortly thereafter, Coffee and Weddington filed suit in federal district court against Dallas District Attorney Henry Wade (1914–2001), seeking to enjoin him from enforcing what was claimed to be an unconstitutional law.

The suit was filed as a class-action i.e., not only on behalf of Jane Roe but on behalf of all women 'similarly situated.' The district court declared the Texas law unconstitutional but refused to issue the injunction, invoking the doctrine of abstention, whereby, federal courts refrain from interfering with state judicial process. As permitted in cases of this kind, Jane Roe appealed directly to the US Supreme Court.[11]

Roe v. Wade, of course, is the key case recognizing a constitutional right to abortion.[12] *Roe* involved a challenge to a Texas law, that prohibited all abortions except those necessary to save the life of the mother. A companion case, *Doe v. Bolton*,[13] presented a challenge to a Georgia law that outlawed abortions except, if, a doctor determined that continuing the pregnancy would endanger a woman's life or health, if the fetus likely would be born with a serious defect, or if the pregnancy resulted from rape.

In *Roe v. Wade*, Justice Harry Blackmun (1908–99),[14] writing for the court, exhaustively reviewed the history of abortion from ancient attitudes through English law, through American history, and to the present day, Justice Blackmun also described the development of medical technology to provide safe abortions. With this as background, Justice Blackmun focused on the right to privacy. After reviewing earlier cases dealing with family and reproductive autonomy, Blackmun concluded:

> 'This right of privacy, whether it be founded in the 14th Amendment's conception of personal liberty and restrictions upon state action, as well feel it is, or,....in the 9th Amendment's reservation of rights to the people, is broad enough to encompass a woman's decision whether or not to terminate her pregnancy.'

It is notable that the US Supreme Court did not find privacy, as Justice William O. Douglas (1898–1980)[15] did in *Griswold*, in the penumbra of the Bill of Rights, but, instead as part of the liberty protected under the Due Process Clause.

The Court then explained why prohibiting abortion infringes on a woman's right to privacy. Justice Harry Blackmun observed that –

> '[m]aternity, or additional off-spring, may force upon the woman a distressful life and future. Psychological harm may be imminent. Mental and physical health may be taxed by child care. There is also the distress, for all concerned, associated with the unwanted child.'

Forcing a woman to continue a pregnancy against her will obviously imposes enormous physical and psychological burdens.

The Court observed, however, that the right to abortion is not absolute and that it must be balanced against other considerations, such as the state's interest in protecting 'prenatal life.' The Court said, that strict scrutiny was to be used in striking the balance because the right to abortion was a fundamental right. The Court reiterated the principle that –

> 'where "fundamental rights" are involved,...regulation limiting these rights may be justified only by "a compelling state interest," and....legislative enactments must be narrowly drawn to express only legitimate state interests at stake.'

The US Supreme Court rejected the state's claim, that fetuses are persons and, that there was a compelling interest in protecting potential life. The Court observed, that there was no indication that the term 'person' in the constitution ever was meant to include fetuses. Moreover, the Court noted, that there was no consensus as to when human personhood begins. There was enormous disagreement among various religions and philosophies on this point. The Court said:

> 'We need not resolve the difficult question of when life begins. When those trained in the respective disciplines of medicine, philosophy and theologies are unable to arrive at any consensus, the judiciary, at this point in the development of man's knowledge, is not in a position to speculate as to the answer.'

The Court said, that in balancing the competing interests, the state had a 'compelling interest' in protecting maternal health after the first trimester because it was then that abortions became more dangerous than childbirth. The Court further concluded that –

> '[w]ith respect to the State's important and legitimate interest in potential life, the "compelling" point is at viability. This is so because the fetus then presumably has the capability of meaningful life outside the mother's womb.'

Thus, the Court divided pregnancy into three trimesters. During the first trimester, the government could not prohibit abortions and could regulate abortions only as it regulated other medical procedures, such as by requiring that they be performed by a licensed physician. During the second trimester, the government also could not outlaw abortions, but the government –

> 'may, if it chooses, regulate the abortion procedure in ways that are reasonably related to maternal health.'

Finally, for the stage subsequent to viability, the government may prohibit abortions except if necessary to preserve the life or health of the mother.

Roe v. Wade was a 7 to 2 decision with only Justices William Rehnquist (1924–2005)[16] and Byron White (1917–2002)[17] dissenting.[18] Both of the dissenting justices emphasized, that the question of abortion was one, that should have been left to the legislative process. Justice White, for example, objected:

> "As an exercise of raw judicial power, the Court perhaps has the authority to do what it does today; but in my view its judgement is an improvident and extravagant exercise of the power of judicial review."

Justice White said, that –

> the issue 'should be left with the people and to the political processes the people have devised to govern their affairs.'

The US Supreme Court relied on its decision in *Roe* to invalidate Georgia's abortion law in *Doe v. Bolton*. Once the Court recognized, that women have a constitutional right to abortions prior to viability, it follows, that a state law is unconstitutional if it prohibits abortion except when pregnancy endangers the mother's health, the fetus is seriously deformed, or the woman has been raped.

The Debate over *Roe v. Wade*

Roe v. Wade has become one of the most controversial constitutional decisions in American history with passions running high on all aspects of the issue. It is as much a political issue as it is a legal or a constitutional one. Many scholarly articles have been written about *Roe*. Three major criticisms of *Roe* are discussed below.

First, as it is already mentioned, that the US Supreme Court was wrong to protect a right to abortion because the right is neither mentioned in the text nor intended by the framers. John Hart Ely (1938–2003),[19] for example, argued:

> 'What is frightening about *Roe* is that this super-protected right is not inferable from the language of the Constitution, the framers' thinking respecting the specific problem in issue, any general value derivable from the provisions they included, or the nation's governmental structure....The problem with *Roe* is not so much that it bungles the question it sets itself, but rather that it sets itself a question the Constitution has not made the Court's business....[*Roe* is] a very ad decision....It is bad because it is bad constitutional law, or rather because it is not constitutional law and gives almost no sense of an obligation to try to be.'

But, defenders of *Roe* answer this criticism by pointing to the other rights that the Court has protected concerning family and reproductive autonomy throughout the 20th century. The Court has safeguarded the right to marry, the right to custody, the right to keep the family together, the right to control the upbringing of children, the right to procreate, and the right to purchase and use contraceptives even though these liberties are not mentioned in the Constitution and were not intended by the framers. Professor Laurence Tribe (1941),[20] for example, notes that –

> 'nearly everyone supposes that at least some of these dimensions of personal autonomy and independence are aspects of the "liberty" which the 14th Amendment says no state may deny to any person "without due process of law".'

Thus, *Roe* cannot be criticized simply because the American Constitution and its framers were silent about abortion. Ultimately, this first objection to *Roe* turns on a much wider ongoing debate over how the Court should interpret the Constitution and when, if at all, it is permissible for the judiciary to protect unenumerated rights.[21]

The second major criticism of *Roe* is, that the Court gave insufficient weight to the state's interest in protecting fetal life. Some who criticize *Roe*, focus less on the issue of judicial methodology and more on the Court's substantive judgement, that protecting the fetus was not a sufficiently compelling interest to justify the prohibition of abortion. Professor (now Judge) John T. Noonan Jr (1926–2017)[22] said that –

> '[t]o judge from the weight the Court gave the being in the womb–found to be protectable in any degree only in the last two months of pregnancy–the Court itself must have viewed the unborn as pure potentiality or a mere theory before viability. The Court's opinion appeared to rest on the assumption that the biological reality could be subordinated or ignored by the sovereign speaking through the Court.'

Those who defend *Roe* respond to this criticism in two ways. One is that the US Supreme Court was correct in not deciding the question of when personhood begins. There are many possibilities for defining the point at which the fetus is a human person entitled to constitutional protection; conception, implantation into the uterine wall, individuation (whether the fetus takes on individual characteristics), quickening (when the mother feels the first movement of the fetus), viability, and birth. Professor Frances Olsen (1945)[23] explains that –

> 'any determination of the beginning of human life can be criticized as arbitrary... The value of life is not a simple attribute of any particular life form, something that can be discovered. Culturally created, the value of life rests on social meanings, and importantly on sexual politics.'

Therefore, the Court acted properly in leaving each woman to decide for herself when human personhood begins.

An alternative response to the argument, that the Court gave too little weight to protecting the fetus, is that even if the fetus is regarded as a person, the law should not force the woman to be an incubator against her will. Professor Judith Jarvis Thomson (1929–2020)[24] argued, that even granting that the fetus is a person from the moment of conception, the law should not force one person to use their body to sustain the life of another. She says, for example, that the law would not require a person to be physically connected with another even if it was the only way to save a life. Parents are not required to donate organs or blood to save their children. By this view, nor should women be forced to donate their wombs and their bodies to sustain fetal life.[25]

The third criticism of *Roe* is, that the Court erred in using Due Process rather than Equal Protection as the basis for its decision. The argument is, that laws prohibiting abortion apply exclusively to women, and thus, they should be declared unconstitutional as gender discrimination. Professor Catharine A. MacKinnon (1946)[26] wrote:

> 'Under this sex equality analysis, criminal abortion statutes of the sort invalidated in *Roe v. Wade* violate equal protection of the laws. They make women criminals for a medical procedure only women need, or make others criminals for performing a procedure on women that only women need, when much of the need for this procedure as well as barriers to access to it has been created by social conditions of sex inequality.'

Forced motherhood in her view is sex inequality. The response to this argument is, that an equality analysis, like a privacy approach, still comes down to the same basic question: Does the government's interest in protecting fetal life justify prohibiting abortion? Under Equal Protection law, gender discrimination is permissible if intermediate scrutiny is met; that is, if the government's action is substantially related to an important government interest. If protecting fetal life is regarded as an important government interest, then laws prohibiting abortion are justified even though they are a form of gender discrimination. The argument is that nothing is gained by shifting to an equal protection analysis; either the state's interest in protecting fetal life is not a sufficient interest, in which case abortion laws are unconstitutional under both privacy and equal protection, or the state has an interest sufficient to justify prohibiting abortion under either approach.[27]

Decisions after *Roe v. Wade*

The US Supreme Court reaffirmed *Roe v. Wade* again in *Thornburgh v. American College of Obstetricians and Gynecologists*.[28] However, in *Thornburgh*, the vote in favour of a constitutional right to abortion was 5 to 4, because Chief Justice Warren E. Burger (1907–95)[29] switched sides and joined the dissenters. Although, Justice Burger retired after the 1985 term, his departure did not strengthen the position of *Roe v. Wade*. President Ronald Reagan (1911–2014)[30] promoted Associate Justice William Rehnquist (1925–2005) to the position of Chief Justice, and appointed Antonin Scalia (1936–2016), a conservative, to fill the vacancy.

In 1987, it appeared, that the opponents of legalized abortion were only one vote away from overturning *Roe v. Wade*. In that year, Justice Lewis F. Powell Jr (1907–98), a member of the *Roe* majority, retired from the Court. It looked as if the Court would be divided 4 to 4 on the abortion issue, possibly making the next appointee to the Court the swing vote on whether to overrule *Roe v. Wade*. To a great extent, this fact explains the furor surrounding President Reagan's nomination of conservative federal judge Robert Bork (1927–2012), to fill the vacancy left by Justice Lewis F. Powell Jr. A well-known critic of *Roe*, and of the right of privacy generally, Bork entered a firestorm of political controversy, when he appeared before the Senate Judiciary Committee. The US Senate, was controlled by the Democrats, ultimately rejected Bork, in no small measure due to his stand on the right of privacy. Eventually, the US Senate confirmed Reagan's nomination of another federal judge, Anthony Kennedy (1936). In his confirmation hearing, Justice Kennedy was asked repeatedly about his views on abortion. He replied,

> 'If I had a …fixed view…I might be obliged to disclose that to you. I don't have such a view.'

The nation would have to wait two years for Justice Kennedy to register his opinion in the abortion debate.[31]

The *Webster* Decision

Without question, the most significant abortion case of the 1980s was *Webster v. Reproductive Health Services.*[32] It was expected by many Americans, that the *Webster* case would be the one in which the US Supreme Court would overturn *Roe v. Wade*. Those who favoured such an outcome were disappointed by the decision. Yet, those who supported legalized abortion found cause for alarm in what they perceived as a significant departure from the philosophy of *Roe*.

The *Webster* case, involved a challenge to a state of Missouri statute containing a number of restrictions on abortions. Most worrisome from the pro-choice perspective was the statement in the preamble of the law that 'the life of each human being begins at conception.' In its various provisions, the law forbade state employees from performing, assisting in, or counseling women to have abortions. It also prohibited the use of any state facilities for these purposes. Finally, it required all doctors who would perform abortions to conduct viability tests on fetuses at or beyond twenty weeks' gestation.

The US Supreme Court, splitting 5 to 4, sustained the constitutionality of the Missouri statutes. Yet, in deciding the issues in *Webster*, the Supreme Court could not agree on a majority opinion. A plurality opinion of Chief Justice Rehnquist (1924–2005) and Associate Justices Byron White (1917–2002), Anthony Kennedy, and Sandra Day O'Connor (1930), expressed the view, that the legislation could be sustained without overruling *Roe v. Wade*. In her separate concurrence, Justice O'Connor stressed the 'fundamental rule of judicial restraint,' which dictates that major issues should only be decided by the courts if they are absolutely necessary. Only Justice Antonin Scalia (1936–2016), in a separate concurrence, called for the explicit overruling of *Roe*, and chided his colleagues in the majority for not facing the issue squarely:

> 'Of the four courses we might have chosen today- to reaffirm *Roe*, to overrule it explicitly, to overrule it *sub silentio*, or to avoid the question- the last is the least responsible.'

Justice Harry Blackmun (1908–99), the author of the Court's opinion in *Roe v. Wade*, accused the plurality of undermining *Roe*:

> With feigned restraint, the plurality announces that its analysis leaves *Roe* "undisturbed," albeit "modif[ied] and narrow[ed],"....But this disclaimer is totally meaningless. The plurality opinion is filled with winks, and nods, and knowing glances to those who would do away with *Roe* explicitly, but turns a stone face to anyone in search of what the plurality conceives as the scope of a woman's right under the Due Process Clause to terminate a pregnancy free from the coercive and brooding influence of the State.

Rust v. Sullivan: Restricting Information about Abortion

During the spring of 1991, supporters of legalized abortion suffered a new setback. In *Rust v. Sullivan*,[33] the US Supreme Court upheld a federal regulation, that barred federally funded birth control clinics from informing their clients about abortion services. The regulation had been imposed in 1987 by the Department of Health and Human Services (HHS),[34] at the direction of the President Reagan administration, which opposed legalized abortion.

The US Supreme Court found the regulation to be a legitimate condition imposed on the receipt of financial assistance from the government. In the Court's view, the regulation was neither an invasion of privacy rights nor of freedom of speech, as plaintiffs in the lawsuit alleged. US Congress, with broad public support, passed a measure designed to overturn the HHS regulation. However, this Act was vetoed by President George H. W. Bush (1924–2018)[35], and Congress was unable to muster the two-thirds vote necessary to override the veto.

The Court Reaffirms *Roe v. Wade*

In *Rust v. Sullivan*, as in the *Webster* decision two years earlier, the US Supreme Court did not face squarely the question of whether *Roe v. Wade* should be maintained as the law of the land. Yet, these decisions did send a strong signal, that the Court was prepared to tolerate greater restrictions on legalized abortion.

On 21 January 1992, on the eve of the 19th anniversary of its landmark decision in *Roe v. Wade*, the US Supreme Court announced, that it would hear a case challenging a Pennsylvania law, that contained a series of restrictions on abortion (*Planned Parenthood of Southeastern Pennsylvania v. Casey*).[36] Among other things, the law required spousal notification, parental consent in cases of minors, and a 24 hour waiting period before an abortion could be performed. Identical requirements had been declared invalid by the Supreme Court in previous decisions, but the Third Circuit Court of Appeals in Philadelphia, upheld most of the provisions of the Pennsylvania statute. The appellate court based its ruling largely on the Supreme Court's 1989 *Webster v. Reproductive Health Services* decision, which it interpreted as a significant retreat from the 'strict scrutiny' to which abortion regulations had been subjected.

On 22 April 1992, the Supreme Court heard oral arguments in *Planned Parenthood v. Casey*. Ernest D. Preate, Jr (1940)[37], Attorney General of Pennsylvania, defended the constitutionality of the statute, contending, among other things, that –

> '*Roe* did not establish an absolute right to abortion on demand, but rather a limited right subject to reasonable state regulations.'

Attacking the statute, Kathryn Kolbert,[38] counsel for the American Civil Liberties Union (ACLU), characterized Pennsylvania's regulations not only as unreasonable but as 'cruel and oppressive.' US Solicitor General Kenneth W. Starr (1946),[39] speaking on behalf of the Bush administration, urged the Court to abandon the 'compelling state interest' test and adopt a more lenient 'rational basis test' for determining the constitutionality of statutes in this area. When asked by Justice Byron White (1917–2002) whether the adoption of such a test would lead to a conclusion that the Pennsylvania laws should be upheld, Starr replied, 'Exactly.'

On 29 June 1992, the Supreme Court handed down its much anticipated decision. To the surprise of many observers, the Court reaffirmed by a 5 to 4 vote the essential holding in *Roe v. Wade*, that the constitutional right of privacy is broad enough to include a woman's decision to terminate her pregnancy. The Court was highly fragmented, however, producing five opinions. Two justices, Harry Blackmun (1908–99) and John Paul Stevens (1920–2019), took the position, that *Roe v. Wade* should be reaffirmed and that all of the challenged provisions of the Pennsylvania statute should be declared invalid. Four justices – William Rehnquist (1924–2005), Antonin Scalia (1936–2016), Byron White (1917–2002), and Clarence Thomas (1948)– took the view that *Roe* should be overruled, and all of the Pennsylvania restrictions upheld. Adopting an extremely unusual method of presentation underscoring the gravity of the case, Justices Sandra Day O'Connor (1930), Anthony Kennedy (1936), and David Souter (1939) jointly authored the controlling opinion of the court. This lengthy joint opinion thoroughly reexamined *Roe v. Wade*, its underlying rationale and formulation, and the line of cases it spawned. While joining Justices Blackmun and Stevens in explicitly reaffirming *Roe*, the joint opinion abandoned the trimester framework and declared a new 'undue burden' test for judging regulations of abortion. Applying this test, the joint opinion upheld the parental consent, waiting period, and record-keeping and reporting provisions but invalidated the spousal notification requirement.

The *Planned Parenthood v. Casey* decision was greeted with dismay and derision from both pro-life and pro-choice groups. Pro-choice groups expressed alarm that the court was willing to overturn previous precedents *Akron v. Akron Center for Reproductive Health*,[40] and *Thornburgh v. American College of Obstetricians and Gynecologists*,[41] and uphold Pennsylvania's restrictions on abortion. Pro-life advocates were disappointed that two President Reagan (1911–2004) appointees Anthony Kennedy and Sandra Day O'Connor, and one President H. W. Bush (1924–2018) appointee David Souter voted to reaffirm *Roe v. Wade*.

In their separate opinions in *Casey*, Chief Justice William Rehnquist and Justice Antonin Scalia, supported by Justices Byron White and Clarence Thomas, made it clear, that four members of the Court are fully prepared to overturn *Roe v. wade*. However, in 1993, with the replacement of Justice Byron White by Justice Ruth Bader Ginsburg (1933–2020), the anti-*Roe* bloc on the court was diminished. In 1994, Justice Harry Blackmun, the author of the *Roe* opinion, resigned from the court. His replacement by Justice Stephen G. Breyer (1938), the second President Bill Clinton (1946)[42] appointee to the court, was not likely to weaken support of the *Roe* precedent.[43]

Undue Burden test on the Right to Abortion?

In *Stenberg v. Carhart*,[44] the majority opinion expressly adopted and applied the 'undue burden' test. The US Supreme Court declared unconstitutional a state law that prohibited the procedure called 'partial birth abortion'. Its greatest significance is, that it is for the first time that a majority of the Court said that the undue burden test is to be used in evaluating laws regulating abortion. Subsequently, in *Gonzales v. Carhart*, the Court again used the undue burden test, though this time to uphold a federal law prohibiting partial birth abortion.[45]

The key question is what constitutes an 'undue burden' on the right to abortion. However, there are some important problems with applying the 'undue burden' test.

First, the 'undue burden' test combines four questions into one inquiry.

— Is there a fundamental right;
— is the right infringed;
— is the infringement justified by a sufficient purpose;
— are the means sufficiently related to the end sought?

The 'undue burden' test combines the latter three questions. Undue burden is thus confusing to apply because it melds together three distinct issues.

Second, the joint opinion's statement of the 'undue burden' test has an internal tension. The joint opinion in *Planned Parenthood v. Casey's* case says that a law is an undue burden –

> 'if its purpose or effect is to place a substantial obstacle in the path of a woman seeking an abortion before the fetus attains viability.'[46]

Third, there is the issue of how many women must be adversely affected by a regulation of abortions in order for it to be considered an undue burden.

In *Planned Parenthood v. Casey*, the plurality found that the requirement for spousal notification before a married women could receive an abortion was an 'undue burden' because *some* women might be adversely affected. By contrast, in *Gonzales v. Carhart*, the Court said, that for a law to be unconstitutional there must be a showing that it would be an undue burden for a 'large fraction of women.' In *Gonzales*, a law regulating abortion is unconstitutional only if it would be an undue burden for a large fraction of women.[47]

Despite these ambiguities in the 'undue burden' test, *Casey* is clear and emphatic in reaffirming, that states may not prohibit abortions prior to viability and that states may prohibit abortions after viability except where necessary to protect the women's life or health. Likewise, in its subsequent decision in *Stenberg*, the Court began its opinion by declaring:

> '[B]efore viability the woman has a right to choose to terminate her pregnancy.'[48]

No Requirement for Government Funding for Abortions

The US Supreme Court repeatedly has held that the government is not constitutionally required to subsidize abortions even if it is paying for childbirth. In 1977, in three cases, the Court upheld the ability of the government to deny funding for 'nontherapeutic abortions'—that is, abortions that were not performed to protect the life or health of the mother.

In *Beal v. Doe*, the Supreme Court held that the federal Medicaid Act did not require, that states fund nontherapeutic first trimester abortions as part of participating in the joint federal-state program.[49] In *Maher v. Roe*, the Supreme Court upheld the constitutionality of a state law, that denied the use of Medicaid funds for nontherapeutic first trimester abortions, although, the law provided funding for medically necessary first trimester abortions.[50] And in *Poelker v. Doe*, the Court found that it was constitutional for a city to refuse to pay for nontherapeutic first trimester abortions in its public hospital.[51]

In 1980, in two cases, the Supreme Court went even further and affirmed the constitutionality of laws that denied public funding for medically necessary abortions except where it was necessary to save the life of the mother. In *Harris v. McRae*, the Court upheld a federal law, the Hyde Amendment (1977), that prohibited the use of federal funds for performing abortions –

> 'except where the life of the mother would be endangered if the fetus were carried to term'

or except for cases of rape or incest,

> 'when such rape or incest has been reported promptly to a law enforcement agency or public health service.'[52]

Similarly, in *Williams v. Zbaraz*, the Supreme Court found constitutional a state law that prohibited the use of state funds for performing abortions except where the mother's life was in danger.[53]

In 1989, *Webster v. Reproductive Health Services*, the US Supreme Court upheld a state law prohibiting the use of public employees and facilities to perform or assist the performance of abortions except where necessary to save the mother's life.[54] The Court said, that this law was indistinguishable from the earlier cases that allowed the government to deny funding of abortions.[55]

In all of these cases, the US Supreme Court gave the same basic reasons as to why it is constitutional for the government to deny funding or facilities for abortions, even though it pays for childbirth. First, the Court often said, that the existence of a constitutional right does not create a duty for the government to subsidize the exercise of the right. For example, in *Harris v. McRae*, the Court said:

> 'It cannot be that because government may not prohibit the use of contraceptives, or prevent parents from sending their children to a private school, government, therefore, has an affirmative constitutional obligation to ensure that all persons have the financial resources to obtain contraceptives or send their children to private schools.'[56]

This is in accord with a more general principle, that the government rarely has an affirmative constitutional duty to provide benefits or to facilitate the exercise of rights.

Second, the Court said, that denial of public funding places a woman in no different position than she would have been if there was no Medicaid program or no public hospital. In *Harris v. McRae*, the Court said, that the prohibition of the use of federal funds for abortions –

> 'leaves an indigent woman with at least the same range of choices in deciding whether to obtain a medically necessary abortion as she would have had if Congress chose to subsidize no health care costs at all.'[57]

Third, the US Supreme Court emphasized that the government constitutionally could make the choice to encourage childbirth over abortion. In *Maher v. Roe*, the Court wrote that –

> *Roe* 'implies no limitation on the authority of a State to make a value judgment favoring childbirth over abortion, and to implement that judgment by the allocation of public funds.'[58]

Latest Verdict of US Supreme Court

In 2016, Donald Trump (1946)[59] in his Presidential election campaign said, that *Roe v. Wade* would 'automatically' be overruled by justices he would appoint to the US Supreme Court. Three years later, with two of his picks in robes and a surge of challenges to *Roe* flying to the court, abortion-rights supporters fear that Trump's prediction may be close to coming true. But, so far, every time a reckoning on *Roe* seems imminent, the Supreme Court takes a step back. Abortion rights are in trouble, but it seems that the conservative justices on the nation's highest court, with the notable exception of Clarence Thomas (1948), are content to plod along rather than rush headlong into a decision, that could spark a dangerous new flashpoint in the culture wars.

States like Georgia and Alabama have passed anti-abortion legislation that is clearly in violation of *Roe v. Wade*. The Supreme Court has been considering whether or not to take up *Box v. Planned Parenthood of Indiana and Kentucky*,[60] a case involving a more insidious type of anti-abortion law. The *Box* case, concerns HEA (House Enrolled Act) 1337, which Mike Pence when he was Governor of Indiana, and recently the 48th Vice-President of US, signed into law in 2016. In a Seventh Circuit Court of Appeals ruling, two of the law's provisions were deemed unconstitutional:

— a requirement that fetal remains from abortions be buried or cremated;
— and a bar on abortions motivated solely by the fetus's race, sex or diagnosed disability such as Down syndrome.

The fetal-remains provision lacks a rational basis, the Seventh Circuit held, while the 'nondiscrimination' rule undermines *Roe's* promise, reaffirmed in 1992 in *Planned Parenthood v. Casey*,[61] that states may place no 'undue burden' on a woman's right to end a pregnancy prior to viability, or before 24 weeks' gestation. To prohibit women with particular motivations from aborting their fetuses is to impose 'far greater than a substantial obstacle' on the constitutional right, the Seventh Circuit ruled. These limits are –

> 'absolute prohibitions on abortions prior to viability which the Supreme Court has clearly held cannot be imposed by the state.'

Searches and Seizures

The 4th Amendment, recognizes a right of personal privacy entitling the American people to protection against arbitrary intrusion by law enforcement officers. The framers of the Bill of Rights were actually sensitive to the need to insulate people from unlimited governmental powers of search and seizure. One of the chief complaints of the American colonists was the power of police and customs officials to conduct 'general' searches under the dreaded 'writs of assistance' authorized by British Parliament in 1662, these writs became controversial when they were issued by courts in British America in the 1760s. In 1761, James Otis Jr (1725–83)[62] reviled the 'writs of assistance' as –

> 'the worst instrument of arbitrary power, the most destructive of English liberty and the fundamental principles of law, that was ever found in an English law book'(quoted in *Boyd v. United States*).[63]

When the 1st American Congress considered the Bill of Rights, most state constitutions already contained limitations on government powers in this area. Thus, there was little objection in Congress to the 'search and seizure' amendment contained in James Madison's proposal for a Bill of rights. After minor changes in language, the 4th Amendment was adopted in the following words:

> 'The right of the people to be secure in their persons, houses, papers, and effects, against unreasonable searches and seizures, shall not be violated, and no Warrants shall issue, but upon probable cause, supported by Oath or affirmation, and particularly describing the place to be searched, and the persons or things to be seized.'

Like many of the broad provisions of the American Constitution, the 4th Amendment raises as many questions as it answers. It is clear that government cannot subject people to unreasonable searches and seizures, but what is meant by 'unreasonable'? What exactly is a search? What is the precise meaning of 'probable cause'? In the American legal system, these are questions for the Supreme Court to answer. However, the answers to these questions can be very complicated and confusing for the ordinary citizens.

Reasonable Expectations of Privacy

One of the most challenging problems in adapting the 18th century language of the 4th Amendment to current circumstances is determining the extent of privacy to be protected. Obviously, the amendment prohibits unreasonable searches of one's dwelling. But what about the search of an individual's automobile, motor home, or boat? What about one's telephone conversations, fax transmissions, or e-mail? Are such communications protected by the 4th Amendment?

In *Olmstead v. United States*,[64] the American Supreme Court took a very strict view of the scope of the 4th Amendment. Roy Olmstead, a suspected bootlegger, was charged with conspiracy to violate the National Prohibition Act (NPA).[65] The government's evidence consisted of transcripts of Olmstead's telephone conversations obtained through a wiretap placed outside his property.

The agents had obtained no warrant authorizing the wiretap. Although, there was no search or seizure of his persons or physical property, Olmstead maintained that the 4th Amendment had been violated. The term 'effects', as used in the 4th Amendment, could have been interpreted to include telephone conversations, The Supreme Court, however opted for a narrower construction. Writing for the majority, Chief Justice William Howard Taft (1857–1930)[66] stated:

> 'The reasonable view is that one who installs in his house a telephone instrument with connecting wires intends to project his voice to those quite outside, and that the wires beyond his house, and messages passing over them, are not within the protection of the 4th Amendment.'

Justice Louis Brandeis (1856–1941), along with three of his colleagues, dissented. In one of his most forward-looking opinions, he asserted the need to keep the American Constitution relevant to changing technological conditions:—

> 'The progress of science in furnishing the government with means of espionage is not likely to stop with wiretapping. Ways may someday be developed by which the government, without removing papers from secret drawers, can reproduce them in court, and by which it will be enabled to expose to a jury the most intimate occurrences of the home .... Can it be that the Constitution affords no protection against such invasions of individual security?'

In 1928, the telephone was already wide use but today it is virtually omnipresent. Perhaps, it was this reality that motivated the US Supreme Court in 1967 to overturn *Olmstead*, in the landmark decision of *Katz v. United States*. Here, the Court reversed a conviction in which government agents, acting without a warrant, were recording his conversations via a 'bug' or listening device, attached to the outside of a public telephone booth, from which Charles Katz, a suspected bookie, often placed calls. Writing for the Court, Justice Potter Stewart (1915–85) stated, that –

> 'the Fourth Amendment protects people, not places.'

Adhering to Justice John M. Harlan II's (1899–1971)[67] concurrence in *Katz*, the Supreme Court has since held that the 4th Amendment extends to any place or anything in which an individual has a reasonable expectation of privacy. The Court has demonstrated a willingness to consider hotel rooms, garages, offices, automobiles, sealed letters, suitcases, and other closed containers as protected by the 4th Amendment. On the other hand, in *Oliver v. United States*, the Court has held, that there is no 4th Amendment protection for abandoned or discarded property or for the open fields except what covers the 'open fields' around a home, even if that area is private property.[68]

Use of Thermal Imagers by Police—In the year 2000, the US Supreme Court heard one of the more interesting problems in this area. In *Kyllo v. United States*,[69] the Court considered whether the use of a thermal imager by law enforcement agents constitutes a 'search' within the meaning of the 4th Amendment.

In this case, the police had used the thermal imaging device without first obtaining a warrant to scan a home, they suspected to be housing an indoor marijuana growing operation. Having discerned the telltale infrared radiation associated with the use of indoor growing lights, and having obtained corroborating information, the police obtained a warrant to search the premises, where they found more than 100 cannabis plants.

The procedure used by police in the *Kyllo* case has been in wide use around the country as part of the national war on drugs. Police and prosecutors typically take the view that the thermal scan is not a search within the meaning of the 4th Amendment, since it merely collects data on heat that is being released into the public space. In a 5 to 4 decision, the Supreme Court disagreed with this perspective. Writing for the Court, Justice Antonin Scalia (1936–2016) opined that –

> '[w]here, as here, the Government uses a device that is not in general public use, to explore details of the home that would previously have been unknowable without physical intrusion, the surveillance is a search and is presumptively unreasonable without a warrant.'

In dissent, Justice John Paul Stevens (1920–2019) noted that –

> '[a]ll that the infrared camera did…was passively measure heat emitted from the exterior surfaces of petitioners home, all that those measurements showed were relative differences in emission levels, vaguely indicating that some areas of the roof and outside walls were warmer than others.'

In Justice Stevens's view, the police did not significantly intrude on the privacy of the occupants. The *Kyllo* case is interesting because it shows how changing technology creates new and difficult 4th Amendment problems. As technology in this area advances, courts will continue to confront such issues.

Probable Cause

The fundamental requirement imposed by the 4th Amendment is that searches and seizures must be 'reasonable'. The amendment presupposes that searches would be authorized by warrants, and that warrants will not be issued without 'probable cause'. The US Supreme Court has recognized exceptions to the warrant requirement, but has for the most part viewed 'probable cause' as an indispensable precondition of a valid search.

'Probable cause' is a term of art that does not have any precise meaning. The US Supreme Court has observed that –

> 'probable cause is a fluid concept-turning on the assessment of probabilities in particular factual contexts- not readily, or even usefully, reduced to a neat set of legal rules', (*Illinois v. Gates*)[70]

As interpreted by the Court, 'probable cause' means in effect that for a search to be valid, a police officer must have good reason to believe that the search will produce evidence of crime. According to the Court's decision in *Brinegar v. United States*,[71] officers have 'probable cause' when –

> 'the facts and circumstances within their knowledge, and of which they had reasonably trustworthy information, [are] sufficient in themselves to warrant a man of reasonable caution in the belief that an offense has been or is being committed.'

The Warrant Requirement

A search warrant is simply an order issued by a judge or magistrate that authorizes a search. To obtain a search warrant, a law enforcement officer must take an oath or sign an affidavit attesting to certain facts that, if true, constitute 'probable cause' to support the issuance of a warrant.

In *Coolidge v. New Hampshire*,[72] the American Supreme Court invalidated a warrant that was issued by the state's attorney general, rather than by a judge or magistrate. Thus, the Court places great importance on the role of the neutral and detached officer in maintaining the integrity of the 4th Amendment. This amendment also requires that search warrants describe with particularity –

> 'the place to be searched, and the persons or things to be seized.'

This provision reflects the framers' distaste for the general warrants used in colonial America.

In *Stanford v. Texas*,[73] the Supreme Court reaffirmed this long-standing distaste for 'dragnet' searches when it invalidated a five-hour search of a Communist Party headquarters resulting in the seizure of some 5000 items, including books by Justice Hugo Black (1886–1971), and Pope John XXIII (1881–1963).

Confidential and Anonymous Informants

One of the most controversial questions concerning the issuance of search warrants involves the use of confidential or anonymous informants. Police often use tips provided by confidential informants to obtain search warrants that lead to the discovery of incriminating evidence.

In *Aguilar v. Texas*,[74] police obtained a warrant simply by saying that they –

> 'had received reliable information from a credible person'

that illegal drugs would be found at a certain location. The Supreme Court ultimately invalidated the warrant, holding that an affidavit must inform the magistrate of the underlying circumstances from which the informant concluded, that the narcotics were where he claimed they were, and some of the underlying circumstances from which the officer concluded that the informant, whose identity need not be disclosed,...was 'credible' or his information 'reliable'.

Five years later, the Court reaffirmed this two-pronged test in the case of *Spinelli v. United States*.[75] The so-called *Aguilar-Spinelli* test made it more difficult for police to obtain warrants based on tips from confidential informants. Accordingly, on this issue, as on several others, the Warren Court was much criticized for 'hand-cuffing the police'. In 1983, a more conservative Supreme Court under Chief Justice Warren E. Burger (1907–95)[76] abandoned the rigorous *Aguilar-Spinelli* test in favour of a 'totality of circumstances' approach, that makes it easier for police to get search warrants.

In *Illinois v. Gates*, Justice William Rehnquist (1924–2005) asserted, that the *Aguilar-Spinelli* test could not 'avoid seriously impeding the task of law enforcement' because 'anonymous tips seldom could survive a rigorous application of either of the *Spinelli* prongs.' Dissenting Justice William J. Brennan Jr (1906–97) argued that:

> the Court [gave] virtually no consideration to the value of insuring that finding of probable cause are based on information that a magistrate can reasonably say has been obtained in a reliable way by an honest or credible person. I...fear that the Court's rejection of *Aguilar* and *Spinelli*... 'may foretell an evisceration of the probable cause standards.'

In 1984, the Court held, that the 'totality of circumstances' standard announced in the *Illinois v. Gates* decision, was to be given a broad interpretation by lower courts (*Massachusetts v. Upton*[77]).

Subsequently, the Court moved beyond *Illinois v. Gates* and manifested an even greater level of permissiveness toward police reliance on anonymous tips (for example, *Alabama v. White*).[78] Critics of these decisions argue, that the Court's interest in facilitating law enforcement is eclipsing its traditional concern for the privacy of citizens subjected to police searches.

Execution of Search Warrants

Under federal law an officer is required to knock and announce upon arrival at the place to be searched. The purpose of this requirement is to reduce the potential for violence as well as to protect the occupants' right of privacy.

In *Wilson v. Arkansas* (1995),[79] the US Supreme Court decided unanimously, that the 4th Amendment requires police, absent a threat of physical violence or other exigent circumstances, to 'knock and announce' when serving a search warrant at a home. The most striking aspect of the Court's decision was, that the opinion was authored by Justice Clarence Thomas (1948), who has generally taken a pro-law enforcement position in criminal cases in keeping with his adherence to the doctrine of 'original intent', Justice Thomas examined the state of the common law at the time when the 4th Amendment was adopted. He concluded that –

> '[a]t the time of the framing, the common law of search and seizure recognized a law enforcement officer's authority to break open the doors of a dwelling, but generally indicated that he first ought to announce his presence and authority.'

Justice Clarence Thomas concluded, that the authors of the Bill of Rights intended for the common law 'knock and announce' requirement to be part and parcel of the 4th Amendment. The *Wilson* case, resolved a conflict among lower courts as to whether the American Constitution requires officers to 'knock and announce' – a requirement that many states already observed under their respective constitutions, statutes, or judicial decisions.

One of the reasons police officers resist compliance with the 'knock and announce' requirement is that by announcing their presence, officers risk losing evidence that is easily destroyed or disposed of. In the *Wilson* case, the Court said that officers facing exigent circumstances could dispense with the 'knock and announce' requirement. But in *Richards v. Wisconsin*,[80] the Court ruled unanimously, that states may not create a blanket 'drug exception' to the requirement that police officers 'knock and announce' prior to executing a search warrant.

Warrantless Searches

Although, the 4th Amendment clearly indicates a preference for search warrants, the US Supreme Court has held that, under exigent circumstances, a warrantless search may nevertheless be 'reasonable.' One example of a legitimate warrantless search is the search incidental to a lawful arrest. In *Chimel v. California*,[81] Justice Potter Stewart's (1915–85) majority opinion stated:

> 'When an arrest is made, it is reasonable for the arresting officer to search the person arrested in order to remove any weapons that the latter might seek to use in order to resist arrest or effect his escape... In addition, it is entirely reasonable for the arresting officer to search for and seize any evidence on the arrestee's person in order to prevent its concealment or destruction. And the area into which an arrestee might reach in order to grab a weapon or evidentiary items must, of course, be governed by a like rule.'

Consent Searches—An obvious example of a legitimate warrantless search is one based on the consent of the individual whose privacy is to be invaded. It is an elementary principle of law that individuals may waive their constitutional rights; 4th Amendment protections are no exception.

In *Schneckloth v. Bustamonte*,[82] the US Supreme Court upheld a search based on consent even though the police failed to advise the individual, that he was not obligated to consent to the police request. In *Florida v. Bostick*,[83] a highly publicized 1991 decision, the Court upheld the controversial police practice of boarding interstate buses in big city terminals, approaching persons matching a drug courier profile, and asking them for permission to search their belongings.

Later, in *Ohio v. Robinette*,[84] the Court held, that police are not required to inform motorists who are stopped for other reasons that they are 'free to go' before asking them to consent to a search of their automobile. To determine whether consent was given voluntarily, and knowingly, the Court looks to the 'totality of circumstances' surrounding the search.

Other Justifications for Warrantless Searches—Other accepted justification for warrantless searches included 'plain view' (*Coolidge v. New Hampshire*),[85] 'hot pursuit' (*Warden v. Hayden*),[86] 'evanescent evidence' (*Schmerber v. California*),[87] and emergency searches (*Michigan v. Tyler*).[88] In each of these examples, compelling exigencies make the warrant requirement itself unreasonable, at least in the view of the US Supreme Court.

Automobile Searches—One of the most interesting and most problematic—exceptions to the warrant requirement is the automobile search. In *Carroll v. United States*,[89] the US Supreme Court upheld the warrantless search of an automobile believed to be carrying illegal liquor. The Court stressed, however, that probable cause was essential to justify a warrantless automobile search. Indiscriminately stopping and searching passing motorists in an effort to discover evidence of crime could never be constitutionally justified.

The case of *Arkansas v. Sanders*,[90] presented the Court with an interesting question. Can warrantless searches of automobiles extend to all the contents of said vehicles, or do police still need a warrant to search luggage taken from the trunk? In *Sanders*, the Court disallowed the search of the luggage, suggesting to some observers that the automobile exception was 'in trouble.'

However, in *United States v. Ross*,[91] the US Supreme Court demonstrated otherwise. In a 6 to 3 decision, the Court upheld a warrantless search of a paper bag and a leather pouch found in the locked trunk of a stopped automobile, a search that produced $3200 in cash and a sizable quantity of heroin. Writing for the Court, Justice John Paul Stevens (1920–2019) clarified the legitimate scope of a warrantless automobile search as that –

> 'no greater than a magistrate could have authorized by issuing a warrant based on the probable cause that justified the search.'

Dissenting vehemently in *Ross*, Justice Thurgood Marshall (1908–93) assailed the majority position as 'flatly inconsistent…with established 4th Amendment principles.'

In 1991, the Court went one step further and formally overruled *Arkansas v. Sanders*, removing any lingering doubts about judicial distinctions between searches of automobiles and closed containers found therein. Thus, under current interpretation of the 4th Amendment, the legitimate scope of a warrantless search, whether of an automobile or any other place, is determined more by the nature of the object of the search than by the nature of the space being searched.

Police Powers of Search and Entry in the UK

There is however, no recognition of the 'right of privacy' in UK despite forceful advocacy by progressive thinkers like late Lord Denning (1899–1999). It was held in *Malone v. Metropolitan Police Commissioner*,[92] that English law does not recognize any general right of privacy. Nevertheless, many rules of common law protect individuals from intrusion on their private lives like laws regarding trespass, confidential information, business secrets or publication of the intimacies of the marriage bed.[93]

Although, the normal rule is that no person may enter private premises without permission from the owner or occupant, police may always enter premises to execute a warrant for arrest or to search a person lawfully arrested. It was also held in the famous case of *Elias v. Pasmore*,[94] that where police lawfully enter private premises to arrest a man, but do not possess a search warrant, they would still be excused if they take documents or search the premises, provided that they discover something which is useful as evidence in the prosecution of the arrested person, or even of some other person altogether. This decision really provides that document, even though illegally seized, may be put in evidence against an accused person.[95] But it may amount to a dangerous accretion of power in the hands of the police, even though it was made clear in the case itself, that the accused would still have a right of civil action against the police for trespass etc., in respect of any documents searched or taken away which proved to be of no use for a prosecution. This decision was to some extent superseded by the provisions in the subsequent Incitement to Disaffection Act 1934, and the Public Order Act 1936, which specify types of case in which it would be lawful for the police to make searches without warrant.

It should be remembered that many of the cases on this subject, and on that of police powers in respect of unlawful assemblies etc., took place in the economically and politically troubled times of the 1930s, when considerable difficulty was experienced in controlling the public meetings and activities of Communists and Fascists. Extensive powers were sometimes sorely needed. Concerning a more general run of criminal activity it is of note that the Theft Act 1968, Section 25(3) provides, that a person who is authorized to search premises for stolen goods may seize any goods he believes to be stolen, and that such seizure is legal whether or not the goods turn out in the end to have been stolen.

But *Kuruma v. The Queen* in 1955,[96] makes it clear that the statutes leave untouched the basic common law provisions concerning admissibility of illegally obtained evidence. In that case, Kuruma son of Kaniu, a Kenyan had been found guilty, under Emergency Regulations in force at the time, of unlawfully possessing ammunition, and had been sentenced to death. Although, he had been lawfully arrested under the Emergency Regulations, the policemen who arrested him had no power to search him, since they were below the rank of officer (assistant inspector), that had such a power to search without warrant in Kenya. Yet, the policemen who arrested him did search him at the time of his arrest and they found two cartridges on him which were used as vital evidence at his trial. On appeal to the Privy Council, it was held that the use of such evidence was lawful, and of course any question of a right of civil action for any part of the search which provided useless for the purposes of a prosecution would have been small comfort to Kuruma. The Board, however, did direct that the sentence should not be carried out until the Secretary of State had had an opportunity of considering the case.

A decision which possibly goes even further in *Chic Fashions (West Wales) Ltd. v Jones*,[97] in which the Court of Appeal held, that a constable who enters premises by virtue of a search warrant for stolen goods may seize not only the goods covered by the warrant, but also any other goods which he believes on reasonable grounds to have been stolen and to be material evidence on a charge of stealing or receiving against the person in possession of them or anyone associated with him. It was further held that subsequent events cannot affect the lawfulness of the original act, so that the fact that the goods were not stolen, and not used as evidence on the prosecution of any criminal charge, did not render the Chief Constable liable in damages for trespass. Clearly, a balance should be struck between protection of the individual from excessive police powers and the desirability of the police being able to use relevant evidence for a prosecution, however, it is obtained.

To take an extreme example, if a policeman chases a man he sees committing a theft, and in catching him happens to put his hand in the man's pocket, and then withdraws his hand which is (unlawfully) grasping a piece of paper, and this paper turns out upon inspection to be a written confession to a murder which the criminal had been carrying round with him for his own private delectation, it would be ridiculous to say that the policeman's only duty as far as the paper was concerned would be to return it and forget he had ever seen it. But on the other hand the police should not be encouraged to go to all sorts of unlawful lengths on the off-chance that some relevant evidence might turn up.

A further possibility of invasion of private premises by the police without warrant is instanced by the case of the *Thomas v. Sawkins*,[98] which provides a limitation at common law upon the general right to hold a public meeting on private property. There it was held, that the police may enter private premises without a warrant if they have reasonable grounds to believe that, if they are not present, seditious speeches will be made or breaches of the peace will take place. It appears, therefore, that a general licence to the public to enter private premises may be revoked as concerns anyone except a policeman, who may in his discretion override such a revocation. Such a police power is, however, limited, for it has also been held,[99] that a power of entry without warrant does not exist where the commission or future commission of merely a summary offence has been suspected.

The cases considered above are all cases at common law, but certain statutory powers of entry and search have also been conferred upon civil servants, public corporation officers, inspectors of gas and electricity meters, health visitors etc. The Criminal Law Act 1967, Section 2(6) also:

— permits a constable, for the purpose of arresting a person for an arrestable offence, to enter and search any place where that person is or where the constable, has reasonable cause, to suspect that person to be.[100]

Post Interception and Telephone Tapping

The interception of letters and particularly of telephone conversations has quite often been used as an aid to the maintenance of law and order. There have often been fears that the use of such a weapon could amount to a dangerous incursion upon normal civil liberties. But, in 1957, a Committee of Privy Councillors reported, that the opening of mail and tapping of telephones in certain circumstances for the defence of the realm was within the royal prerogative, as afforded by early statutory powers. The practice is under the control of the Home Secretary and requires his warrant. The Committee recommended that telephone messages should only be intercepted to detect serious crime or to safeguard the security of the state.

In 1981, Lord Diplock (1907–85),[101] who had been asked by the Home Secretary to monitor the interception procedures, reported that they had been consistently being used only within the limits suggested in 1957, and he recommended that no change in procedures or safeguards was required.[102]

Right of Privacy in Pakistan and India

Article 14 of the Pakistan Constitution provides that –

> 'the dignity of man and, subject to law, privacy of home, shall be inviolable'

This protection however, has been made subject to law which does not mean that the guarantee can be taken away by law. It only means that the 'right of privacy' may be regulated by law.

For example, a police official may be permitted by law to enter a house for making an arrest or a search. Of course, such entry would be subject to warrants for search issued under the law by the competent authority. In any case, the police officials would have to execute the warrants very discreetly or cautiously keeping in view the human dignity of the inmates and modesty of the females living inside the house. In either case, the right to privacy in Pakistan is limited to the privacy of house and rather than the privacy of person, the way it has developed in the United States of America.

The courts in Pakistan have to define and develop this right particularly in the context of searches and seizures of articles by the police officials after forcing their entry into the house of someone ostensibly to collect evidence in a criminal case. Thus, there is frequent misuse of this practice in Pakistan which has become a cause for harassment of the people at the hands of highhanded police officials.

Article 14 embodies within itself the Islamic concept of *Purdah* because *Purdah* is inherent in the idea of privacy of home.[103] Right to privacy, however, cannot be claimed by a person whose house is distantly situated from the proposed building.[104] The Supreme Court of Pakistan held, that the inviolability of privacy is directly linked with the dignity of man.

> If a man is to preserve his dignity, if he is to live with honour and reputation, his privacy whether in home or outside the home, has to be saved from invasion and protected from illegal intrusion.[105]

The dignity of man is an absolute right and is not subject to law. It is an unqualified guarantee. But the right to privacy of home is subject to law and is therefore not absolute.[106]

In *Mehram Ali v. Federation of Pakistan*, Section 10 of the Anti-Terrorism Act 1997, was held to be invalid and the same was required to be suitably amended so as to provide that before entering a premises, the concerned officer should record his reasons in writing for such belief and serve on the person or premises concerned a copy of such reason before conducting the search.[107]

In India, there is no constitutional guarantee of the 'right of privacy'. If the Indian Supreme Court has to develop a fundamental right to privacy, it can do so only by a liberal interpretation of the guarantee of 'personal liberty' in Article 21 of the Indian Constitution.[108] This question was partly raised, though not resolved in *Kharak Singh v. State of U.P.*[109] The question raised was whether domiciliary visits or 'surveillance' by police over a person at his house, without authority of law constituted a contravention of Article 21 of the Constitution. The answer of the majority was not clear enough but, Justice Koka Subba Rao (1902–76),[110] speaking for the minority, held that the right of privacy was included in the freedom of 'personal liberty' guaranteed by Article 21 of the Constitution.

The right to privacy also protects the autonomy of individuals to make choices with regard to decisions on sexual orientation.[111] In *District Registrar & Collector, Hyderabad v. Canara Bank*,[112] the Indian Supreme Court struck down a provision allowing authorities to inspect banking records that could lead to proof of an offence, holding that the right to privacy protected documents handed over by customers on a confidential basis.

Wiretapping has been condemned universally as invasion of privacy. However, Pakistan and India have lagged behind in this context. Both countries need to develop law through interpretation of the fundamental rights in order to expand on the 'right of privacy' as it is recognized throughout the democratic world.

Notes

1. Hugo Black served as Associate Justice of the US Supreme Court from 1937 to 1971.
2. Robert Bork served as a judge of the United States Court of Appeals for the District of Columbia Circuit from 1982 to 1988.
3. 410 U.S. 113 (1973).
4. Otis H. Stephens, John M. Scheb II, *American Constitutional Law*, (California, Belmont: Thomson/West, 2003), pp. 660–1.
5. 501 U.S. 560 (1991).
6. 381 U.S. 479 (1965).
7. 389 U.S. 347 (1967).

8. 277 U.S. 438 (1928).
9. Louis Brandeis was former Associate Justice of the US Supreme Court from 1916 to 1939.
10. Sarah Weddington is an American attorney, law professor and former member of the Texas House of Representatives.
11. Supra Note 4, pp. 666–7.
12. 410 U.S. 113 (1973).
13. 410 U.S. 179 (1973).
14. Harry Blackmun served as Associate Justice of the US Supreme Court from 1970 until 1994.
15. William O. Douglas served as Associate Justice of the US Supreme Court from 1939 to 1975.
16. William Rehnquist was the 16th Chief Justice of the United States from 1986 to 2005.
17. Byron White served as Associate Justice of the US Supreme Court from 1962 to 1993.
18. Several Justices—Chief Justice Warren E. Burger, Justice William O. Douglas, and Justice Potter Stewart- wrote separate concurring opinions. Chief Justice Burger said, that he would allow a state to require that 2 physicians certify an abortion before one could be performed. Justice Douglas argued that prohibiting abortions threatens women's lives and thus, is unconstitutional. Justice Stewart wrote separately to emphasize, that the right to abortion was properly protected under the liberty of the Due Process Clause.
19. John Hart Ely was an American legal scholar known for his studies of constitutional law.
20. Laurence Tribe is a American legal scholar who is the Carl M. Loeb University Professor at the Harvard Law School.
21. Erwin Chemerinsky,; *Constitutional Law: Principles and Policies*, 2nd ed. (New York: Aspen Law & Business, 2002), pp. 792–3.
22. John T. Noonan Jr was also a United States Circuit Judge of the United States Court of Appeals for the Ninth Circuit.
23. Frances Olsen is Professor of Law at UCLA and a noted member of the school of Feminist Legal Theory.
24. Judith Jarvis Thomson was an American philosopher who studied and worked on ethics and metaphysics.
25. Supra Note 21, p. 793.
26. Catharine A. MacKinnon is the Elizabeth A. Long Professor of Law at the University of Michigan Law School.
27. Supra Note 21, p. 794.
28. 476 U.S. 747 (1986).
29. Warren E. Burger was the 15th Chief Justice of the US Supreme Court, serving from 1969 to 1986.
30. Ronald Reagan served as the 40th president of the United States from 1981 to 1989.
31. Supra Note 4, p. 670.
32. 492 U.S. 490 (1989).
33. 500 U.S. 173 (1991).
34. The US Department of Health and Human Services (HHS) is the nation's principal agency for protecting the health of all Americans and providing essential human services.
35. George H. W. Bush served as the 41st President of the United States from 1989 to 1993.
36. 505 U.S. 833 (1992).
37. Ernie D. Preate Jr served as the 41st Attorney General of Pennsylvania.
38. Kathryn Kolbert served as the State Coordinating Counsel of the American Civil Liberty Union's Reproductive Freedom Project in New York City from 1988 to 1992.
39. Kenneth W. Starr served as a United States circuit judge and 39th solicitor general of the United States.
40. 462 U.S. 416 (1983).
41. 476 U.S. 747 (1986).
42. Bill Clinton served as the 42nd President of the United States from 1993 to 2001.
43. Supra Note 4, pp. 671–2. 476 U.S. 747 (1986).
44. 530 U.S. 914 (2000).
45. 550 U.S. 124 (2007).
46. 505 U.S. 833 (1992).
47. 550 U.S. 124 (2007).
48. 530 U.S. 914 (2000).
49. 432 U.S. 438 (1977).
50. 432 U.S. 464 (1977).
51. 432 U.S. 519 (1977).
52. 448 U.S. 297 (1980).
53. 448 U.S. 358 (1980).
54. 492 U.S. 490 (1989).
55. In *Rust v. Sullivan*, 500 U.S. 173 (1991), the Court held that the government does not violate the First Amendment if it denies funding to Planned Parenthood clinics, that perform abortion counseling or make abortion referrals.

56. 448 U.S. 297 (1988).
57. Ibid at p. 317.
58. 432 U.S. 464 (1977).
59. Donald Trump served as the 45th President of the United States from 2017 to 2021.
60. 139 S. Ct. 1780 (2019).
61. 505 U.S. 833 (1992).
62. James Otis Jr. was a political activist, pamphleteer, legislator in Boston, a member of the Massachusetts provincial assembly during the period leading upto the American Revolution.
63. 116 U.S. 616 (1886).
64. 277 U.S. 438 (1928).
65. The National Prohibition Act (NPA), known informally as the Volstead Act, was adopted by Congress in 1919 to implement the recently ratified 18th Amendment to the US Constitution.
66. William Howard Taft was the 27th President of the United States (1909–1913) and the 10th Chief Justice of the United States (1921–1930).
67. John Marshall Harlan II served as Associate Justice of the US Supreme Court from 1955 to 1971.
68. 466 U.S. 170 (1984).
69. 533 U.S. 27 (2001).
70. 462 U.S. 213 (1983).
71. 338 U.S. 160 (1949).
72. 403 U.S. 43 (1971).
73. 379 U.S. 476 (1965).
74. 378 U.S. 108 (1964).
75. 393 U.S. 410 (1969).
76. Warren E. Burger was the 15th Chief Justice of the United States Supreme Court, serving from 1969 to 1986.
77. 466 U.S. 727 (1984).
78. 496 U.S. 325 (1990).
79. 514 U.S. 927 (1995).
80. 520 U.S. 385 (1997).
81. 395 U.S. 752 (1969).
82. 412 U.S. 218 (1973).
83. 501 U.S. 429 (1991).
84. 519 U.S. 33 (1996).
85. 403 U.S. 443 (1971).
86. 387 U.S. 294 (1967).
87. 384 U.S. 757 (1966).
88. 436 U.S. 499 (1978).
89. 267 U.S. 132 (1925).
90. 442 U.S. 753 (1979).
91. 456 U.S. 798 (1982).
92. [1979] CLY 2098.
93. *Schering Chemical Ltd v. Falkman Ltd*, (1982) Q.B. 1; *Duchess of Argyll v. Duke of Argyll*, (1967) Ch 302.
94. (1934) 2 KB 164.
95. An earlier case was *Jones v. Owen* (1870) 34 JP 759. Later cases are *Herman King v. The Queen* (1969) AC 304, (1968) 2 All ER 610; *Ghani v. Jones* (1970) 1 QB 693, (1969) 3 All ER 1700; and *R v. Sang* (1980) AC 402, (1979) 2 All ER 1222. *see also Regina v. Leatham* (1861) 8 Cox CC 498 at 503, where Crompton J said: 'It matters not how you get it; if you steal it even, it would be admissible in evidence.'
96. (1955) AC 197, (1955) 1 All ER 236.
97. (1968) 2 QB 299, (1968) 1 All ER 229; *see also Malone v. Metropolitan Police Commissioner* (1980) QB 49, (1979) 2 All ER 620.
98. (1935) 2 KB 249.
99. *Davis v. Lisle* (1936) 2 KB 434, (1936) 2 All ER 213.
100. D.C.M. Yardley, *Introduction to British Constitutional Law*, 6th ed. (London: Butterworths, 1984), pp. 93–6.
101. Lord Diplock served as Lord of Appeal in Ordinary from 30 September 1968 – 14 October 1985.
102. Supra Note 100, pp. 96–7.
103. *Suleman Mala v. Karachi Building Control Authority*, 1990 CLC 448; *Akhtar Hamid Ghori v. Saima Estate Developer*, 1989 CLC 2173, *Sardar Begum Faruqui v. Rashida Khatoon*, 1990 CLC 83.

104. *Ardeshir Cowasji v. Multiline Associates, Karachi,* PLD 1993 Karachi 237.
105. *Benazir Bhutto v. President of Pakistan,* PLD 1998 S.C. 388.
106. *In re: Suo Moto Constitutional Petition,* 1994 SCMR 1028.
107. PLD 1998 S.C. 1445.
108. Durga Das Basu, *Comparative Constitutional Law,* 3rd ed., (New Delhi: Prentice-Hall of India, 1984), p. 297.
109. AIR 1963 S.C.1295.
110. Koka Subba Rao served as 9th Chief Justice of India from 1966 to 1967.
111. *Gobind v. State of Madhya Pradesh,* (1975) 2 SCC 148.
112. (2005) 1 SCC 496.

19 Self-Incrimination

Historical background and rationale

The development of the privilege against self-incrimination in the UK

The privilege against 'self-incrimination' can only be understood against the background of English history that gave rise to it.

Early during the reign of Henry VIII (1491–1547), in the 16th century, England was a Roman Catholic state. Protestants were vigorously persecuted. Later, Henry VIII (1491–1547) broke ties with the Roman Catholic Church following which the British Parliament established the Church of England and the Protestants reversed the situation and began to persecute the Catholics.

This situation continued until the reign of Mary I of England (1516–58), known as Bloody Mary by her Protestants opponents, when once again the Catholics persecuted the Protestants. After Mary I of England's death in 1558, her half-sister Elizabeth I (1533–1603) took the throne and reversed Roman Catholicism. From 1560 onward, Elizabeth's Church began persecuting (in addition to the Catholics) dissident Protestants called Puritans.[1] This continued under James I (1566–1625)[2], and Charles I (1600–49)[3], and helped provoke the Revolution (1642–1651), in which the Puritans and their allies were victorious.

After the Puritan's victory, the authorities continued to persecute the Catholics, while also persecuting both the Anglican clergy who were less reform-minded than themselves, and the 'left wing' dissenters who broke away from the main body of the Puritans. Then, after the accession to power of Oliver Cromwell (1599–1658)[4], the center of the Puritan establishment moved left and began its own campaigns against the 'ungodly', persecuting the Catholics, the High Anglicans[5] and the right-wing Puritans. By the time of the Restoration of the monarchy under Charles II (1630–85)[6], all England was sick of religious persecution and for the most part it ceased.

This history is quite remarkable. In the course of about 150 years, members of every major religious group in England had been both the initiators and the victims of persecution and the roles had changed with bewildering rapidity. The oath was a significant instrument used in these persecutions. During the persecution of the Puritans by the Church of England under Elizabeth I (1533–1603), and James I (1566–1625), for example, Puritan ministers were called before the High Commission and asked questions under oath about their beliefs. Being men of God, they could not lie and, if they admitted to their deviant and nonconformist views, they could be seriously punished. As a result, increasingly, they claimed the right not to answer and the existence or non-existence of such a right gradually became a major issue in 17th century England. One of the most celebrated cases involving the right was that of John Lilburne also known as 'Freeborn John' (1614–57).[7]

In 1637, Lilburne, a Puritan dissenter, was brought before the Court of Star Chamber.[8] Having just returned from Holland, he was charged with sending 'factitious and scandalous books' to England. Lilburne repeatedly contended that he was entitled to notice, indictment, and court trial under the known laws of England;

- — that he had a right to be represented by counsel;
- — that he had a right to have witnesses summoned in his behalf and be confronted by witnesses against him;
- — and that he could not be compelled to testify against himself.

For refusing to respond to the questions, Lilburne was fined, was tied to a cart and, his body bared, was whipped through the streets of London. At Westminster he was placed in a pillory—his body bent down, his neck in a hole, and his lacerated back bared to the midday sun; there he stood for 2 hours and exhorted all who would listen to resist the tyranny of the bishops. Refusing to be quiet, he was gagged so cruelly that his mouth bled. After all this, he was kept in solitary confinement in Fleet Prison[9] with irons on his hands and legs and without anything to eat for 10 days. After Lilburne's release, his cruel treatment and bold resistance had two consequences. The first was the vote of the Long Parliament,[10] that his sentence was illegal and that he be paid reparations. The second was the abolition of both the Star Chamber and the Court of the High Commission by the same Parliament.

The development of the privilege was by no means complete at this point. As has been pointed out, [the] objection to compulsory self-incrimination were not, however, aimed at the practice in the regular criminal courts but, rather, at the practice as it was carried out by the Star Chamber and the High Commission. [After the abolition of the Courts of the Star Chamber and of the High Commission,] [q]uestioning of the accused at his trial continued unaltered for nearly two decades; the examination of the prisoner by the committing magistrate continued for as long as two centuries.

Nevertheless, a gradual repugnance to compulsory self-incrimination developed. By the end of the reign of Charles II (1630–85), the privilege was recognized in all courts when claimed by defendant or witness.[11]

Privilege against Self Incrimination in the USA

The 5th Amendment

By the close of the 17th century, the right against 'self-incrimination' was shakily or unevenly established in the USA. But a perceptible change was occurring in the legal development of all the colonies; English common law was increasingly becoming American law. The degree to which that was true varied from colony to colony, but the pace was not the same in each colony. Overall, as their political and economic systems matured, their legal systems, most strikingly in the field of criminal procedure, began to increasingly resemble that of England. The result was a greater familiarity with and respect for the right against 'self-incrimination'.

The fact must be emphasized that the right in question, was a right against compulsory 'self-incrimination', and, excepting rare occasions when judges intervened to protect a witness against incriminating interrogatories, the right had to be claimed by the defendant. Historically, it has been a fighting right: unless invoked, it offered no protection. It vested an option to refuse answer but did not bar interrogation nor taint a voluntary confession as improper evidence. Incriminating statements made by a suspect at the preliminary examination, or even at arraignment could always be used with devastating effect at his trial. That a man might unwittingly incriminate himself when questioned in no way impaired his legal right to refuse answer. He lacked the right to be warned that he need not answer, for the authorities were under no legal obligation to apprise him of his right.

That reform did not come in England until Sir John Jervis (1802–56)[12] drafted an Act in 1848, known as Justices Protection Act 1848, and in the United States, more than a century later the matter was still a subject of acute constitutional controversy. Yet, if the authorities in 18th century Britain, and in her colonies were not obliged to caution the prisoner, he in turn was not legally obliged to reply.

As originally proposed by James Madison (1751–1836),[13] the 5th Amendment's 'Self-Incrimination' Clause was part of a miscellaneous article that read:

> 'No person shall be subject, except in cases of impeachment, to more than one punishment or trial for the same offence; nor shall be compelled to be a witness against himself; nor be deprived of life, liberty, or property, without due process of law; nor be obliged to relinquish his property, where it may be necessary for public use, without a just compensation.'

This proposal reflects the research and novelty that characterized Madison's work....[N]o state, either in its own constitution or in its recommended amendments, had a 'Self-Incrimination' Clause phrased like that introduced by James Madison (1751–1836):

> 'no person....shall be compelled to be a witness against himself.'

Not only was Madison's phrasing original; his placement of the clause was also unusual. In the widely imitated model of his own state, the clause appeared in the midst of an enumeration of the procedural rights of the criminally accused at his trial. Only the state of Delaware and Maryland had departed from this precedent, by giving the Clause independent status and applicability in all courts, thereby extending it to witnesses as well as parties and to civil as well as criminal proceedings.

In presenting his amendments, James Madison (1751–1836) said nothing whatsoever that explained his intentions concerning the 'Self-Incrimination' Clause. Nor do his papers or correspondence illuminate his meaning. The language of his proposal revealed the intent to incorporate into the American Constitution the whole scope of the common law right. From the very meaning of its terms, Madison's proposal seemed as broad as the old *nemo tenetur seipsum accusare* maxim[14] in which it had its origins.

Madison's proposal certainly applied to civil as well as criminal proceedings and in principle to any stage of a legal inquiry, from the moment of arrest in a criminal case, to the swearing of a deposition in a civil one. And not being restricted to judicial proceedings, it extended to any other kind of governmental inquiry such as a legislative investigation. Moreover, the unique phrasing, that none could be compelled to be a witness against himself, was far more comprehensive than a prohibition against 'self-incrimination'. By its terms the clause could also apply to any testimony that fell short of making one vulnerable to criminal jeopardy or civil penalty or forfeiture, but, that nevertheless, exposed him to public disgrace or obloquy, or other injury to name and reputation.

Finally, Madison's phrasing protected third parties, those who were merely witnesses, called to give testimony for one side or the other, whether in civil, criminal, or equity proceedings.

According to customary procedure, witnesses, unlike parties, could in fact be compelled to give evidence, under oath, although, they were safeguarded against the necessity of testifying against themselves in any manner, that might open them to prosecution for a criminal offense or subject them to forfeiture or civil penalties. James Madison (1751–1836), going beyond the recommendations of the states and the Constitution of his own State of Virginia, phrased his own proposal to make it co-extensive with the broadest practice.[15]

Madison's proposed amendments were sent to a select committee of which he was a member. The committee, when reporting to the United States House of Representatives,[16] made no change in the positioning or language of the clause protecting persons from being witnesses against themselves. The report was taken up by the US House of Representatives, after James Madison (1751–1836), fought off further delaying tactics, and debate followed seriatim on each proposed amendment. There was no debate, however, on the clause in question. Only one speaker, John Laurence (1750–1810),[17] a Federalist lawyer of New York, addressed himself to what he called the proposal, that –

> 'a person shall not be compelled to give evidence against himself.'

John Laurence thought that [the provision] should 'be confined to criminal cases,' and he moved an amendment for that purpose. The amendment was adopted, apparently without discussion, not even by James Madison (1751–1836), and then the clause as amended was adopted unanimously. It is not known whether the US House of Representatives, debated Laurence's motion or what the vote on it was. The speed by which the US House of Representatives seems to have acted, without the record showing any controversy over the significant restriction of the scope of the clause, is bewildering.

Simple respect for the House's own distinguished select committee, a nonpartisan group that included one member from each state, 5 of whom had been delegates to the Philadelphia Constitutional Convention of 1787, ought to have required some explanation. The select committee, following Madison, had intended what Laurence rightly called 'a general declaration.' Taken literally, the amended clause,

> 'No person shall....be compelled in any criminal case, to be a witness against himself,'

excluded from its protection parties and witnesses in civil and equity suits as well as witnesses before non-judicial governmental proceedings such as legislative investigations. It now applied only to parties and witnesses in criminal cases, presumably to all stages of proceedings from arrest and examination to indictment and trial.

In the US Senate, the House of Representatives's proposed amendments to the American Constitution underwent further change. However, the US Senate accepted the 'Self-Incrimination' Clause without change. The 5th Amendment, even with the 'Self-Incrimination' Clause restricted to criminal cases, still put its principle broadly enough to apply to witnesses and to any phase of the proceedings.

The clause by its terms also protected against more than just 'self-incrimination,' a phrase that had never been used in the long history of its origins and development. The 'right against self-incrimination' is a short-hand gloss of modern origin that implies a restriction not in the constitutional clause. The right not to be a witness against oneself imports a principle of wider reach, applicable, at least in criminal cases, to the self-production of any adverse evidence, including evidence that made one the herald of his own infamy, thereby publicly disgracing him. The clause extended, in other words, to all the injurious as well as incriminating consequences of disclosure by witness or party.

Whether the framers of the 5th Amendment intended it to be fully co-extensive with the common law cannot be proved or disproved. The language of the clause and its framers' understanding of it may not have been synonymous. The difficulty is that its framers, from George Mason (1725–92)[18] to James Madison (1751–1836), and John Laurence (1750–1810), left too few clues. Nothing but passing explication emerged during the process of state ratification of the Bill of Rights from 1789 through 1791.

Indeed, in legislative and convention proceedings, in letters, newspapers, and tracts, in judicial opinions and law books, the whole period from 1776 to 1791 reveals neither sufficient explanation of the scope of such a clause nor the reasons for it. That it was a ban on torture and a security for the criminally accused were the most important of its functions, as had been the case historically, but these were not the whole of its functions. Still, nothing can be found of a theoretical nature expressing a rationale or underlying policy for the right in question or its reach.

By 1776, the principle of the *nemo tenetur seipsum accusare* (no man has to accuse himself) maxim was simply taken for granted and so deeply accepted, that its constitutional expression had the mechanical quality of a ritualistic gesture in favour of a self-evident truth needing no explanation....[C]onstitution-makers, in that day at least, did not regard themselves as framers of detailed codes. To them the statement of a bare principle was sufficient, and they were content to put it spaciously, if somewhat ambiguously, in order to allow for its expansion as the need might arise.[19]

The purposes of the privilege against Self-Incrimination

Despite its honourable lineage, one might wonder if the privilege against self-incrimination serves any modern purpose. After all, most of the practices that led to the establishment of privilege, would now be forbidden by the First Amendment. Nevertheless, there have been numerous justifications for keeping the privilege as an important safeguard for the individual.

The privilege has been defended as a means of safeguarding the right to privacy. It ensures that the government in investigating a person, cannot force a person to give up this privacy in the most coercive form of state action—the criminal process. To be sure, the citizen's privacy can be invaded in various other ways. Moreover, the privilege protects only one kind of privacy—being forced to reveal things about one's self. Nonetheless, the privilege at least puts one major method of invading the citizens' privacy beyond the reach of the government. The citizen can be forced to answer questions, if he/she is given immunity from criminal prosecution. It, however, negates the major reason why the government is pressing the inquiry i.e. punishment of the involuntary witness.

Another defence of the privilege is that it prevents a type of weakening of law enforcement. The privilege against self-incrimination would appear to be a significant impediment to law enforcement, and it is in many ways. Nonetheless, some have defended the privilege by pointing out that its neglect by the British Government in India, produced the famous comment of one British official that,

> 'There is a great deal of laziness in it...It is far pleasanter to sit comfortably in the shade rubbing red pepper into some poor devil's eyes, than to go about in the sun hunting up evidence.'[20]

What he meant is that a police force that tends to rely on getting all information out of the mouths of criminal suspects gradually loses the ability to develop information and clues in any other way. The privilege, thus, prevents this type of debilitation of law enforcement.

An additional justification is that the privilege prevents certain kinds of threats to the dignity and welfare of citizens. The government cannot, consistent with the privilege, subject the citizen to torture to extract information about his criminality because of its effect on the citizen himself. It is true, that the privilege historically is far broader than merely a prohibition against torturing confessions out of an accused. Nonetheless, the privilege stands to prevent torture at the hands of the government.

A related justification for the privilege is that it is basically unseemly to use an accused to prove a case against himself. In the words of Justice Felix Frankfurter's (1882–1965)[21] that a prisoner is not to be made 'the deluded instrument of his own conviction.'[22]

The analogy drawn here is that even when a man is executed, he is not made to dig his own grave as well. The privilege has been defended as an impediment to this type of assault upon human dignity—using of men as means rather than ends, and of forcing people to do themselves injury.

Perhaps, the most interesting justification for the privilege is as an impediment to 'total' law enforcement. When one thinks about armed robbery, mugging, rape and murder, it seems only natural that a desirable society is the one in which everybody obeyed the law. There are, however, all kinds of laws in a society and, according to this view, the only reason we do not have a great many more of them than we do is that the legislature doubts that it can enforce any more of them or even those we have. The view implied here is that human government is insatiable and will meddle in its citizens' private lives as much as it can. One author has commented:

> If we had had a method of perfect law enforcement we would still have Prohibition and we probably would have laws against masturbation, smoking in bed, and 150 other things the legislature would decide were not good for people. It is no coincidence that the countries which come closest to being able to enforce their criminal laws completely are also those which most regiment their citizens, most restrict their behaviour and interfere most with their private lives.[23]

Exchanging immunity from criminal prosecution for the privilege against Self-Incrimination

It might be thought from the simple wording of the 5th Amendment –

> '[N]or shall [any person] be compelled in any criminal case to be a witness against himself'

that the privilege against 'self-incrimination' could only be exercised in a criminal trial. The 5th Amendment privilege however, like the common law privilege existing at the time of adoption of the Bill of Rights, is broader than this. The privilege developed almost completely as a result of questioning, not in trials, but before investigative bodies. Moreover, the privilege would not be of much value if testimony could be obtained under compulsion by a grand jury or legislative committee, and then used against the former witness as an admission or confession in his subsequent criminal trial.

Suppose, then, that the government guaranteed that any information compelled by an investigator's questions would not be used against the witness in a subsequent criminal trial. Would the privilege against 'self-incrimination' still prevent compelling the witness to answer the questions? The first US Supreme Court case in which this issue was raised was *Counsel-man v. Hitchcock*.[24] The court held, that a statute providing that testimony compelled from a witness could not be used against him in any subsequent criminal trial, was not an adequate substitute for a privilege not to answer at all. The rationale was that, so long as leads or evidence developed from the compelled testimony might be used against the witness at a later criminal trial, the guarantee of the 5th Amendment against compulsory self-incrimination was not satisfied. The court in *dictum* stated that the only method of protecting the witness against compulsory self-incrimination was immunity from conviction on any charge relating to the subject matter of compelled testimony. As a reaction to this, the US Congress passed the broader 'transactional' immunity statute at issue in the decision that follows.

Leading Cases:

Brown v. Walker[25]

Brown had pleaded the privilege against self-incrimination and refused to answer certain questions before a grand jury investigating alleged violations of the Interstate Commerce Act 1887, by the Alleghany Valley Railway company for which he worked. Congress had provided that the privilege against self-incrimination would not be available to any witness in an Interstate Commerce Commission investigation. Instead, immunity from criminal prosecution would be granted for any 'transaction, matter or thing concerning which he may testify.' The lower courts found Brown in contempt of court for his refusal to testify.

Justice Brown[26]...delivered the opinion of the court

The clause of the (American) Constitution in question is obviously susceptible of two interpretations. If it be construed literally, as authorizing the witness to refuse to disclose any fact which might tend to incriminate, disgrace or expose him to unfavorable comments, then as he must necessarily to a large extent determine upon his own conscience and responsibility, whether his answer to the proposed question will have that tendency,....the practical result would be, that no one could be compelled to testify to a material fact in a criminal case, unless he chose to do so, or unless it was entirely clear that the privilege was not set up in good faith. If, upon the other hand, the object of the provision be to secure the witness against a criminal prosecution, which might be aided directly or indirectly by his disclosure, then, if no such prosecution be possible—in other words, if his testimony operate as a complete pardon for the offence to which it relates–a statute absolutely securing to him such immunity from prosecution would satisfy the demands of the clause in question.

...It can only be said in general that the clause should be construed, as it was doubtless designed, to affect a practical and beneficent purpose–not necessarily to protect witnesses against every possible detriment which might happen to them from their testimony, nor to unduly impede, hinder or obstruct the administration of criminal justice. That the statute should be upheld, if it can be construed in harmony with the fundamental law, will be admitted....

The maxim *nemo tenetur seipsum accusare* had its origin in a protest against the inquisitorial and manifestly unjust methods of interrogating accused persons.... While the admission or confessions of the prisoner, when voluntarily and freely made, have always ranked high in the scale of incriminating evidence, if an accused person be asked to explain his apparent connection with a crime under investigation, the case with which the questions put to him may assume an inquisitorial character, the temptation to press the witness unduly, to browbeat him if he be timid or reluctant, to push him into a corner, and to entrap him into fatal contradictions,...made the system so odious as to give rise to a demand for its total abolition... So deeply did the iniquities of the ancient system impress themselves upon the minds of the American colonists that the states, with one accord, made a denial of the right to question an accused person a part of their fundamental law, so that a maxim, which in England was a mere rule of evidence, became clothed in this country with the impregnability of a constitutional enactment.

Stringent as the general rule is, however, certain classes of cases have always been treated as not falling within the reason of the rule, and, therefore, constituting apparent exceptions. When examined, these cases will all be found to be based upon the idea that, if the testimony sought cannot possibly be used as a basis for, or in aid of, a criminal prosecution against the witness, the rule ceases to apply, its object being to protect the witness himself and no one else- much less that it shall be made use of as a pretext for securing immunity to others.

1. Thus, if the witness himself elects to waive his privilege, as he may doubtless do, since the privilege is for his protection and not for that of other parties, and discloses his criminal connections, he is not permitted to stop, but must go on and make a full disclosure. So, under modern statutes permitting accused persons to take the stand in their own behalf, they may be subjected to cross-examination upon their statements.
2. For the same reason if a prosecution for a crime, concerning which the witness is interrogated, is barred by the statute of limitations, he is compellable to answer...
3. If the answer of the witness may have a tendency to disgrace him or bring him into disrepute, and the proposed evidence is material to the issue on trial, the great weight of authority is that he may be compelled to answer ....
4. It is almost a necessary corollary of the above propositions that, if the witness has already received a pardon, he cannot set up his privilege, since he stands with respect to such offence as if it had never been committed...

All of the [propositions] above cited proceed upon the idea that the prohibition against his being compelled to testify against himself presupposes a legal detriment to the witness arising from the exposure...

The danger of [allowing a witness the absolute privilege of remaining silent under all circumstances] is that the privilege may be put forward for a sentimental reason, or for a purely fanciful protection of the witness against an imaginary danger, and for the real purpose of securing immunity to some third person, who is interested in concealing the facts to which he would testify. Every good citizen is bound to aid in the enforcement of the law, and has no right to permit himself, under the pretext of shielding his own good name, to be made the tool of others, who are desirous of seeking shelter behind his privilege.

It is entirely true that the statute does not purport, nor is it possible for any statute, to shield the witness from the personal disgrace or opprobrium attaching to the exposure of his crime; but, the authorities are numerous and very nearly uniform to the effect that, if the proposed testimony is material to the issue on trial, the fact that the testimony may tend to degrade the witness in public estimation does not exempt him from the duty of disclosure. A person who commits a criminal act is bound to contemplate the consequences of exposure to his good name and reputation and ought not to call upon the courts to protect that which he has himself esteemed to be of such little value. The safety and welfare of an entire community should not be put into the scale against the reputation of a self-confessed criminal, who ought not, either in justice or in good morals, to refuse to disclose that which may be of great public utility, in order that his neighbor may think well of him. The design of the constitutional privilege is not to aid the witness in vindicating his character, but to protect him against being compelled to furnish evidence to convict him of a criminal charge. If he secures legal immunity from prosecution, the possible impairment of his good name is a penalty which it is reasonable he should be compelled to pay for the common good...

...While the constitutional provision in question is justly regarded as one of the most valuable prerogatives of the citizen, its object is fully accomplished by the statutory immunity, and we are, therefore, of opinion that the witness was compellable to answer...

Justice Field[27] dissenting

This Court has declared...that:

> 'no attempted substitute for the constitutional safeguard is sufficient unless it is a *complete* substitute. Such is not the nature and effect of this statute of Congress under consideration. A witness, as observed by counsel, called upon to testify to something which will incriminate him, claims the benefit of the safeguard; he is told that the statute fully protects him against prosecution for his crime; 'but,' he says, 'it leaves me covered with infamy and unable to associate with my fellows;' he is then told *that under the rule of the common law* he would not have been protected against mere infamy, and that the constitutional provision does not assume to protect against infamy *alone*, and that it should not be supposed that its object was to protect against infamy even when associated with crime. But he answers: 'I am not claiming any common law privilege, but this particular constitutional safeguard. What its purpose was does not matter. It saves me from infamy and you furnish me with no *equivalent*, unless by such equivalent I am equally saved from infamy.'...

The Act of Congress [involved here], very materially qualifies the constitutional privilege of exemption of a witness in a criminal case from testifying...

...The constitutional safeguards for security and liberty cannot be thus dealt with. They must stand as the Constitution has devised them. They cannot be set aside and replaced by something else on the ground that the substitute will probably answer the same purpose. The citizen, as observed by counsel, is entitled to the very thing which the language of the Constitution assures to him.

Later Developments in the USA

During 1950s, Senator Joseph McCarthy (1908–57)[28] summoned witnesses before the Houses of Congress, to answer about their own acts and those of others in regard to the Communist Party of United States of America (CPUSA)[29] activities. This was McCarthy era witch hunt also known as McCarthyism.

Sometime the US Supreme Court would step in on behalf of witnesses during the period. In *Watkins v. United States*,[30] a witness subpoenaed by the House of Representatives Committee on Un-American Activities, refused to answer questions about the activities of others; he said that he would answer all questions about his own activities.

The Court overturned the contempt citation against him based on the concerns of the effect of the investigation on First Amendment rights of freedom of speech and association.

A key protection for witnesses is their ability to invoke the privilege against self-incrimination. It is firmly established that a witness may invoke the 5th Amendment before Congress or one of its committees, just as a witness may invoke it in a court.[31] However, Congress can overcome the 5th Amendment privilege, by granting the witness immunity, providing a legally binding promise that the testimony will not be used against the person.[32]

In *Watkin's* case, the court recognized a First Amendment limit on congressional investigation because it is implicated when a witness is forced to answer questions about his speech or associational activities. However, in a later case, the Court rejected a First Amendment defence to a congressional investigation into the Communist Party. The Court said that in evaluating a 5th Amendment claim it would engage in a balancing of the competing private and public interests at stake. The court held that the need to investigate the Communist Party of the United States of America (CPUSA), and its alleged infiltration into education, outweighed the infringement of First Amendment rights.[33]

During the last half century, the congressional power to investigate is an important power that can discover and publicize any wrongdoing, such as with the Watergate scandal and the Iran-Contra affair. At the same time, the McCarthy era witch hunts show how the power can be abused. The US Supreme Court decisions indicate that the primary check on this power must come from the political process. Courts are generally reluctant to get involved, so long as there is properly delegated authority and so long as the 5th Amendment privilege against self-incrimination is protected.[34]

Miranda v. Arizona[35] and Later Rulings

Prior to the decision in *Miranda*, the admissibility of a confession in a state criminal case was governed by the due process 'voluntariness' or 'totality of the circumstances' test. Under this approach, the courts decided on a case-by-case basis whether the will of the person who confessed had been 'broken' or 'over-borne' or whether the confession had been voluntary.

But, it soon became clear, that these terms were not being used as tools of analysis, but as mere conclusions. When a court concluded that the 'totality' of a suspect's treatment had not been too bad (e.g., although the police had exerted considerable pressure and used some trickery, they had given the suspect a sandwich and permitted him to have a normal night's sleep), it called the resulting confession 'voluntary'. On the other hand, when a court concluded that police methods were too offensive or too heavy-handed (in consideration of such factors as the suspect's youth, poor education, or low intelligence), it labelled the resulting confession 'involuntary' or 'coerced'.

The vagueness and unpredictability of the 'voluntariness' test, its application (or manipulation) by lower courts so as to validate confessions of doubtful constitutionality, and the inability of the US Supreme Court, because of its heavy workload, to review more than one or two state confession cases a year, led a growing number of the justices to search for a more meaningful and more manageable alternative approach. *Miranda v. Arizona* was the culmination of these efforts.

Ernesto Miranda (1941–76), an indigent 23 year old who had not completed his 9th grade, was arrested at his home and taken directly to Phoenix, Arizona police station. There, after being identified by the victim of rape and kidnapping, he was taken to an 'interrogation room', where he was questioned about the crimes. At first, Ernesto Miranda maintained his innocence, but after 2 hours of questioning, the police emerged from the room with a signed written confession of guilt. At his trial, the written confession was admitted into evidence and Miranda was found guilty of kidnapping and rape.

Whether Miranda had been told, that anything he said could be used against him was unclear. But the police admitted that neither before nor during the questioning had Miranda been advised of his right to consult with an attorney before answering any questions or his right to have an attorney present during the interrogation. Miranda's confession plainly would have been admissible under the 'voluntariness' test. His questioning had been quite mild compared to the objectionable police methods that had rendered a resulting confession involuntary or coerced in previous cases. But the confession was obtained from Miranda under circumstances that did not satisfy the new constitutional standards the Court was to promulgate in this very case.

A remarkable feature of the American history of confessions law is that, until the mid-1960s the privilege against self-incrimination did not apply to the proceedings in the interrogation room or to in-custody police interrogation. One reason for this situation was that the privilege was not deemed applicable to the states until 1964 and by that time a large body of law pertaining to involuntary or coerced state confessions had developed.

Furthermore, and more importantly, the prevailing pre-*Miranda* view was that 'compelling' someone to testify against him or herself meant legal compulsion. Since a suspect was threatened neither with perjury for testifying falsely nor contempt for refusing to testify at all, it could not be said, ran the argument, that a person undergoing police interrogation was being 'compelled' to be 'a witness against himself' within the meaning of the privilege—even though under such circumstances a person is likely to assume or to be led by the police to believe that there are legal sanctions for 'refusing to cooperate.'

Decision

There are three parts to the *Miranda* decision:

First, the 5th Amendment privilege is available outside of court proceedings and other formal proceedings and serves to protect persons in all settings from being compelled to incriminate themselves. Thus, the privilege applies to informal compulsion exerted by law-enforcement officers during 'custodial interrogation,' that is, questioning initiated by the police after a person has been taken into custody.

Second,

> '[A]n individual swept from familiar surroundings into police custody, surrounded by antagonistic forces, and subjected to the techniques of persuasion described in the [standard police interrogation manuals] cannot be otherwise than under compulsion to speak.'.

Because the custodial interrogation environment 'carries its own badge of intimidation' that is at odds' with the privilege,

> '[u]nless adequate protective devices are employed to dispel the compulsion inherent in custodial surroundings,'

no statement obtained from a person under these circumstances is admissible.

Third, the Constitution does not require adherence to any particular system for dispelling the coercion of custodial interrogation. However, unless the government utilizes other procedures that are at least as effective, in order for a statement to be admissible, a suspect must be given the now familiar four-fold *Miranda* warnings before being subjected to custodial interrogation and must effectively waive his or her rights before any questioning.

According to *Miranda*, advising a suspect that he has a right to remain silent and that anything he says can be used against him is not enough to assure that the suspect's right to choose between silence and speech will remain unfettered throughout the interrogation process. Therefore, a suspect must also be told of her right to counsel, either retained or (if she is indigent) appointed.

Although the warnings need not be given in the exact form described in the *Miranda* opinion—indeed, they are not described the same way throughout the opinion—the substance of each of the following four warnings must be effectively given:

(1) You have the right to remain silent;
(2) anything you say can and will be used against you;
(3) you have the right to talk to a lawyer before being questioned and to have him or her present when you are being questioned; and
(4) if you cannot afford a lawyer, one will be provided for you before any questioning if you so desire.

CONCERNS ABOUT *MIRANDA'S* FUTURE.

For supporters of Miranda, an ominous note was struck in *Michigan v. Tucker*,[36] in which the Court, speaking through Justice William Rehnquist (1924–2005), viewed the *Miranda* warnings as 'not themselves rights protected by the Constitution,' but only 'prophylactic standards' designed to 'safeguard' or to 'provide practical reinforcement' for the privilege against self-incrimination.

A decade later, first in *New York v. Quarles*,[37] recognizing a 'public safety' exception to *Miranda*, and then in *Oregon v. Elstad*[38] indicating that the prosecution may make considerable derivative use of *Miranda* violations, the Court reiterated *Tucker's* way of looking at and thinking about *Miranda*. Both *Quarles* and *Elstad* cases underscored the distinction between statements that are actually 'coerced' or 'compelled' and those obtained merely in violation of *Miranda's* 'prophylactic rules.'

THE REAFFIRMATION OF *MIRANDA*

In *Dickerson v. United States*,[39] the US Supreme Court struck down a federal statute purporting to abolish *Miranda* and to reinstate the pre-*Miranda* 'voluntariness' or 'totality of the circumstances' test for the admissibility of confessions in federal cases. Speaking for a 7 to 2 majority, Chief Justice William Rehnquist (1924–2005), removed any doubt that '*Miranda* is a constitutional decision' and thus a decision that 'may not be in effect overruled by an Act of Congress.'

Nor did the Court see any good reason to overrule *Miranda* on its own: –

> '*Miranda* has become embedded in routine police practice to the point where the warnings have become part of our natural culture. [While] we have overruled our precedents when subsequent cases have undermined their doctrinal underpinnings, we do not believe that this has happened to the *Miranda* decision. If anything, our subsequent cases have reduced the impact of the *Miranda* rule on legitimate law enforcement while reaffirming the decision's core ruling that unwarned statements may not be used as evidence in the prosecution's case in chief.'

MIRANDA WARNINGS

Miranda warnings apply when suspects are in police custody and under interrogation. In decisions subsequent to *Miranda*, the Court has emphasized that custody consists of the restriction of freedom of movement by police. This can occur in one's home (*Orozco v. Texas*),[40] or in jail on an unrelated offense (*Mathis v. United States*).[41] Public safety concerns, however, constitute an exemption to this requirement as the Court emphasized in *New York v. Quarles*[42] when it ruled that emergency circumstances (e.g., the officer's immediate protection) do not require *Miranda* warnings, even if these situations could be describe as interrogations. Suspects who voluntarily go to a police station are not entitled to *Miranda* warnings unless arrested and drivers who are stopped by police for a routine traffic violation are also not entitled to *Miranda* warnings (*California v. Beheler*[43] and *Berkemer v. McCarty*[44]).

The US Supreme Court considered the applicability of *Miranda* to juveniles. Of central interest in *Yarborough Warden v. Alvarado*[45] as the use at trial of testimony obtained in a 2-hour interview that police in Los Angeles conducted with a 17 year old who was implicated in an attempted robbery and murder case. At trial, Alvarado moved to suppress the interview on the grounds that no *Miranda* warnings were issued, a claim unchallenged by the prosecution. The trial court and the state appellate court concluded that Alvarado was not in custody at the time of the interview.

The Ninth Circuit reversed and took issue with the application of the custody test, and called particular attention to Alvarado's youth and inexperience. The US Supreme Court reversed the Ninth Circuit ruling and concluded that Alvarado was not in custody for purposes of *Miranda* and that the trial court's application of the custody test was not unreasonable.

One of the most important questions related to the continued validity of *Miranda* is the indirect use of information obtained in violation of the warning requirement. In 1971, the Burger Court[46] concluded that statements made in violation of *Miranda* could be used to impeach the credibility of the defendant if he/she took the stand in his/her own defense. *Harris v. New York*[47] verdict has sometimes been described as a 'back-door' reversal of the famous 1966 precedent.

However, the US Supreme Court continues to uphold the constitutionality of the Court's famous 1966 decision and the warnings requirement that it set out. An appropriate illustration is the 2000 decision in *Dickerson v. United States*[48] where the US Supreme Court rejected a 1999 Fourth Circuit ruling that upheld the admissibility of a voluntary confession in the face of an acknowledged failure of police to issue *Miranda* warnings. In this decision, the Court emphasized, among other arguments, that 'the *Miranda* warnings have become part of our national culture.'[49]

Conclusion: *Miranda* Has Survived

While Chief Justice Earl Warren's (1891–1974) period as Chief Justice has been described as an era of judicial revolution, *Miranda* has been described as –

> 'the centerpiece of the Warren Court's revolution in American criminal procedure.'

Miranda has been the most famous, the most cited and at the same time the most criticized case in America. Following *Miranda*, public outcry against the Warren Court[50] intensified. The debate was confined not to the police stations and the halls of academia, but also filtered into presidential politics. In 1968, Richard Nixon, in his presidential bid, said that –

> 'the cumulative effect of these decisions has been to very nearly rule out the confession as an effective and major tool in prosecution and law enforcement.'

Congress also reacted and quickly enacted 18 USC §3501, an Act designed to confine the law of confessions solely to the pre-*Escobedo*, due process voluntariness test. Essentially, Congress attempted to overrule the Warren Court's *Miranda* ruling. Yet, *Miranda* remained intact. When the Supreme Court came under the leadership of the conservative Chief Justice Warren Burger (1907–95), many began to wonder if *Miranda* would survive. In a series of decisions, the Burger Court began to peel away at the scope of the Warren Court's holding (as discussed above).

However, as the 1970s gave way to the 1980s, the Court's position seemed to be changing, and Chief Justice Burger (1907–95) commented that –

> –'law enforcement practices had adjusted to *Miranda's* stricture'

and that he had no intention of overruling it.

Then, in *Dickerson v. United States* in 2000, the Rehnquist Court[51] was faced with the difficult decision to overrule *Miranda* or hold the Congress enactment unconstitutional. The conservative Chief Justice Rehnquist, in a 6 to 3 majority opinion, refused to overrule *Miranda*.

Self-Incrimination in India

Clause (3) of Article 20 provides:

> 'No person accused of any offence shall be compelled to be a witness against himself.'

This Clause is based on the maxim *nemo tenetur prodere accusare seipsum*, which means that 'no man is bound to accuse himself.'[52] The Clause embodies the general principle of English and American jurisprudence according to which no person would be compelled to give testimony which might expose him to prosecution for a crime. The characteristic feature of Common Law criminal jurisprudence are that –

- — an accused must be presumed to be innocent till the contrary is proved;
- — that it is the duty of the prosecution to establish the guilt of the accused;
- — and that the accused need not make any admission or statement against his own free will.[53]

The protection contained in Article 20(3) is available to every person. The term 'person' in Article 20(3) includes not only natural individuals but also companies and unincorporated bodies.[54] The protection is available only if the following ingredients are present:—[55]

(i) It is a protection available to a person accused of an offence;
(ii) It is a protection against compulsion to be a witness; and
(iii) It is a protection against such 'compulsion' resulting in his giving evidence against himself.

(i) *Person accused of an offence*

The protection against self-incrimination is available only to a person accused of an offence. A person 'accused of an offence' means a person against whom a formal accusation relating to the commission of an offence has been leveled, which in the normal course, may result in a prosecution.[56] 'Formal accusation' is ordinarily brought into existence by lodging of an F.I.R. (First Information Report)[57] or a formal complaint to the appropriate authority or court against the specific individual accusing him of the commission of a crime.[58] It is, however, not necessary, to avail the privilege contained in Article 20(3), that actual trial or inquiry should have commenced before a Court or a judicial tribunal.

The words 'accused of an offence' indicate an accusation made in a criminal prosecution before the Court or a judicial tribunal where a person is charged with having committed on act which is punishable under the Indian Penal Code 1860, or any special or local law.[59] It is only on the making of such formal accusation that Clause (3) of Article 20 becomes operative covering that person with its protective umbrella against testimonial compulsion.[60] It follows that a person cannot claim the protection if at the time he made the statement, he was not an accused but become an accused thereafter.[61]

The mere fact that at the relevant time, the person was arrested on suspicion of having committed an offence, would be immaterial, when neither the case is registered nor an F.I.R. (First Information Report) is recorded.[62]

Likewise, where a customs officer arrested a person, and informed him of the ground of his arrest for the purpose of holding an inquiry into the violation of the provisions of the Sea Customs Act 1978, there being no formal accusation of an offence, it was held that Article 20(3) would not apply.[63] In *Raja Narayanlal Bansilal v. Maneck Phiroz Mistry*,[64] the Registrar of Companies acting under Section 240 of the Banking Companies Act 1949, called upon the managing agents of the company to give evidence and produce documents from their possession. It was held that the proceedings did not partake the character of a criminal prosecution and the managing agents were not persons accused of any offence, therefore, Article 20(3) would not apply.

A person charged with contempt of court has been held to be not accused of any offence within the meaning of Article 20(3).[65] Article 20(3) does not apply to departmental inquiries into allegations against a government servant, since, there is no accusation of any offence within the meaning of Article 20(3).[66]

In *Nandini Satpathy v. Dani (P.L.)*,[67] the appellant, a former Chief Minister of Orissa, was directed to appear at Vigilance Police Station, Cuttack, for being examined in connection with a case registered against her under the Prevention of Corruption Act 1947, and under Sections 161/165 and 120-B and 109 of Indian Penal Code 1860. On the strength of this first information report, investigation was commenced against her.[68] During the course of the investigation, she was interrogated with reference to a long list of questions given to her in writing. She refused to answer those questions claiming the protection of Article 20(3). On this, she was prosecuted under Section 179 of Indian Penal Code 1860, which punished a person for refusing to answer questions demanded by any public servant. It was contended that she was justified in refusing to answer the questions on the ground of Article 20(3) as well as Section 161(2)[69] of the Criminal Procedure Code 1973.

The Indian Supreme Court held that Section 160(1) of Cr.P.C. (Criminal Procedure Code), which barred the calling of a woman to a police station was violated in the case. Further, the question related to the scope of the protection contained in Article 20(3). The Court ruled that Article 20(3) extended back to the stage of police investigation not commencing in court only, since such inquiry was of an accusatory nature and could end in prosecution. The ban on self-accusation and the right to silence while an investigation or trial was underway, the Court viewed, extended beyond that case and protected the accused in regard to other offences, pending or imminent, which might deter him from voluntary disclosure of criminatory matter.

It follows that the protection contained in Article 20(3) is also available at the stage of police investigation. Further, that the right of silence guaranteed by Article 20(3) is not limited to the case for which the person is examined, but extends to other offences pending or imminent, which may deter him from voluntary disclosure of criminatory matter. It was also held that the protection could be claimed by a suspect also.

(ii) *Protection Against compulsion to be a Witness*

The protection contained in Article 20(3) is against compulsion 'to be a witness'. In *M.P. Sharma v. Satish Chandra,*[70] the Indian Supreme Court gave a wide connotation to the expression 'to be a witness' so as to include oral, documentary and testimonial evidence. The protection contained in Article 20(3), the court held, covered not merely testimonial compulsion in the court room but also compelled testimony previously obtained from him. It would extend to any compulsory process for production of evidentiary documents which, the Court said, were reasonably likely to support a prosecution against the accused. The administration of caution to a person summoned in the Court that not making truthful statement would be an offence, does not amount to use of pressure within the meaning of Article 20(3).[71]

To be a Witness – Furnishing Evidence

The proposition laid down in *M.P. Sharma*'s case[72] that the protection of Article 20(3) extended to documentary evidence which the accused might be compelled to produce was narrowed down in *State of Bombay v. Kathi Kalu Oghad.*[73] The Indian Supreme Court stated that the interpretation of the expression 'to be a witness' given in *M.P. Sharma*'s case[74] was too broad and required a qualification. The Court observed:

> 'It is well established that Clause (3) of Article 20 is directed against self-incrimination by the accused person. Self-incrimination must mean conveying information based upon the personal knowledge of the person giving the information and cannot include merely the mechanical process of producing documents in Court which may throw a light on any of the points in the controversy, but which do not contain any statement of the accused based on his personal knowledge. For example, the accused person may be in possession of a document which is in his writing or which contains his signature or his thumb-impression. The production of such a document, with a view to comparison of the writing or the signature or the impression, is not the statement of an accused person which can be said to be of the nature of a personal testimony.'

It follows that giving thumb impression or impression of foot or palm or fingers or specimen of writings or exposing parts of the body by way of identification are not covered by the expression 'to be a witness' under Article 20(3).[75] In these cases, the accused is not giving any personal testimony. They are merely materials for comparison.

The Supreme Court distinguished 'to be a witness' from 'furnishing evidence'. 'To be a witness', the Court held, meant making of oral or written statements in or out of court by a person accused of any offence. It means imparting knowledge in respect of relevant facts by an oral statement or statement in writing made or given in court or otherwise. While, 'furnishing evidence' in its widest significance included production of documents or giving materials which might be relevant at a trial to determine the guilt or innocence of the accused.

Thus, self-incrimination in the context of Article 20(3) only means conveying information based upon personal knowledge of the person giving information.[76] Therefore, where an accused is compelled to produce a document in his possession, which is not based on the personal knowledge of the accused, there is no violation of Article 20(3), because he does not become a witness by the mere fact that he has produced it.[77] Directing the accused to give his specimen signatures and handwriting does not amount to testimonial compulsion offending Article 20(3).[78]

It has been held, that the protection of Article 20(3) does not extend to searches made in pursuance of a warrant issued under Section 96 of the Criminal Procedure Code 1898.[79] In Indian law, there is no basis for the assumption that a search or seizure of a thing or document, was in itself to be treated as a compelled production of it.[80] Since the search warrant is addressed to an officer of the government generally, a police officer, and not to the person whose premises or property is to be searched, it is not the act of the accused but of a third person, the police officer to which the accused is obliged to submit and is therefore, not his testimonial act in any sense and does not involve a violation of Article 20(3).[81] Again in *V.S. Kuttan Pillai v. Ramakrishnan,*[82] the Supreme Court held that search of the premises occupied by the accused without the accused being compelled to be a party to such search would not be violative of the constitutional guarantee enshrined in Article 20(3).

The plea that once the police accosted a person who was suspected of possessing contraband opium, he must be deemed to be under arrest and therefore, any confession made by him could not be used against him, was held to be unsustainable.[83] Article 20(3) is not violated when a police officer investigating a case seeks direction through the court of a competent Magistrate for obtaining samples of handwriting, fingerprints, footprints, photographs, blood, saliva, semen, hair, voice of any accused person reasonably suspected to be involved in the commission of an offense under Section 27 of the Prevention of Terrorism Act 2002.[84]

Section 27 of Evidence Act 1872 and Article 20(3)

Section 27 of the Evidence Act 1872, provides that when at a trial evidence is led to the effect that some fact was discovered in consequence of the information given by the accused in custody, so much of the information as relates to the facts discovered, may be proved irrespective of the fact whether that information amounts to confession or not. It has been held that the provisions of this section are not within the prohibition of Article 20(3), unless compulsion had been used in obtaining the information.[85]

In *Parshadi v. State of U.P.*,[86] the accused while in police custody stated that he killed the deceased with a dagger and had concealed the dagger and blood-stained clothes of the deceased in a pit. He led the police to the pit from where, the dagger and the clothes of the deceased were recovered. The Court held that the statement of the accused leading to the recovery of the dagger and the clothes of the deceased was admissible and could not be held to be compelled testimony within the meaning of Article 20(3). But, where the statement leading to the discovery of some facts was obtained by employing third degree methods, the statement would be hit by Article 20(3).[87]

(iii) *Compulsion to give Evidence 'against himself'*

The protection under Article 20(3) is available only against compulsion of the accused to give evidence against himself/herself. Thus, if the accused voluntarily makes an oral statement or voluntarily produces documentary evidence, incriminatory in nature, Article 20(3) would not be attracted.[88] In *Smt. Kalawati v. State of Himachal Pradesh*,[89] the appellant was accused of committing the murder of her husband. The Indian Supreme Court held that Article 20(3) would not apply to a case where the confession was made by an accused without any inducement, threat or promise.

The expression 'compelled to be a witness' in Article 20(3) indicates that the evidence given by the accused must be shown to have been given under compulsion. The term 'compulsion' in the context of Article 20(3) means 'duress'.

Compulsion may take many forms. Person accused of an offence may be subjected to physical or mental torture. He may be starved or beaten, and a confession may be extracted from him. By deceitful means he may be induced to believe that his son is being tortured in an adjoining room and by such inducement he may be compelled to make an incriminating statement.[90]

In *Nandini Satpathy v. Dani (P.L.)*,[91] the Indian Supreme Court observed that the phrase 'compelled testimony' must be read as evidence procured not merely by physical threats or violence, but by psychic torture, atmospheric pressure, environmental coercion, tiring interrogative prolixity, overbearing and intimidatory methods and the like, not legal penalty for violation. In this case, the Court tried to introduce through interpretation the protection under *Miranda v. Arizona*,[92] which requires a police officer to inform the person arrested of his right to consult a legal practitioner immediately upon arrest.

However, Article 20(3) would have no application where the accused is not in any manner compelled to give evidence against himself. In *Mohamed Dastagir v. State of Madras*,[93] the appellant went to the residence of the Deputy Superintendent of Police (D.S.P.) and offered him a closed envelope. The police officer on opening the envelope found it containing currency notes and realized that the appellant had come to offer him a bribe. The D.S.P. (Deputy Superintendent of Police) threw the envelope on the appellant's face and in that process the envelope and some currency notes fell on the floor. Thereafter, the D.S.P. (Deputy Superintendent of Police) asked the appellant to place the envelope and currency notes on the table, which he did. The envelope and the currency notes were seized by the police officer and the appellant was prosecuted for offering bribe to the D.S.P. (Deputy Superintendent of Police). The Indian Supreme Court held, that the accused was not compelled to produce the currency notes as no duress was applied on him. Moreover, the appellant was not an accused at the time when the currency notes were seized from him and, therefore, there was no infringement of Article 20(3).

In *C. Sampath Kumar v. Enforcement Officer, Enforcement Directorate, Madras*,[94] the Indian Supreme Court held that administration of caution to person summoned that not making truthful statement was an offence, did not amount to use of pressure within the meaning of Article 20(3). Administration of such a caution, the Court said, was in fact, in the interest of the person who was making the statement.

Under Section 15 of TADA [The Terrorist and Disruptive Activities (Prevention) Act 1987], confession made by the accused was made admissible in evidence. The Indian Supreme Court ruled in *Ayub v. State of Uttar Pradesh*,[95] that under Article 20(3), the accused person has a protection to being a witness against himself. Therefore, the confession made must be strictly according to the procedure laid down in the Act for recording confession. The confession should appear to have been made voluntarily, and the police officer who records the confession, should satisfy himself that the same was being made voluntarily by the maker of that statement. The recorded confession must indicate that these safeguards had been fully complied with. However, non-compliance of with procedural safeguards against involuntary confession need not necessarily or automatically had to the rejection of the confession although 'the breach thereof will normally result in eschewing the confession from consideration.'[96]

Tape-recording of Statements made by the Accused

It has been held that the tape-recording of statements made by the accused, though the recording was done without his knowledge, but without force or oppression, is not hit by Article 20(3),[97] since there is no element of compulsion within the meaning of this clause.

Scope of the Protection contained in Article 20(3)

The protection under Article 20(3) is confined to an accused in a criminal proceeding, and does not apply to witnesses or to civil proceedings[98] or proceeding other than criminal.[99] In America, the privilege against self-incrimination is not confined to accused only but it extends to witness also. Same is the position under the English Law.

Protection Against Self-Incrimination in Pakistan

Article 13(b) of the 1973 Constitution of Pakistan provides that –

> 'no person shall, when accused of an offence, be compelled to be a witness against himself.'

However, the construction of Article 20(3) of the Indian Constitution that –

> 'no person accused of any offence shall be compelled to be a witness against himself'

is somewhat different.

This provision embodies the principle of protection against compulsion which is one of the fundamental canons of the British system of criminal jurisprudence and which has been adopted by the American system and incorporated in the Federal Constitution. It has also, to a substantial extent, been recognized in the criminal administration of justice in Pakistan by incorporation of the same into Sections 5 and 6 of the Oaths Act 1873, and Section 342 of the Code of Criminal Procedure 1898.

However, Sub-section (2) of Section 340, as substituted with effect from 22 February 1982, by the Code of Criminal Procedure (Amendment) Ordinance, XII of 1982, and Article 44 of the *Qanun-e-Shahadat* 1984, tend to make the accused not only a competent, but also a compellable witness. Sub-section (2) of Section 340 reads as follows:

> Any person accused of an offence before a Criminal Court, or against, whom proceedings are instituted under this Code in any such Court shall, if he does not plead guilty, give evidence on oath in disproof of the charge or allegations made against him or any person charged or tried together with him at the same trial:

Provided that he shall not be asked, and, if asked, shall not be required to answer, any question tending to show that he has committed or been convicted or any offence other than the offence with which he is charged or for which he is being tried, or is of bad character unless—

(i) the proof that he has committed or been convicted of such offence is admissible in evidence to show that he is guilty of the offence with which he is charged or for which he is being tried; or
(ii) he has personally or by his pleader asked questions of any witness for the prosecution with a view to establishing his own good character. or has given evidence of his good character; or
(iii) he has given evidence against any other person charged with or tried for the same offence.

Article 44 of *Qanun-e-Shahadat*, 1984 lays down that –

> 'all accused, including an accomplice, shall be liable to cross-examination.'

Both, these provisions in so far as they make an accused person compellable witness and liable to compulsory cross-examination are *ultra vires* Article 13 of Pakistan's Constitution, for if any law compels an accused person to give evidence and such evidence will tend, directly or indirectly, to be self-incriminatory, that law to that extent would be unconstitutional by reason of this Article.[100]

It may also be noted that Article 15 of the *Qanun-e-Shahadat* 1984, (Section 132 of the Evidence Act 1872) lays down that –

> A witness is not excused from answering on the ground that the answer will criminate him. The Article says that a witness shall not be excused from answering any question as to any matter in issue in any suit or in any civil or criminal proceeding, upon the ground that the answer to such question will criminate, or may tend directly or indirectly to criminate, such witness, or that it will expose, or tend directly or indirectly to expose, him to a penalty or forfeiture of any kind.
>
> This rule is subject to the proviso that no such answer, which a witness shall be compelled to give, shall subject him to any arrest or prosecution, or be proved against him in any criminal proceeding, except a prosecution for giving false evidence by such answer.

And accused person is now a competent, though not compellable, witness. If he voluntarily appears as his own witness in his defence he may be cross-examined by the prosecutor subject to the provision of Article 15 of *Qanun-e-Shahadat* 1984.

Section 340(2) Cr.P.C. is inconsistent with Article 13(b) or not

Section 340(2) Cr.P.C. (Criminal Procedure Code) has been held by Federal *Shariat* Court not as *ultra vires* of Article 13(b). Sub-section (2) and only gives an opportunity to an accused to make a statement on oath in disproof of the charge/allegation against him.[101]

Sub-section (2) of Section 340 Cr.P.C. (Criminal Procedure Code), should be interpreted as only conferring a duty or power on the court to inform the accused that he has a right under the law to make a statement on oath of it his option with no risk attaching it to either make that statement or not to make that statement.[102]

In *Mehram Ali v. Federation of Pakistan*,[103] Section 26 of the Anti-Terrorism Act 1997, which made a confession of guilt made before a police officer admissible was held to be against Article 13(b). The opinion proceeds on the basis that a confession before the police, in view of the special circumstances obtaining in this country, cannot be a voluntary confession; it must have been processed by compelling the accused to be a witness against himself.

Person accused of an offence

The Supreme Court of Pakistan in *F.B. Ali v. The State*[104] held, that the protection conferred by Article 13 of the Constitution, is confined only to an accused person, that is, a person against whom a formal accusation relating to the commission of an offence has been leveled which in the normal course may result in the prosecution, and the mere lodging of information or conducting investigation by the police against a person does not make him an accused person.

The holding of the Full Bench of the Lahore High Court in *Noor Muhammad v. Commissioner, Sargodha Division*,[105] that an accused placed in Column No. 2 of the police challan is an accused person within the meaning of Section 3 of the West Pakistan Criminal Law (Amendment) Act 1963, has to be distinguished from *Muhammad Ilyas v. Ijaz Ahmad Butt*,[106] in which it has been held, that a person placed in Column No. 2 of the police challan is not an accused person within the meaning of Section 497 of the Code of Criminal Procedure 1898. Whereas, *Noor Muhammad v. Commissioner, Sargodha Division*, held that a person against whom an F.I.R. (First Information Report) has been lodged, is an accused person.[107] In *Muhammad Ilyas v. Ijaz Ahmad Butt*,[108] it has been held that a person placed in Column No. 2 of the challan is not an accused person within the meaning of Section 497 of the Code of Criminal Procedure, 1898.

Compulsion to be a witness

The words 'to be a witness' used in Article 13 of Pakistan's Constitution, means imparting knowledge in respect of relevant facts by an oral or written statement made before a court of law or otherwise. Such statements are not confined to confessions but also cover incriminatory statements, i.e., statements which have a reasonable tendency to point out to the guilt of the accused.

Notes

1. A member of a group of English Protestants of the late 16th and 17th centuries who regarded the Reformation of the Church under Elizabeth I as incomplete and sought to simplify and regulate forms of worship.
2. James I was King of England and Ireland and King of Scotland as James VI from 24 July 1567, from the union of the Scottish and English crowns on 24 March 1603 until his death in 1625.
3. Charles I of England was King of England, Scotland, and Ireland from 27 March 1625 until his execution in 1649.
4. Oliver Cromwell was Lord Protector of the Commonwealth of England, Scotland and Ireland from 1653–58.
5. High Anglicans one of the major branches of the 16th century Protestant Reformation and a form of Christianity that includes features of both Protestantism and Roman Catholicism.
6. Charles II of England king of Great Britain and Ireland (1660–85), who was restored to the throne after years of exile during the Puritan Commonwealth.
7. William Cohen, David J. Danelski, David Yalof, *Constitutional Law, Civil Liberty and Individual Rights (University Casebook Series)*, 5th ed., (New York: Foundation Press, 2002), pp. 809–10.
8. an English court of civil and criminal jurisdiction that developed in the late 15th century, trying especially those cases affecting the interests of the Crown.
9. Fleet Prison was a notorious London prison by the side of the River Fleet.
10. The Long Parliament was an English Parliament which lasted from 1640 until 1660.
11. Supra Note 7.
12. Sir John Jervis was an English lawyer, law reformer and served as Attorney General for the Crown.
13. James Madison was Founding Father who served as the 4th President of the United States from 1809 to 1817.
14. It states that no one is bound to incriminate or accuse himself.
15. Supra Note 7, pp. 811–2.
16. The United States House of Representatives is the lower house of the United States Congress, with the Senate being the upper house.
17. John Laurance was a New York delegate to the 6th, 7th and 8th Congresses of the Confederation, and a judge who served as Judge Advocate General during the American Revolution.
18. George Mason participated in the American Revolution, was the author of the Virginia Declaration of Rights, Founding Framer and influential delegate to the Constitutional Convention, co-father of the United States Bill of Rights.

19. Supra Note 7, pp. 813–4.
20. James Fitzjames Stephen, *A History of the Criminal Law of England*, (London: MacMillan & Co., 1883) p. 442.
21. Felix Frankfurter former Associate Justice of the Supreme Court of the United States from 1939 to 1962.
22. *Culombe v. Connecticut*, 367 U.S. 568 (1961), 581.
23. *Ibid*, pp. 814–5.
24. 142 U.S. 547 (1892).
25. 161 U.S. 591 (1896).
26. Henry Billings Brown (1836–1913) was Associate Justice of the Supreme Court of the United States from 1890 to 1906.
27. Stephen Johnson Field (1816–99) was Associate Justice of the US Supreme Court from 1863 to 1897.
28. Joseph McCarthy was a Republican Senator from the state of Wisconsin and was also Former Chair of Senate Government Operations Committee from 1953–55.
29. Communist Party USA is a far-left communist party in the United States established in 1919 after a split in the Socialist Party of America following the Russian Revolution.
30. 354 U.S. 178 (1957).
31. *Quinn v. Unites States*, 349 U.S. 155 (1955).
32. *Kastigar v. United States*, 406 U.S. 441 1972).
33. *Barenblatt v. United States*, 360 U.S. 109 (1959).
34. Erwin Chemerinsky, *Constitutional Law: Principles and Policies*, 4th ed. (New York: Wolters Kluwer Law & Business, 2011), pp. 318–19.
35. 384 U.S. 436 (1966).
36. 417 U.S. 433 (1974).
37. 467 U.S. 649 (1984).
38. 470 U.S. 298 (1985).
39. 530 U.S. 428 (2000).
40. 394 U.S. 324 (1969).
41. 391 U.S. 1 (1968).
42. 467 U.S. 649 (1984).
43. 463 U.S. 1121 (1983).
44. 468 U.S. 420 (1984).
45. 541 U.S. 652 (2004).
46. The Burger Court was the period in the history of the US Supreme Court from 1969 to 1986, when Warren Burger served as Chief Justice of the United States.
47. 401 U.S. 222 (1971).
48. 530 U.S. 428 (2000).
49. *The Oxford Companion to the Supreme Court of the United States*, 2nd ed. (New York: Oxford University Press, 2005), pp. 641–5.
50. The Warren Court was the period in the history of the US Supreme Court from 1953 to 1969 when Earl Warren served as Chief Justice.
51. The Rehnquist Court refers to the US Supreme Court from 1986 to 2005, when William Rehnquist served as Chief Justice of the United States.
52. *P. Rajangam v. State of Madras*, AIR 1959 Mad 294.
53. Narender Kumar, *Constitutional Law of India*, 3rd ed., (Delhi: Pioneer Publications, 2003), p. 222.
54. *State of Maharashtra v. N.E. & P. Co.*, AIR 1951 Bom 242; *M.P. Sharma v. Satish Chandra*, AIR 1954 SC 300.
55. *M.P. Sharma v. Satish Chandra*, AIR 1954 SC 300; *Delhi Judicial Service Association v. State of Gujarat*, AIR 1991 SC 2176.
56. *M.P. Sharma v. Satish Chandra*, AIR 1954 SC 300.
57. F.I.R. (First Information Report) The first information report means an information recorded by a police officer on duty given either by the aggrieved person or any other person to the commission of an alleged offence.
58. *Balkishan A. Devidayal v. State of Maharashtra*, AIR 1981 SC 379.
59. *Amin v. The State*, AIR 1958 All 293, 1958 CriLJ 462.
60. *Balkishan A. Devidayal v. State of Maharashtra*, AIR 1981 SC 379; *M.P. Sharma v. Satish Chandra*, AIR 1954 SC 300.
61. *State of Bombay v. Kathi Kalu Oghad*, AIR 1961 SC 1808; *K. Joseph Augusthi v. M.A. Narayanan*, AIR 1964 SC 1552; *Romesh Chandra Mehta v. State of West Bengal*, AIR 1970 SC 940; *Ramanlal Bhogilal Shah v. D.K. Guha*, 1970 AIR 940.
62. *Balkishan A. Devidayal v. State of Maharashtra*, AIR 1981 SC 379; *Amin v. The State*, AIR 1958 All 293.
63. *Ibid. See also Veera Ibrahim v. State of Maharashtra*, AIR 1976 SC 1167.
64. AIR 1961 SC 29.

65. *Delhi Judicial Service Association v. State of Gujarat*, AIR 1991 SC 2176.
66. *Srikant Upadhya v. Union of India*, AIR 1963 Pat. 38.
67. AIR 1978 SC 1025.
68. She was at that stage merely a suspect and not yet an accused.
69. Section 161(2) Cr.P.C. also entitles a person not to answer questions which tend to expose him to a criminal charge or to a penalty.
70. AIR 1954 S.C.300.
71. *C. Sampath Kumar v. The Enforcement Officer, Enforcement Directorate, Madras*, [1997] INSC 736 (16 September 1997).
72. *M.P. Sharma v. Satish Chandra*, AIR 1954 SC 300.
73. AIR 1961 SC 1808.
74. AIR 1954 SC 300.
75. *Shyam Sunder Chowkhani v. Kajal Kanti Biswas*, AIR 1999 Gauheti 101.
76. *State of Bombay v. Kathi Kalu Oghad*, AIR 1961 SC 1808.
77. *State of Gujarat v. Shyamlal Mohanlal*, AIR 1963 Guj 178.
78. *State of U.P. v. Boota Singh*, AIR 1978 SC 1770; *T. Subbiah v. S.K.D. Ramaswamy Nadar*, AIR 1970 Mad 85.
79. *M.P. Sharma v. Satish Chandra*, AIR 1954 SC 300; *State of Gujarat v. Shyamlal Mohanlal*, AIR 1965 SC 1251.
80. *Ibid.*
81. *M.P. Sharma v. Satish Chandra*, AIR 1954 SC 300; *State of Gujarat v. Shyamlal Mohanlal*, AIR 1965 SC 1251; *K.A Kunhi v. Pudiya Purayil*, AIR 1956 Madras 685.
82. AIR 1980 S.C. 185.
83. *State of Rajasthan v. Daulat Ram*, AIR 1980 SC 1314.
84. *Peoples Union for Civil Liberties v. Union of India*, (2004) 9 SCC 580. Contrary view express in *Amrit Singh v. State of Punjab*, AIR 2007 SC 132.
85. *State of Bombay v. Kathi Kalu Oghad*, AIR 1961 S.C. 1808.
86. AIR 1957 S.C. 211.
87. *Ghazi v. State of U.P.*, AIR 1966 All 142; *Amrut Soma Kunbi v. State of Bombay*, AIR 1960 Bom 488; *Niranjan Prasad v. State*, AIR 1960 All 323.
88. *Mohamed Dastagir v. State of Madras*, AIR 1960 SC 756; *Gulam Nabi Zaki v. State of Jammu & Kashmir*, AIR 1957 J & K 44.
89. AIR 1953 SC 131.
90. *Yousufalli Esmail Nagree v. State of Maharashtra*, AIR 1968 SC 147, 1967 SCR (3) 720.
91. AIR 1978 S.C. 1025, (1978) 2 SC 424.
92. 384 U.S. 436 (1966).
93. AIR 1960 S.C. 756.
94. [1997] INSC 736 (16 September 1997).
95. AIR 2002 SC 1192.
96. *State (N.C.T. of Delhi) v. Navjot Sandhu*, AIR 2005 S.C. 3820, (2005) 11 SCC 600 at 720.
97. *Yusufalli Esmail Nagree v. State of Maharashtra*, AIR 1968 SC 147; *Shiv Kirpal Singh v. Shri V.V. Giri*, AIR 1970 SC 2097; *R. M. Malkani v. State of Maharashtra*, AIR 1973 SC 157.
98. *Capt. Dushyant Somal v. Smt. Sushma Somal*, AIR 1981 SC 1027; *In Re: Pappathi Ammal v. Unknown*, AIR 1959 Mad 239, 1959 CriLJ 724.
99. *Shyam Sunder Chowkhani v. Kajal Kanti Biswas*, AIR 1999 Gau 101; *Popular Bank Ltd. v. K. Madhava Naik*, 1965 KLT 469.
100. A.G. Chaudhry, *Lectures on Constitutional Law*, (Lahore: Irfan Law Book House, 1994), pp. 138–40.
101. *Muhammad Siddique v. State*; PLD 1983 FSC 173.
102. *Amir Khatoon v. Faiz Ahmad*, PLD 1991 S.C. 787.
103. PLD 1998 S.C.1445.
104. PLD 1975 S.C. 506.
105. PLD 1968 Lahore 1441.
106. 1992 SCMR 1857.
107. PLD 1968 Lahore 1441.
108. 1992 SCMR 1857.

20 Double Jeopardy

The 5th Amendment of the American Constitution provides that –

> 'no person shall ....be subject for the same offence to be twice put in jeopardy of life or limb.'

This protection against 'double jeopardy' has deep roots in the soil of the common law. To allow the government to continue to prosecute a defendant on the same charge, using the same evidence that had previously resulted in acquittal, would seem to violate 'fundamental canons of decency and fairness.'

The US Supreme Court, however, disagreed in *Palko v. Connecticut*,[1] declining to incorporate the Double Jeopardy Clause into the 14th Amendment. But, in *Benton v. Maryland*, this judgment has since been overruled,[2] and the Double Jeopardy Clause has taken its place among those protections deemed 'essential to a scheme of ordered liberty.' However, the question of what exactly constitutes 'double jeopardy' remains open. Essentially, the clause prevents the government from attempting to convict the accused of an illegal act after it has once failed to do so. There are, however, a number of exceptions to this general rule.

Where 3 persons were tried together, 2 were convicted and 1 acquitted. The US Supreme Court set aside the conviction because of defective indictment. All 3 were tried again and all 3 were convicted. The Supreme Court set aside the conviction of the 1 acquitted earlier, on the principle of 'double jeopardy' but, held that there was no bar to the prosecution and conviction of other 2 who had earlier been convicted.[3] Where a defendant pleaded insanity before the trial court but the later denied the plea of insanity, the Appeal Court accepted the plea of insanity, but, remanded the case instead of acquitting the accused. The US Supreme Court reversed and held that Double Jeopardy Clause precluded a second trial once the evidence has been found sufficient about insanity. The appellate court had no choice but to enter judgment of acquittal.[4]

The US Supreme Court has declared in *Kepner v. United States*,[5] –

> 'the weight of authority, as well as decisions of this court, have sanctioned the rule that a person has been in jeopardy when he is regularly charged with a crime before a tribunal properly organized and competent to try him, even though the trial did not result in any verdict.'

In *Serfass v. Jenkins*,[6] it was held that the jeopardy attaches to the merits, if the same facts are 'put to trial before the triers of facts.' In *Benton v. Maryland*,[7] the US Supreme Court said that –

> 'the underlying idea....is that the State, with all its resources and power, should not be allowed to make repeated attempts to convict an individual for an alleged offence, thereby subjecting him to embarrassment, expense and ordeal compelling him to live in a continuing state of anxiety and insecurity, as well as enhancing the possibility that even though innocent he may be found guilty.'

Successive State and Federal Prosecutions

Under the American system of federalism, a single set of actions can lead to separate criminal prosecutions in the state and federal courts. In *United States v. Lanza*,[8] the US Supreme Court upheld successive state and federal prosecutions for the same offense, the Double Jeopardy Clause notwithstanding. Writing for the court in *United States v. Lanza*, Chief Justice William Howard Taft (1857–1930)[9] observed:

> We have here two sovereignties, deriving power from different sources, capable of dealing with the same subject matter within the same territory...Each government in determining what shall be an offense against its peace and dignity is exercising its own sovereignty, not that of the other.

It follows that, an act denounced as a crime by both national and state sovereignties is an offense against the peace and dignity of both and may be punished by each.

Of course, the *Lanza* decision was rendered prior to the incorporation of the Double Jeopardy Clause in *Benton v. Maryland*. But, the Court has held that application of the Clause to the states does not abrogate the dual sovereignty principle articulated in *United States v. Lanza*. Were it otherwise, the Court noted in *United States v. Wheeler*,

> 'Prosecution by one sovereign for a relatively minor offence might bar prosecution by the other for a much graver one, thus effectively depriving the latter of the right to enforce its own laws.'

Thus, double jeopardy does not prevent a separate sovereignty from prosecuting again for the same offence. In *Heath v. Alabama*,[10] the US Supreme Court held that federal prosecution is not barred by previous state prosecution for the same offense.

A good example of a successive prosecution by the federal government after an acquittal in state court is provided by the case of the Los Angeles police officers involved in the videotaped beating of African-American motorist Rodney King (1965–2012) in 1992. The California Superior Court's verdict finding the police officers not guilty of criminal misconduct was followed by considerable outrage and large-scale destructive rioting in Los Angeles. Despite the officer's acquittal on state charges, the federal government brought new charges against them for violating King's civil rights. On appeal, the officers argued that the new federal charges were barred by the Double Jeopardy Clause.[11]

In *United States v. Koon*,[12] the Ninth Circuit rejected this claim, saying that –

> 'there is no evidence that the federal prosecution was a "sham" or a "cover" for the state prosecution.'

Ultimately, the defendants were convicted and served time in federal prison.

Mistrials

Another legitimate deviation from the double jeopardy principle occurs in the case of a mistrial granted on the request of the defense. Judges often declare a mistrial if some extraordinary event occurs, such as the death of a juror or attorney; if some prejudicial error cannot be corrected; or if a hung jury (that is, a jury unable to reach a verdict) results. The declaration of a mistrial, at least on the motion of the defendant, has the effect of 'wiping the slate clean', of declaring that no trial took place. Thus, the state's renewal of its prosecution of the accused does not violate the Double Jeopardy Clause.

Confinement of Sexual Predators in Mental Institutions

In *Kansas v. Hendricks*,[13] the US Supreme Court upheld the Kansas Sexually Violent Predator Act 1994, which permits the state to continue to institutionalize certain sex offenders after they have completed their prison sentences. The Court concluded that the law, which provides for involuntary confinement in mental institutions, did not inflict 'punishment' and was, therefore, beyond the scope of the Double Jeopardy Clause.

Justice Clarence Thomas (1948)[14] wrote the opinion of the Court, joined by Chief Justice William Rehnquist (1924–2005)[15], and Justices Sandra Day O'Connor (1930)[16], Anthony Kennedy (1936)[17], and Antonin Scalia (1936–2016)[18]. Dissenting Justice Stephen Breyer (1938)[19], joined by Justices John Paul Stevens (1929–2019)[20], David Souter (1939)[21], and Ruth Bader Ginsburg (1933–2020)[22] argued that the confinement amounted to an unconstitutional *ex post facto* law. The Court, however, rejected this argument on the grounds that the confinement resulted from a civil commitment preceding not a criminal prosecution.

Ever since *Calder v. Bull*,[23] the *ex post facto* Clause has been limited to criminal punishments. Technically, civil confinement is not criminal punishment, although the result may be indistinguishable from the point of view of the person who loses his freedom. In *Kansas v. Crane*,[24] the Court held, that substantive due process prohibits civil commitment of sex offenders, unless, the state can show that the offender has at least some difficulty controlling his or her impulses. The Court was attempting to make states distinguish between sex offenders who pose real harm to others and those who do not pose such harm after their sentences are completed.

Civil Forfeitures, Double Jeopardy, and Excessive Fines

US Federal Law provides for the forfeiture of real estate and other property used in illegal drug trafficking. In *United States v. Ursery,*[25] the Court held that such forfeitures do not constitute 'punishment' for purposes of the Double Jeopardy Clause. Two federal circuit courts had held, that the Double Jeopardy Clause prohibits both punishing a defendant for a criminal offense, and forfeiting his property for that same offense in a separate civil proceeding.

The US Supreme Court reversed, with Chief Justice William Rehnquist (1924–2005), noting that

> 'Congress long has authorized the Government to bring parallel criminal proceedings and civil forfeiture proceedings, and this Court consistently has found civil forfeitures not to constitute punishment under the Double Jeopardy Clause.'

In this regard, two cases decided by US Supreme Court are important, namely, *Austin v. United States,*[26] and *Department of Revenue of Montana v. Kurth Ranch.*[27]

In *Austin v. United States*, the Court decided that a property forfeiture stemming from a drug crime is subject to limitation under the 8th Amendment. In *Department of Revenue of Montana v. Kurth Ranch,* the Court invoked the Double Jeopardy Clause in striking down a state tax imposed on a quantity of marijuana, when the taxpayer had already been convicted of possessing the same contraband. In Justice John Paul Stevens's (1920–2019) view, these decisions dictated 'a far different conclusion' from that reached by the Court.[28]

Double Jeopardy in India

Clause (2) of Article 20 of the Indian Constitution, provides protection against 'double jeopardy'. The Clause lays down –

> 'No person shall be prosecuted and punished for the same offence more than once.'

This Clause enacts the well-known principle of criminal jurisprudence that –

> 'no one should be put in jeopardy twice for the same offence.'[29]

The Clause is based on the Common Law Maxim '*Nemo debet bis vexari*', which means that a man must not be put twice in peril for the same offence.

Where a person has been convicted for an offence by a competent court, the conviction operates as a bar to any further criminal proceedings against him for the same offence. The object is to avoid the harassment which must be caused to a person for successive criminal proceedings where only one crime has been committed.

The protection contained in Article 20(2) of the Indian Constitution, would be available only if the following essential are complied with—

- (i) The person must be accused of an 'offence'—The term 'offence' means 'any act or omission made punishable by any law for the time being in force.'[30]
- (ii) The person must have been prosecuted before a Court or a judicial tribunal. The term 'Prosecution' means initiation or starting of any proceeding, criminal in nature, before a court, or a judicial tribunal.[31] It means that Article 20(2) would have no application where the proceedings are held under any revenue authorities.

The American Constitution incorporates the same rule in the 5th Amendment that –

> 'no person shall be twice put in jeopardy of life or limb.'

The protection under Clause (2) of Article 20 of the Indian Constitution is narrower than that given in American and British laws. Under the American and the British Constitution, the protection against 'double jeopardy' is given for the second prosecution for the same offence irrespective of whether an accused was acquitted or convicted in the first trial. But, under Article 20(2) the protection against double punishment is given only when the accused has not only been 'prosecuted' but also 'punished', and is sought to be prosecuted second time for the same offence. The use of the word 'prosecution' thus limits the scope of the protection under Clause (1) of Article 20. If there is no punishment for the offence as a result of the prosecution, Clause (2) of Article 20 has no application and an appeal against acquittal, if provided by the procedure is in substance a continuance of the prosecution.[32]

The word 'prosecution' as used with the word 'punishment' embodies the following essentials for the application of double jeopardy rule. They are:

1) The person must be accused of an "offence'. The word 'offence' as defined in General Clauses Act 1897, means 'any act or omission made punishable by law for the time being in force.'
2) The proceeding or the prosecution must have taken place before a 'court' or 'judicial tribunal.'
3) The person must have been 'prosecuted and punished' in the previous proceeding.
4) The 'offence' must be the same for which he was prosecuted and punished in the previous proceedings.

In *Maqbool Hussain v. State of Bombay*,[33] the appellant, a citizen of India, brought from a foreign country some gold without making a declaration. The Sea Customs Authorities took action against him under Section 167 of the Sea Customs Act 1878 and confiscated the gold. Subsequently, he was charged under Section 8 of the Foreign Exchange Regulation Act 1947, and prosecution was initiated against him under the said law.

The Indian Supreme Court held that the Sea Customs Authorities were not a court or a judicial tribunal and the adjudging of confiscation under the Sea Customs Act 1878, did not constitute a judgment or an order of a Court or a judicial tribunal necessary for the purpose of supporting a plea of double jeopardy. The proceeding taken before the Sea Customs Authorities, therefore, did not amount to prosecution of the appellant nor the order of confiscation constitute a punishment imposed by a Court or a judicial tribunal. It was, therefore, held that the prosecution under the Foreign Exchange Regulation Act 1947, was the first prosecution not barred by Article 20(2).[34]

In *S.A. Venkataraman v. Union of India*,[35] the appellant, a government servant, was charged for corruption. An inquiry was held against him under the Public Servants (Inquiries) Act 1850. As a result of the report of the Enquiry Commissioner, he was dismissed from service. Thereafter, he was prosecuted before the Court for having committed offences under Sections 161 and 165 of the Indian Penal Code, 1860, and Section 5(2) of the Prevention of Corruption Act 1947.

The Indian Supreme Court held, that the proceeding taken before the Enquiry Commissioner did not amount to a prosecution for an offence. It was in the nature of a fact-finding inquiry held to advise the government for taking any disciplinary action against the appellant, if so called for. Therefore, the prosecution under the India Penal Code 1860, and the Prevention of Corruption Act 1947, was the first prosecution not barred by Article 20(2). The same result would follow if the departmental inquiry is held after the prosecution of the accused in a criminal proceeding before a court.[36]

In *Union of India v. Subedar Ram Narain*,[37] the Indian Supreme Court held that withholding of pension under Regulation 113(a) of the Army Act 1950, when a junior commissioned officer (JCO) was court-martialed and dismissed [under Section 71(e) of the Army Act 1950], did not amount to double jeopardy. It was because the order of dismissal under the provisions of the Army Act 1950, in case of junior commissioned officer, made him ineligible, for pension or gratuity.

(iii) The person must have been punished after his prosecution before a court or a judicial tribunal.

The protection against 'double jeopardy' contained in Article 20(2) would be available only when the accused has been not only prosecuted but also punished after such prosecution. Therefore, if there is no punishment for the offence as a result of the prosecution, Clause (2) of Article 20 would have no application. Both prosecution and punishment must co-exist for the operation of Article 20(2). It, thus, follows that where a person having been prosecuted for an offence is acquitted, he can be prosecuted for the 'same offence' again.[38] It must be noted that an appeal against an acquittal is, in substance, a continuance of the prosecution. A prosecution starts at the court of first instance and concludes at the final court of appeal.

In *Kalawati v. State of Himachal Pradesh*,[39] the appellant Kalawati, being accused of committing murder of her husband was prosecuted but acquitted by the District Judge. The State of Himachal Pradesh preferred an appeal against the acquittal. The accused contended that the appellate proceedings before the High Court against the acquittal by the District Judge, contravened Article 20(2). The Indian Supreme Court held, that appeal against the acquittal was not the second prosecution, but a continuation of the original prosecution and, therefore, Article 20(2) would not be attracted. Besides, there was no punishment for the offence in the earlier prosecution. Likewise, where a prosecution was a nullity and as a result, the accused was discharged, a fresh prosecution for the 'same offence' would not be violative of Article 20(2).

In *Baij Nath Prasad Tripathi v. State of Bhopal*,[40] the accused Baij Nath Prasad Tripathi, a government servant, was prosecuted under Section 161[41] of the Indian Penal Code 1860 and was punished. In the High Court, the trial was quashed for want of proper sanction as required under Section 6 of the Prevention of Corruption Act 1947. Subsequently, the accused was again prosecuted on getting sanction from the competent authority for his prosecution. It was held that the earlier prosecution was void *ab initio* and no prosecution at all. The prosecution started after obtaining the proper sanction was held to be the first prosecution. Again, enhancement of punishment by the revising authority, has been held not a second punishment.[42]

It may be noted, that the ambit of protection against 'double jeopardy' embodied in Article 20(2) is narrower than that under the English and the American rule. Under the English common law, the maxim *nemo debet bis vexari* explains that, a person can plead as a complete defence, his formal acquittal or conviction if he is indicted again for the same offence in a court, i.e. he can take the plea of *autrefois acquit* or *autrefois convict*. Similarly, the 5th Amendment under the US Constitution which provides *inter alia*:

> 'nor shall any person be subject for the same offence to be twice put in jeopardy of life or limb,'[43]

the protection is available not only against a second punishment, but even against the second trial for the same offence, irrespective of whether the accused was acquitted or convicted in the first trial.

(iv) The person must be prosecuted for the second time before a court or a judicial tribunal. Article 20(2) would have no application where the person is prosecuted and punished for the second time, but the subsequent proceedings is merely the continuation of the previous proceeding, as is the case of an appeal against acquittal,[44] or an appeal against conviction.[45]

(v) The 'Offence' must be the same in both the proceedings—

In *Leo Roy Frey v. Superintendent, District Jail, Amritsar*,[46] the accused Leo Roy Frey, was prosecuted and punished under the Sea Customs Act 1878. Later on, he was prosecuted under Section 120 of the India Penal Code 1860, for conspiracy to commit the act for which he was already convicted under the Sea Customs Act, 1878. It was held that the second prosecution was not barred by Article 20(2), since it was not for the same offence. Committing an offence and conspiracy to commit that offence has been held to be two distinct offences.

It, thus, follows that, when one and the same act of a person constitutes two different offences, the punishment for one offence does not bar prosecution and punishment for the other offence. It has been held that offences may be distinct although some ingredients of two offences are common.[47]

In *Mohinder Singh v. State of Punjab*,[48] the Indian Supreme Court held that offence of attempted dacoity under Sections 399 and 402 of I.P.C. (India Penal Code), and Section 3 of T.A.D.A. Act 1985 (Terrorist and Disruptive Activities [Prevention] Act), and offence of possession of fire-arms without a valid licence under Section 25 of the Arms Act 1959; and Section 5 of the T.A.D.A. Act 1985 (Terrorist and Disruptive Activities [Prevention] Act), were distinct offences, and therefore, trial for the former offence would not be a bar to trial for the later offence. The Court further ruled, that Section 220 of the Cr.P.C. (Criminal Procedure Code) 1973, which provided for joint trial for all the offences a person was accused of, was an enabling provision. The Court may or may not try all the offences together in one trial. By trying separately the offences, the Court said, that the designated Court had committed no illegality.

In *Union of India v. Sunil Kumar Sarkar*,[49] the respondent, a superintendent in Boarder Road Organization, was found guilty of defrauding the organization. He was sentenced to 6 months R.I. (rigorous imprisonment) under the Army Act 1950. After the respondent had undergone the sentence, a disciplinary proceeding was initiated against him under the Central Civil Services (Classification, Control and Appeal) Rules 1965, and as a result, he was dismissed from service. Since, the two proceedings operated in two different fields though, the crime or the misconduct might have arisen out of the same act, and the Court held Article 20(2) inapplicable. It was observed that the court-martial proceedings dealt with the penal aspect, while the proceedings under the Central Rules dealt with disciplinary aspect of the misconduct. So Article 20(2) does not apply to departmental proceedings. An employee, punished by a reduction of pay because of rash and negligent driving, can subsequently be dismissed from service upon his conviction by a criminal court in respect of the same incident.[50]

Article 20(2) would have no application to a 'continuing offence'.[51] Breach of a covenant to keep the premises in good repair, breach of a continuing guarantee, continued wrongful or unauthorized possession of the land, obstruction to a right of way, refusal by a man to maintain his wife and children whom he is bound to maintain under law, the running of a factory without complying with the measures intended for the safety and well-being of workmen, have been held to be illustrations of continuing breaches giving rise to civil or criminal liability, as the case *may be*.[52]

Article 20(2), prohibits the imposition of punishment twice for the same offence. In *State of Haryana v. Ghaseeta Ram*,[53] the respondent, while undergoing sentence of life imprisonment, committed an offence under the Prisons Act 1894, for which he was punished by the trial Court as well as by the Superintendent of Jail, District Jail, Bhiwani. The Supreme Court quashed the punishment imposed by the Jail Superintendent as not permissible.

In a case of kidnapping and extortion, the accused was booked under the Arms Act 1959, and T.A.D.A. (Terrorist and Disruptive Activities [Prevention] Act). He was acquitted in the kidnapping case. The Indian Supreme Court set aside the sentence under T.A.D.A. (Terrorist and Disruptive Activities [Prevention] Act), as also under the Arms Act 1959, on the ground that –

> 'once the accused was acquitted in kidnapping case the doctrine of *autrefois acquit* gets attracted.'[54]

When a person is neither convicted nor acquitted of the charges against him in the first trial, a retrial in such a case would not amount to double jeopardy.[55] When a trial has for some reason become abortive either, because of some inherent defect or illegality affecting, the validity of the trial itself, a second trial is not barred by Article 20(2).[56]

Double Jeopardy and Issue Estoppels

The plea of 'double jeopardy' may be distinguished from the rule of 'issue estoppels'. The rule of 'issue estoppels' precludes evidence being led to prove a fact in issue as regards which evidence has already been led and a specific finding recorded at an earlier criminal trial before a competent Court. The rule relates only to the admissibility of evidence.[57]

If it is proved by proper evidence that the same point was determined in favour of a prisoner in a previous criminal trial which is brought in issue on a second criminal trial of the same prisoner, there is an 'issue estoppels'. For the operation of the rule, the parties as well as the facts is issue, in the two trials, must be the same.[58]

In *Pritam Singh v. State of Punjab*,[59] the accused made a statement leading to the recovery of a fire-arm which he was alleged to have used against the victims. He was prosecuted for the possession of the fire-arm but was acquitted. Later on, in the trial of murder charge against the same accused, the evidence of the possession of the fire-arm was pleaded. It was held that the evidence was precluded by the rule of 'issue estoppels'. It has been held that the prosecution cannot adduce evidence to set aside the finding of fact arrived at in the previous criminal trial of the accused.[60]

While Article 20(2) bars double punishment, the rule of 'issue estoppels' bars reception of evidence on an issue on which the finding was in favor of the accused at a previous trial. Article 20(2) has no direct bearing on the question at issue, while the rule of 'issue estoppels' relates to evidence on the question in issue at the two trials. What are required for the application of the rule of 'issue estoppels' are the identity of issue and the acquittal of the accused at a previous trial on the same issue, while Article 20(2) would be attracted, if, the 'offence' is the same in the second prosecution for which the accused has earlier been prosecuted and punished.[61]

Double Jeopardy in Pakistan

Article 13(a) of the 1973 Pakistan Constitution provides that –

> 'no person shall be prosecuted or punished for the same offence more than once.'

The only difference between the provisions of the Pakistan and the Indian Constitutions is that, in Article 13 of the Pakistan Constitution, the word 'or' appears whereas in the Indian Constitution the word 'and' is used. This difference is of great significance. The words 'shall be prosecuted' in Article 13(a) refer to initiation of proceedings of a criminal nature before a court of law or a judicial tribunal in accordance with the procedure prescribed in the statute which creates the offense and regulates the procedure.[62]

Article 13(a) raises to constitutional status the principle of *autrefois convict* and *autrefois acquit* embodied in Section 403 of the Code of Criminal procedure 1898, which provides that –

> A person who has once been tried by a competent Court for an offence and convicted or acquitted of such offence shall, while such conviction or acquittal remains in force, not be liable to be tried again for the same offence, nor on the same facts for any other offence for which a different charge from the one made against him might have been made under Section 236, or for which he might have been convicted under Section 237 of the Code of Criminal Procedure, 1898.

The principle also finds place in a modified form in Section 26 of the General Clauses Act 1897, which provides that –

> Where an act or omission constitutes an offence under two or more enactments, then the offender shall be liable to be prosecuted and punished under either or anyone of those enactments, but shall not be liable to be punished twice for the same offence.

These provisions, however, not, bar subsequent trial for a 'distinct' or 'different' or 'other' offence as described in subsections (2) and (3) of Section 403 of the Criminal Procedure Code 1898.

Americans refer to this principle as the rule against double jeopardy, which is based on the common law maxim of *nemo debet bis vexari pro una et eadem causa*, which means 'a man shall not be twice vexed for one and the same cause.'

The rule serves as the basis for the special pleas of *autrefois acquit* and *autrefois convict.* When a criminal charge has been once adjudicated upon by a Court of competent jurisdiction, that adjudication is final, whether it takes the form of an acquittal or a conviction, and it may be pleaded in bar of a subsequent prosecution for the same offence, whether charged with or without matters of mere aggravation, and whether such matters relate to the intent with which the offence was committed or to the consequences of the offence. The rule against double jeopardy is embodied in that part of the 5th Amendment of the American Constitution which declares that –

> 'no person shall be subject for the same offence to be twice put in jeopardy of life or limb.'

In the American system, the constitutional barrier applies to the second prosecution irrespective of the result of the first prosecution, because double jeopardy commences with the commencement of the second prosecution. The constitutional safeguard, therefore, can be pleaded to the second prosecution whether the accused was acquitted or convicted in the first prosecution. The Common Law principle is also the same.

Article 13 (a) of the Pakistan Constitution, also follows the American and the common law rule by providing that –

> 'no man shall be prosecuted or punished for the same offence more than once.'

In *Alamdar Hussain Shah v. Abdul Bashir Qureshi*,[63] Justice Dr Nasim Hasan Shah (1929–2015)[64], of the Supreme Court of Pakistan conforming to the corresponding provision of the Indian Constitution held that the word 'prosecution' in Article 13(a) of the Pakistan Constitution includes 'punishment' with the result that fresh prosecution for the same offence would be barred only where prosecution finally concluded and ended either in acquittal or conviction.

This interpretation runs counter to the principle of *autrefois acquit* or *autrefois convict* but is in accordance with the Indian constitution. *Autrefois acquit* (formerly acquitted) means when a person in indicted for an offence and acquitted, he cannot be afterwards, indicted for the same offence, and if he be thus, indicted a second time, he may plead *autrefois acquit*, which will be a good bar to the indictment. *Autrefois convict* (formerly convicted) is defense of a person charged with any crime that he has been already convicted of the same crime and therefore, cannot be indicted again for the same offence. It is certainly contrary to the provisions of Article 13(a) of the Pakistan Constitution which uses the word 'or' unlike the Indian Constitution which uses the word 'and'.

Thus, in the Pakistan Constitution, the words 'prosecution' and 'punishment' have been disjunctively used. Pakistani Article 13(a), clearly, means that if a person has been prosecuted once, he cannot be again prosecuted, and if a person has been once punished, he cannot be prosecuted or punished again. Therefore, under the Pakistan Constitution, second prosecution is barred irrespective of the result of the first prosecution, that is, irrespective of the fact whether or not the accused was convicted or acquitted pursuant to the prosecution. If 'prosecution' includes within its ambit 'punishment' there was no necessity of using the words 'or punished'. It is acknowledged that Pakistan's Constitution constitutionalizes the two maxims of *autrefois acquit* or *autrefois convict*, and it has to be treated at par with Constitution of the United States and the common law principle of England.[65]

The constitutional protection contained in Article 13(a) of the 1973 Constitution is available only if the accused is convicted and punished. If the first prosecution results in acquittal, the second prosecution is not prohibited. If an accused is tried twice, simultaneously, for the same offence and the judgment of conviction in point of time is rendered first, and the judgment of acquittal later, the judgment of conviction will hold the field. The provision of Section 26, General Clauses Act 1897, does not bar 'duplicate trial'; it only prohibits 'duplicate punishment'.

These three propositions were laid down by Justice Muhammad Afzal Lone (1928–2020)[66], with whom the other two learned judges, namely, Justice Dr Nasim Hasan Shah (1929–2015) (Later 12th Chief Justice of Pakistan) and Justice Rustam S. Sidhwa (1927–94)[67] agreed, in *Muhammad Ashraf v. The State* case.[68] All the three propositions are of highly doubtful validity.

The provisions of Article 13(a) did not find place in the Constitution, because it was not included in the Constitutions of 1956, 1962 and 1972; moreover, it does not replicate the provision of Article 20(2) of the Indian Constitution, because Article 13(a) says,

> 'no person shall be prosecuted or punished' twice for the same offence,

and the Indian Article says,

> 'no person shall be prosecuted and punished' twice for the same offence.

Article 13(a) of the Pakistan Constitution is based in fact, though using the modern language adopted by the Indian Constitution, on a clause of the 5th Amendment of the US Constitution, which lays down that –

> 'no person shall be subject for the same offence to be twice put in jeopardy or life and limb.'

As commonly described, the constitutional guarantee is against double jeopardy and what constitutes 'jeopardy' is to be determined in accordance with the common law which these constitutional clauses incorporate. It has been ruled in *ex parte Lange, 18 Wall 163*, that by the common law not only was a second punishment for the same offence prohibited but a second trial forbidden whether or not the accused had suffered punishment or had been acquitted or convicted. Therefore, it is not necessary in order to plead the bar of prior jeopardy that there should have been a verdict of guilty or acquittal in the formal trial.

According to Muhammad Munir,[69] Article 13(a) –

> 'raises to a constitutional status the principle of *autrefois convict* and *autrefois acquit* embodied in section 403 of the Code of Criminal Procedure 1898 and a part of section 132 of the Evidence Act, 1872.'

He further said,

> 'the present Article prohibits both double prosecution and punishment for the same offence.'

The principle of 'double jeopardy' is in turn based on the maxim, '*nemo bis debet puniri pro uno delicto*' which means 'no person shall be prosecuted or punished for the same offence more than once' includes within its ambit the following three situations:

(i) A person who has been prosecuted once for an offence cannot be prosecuted again for the same offence even though no final judgment of conviction or acquittal was recorded in the first trial.
(ii) A person who has been prosecuted and consequently punished once for an offence cannot be prosecuted again for the same offence.
(iii) A person who has been prosecuted and consequently acquitted for an offence cannot be prosecuted again for the same offence.

If a person who has been prosecuted once cannot be prosecuted again for the same offence irrespective of the result of the first prosecution, there is no reason why under Article 13(a), second prosecution should not be a bar, if the person has been prosecuted and consequently acquitted in the first trial.

The Indian Supreme Court while construing Article 20(2), couched in exactly the same language (except the word 'and') has never held that the provisions of the Article only contains one-half (rather one-third) of the principles, or double jeopardy, and the other half (or two-third) has to be searched in the body of statutory law.

The Indian Supreme Court, since the commencement of the Indian Constitution on 26 January 1950, has had umpteen occasions to construe Article 20(2) of the Indian Constitution, and has decided cases in hundreds, but, nowhere has it ruled that Article 20(2) does not protect a person against double jeopardy who had been acquitted in the first trial.

The decision of Justice Muhammad Afzal Lone (1928–2020), would amount to saying that in the absence of Section 403(1), Criminal Procedure Code (C. Pr. C), an accused is liable to be prosecuted and tried again and again for the same offence, till possibly he is convicted in order to prohibit the state from further prosecuting him. Was this the intention of the constitution makers?

The holding of Justice Lone, in *Muhammad Ashraf v. the State*,[70] that –

> 'under section 26 of the General Clauses Act 1897, there is no bar on the simultaneous prosecution and what is prohibited is duplicate punishment and not the "duplicate trial" is to say the least a misconceived interpretation of the section.'

The section merely laid down that, where a transaction is made offence under more than one enactments then the offender may be charged under one or more enactments, but, the punishment can only be awarded under one of those enactments. It does neither authorize nor envisage expressly or implicitly multiplicity of trials for the same offence. If, facts constituting the offence fall under ten different enactments, can the accused be tried ten times separately.

There must be a previous prosecution or punishment to attract the prohibition. In *S.A. Venkataraman v. Union of India*,[71] it was held that an enquiry held against a public servant under the Public Servants (Inquiries) Act 1850, for corruption resulting in his dismissal from service, was not a bar against his prosecution under Sections 161 and 165 of the Indian Penal Code 1860, read with Section 5 (2) of the Prevention of Corruption Act 1947; because the proceeding taken under the Inquiries Act 1850, was not prosecution and the dismissal was not a punishment for an offence. The rule is the same, if the departmental enquiry is held after the acquittal of the accused in a criminal prosecution on the same facts as held by the Supreme Court of Pakistan in *Muhammad Ayub v. The Chairman, Electricity Board, WAPDA, Peshawar*.[72]

Where a case was still at the investigation stage, it could not be said that the second prosecution has been launched. If, during investigation stage, a non-bailable warrant was issued by a magistrate, it was merely an act in aid of investigation, and Article 13 was not attracted.[73]

NOTES

1. 302 U.S. 319 (1937).
2. 395 U.S. 784 (1969).
3. *Ball v. United States*, 163 U.S. 662 (1896).
4. *Burks v. United States*, 437 U.S. 1 (1978).
5. 195 U.S. 100 (1905).
6. 420 U.S. 377 (1975).
7. 395 U.S. 784 (1969).
8. 260 U.S. 377 (1922).
9. William Howard Taft was the 27th president of the United States (1909–1913) and the 10th Chief Justice of the US Supreme Court (1921–1930).
10. 474 U.S. 82 (1985).
11. 16 F.3d 992 (9th Cir. 1994).
12. Otis H. Stephens Jr, John M. Scheb II, *American Constitutional Law*, (California, Belmont: Thomson/West, 2003), pp. 598–9.
13. 521 U.S. 346 (1997).
14. Clarence Thomas is Associate Justice of US Supreme Court.
15. William Rehnquist served as 16th Chief Justice of the United States.
16. Sandra Day O'Connor was the first female Associate Justice of US Supreme Court from 1981 to 2006.
17. Anthony Kennedy served as Associate Justice of the Supreme Court of the United States from 1988 to 2018.
18. Antonin Scalia served as Associate Justice of the US Supreme Court from 1986 to 2016.
19. Stephen Breyer is serving Associate Justice of the US Supreme Court.
20. John Paul Stevens served as Associate Justice of the Supreme Court of the United States from 1975 to 2010.
21. David Souter served as Associate Justice of the Supreme Court of the United States from 1990 to 2009.
22. Ruth Bader Ginsburg served as Associate Justice of the Supreme Court of the United States from 1993 to 2020.
23. 3 U.S. 386 (1798).
24. 534 U.S. 407 (2002).
25. 518 U.S. 267 (1996).
26. 509 U.S. 602 (1993).
27. 511 U.S. 767 (1994).
28. Supra Note 12, pp. 599–600.
29. *Maqbool Hussain v. State of Bombay*, AIR 1953 S.C. 325; *A.L. Kalara v. The Project & Equipment Corporation of India Ltd.*, AIR 1984 S.C. 1361; *Sunil Batra v. Delhi Administration*, AIR 1978 S.C. 1675.
30. Section 26 of the General Clauses Act 1897; *S.A. Venkataraman v. Union of India*, AIR 1954 S.C. 375.
31. *Thomas Dana v. State of Punjab*, AIR 1959, S.C. 375; *Raja Narayanlal Bansilal v. Maneck Phiroz Mistry*, AIR 1961 S.C. 29; *Shewpujanrai Indrasanrai Ltd. v. The Collector of Customs*, AIR 1958 S.C. 845.
32. *Kalawati v. State of Himachal Pradesh*, AIR 1953 S.C. 131.
33. AIR 1953 SC 325.
34. *See also Assistant Collector of Customs v. U.L.R. Malwani*, AIR 1970 SC 962; *In Re: P. Bapanaiah v. Unknown*, AIR 1970 AP 47.
35. AIR 1954 SC 375.
36. *Motising Chhagasing Vaghela v. S.D. Mehta*, AIR 1966 Guj 233, 1966 CriLJ 1001.
37. (1998) 8 SCC 52, AIR 1998 SC 3225.
38. *State of Madhya Pradesh v. Veereshwar Rao Agnihotry*, AIR 1957 SC 592.
39. AIR 1953 SC 131.
40. AIR 1957 SC 494.
41. Section 161 of Indian Penal Code punishes 'public servant committing acts of corruption.'
42. *D.A. Kelshikar v. State of Bombay*, (1959) 61 BOMLR 1625, (1960) ILLJ 66 Bom.
43. 5th amendment of the US Constitution.
44. *Kalawati v. State of Himachal Pradesh*, AIR 1953 SC 131; *State of M.P. v. Veereshwar Rao Agnihotry*, AIR 1957 SC 592.

45. *State of Maharashtra v. Shriram*, (1991) CrLJ 1631; *D.A. Kelshikar v. State of Bombay*, (1959) 61 BOMLR 1625.
46. AIR 1958 SC 119.
47. *Mohinder Singh v. State of Punjab*, AIR 1999 SC 211; *M. M. Gandhi v. State of Mysore*, 1960 CriLJ 934; *Om Prakash Gupta v. State of U.P.*, AIR 1957 SC 458; *State of Madhya Pradesh v. Veereshwar Rao Agnihotry*, AIR 1957 SC 592.
48. AIR 1999 SC 211. *See also A.A. Mulla v. State of Maharashtra*, AIR 1997 SC 1441; *P.V. Mohammad Barmay Sons v. Director of Enforcement*, AIR 1993 SC 1188; *V.K. Agarwal, Assistant Collector of Customs v. Vasantaraj Bhagwanji Bhatia*, AIR 1988 SC 1106.
49. AIR 2001 SC 1092. *See also R. Viswan v. Union of India*, 1983 SCR (3) 60, 1983 SCC (3) 401, AIR 1983 SC 658.
50. *State of Haryana v. Balwant Singh*, AIR 2003 S.C. 1253; (2003) 3 SCC 414.
51. *Jain Singh v. State of Haryana*, AIR 1995 P H 243; *In re: Meenapati Daveed And Anr. v. Unknown*, AIR 1959 AP 137; *Mohammad Ali v. Sri Ram Swarup*, AIR 1965 All 161; *Saharanpur Municipal Board v. Kripa Ram*, AIR 1965 All 160; *Emperor v. Chhotalal Amarchand*, (1936) 38 BOMLR 1164; *Balkrishna Savalram Pujari v. Shree Dnyaneshwar Maharaj Sansthan*, AIR 1959 SC 798; *Commissioner of Wealth Tax v. Suresh Seth*, AIR 1981 SC 1106.
52. *Commissioner of Wealth Tax v. Suresh Seth*, AIR 1981 SC 1106.
53. AIR 1997 SC 1868.
54. *Mukhtar Ahmad Ansari v. State* (NCT of Delhi), AIR 2005 S.C. 2804, (2005) SCC 258.
55. *O.P. Dahiya v. Union of India*, AIR 2003 S.C. 4464, (2003) 1 SCC 122.
56. *Muhammad Safi v. State of West Bengal*, AIR 1966 S.C. 69; *State of Karnataka through CBI v. C. Nagarajaswamy*, AIR 2005 S.C. 4308, (2005) 8 SCC 370.
57. *Piara Singh v. State of Punjab*, AIR 1969 SC 961; *State of Andhra Pradesh v. Kokkiliagada Meerayya*, AIR 1970 SC 771.
58. *Ravinder Singh v. State of Haryana*, AIR 1975 S.C. 856.
59. AIR 1956 S.C. 415.
60. *Manipur Administration v. Thokchom Bria Singh*, AIR 1964 S.C. 87; *Mohinder Singh v. State of Punjab*, AIR 1965 S.C. 79.
61. *Assistant Collector of Customs v. U.L.R. Malwani*, AIR 1970 SC 962.
62. *Tasawar Hussain v. State*, 1986 P. Cr. L. J. 2218.
63. PLD 1978 S.C. 121.
64. Dr Nasim Hasan Shah was the 12th Chief Justice of Pakistan.
65. A.G. Chaudhry, *Lectures on Constitutional Law*, (Lahore: Irfan Law Book House, 1996), pp. 131–3.
66. Muhammad Afzal Lone was a Judge in Supreme Court of Pakistan.
67. Rustam S. Sidhwa served as a Judge in Supreme Court of Pakistan from 1989 to 1992.
68. 1995 SCMR 626.
69. Muhammad Munir, *Constitution of Islamic Republic of Pakistan: being a commentary on the Constitution of Pakistan*, (Lahore: PLD Publishers, 1975), p. 128.
70. 1995 SCMR 626.
71. AIR 1954 S.C. 375.
72. PLD 1987 S.C. 195.
73. *Nazir Ahmad v. Muhammad Shafi*, PLD 1980 S.C. 6.

Part VI

Political Rights and Civil Liberties

21 Freedom of Speech and Press

'Congress shall make no law abridging the freedom of speech, or of the press'

is part of the statement contained in the First Amendment to the Constitution of the United States of America. US Supreme Court developed a constitutional doctrine effectively defining 'freedom of expression', which encompasses both freedom of speech and freedom of the press. It cannot be denied that freedom of expression is the fundamental freedom in a democracy.

INTERPRETIVE FOUNDATIONS OF EXPRESSIVE FREEDOM

The idea of free speech is a largely modern notion that correlates with the emergence of democracy. Freedom of speech, particularly in religious and political matters, was unthinkable in ancient and medieval world. In England the idea of freedom of speech emerged gradually, coincident with the development of parliamentary form of government. Since free speech was so important in galvanizing the American Revolution (1775–83), it was enshrined in the constitutions of the new American States.

The constitutional commitment to freedom of the press also has its roots in English history and in American colonial experience, especially during the decades immediately preceding the American Revolution (1775–83). Small independent newspaper and pamphlet publishers, who dominated the mass media of that period, played a vital role in facilitating political debate and in disseminating information. The ratification of the constitution was vigorously debated not only in the state ratifying conventions, but in the press as well. '*The Federalist Papers*,'[1] were collection of essays, which first appeared as a series of newspaper articles analyzing and endorsing the new constitution. Anti-Federalists also made wide use of newspapers to express opposition to ratification.

Despite the obvious importance of freedoms of speech and press in the establishment of American democracy, the US Supreme Court did not pay major attention to these values during the early days of the republic. For a brief period during the administration of President John Adams (1735–1826),[2] the national government sought to suppress public criticism through enforcement of the Sedition Act, passed by Congress in 1798. The Sedition Act 1798, prohibited 'any false, scandalous and malicious' writing against the federal government. This legislation was used to punish a few of Thomas Jefferson's (1743–1826)[3] partisans, and it may have had a chilling effect on criticism of the government. Nevertheless, the provision expired on 3 March 1801, just before Thomas Jefferson and his newly victorious party took power. Jefferson pardoned those convicted under the statute, and no occasion arose for the US Supreme Court to determine its constitutionality.

During the American Civil War (1861–65), a number of limits were imposed on freedom of expression. This included newspaper censorship and the prosecution of some of the more vociferous critics of the Abraham Lincoln[4] administration. However, no constitutional challenges raising First Amendment issues reached the US Supreme Court.[5]

(i) *Incorporation of the Freedoms of Speech and Press*

The principal reason that First Amendment controversies did not reach the US Supreme Court during the 19th century was that, by design, the First Amendment did not apply to the state and local governments. Not until *Gitlow v. New York*,[6] did the US Supreme Court recognize that the First Amendment freedoms of speech and press were applicable to the states via the 14th Amendment. In addition to the incorporation of the First Amendment, changes in the national political environment brought questions of freedom of speech to the forefront. The national government's efforts to deal with political dissent in the early decades of the 20th century produced a series of cases that required the Court to interpret the scope of First Amendment protection. By the 1920s, the First Amendment emerged as an important field of constitutional interpretation.

(ii) *Preferred Freedoms?*

Following the late-1930s constitutional revolution, the US Supreme Court shifted its focus away from protecting private property rights and toward promoting personal liberty. The First Amendment figured prominently in the Court's newfound emphasis. Justice Benjamin N. Cardozo (1870–1938),[7] writing for the Court in *Palko v. Connecticut*,[8] characterized freedom of speech as –

> 'the matrix, the indispensable condition, of nearly every other form of freedom.'

During the 1940s, several members of the US Supreme Court went so far as to suggest that the First Amendment freedom of speech and press enjoy a 'preferred position' in relation to other constitutional guarantees for example, Justice William O. Douglas's (1898–1980),[9] majority opinion in *Murdock v. Pennsylvania*.[10]

Although, the Court soon abandoned the preferred freedom language, 'freedom of expression' was accorded high priority during the Warren Court era (1953–1969). The Warren Court established a number of important precedents in this area, and the more conservative Burger and Rehnquist Courts have, for the most part, adhered to these precedents. Clearly, First Amendment questions of increasing complexity and difficulty continue to be among the most important concerns of the US Supreme Court.

(iii) *Are the Protections of the First Amendment Absolute?*

Although, the First Amendment begins with the seemingly absolute injunction, 'Congress shall make no law....' the US Supreme Court has never taken the view that First Amendment protections are absolute in character. Indeed, only a few justices who have served on the court have argued for an absolutist interpretation. Hugo Black (1886–1971),[11] the best known and most forceful of the 1st Amendment absolutists, believed that all speech and writing, regardless of its purpose, content, or impact, should be absolutely protected against censorship or sanction. Thus, Justice Black believed that criminal laws prohibiting obscenity, profanity, and seditious speech were inherently unconstitutional. Justice Black also believed that laws that permitted civil suits for libel or slander could not be reconciled with the 1st Amendment.

In Justice Black's view, the First Amendment gives everyone the right to say or write anything, regardless of its impact on other individuals or society in general. However, Justice Black believed that the protections of the First Amendment were limited to pure speech and pure writing. In his view, picketing and other forms of expressive conduct were not covered by the First Amendment.

Although, Justice Hugo Black wrote a number of important opinions for the Court on questions of freedom of speech and freedom of the press, most of his colleagues and most of the justices who came after him refused to accept Black's First Amendment absolutism. The Court has never taken the position that the protections of the First Amendment are absolute. Indeed, the Court has recognized that certain types of expression, including obscenity, fighting words, and defamation, are outside the scope of the First Amendment. It has also held that speech that is normally protected by the American Constitution might not be protected depending on the circumstances in which it takes place.

On the other hand, the Court has recognized that the protections of the First Amendment are not limited to pure speech and writing. Rather, the First Amendment potentially protects communication of any kind. Protests, demonstrations, performances, advertisements, artistic endeavours all of these are within the ambit of expression. So too are records, films, videos, software, e-mail, broadcasts, cablecasts, and sites on the Internet. In short, the First Amendment protects communication, regardless of its nature or medium. Whether specific instances of expression merit First Amendment protection or may be censored or sanctioned by government depends on a number of factors.

The American Government can infringe on 'freedom of expression' in two ways. It can employ censorship to prevent a specific instance of expression from reaching the public. Alternatively, it can punish someone after the fact, usually through criminal prosecution.[12]

Restrictions on Freedom of Speech

(i) *The clear and present danger doctrine*

Even though, a specific instance of expression may not be censored prior to its utterance or publication, it may still be subject to sanctions after the fact. Individuals may be subjected to criminal prosecution or civil suit for instances of expression that violate specific legal prohibitions. Whether, such instances of expression are protected by the First Amendment depends on a number of factors including the nature of the expression and context in which it takes place.

In *Schenck v. United States,*[13] the first major US Supreme Court decision interpreting the scope of free speech, the Court made plain that there are instances in which speech that is normally subject to constitutional protection may be suppressed by the government. Writing for the Court, Justice Oliver Wendell Holmes Jr (1841–1935),[14] flatly rejected an absolutist interpretation of the First Amendment. In what has become a stock phrase in the American political lexicon, Justice Holmes observed that –

> 'the most stringent protection of free speech would not protect a man in falsely shouting fire in a theater, and causing a panic.'

Justice Holmes went on to articulate the famous 'clear and present danger' test, saying that –

> 'the question in every case is whether the words used are used in such circumstances and are of such a nature as to create a clear and present danger that they will bring about the substantive evils that Congress has a right to prevent.'

For example, government has a right, indeed an obligation, to protect the national security. If an instance of expression creates a 'clear and present danger' to national security, then government has the right to prohibit the speech or punish the speaker.

In the *Schenck* case, Charles Schenck was general secretary of the Socialist Party of America, he was convicted for conspiring to print and circulate leaflets, urging resistance to the military draft. The leaflets urged resistance to the draft on the grounds that it violated the 13th Amendment. Although, sharply critical of the war effort, Schenck's message was confined to the advocacy of peaceful measures, such as petition for repeal of the draft. Nevertheless, a unanimous US Supreme Court believed that Schenck's activities amounted to a clear and present danger. One must remember, though, that Schenck's prosecution occurred during World War I (1914–18). As Justice Holmes observed,

> 'When a nation is at war many things that might be said in time of peace are such a hindrance to its effort that their utterance will not be endured so long as men fight, and that no Court could regard them as protected by any constitutional right.'

A week after *Schenck,* the US Supreme Court upheld convictions under the Espionage Act 1917, in *Frohwerk v. United States*[15] and *Debs v. United States.*[16] In *Frohwerk v. United States*, two individuals were convicted and sentenced to 10 years in prison because of their articles criticizing the war. The Court acknowledged, that there was no evidence that the articles had any adverse effect on the war effort, but the articles in certain quarters could have kindled a flame. In *Debs v. United States*, the Court affirmed the conviction of the Leader of the Socialist Party of America, Eugene Debs, who had been sentenced to jail for 10 years. His speech was primarily on advocacy of Socialism, but, mildly criticized the war which was small part of the speech. The Court held that speech was not protected because one purpose of the speech was to oppose the war.

It is also noteworthy that the Court's decision came at a time when the threat of international Communism was looming large. For the next 4 decades, the 'clear and present danger' doctrine competed with other approaches to First Amendment interpretation in the area of political dissent.[17]

(ii) *The Bad Tendency Test*

The standard that Justice Oliver Wendell Holmes Jr (1841–1935) articulated, in the *Schenck* case was ignored by a US Supreme Court majority some 8 months later in *Abrams v. United States.*[18] Here, the Court affirmed the convictions of Jacob Abrams, a self-styled 'anarchist-Socialist,' and several associates for distributing leaflets in New York City urging the 'workers of the world' to resist, among other things, American intervention in Russia against the newly formed Bolshevik government.[19]

For Justice John Hessin Clarke (1857–1945)[20], the US Supreme Court's majority spokesman, it was enough that Abrams was advocating a general strike 'in the greatest port of our land' for the purpose of –

> 'curtailing the production of ordnance and munitions necessary and essential to the prosecution of the war.'

In effect, Justice Clarke was reverting to the traditional common law 'bad tendency' test, according little importance to the free speech question and focusing on the possibility that Abrams's circular might in some way hinder the war effort.

In a powerful dissenting opinion, Justice Oliver Wendell Holmes Jr, joined by Justice Louis D. Brandeis (1856–1941)[21], again resorted to the 'clear and present danger' test, but this time he used it as a basis for challenging, rather than endorsing, governmental interference with free speech:

> '[T]he ultimate good desired is better reached by free trade in ideas…I think that we should be eternally vigilant against attempts to check the expression of opinions that we loathe and believe to be fraught with death, unless they so imminently threaten immediate interference with the lawful and pressing purposes of the law that an immediate check is required to save the country.'

Through the 1920s, a court majority continued to adhere to the 'bad tendency test', while Justices Holmes and Brandeis, further developed the 'clear and present danger' doctrine as a rationale in support of freedom of expression and association.

In *Gitlow v. New York*,[22] the US Supreme Court upheld a conviction under New York's Criminal Anarchy Act 1902, that prohibited advocating for the overthrow of government 'by force or violence.' Prior to this decision, the Court had addressed issues of freedom of expression arising from the states strictly on the basis of the 'Due Process Clause' of the 14th Amendment, without specific reference to the First Amendment.

In fact, as late as 1922 the Court observed that –

> 'the Constitution of the United States imposes upon the States no obligation to convey upon those within their jurisdiction…the right of free speech' (*Prudential Insurance Company v. Cheek*).[23]

In 1923, in *Meyer v. Nebraska*, the US Supreme Court invalidated on 'due process' grounds, a Nebraska law prohibiting the teaching of the German language in primary schools.[24] Similarly, in *Pierce v. Society of Sisters*,[25] the Court struck down an amendment to the State of Oregon Constitution, aimed at prohibiting parents from sending their children to private schools. In the *Meyer* and *Pierce* cases, the Court focused on the deprivation of liberty and property rights protected by the 14th Amendment 'Due Process Clause.' In the *Gitlow* case, however, Justice Edward Terry Sanford (1865–1930),[26] writing for the majority, stated without elaboration:

> 'For present purposes we may and do assume that freedom of speech and of the press- which are protected by the First Amendment from abridgment by Congress—are among the fundamental personal rights and 'liberties' protected by the Due Process Clause of the Fourteenth Amendment from impairment by the states.' (The Court first invalidated a state law on First Amendment freedom of speech grounds two years later in *Fiske v. Kansas*).[27]

The incident giving rise to the *Gitlow* case[28] was publication of the 'Left Wing Manifesto,' a statement of beliefs held by what the Court characterized as the most radical section of the Socialist Party of America. In essence, the manifesto called for the destruction of established government and its replacement by a 'revolutionary dictatorship of the proletariat.' In affirming the conviction of Benjamin Gitlow, business manager of *The Revolutionary Age*, the Socialist Party of America newspaper that published the 'Left Wing Manifesto,' Justice Edward Terry Sanford stated the essence of the bad tendency test:

> 'That a state, in the exercise of its police power, may punish those who abuse [freedom of speech and press] by utterances inimical to the public welfare, tending to corrupt public morals, incite to crime, or disturb the public peace, is not open to question.'

Justice Sanford continued:

> 'The state cannot reasonably be required to measure the danger from every such utterance in the nice balance of a jeweler's scale. A single revolutionary spark may kindle a fire that, smoldering for a time, may burst into a sweeping and destructive conflagration. It cannot be said that the state is acting arbitrarily or unreasonably when, in the exercise of its judgement as to the measures necessary to protect the public peace and safety, it seeks to extinguish the spark without waiting until it has enkindled the flame or blazed into the conflagration.'

Again Justices Holmes and Brandeis dissented. They could find no 'clear and present danger' of an effort–

> 'to overthrow the government by force on the part of the admittedly small minority who shared the defendant's views.'

In response to the contention that the 'Left Wing Manifesto' was an incitement, Justice Holmes asserted:

> 'Every idea is an incitement. It offers itself for belief and if believed it is acted on unless some other belief outweighs it or some failure of energy stifles the movement at its birth. The only difference between the expression of an opinion and an incitement in the narrower sense is the speaker's enthusiasm for the result. Eloquence may set fire to reason. But whatever may be thought of the redundant discourse before us it had no chance of starting a present conflagration. If in the long run the beliefs expressed in proletarian dictatorship are destined to be accepted by the dominant forces of the community, the only meaning of free speech is that they should be given their chance and have their way.'

This rising endorsement of the concept of a free marketplace of ideas contrasts sharply with Justice Holmes's earlier deference, in the *Schenck* case,[29] to governmental control of dissident expression. As we have seen in connection with judicial review of economic regulation, Justice Holmes was inclined to give wide latitude to legislative discretion in matters of public policy. But, his dissent in *Gitlow*, like his dissent in *Abrams v. United States*,[30] reflected a decided shift in emphasis where 1st Amendment values were concerned. This change was probably influenced by Holmes's association on the Court with Justice Louis Brandeis (1846–1941), a dedicated and articulate defender of civil rights and liberties, and his acquaintance with Harvard University law Professor Zechariah Chafee Jr (1885–1957), a widely recognized authority on the 1st Amendment.

Justice Brandeis himself had occasion to discuss the 'clear and present danger' formula in a concurring opinion in *Whitney v. California*.[31] In this case, the majority, speaking again through Justice Sanford, adhered to the 'bad tendency' test in affirming the conviction of Charlotte Anita Whitney (1867–1955)[32] for violating California's Criminal Syndicalism Act 1919. The statute defined 'criminal syndicalism' as –

> 'any doctrine or precept advocating, teaching or aiding and abetting the commission of crime, sabotage…or unlawful acts of force and violence or unlawful methods of terrorism as a means of accomplishing a change in industrial ownership or control, or effecting any political change.'

Whitney's conviction was based on her participation in the organizing convention of the Communist Labor Party of California. The jury rejected her contention, that at this meeting she advocated lawful, non-violent political reform. She maintained that her conviction was a deprivation of liberty without due process of law, but she did not contend specifically that her participation in organizing the Communist Labor Party constituted no clear and present danger. Justice Sanford rejected the view that the act, as applied in this case, was –

> 'an unreasonable or arbitrary exercise of the public power of the state, unwarrantably infringing any right of free speech, assembly, or association, or that those persons are protected by the Due Process Clause who abuse such rights by joining and furthering an organization...menacing the peace and welfare of the state.'

Because, *Whitney v. California* did not raise the 'clear and present danger' issue, Justices Brandeis and Holmes felt compelled to concur. The jury was presented with evidence of a conspiracy, and under the circumstances, they concluded, its verdict should not be disturbed. Nevertheless, Justice Brandeis took sharp issue with the majority's narrow view of the constitutional protection that should be afforded political dissent. The crux of the Brandeis-Holmes position is contained in the following excerpts:

> 'Those who won our independence believed that the final end of the state was to make men free to develop their faculties; and that, in its government, the deliberative forces should prevail over the arbitrary. They valued liberty both as an end, and as a means. They believed liberty to be the secret of happiness, and courage to be the secret of liberty. They believed that...public discussion is a political duty, and that this should be a fundamental principle of the American government...'
>
> '....To justify suppression of free speech, there must be reasonable ground to fear that serious evil will result if free speech is practiced. There must be reasonable ground to believe that the danger apprehended is imminent. There must be reasonable ground to believe that the evil to be presented is a serious one.'

A Supreme Court majority first used the 'clear and present danger' test, in defense of free speech in the 1937 case of *Herndon v. Lowry.*[33] This decision reversed a conviction for violation of a Georgia statute prohibiting 'any attempt, by persuasion or otherwise,' to incite insurrection. Following this decision, the Court began to apply the 'clear and present danger' test not only to 'seditious' speech but to other First Amendment issues as well.[34]

(iii) *Clear and Probable Danger*

The Cold War (1947–91), which had begun after World War II (1939–45), deepened after the United States became embroiled in the Korean conflict (1950–53)—and by the early 1950s, McCarthyism, with its emphasis on the 'communist menace', had achieved substantial national influence.

Against this background of Cold War paranoia, the US Supreme Court reviewed and affirmed the convictions of 11 leaders of the American Communist Party in *Dennis v. United States.*[35] Eugene Dennis (1905–61) and his 10 co-defendants had been convicted after a highly publicized 9 month federal trial for violation of the Internal Security Act of 1940, more commonly known as the Smith Act.

The Smith Act[36] made it a crime –

> 'to knowingly or willfully advocate, abet, advise, or teach the duty, necessity, desirability, or propriety of overthrowing or destroying any government in the United States by force or violence.'

In essence, the defendants' convictions resulted from their activities in organizing and furthering the purposes of the Communist Party in the United States.

The Court of Appeals for the Second Circuit upheld these convictions. In his opinion for that Court, Chief Judge Learned Hand (1872–1961),[37] substituted a more limited defense of First Amendment freedoms than that of 'clear and present danger'. This doctrine, popularly known as the 'clear and probable danger' test, was adopted by Chief Justice Frederick Moore Vinson (1890–1953)[38] in a plurality opinion announcing the Supreme Court's judgment affirming the convictions. The new standard that Justice Hand articulated required courts in each case to –

> 'ask whether the gravity of the "evil", discounted by its improbability, justifies such invasion of free speech as is necessary to avoid the danger.'

Two members of the *Dennis v. United States* majority, Justices Felix Frankfurter (1882–1965)[39] and Robert H. Jackson (1892–1954),[40] wrote separate concurring opinions, neither of which endorsed Justice Hand's formula or the 'clear and present danger' test. Justice Frankfurter maintained that the Court should defer to the legislative balancing of competing interest in the free speech area no less than in other areas of policy making. Justice Jackson differentiated between isolated, localized protest and what he saw as a highly organized conspiracy of international dimensions aimed at subverting American Government. He regarded the 'clear and present danger' test as an inadequate standard for assessing a conspiracy of this magnitude. Justice Jackson found –

> 'no constitutional right to "gang up" on the Government.'

Justice Hugo Black (1886–1971),[41] who dissented along with Justice William O. Douglas (1898–1980),[42] expressed the hope that –

> 'in calmer times, when present pressures, passions and fears subside, this or some later Court will restore the First Amendment liberties to the high preferred place where they belong in a free society.'

Changes in public opinion and in US Supreme Court personnel did, in fact, result in a gradual movement away from the restrictive First Amendment interpretation symbolized by the *Dennis* decision. Although, as previously indicated, the Court did not resurrect the phrase 'preferred position' and did not formally overrule *Dennis v. United States*, it narrowed the scope of the Smith Act 1940, and offered greater protection to advocacy of ideas, including the forcible overthrow of government. The Court raised evidentiary standards for Smith Act prosecutions and confined its 'membership clause' to 'active' as distinguished from 'nominal' membership in an organization advocating forcible overthrow of the government (for example, *Yates v. United States*,[43] *Scales v. United States*,[44] *Noto v. United States*,[45] and *Communist Party v. Subversive Activities Control Board*.[46])

(iv) *Fighting words*

The 'fighting words' include the lewd and obscene, the profane the libelous and the insulting or 'fighting' words—those which by their utterance inflict injury or tend to incite an immediate breach of the peace.

The definition from *Chaplinsky v. New Hampshire*,[47] provides the original statement of the 'fighting words' doctrine. Under *Chaplinsky*, speech could be punished if it inflicts injury or created a danger that the person addressed would resort to violence. The US Supreme Court probably underestimated the social value of what some would regard as 'fighting words', and no consideration was given to the question of whether police should be expected to exercise more restraint than the average person in responding to such epithets. For several decades, State Courts routinely used the 'fighting words' doctrine, and the *Chaplinsky* precedent, to justify prosecutions of intemperate street-corner orators for incitement to riot or breach of the peace.

In 1971, the US Supreme Court significantly narrowed the 'fighting words' exception. In *Cohen v. California*,[48] the Court refused to classify as fighting words the message 'Fuck the Draft' emblazoned on the back of a jacket worn by 19-year-old Paul Robert Cohen in the corridors of the Los Angeles County Courthouse. Reversing Cohen's conviction for breach of the peace, the Court, through Justice John Marshal Harlan (1899–1971), reasoned as follows:

> 'While the four-letter word displayed by Cohen in relation to the draft is not uncommonly employed in a personally provocative fashion, in this instance it was clearly not "directed to the person of the hearer"… No individual actually or likely to be present could reasonably have regarded the words on appellant's jacket as a direct personal insult. Nor do we have here an instance of the exercise of the State's police power to prevent a speaker from intentionally provoking a given group to hostile reaction.'

Although, the Court still gives formal recognition to the 'fighting words' exception, it has not in recent years found any specific instances of expression to qualify as 'fighting words.'

(v) *Hate Speech*

During the 1980s, a number of communities adopted laws aimed at protecting African-Americans and other minority groups from so-called hate crimes, crimes motivated by racial, or other group-related hatred. One such ordinance was enacted by the city of St. Paul, Minnesota:

> 'Whoever places on public or private property a symbol, object, appellation, characterization or graffiti, including, but not limited to, a burning cross or Nazi swastika, which one knows or has reasonable grounds to know arouses anger, alarm or resentment in others on the basis of race, color, creed, religion or gender commits disorderly conduct and shall be guilty of a misdemeanor.'

In the widely publicized case of *R.A.V. v. City of St. Paul*,[49] the US Supreme Court declared the ordinance unconstitutional. Justice Antonin Scalia (1936–2016) summarized the rationale of the majority as follows:

> 'Assuming *arguendo*, that all of the expression reached by the ordinance is proscribable under the "fighting words" doctrine, we nonetheless conclude that the ordinance is facially unconstitutional in that it prohibits otherwise permitted speech solely on the basis of the subjects the speech addresses.'

The Court's decision in *R.A.V. v. City of St. Paul*, raised serious questions as to whether, hate crimes legislation can be made to conform to constitutional standards. Nevertheless, states and communities have a number of legal means at their disposal for combating hate crimes. For example, an individual who burns a cross on someone else's front lawn may be charged with criminal trespass and possibly with malicious mischief or vandalism.

Another approach to deterring hate crimes is enhancing or extending criminal penalties based on characteristics of the crime or the victim. In *Wisconsin v. Mitchell*,[50] the US Supreme Court upheld a Wisconsin statute, that increases the severity of punishment, if a crime victim is chosen on the basis of race or other designated characteristics. Stressing the fact that the statute was aimed at conduct rather than belief, the Court held, that increasing punishment because the defendant targeted the victim on the basis of his race does not infringe the defendant's freedom of conscience protected by the First Amendment. Many commentators, however, thought that *Wisconsin v. Mitchell* could not be squatted with the Court's earlier decision in *R.A.V.*[51]

(vi) *Profanity*

Although, in *Chaplinsky v. New Hampshire*,[52] the US Supreme Court specifically enumerated profanity as being among those categories of speech so lacking in values as not to merit First Amendment protection, this view no longer prevails.

In *Cohen v. California*, the US Supreme Court overturned the conviction of a man who entered a Los Angeles Courthouse wearing a jacket emblazoned with the slogan 'Fuck the Draft'. Speaking for the Court, Justice John Marshal Harlan (1899–1971) opined that:

> 'while the particular four-letter-word being litigated here is perhaps more distasteful than others of its genre, it is nevertheless often true that one man's vulgarity is another's lyric. Indeed, we think it is largely because government officials cannot make principled distinctions in this area that the Constitution leaves matters of taste and style so largely to the individual.'

Despite the Supreme Court's decision in *Cohen v. California*,[53] most states and many cities retain laws proscribing profanity. But, these laws are seldom enforced and even more rarely challenged in court. One notable exception is the case of the 'cussing canoeist'[54] that made national news in 1998. When Timothy Boomer fell from his canoe into Michigan's Rifle River, he unleashed a tirade of profanities in a very loud voice. He was convicted of violating a 19th century state law that prohibited the utterance of profanity in the presence of children. Boomer was fined $75 and ordered to perform 4 days of community service. With the assistance of the American Civil Liberties Union (ACLU),[55] Boomer appealed his conviction to the Michigan Court of Appeals. On 1 April 2002, the Michigan Appellate Court reversed Boomer's conviction and struck down the statute on which the conviction was based. Writing for the Court, Judge William B. Murphy[56] observed that the law,

> 'as drafted, reaches constitutionally protected speech, and it operates to inhibit the exercise of First Amendment rights.'

Symbolic speech and expressive conduct

As *Cohen v. California* and *R.A.V. v. City of St. Paul* make clear, the protection of the First Amendment is not limited to pure speech. The term symbolic speech is applied to a wide range of non-verbal communication that is subject to First Amendment protection. Of course, not every symbol is entitled to constitutional protection; it depends on the circumstances in which the symbol is displayed.

(i) *The Flag Salute Controversy*

US Supreme Court's willingness to protect symbolic speech is provided by the flag salute cases of *Minersville School District v. Gobitis*[57] and *West Virginia State Board of Education v. Barnette.*[58]

In *Minersville School District v. Gobitis*, the Court upheld a local school board directive requiring public school students to salute the American flag as part of the daily class routine. Then, in one of the most dramatic turnabouts in its history, the court overruled this precedent 3 years later in the second flag salute case i.e. *West Virginia State Board of Education v. Barnette.*

In *Barnette* case, a 6-member majority recognized the right of schoolchildren who were members of Jehovah's Witnesses to refrain from participation in the flag salute ritual. Writing for the Court, Justice Robert H. Jackson (1892–1954) observed that –

> 'no official, high or petty, can prescribe what shall be orthodox in politics, nationalism, religion, or other matters of opinion or force citizens to confess by word or act their faith therein.'

(ii) *Symbolic Speech in the Vietnam Era*

Protests against the Vietnam War (1955–75) produced a number of controversies over symbolic speech. For example, in *United States v. O'Brien* (1968),[59] the US Supreme Court rejected the First Amendment claim of a Vietnam War protester that publicly burning his 'draft card' was a form of constitutionally protected symbolic speech.

David Paul O'Brien, who had burned his Selective Service registration certificate, also known as 'draft cards', on the steps of the South Boston Courthouse in the presence of a 'sizable crowd,' was convicted for violation of a federal law providing that an offense was committed by any person –

> 'who forges, alters, knowingly destroys, knowingly mutilates, or in any manner changes any such certificate.'

Chief Justice Earl Warren (1891–1974), writing for a 7 member majority, determined that Congress had ample constitutional authority to prohibit the destruction or mutilation of 'draft cards'. The 'draft card', after all, belonged to the government, and not to Mr O'Brien.

A less defiant form of symbolic speech in opposition to the Vietnam War (1955–75) was afforded First Amendment protection in *Tinker v. Des Moines Independent Community School District.*[60] High school students John F. Tinker and Christopher Eckhardt, along with Tinker's sister Mary Beth, wore black armbands to school to protest American involvement in the Vietnam War (1955–75). Anticipating this protest, school officials had adopted a policy that students refusing to remove such armbands would be suspended until they agreed to return to school without them. The Tinker siblings and Eckhardt, refused to remove their armbands when requested, and were sent home under suspension. They then brought suit to recover nominal damages and to enjoin school officials from enforcing the regulation. The case eventually reached the American Supreme Court, which rejected the lower Court's view that the action of school officials was 'reasonable' because it was based on fear that a disturbance would result from the wearing of armbands. Writing for the majority, Justice Abe Fortas (1910–82)[61] concluded that the wearing of armbands in this instance –

> 'was divorced from actual or potential disruptive conduct' and as such was 'closely akin to "pure speech" which…is entitled to comprehensive protection under the 1st Amendment.'

For public school officials to justify prohibiting the 'particular expression of opinion,' Justice Fortas asserted, they must be able to show that such action –

> 'was caused by something more than a mere desire to avoid the discomfort and unpleasantness that always accompany an unpopular viewpoint.'

(iii) *Flag Burning*

The US Supreme Court, in *Street v. New York*,[62] addressed the question of whether burning of the American flag is protected by the Constitution as symbolic speech during the same year in which it decided the *Tinker v. Des Moines Independent Community School District* case. The Court focused on the element of verbal expression also presented in this case, however, it effectively avoided the symbolic speech issue.

After hearing of the news of an assassination attempt against civil rights leader James Meredith (1933) in Mississippi; Sidney Street, the defendant, burned his American flag on a Brooklyn street corner. The arresting officer testified that he heard Sidney Street say to a small crowd of onlookers. 'We don't need no damn flag.' Street was convicted of 'malicious mischief' in violation of a New York State statute § 1425, subd. 16, par. d, making it a misdemeanor to –

> 'publicly mutilate, deface, defile, or defy, trample upon or cast contempt upon, either by words or act [any flag of the United States].'

Because a general verdict was rendered by the trial court, the US Supreme Court, in an opinion by Justice John Marshall Harlan (1899–1971), observed that Sidney Street might have been punished for his speech as well as for burning the flag. The Court concluded, that under the circumstances, he could not be constitutionally punished for his words alone. Justice Harlan emphasized that the court was not ruling on the question of whether Sidney Street could be punished for flag burning, 'even though the burning was an act of protest.' The Warren Court's decision left open the question of whether flag burning *per se* was a form of symbolic speech protected by the 1st Amendment.

The Rehnquist Court, surprising many observers, answered that question in the affirmative in the highly publicized case of *Texas v. Johnson*.[63] Gregory Johnson after publicly burning the American flag during the 1984 Republican National Convention in Dallas, against the Reagan Administration and certain companies based in Dallas, was prosecuted under a Texas law prohibiting flag desecration. Gregory Johnson was convicted at trial, but his conviction was reversed by the Texas Court of Criminal Appeals, which held that Johnson's conduct was protected by the First Amendment. In an extremely controversial decision, the US Supreme Court agreed, splitting 5 to 4. Perhaps, most surprising to court watchers was the fact that two President Reagan appointees, Justices Antonin Scalia (1936–2016) and Anthony Kennedy (1936), joined the majority. On the other hand, Justice John Paul Stevens (1920–2019), generally considered a liberal on civil liberties issues, was among the dissenters.[64]

Writing for the Court in *Texas v. Johnson*, Justice William J. Brennan Jr (1906–97) observed that –

> '"[t]he expressive, overtly political nature of [Johnson's] conduct was both intentional and overwhelmingly apparent.'

In Justice Brennan's view,

> 'Johnson was convicted for engaging in expressive conduct. The State's interest in preventing breaches of the peace does not support his conviction because Johnson's conduct did not threaten to disturb the peace. Nor does the State's interest in preserving the flag as a symbol of nationhood and national unity justify his criminal conviction for engaging in political expression.'

Dissenting, Chief Justice William Rehnquist (1924–2005) challenged the majority's conclusion that Johnson's act of flag burning was a form of political speech, saying that –

> 'flag burning is the equivalent of an inarticulate grunt or roar that....is most likely to be indulged in not to express any particular idea, but to antagonize others.'

Chief Justice Rehnquist stressed the –

> 'unique position' of the flag 'as the symbol of our Nation, a uniqueness that justifies a governmental prohibition against flag burning.'

But, for Justice Brennan and the majority,

> '[t]he way to preserve the flag's special role is not to punish those who feel differently.'

In the wake of the *Texas v. Johnson* decision, conservatives called for a constitutional amendment to place flag burning beyond the pale of First Amendment protection. In an attempt to address the issue by less drastic means, US Congress passed the Federal Flag Protection Act of 1989, making flag burning a federal crime. In *United States v. Eichman*,[65] the US Supreme Court struck down the Flag Protection Act 1989, as applied to flag burning as a means of political protest.

Prior restraint or censorship

The authors of the Bill of Rights saw the 1st Amendment as necessary because the common law, which this nation inherited from England, had no protection for 'freedom of expression.' However, through judicial interpretation, one common law doctrine has been grafted onto the First Amendment. This is the 'prior restraint' rule.

In *Commentaries on the Laws of England, Vol. IV (1769)*, Sir William Blackstone (1723–80),[66] stated the rule against 'prior restraint' in the context of freedom of the press.

> 'The liberty of the press is indeed essential to the nature of a free state; but this consists in laying no previous restraints upon publications, and not in freedom from censure for criminal matter when published.'

In the United States, the concept of 'prior restraint' has been of great importance to the US Supreme Court in defining both freedom of the press and freedom of speech under the First Amendment. The concept was first discussed by the Court, however, in the context of a dispute over publication of a newspaper.

(i) *The Court Adopts the Rule against Prior Restraint*

In *Near v. Minnesota*,[67] the US Supreme Court struck down a Minnesota State law that permitted public officials to seek an injunction to stop publication of any –

> 'malicious, scandalous and defamatory newspaper, magazine or other periodical.'

The statute was invoked to suppress publication of a small Minneapolis city newspaper, *The Saturday Press*, which had strong anti-Semitic overtones and maligned local political officials, particularly the chief of police. The State of Minnesota law provided, that once a newspaper was enjoined, further publication was punishable as contempt of court. Writing for the court in *Near v. Minnesota*, Chief Justice Charles Evans Hughes (1862–1948),[68] characterized this mode of suppression as 'the essence of censorship' and declared it unconstitutional. With its decision in *Near v. Minnesota*, the Court specifically incorporated the First Amendment freedom of the press into the 'Due Process Clause' of the 14th Amendment, thus, making it fully applicable to the states.

In commenting with general approval on the rule against prior restraint, Chief Justice Charles Evans Hughes (1862–1948), acknowledged that this restriction is not absolute. It would not, for example, prevent the government in time of war from prohibiting publication of 'the sailing dates of transports or the number and location of troops.' In these and related situations, national security interests are almost certain to prevail over freedom of the press. But where is the line to be drawn? How far can the 'national security' justification be extended in suppressing publication?

(ii) *The Pentagon Papers Case*

In *New York Times Company v. United States*, the US Supreme Court revisited the question of 'prior restraint' on the press in the much-heralded *Pentagon papers* case of 1971.[69] The federal government attempted to prevent the *New York Times* and the *Washington Post* from publishing excerpts from a classified study titled '*History of US Decision-Making Process on Vietnam Policy*' known as the *Pentagon papers*.

By a 6 to 3 vote, the US Supreme Court, in a brief *per curiam* opinion, held that the government's effort to block publication of this material amounted to an unconstitutional 'prior restraint.' The majority of the judges was simply not convinced that such publication, several years after the events and decisions discussed in the *Pentagon papers*, constituted a significant threat to national security. The furor produced by this highly publicized case and the great pressure brought to bear on the Court for a speedy decision help explain why no detailed majority opinion was produced. The justices in fact wrote 9 separate opinions, advancing a wide variety of rationales for and against application of the 'prior restraint' concept.

(iii) *May the Government Prevent Publication of How to Make a Hydrogen Bomb?*

The issue of 'prior restraint' emerged again in 1979 in the case of *United States v. Progressive*,[70] which included the publication of a magazine article purporting to describe the process of making a hydrogen bomb. The federal government obtained a preliminary injunction against *The Progressive* magazine, blocking publication of the article pending a hearing. In the meantime, however, another newspaper, *Madison Press Connection*, published a similar article, with no apparent damage to national security. As a result, the case against *The Progressive* was dismissed and the injunction lifted. *The Progressive's* hydrogen bomb article was ultimately published in November 1979.

In light of the *Pentagon papers* and *Progressive* cases, it can be concluded that, although national security may justify a departure from the rule against 'prior restraint', in the real world of American constitutional law, such departures tend to be rare and short-lived.

(iv) *Does the Prior Restraint Doctrine Apply to Student Newspapers?*

The case of *Hazelwood School District v. Kuhlmeier*,[71] which involved the publication of student-run school newspaper, is a notable exception to the protection of press freedom against 'prior restraint'. The US Supreme Court voted 5 to 3 to uphold a public school principal's decision to excise certain controversial material from the school newspaper. The principal objected to certain articles dealing with divorce and teenage pregnancy on the grounds that they were written in such a way as to permit students to identify classmates who had encountered such difficulties.

The student newspaper staff hired a lawyer and challenged the principal's action in Federal Court. Writing for the majority, Justice Byron White (1917–2002) concluded that –

> 'educators do not offend the First Amendment by exercising editorial control over the style and content of student speech in school-sponsored expressive activities so long as their actions are reasonably related to legitimate pedagogical concerns.'

Dissenting, Justice William J. Brennan Jr (1906–97), accused the majority of eviscerating *Tinker v. Des Moines Independent Community School District*,[72] in which the US Supreme Court had accorded First Amendment protection to certain expressive activities by students in public schools. According to Justice Brennan, the majority opinion in *Hazelwood* –

> 'denudes high school students of much of the First Amendment protection that *Tinker* itself prescribed.'

The controversy in *Hazelwood* centered around a student newspaper at a public high school. Would the federal courts permit officials at a state college or university to censor student-run campus newspapers? Could legitimate pedagogical concerns at this level ever justify such interference? Most observers doubt the courts would permit this type of censorship.[73]

The obscenity problem

During the recent decade's sexually explicit magazines, books, videotapes, and films have become increasingly available in the marketplace in the US. These are available at bookstores other than 'adult' bookstores. Soft-core pornography like *Hustler* is readily available at most convenience stores and magazine stands. Many cable and satellite television companies also provide adult entertainment in varying degrees of explicitness. Even hard-core pornography is easily obtained in the back rooms of many local video rental stores. The commercial success of such ventures obviously indicates a degree of social acceptance, but many critics continue to regard pornography as an evil that should be curtailed if not eliminated altogether.

Of course, anyone accused of producing or selling obscene materials will argue that the First Amendment protects his or her right to engage in such activities. One of the most difficult tasks the US Supreme Court has undertaken in recent decades is that of determining the degree to which the First Amendment protects pornography.

Prior to the US Supreme Court's entry into this field in 1957, most American courts adhered to a legal definition of obscenity derived from the 1868 English case of *Regina v. Hicklin*.[74] The *Hicklin* test was –

> 'whether the tendency of the matter charged as obscenity is to deprave and corrupt those whose minds are open to such immoral influences, and into whose hands a publication of this sort may fall.'

By the mid-20th century, this standard was widely regarded as unduly restrictive of artistic and literary expression. The principal objection to the *Hicklin* test, was that it sought to measure obscenity with reference to its supposed impact on the most vulnerable members of society.

(i) *The Prurient Interest Test*

In *Roth v. United States*,[75] the US Supreme Court handed down new legal guidelines for obscenity. Writing for the majority, Justice William J. Brennan Jr (1906–97) expressed the view that obscenity is 'utterly without redeeming social importance' and thus, entitled to no First Amendment protection. Rejecting the essence of the *Hicklin* standard, he stated the new test as –

> 'whether to the average person, applying contemporary community standards, and the dominant theme of the material taken as a whole appeal to a prurient interest.'

Roth v. United States, a federal case, was consolidated with the state case of *Alberts v. California*, thus, making the new test applicable to every level of government in the country. But, in spite of its uniform applicability and apparent simplicity, the *Roth-Alberts* test drew the Court into an interpretive quagmire from which it has not yet emerged. Virtually every term contained in the new obscenity test proved elusive. The Court could never reach full agreement on what constitutes a prurient interest. The term redeeming social importance also failed to generate consensus.

A majority of the Court, in the years immediately following *Roth v. United States*, could not even agree on whether 'community' referred to the nation as a whole or to individual states or localities. Although, most of the justices believed that hard-core pornography was not entitled to First Amendment protection, they were unable to define its meaning. Justice Potter Stewart's (1915–85) well-known remark 'I know it when I see it' (*Jacobellis v. Ohio*,[76] concurring opinion) points up the difficulty of precise definition in this area.

(ii) *The Miller Test*

Partly because of the complexity of the problem and partly as a result of the refusal of Justice Hugo Black (1886–1971), and William O. Douglas (1898–1980) to recognize the legitimacy of any limitations on expression in the obscenity field, the Warren Court was unable to muster a clear majority in support of all aspects of the *Roth-Alberts* test during the 1960s. The Burger Court was also sharply divided, but, ultimately achieved a bare majority in restating the constitutional test of obscenity. Writing for the court in *Miller v. California*,[77] Chief Justice Warren E. Burger (1907–95) stated that 'the basic guidelines for the trier of fact' in obscenity cases are as follows:—

(a) whether 'the average person, applying contemporary community standards' would find that the work, taken as a whole, appeals to the prurient interest,
(b) whether the work depicts or describes, in a patently offensive way, sexual conduct specifically defined by the applicable state law, and
(c) whether the work, taken as a whole, lacks serious literary, artistic, political, or scientific value.

The *Miller* test, was somewhat more restrictive of free expression than was the original *Roth-Alberts* test, as embellished and applied by the Warren Court. The Burger Court in *Memoirs v. Massachusetts*, explicitly rejected the 'utterly without redeeming social value' standard advanced by a minority of justices in the 1960s.[78] Nevertheless, the new guidelines were far from clear. Exactly, what is patently offensive material? Precisely, how does a prurient interest in sex differ from a normal, healthy interest? What constitutes serious literary, artistic, political, or scientific value? And, perhaps most importantly, whose standards are to prevail in making these determinations?

In *Miller v. California*, the Court indicated that the applicable community standards under the new test were local or at most statewide standards. But, when authorities in Albany, Georgia, purportedly applying 'community standards', attempted to ban the movie *Carnal Knowledge*, the court, in *Jenkins v. Georgia*, ruled that the test had been improperly applied. Only material showing 'patently offensive hard-core sexual conduct' could be proscribed under the new rules.[79]

In 1987, a 5 to 4 majority of the US Supreme Court modified the 'contemporary community standards' yardstick. Writing for the majority in *Pope v. Illinois*,[80] Justice Byron White (1917–2002) declared that –

> 'the proper inquiry is not whether an ordinary member of any given community would find serious literary, artistic, political and scientific value in allegedly obscene material, but whether a reasonable person would find such value in the material, taken as a whole.'

Whether this 'reasonable person' alternative represents a liberalization of the obscenity test or fosters 'intolerable orthodoxy,' as Justice John Paul Stevens (1920–2019), predicted in a dissenting opinion, it is clear that First Amendment issues in the field of obscenity are far from resolved.

(iii) *Pornography on the Internet*

As a practical matter, one must recognize that pornography has become much more widely available in recent years. This is due to several factors. Most fundamentally, society's attitudes in this area have become more permissive. Second, prosecutions in this area have become increasingly rare. In the absence of a public outcry, prosecutors tend to avoid this area in favour of more 'ordinary' types of crime.

Finally, one must recognize the effect of the Internet, which has made pornography easily accessible to people who might not wish to enter an adult bookstore or place an order from the back of an adult magazine. The World Wide Web (WWW) has thousands of sites devoted to 'adult entertainment', many of which feature extremely graphic, hard-core pornography. One of the principal concerns about pornography on the Internet is its availability to children.

In 1996, US Congress passed the Communications Decency Act, which made it a crime to display 'indecent' material on the Internet, in a manner that might make it available to minors. In *Reno v. American Civil Liberties*

Union,[81] the US Supreme Court declared the statute unconstitutional on 1st Amendment grounds. Writing for the Court, Justice John Paul Stevens (1920–2019) concluded that, with respect to cyberspace,

> 'the interest in encouraging freedom of expression in a democratic society outweighs any theoretical but unproven benefit of censorship.'

The Court's opinion in *Reno*, left open the possibility that a more narrowly tailored statute—that is, one limited to prohibiting obscenity as distinct from indecency—might pass constitutional muster.

(iv) *Child Pornography*

It is established that government may criminalize the production and distribution of material depicting children engaged in sexual activities, irrespective of whether the material meets the legal test of obscenity.

In *New York v. Ferber*,[82] the US Supreme Court held that a state has a compelling interest in protecting children from sexual abuse and found a close connection between such abuse and the use of children in the production of pornographic materials.

But, in 2002 the Court surprised some observers by limiting government's efforts to ban child pornography. In *Ashcroft v. Free Speech Coalition*,[83] the Court struck down as 'overbroad' a provision of federal law that banned virtual child pornography as well as that employing live subjects. Dividing 6 to 3, the Court, speaking through Justice Anthony Kennedy (1936), held that the challenged provision of the Child Pornography Prevention Act of 1996 –

> 'covers materials beyond the categories recognized in *Ferber* and *Miller*, and the reasons the Government offers in support of limiting the freedom of speech have no justification in our precedents or in the law of the 1st Amendment.'

(v) *Nude Dancing*

In *Schad v. Borough of Mount Ephraim*, the American Supreme Court indicated that nude dancing was protected by the First Amendment.[84] The Court declared unconstitutional, a city's ordinance, that prohibited all live entertainment and was used to close down a nude dancing establishment. The Court said that –

> 'nude dancing is not without its First Amendment protections from official regulation.'

The US Supreme Court upheld government regulation of nude dancing in a series of cases involving liquor licenses. In *California v. LaRue*, the Court held that the government could regulate live performances in establishments licenced to sell liquor.[85] The Court said that the government could constitutionally conclude –

> 'that certain sexual performances and the dispensation of liquor ought not to occur [together].'

Similarly, in *City of Newport v. Iacobucci*, the US Supreme Court upheld a city ordinance banning nude dancing in bars.[86] The Court accepted the city's rationale that –

> 'nude dancing in establishments serving liquor was 'injurious to the citizens of the city.'

In *Barnes v. Glen Theatre, Inc.*, the US Supreme Court went on further holding that the government may completely ban nude dancing.[87] There was no majority opinion for the Court in its 5 to 4 decision. The plurality, saw nude dancing as a form of conduct that communicates and applied the test used for regulating symbolic speech, and upheld the prohibition of nude dancing because it served the goal of protecting societal order and morality. Justice Byron White dissented and emphasized, that stopping nude dancing was suppressing the message because the nudity of the dancer is an integral part of the emotions and thoughts that a nude dancing performance evokes.

The Court affirmed *Barnes v. Glen Theatre, Inc.*, in *City of Erie v. PAP's A.M*, though under different reasoning. The City council of Erie, Pennsylvania, adopted an ordinance prohibiting nudity, with the clear objective of shutting down Kandyland, a nude dancing club. In a 6 to 3 decision, but, without a majority opinion, the court upheld the ordinance.[88] Justice Sandra Day O'Connor (1930), writing for the plurality, emphasized that the city was justified in prohibiting nude dancing, so as to stop the undesirable secondary effects, such as crime, associated with the activity. The dissenters, Justices John Paul Stevens (1920–2019) and David Souter (1939), stressed the absence of any proof that nude dancing increases or causes undesirable secondary effects. Since, the Ordinance allowed dancers wearing pasties and a G-string, therefore, it was reasoned that there was no evidence that fully nude dancers cause any more crime than those minimally clothed. However, the plurality opinion of Justice O'Connor said that such proof was unnecessary.

(vi) Speech materially assisting a Foreign Terrorist Organization

In *Holder v. Humanitarian Law Project*, the US Supreme Court considered a Federal law that prohibits providing 'material assistance' to a 'foreign terrorist organization'. Material assistance was defined to include such activities as 'training', 'personnel' and 'expert advice or assistance'.[89] Two groups of Americans brought a law suit seeking to establish First Amendment protection for groups that had been designated by the US Department of State as foreign terrorists organizations. One group of Americans, sought to help a Kurdish group, which sought to form a separate country, use international law and the United Nations to peacefully resolve disputes. The other group of Americans sought to help a group in Sri Lanka, seeking to form a separate nation, to apply for humanitarian assistance.

The Court, in a 6 to 3 decision ruled that this speech could be punished so long as it was done in co-ordination with a foreign terrorist organization. The plaintiffs could speak out on any topic they wished, but if the speech was done in concert with a foreign terrorist organization, it was not protected by the 1st Amendment. The dissenting opinion criticized the majority for allowing punishment of speech without any proof that it was likely to cause harm.

Electronic media and the First Amendment

The authors of the First Amendment could not have foreseen the invention of radio and television, let alone the prevalence of electronic media in contemporary society. Nevertheless, because television and radio are used to express ideas in the public forum, most observers would agree that these electronic media, deserve First Amendment protection, at least to some extent. Yet, since their inception, radio and television have been regulated extensively by the federal government.

To operate a television or radio station, one must obtain a license from the Federal Communications Commission (FCC); to broadcast without a license from the FCC is a federal crime (as operators of 'pirate' radio stations have often discovered). In granting licenses, the FCC is authorized to regulate the station's frequency, wattage, and hours of transmission. To a lesser extent, it also has the power to regulate the content of broadcasts. For example, the FCC has developed regulations to keep the airwaves free of 'obscene' or 'indecent' programming. Moreover, station licenses come up for renewal every 3 years, and the FCC is invested with tremendous discretion to determine, whether a given station has been operating 'in the public interest.'

Clearly, government regulations that apply to the electronic media would be unconstitutional, if applied to books, newspapers, and magazines. The more permissive approach to government control of television and radio, was originally predicated in the scarcity rationale theory, which held that due to the limited number of available broadcast spectrum, the government must regulate this scarce resource, in the public interest. The proliferation of cable, TV, and radio, has undermined the controlling influence of the 'scarcity' doctrine. Moreover, changing societal norms have Communications Decency Act of 1996 (CDA), which made it a crime to display 'indecent' material on the Internet, led to a relaxation of earlier restrictions on sexual content and profanity on radio and TV.

Nevertheless, the US Supreme Court continues to recognize the FCC's authority to impose restrictions on broadcast media, that would not be tolerated if they were applied to the print medium.[90]

(i) *Restrictions of 'Indecent' Programming on Television and Radio*

In a broad regulation that would almost certainly be declared unconstitutional, if applied to a magazine or newspaper, the FCC (Federal Communications Commission), has prohibited radio and television stations, whether public or private, from broadcasting 'indecent' or 'obscene' programs.

In April 1987, the FCC made national news when it threatened not to renew the licenses of certain radio stations in New York and California. These stations were engaged in so-called 'shock radio,' which featured talk programs that were intentionally tasteless and given to heavy doses of profanity and frequent sexual references. Although, the FCC's threats made headlines, there was little talk of litigation to challenge the agency's regulations. The US Supreme Court had previously upheld restrictions on indecent broadcasting in *Federal Communications Commission v. Pacifica Foundation.*[91]

In *Federal Communications Commission v. Pacifica Foundation* case, the Court reviewed FCC regulations, as applied to a radio broadcast of a monologue by comedian George Carlin (1937–2008)[92] that examined 'seven dirty words you can't say on the radio.' Attorneys for the Pacifica Foundation[93] argued, that the monologue in question did not meet the legal test of obscenity, and therefore, could not be banned from the radio by the FCC. Writing for the Court, Justice John Paul Stevens (1920–2019) disagreed, observing that –

> 'when the Commission finds that a pig has entered the parlor, the exercise of its regulatory power does not depend on proof that the pig is obscene.'

(ii) *Indecent Programming on Cable Television*

The so-called 'Helms Amendment' to the Cable Television Consumer Protection and Competition Act of 1992 (also known as the 1992 Cable Act), required cable system that lease channels to commercial providers of 'patently offensive' programming to scramble the signals of those channels and make them available only to subscribers who specifically request access.

In *Denver Area Educational Telecommunications Consortium v. Federal Communications Commission,*[94] the US Supreme Court struck down this provision. Writing for the court, Justice Stephen Breyer (1938) observed, that the provision was not carefully drafted, failed to consider less intrusive alternatives, and was not a 'narrowly or reasonably tailored effort to protect children.' In Breyer's view the provision was –

> 'overly restrictive, "sacrific[ing]" important 1st Amendment interests for too "speculative a gain".'

In dissent, Justices Clarence Thomas (1948), joined by Antonin Scalia (1936–2016) and William Rehnquist (1924–2005), argued that the requirement that indecent programming be scrambled was supported by the government's compelling interest in protecting children. In Justice Thomas's view, the provision at issue was in keeping with –

> 'precedents [which] establish that government may support parental authority to direct the moral upbringing of their children.'

Some commentators were disappointed, that the Court failed in the *Denver Area Educational Telecommunications Consortium* decision, to articulate a coherent general theory of the 1st Amendment, as it relates to new technology and media. Indeed, the various opinions produced by the justices manifested uncertainty, even confusion, as to the fundamental First Amendment issues involved. This is often the case when the law is confronted by rapid technological change.

By 1997, however, the court achieved greater clarity in addressing the question of whether the government could regulate 'indecency' on the Internet. While recognizing the government's legitimate role in shielding children from inappropriate expression, the Court insisted that this objective cannot justify limiting adults' access to the Internet only to material that is appropriate for children.

(iii) *Editorializing by Public Television and Radio Stations*

Public radio and television, as distinguished from commercial stations and networks, have long been subject to more restrictive government regulations on editorializing. Based on a Section 399 of Public Broadcasting Act 1967, enacted by US Congress; the FCC (Federal Communications Commission) prohibited public radio and television stations from engaging in editorializing altogether.

However, in *Federal Communications Commission v. League of Women Voters*,[95] the US Supreme Court declared this ban unconstitutional. Writing for a sharply divided court, Justice William J. Brennan Jr (1906–97), concluded that the ban failed to meet a least restrictive means test. In Brennan's view, the ban –

> 'far exceeds what is necessary to protect against the risk of governmental interference or to prevent the public from assuming that editorials by public broadcasting stations represent the official view of government.'

The Court's general expansion of 'freedom of expression' since the mid-20th century is reflected not only in areas of political, social, and cultural dialogue, but in the Court's growing awareness that we live in an information age. The emergence and dynamic growth of electronic media, most recently, the Internet, have stimulated the Court's development of a 1st Amendment jurisprudence, that elevates communication to an almost hallowed status.

Commercial speech

The US Supreme Court, until the mid 1970s, regarded the regulation of commercial speech (a broad category, including but not limited, to the advertising of products and services) as simply an aspect of economic regulation, entitled to no special 1st Amendment protection.

In *Virginia State Board of Pharmacy v. Virginia Citizens Consumer Council*, an important 1976 decision, however, the court struck down Virginia's ban on the advertisement of prescription drug prices.[96] Writing for the Court, Justice Harry Blackmun (1908–99) stated, that although reasonable time, place, and manner restrictions on commercial speech are legitimate, and although, the state is free to proscribe 'false and misleading' advertisements, consumers have a strong 1st Amendment interest in the free flow of information about goods and services available in the marketplace.

(i) *A Test for Judging Regulations of Commercial Speech*

Justice Lewis F. Powell Jr (1907–98) in his opinion for the US Supreme Court, in *Central Hudson Gas & Electric Corporation v. Public Service Commission of New York*,[97] articulated the general rationale for 1st Amendment protection in this area.

Commercial expression not only serves the economic interest of the speaker, but also assists consumers and furthers the societal interest in the fullest possible dissemination of information. In applying the First Amendment to this area, we have rejected the 'highly paternalistic' view that government has complete power to suppress or regulate commercial speech.

In the same opinion, Justice Powell outlined a 4-part test for evaluating regulations of commercial speech. To begin with, commercial speech must 'concern lawful activity and not be misleading' if it is to be protected under the First Amendment. If this prerequisite is met, then 3 additional questions must be considered:

(1) Is the 'asserted governmental interest' in regulation substantial?
(2) Does the regulation directly advance the asserted governmental interest?
(3) Finally, is the regulation more extensive than is necessary to serve that purpose?

This test is an attempt to balance the need for consumer protection on one hand with the value of a free marketplace of ideas on the other.

(ii) *Conflicting Applications of the Test*

In a landmark decision in 1986, a narrowly divided US Supreme Court opted for consumer protection over the free marketplace of ideas.[98] In *Posadas de Puerto Rico Associates v. Tourism Company of Puerto Rico*,[99] the Court upheld a law prohibiting advertisements inviting residents of the territory of Puerto Rico, to gamble legally in local casinos. In his majority opinion, Justice William Rehnquist (1924–2005), emphasized Puerto Rico's substantial interest in reducing the demand for casino gambling among its citizens and noted that the regulation at issue directly advanced this objective. He maintained that the legislature of Puerto Rico –

> 'surely could have prohibited casino gambling by the residents of Puerto Rico altogether.'

He concluded that this –

> 'greater power to completely ban casino gambling necessarily includes the lesser power to ban advertising of casino gambling.'

In a strongly worded dissent, Justice John Paul Stevens (1920–2019), contended that Puerto Rico had not merely banned the advertising of casino gambling, it had 'blatantly' discriminated in punishing speech 'depending on the publication, audience and words employed.' In his view, the challenged prohibition established 'a regime of prior restraint' and articulated a 'hopelessly vague and unpredictable' standard.

(iii) *Commercial advertising of Alcoholic Beverages*

Under the 21st Amendment, states have broad authority to regulate the sale of alcoholic beverages. Does this authority extend to the ban of advertising in this area?

In *44 Liquormart, Inc. v. Rhode Island*,[100] the Court struck down Rhode Island's –

> 'statutory prohibition against advertisements that provide the public with accurate information about retail prices of alcoholic beverages.'

Speaking for a unanimous Court, Justice John Paul Stevens (1920–2019) concluded that –

> 'such an advertising ban is an abridgment of speech protected by the 1st Amendment and....is not shielded from constitutional scrutiny by the 21st Amendment.'

In a concurring opinion, Justice Clarence Thomas (1948) wrote that –

> '[a]ll attempts to dissuade legal choices by citizens by keeping them ignorant are impermissible.'

(iv) *Restrictions on Advertising of Tobacco Products*

In 1965, US Congress passed the Federal Cigarette Labeling and Advertising Act (also known as the Cigarette Act), which mandates warning labels on cigarette packages. In 1970, US Congress adopted the Public Health Cigarette Smoking Act, which prohibits cigarette advertising on any medium of electronic communication under the jurisdiction of the Federal Communications Commission (FCC). In 1984, Congress enacted the Comprehensive Smoking Education Act (also known as the Rotational Warning Act), which, among other things, established a series of strong health warning to appear in print and billboard advertisements of cigarettes.

While these measures have been criticized by libertarians and various interest groups, they have come to be widely accepted by the courts, by the society, and even by the tobacco industry. In 2001, however, the US Supreme Court held, that the state of Massachusetts had gone too far, in its attempt to regulate advertising of tobacco products. In *Lorillard Tobacco Company v. Reilly*,[101] the court held that Massachusetts's regulation of cigarette advertising was pre-empted by federal law. It further held, that regulations with respect to other tobacco products (including cigars and smokeless tobacco) violated the First Amendment. Writing for a majority of 5, Justice Sandra Day O'Connor (1930) observed that –

> 'so long as the sale and use of tobacco is lawful for adults, the tobacco industry has a protected interest in communicating information about its products and adult customers have an interest in receiving that information.'

(v) *Attorney Advertising and Solicitation*

Until the late 1970s, attorneys were prohibited by their state bar associations from advertising. These prohibitions reflected a desire by the elite elements of the bar to maintain lawyering as a noble and learned profession. But, critics of the prohibition, including many newly licensed attorneys, viewed it as an unwarranted restriction on the dissemination of important information in the marketplace.

In *Bates v. State Bar of Arizona*,[102] the US Supreme Court sided with the critics, and extended 1st Amendment protection to attorney advertising. As a consequence, it is now common to see ads for legal services on TV, in newspapers, and on buses.

Despite the relaxation of the ban on attorney advertising, many states still maintain restrictions on solicitation by lawyers. For example, the Florida Bar, a state-sanctioned organization, prohibits lawyers from sending targeted direct small solicitations to personal injury victims and their relatives for 30 days following an accident or disaster. The rule was challenged by a number of personal injury lawyers who argued that it violated the 1st Amendment.

In *Florida Bar v. Went for It, Inc.*,[103] the US Supreme Court divided 5 to 4 in upholding the challenged restriction. Justice Sandra Day O'Connor (1930), delivered the opinion of the Court, concluding that the Florida Bar –

> 'has substantial interest both in protecting injured Floridians from invasive conduct by lawyers and in preventing the erosion of confidence in the profession that such repeated invasions have engendered.'

In an unusually caustic dissent, Justice Anthony Kennedy (1936) attacked the majority opinion as –

> 'a serious departure, not only from our prior decisions involving attorney advertising, but also from the principles that govern the transmission of commercial speech.'

Kennedy accused the majority of unsettling precedents –

> 'at the expense of those victims most in need of legal assistance.'

In spite of the somewhat restrictive (some would say paternalistic) ruling in *Florida Bar v. Went for It Inc.*, it is clear that a great many commercial messages today are entitled to 1st Amendment protection that was nonexistent two decades ago. The US Supreme Court has even gone so far as to protect commercial interests against 'compelled speech'.

Thus, in *United States v. United Foods Inc.*[104] in 2001, Justice Anthony Kennedy (1936), writing for a 6 member majority, concluded that a federal assessment on mushroom growers used to fund mushroom advertising violated the First Amendment. The enlargement of freedom of expression in the commercial realm underscores the recognition, that First Amendment freedoms are by no means limited to the traditional categories of political debate and social protest, important as these concerns are in a constitutional democracy.

Despite, the Court's recognition of commercial speech, this type of expression is still not accorded the degree of First Amendment protection extended to political and social communication. Indeed, numerous restrictions on commercial speech still abound. For example, truth-in-lending laws require creditors to disclose accurate information regarding all the terms of loans. Various state laws prohibit false advertising. In spite of enhanced legal protections of 'adult expression', the advertising of adult-oriented material is often restricted. Some scholars have urged the abandonment of any distinction between commercial speech and other forms of expression. Thus, far, however the US Supreme Court has been unwilling to place commercial speech alongside political speech in the hierarchy of 1st Amendment values.[105]

Freedom of Speech and Press in the United Kingdom

In the United Kingdom, there are no guarantees of free speech and free press; nonetheless, the British citizen is free to say or publish anything he wants about anybody or anything, subject to laws governing blasphemy, obscenity, incitement to mutiny, defamation, and sedition.

— He/she may criticize the government or the Church of England;
— he/she may advocate the formation of a new political party or a new religion;
— he/she may write a novel, a play, or a poem.

In time of war, speech and press are subject to additional restrictions in the interests of national security and the effective prosecution of the war. Because it was constantly publishing material prejudicial to the war effort, the Communist '*Daily Worker*' was suppressed in 1941.[106]

In the United Kingdom, freedom of speech or expression is, like other freedoms, residual and subject to limitation by common law and statute. Even, where freedom of expression is constitutionally guaranteed the question may arise, what is meant by such freedom? It must no doubt include writings and words meant to influence political views, for example, the desirability of proportional representation as a method of electing members of the House of Commons. But, does freedom of expression include symbolic gestures intended to convey a political message; the wearing of a particular coloured shirt to indicate support for a political party; the vulgar sign in the presence of royalty intended to indicate a profound conviction of the need for a republican form of government? There may be doubts too about whether the right is confined to communicating political ideas, and what is meant by communication? Does the freedom to publish books criticizing Marxism extend to the freedom to publish books criticizing conventional views on matrimony or sexual mores in general? Are collections of pornographic photographs (assuming agreement could be reached on the meaning of pornographic) also expressions of views about morality which are therefore entitled to claim the protection of the law?

While agreeing on the importance of the freedom of expression, there may be doubts about the propriety of limiting that freedom to achieve other ends, for example to protect the young from corruption or to prevent public disorder. The extent to which such limitations are appropriate is likely to depend on why freedom of expression is believed to be important. Some may wish to argue that restrictions on free expression may prevent society from ascertaining the truth on matters of debate. Others may see freedom to speak, write and read as an aspect of each individual's right to moral independence.

The British Parliament and the English and Scottish Courts have, however, no entrenched constitutional rights to concern themselves when dealing with issues of freedom of expression. Parliament places no particular value on free speech in competition with the claims, real or alleged, of public order. In the area of censorship on grounds of obscenity, it is willing to legislate hastily and with little though, at the instigation of the latest pressure groups.

The importance of freedom of speech, particularly in the political sphere, may be recognized by the courts as was done in *Verrall v. Great Yarmouth Borough Council*.[107] But, the wider meaning, which they give or allow magistrates to give, to 'insulting' and their willingness to foresee the likelihood of words leading to a breach of the peace reflect a different attitude. In the *Bognor Regis Urban District Council v Campion* decision,[108] that a local authority has a reputation, which it can protect by suing its critics in defamation, as a trading company can sue to protect its reputation, may also be thought to show little respect for the right to criticize freely political institutions.

In England, the test of obscenity, is that of probable effect on those who may happen to read the material. This was held in *R. v. Reiter*.[109] In this case, the test laid down by the Queen's Bench Division (QBD) earlier in *R. v. Hicklin*,[110] to be whether the publication has a tendency to deprave and corrupt its readers whose minds are open to immoral influences, was discarded by the Court of Appeal.

Limitations on the freedom of expression include treason, sedition, incitement to racial hatred, official secrets, contempt of court or Parliament, and incitement to mutiny or disaffection among the armed forces and police. The other limitations are defamation, civil and criminal seditious libel, blasphemy, obscenity, and the application of the restriction imposed by these areas of law on newspapers, wireless, television and theatres.[111]

FREEDOM OF SPEECH AND PRESS IN INDIA

Article 19(1)(a) of the Indian Constitution lays down that –

> 'all citizens shall have the right to freedom of speech and expression.'

Article 19(2) provides that –

> 'nothing in Sub-clause (a) of clause (1) shall affect the operation of any existing law, or prevent the State from making any law, insofar as such law imposes reasonable restrictions on the exercise of the right conferred by the said Sub-clause in the interests of the sovereignty and Integrity of India, the security of the State, friendly relations with foreign States, public order, decency or morality or in relation to contempt of court, defamation or incitement to an offence.'

Meaning and scope—Freedom of Speech and expression means the right to express one's own convictions and opinions freely by words of mouth, writing, printing, pictures or any other mode. It, thus, includes the expression of one's ideas through any communicable medium or visible representation, such as, gesture, signs and the like. The expression connotes also publication, and thus, the freedom of the press is included in this category. Free propagation of ideas is the necessary objective, and this may be done on the platform or through the press. The freedom of propagation of ideas is secured by freedom of circulation. Liberty of circulation is essential to that freedom as the liberty of publication. Indeed, without circulation the publication would be of little value.[112]

The freedom of speech and expression includes liberty to propagate not one's views only. It also includes the right to propagate or publish the views of other people,[113] otherwise this freedom would not include the freedom of the press.

The right to speech implies right to silence. It implies freedom, not to listen, and not to be forced to listen. The right comprehends the freedom to be free from what one desires to be free from. A loudspeaker forces a person to hear what he wishes not to hear. The use of a loudspeaker may be incidental to the exercise of the right but, its use is not a matter of right or part of the rights guaranteed by Article 19(1).[114]

Freedom of expression under Article 19(1)(a) has manifold meanings. It need not and ought not to be confined to expressing something in words orally or in writing. Even a manifestation of an emotion or feeling without words would amount to expression. Communication of emotion or display of talent through music, painting etc., is also a sort of expression. The Court observed that ballot is the instrument by which the voter expresses his choice between candidates.[115]

Freedom of expression has four broad special purposes to serve:

(1) it helps an individual, to attain self-fulfillment;
(2) it assists in the discovery of truth;
(3) it strengthens the capacity of an individual in participation in decision making; and
(4) it provides a mechanism by which it would be possible to establish a reasonable balance between stability and social change. All members of society should be able to form their own beliefs and communicate them freely to others.

In sum, the fundamental principle involved here is the people's right to know. Freedom of speech and expression should, therefore, receive generous support from all those who believe in the participation of people in the administration. It is on account of this special interest, which society has in the freedom of speech and expression that the approach of the government should be more cautious, while levying taxes on matters of concerning newspaper industry than while levying taxes on other matters.[116]

In *Prabha Dutt v. Union of India*,[117] the Supreme Court of India, held that the right to have news and information regarding administration of the government is included in the freedom of press. But, this right is not absolute and restrictions can be imposed on it in the interest of society and the individual from which the press obtains the information. They can obtain information from an individual when he voluntarily agrees to give such information. In the instant case the court directed the Superintendent of the Tihar Jail, to permit the Chief Reporter of the

Hindustan Times newspaper to interview Ranga and Billa, the two death sentence convicts, under Article 19(1)(a) as they were willing to be interviewed.

In *State v. Charita*,[118] the Indian Supreme Court has held, that the press does not have an unfettered right to interview an under-trial prisoner in jail. Thus, where the trial of the accused was pending before the Additional Session Judge, he had authority to grant permission to the press to interview an under-trial prisoner inside the jail. However, the permission to the press to interview an under-trial prisoner cannot be granted mechanically without application of mind. The Court, while granting permission, will have to weigh the competing interest between the right of the press, and the right of the authorities prohibiting such interview in the interest of administration of justice. The permission granted by the Court would be subject to the relevant rules and regulations contained in the Jail Manual.

In *Life Insurance Corporation of India v. Professor Manubhai D. Shah*,[119] the Indian Supreme Court got an opportunity to examine the scope and extent of the freedom of speech and expression guaranteed by Article 19(1)(a) of the Constitution of India. In the first case, the respondent Professor Manubhai D. Shah, the executive trustee of the Consumer Education & Research Centre (CERC), Ahmedabad, after undertaking research into the working of the Life Insurance Corporation of India (LIC) published a study paper entitled '*Fraud on Policy Holders*' – *A shocking story*. This study paper depicted the discriminatory practice adopted by the LIC (Life Insurance Corporation of India), which adversely affected the interest of a large number of policy holders.

A member of the LIC published a counter in a magazine called '*Yogakshema*' published by the LIC. The respondent, Professor Manubhai D. Shah requested the LIC to publish his rejoinder to the said article, in the said magazine, but his request was not accepted. The LIC (Life Insurance Corporation of India) contended, that the magazine *Yogakshema*, is a house magazine, and not put in the market for sale to the general public. It was meant only for informing its members, staff and agents about its activities. The respondent contended, that the refusal to publish his rejoinder in the magazine violated his fundamental right under Articles 14 and 19(1)(a) of the constitution.

The High Court accepted the contention on two grounds *viz.*,

(i) it is available to anyone on payment of subscription and
(ii) members of public are invited to contribute articles for publication.

The Court directed LIC (Life Insurance Corporation of India), to publish the article in the next issue.

In the other case, the managing trustee of the respondent's trust had produced a documentary film on Bhopal Gas Disaster titled '*Beyond Genocide*'. This film was awarded the Golden Lotus being the best non-feature film of 1987. At the time of the presentation of awards the Minister for Information and Broadcasting (MIB), had made a declaration that the award-winning short films would be telecast on *Doordarshan* (DD).

The respondent submitted for telecast his film to *Doordarshan* (DD), but, it refused to telecast the film on the ground that its contents were outdated and did not have relevance for the telecast. The respondent challenged the refusal on the ground of violation of his fundamental right under Article 19(1)(a) of the Indian Constitution and for a *mandamus* to *Doordarshan* (DD) to telecast the same. The High Court held, that the respondent's right under Article 19(1)(a) obligated *Doordarshan* (DD) to telecast the film, since the refusal was based purely on an executive order, and not law within the meaning of Article 19(2). The LIC appealed against both the orders of the High Court to the Supreme Court.

The Indian Supreme Court rejected the appeal of LIC on both points. It held, that the LIC is a 'State' within the meaning of Article 12 and 'therefore' it must function in the best interest of the community. The community is entitled to know, whether or not this requirement of the statute is complied with, by the LIC in its functioning. The LIC's house magazine *Yogakshema*, is financed from public funds, and therefore, its refusal to publish the respondent's rejoinder was unfair, and unreasonable, and arbitrary, and was violative of the respondent's fundamental right of speech and expression, entitled him to insist that his views on the subject should reach those who read the magazine. The LIC's argument, that the rejoinder has become stale by passage of time and lost relevance for publication cannot be accepted. If the respondent thinks that the view raised by him regarding high premium rates is still live, and desires its publication, the court accept his assessment.

Accordingly, the Court directed the LIC to publish the respondent's rejoinder. But the Court made it clear that this ruling will not entitle all citizens to get their article published in the LIC magazine, on the ground that it is being financed from public funds. It applies in a particular situation like this one only. Explaining the scope of the freedom, the Court said, the words 'freedom of speech and expression' must be broadly construed to include the freedom to circulate one's views by words of mouth or in writing or through audio visual instrumentalities. It, therefore, includes the right to propagate one's view through the print media or through any other communication channel e.g. the radio and the television.

In the second connected case, regarding the refusal to telecast the film of the respondent Professor Manubhai D. Shah, the Court held that a film maker has a fundamental right under Article 19(1)(a) to exhibit his film and the party, which claims the right to refuse the telecast of the film on the ground that the film did not conform to the requirements of law made under Article 19(2), has the onus to prove that he is entitled to refuse this right. It was held that *Doordarshan* (DD) being a state-controlled agency funded by public was not justified to refuse to telecast the film. The Court upheld the decision of the High Court directing *Doordarshan* (DD) to telecast respondent's award-winning film. The grounds that the list of award-winning film was long and 'therefore' it was not possible to telecast the film cannot be justified under Article 19(2) of the Constitution. The respondent had a right to convey his perception of the gas disaster in Bhopal, through the documentary film, and merely, because it was critical of the State Government was no reason to deny selection and publication of the film. In fact, the community was keen to know what actually had happened, what is happening, which remedial measures the state authorities are taking, and what are the likely consequences of the gas leak.

The Indian Supreme Court also held that 'prior restraints,' regardless of their form, are considered as threats to 'freedom of expression' since they contain within themselves forces which if released have the potential for imposing arbitrary and at times irrational decisions. Movie is a powerful mode of communication and has the capacity to make profound impact on the minds of the viewers and it is therefore essential to ensure that the message that it conveys is not harmful to the society or even a section of the society. Censorship by 'prior restraint,' is therefore, justified for the protection of the society from the ill effects that the motion picture may produce if unrestricted exhibition is allowed. Censorship is thus permitted to protect social interests enumerated in Article 19(2) and Section 5-B of the Censorship Act.

In the *National Anthem* case,[120] the Indian Supreme Court has held, that no person can be compelled to sing the National Anthem, 'if he has genuine conscientious objections based on his religious faith.' In this case, the 3 children belonging to Jehovah's Witness group, were expelled from the school for refusing to sing the national anthem. The circular issued by the Director of Public Instructions Kerala, had made it obligatory for students in the schools to sing the national anthem. The children in this case stood up respectfully when the national anthem was being sung at their school, but they did not join in singing it. They refused to sing the national anthem, as according to them it was against their religious faith, which does not permit them to join in any rituals except, if be in their prayer to Jehovah, their God. They challenged the validity of their expulsion before the Kerala High Court, which upheld their expulsion as valid on the ground that it was their fundamental duty to sing the national anthem.

On appeal, the Supreme Court of India held, that there was no law under which their fundamental right under Article 19(1)(a) could be curtailed. The right under Article 19(1)(a) can only be regulated by law and on the grounds mentioned in the Constitution and not by executive instructions. They did not commit any offence under the Prevention of Insults to National Honour Act 1971, because they stood up respectfully when the national anthem was being sung. Accordingly, it was held that the children's expulsion from the school was a violation of their fundamental right under Article 19(1)(a), which also includes the freedom of silence.

New dimension to freedom of speech and expression – Government has no monopoly on electronic media

In a historic judgment in *Secretary, Ministry of Information & Broadcasting v. Cricket Association of Bengal (CAB)*,[121] the Supreme Court of India, has considerably widened the scope and extent of the right to freedom of speech and expression and held that the government has no monopoly on electronic media, and a citizen has under Article 19(1)(a) a right to telecast and broadcast to the viewers/listeners through electronic media, television and radio, any important event. The government can impose restrictions on such a right only on grounds specified in Clause (2) of Article 19, and not on any other ground. State monopoly on electronic media is not mentioned in Clause (2) of Article 19. The Court directed the government to set up an independent autonomous broadcasting authority, which will free *Doordarshan* (DD) and *Akashvani*[122] from the shackles of government control and ensure conditions in which the freedom of speech and expression can be meaningful and effectively enjoyed by one and all.

In the instant case, the petitioner the Cricket Association of Bengal (CAB), wrote a letter to the Director General of *Doordarshan* that a Six-nations International Cricket Tournament would be held in November 1993, as a part of its Diamond Jubilee celebration, and requested the DD (*Doordarshan*) to make necessary arrangements for telecasting of all matches in the said tournament in India. The CAB made it clear that the foreign TV rights would remain with it. The CAB had agreed to pay the requisite royalty amount to the DD (*Doordarshan*). Meanwhile, the CAB without permission from the government entered into an agreement with a foreign TV channel – TWI (Trans World International) for telecasting all the matches out of India and asked the DD (*Doordarshan*) to make available its TV signals for telecasting the matches. The TWI had agreed to pay more royalty to the CAB. The DD (*Doordarshan*) refused the permission.

The CAB filed a writ petition in the Calcutta High Court and requested the court to issue a direction for telecasting the matches in India, and also to provide signals to foreign TV for telecasting the matches to foreign viewers. The Court directed the DD (*Doordarshan*) to provide all the facilities for telecasting the matches by the agency appointed by the CAB. The government filed an appeal in the Supreme Court of India, against the order. It contended before the Court that it had monopoly on it under Section 4 of the Indian Telegraph Act 1885. The word 'telegraph' includes telecast. It was submitted that the CAB and TWI had not obtained a licence or permission under the Indian Telegraph Act 1885, and therefore, they could not telecast the matches from any place in Indian territory. The CAB argued, that the game of cricket provides entertainment to public. It is a form of expression, and therefore, included within the expression of speech and expression guaranteed by Article 19(1)(a) of the Indian Constitution. The right includes the right to telecast and broadcast matches, and this right belongs to the organizers, which cannot be interfered with by anyone. The organizer is free to choose any agency as it thinks appropriate for this purpose.

The Supreme Court of India, confirming the order of the Calcutta High Court, held that the fundamental right to freedom of speech and expression includes the right to communicate effectively, and to a large population not only in this country but also abroad. There are no geographical barriers on communication. A citizen has a fundamental right to use the best means of imparting and receiving communication and as such have access to telecasting for the purpose. At present electronic media *viz*., TV and radio is the most effective means of communication. However, since airwaves are public property and they must be used for public good. They are, therefore, subject to certain limitations. The Court directed the government to establish an independent autonomous public authority representing all sections of society to control and regulate the use of airwaves. A monopoly over electronic media is inconsistent with the right to freedom of speech and expression. Broadcasting media must be under the control of public. Justice B.P. Jeevan Reddy (1932)[123] in his concurring judgment suggested that suitable amendments should be made to the Indian Telegraph Act 1885, keeping in view of modern technological developments in the field of information and communication.[124]

Commercial Advertisement – Part of Freedom of Speech and Expression

In a landmark judgment in *Tata Press Ltd. v. Mahanagar Telephone Nigam Ltd.*,[125] a 3 judges bench held that commercial speech (advertisement) is a part of the freedom of speech and expression granted under Article 19(1)(a) of the Indian Constitution. It can only be restricted on the grounds specified in Clause (2) of Article 19. The Supreme Court of India, however, made it clear that the commercial advertisements which are deceptive, unfair, misleading and untruthful could be regulated by the Government of India.

Tata Press Ltd. (Tatas), were engaged in publication of the '*Tata Press Yellow Pages*'. The Union of India filed a civil suit before Civil Court at Bombay, for a declaration that they alone have the right to print publish the list of telephone subscribers, and Tata Press Ltd. have no right to print and publish without its permission, as it was violative of the Indian Telegraph Act 1885, and they should therefore, be restrained from publishing the 'yellow pages'. The City Civil Court dismissed the suit. But, a single judge of the Bombay High Court allowed the appeal. Tata's Letters Patent Appeal was dismissed by the Division Bench of the High Court. Tatas (Tata Press Ltd.) filed an appeal in the Supreme Court. The Supreme Court of India held, that the Union Government had no right to restrain the appellant Tata Press Ltd. (Tatas) from publishing '*Tata Yellow Pages*' comprising paid advertisements from businessmen, traders and professionals. The Court said that, the advertisement as a 'commercial speech' has two facets; Advertising, which is no more than a commercial transaction, is nonetheless dissemination of information regarding the product and that when – advertised, public at large would benefit by the information made available through the advertisements. In a democratic economy, free flow of commercial information is indispensable. There cannot be honest and economical marketing by the public at large without being educated by the information disseminated through advertisements. The economic system in a democracy would be handicapped, without there being freedom of 'commercial speech'. The other facet according to the court is that the public at large has a right to receive the 'commercial speech'. Article 19(1)(a) of the Indian Constitution, not only guarantees freedom of speech and expression, but it also protects the rights of an individual to listen, read and receive the said speech.

In an earlier case, *Hamdard Dawakhana v. Union of India*,[126] the validity of the Drug and Magic Remedies (Objectionable Advertisement) Act 1954, which put restrictions on advertisement of drugs in certain cases, and prohibited advertisements of drugs having magic qualities for curing diseases was challenged on the ground that the restriction on advertisement abridged the freedom of speech. The Supreme Court of India held, that an advertisement is no doubt a form of speech, but every advertisement was not a matter dealing with the freedom of speech and expression of ideas. In that case, the advertisement was held to be dealing with commerce or trade, and not for propagating ideas. Advertisement of prohibited drugs would thus, not fall within the scope of Article 19(1)(a).

In view of the Supreme Court of India's decision in the case of *Tata Press Ltd.*, the ruling in *Hamdard Dawakhana* case, has a limited application that is prohibiting an obnoxious advertisement and cannot be applied to general advertisement as such.

Telephone Tapping – Invasion on Right to Privacy

People's Union for Civil Liberties Union v. Union of India[127] was a landmark decision that had far-reaching implications. The petitioner, Peoples Union for Civil Liberties, a voluntary organization filed a petition under Article 32 of the Indian Constitution, by way of public interest litigation highlighting the incidents of telephone tapping in recent years.

The petitioner challenged the validity of Section 5(2) of the Indian Telegraph Act 1885, which permits the interception of messages under the provisions of the said section. It was argued that 'Occurrence of any public emergency' or 'in the interest of public safety' are the *sine qua non* for the application of the provisions of Section 5(2), unless these two conditions were satisfied, the Indian Government could not exercise its power under the said Section. The expression 'public safety' means the state or condition of freedom from danger or risk for the people at large, and unless these two conditions were in existence, the government could not resort to telephone tapping, even though there is satisfaction that it is necessary or expedient to do so in the interest of sovereignty of India etc.

The Supreme Court of India, laid down exhaustive guidelines to regulate the discretion vested in the state under said Section 5(2), for the purposes of phone tapping and interception of other messages, so as to safeguard public interest against arbitrary and unlawful exercise of power by the government. The Court expressed its displeasure, that the state has so far not framed any rules to prevent misuse of the power and the CBI (Central Bureau of Investigation) investigation had revealed several lapses in the execution of the orders passed by the state while exercising powers under the Indian Telegraph Act 1885.

Under the guidelines laid down by the Indian Supreme Court, an order for telephone tapping can only be issued by the Home Secretary of the Centre and State Governments. The order is subject to review by a high power review committee and the period for telephone tapping cannot exceed 2 months unless approved by the reviewing authority, which can extend it up to 6 months. At the Centre, the review committee consists of the Cabinet Secretary, the Law Secretary and the Secretary Communications. Similarly, at the State level the committee consists of the Chief Secretary, the Law Secretary and another member other than Home Secretary.

Telephone tapping also violates Article 19(1)(a), unless it comes within grounds of restrictions under Article 19(2). The freedom means the right to express one's convictions and opinions freely by words of mouth, writing, printing, picture, or in other manner. When a person is talking on telephone, he is exercising his right to freedom of speech and expression. Telephone tapping unless comes within the grounds of restrictions under Article 19(2), would violate Article 19(1)(a) of the Indian Constitution.

Calling for and holding '*Bandh*' illegal and unconstitutional being violative of fundamental Rights of Citizens

In a judgment of far reaching importance in *Communist Party of India (M) v. Bharat Kumar and others,*[128] a 3 judge bench of the Supreme Court of India, upholding the Full Bench judgment of the Kerala High Court, held that calling for and holding of '*Bandh*'[129] by a political party or organization is unconstitutional, and is hence illegal, as it violates the fundamental rights of the citizens guaranteed by Article 19(1)(a) and 21 of the Constitution of India, in addition to causing national loss.

The petitioners contended that by holding a *Bandh*, citizens were prevented from attending their avocations, and traders are prevented from keeping their business activities, and workers are prevented from attending to work in the factories. The right of political parties to hold demonstration or to show protest cannot extend to preventing citizens from exercising their fundamental rights of attending to their business, their studies and their avocations. It was said that, neither the stationer, nor the police force take any step to prevent violence and coercion. So that whenever a *Bandh* is called, a citizen out of fear of his life and his property, is forced to remain indoors. On the other hand, the Communist Party of India (M) claimed, that the right to call for a *Bandh* is the fundamental right of a political party under Article 19(1)(a) and (b) of the Indian Constitution.

The Kerala High Court held, that no political party has right to call for *Bandh* on the ground, that it is part of its fundamental right of freedom of speech and expression under Article 19(1)(a). Nothing stands in the way of political parties calling for a general strike or *hartal* unaccompanied by express or implied threat of violence to enforce it. The Court held that the call for a *Bandh* implies a threat to the citizen that any failure on his part to honour the call, would result in either injury to person or property, and involves preventing a citizen by instilling into him the psychological fear that if he defies the call for *Bandh*, he would be dealt by those who are allegedly supporter of the *Bandh*. When a citizen is coerced into not acceding to his work or prevented from going out for his work or from practicing his profession or carrying on his business, there is involved a violation of his fundamental right. The Court held that no political party or organization can claim that it is entitled to paralyze the industry and commerce in the entire state or nation and is entitled to prevent the citizens not in sympathy with its view point, from exercising their fundamental rights or from performing their duties for the benefit of the state, or the nation.

The Supreme Court upheld the Kerala High Court's decision. The Supreme Court agreed with the distinction drawn by the High Court between '*Bandh*' and a call for general strike or '*Hartal*'. There cannot be any doubt, it was held, that fundamental rights of the people as a whole cannot be subservient to the claim of fundamental right of an individual or only a section of the people.

Territorial extent of freedom—There are no geographical limitation to freedom of speech and expression guaranteed under Article 19(1)(a), and this freedom is exercisable not only in India but outside, and if state action sets up barriers to its citizens, freedom of expression in any country in the world, it would violate Article 19(1)(a), as much as if it inhibited such expression within the country. In *Maneka Gandhi v. Union of India,*[130] the Union of India contended that the fundamental rights guaranteed by the constitution were available only within the territory of India. How could the fundamental rights be intended to be operative outside the territory of India when their exercise in the foreign territory could not be protected by the state?

The Supreme Court of India rejected these conditions and held, that the right to freedom of speech and expression has no geographical limitations. Freedom of speech and expression carries with it the right to gather information as also to speak and express oneself at home and abroad and to exchange thoughts and ideas with others not only in India but also outside.

Freedom of the press—The fundamental right of the freedom of the press implicit in the right the freedom of speech and expression, is essential for political liberty and proper functioning of democracy.

> 'Freedom of the press is essential to political liberty. When men cannot freely convey their thoughts to one another, no freedom is secured, where freedom of expression exists the beginning of a free society and means for every retention of liberty are already present. Free expression is therefore, unique among liberties.'[131]

Unlike the American Constitution, Article 19(1)(a) of the Indian Constitution does not expressly mention the liberty of the press, but it has been held, that liberty of the press is included in the freedom of speech and expression.

> 'The press has no special rights which are not to be given or which are not to be exercised by the citizen in his individual capacity. The editor of a press and the manager are all citizens and therefore when they choose to write in newspapers, are merely exercising the right of the expression, and therefore, no special mention is necessary of the freedom of the press.'[132]

In *Indian Express Newspapers v. Union of India,*[133] speaking about the utility of freedom of press the court observed:

> 'The expression "freedom of the press" has not been used in Article 19 but it is comprehended within Article 19(1)(a). The expression means freedom from interference from authority which would have the effect of interference with the content and circulation of newspapers. There cannot be any interference with that freedom in the name of public interest. The purpose of the press is to advance the public interest by publishing facts and opinions without which a democratic electorate cannot make responsible judgments. Freedom of the press is the heart of social and political intercourse. It is the primary duty of the courts to uphold the freedom of the press and invalidate all laws or administrative actions which interfere with it contrary to the constitutional mandate.'

In *Printers (Mysore) Ltd. v. Asstt. Commercial Tax Officer,*[134] the Indian Supreme Court held, that no sales tax can be imposed on sale of newspapers in the country. However, the Court clarified that this does not mean that the press is immune either from taxation or from general law relating to industrial relations or from the state regulation of condition of service of its employees. The prohibition is upon the imposition of any restriction to disseminate information and to the circulation of newspaper. Freedom of press has always been a cherished right in all democratic countries. The newspaper not only survey news but also ideas, opinion and ideologies, besides much else. They are supposed to guard public interest by bringing to fore the misdeeds, failing and lapses of the government and other bodies exercising governing power. Rightly, therefore, it has been described as the *Fourth Estate.*

A citizen's right to propagate and publish extends not merely to the matter to which he was entitled to circulate but also to the volume of circulation. Freedom of speech could not be restricted for the purpose of regulating commercial aspect of the activities of the newspapers. A newspaper cannot survive and sell itself at a price, which is not within the reach of a common man unless it is allowed to take in advertisements.

The Court held that the freedom of press stands at a higher footing than other enterprises. In view of this, the test for determining the *vires* of a statute taxing newsprint have, therefore, to be different from the test usually adopted for testing the *vires* of other taxing statutes. The judges held, that the newspapers are entitled to the benefit of concessional Central Sales Tax of 4 per cent on purchase of raw materials which they require for printing and publishing of the newspapers. The definition of 'goods' in Section 2(d) of the Central Sales Tax Act was amended to bring the said definition in accord with the amendments brought in the Constitution 6th (Amendment) Act 1956, by which Entry 92A was introduced in List I, which prohibits imposition of sales tax on sale of newspapers; it was aimed at exempting the sale of newspapers from the levy of Central Sales Tax. The amendment in the Act was not intended to create a burden but to remove the burden.

Pre-Censorship invalid—The imposition of censorship on a journal previous to its publication would amount to an infringement of Article 19(1)(a). The question of validity of censorship came up for consideration in the case of *Brij Bhushan v. State of Delhi.*[135] In that case, the Chief Commissioner of Delhi, in pursuance of Section 7 of the East Punjab Safety Act 1949, issued an order against the printer, publisher, editor of an English weekly of Delhi, called the *Organizer,* directing them to submit for scrutiny in duplicate before publication till further orders, all communal matters and news and views, about Pakistan including photographs and cartoons other than those derived from official sources or supplied by the news agencies. The Indian Supreme Court struck down the order, observing:

> '... the imposition of pre-censorship of a journal is a restriction on the liberty of the press which is an essential part of the freedom of the speech and expression declared by Article 19(1)(a).'

Similarly, prohibiting newspaper from publication of its own views or the views of correspondents about the burning topic of the day is a serious encroachment on the valuable right of freedom of speech and expression.[136]

In *Express Newspapers (Pvt.) Ltd. v. Union of India*,[137] the Indian Supreme Court held, that a law which imposes pre-censorship or curtails the circulation or prevents newspapers from being started or require the concerned person to seek government aid in order to survive was violative of Article 19(1)(a). In this case the validity of the Working Journalists Act 1955, was challenged. The Act was enacted to regulate conditions of service of persons employed in newspaper industry, e.g. payment of gratuity, hours of work, leave, fixation of wages etc. It was contended that the Act would adversely affect financial position of newspaper which might be forced to close down and would curtail circulation and thereby narrow the scope for dissemination of information and hence violative of Article 19(1)(a). The Court held the Act valid. It said that press was not immune from laws of general application or ordinary forms of taxation, or laws of industrial relations. The Act was passed to ameliorate the service conditions of workmen in the newspaper industry and, therefore, impose reasonable restriction on the right guaranteed by Article 19(1)(a).

In *Romesh Thappar v. State of Madras*,[138] a law banning entry and circulation of journal in a state was held to be invalid. The petitioner was printer, publisher and editor of a weekly journal in English called '*Cross Road*' printed and published in Bombay. The Government of Madras, in exercise of their powers under Section 9(1-A) of the Maintenance of Public Order Act 1949, issued an order prohibiting the entry into or the circulation of the journal in that state. The Court said, that there can be no doubt that freedom of speech and expression includes freedom of propagation of ideas, and that freedom is ensured by the freedom of circulation. Liberty of circulation is essential to that freedom as the liberty of publication. Indeed, without circulation the publication would be of little value. Restrictions on freedom of speech and expression can only be imposed on grounds mentioned in Article 19(2) of the Indian Constitution. A law which authorizes imposition of restrictions on grounds of 'public safety' or the 'maintenance of public order' falls outside the scope of authorized restrictions under Clause (2) and therefore, void and unconstitutional.

In *Sakal Papers (Pvt.) Ltd. v. Union of India*,[139] the Daily Newspapers (Price and Control) Order 1960, which fixed a minimum price and number of pages which a newspaper was entitled to publish was challenged as unconstitutional by the petitioner on the ground that it infringed the liberty of the press. The petitioners were required to increase the price of their newspaper without increasing the pages. An increase in price without any increase in number of pages would reduce the volume of circulation. On the other hand, any decrease in the number of pages would reduce the column, space for news, views or ideas. The order, therefore, acted as double-edged knife. It cut circulation by a price rise or publication or dissemination of news, ideas and knowledge by restricting column space consequent to decrease in the number of pages. The state justified the law as a reasonable restriction on a business activity of a newspaper in the interests of the general public. The Court struck down the order rejecting the state's argument. It said that the right of freedom of speech and expression cannot be taken away with the object of placing restrictions on the business activity of a citizen.

In *Bennett Coleman and Co. v. Union of India*,[140] the validity of the Newsprint Control Order 1962, which fixed the maximum number of pages (10 pages which a newspaper could publish) was challenged as violative of fundamental rights guaranteed in Article 19(1)(a) and Article 14 of the Indian Constitution. The government defended the measure on the ground that it would help small newspapers to grow and to prevent a monopolistic combination of big newspapers. The Court held, that the newsprint policy was not reasonable restriction within the ambit of Article 19(2). The newsprint policy abridges petitioner's right of the freedom of speech and expression. The newspapers were being denied their right of circulation. In the garb of distribution of newsprint, the government has tended to control the growth and circulation of newspapers. Freedom of the press is both quantitative and qualitative. Freedom lies both in circulation and in content. The newsprint policy, which permits newspapers to increase circulation by reducing the number of pages, page area and periodicity, or prohibits them to increase the number of pages, page area and periodicity by reducing circulation constitutes unreasonable restrictions.

In *Indian Express Newspaper v. Union of India*,[141] the petitioners, publishers, of daily newspapers and periodicals, challenged the imposition of import duty and the levy of auxiliary duty on the newsprint on the ground of infringement of the freedom of press as it imposed a burden beyond capacity of the industry, and also affected the circulation of the newspapers and periodicals. The Court held, that the press industry was not free from taxation. Taxes have to be levied by reason of public services, facilities and amenities enjoyed by the newsprint industry, the burden of maintaining which falls on the government. They must contribute a fair and reasonable amount to the public exchequer. As long as such tax is within reasonable limits, and does not impede freedom of expression, it will not be beyond the limit of Article 19(2). But, when such taxes, transgress into the field of freedom of expression and stifles that freedom. They become unconstitutional.

In *Express Newspaper Pvt. Ltd. v. Union of India*,[142] the petitioners challenged the constitutional validity of a notice of re-entry upon the forfeiture of lease, and of threatened demolition of the Express Buildings on the ground, that it was violative of Articles 14, 19(1)(a) and (g). By an agreement of lease the petitioner was allotted certain plots for construction of its press building by the Government of India. The Express Newspapers then constructed its new Express Building. The Lt. Governor of Delhi alleged, that the new Express Building was constructed in contravention of municipal corporation laws and served a notice for re-entry and for its demolition. The construction of new building was in conformity with the lease deed, and with the express sanction of the lessor, i.e. the Union of India. It was contended that the impugned notices have a direct impact on the freedom of press under Article 19(1)(a). The Court held, that the impugned notices constituted direct and immediate threat to the freedom of the press and were thus, violative of Article 19(1)(a) and Article 14 and thus, invalid. They were intended to silence the voice of the Indian Express.

In *Odyssey Communication Pvt. Ltd. v. Lokvidayan Sanghatana*,[143] the respondents, a registered social organization of Pune, filed a public interest litigation under Article 226, to restrain the Union of India, Ministry of Information and Broadcasting (MIB), and the State of Maharashtra, from telecasting the serial '*Hony Anhoni*' on the ground, that it was likely to spread false or blind beliefs and superstition amongst the members of the public. It was, however, held that the rights of a citizen to exhibit films on the *Doordarshan* (DD), on the terms and conditions imposed by the *Doordarshan* (DD) is a part of the fundamental right of freedom of expression guaranteed under Article 19(1)(a), which can be curtailed only on the grounds mentioned in Article 19(2). The right is similar to the right of a citizen to publish his views through any other media such as newspapers, magazines, advertisement hoarding etc., subject to the terms and conditions of the owners of the media. The respondents failed to show that exhibition of the serial was *prima facie* prejudicial to the community. It was also not likely to endanger public morality.

Decency or morality

The freedom of speech and expression does not extend to indecent or immoral publications and utterances. But, as the concepts of decency and morality differ historically and geographically, the Courts must decide the matter in the light of the existing and generally accepted notions of decency and morality, in a given society.

Reasonableness of restrictions

The restriction, apart from having a rational nexus with public order, must also be reasonable. It is for the Courts to decide if a restriction is reasonable both substantively and procedurally. *Virendra v. State of Punjab*,[144] is an important decision of the Supreme Court of India illustrating the scope of permissible restriction. The law impugned in that case was the Punjab Special Powers (Press) Act 1956. It provided for –

(i) the prohibition of printing or publication of any article, report, news item, letter or any other material relating to or connected with 'Save Hindi Agitation';
(ii) the imposition of ban against the entry and the circulation of the said papers published from New Delhi in the State of Punjab and
(iii) authorizing the state government or its delegate to impose pre-censorship.

The first provision relating to ban on publication of news, etc., was upheld in the time of tension brought about or aided by the 'Save Hindi Agitation', taking into consideration the safeguards provided therein, as being a reasonable restriction, substantively and procedurally on the liberty of the press.

The second provision of the Act namely, the power to impose a ban against the entry, and the circulation of the paper, was not sustained as a reasonable restriction because there was no time-limit for the operation of an order made against a paper and also because there was no provision made for any representation to the state government.

Government cannot impose prior-restraint on publication of defamatory material against its officials- Auto Shankar case

In a historic judgment in *R. Rajagopal v. State of Tamil Nadu*[145] the Supreme Court of India held, that the government had no authority in law to impose a 'prior-restraint' upon publication of defamatory material against its officials. Public authorities who apprehend that they or their colleagues may be defamed could not prevent the press from publication of such material but could take action for damages after the publication of such material, if they prove, that the publication was based on false facts. The Court held that no action could be initiated against the press if the publication was based on public records including court records. Freedom of the press, the Court said, means absence of interference by the state except, insofar, as it is authorized by the Constitution of India and by laws.

The ruling was given by the Court while allowing a writ petition by a Tamil Weekly Magazine '*Nakkheeran*' seeking a direction to the Tamil Nadu Government from interfering with the publication of the autobiography of the condemned prisoner, Auto Shankar, in the magazine who had been charged and tried for as many as 6 murders. His mercy petition to the President of India was pending consideration. The first petitioner was editor, printer and publisher of the magazine '*Nakkheeran*' published from Madras. The second petitioner was the associate editor of the magazine. Their case was that the condemned prisoner Auto Shankar, who was convicted for 6 murders and sentenced to death, had written his autobiography in jail and had handed over the same to his wife with the knowledge and approval of the jail authorities, for being delivered to his advocate with a request to publish it in the petitioner's magazine.

The autobiography depicted a close nexus between the prisoner and several IAS (India Administrative Service), IPS (India Police Service) and other officers, some of whom were indeed his partners in several crimes. The petitioners, decided to commence the serial publication of the autobiography, and for this purpose they announced, that very soon the magazine would be coming out with the sensational life history of Auto Shankar. This announcement sent shock waves among several police and prison officials who were afraid that their links with the condemned prisoner would be exposed. They forced Auto Shankar, by applying third degree methods, to write letters addressed to the Inspector General of Prisons (IG Prison), State of Tamil Nadu, and the editor of the magazine requesting that his life story should not be published in the magazine. The Inspector General of Prisons (IG Prison), State of Tamil Nadu, wrote a letter to the editor on 15 July 15 1994, informing him that the autobiography was false and Auto Shankar had denied that he had written any such book, and therefore, asked him to stop the publication of serial.

The Indian Supreme Court held, that the petitioners have a right to publish the autobiography of Auto Shankar, in so far, as it appears from the public records even without his consent or authorization. But, if they go beyond that and publish his life story, they may be invading his right to privacy and will be liable for the consequences in accordance with law. Similarly, the State of Tamil Nadu, and its officials who apprehend, that they may be defamed cannot impose 'prior restraint' upon the publication of the alleged autobiography. The remedy of the affected officials, if any, is after the publication.

The Court made it clear, that any publication concerning the privacy aspects would become unobjectionable if, such publication was based upon public records including Court record. It is for this reason, that once a matter becomes a matter of public record, the right to privacy no longer subsists, and it becomes a legitimate subject for comment by press and media and others. It is enough for the press to prove that it acted after a reasonable verification of the facts; it is not necessary for the press to prove that what is published was true. But, in the interest of decency an exception has to be carried out to this rule, that is, the name of a female who was victim of sexual assault, kidnapping, abduction or a like offence should not be published in the press. The right of privacy of public servants, however, stands on different footing. In a free democratic society, public officials must always be open to criticism.

Test for determining whether legislation infringes fundamental right?—The test in determining the question whether a legislation or executive action infringes the fundamental right is to examine its 'effect', and not its object or subject matter. In *Bennett Coleman's* case, it was held that the direct and inevitable effect of the rationing of newsprint was to control newspapers.[146] In other words, it was urged that the test to be applied to ascertain whether a law violates Article 19(1)(a) is to look into the subject matter of a law, and not its effect on a particular right. The Supreme Court of India rejected this contention and approved the 'effect' test *viz.*, whether the 'effect' of the impugned law is to abridge a fundamental right. The Court held, that if the direct effect of the impugned law is to abridge a fundamental right, its object or subject matter will be irrelevant. In the instant case, the Court held, that although, the subject matter of the newsprint policy was different, its direct effect was newspaper control and hence violative of article 19(1)(a).

'Although, the freedom of the press is implicit in the freedom of speech' it does not stand on higher footing than the freedom of speech and expression of a citizen. It is subject to some limitations as are imposed by Article 19(2) of the Indian Constitution. In *Express Newspaper Ltd. v. Union of India*,[147] the Indian Supreme Court, while upholding the validity of the Working Journalists Act 1955, observed,

> 'The press was not immune from ordinary forms of taxation for the general support of the Government or from the application of general laws relating to industrial relations or laws regulating the payment of wages.'

Demonstration or 'Picketing'—Demonstration or picketing are visible manifestation of one's ideas and in effect a form of speech and expression. Demonstrations or picketing are protected under Article 19(1)(a), provided they are not violent and disorderly.[148] It has been held, that there is no fundamental right to resort to strike. Right to strike is not included within the ambit of freedom of speech.[149]

Film censorship valid—*K. A. Abbas v. Union of India*,[150] is the first case in which the question, whether prior censorship of films is included in Article 19(2), came for the consideration of the Supreme Court of India. The petitioner had challenged the validity of censorship as violative of his fundamental right of freedom of speech and expression, as according to him it imposed unreasonable restriction.

Under the Cinematograph Act 1952, films are divided into 2 categories, i.e. 'U' films are meant for unrestricted exhibition, while 'A' films can be shown to adults only. The petitioner's film '*Tale of Four Cities*' was refused 'U' certificate. He also contended, that there were other forms of speech and expression, besides the films and none of them were subjected to any 'prior restraint' in the form of pre-censorship and claimed equality of treatment with such other forms. The Court, however, held that pre-censorship of films was justified under Article 19(2) on the ground, that films have to be so treated separately from other forms of art and expression because a motion picture was able to stir up emotions more deeply than any other product of art. Hence, classification of films between two categories i.e., 'A' (for adults only) and 'U'(for all) was held to be valid.

In *Bobby Art International v. Om Pal Singh Hoon*,[151] popularly known as '*Bandit Queen* case' the respondent filed a writ petition in the Court for quashing the certificate of exhibition given to the film 'Bandit Queen', and restraining its exhibition in India. The film 'Bandit Queen', was the story of Phoolan Devi, a village child, who was exposed to from an early age to the brutality and lust of men. Phoolan Devi was married to a man old enough to be her father. She was beaten and raped by him. The village boys made advances which was repulsed by her, but the village *Panchayat* found her guilty of the enticement of a village boy because he was of high class, and she had to leave the village. She was arrested by the police and subjected to indignity and humiliation in the police station. She was kidnapped by dacoits and raped by their leader, Babu Singh Gujjar. Another member of the gang, Vikram Mallah shot Babu Gujjar dead, while he was assaulting Phoolan Devi and she found an ally to secure her. With his assistance she took revenge from her husband. Her rescuer Vikram Mallah, was shot dead by the leader of a gang of Thakur who made advances to her and was spurned. She was then gang raped by him and his accomplices who humiliated her in the sight of the village by being stripped naked and made to fetch water from the village well under the gaze of the villagers, but no one came to her rescue. To take revenge from her persecutors she joined a dacoit's gang headed by Babu Mustkin and killed 20 Thakurs of the village of Bahmain. Ultimately, she surrendered and was in jail for a number of years.

The film was presented for certification to the Censor Board of Film Certification (CBFC). The Examining Committee of the Censor Board referred it to the Revision Committee, recommended that the film be granted an 'A' certificate (for adults only), subject to certain modifications and cuts. Aggrieved by the decision of the Revision Committee, an appeal was filed before the Appellate Tribunal. The tribunal consisted of a chairman and 3 other members who were ladies. The tribunal granted the film an 'A' certificate.

The respondent, then, filed the writ petition in the Delhi High Court, seeking to quash the certificate granted to the film and restrain its exhibition in India. He contended, that though the audiences were led to believe that the film depicted the character of 'a former queen of ravines' also known as Phoolan Devi, the depiction was 'abhorrent and unconscionable and a slur on the womanhood of India.' The respondents and his community had been depicted in a most depraved way specially in the scene of rape by Babu Gujjar, 'which scene was suggestive of the moral depravity of the Gujjar community.' The High Court held that the film was obscene and quashed the order of the Appellate Tribunal.

The Supreme Court of India allowing the appeal, held that the certificate issued to the film 'Bandit Queen' upon conditions imposed by the Appellate Tribunal is valid and was, therefore, restored. The Court held that the film must be –

> 'judged in its entirety from the point of view of its overall impact.' The story of the film is a serious and sad story of a village born female child becoming a dreaded dacoit. The film levels an accusing finger at the members of society who compelled her to become a dreaded dacoit. The scene where she is humiliated stripped, naked, paraded, made to draw water from the well within the circle of hundreds of men, the exposure of her breasts and genitals to those men was intended by those who strip her to demean her. This did not arouse the cinemagoer's lust but aroused in him sympathy for the victim and disgust for the perpetrators. Nakedness does not always arouse the baser instinct. 'Bandit Queen' told a powerful human story and to that story the scenes of Phoolan Devi's enforced naked parade was central. It helped to explain why Phoolan Devi became what she did, her rape and vendetta against the society that had heaped indignities upon her. It shows what a terrible and terrifying effect rape and lust can have upon the victim. A film that illustrates the consequences of a social evil necessarily must show that social evil. The guidelines in the Cinematograph Act 1952, must be interpreted in that light.

An exhibitor of video films cannot claim protection of Article 19(1)(a), as he/she is not propagating or circulating any of his own views. The producer of a film can, but a mere exhibiter of video films cannot, claim protection of Article 19(1)(a). A right of a film maker to make and exhibit his film is a part of his fundamental right of freedom of speech and expression under Article 19(1)(a), and the restrictions under Cinematograph Act 1952, relating to certification by Censor Board are reasonable restrictions contemplated under Article 19(2). The exhibitor shows films or videos merely to earn profit and not to propagate any idea or arousing any public opinion.[152]

Grounds of Restrictions—Clause (2) of Article 19, contains the grounds on which restrictions on the freedom of speech and expression can be imposed:

(a) Security of the State
(b) Friendly Relations with foreign States
(c) Public Order
(d) Decency or Morality
(e) Contempt of Court
(f) Defamation
(g) Incitement of an offence
(h) Sovereignty and integrity of India

(a) *Security of the State*—Under Clause (2) of Article 19, reasonable restrictions can be imposed on freedom of speech and expression in the interest of security of the state. In *Romesh Thappar v. State of Madras.*[153] The Supreme Court of India, had occasion to interpret the meaning of the words 'security of the State'. The Court said, that there are different grades of offences against 'public order'. Every public disorder cannot be regarded as threatening the security of the state. The term 'security of the State' refers only to serious and aggravated forms of public disorder e.g., rebellion, waging war against the state, insurrection and not the ordinary breaches of public order and public safety, e.g., unlawful assembly, riot, affray. Thus, speeches or expression on the part of an individual which incite to or encourage the commission of violent crimes, such as, murder are matters which would undermine the security of the state.[154]

The words 'in the interests of' before the words 'security of the State', clearly imply that the actual result of the act is immaterial. Thus, acts which may indirectly bring about an overthrow of the state would come within the expression. An incitement to an armed revolution, though infructuous, ultimately, is enough to attract the term 'security of the State'.

(b) ***Friendly relation with Foreign States***—This ground was added by the Constitution (1st Amendment) Act 1951. The object behind the provision is to prohibit unrestrained malicious propaganda against a foreign friendly state, which may jeopardize the maintenance of good relations between India and that state. Similar provision is present in the Constitution of Pakistan. The laws of every country have adequate provisions to safeguard peaceful relations with foreign states.

In India, the Foreign Relations Act (XII of 1932), provides punishment for libel by India citizens against foreign dignitaries. Again, the Foreign Recruiting Act (IV of 1874), empowers the executive to prohibit recruitment of any citizen of India to the army of foreign states. But, the interests of friendly relations with foreign states, would not justify the suppression of fair criticism of foreign policy of the government.

(c) ***Public Order***—This ground was added by the Constitution (1st Amendment) Act 1951, in order to meet the situation arising from the Indian Supreme Court's decision in *Romesh Thappar*'s case.[155] In that case, it was held that ordinary or local breaches of public order were no grounds for imposing restriction on the freedom of speech, and expression guaranteed by the Constitution.

The Indian Supreme Court said, that –

> 'public order' is an expression of wide connotation and signifies that state of tranquility which prevails among the members of political society as a result of internal regulations enforced by the government which they have established.

In that case, the Supreme Court of India, struck down a law, banning the entry and circulation of the petitioner's journal in the State of Madras in the interest of 'public order', because Article 19(2) did not contain the expression 'public order'. It was held, that restrictions could only be imposed on the grounds mentioned in Article 19(2). As a result of this decision the expression 'public order' was added to Article 19(2), as one of the grounds for imposing restrictions on the freedom of speech and expression.

'Public order' is something more than ordinary maintenance of law and order. 'Public order' is synonymous with public peace, safety and tranquility. The test for determining, whether an act affects law and order or public order is to see, whether the act leads to the disturbances of the current of life of the community so as to amount to a disturbance of the public order or whether it affects merely an individual leaving the tranquility of the society undisturbed.[156]

In *Kishori Mohan Bera v. State of West Bengal*,[157] the Supreme Court of India, explained the differences between 3 concepts;

— law and order,
— public order,
— security of state.

The difference between these concepts, the court said, can be explained by 3 functional concentric circles, the largest representing law and order, the next public order, and the smallest, the security of the state. Every infraction of law must necessarily affect law and order, but not necessarily public order, and an act may affect public order, but not necessarily security of the state, and an act may fall under two concepts at the same time, affecting public order and security of the state. One act may affect individual, in which case it would affect law and order, while another act though of a similar kind may have such an impact that it would disturb even the tempo of the life of the community, in which case it would be said to affect public order, the test being the potentiality of the act in question.

Anything that disturbs public tranquility or public peace disturbs public order.[158] The communal disturbances[159] and strikes, promoted with the sole object of causing unrest among workmen,[160] are offences against public order. 'Public Order' thus, implies absence of violence and an orderly state of affairs in which citizens can peacefully pursue their normal avocation of life.[161] 'Public order' also includes public safety.[162] Public safety means the safety of the community from the external and internal dangers. Thus, creating internal disorder or rebellion would affect public order and public safety.[163] But, mere criticism of government does not necessarily disturb public order.[164] In its external aspect 'public safety' means protection of the country from foreign aggression. Under 'public order' the state would be entitled to prevent propaganda for a state at war with India.[165]

The words 'in the interest of public order', include not only such utterances as are directly intended to lead to disorder, but also, those that have the tendency to lead to disorder. Thus, a law punishing utterances made with deliberate intention to hurt the religious feelings of any class of persons is valid, because it imposes a restriction on the right of free speech in the interest of public order, since such speech or writing has the tendency to create public disorder, even if in some case those activities may not actually lead to a breach of peace.[166] But, there must be reasonable and proper nexus or relationship between the restriction and the achievement of public order.

In *Superintendent, Central Prison, Fatehgarh v. Ram Manohar Lohia*,[167] Section 3 of U.P. Special Powers Act 1932; which punished a person if he incited a single person not to pay or defer the payment of government dues was held to be invalid, because there was no proximate nexus between the speech and public order. The Court said, that fundamental right cannot be controlled on such 'hypothetical and imaginary considerations'. The Court rejected the argument that instigation of a single individual not to pay tax would itself destroy public order.

In *Sodhi Shamsher Singhv. State of PEPSU*,[168] a vitriolic attack upon the character and integrity of the Chief Justice of a High Court, was held to have no rational connection with the maintenance of law and order. An action in advance to maintain public order is not prohibited. In *Babulal Parate v. State of Madras*,[169] Section 144 of the Cr.P.C. (Code of Criminal Procedure), was challenged on the ground that it imposed unreasonable restriction on the right of freedom of speech and expression. The Court upheld validity of Section 144, holding that anticipatory action to prevent disorder is within the ambit of Clause (2) of Article 19. Under Section 144, Cr.P.C. (Code of Criminal Procedure), if a magistrate is of the opinion that there is sufficient ground for immediate danger of breach of peace, he can, by a written order direct a person or persons to abstain from certain acts, if, he considers, that such direction is likely to prevent or tend to prevent a disturbance of public tranquility, or a riot or affray.

(d) *Decency or morality*—The words 'morality or decency' are words of wide meaning. The word 'obscenity' of English law is identical with the word 'indecency' under the Indian Constitution. The test of obscenity is –

> 'whether the tendency of matter charged as obscene is to deprave and corrupt those whose minds are open to such immoral influences,'

and into whose hands a publication of this sort is likely to fall. Thus, a publication is obscene, if it tends to produce lascivious thoughts and arouses lustful desire in the minds of substantial numbers of that public, into whose hands the book is likely to fall. This test was laid down in an English case of *R. v. Hicklin*.[170]

Sections 292 to 294 of the Indian Penal Code (I.P.C.), provide instances of restrictions on the freedom of speech and expression in the interest of decency and morality. These sections prohibit the sale or distribution or exhibition of obscene words, etc., in public places. But, the Indian Penal Code (I.P.C.), does not lay down any test to determine obscenity.

In *Ranjit D. Udeshi v. State of Maharashtra*,[171] the Indian Supreme Court accepted the test laid down in the English case of *R. v. Hicklin*, to judge the obscenity of a matter. In this case, the court upheld the conviction of the appellant, a book seller, who was prosecuted under Section 292, I.P.C., for selling and keeping the book '*The Lady Chatterley's Lover*'. Applying the above test, the court held the novel as obscene.

It has rightly been submitted, that the Court has erred in not rejecting *Hicklin* rule, which has become obsolete. It lays down a vague and arbitrary standard for judging obscenity and has a tendency to curtail the guaranteed right to freedom of speech. No fixed standard can be laid down as to what is moral and indecent. The standard of morality varies from time to time and from place to place. Birth control, which was once considered immoral is now considered proper as a means to check over-population. On these considerations, it is time that the Court should revise its opinion as soon as it gets an opportunity to do so and reject the rule laid nearly hundred years ago by Lord Chief Justice Sir Alexander Cockburn (1802–82).[172]

In *Dr Ramesh Yeshwant Prabhoo v. Shri Prabhakar Kashinath Kunte,* the Supreme Court of India, has given somewhat wider meaning to the term 'decency' and 'morality'. These terms are not confined to sexual morality alone. 'Decency' means that the action must be in conformity with the current standards of behavior or propriety.[173]

(e) *Contempt of Court*—Restriction on the freedom of speech and expression can be imposed, if it exceeds the reasonable and fair limit and amounts to contempt of Court.

The Contempt of Court Act 1971 defines the expression 'Contempt of Court' as follows: 'Contempt of Court' may be either 'civil contempt' or 'criminal contempt'. 'Civil contempt' means willful disobedience to any judgment, decree, direction, order, writ or other process of a Court or willful breach of an undertaking given to a Court. 'Criminal contempt' means the publication (whether by words spoken or written, or by signs or by visible representations or otherwise) or any matter or the doing of any other act whatsoever, which—

(i) scandalizes or tends to scandalize, or lowers or tends to lower the authority of any court;
(ii) prejudices, or interferes or tends to interfere with the due course of any judicial proceedings; or
(iii) interferes or tends to interfere with, or obstructs or tends to obstruct, the administration of justice in any other manner.

The following acts are, however, not contempt of courts:

(a) Innocent publication and distribution of any matter;
(b) Publication of fair and accurate report of judicial proceedings;
(c) Fair criticism of judicial act;
(d) Complaint against Presiding Officers made in good faith; and
(e) Publication of fair information relating to proceedings in chambers or in *camera.*

Under the Act, contempt of court is punishable with simple imprisonment for a term of 6 months, or with fine which may extend to Rs 2000, or with both. A judge, magistrate or any person acting judicially is also liable for contempt of his court in the same manner as any other individual is liable under this Act. Thus, judges have no general immunity from criticism of their judicial conduct provided it is made in good faith and is a fair criticism of his judicial act.

The terminology used in the definition is borrowed from the English law of contempt and embodies concepts which are familiar to that law which by and large, was applied in India. The expressions 'scandalize', 'lowering the authority of the Court', 'interference', 'obstruction' and 'administration of justice' are therefore, to be understood by Indian Courts with the aid of English law. Free expression cannot be equated or confused with a license to make unfounded and irresponsible allegations against the judiciary.[174]

In *Baradakanta Mishra v. Registrar of Orissa High Court,*[175] the appellant, senior Judicial Officer, was convicted and sentenced under the Contempt of Courts Act 1971, by a Full Bench of Orissa High Court. The facts of the case were that on 28 March 1971, a disciplinary proceeding was started against him and he was placed under suspension. On receiving the suspension order, the appellant, wrote 3 letters to the High Court and one to the government. It was the contents of these letters on which the contempt proceedings were launched against him and he was punished. The Indian Supreme Court held, that contemptuous allegations made with reference to the administrative functions of High Court amount to criminal contempt. Administration of justice is closely associated with the court of justice, which have to perform multifarious functions for due administration of justice. Any lapse from the strict standards of rectitude in performing these functions is bound to effect administration of justice. The whole set up of courts, is for the purpose of justice, and the control exercised by a judge over his assistants, has also the object of maintaining the purity of justice. It is, therefore, important for the superior court to be vigilant about the conduct and behavior of the subordinate judge, as a judge to administer the law. Adjudication of cases between parties is not the whole administration of justice. Disciplinary control is a function, as conducive to proper administration of justice as laying down the law or doing justice between the parties. Thus, when the High Court under Article 235 functions in disciplinary capacity, it does so in furtherance of administration of justice.

It was held that the defamatory criticism of a judge, functioning as a judge even in purely administrative or non-adjudicatory matters, amounted to criminal contempt. The imputations in the above-mentioned letters grossly vilified the High Court and had substantially interfered with the administration of justice, and therefore, the appellant was rightly convicted of the offence of the criminal contempt.

Where an article was published, on the basis of an interview of father, of woman, who had committed suicide, apparently, due to harassment over diary and the matter was pending adjudication before the courts, the Supreme Court of India, took the view that such articles appearing in the media would interfere with the administration of justice and deprecated the practice and cautioned the publisher, editor and the journalist, responsible for the article not to indulge in trial by media specially when the issue was sub judice.[176] While the media can, in the public interest, resort to reasonable criticism of a judicial act or judgment of a court, in the public interest, the media should however refrain from casting aspersions or impute improper motives or personal bias to a judge. Nor should they scandalize the Court or the judiciary as a whole or make personal allegation of lack of ability or integrity against a judge. The judgments of the courts are public documents and can be commented upon, analyzed or criticized but in a dignified manner without attributing motives.

(f) *Defamation*—A statement which injures a man's reputation amounts to defamation. Defamation consists in exposing a man to hatred, ridicule, or contempt. In India, Section 499 of the I.P.C. (India Penal Code), contains the criminal law relating to defamation. It recognizes no distinction between the defamatory statement addressed to the ear or eyes, i.e., slander and libel. These sections are saved as being reasonable restrictions on the freedom of speech and expression.[177] The civil law relating to defamation is still uncodified in India and subject to certain exceptions follows generally the English law.

(g) *Incitement to an offence*—This ground was also added by the Constitution (First Amendment) Act 1951. Obviously, freedom of speech and expression cannot confer a licence to incite people to commit offence. The word 'offence' used here is not defined in the Indian Constitution. It is, however, defined in the General Clauses Act as meaning –

> 'Offence shall mean any act or omission made punishable by any law for the time being in force.'

What constitutes incitement will, however, have to be determined by the Court with reference to the facts and circumstances of each case. In *State of Bihar v. Shailabala Devi*,[178] the Indian Supreme Court held, that incitement to murder or other violent crimes would generally endanger the security of the state; hence a restriction against such incitement would be a valid law.

(h) *Integrity and Sovereignty of India*—This ground was added to Clause (2) of Article 19 by the Constitution (16th Amendment) Act 1963. Under this clause freedom of speech and expression can be restricted, so as not to permit to anyone to challenge the integrity or sovereignty of India, or to preach cession of any part of India from the Union.

Sedition—As understood in English law, sedition embraces all those practices whether by word of mouth or writing which are calculated to disturb the tranquility of the state and lead ignorant persons to subvert the government.[179] Thus, the gist to the offence of sedition is incitement to violence. Mere criticism of the government is no offence.

In India, Section 124-A of the Indian Penal Code (I.P.C.), defines the offence of sedition as follows:

> 'Whoever by words either spoken or written, or by signs, or by visible representation or otherwise brings or attempts to bring into hatred or contempt or excite or attempts to excite disaffection towards the Government established by law in India shall be punished.'
>
> 'Explanation 3 to Section 124-A states, that mere comment expressing misappropriation of Government is no offence if it does not excite or attempt to excite disaffection towards Government established by law.'

In *Niharendu Dutt Majumdar v. Emperor,*[180] the federal court held, that mere criticism, or even ridicule of the government was no offence, unless it was calculated to undermine respect for the government in such a way as to make people cease to obey it, or obey the law, so that only anarchy can follow. Public disorder is the gist of the offence. But, the Privy Council overruled this decision and held, that the offence of sedition was not confined to only incitement to violence or disorder.

It is to be noted that sedition is not mentioned in Clause (2) of Article 19, as one of the grounds on which restriction on freedom of speech and expression may be imposed. But, it has been held in *Debi Soren v. State,*[181] that Section 124-A and 153-A, of I.P.C. (India Penal Code), impose reasonable restriction in the interest of public order and is saved by Article 19(2). In *Kedar Nath Singh v. State of Bihar,*[182] the constitutional validity of Section 124-A, I.P.C. (India Penal Code), was considered by the Indian Supreme Court. The Court upheld the view taken by the federal court in *Niharendu's* case, that the gist of the offence of sedition is that the words written or spoken have tendency or intention of creating public disorder and held the section constitutionally valid.

Freedom of Speech and Press in Pakistan

Article 19 of the 1973 Pakistan Constitution provides that –

> 'every citizen shall have the right to freedom of speech and expression, and there shall be freedom of the press, subject to any reasonable restrictions imposed by law in the interest of the glory of Islam or the integrity, security or defence of Pakistan or any part thereof, friendly relations with foreign States, public order, decency or morality, or in relation to contempt of Court, defamation, commission of or incitement to an offence.'

Speech is thus, the outward expression of ideas, beliefs and free conscience. The concept of freedom of expression implies –

> 'that every citizen is free to say or publish what he wants, provided that he does not trample upon the rights of others and this freedom could become mockery and delusory if every man was at liberty to publish what he pleased.........'[183]

Freedom of Press

Freedom of press is highly valued in Pakistan as is obvious from the observations in *Masroor Ahsan v. Ardeshir Cowasjee* –[184]

> 'The freedom of press is only a specific instance of general right of freedom of speech; persons engaged in newspaper business cannot claim any other or greater right than that possessed by the persons not in that business.'

It was further observed that –

> 'The freedom of press is not absolute, unlimited and unfettered. The protective cover must not be thrown open for wrong doings. The person is expected to recognize its duties and responsibilities towards the society and in discharging their functions/duties, they should not compromise on public order, decency and morality.'

In *Mahmud Zaman v. District Magistrate, Lahore,*[185] an order was passed under the Press (Emergency Powers) Act 1931, requiring the publisher of a newspaper to deposit Rs 1000 as security against use for 'objectionable purposes'. It was held, that Article 8 of the 1956 Constitution (which was predecessor of Article 19) required that, every person should have the right to express himself freely, which did not mean that he could be restrained before he had actually expressed himself. If, he was required to fulfill a condition before expressing himself, the restraint would be of a preventive nature which was not contemplated by Article 8. Thus, the Court held against imposing 'prior restraint' on a publication.

In *Independent Newspapers Corporation v. Chairman Fourth Wage Board,*[186] the Supreme Court of Pakistan held that, freedom of expression includes the right to receive information through organs of public opinion, and the freedom of press on its turn rests on the assumption that there is a wide dissemination of information. Such dissemination inevitably contemplates absence of restraints. The question of 'prior restraint', being reasonable or not, depends upon the restriction which must have been imposed by a positive law made by a competent law-making authority.[187]

Reasonableness of Restrictions

The freedom of speech and expression, including the liberty of the press under the Pakistan Constitution, is subject to any reasonable restrictions that may be imposed by law in the interests of the glory of Islam, the security of Pakistan, friendly relations with foreign states, public order, decency or morality, or in relation to contempt of Court, defamation or incitement to an offence.

Reasonable restrictions under these heads in Pakistan can be imposed only by a duly enacted law and not by executive action. An absolute test of 'reasonableness of restrictions' cannot be laid down. In the United States, the question that arises in every case of the alleged infringement of the constitutional right of freedom of speech and press is –

> 'whether the words used are used in such circumstances and are of such a nature as to create a clear and present danger that they will bring about the substantive evils that Congress or the State has a right to prevent. It is a question of proximity and degree.'[188]

In *Nawabzada Nasrullah Khan v. Government of West Pakistan*,[189] the Lahore High Court held, that freedom of speech and press is not absolute at all times and in all circumstances, and it does not mean that one can talk or distribute where, when and how one chooses.

The privilege of free speech does not confer on an individual the right to use that privilege to the injury of another. Thus, the lewd and obscene, the profane and the blasphemous, the slanderous and the libelous, and the insulting or fighting words, which by their very utterance inflict injury and tend to incite an immediate breach of the peace are not protected.

(a) *Security of State*

Freedom of speech and expression being an essential feature of a democratic society, those who believe in and live by such freedom cannot complain of a restriction on that freedom, where the very existence of the state in which they enjoy such freedom is threatened by external attack or internal rebellion, which may destroy their freedom in every respect. There can, of course, be no valid objection to people desiring and working for a change of government by constitutional means, and no democratic government will use its law-making power to restrict freedom of speech with a view to preventing them from attaining that object by peaceful means. But, every government has the inherent right of self-preservation and, therefore, has the concomitant power to make it unlawful the overthrowing of the existing form of government by violence, or other unlawful means.

The constitutional guarantee of freedom of speech protects all utterances, individual or concerted, seeking constitutional changes, however revolutionary, by the processes which the constitution provides. A mere advocacy of a political change, to be accomplished by lawful means, is not a crime, and to prohibit such means would be a violation of the guarantee of freedom of speech. Such freedom permits the advocacy or promotion of Communism or Socialism by peaceful means. But, the freedom does not authorize the violent overthrow of the government.

The Courts, have, therefore, upheld the authority of statutes passed by the legislature in order to prevent the overthrowing of government by violent means. All laws relating to the defence and security of the country, including laws for the prosecution of war, laws relating to constrictive recruitment and the maintenance of discipline in the armed forces, laws relating to foreigners including enemy aliens, laws relating to suppression of mutiny and internal rebellion, and laws relating to sedition, treason, espionage, official secrets, will be held to be constitutionally valid even if they impose restrictions on freedom of speech, provided the Court is satisfied that the restrictions imposed have a reasonable relation with the preservation of security of the state. Reasonable restrictions must be based on an intimate and proximate relation between the law and the security of the state.[190]

(b) *Friendly relations with Foreign States*

The state, can impose reasonable restrictions on the freedom of speech in the interest of friendly relations with foreign states. V.N. Shukla wrote that –

> 'it may be pointed out that it is a recognized principle of international law that States in their relation with other states are responsible for acts committed by persons within their jurisdiction.'[191]

In accordance with this principle, most modern systems of law have made provisions for the punishment of libels against the heads of foreign states. The English common law punishes such libels on the ground that they imperil the peaceful relations of Her Majesty with foreign states. Accordingly, a law which makes it an offence to publish any libel tending to degrade, or revile, or expose to hatred, or contempt any foreign prince, ambassador or other foreign dignitaries, will fall within this expression and will be held valid provided that the restrictions are not unreasonable.[192]

(c) *The Glory of Islam*

How does a legislature impose restrictions imposed by law in the interests of the glory of Islam? According to former Chief Justice Muhammad Munir (1895–1979)[193], the meaning one can attribute to this part of the Article is that no propaganda against Islam can be permitted.[194]

In this behalf, it was held in *Agha Abdul Karim Shorish Kashmiri v. Province of West Pakistan*,[195] that a speech in which it is alleged that a particular sect *Ahmadis*, in this case before they were declared 'non-Muslim' under the 2nd Amendment to the 1973 Constitution, is not a sect of Islam is covered by the constitutional guarantee of freedom of speech.

(d) *Decency or Morality*

The right of freedom of speech and expression does not extend to indecent or immoral utterances and publications. In other words, obscenity is not part of the permissible speech. There are few cases dealing with question of obscenity.

The Lahore High Court relied on *Hicklin* test in *Crown v. Saadat Hassan Manto.*[196] In this case the well-known writer, Saadat Hassan Manto (1912–55), had contributed a short story titled '*Thanda Gosht*' in an Urdu magazine called *Jawed.* The accused persons, Saadat Hassan Manto, editor and publisher, were convicted and sentenced under section 292 PPC (Pakistan Penal Code). In the words of Chief Justice Muhammad Munir (1895–1979), –

> 'judged by every standard of decency' the passage in question was 'definitely obscene.'

In that connection, he observed:

> 'It is true that morality and obscenity are comparative terms and what is obscene or immoral in one society may be considered to be quite decent and moral in another. But while considering the question whether certain words or representations are obscene or not, one has to apply standards that are current in the society in which those words have been uttered or anywhere else in the civilized world, there can be no doubt that a description of the actions preparatory to sexual intercourse, however graphic or life-like that description may be, would be considered obscene.'[197]

It is to be noted, that what is obscene cannot be determined by the opinions of the majority of the witnesses, nor is the opinion of any particular witness a true test, whether a particular book/material is obscene or not. It is the duty of the Court to decide on the facts of each case, whether the material is obscene or not. Whether a picture/photograph/article is obscene depends upon surrounding circumstances and facts in each and every case.[198]

(e) *Public Order*

The phrase 'public order' is synonymous with public peace, safety and tranquility and is of local significance as distinguished from national upheavals like 'law and order' and 'security of state'. An act prejudicial to public order must affect the public at large. An act, which concerns only an individual and does not amount to an activity prejudicial to the public peace and tranquility cannot fall within the ambit of Article 10(4) and (7) of the 1973 Constitution.[199]

The phrase 'public order' or the preservation of public order is one of the grounds for imposing restrictions on the freedom of speech and expression. In *Begum Zeb-un-Nissa Hamidullah v. Pakistan*,[200] it was held that the Security of Pakistan Act 1952, Section 12 conflicts with Article 8 of the 1956 Constitution, embodying the fundamental right of freedom of speech and expression and therefore, is unenforceable after coming in force of the constitution. In this case, the petitioner, editor and publisher of an illustrated English monthly *The Mirror*, Karachi, filed a writ petition under Article 22 of the 1956 Constitution, in the Supreme Court of Pakistan, challenging the order of the central government made under Section 12(1)(i)(c) of the Security of Pakistan Act 1952, prohibiting for 6 months the publication of *The Mirror*, on the ground that the magazine, in its issue of November 1957, had printed under the caption '*MATTERS OF MOMENT*,' an article which was

> 'defamatory in the first place, and the second, trespasses beyond limits of legitimate comments and is of a nature which tends to bring or attempts to bring the Government into hatred and contempt.'

The grounds of attack of the impugned order were, first and foremost, that the life of the Security Act was extended 3 times by consecutive ordinances, which was not possible under the Constitution; and secondly, that Section 12 of the Act was void, as it violated Article 8 of the Constitution, embodying the fundamental right of freedom of speech and expression.

The Pakistan Supreme Court did not consider it necessary to decide the first objection because it found that Section 12 of the Act ceased to be operative on the promulgation of Fundamental rights. Chief Justice Muhammad Munir (1895–1979), held that –

> 'Unlike the other provisions of the Act to which... Section 12 does not require to the making of any order under this Section, the condition precedent that the person against whom action is to be taken should be likely to endanger the defence, or external affairs, or security of Pakistan or any part thereof, or the maintenance of public order in the Federal Capital. The powers of the Central Government, when it acts under Section 12, are circumscribed by no qualifications, limitations or conditions except that it should "consider it necessary or expedient to make the order". On this construction, the section clearly comes in conflict with Article 8 of the Constitution which guarantees to every citizen the freedom of speech and expression "subject to any reasonable restrictions imposed by law in the interest of the security of Pakistan, friendly relations with foreign States, public order, decency or morality, or in relation to contempt of Court, defamation or incitement to an offence"....
>
> The Security of Pakistan Act was a pre-Constitution Act, having been passed in May 1952 when no basic rights had been guaranteed by the Constitution and the government had absolute authority to restrict the freedom of speech and expression by securing legislation to enable it to act in the manner it considered expedient. After the Constitution; however, these powers no longer exist and neither the legislature nor the Government can impose any restriction on freedom of speech and expression except for purposes mentioned in Article 8. In this case, defamatory character of the publication was alleged, but neither that ground nor the ground "exceeding the limits of legitimate comment", nor the ground "bring or attempting to bring the Government into hatred or contempt" is to be found in the act under which action was taken. It is, therefore, obvious that, this action was taken by the Government in complete ignorance of the constitutional right to freedom of speech and expression and was therefore in excess of the authority possessed by the Government.
>
> Section 12 of the Security of Pakistan Act, insofar as it permits the Government to prohibit the publication of a newspaper for any reason whatsoever, has after the Constitution, become unenforceable and that accordingly action under that section could not be taken in the present case.'

The expression 'public order' is synonymous with public peace, safety, and tranquility. It signifies absence of disorder involving breaches of local significance in contradistinction to national upheavals as revolution, civil strife or war, affecting the security of the state. The state may, in the interest of public order, prohibit and punish the causing of loud and raucous noise in streets and public places by means of sound amplifying instruments; regulate the hours and place of public discussions and the use of public streets for the purpose of exercising freedom; provide for expulsion of hecklers from meeting and assemblies; punish utterances tending to incite breach of the peace or riot and use of threatening, abusive or insulting words or behavior in any public place or at any public meeting with intent to cause a breach or whereby breach of the peace is likely to be caused, and because all such acts would endanger public safety.[201]

In Pakistan, in *Khawaja Muhammad Safdar v. West Pakistan*,[202] the decision of the Lahore High Court that Section 2 of the West Pakistan Use of Loudspeakers (Prohibition) Ordinance 1963, requiring a permit from a Deputy Commissioner (DC), for the use of a loudspeaker in a public place was held invalid. The case seems to have been wrongly decided for the reason that a law may impose reasonable restriction to prevent loud and raucous noise in public place amounting to public nuisance. The expression 'in the interests of public order' does not mean 'for the maintenance of public order'.

There must be reasonable and proper nexus or relationship between the restriction and the achievement of public order. If the restriction has no proximate relationship to the achievement of public order, it cannot be said that the restriction is a reasonable restriction. The restriction must not be far-fetched, hypothetical or problematical or too remote in its relationship with the public order.

Subject to the condition of proximate relationship, the legislature is competent to pass a law permitting an appropriate authority to place anticipatory restrictions upon particular kinds of acts in an emergency for the purpose of maintaining public order.[203]

Contempt of Court

Article 204 of the 1973 Pakistan Constitution, and the Contempt of Courts Act 1976, make provisions and confer jurisdiction on the Supreme Court and the High Courts to punish any person who:

(a) abuses, interferes with or obstructs the process of the Court in any way or disobeys any order of the Court; or
(b) scandalizes the Court or otherwise does anything which tends to bring the Court or a judge in relation to his office into hatred, ridicule or contempt; or
(c) does anything which tends to prejudice the determination of a matter pending before the Court; or
(d) does any other thing which, by law constitutes contempt of the Court.

The constitutional right to freedom of speech would not prevent the Courts to punish, as contempt of themselves, spoken or printed words calculated to have that effect. However, judges have no general immunity from criticism of their judicial conduct provided that it is made in good faith and does not impute any private motive to those taking part in the administration of justice; it must be genuine criticism and not malicious or attempt to impair the administration of justice. 'Justice is not a cloistered virtue', said the Privy Council in *Andre Paul Terence Ambard v. Attorney-General for Trinidad and Tobago*,[204]

> 'She must be allowed to suffer the scrutiny and respectful, though outspoken, comments of ordinary men.'

The fundamental right to freedom of speech and expression allows people to express themselves about judiciary.

The contempt of Court has always been a delicate matter for the lawyer, litigant and the press. Anything published by them in any form having tendency:

(i) to interfere with the due course of justice
(ii) to prejudice the determination of a *sub judice* matter, and
(iii) to scandalize the Court, has always been punished as contempt of Court.

The first of the above categories do not pose any particular problem because by applying the test: whether the publication complained of was calculated to interfere with the course of justice in any substantial manner, it can easily be determined that contempt of Court has been committed. If the Court comes to the conclusion, by applying this test, that contempt has been committed it would punish the contemnor on the principle that the courts would not permit any one to poison the fountain of justice before it begins to flow. This test can very easily be applied to a set of particular facts found by the Court.

But, the real difficulty arises in the case of third category that is, scandalizing the Court means lowering the Court in general esteem or creating feelings of hatred or ridicule against the Court. The *St. James's Evening Post* case,[205] which came before Lord Hardwick Lord High Chancellor (1690–1764)[206] in 1742, classified contempt into 3 categories, one of the categories being the scandalizing the court.

But in 1899, it was declared by the Privy Council in *Mcleod v. St. Aubyn*,[207] that –

> 'committals of contempt of Court by scandalizing the Court itself have become obsolete in this country. Courts are contented to leave to public opinion attacks or comments derogatory or scandalous to them.'

In 1928, however, it was revived in *R. v. Editor of New Statesman*.[208] In this case, in an action for libel, damages in the sum of £200 were awarded against Dr Stopes, an advocate of birth control. The action was tried by Mr Justice Sir Horace Edmund Avory (1851–1935),[209] with jury. *The New Statesman* denounced the case by publishing the following remarks:

> 'The serious point in this case, however, is that an individual owing to such views as those of Dr Stopes cannot apparently hope for a fair hearing in a Court presided over by Mr Justice Avory and there are so many Avorys.'

The publication clearly imputed injustice, unfairness and partiality to Justice Avory for giving judgement against Dr Stopes merely because of his views on birth control different from Mr Justice Avory, though Dr Stopes was found guilty by the jury and not by the judge. Proceedings were taken against the editor of the *New Statesman* for contempt of Court. Objection was taken by the counsel for the editor that since 1899, committals for contempt of Court by scandalizing the Court have become obsolete, therefore, proceedings were incompetent. The counsel for the editor however, felt that the judges of the Court were against him. So, he submitted, that the editor had committed no contempt. He sought for excuse the article by reason of the haste in which it was written, and apologized humbly, if it were held to be a contempt. The Court was so pleased to hear this plea that they did not fine him, though, found him guilty of contempt. They only ordered him to pay the costs.

Under Article 204 of the 1973 Constitution of Pakistan, the High Courts and the Supreme Court, are empowered to punish any person who scandalizes the Court, or otherwise does anything, which tends to bring the Court or a judge of the Court into hatred, ridicule or contempt. On various occasions, a number of persons have been convicted by the High Courts for committing this category of offence. An outstanding instance is that of Syed Mohsin Tirmizey, who in 1964 was posted as a District and Session Judge at Dera Ghazi Khan. He had the misfortune of being placed under disciplinary enquiry at the instance of the High Court for –

(i) absenting himself from his station
(ii) submitting delayed annual reports, and
(iii) making insolent observations about Judges of the High Court.

In his reply to the show cause notice sent to the Chief Secretary, Government of West Pakistan, Lahore, he attributed to the Judges of the High Court 'mean machinations' and 'malicious prosecution', 'wreaking private vengeance through public offices' and described them as 'evil designers'. He was found guilty of 'a contempt of the grossest kind' for his attack on the 'impartiality and fair-mindedness' of the Judges of the High Court. He was sentenced to imprisonment, till the rising of the Court, and a fine of Rs 2000 by the Full Bench of the High Court. His appeal to the Supreme Court of Pakistan was dismissed. The judgement of the Supreme Court is reported in *Mohsin Tirmizey v. The State*.[210]

Invariably, the scandalization of the Court pertains to a decision or judgement of the Court. The contemnor imputes partiality, dishonesty, or unfairness to the Court in giving such judgement. In *Mohsin Tirmizey*, it was the administrative decision of the High Court, which was the subject-matter of the contempt proceedings. But, honest criticism of a judgment in temperate language and without any ulterior motive does not amount to contempt.

Accordingly, it was held in *Ashfaque Ahmad Sheikh v. The State*,[211] by the Pakistan Supreme Court that, it is true that judicial acts of judges are not above criticism. The members of the public may, in good faith, criticize judicial acts. This is their ordinary right of criticism. But, this right must be genuinely exercised, and not in pursuance of improper motive or malice, or in an attempt to impair or impede the course of administration of justice. It is in the exercise of this ordinary right of criticism in good faith that the judgments of Courts are often commented upon in law journals, and before higher courts in appeal or revision. But, where a person not only challenges the validity of the court's order in the loudest voice and in an insolent manner, on the face of the judge, but also, incites its disobedience, it cannot be held that he genuinely exercised the ordinary right of criticism in good faith.

The Supreme Court of Pakistan in *M. Inayat Khan v. M. Anwar*,[212] made the following observation while discussing 'fair comment' in the context of Contempt of Court law:

> 'While, in a civilized and democratic society, the need and value of a free and informed discussion of issues of public importance cannot be denied, it is also in the public interest that the administration of justice must be kept free from all extraneous influence so that public confidence in the independence and impartiality of the Courts is not impaired, and litigants are not deterred in any manner from seeking the enforcement of their legal rights through the Courts of justice, nor is the determination of their causes pre-judged or prejudiced by public utterances and newspaper publications. It is, therefore, imperative that a balance should be struck between these competing demands of public interest and public policy. It seems to the Court that this balance is adequately ensured by allowing fair comment made in good faith and in the public interest on the working of the Courts or any of their final decisions after the expiry of the period of limitation for appeal, if any.'

A 'fair comment' made in good faith in the public interest relating to a case decided finally by the Court is not contempt. This has not always been the case. An explanation was added to Article 204 of the 1973 Constitution, which was doubtlessly based on the previous state of the law, but surprisingly, when this article was totally substituted by General Ziaul Haq (1924–1988), by promulgating the Revival of the Constitution 1973 Order, President's Order No. 14 of 1985, the explanation was omitted. No other reason for this omission seems to be plausible, except that the explanation was unnecessary. Be that as it may, the principle of law remains as it always has been.[213]

In *R. v. Metropolitan Police Commissioner, ex parte Blackburn*,[214] the judgment of Lord Denning (1899–1999), Master of Rolls,[215] was attacked by Barrister Quintin Hogg (1907–2001),[216] in an article in '*Punch*' magazine. Mr Hogg was issued contempt of court notice and Lord Denning sitting in judgment in this case made the following historic observation:

> 'This is the first case, so far as I know, where this Court has been called on to consider an allegation of contempt against itself. It is a jurisdiction which undoubtedly belongs to us but which we will most sparingly exercise; more particularly as we ourselves have an interest in the matter. Let me say at once that we will never use this jurisdiction as a means to uphold our own dignity. That must rest on surer foundations. Nor will we use it to suppress those who speak against us. We do not fear criticism, nor do we resent it for there is something far more important at stake. It is no less than freedom of speech itself. It is the right of every man, in Parliament or out of it, in the Press or over the broadcast, to make fair comment, even outspoken comment, on matters of public interest. Those who comment can deal faithfully with all that is done in a Court of Justice. They can say that we are mistaken, and our decisions erroneous, whether they are subject to appeal or not. All we would ask is that those who criticize us will remember that, from the nature of our office, we cannot reply to their criticisms. We must rely on our conduct itself to be its own vindication.'[217]

The Supreme Court of Pakistan in *Yousaf Ali Khan v. The State*,[218] not only found the aforementioned test laid down by Lord Denning, Master of Rolls, as relevant in Pakistan, but also praised his judgment in unmistakable terms. Justice Dorab Patel (1924–1997),[219] In this respect said:

> 'The judgement is a milestone in the development of the law of contempt. Instead of limiting the exercise of the summary power of contempt to serious cases, it redefines the concept of contempt, sweeping away thereby the case-law which had become obsolete with changing times, and a question which arises for consideration is whether we should follow the view taken by one of the great Judges of our generation. As the development of the law must have reference to the conditions of society, in my humble opinion, the test laid down by "Lord

> Denning for determining what is contempt is obviously relevant in a country with a Constitution which enjoins the right of free speech".'

Justice Dorab Patel made similar observations as those of Lord Denning MR. He said:

> 'If respect for the Courts rests only on the law of contempt, then it is resting on foundations of sand. In the long run, if public confidence in the Courts is to be maintained, it must rest on surer foundations than the sanctions available to us under the law of contempt, and in the ultimate analysis, public opinion is the only sure foundation both for respect for the law and for maintaining public confidence in the Courts.

Writing to a Judge, after the case has finished, criticizing his judgment and imputing partiality to him was held by the Calcutta High Court not to be contempt of Court, *In Re: Sudhir Chandra Ray*,[220] and by Justice Shabbir Ahmad,[221] in *The State v. Abdul Latif*.[222] In *Andre Paul Terence Ambard v. Attorney General Of Trinidad*,[223] a soldier in Port of Spain had fired at his superior officer but missed him, and had been awarded a sentence of 8 years' imprisonment for attempting murder. In the same session, another judge had awarded a sentence of 7 years for the same offence to a person who had slashed an expectant woman with a razor and had seriously mutilated her. She was not even the person intended. Thereupon, a newspaper published an article, merely pointing out the absence of proportion in the 2 sentences. The Privy Council, holding that this was not a contempt of Court, made the following observation:

> 'The path of criticism is a public way; the wrong-headed are permitted to err therein; provided that members of the public abstaining from imputing motives to those taking part in the administration of justice and are genuinely exercising a right of criticism and not acting in malice. Justice is not a cloistered virtue: she must be allowed to suffer the scrutiny and respectful, even though outspoken, comments of ordinary men.'

It may be concluded by citing a philosophical observation made by Chief Justice M. R. Kayani (1902–62),[224] in *The State v. Abdul Latif* case. He said, –

> 'consider the effect on the mind of the Judge himself. We are human beings like others, and although we are constantly striving towards the attainment of an ideal, we are not all on the same philosophical level. When injustice is imputed to me in a private treatise, even though it be marked secret and not negotiable, I do get a throbbing of the heart, which, I hope and believe, is at no great distance from my mind; a feeling that there is at least one person who is dissatisfied with my sense of justice.'

Article 204 (Contempt of Court) of the Pakistan Constitution, is to be construed in conjunction with Article 19, thereof in a manner, which should deter the commission of contempt of Court, but, at the same time it should preserve and protect the freedom of speech and expression and freedom of press. A balance is to be maintained between the above two objectives.[225] In *M. H. Khondkar v. The State*,[226] Chief Justice A.R. Cornelius (1903–91)[227] held that, litigant and his counsel were entitled, in certain circumstances, to advance the plea of bias against a judge even in the face of a superior court, but, such a plea could amount to contempt if it was false.

In a case arising out of the banning of National Awami Party (NAP), the question of Prime Minister Zulfiqar Ali Bhutto (1928–79),[228] committing contempt of court was considered. He made a public speech in which he stated,

> 'We have now banned them, and this ban can under no circumstances be withdrawn. If the Supreme Court gives a decision to the contrary it is a different matter but even, then it will not be my decision. It will not be the decision of the people, and if in consequence of that decision, anything happens, the responsibility will be of the Supreme Court...'

A contempt application was filed against Mr Bhutto before the Supreme Court of Pakistan, which observed that in a parliamentary democracy, where a leader of a political party becomes the Prime Minister, it is not easy to define the exact source of his powers and functions. But, it is certain that his powers and functions are derived from the Constitution and must, therefore, be referable, to the Constitution. Neither, the Constitution nor any law can possibly authorize him to commit a criminal act or do anything which is contrary to law.

The immunity to Prime Minister cannot extend to illegal or unconstitutional acts. The Prime Minister is bound to obey the Constitution under Article 5(2) of the Pakistan Constitution, like every citizen. His powers and functions cannot possibly extend to committing contempt of court punishable under the Constitution itself, and thus, prohibited. His speech did prejudice the pending proceedings against NAP (National Awami Party), and also contained a veiled threat to the court. It amounted to contempt and was not protected by Article 248 (Immunity clause) of the Constitution of Pakistan. However, the Pakistan Supreme Court exercised restraint and did not punish the Prime Minister for contempt, applying the test as to whether the Court before which the matter is pending would be so influenced by the article or speech that its impartiality might be consciously or even unconsciously affected. The Pakistan Supreme Court regarded otherwise.[229]

(f) *Defamation*

Defamatory utterances are not within the area of constitutionally protected speech and writing, and freedom of speech and of the press does not establish an exemption from the common law liability for liable and slander. This part of the exception saves the law of libel and slander as well as that of defamation and criminal intimidation insofar as it relates to communication of threats to reputation. The privilege of freedom of press is not absolute or unbridled. The newspapers should not print any libelous or defamatory material because the society for which they cater has the right to maintain a minimum standard of decency and protect its members from publication of scandalous or obscene materials.[230]

(g) *Incitement to an offence*

'Offence' is defined by Section 3(37) of the General Clauses Act 1897, as –

> 'any act or omission made punishable by any law for the time being in force,'

and slightly differently by Section 40 of the Pakistan Penal Code (PPC). The principle, underlying this restriction is that the right of freedom of speech and expression does not extend to an incitement to commit an offence, whether the offence intended to be committed is major or minor, cognizable or non-cognizable. The legislature has the power to impose restrictions on the freedom of speech and expression, provided the court holds that the restriction imposed is reasonably necessary to prevent incitement to crime. The decision of this issue is of the very essence of the judicial function, and while deciding it what the Court has to consider is the nature, extent and duration of the restriction and its relationship with the avowed object, i.e., the prevention of the incitement to crime, and all the surrounding circumstances.

Leading Cases:

Certain leading cases decided by the US Supreme Court on the interpretation of freedom of speech and press are discussed below.

Schenck v. United States[231]

Charles T. Schenck, general secretary of the Socialist Party of America, was convicted of 'causing and attempting to cause insubordination in the military and naval forces of the United States,' in violation of the Espionage Act of 1917. The conviction stemmed from the Socialist Party's activities in printing and distributing leaflets attacking American participation in the First World War (1914–18) and urging young men to oppose the military draft.

Justice Oliver Wendell Holmes Jr (1841–1935), delivered the opinion of the American Supreme Court:

> This is an indictment in three counts. The first charges a conspiracy to violate the Espionage Act of 15 June 1917.... by causing and attempting to cause insubordination, etc., in the military and naval forces of the United States, and to obstruct the recruiting and enlistment service of the United States, when the United States was at war with the German Empire; to-wit, that the defendant willfully conspired to have printed and circulated to men who had been called and accepted for military service, a document set forth and alleged

> to be calculated to cause such insubordination and obstruction. The court alleges overt acts in pursuance of the conspiracy, ending in the distribution of the document set forth. The second count alleges a conspiracy to commit an offense against the United States; to-wit, to use the mails for the transmission of matter declared to be non-mailable, ... to-wit, the above-mentioned document, with an averment of the same overt acts. The third count charges an unlawful use of the mails for the transmission of same matter and otherwise as above. The defendants were found guilty on all the counts. They set up the 1st Amendment to the Constitution, forbidding Congress to make any law abridging the freedom of speech or of the press...

According to the testimony Schenck said, he was general secretary of the Socialist Party and had charge of the Socialist headquarters from which the documents were sent. He identified a book found there as the minutes of the executive committee of the party. The book showed a resolution of 13 August 1917, that 15000 leaflets should be printed ... to be mailed to men, who had passed exemption boards, and for distribution. Schenck personally attended to the printing.

On 20 August the general secretary's report said, 'Obtained new leaflets from the printer and started work addressing envelopes,' etc.; and there was a resolve that Comrade Schenck be allowed $125 for sending leaflets through the mail. He said that he had about 15 or 16 thousand printed. There were files of the circular in question in the inner office... Copies were proved to have been sent through the mails to men who had been drafted. Without going into confirmatory details that were proved, no reasonable man could doubt that the defendant Schenck was largely instrumental in sending the circulars about...

The document in question, upon its first printed side, recited the 1st section of the 13th Amendment, said that the idea embodied in it was violated by the Conscription Act,[232] and that a conscript is little better than a convict. In impassioned language it intimated that conscription was despotism in its worst form and a monstrous wrong against humanity, in the interest of Wall Street's chosen few. It said: 'Do not submit to intimidation,' but in form at least confined itself to peaceful measures, such as a petition for the repeal of the act. The other and later printed side of the sheet was headed, 'Assert Your Rights.' It stated reasons for alleging that anyone violated the Constitution when he refused to recognize 'your right to assert your opposition to the draft,' and went on:

> 'If you do not assert and support your rights, you are helping to deny or disparage rights which it is the solemn duty of all citizens and residents of the United States to retain.'

It described the arguments on the other side as coming from cunning politicians and a mercenary capitalist press, and even silent consent to the Conscription Law as helping to support an infamous conspiracy. It denied the power to send our citizens away to foreign shores to shoot up the people of other lands, and added that words could not express the condemnation such cold-blooded ruthlessness deserves, etc., etc., winding up, 'You must do your share to maintain, support, and uphold the rights of the people of this country.' Of course, the document would not have been sent unless it had been intended to have some effect, and we do not see what effect it could be expected to have upon persons subject to the draft except to influence them to obstruct the carrying of it out. The defendants do not deny that the jury might find against them on this point.

But it is said, suppose that that was the tendency of this circular, it is protected by the 1st Amendment to the Constitution of United States. Two of the strongest expressions are said to be quoted respectively from well-known public men. It may well be that the prohibition of laws abridging the freedom of speech is not confined to previous restraints, although to prevent them may have been the main purpose....

We admit that in many places and in ordinary times, the defendants, in saying all that was said in the circular, would have been within their constitutional rights. But the character of every act depends upon the circumstances in which it is done. ... The most stringent protection of free speech would not protect a man in falsely shouting fire in a theater and causing a panic. It does not even protect a man from an injunction against uttering words that may have all the effect of force... The question in every case is whether the words used are used in such circumstances and are of such a nature as to create a clear and present danger that they will bring about the substantive evils that Congress has a right to prevent. It is a question of proximity and degree. When a nation is at war, many things that might be said in time of peace are such a hindrance to its effort that their utterance will not be endured so long as men fight, and that no court could regard them as protected by any constitutional right. It seems to be admitted that, if an actual obstruction of the recruiting service were proved, liability for words that produced that effect might be enforced. The Statute of 1917 punishes conspiracies to obstruct, as well as actual obstruction. If the act (speaking, or circulating a paper), its tendency and the intent with which it is done are the same, we perceive no ground for saying that success alone warrants making the act a crime…

New York Times Company v. United States (The Pentagon Papers Case)[233]

In June 1971, Daniel Ellsberg (1931), a disaffected Pentagon employee, turned over to the *New York Times* a 7000-page top secret study titled '*History of US Decision-Making Process on Vietnam Policy*.' Excerpts from the study, popularly known as the *Pentagon papers*, appeared in the *New York Times* beginning on 13 June 1971. After the *Times* refused a request to cease publishing excerpts from the study, the Justice Department filed a motion for an injunction in federal court.

On Tuesday, 16 June 1971, Judge Murray Gurfein (1907–79)[234] issued the first federal court injunction against a newspaper in this nation's history. Three days later, a federal district court in Washington, D.C., refused to issue a similar injunction against the *Washington Post*. Thereupon, Judge Gurfein lifted the injunction against the *New York Times*. On appeal to the circuit courts, the injunctions were quickly reinstated. The US Supreme Court granted *certiorari* and heard the case immediately.

Per Curiam.

We granted *certiorari* in these cases in which the United States seeks to enjoin the *New York Times* and the *Washington Post* from publishing the contents of a classified study entitled '*History of US Decision Making Process on Vietnam Policy*.'

'Any system of prior restraints of expression comes to this Court bearing a heavy presumption against its constitutional validity.' … The Government 'thus carries a heavy burden of showing justification for the imposition of such a restraint.' … The District Court for the Southern District of New York, in the *New York Times* case, and the District Court for the District of Columbia and the Court of Appeals for the District of Columbia Circuit, in the *Washington Post* case held that the Government had not met that burden. We agree.

The judgment of the Court of Appeals for the District of Columbia Circuit is therefore affirmed. The order of the Court of Appeals for the Second Circuit is reversed, and the case is remanded with directions to enter a judgment affirming the judgment of the District Court for the Southern District of New York. The stays entered 25 June 1971, by the Court are vacated. The judgments shall issue forthwith.

Justice Hugo Black (1886–1971), with whom Justice William O. Douglas (1898–1930) joins, concurring.

… I believe that every moment's continuance of the injunctions against these newspapers amounts to a flagrant, indefensible, and continuing violation of the 1st Amendment…. In my view it is unfortunate-that some of my Brethren are apparently willing to hold that the publication of news may sometimes be enjoined. Such a holding would make a shamble of the First Amendment …

In seeking injunctions against these newspapers and in its presentation to the Court, the Executive Branch seems to have forgotten the essential purpose and history of the First Amendment ….

In the First Amendment the Founding Fathers gave the free press the protection it must have to fulfill its essential role in our democracy. The press was to serve the governed, not the governors. The Government's power to censor the press was abolished so that the press would remain forever free to censure the Government. The press was protected so that it could bare the secrets of government and inform the people. Only a free and unrestrained press can effectively expose deception in government. And paramount among the responsibilities of a free press is the duty to prevent any part of the government from deceiving the people and sending them off to distant lands to die of foreign fevers and foreign shot and shell. In my view, far from deserving condemnation for their courageous reporting, the *New York Times*, the *Washington Post*, and other newspapers should be commended for serving the purpose that the Founding Fathers saw so clearly. In revealing the workings of government that led to the Vietnam war, the newspapers nobly did precisely that which the Founders hoped and trusted they would do ….

[W]e are asked to hold that despite the 1st Amendment's emphatic command, the Executive Branch, the Congress, and the Judiciary can make laws enjoining publication of current news and abridging freedom of the press in the name of 'national security.' The Government does not even attempt to rely on any act of Congress, Instead it makes the bold and dangerously far-reaching contention that the courts should take it upon themselves to 'make' a law abridging freedom of the press in the name of equity, presidential power, and national security, even when the representatives of the people in Congress have adhered to the command of the 1st Amendment and refused to make such a law...

To find that the President has 'inherent power' to halt the publication of news by resorting to the courts would wipe out the First Amendment and destroy the fundamental liberty and security of the very people the Government hopes to make 'secure.' No one can read the history of the adoption of the First Amendment without being convinced beyond any doubt that it was injunctions like those sought here that James Madison and his collaborators intended to outlaw in this Nation for all time.

The word 'security' is a broad, vague generality whose contours should not be invoked to abrogate the fundamental law embodied in the First Amendment. The guarding of military and diplomatic secrets at the expense of informed representative government provides no real security for our Republic. The Framers of the First Amendment, fully aware of both the need to defend a new nation and the abuses of the English and Colonial Governments, sought to give this new society strength and security by providing that freedom of speech, press, religion, arid assembly should not be abridged....

Justice Douglas, with whom Justice Black joins, concurring:

... The Government says that it has inherent powers to go into court and obtain an injunction to protect the national interest, which, in this case is alleged to be national security. *Near v. Minnesota* (1931)[235] ... repudiated that expansive doctrine in no uncertain terms.

The dominant purpose of the First Amendment was to prohibit the widespread practice of governmental suppression of embarrassing information. It is common knowledge that the First Amendment was adopted against the widespread use of the common law of seditious libel to punish the dissemination of material that is embarrassing to the powers-that-be ... The present cases will, I think, go down in history as the most dramatic illustration of that principle. A debate of large proportions goes on in the Nation over our posture in Vietnam. That debate antedated the disclosure of the contents of the present documents. The latter are highly relevant to the debate in progress.

Secrecy in government is fundamentally antidemocratic, perpetuating bureaucratic errors. Open debate and discussion of public issues are vital to our national health. On public questions there should be 'uninhibited, robust, and wide-open' debate.

Justice William J. Brennan Jr (1906–97), concurring:

... I write separately in these cases only to emphasize what should be apparent: that our judgments in the present cases may not be taken to indicate the propriety, in the future, of issuing temporary stays and restraining orders to block the publication of material sought to be suppressed by the Government. So far as I can determine, never before has the United States sought to enjoin a newspaper from publishing information in its possession. The relative novelty of the question presented, the necessary haste with which decisions were reached, the magnitude of the interests asserted, and the fact that all the parties have concentrated their arguments upon the question whether permanent restraints were proper may have justified at least some of the restraints heretofore imposed in these cases. Certainly, it is difficult to fault the several courts below for seeking to assure that the issues here involved were preserved for ultimate review by this Court. But even if it be assumed that some of the interim restraints were proper in the two cases before us, that assumption has no bearing upon the propriety of similar judicial action in the future. To begin with, there has now been ample time for reflection and judgment; whatever values there may be in the preservation of novel questions for appellate review may not support any restraints in the future. More important, the 1st Amendment stands as an absolute bar to the imposition of judicial restraints in circumstances of the kind presented by these cases ...

The error that has pervaded these cases from the outset was the granting of any injunctive relief whatsoever, interim or otherwise. The entire thrust of the Government's claim throughout these cases has been that publication of the material sought to be enjoined 'could,' or 'might,' or 'may' prejudice the national interest in various ways. But the First Amendment tolerates absolutely no prior judicial restraints of the press predicated upon surmise or conjecture that untoward consequences may result.

Chief Justice Warren E. Burger (1907–95), dissenting.

... I suggest ... these cases have been conducted in unseemly haste... The chronology of events demonstrating the hectic pressures under which these cases have been processed, and I need not restate them. The prompt setting of these cases reflects our universal abhorrence of prior restraint. But prompt judicial action does not mean unjudicial haste.

Here, moreover, the frenetic haste is due in large part to the manner in which the *Times* proceeded from the date it obtained the purloined documents. It seems reasonably clear now that the haste precluded reasonable and deliberate judicial treatment of these cases and was not warranted. The precipitate action of this Court aborting trials not yet completed is not the kind of judicial conduct that ought to attend the disposition of a great issue.

The newspapers make a derivative claim under the First Amendment; they denominate this right as the public 'right to know'; by implication, the *Times* asserts a sole trusteeship of that right by virtue of its journalistic 'scoop.' The right is asserted as an absolute. Of course, the First Amendment right itself is not an absolute, as Justice Oliver Wendell Holmes Jr so long ago pointed out in his aphorism concerning the right to shout 'fire' in a crowded theater if there was no fire. There are other exceptions, some of which Chief Justice Charles Evans Hughes mentioned by way of example in *Near v. Minnesota*. There are no doubt other exceptions no one has had occasion to describe or discuss. Conceivably such exceptions may be lurking in these cases and, would have been flushed had they been properly considered in the trial courts, free from unwarranted deadlines and frenetic pressures. An issue of this importance should be tried and heard in a judicial atmosphere conducive to thoughtful, reflective deliberation, especially when haste, in terms of hours, is unwarranted in light of the long period the *Times*, by its own choice, deferred publication.

It is not disputed that the *Times* has had unauthorized possession of the documents for 3 to 4 months, during which it has had its expert analysts studying them, presumably digesting them and preparing the material for publication. During all of this time, the *Times*, presumably in its capacity as trustee of the public's 'right to know,' had held up publication for purposes it considered proper, and thus public knowledge was delayed. No doubt this was for a good reason; the analysis of 7000 pages of complex material drawn from a vastly greater volume of material would inevitably take time, and the writing of good news stories takes time. But why should the United States Government, from whom this information was illegally acquired by someone, along with all the counsel, trial judges, and appellate judges be placed under needless pressure? After these months of deferral, the alleged 'right to know' has somehow and suddenly become a right that must be vindicated instanter.

Would it have been unreasonable, since the newspaper could anticipate the Government's objections to release of secret material, to give the Government an opportunity to review the entire collection and determine whether agreement could be reached on publication? Stolen or not, if security was not, in fact, jeopardized, much of the material could no doubt have been declassified, since it spans a period ending in 1968. With such an approach—one that great newspapers have in the past practiced and stated editorially to be the duty of an honorable press—the newspapers and Government might well have narrowed the area of disagreement as to what was and was not publishable, leaving the remainder to be resolved in orderly litigation, if necessary. To me it is hardly believable that a newspaper long regarded as a great institution in American life would fail to perform one of the basic and simple duties of every citizen with respect to the discovery or possession of stolen property or secret government documents. That duty, I had thought—perhaps naively—was to report forthwith, to responsible public officers. This duty rests on taxi drivers, Justices and the *New York Times*. The course followed by the *Times*, whether so calculated or not, removed any possibility of orderly litigation of the issues. If the action of the judges up to now has been correct, that result is sheer happenstance ...

Roth v. United States[236]

The US Supreme Court in *Roth v. United States*, along with its companion case *Alberts v. California*,[237] sustained the validity of federal and state obscenity laws without reaching the question of whether any particular materials to which the laws were applied were obscene.

Samuel Roth (1893–1974), a New York publisher and seller, was convicted of mailing obscene advertising and an obscene book in violation of a federal statute barring the mailing of 'obscenity.' David Alberts, who ran a mail order business, was convicted under a California law for 'lewdly keeping for sale obscene and indecent books' and 'publishing an obscene advertisement of them.

Justice William J. Brennan Jr delivered the opinion of the Court.

The dispositive question is whether obscenity is utterance within the area of protected speech and press. Although, this is the first time the question has been squarely presented [here], expressions found in numerous opinions indicate that this Court has always assumed that obscenity is not protected by the freedoms of speech and press.

In light of history, it is apparent that the unconditional phrasing of the 1st Amendment was not intended to protect every utterance. [T]here is sufficiently contemporaneous evidence to show that obscenity [like libel law, *see also Beauharnais v. Illinois*[238]] was outside the protection intended for speech and [press].

All ideas having even the slightest redeeming social importance—unorthodox ideas, controversial ideas, even ideas hateful to the prevailing climate of opinion—have the full protection of the guaranties, unless excludable because they encroach upon the limited area of more important interests. But implicit in the history of the 1st Amendment is the rejection of obscenity as utterly without redeeming social importance. This rejection for that reason is mirrored in the universal judgment that obscenity should be restrained, reflected in the international agreement of over 50 nations, in the obscenity laws of all of the 48 States, and in the 20 obscenity laws enacted by the Congress from 1842 to 1956. This is the same judgment expressed [in *Chaplinsky v. New Hampshire*[239]]. [We] hold that obscenity is not within the area of constitutionally protected speech or press.

It is strenuously urged that these obscenity statutes offend the constitutional guaranties because they punish incitation to impure sexual *thoughts*, not shown to be related to any overt antisocial conduct which is or may be incited in the persons stimulated to such *thoughts*.

[It] is insisted that the constitutional guaranties are violated because convictions may be had without proof either that obscene material will perceptibly create a clear and present danger of antisocial conduct, or will probably induce its recipients to such conduct.

However, sex and obscenity are not synonymous. Obscene material is material which deals with sex in a manner appealing to prurient interest. The portrayal of sex, e.g., in art, literature and scientific works, is not itself sufficient reason to deny material the constitutional protection of freedom of speech and press. Sex, a great and mysterious motive force in human life, has indisputably been a subject of absorbing interest to mankind through the ages; it is one of the vital problems of human interest and public [concern].

The fundamental freedoms of speech and press [are] indispensable to [our free society's] continued growth. [It] is therefore vital that the standards for judging obscenity safeguard the protection of freedom of speech and press for material which does not treat sex in a manner appealing to prurient interest.

The early leading standard of obscenity allowed material to be judged merely by the effect of an isolated excerpt upon particularly susceptible persons. *Regina v. Hicklin*, (*[1868] L.R. 3 Q.B. 360* [which defined obscenity as material tending 'to deprave and corrupt those whose minds are open to such immoral influences']). Some American courts adopted this standard but later decisions have rejected it and substituted this test:

> whether to the average person, applying contemporary community standards, the dominant theme of the material taken as a whole, appeals to prurient interest.

The *Hicklin* test, judging obscenity by the effect of isolated passages upon the most susceptible persons, might well encompass material legitimately treating with sex, and so it must be rejected as unconstitutionally restrictive of the freedoms of speech and press. On the other hand, the substituted standard provides safeguards adequate to withstand the charge of constitutional infirmity.

Both trial courts below sufficiently followed the proper [standard]. [W]e hold, that these statutes, applied according to the proper standard for judging obscenity, do not offend constitutional safeguards against convictions based upon protected material, or fail to give men in acting adequate notice of what is [prohibited].

Affirmed.

Notes

1. *The Federalist Papers* was a collection of essays written by John Jay, James Madison, and Alexander Hamilton in 1788 to promote the ratification of the United States Constitution.
2. John Adams was a Founding Father and the 2nd President of the United States from 1797 to 1801.
3. Thomas Jefferson was a Founding Father and the 3rd President of the United States from 1801 to 1809.
4. Abraham Lincoln was the 16th president of the United States from 1861 until his assassination in 1865.
5. Otis H. Stephens Jr, John M. Scheb II, *American Constitutional Law*, (California, Belmont: Thomson/West, 2003), p. 428.
6. 268 U.S. 652 (1925).
7. Benjamin N. Cardozo served as Associate Justice of the US Supreme Court from 1932 to 1938.
8. 302 U.S. 319 (1937).
9. William O. Douglas served as Associate Justice of the US Supreme Court from 1939 to 1975.
10. 319 U.S. 105 (1943).
11. Hugo Black served as Associate Justice of the US Supreme Court from 1937 to 1971.
12. Supra Note 5, pp. 429–30.
13. 249 U.S. 47 (1919).
14. Oliver Wendell Holmes Jr served as Associate Justice of the US Supreme Court from 1902 to 1932.
15. 249 U.S. 204 (1919).
16. 249 U.S. 211 (1919).
17. Supra Note 5, pp. 432–3.
18. 250 U.S. 616 (1919).
19. Bolshevik, (English meaning One of the Majority), were member of a wing of the Russian Social-Democratic Workers' Party, which, led by Vladimir Lenin, seized control of the government in Russia (October 1917) and became the dominant political power.
20. John Hessin Clarke was Associate Justice of the US Supreme Court from 1916 to 1922.
21. Louis Brandeis was Associate Justice of the US Supreme Court from 1916 to 1939.
22. 268 U.S. 652 (1925).
23. 259 U.S. 530 (1922).
24. 262 U.S. 390 (1923).
25. 268 U.S. 510 (1925).
26. Edward Terry Sanford was Associate Justice of the US Supreme Court from 1923 until his death in 1930.
27. 274 U.S. 380 (1927).
28. 268 U.S. 652 (1925).
29. 249 U.S. 47 (1919).
30. 250 U.S. 616 (1919).
31. 274 U.S. 357 (1927).
32. Charlotte Anita Whitney was an American women's rights and political activist, suffragist and Communist Party USA organizer in California.
33. 301 U.S. 242 (1937).
34. Supra Note 5, pp. 434–5.
35. 341 U.S. 494 (1951).
36. Smith Act, formally Alien Registration Act of 1940, US federal law passed in 1940.
37. Learned Hand was an American judge and judicial philosopher.
38. Frederick Moore Vinson was the 13th Chief Justice of the United States.
39. Felix Frankfurter served as Associate Justice of the US Supreme Court from 1939 to 1962.
40. Robert H. Jackson served as Associate Justice of the US Supreme Court from 1941 to 1954.

41. Hugo Black served as Associate Justice of the US Supreme Court from 1937 to 1971.
42. William O. Douglas served as Associate Justice of the US Supreme Court from 1939 to 1975.
43. 354 U.S. 298 (1957).
44. 367 U.S. 203 (1961).
45. 367 U.S. 290 (1961).
46. 367 U.S. 1 (1961).
47. 315 U.S. 568 (1942).
48. 403 U.S. 15 (1971).
49. 505 U.S. 377 (1992).
50. 508 U.S. 476 (1993).
51. Supra Note 1, pp. 438–9.
52. 315 U.S. 568 (1942).
53. 403 U.S. 15 (1971).
54. 655 N.W.2d 255 (2002), 250 Mich. App. 534.
55. American Civil Liberties Union (ACLU) is a nonprofit organization founded in 1920.
56. William B. Murphy was a judge on the Third District Court of Appeals in Michigan from 1988 to 2019.
57. 310 U.S. 586 (1940).
58. 319 U.S. 624 (1943).
59. 391 U.S. 367 (1968).
60. 383 U.S. 503 (1969).
61. Abe Fortas served as Associate Justice of the US Supreme Court from 1965 to 1969.
62. 394 U.S. 576 (1969).
63. 491 U.S. 397 (1989).
64. Supra Note 5, pp. 440–1.
65. 496 U.S. 310 (1990).
66. Sir William Blackstone was a British jurist, judge and Tory politician of the 18th century.
67. 283 U.S. 697 (1931).
68. Charles Evans Hughes was the 11th Chief Justice of the US Supreme Court from 1930 to 1941.
69. 403 U.S. 713 (1971).
70. 467 F. Supp. 990 (D.C. Wis. 1979).
71. 484 U.S. 260 (1988).
72. 393 U.S. 503 (1969).
73. Supra Note 1, pp. 430–2.
74. (1868) L.R. 3 Q.B 360.
75. 354 U.S. 476 (1957).
76. 378 U.S. 184 (1964).
77. 413 U.S. 15 (1973).
78. 383 U.S. 413 (1966).
79. 418 U.S. 153 (1974).
80. 481 U.S. 497(1987).
81. 521 U.S. 844 (1997).
82. 458 U.S. 747 (1982).
83. 535 U.S. 234 (2002).
84. 452 U.S. 61 (1981).
85. 409 U.S. 109 (1972).
86. 479 U.S. 92 (1986).
87. 501 U.S. 560 (1991).
88. 529 U.S. 277 (2000).
89. 561 U.S. 1 (2010).
90. Supra Note 5, p. 453.
91. 438 U.S. 726 (1978).
92. George Carlin was an American stand-up comedian, actor, social critic, and author.
93. Pacifica Foundation is an American left-wing non-profit organization that owns 5 independently operated, non-commercial, listener-supported radio stations.
94. 518 U.S. 727 (1996).
95. 468 U.S. 364 (1984).

96. 425 U.S. 748 (1976).
97. 447 U.S. 557 (1980).
98. The marketplace of ideas refers to the theory of speech therefore condemns censorship and encourages the free flow of ideas as a way of viewing the 1st Amendment.
99. 478 U.S. 328 (1986).
100. 517 U.S. 484 (1996).
101. 533 U.S. 525 (2001).
102. 433 U.S. 350 (1977).
103. 515 U.S. 618 (1995).
104. 533 U.S. 405 (2001).
105. Supra Note 1, pp. 455–7.
106. C. Gordon Post, *Significant Cases in British Constitutional Law,* (New York: The Liberal Arts Press, 1957), pp. 205–6.
107. (1981) Q.B. 202.
108. (1972) 2 Q.B. 169.
109. (1954) All E.R. 741 (C.C.A.), (1954) 2 QB 16.
110. (1868) L.R. 3 Q.B. 360.
111. A.G. Chaudhry, *Lectures on Constitutional Law,* (Lahore: Irfan Law Book House, 1994), pp. 178–80.
112. *Romesh Thappar v. State of Madras,* AIR 1950 SC 124; *Life Insurance Corpn. of India v. Prof. Manubhai D. Shah,* (1992) 3 SCC 637.
113. *W.N. Srinivasa Bhat v. State of Madras,* AIR 1931 Mad. 70.
114. *In re: Noise Pollution v. Unknown,* AIR 2005 SC 3136, (2005) 5 SCC 733.
115. *PUCL v. Union of India,* AIR 2003 S.C. 2363, (2003) 4 SCC 399.
116. *Indian Express Newspaper v. Union of India,* (1985) 1 SCC 641.
117. AIR 1982 SC 6.
118. AIR 1999 SC 1379.
119. (1992) 3 SCC 637.
120. *Bijoe Emmanuel v. State of Kerala* (1986) 3 SCC 615.
121. (1995) 2 SCC 161.
122. All India Radio (AIR), officially known since 1957 as *Akashvani* ('Voice from the Sky'), is the national public radio broadcaster of India.
123. B.P. Jeevan Reddy was a Judge of Supreme Court of India from 1991 to 1997.
124. J.N. Pandey, *Constititutional Law of India,* 38th ed., (Allahabad: Central Law Agency, 2002), pp. 155–9.
125. (1995) 5 SCC 139.
126. AIR 1960 SC 554.
127. AIR 1997 SC 568.
128. AIR 1998 SC 184.
129. Literally means shutting down, it is a form of protest used by political activists. It is similar to a general strike.
130. AIR 1978 SC 597.
131. *Brij Bhushan v. State of Delhi,* AIR 1950 SC 129.
132. Dr Ambedkar's Speech in Constituent Assembly Debates, VII, 7.65.168.
133. (1985) 1 SCC 641.
134. (1994) 2 SCC 434.
135. AIR 1950 SC 129.
136. *Virendra v. State of Punjab,* AIR 1957 SC 896.
137. AIR 1958 SC 578.
138. AIR 1950 SC 124.
139. AIR 1962 S.C. 305.
140. AIR 1973 SC 106.
141. (1985) 1 SCC 641.
142. (1986)1 SCC 133.
143. (1988) 3 SCC 410.
144. AIR 1957 S.C. 896.
145. (1994) 6 SCC 632.
146. AIR 1973 S.C. 106, (1972) 2 SCC 788.
147. AIR 1958 SC 578.
148. *Kameshwar Prasad v. State of Bihar,* AIR 1962 SC 1166; *O. K. Ghose v. E. X. Joseph.* AIR 1963 SC 812.

149. *O. K. Ghose v. E. X. Joseph*. AIR 1963 812; *Radhey Shyam Sharma v. Post Master General, Central Circle Nagpur*, AIR 1965 SC 311.
150. AIR 1971 SC 481; *see also Life Insurance Corporation of India v. Prof. Manubhai D. Shah*, (1992) 3 SCC 637.
151. AIR 1996 S.C. 1846, (1996) 4 SCC 1.
152. *Directorate of Film Festivals v. Gaurav Ashwin Jain*, AIR 2007 SC 1640, (2007) 4 SCC 737.
153. AIR 1950 SC 124.
154. *State of Bihar v. Shailabala Devi*, AIR 1952 SC 329.
155. AIR 1950 SC 124.
156. *Kanu Biswas v. State of West Bengal*, AIR 1972 SC 1656.
157. AIR 1972 SC 1749; *Dr Ram Manohar Lohia v. State of Bihar*, AIR 1966 SC 740.
158. *Om Prakash v. Emperor*, AIR 1948 Nag. 199.
159. *Noor Mohammad v. Rex*. AIR 1949 All 120, 1949 CriLJ 131.
160. *Om Prakash v. Emperor*, AIR 1948 Nag. 199.
161. *Basudeva v. Rex*, AIR 1949 All 513 (FB).
162. *Romesh Thappar v. State of Madras*, AIR 1950 S.C. 124.
163. *Brij Bhushan's* case, AIR 1950 S.C. 129.
164. *Raj Bahadur Goud v. State of Hyderabad*, AIR 1953 AP 277, AIR 1953 Hyd 124.
165. *Amir Hasan And Ors. vs Rex Through Ram Sarup*, AIR 1948 All 405.
166. *Ramji Lal Modi v. State of U.P.*, AIR 1957 SC 620.
167. AIR 1960 SC 633.
168. AIR 1954 SC 276. *See also* Patiala and East Punjab States Union (PEPSU) was a state of India, uniting eight princely states between 1948 and 1956.
169. AIR 1961 SC 884.
170. LR 3 QB 360.
171. AIR 1965 SC 881.
172. Sir Alexander Cockburn was the Lord Chief Justice of the Queen's Bench from 1859 to 1880.
173. AIR 1996 S.C. 1113, (1996) SCC 130.
174. *Radha Mohan Lal v. Rajasthan High Court*, AIR 2003 S.C. 1467, (2003) 3 SCC 427.
175. AIR 1974 SC 710.
176. *M. P. Lohia v. State of West Bengal*, AIR 2005 S.C. 790, (2005) 2 SCC 686.
177. *Dr Suresh Chandra Banerji v. Punit Goala*, AIR 1958 Cal. 176.
178. AIR 1952 S.C. 329.
179. *R v. Sullivan*, (1868) 11 Cox CC 44.
180. AIR 1942 F.C. 22.
181. AIR 1954 Patna 254.
182. AIR 1952 SC 955.
183. *Muzaffar Qadir v. District Magistrate*, PLD 1975 Lahore 1198 (1204).
184. PLD 1998 S.C.823.
185. PLD 1958 Lahore 651.
186. 1993 SCMR 1533.
187. *Ghulam Sarwar Awan v. Government of Sindh*, PLD 1988 Karachi 414.
188. *Schenck v. United States*, 249 U.S. 47 (1919).
189. PLD 1965 Lahore 642.
190. Supra Note, 111 pp. 187–8.
191. V.N. Shukla, *Constitution of India*, 10th ed., (Lucknow: Eastern Book Company, 2001), p. 114.
192. Supra Note 111, p. 188.
193. Muhammad Munir was the 2nd Chief Justice of Pakistan serving from 1954 to 1960.
194. M. Munir, *Constitution of the Islamic Republic of Pakistan*, (Lahore: Law Publishing Company,1976), pp. 154–5.
195. PLD 1969 Lahore 289.
196. PLD 1952 Lahore 384.
197. *Ibid* at p. 386.
198. *Naimat v. Summary Military Court*, PLD 1979 Lahore 279.
199. *Mrs Arshad Ali Khan v. Government of the Punjab*, 1994 SCMR 1532.
200. P L D 1958 Supreme Court (Pak.) 35.
201. Supra Note 191, p. 114–5.
202. PLD 1964 Lahore 718.

203. Supra Note 111, p. 191.
204. [1936] AC 322.
205. (1772) 2 Atk. 469.
206. Philip Yorke, First Earl of Hardwicke served as Lord High Chancellor of Great Britain from 1737 to 1756.
207. (1899) A.C. 549.
208. (1928) 44 T.L.R. 301.
209. Sir Horace Edmund Avory served as senior judge of the King's Bench Division in 1910.
210. P L D 1964 (W. P.) Lahore 434.
211. P L D 1967 Lahore 1231.
212. PLD 1976 S.C. 354 at 368.
213. Supra Note 111, pp. 197–8.
214. (1968) No. 2 ALL ER 319.
215. Lord Denning served as Master of the Rolls in Court of Appeal from 1962 to 1982.
216. Quintin Hogg, Baron Hailsham of St Marylebone served as Lord High Chancellor of Great Britain from 1979 to 1987.
217. Supra Note 214 at p. 320.
218. PLD 1977 S.C. 482.
219. Dorab Patel served as Justice of the Supreme Court of Pakistan from 1976 to 1981.
220. AIR 1952 Cal 258.
221. Justice Shabbir Ahmad was a judge of the Lahore High Court and later a judge of the High Court of West Pakistan. He retired as such in the year 1963.
222. PLD 1961 Lahore 51.
223. AIR 1936 P.C. 141.
224. M. R. Kayani served as Chief Justice of West Pakistan from 1958 to 1962.
225. *Masroor Ahsan v. Ardeshir Cowasjee*, PLD 1998 S.C. 823.
226. 1971 SCMR 743.
227. A.R. Cornelius served as the 4th Chief Justice of Pakistan from 1960 until 1968.
228. Zulfiqar Ali Bhutto served as the 9th Prime Minister of Pakistan from 1973 to 1977.
229. *Ch. Zahur Elahi v. Zulfiqar Ali Bhutto*, PLD 1975 S.C. 383.
230. *Majid Nazam v. Sheikh Muhammad Rashid*, PLD 1996 Lahore 410.
231. 249 U.S. 47 (1919).
232. In 1863, the United States Government implemented the Conscription Act, which was also known as the Enrollment Act.
233. 403 U.S. 713 (1971).
234. Murray Gurfein served as Judge of the United States Court of Appeals for the Second Circuit from 1974 to 1979.
235. 283 U. S. 697.
236. 354 U.S. 476 (1957).
237. 354 US 476 (1957).
238. 343 U. S. 250 (1952).
239. 315 U. S. 568 (1942)

22 Freedom of Association

Introduction:

Protection as a Fundamental Right

The US Supreme Court has expressly held that 'freedom of association' is a fundamental right protected by the First Amendment. Although, 'association' is not listed among those freedoms enumerated in the amendment, the Court has nonetheless declared that –

> 'freedom to engage in association for the advancement of beliefs and ideas is an inseparable aspect of the "liberty" assured by the Due Process Clause of the 14th Amendment, which embraces freedom of speech.'[1]

'Freedom of association' is regarded as integral to the freedom of speech, and assembly, and press, which is protected by the First Amendment. The US Supreme Court explained, that:

> '[e]ffective advocacy of both public and private points of view, particularly controversial ones, is undeniably enhanced by group association.'[2]

Groups have human capital and financial resources that a single person lacks. The Court has observed that an –

> 'individual's freedom to speak, to worship, and to petition the Government for the redress of grievances could not be vigorously protected from interference by the state unless a correlative freedom to engage in group effort toward those ends were not also guaranteed.'[3]

Additionally, the very existence of group support for an idea conveys a message. Association is also important as people benefit from being with others in many ways.[4]

Issues Concerning Freedom of Association

There are several issues concerning 'freedom of association,' like issue of compelled association, such as requiring employees to pay union dues or attorneys to pay bar dues. In addition, several questions of 'freedom of association' arise in the context of government regulation of campaign financing. Several questions concerning 'freedom of association' involve the 1st Amendment rights of government employees.

There are three issues concerning regulation of the 'freedom of association.' First, considers when the government may prohibit or punish membership in a group. Second, focuses on when the government may require disclosure of membership, particularly where disclosure will chill association. Third, looks at when 'freedom of association' protects a right of groups to discriminate.

Laws Prohibiting or Punishing Membership

When may the government prohibit or punish group membership?

Obviously, freedom of association is most directly violated when the government outlaws and punishes membership in a group. The US Supreme Court has held, that the government may punish membership only if it proves that a person is actively affiliated with a group, knowing of its illegal objectives, and with the specific intent to further those objectives.

For example, in *Scales v. United States*,[5] the Court affirmed the conviction of the chairman of the North Carolina and South Carolina Districts of the Communist Party of the United States (CPUSA), under the 'membership clause' of the Smith Act,[6] that made a felony –

> 'the acquisition or holding of knowing membership in any organization which advocates the overthrow of the Government by force or violence.'

The Court said, that earlier precedents had established that –

> 'the advocacy with which we are here concerned is not constitutionally protected speech, and it was further established that a combination to promote such advocacy, *albeit* under the aegis of what purports to be a political party, is not such association as is protected by the 1st Amendment.'

Justice John Marshall Harlan (1899–1971),[7] writing for the Court, said that the government's ability to prohibit such speech meant that it also had the authority to forbid associations to further these ideas and activities. Justice Harlan wrote –

> 'We can discern no reason why membership, when it constitutes a purposeful form of complicity in a group engaging in this same forbidden advocacy, should receive any greater degree of protection from the guarantees of the Amendment.'

The Court emphasized that Junius Scales (1920–2002),[8] was being punished for his active affiliation with the Communist Party, with knowledge of its illegal objectives, and with proof that he –

> 'specifically intends to accomplish the aims of the organization by resort to violence.'

In contrast, in *Noto v. United States*,[9] decided the same day, the court reversed a conviction for membership in the Communist Party of the United States of America (CPUSA), because of the absence of 'illegal advocacy'. The Court stressed that the speech was advocacy of abstract ideas, and that there was not proof that the individual had the specific intent to further any illegal activities.

Public Employment

The Court has applied this test for punishing association in many contexts.[10] For example, the Court has held, that the government may deny public employment to an individual based on group affiliation, or require that an individual take an oath concerning group affiliation, only if it is limited to situations where the individual activity affiliated with the group, knowing of its illegal activities, and with the specific intent to further those illegal goals.

In *Elfbrandt v. Russell*, the US Supreme Court declared unconstitutional a State's loyalty oath and law that prohibited anyone from holding office, if they were a member of a group such as the Communist Party of the United States of America (CPUSA).[11] The Court applied the *Scales* test, and said that it was impermissible for the government to punish individuals for being a member of a group without proof that the individual joined the organization knowing of its illegal objectives and with the specific intent to further them. The Court said that the law was unconstitutional because it –

> 'threatens the cherished freedom of association protected by the First Amendment.'

Similarly, in *Keyishian v. Board of Regents*, the US Supreme Court declared unconstitutional a state law, that denied employment as teachers to those who were part of organizations that advocated the overthrow of the government.[12] The Court emphasized, that the law punished mere membership in a 'subversive' group, without any requirement for proof that the individual knew of the illegal objectives or intended to further them.

Similarly, in *United States v. Robel*, the Court invalidated a federal statute that denied employment to individuals who were members of designated Communist group.[13] The Court explained that the statute created guilt by association because membership alone was enough to deny employment. The Court ruled that the government could deny employment to an individual only if the person was actively affiliated with a group, knowing of its illegal objectives, and with the specific intent to further those objectives.

Bar Membership

The same standards have been applied with regard to the ability of states to deny bar membership to individuals based on their group affiliations. In *Konigsberg v. State Bar of California*, the US Supreme Court held, that the government could deny bar membership to an individual who refused to answer questions concerning membership in the Communist Party of the United States of America (CPUSA).[14] But a decade later, the Court said, that the government may require individuals to answer such questions only if they are narrowly focused on whether the individual actively affiliated with a group, knowing of its illegal objectives, and with the specific intent to further those goals.

In *Baird v. State Bar of Arizona*,[15] and *In re Stolar*,[16] the US Supreme Court invalidated bar questions that asked, whether a person was or ever had been a member of the Communist Party of the United States of America (CPUSA), or any organization that advocated the overthrow of the government by force or violence. In contrast, in a companion case, *Law Students Civil Rights Research Council v. Wadmond*,[17] the Court upheld a bar question that asked, whether a person ever had joined a group knowing that its objective was the overthrow of the government by force or violence and, if so, whether the individual had the specific intent to advance those goals.

The difference among these cases is obviously the specificity of the questions. The inquiry is allowed only if it is narrowly focused on whether a person actively affiliated with a group that advocated the overthrow of the government, knowing of its goals, and with the specific intent to further them.

Laws Requiring Disclosure of Membership

The US Supreme Court has held, that the government may require disclosure of membership, where disclosure will chill association, only if it meets strict scrutiny.[18] In *NAACP v. Alabama*,[19] in 1958, the Court declared unconstitutional an Alabama law, which required that out-of-state corporations meet certain disclosure requirements. In connection with this law, State of Alabama required that the NAACP (National Association for the Advancement of Colored People) disclose its membership lists. The Court, in an opinion by Justice John Marshall Harlan (1899–1971), found the law unconstitutional and explained:

> 'It is hardly a novel perception that compelled disclosure of affiliation with groups engaged in advocacy may constitute [an] effective…restraint on freedom of association…. This Court has recognized the vital relationship between freedom to associate and privacy in one's associations…. Inviolability of privacy in group association may in many circumstances be indispensable to preservation of freedom of association, particularly where a group espouses dissident beliefs.'

Similarly, in *Shelton v. Tucker*,[20] the Court declared unconstitutional a state law that required that all teachers disclose their group memberships on an annual basis. The Court again stressed the impact of such disclosures in chilling constitutionally protected association. The Court explained:

> '[To] compel a teacher to disclose his every associational tie is to impair that teacher's right of free association. [The] statute does not provide that the information it requires be kept confidential…. Even if there were no disclosure to the general public, the pressure upon a teacher to avoid any ties which might displease those who control his professional destiny would be constant and heavy.'

Although, the Court recognized the government's important interest in having competent teachers, it concluded that the state cannot pursue the goal, –

> 'by means that broadly stifle fundamental personal liberties when the end can be more narrowly achieved.'

Campaign Finance Disclosure

A crucial aspect of many campaign finance laws is a requirement that candidates disclose their contributors. Such disclosures may adversely affect contributions. Nonetheless, the Court generally has upheld such requirements because of the government's compelling interest in stopping corruption, except where there is reason to believe that the disclosure will chill contributions to a minor party or candidate.

In *Buckley v. Valeo*,[21] the US Supreme Court upheld a provision in the Federal Election Campaign Act of 1971, that required that every political candidate and political committee keep records of the names and addresses of all who contributed more than $10. These records were required to be available to the Federal Election Commission (FEC), and for public inspection and copying. There is no doubt, that in some context people might be discouraged from making a contribution because of the disclosure requirement. But the Court found that the requirement served significant government interests. The Court said that

> 'disclosure provides the electorate with information "as to where political campaign money comes from"... in order to aid the voters in evaluating those who seek federal office.'

The Court also observed that the disclosure requirements discourage corruption and the appearance of corruption because of the "light of publicity." Finally, the Court explained that such –

> 'requirements are an essential means of gathering the data necessary to detect violations of the contribution limitations.'

The Court in *Buckley v. Valeo* recognized, that disclosure might have a particularly harmful effect on a minor party and –

> '[i]n some instances fears of reprisal may deter contributions to the point where the movement cannot survive.'

The Court said that for a minor party there was much less need for disclosure to prevent corruption 'for it is less likely that the candidate will be victorious.' Although, no such parties were involved in *Buckley v. Valeo*, but in *Brown v. Socialist Workers '74 Campaign Committee*,[22] the Court held that it was unconstitutional to require the Socialist Workers Party (SWP), to comply with a state campaign disclosure law. The Court applied its *dicta* from *Buckley v. Valeo*, and concluded that the Socialist Workers Party (SWP), was a minor party, that was historically unpopular, so that disclosure requirements would serve little purpose, and would likely chill contributions, and associational activity.

In *Citizens United v. Federal Election Commission (FEC)*,[23] the US Supreme Court invalidated restrictions on independent expenditures by corporations and labor unions, but once more upheld disclosure requirements. The Court explained –

> 'that disclosure is a less restrictive alternative to more comprehensive regulation of speech.... The First Amendment protects political speech and disclosure permits citizens and shareholders to react to the speech of corporate entities in a proper way. This transparency enables the electorate to make informed decisions and give proper weight to different speakers and messages.'

Laws Prohibiting Discrimination

Freedom of Association Generally Does Not Protect Discrimination

Many American States and local governments have adopted laws that prohibit discrimination by private groups and clubs. Frequently, challenges are brought to these laws by those wishing to discriminate; the claim is that freedom of association protects their right to discriminate and exclude whomever they want from their group. The US Supreme Court has held, that the compelling interest in stopping discrimination justifies interfering with such associational freedoms. The Court has indicated that 'freedom of association' would protect a right to discriminate only, if it is intimate association, or where the discrimination is integral to express activity.

Roberts v. United States Jaycees is the leading case.[24] The Jaycees,[25] a national organization of young men between ages 18 and 35, challenged the Minnesota Human Rights Act, which prohibited private discrimination based on characteristics such as race and sex. The Jaycees claimed, that 'freedom of association' protected their right to exclude women and to be a place where men associated with each other. The US Supreme Court reaffirmed that 'freedom of association' is a fundamental right and agreed that –

> '[t]here can be no clearer example of an intrusion into the internal structure or affairs of an association than a regulation that forces the group to accept members it does not desire.'

However, the Court said that 'freedom of association' is not absolute and that –

> '[i]nfringements on that right may be justified by regulations adopted to serve compelling state interests, unrelated to the suppression of ideas that cannot be achieved through means significantly less restrictive of associational freedoms.'

The Court concluded that the state's goal of prohibiting discrimination was unrelated to the suppression of any message and 'plainly serves compelling state interests of the highest order.' The Court found no evidence that requiring the Jaycees to include women would undermine its expressive activities and the Jaycees obviously was too large to be considered 'intimate association.'

Similarly, in *Board of Directors of Rotary International v. Rotary Club of Duarte*,[26] the US Supreme Court held, that it did not violate the First Amendment rights of the Rotary Club,[27] to force them to admit women in compliance with a California law, that prohibited private business establishments from discrimination based on characteristics such as gender. In *New York State Club Association, Inc. v. City of New York*,[28] the Court upheld the constitutionality of a city's ordinance that prohibited discrimination by clubs, that have more than 400 members, and that provide regular meal service.

The Court in these cases acknowledged that the laws interfered with 'freedom of association.' The Court, however, concluded that the government had a compelling interest in stopping discrimination that justified the infringement. Private clubs are places where business contracts are made, clients are recruited, and deals are done. If women and racial minorities are allowed to be excluded from these places, they will suffer in their careers.

The Court has recognized, however, that 'freedom of association' would protect a right to discriminate in limited circumstances. For instance, if the activity is 'intimate association' - a small private gathering - freedom of association would protect a right to discriminate. Also, 'freedom of association' would protect a right to discriminate, where discrimination is integral to expressive activity. For example, the Ku Klux Klan (KKK) likely could exclude African-Americans, or the Nazi party could exclude Jews because discrimination is a key aspect of their message.[29]

The US Supreme Court applied these exceptions in a very important decision: *Boy Scouts of America v. Dale*.[30] In *Dale*, the Court, in a 5 to 4 decision, held that 'freedom of association' protects the right of the Boy Scouts of America (BSA), to exclude gays in violation of a state's antidiscrimination statute. James Dale (1970), was a lifelong Scout, who had reached the rank of Eagle Scout,[31] and had become an assistant Scoutmaster. While in college he became involved in gay rights activities. James Dale was quoted in a newspaper article after attending a seminar on the psychological needs of gay and lesbian teenagers, and was identified in the article as the co-president of the Lesbian, Gay and Bisexual Alliance at Rutgers University. After reading this post, a scout official sent Dale a letter stating that he would no longer be able to participate in the Boy Scouts of America (BSA). Dale sued under the New Jersey law that prohibits discrimination by places of public accommodation. The New Jersey Supreme Court found that the Boy Scouts of America (BSA) are a 'public accommodation' within the meaning of the law and rejected the Boy Scouts of America (BSA) claim that 'freedom of association' protected their right to discriminate based on sexual orientation.[32]

The issue before the US Supreme Court was whether the Boy Scouts' desire to exclude gays, fit within either of the exceptions recognized in Jaycees. Since the Boy Scouts of America (BSA) are a large national organization, they could not realistically claim to be 'intimate association.' Instead, their central argument was that they had an expressive message that was antigay and that forcing them to include homosexuals undermined this communicative goal. The key question, then, was how to determine the expressive message of the Boy Scouts of America (BSA), and whether forced inclusion harms this First Amendment right. In answering this question, the Court held, that a group gets to determine its own expressive message, including during litigation, and that forced association undermines the expressive message of the group.

Determining a group's expressive message obviously is crucial in evaluating, whether discrimination is integral to it. The Boy Scouts of America (BSA), claimed to have an antigay expressive message, but as Justice John Paul Stevens (1920–2019)[33] pointed out in a lengthy dissent, there is virtually nothing in the organization's literature communicating this.[34] Justice Stevens carefully reviewed the Boys Scouts' mission statement, Handbook, and publications and found nothing expressing an antigay message. There is one line stating that Boy Scouts should be 'morally straight.' But, this obviously had nothing to do with sexual orientation when it was written. In fact, the Boy Scouts' literature instructs scout leaders and their assistants to refrain from discussing matters of sexuality.

Chief Justice William Rehnquist's (1924–2005),[35] majority opinion acknowledged that:

> '[o]bviously, the Scout Oath and Law do not expressly mentione sexuality or sexual orientation.'

But Chief Justice Rehnquist was willing to find such a goal based on the Boy Scouts' interpretation of its own words, such as its command that scouts be 'morally straight,' and from the position it had taken during litigation.

In other words, the US Supreme Court in *Boy Scouts of America v. Dale* essentially held, that during litigation a group can define its own expressive message. Chief Justice Rehnquist said that its failure to clearly state such a communicative goal in advance is not determinative:

> 'The fact that the organization does not trumpet its views from the housetops, or that it tolerates dissent within its ranks, does not mean that its view received no First Amendment protection. Even if it is assumed that the Boy Scouts had an expressive message that was antigay, there still must be a determination of whether stopping it from discriminating undermined this communication. The Supreme Court in *Dale* recognized that this is crucial to any First Amendment claim. Chief Justice Rehnquist explained: "The forced inclusion of an unwanted person in a group infringes the group's freedom of expressive association if the presence of that person affects in a significant way the group's ability to advocate public or private viewpoints."'

But James Dale being a Scout leader does not keep the Boy Scouts of America (BSA) from expressing and advocating any message that they choose. The Boy Scouts of America (BSA) can advocate any viewpoint it wants with regard to sexual orientation in its publications, its legal briefs, its legislative testimony, and its statements to the media. Chief Justice Rehnquist said that –

> 'we give deference to an association's view of what would impair its expression.'

Chief Justice Rehnquist explained that –

> 'Dale's presence in the Boy Scouts would, at the very least, force the organization to send a message, both to youth organization and the world, that the Boy Scouts accepts homosexual conduct as a legitimate form of behavior.'

On the one hand, *Boy Scouts of America v. Dale* can be defended as protecting 'freedom of association.' The Court upheld the right of a group to determine its members and its message. But critics, such as the 4 dissenting Justices, argued that the Court has opened the door to discrimination. Any group that wants to discriminate and exempt itself from state anti-bias law can do so by claiming, during litigation, that it has a discriminatory purpose. Moreover, critics argue that the Court erred in finding that requiring the Boys Scouts to include Dale would undermine their ability to express their antigay views.

'Freedom of association' is unquestionably a fundamental right, and one of its core aspects is the right of a group to choose who is in and who is out. But anti-discrimination laws seek to keep people from being excluded based on invidious characteristics such as race, gender, religion, disability, and sexual orientation. Enforcing anti-discrimination laws against groups that want to exclude on such grounds intrudes on associational decisions. Refusing to apply anti-discrimination laws on this basis compromises the commitment to equality. *Boy Scouts of America v. Dale* is certainly not going to be the Court's last struggle with this difficult question. *Dale* case, is important because it is the first time that the Court has found that 'freedom of association' protects a right to discriminate. Future cases will determine whether this is a limited exception or a basis for many groups to exempt themselves from anti-discrimination laws.

Freedom of Association in United Kingdom

In English law, 'freedom of association' includes forming and belonging to political parties, trade unions, societies and other organizations. A person is at liberty to join an association provided, it does not amount to criminal conspiracy under the Criminal Law Act 1977, or a tort of civil conspiracy, provided that the association is not organized to usurp the functions of the police or armed forces, or for the purpose of using force for a political object. It is important to notice that 'force' does not necessarily mean armed force. Conversely, no one is obliged by law to join any association against his will, although, in practice it may be impracticable for a person to get a certain kind of employment or to engage in a particular occupation or trade, unless, he joins a trade union or professional association.

The United Kingdom has ratified the International Labour Organization (ILO) Convention on 'freedom of association.'[36]

Right to Form 'Union' in United Kingdom

A union is an organization of employees, furthering the interest of workers with respect to higher wages, improved labour conditions and bettering the working hours of labour. In other words, it is a combination of workmen, for the purpose of securing by united action, favourable conditions as regards wages, hours and terms of employees by bargaining on behalf of the workers with the employers. A union may be a corporate body or an unincorporated body.

There were observations in two cases from the English jurisdiction, titled *Taff Vale Railway Co v. Amalgamated Society of Railway Servants*,[37] and *Bonsor v. Musicians' Union*,[38] to the effect that registration differentiates a union from other voluntary associations, in that a registered union may be entitled to be called a legal entity, while at the same time remaining an unincorporated society of individuals.

> 'As an association its membership is constantly changing, but as a registered union, it has a permanent identity and represents its members at any moment of time.'

In the *Bonsor v. Musicians' Union* case, Lord Keith of Avonholm (1886–1964) stated that calling it a legal entity would not be incorrect…

Freedom to Form Associations or Unions in India

Article 19(1) (c) guarantees to the citizens of India 'the freedom to form associations or unions.' Article 19(4) provides that the state may impose reasonable restrictions on the exercise of this freedom in the interest of 'public order,' 'morality' or 'the sovereignty and integrity of India.' The grounds of 'the sovereignty and integrity of India' was inserted in Article 19(4) by the Constitution (16th Amendment) Act 1963.

The right to form association may be said to be a corollary of the right to free speech contained in Article 19(1) (a). This freedom is as essential to democracy as the free discussion.[39] Or the freedom to meet for consultation with others.[40] It is the very lifeblood of democracy, for without 'freedom of association', no political parties so essential for the proper functioning of parliamentary democracy, can be formed. It is not merely for political purposes, but also, for the protection of other rights guaranteed by the Indian Constitution, that the 'freedom of association', is essential.

Scope of the Right to Form Associations or Unions

An association means –

> 'a collection of persons who have joined together for a certain object, which may be for the benefit of the members or the improvement, welfare or advantage of the public or some scientific, charitable or similar purpose.'[41]

It is a term of widest connotation. Therefore, the right to form associations or unions guaranteed by Article 19(1)(c) includes, the right to form companies, societies, partnership firms, trade unions, clubs, political parties and the like body of persons. It is the right of every citizen, to be a member of or to associate himself, with any organization, association, union, club, company or society.

Article 19(4) empower the state to impose reasonable restrictions in the interests of—

(i) the sovereignty and integrity of India;
(ii) public order; or
(iii) morality

The right guaranteed by Article 19(1)(c) must therefore, be read with Article 19(4).

Right To Be a Member Voluntarily

The right to form associations means, the right voluntarily to be a member of an association. It includes the right not to be a member or the right to continue to be or not to continue to be a member of the association.[42]

In *Damayanti Naranga v. Union of India*,[43] the petitioner was a member of the *Hindi Sahitya Sammelan*, a society, registered under the Societies Registration Act 1860, formed to promote and propagate Hindi language. Subsequently, Indian Parliament enacted the *Hindi Sahitya Sammelan* Act 1962, for regulating the affairs of the society. The Act changed the composition of the society, and introduced new members. The Act further provided, that the original members would continue to be the members of the newly constituted society. As a result, the members who voluntarily formed the association were now compelled to act in the association with other members in whose admission they had no say.

The Supreme Court of India held that the right guaranteed by Article 19(1)(c) could be effective only if it was held to include within it the right to continue the association/society with its composition as voluntarily agreed upon by the persons forming the association. The Court thus held, that the Act violated the right of the original members of the society to form an association guaranteed under Article 19(1)(c).

Right of the State to Nominate Members to Societies

It has been held that Article 19(1)(c) does not prohibit the state from making reservation, or nomination of weaker sections into the cooperative societies and their managing committees.

In *State of Uttar Pradesh v. C.O.D. Chheoki Employees Co-operative Society Ltd.*,[44] the Indian Supreme Court upheld the validity of the Uttar Pradesh Co-operative Societies Act 1965, and the Uttar Pradesh Co-operative Societies Rules 1968, which empowered the state to provide for reservation for or nomination of weaker sections into the co-operative societies and their managing committees. This power, the Court said, was contained in Clause (4) of Article 15, the object of which was to lift the prohibition of general equality guaranteed in Articles 15(2) and 29(2) of the Indian Constitution.

The Court explained, that though Article 19(1)(c) gave freedom to form association/society, but once a society/association had been registered under the Act, its management, under the Act and the rules, would be regulated by duly elected members. In the absence of the elected members belonging to the weaker sections and women, nomination of them by the government, was the alternative dispensation envisaged as one of the policies of the Act, in which matter, the Court would not interfere.

Earlier, in *Toguru Sudhakar Reddy v. Government of Andhra Pradesh*,[45] the Indian Supreme Court had upheld the nomination, by the government, of women, to co-operative societies, under the Andhra Pradesh Co-operative Societies Act 1964.

Right subjected to Reasonable Restrictions [Article 19(4)]

The right guaranteed under Article 19(1)(c) is not absolute. Article 19(4) specifically empowers the state to make any law to fetter, abridge or abrogate the right by imposing reasonable restrictions.

In *State of Madras v. V.G. Row*,[46] the respondent, the secretary of the People's Education Society, a society registered under the Registration of Societies Act 1860, challenged the validity of the Criminal Law (Amendment) Act 1908, as amended by the Madras Amendment Act 1950. The society was declared unlawful under the Madras Act. The Madras State Government could declare by notification in the Official Gazette, an association unlawful on the ground that –

(i) it constituted a danger to the public peace, or
(ii) interfered with the maintenance of public order.

The Government of Madras was required to give reasons for such declaration. The association so declared unlawful had the right to make a representation against such action within a reasonable period. The notification as well as the representation made by the association declared unlawful, had to be placed before an Advisory Board to be constituted by the government. The decision of the Advisory Board on the matter, as to whether there were sufficient grounds or not for declaring the association as unlawful, would be final and conclusive. There was thus, no provision in the Madras Act 1950, for judicial review of the order of the government. The respondents contended that the Madras Act 1950, imposed unreasonable restrictions on their right guaranteed by Article 19(1)(c).

The Supreme Court held the Madras Act 1950, as violative of Article 19(1) (c) as it had imposed unreasonable restriction on the guaranteed right. The Court said that the existence of the Advisory Board could not be a substitute for judicial inquiry. The test under the Madras Act 1950, was subjective satisfaction of the government, the factual existence of the grounds was not a justiciable issue, which made the restriction as unreasonable and hence violative of the right contained in Article 19(1)(c).

Right Not to be a Member of an Association

The right to form an association or union necessarily implies a right not to be a member of the association. In *Sitaramacharya v. Senior Dy. Inspector*,[47] a circular was issued requiring the teachers to join an association sponsored and recognized by the government at the pains of disciplinary action. The Andhra Pradesh High Court (APHC) struck down the circular as violative of Article 19(1)(c) and laid down that the right to form an association included the right not to be a member of an association.

In *Hazi Mohd. Ibrahim v. District School Board Malda*,[48] teachers were required to take prior permission to engage themselves in politics or to participate in political activities. The Calcutta High Court upheld the restriction as reasonable one. It was held that a teacher in service in a school is not merely a citizen but is also under certain terms and discipline of employment. The restriction was aimed at preventing teachers from getting involved with political institutions.

The right to form association implies the right not to form an association. But it does not follow that the negative right must also be regarded as a fundamental right. In *Ch. Tika Ramji v. State of Uttar Pradesh*,[49] the Uttar Pradesh Sugar-Cane (Regulation of Supply and Purchase) Act 1953, required that the sugar-cane growers could sell their sugar-cane to the sugar mills only through co-operative societies consisting of sugar-cane growers. Thus, a grower of the sugar-cane had to become a member of the society if he wanted to sell the cane to the sugar mills. The restriction was imposed with a view to ensuring fair price of the cane to the growers. The Supreme Court of India held, the Act as imposing reasonable restriction. It was held that the right not to be a member of the society had not been regarded as a fundamental right.

No right to continue in Government Service

In *P. Balakotaiah v. Union of India,*[50] the Supreme Court of India, distinguished between the right to be a member of an association and the right to continue in the government service. The Railway Service (Safeguarding of National Security) Rules 1949, enabled the Indian Government to terminate the services of government servants at their pleasure. The services of the appellant were terminated under the said Rules for his being a member of the Communist Party of India (CPI) and a trade unionist. The appellant contended that the termination of his service amounted, in substance, to a denial to him the right to form association.

The Indian Supreme Court held, that the order/notification terminating his services was not in contravention of his right guaranteed under Article 19(1)(c). The Court said that the appellant, no doubt, had the fundamental right to form association, but he had no fundamental right to be continued in the government service. The order/notification terminating his service, the Court held, did not prevent him from continuing to be a member of the Communist Party and a trade unionist.

The Indian Supreme Court reiterated with approval the decision in *P. Balakotaiah*, and upheld it in *M. H. Devendrappa v. The Karnataka State Small Industries Development Corpn.,*[51] the dismissal from service of an employee of the corporation, on the ground of misconduct under the Service Rules of the Corporation. The Court held, that a proper balancing of interests of an individual as a citizen and the right of the state to frame a code of conduct for its employees in the interest of proper functioning of the state, was required. Making allegations against various officers and making public statements against the head of the administration on a political issue, the Court held, amounted to lowering the prestige of the organization.

No Prior Restraint on the Right to Form Association

The state may impose restrictions on the right to form association, but the restrictions must not be unreasonable. In *O. K. Ghosh v. E. X. Joseph,*[52] Rule 4-B of the Central Civil Service (Conduct) Rules 1955, provided that no government servant would join or continue to be a member of any association or union not recognized by the government or the recognition of which had been withdrawn.

Thus, the right to form as association was conditioned on the existence of recognition of the said association by the government. The Indian Supreme Court struck down Rule 4-B as imposing unreasonable restriction, and therefore violative of Article 19(1)(c). The Court said, that the said Rule had made the guaranteed right under Article 19(1)(c) ineffective and even illusory. It follows that no 'prior restraint' on the right to form an association can be imposed.

No Right to Recognition by State

On the other hand, it has been held that the right to the recognition of the association or the union by the government is not a fundamental right. In *Delhi Police Non-Gazetted Karmchari Sangh v. Union of India,*[53] under the statutory rules, the government was empowered to revoke the recognition granted to an association. The recognition of the appellant association was revoked. The Supreme Court of India held, that the statutory rules regarding recognition and revocation of the recognition of an association were not violative of the right guaranteed under Article 19(1)(c), and that the provisions merely imposed reasonable restrictions on the right so guaranteed which were permitted under Articles 19(4) and 33. The Court further said that the appellants, the members of Police Force, came within the ambit of Article 33, which empowered the Indian Parliament to modify the fundamental rights in their application to certain forces charged with the maintenance of public order, and thus these persons stood on a different footing.

In *Ous Kutilingal Achudan Nair v. Union of India,*[54] the Supreme Court of India, declared that the civilian employees in Defence Establishment, answered the description of the members of the Armed Force within the meaning of Article 33, and therefore, they were not entitled to form trade unions.

In *Raja Kulkarni v. State of Bombay,*[55] Section 27 of the Industrial Disputes (Appellate Tribunal) Act 1950, was upheld as not impinging upon the right to form an association. The impugned section provided, that only a trade union with a certain percentage of membership would be allowed, to the exclusion of others, to represent the workers as a class before the Appellate Tribunal. It was held, that the right to form a union did not carry with it any right of every individual union to represent its members in an industrial dispute.

No Right to Achieve the Objects of Association

Again, the right to form an association does not carry with it the right to achieve the objects for which the association is formed.[56] Thus, the right does not include the right of the union to an effective collective bargaining or to strike either as a part of collective bargaining or otherwise. Such matters may be regulated by the appropriate authority. These matters are based on totally different considerations and provisions regulating these matters have not to be tested with reference to the criteria laid down under Article 19(4).[57]

Freedom of Association in Pakistan

In English law, 'freedom of association' includes forming and being a member of political parties, trade unions, societies, and other organizations. A person is at liberty to join an association provided it does not amount to criminal conspiracy under the Criminal Law Act 1977, or a tort of civil conspiracy, or that the association is not organized to usurp the functions of the police or armed forces, or for the purpose of using force for a political object. It is important to notice that 'force' does not necessarily mean armed force. Conversely, no one is obliged by law to join any association against his will, although, in practice it may be impracticable for a person to get a certain kind of employment, or to engage in a particular occupation or trade unless he joins a trade union or professional association. The United Kingdom has ratified the International Labour Office (ILO) Convention on freedom of association.[58]

Article 17 of the 1973 Constitution of Pakistan provides that:

(1) 'every citizen shall have the right to form associations or unions, subject to any reasonable restrictions imposed by law in the interest of sovereignty or integrity of Pakistan, public order or morality' and
(2) 'every citizen, not being in the service of Pakistan, shall have the right to form or be a member of a political party, subject to any reasonable restrictions imposed by law in the interest of the sovereignty or integrity of Pakistan and such law shall provide that where the Federal Government declares that any political party has been formed or is operating in a manner prejudicial to the sovereignty or integrity of Pakistan, the Federal Government shall, within 15 days of such declaration, refer the matter to the Supreme Court whose decision on such reference shall be final.'
(3) 'every political party shall account for the source of its funds in accordance with law.'

Both the Articles of the Pakistan and Indian Constitutions provide for the following three freedoms:

(i) freedom to form associations;
(ii) freedom to form unions; and
(iii) freedom to form political parties, though Indian Constitution does not specifically mentions the political parties.

The first two freedoms under the Pakistan Constitution namely, mentioned above are subject to reasonable restrictions imposed by law in the interest of sovereignty or integrity of Pakistan, public order or morality. But the third freedom, is subject only to reasonable restrictions imposed by law in the interest of sovereignty or integrity of Pakistan.

However, Article 17 further lays down, that the law that imposes reasonable restrictions –

> 'shall provide that where the Federal Government declares that any political party has been formed or is operating in a manner prejudicial to the sovereignty or integrity of Pakistan, the Federal Government shall,

> with 15 days of such declaration, refer the matter to the Supreme Court whose decision on such reference shall be final.'

The Political Parties Act 1962 is one of such laws which prescribe reasonable restrictions on the political parties. The provisions of Article 17(2) of the Constitution, and Section 6 of the Political Parties Act 1962, came up for interpretation in *Islamic Republic of Pakistan v. Abdul Wali Khan*,[59] before the Supreme Court of Pakistan. It was held, that the dissolution of a party takes place not on the declaration and publication by the Federal Government's satisfaction but on the decision of the Supreme Court given under Section 6(2) of the 1962 Act, and the dissolution by operation of law is merely in the nature of *ad interim* measure pending decision of the Supreme Court. Under Clause (3) every political party is under an obligation to 'account for the source of its funds in accordance with law.'

Freedom of Association

The right to form associations, unions and political parties for lawful purposes flows from the right to freedom of movement, the right to enter upon any lawful profession or occupation, the right to freedom of speech and expression, and the right to freedom of religion. What a person may legally do alone, he may do with the assistance and co-operation of others. Individuals have the right to organize themselves into parties and even into special groups to advance causes and to circulate their views and difficulties and to advocate their cause in public assemblies. It is only when people combine together for illegal purposes that the law prohibits their association and creates vicarious liability for acts done by others.

An association may take the form of a political party, company, an institute, a firm, union, society or club, or it may just be an association of persons. When persons combine together for a common purpose, they generally set out their aims and objects in a document and set up some sort of organizational structure to regulate their activities. They may associate for a political, economic or social purpose or their objective may be no more than the promotion of science, religion, art, literature, or charity. So long, as the purpose for which they associate is lawful, law imposes no restriction on their association.

The right to 'freedom of association' is, therefore subject to this important qualification that reasonable restriction on its exercise may be imposed by law in the interest of morality or public order or the sovereignty or integrity of Pakistan. Thus, associations, the object of which is to advocate or carry on some immoral purpose, e.g., gambling, or illegal activity, or overthrowing the government by unlawful means, may be prohibited by law. The dissolution of *Imdadi Scheme* companies by the Undesirable Companies Act 1958, was upheld by the Lahore High Court in *The Progress of Pakistan Co. Ltd. v. Registrar, Joint Stock Companies, Karachi*,[60] on the ground that the companies encouraged immoral gambling.

In *Syed Abul A'la Maudoodi v. Government of West Pakistan*,[61] Section 16 of the Criminal Law Amendment Act 1908, which authorized the provincial government to declare an association unlawful, if in its opinion it had as its object interference with the maintenance of law and order, was held to be an unconstitutional interference with the right of 'freedom of association' on the ground that the provision gives to the provincial government an arbitrary and unqualified power to declare an association unlawful, the making of the declaration depending upon the subjective satisfaction of the government. It was also held, that the question, whether a restriction is reasonable or unreasonable is for the court to determine and, in determining it, the Court has to examine not only the reasonableness of the law itself but also the reasonableness of the mode of application of the restriction, whether or not such mode be prescribed by law or not.

In *Nawbzada Nasrullah Khan v. Government of West Pakistan*,[62] it was held that a law which authorizes a District Magistrate (DM), to depute a person to attend a public meeting, for the purpose of causing a report to be made of its proceedings and direct the persons convening or conducting the meeting to admit the person so deputed, is an unjustified invasion of the right of free assembly and association. The right to form associations also implies that the persons forming an association have the right to continue to be associated with only those whom they voluntarily admit in the association. This right can be effective only if it is held to include within the right to continue the association with its composition as voluntarily agreed upon by the persons forming the association.[63]

Right to form Unions

The object of a trade union is to engage in collective bargaining; this is the object with which a trade union or association is formed by workmen or employees, just as, an association may be formed with a religious, cultural or educational object, by persons belonging to different groups inspired with religious, cultural or educational interests or ideas.

It was held by the Supreme Court of Pakistan, in *Civil Aviation Authority, Islamabad v. Union of Civil Aviation Employees*,[64] that union or unions of the employees of a statutory authority or a corporation can act as collective bargaining agent, which is inherent right in a union, but they cannot go on strike or to go slow in the absence of statutory backing.

Right under Article 17 is not absolute

The general right to form associations or unions under Clause (1) of Article 17, is subject to reasonable restrictions imposed by law in the interest of sovereignty or integrity of Pakistan, public order or morality and the right to form and be a member of a political party under Clause (2) of Article 17 is subject to reasonable restrictions imposed by law in the interest of the sovereignty or integrity of Pakistan. In other words, these rights are not absolute rights.

As to the connotation of the expression 'reasonable restrictions', ordinarily the power to impose restrictions is not a power to kill or destroy. In the context of Article 17, Clause (1), this view was expressly adopted in *Civil Aviation Authority, Islamabad v. Union of Civil Aviation Employees*.[65]

After referring to the ordinary dictionary meanings of the words 'restrict' and 'restriction', it was held that the predominant meanings of these words do not admit of total prohibition. They connote the imposition of limitations or the bounds within which one can act.

> 'It is, therefore, evident that under Clause (1) of Article 17 of the Constitution, there cannot be total prohibition, but the right can be regulated/restricted by law if any of the four ingredients is present.'

In this behalf, reference was made to the well-known case of *Jibendra Kishore v. Province of East Pakistan*,[66] where Chief Justice Muhammad Munir (1895–1979),[67] *inter alia*, said that –

> 'the very conception of a fundamental right is that it being a right guaranteed by the Constitution cannot be taken away by the law, and it is not only technically inartistic but a fraud on the citizens for the makers of a Constitution to say that a right is fundamental but that it may be taken away by the law.'

In *Islamic Republic of Pakistan v. Abdul Wali Khan*,[68] a reference made by the Government of Pakistan against the National Awami Party (NAP), which fell to be decided under Article 17, Clause (2), it was held –

> '... What is unreasonable in one given set of circumstances may well be reasonable in another different set of circumstances. In order to test the reasonableness of such restrictions, therefore, no general standard exists. It will depend upon a variety of circumstances including the interest and urgency of the action proposed and the nature of the safeguard, if any, provided to prevent possibilities of abuse of power. The investment of arbitrary power in the executive to put to an end to the existence of a political party on the basis of its own satisfaction which may or may not be capable of being proved in a Court of Law may well be an unreasonable restriction having regard to the importance of the right of association guaranteed by the Constitution. The safeguard that such a declaration by the Executive will be subject to the decision of the Supreme Court is, however, a sufficient safeguard of the interest of the political party and adequately protects it from being dealt with either arbitrarily or whimsically or out of political vengeance. This can, in so sense, be considered to be an unreasonable restriction.'

Compulsory registration of and rendition of accounts by political parties

Compulsory registration of political parties was struck down as violative of Article 17(2) of the 1973 Constitution of Pakistan, but the provisions regarding the rendition of accounts for the purpose of audit by the political parties was held to be in consonance with Article 17(3), which provides that every political party should account for the source of its funds in accordance with law.

This principle is illustrated by *Benazir Bhutto v. Federation of Pakistan*.[69] In this case, by a Constitution petition filed under Article 184(3) of the Constitution of Pakistan, the petitioner, Chairperson of the Pakistan Peoples' Party challenged the amendments made in the Political Parties Act 1962, as violative of Articles 17 and 25 of the Constitution of Pakistan. The *vires* of the Freedom of Association Order 1978 (President's Order No. 20 of 1978), was also challenged as being unconstitutional. She further challenged the constitutionality of Article 270-A of the Constitution of Pakistan as 'affirmed and purportedly validated' by the Constitution (8th Amendment) Act 1985, in so far as it curtailed the power to judicially review its content and restricted the jurisdiction of the superior courts to protect fundamental rights of the citizens including the right to form or be a member of a political party guaranteed under Article 17(2) of the Constitution of Pakistan.

It was further contended that the provisions of Article 270-A were repugnant to the provisions of Article 2-A of the Constitution of Pakistan, which relates to the concept of legal sovereignty in Pakistan and the independence of the judiciary. The Supreme Court of Pakistan accepted the petition and held that Article 17(3) requires every political party to account for the sources of its funds in accordance with law. The purpose obviously is to seek out foreign aided parties whose activities are prejudicial to the interests of sovereignty or integrity of Pakistan, as the source of funds provides a guideline amongst others, in determining the true character of a political party and the nature of its activities. The source of funds also reveals information of how the funds are collected, and identifies those who subscribe to it to assess not only the financial status of the political party, but that the funds are not collected in an unlawful manner. The words 'account for the source of its funds' would also include the expenditure as that provides a check for determining actual amounts received and disbursed in the context of the political activities carried out and whether the funds were being utilized for lawful political activities, or for promoting prejudicial activities against the sovereignty or integrity of Pakistan.

The rendition of accounts for audit, therefore, could not be regarded as an unreasonable restriction or outside the ambit of this sub-Article. However, the provisions of Section 3-B of the Political Parties Act 1962, requiring compulsory registration of political parties were held to be violative of Article 17(2) of the Constitution.[70]

Denial of election symbols to political parties

Election symbols allocated to political parties play an invaluable role, in a predominantly illiterate society, in identifying the political parties, their candidates, and the issues involved in facilitating the casting of votes by the voters.

Therefore, any law that allows the allocation of symbols to only individual candidates and not to the political parties is violative of a fundamental right 'to form or be a member of political party' enshrined in Article 17(2) of the 1973 Constitution, in so far as such law fails to recognize the existence and participation of the political parties in the process of elections, particularly in the matter of allocation of symbols and is, for that reason void to that extent.

This is the ratio of *Benazir Bhutto v. Federation of Pakistan*.[71] The facts of the case were that Section 21(1)(b) of the Representation of the People Act 1976, provided for allocation of prescribed symbols to each contesting candidate only, and no reference whatever was contained in the section to allocation of a symbol to a political party. Rule 9(2) of the Representation of the People (Conduct of Election) Rules 1977, however, provided that the –

> 'Election Commission may allot any one of the symbols…to any political parties who have agreed to put up joint candidates for election.'

Benazir Bhutto (1953–2007)[72] challenged the validity of the provisions of Section 21(1)(b), by filing a constitutional petition under Article 184(3) of the Constitution of Pakistan, in the Pakistani Supreme Court, contending that the Supreme Court had recently held in *Benazir Bhutto v. The Federation of Pakistan*,[73] that –

> 'citizens of Pakistan enjoy fundamental right not only of forming a political party but also of its functioning as such. This right necessarily extends to its participation at all stages of the constitutional process of elections culminating in the formation of the government in a parliamentary system.'

It was further contended that the provisions of the said Section 21(1)(b), were violative of Article 17(2) of the Constitution in so far as the provisions did not allow the allocation of symbols to political parties.

It was also argued that under Article 17(2) as interpreted by the Supreme Court of Pakistan –

> 'That every political party was eligible to participate in election to every seat in the Houses of Parliament or Provincial Assemblies, and to nominate and put up candidates at any such election under party manifesto, party ticket, party flag and party symbol and under the discipline of the political party nominating the candidates.'

It was pointed out by the petitioner Benazir Bhutto, that the Representation of the People (Conduct of Election) Rules 1977, has been left unamended. Which explains why Sub-rule (2) of Rule 9 still authorizes the Commission to allot any 'one of the symbols' specified in Sub-rule (1) to any political parties; who have agreed to put up joint candidates for election on an application made by it in 'this behalf'. This rule, according to the petitioner, was in direct conflict with Section 21(1)(b) of the Act where the Returning Officer has a statutory duty in case of a contested election to allot the symbols by drawing of lots.

The Supreme Court of Pakistan accepted the petition holding that –

(i) the provisions of section 21(1)(b) of the Representation of the People Act 1976, were violative of Fundamental Right enshrined in Article 17(2) of the Constitution in so far it fails to recognize the existence and the participation of the political parties in the process of elections particularly in the matter of allocation of symbols and is for that reason void to that extent, and
(ii) the obvious repugnancy between Section 21(1)(b) and Rule 9(2) can be resolved in favour of the former for, it is a principle of interpretation of statutes that repugnancy between a statute and the rules made thereunder must be resolved in favour of the statute.

Acts Completed and Continuing

In *Inamur Rehman v. Federation of Pakistan*,[74] the Supreme Court of Pakistan held that the Acts done and completed before the coming into existence of the Fundamental Rights cannot be re-opened on the ground of inconsistency, nor can proceedings already commenced be stopped.

But the position, would be different if the right was to be found to be still subsisting and capable of being enforced or there was something still left to be done to complete the extinction of the right after the conferment of the fundamental rights. Thus, if a person is detained under a law, which provides for preventive detention without trial, before the coming into existence of the fundamental rights, he would be entitled to challenge the detention order, if his detention continues even after the coming into force of the fundamental rights on the ground that the law under which his detention was ordered is inconsistent with the security of person guaranteed to him.

Where rights which were violated were still capable of being in force and there is something still left to be done under the impugned legislation after the restoration of fundamental rights, then the Court is bound to give effect to such fundamental rights.

Notes

1. *NAACP (National Association for the Advancement of Colored People) v. Alabama ex rel. Patterson, Attorney General*, 357 U.S. 449 (1958) at p. 460.

2. *Ibid.*
3. *Roberts v. United States Jaycees*, 468 U.S. 609 (1984) at p. 622.
4. The Court, however, generally has been unwilling to extend protection of freedom of association outside situations where it relates to First Amendment purposes. For instance, in *City of Dallas v. Stanglin*, 490 U.S. 19 (1989), the Court upheld a city ordinance which limited the ability of adults to gain access to teenage dance halls. The Court rejected a challenge based on freedom of association and emphasized that the restriction did not limit association for expressive purposes.
5. 367 U.S. 203 (1961).
6. An Act to prohibit certain subversive activities; to amend certain provisions of law with respect to the admission and deportation of aliens; to require the fingerprinting and registration of aliens; and for other purposes.
7. John Marshall Harlan was Associate Justice of the US Supreme Court from 1955 to 1971.
8. Junius Scales was leader of the Communist Party of the United States of America (CPUSA).
9. 367 U.S. 290 (1961).
10. *Communist Party of Indiana v. Whitcomb*, 414 U.S. 441 (1974), (declaring unconstitutional a state law that said that political parties could not be listed on the ballot unless they filed an affidavit that they did not advocate the overthrow of the government by force or violence); *Aptheker v. Secretary of State*, 378 U.S. 500 (1964), (declaring unconstitutional a law that prohibited the use of a passport by a member of the Communist organization).
11. 384 U.S. 11 (1966).
12. 385 U.S. 589 (1967).
13. 389 U.S. 258 (1967).
14. 366 U.S. 36 (1961). *See also in re Anastaplo*, 366 U.S. 82 (1961).
15. 401 U.S. 1 (1971).
16. 401 U.S. 23 (1971).
17. 401 U.S. 154 (1971).
18. *Communist Party of the United States v. Subversive Activities Control Board*, 367 U.S. 1 (1961); *New York ex rel. Bryant v. Zimmerman*, 278 U.S. 63 (1928) (upholding disclosure requirements).
19. 357 U.S. 449 (1958).
20. 364 U.S. 479 (1960).
21. 424 U.S. 1 (1976).
22. 459 U.S. 87 (1982).
23. 558 U.S. 310 (2010).
24. 468 U.S. 609 (1984).
25. The United States Junior Chamber, also known as the Jaycees, JCs or JCI USA, is a leadership training and civic organization for people between the ages of 18 and 40.
26. 481 U.S. 537 (1987).
27. Rotary is an organization of business and professional persons united worldwide who provide humanitarian service, encourage high ethical standards in all vocations and help build goodwill and peace in the world.
28. 487 U.S. 1 (1988).
29. In *Hurley v. Irish-American Gay, Lesbian, and Bisexual Group of Boston*, 515 U.S. 557 (1995), the Court held that a private group that organized a St. Patrick's Day Parade could exclude a gay, lesbian and bisexual group from participation. The unanimous decision said that organizing a parade is an inherently expressive activity and those doing so have a right to exclude messages inimical to their own.
30. 530 U.S. 640 (2000).
31. Eagle Scout is the highest achievement or rank attainable in the Scouts BSA program of the Boy Scouts of America (BSA).
32. 160 N.J. 562; 734 A. 2nd 1196 (1999).
33. John Paul Stevens was Associate Justice of the US Supreme Court from 1975 to 2010.
34. 530 U.S. 640 (2000) at 665–671 (Justice John P. Stevens, dissenting).
35. William Rehnquist was the 16th Chief Justice of the United States from 1986 to 2005.
36. A.G. Chaudhry, *Lectures on Constitutional Law*, (Lahore: Irfan Law Book House, 1994), p. 159.
37. (1901) AC 426, 442.
38. (1956) AC 104; (1955) 3 All ER 518.
39. *Thornhill v. Alabama*, 310 U.S. 88 (1940).
40. *United States v. Cruikshank*, 92 U.S. 542 (1875).
41. Narinder Kumar, *Constitutional Law of India*. 3rd ed.(Delhi: Pioneer Publications, 2002), pp. 191–2.
42. *Raja Suryapal Singh v. State of U.P.*, AIR 1951 All 674.
43. AIR 1971 SC 966.
44. AIR 1997 SC 1413, (1997)3 SCC 681.

45. AIR 1994 SC 544, (1993) Supp (4) SCC 439.
46. AIR 1952 SC 196.
47. AIR 1958 AP 78.
48. AIR 1958 Cal 401.
49. AIR 1956 SC 676.
50. AIR 1958 SC 232.
51. AIR 1998 SC 1064.
52. AIR 1963 SC 812.
53. AIR 1987 SC 379, (1987) 1 SCC 115.
54. AIR 1976 SC 1179.
55. AIR 1954 S.C. 73.
56. *All India Bank Employees Association v. National Industrial Tribunal*, AIR 1962 SC 171; *Raghubar Dayal Jai Prakash v. Union of India*, AIR 1962 SC 263.
57. Supra Note 41, pp. 195–6.
58. Supra Note 36, p. 159.
59. PLD 1976 S.C. 57.
60. PLD 1958 Lahore 887.
61. PLD 1964 SC 673.
62. PLD 1965 Lahore 642.
63. Supra Note 28, pp. 161–2.
64. PLD 1997 SC 781, 812, PLD 1993 Lahore 306.
65. PLD 1997 SC 781, 820.
66. PLD 1957 SC (Pak) 9.
67. Muhammad Munir was the 2nd Chief Justice of Pakistan serving from 1954 to 1960.
68. PLD 1976 SC 57.
69. PLD 1988 S.C. 416.
70. Supra Note 36, pp. 164–5.
71. PLD 1989 S.C. 66.
72. Benazir Bhutto was the 11th and 13th Prime Minister of Pakistan and was also the first Pakistani female to hold office.
73. PLD 1988 S.C. 416.
74. 1992 SCMR 563.

23 Freedom of Assembly

'Freedom of Assembly' means that there is no law which forbids people to assemble. The 'freedom of assembly' includes taking part in public meetings, processions and demonstration. Under English law, all the privileges, including the 'freedom of assembly', are neither liberties nor rights; they are residual. It is not illegal if a group of people choose to go to the same location at the same time, provided they keep within the limits of the law, individually and collectively.

An assembly convened for the purpose of affecting a breach of the peace is unlawful at common law; and there are various statutory offences, notably under Public Order Acts, Highways Act, the Police Act 1964 and local by-laws. Britain is a party to the European Convention, which provides that everyone has the right to freedom of peaceful assembly.[1]

A meeting with lawful purpose and conducted in lawful manner may in certain circumstances be liable to be prevented or regulated if it provokes public disorder. In *Beatty v. Gillbanks*,[2] it was held that the mere knowledge that opponents are likely to cause disorder, does not turn an otherwise lawful assembly into an unlawful assembly. The decision proceeded on the basis that an act does not become unlawful because doing it may cause another to commit an unlawful act. In a later decision of *Duncan v. Jones*,[3] it appears to have modified that law laid down in *Beatty v. Gillbanks*. The effect of that decision is that a magistrate or the police may take any steps that are necessary to prevent a breach of peace if reasonably apprehended.

The US Supreme Court held in *Cox v. Louisiana*,[4] that the notion that the First and 14th Amendments which guarantee, among others, the freedom of speech and press; the right to life, liberty or property; and the right to equal protection of laws,

> 'afford the same kind of freedom to those who would communicate ideas by conduct such as patrolling, marching and picketing on streets and highways as these amendments afford to those who communicate ideas by pure speech'

has been rejected.

This freedom has its roots in the tradition of petitioning to the legitimate government for redress within the democratic process. The American Constitution, by its First Amendment, provides:

> 'Congress shall make no law … abridging the freedom of speech, or of the press, or the right of the people to peaceably assemble, and to petition the Government for a redress of grievances.'

The United States Supreme Court has held' that –

> 'the very idea of government, republican in form, implies a right on the part of its citizens to meet peaceably for consultation in respect of public affairs and to petition for a redress of grievances.'[5]

Decided cases in the US indicate that it is not significant, whether one is engaged in speech, association, assembly or petition. All four rights are now considered to be elements of a broad right to freedom of expression. Lord Alfred Denning MR (1899–1999) has said:

> 'If men are ever to be able to break the bonds of oppression or servitude, they must be free to meet and discuss their grievances and to work out in unison a plan of action to see things right.'[6]

While the US Supreme Court in the case of *American Communications Assn. v. Douds*[7] observed –

> 'it goes without saying that the right of assembly is a very important right for the preservation of a democratic political system, yet it cannot be denied that no state can tolerate utterances or actions which threaten to overthrow the government established by law in that state by unlawful or unconstitutional means.

The Supreme Court of Pakistan in *Islamic Republic of Pakistan v. Abdul Wali Khan* stated:

> 'Freedoms of speech, press, and assembly are dependent upon the power of the constitutional government to survive. If it is to survive, it must have the power to protect itself against unlawful conduct and under some circumstances, against incitements to commit unlawful acts.'[8]

The place of assembly may be a private place or a public place. But whether it is one or the other, the courts have recognized the vital relationship between the freedom to associate and privacy of one's associations... inviolability of privacy in group association may in many circumstances be indispensable to preservation of freedom of association, particularly, where a group espouses dissident belief. Indeed, this applies with greater force when the meeting is in a private place.[9]

In *Walker v. City of Birmingham*,[10] provides an illustration with regard to the right to assemble in a public place. Here, Birmingham officials filed a bill of complaint in a state circuit court against certain individuals and organizations alleging, that their conduct was calculated to provoke breaches of the peace, threatened the safety, peace and tranquility of the city and asking for an injunction restraining them from holding demonstrations, mass street parades etc., in a public place. The injunction was granted; yet the demonstrations were held, and consequently those persons were charged with contempt of court. The question arose was whether the law under which the injunction was sought and issued violated the First and 14th Amendments rights to free speech and peaceful assembly. While the majority did not go into this question, Chief Justice Earl Warren (1891–1974)[11] speaking for the minority observed:

> 'Our decisions have consistently held that picketing and parading are means of expression protected by the First Amendment and that the right to picket or parade may not be subjected to the unfettered discretion of local officials.... Although a city may regulate the manner of use of its streets and sidewalks in the interest of keeping them open for the movement of traffic, it may not allow local officials unbridled discretion to decide who shall be allowed to parade or picket and who shall not. "Wherever the title of streets and parks may rest, they have immemorially been held in trust for the use of the public and time out of mind, have been used for purposes of assembly, communicating thoughts between citizens and discussing public questions. Such use of the streets and public places has, from ancient times, been a part of the privileges, immunities, rights and liberties of citizens. The privilege of a citizen of the United States to use the streets and parks for communication of views on national questions may be regulated in the interest of all; it is not absolute, but relative, and must be exercised in subordination to the general comfort and convenience and in consonance with peace and good order; but it must not, in the guise of regulation, be abridged or denied."
>
> When local officials are given totally unfettered discretion to decide whether a proposed demonstration is consistent with "public welfare, peace, safety, health, good order, morals or convenience," as they were in this case, they are invited to act as censors over the views that may be presented to the public. The unconstitutionality of the ordinance is compounded, of course, when there is convincing evidence that the officials have, in fact, used their power to deny permits to organizations whose views they dislike.'

These views had earlier been expressed in *Hague v. Committee for Industrial Organization*,[12] which was relied upon by the Full Bench in *Khawaja Muhammad Safdar v. The Province of West Pakistan*,[13] adding:

> 'therefore, the right to use parks for discussion or communication of views on public matters, especially those relating to national affairs, cannot be denied by the state to the citizens, though these rights are subject to the exigencies of law and order and maintenance of peace and tranquility.'

It is a relative right, subject to imposition of restrictions with necessary conditions, to safeguard the public interest. But, according to American law there must be grave and immediate danger to the interest of public order to restrict the right. In other words, any attempt to restrict 'freedom of assembly' must be justified by clear public interest threatened, not doubtfully or remotely, but by clear and present danger and only the gravest abuses, endangering paramount interests, give occasion for permissible limitations on the right.

The American law on the subject is that without abridging the right of assembly, the government may reasonably and without discrimination regulate the use of places wholly within its control by requiring permits for public assemblies in the streets or parks; but any requirement of a permit would violate the Constitution, where absolute discretion to deny a permit is vested in a public official. While the public have the right to move peacefully in a highway or other public places, and to parade the streets, the right may be regulated in the interest of all and must be exercised in subordination to the general comfort and convenience and in consonance with peace and good order. So, the state may in a proper manner regulate the use of the streets by requiring a permit.[14]

Freedom of Assembly in India and Pakistan

Article 16 of the 1973 Constitution of Pakistan provides –

> 'every citizen shall have the right to assemble peacefully without arms, subject to any reasonable restrictions imposed by law in the interest of public order.'

Article 19(1)(b) of the Indian Constitution provides that –

> 'all citizens shall have the right to assemble peaceably and without arms.'

But Clause (3) of this Article lays down that nothing in sub-Clause (b) –

> 'Shall affect the operation of any existing law in so far as it imposes, or prevent the State from making any law imposing, in the interests of the sovereignty and integrity of India or public order, reasonable restrictions on the exercise of the right conferred by the said sub-Clause.'

The fundamental right guaranteed to a citizen of Pakistan by the Constitution of 1973 is confined to unarmed gatherings and for peaceful purposes, which can only be restricted by laws, which have as their object the maintenance of public order. The restrictions imposed must, however, be reasonable, and it is for the Court to decide in each case, whether the restriction is or is not reasonable. In deciding this, the Court will have to take into consideration the conditions prevailing at the time, the nature, the extent and the duration of the restrictions, and all the other surrounding circumstances.

In *Qari Abdul Hameed Qadri v. District Magistrate, Lahore*,[15] it was held that –

> 'the danger to human life and safety and disturbance of the public tranquility fall within the purview of the expression "Public Order", and if an order is passed by the District Magistrate to prevent danger to Human life and safety and the disturbance of public tranquility, it is an order passed in the interest of public order, if the restrictions imposed by the District Magistrate are reasonable restrictions. If they are unreasonable, the order, although it may be perfectly legal under Section 144 of the Code of Criminal Procedure, will be illegal. But if they are reasonable then the order cannot be challenged on this ground. Restrictions may be complete or partial. In the circumstances of a case, total prohibition of the exercise of such a right may be legal and valid. Drastic remedies may be necessary to meet conditions in an emergency giving rise to serious and urgent problems.
>
> In determining the reasonableness of restrictions, several circumstances would have to be taken into consideration, including the conditions prevailing at the time, and the nature; extent and duration of the restrictions of the fundamental right having regard to all the surrounding circumstances, the restrictions imposed may be quite unreasonable while in a different set of circumstances they may be reasonable. There cannot be any absolute and fixed standard laid down by which the reasonableness of restrictions upon fundamental rights may be tested, but it can be safely assumed that in judging the same an objective standard that is the standard of the average prudent man would have to be applied. The concept of reasonableness is nothing but that of harmonising rights of the individuals with that of collective interest.
>
> If it was clear that there was danger to public peace and tranquility if a meeting of a political nature was allowed to be held, the District Magistrate after having been satisfied about the urgency of the matter could not have abdicated his powers or confessed helplessness until the disturbance had actually occurred. In times of danger and crisis it is clearly his duty to act and to act with promptitude. The maintenance of peace and order, being the special responsibility of the District Magistrate, it is his duty to exercises his power under Section 144 of the Code of Criminal Procedure if and when he feels satisfied that it is necessary to exercise such powers.'

'Freedom of assembly' may be restricted to a large extent in times of national emergency than in normal times. The restriction should be certain and well defined and imposed directly by the law rather than by the discretionary authority of the police or other executive authority. The principles governing the right of free assembly and of free speech are the same; both rights, although not identical, are inseparable and cognate. This was held in *Nawabzada Nasrullah Khan v. Govt of West Pakistan*,[16] in which it was ruled that 'freedom of assembly' is not in its nature absolute.

In *Babulal Parate v. The State of Maharashtra*,[17] the Indian Supreme Court observed that the –

> 'public order has to be maintained in advance in order to ensure it, and, therefore, it is competent for a legislature to pass a law permitting anticipatory restrictions upon particular kinds of acts in an emergency for the purpose of maintaining public order.'

The expression 'public order' is not defined anywhere, but it was held in *Qari Abdul Hameed Qadri v. District Magistrate, Lahore*,[18] and *Shukar Din v. Govt. of West Pakistan*,[19] that danger to property, human life and safety and the disturbance of public tranquility fall within the purview of reasonable restrictions that may be imposed in the public interest to avert danger or disturbances.

The Prevention of Seditious Meetings Act 1911, is an Act to consolidate and amend the law relating to the prevention of public meetings likely to promote sedition or to cause disturbance of public tranquility.

1) It enjoins the provincial government to declare the whole or any part of a province to be a proclaimed area.
2) After such declaration, no public meeting for the furtherance or discussion of any subject likely to cause disturbance or public excitement or for the exhibition or distribution of any written or printed matter relating to any such subjects can be held in any such proclaimed area,
   a) unless written notice of the intention to hold such meeting and of the time and place of such meeting has been given to the District Magistrate (DM) at least three days in advance and
   b) unless permission to hold such meeting has been obtained in writing from the District Magistrate (DM).

Under Section 30 of Police Act 1861, the police officers had power to issue licences defining the conditions on which assemblies or processions were to take place; so as to avert a breach of the public peace and to disperse any assembly or procession conducting itself contrary to the conditions of the licence. They are also bound to maintain order on the public streets in the neighborhood of places of worship during the time of worship. Further, in cases of emergency certain specified class of magistrates have the power to issue orders under Section 144 of the Code of Criminal Procedure 1898 (Cr.P.C.), imposing restrictions on holding of public meetings.

Section 107 of the Code of Criminal Procedure 1898 (Cr.P.C.), empowers a magistrate to obtain security for keeping the peace, from any person who is likely to commit a breach of the peace. It is not necessary that the person bound over should have actually committed the breach of the peace. Section 112 of the Code of Criminal Procedure 1898 (Cr.P.C.), provides that the magistrate acting under Section 107, has to make an order in writing, setting forth the substance of the information received, the amount of the bond to be executed, the term for which it is to be in force, and the number, character and the class of 'sureties' (if any) required.

All these three restrictions were held reasonable and in the interest of public order in *Madhu Limaye v. Sub-Divisional Magistrate, Monghyr.*[20]

In the interest of 'public order'

The right of assembly may be regulated in the interest of 'public order', but an assembly cannot be prohibited. In *Himat Lal K. Shah v. Commissioner of Police, Ahmedabad*,[21] the Indian Supreme Court upheld Section 33(1)(o) of the Bombay Police Act 1951, which enables the commissioner to make rules to regulate assemblies and processions. The Supreme Court of India held, that –

> power to regulate would include the power to give prior permission to be obtained for holding assemblies or processions as it becomes necessary to regulate the conduct and behaviour or action of persons constituting such assemblies or processions in order to safeguard the rights of citizens and in order to preserve public order.

However, no rule can be prescribed prohibiting all meetings or processions. The state can only make regulations in aid of the right of assembly of each citizen and can impose reasonable restrictions in the interest of 'public order.' A rule which empowered the commissioner to refuse permission to hold a public meeting was struck down as being *ultra vires* of a statute, which does not authorize framing of rules to regulate the conduct, behaviour or action of persons before an assembly is constituted.

Although, in *Himat Lal* held that a meeting cannot be totally prohibited, the Lahore High Court in *Qari Abdul Hameed Qadri* case, took the view that a District Magistrate (DM) may prohibit a public meeting, if in the circumstances, he considers it necessary in the interest of public order.

A public meeting is a meeting, which is open to the public or a class or a portion of the public in its capacity as such. It does not cease to be a public meeting because its conveners have levied an entry fee to raise public funds or have regulated the entry of the public by passes in view of the limited accommodation available at the venue of the meeting or have excluded some known mischief mongers from the meeting. Therefore, notwithstanding the fact that the entry to the meeting is controlled by a certain regulation, it will constitute a public meeting in every sense, if otherwise, it is open to the public or a class or portion of the public. On the other hand, if a political organization convenes a meeting; for example, of its executive to which the admission, is restricted to its chosen members by name and which is not accessible to the public or a class or portion of the public as such, it will be a private meeting.[22]

The expression 'in the interest of' as used in this Article 16 and various other Articles guaranteeing fundamental rights is of great amplitude; it is much wider than, for example, the words 'for the maintenance of'. A law may not have been designed to directly maintain the public order or to directly protect the general public against any particular evil and yet it may have been enacted 'in the interest of' the public order or the general public as the case may be. It is in this sense that any law which is enacted in the interest of public order is saved from the vice of constitutional invalidity.[23]

The provisions of amended Section 30 of the Police Act [Punjab Amendment Ordinance (8 of 1984)], were held to be repugnant and violative of Articles 16 and 20(a) of the Constitution of Pakistan, in so far as it relates to 'public interest' which is much wider phrase than the 'public order' used in Articles 16 and 20 of the Constitution and to that extent it is *ultra vires*.[24]

The collective interests of the society, the peace and security of the state and the maintenance of public order are of vital importance in any organized society. Fundamental rights have no real meaning if the state itself is in danger or under threat of being disorganized. It is for these reasons that an equilibrium has to be maintained by the two contending interests at stake: one, the individual liberties and the positive rights of the citizens which are declared by the Constitution to be fundamental, and second, the need to impose social control and reasonable limitations on the enjoyment of those rights in the interest of the collective good of the society.

Thus, the right of assembly as guaranteed by the Constitution is a right to assemble peacefully and without arms, but at the same time this right is not without its limitations imposed by the Constitution. The right is subordinate to any reasonable restrictions imposed by law in the interest of public order. It is here that the Court is –

> 'called upon to hold the balance between the contending interests as its sacred duty and adjudicate upon the reasonableness of the restrictions imposed by law which have encroached upon the right.'

And in case, the Court finds that the legislature in promulgating the law, has transgressed the reasonable limits envisaged by the Constitution, it will not hesitate to strike it down as *ultra vires*. Thus, in *Nawabzada Nasrullah Khan v. District Magistrate, Lahore*,[25] Section 8 of the West Pakistan Maintenance of Public Order Ordinance 1960, was held to be *ultra vires* being in contravention of fundamental rights of assembly and association, because the powers conferred on the District Magistrate (DM) under that section were not subject to any restrictions, the discretion vested in him to depute any person to attend any public meeting for the purposes of causing a report to be made of the proceedings was absolute and he was free to act under any circumstances he liked, not necessarily in the interest of the public order alone, and there was no provision in Section 8 to control and regulate the exercise of this naked power given to the District Magistrate (DM) and to keep it under check within reasonable limits in the interest of public order.

In *Qari Abdul Hameed Qadri v. District Magistrate, Lahore*,[26] the District Magistrate (DM) had by an order made in the exercise of his powers under Section 144 of the Code of Criminal Procedure 1898 (Cr.P.C.), prohibited within the limits of the Lahore Cantonment area, the assembly of 5 or more persons, or the taking out of any procession or holding of public demonstrations in any public place. The order was not applicable to any gathering of persons permitted by the District Magistrate (DM), a genuine marriage or mourning procession, purely religious assembly within a place acknowledged for such assembly and to the members of police and armed forces. The order was to remain in force for 2 months. It was held that as the restrictions imposed were confined to the Lahore Cantonment area, where armed forces were stationed, 'it requires special consideration for determining the nature of reasonable restrictions,' and that if the District Magistrate (DM) was satisfied that there was apprehension of breach of the peace and the disturbance of public tranquility, the restrictions imposed were not unreasonable so as to contravene the fundamental right of assembly.[27] The judgment in *Qari Abdul Hameed Qadri* case, is also an authority for the view that the restrictions imposed by Section 144 of the Code of Criminal Procedure 1898 (Cr.P.C.), are reasonable restrictions and that the section does not violate the right of assembly conferred by Article 16.

In *Babulal Parate v. State of Maharashtra*,[28] constitutional validity of Section 144 of the Code of Criminal Procedure (Cr.P.C.), was directly challenged, but the challenge was repelled. It was held that the section was intended to be availed of for preventing obstructions and annoyances and to secure the public weal. The powers are exercisable by responsible magistrates who have to act judicially. Moreover, the restrains permissible to be placed under that section are of a temporary nature and can only be imposed in an emergency.[29]

Right to Take Out Processions

The right to take out procession flows from the right of 'free assembly'. But this right may only be exercised subject to the right of others to use public roads and streets. There is always apprehension of breach of the peace during the procession, and the law may empower the authorities responsible for the maintenance of law and order to impose restrictions on the exercise of the right.

In *Mathai Manjooran v. The State*,[30] it was held that an order imposing total prohibition on a procession was unreasonable, but in *Inderdeo Singh v. The State*,[31] it was held that imposition of a pre-condition of obtaining a permit for taking out a procession is reasonable.

In *Syed Manzur Hasan v. Syed Muhammad Zaman*,[32] the Privy Council held that there is always a right to conduct a religious procession along highways, but it should be done in a way as not to obstruct the general public user, and subject to restrictions imposed by the state. No one section of the community can claim the exclusive right of using the roads. Further, in *Martin & Co. v. Faiyaz Hussain*,[33] the Privy Council held that once an electric company was granted a licence to install wires at a particular height, it implied that they had been given the power to abridge the public' right to carry through the streets (*Tazias*) of a greater height.

Notes

1. A. G. Chaudhry, *Lectures on Constitutional Law*, (Lahore: Irfan Law Book House, 1994), p. 154.
2. (1882) 9 Q. B.D. 308.
3. (1936) 1 K.B. 218.
4. 379 US 536, (1965).
5. *United States v. Cruikshank*, 92 US 542 (1875).
6. Lord Justice Alfred Denning, *The Road to Justice*, (London: Stevens & Sons, 1955), p. 98; quoted in *Benazir Bhutto v. Federation*, PLD 1988 SC 416, at p. 518.
7. 339 US 382 (1950).
8. Quoted by Chief Justice Hamoodur Rahman in *Islamic Republic of Pakistan v. Abdul Wali Khan*, PLD 1976 SC 57 at p. 104.
9. Justice (R) Fazal Karim, *Judicial Review of Public Actions* (Karachi: Pakistan Law House, 2006), p. 692.
10. 388 US 307 (1967).
11. Earl Warren was the 14th Chief Justice of the United States from 1953 to 1969.
12. 307 US 496 (1939).
13. PLD 1964 Lah. 718.
14. Supra Note 1, p. 158.
15. PLD 1957 Lahore 213.

16. PLD 1965 Lahore 642.
17. AIR 1961 SC 884.
18. PLD 1957 Lahore 213.
19. PLD 1965 Lahore 522.
20. AIR 1971 SC 2486.
21. AIR 1973 S.C. 87.
22. Justice Muhammad Akram, in *Nasrullah Khan v. District Magistrate*, PLD 1965 Lah 642.
23. *Virendra v. State of Punjab*, AIR 1957 SC 896, 899; *Kedar Nath Singh v. State of Bihar*, AIR 1962 SC 955.
24. *Manzoor Husain Bukhari v. S.P. City, Lahore*, 1990 MLD 1807.
25. PLD 1965 Lah 642.
26. PLD 1957 (WP) Lah 213.
27. Supra Note 9, pp. 695–6.
28. AIR 1961 SC 884.
29. Supra Note 9, p. 696.
30. AIR 1954 TC(Travancore-Cochin) 47.
31. AIR 1951 Patna 242.
32. AIR 1925 PC 36.
33. AIR 1944 PC 33, (1945) 47 BOMLR 575.

24 Freedom of Movement

Introductory

Article 15 of the 1973 Constitution of Pakistan provides that:

> 'Every citizen shall have the right to remain in, and subject to any reasonable restriction imposed by law in the public interest, enter and move freely throughout Pakistan and to reside and settle in any part thereof.'

Article 19(1)(d) & (e) of the 1949 Indian Constitution provides that:

(d) 'all citizens shall have the right to move freely throughout the territory of India,' and
(e) 'to reside and settle in any part of the territory of India.'

Article 19(5), however, lays down that:

> 'Nothing in sub-clauses (d) & (e) shall effect the operation of any existing law in so far as it imposes or prevents the State from making any law imposing reasonable restrictions on the exercise of any of the rights conferred by the said sub-clauses either in the interests of the general public or for the protection of the interests of any Scheduled Tribe.'

The right to enter and move freely throughout Pakistan and to reside anywhere, therein has been, unlike the American Constitution, expressly granted by the Constitutions of India and Pakistan. In the American Constitution, the right to travel throughout the length and breadth of America finds no explicit mention in the Constitution.

> 'The reason, it has been suggested, is that a right so elementary was conceived from the beginning to be a necessary concomitant of the stronger union that the Constitution created. In any event, freedom to travel throughout the United States has long been recognized as a basic right under the Constitution.'[1]

Similarly, the Constitutions of India and Pakistan allow every citizen the right to remain in the country. This right is absolute and unqualified.

However, in *Nasrullah Khan Henjra v. Government of Pakistan, Ministry of Interior and Narcotics Control, Islamabad*,[2] the Supreme Court of Pakistan held that 'the right to remain in the country' does not afford protection against their extradition, of Pakistan nationals who are accused of committing serious crimes in other countries. Therefore, the Extradition Act 1972, allowing the extradition of Pakistan nationals, is not inconsistent with the fundamental right to remain in Pakistan as embodied in Article 15. It was further held, that this would be in consonance with the provisions of the Objectives Resolution 1949, laying down that people of Pakistan will attain their rightful and honoured place amongst the nations of the world and make their full contribution towards international peace, and progress, and happiness of humanity.

In India, it was held in *Ebrahim Vazir Mavat v. The State of Bombay*,[3] that a punishment involving removal of a citizen from his own country would be unconstitutional. Prior to 1947, criminals convicted of serious offenses such as murder were sentenced to transportation for life, which meant they were transported to a foreign territory and would spend the rest of their lives there. In view of the right to remain in Pakistan, guaranteed by Article 15, this cannot be done now. In fact, the law has been amended and there is no such thing as transportation for life now. That this right is an absolute and unqualified right was made plain by providing, that the right to move freely throughout Pakistan and to reside and settle in any part, thereof, is subject to any reasonable restriction imposed by law in the public interest.[4]

Many countries of the world especially the civil law countries do not extradite their citizens to foreign countries. There has always been, in this regard, a conflict between the common law countries and the civil law countries.

The common law countries allow extradition even of the nationals of the state, which is required to extradite. But, the civil law countries, such as France, Italy and Germany have adopted the principle of never extraditing any of their subjects to foreign states, prefer punishing their own subjects for grave crimes committed abroad. The constitutions of these civil law countries have made specific provisions in this respect.[5]

A citizen cannot be expelled or banished from the country. But his right to enter the country if he is leaving it or has gone abroad and his rights to step out and step into the country, move freely throughout Pakistan and to reside and settle in any part thereof, are subject to reasonable restrictions imposed by the law in the public interest.

In *Saiyyad Abul A'la Maudoodi v. The Central Government of Pakistan*,[6] it was held that the purpose behind this safeguard –

> 'is to remove all territorial barriers within the country for the citizens of Pakistan. It is designed to be a check against provincialism, regional discrimination and all parochial considerations. To a citizen of Pakistan, the whole of this country, is his cherished home freely and equally accessible to him. Subject to any reasonable restrictions imposed by law in the public interest, he is free to move about, settle and reside in any part of the territory throughout Pakistan. But the converse of it may not be true and it does not necessarily follow that a citizen of Pakistan has no freedom of movement at all to leave his country.'

Externment or Internment Orders

Externment or internment orders, such as orders requiring a person to leave a certain area, or not to enter certain area, or not to leave a certain area, would undoubtedly curtail the freedom of movement. And a law authorizing externment or internment to be valid, must fall within the limits of permissible legislation, and the restrictions on the exercise of the right of freedom of movement must be reasonable and in public interest.

In *Ebrahim Vazir Mavat v. State of Bombay*,[7] the appellant, a citizen of India, who returned to the country without a permit, was arrested and ordered to be deported to Pakistan. It was contended that Section 7 of the Influx from Pakistan (Control) Act 1949, which permitted the Indian Government to deport a citizen to Pakistan was unconstitutional, for it imposed unreasonable restrictions on the freedom of movement. The Supreme Court of India, by a majority, held Section 7 of the Act, invalid and ruled that a law which subjects a citizen to the extreme penalty of a virtual forfeiture of his citizenship upon conviction for a mere breach of the permit regulations or upon a reasonable suspicion of having committed such a breach can hardly be justified upon the ground that it imposes a reasonable restriction upon the fundamental right to reside and settle in the country in the interests of the general public.

In *State of Madhya Pradesh v. Baldeo Prasad*,[8] the petitioner, by an order passed by the State of Madhya Pradesh under Section 4(a) of the Central Provinces and Berar Goondas Act 1946, was externed from district of Chhindwara. He filed a writ petition in the High Court challenging the validity of the order on the ground that the Act itself was *ultra vires*. The Supreme Court of India accepted the plea of the petitioners and held, that where a statute empowers the specified authorities to take preventive action against the citizens, it is essential that it should expressly make it the duty of the said authorities to satisfy themselves of the existence of conditions precedent to the exercise of the power. Under Section 4, the District Magistrate (DM) can proceed against a person without being required to come to a formal decision, as to whether the said person is a *goonda* or not and no opportunity is given to such person to show that he is not a *goonda*. Moreover, the Act nowhere indicated the test to be applied in determining, whether a person is a *goonda* or not. It was held that the operative part of the Act, namely, Sections 4 and 4-A imposed unreasonable restrictions on the right of movement.

In *State of Madhya Pradesh v. Thakur Bharat Singh*,[9] Section 3(1)(b) of the Madhya Pradesh Public Security Act 1959, which authorized the Madhya Pradesh State Government to order the respondent not to reside or remain in such place, or within such area in Madhya Pradesh, as may be specified in the order, it was challenged as being violative of the right guaranteed by Article 19(1)(d). Under the Act, if the person so ordered failed to carry out the directions, he could be removed to the area or place designated and could also be punished with imprisonment. The Act did not give any opportunity to the person concerned, of being heard before the place where he was to reside or remain was selected. The place selected could be one in which the person might have no residential accommodation and no means of subsistence. He might not be able to secure the means of subsistence in the place selected. Further, the section did not indicate the extent of the place or the area, its distance from the residence of the person externed or whether it was inhabited or uninhabited. It also nowhere laid that the person directed to be removed would be provided with any residence, maintenance or means of livelihood in the place selected. It was held that the restriction was unreasonable and therefore void.

In *Kharak Singh v. State of Uttar Pradesh,*[10] Regulation 236 of the Uttar Pradesh Police Regulations permitted surveillance of suspects. Some of its aspects were held unconstitutional, but, it was held that the watching and shadowing of suspects for the purpose of keeping a record of their movements and activities did not infringe the right to move freely.

In *Guru Datta Sharma v. State of Bihar,*[11] the Supreme Court of India upheld the validity of the provisions of the Official Secrets Act 1923, because the restrictions on the free movement were imposed in public interest, namely, the security of the state.

In *Bazal Ahmed Ayubi v. The West Pakistan Province,*[12] the petitioners were declared '*goondas*' under the Punjab Control of Goondas Act 1951, and their movements were restricted on the ground that their activities were anti-social. The restrictions were in the nature of preventive detention, but the law, in so far as it permitted the possibility of exclusion of a proper defence through counsel and the keeping of a secret record, was not in consonance with the principles of natural justice and, therefore, imposed unreasonable restrictions.

In *Rao Mahroz Akhtar v. District Magistrate, Dera Ghazi Khan,*[13] movements of the petitioners were restricted under the Punjab Public Safety Act 1949, to a particular area. It was held that the provisions of the Act, which permitted an order of internment to be made against a Pakistani citizen, without communicating the ground, therefore, to him or according him an opportunity to represent against such an order imposed unreasonable restrictions on the freedom of movement possessed by him and therefore, offended Article 11, which was the predecessor of Article 15, of the present Constitution. Another factor that was considered was the statute's grant of the authority to issue an order of indefinite duration of internment…

Public Interest

The restrictions imposed under Article 15 of the Pakistan Constitution must not only be reasonable, but they must also be in the public interest. A discussion on the connotation of the word 'public' will be found under Article 184(3), under the heading 'question of public importance'. Suffice it to say here that the term 'public' is used in contrast to 'private', and that to be in the 'public interest' the restriction must be to protect the public at large.

The phrase 'public interest' has never been defined. But, it is well settled that it is not to be confined within narrow limits. Lord Alfred Denning MR (1899–1999) said in *London Artists Limited v. Littler,*[14]–

> 'Whenever a matter is such as to affect people at large so that they may be legitimately interested in, or concerned at, what is going on, or what may happen to them or others, then it is a matter of public interest on which everyone is entitled to make fair comments.'

This definition of 'public interest' was cited with approval in *Reynolds v. Times Newspapers.*[15]

What has been sanctioned by Islam cannot be against public interest. Thus, in *Allah Ditta v. Fateh Ali Khan,*[16] the law of preemption, it was argued, was an unreasonable restriction on the sale and purchase of property; it was held that –

> 'law of preemption is recognized by Islam and such restrictions, therefore, cannot be declared against public interest.'

Indeed, the question whether a restriction is in the public interest is to be determined with reference to the facts and circumstances of each case.

Mehtab Jan v. Municipal Committee, Rawalpindi,[17] was a case in which Municipal Committee, Rawalpindi, had in exercise of the power vesting in it under Section 152 of the Punjab Municipal Committee Act 1911, directed all owners, tenants, residents and prostitutes of a particular area to vacate their premises for the reason that the use of the locality in question as '*chakla*' was injurious to the morals of the residents. This was a restriction on the residence of a particular class of citizens in a particular locality. It was held that this was in recognition of the injurious effect of prostitution on morals. A certain locality may be particularly susceptible to injury, where, for instance, there is a school or college, and there can be no doubt that on general grounds, so long as prostitution is not totally prohibited, it should be confined to an out of the way locality. The law was held valid, but if such a law be so administered as to turn out prostitutes from one locality after another, then Article 11 (which was the predecessor of Article 15 of the present Constitution) would, it was held apply.

In *Kamla China v. The State,*[18] *Begum and others v. The State,*[19] and *Smt. Kaushailiya v. The State,*[20] and *State of Uttar Pradesh v. Kaushaliya,*[21] it has been held that prostitutes may be confined to any particular area and can be required to be removed from a particular area, but a prostitute cannot be exiled from the whole municipal area or the magistrate's jurisdiction.

In *Kamla Kant Mishra v. State of Bihar,*[22] it was held that an order under Section 144 of the Code of Criminal Procedure 1898 (Cr.P.C.), may be violative of the right of freedom of movement.

Inter-Provincial Travel

The right of inter-state travel was described by Justice John Marshall Harlan (1899–1971)[23] 'as a nebulous judicial construct.' This right of inter-state travel has been relied upon in US Supreme Court's opinion as a basis for –

(1) upholding the validity of federal legislation prohibiting states from disqualifying persons from voting in presidential and vice-presidential elections because of failure to meet state residency requirements,
(2) invalidating state and District of Columbia residency requirements for recipients of welfare benefits,
(3) invalidating a state tax imposed on interstate travelers,
(4) invalidating state legislation prohibiting the transportation of indigent persons into the state,
(5) upholding the validity of federal legislation which, as applied, prohibited private parties from conspiring to interfere with a citizen's free exercise of his federal constitutional rights.

On the other hand, the US Supreme Court has held that no federal constitutional right of inter-state travel was violated where –

(1) state statutes' imposed taxes or fees which were deemed to have had merely an indirect effect upon interstate travel, or
(2) a state statute authorized a person to be compelled to appear as a witness in judicial proceedings in another state.

Right to Enter, Remain and Reside anywhere in the Country

As observed above, the right to reside anywhere in the country does not find express mention in the United States Constitution. In *Edwards v. California,*[24] some of the justices relied upon the Commerce Clause of the US Constitution as the basis of this right. Justice Robert H. Jackson (1892–1954)[25] thought that –

> 'This Court should, however, hold squarely that it is a privilege of citizenship of the United States, protected from state abridgment, to enter any state of the Union, either for temporary sojourn or for the establishment of permanent residence therein and for gaining resultant citizenship thereof. If national citizenship means less than this, it means nothing.'

In his view,

> 'State citizenship is ephemeral; it results only from residence and is gained or lost there-with. That choice of residence was subject to local approval is contrary to the inescapable implications of the westward movement of our civilization.'

In that case, 'indigence' as defined in the statute in question, constituted a basis for restricting the freedom of a citizen, as crime or contagion warrants its restriction. Justice Jackson said,

> 'We should say now, and in no uncertain terms, that a man's mere property status, without more, cannot be used by a statute to test, qualify or limit his rights as a citizen of the United States. Indigence in itself is neither a source of rights nor a basis for denying them. The mere state of being without funds is a neutral fact – constitutionally an irrelevance, like race, creed or colour.'

The right to remain in Pakistan under Article 15 appears to be an absolute right, as distinguished from the other rights guaranteed by this Article, which are subject to reasonable restrictions imposed by law. Former Chief Justice Muhammad Munir (1895–1979), in his book on *Constitution of the Islamic Republic of Pakistan*,[26] stated that the right is absolute and unqualified, and a citizen cannot, therefore, be expelled or banished from the country. This view also receives support from the way the right to remain in Pakistan and the other rights guaranteed by Article 15 have been treated.

The right to move freely throughout Pakistan and to reside and settle in any part thereof is subject to reasonable restrictions imposed by law, but the right to remain in Pakistan is not so subject. However in *Nasrullah Khan Henjra v. Government of Pakistan, Ministry of Interior and Narcotics Control, Islamabad*,[27] it was held that this right too is not an absolute right. It was a case in which the petitioners were sought to be extradited to the USA (United States of America) under a treaty between Pakistan and USA, for being tried there on some serious charges. A magistrate found that the evidence laid before him *prima facie* supported the charges and allowed extradition. This amounted to sending the petitioner Nasrullah Khan Henjra, to USA against his will, and the contention before the Supreme Court of Pakistan was that, that would be in violation of his right to remain in Pakistan. At first sight, so observed Justice Saad Saood Jan (1931–2005)[28] writing for the Court,

> 'the argument advanced on behalf of the petitioners seems unanswerable for the forcible deportation of a citizen will come in conflict with his fundamental right to remain in Pakistan.'

Justice Saad Saood Jan, however, rejected the contention. He referred to the Objectives Resolution 1949, to point out that the ultimate goal of the people of Pakistan is that the people of Pakistan will prosper and attain their rightful and honoured place amongst the nations of the world and make their full contribution towards international peace and progress and the happiness of humanity.

Mian Muhammad Nawaz Sharif (1949), who had been the Prime Minister of Pakistan twice, was removed by General Pervez Musharraf (1943) in a military *coup*, and was put in jail, tried for a criminal offence and sentenced to imprisonment. Later, he and his family, including Muhammad Shahbaz Sharif (1951), were allowed to leave Pakistan and go to Saudi Arabia, on the condition that he would reside in Saudi Arabia and would not take part in political activities for 10 years. The case of Muhammad Shahbaz Sharif arose when he tried to return to Pakistan. In *Mian Muhammad Shahbaz Sharif v. Federation of Pakistan*,[29] the petitioner being a citizen of Pakistan was held to have –

> 'a constitutional right to enter and remain in the country..... Article 15 of the Constitution bestows a right on every citizen of Pakistan to enter or move freely throughout the country and to reside and settle in any part thereof. It is a settled proposition of law that the right to enter in the country cannot be denied but a citizen can be restrained from going out of country.'

Another case arose when Mian Muhammad Nawaz Sharif attempted to return to Pakistan, before the expiry of 10 years.[30] In this case, it was held:

> '... the petitioners being citizens of Pakistan can return to their country as no restraint can be placed on a Pakistani citizen to return to his country and the undertaking given by the petitioner had no constitutional legitimacy as such the petitioners cannot be prohibited from coming to Pakistan. Every citizen has undeniable right vested in him as conferred under Article 15 of the Constitution to go abroad and return back to Pakistan without any hindrance and restraint but it must be kept in view that it is neither absolute nor unqualified....'

The petitioners Mian Muhammad Nawaz Sharif and Mian Muhammad Shahbaz Sharif, were therefore, held to have, under Article 15 of the 1973 Constitution of Pakistan, –

> 'an inalienable right to enter and remain in country, as citizens of Pakistan. Their return/entry into country shall not be restrained, hampered or obstructed by the Federal Government or Provincial Government agencies in any manner.'

Right to Travel Abroad

The right to travel abroad is not one of the rights expressly guaranteed by Article 15 or, for that matter, by other provisions of the 1973 Constitution. To support this right, sometimes Article 4 and sometimes Article 9 are invoked. But as was said in *Government of Pakistan v. Dada Amir Haidar Khan*,[31] Article 15 is of greater relevance.

In the US, while the constitutional right of inter-state travel is virtually unqualified, the right of international travel has been considered to be no more than an aspect of liberty protected by the 'due process clause' of the 5th Amendment. As such, this right, the US Supreme Court has held, can be regulated within the bounds of due process.[32]

In Pakistan, every citizen has the liberty to go abroad and to re-enter Pakistan unless he is precluded from doing so under some law made in the public interest. As was held in *Muhammad Shahbaz Sharif v. Federation of Pakistan*, referred to above, –

> 'the right to enter in the country cannot be denied, but a citizen can be restrained from going out of the country.'

His right to enter the country, if he is leaving it, or has gone abroad, and his right to step out and step into the country, are subject to reasonable restrictions imposed by law in the public interest. The Passport Act 1974, is a law made in the public interest regulating the right of a citizen to travel abroad and to return home. The issuance of a passport is incidental to the power to regulate the exit of any person out of Pakistan and his return thereafter.

In the *Superintendent of Police v. Abubakar*,[33] which was decided before the enactment of the Passport Act 1974, it was said that no citizen could go out of the country without a valid passport. In *Dada Amir Haidar Khan's* case referred to above,[34] the respondent was refused passport on the ground, that he was a political worker having 'communist thought.' While up-holding the validity of the Passport Act 1974, the Supreme Court of Pakistan proceeded to consider the question, whether, in refusing the passport, the discretion vested in the authorities to issue or refuse a passport was properly exercised. It was held that the reason that the respondent was an old political worker having communist thoughts was not a reasonable ground on which the liberty of a citizen to travel abroad could be curtailed. Further, the order refusing to issue the passport did not give any reasons. In the view of the Supreme Court, –

> 'Undoubtedly, to travel abroad could be barred if it was shown that the applicant was going abroad to meet the enemies of the country and his foreign visit could endanger the security of the state or was against the public interest. Nothing of the kind has been stated and the only reason given while refusing the passport to the respondent is that he was a person of "communist thought." The world, however, is filled with "communist thought" and communist regimes are existing on more than one continent. They are part of the world spectrum and if we are to know them and understand them we must mingle with them. Keeping alive intellectual intercourse between opposing groups is important and this should not be curbed unless in so doing some interest of the State is imperiled.'

Further, before a person is finally refused the grant of a passport he must be given an opportunity of being heard.[35]

Indeed, as was noticed in *Dada Amir Haidar Khan* case, there may be cases in which it may not be in the public interest to disclose the full reasons for refusal to issue passport but –

> 'in such cases, while refusing to issue the passport it should be stated that in view of the sensitivity of the matter, the disclosure of detailed reasons for refusal of the passport was not in the public interest.'

Wajid Shamsul Hassan v. Federation of Pakistan,[36] and *Malik Mushtaq Awan v. Government of Pakistan*,[37] are cases under the Exit from Pakistan (Control) Ordinance 1981, which is another law placing restrictions on travel abroad. In the *Wajid Shamsul Hassan* case, the validity of Section 2 of the Ordinance was doubted because it fails to provide any guidelines, or reasonable classification for taking action against a person prohibiting him/her from traveling abroad and denying him/her the valuable right of being heard and of knowing the reasons for such an action. In both of these cases, the petitioner's right to travel abroad made under the Ordinance of 1981 was deemed to have been violated.

In *Maneka Gandhi v. Union of India*,[38] the petitioner's passport was impounded under Section 10(3)(c) of the Passport Act 1967, which authorized the passport authority to impound a passport in the interest of the general public. The action was challenged, *inter alia*, on the ground that it violated Article 21 of the Indian Constitution, which guarantees 'personal liberty.' In view of a statement by the Attorney General, it was not thought necessary to formally interfere with the impugned action. Opinions were, however, expressed that, in the circumstances of the case, the right to go abroad was not a fundamental right.

'Reasonable Restrictions' their Nature and Justiciability

Generally speaking, the validity of primary legislation, for e.g., an Act of Parliament, is not open to challenge on the ground of reasonableness, but 'reasonableness' is a recognized ground to challenge the validity of subordinate legislation such as rules, regulations etc.[39] But, this general rule does not apply where, under the constitution, a right is subject to 'reasonable restrictions' imposed by the law.

The term 'law' here embraces the law made by both primary and subordinate legislation, and the question of the 'reasonableness' of a restriction, even if imposed by primary legislation, is justiciable.

Power to Impose Restrictions is Legislative

The fundamental rights guaranteed by this Article and Articles 16, 17, 19 & 23 of the Constitution of Pakistan are subject to any 'reasonable restrictions' imposed by law. This means clearly an authority in the legislature to make law, within its legislative limits, imposing any 'reasonable restriction.' It has long been settled that –

> 'with respect to this there must necessarily be a large discretion on the part of the legislature. In determining the question of reasonableness, it (the legislature) is not likely to act with reference to he established usages, customs, and traditions of the people, and with a view to the promotion of their comfort, and the preservation of the public peace and good order.'[40]

The question, whether a restriction is or is not reasonable is justiciable, that is to say, amenable to judicial determination.[41] As was said by Chief Justice A.R. Cornelius (1903–91),[42] in the leading case on the subject namely *Saiyyad Abul A'la Maudoodi v. Government of West Pakistan*,[43] –

> 'the Constitution ... expressly gave the courts power of judicial review of legislation, and reason in such affairs being peculiarly the province of the judiciary, it is surely within judicial review to examine both as to the reasonableness of the law itself, as well as the reasonableness of the mode of application, of the restriction, whether such mode be prescribed by the statute or not.'

Thus, the very word 'reasonable' itself attracts the judicial process of ascertainment of the quality of consistency with reason. This excludes subjective satisfaction and, in judging whether a restriction is reasonable, an objective standard, that is, the standard of the average prudent man, should have to be applied.[44]

'Reasonableness' – Its Connotation and Test

The word 'reasonable' is a relative generic term difficult of adequate definition. It *inter-alia* connotes agreeable to reason, conformable to reason; having the faculty of reason; rational; thinking, speaking or acting rationally; or according to dictates of reason; sensible; just; proper and equitable or to act within the constitutional bounds.[45]

The question of whether a restriction is a reasonable restriction cannot be resolved by a 'litmus – paper test' that will separate valid from invalid restrictions. 'Instead, a Court must,' as was said in an American case,[46] resolve such a challenge by an analytical process that parallels its work in ordinary litigation.

> 'It must first consider the character and magnitude of the asserted injury to the rights protected by the First and Fourteenth Amendments that the plaintiff seeks to vindicate. It then must identify and evaluate the precise interests put forward by the state as justification for the burden imposed by its rule. In passing judgment, the court must not only determine the legitimacy and strength of each of those interests; it also must consider the extent to which those interests make it necessary to burden the plaintiff's rights. Only after weighing all those factors is the reviewing court in a position to decide.... whether the challenged provision is unconstitutional....... The results of this evaluation will not be automatic, as we have recognized, there is no substitute for the hard judgments that must be made.'

In *Saiyyad Abul A'la Maudoodi* case,[47] Justice Hamoodur Rehman (1910–81),[48] observed:

> '... from the very nature of things, no hard and fast rule can be laid down as to what matters are relevant or irrelevant for the purposes of determining the reasonableness of an act or restriction. Reasonableness is itself a relative term. What is unreasonable in one given set of circumstances may well be reasonable in another different set of circumstances. In my view, it will neither be possible nor advisable to lay down any exact or precise enumeration of the matters which may be taken into consideration for testing the reasonableness of such a restriction, for there can be no general standard of reasonableness applicable to all classes. It will certainly depend upon the nature of the right sought to be restricted, the nature and the extent of the restrictions sought to be imposed, the nature of the circumstances in which the restriction is to be imposed, the evil sought to be prevented or remedied, the necessity or urgency of the action proposed to be taken and the nature of the safeguards, if any, provided to prevent possibilities of abuse of power All these and there may well be other consideration, such as the objectives of the legislation and the prevailing conditions at the time, in the light of which the reasonableness has to be considered. This much, however, appeals from decided cases that the courts both in this country and in other foreign jurisdictions have treated a restriction as unreasonable if the restriction is for an indefinite or an unlimited period or disproportionate to the mischief sought to be prevented or if the law imposing the restriction has not provided any safeguard at all against arbitrary exercise of power. I am not prepared to go the extent of saying that if a law merely confers an unfettered discretion, then the law must necessarily be bad. It is not difficult to conceive of situations where power must be vested in some authority to take immediate action to prevent acts fraught with imminent danger, even though such prevention encroaches upon the fundamental rights guaranteed to citizens by the Constitution of the country. But here again the reasonableness of it would be dependent upon the circumstances which necessitate the taking of such drastic action, the duration for which it is to be taken and the safeguards provided against abuse of power. If the circumstances do not demand such action or the action is disproportionate to the mischief to be prevented and can be exercised without any check, then the restriction will certainly be unreasonable.'[49]

The test of reasonableness is to be applied in every case individually and not with reference to any abstract standard or general pattern of reasonableness. The proposition that emerges from decided cases is that –

> 'in deciding whether any particular law provides for reasonable restrictions on a fundamental right, not only the substantive portion of the law but also the procedural part by which the eventual result is secured has to be scrutinized.... The Court in such cases has to consider the nature of the restrictions, the manner in which they are imposed and their extent both territorial and temporal.'[50]

Chief Justice A.R. Cornelius in *Saiyyad Abul A'la Maududi's* case observed as under:[51]

> 'The courts cannot regard themselves as satisfied that the citizens' freedom has been subjected to a reasonable restriction unless it is proved to their satisfaction that not only the grounds of the restrictions as stated by *the law* are reasonable in themselves, but they have been applied reasonably as required by the Constitution. The only manner which the courts themselves would regard as reasonable – is that existence of the factual grounds of the restriction should have been established in the mode which the courts recognize as essential where a right to life or liberty or property is concerned, namely, after a proper hearing given to the person concerned.... Any presumption that the authority in question has acted in accordance with justice or reason or equity, if made by the courts in respect of such actions would, *in* my opinion, amount to a denial of the

> duty which the courts are called upon to discharge in respect of these fundamental matters. The duty of the courts would be thus to apply the principles of reason and justice according to the procedures with which they are familiar, to the ascertainment of the questions whether the restrictions in themselves are consistent with justice and reason, whether the conditions for their application have in fact been established, and whether they have been applied by competent authority. These are matters falling within the large principle of judicial review as a power possessed by the courts for the correction of excesses in action under law.'

As a result, in deciding if a restriction is a 'reasonable restriction,' the court has to engage in a balancing exercise. It begins with the presumption that the fundamental right in question is itself a matter of high public importance, that the power is to impose reasonable restrictions only, that nothing less than necessity will suffice to override the right, and that the necessity arises out of concern for the interests or interests listed in the article which provides for the fundamental right.

It may be a clear case of the restriction being reasonable, or it may be a clear case of the restriction being unreasonable, or it may be doubtful whether the restriction is or is not reasonable. The way to approach these issues was stated in the *Sardar Ram v. Haji Abdul Majid* case[52] as follows:

> 'What is reasonable is primarily for the decision of the legislature and ultimately for that of the Court. If the Court is satisfied that the restriction is reasonable it should have no difficulty in upholding the validity of the statute. If it is in doubt whether the restriction is or is not reasonable the Court must defer to the legislative wisdom and resolve the doubt in favour of the validity of the statute. If, however, the Court comes to entertain the view that the restriction is unreasonable beyond a reasonable doubt or if it is satisfied that the statute is manifestly in contravention of the Constitution it would plainly be the duty of the Court to interfere.'

Notes

1. *United States v. Guest*, 383 US 745 (1966).
2. PLD 1994 S.C. 23, 1998 SCMR 1072.
3. AIR 1954 SC 229.
4. Justice (R) Fazal Karim, *Judicial Review of Public Actions*, (Karachi: Pakistan Law House, 2006), p. 678.
5. A.G. Chaudhry, *Lectures on Constitutional Law*, (Lahore: Irfan Law Book House, 1994), pp. 149–150.
6. PLD 1969 Lahore 908.
7. AIR 1954 S.C. 229.
8. AIR 1961 S.C. 293.
9. AIR 1967 S.C. 1170.
10. AIR 1963 S.C. 1295.
11. AIR 1961 S.C. 1684.
12. PLD 1957 (W.P.) Lahore 388.
13. PLD 1957 (W.P.) Lahore 676.
14. (1969) 2 All ER 193 at p. 198.
15. (1999) 4 All ER 609 at p. 615.
16. PLD 1970 Lahore 168.
17. PLD 1958 (W.P.) Lahore 929, the Judgment is by Chief Justice M.R. Kiyani, on a difference of opinion between Justices Badi-uz-Zaman Kaikaus, and Akhlaq Hussain.
18. AIR 1963 Punjab-Haryana 36, 1963 CriLJ 59.
19. AIR 1963 Bombay 17, 1963 CriLJ 148.
20. AIR 1963 Allahabad 71, 1963 CriLJ 138.
21. AIR 1964 S.C. 416.
22. AIR 1971 S.C. 1667.
23. *Oregon v. Mitchell*, 400 US 112 (1970).
24. 314 US 160 (1941).
25. Robert H. Jackson was Associate Justice of the US Supreme Court from 1941 to 1954.
26. Muhammad Munir, *Constitution of the Islamic Republic of Pakistan: Being a Commentary on the Constitution of Pakistan, 1973*, (Lahore: PLD Publishing Company, 1975).
27. PLD 1998 SCMR 1072.
28. Saad Saood Jan was a judge of the Supreme Court of Pakistan.

29. PLD 2004 SC 583.
30. *Pakistan Muslim League(N) through Khawaja Muhammad Asif, M.N.A. and others v. Federation of Pakistan through Secretary Ministry of Interior*, PLD 2007 S.C. 642.
31. PLD 1987 S.C. 504.
32. *Califano v. Aznavorian*, 439 US 170 (1978).
33. 1972 SCMR 154.
34. PLD 1987 S.C. 504.
35. *Mumtaz Ali Bhutto v. Government of Pakistan*, PLD 1981 Karachi 98, approved in *Dada Amir Haidar Khan* case.
36. PLD 1997 Lahore 617.
37. PLD 1999 Lahore 372.
38. AIR 1978 SC 597.
39. *Government of Pakistan v. Akhlaque Hussain*, PLD 1965 SC 527.
40. Justice Henry Billings Brown Speaking for the court in *Plessy v. Ferguson*, 163 US 537 (1896).
41. Justice S.A. Rehman, in *Abul A'la Maudoodi v. Government of West Pakistan*, PLD 1964 SC 673, 730.
42. Alvin Robert Cornelius/A.R. Cornelius was the 4th Chief Justice of Pakistan from 1960 until 1968.
43. PLD 1964 SC 673.
44. Justice A.R. Changez, in *Qari Abdul Hameed Qadri v. District Magistrate*, PLD 1957 (W.P.) Lahore 213, and Justice Hamoodur Rehman in *Saiyyad Abul A'la Maudoodi* case – PLD 1964 SC 673.
45. Justice Ajmal Mian in *Elahi Cotton Mills v. Federation of Pakistan*, PTD 1997 SC 1555 at p. 678. This is based on a number of foreign and Pakistani cases.
46. *Anderson v. Celebrezze* 460 US 780, (1983).
47. PLD 1964 SC 673.
48. Hamoodur Rahman was the 7th Chief Justice of Pakistan from 1968 to 1975.
49. Relied upon by Chief Justice Muhammad Haleem in *Benazir Bhutto v. Federation of Pakistan*, PLD 1988 SC 416.
50. *Bazal Ahmed Ayubi v. West Pakistan Province*, PLD 1957 Lah 388.
51. PLD 1964 S.C. 673 at p. 700.
52. *Sardar Ram v. Haji Abdul Majid*, AIR 1960 PB 196.

25 Right to Counsel

Introductory

Historically, the 6th Amendment to the US Constitution guaranteed the right to counsel in 'all criminal prosecutions,' which meant that the government could not prevent a person accused of a crime from hiring a lawyer if he or she could afford to do so.

The US Supreme Court moved significantly away from this traditional view in the celebrated *Scottsboro* case of the 1930s. Here, the Court reversed the convictions of a group of young African-American men who had been sentenced to death in an Alabama court for allegedly raping two white women. During the rushed investigation and trial, conducted in an atmosphere of extreme racial animosity, the defendants were not represented by counsel in any meaningful sense. In *Powell v. Alabama*,[1] the US Supreme Court found that the defendants had been denied due process of law in violation of the 14th Amendment. The majority opinion of Justice George Sutherland's (1862–1942)[2] emphasized the trial judge's failure to ensure effective representation and adequate time to prepare a defense. Justice Sutherland laid stress on the essential relationship between 'the right to be heard' and 'the right to be heard by counsel'. The Court observed:

> 'All that is necessary now to decide, ... is that in a capital case where the defendant is unable to employ counsel, and is incapable adequately of making his own defence because of ignorance, feeble mindedness, illiteracy or the like, it is the duty of the court, whether requested or not, to assign counsel for him as a necessary requisite of due process of law....'

The *Gideon* Decision

Under Chief Justice Earl Warren (1891–1974), the US Supreme Court placed enormous stress on the need for professional representation of people who were suspected or accused of crimes. In the *Escobedo v. Illinois*[3] and *Miranda v. Arizona*[4] decisions, for example, the Warren Court was obviously concerned about the absence of defense counsel during custodial police interrogations.

In *Gideon v. Wainwright*,[5] the Court overruled precedent and held that the 6th Amendment 'right to counsel' as applied to the states via the 'Due Process Clause' of the 14th Amendment requires states to provide counsel to defendants who cannot afford to hire attorneys on their own. The *Gideon* Court recognized that –

> 'in our adversary system of criminal justice, any person hauled into court, who is too poor to hire a lawyer, cannot be assured a fair trial unless counsel is provided for him.'

In a related case decided on the same day as *Gideon*, (*Douglas v. California*)[6] [1963], the Court held that a state must provide counsel to an indigent defendant who has a right under state law to appeal a conviction to a higher court.

However, in *Pennsylvania v. Finley*,[7] the Court made clear what had been only implicit in *Douglas v. California*[8] – namely, that –

> 'the right to appointed counsel extends to the first appeal ... and no further.'

The aforementioned case law establishes –

(1) that appointment of counsel at state expense, in cases in which the accused cannot afford to hire a counsel, is a constitutional right in all criminal prosecutions, capital or non-capital;
(2) that the right is essential to fair trial; and

(3) that although the 'right to counsel' may not be expressly granted by the US Constitution, yet, it will be read as part of the right to due process of law.

As held in *Powell v. Alabama*, the fact that the right of an accused to have counsel was guaranteed expressly by the 6th Amendment, notwithstanding the 'Due Process Clause' in the 5th Amendment, does not exclude that right from the concept of 'due process of law'.[9]

When can the right to counsel invoked

It is because of the 6th Amendment to the US Constitution, that the right to 'have the assistance of counsel for his defence' is available to the accused persons 'in all criminal prosecutions,' the US Supreme Court has naturally remained concerned with the question of what may be described as 'criminal prosecution.'

A trial has always been held to be a 'criminal prosecution,' and there is therefore, no doubt that the 'right to counsel' is available at that critical and decisive stage of criminal proceedings. In *Massiah v. United States*,[10] the US Supreme Court noted that –

> 'under our system of justice the most elemental concepts of due process of law contemplates that an indictment be followed by a trial in an orderly courtroom, presided over by a judge, open to the public, and protected by all the procedural safeguards of the law.'

It was noted further that –

> 'during perhaps the most critical period of the proceedings…, that is to say, from the time of their arraignment until the beginnings of their trial, when consultation, thorough going investigation and preparation [are] vitally important, the defendants… [are] as much entitled to such aid [of counsel] during that period as at the trial itself.'

Massiah was a case in which the accused was, during investigation, under interrogation by the police and the US Supreme Court held that –

> 'a constitution which guarantees a defendant the aid of counsel at trial could surely vouchsafe no less to an indicted defendant under interrogation by the police in a completely extrajudicial proceeding. Anything less, might deny a defendant effective representation by counsel at the only stage when legal aid and advice would help him.'

In *Escobedo v. Illinois*,[11] the petitioner's request to be allowed to speak to his lawyer before he was interrogated was denied, and following *Massiah v. United States*, it was held that the 'guiding hand' of counsel was essential to advise him of his rights 'in this delicate situation':

> 'We hold, therefore, that where, as here, the investigation is no longer a general enquiry into an unsolved crime, but has begun to focus on a particular suspect, the suspect has been taken into police custody, the police carry out a process of interrogations that lends itself to eliciting incriminating statements, the suspect has requested and been denied an opportunity to consult with his lawyer, and the police have not effectively warned him of his absolute constitutional right to remain silent, the accused has been denied "the Assistance of Counsel" in violation of the 6th Amendment to the Constitution as made obligatory upon the states by the 14th Amendment (due process of law), and that no statement elicited by the police during interrogation may be used against him at a criminal trial.'

In one of the most famous American cases on the point–due to what is commonly known as '*Miranda Warnings*' – viz. *Miranda v. Arizona*,[12] which 'is an application of principles long recognized and applied in other settings,' and which held that –

> 'the prosecution may not use statements, whether exculpatory or inculpatory, stemming from custodial interrogation of the defendant unless it demonstrates the use of procedural safeguards effective to secure

> the privilege against self-incrimination .... As for the procedural safeguards to be employed.... the following measures are required. Prior to any questioning, the person must be warned that he has a right to remain silent, that any statement he does make may be used as evidence against him, and that he has a right to the presence of an attorney, either retained or appointed....'

In *Rothgery v. Gillespie County,*[13] the petitioner was indicted, arrested, and jailed without being provided a counsel at state expense. When he was finally assigned a lawyer, the lawyer's work led to the dismissal of the indictment. He sued for damages, and the question was whether he had been denied the 'right to counsel' and that turned on the point of time when the 'right to counsel' began. The US Supreme Court affirmed that –

> 'What we have held before and what an overwhelming majority of American jurisdictions understand in practice: a criminal defendant's initial appearance before a judicial officer, where he learns the charge against him and his liberty is subject to restriction, mark the start of adversary judicial proceedings that trigger attachment to the 6th Amendment right to counsel....'

Because *Gideon v. Wainwright*[14] was made retroactive, it had a tremendous impact on the criminal justice system. For example, in Florida State, where the *Gideon* case originated, the state was required to retry hundreds of convicted felons who had not been represented by counsel at their first trials. In many cases, the key witnesses were no longer available, and the state was forced to drop its charges. In the wake of *Gideon*, many states decided it would be more economical in the long run to set up permanent offices to handle indigent defense, rather than to have judges appoint counsel *ad hoc*. Most states now have public defenders to make good on the state's responsibility under the 'Due Process Clause' of the 14th Amendment. Although many state judges, legislators, governors, and law enforcement officers resented the Court's 'meddling' in their affairs, the *Gideon* decision has come, like so many other Supreme Court rulings, to be accepted and even praised by state officials.

For the most part, the Burger Court maintained this commitment to providing counsel to indigent defendants. In *Argersinger v. Hamlin,*[15] the US Supreme Court extended the *Gideon* ruling to cover misdemeanor trials (*Gideon v. Wainwright* applied only to felonies). The *Argersinger* decision was ambiguous, however, on the issue of whether misdemeanor defendants were entitled to counsel, if they faced possible jail terms or only if their convictions actually resulted in incarceration.

In *Scott v. Illinois,*[16] the US Supreme Court clarified the situation, holding that counsel had to be provided to indigent misdemeanants only if conviction would actually result in imprisonment. Writing for the Court, Justice William Rehnquist (1924–2005),[17] thus, opted for a narrow interpretation of *Argersinger*, arguing that –

> 'whereas any extension would create confusion and impose unpredictable, but necessarily substantial costs on 50 quite diverse states.'

In *Griffin v. Illinois,*[18] the defendant was denied transcript for appeal purposes because he could not afford to pay, Justice Hugo Black (1886–1971) said –

> 'there can be no equal justice where the kind of trial a man gets depends on the amount of money he has....'

Effectiveness of Appointed Counsel

One of the most elusive contemporary issues in the 'right to counsel' area is that of ineffective representation. As the US Supreme Court recognized in *Powell v. Alabama*, the 'right to counsel' is useless unless a defendant is competently represented. Until recently, most federal courts followed the mockery of justice test in determining the competency of appointed counsel.

The question was whether the attorney was so ineffective as to constitute 'a farce or mockery of justice,' for example, *Edwards v. United States.*[19] This permissive standard was rapidly adopted by most of the State Supreme Courts. However, the Federal Circuit Courts have adopted different standards of varying strictness. In 1984, the US Supreme Court finally standardized the test that courts must follow to comply with the 6th Amendment.

In *Strickland v. Washington,*[20] the Court held that an indigent appellant must show –

(1) that his or her trial lawyer was less than reasonably effective and
(2) that there is a reasonable probability that the outcome of the trial would have been different had counsel been more effective.

Obviously, this is a difficult test to meet, allowing for reversal only in cases of egregious incompetence.

Self-Representation

Although decisions such as *Powell v. Alabama*[21] and *Gideon v. Wainwright*,[22] stressed the importance of counsel in ensuring a fair trial, the US Supreme Court has made it quite clear that a defendant has a constitutional right to refuse counsel, as long as the waiver is made 'knowingly and intelligently.'

In *Faretta v. California*,[23] the Court decided a case in which Anthony Faretta, accused of grand theft, requested permission from the trial court to represent himself, arguing that the public defender's office was too busy to provide him with effective representation. The trial judge refused the request and appointed an assistant public defender to represent him. Faretta's conviction was ultimately vacated by the Supreme Court by a 6 to 3 vote. The majority asserted that –

> '[t]he language and spirit of the 6th Amendment contemplate that counsel, like the other defense tools guaranteed by the Amendment, shall be an aid to a willing defendant – not an organ of the state interposed between an unwilling defendant and his right to defend himself personally.'

Although the *Faretta* decision did not produce a rash of *pro se defenses* (those in which the defendant conducts his or her own defense), occasionally a defendant will 'go it alone' in the courtroom. In the early 1980s, a notable example of self-representation occurred during the trial of serial killer Ted Bundy in Florida. Bundy, a former law student, insisted on representing himself, despite the fact the trial judge appointed a lawyer as standby counsel. Although most analysts thought that Bundy did a reasonably effective job of representing himself, he still claimed on appeal that his conviction was invalid because he had ineffective representation at the trial. Not surprisingly, the Appellate Court was unmoved by this attempt to have it both ways.

Right to Counsel in India

Clause (1) of Article 22 of Indian Constitution further provides that the person arrested –

> 'shall not be denied the right to consult and to be defended by a legal practitioner of his choice.'

The right to consult and be defended by a legal practitioner of his choice is guaranteed with a view to enabling the defendant to prepare for his defence. This right belongs to the arrested person not only at the pre-trial stage, but also at the trial before a criminal court or before a special tribunal/court, and whether the arrest is made under a general law or under a special statute.[24]

In *Janardhan Reddy v. State of Hyderabad*,[25] the Indian Supreme Court taking the traditional view of Article 22(1) ruled that –

> 'the right to be defended by a legal practitioner of his choice.'

It could only mean a right of the accused to have the opportunity to engage a lawyer and does not guarantee an absolute right to be supplied with a lawyer by the state.

Since then, Article 39A, a Directive Principle of State Policy (DPSP), has been added to the Indian Constitution by the 42nd Constitutional Amendment, which enjoins the state to provide free legal aid and opportunities forthe accused to secure justice. This has also led to a new judicial view as to providing legal aid to an accused at his trial through an amendment to the Criminal Procedure Code (Cr.P.C.).[26]

Earlier, it was held that a demand to consult a lawyer must be made by the person arrested and that the Court was not bound to provide to him the help of a lawyer unless a request was made by him.[27] But, it is now held that it is the constitutional duty of the state to provide a lawyer to the detinue to defend him.

In *Hussainara Khatoon v. Home Secretary, State of Bihar*,[28] the Supreme Court of India, has laid down that it is the constitutional right of every accused person under Article 21, who is unable to engage a lawyer and secure legal service on account of reasons such as poverty, indigence or incommunicado situation, to have free legal services at state's expenses.

In *Joginder Kumar v. State of Uttar Pradesh*,[29] the Supreme Court of India has ruled that the right of an arrested person to have someone informed about his arrest and to consult privately with his lawyer is inherent in Articles 21 and 22. Thus, the right to consult a lawyer means the right to consult him away from the hearing of the police.[30] The right to be defended by a legal practitioner cannot be excluded by a statute because of the constitutional mandate under Article 22 (1).

In *State of Madhya Pradesh v. Shobharam*,[31] certain people were arrested under the provisions of the Criminal Procedure Code (C.Pr.C.), for committing the offence of criminal trespass and were prosecuted under the Madhya Bharat Panchayat Act 1949, by the Court of *Nyaya Panchayat*. Section 63 of the Panchayat Act has excluded legal practitioners from practicing before the Court of the *Nyaya Panchayat*. The Court imposed a fine of Rs 76/- on each accused. The Indian Supreme Court struck down Section 63 of the Madhya Bharat Panchayat Act 1949, as a violation of Article 22(1).

Prior to *Maneka Gandhi's*[32] decision in India, the Court held that it was not bound to provide legal assistance unless requested by the accused. But, as a result of the ruling of the Indian Supreme Court in *Maneka Gandhi's* and a series of cases following that case, it is clear that the courts are bound to provide the assistance of a lawyer to a person arrested under an ordinary law also.

The Supreme Court of India held in *Hussainara Khatoon v. Home Secretary, State of Bihar*, that it is the constitutional right of every accused person who is unable to engage a lawyer and secure legal services for reasons such as poverty, indigence or incommunicado situation, to have free legal services provided to him by the state and the state is under constitutional duty to provide a lawyer to such person if the needs of justice so require.[33] If free legal services are not provided, the trial itself may be vitiated by contravening Article 21. The protection of this Article is also not available to a person who has been convicted by a competent court and detained.[34]

A lawyer whom an accused has engaged for his defence cannot be put under a threat of criminal prosecution, because he would not be able to discharge his professional duty of defending his client in a fearless manner.[35]

The 'right to consult' a legal practitioner begins right from the day of arrest.[36] The right arises as soon as a person is arrested. According to Justice V. R. Krishna Iyer (1915–2014),[37] in *Nandini Satpathy v. Dani (P.L.)*,[38] Article 22(1) does not mean that a person who is not under arrest or custody can be denied the right to consult an advocate of his choice. The spirit and sense of Article 22(1) is that it is fundamental to the rule of law that the services of a lawyer should be available for consultation to any accused person under 'circumstances of near custodial interrogation.'

Right to be represented by a Lawyer before Review Board

The observation of the Supreme Court of India in *Francis Coralie v. Union Territory of Delhi*,[39] that a detainee has the right to consult a legal advisor of his choice for any purpose, including his release from preventive detention, which was left open by the Indian Supreme Court in *A.K. Roy v. Union of India*[40] without confirmation or rejection. But it held in this case that –

> 'if the detaining authority or the government takes the aid of legal practitioner or advisor before the Review Board, the detenue must be allowed the facility of appearing before the Board through a legal practitioner,'

and denial of such facility would invalidate detention. It was further held that the detenue is entitled to be aided or assisted, if he so demands, 'by a friend, who in truth and substance, is not a legal practitioner' in the proceedings before the Board.

Right to Counsel in Pakistan

The constitutional provisions that give an accused person the right to be defended by counsel must be read as part of the law, irrespective of whether the law gives or denies such a right. This was held by the Dacca High Court in *Mrs Rowshan Bijaya Shaukat Ali Khan v. Govt. of East Pakistan*,[41] and by the Lahore High Court in *Malik Muhammad Usman v. The State, through E.A.C. and A.D.M., Quetta and another*,[42] which held that the provision of the law, which deny to such person the right to be defended by a legal practitioner are void, unless the arrest is under a law relating to preventive detention. The person arrested must be given, as held in *Moslemuddin Sikadar v. Chief Secretary, Govt. of East Pakistan*,[43] a reasonable opportunity to engage a counsel and the counsel engaged must be given reasonably opportunity to defend the arrested person.

Pakistan's Constitution, in granting the 'right to counsel' in its Article 10, Clause (1) is more definitive and explicit. It grants not only the right 'to be defended' by counsel, which is the same thing as the 6th Amendment of the US Constitution providing 'to have the assistance of counsel for his defence,' but also, in express terms, the right to consult with a counsel. As the case law discussed above shows demonstrably and clearly, the right 'to consult' is relevant more appropriately at the investigation stage, when the suspect needs advice on his constitutional rights, particularly on his right to silence or right against self-incrimination. The whole purpose of the police interrogation of a suspect is to extract evidence from him and that, as regard to him, is, therefore, the most critical stage of criminal proceedings.[44]

Right of a government servant to counsel in Inquiry Proceedings

The law of civil servants in Pakistan prohibited engaging a lawyer to represent a civil servant facing disciplinary action before enquiry officer or enquiry tribunal.[45]

On challenge, the Lahore High Court held that the 'right to counsel' grows out of Article 4 of the 1973 Constitution, because it provides every individual the right to enjoy the protection of the law and to be treated in accordance with the law. The rule disallowing the appearance of lawyer in inquiry proceedings was struck down as unconstitutional.[46] Representation through lawyers is necessary for an effective defence in the inquiry proceedings, particularly for the exercise of the right to cross examine the witnesses being produced against the accused government servant.[47] However, when one of these judgments was challenged before the Supreme Court of Pakistan, it did not give any findings and decided the case at a different point.[48]

The Supreme Court of Pakistan has given its view in a recent case titled *Ishtiaq Ahmad v. Honorable Competent Authority*.[49] In this case, the petitioner, who had served as a private secretary at the Supreme Court, was dismissed from service on the orders of the Chief Justice of Pakistan. The petitioner filed an appeal against the order of the dismissal before the tribunal consisting of the Chief Justice and two most senior judges of the Supreme Court. This Appeal was filed under Rule 13 of the Supreme Court (Appointment of Officers and Servants and Terms and Conditions of Service) Rules 1982. His appeal was dismissed by the tribunal. One of the difficulties faced by the petitioner was that, under the aforesaid Rule 13, he could not be represented by a counsel of his choice. Rule 13 is reproduced below:

> 'Rule 13: Advocates Bar to appear. At no stage of the proceedings under these Rules, the person concerned shall be represented by an Advocate.'

Subsequently, these rules of 1982 were repealed and substituted by the Supreme Court (Establishment) Rules 2015. Rule 17 of 2015, the new rules, also barred an advocate from appearing in the proceedings. Rule 17 is reproduced as below:

> 'Rule 17: Bar against appearance of counsel. At no stage of the proceedings under these Rules, the, person concerned shall be represented by an Advocate.'

The petitioner challenged both the rules in a petition under Article 184(3) of the Pakistan Constitution, pleading that these rules were against the fundamental right of representation through counsel, and therefore, be declared as *ultra vires* and that his appeal be relisted for hearing on the merits, so that the petitioner could present an advocate on his behalf as his counsel. This petition was heard at length, but was eventually dismissed by a bench of 3 judges of the Supreme Court headed by the then Chief Justice Anwar Zaheer Jamali (1951).[50] It was determined that the petitioner had failed to address how the Appellate forum comprising of three senior judges of the Supreme Court had prejudiced him. It would not suffice to grant relief solely because he had been denied the right to representation through counsel.

Another judge on the bench wrote a concurring note, in which he held that the issue before the Appellate forum was whether there was any justification available for petitioner's long absence from the duty. Seeing the documents produced by the parties and after taking into consideration the order of dismissal passed by the Chief Justice of Pakistan imposing a major penalty, it is to be noted that the petitioner had not alleged any bias, prejudice or partisanship against any member of the tribunal who had heard his appeal.

He also held that the constitutional rights of fair trial, due process and access to justice or inherent rights that predicated every proceeding that may conclude in a penalty being imposed on an accused person, did not lay down any requirement that an affected accused officer before any 'domestic fora' in disciplinary proceedings must be represented by counsel. The constitutional right of consultation with and be represented by counsel under Article 10(1) of the Constitution, or the right of representation, was limited to cases involving arrest, detention, and confinement under the law of the land, whether it was criminal law, a detention law, or any other law imposing penalty of confinement on an offender. None of the penalties that could be imposed under the Supreme Court (Appointment of Officers and Servants and Terms and Conditions of Service) Rules 1982 [since repealed and replaced by the Supreme Court Establishment Service Rules 2015] inflicted personal restraints on an accused person's liberty that were envisaged by Article 10(1) of the Constitution of Pakistan. It was therefore clear that the express exclusion of the right of representation of an accused by counsel under Rule 13 of the Rules of 1982, or Rule 17 of the Rules of 2015, did not violate any of his rights conferred by the Constitution or the law. Equally, the procedural statutes, which regulated Court proceedings and granted the right of representation to an accused or a defendant, did not apply to the proceedings of a domestic appellate forum in disciplinary proceedings. These statutes were the Code of Criminal Procedure 1898 (Pak. Code Crim. Proc.), and the Code of Civil Procedure 1908 (Pak. Code Civ. Proc.). Exclusion of the said statutes did not offend or violate any higher right conferred on an accused person in disciplinary proceedings by the law or the Constitution.

It was further held that there was significant difference between the substantive nature 'of trial by a Court of law' as against the proceedings in a domestic disciplinary forum. Consequently, the entitlement to representation of an accused by counsel before a trial court could not, by analogy, be imported into the proceedings of a domestic appellate disciplinary forum constituted by Rule 11 of the Rules of 1982 (since repealed). The relief of representation through counsel claimed by the petitioner was neither apt nor appropriate for the *fora* established under disciplinary laws governing the service rights of officers and staff (of the Supreme Court) that were governed by rules having the force of law. As a result, the constitutional petition was dismissed.

With due respect, the Supreme Court's position appears to be *ex facie* erroneous and misconceived. Firstly, the Court failed to appreciate that the very denial of representation through counsel is violative of the fundamental rights guaranteed under the constitution. Secondly, the Court should not have gone into the merits of the case, which the petitioner was forced to present himself personally. The Court failed to appreciate that a former employee of the Supreme Court and also of the level of private secretary cannot be expected to present his case forcefully and effectively before the Chief Justice and the senior judges of the Supreme Court. He would obviously be overwhelmed by the mere presence of the senior judges. Thirdly, even in the matter of domestic enquiry, it cannot be denied that the same thing is before the judges of the country's highest Court, which would necessitate the intervention of a lawyer of standing who could effectively argue the case. Fourthly, the reliance on Article 10(1) of the Pakistan Constitution, which deals with orders of detention, was clearly misconceived. The argument regarding the right of representation in a service matter was based on Article 10A of the Constitution, which guarantees the right of fair trial and due process to every citizen. For all intents and purposes, a domestic enquiry against a Supreme Court employee would fall within the general principles of fair trial and due process. Thus, depriving the presentation of his case through counsel of his choice would be violative of due process under the Constitution.

The Supreme Court of Pakistan ought to have taken a liberal and wider view of the interpretation of the 'right to counsel' rather than a narrow and pedantic view of the same thing.

NOTES

1. 287 U.S. 45 (1932).
2. George Sutherland was Associate Justice of the US Supreme Court between 1922 and 1938.
3. 378 U.S. 478 (1964).
4. 384 U.S. 436 (1966).
5. 372 U.S. 335 (1963).
6. 372 U.S. 353 (1963).
7. 481 U.S. 551 (1987).
8. 372 U.S. 353 (1963).
9. Justice Fazal Karim, *Judicial Review of Public Actions, Volume 2*, 2nd ed., (Karachi: Pakistan Law House, 2018), pp. 848–50.
10. 377 U.S. 201 (1964).
11. 378 U.S. 478 (1964).
12. 384 U.S. 436 (1966).
13. 554 U.S. 191 (2008).
14. 372 U.S. 335 (1963).
15. 407 U.S. 25 (1972).
16. 440 U.S. 367 (1979).
17. William Rehnquist was the 16th Chief Justice of the United States from 1986 to 2005.
18. 351 U.S. 12 (1956).
19. 358 U.S. 847 (1958).
20. 466 U.S. 668 (1984).
21. 287 U.S. 45 (1932).
22. 372 U.S. 335 (1963).
23. 422 U.S. 806 (1975).
24. *State of Madhya Pradesh v. Shobharam*, AIR 1966 SC 1910.
25. AIR 1951 SC 217: 1951 SCR 344.
26. Section 304(1), Cr.P.C., has now been added which runs as:
    'WHERE, in a trial before the court of session, the accused is not represented by a pleader, and where it appears to the court that the accused has not sufficient means to engage a pleader, the court shall assign a pleader for his defence at the expense of the State.'
27. *Ram Sarup v. Union of India*, AIR 1965 SC 247.
28. 1979 AIR 1369, 1979 SCR (3) 532.
29. AIR 1994 SC 1349.
30. *Moti Bai v. State of Rajasthan*, AIR 1954 Raj 241.
31. AIR 1966 SC 1910.
32. *Maneka Gandhi v. Union of India*, AIR 1978 S.C. 597.
33. AIR 1979 S.C. 1377.
34. *Keshar Singh v. Speaker of Uttar Pradesh Assembly*, AIR 1965 Allahabad 349.
35. *Sri Jayendra Saraswathy v. State of Tamil Nadu*, AIR 2006 S.C. 6; (2005) 8 SCC 771.
36. *Moti Bai v. State of Rajasthan*, AIR 1954 Raj. 241.
37. V. R. Krishna Iyer served as the Justice of the Supreme Court of India from 1973 to 1980.
38. *Nandini Satpathy v. P.L. Dani*, AIR 1978 SC 1025 (1978), 2 SCC 424.
39. AIR 1981 S.C 746.
40. AIR 1982 S.C. 710.
41. PLD 1965 Dacca 241.
42. PLD 1965 (W. P.) Lahore 229.
43. PLD 1957 S.C. 101.
44. Supra Note 5, p. 853.
45. Rule 10A of the Government Servant (Efficiency and Discipline) Rules 1973; and Rule 7-B of the Punjab Civil Servant (Efficiency and Discipline) Rules 1975.
46. *Aslam Ali Shah v. Collector of Central Excise and Land Customs*, 1983 P.L.C. (C.S.) 498.
47. *Muhammad Saeed Ahmed Khan v. Secretary to Govt. of Pb., Housing and Planning Deptt.*, PLD 1983 Lahore 206.
48. *Collector, Excise and Land Customs v. Aslam Ali Shah*, PLD 1985 S.C. 82.
49. 2016 SCMR 943.
50. Anwar Zaheer Jamali served as the 24th Chief Justice of Pakistan from 2015 to 2016.

Part VII

Evolving Constitutional Concepts

26 Doctrine of Necessity

INTRODUCTORY

> 'Necessity is the plea for every infringement of human freedom, it is the argument of every tyrant; it is the creed of slaves.'[1]

Legal precepts include laws and rules made by the legislature, customs, usages and judicially evolved doctrines and precedents. Necessity is one of those judicially created elusive doctrine that is applied to cases before courts but its scope remains undetermined. In criminal law, necessity has been accepted as a defence since very recent times. If an act is done or omitted under necessity, then the law does not apply to that act or omission. It is no longer a defence against murder, sedition and treason. Similarly, an act may be a civil wrong, but if done out of necessity, it creates an exception to the liability.

In public law, too, there are rules enshrined in the Constitution or Acts of Parliament. These rules govern and apply to specific situations, but when there is a mismatch between the public law and the political fact,[2] the courts have evolved and applied the doctrine of necessity to bridge the gap. Two Latin legal maxims, *'Necessitas non habet legem'* 'Necessity knows no law' and *Salus populi est suprema lex* 'welfare of the people is the supreme law' provided legal basis to justify the dissolution of assembly as argued by Sir Ivor Jennings (1903–65),[3] who defended the dissolution of Pakistan's first Constituent Assembly by the then Governor General, Ghulam Muhammad (1895–1956)[4]. Chief Justice Muhammad Munir (1895–1979)[5] was able to introduce this legal concept by giving it doctrinal shape, which became a feature of jurisprudence in Pakistan. It is now called the Doctrine of State Necessity. Its precise legal form is not without ambiguity, but so far it is certain that necessity is not merely a political fact to which normal rules of public law do not apply, but also a legal concept which is a rule or doctrine which is applied by the courts to justify a clear violation of the Constitution or law. Muhammad Munir left an immutable footprint on Pakistan's constitutional and political history with his own ideas of government. Because he dominated the Court, he wrote the majority of significant decisions of the Pakistan Federal Court (now Supreme Court) until his retirement as Chief Justice of Pakistan in 1960. His judgments reflect his political philosophy, favouring a strong executive.[6]

Muhammad Munir and Chief Justice John Marshall (1755–1835)[7] can be compared to one another due to their legal genius. Marshall had played no role in the Constitution making process. But on becoming Chief Justice of the United States Supreme Court, he used judicial review against James Madison (1755–1836)[8], a litigant in *Marbury v. Madison*[9], the first case in which the 'doctrine of judicial review' was articulated. Despite the fact that Madison was one of the most influential members of the Constitutional Convention (1787) in shaping the ideas of the US Constitution, it was Marshall who decided the true meaning of the Constitution. Justice Munir did the same in *Moulvi Tamizuddin's* case, holding that it was his understanding of Pakistan's Dominion Constitution which made it necessary to strike down a law that had been passed in violation of the Dominion Constitution notwithstanding the fact that Munir had played no part in deliberations led by Muhammad Ali Jinnah (1876–1948) for Interim Constitution of Pakistan. In the case of both Munir and Marshall, it was a judge who assumed the power of determining the intent of the Constitution, not Jinnah and Madison, who participated in the making of the Constitution.[10]

The difference lies somewhere else. Chief Justice Munir used his genius, which proved to be a genius, to demolish Pakistan's constitutionalism, but Chief Justice Marshall demonstrated great legal statesmanship. Chief Justice Munir's decision in *Moulvi Tamizuddin's* case[11] served the obvious purpose of making the Governor General happy, but it also cast a long shadow over Pakistan's subsequent legal history and sowed the seeds of thorny weeds that have forever weakened the country's democracy.

The consequences of the mistakes committed in *Moulvi Tamizuddin's* case soon began to appear. It was held in *Moulvi Tamizuddin's* case that the assent of the Governor General was necessary for the validity of every piece of legislation. The immediate consequence was that all the legislative instruments, whether constitutional or ordinary laws, became void. When the Federal Court was confronted with its findings in *Moulvi Tamizuddin's* case, it did not hesitate to state the legal position more clearly in the case of *Usif Patel v. Crown.*[12] Justice Munir, despite knowing the consequences, did not provide the solution through the same judgment as he did in a later case, for reasons best known to him. The constitutional and legal impasse was thus created in *Usif Patel's* case when the Governor General attempted to undo the wrong committed by him when the appellants in the said case relied on *Moulvi Tamizuddin's* case that Governor General's assent for legislation including the Sind Control of *Goondas* Act 1952, whereunder the appellant and others were detained and thus their detention was illegal. Caught between the devil and the deep blue sea, the Governor General again resorted to the Federal Court headed by Justice Munir to find a legal bridge to cross the deep legal gulf dug by them together.

It is in this background that the Governor General filed a reference under Section 42 of the Government of India Act 1935, (which, with necessary amendments, was adopted as the Interim Constitution of Pakistan) for the advice of the Federal Court.

Four (4) questions were raised in the *Governor General's Reference No. 1,*[13] but out of these, only question No. 2 would be relevant for the present purpose. Question No. 2 was formulated as under:

> 'The Federal Court having held in *Usif Patel*'s case that the laws listed in the Schedule to the Emergency Powers Ordinance could not be validated under Section 42 of the Government of India Act 1935, nor retrospective effect given to them and no legislature competent to validate such laws being in existence is there any provision in the Constitution or any rule of law applicable to the situation by which the Governor General can by Order or otherwise declare that all orders made, decisions taken and other acts done under those laws shall be valid and enforceable and those laws which cannot without danger to the state be removed from the existing legal system shall be treated as part of the law of the land until the question of their validation is determined by the new Constituent Convention?'

The opinion given by Munir on the above question (and with him agreed Justice A.S.M. Akram (1888–1968)[14] and Justice S.A. Rehman (1903–90)[15] by adding their separate notes) was in the following words:

> 'That in the situation presented by the Reference the Governor General has, during the interim period, the power under the common law of civil and state necessity retrospectively validating the laws listed in the Schedule to the Emergency Powers Ordinance 1955, and all those laws, until the question of their validation is decided by the Constituent Assembly are, during the aforesaid period valid and enforceable in the same way as if they had been valid from the date on which they purported to come into force.'

Before proceeding further, it would be appropriate to give *in exentio* the particular finding given by Munir on the doctrine of civil and state necessity. He stated:

> 'The principle clearly emerging from this address of Lord Mansfield[16] is that subject to the conditions of absoluteness, extremeness, and imminence, an act which would otherwise be illegal becomes legal if it is done *bona fide* under the stress of necessity, necessity being referable to an intention to preserve the constitution, the State or the Society and to prevent it from dissolution and affirms Chitty's[17] statement that necessity knows no law and the maxim cited by Bracton[18] that necessity makes lawful which otherwise is not lawful. Since the address expressly refers to the right of private person to act in necessity, in the case of Head of the State justification to act must *a fortiori* be clearer and more imperative.
>
> This being the position regarding the individual acts, the next question is whether the Head of the State can, in the circumstances postulated, legislate for the society. The Court has held in *Usif Patel's* case that the Governor General has no power to make such laws as are mentioned in the subsection (1) of Section 8 of the Indian Independence Act, 1947, but that decision was limited to the Governor General's powers under Section 42 of the Government of India Act, 1935, no other source for the power to pass such laws having been claimed for him in that case. If it once be conceded that the power to act in an emergency of the nature just indicated exists, the conclusion is inescapable that the act may be done by a general order which as admitted by the Mr Pritt[19] would amount to legislation. If, the law as stated by Chitty that the Crown is the only branch of legislature that is capable of performing any act at a time when Parliament is not in being is correct, legislative powers of the Crown in an emergency are necessary corollary from that statement, and the same result flows from Dicey's[20] statement that the free exercise of a discretionary or prerogative powers at a critical juncture is essential to the executive Government of every civilized country, the indispensable condition being that the exercise of that power is always subject to the legislative authority of Parliament, to be exercised *ex post facto.*

> The manner in which such power is exercised, whether in individual cases or by positive directions or restraint order of general character, is essentially a question of method and detail, not affecting the main principle. The emergency legislative power, however cannot extend to matter which are the product of necessity, as for instance, changes in the constitution which are directly referable to emergency.'

The above paragraphs are reproduced from Justice Munir's opinion in *Governor General's Reference No. 1.*[21] Since this discourse is not directly concerned with the correctness or otherwise of the advisory opinion rendered by the Federal Court, suffice to say that, as a whole, the opinion is not free from legal flaws. Professor Stanley Alexander De Smith (1922–74)[22] commented as follows:

> 'It is clear ... the leading Pakistan decision in 1955 was not very well disguised act of political judgment. By normal cannons of construction, what the Governor General had done was null and void. But the judges steered between Scylla and Charybdis and chose what seemed to them to be the least of evils.'[23]

Since this discourse is focused on the Doctrine of State Necessity, therefore a few points are noticeable:

1. The fundamental conditions for the application of the doctrine were the absoluteness, extremeness and imminence and the *bona fide.*
2. In the case of the Head of the State (whose legitimacy is not an issue) justification to act under necessity must *a fortiori* be clearer and more imperative.
3. The act of acting under necessity cannot extend to acts, which are not the product of necessity, as for instance changes in constitution, which are directly referable to the emergency.
4. The legitimacy granted to the acts of the Governor General was only temporary and the Governor General was advised to convene the Constituent Assembly at the earliest and that those laws were to be legitimized by the Constituent Assembly.

The next case in Pakistan wherein the doctrine of necessity was applied was *Asma Jilani's* case.[24] In this case, the Supreme Court heard two criminal appeals challenging the detention of certain persons under General Yahya Khan (1917–80)[25] martial law regulations. Consequently, the martial law regulations and the regime of Yahya Khan were challenged in those appeals. The Supreme Court of Pakistan, in its unanimous judgment, declared General Yahya Khan to be a usurper. The obvious consequence of such a ruling was that all legal instruments and Acts done (like the Legal Framework Order and other Orders where under the general elections were held in 1970) were bound to be declared illegal and void. Such a decision without finding 'a legal bridge' would have created disastrous consequences. Faced with this dilemma, the Supreme Court adopted the Doctrine of State Necessity (since the precedent at home was available) to resolve the legal impasse. Chief Justice Hamoodur Rehman (1910–81)[26] was, however, mindful of the consequences and, therefore, he attempted to write his opinion with great caution in the following words:

> 'This does not however dispose of the case for we were again presented by the learned Attorney General with the argument that a greater chaos might result by the acceptance of this principle of legitimacy. He has reminded the Court of the grave consequences that followed when in *Moulvi Tamizuddin's* case a similar argument was spurned by the Federal Court and "disaster brought in" I am not unmindful of the grave responsibility that rests upon courts not to do anything which might make confusion worse confounded or create a greater state of chaos if that can possibly be avoided consistently with their duty to decide in accordance with law.'[27]

Having stated the problem in its right context, the Chief Justice proceeded to examine the ways out and came to a conclusion, as under:

> 'I am too of the opinion that recourse has to be taken to the doctrine of necessity where ignoring of it would result in disastrous consequences to the body politic and upset the social order itself but I respectfully beg to disagree with this doctrine as a doctrine of validating the illegal act of usurpers. In my humble opinion, this doctrine can be invoked in aid only after the court has come to the conclusion that the acts of the usurper were illegal and illegitimate. It is only then that the question arises as to how many of his acts,

legislative or otherwise, should he condoned or maintained. I would call this principle of condonation and not legitimization.'

Before proceeding further, it is necessary to refer to the other leading judgment in the case given by Justice Muhammad Yaqoob Ali (1912–94),[28] who, while dealing with the question of condoning the acts of the usurper, held as follows:

> 'The next question which arises for determination is whether these illegal legislative acts are protected by the doctrine of state necessity. The laws saved by this rule do not achieve legitimacy. They remain illegal, but acts done, and proceedings undertaken under invalid laws may be condoned on the conditions that recognition given by the Court is proportionate to the evil averted, it is transitory and temporary in character—does not imply abdication of judicial review.'

What was held by the courts in the above two cases can be summed up as under:

What the Governor General was asking was constitutional power to validate the laws declared void as a result of the decision of the Federal Court.

1. The doctrine of civil and state necessity was essentially a common law doctrine and as admitted by Chief Justice Munir, it could not be extended to the constitutional domain. The very extension of the doctrine to the facts of the situation arisen in 1955 was by no means free from legal flaws.
2. In *Asma Jilani's* case Chief Justice and the senior puisne judge did not agree with Munir, that through the doctrine of necessity what is illegal could become legal. They rather accepted it as only a doctrine, which condoned the illegal acts and that too for acts, which were in conformity with the previous Legal Order and necessary for the smooth running of the state. In *Asma Jilani's* case, the regulation under which the appellants were detained was not condoned and they were set free.

DOCTRINE OF NECESSITY AND MILITARY TAKE OVERS; THE CASE OF PAKISTAN

It is clear from the decision in *Asma Jilani's* case and also from the advisory opinion by the Federal Court that the Doctrine of State Necessity has been established and accepted by the courts in Pakistan. However, its exact scope was not clear and, though applied in *Asma Jilani's* case, it differed in its scope from what was held in the *Governor General's Reference No. 1* of 1955. It was, however, common and clear that this doctrine could not be used to override the constitution.

At midnight of 4 and 5 July 1977, the Chief of Army Staff General Ziaul Haq (1924–88) seized power and declared Martial Law throughout Pakistan. The sitting Prime Minister Zulfikar Ali Bhutto (1928–1979), and other members of his cabinet and party workers, were arrested and detained. The wife of the deposed Prime Minister, Begum Nusrat Bhutto (1929–2011), challenged the detention through a direct constitutional petition under Article 184(3) of the Pakistan Constitution, praying for the issuance of a writ in the nature of *Habeas Corpus*. Since the detenue was kept under the Martial Law Regulations issued by the new regime, the essential question was the constitutionality and legality of those regulations. The writ was filed against the Chief of Army Staff and the Federation of Pakistan was arrayed as a party at the Court's notice. It is also important to point out that soon after the takeover by the Military, the 5th and 6th Amendments to the Constitution were annulled by the new regime, resulting in the retirement of the Chief Justice Muhammad Yaqoob Ali (1912–94) and in his place Justice Anwarul Haq (1917–95)[29] was sworn in as the Chief Justice. Chief Justice Haq after grappling with various legal concepts, came to the following conclusion as far as the Doctrine of State Necessity was concerned:

> 'a review of the concept of the law of necessity, as recognized in the various jurisdictions clearly confirms the statement made in this behalf by Muhammad Munir, C.J. in *Reference by H.E. Governor General PLD 1955 FC 435*, to the effect that an act which would otherwise be illegal becomes legal if it is done *bona fide* under the stress of necessity, the necessity being referable to an intention to preserve the Constitution, the State or the society and to prevent it from dissolution. The principle has been reiterated by the Supreme Court in *Asma Jilani's* case with the difference that where the Court is dealing with the acts of a usurper, such acts may be condoned and not validated by the application of the law of necessity. It seems to me, therefore, that on

> facts, of which we have taken judicial notice, namely the imposition of the Martial Law was impelled by high considerations of State Necessity and welfare of the people, the extra-constitutional step taken by the Chief of the Army Staff to overthrow the Government of Mr Z. A. Bhutto as well as the Provincial Governments and to dissolve the Federal and Provincial/Legislatures stands validated in accordance with the doctrine of necessity.

Now, after accepting the Doctrine of Necessity as a valid legal principle to validate the illegal acts of the Chief Martial Law administrator, it was contended by the Attorney General that once the takeover was validated on the principle of necessity, then the Chief Martial Law Administrator would have the right to govern the country in any manner he thought best and the Courts in Pakistan would be bound by the provisions of the Laws (continuance in Force) Order 1977, which must henceforth be treated as a supra-constitutional instrument, binding on all authorities in Pakistan.[30]

The submissions of the Attorney General were a clear indication of the Chief of the Army Staff intentions to remain in power indefinitely. But Chief Justice Anwarul Haq articulated his viewpoint as follows:

> 'It will be seen that the declared objectives of the imposition of Martial Law are to create conditions suitable for the holding of free and fair elections in terms of the 1973 Constitution, which was not being abrogated, and only certain parts of which being held in abeyance, namely the parts dealing with the Federal and Provincial executives and legislatures. The President of Pakistan was to continue to discharge his duties as heretofore under the same Constitution. Soon after the polls the power is to be transferred to the elected representatives of the people. It is true that owing to the process of completing the process of accountability of holders of public offices, the holding of elections had to be postponed for the time being but the declared intention of the Chief Martial Law Administrator still remains the same, namely that he has stepped in for temporary period and for the limited purpose of arranging free and fair elections so as to enable the country to return to a democratic way of life.
>
> In the presence of these unambiguous declarations, it would be highly unfair and uncharitable to attribute any other intention to the Chief Martial Law Administrator, and to insinuate that he has not assumed power for purposes stated above by him, or that he does not intend to restore democratic institutions in terms of the 1973 Constitutions.'

Finally the learned Chief Justice came to the conclusion:

> 'As a result, the true legal position which, therefore, emerges:
>
> i) That the 1973 Constitution still remains the Supreme law of the land, subject to the condition that certain parts thereof have been held in abeyance on account of state necessity;
> ii) That the President of Pakistan and the superior courts continue to function under the Constitution. The mere fact that the judges of superior courts have taken a new oath after the proclamation of Martial Law, does not in any manner derogate from this position, as the Courts had been originally established under 1973 Constitution, and have continued in their functions in spite of the proclamation of Martial Law;
> iii) That the Chief Martial Law Administrator, having validly assumed power by means of an extra-Constitutional step, in the interest of the State and for the welfare of the people, is entitled to perform all such acts and promulgate all legislative measures which have been consistently recognized by judicial authorities as falling within the scope of the law of necessity, namely:—
>
> a) All acts, all legislative measures which are in accordance with, or could have been made under the 1973 Constitution, *including the power to amend it*;[31]
> b) All acts which tend to advance or promote the good of the people,
> c) All acts required to be done for the ordinary orderly running of the State; And
> d) All such measures as would establish or lead to the establishment of the declared objectives of the proclamation of Martial Law, namely, restoration of law and order, and normalcy in the country, and earliest possible holding of free and fair election for the purpose of restoration of democratic institutions under the 1973 Constitution;
>
> iv) That these acts, or any of them, may be performed or carried out by means of Presidential Orders, Ordinances, Martial Law Regulations, or Orders as the occasion may require; and
> v) That the superior Courts continue to have the power of judicial review to judge the validity of any act or action of the Martial Law Authorities, if challenged, in light of the principles underlined the law of

> necessity as stated above. Their powers under Article 199 of the Constitution thus remains available to their full extent, and may be exercised as heretofore, notwithstanding anything to the contrary contained in any Martial Law Regulation or Order, Presidential Order or Ordinance.
>
> (the *italics* are by the authors)
>
> This last point needs a little explanation. In the body of this judgment, opinions of certain text book writers and contemporary jurists have been quoted in support of the proposition that the Courts established under the pre-existing Legal Order continue to have the power and jurisdiction to adjudicate upon the validity and effectiveness of the new Legal Order. As it was held that the new Legal Order would only be for a temporary period, and for a specified and limited purpose and did not seek to destroy the old Legal Order but merely to hold certain parts thereof in abeyance or to subject it to certain limitations on the ground of state necessity or on the principle of *salus populi supreme lex*, the superior Courts continued to remain the judges of the validity of the actions of the new regime in the light of the doctrine of necessity, for the new regime then represented not a new legal Order, but only a phase of constitutional deviation dictated by necessity.
>
> There is yet another, and a stronger reason for holding that the power of judicial review continues. The 1973 Constitution provides for clear trichotomy of powers between the executive; legislative and judicial organs of the state. However, owing to reasons of necessity, the executive and the legislative powers now stands combined in one authority, for the reason that these two organs of the state had lost their constitutional and moral authority in the circumstances arising since the 7th of March 1977, but no such considerations arose in regard to the judicial organ of the state. Accordingly, on no principle of necessity could powers of judicial review vested in the superior courts under the 1973 Constitution be taken away.
>
> Next, even if for any reason the principle or power of judicial review embodied in the relevant provisions of the 1973 Constitution be held not to be available under the new dispensation, the fact remains that the ideology of Pakistan embodying the doctrine that sovereignty belongs to Allah and is to be exercised on his behalf as a sacred trust by the chosen representatives of the people, strongly militates against placing the ruler for the time being above the law, and not accountable to anyone in the realm. Muslim rulers have always regarded themselves as being accountable to the courts of the land for all their actions and have never claimed exemption even from personal appearance in the courts. The Courts of Justice or an embodiment and a symbol of the conscience of the *Millat* (Muslim community) and provide an effective safeguard for the rights of the subjects. On this principle as well, the power of judicial review for judging the validity of the actions of the Martial Law Authorities must continue to remain in the superior Courts.
>
> Lastly, the Court is bound to take note of the fact that already several instances have been brought to its notice where the ordinary civil rights of the people are being interfered with by the subordinate Martial Law authorities even though laws of the land, which have been kept alive under the Laws (Continuance in Force) Order, 1977, make full provision for their adjudication. In some cases, interference has occurred even when the contending parties had already been litigating in the civil courts regarding the same disputes. The necessity, which justified the proclamation of Martial Law, did not arise owing to the failure of the Courts to adjudicate on these matters. Such matters must, therefore, continue to fall outside the purview of the Martial Law Authorities, and the only remedy to the citizens against any such encroachment can be by way of judicial review in the superior Courts.'[32]

The above is the reproduction of Chief Justice Anwarul Haq detailed opinion in the *Nusrat Bhutto's* case. There were separate opinions from other judges except Justice Wahiduddin Ahmed It may be mentioned that Justice Wahiduddin was party to the judgment in *Asma Jilani's* case in 1972. He, however, stated in the judgment that the principles laid down in *Asma Jilani's* case were not applicable to the facts of this case. In those circumstances, he opined that the principles enunciated in the *Governor General's Reference* would have to be invoked to solve the constitutional deadlock at hand. He, however, gave no reason for arriving at this conclusion.[33] Other judges, particularly Nasim Hassan Shah (1929–2015)[34] wrote a separate opinion, but in substance, he repeated what was already held by the Chief Justice Haq.

Now, before a critical appraisal of *Begum Nusrat Bhutto's* case is undertaken, it is necessary to put in perspective some important facts. Firstly, soon after taking over, Ziaul Haq annulled the 5th and 6th Amendments of the Constitution resulting in the immediate retirement of Chief Justice Muhammad Yaqoob Ali (1912–94) and as a consequence thereof, Anwarul Haq became the Chief Justice, and was directly an interested party and a beneficiary. Propriety demanded that he should not have sat on the Bench. Somehow, no objection was taken to that effect and the learned Chief Justice did not find it appropriate to exclude himself from the Bench when hearing the case.

When Martial Law was imposed on 5 July 1977, the main justification that was given was that Zulfikar Ali Bhutto (1928–79) had rigged the elections and, therefore, he was holding power illegally. The Pakistan National Alliance (PNA) refused to accept the results of the election and there were countrywide agitations, rioting and killings and, therefore, the armed forces could not sit as spectators and they had to intervene to save the state and that was done for the welfare of the people. That it was only a temporary intervention and that the Chief of Army Staff had given a solemn assurance to hold free and fair elections. Most importantly, the Constitution did not provide any solution to meet the situation and, therefore, under the doctrine of necessity the acts of the Chief of Army Staff were held valid.

With the benefit of hindsight, the opinion of the Supreme Court appears to be erroneous and based on unfounded assumptions, like the finding that:

> 'in the presence of these unambiguous declarations it would he highly unfair and uncharitable to attribute any other intention to the Chief Martial Administrator, and to insinuate that he has not assumed power, for the purposes stated by him.'

Subsequent events proved that these assumptions were wrong and General Ziaul Haq had other motives to cling on to power, as a result of which the army's rule was prolonged for 11 long years.

The findings can be analyzed as under:

There was no justification for holding that the Constitution, did not provide any solution to the alleged problems of rigging of elections and to curtail the law and order situation, and that the armed forces had to intervene to save the state from dissipation. If it is assumed that there was a flaw in the Constitution as the Constitution makers failed to contemplate such an eventuality or to provide for a remedy for such problems, then, obviously, the Constitution was unworkable. In these circumstances, holding that the 1973 Constitution was still the supreme law of the land was, to put it mildly, a contradiction in terms.

In view of the rulings in *Governor General's Reference No. 1* of 1955, the tests laid down for applying the Doctrine of Necessity clearly stated that necessity had to be extreme, absolute and imminent and that the action taken was *bona fide* and, moreover, above all, it could not be extended to constitutional matters. In *Asma Jilani's* case, that the Doctrine of Necessity was only a doctrine for condonation and not a doctrine of validity. There was no precedent of direct relevance cited before the court wherein the army's intervention was justified under the Doctrine of Necessity. In *Nusrat Bhutto's* case, *Mustafa Ibrahim's* case[35] in Cyprus was not a direct authority issue. The Constitution was put in abeyance there. It is now clear that the Doctrine of State Necessity was misapplied to justify the takeover by the armed forces.

That Court, despite having laid down in a rhetorical way the availability of judicial review, also gave the power of amendment of the Constitution to the Chief Martial Law Administrator (CMLA). By giving such a power, the Court gave him *power to deprive courts from judicially reviewing the acts of the Chief Martial* Administrator and other Martial Law Authorities. Thus the Court contradicted itself. On the one hand, it assumed unto itself the power of judicial review against the acts of CMLA and, on the other hand, it gave CMLA the power to amend the Constitution to deprive the courts of such power of judicial review.

Before the judgment was delivered, the 'solemn undertaking' given by the CMLA had already been violated and the elections were postponed. The so-called objectives to stabilize the economy, holding accountability, and creating a 'conducive atmosphere' for free and fair elections were rather vague propositions that served as the basis for the constitutional court's decision. The cases of election rigging had already been investigated, and those found guilty had been disqualified. Judicial notice was taken of these facts by the Supreme Court in the same judgement. The finding of the Supreme Court that the Constitution did not provide any solution to the situation prevailing since March 1977 was thus negated by the fact that the main reason for finding favour with the Supreme Court was remediable under the Constitution i.e., through election petitions.

The extension of the Doctrine of State Necessity to validate the illegal acts of an illegal authority was not only novel but also unprecedented. The Supreme Court, which had taken an oath to uphold the Constitution, sacrificed it on the altar of expediency and compromise.

It was incorrect to assume that the Supreme Court did not have any alternative options for dealing with this issue. It was possible for the court to hold the action of imposing Martial Law by the Chief of Army Staff illegal and then condone some of his actions under the doctrine of necessity, as it was done in *Asma Jilani's* case. A judicial commission could have been appointed to hold an inquiry into the allegations of the PNA and, being the third organ of the government, elections could be held under the supervision of the Supreme Court by the judiciary.

1) Chief Justice Anwarul Haq heavily relied upon *Mustafa Ibrahim's* case[36] in Cyprus, but it could be shown that the said case was absolutely distinguishable from the facts. The authority (the legislature), therein taking the plea of doctrine of civil necessity, was a legitimately elected legislature, and it was only an Act passed by it which was not in accordance with the Constitution.

The judgement of the Supreme Court validating the military takeover in 1977 caused incalculable harm to the constitutional history of Pakistan. All the basic assumptions were nullified by the Martial Law regime. When, after nearly three years, certain people attempted to remind the Supreme Court of its duties under the judgment in *Nusrat Bhutto's* case, it took unnecessary offence and abdicated its duty to enforce its judgment.[37] The most important consequence of the judgement in this case was that it set a precedent where the military could take over power at any time and, for its recognition/validation, a tailor-made constitutional solution was offered by the Supreme Court.

In *Nawaz Sharif v. President of Pakistan*, the Supreme Court upheld all orders passed, acts done, and measures taken by the caretaker government as valid and legally done, despite declaring the President of Pakistan's order dissolving the National Assembly, dismissing the Nawaz Sharif government, and appointing a caretaker government as invalid and of no legal effect. This was obviously held on the basis of the Doctrine of Necessity, because the justification of such orders, acts and measures was that these were valid if taken and given effect to in accordance with the terms of the Constitution and were required to be done or taken for the ordinary orderly running of the state.

Next in line is the case of *Zafar Ali Shah v. General Pervez Musharraf.*[38] On the evening of 12 October 1999, the Prime Minister removed the Chief of Army Staff, General Pervez Musharraf (1943), and a new Chief of Army Staff, Ziauddin Butt, was appointed in his place. General Musharraf was on an official visit to Sri Lanka. On learning this news, the Corps Commanders seized power and the Prime Minister and some other Cabinet Ministers were put under house arrest. General Musharraf appeared on television late at night and declared that the military had taken over power in Pakistan. On 14 October 1999, General Musharraf issued a Proclamation in the following terms:

> 'In pursuance of the deliberations and decisions of the Chiefs of Staff of the Armed Forces and Corps Commanders of Pakistan Army, I, General Pervez Musharraf, Chairman, Joint Chiefs of Staff Committee and the Chief of the Army Staff proclaim Emergency throughout Pakistan and assume the office of the Chief Executive of Islamic Republic of Pakistan.
>
> I hereby order as follows:
>
> (a) The Constitution of Islamic Republic of Pakistan shall remain in abeyance;
> (b) President of Pakistan shall continue in office;
> (c) The National Assembly, the Provincial Assemblies and the Senate shall remain suspended;
> (d) The Chairman, the Deputy Chairman of the Senate, Speakers and Deputy Speakers of the National Assembly and the Provincial Assemblies shall remain suspended;
> (e) The Prime Minister, the Federal Ministers, Ministers of State, Advisors to the Prime Minister, Parliamentary Secretaries, the Provincial Governors, the Provincial Chief Ministers, the Provincial Ministers and Advisors to the Chief Ministers shall cease to hold office; and
> (f) The whole of Pakistan will come under the control of the Armed Forces of Pakistan.'

This was followed by the Provisional Constitutional Order I of 1999 (PCO). This PCO was based on the above proclamation. After the above PCO, the Oath of Office (Judges) Order 2000, was promulgated on 25 January 2000, which provided for a new oath of office for the judges. Consequently, six judges of the Supreme Court of Pakistan, did not take the oath and certain High Courts judges refused the oath and they all had to vacate their offices.

In the meantime, several constitutional petitions have been filed with the Supreme Court, challenging the legality or otherwise of the proclamation of 14 October 1999 and the PCO. It is interesting to note that some petitions were also filed at the behest of the intelligence agencies by people on their payroll. In these petitions, the petitioners asked the Supreme Court to uphold the military takeover.

These petitions were filed in November 1999 and two hearings on the petitions took place by a Bench headed by Chief Justice Saeeduzzaman Siddiqui (1937–2017).[39] But before the next hearing could take place on 31 January 2000, six of the Supreme Court judges, including the Chief Justice, had vacated their offices and only seven judges had taken the oath, resulting in the constitution of a new Supreme Court under Chief Justice Irshad Hassan Khan (1937).[40] To hear the petitions, five judges were later appointed and added to the Bench. However, all 12 judges hearing the cases had taken the oath under the PCO. As a result, the proceedings in the case have turned into a sham and a fraud on the constitution and the nation, because the people who had taken the oath under the PCO were to judge the constitutionality, legality, or otherwise of the PCO and the proclamation thereunder. Had they decided against the General, it would have been a negation of the oath they had taken.

The Supreme Court in this case used the precedent of *Nusrat Bhutto's* case. During the course of the arguments, the petitioners attempted to show that the Doctrine of Necessity was not a correct doctrine. Their critics argued that since the Constitution was in abeyance as was the case when *Nusrat Bhutto's* case was decided, the Supreme Court was bound by its own precedent.

Chief Justice Irshad Hassan Khan (1937), who presided over the Bench, announced a short order on 12 May 2000. The following passage of the order is reproduced as under:

> 'National Assembly is the highest representative body, which reflects the will and aspirations of the people of Pakistan. Similar is the status of a Provincial Assembly in a province. Senate, being a symbol of unity of the federating units has its own utility for the country as a whole. It is, therefore, of utmost importance that the impugned; suspension of the above democratic institutions is examined with great care and caution, otherwise it would affect the democratic process adversely in the country, which may cause instability, impair the economic growth, and resultantly prove detrimental to the general well-being of the people. However, where the representatives of the people, who are responsible for running the affairs of the State are themselves accused of massive corruption and corrupt practices and in the public as well as private sectors are benefiting therefrom and resist establishing good governance; where a large number of references have been filed against the former Prime Minister, Ministers, Parliamentarians and members of the Provincial Assemblies for their disqualification on account of corruption and corrupt practices; where there is general perception that corruption is being practiced by diversified strata including politicians, Parliamentarians, public officials and ordinary citizens and that a number of Parliamentarians and members of the Provincial Assemblies who had mis-declared their assets before Election Commission and Tax Authorities; where there was no political and economic instability and bank loan defaults were rampant and that per report of the Governor State Bank of Pakistan Rs 365 billion are payable by the bank defaulters up to 12.10.1999, having no accountability and transparency; where economic stability in Pakistan was highly precarious and, there was an overall economic slowdown as GDP growth during the past three years had not kept pace with the growth of the population; where Pakistan has debt burden of which equals the entire national income; where all institutions of the State were being systematically destroyed and the economy was in state of collapse due to self-serving policies of the previous government, which had threatened the existence, security, economic life, financial stability, and credit of Pakistan; where a situation had arisen under which the democratic institutions were not functioning in accordance with the provisions of the Constitution, inasmuch as, the Senate and the National and Provincial Assemblies were closely associated with the former Prime Minister and there was no real democracy because the country was, by and large, under one man rule; where attempts were made to politicize the Army, destabilize it and create dissention within its ranks and where the judiciary was ridiculed, leaving no stone unturned to disparage and malign it by making derogatory and contemptuous speeches by some of the members of the previous ruling party inside and outside the Parliament and no Reference was made to the Chief Election Commissioner for their disqualification as members of the Parliament under Article 63(2) of the Constitution; where the disparaging remarks against the judiciary crossed all limits with the rendering judgement by this Court in the case of *Sh. Liaquat Hussain v Federation of Pakistan PLD 1999*

> *SC 504*, declaring the establishment of Military Courts as *ultra vires* of the Constitution, which resulted into a slanderous campaign against the judiciary by the former Prime Minister registering his helplessness in the face by the judiciary not allowing him the establishment of Military Courts as a mode of speedy justice; where image of the judiciary was tarnished under a well-conceived design; where the telephones of the judges of the Superior Courts and other personalities were tapped in spite of the law laid down by this Court in *Benazir Bhutto v. President of Pakistan, PLD 1998 S.C. 388*, "that tapping of the telephones and eavesdropping was immoral, illegal and unconstitutional;" where storming of the Supreme Court was resorted to allegedly by some of the leaders and activists of the Muslim League which ultimately—led to issuance of contempt notices against them/contemners by the Full Bench of this Court in a pending appeal; where Mian Nawaz Sharif's constitutional and moral authority stood completely eroded, and where situation was somewhat similar and analogous to the situation that was prevalent in July 1977, the extra–constitutional step of taking over the affairs of the country by the Armed Forces for transitional period to prevent any further destabilization, to create corruption free atmosphere at national level through transparent accountability and revive the economy before restoration of democratic institutions under the Constitution, is validated, in that the Constitution offered no solution to the present crisis.
>
> ...therefore, constitutional deviation made by the Chief of the Army Staff, General Pervez Musharraf for the welfare of the people rather than abrogating the Constitution or imposing Martial Law by means of extra constitutional measure is validated for transitional period on ground of State necessity and on the principle of that it is in the public interest to accord legal recognition to the present regime with a view to achieving his declared objectives and that it is in the interest of the community that order be preserved. Legal recognition/legitimacy can be accorded to the present regime also on the principle that the Government should be by consent of the governed, whether voters or not. Here there is an implied consent of the governed i.e. the people of Pakistan in general including politicians/parliamentarians, etc., to the army take over, in that no protests worth the name or agitations have been launched against the army take-over/and or its continuance. The Court can take judicial notice of the fact that the people of Pakistan have generally welcomed the Army takeover due to their avowed intention to initiate the process of across the board and transparent accountability against those, alleged of corruption in every walk of life, of abuse of national wealth, and of not taking appropriate measures for stabilizing the economy and democratic institutions. Another principle, which is attracted is that since an extra-constitutional action has been taken by General Pervez Musharraf wielding effective political power, it is open to the Court to steer a middle course so to ensure that the frame-work of pre-existing Order survives but the constitutional deviation therefrom be justified on the principle of necessity, rendering lawful what would otherwise be unlawful ....
>
> On 12 October 1999, a situation arose for which the Constitution provided no solution and the intervention of the Armed Forces through an extra- constitutional measure became inevitable, which is hereby validated on the basis of doctrine of state necessity and the principle of *Salus populi supremo lex* as embodied in *Nusrat Bhutto's* case. The doctrine of state necessity is recognized not only in Islam and other religions of the world but also accepted by the eminent jurists including Hugo Grotius,[41] Chitty and De Smith and some Superior Courts from the foreign jurisdictions to fill a political vacuum and bridge the gap.'

The Supreme Court of Pakistan not only validated the army's takeover but also gave the Chief of Army Staff the power to amend the constitution, and although some conditions were attempted to be prescribed for exercising that power, they proved to be ineffective. General Musharraf amended the Constitution, like his predecessor, with impunity and when those amendments were challenged, the Supreme Court readily granted its approval and validity to them.

The short order merged into the detailed judgment and more reasons were advanced to justify the army takeover.

General Musharraf was given a 3 year period to carry out his plan, according to the ruling. Corruption, economy, the attack on the Supreme Court etc., were all those grounds which were accepted on their face. As seen above, the short order runs like a charge sheet against the ousted government. The Court wholly missed the point. Almost 99% of the allegations leveled against the Prime Minister and other politicians existed on the evening of 11 October 1999 or even earlier. Could any court of law on its own hold that the constitutional machinery had broken down and that the government was not being run in accordance with the constitution (the language borrowed from the Government of India Act 1935, and adopted in Article 58 (2) (b) before its repeal through the 13th Amendment? The answer is No. As previously stated, the fundamental issue before the court was whether the army's takeover as a result of the dismissal of the Chief of Army Staff was unconstitutional and therefore had no legal effect?

Discussing a pure legal issue, it can be said that the prime minister was the constitutionally elected head of the government, who, while exercising his constitutional power, could dismiss a person in the service of Pakistan. That person refused to accept the order for his dismissal and seized tpower through force and issued a proclamation of the assumption of power. The force behind the proclamation was the support of the chiefs of the Air, Naval Staff and Corps Commanders of the Pakistan Army. Is it possible to justify such a person's actions under any doctrine of necessity?

There was no similarity between *Nusrat Bhutto's* case and this one. The Supreme Court simply recognized the naked exercise of force of the armed forces, who could violate the Constitution at their will.

The Judgement could be analyzed as follows:—

> The Court was biased and helpless, having taken the oath and having sworn allegiance to the chief of army staff. The judges on the Bench had already recognized the regime and had disqualified themselves from exercising any constitutional powers.

It appears that the judgement was the result of an implicit bargain between the military junta and the judiciary, which, because of its perks and privileges, had compromised its oath to defend the Constitution. The paradoxical reasoning in the judgement only reflects the Supreme Court's intellectual bankruptcy in coming up with a sound reasoning to defend the constitution.

1. The Court took into consideration such materials and facts, while deciding the petitions, which were totally inadmissible in such proceedings. The so-called allegations of corruption, the storming of the Supreme Court by the party workers of the ousted government, economic conditions and such other factors as were enumerated in the judgement, were totally irrelevant for the purposes of deciding the issue at the bar. In a civilized world, even if all those allegations were correct, the fundamental law of the land could not be suspended and a military regime could not be allowed to run the government even for a day. In this case, three years period was given.
2. The Court went beyond the Doctrine of Necessity and attracted other principles, like the principles that the government should be by consent of the governed, whether voters or not, and also that since the General had wielded effective political power, the army's takeover was justified. Now all these grounds and reasons are beyond the rationale of any constitutional expert to justify the army's takeovers. The Court in this case paved the way for future adventures to over-throw legitimate governments in Pakistan. It was a reincarnation of Justice Munir's (1895–1979) jurisprudence in *Dosso's* case,[42] that still haunts the Supreme Court and the country.
3. The Chief Justice Irshad Hassan Khan (1937), in his earlier judgement in *Liaquat Hussain's*[43] case had already twisted the Doctrine of Necessity (though he rejected it in that case and accepted it is as doctrine of condonation rather than a doctrine of validation as held in *Asma Jilani's* case) and thus relied upon the same judgement validating the illegal military takeover in this case. Although, Chief Justice Ajmal Mian (1934–2017) later wrote in his autobiography[44] that, by rejecting the Doctrine of Necessity in *Liaquat Hussain's* case, we thought we had buried it forever, but in a period less than a year later, it was again brought out by the Supreme Court. Even Justice Irshad in *Liaquat Hussain's* case had reiterated the preconditions for the applicability of Doctrine of Necessity[45] but he forgot all those conditions while deciding the instant case and proceeded to give three years to the military regime.
4. The whole line of reasoning in the judgement was that the former prime minister was at fault. This kind of reasoning was the result of the mindset of the judges in the dissolution cases [Article 58 (2) (b)][46] and these cases were cited at the bar. The fundamental error, however, was committed in this whole process. It was the unconstitutional acts of General Musharraf that were challenged before the Court and validation was sought to be given to his unconstitutional act of taking over power in Pakistan. As stated earlier, this time the Court was not only bent upon validating the unconstitutional act of General Musharraf, but also on finding all sorts of reasons to give him time to rule over the country. This was indeed unprecedented, even in the application of the Doctrine of Necessity in the annals of Pakistan's judicial history.
5. The proclamation which suspended the Constitution and which provided the 'legal source' for the Provisional Constitutional Order (PCO) was issued by the Chief of Army Staff, who was in the service of Pakistan, in pursuance of Article 260 of the Constitution of 1973. The Court held that putting the Constitution in abeyance was an act valid under the Doctrine of Necessity. Now, if the abeyance was valid, the person(s)

who performed this act would, at that time, be no longer in the service of Pakistan because the Constitution was in abeyance. As a result, the entire act amounted to usurpation of power by a stranger, similar to that of General Yahya Khan (1917–80).

6. The fundamental requirement for the applicability of the doctrine of civil and state necessity was the *bona fides* of the person taking such steps. Here the entire act was *malafide* but the Court proceeded to assume his *bona fides* which was again the result of implicit bargain.
7. Commenting on the judgement, N.W. Barber in his article stated:[47]

> 'There is cost, however, to acknowledging the principle of state necessity as a feature of Pakistani constitutional law. It effectively raises the Army to an institution of government; it acknowledges that the military has a role to play as part of the checks and balances of the Pakistani system. The long-term cost of this is considerable. Once democratic government is resumed there will always be the fear that, at times of strain, the military will decide to intervene. A consequence of the existence of the state necessity is that in some circumstances the Army will be legally entitled, or permitted to act. This is a risk that this may serve to encourage military rule.'

Subsequent events have proved beyond doubt that the so-called limitations put on the power of amendment of the Constitution were only a fig leaf. In the judgment on the review petitions filed against the said judgement, the Court further mutilated the constitutional norms and principles and re-affirmed the findings given in *Zafar Ali Shah's* case.[48]

However, the Supreme Court of Pakistan, while adjudicating upon the principle that 'no man can be a judge in his own cause', did apply the Doctrine of Necessity in exceptional circumstances. The Court applied the Doctrine of Necessity in the case of adjudicators in the following words:

> 'An adjudicator who is subject to disqualification at common law may be required to sit if there is no other competent tribunal or if a quorum cannot be formed without him. Here the doctrine of necessity is applied to prevent a failure of justice. So, if proceedings were brought against all the superior Judges, they would have to sit as Judges in their own cause. Similarly, a Judge may be obliged to hear a case in which he has a pecuniary interest.'[49]

The Doctrine of Necessity was again applied to protect General Musharraf's regime. In order to avoid being disqualified from running for President while wearing an army uniform, he declared an emergency (beyond the Constitution as Chief of Army Staff) and imposed the Provisional Constitution Order (PCO) on 3 November 2007. Consequently, 13 out of the 18 judges of the Supreme Court were deposed and kept under house arrest. The deposed judges were replaced by the judges of Musharraf's choice. A case for validation of the actions of Musharraf on 3 November 2007 was filed before the newly constituted Supreme Court. These actions were upheld by the 7-member of the Bench of the Court on the basis of the Doctrine of State Necessity.[50] This judgment was upheld on review by 13 member bench (including 5 newly appointed judges) on the Doctrine of State Necessity.[51]

On the restoration of the Chief Justice of Pakistan and the judges of the Supreme Court and the High Courts, the judgment in *Tika Iqbal's* case was revisited by the 14-member Bench of the Supreme Court of Pakistan in the case titled *Sindh High Court Bar Association v. Federation of Pakistan*.[52] The judgment in *Tika Iqbal's* case was declared illegal, *mala fide, coram non judice* and *void ab initio*. It was declared that the doctrine of necessity and the maxim *salus populi est suprema lex esto*, as elucidated in the cases of *Begum Nusrat Bhutto* and *Zafar Ali Shah* cases, had no application for an unconstitutional and illegal assumption of power by an authority not mentioned in the Constitution.[53] This judgment favourably mentioned the view taken by one of the judges, Justice Sardar Muhammad Raza Khan (1945), in an earlier judgment regarding the doctrine of necessity. The learned judge, having alluded to the writings of philosophers, scholars and intellectuals, and having referred to various verses of the Quran, held that the Doctrine of Necessity, as used to prevent the decision of cases on merit in the name of achieving a smooth transition in the interest of state necessity, was neither just nor fair nor legal and was violative of the injunctions of the Quran.[54]

Doctrine of Necessity and The Indian Supreme Court

There is no doubt that the Doctrine of Necessity dates back to antiquity and has been drawn to solving difficult situations where the existing laws fail to provide a solution to problems arising under the Constitution or when other laws fail to provide an answer.

The Indian Supreme Court read this doctrine into the Constitution on a number of occasions and the first case in reference is the *State of Maharashtra v. Ramdas Shrinivas Nayak.*[55] In this case, the prosecution for corruption was started against the former Chief Minister Abdul Rehman Antulay (1929–2014),[56] without the previous sanction of the governor of the province, which was a precondition under the Prevention of Corruption Act 1947 (Act I of 1947). In the meantime a writ petition was filed in the High Court where the attorney general for India Mr A. K. Sen made the following statement:

> 'If in the existing case, the entire Council of Ministers becomes interested in the use of the statutory power one way or the other, the doctrine of necessity will fill up the gap by enabling Governor dispensing with the advice of his Council of Ministers and take a decision of his own on the merits of the case. Such a discretion of the Governor must be implied as inherent in his constitutional powers. The doctrine of necessity will supply the necessary power to the Governor to act without the advice of the Council of Ministers ....'

The High Court agreed with the Attorney General and when the petition for leave to appeal was filed in the Indian Supreme Court, the Supreme Court up-held the judgement of the High Court.

The next Indian case in line is *Sub-Committee on Judicial Accountability v. Union of India.*[57] The Indian Supreme Court held:

> 'But a point was made that the Speaker not having entered appearance and denied these allegations on oath must be deemed to have admitted them. It appears to us that even on allegations made in the petition and plea of *mala fides* which require to be established on strong grounds, no such case is made out. A case of *mala fides* cannot be made out merely on the ground of political affiliation of the Speaker either. That may not be a sufficient ground in the present context. At all events as the only statutory authority to deal with the matter, the doctrine of statutory exception or necessity might be invoked.'

The acceptance of the above doctrine in the above case has not been criticized by any legal experts in India.[58]

Doctrine of Civil Necessity in England

England, the birthplace of the Common Law, is the seat of novel doctrines, including the Doctrine of Civil Necessity. It may, however, be stated that no author or Court in England has ever justified the usurpation of power or that it can be validated forever on the basis of the Doctrine of Necessity. The survey of the origin and application of the Doctrine of Civil Necessity in the constitutional scheme of England has been pointed out in two incidents in a paragraph in Joseph Chittys'(1775–1841) celebrated work on the *Treatise on the Law of the Legal Prerogatives of the Crown.*

The whole paragraph can be quoted to show the real context in which the doctrine was mentioned. Chapter VI from where this paragraph has been taken deals with Crown's Prerogative with respect to the Houses of Parliament. Now it is the prerogative of the Crown to summon the Parliament. The learned author writes:

> 'the King alone is entitled by the constitution to summon a Parliament, nor can this power be vested in any other department of the State with equal propriety; because, to borrow the words of Sir William Blackstone,[59] the King is a single person, whose will maybe uniform and steady; the first person in the nation, being superior to both Houses in dignity, and the only branch of legislature that has separate existence, and is capable of performing any act at a time when no Parliament is in being.
>
> There are indeed two memorable instances on record, in which Parliament have assembled without the authority of the King; and have, when so assembled, effected most momentous revolutions in the governments. I allude to the Parliaments, which restored Charles II;[60] and the Parliament of 1688, which disposed of British Crown to William III.[61] But in both these instances the necessity of the case rendered it for the Parliament to meet as they did, there being no King to call them together, and necessity supersedes all laws.'[62]

Before proceeding further, reference may also be made to an observation made by Frederic William Maitland (1850–1906)[63] in his celebrated book *The Constitutional History of England* wherein he stated that the summoning of the Parliament was illegal and that it could only be justified under the principle, what Joseph Chitty called, necessity.

The above constitutional position stated by Joseph Chitty (1775–1841) in 1820 is in particular reference to the English constitutional history of 1680's. There was no written Constitution in England and, after Oliver Cromwell's revolution (1599–1658),[64] the King and the Parliament were disbanded. After the death of Oliver Cromwell the English people resolved to resume the constitutional government. When Charles I of England (1600–49)[65] fled, he dropped the Great Seal into the River Thames. The Great Seal was required for summoning the Parliament. A Parliament summoned without affixing the Great Seal was therefore illegal. It is in this context that the above paragraphs were written.

But how is it possible to allude to this episode in 17th century England to justify that, in 21st century Pakistan, a military dictator can usurp political power and hold in 'abeyance' the Constitution? It is therefore pertinent to point out that the reliance on the above paragraphs in *Zafar Ali Shah's* case and even earlier in the *Governor General's Reference* (1955) by Chief Justice Muhammad Munir, was utterly misconceived and misplaced.

Glanville Williams (1911–97),[66] in his essay on *The Defence of Necessity* deals with the doctrine in the English context as follows:—[67]

> 'A further element of confusion arose in public law. At first sight the doctrine of necessity is somewhat difficult to separate from the prerogative. The difference is that the defence of necessity is open to everybody, while the prerogative relates only to the King. The old books take it as settled law that everyone may in time of emergency go upon land throw up bulwarks against the enemy. If the King chooses to do this, he does so by necessity, not by prerogative, for it is no special prerogative of his. On the other hand, there were some politically necessary things that only the King could do; these belonged to his prerogatives. Thus, he could (and can) erect sea walls and embankments against sea or tide, and enter the land of a subject to do so. It was said that before *Magna Carta*, he could take wood for the repair of his castles. He requisitioned ships, subject to the payment of compensation and, by the prerogative of purveyance, similarly requisitioned provisions for his household and armed forces, including even the impressment of labour. Such powers rested upon the prerogative justified by necessity. In the case of the King's prerogative Saltpeter, the judges declared the King had a prerogative to dig for saltpeter, for the necessary defence of the realm, notwithstanding that gunpowder had been invented within time of memory. The opinion, which was an advisory one, was hedged about with various qualifications, and reads more like a piece of legislation than a statement of existing law. The King was required to restore the place afterwards, and in practice compensation was paid.
>
> This doctrine of state necessity was brought into bad odour by the excesses of Charles I, trying to govern without a Parliament; Charles justified the exactions of ship-money on ground of public necessity. Now, if it were to assumed as a premise that Parliament was not there to grant money, the exaction was necessary, and might reasonably have been regarded as lawful. The weakness in the King's case was that he was deliberately refraining from summoning the constitutional organ for taxation. The necessity was therefore self-induced necessity, which in law is not one at all. Although, Hampden lost, when he challenged the tax, it is the subsequent reversal of the decision by a special statute of 1640, that was taken to settle the legal principle.
>
> Since the Revolution the law may be stated as follows. The King cannot acquire new prerogatives by reference to the state necessity.... However, necessary the behaviour, the Government must today invoke the aid of the Parliament if the behaviour involves breaking the letter of the law. It can act under the doctrine of necessity only to the same extent as a private person. Parliament's alleged failure to give adequate powers cannot be an excuse for conduct, because the necessity of the powers claimed is for Parliament to decide, not for the judges over the head of Parliament. The question is not whether it is necessary to do the act, but whether it is necessary to do it without the sanction of Parliament.
>
> This does not altogether excludes public necessity in public affairs. At one time, the Parliamentarians might have wished to confine it in this way, for they were impressed more by the danger of the notion than by its utility. John Milton[68] called necessity the tyrant's plea; and John Selden[69] said: "there is not anything in the world more abused than this sentence, *salus populi suprema lex esto*.' Cromwell declared: "necessity hath no law."
>
> It is this attitude of mind that explains such sweeping judicial utterances as that of John Pratt,[70] C.J, in *Entick v. Carrington* (1765):

> "With respect to the argument of state necessity, or a distinction that has been aimed at between state offences and others, the common law does not understand that kind of reasoning, nor do our books take notice of any such distinctions."

Notwithstanding, the esteem in which this pronouncement is commonly held, it does not seem to represent the law. Our books do take notice of State necessity in the particular matter of throwing up bulwarks against the enemy, to mention only one. The view of all lawyers who have considered the subject is that the Crown may by necessity use force to quell insurrection or repel invasion; and this is about all that a so called declaration of Martial Law with the realm amounts to. It is also clear from *Humphries v. Connor* (1864), that a constable may commit what would otherwise be an assault upon an innocent person if that is the only way of preserving the peace.

A more difficult case of state necessity was presented in *Rex v. Stratton* (1779). Wherein Lord Mansfield[71] directed the jury that the defence was one of civil or state necessity. He remarked:

> "In India you may suppose a possible case but in that case, it must be imminent, extreme necessity; there must be no other remedy to apply for redress; and in the whole they do, they must appear clearly do it with the view of preserving the society and themselves…."

What immense mischief, would have arisen to have waited for the interposition of the council at Bengal?'[72]

It is however interesting to note that the jury returned a verdict of guilty.

Now, these are the cases, which were cited in the *Governor General's Reference No. 1* of 1955, by the Chief Justice Muhammad Munir (1895–1979). But most of them are related to military necessity.

In English law, it has been stated that the executive, acting out of an actual and immediate necessity arising in the face of the enemy and in circumstances where the rule of *salus populi suprema lex* was clearly applicable, may take possession of a citizen's property for the defense of the realm without payment of compensation unless by statute compensation is to be paid.[73]

It can thus be safely stated that the doctrine of civil or state necessity has never been invoked to abrogate or put in abeyance the Constitution in England. The invocation of the doctrine in the 1680s, as pointed out by Joseph Chitty (1775–1841), was a matter of fact, towards the revival of a constitutional and civilian government.

Doctrine of Civil Necessity in The United States

The American Constitution prohibits the deprivation of life, liberty or property 'without due process of law.' This leaves it to the Court to determine in what circumstances a deprivation might be justified in accordance with the due process of law.

It cannot be questioned that war is one of such justifying circumstances; such an emergency, which threatens the very existence of the state and of society, creates, indeed, a compelling necessity for drastic action, overriding the individual's civil liberties. The extent of this over-riding effect of total war was the question the US Supreme Court had to decide in the series of cases involving Japanese living on the west coast of the United States during the Second World War. The protective measures implemented by the military with the approval of the executive and legislature were curfews and, later, segregation of Japanese Americans, which amounted to concentration camps. Unquestionably, these orders infringed on the Japanese Americans' constitutional rights, and the question was whether this was legally justified by the danger against which it was meant to be a protection.

The US Supreme Court sustained the validity of the curfew order on the ground that it was necessary to meet the threat of sabotage and espionage which would substantially affect the war efforts.[74] The Court also upheld the validity of the segregation order.[75]

In addition to these cases of war, there are some other cases where the United States Supreme Court adopted such a principle in cases that arose after the suppression of the rebellion in the southern states. These cases were cited in *Asma Jilani's* case in order to show that illegal acts could be justified under the Doctrine of Necessity and Hamoodur Rehman (1910–81) observed as follows:

> 'such principle, it appears, has also been adopted in America in various cases which came up after the suppression of the rebellion of Southern States and the American Courts too adopted the policy that where acts done by the usurper were "necessary to peace and good order among citizens and had affected property or contractual rights they should not be invalidated," not because they were legal but because they would cause inconvenience to innocent persons and lead to further difficulties.'[76]

In his book, Fazal Karim, a former judge of the Supreme Court of Pakistan, cites *Ex parte Milligan*,[77] to demonstrate that the Doctrine of State Necessity has no place in American jurisprudence. It is true that, in the particular context of military tribunals trying civilians, the finding seems to be stated by the correct law. However, the principle was later adopted by the US Supreme Court in subsequent cases.

As previously stated, one of the most challenging aspect of this elusive doctrine and that is in what cases it can be applied?

Attorney General of Cyprus v. Mustafa Ibrahim[78]

The above-mentioned case can be explained in some detail for two reasons. Firstly, it is a case heavily relied on by Chief Justice Anwarul Haq (1917–95) in *Nusrat Bhutto's* case.[79] And secondly, it is the case that, for the first time, the Doctrine of State Necessity was extended to validate an illegal act of takeover of power by a military general.

The application of the doctrine in Cyprus was a case of the legislature exceeding the limits of its constitutional power in the matter of the re-constitution of the Supreme Constitutional Court, but the Cypriot precedent can only be understood in light of the nature of society and of the constitution. The island state of Cyprus comprises both Turkish and Greek populations under the constitutional arrangement that arrived in Zurich in 1958–59.

This arrangement was incorporated into the Constitution under which the president and one judge would be Greek-Cypriots, while the vice-president and one judge would be Turkish, while the third judge, the president of the court, would be from a neutral country. As a result of this constitutional arrangement, a German was appointed as the president of the Supreme Constitutional Court. As a result of the turmoil that ensued, the German judge resigned and his successor, an Australian, was appointed, who had to take charge in January 1964. Meanwhile, trouble flared up, thus making it impossible for the new president of the Court to assume his duties. Meanwhile, the Canadian Court's neutral president also resigned. The appointment of the judges was the joint responsibility of both the president and the vice-president and neither of them could over-rule the other in the matter of such appointments and it reached a dead lock. The Court thus became non-functional. The non-functioning of the Supreme Constitutional Court affected the governmental structure in other respects, since the court was the pivot of the constitutional system in the government.

It was in these circumstances that the House of Representatives, sitting with only its Greek-Cypriot members, on 9 July 1964, passed a law, the Administration of Justice (Miscellaneous Provisions) Law, to enable justice to continue to be administered pending a political settlement of the controversy. Under the new law, a supreme court was established comprising three Greek and two Turkish judges of the Supreme Constitutional Court and the High Court, and vested with the jurisdiction and power of those two courts. It also empowered the new Court to determine the composition of sub-ordinate courts without the requirement that in mixed cases, such courts should contain Greek and Turkish judges.

The constitutionality of this law was challenged on the ground that it contravened the basic provisions of the Constitution relating to the administration and jurisdiction of the courts, which articles were unalterable by the house representatives or even at all. The other ground of attack was that the law was not enacted as provided by the Constitution, because under the constitution, it had to be passed by the House of Representatives and assented to by the president and the vice-president.

It was in these circumstances where the state itself was in danger that the Doctrine of Necessity was invoked to validate an act of the legislature.

Doctrine of Necessity in Canada

The issue before the Supreme Court of Canada on a reference from the Governor General was:

> Whether a provincial Act that had not been published in French language as required by the Constitution was valid as it violated Section 133 of the Constitution Act 1867, giving a guarantee of language, and Section 23 of the Manitoba Act 1870, requiring printing, publication and circulation of laws in English and French?

The Court, after reviewing case law on the Doctrine of Necessity from various jurisdictions, concluded that from the date of the judgement until the translation and publication of those laws by the Manitoba Legislature, all rights, obligations, and actions taken are temporarily valid, and all rights, obligations, and actions taken are also protected.[80]

The second case also arose from a reference to a reference filed by the Governor General under Section 18 of the Supreme Act, R.S.P.E.I. 1988, ch. S-10, which related to the independence of provincial judges who, having insufficient salaries, were declared by the Court to be not independent. The Court on rehearing applied the Doctrine of Necessity and held that an otherwise disqualified, biased and not impartial judge could hear a matter if no other judge was available.[81]

Conclusions

The fundamental problem with the doctrine of civil and state necessity in the context of military takeovers in developing countries, particularly Pakistan and countries on the Asian, African and Latin American continents that are part of the Commonwealth of Nations,[82] is that it has been stretched too far to justify military rule. The courts have found it convenient to adopt and adapt this doctrine to legitimize military regimes.

It is true that 10 or 17 members sitting in the Supreme Courts are not expected to take up a fight with the military junta, because the real guardians of democratic institutions in a country are its people. At the same time, the judges owe them a special duty as they have taken upon themselves to defend the constitution and that is the only institution that survives under the abrogated Legal Order. It is the only organ of the state left intact. That is, of course, for a reason, as the new regime requires a certificate of legitimacy from the court.

Neither in 1977 nor in 1999, however, the Supreme Court of Pakistan, while bargaining with the military junta, took into consideration the people of Pakistan. It is the only time that the court can bargain with the military junta if it is going to grant such a certificate, and that is the least it can do.

In addition to the above, it is high time that when civilian rule returns, such governments should make a move for the amendment of the Charter of the United Nations and other international forums, so that no military regime will ever be recognized. If sanctions can be imposed for having nuclear arms and for other things, the right to be governed under civilian rule, as enshrined in Article 21 of the United Nations Declaration of Human Rights, should also be implemented and non-civilian governments must not be allowed to represent the states before international bodies.

The unconstitutional and extra constitutional events of November/December 2007 in Pakistan led to the remarkable judgment in the case of *Sindh High Court Bar Association v. Federation of Pakistan*,[83] wherein the Supreme Court has attempted to prevent future adventurers from an unconstitutional and illegal takeover of State power. The following judgment stated, as under:[84]

> 'However we are inclined to take the view that in situation where people did not show any reaction or failed to hold even peaceful rallies or protests against the unconstitutional, illegal and *void ab initio* acts of usurper of power, such inaction and apathy could not be pressed into service to justify such unconstitutional and illegal acts, as was done in the previous cases.'

Notes

1. Susan Ratcliffe, ed., *Oxford Essential Quotations*. 4th ed. (Oxford University Press; 2016); William Pitt the Younger, *Speech in the House of Commons 18 November 1783*.

2. Giorgio Agamben, *State of Exception*, (Chicago, USA: University of Chicago Press, 2005).
3. Sir Ivor Jennings was a British lawyer and academic.
4. Ghulam Muhammad served as the 3rd Governor-General of Pakistan from 1951 to 1955.
5. Muhammad Munir was the 2nd Chief Justice of Pakistan from 1954 to 1960.
6. Allen McGrath, *The Destruction of Pakistan's Democracy* (Karachi: Oxford University Press, 1999) p. 201.
7. John Marshall was the 4th Chief Justice of the United States from 1801–1835.
8. James Madison was the 4th President of the United States from 1809 to 1817.
9. 5 U.S. 137 (1803).
10. Supra Note 6, at page 281.
11. PLD 1955 FC 240.
12. PLD 1955 5 F.C. 387.
13. *Reference by His Excellency the Governor-General*, PLD 1955 F.C. 435.
14. A.S.M. Akram was the first Chief Justice of Dacca High Court and a former justice of the Federal Court of Pakistan (now Supreme Court of Pakistan).
15. S. A. Rahman was the 5th Chief Justice of Pakistan.
16. Lord Mansfield (1705–93) was the Lord Chief Justice of the King's Bench from 1756 to 1788.
17. Joseph Chitty (1775–1841) was an English lawyer and legal writer.
18. Henry de Bracton (c.1210–c.1268) was an English cleric and jurist.
19. Denis Nowell Pritt (1887–1972) was a British barrister and left-wing Labour Party politician.
20. A. V. Dicey (1835–1922) was a British Whig, jurist, and constitutional theorist.
21. Supra Note 13.
22. Stanley Alexander de Smith was an English academic lawyer and author.
23. WOLR (7) 1968 page 98.
24. *Asma Jilani v. Government of the Punjab*. PLD 1972 SC 139.
25. General Yahya Khan served as the 3rd President of Pakistan and Chief Martial Law Administrator from 1969 to 1971.
26. Hamoodur Rahman was the 7th Chief Justice of Pakistan from 1968 to 1975.
27. Supra Note 24 at page 204.
28. Muhammad Yaqoob Ali was the 8th Chief Justice of Pakistan from 1975 to 1977.
29. Sheikh Anwarul Haq was the 9th Chief Justice of Pakistan from 1977 to 1981.
30. *Nusrat Bhutto v. Chief of Army Staff*, PLD 1977 S.C. 657.
31. There is serious controversy that the words underlined above were added by Chief Justice Anwarul Haq, in his own hand and were not part of the original draft of the opinion circulated amongst the judges.
32. *Nusrat Bhutto v. Chief of Army Staff*, PLD 1977 SC 657 at pp. 716–17.
33. *Ibid*, p. 723.
34. Nasim Hassan Shah wasthe 12th Chief Justice of Pakistan from 1993 to 1994.
35. *Attorney General of the Republic v. Mustafa Ibrahim and others*, [1964] CLR 195.
36. Ibid.
37. *Hamid Sarfraz v. Federation of Pakistan*, PLD 1979 S.C. 991.
38. PLD 2000 SC 869.
39. Saeeduzzaman Siddiqui served as the 15th Chief Justice of Pakistan from 1999 to 2000.
40. Irshad Hassan Khan served as the 16th Chief Justice of Pakistan from 2000 to 2002.
41. Hugo Grotius (1583–1645) was the greatest contributor to the development of International law.
42. PLD 1958 SC 553.
43. PLD 1999 SC 504.
44. Ajmal Mian, *A Judge Speaks Out*, (Karachi: Oxford University Press, 2004).
45. *Liaquat Hussain v. Federation of Pakistan* PLD, 1999 SC 504, at page 806.
46. There is a long list of these cases beginning with *Federation of Pakistan v. Haji Muhammad Saifullah Khan*, PLD 1989 S.C. 166; and ending with *Benazir Bhutto v. President of Pakistan Farooq Ahmad Khan Leghari*, PLD 1998 S.C. 388.
47. N. W. Barber, *The Doctrine of State Necessity in Pakistan*, (2000) 116 Law Quarterly Review 332.
48. *Wasim Sajjad v. Federation of Pakistan*, PLD 2001 SC 233.
49. *Federation of Pakistan v. Mohammad Akram Sheikh*, PLD 1989 S.C. 689.
50. *Tika Iqbal Muhammad Khan v. General Pervez Musharraf*, PLD 2008 SC 178.
51. *Tika Iqbal Muhammad Khan v. General Pervez Musharraf*, PLD 2008 SC 615.
52. PLD 2009 S.C. 879.
53. *Ibid* at p. 1082.
54. *Jamaat-e-Islami v. Federation of Pakistan*, PLD 2009 S.C. 549.

55. AIR 1982 SC 1249.
56. Abdul Rahman Antulay was the 8th Chief Minister of Maharashtra from 1980 to 1982.
57. (1991) 4 SCC 699.
58. B.N. Kirpal, Ashok H. Desai, Gopal Subramanian, Rajeev Dhavan, Raju Ramchandran, *Supreme But Not Infallible: Essays in Honour of the Supreme Court of India*, (Delhi: Oxford University Press, 2000) pp. 31.
59. Sir William Blackstone (1723–80) was an English jurist, judge and Tory politician of the 18th century.
60. Charles II of England (1630–1685) byname The Merry Monarch, King of Great Britain and Ireland (1660–85), who was restored to the throne after years of exile during the Puritan Commonwealth.
61. William III (1650–1702) byname William of Orange, A Dutchman by birth, he would later reign as King of England, Scotland and Ireland until his death in 1702.
62. Joseph Chitty, *A Treatise on The Law of Prerogatives of the Crown*, (London, Dublin: Joseph Butterworth & Son, 1820) page 68.
63. Frederic William Maitland was an English historian and lawyer who is regarded as the modern father of English legal history.
64. Oliver Cromwell was a political and military leader in 17th century England who served as Lord Protector of the Commonwealth of England, Scotland and Ireland from 1653 to 1658.
65. Charles I of England was King of England, Scotland, and Ireland from 27 March 1625 until his execution in 1649.
66. Glanville Williams was a Welsh legal scholar. He has been described as Britain's foremost scholar of criminal law.
67. Glanville Williams, *11 The Defence of the Necessity, Current Legal Problems*, Vol. 6, Issue 1, (Oxford: Oxford University Press, 1953), page 216 at page 229.
68. John Milton (1608–1674) was an English poet, polemicist, man of letters, and a civil servant under Oliver Cromwell.
69. John Selden (1584–1654) was an English jurist, a scholar of England's ancient laws and constitution and scholar of Jewish law.
70. Sir John Pratt (1657–1725) was Lord Chief Justice of England from 1718 until 1725.
71. Lord Mansfield (1705–1793) was a British barrister, who served as Lord Chief Justice of the King's Bench from 1756 until 1788.
72. Supra Note 67 at page 222–231.
73. *Attorney General v. De Keyser's Royal Hotel*, 1920 A.C. 508; per Lord Moulton. *Also see* B. O. Nwabueze, *Constitutionalism in the Emergent States*, (London: C. Hurst & Co [publishers] Ltd., 1973). page 182.
74. *Hirabayshi v. U.S.*, 320 U.S. 81 (1943).
75. *Korematsu v. U.S.*, 323 U.S. 214 (1944).
76. *Asma Jilani v. Government of the Punjab*, PLD 1972 S.C. 139 at pages 205–06.
77. 71 U.S. 2 (1866).
78. 1964 CLR 195.
79. PLD 1977 S C 657.
80. [1985] 1 RCS 721.
81. [1998] 1 RCS 3.
82. Commonwealth of Nations is a political association of 54-member states, almost all of which are former territories of the British Empire.
83. PLD 2009 S.C. 879.
84. *Ibid*, para 120 at p. 1107.

27 Theory of Basic Structure of Constitution

Introduction

Power of Amendment of Constitution

The Constitution of Pakistan, by virtue of its Article 239, may be amended by an Act of Parliament passed by the National Assembly and the Senate, by votes of not less than two-thirds of the total membership of each House, and given assent by the President.

Article 368 of the Indian Constitution provides that Parliament may, in exercise of its constitutional power, amend by way of addition, variation or repeal any provision of the Constitution by a majority of the total membership of each House of Parliament as well as by a majority of not less than two-thirds of the members of that House present and voting.

However, amendments in:

a. Article 54 (Election of President),
b. Article 55 (Manner of election of President),
c. Article 73 (Extent of Executive Power of the Union),
d. Article 162 (Extent of Executive Power of State),
e. Chapter IV of Part V (provisions dealing with the High Courts for Union Territories),
f. Chapter I of Part XI (Distribution of Legislative Powers between the Union and the States),
g. Fourth Schedule (Representation of States in Parliament),
h. Seventh Schedule (Legislative Lists I, II, and III),
i. Article 368 (Amendment of the Constitution),

requires, in addition to the two-third majority, a ratification resolution passed by not less than one-half of the legislatures of the States.

Article 368 in its original form reads as under:

> An amendment of this Constitution may initiated only by the introduction of a Bill for purpose in either House of Parliament, and when the Bill is passed in each House by a majority of the total membership of that House and by a majority of not less than two-thirds of the Members of that House present and voting, it shall be presented to the President who shall give his assent to the Bill and thereupon the Constitution shall stand amended in accordance with the terms of the Bill:
>
> Provided that if such amendment seeks to make any change in:
>
> (a) Article 54, Article 55, Article 73, Article 162 or Article 241 or
> (b) Chapter IV of Part V, Chapter V of Part VI or Chapter I of Part XI, or
> (c) Any of the lists in, the seventh schedule, or
> (d) The representation of States in Parliament, or
> (e) The provisions of this Article.
>
> The amendment shall also require to be ratified by the Legislatures of not less than one-half of the States by resolutions to that effect passed by those Legislatures before the Bill making provision for such amendment is presented to the President for assent.

The amendment of the US Constitution may be brought about by the US Congress, with the approval of two-thirds of the majority of both Houses (i.e. the Senate and the House of Representatives) or by a convention summoned on an application from two-thirds of the members of both Houses. The proposed amendments must subsequently be ratified by at least three-fourths of the total number of state legislatures or by conventions in three-fourths of the total number of states.

The question of whether or not the fundamental rights guaranteed expressly in a written Constitution can be abridged or taken away under the procedure prescribed for amendment of the Indian Constitution by Article 368 arose for the first time in India as a consequence of the decision in *Sir Kameshwar Singh v. State of Bihar*,[1] in which the Patna High Court declared that the Bihar Land Reforms Act 1950, was unconstitutional on the ground that the classification of land owners made for the purpose of paying compensation to the expropriated land owners violated the Equal Protection Clause of the Indian Constitution. In order to meet the situation created by the Patna High Court, the First Amendment of the Indian Constitution was passed in 1951. The amendment added two new Articles, 31-A and 31-B, and the 9th Schedule, with the result that a law acquiring the interests of tenure holders in land could not be challenged in a court of law.

In *Sankari Prasad Singh Deo v. Union of India*,[2] the constitutional validity of the First Amendment was challenged. It was contended before the Indian Supreme Court that the term 'Law' used in Article 13 (2) of the Indian Constitution, which states:

> The State shall not make any law which takes away or abridges the fundamental rights and any law made in contravention of that provision was void.

Included in its meaning and significance was an Act amending the Constitution, with the result that the fundamental rights enumerated in the Constitution could not be abridged or repealed. The Supreme Court of India did not accept the argument and held that the word 'law' used in Article 13 (2) referred to sub-constitutional laws made in the exercise of ordinary legislative powers and did not include the Constitution (Amendments) Acts made in the exercise of the Constituent power under Article 368 of the Indian Constitution. It was, therefore, held that Article 13 (2) did not govern or affect the amendments made to the Constitution.

Further, in *Karimbil Kunhikoman v. State of Kerala*,[3] the Supreme Court of India struck down the Kerala Agrarian Relations Act 1961, on the ground that acquisition of *Ryotwari*[4] tenures was not protected by Article 31-A (1) (a) of the Indian Constitution. In order to address the issue created by this judgment, the 17th Amendment of the Constitution was passed in 1964. The amendment changed the definition of the term 'estate' in such a way as to include *Ryotwari* land as well as other lands. The 9th Schedule of the Constitution of India was also extended, and a number of laws passed by the states were included in it so that they could not be challenged in a court of law.

The validity of the 17th Amendment of the Indian Constitution was challenged in *Sajjan Singh v. State of Rajasthan*,[5] on the ground that the Amendment, by including a number of enactments in the 9th Schedule, made them immune from the writ jurisdiction of the High Court. Therefore, the constitutional jurisdiction of the High Courts was affected. As Article 226 (writ jurisdiction) was affected, it was necessary that the special procedure laid down in the proviso to Article 368 should have been followed and the concurrence of at least half of the state legislatures should have been secured for passing the 17th Amendment. By a majority of 3 to 2, the Indian Supreme Court followed the interpretation made by *Sankari Prasad* of the word 'law' used in Article 13 (2) and held that, in pith and substance, the 17th Amendment sought to amend Article 31A only in order to facilitate agrarian reform and to make such legislation immune from attack in a court of law. If the 17th Amendment affected Article 226 dealing with the powers of the writ of the High Court, the effect was only incidental. However, Justice Mohammad Hidayatullah (1905–92),[6] in his dissenting judgment, observed:

> 'I would require stronger reasons than those given in *Sankari Prasad* case to make me accept the view that Fundamental Rights were not really fundamental but were intended to be within the powers of amendment in common with other parts of the Constitution.'

The majority judgment of 3 to 2 in the *Sankari Prasad* case was reversed in *Golak Nath v. State of Punjab*[7] in which the Indian Supreme Court, by a majority of 6 to 5, held that fundamental rights were outside the amendatory process, if the amendment took away or abridged any fundamental right. In this case, three petitions challenged the validity of the First, the 4th and the 17th Amendments of the Indian Constitution; whereby the Punjab Security of Land Tenures Act 1953, and the Mysore Land Reforms Act 1962, were included in the 9th Schedule pursuant to Article 31-B, which is a constitutional device to place the specified statutes beyond any attack on the ground that they are violative of fundamental rights. The Supreme Court by majority of 6 to 5 declared the offending parts of the amendments unconstitutional as they abridged the fundamental rights holding that *Sankari Prasad* and *Sajjan Singh* cases did not lay down good law. The reasons, advanced by the majority are summarized as follows:[8]

(a) The Constitution incorporates an implied limitation that the fundamental rights are out of reach of Parliament. The Constitution has given by its scheme a place of permanence to the fundamental freedoms. In other words, the people, by giving to themselves the Constitution, have reserved the fundamental freedoms to themselves. The importance attached to the fundamental freedoms is so transcendental that a bill enacted by unanimous vote of all the members of both the Houses is ineffective.
(b) Article 368 does not contain the power to amend but merely provides procedure for amending the Constitution. The power to amend the Constitution is a legislative process and is included within the plenary legislative power of Parliament
(c) The word 'law' mentioned in Article 13(2) would cover a constitutional amendment. The provisions of other conditions such as larger majority and in the case of articles mentioned in the proviso, a ratification by states' legislatures, does not make the amendment any the less a law. Therefore, Parliament under Article 368 cannot, by an amendment, abridge or take away any of the fundamental rights.
(d) There is nothing in the nature of the amending power which enables Parliament to override all the express or implied limitations on that power. The fundamental rights can only be curtailed by the plenary power of Constitution making and not by the constituent power of amending the Constitution.

The decision by *Golak Nath* led to the passing of the Constitution (24th Amendment) Act 1971, which made significant changes to Article 368. Firstly, it sought to nullify the effect of *Golak Nath* by adding Clause (4) to Article 13, which provides that–

> 'Nothing in Article 13 shall apply to any amendment of the Constitution made under Article 368.'

It means that the meaning of the word 'law' in terms of Article 13 will not, after the 24th Amendment, extend to an amendment made under Article 368. This position was reassured by adding Clause (3) to Article 368 which provides that–

> 'Nothing in Article 13 shall apply to an amendment made under this Article.'

Secondly, the 24th Amendment made changes in the marginal head of Article 368 by substituting 'Procedure for Amendment of the Constitution' for 'Power of Parliament to amend the Constitution and procedure therefore.' The amended Clause (1) of Article 368 was inserted, which now states that–

> 'Notwithstanding anything in this Constitution, Parliament may in the exercise of its constituent power amend by way of addition, variation or repeal any provision of the Constitution in accordance with the procedure laid down in that Article.'

Parliament was thus empowered to amend any provision of the Constitution, including the fundamental rights. Thirdly, in the next paragraph, now numbered as Clause (2), the 24th Amendment words

> 'it shall be presented to the President who shall give his assent to the Bill.'

are replaced by

> 'it shall be presented to the President for his assent and upon such assent being given to the Bill.'

This change removes the president's discretion in granting his assent to a Bill seeking an amendment to any provision of the Constitution.

Concept of Basic Structure or framework of the Constitution in India

The validity of the 24th Amendment came up for decision in *Kesavananda Bharati v. State of Kerala*,[9] wherein a writ petition was filed initially to challenge the validity of the Kerala Land Reforms Act 1971. But as the Act was amended during the pendency of the petition and was placed on the 9th Schedule by the 29th Amendment, the petitioner was permitted to also challenge the validity of the 25th and 29th Amendments to the Constitution of India.

The petition was heard by a bench consisting of all the 13 judges of the Supreme Court of India. It was urged by the petitioner that if the power of an amendment is to be construed as empowering Parliament to exercise the full constitutional power of the people and authorizing it to destroy or abrogate the essential features, basic elements and fundamental provisions of the Constitution, such a construction must be held illegal and void, because:

(i) have only such constituent power as is conferred on it by the Constitution, which is given by the people unto themselves, Parliament cannot enlarge its own power so as to abrogate the limitation in the terms on which the power to amend was conferred;
(ii) being a functionary created under the Constitution, Parliament cannot arrogate to itself the power of amendment so as to alter or destroy any of the essential features of the Constitution;
(iii) purporting to empower itself to take away or abridge all or any of the fundamental rights, Parliament does not become competent to destroy the basic human rights like liberty and equality and the fundamental freedoms which were reserved by the people for themselves when they gave to themselves the Constitution; and
(iv) Initially having no power to alter or destroy any of the 'essential features' of the Constitution, and also recognizing implied and inherent limitations on the amending power, Parliament has no power to alter or destroy all or any one of the fundamental rights.

All the judges overruled *Golak Nath* and were of the — view that the 24th Amendment, which inserted Clause (4) in Article 13, and Clause (3) in Article 368, was valid. Parliament therefore, under Article 368, as amended by the 24th Amendment, has the power to amend the provisions of the Constitution, including those enshrining fundamental rights.

However, 7 of the 13 judges held that in the exercise of its amending power, Parliament cannot amend the provisions embodying the basic structure or framework of the Indian Constitution. Six of them believed that the fundamental rights related to the basic structure or framework of the Constitution, and thus cannot be amended. The 6 minority judges were, by and large, not prepared to accept any limitation on the plenary power of Parliament to amend the Constitution.

According to Chief Justice Sarv Mittra Sikri (1908–92),[10] one of the majority judges, the basic structure or framework of the Constitution was:

(i) The supremacy of the Constitution.
(ii) A republican and democratic system.
(iii) The secular character of the Constitution.
(iv) The separation of powers between the legislature, the executive and the judiciary.
(v) The federal character of the Constitution.

Justices K. S. Hegde (1909–90)[11] and A.K. Mukherjea (1915–73)[12], illustrated the basic elements or fundamental features of the Indian Constitution as:

(i) Sovereignty of India.
(ii) The democratic character of the Indian polity.
(iii) The unity of India.
(iv) Essential features of the individual freedoms secured to the citizens.
(v) The mandate to build a welfare state and egalitarian society.

However, the individual freedoms secured for the citizens were regarded by all the 6 judges as a basic structure or framework of the Constitution which may not be altered or destroyed by invoking the power of amendment under Article 368 of the Indian Constitution.

According to the 'summary' signed by 9 out of 13 judges in *Kesavananda Bharati*, the majority of judges overruled *Golak Nath*,[13] but held that Article 368 did not allow Parliament to alter the basic structure or framework of the Indian Constitution.[14]

In *Indira Nehru Gandhi v. Shri Raj Narain*,[15] the Supreme Court of India accepted the majority opinion in *Kesavananda Bharati* on the doctrine of the basic structure or framework of the Constitution. In this case, an appeal was filed by Indira Gandhi (1917–84)[16] to the Supreme Court against the decision of the Allahabad High Court invalidating her election on the ground' of corrupt practices.

Meanwhile, Parliament enacted the 39th Amendment to overcome the effect of the High Court judgment by withdrawing the jurisdiction of all courts over election disputes involving the Prime Minister. Following *Kesavananda Bharati*, it was argued that the 29th Amendment could not affect free and fair elections and the power of judicial review of the judiciary as these constituted the basic structure or framework of the Constitution. It was further argued that Parliament, in the exercise of the constituent power of amendment under Article 368, was not competent to validate an election declared void by the High Court.

This challenge was unanimously upheld by the Supreme Court. Two of the judges held that democracy was an essential feature forming part of the basic structure or framework of the Constitution and the exclusion of judicial review in election disputes also damaged the basic structure or framework of the Constitution. Justice Y.V. Chandrachud (1920–2008)[17] identified 4 unamendable features as forming part of the basic structure or framework, namely:

(i) A sovereign, democratic, republic status.
(ii) Equality of status and opportunity of an individual.
(iii) Secularism and freedom of conscience and religion.
(iv) Government of laws and not of men i.e. the rule of law.

He held that the exclusion of judicial review by the amendment was an outright negation of the right to equality. Another judge maintained that Parliament should not perform judicial and quasi-judicial functions as judicial powers are vested in the Supreme Court and the High Courts. Otherwise, it would be a violation of the basic structure or framework of the constitution. Another judge, while not fully supporting the theory of separation of powers, acknowledged the conscious adherence to checks and balances and said that because the courts should not enter into problems entwined with 'political thicket', Parliament must also respect the preserve of courts. However, all the judges seemed to rely in varying degrees, either expressly or impliedly, upon the basic structure theory, as revealed by the express provisions of the Constitution to hold that under the guise of exercising a legislative power Parliament could not adjudicate on merits in an election dispute.

Section 55 of the Constitution (42nd Amendment) Act 1976, inserted Clauses (4) and (5) in Article 368, nullifying the effect of the *Indira Gandhi* case.

Clause (4) provided that:

> No amendment of this Constitution (including the provisions relating to Fundamental rights) made or purporting to have been made under Article 368 whether before or after the commencement of Section 55 of the Constitution (42nd) Amendment 1976, shall be called in question in any court on any ground.

Clause (5) provided that:

> 'For the removal of doubts, it is hereby declared that there shall be no limitation whatever on the constituent power of Parliament to amend by way of addition, variation or repeal the provisions of this Constitution under this article.'

The validity of Clauses (4) and (5) of Article 368 as inserted by Section 55 of the 42nd Amendment 1976, and the scope and extent of the application of the Doctrine of Basic Structure again came up for discussion before the Indian

Supreme Court in *Minerva Mills Ltd v. Union of India*,[18] in which a petition was filed challenging the takeover by the Central Government of the management of the mill under the Sick Textile Undertakings (Nationalization) Act 1974, and an order made under Section 18-A of the Industrial (Development and Regulations) Act 1951. The petitioner, inter alia, challenged the constitutional validity of Clauses (4) and (5) of Article 368 as inserted by section 55 of the 42nd Amendment 1976. These clauses stood in the way of the petitioners challenging the constitutional validity of the 39th Amendment, which included the Nationalization Act 1974, in the 9th Schedule. The Supreme Court unanimously held Clauses (4) and (5) of Article 368 and Section 55 of the 42nd Amendment as unconstitutional, transgressing the limits of the amending power and damaging or destroying the basic structure or framework of the Indian Constitution. The Chief Justice Y. V. Chandrachud (1920–2008) and 3 other judges, held that, according to the majority view in *Kesavananda Bharati v. State of Kerala*,[19] Article 368 did not enable Parliament to alter or destroy the basic structure or framework of the constitution.

In *Waman Rao v. Union of India*,[20] the Indian Supreme Court held that all amendments to the Indian Constitution which were made before 24 April 1973, that is, the day on which judgment in *Kesavananda Bharati v. State of Kerala* was rendered, including those by which the 9th Schedule was amended from time to time, were valid and constitutional and, therefore, the Parliament could, in the exercise of its constituent power under Article 368, validate the state law by including it in the 9th Schedule.

In *Sanjeev Coke Mfg. Co. v. Bharat Coking Coal*,[21] the court expressed reservations about the *Minerva Mills* case insofar as it invalidated the amendment to Article 31-C of the Coking Coal Mines (Nationalization) Act 36 of 1972. It was said that *Minerva Mills* was concerned with a law passed before the amendment of Article 31-C by the 42nd Amendment and, therefore, any decision on the validity of the amendment of that article was purely hypothetical and academic and, by the logic of *Kesavananda Bharati v. State of Kerala*, Article 31-C, as amended by the 42nd Amendment, was constitutionally valid.

In *Shri Raghunathrao Ganpatrao v. Union of India*,[22] the Supreme Court of India upheld the Constitution (26th Amendment) Act 1971, which derecognized the former Indian rulers and abolished their privy purses and other privileges by repealing Articles 291 and 362 and inserting Article 363-A. The court, however, found that the repealed provisions were an integral part of the Constitution. It did not agree that every integral provision constituted the basic structure or framework of the Constitution. It also found the amendment to be consistent with the preamble's and the Constitution's declarations of republicanism, human dignity and equality.

The Indian Supreme Court unanimously upheld the theory of basic structure or framework of the Constitution in *I.R. Coelho v. State of Tamil Nadu*.[23] It was held that the jurisdiction conferred on the Supreme Court under Article 32 (writ jurisdiction) is an integral part of the basic structure or framework of the Constitution of India and no Parliament can abrogate it or take it away. These, the Supreme Court held, are settled propositions of Indian jurisprudence. If the Doctrine of Basic Structure provides a touchstone to test the amending power or its exercise, there can be no doubt and it has to be so accepted that Part III (Fundamental Rights) of the Constitution has a key role to play in the application of the said doctrine.

The Doctrine of Basic Structure or framework in Indian constitutional law is now established, although its contents are still debated. The cases of *Kesavananda Bharati, Indira Gandhi, Minerva Mills, Waman Rao, Sanjeev Coke, Shri Raghunathrao and I.R. Coelho* establish that the superior courts of India do possess the power of judicial review of constitutional amendments affecting the basic structure or framework of the Constitution.

99th Constitutional Amendment Declared

Ultra Vires by the Supreme Court of India

The Supreme Court of India has exerted itself aggressively in the question of the appointment of judges of India's superior courts, as detailed in a previous chapter on 'Independence of Judiciary', In its judgment of *Supreme Court Advocates-on-Record v. Union of India*,[24] it was held that consultation with and opinion of the Chief Justice of India would have primacy in the matter of appointment of judges of the Supreme Court and the High Courts of India. The opinion of the Chief Justice of India would be binding on the executive (the President/Prime Minister) and, in case of a difference of opinion, the Executive would have to give the reasons for the same.

This judgment resulted in difficulties faced by the Executive in India in the matter of the appointment of judges and, in 1998, a Presidential Reference was sent to the Supreme Court of India seeking its advisory opinion on the working of the system of the appointment of judges could be improved.

This reference was answered by the Supreme Court of India, in the case of *Special Reference No. 1 of 1998.*[25] In this judgment, the Supreme Court advised the formation of a collegium of judges consisting of the Chief Justice and four senior judges of the Supreme Court who would have to be consulted in the matter of the appointment of judges by the President of India (on the advice of the Prime Minister).

In this way, the judiciary had the final say in the matter of the selection of judges for appointment to the Supreme Court and High Courts in India. Obviously, this led to resentment by the Executive and the Parliament in India, which finally came up with the Constitution (99th Amendment) Act 2014, which, amongst others, added Article 124A to the Constitution providing for the constitution and composition of the National Judicial Appointments Commission (NJAC). NJAC was composed of the following 6 persons:-

— The Chief Justice of India–Chairperson, *ex officio.*
— Two other of senior judges of the Supreme Court next to the Chief Justice of India,–*ex officio.*
— The Union Minister of Law and Justice,–*ex officio.*
— Two eminent persons, to be nominated–Members.

The 99th Constitutional Amendment was challenged before the Supreme Court of India as violative of 'independence of judiciary' which had earlier been declared as basic features/basic structure of the Constitution. In the case of *Supreme Court Advocates-on-Record Association v. Union of India,*[26] A 5 member bench headed by Justice Jagdish Singh Khehar (1952),[27] concluded that Article 124A is *ultra vires* the provisions of the Constitution because of the inclusion of the Union Minister in charge of Law and Justice as an *ex officio* Member of NJAC (National Judicial Appointments Commission) because it violated the principles of independence of the judiciary as well as separation of powers.

The 5-member bench included Justices Jagdish Singh Khehar (1952), Jasti Chelameswar (1953),[28] Madan Bhimrao Lokur (1953),[29] Kurian Joseph (1953)[30] and Adarsh Kumar Goel (1953).[31] Justice Khehar wrote the opinion of the Supreme Court and other judges on the bench wrote separate but mostly concurring opinions. Furthermore, it was concluded that the inclusion of two eminent persons as members of the NJAC (National Judicial Appointments Commission) was also *ultra vires* to the provisions of the Constitution, being violative of the structure of the Constitution. It was also held that because Article 124A had been struck down, the entire Constitution (99th Amendment) Act 2014 stands struck down as being *ultra vires* to the provisions of the Constitution.

It was reasoned by the Court that if primacy was not vested in the judiciary in the matter of the appointment of judges, the executive and the legislature could exert political pressure on the appointment of judges and would continue to unduly influence judges even after appointment through the psychological mechanism of 'power of reciprocity' and 'loyalty to appointor', coupled with the fact that the executive is by far the biggest litigant. Such a conclusion could not be avoided because historical evidence would shows that executive interference in the appointment of judges has continually undermined judiciary's independence. This conclusion could be further strengthened further by the weak moral fibre of Indian civil society and polity as evidenced over a time, as well as the existence of a veritable spoils system in Indian polity. It was also stated that psychological studies have explained and provided evidence of the subtle interplay of doctrines of 'reciprocity' and 'loyalty to appointor' in making judges susceptible to influence by those who appoint them, even after such appointment. Thus, preventing them from acting without fear or favour. It destroys the independence of the judiciary as a consequence. Weak moral fibre of the Indian polity and insufficient strength of civil society would be unable to manoeuvre its leaders towards national interest with the consequence that society would lack capacity to deter overreach by political executive. Such a situation would imply and compel that the higher judiciary alone should continue to act as the protector of civil society. Therefore, conferring primacy on the judiciary is the only safeguard.

The Supreme Court also held that the primacy of the judiciary in the matter of the appointment of the judges of the Supreme Court and High Courts is part of the basic structure or framework of the Constitution. This primacy extends not only to rejecting unworthy candidates, but also to ensuring the appointment of worthy candidates. The scheme of NJAC (National Judicial Appointments Commission) gave veto power to any two members of the

NJAC. The same would be clearly unsustainable in the scheme of independence of the judiciary. The Court took exception to the participation of two eminent people only because such a system of including 'lay persons' in the judicial appointment commission was taken from some advanced countries, like the UK or South Africa. The Court was of the opinion that such a system should not be copied in India because such advanced countries have evolved societies.

Basic Structure Theory in Pakistan

Fazlul Quader Chowdhry v. Muhammad Abdul Haque was the first case in Pakistan involving the basic structure doctrine, which occurred shortly after the promulgation of the 1962 Constitution in.[32]

President General Ayub Khan (1907–74), in order to accommodate a Central Council of Ministers; who was a member of the National Assembly, allowed him to retain his seat in the National Assembly under the Removal of Difficulties (Appointment of Ministers) President's Order No. 34 of 1962. The Supreme Court of Pakistan declared it void and *ultra vires* of the Constitution.

By allowing members of the National Assembly to become ministers while implementing the provisions of the Constitution, they were being altered in a fundamental way so as to change the form of government from the pure presidential form to an anomalous parliamentary form. The Supreme Court of Pakistan ruled that the presidential form of government requires the executive to be completely separate from the legislature. In *Islamic Republic of Pakistan v. Abdul Wali Khan*,[33] the question of whether an existing provision in the Constitution relating to fundamental rights could be amended to abridge or take away the fundamental right, was for the first time raised before the Supreme Court of Pakistan. It was submitted that the Supreme Court of India, by a majority of 6 to 5 in *Golak Nath v. State of Punjab*,[34] actually took the view that fundamental rights cannot be abridged and taken away by amending the Constitution, though this view was modified subsequently by a larger bench of 7 to 6 in *Kesavananda Bharati v. State of Kerala*[35] to the extent that:

> 'While fundamental rights cannot be abrogated, reasonable abridgements of fundamental rights can be effected in the public interest.'

The Supreme Court of Pakistan held:

> 'It is not necessary for us to enter into this controversy, as this Court is committed to the view that "the judiciary cannot declare any provision of the Constitution to be invalid or repugnant" and the validity of a constitutional amendment can only be challenged if it is adopted in a manner different to the one prescribed by the Constitution or is passed by a lesser number of votes than those specified in the Constitution.'

In *State v. Zia-ur-Rehman*,[36] the validity of military court detentions and convictions, as well as the validity of the 1972 Interim Constitution, and the competence of the National Assembly to frame such a Constitution, was challenged. The defendant contented that because the regime of General Muhammad Yahya Khan (1917–80)[37] had been declared a usurper by this Court in *Asma Jilani's*[38] case. As a consequence, the 1962 Constitution remained in force and the National Assembly, as it was then constituted, could not frame the Interim Constitution. The Supreme Court of Pakistan held:

> 'The Supreme Court has never claimed to be above the Constitution nor to have the right to strike down any provision of the Constitution. It has accepted the position that it is a creature of the Constitution; that it derives its powers and jurisdictions from the Constitution; and that it will even confine itself within the limits set by the Constitution which it has taken oath to protect and preserve but it does claim and has always claimed that it has the right to interpret the Constitution and to say as to what a particular provision of the Constitution means or does not mean, even if that particular provision is a provision seeking to oust the jurisdiction of this Court.'

The *Federation of Pakistan v. United Sugar Mill* case[39] was the second case in which an argument based on *Golak Nath*[40] was made. In this case, the validity of the Constitution (4th Amendment) Act 1975, whereby Clause (4-A) was added to Article 199 providing that an interim order made by the High Court in a writ petition relating to the assessment or collection of public revenue would cease to have effect on the expiration of 60 days following the day on which it was made, was challenged on the ground that the amendment had stultified the judicial power of the High Court and that the amendment was unconstitutional on the authority of *Golak Nath*. The Supreme Court of Pakistan rejecting the argument held:

> 'In that case (*Golak Nath*) a narrowly divided Supreme Court ruled that the Indian Parliament' lacked the power to amend Part III of the Indian Constitution which provided for fundamental rights. However, the majority view in that case was modified later in the case of *Kesavananda*, AIR 1973 SC 1461 again by a narrow majority. In Pakistan, this Court in the case of Ziaur Rehman, PLD 1973 SC 49 has however firmly laid down the principle that a constitutional provision, cannot be challenged on the ground of being repugnant to what are sometimes stated as "national inspirations" or an "abstract concept" so long as the provision is passed by the competent Legislature in accordance with the procedure laid down by the Constitution. In the instant case, the two amendments are not questioned for want of competency or any other formal defect.'

The third case is the *Fauji Foundation v. Shamimur Rahman*.[41] In this case, the validity of Martial Law Regulation No. 103, whereby a company was dissolved and its rights, properties, assets, debts, liabilities and obligations were transferred to the appellant, a shareholder of the company, was challenged on the ground that the regulation amounted to a legislative judgment.

After citing cases such as *Golak Nath*, *Kesavananda Bharati*,[42] and *Indira Gandhi*,[43] Justice K. K. Mathew (1911–92)[44] stated that separation of powers between the legislature, executive, and judiciary was the fundamental structure of the Constitution. After attempting to find *Nehru Gandhi v. Shri Rai Raj Narain*'s *ratio decidendi* and citing H. M. Seervai's (1906–96) criticism of the decision in his book *Constitutional Laws of India*, Chief Justice Muhammad Haleem (1925–2006),[45] expressed his view, though not in so many words, that there is a difference between the constituent power of amending the constitution and the plenary power of making a Constitution and that the legislature had the power to dissolve the company and transfer its assets and liabilities in favour of the Fauji Foundation.[46]

The next important case in Pakistani jurisdiction is *Mahmood Khan Achakzai v. Federation of Pakistan*,[47] in which the theory of the basic structure of the Constitution was somewhat recognized. For a long time, the 8th Amendment to the Constitution, ratified in 1985, had been the subject of political controversy, particularly in respect to the president's discretionary powers to dissolve the National Assembly and dismiss the federal government. This power was exercised on 4 occasions, and each time was thoroughly judicially reviewed by the superior courts. On two occasions, the exercise of such presidential power was upheld but on the other two occasions, it was held that the power was exercised invalidly.[48] However, on one occasion, only the National Assembly and the federal government were restored.

A number of citizens, or their organizations, had challenged the 8th Amendment as unconstitutional. The main arguments raised by the petitioners were as under:

(a) The decision of the Supreme Court in *Nusrat Bhutto* case[49] was violated by General Ziaul Haq (1924–88) in promulgating and enforcing, amongst others, the Provisional Constitution Order 1981, and the Referendum Order 1984. This being so, the National Assembly and the provincial assemblies elected in 1985 and their functioning thereafter could not be taken to be duly elected bodies under the constitution. Consequently, the 8th Amendment passed by such a National Assembly would be invalid.

(b) The basic structure of the Constitution of Pakistan has been given in the Objectives Resolution and any amendment that violates such a basic structure would itself be invalid. The 8th Amendment being violative of such a basic structure by having altered its parliamentary character was liable to be struck down as invalid.

(c) The National Assembly, elected on a non-party basis in 1985, was unconstitutional and illegal and could not thus amend the Constitution.

The federation raised the following objections in response:

(i) That the judges hearing the cases had taken oath under the Constitution as amended by the 8th Amendment. Therefore, they could not question it or allow it to be questioned.

(ii) That all the petitions were hit by the doctrine of political question. Since the question of balance of power between the President and the Prime Minister, because of its political sensitivity, is a political question, therefore, the Court could not determine the same.
(iii) That doctrine of *de facto* would favour the validation of the 8th Amendment as it has been in force for so long. Its invalidation after more than 12 years would affect large number of orders made or actions taken there under.

The Supreme Court upheld the validity of the 8th Amendment. The main findings of the Court were as under:

1. Although Article 239 confers unlimited power to the Parliament to amend the Constitution, yet it cannot amend in complete violation of Islam, nor can it convert democratic form into undemocratic. Similarly, courts cannot be abolished through amendment in the Constitution. It is an emerging legal theory that even if the Constitution is suspended or abrogated, the judiciary continues to hold its position to impart justice and protect rights of the people.
2. The salient features of the Constitution as reflected in the Objectives Resolution are federation and parliamentary form of government blended with Islamic provisions. As long as such salient features are retained and not altered in substance, amendments can be made as per procedure prescribed in Article 239 of the Constitution. The Court held that the 8th Amendment did not alter the basic features of the Constitution and was, therefore, valid.
3. The National Assembly elected on a non-party basis was held to be constitutional and legal. Parliament having been validly constituted, Constitution (8th Amendment) Act 1985, introduced in and passed by such Parliament was a competently enacted piece of legislation.
4. Article 58(2)(b) of the Constitution only brought about balance between the powers of the president and the prime minister in parliamentary form of government as is contemplated under a parliamentary democracy. There was nothing unusual about it and such provisions enabling the president to exercise such power could be found in various parliamentary democratic constitutions like those of Australia, Italy, India, France, and Portugal.
5. By recognizing certain basic features and characteristics of the Constitution, it does not mean that the Supreme Court has impliedly accepted the theory of the basic structure of the Constitution. Only a limited application of the theory has been made to save prominent features found within the realm of the Constitution itself.
6. On the objection regarding the doctrine of political question, it was held that any question being a political question would not deter the Court from determining it on the touchstone of the Constitution. Courts should not adopt a 'political question doctrine' for refusing to determine difficult and knotty problems barring political overtures. It would amount to abdication of judicial power which neither the Constitution permits nor the law allows. The crucial factor is that the action impugned is shown to be violative of the Constitution.
7. The 8th Amendment was incorporated into the Constitution in 1985, after which three elections were held on a party basis and the resultant Parliaments did not touch this amendment. It amply demonstrated that this amendment was ratified by implication and had come to stay in the Constitution unless amended in the manner prescribed in Article 239.

The judgment in *Mahmood Khan Achakzai's* case was partly followed by the Supreme Court of Pakistan in *Zafar Ali Shah v. Pervez Musharraf.*[50] In this case, while conferring power on General Pervez Musharraf, Chief of Army Staff (COAS) who had sacked the civilian government and taken over power himself, to amend the Constitution forbade him from making any amendment in the salient features of the Constitution, i.e.

(i) independence of judiciary,
(ii) federalism,
(iii) parliamentary form of government blended with Islamic provisions.

In *Pakistan Lawyers Forum v. Federation of Pakistan,*[51] Clauses (7) and (8) of Article 41 of the Constitution added by the 17th Amendment were challenged before the Supreme Court of Pakistan. It was argued that these clauses, which recognized the election of General Pervez Musharraf as president through a referendum and provided for a vote of confidence by the Parliament and provincial assemblies for General Musharraf, were liable to be struck down being against basic structure/basic features of the Constitution. The Constitution, it was contended, has made clear provisions for election to the office of President of Pakistan through an Electoral College and has also laid down the clear provisions for determining the qualifications and disqualifications of persons desiring to run for the office of President. Therefore, the new Clauses (7) and (8) being introduced in Article 41 of the Constitution were against the basic structure/basic features of the Constitution.

These arguments were repelled by the Supreme Court. It was held that so far as the argument that Article 41(7) and Article 41(8) should be struck down as violative of the basic structure of the Constitution. The Supreme Court would have no jurisdiction to strike down provisions of the Constitution on substantive grounds.

There is a significant difference between the position that Parliament cannot amend salient features of the Constitution and the position that if Parliament does amend these salient features, it would then be the duty of the superior judiciary to strike down such amendments. The superior courts in Pakistan have consistently acknowledged that while there may be a basic structure to the Constitution, and while there may also be limitations on the power of Parliament to make amendments to such a basic structure, such limitations are to be exercised and enforced not by the judiciary (as in the case of conflict between a statute and Article 8), but by the body politic, i.e., the people of Pakistan.

The theory of basic structure or salient features, as far as Pakistan is concerned, has been used only as a doctrine to identify the basic features of the Constitution. Prior to *Zafar Ali Shah's* case, there was almost three decades of settled law to the effect that even though there were certain salient features of the Constitution, no constitutional amendment could be struck down by the superior judiciary as being violative of those features. The remedy lay in the political and not the judicial process. The appeal in such a case was to be made to the people, not the courts. Constitutional amendments always pose a political question, which can be resolved only through the normal mechanisms of parliamentary democracy and free elections.

The Supreme Court in this case nullified the doctrine of unamendability of basic features of the constitution recognized in *Mahmood Achakzai's* case.

The 18th Amendment to the Constitution in 2010 provided for procedure and process of appointment of the judges of the Supreme Court and the High Courts' by introducing Article 175A in the Constitution. Article 175A was challenged before the Supreme Court in a number of petitions on the touchstone of the theory of the basic structure of the Constitution contending that it was repugnant to the basic features of the Constitution, particularly, independence of the judiciary and separation of powers.[52]

The Supreme Court of Pakistan, after hearing the case over several months, did not decide it and made certain recommendations to the Parliament, including the addition of 2 more judges of the Supreme Court for future amendments which were duly carried out by the Parliament under the 19th Amendment to the Constitution. However, the question of the application of the theory of basic structure for judicial review of constitutional amendment remained open and undecided.

In the year 2015, the Constitution (21st Amendment) Act was passed by Parliament, under which military courts were introduced for a period of 2 years. Subsequently, the military courts were extended for another period of 2 years under the Constitution (22nd Amendment) Act 2017. This amendment introducing military courts was challenged by a number of Bar Associations throughout Pakistan and eventually the pending cases against the 18th Amendment and the new cases against the 21st Amendment were heard together in the year 2015 by a full court of 17 judges of the Supreme Court of Pakistan, headed by the Chief Justice Nasirul Mulk (1950).[53] The petitions against the 18th Amendment were dismissed by a majority of 14 to 3. Although the petitions against the 21st Amendment and Pakistan Army (Amendment) Act 2015, were dismissed by a majority of 11 to 6, yet by a majority of 13 to 4 the Supreme Court recognized and accepted the theory of basic structure/basic features of the constitution.

The 17 members of the bench wrote nine different opinions. Most of the opinions are very detailed and can be discussed separately. The Chief Justice Nasirul Mulk (1950), with whom Justice Iqbal Hameedur Rahman (1956)[54] agreed, dismissed the petitions on the ground of non-maintainability. It was held that there are no limitations, express or implied, on the powers of the Parliament to amend the Constitution and the amendments brought about in exercise of such powers are not liable to be challenged on any ground whatsoever before any Court. Because the Court lacked jurisdiction to strike down any amendment in the Constitution, it was not necessary to examine the grounds on which the 18th and 21st Amendments were challenged.

The next senior judge of the Court, Justice Jawwad S. Khawaja (1950)[55] wrote a separate opinion in which he accepted the petitions against the 21st Amendment and held the same to be liable to be struck down. His conclusions were as under:

> (i) That Parliament is not sovereign or supreme in the sense that there are no limitations on its power to amend the Constitution;
> (ii) The limitations on Parliament are not only political, but are borne out from the Constitution itself;
> (iii) This Court has the power to judicially review a Constitutional Amendment passed by Parliament and to strike it down where appropriate; and
> (iv) The 21st Amendment is liable to be struck down.

Hence, he accepted the propositions that Constitutional Amendments can be judicially reviewed by the superior courts and can be struck down if found to be violative of the basic structure/basic features of the Constitution.

Justice Mian Saqib Nisar (1954)[56] wrote a separate lengthy opinion. Most of the opinion is an anti-thesis to the theory of the basic structure of the Constitution propounded by the Supreme Court of India. He concluded that constitutional amendment power should vest only in the hands of chosen representatives of the people and not in the hands of an unelected judiciary even though it acts in good faith. He accordingly dismissed the petitions.

The next senior judge, Justice Asif Saeed Khan Khosa (1954)[57] accepted the petitions against the 21st Amendment but did not go into the question of validity of judicial review of constitutional provisions. His conclusions were as under:-

> 'As a result of the discussion made above I have concluded as follows:
>
> (i) In view of the clear and categorical provisions of Article 175(2) and Article 239(5) and (6) of the Constitution I have not felt persuaded to accept the academic theory of basic features or basic structure of the Constitution as conferring jurisdiction upon this Court for striking down an amendment of the Constitution.
> (ii) The Constitution Petitions assailing the Constitution (21st Amendment) Act (Act I of 2015) and the Pakistan Army (Amendment) Act (Act II of 2015) are partially allowed and the Pakistan Army (Amendment) Act (Act II of 2015) is declared to be unconstitutional, without lawful authority and of no legal effect. As a consequence of this declaration all the trials conducted, and the appeals decided by the military courts deriving authority from the Pakistan Army (Amendment) Act (Act II of 2015) are to be treated as *non est* and all the judgments delivered by invoking that law are rendered incapable of implementation and execution.
> (iii) As an outcome of the declaration made above in respect of the Pakistan Army (Amendment) Act (Act II of 2015) the Constitution (21st Amendment) Act (Act I of 2015) has lost its *raison* d'être, efficacy and utility and, therefore, no determination needs to be made about its fate or continued existence.'

Justice Azmat Saeed (1954)[58] wrote an opinion with which 7 other judges; namely Justices Anwar Zaheer Jamali (1951),[59] Sarmad Jalal Usmani (1950),[60] Amir Hani Muslim (1952),[61] Gulzar Ahmed (1957),[62] Mushir Alam (1956),[63] Umar Ata Bandial (1958)[64] and Maqbool Baqar (1957)[65] concurred. Justices Sarmad Jalal Usmani (1950) and Umar Ata Bandial (1958), however, wrote separate concurring opinions as well. In this way, the opinion authored by Justice Azmat Saeed became an opinion of 8 out of 17 judges, which virtually became the majority judgment. He stated as under:

> 'In view of the aforesaid, it is held that:
>
> (i) The Constitution contains a scheme reflecting its salient features which define the Constitution. Such salient features are obvious and self-evident upon a harmonious and holistic interpretation of the Constitution. In an effort to discover such salient features material outside the Constitution cannot be safely relied upon.
> (ii) The salient features, as are ascertainable from the Constitution, include democracy, parliamentary form of government and independence of the judiciary.
> (iii) The amendatory powers of the Parliament are subject to implied limitations. The Parliament, in view of Articles 238 and 239, is vested with the power to amend the Constitution as long as the salient features of the Constitution are not repealed, abrogated or substantively altered.

(iv) This Court is vested with the jurisdiction to interpret the Constitution in order to ascertain and identify its defining salient features. It is equally vested "with jurisdiction to examine the *vires* of any constitutional amendment so as to determine whether any of the salient features of the Constitution has been repealed, abrogated or substantively altered as a consequence thereof".'

Thus, this opinion of 8 judges upheld the principles of basic structure/salient features of the constitution which would be beyond the reach of amendatory power of the Parliament.

Another opinion was authored by Justice Ejaz Afzal Khan (1953)[66] with whom Justice Ijaz Ahmad Chaudhry (1950)[67] agreed. Justice Ejaz Afzal Khan (1953) concluded as under:

(i) We have jurisdiction to examine the *vires* of any amendment and annul it if it impairs, undermines or alters any of the parts forming the basic structure of the Constitution;
(ii) The Constitution (21st Amendment) Act 2015, impairing, undermining and altering the parts forming the basic structure of the Constitution is *ultra vires* and thus *non est*; and
(iii) That once the amendment in the Constitution enabling amendment in the Acts is declared *ultra vires* and *non est*, the latter automatically becomes *ultra vires* and *non est*.

Thus, two judges fully endorsed theory/principle of basic structure/basic features of the constitution.

Another judge, Justice Dost Muhammad Khan (1953),[68] wrote a separate opinion in which he concluded that—

> 'the 18th Constitutional Amendment and 19th Constitutional Amendment inserting Article 175A, the 21st constitutional amendment inserting a proviso in Article 175 and amendment in the Army Act 1952, the Pakistan Air Force Act 1953, the Pakistan Navy Ordinance 1961, and the Protection of Pakistan Act 2014, and all subsequent amendments, made through ordinary legislation are declared null and void being unconstitutional and shall be deleted from the Constitution as a whole.'

The 17th judge, Justice Qazi Faez Isa (1959)[69] wrote a separate opinion in which he concluded as under:

(i) Article 239(5) of the Constitution does not oust the jurisdiction of the Supreme Court to examine an amendment made to the Constitution.
(ii) The Supreme Court also has the jurisdiction to examine an amendment made to the Constitution under Clause (3) of Article 184 read with Clause (2) of Article 175 of the Constitution.
(iii) The 21st Amendment does not succeed in its attempt to try civilians by the military.
(iv) The military, which is a part of the Executive, cannot conduct criminal trials because judicial power can only be exercised by the Judiciary.
(v) The Pakistan Army (Amendment) Act 2015, takes away and abridges Fundamental Rights mentioned in Chapter 1 of Part II to the Constitution therefore the same is void.
(vi) All convictions, sentences passed or acquittals made of civilians tried by the military pursuant to the Pakistan Army Act 1952, the Pakistan Air Force Act 1953, the Pakistan Navy Ordinance 1961, and the Protection of Pakistan Act 2014, are set aside and all such cases to be adjudicated afresh by the Anti-Terrorism Courts.

As a result of this judgment, it can be said that only 4 judges of the Supreme Court, namely; Chief Justice Nasirul Mulk (1954), Justices Mian Saqib Nisar (1954), Asif Saeed Khan Khosa (1954) [who did not go into question of basic structure/basic features of the Constitution] and Justice Iqbal Hameedur Rehman (1956) rejected the Doctrine of the Basic Structure of the Constitution. Other 13 judges, directly or indirectly, upheld the theory of basic structure of the Constitution.

Basic Structure Theory in Bangladesh

Under the Constitution (8th Amendment) Act 1988, several benches of the High Court of Bangladesh were created at various places in Bangladesh, including Chittagong, Rajshahi and Sylhet. The Constitution of these benches of the High Court was challenged before the Supreme Court of Bangladesh on the ground of being violative of 'independence of judiciary' which is a basic feature/structure of the Constitution of Bangladesh.

In *Anwar Hossain v. Bangladesh*,[70] the Supreme Court of Bangladesh upheld the theory of basic structure and struck down the benches formed under the constitutional amendment, relying on the reasonings in *Kesavananda Bharati*[71] and other cases. Hence, the basic structure theory was upheld in Bangladesh and this view has remained unchanged ever since.

Basic Structure Theory in Malaysia

In *Phang Chin Hock v. Public Prosecutor*, the Federal Court of Malaysia initially held that the basic feature doctrine was inapplicable.[72] The Court held that the Indian Constitution was drafted by a constituent assembly of the Indian people in territorial, racial and community terms, while both the Malaysian and Singapore Constitutions were by ordinary legislature.

However, the Basic Structure Doctrine was cited with approval by Federal Court of Malaysia in *Sivarasa Rasiah v. Badan Peguam Malaysia*.[73] Subsequently, the theory of basic structure was applied by the Federal Court in *Semenyih Jaya Sdn Bhd v. Pentadbir Tanah Daerah Hulu Langat*.[74]

In those cases, the Federal Court held that the vesting of judicial power of the federation in the civil courts formed part of the basic structure of the Constitution and could not be removed even by constitutional amendment.

Criticism of the Concept of Basic Structure of Constitution

The principle stated in written constitutions is that legislation that is inconsistent with or violates fundamental rights, such as Article 8 of the Pakistan Constitution and Article 13 of the Indian Constitution are void. And all legislations and executive actions must conform to the provisions of the constitution, or they will be declared unconstitutional and void by the courts exercising judicial review of legislative and administrative actions, as stated by Chief Justice John Marshall (1755–1835)[75] of the United States in *Marbury v. Madison*.[76] He observed:

> 'It is a proposition too plain to be contested, that the Constitution constructs any legislative act repugnant to it, or that the Legislature may alter the Constitution by an ordinary act.
>
> Between these alternatives there is no middle ground. Certainly all those who have framed written Constitutions contemplate them as forming the fundamental and paramount law of the nation, and consequently the theory of every such government must be that an act of the Legislature repugnant to the Constitution is void.'

In the US Constitution, there is no such provision as Article 8 of the Pakistan Constitution and Article 13 of the Indian Constitution expressly declaring laws in conflict with the constitution to be void.

Nevertheless, Chief Justice Marshall (1755–1835) by an unanswerable process of reasoning arrived at the same result as is expressly stated in Article 8 or Article 13 and the word 'void' has undoubtedly been borrowed both by Pakistan and the Indian Constitution from his judgment. It is, however, obvious from his judgment that the judicial review expounded by him is confined only to the legislative enactments of inorganic nature and administrative actions. It has never been extended by the US Supreme Court to the amendments made to the US Constitution. No judge has even thought of declaring a constitutional amendment as unconstitutional on the ground that it is inconsistent with or in derogation of the existing provisions of the Constitution.

By recognizing constitutional amendments as an ordinary law within the meaning of Article; Article 8 of the Pakistan Constitution and Article 13 of the Indian Constitution, in order to bring such amendments within the purview of judicial review of the Courts, it is tantamount to negation of the principle that the constitution is a supreme law standing higher in position than the ordinary or sub-constitutional laws of the country. Chief Justice Hamoodur Rahman (1910–81)[77] in *State v. Zia-ur-Rehman*[78] said in this respect:

> 'In countries which adopt a detailed Constitution, the Constitution is thought of as an instrument by which Government can be controlled, and it is for this reason that generally some measure of rigidity in the procedure for the amendment of the Constitution is also introduced, and the Constitution is conceived, of as a fundamental or an organic or a Supreme law standing in a somewhat higher position than the other laws of the country. It then assumes the position of a law on the basis of which the *vires* of all other sub-Constitutional

> laws and the validity of Governmental actions can be judged. Thus, even non-Constitutional provisions, if incorporated in a Constitution, acquire a higher sanctity and stand on the same footing as strictly constitutional provisions. No differentiation can be made between them, once they have been given a constitutional status by being incorporated in the Constitution itself.'

The Indian Supreme Court, by treating a constitutional amendment on a par with the sub-constitutional law, has deprived the constitutional provisions of their higher status. Once an amendment has been incorporated into the Constitution, it acquires the same status as that of the Constitution itself and, therefore, it cannot be treated as an ordinary law. It cannot be denied that amendment of the Constitution is not an ordinary legislative process; it is in fact a constituent power. A constitutional amendment is made in exercise of the sovereign power and not the legislative power of the Parliament, and therefore, it partakes of the quality and character of the Constitution itself.

Nevertheless, the theory of the basic structure of the Constitution is a developing constitutional concept which has the effect of empowerment of the judiciary as the ultimate arbiter of the constitution. It has been held in *Sindh High Court Bar Association v. Federation of Pakistan,*[79] that the courts' 'expand' jurisdiction to protect the rights of the people against arbitrary violations by the executive.

Justice Fazal Karim[80] in his book *Judicial Review of Public Actions,*[81] has severely criticized the Doctrine of Basic Structure. According to him, since the power to amend the Constitution was given to the Parliament by the people, therefore, it is simple and inexorable logic that it can be taken away only by the people and not by anybody else, including the judiciary. The power to amend the Constitution has been given to the representatives of the people in Parliament and it must remain over there. So he thinks that cases challenging constitutional amendments are not 'justiciable'. He feels that with the decision in *District Bar Association, Rawalpindi v. Federation of Pakistan,*[82] the system of government in Pakistan has ceased to be one of checks and balances. The balance has tilted in favour of the judiciary.

Conclusions

Much can be written about the validity of the theory/doctrine of the basic structure of the Constitution. However, it is now an accepted legal doctrine throughout the South Asian sub-continent. As explained in this chapter, this theory/doctrine has undergone a thorough debate during the last 70 years, both in legal and academic circles, particularly in India and Pakistan. It has now finally stood as established law throughout South Asia.

It is impossible to deny that several general elections, particularly in Pakistan and Bangladesh, have sparked considerable debate about their fairness. Except for the 1970 general elections, all other general elections in Pakistan have been marred by serious controversies.

The same is true for Bangladesh's elections. With controversial elections, it is impossible to say that the so called 'chosen representatives' are truly elected. Therefore, their legitimacy has always been under serious doubts, and it might not be advisable to allow dubiously elected representatives to play havoc with the basic features of the Constitution, which are regarded as sacrosanct by the people. The judiciary, though an unelected body, is the guardian of the Constitution and is generally called upon to perform its fundamental role of exercising checks and balances against the possibility of excesses and overreach on the part of other organs of the state, the executive and the legislature.

It is common knowledge in South Asia that politically powerful leaders can easily implement constitutional amendments. The dominance of the will of political leaders like Indira Gandhi (1917–84)[83] and Narendra Modi (1950)[84] cannot be lost sight of and they have been/or are in a position to have the Constitution amended to suit their narrow ends and objectives.

Similarly, during the military regimes in Pakistan, the military rulers had no difficulty in having the Constitution amended to suit their convenience or interests. Similarly, Bangladesh has bitter experience with strong military rulers like Ziaur Rehman (1936–81)[85] and Hussain Muhammad Ershad (1930–2019)[86] and now with an autocrat like Sheikh Haseena Wajed (1947).[87] They could get the Constitution amended.

In the face of such situations, it is imperative that the judiciary should be empowered as a check on wanton exercise of manipulating the Constitution at the hands of autocratic leaders.

Notes

1. AIR 1951 Patna 246.
2. AIR 1951 S.C. 458.
3. AIR 1962 S.C. 723.
4. This system of land revenue was introduced by Sir Thomas Munro, Governor of Madras, in 1820. In this system, the peasants or cultivators ('ryots') were regarded as the owners of the land. They had ownership rights, and could sell, mortgage or gift the land. The taxes were directly collected by the government from the peasants.
5. AIR 1965 S.C. 845.
6. Mohammad Hidayatullah was the 11th Chief Justice of India serving from 1968 to 1970, and the 6th Vice President of India, serving from 1979 to 1984.
7. AIR 1967 S.C. 1643.
8. A.G. Chaudhry, *Lectures on Constitutional Law*, (Lahore: Irfan Law Book House, 1996), pp. 314–5.
9. AIR 1973 S.C. 1461.
10. Sarv Mittra Sikri was the 13th Chief Justice of the Supreme Court of India from 1971 until his retirement in 1973.
11. Kowdoor Sadananda Hegde served as a judge in the Supreme Court of India from 1967 to 1973.
12. Arun Kumar Mukherjea served as a judge of the Supreme Court of India from 1972 until his death in 1973.
13. AIR 1967 S.C 1643.
14. Supra Note 8, p. 317.
15. AIR 1975 S.C. 2299.
16. Indira Gandhi was the 3rd prime minister of India from 1966 to 1977 and again from 1980 until 1984.
17. Justice Y.V. Chandrachud was the 16th Chief Justice of India, serving from 1978 until his retirement in July 1985.
18. AIR 1980 S.C. 1789.
19. AIR 1973 SC 1461.
20. AIR 1981 S.C. C. 362.
21. AIR 1983 S.C. 239.
22. AIR 1993 S.C. 1267.
23. AIR 2007 S.C. 861.
24. AIR 1994 S.C. 268.
25. AIR 1999 S.C. 1.
26. (2016) 5 SCC 1.
27. Jagdish Singh Khehar was the 44th Chief Justice of India in 2017 retiring on reaching superannuation.
28. Jasti Chelameswar was a judge of the Supreme Court of India from 2011 to 2018.
29. Madan Bhimrao Lokur was a judge of the Supreme Court of India from 2012 until 2018.
30. Kurian Joseph was a judge of the Supreme Court of India from 2013 until 2018.
31. Adarsh Kumar Goel was a judge of the Supreme Court of India from 2014 until 2018.
32. PLD 1963 S.C. 486.
33. PLD 1976 S.C. 57.
34. AIR 1967 S.C. 1643.
35. AIR 1973 SC 1461.
36. PLD 1973 S.C. 49.
37. General Muhammad Yahya Khan was the 3rd President of Pakistan and Chief Martial Law Administrator from 1969 to 1971.
38. PLD 1972 S.C. 139.
39. PLD 1977 S.C. 397.
40. AIR 1967 S.C. 1643.
41. PLD 1983 S.C. 457.
42. AIR 1973 SC 1461.
43. 1975 AIR 2299.
44. K. K. Mathew was a judge of the Supreme Court of India from 1971 to 1976.
45. Mohammad Haleem was the 10th Chief Justice of Pakistan from 1981 to 1989.
46. Supra Note 8, p. 323–4.
47. PLD 1997 S.C. 426.

48. See also *Federation of Pakistan v. Haji Muhammad Saifullah*, PLD 1989 S.C. 166; *Khawaja Ahmad Tariq Rahim v. Federation of Pakistan*, PLD 1992 S.C. 646; *Muhammad Nawaz Sharif v. President*, PLD 1993 S.C. 473; *Benazir Bhutto v. President*, PLD 1998 S.C. 388.
49. PLD 1977 S.C. 657.
50. PLD 2000 S.C. 869.
51. PLD 2005 S.C. 719.
52. *Nadeem Ahmad v. Federation of Pakistan*, PLD 2010 S.C. 1165.
53. Nasirul Mulk served as the 7th caretaker prime minister of Pakistan who had previously served as the 22nd Chief Justice of Pakistan.
54. Iqbal Hameedur Rahman was a senior judge of the Supreme Court of Pakistan from 2013 until 2016.
55. Jawwad S. Khawaja served as the 23rd Chief Justice of Pakistan from 17 August 2015 until 9 September 2015.
56. Mian Saqib Nisar served as the 25th Chief Justice of Pakistan from 2016 till 2019.
57. Asif Saeed Khan Khosa served as the 26th Chief Justice of Pakistan from 18 January 2019 to 20 December 2019.
58. Justice Azmat Saeed Sheikh wasa judge of the Supreme Court of Pakistan from 2012 until 2019.
59. Anwar Zaheer Jamali was the 24th Chief Justice of Pakistan from 2015 to 2016.
60. Sarmad Jalal Usmani was a judge of the Supreme Court of Pakistan from 2011 to 2015.
61. Amir Hani Muslim served as a judge of the Supreme Court of Pakistan from 2011 to 2017.
62. Gulzar Ahmed was the 27th Chief Justice of Pakistan from 2019 to 2022.
63. Mushir Alam served as a judge of the Supreme Court of Pakistan from 2013 until 2013.
64. Umar Ata Bandial is the 28th and current Chief Justice of the Supreme Court of Pakistan from 2022.
65. Maqbool Baqar became judge of the Supreme Court of Pakistan from 2015.
66. Ejaz Afzal Khan was a judge of the Supreme Court of Pakistan from 2011 to 2018.
67. Ijaz Ahmad Chaudhry was a judge in the Supreme Court of Pakistan from 2011 to 2015.
68. Dost Muhammad Khan served as a judge of the Supreme Court of Pakistan from 2014 to 2018.
69. Qazi Faez Isa is a judge of the Supreme Court of Pakistan, who assumed office on 5 September 2014.
70. 41 DLR 1989 App, Div 165; 1989 BLD (Spl) 1.
71. AIR 1973 SC 1461.
72. (1980) 1 MLJ 70.
73. (2010) 2 MLJ 333.
74. (2017) 3 MLJ 561.
75. John Marshall was the 4th Chief Justice of the United States from 1801 to 1835.
76. 5 U.S. 137 (1803).
77. Hamoodur Rahman was the 7th Chief Justice of Pakistan from 1968 till 1975.
78. PLD 1973 S.C. 49.
79. PLD 2009 S.C. 879.
80. Fazal Karim was a judge of the Supreme Court of Pakistan from 1994 to 1996.
81. Fazal Karim, Vol 3, 2nd ed., (Karachi: Pakistan Law House,2018), pp. 1820–22.
82. PLD 2015 S.C. 401.
83. Indira Gandhi was the first female and 3rd prime minister of India from 1966 to 1977 and again from 1980 until 1984.
84. Narendra Modi is the 14th and current prime minister of India since 2014.
85. Ziaur Rahman was a Bangladesh Army officer who served as the 7th president of Bangladesh during 1977–1981.
86. Hussain Muhammad Ershad was Bangladesh Army Chief who served as the 10th president of Bangladesh from 1983 to 1990.
87. Sheikh Haseena Wajed is the 11th prime minister of Bangladesh.

Index

A

Ahmad, Justice Shabbir, 478
Ahmed, Chief Justice Gulzar, 564
Ahmed, Justice Wahiduddin, 539
Akram, Justice A.S.M., 535
Alam, Justice Mushir, 564
Ali, Chief Justice Muhammad Yaqoob, 537, 539
Ali, Justice Shaukat, 208
Ali, Justice Sir Saiyid Fazal, 52, 282
Alito, Justice Samuel, 78, 166
Ambedkar, Dr B. R., 136
Amendment, 2–4 *see also* India; Pakistan; United Kingdom, United States of America
Aristotle, 32
Atkins, Lord, 139
Australia, 4, 6, 26, 114, 117, 129, 131, 133, 143, 193, 562
Australia, Constitution of, 6, 129, 145, 159; Article 109, 145; Article 114, 145
Avonholm, Lord Keith of, 496
Avory, Justice Sir Horace Edmund, 476
Ayyangar, Justice N. Rajagopala, 38

B

Badinter, Robert, 193
Bagehot, Walter, 117
Bandial, Justice Umar Ata, 564
Bangladesh, 12, 566–67
Bangladesh, Constitution of, 565; Constitution (8th Amendment) Act 1988, 565
Baqar, Justice Maqbool, 564
Barber, N.W., 545
Barrett, Justice Amy Coney, 196
Beg, Justice Mirza Hameedullah, 205
Bhagwati, Justice P.N., 101–02, 282–84, 286
Bhutto, Benazir, 125, 235, 504
Bhutto, Nusrat, 537
Bhutto, Zulfikar Ali, 39, 40, 537–38, 540
Bingham, Lord Tom, 35, 37
Black, Justice Hugo, 72, 164, 178, 249, 343, 347, 381, 393, 435, 440, 447, 482, 526
Blackmun, Justice Harry, 80, 350, 354, 383, 387–88, 451
Blackstone, Sir William, 7, 32, 444, 546
Bork, Judge Robert, 163, 193, 196, 252, 381, 386
Bradley, Justice Joseph P., 47
Brandeis, Justice Louis, 157, 175, 220, 222, 224, 229, 263, 383, 392, 437–39,
Brennan Jr, Justice William Joseph, 80, 162, 177, 194, 220, 255, 274, 345, 349, 350, 354, 394, 443, 445–46, 451, 482, 484
Brewer, Justice David Josiah, 74
Breyer, Justice Stephen, 78–9, 164, 182, 196, 228–29, 272, 345–47, 349, 351, 388, 422, 450
Bridge, Lord Nigel, 36
Brown, Justice Henry Billings, 74, 103, 407
Browne-Wilkinson, Lord, 232
Burger, Justice Warren E., 80–2, 84, 162–63, 350–51, 386, 394, 411–12, 435, 447, 483, 526
Burton, Justice Harold Hitz, 344
Bush, George W., 169, 171, 181

C

Canada, 26, 63, 114, 117, 129, 138–39, 255, 549, 550
Canada, Constitution of 27, 117, 129, 138–39; Balfour Declaration 1926, 26; British North America Act 1867 26, 28, 117, 129, 146; Canadian Citizenship Act 1946, 8;Canadian Constitution Act 1867, 28, 117, 131; Constitution Act 1867, 550
Cardozo, Justice Benjamin N., 213, 435
Carson, Lord Edward, 194
Carswell, Judge George Harrold, 196
Ceylon Independence Act 1947, 161
Chandrachud, Chief Justice Y.V., 557–58
Chaudhry, Chief Justice Iftikhar Muhammad, 208
Chaudhry, Justice Abdul Qadeer, 369
Chaudhry, Justice Ijaz Ahmad, 565
Chelameswar, Justice Jasti, 559
Chitty, Joseph, 535, 543, 546–48
Claiborne, Judge Harry, 196
Clark, Justice Tom C., 341, 374
Clarke, Justice John Hessin, 437
Clinton, Bill, 169, 172, 174, 196, 221, 253, 388
Cockburn, Lord Chief Justice Sir Alexander, 469
Coke, Chief Justice Sir Edward, 43, 116
Constitution, 2–3 *see also* Australia; Bangladesh; India; Germany; Japan; Pakistan; Switzerland; United Kingdom; United States of America
Constitutional convention, 24–8, 30, 57, 119, 120, 169, 170, 194–95, 236, 351, 404, 534
Constitutional interpretation, 28, 46, 82, 156, 162, 177, 212–13, 224, 226, 236, 244–45, 247, 249, 250, 264, 356, 381, 434
Cooley, Chief Justice Thomas McIntyre, 336
Cornelius, Chief Justice A.R. (Alvin Robert), 478, 520–21
Curtis, Justice Benjamin R., 50

D

Das, Justice Sudhi Ranjan, 87, 238
Davis, Justice David, 179
Denning, Lord Tom, 27, 261, 396, 477–78
De Smith, Stanley Alexander, 536, 543
Dicey, A.V., 24, 26, 32–5, 62–3, 114–19, 132–33, 282, 535
Diplock, Lord Kenneth, 231, 397
Discrimination, 9, 62–9, 71–7, 79, 80–1; based on gender 67–9, 81–6, 251, 386, 494; based on sex 81–5; based on racial 73–4, 81, 212, 225, 230; judicial scrutiny of 65, 73, 82
Doctrine of necessity, 204, 267, 534, 536–39, 540–42, 544–49, 550 *see also* Pakistan
Doctrine of Original Package, 254 *see also* United States of America
Doctrine of precedents, 222 *see also* Pakistan; United States of America
Doctrine of Saving Construction, 221 *see also* United States of America
Donaldson, Lord John, 35–6, 194
Double jeopardy clause, 421–29
Douglas, Justice William O., 84, 145, 220, 344, 352, 383, 435, 440, 447, 481–82
Dowling, Noel T., 3
Due process clause, 17, 46–9, 50–1, 54, 59, 65, 81, 108, 165, 270, 272–75, 383, 387, 437, 439, 444, 490, 519, 524–26
Dunedin, Lord, 261, 330

E

Equal protection of law, 7, 62, 67, 86, 89, 91–4, 96–7, 507
Equality before law, 7, 37, 62, 86–7, 92–4, 97–8, 100
Ershad, Hussain Muhammad, 567

F

Federal Constitutional Court (*Bundesverfassungsgericht*), 146, 193–94,
Federalism, 132–33, 139, 140, 142, 147–48, 156
Federation, 6, 124, 126, 129, 131–36, 138, 142–49, 158, 207, 537, 561–62, 566
Field, Justice Stephen Johnson 56, 340
Fortas, Judge Abe, 196, 349, 442
Fortescue, Chief Justice John, 32
Frankfurter, Justice Felix, 175, 178, 213, 226, 344, 405, 439
Freedom of assembly, 7, 18, 362, 507–08, 510
Freedom of association, 7, 19, 135, 331, 382, 490–96, 500–01, 503, 508
Freedom of movement, 7, 18–9, 52, 92, 282, 300, 411, 501, 515–17
Freedom of religion, 7, 353, 361–62, 364–65, 367, 369, 371, 501
Freedom of speech and press, 212, 435, 438, 472, 479, 484, 507

G

Gajendragadkar, Chief Justice P. B., 238
Gandhi, Indira, 28, 204–05, 303, 557, 567
Germany, 4, 6, 26, 62, 114, 129, 131, 133, 146, 183, 193–95, 515
Germany, Constitution of 4, 26, 62; Article 28(1), 146; Article 31, 146; Article 92, 146; Article 93, 146; Article 95, 146
Gibson, Chief Justice John Bannister, 218
Ginsburg, Douglas H., 196
Ginsburg, Justice Ruth Bader, 78–9, 85, 165, 182, 196, 228–29, 345–46, 349, 351, 388, 422
Goel, Justice Adarsh Kumar, 559
Goff, Lord Robert, 59
Gorsuch, Neil, 196
Government of India Act 1935, 10–1, 123, 147, 157–58, 164–65, 202, 256, 263–64, 535, 543 *see also* India
Green, Lord, 27
Grier, Justice Robert Cooper, 179
Griffith, Chief Justice Sir Samuel Walker, 233
Griffiths, Lord William Hugh, 232
Grotius, Hugo, 543
Gul, Justice Muhammad, 167
Gurfein, Judge Murray, 481
Gwyer, Chief Justice Sir Maurice, 256, 263

H

Hale, Lord Chief Justice Sir Matthew, 55, 57
Haleem, Chief Justice Muhammad, 39, 54, 167, 235, 561
Hand, Chief Judge Learned, 439
Haq, Chief Justice Sheikh Anwarul, 537–39, 541, 549
Haq, Ziaul, 125, 537, 539, 540, 561
Harlan II, Justice John Marshall, 51, 74, 80–1, 104, 392, 440–41, 443, 491–92, 517
Harwich, Lord Bridge of, 233
Haynsworth Jr, Judge Clement F., 196
Hegde, Justice K.S. (Kowdoor Sadananda), 556
Hewart, Lord Chief Justice Gordon, 279
Hidayatullah, Chief Justice Mohammad, 554
High Court of Australia, 143, 368, 370
Hobhouse, Lord John, 59
Holmes Jr, Justice Oliver Wendell, 84, 131, 157, 161, 175, 179, 220, 252, 263, 436–37, 479, 483
Hope, Lord David, 37
House of Commons, 25, 114, 116–19, 120, 190, 195, 197, 233, 454
House of Lords, 27, 36, 114–16, 118–19, 120, 192–94, 198–99, 202, 231–33, 260, 263, 317, 330
Hughes Sr, Chief Justice Charles Evans, 2, 221, 253, 444, 483
Husain, Justice Ikhlaq, 208

I

India, 3–4, 6–7, 9, 10–6, 29, 30, 38, 53, 92, 122–23, 129, 131, 133, 136–38, 142, 157, 160–61, 202–03, 205–06, 233, 239, 240, 255–56, 263, 284, 290, 292–93, 301–02, 333, 360, 364, 367, 398, 458–59, 460, 464, 467, 470, 496, 509, 546, 548, 554, 558–59, 560, 567
India, Constitution of, 4, 7–9, 10–5, 28–9, 52, 86, 123, 136–38, 147–48, 158, 161, 166, 202, 238–39, 263, 265, 281–82,

284–86, 288–89, 291–94, 296–98, 300, 302–04, 307, 310, 317–18, 331, 335, 356–59, 360–62, 364–67, 370, 398, 416, 423–24, 427–29, 455–56, 458–59, 460–62, 464–65, 468, 470, 496–97, 500, 509, 514, 520, 527, 553–54, 556–58, 561, 566; 16th Amendment, 470, 496; Article 1(3), 10; Article 10, 12; Article 103, 122; Article 11, 12, 517; Article 12, 101–02, 290, 456; Article 124, 158; Article 131, 147; Article 14, 86–7, 89, 101–03, 284–85, 287, 289, 292, 462–63; Article 15, 86, 497; Article 16, 86; Article 162, 553; Article 17, 86, 366; Article 19, 52, 282, 295, 461, 470; Article 207, 138; Article 21, 52–3, 281–89, 291–99, 300–01, 304, 308, 310, 332, 398, 520, 528; Article 22, 298–99, 300–02, 304–09, 314, 527–28; Article 226, 38, 309, 318, 331, 463, 554; Article 245, 158; Article 249, 137; Article 25, 356–57, 359, 360–66; Article 250, 137; Article 252, 137; Article 253, 137, 333, 335–36; Article 254, 239; Article 256, 137; Article 257, 137; Article 27, 367, 370; Article 28, 367–68; Article 3, 138, 334; Article 31, 300, 331–33, 554, 558; Article 32, 290, 296, 331, 360, 459, 558; Article 329-A, 160; Article 353, 137; Article 356, 137–38; Article 357, 137; Article 360, 138; Article 367(3), 12; Article 368, 4, 239, 331, 553–58; Article 392(3), 12; Article 5, 9, 11, 14; Article 51-A, 360; Article 53, 158; Article 53(1,) 29; Article 6, 10–1, 14; Article 7, 7, 12; Article 73, 553; Article 75, 28–9; Article 8, 11; Article 9, 11–2, 14–5; Abducted Person (Recovery and Restoration) Act 1949, 301, 314; Acquisition of Certain Area at Ayodhya Act 1993, 360; Aligarh Muslim University Act, No. XL of 1920, 365; Andhra Pradesh Charitable and Hindu Religious and Endowments Act 1987, 361; Andhra Pradesh Co-operative Societies Act 1964, 498; Andhra Pradesh Objectionable Performances Prohibition Act 1956, 286; Arms Act 1959, 425–26; Army Act 1950, 424, 426; Auroville (Emergency Provisions) Act 1980, 90, 364; Banking Companies Act 1949, 413; Bengal Money Lenders Act 1940, 256; Bengal Suppression of immoral Traffic Act 1923, 301; Bihar Land Reforms Act 1950, 554; Bihar Sathi Lands (Restoration) Act 1950, 89; Bombay Municipal Corporation Act 1888, 288; Bombay Police Act 1951, 510; Bombay Prevention of Ex-Communication Act 1949, 365; Bombay Provincial Municipal Corporation Act 1949, 361; Central Provinces and Berar Goondas Act 1946, 515; Central Sales Tax Act, 461; Cinematograph Act 1952, 465–66; Citizenship (Amendment) Act 1986, 12–3; Citizenship (Amendment) Act 1992, 15; Citizenship Act 1955, 11–5; Coking Coal Mines (Nationalization) Act 36 of 1972 558; Constitution (16th Amendment) Act 1963, 470, 496; Constitution (1st Amendment) Act 1951, 467; Constitution (24th Amendment) Act 1971, 555; Constitution (26th Amendment) Act 1971 558; Constitution (42nd Amendment) Act 1976, 138, 357, 557–58; Constitution (86th Amendment) Act 2002, 282; Constitution (99th Amendment) Act 2014, 559; Constitution 42nd Amendment Act 1976, 357, 557; Constitution 44th (Amendment) Act 1978, 05, 331; Constitution 6th (Amendment) Act 1956, 461; Contempt of Court Act 1971, 469; Criminal Law (Amendment) Act 1908, 498; Daily Newspapers (Price and Control) Order 1960, 462; Drug and Magic Remedies (Objectionable Advertisement) Act 1954, 459; East Punjab Safety Act 1949, 461; Environmental (Protection) Act, 290; Evidence Act 1872, 415, 417, 429; Foreign Recruiting Act (IV of 1874), 467; Foreign Relations Act (XII of 1932), 467; *Hindi Sahitya Sammelan* Act 1962, 497; Hindu Marriage Act 1955, 362; Indian Telegraph Act 1885, 458–59; Industrial (Development and Regulations) Act 1951, 558; Industrial Disputes (Appellate Tribunal) Act 1950, 499; Influx from Pakistan (Control) Act 1949, 515; Judges Enquiry Act 1966, 204; Karnataka Educational Institutions (Prohibition of Capitation Fee) Act 1984, 292; Kerala Agrarian Relations Act 1961, 554; Kerala Land Reforms Act 1971, 556; Madhya Bharat Panchayat Act 1949, 528; Madhya Pradesh Public Security Act 1959, 515; Madras Amendment Act 1950, 498; Maintenance of Internal Security Act 1971 (MISA), 303, 308–09, 310; Maintenance of Public Order Act 1949, 462; Mysore Land Reforms Act 1962, 554; National Judicial Appointments Commission (NJAC), 559, 560; National Security Act (NSA), 303, 306–07, 309; Nationalization Act 1974, 558; Newsprint Control Order 1962, 462; Official Secrets Act 1923, 516; Orissa Freedom of Religion Act 1967, 362; Orissa Hindu Religious Endowments Act 1939, 367; Passport Act 1967, 284–85, 520; Police Act 1861, 362; Prevention of Black-marketing and Maintenance of Supplies of Essential Commodities Act 1980, 285, 303; Prevention of Corruption Act 1947, 413, 424–25, 429, 546; Prevention of Corruption Act, 204; Prevention of Insults of National Honour Act 1971, 360, 457; Prevention of Terrorism Act 2002, 415; Preventive Detention Act 1950, 282, 302–03, 307, 310; Prisons Act 1894, 294, 426; Public Servants (Inquiries) Act 1850, 424, 429; Railway Property (Unlawful Possession) Act 1966, 309; Registration of Societies Act 1860, 498; Sholpur Spinning and Weaving Company (Emergency Provisions) Act 1950, 84; Shri Jagannath Temple Act 1954, 366; Sick Textile Undertakings (Nationalization) Act 1974, 558; Societies Registration Act 1860, 497; Terrorist and Disruptive Activities (Prevention) Act 1987 (TADA), 296, 304, 416; U.P. Special Powers Act 1932, 468; Uttar Pradesh Co-operative Societies Act 1965, 497; Uttar Pradesh Sugar-Cane (Regulation of Supply and Purchase) Act 1953, 498; Wakf Act 1954, 293; *Wali-ud-Dowla* Act 1950 88–9; Water (Prevention and Control of Pollution) Act, 290; West Bengal Animal Slaughter Control Act 1950, 363; West Bengal Societies Registration Act 1961, 364; Working Journalists Act 1955, 462, 465; Indian Independence Act 1947 123, 535

Inequality, 66, 101, 107, 364, 386

International Labour Office (ILO) Convention, 496, 500

Isa, Justice Qazi Faez, 565

Iyer, Justice V.R. Krishna, 53, 295, 528

J

Jackson, Justice Robert H., 344, 373, 439, 440, 442, 517
Jamali, Chief Justice Anwar Zaheer, 530, 564
Jan, Justice Saad Saood, 518
Japan, 144, 181, 183
Japan, Constitution of, 122; Article 67, 122; Article 69, 122; Article 7, 122
Jennings, Sir Ivor, 25–6, 63, 87, 534
Jessel, Sir George, 259
Joseph, Justice Kurian, 559
Judicial activism, 208, 213, 220, 239, 240, 264
Judicial power, 141, 152, 155–56, 158, 161, 165, 167, 191–93, 195–96, 212–13, 217, 219, 220, 230, 236, 259, 561–62, 565–66
Judicial power, 4, 49, 50, 54, 114, 136, 141, 143, 152, 155–56, 158, 161, 165–67, 190–93, 195–96, 212–13, 217, 219, 220, 230, 236, 259, 285, 313, 350, 384, 557, 561–62, 565–66
Judicial restraint, 66, 219, 220–24, 239, 253, 387
Judicial review, 2–3, 17, 45, 47, 49, 122, 131, 142–47, 157–58, 164, 173, 182, 192, 194, 204, 212, 215–16, 218–19, 220–25, 230, 239, 246, 251–52, 254, 276, 303, 306, 309, 318, 384, 438, 498, 520, 522, 534, 537–39, 540, 557–58, 563–64, 566
Judiciary, independence of, 37, 39, 126, 160, 190, 196, 198, 200, 207, 239, 240, 558–59, 562, 565
Junejo, Muhammad Khan, 125

K

Kania, Chief Justice Sir Harilal Jekisundas, 238
Karim, Justice Fazal, 549
Kavanaugh, Justice Brett, 196
Kayani, Chief Justice M. R., 478
Kelsen, Hans, 153–54
Kennedy, Justice Anthony, 78–9, 165, 182, 227, 272, 276, 345, 356, 386–88, 422, 443, 448, 453
Kerner Jr, Judge Otto, 196
Khan, Ayub, 184, 186, 208, 560
Khan, Chief Justice Irshad Hassan, 542, 544
Khan, Ghulam Ishaq, 125
Khan, Justice Dost Muhammad, 565
Khan, Justice Ejaz Afzal, 565
Khan, Justice Sardar Muhammad Raza, 545
Khan, Yahya, 186, 208, 536, 545, 560
Khanna, Justice Hans Raj, 205, 309
Khawaja, Chief Justice Jawwad S., 564
Khehar, Chief Justice Jagdish Singh, 559
Khosa, Chief Justice Asif Saeed Khan, 564–65
Kinkel, Lord Keith of, 231

L

Latham, Chief Justice John, 370
Leghari, Farooq, 125
Lokur, Justice Madan Bhimrao, 559
Lone, Justice Muhammad Afzal, 428–29

M

Mahajan, Justice Mehr Chand, 52
Mansfield, Lord, 535, 548
Marshall, Chief Justice John, 63, 129, 140, 144, 153, 161, 212–19, 225, 233, 238, 244, 246–49, 250, 254–55, 534, 566
Marshall, Justice Thurgood, 69, 80, 194, 274, 354, 396
Mathew, Justice K. K., 160, 561
Matravers, Lord Phillips of Worth, 191
Matthews, Justice Thomas Stanley, 50
Maugham, Lord Frederic 317
McReynolds, Justice James Clark, 175
Meiji Constitution, 122 *see also* Japan
Mian, Chief Justice Ajmal, 159, 160, 230, 544
Miller, Justice Samuel Freeman, 46–7, 51
Millett, Lord Peter, 59
Mills, John Stuart, 381
Mirza, Justice Zafar Hussain, 134
Modi, Narendra, 361, 567
Muhammad, Ghulam, 205–06, 534
Mukherjea, Justice A.K. (Arun Kumar), 556
Mulk, Justice Nasirul, 563, 565
Munir, Chief Justice Muhammad, 39, 206, 234, 236, 264–65, 429, 473–74, 502, 518, 534–37, 544, 547–48
Murphy, Justice Frank, 180
Murphy, Judge William B., 441
Musharraf, Pervez, 126, 208, 518, 541, 543–45, 562
Muslim, Justice Amir Hani, 564

N

Nisar, Chief Justice Mian Saqib, 564–65
Nixon Jr, Judge Walter L., 196
Nixon, Richard, 76, 79, 162–64, 172, 174, 176, 213, 216, 225, 412

O

O'Connor, Justice Sandra Day, 78, 84, 182, 227, 271, 276, 345–47, 349, 351, 354, 387–88, 422, 449, 453

P

Pakistan, 3–4, 6–9, 10–2, 19, 29, 30, 39, 40, 53–4, 94–5, 114, 123, 131, 133–34, 148, 158, 160, 186, 205, 208, 240, 266, 311–13, 398, 427, 461, 471–72, 500, 503–04, 509, 514–15, 518–19, 529, 536, 539, 541–43, 545, 550, 560, 563, 567
Pakistan, Constitution of, 6–8, 19, 20, 98, 124–25, 135, 158–59, 166, 206, 240, 264–65, 310–11, 314–15, 467, 479, 503–04, 520, 530, 553, 561; 13th Amendment, 126, 543;

17th Amendment, 126, 554, 562; 18th Amendment, 126, 135, 207–08, 563; 21st Amendment, 207–08, 563–65; 22nd Amendment, 563; Article 1, 6, 134, 148; Article 106, 135; Article 10A, 54, 530; Article 137, 135; Article 170, 318; Article 175, 93, 311, 565; Article 18, 7, 86, 91, 333; Article 190, 190; Article 203, 93; Article 22(3)(b), 97–9; Article 226, 135; Article 232(2)(a), 135; Article 232, 95; Article 234, 94; Article 235, 470; Article 239, 4, 553, 562, 564, 565; Article 248, 40; Article 27, 9; Article 3, 19; Article 43, 134; Article 6, 11, 95; Article 7, 7, 99, 313; Article 70(4), 134; Article 90, 158; Anti-Terrorism Act 1997, 314, 398, 417; Associated Cement (Vesting) Ordinance 1974, 96; Capital Development Authority Ordinance 1960, 336; Civil Procedure (Special Provisions) Ordinance 1968, 93; Code of Criminal Procedure (Amendment) Ordinance XII of 1982, 416; Constitution (18th Amendment) Act 2010, 54, 207; Constitution (19th Amendment) Act 2010, 207; Constitution (21st Amendment) Act, 563–65; Constitution (22nd Amendment) Act 2017, 563; Constitution (4th Amendment) Act 1975, 560; Constitution (8th) Amendment Act 1985, 125, 503; Contempt of Courts Act 1976, 475; Control of Shipping Act 1947, 91–2; Criminal Law (Special Provisions) Ordinance 1968, 93; Criminal Law Amendment Act 1908, 501; Customs Act 1969, 266; Defence of Pakistan (Amendment) Ordinance 1968, 318; Defence of Pakistan Ordinance 1965, 318; East Bengal State Acquisition and Tenancy Act 1950, 90–1; Emergency Powers Ordinance 1955, 535; Exit from Pakistan (Control) Ordinance 1981, 519; Extradition Act 1972, 514; Foreign Exchange (Prevention of Payments) (Amendments) Act 1974, 93; Foreign Exchange (Prevention of Payments) Act 1972, 93; Foreign Exchange Regulation Act 1947, 92; General Clauses Act 1897 424, 427–29, 470, 479; Guardians and Wards Act (1890), 336; Land Acquisition Act (1894), 336; Legal Framework Order (LFO), 126, 536; Motor Vehicles Act 1939, 102; Naturalization Act 1926, 9; Oaths Act 1873, 416; Pakistan (Control) Act 1949, 11, 515; Pakistan (Control) Ordinance 1948, 11; Pakistan (Recovery of Abducted Persons) Act 1949, 310; Pakistan Air Force Act 1953, 565; Pakistan Army (Amendment) Act 2015, 563–65; Pakistan Army Act 1952, 94–5, 565; Pakistan Citizenship Act 1951, 8–9; Pakistan Navy Ordinance 1961, 565; Passport Act 1974, 519; Police Act [Punjab Amendment Ordinance (8 of 1984)], 511; Police Act 1861, 510; Press (Emergency Powers) Act 1931, 471; Prevention of Seditious Meetings Act 1911, 510; Protection of Pakistan Act 2014, 565; Provisional Constitution Order (PCO), 542, 544–45; Punjab Control of *Goondas* Act 1951, 516; Punjab Municipal Committee Act 1911, 516; Punjab Public Safety Act 1949, 516; Punjab Security of Land Tenures Act 1953, 554; Quetta and Kalat (Civil and Criminal law) Ordinance 1965, 93; Representation of the People Act 1976, 503–04; Sales Tax Act 1990, 266; Sea Customs Act 1878, 424–25; Sea Customs Act 1978, 413; Security of Pakistan Act 1952, 474; Sind Control of *Goondas* Act 1952, 535; Undesirable Companies Act 1958, 501; West Pakistan Criminal Law (Amendment) Act 1963, 93, 418; West Pakistan Employee's Social Security Ordinance 1965, 100; West Pakistan Maintenance of Public Order Ordinance 1960, 511; West Pakistan Use of Loudspeakers (Prohibition) Ordinance 1963, 475

1956 Constitution of, 90–2, 124, 134, 206, 208, 265, 318, 428, 471, 474; Article 11, 92, 516–17; Article 12, 91–2; Article 15, 7, 92, 417, 514, 516–19; Article 22, 91, 98, 371, 474; Article 5, 40, 91–2, 478; Article 8, 7, 93, 99, 471, 474, 566; Punjab Special Powers (Press) Act 1956, 463

1962 Constitution of, 7, 53, 58, 95, 124, 134, 184, 186, 206, 208, 265, 318, 320, 428, 560; Article 17, 7, 235, 500, 502–04; Article 2, 17, 53–4, 319; Article 63, 9, 265, 542; Article 98, 53, 318–19; Criminal Law (Special Provisions) Act 1962, 161; Criminal Law Act 1962, 161; Fundamental Right No. 15, 95; Political Parties Act 1962, 39, 90, 501, 503; Removal of Difficulties/Appointment of Ministers) Order 1962, 186, 560

1973 Constitution of, 19, 39, 53, 86, 90, 94–9, 124–25, 134, 158–59, 166, 197, 206, 208, 265, 310–11, 315, 317, 320, 333, 335–36, 368–69, 370–71, 416, 427–28, 471, 473–77, 500, 503, 509, 514, 518–19, 529, 538–39, 540, 544; 2nd Amendment, 473; Article 10, 311–13, 315, 317, 320, 529; Article 10(4) and (7), 369, 474; Article 13(a), 427–29; Article 13(b), 416–17; Article 14, 19, 397–98; Article 16, 7, 86, 509, 511–12; Article 165, 96–7; Article 17, 500; Article 17(2), 235, 501, 503–04; Article 184(3), 90, 95, 503–04, 516, 529, 537, 565; Article 186, 197; Article 189, 265; Article 19, 7, 471; Article 199, 41, 166, 317, 539, 560; Article 20, 7, 368; Article 204, 475–78; Article 21, 370; Article 23, 7, 333–34; Article 233, 95; Article 24(2), 336; Article 25, 7, 86, 93–9, 100, 103; Article 25(3), 7, 97–9; Article 260, 369, 544; Article 4, 39, 47, 53, 519, 529; Article 89, 159; Article 9, 93, 310–11, 519; Article 280, 95

Parker, Judge John J., 196
Parliamentary government, 28, 237
Parliamentary supremacy, 32, 114, 116, 118–19, 120, 152
Patel, Justice Dorab, 477–78
Pearce, Lord Edward, 191
Phillips, Owen Hood, 2
Physical restraint, freedom from, 57, 271, 282
Pickering, Judge John, 196
Political question doctrine, 224–27, 229, 230, 562–63
Powell Jr, Justice Lewis Franklin, 49, 85, 176, 226, 252, 386, 451
Pratt, Chief Justice Sir John, 547
Presidential system, 4, 29, 122, 169, 186
Preventive detention law, 300, 302–04, 306, 309, 310–17, 504, 516, 528–29

R

Rahman, Justice Iqbal Hameedur, 563, 565
Rahman, Justice Shafiur, 235–36, 369

Ramaswamy, Chief Justice Veeraswamy, 203–04
Rao, Justice Koka Subba 398
Rashid, Chief Justice Mian Abdul, 205
Rational basis test, 65–9, 70–3, 83, 388; underinclusiveness 70, 72; overinclusiveness 70–1
Ray, Justice Ajit Nath, 205
Reagan, Ronald, 169, 170, 193, 196, 252, 348, 386–88, 443
Reddy, Justice B.P. Jeevan, 458
Reddy, Justice P. Jaganmohan, 123
Rehman, Chief Justice Hamoodur, 40, 53–4, 236, 536, 548, 566
Rehman, Chief Justice S. A., 54, 370, 535
Rehman, Ziaur, 567
Rehnquist, Chief Justice William, 46, 48, 76–7, 80–5, 141, 145, 162, 176, 178, 182–83, 227–28, 275, 327, 345–47, 351, 355, 384, 386–88, 394, 411–12, 422–23, 435, 443–44, 450, 452, 495, 526
Reid, Lord James, 117, 231
Right of privacy, 222, 283, 381–83, 386, 388, 394, 396, 398, 464
Right to counsel, 410, 524–26, 529, 530
Right to liberty, 277
Right to property, 328, 331, 335
Right to speedy trial, 294–95
Rhodesia 117–18 *see also* Southern Rhodesia Act 1965
Roberts, Chief Justice John, 78–9, 166
Rule of law, 19, 25, 28, 32–9, 41, 59, 62–3, 69, 101, 103, 160, 166, 180, 199, 222, 228, 260, 265, 296, 298, 528, 535, 557
Rutledge, Justice Wiley Blount, 180, 344

S

Sanford, Justice Edward Terry, 437–38
Scalia, Justice Antonin, 78, 86, 166, 182–83, 227, 272, 276, 345, 354, 382, 386–88, 392, 422, 441, 443, 450
Seervai, H. M., 331, 561
Self-incrimination, 44, 51–2, 174, 382, 402–06, 409, 410–11, 413–14, 416, 526, 529
Separation of powers, 37, 123, 131–32, 139, 152–59, 160–67, 175, 190–94, 207, 213, 226, 356, 556–57, 559, 561, 563
Shah, Chief Justice Dr Nasim Hasan, 235, 428
Shah, Justice Sajjad Ali, 207
Sharif, Mian Muhammad Nawaz, 518, 541, 543
Sharif, Muhammad Shahbaz, 518
Shastri, Chief Justice M. Patanjali, 302
Sheikh, Justice Azmat Saeed, 564
Siddiqui, Justice Saeeduzzaman, 160, 207, 233, 542
Sidhwa, Justice Rustam, S. 428
Sikri, Chief Justice Sarv Mittra, 556
Simonds, Viscount Gavin, 193
Sinha, Chief Justice Bhuvaneshwar Prasad 366
Souter, Justice David, 68, 78–9, 165, 182, 228–29, 345–47, 349, 351, 388, 422, 449
Southern Rhodesia Act 1965, 117
Stevens, Justice John Paul, 69, 78–9, 80–1, 165, 182–84, 228, 274, 345–47, 349, 351, 388, 393, 396, 422–23, 443, 447–49, 450, 452, 495
Stewart, Justice Potter, 80–1, 347, 376, 392, 395, 446
Steyn, Law Lord, 37
Strong, Justice William, 58
Supreme Court of Bangladesh, 565–66
Supreme Court of Canada, 25–6, 63, 146, 550
Supreme Court of Delaware, 106
Supreme Court of Florida, 228
Supreme Court of Illinois, 58
Supreme Court of India, 62, 87–8, 101–02, 123, 137, 160, 202–03, 205, 238–39, 263, 282–83, 285, 287, 291–92, 297–99, 317, 319, 358, 361–62, 455–59, 460–69, 470–71, 497–99, 510, 515–16, 527–28, 546, 554, 556–59, 560, 564, 567
Supreme Court of Judicature, 199
Supreme Court of Pakistan, 30, 87, 90, 97, 102, 125–26, 135, 148–49, 160, 206–07, 230, 237, 239, 265, 311–13, 317–18, 369, 370, 398, 418, 428–29, 471, 474, 476–78, 501–04, 508, 514, 518–19, 529, 530, 536, 541–43, 545, 549, 550, 560–63
Supreme Court of the Philippines, 157
Supreme Court of the United Kingdom, 199, 200
Supreme Court of United States, 233 *see also* US Supreme Court
Sutherland, George, 156–57, 177, 524
Swiss Federal Tribunal (Federal Supreme Court of Switzerland), 131, 146–47
Switzerland, 3–4, 147, 174
Switzerland, Constitution of, 130, 146–47; Article 102(2), 147; Article 113, 146; Article 71, 146; Article 89, 147

T

Taft, Chief Justice William Howard, 175, 194, 392, 421
Taney, Chief Justice Roger B., 180
Taylor, Judge Robert, 76
Thomas, Justice Clarence, 78, 166, 182, 196, 227–28, 249, 251, 276, 345–48, 388, 390, 394–95, 422, 450, 452

U

U, Chief Justice Sir Ba, 234
UN (United Nations,) 17–8, 63, 134, 449, 550
United Kingdom, 8, 17, 24–8, 33–5, 37, 63, 115–17, 119, 120, 131–34, 190–95, 198–99, 200–01, 277, 454, 496, 500;
United Kingdom, Constitution of 2, 24, 32–4, 152, 197, 424; Acquisition of Land (Authorization Procedure) Act 1946, 329; Act of Settlement 1701, 194; Act of Union 1707, 116; Appellate Jurisdiction Act 1876, 197, 199; Betting Act 1853, 281; Bill of Rights 1688, 232; Article 9 of 232; British Nationality Act 1981, 7–8; British Nationality and Status of Aliens Act 1914, 8; Children and Young Persons (Harmful Publications) Act 1955, 281; Coal Industry Nationalization Act 1946, 330; Compensation (Defence) Act 1939, 330; Constitutional Reform Act 2005, 198–99; Consumer Protection Act 1987, 233; Courts Act 1971, 260, 469; Criminal Law Act 1967, 397; Criminal Law Act 1977, 496, 500; Crown

Proceedings Act 1947, 34; Dangerous Drugs Act 1951, 281; Defence of the Realm Act 1914 (DORA), 302, 314, 330; Employment Act 1982, 34; Equal Pay Act 1970, 64; European Communities Act 1972, 26; Gaming Act 1845, 281; Incitement to Disaffection Act 1934, 280, 396; Judicature Act 1873, 260; Judicial Pensions and Retirement Act 1993, 200; Justices Protection Act 1848, 403; Larceny Act 1916, 280; Law Commission Act 1965, 231; Law Reform (Limitation of Actions) Act 1954, 233; Licensing Act 1662, 279; Mental Health Act 1959, 278, 281; Merchandise Marks Act 1887, 280; National Economy Act 1933, 194; Naturalization Act 1870, 8; Obscene Publications Act 1959, 281; Official Secrets Act 1911, 280; Parliament Acts 1911 and 1949, 26, 115–16, 118–19, 120; Petroleum (Production) Act 1934, 330; Pipe-lines Act 1962, 328; Police Act 1964, 507; Privy Council (Limitation of Appeals) Act 1968, 146; Privy Council Act 1833, 202; Public Order Act 1936, 396; Race Relations Act 1976, 64; Sex Discrimination Act 1975, 64; Smith Act, 439, 440, 491; Social Security Act 1936, 233; Statute of Westminster 1931, 26; Supreme Court Act 1981, 197, 201; Theft Act 1968, 396; Town and Country Planning Act 1962, 328, 330; Trades Disputes Act 1906, 34

United States of America/US, 3, 6, 59, 130, 143, 155, 169, 170, 180–82, 223, 301–02, 332, 336, 355, 398, 403, 408–09, 434, 491–92, 518

United States of America, Constitution of 3, 17, 24, 27, 46–7, 49, 106, 115, 129, 130–31, 133, 140, 144, 157, 161, 166, 169, 184, 195–96, 217–18, 224, 235, 238, 244, 246–49, 250, 252, 262, 270, 310, 381–82, 425, 428, 517, 524–25, 529, 534, 553, 566; First/1st Amendment, 222, 224, 250, 339, 341–42, 344–45, 347, 349, 351–56, 372–76, 382, 405, 409, 434–39, 440–49, 450–53, 480–84, 490–91, 493–95, 507–08; 10th Amendment, 133, 140, 144–45; 11th Amendment, 141; 12th Amendment, 170; 13th Amendment, 436, 480; 14th Amendment, 16, 44–8, 50–2, 57, 62, 65–6, 73, 81, 103–04, 107, 141, 229, 250–51, 253, 270, 273, 372, 385, 437, 524–25; 16th Amendment, 18; 21st Amendment, 452; 22nd Amendment, 27, 170; 25th Amendment, 171; 5th Amendment, 44, 46, 50–1, 65, 75, 81–2, 174, 270, 382, 403–06, 409, 410, 421, 423, 425, 427–28, 519, 525; Article 1, 17, 158, 165, 167, 180; Article 8, 43–4; Article I, 115, 133, 155, 172–73, 179, 196, 244–45, 247; Article I Section 8, 144, 179, 244, 248; Article II, 130, 155, 164, 172–73, 179, 182; Article II Section 1, 170; Article II Section 2, 195; Article II Section 2 Clause 1, 174, 179; Article II Section 2 Clause 2, 175; Article II Section 4, 171; Article III, 130, 140, 155, 164, 195–96, 217, 221, 253; Article III Section 2, 144; Article III Section 2(1), 143, 147; Article V, 3, 130, 145; Article VI, 130–31, 141, 144, 218, 262; Article VI, (2) 143, 148; Cable Television Consumer Protection and Competition Act 1992, 450; Child Pornography Prevention Act 1996, 448; Civil Rights Act of 1866, 73; Civil Rights Act of 1875, 73; Civil Rights Act of 1964, 74, 82; Communications Decency Act 1996, 447, 449; Comprehensive Smoking Education Act, 452; Creationism Act, 349; Criminal Anarchy Act 1902, 437; Criminal Syndicalism Act 1919, 438; Detainee Treatment Act 2005 (DTA), 184; Equal Access Act 1984, 344; Equal Pay Act 1963, 82; Espionage Act 1917, 436, 479; Federal Cigarette Labeling and Advertising Act 1965, 452; Federal Education Act 1972, 82; Federal Election Campaign Act 1971, 493; Federal Flag Protection Act 1989, 444; Gramm-Rudman-Hollings Act, 222; HEA (House Enrolled Act) 1337, 391; Immigration and Nationality Act, 223; Internal Security Act 1940, 439; Interstate Commerce Act 1887, 406; Judiciary Act 1789, 144, 214, 216–18; Judiciary Act 1801, 214; Kansas Sexually Violent Predator Act 1994, 422; Medicaid Act, 389; Military Commission Act, 165–66; Minnesota Human Rights Act, 494; Morrill Anti-Bigamy Act, 353; National Prohibition Act (NPA), 392; Non-Detention Act 1971, 182; Organic Act of the District of Columbia 1801, 201, 219; Presidential Recordings and Materials Preservation Act 1974, 162; Public Broadcasting Act 1967, 451; Public Health Cigarette Smoking Act 1970, 452; Religious Freedom Restoration Act (RFRA) 1993, 339, 356; Sedition Act 1789, 434; Sherman Antitrust Act 1890, 249; Universal Military Training and Service Act 1940, 340; Wagner Act 1935, 221, 253; War Claims Act, 175

US Supreme Court, 24, 45, 52, 68–9, 72, 83, 103, 140, 143, 147, 176, 181–82, 194–95, 202, 212–17, 220–25, 227, 229, 235, 244, 246–47, 253–54, 262, 270–71, 273, 285, 310, 326–27, 339, 340–44, 347–49, 351–56, 371–72, 381–89, 390, 392–96, 406, 408–09, 411–12, 421–23, 434–37, 439, 440–49, 450–53, 479, 481, 484, 490–95, 507, 517, 519, 524–26, 548–49, 566

Usmani, Justice Sarmad Jalal, 564

V

Veeraswamy, Chief Justice Kuppuswami Naidu, 204

Verma, Chief Justice Jagdish Sharan, 289

Vinelott, Justice Sir John, 232

Vinson, Chief Justice Fred Moore, 75, 153, 439

W

Waite, Chief Justice Morrison, 47, 55, 353

Wajed, Sheikh Haseena, 567

Warren, Chief Justice Earl, 75, 106, 196, 212–13, 350, 417, 442, 508, 524

Washington, Justice Bushrod, 47

Wheare, Dr Kenneth Clinton, 3, 138

White, Justice Byron, 80, 176, 345, 384, 387–88, 445, 447–48

Widgery, Lord Chief Justice John, 26–7

Wilmot, Chief Justice John Eardley, 41

Y

Yates, Justice Robert, 213